Hybrid Threats and Grey Zone Conflict

THE OXFORD SERIES IN ETHICS, NATIONAL SECURITY, AND THE RULE OF LAW

Series Editors Claire O. Finkelstein and Jens David Ohlin
Oxford University Press

About the Series

The Oxford Series in Ethics, National Security, and the Rule of Law is an interdisciplinary book series designed to address abiding questions at the intersection of national security, moral and political philosophy, and the law. It seeks to illuminate both ethical and legal dilemmas that arise in democratic nations as they grapple with contemporary national security challenges. The series also seeks to create a synergy between academic researchers and practitioners as they focus on common problems in national security theory and practice. The aim of the series is ultimately to advance thinking about how to protect and augment the rule of law in the context of contemporary armed conflict and national security.

The book series grew out of the work of the Center for Ethics and the Rule of Law (CERL) at the University of Pennsylvania. CERL is a nonpartisan interdisciplinary institute dedicated to the preservation and promotion of the rule of law in twenty-first-century warfare and national security. The only centre of its kind housed within a major research university, CERL draws from the study of law, philosophy, and ethics to answer the difficult questions that arise in times of war and contemporary transnational conflicts.

Hybrid Threats and Grey Zone Conflict

The Challenge to Liberal Democracies

Edited By

MITT REGAN AND AUREL SARI

OXFORD
UNIVERSITY PRESS

Oxford University Press is a department of the University of Oxford. It furthers the University's objective of excellence in research, scholarship, and education by publishing worldwide. Oxford is a registered trade mark of Oxford University Press in the UK and certain other countries.

Published in the United States of America by Oxford University Press
198 Madison Avenue, New York, NY 10016, United States of America.

© Oxford University Press 2024

All rights reserved. No part of this publication may be reproduced, stored in a retrieval system, or transmitted, in any form or by any means, without the prior permission in writing of Oxford University Press, or as expressly permitted by law, by license, or under terms agreed with the appropriate reproduction rights organization. Inquiries concerning reproduction outside the scope of the above should be sent to the Rights Department, Oxford University Press, at the address above.

You must not circulate this work in any other form
and you must impose this same condition on any acquirer.

Library of Congress Cataloging-in-Publication Data
Names: Regan, Milton C., Jr., 1952– author. | Sari, Aurel, author.
Title: Hybrid threats and grey zone conflict : the challenge to liberal
democracies / Mitt Regan and Aurel Sari.
Description: New York : Oxford University Press, 2024. |
Series: Oxford series in ethics, national security, and the rule of law |
Includes bibliographical references and index.
Identifiers: LCCN 2023039621 (print) | LCCN 2023039622 (ebook) |
ISBN 9780197744772 (hardback) | ISBN 9780197744796 |
ISBN 9780197744789 (epub) | ISBN 9780197744802
Subjects: LCSH: Legal ethics. | International law—Political aspects. |
National security—Law and legislation. | Rule of law. |
Democracy—Philosophy. | Liberalism. | Globalization—Political aspects.
Classification: LCC KZ1250 .R44 2024 (print) | LCC KZ1250 (ebook) |
DDC 341.5—dc23/eng/20231003
LC record available at https://lccn.loc.gov/2023039621
LC ebook record available at https://lccn.loc.gov/2023039622

DOI: 10.1093/oso/9780197744772.001.0001

Printed by Integrated Books International, United States of America

Note to Readers
This publication is designed to provide accurate and authoritative information in regard to the subject matter covered. It is based upon sources believed to be accurate and reliable and is intended to be current as of the time it was written. It is sold with the understanding that the publisher is not engaged in rendering legal, accounting, or other professional services. If legal advice or other expert assistance is required, the services of a competent professional person should be sought. Also, to confirm that the information has not been affected or changed by recent developments, traditional legal research techniques should be used, including checking primary sources where appropriate.

(Based on the Declaration of Principles jointly adopted by a Committee of the American Bar Association and a Committee of Publishers and Associations.)

You may order this or any other Oxford University Press publication
by visiting the Oxford University Press website at www.oup.com.

Contents

Acknowledgements	ix
Contributors	xi

1. Introduction   1
   Aurel Sari and Mitt Regan

I WHAT ARE HYBRID THREATS AND GREY ZONE CONFLICT?

2. The Grey Zone and Hybrid Conflict: A Conceptual Introduction   31
   Christopher Marsh

3. Grey Zone Conflict and Military Affairs: Questioning the Premise   45
   Melanie W. Sisson

4. We Have Met the Grey Zone and He Is Us: How Grey Zone
   Warfare Exploits Our Undecidedness about What Matters to Us   61
   Duncan MacIntosh

5. Legal Aspects of Grey Zone and Hybrid Threats: A Primer   87
   Hitoshi Nasu

6. The Divide between War and Peace   103
   Tobias Vestner

7. Rethinking Coercion in Cyberspace   129
   Ido Kilovaty

II ARENAS OF HYBRID AND GREY ZONE COMPETITION

8. A Topography of Information-Based Foreign Influence   157
   Beba Cibralic

9. In Pursuit of Geopolitical Advantage: Hacking Below the
   Threshold of War   179
   Melissa K. Griffith

10. Lawfare, China, and the Grey Zone   207
    Orde F. Kittrie

vi CONTENTS

11. Emerging Bio-Technologies for Disruptive Effects in Grey Zone Engagements 237
Joseph DeFranco, Diane DiEuliis, L. R. Bremseth, and James Giordano

12. The Maritime Domain 251
David Letts

13. The Evolving Chinese Strategy in the Arctic: Entering the Grey Zone? 271
Camilla T. N. Sørensen

14. Hybrid and Grey Zone Operations in Outer Space 289
Melissa de Zwart

III INSTRUMENTS, TACTICS, AND METHODS IN THE GREY ZONE

15. Decoding Grey Zone Environments 319
Andrés B. Muñoz Mosquera and Nikoleta Chalanouli

16. Coercing Well: The Logic, Grammar, and Norms of the Grey Zone 339
C. Anthony Pfaff

17. Lying in the Grey Zone 373
Steven Wheatley

18. Rethinking the International Law of Interference in the Digital Age 393
Steven J. Barela and Samuli Haataja

19. Trapped in the Grey Zone: International Law Applicable to Non-State Actors 425
Agata Kleczkowska

20. From Red Scare to Red Scare, Grey Zone to Grey Zone: Weaponizing Dissent and Civil Society 447
Tyler Wentzell and Barbara J. Falk

21. A Grey Zone Analytic Framework for Military Operations 469
Maegen Nix and Welton Chang

IV COUNTERING HYBRID AND GREY ZONE THREATS: HOW CAN LIBERAL DEMOCRACIES RESPOND?

22. An Ethical Framework for Assessing Grey Zone Responses 495
Edward Barrett

CONTENTS vii

23. Winning at the Strategic Seams 513
   Michael A. Newton

24. Legal Resilience: Just a Warm and Fuzzy Concept? 533
   Aurel Sari

25. How to Involve Civil Society in Grey Zone Defence 557
   Elisabeth Braw

26. Security Assistance by Liberal Democracies: Tensions
   in the Grey Zone 577
   Mitt Regan and Sarah Harrison

27. The Practice of Legal Resilience: Insights from the Maritime
   Incident of 31 May 2010 601
   Marlene Mazel

28. Legal Resilience from a Finnish Perspective 631
   Tiina Ferm

29. The Path to Legal Resilience 649
   *Andrés B. Muñoz Mosquera, Jean Emmanuel Perrin, Panagiotis
   Sergis, Rodrigo Vázquez Benítez, and Borja Montes Toscano*

Index 673

Acknowledgements

In publishing this volume, we are grateful to several organizations and institutions that have supported, in different ways, the conferences and workshops on which this work is based, including the

British Academy (London, United Kingdom)

Center for Ethics and the Rule of Law (University of Pennsylvania, Philadelphia, PA)

European Centre of Excellence for Countering Hybrid Threats (Helsinki, Finland)

Exeter Centre for International Law (University of Exeter, United Kingdom)

Geneva Centre for Security Policy (Geneva, Switzerland)

Judge Advocate General's Legal Center and School (Charlottesville, VA)

Lieber Institute for Law and Warfare (United States Military Academy, West Point, NY)

Middle East Center (University of Pennsylvania, Philadelphia, PA).

Special thanks are due to the Center for Ethics and the Rule of Law for providing the volume with an intellectual home as part of the Oxford Series in Ethics, National Security, and the Rule of Law.

Mitt Regan
Aurel Sari

Contributors

Steven J. Barela Senior Research Fellow, Geneva Academy of International Humanitarian Law and Human Rights, University of Geneva

Edward Barrett Colonel USAFR (ret.); Volgenau Director of Strategy and Research, Stockdale Center for Ethical Leadership, US Naval Academy

Elisabeth Braw Senior Associate Fellow, European Leadership Network

L. R. Bremseth Institute for Biodefense Research

Nikoleta Chalanouli Visiting Professor, Universidad Católica San Antonio de Murcia

Welton Chang Co-founder and CEO, Pyrra Technologies Inc.

Beba Cibralic Associate Fellow, Leverhulme Centre for the Future of Intelligence, University of Cambridge

Melissa de Zwart Deputy Director, ARC Centre of Excellence in Plants for Space; Professor of Space Law and Governance, Andy Thomas Centre for Space Resources, University of Adelaide

Joseph DeFranco Department of Microbiology, Immunology, and Pathology, Colorado State University

Diane DiEuliis Distinguished Research Fellow, Center for the Study of Weapons of Mass Destruction, National Defense University

Barbara J. Falk Professor, Department of Defence Studies at the Royal Military College of Canada

Tiina Ferm Senior Ministerial Adviser, Ministry of the Interior, Finland

James Giordano Departments of Neurology and Biochemistry Sub-program in Military Medicine, Georgetown University Medical Center; Defense Medical Ethics Center, Uniformed Services University of Health Sciences

Melissa K. Griffith Lecturer in Technology and National Security, Johns Hopkins University School of Advanced International Studies (SAIS); Non-Resident Research Fellow at the University of California, Berkeley's Center for Long-Term Cybersecurity (CLTC)

Samuli Haataja Senior Lecturer, Griffith Law School, Griffith University, Australia

xii CONTRIBUTORS

Sarah Harrison Senior Fellow, Center in Ethics and the Legal Profession, Georgetown Law Center

Ido Kilovaty Associate Professor of Law, University of Arkansas School of Law

Orde F. Kittrie Professor, Arizona State University; Senior Fellow, Foundation for Defense of Democracies

Agata Kleczkowska Institute of Law Studies, Polish Academy of Sciences

David Letts Australian National University College of Law; Australian National Centre for Ocean Resources and Security, University of Wollongong

Duncan MacIntosh Professor, Philosophy Department, Dalhousie University; Executive Board Member, Center for Ethics and the Rule of Law, Annenberg Public Policy Center, University of Pennsylvania

Christopher Marsh Professor of International Security Studies, National Defense University, Fort Liberty, North Carolina

Marlene Mazel Director, Foreign Litigation Division, Ministry of Justice, Israel

Borja Montes Toscano e-LAWFAS Legal Content Manager, NATO Allied Command Operations Office of Legal Affairs

Andrés B. Muñoz Mosquera Director, NATO Allied Command Operations Office of Legal Affairs

Hitoshi Nasu Professor of Law, United States Military Academy, West Point, and Lieber Institute for Law and Warfare; Senior Fellow, Stockton Center for International Law, United States Naval War College; Principal Visiting Research Fellow, University of Reading School of Law

Michael A. Newton Director, International Legal Studies Program; Professor of the Practice of Law and Professor of the Practice of Political Science, Vanderbilt University Law School

Maegen Nix Director, Decision Science Division Virginia Tech Applied Research Corporation

Jean Emmanuel Perrin Deputy Chief 'State Action at Sea' to the Chief of Naval Operations, French Navy Headquarters

C. Anthony Pfaff Research Professor for Strategy, the Military Profession, and Ethics, US Army War College's Strategic Studies Institute; Distinguished Senior Research Fellow, Institute for Philosophy and Public Policy

Mitt Regan McDevitt Professor of Jurisprudence; Co-Director, Center on National Security, Georgetown Law Center

Aurel Sari Associate Professor of Public International Law, University of Exeter; Fellow, Supreme Headquarters Allied Powers Europe

Panagiotis Sergis Hellenic National Defense College

Melanie W. Sisson Fellow, Brookings Institution Strobe Talbott Center for Security, Strategy, and Technology

Camilla T. N. Sørensen Associate Professor, Institute for Strategy and War Studies, Royal Danish Defence College

Rodrigo Vázquez Benítez Assistant Legal Advisor, NATO Allied Command Operations Office of Legal Affairs

Tobias Vestner Head, Research and Policy Advice Department and Security and Law Programme, Geneva Centre for Security Policy (GCSP); Honorary Senior Research Fellow, University of Exeter; Fellow, Supreme Headquarters Allied Powers Europe

Tyler Wentzell SJD candidate, Faculty of Law, University of Toronto; Canadian Forces College

Steven Wheatley Professor of International Law, University of Lancaster

1

Introduction

Aurel Sari and Mitt Regan

1. The context: persistent competition

Over the past two decades, great power competition has entered a more intense and openly antagonistic phase. This development is one of the great strategic challenges that liberal democracies are facing, alongside others such as climate change. How they manage this challenge will determine not only the political future of individual nations but also the shape of the international order in years to come.

Great power competition is not a new feature of the international system. Contestation is endemic in international relations. In the modern era, periods of relative stability marked by moderate forms of competition for power, influence, and prosperity were repeatedly interspersed with bouts of more intense rivalry and war, such as the Napoleonic Wars at the start of the nineteenth century, often followed by periods of institution-building and other efforts at peaceful ordering, such as the creation of the League of Nations after World War I. Great power competition is constant, but its intensity ebbs and flows.

The end of the Cold War gave rise to a sense of optimism that the geopolitical and ideological rivalry of that era would make way for a gradual convergence around liberal and democratic values. Most famously, Francis Fukuyama proclaimed that history itself would come to an end with the universalization of Western-style liberal democracy.[1] More recently, a long line of authors have argued that this optimism was misplaced. In the words of Robert Kagan, the unique geopolitical circumstances of the 1990s were not the beginning of some fundamental transformation in international relations, but merely a temporary 'pause in the endless competition of nations and peoples'.[2] Today, that pause has come to an end.

The National Security Strategy of the United States published by the Biden Administration in October 2022 identifies two overarching challenges that define the present strategic environment.[3] The first is geopolitical competition.

---

[1] Francis Fukuyama, *The End of History and the Last Man* (Free Press 1992).
[2] Robert Kagan, *The Return of History and the End of Dreams* (Knopf 2008) 11.
[3] The White House, *National Security Strategy* (2022) 6.

Aurel Sari and Mitt Regan, *Introduction* In: *Hybrid Threats and Grey Zone Conflict.* Edited by: Mitt Regan and Aurel Sari, Oxford University Press. © Oxford University Press 2024. DOI: 10.1093/oso/9780197744772.003.0001

2   INTRODUCTION

Democracies and autocracies are engaged in a contest to shape the international order of the future. As a result, the risk of conflict among major powers has increased, while space for cooperation on issues of shared concern has diminished. According to the National Security Strategy, the most pressing challenges are presented by nations that combine authoritarian governance at home with revisionist foreign policy goals abroad, a combination that leads them to subvert democratic processes in other countries, leverage technology for coercive effect, and promote an illiberal model of international order.[4] The Strategy points to Russia and China as the main competitors, though it is quick to underline that these two nations present different types of difficulties. While Russia 'poses an immediate threat to the free and open international system', as shown by its war of aggression against Ukraine, the People's Republic of China 'is the only competitor with both the intent to reshape the international order and, increasingly, the economic, diplomatic, military, and technological power to advance that objective'.[5] The second overarching strategic challenge are a set of transnational challenges playing out against the backdrop of great power rivalry. They include climate change, food insecurity, terrorism, communicable diseases, energy shortages, and inflation. As the National Security Strategy underlines, these transnational challenges are not secondary in importance but lie at the heart of national and international security.[6] Solving them requires close international cooperation, yet such cooperation will be more difficult to realize in an environment of heightened geopolitical competition.

The *Integrated Review of Security, Defence, Development and Foreign Policy* published by the British Government in March 2021 strikes a similar note.[7] It identifies four trends that will be of particular significance over the next decade as the nature and distribution of global power is changing.[8] First, the *Integrated Review* forecasts that by 2030, the world will have moved further towards multipolarity, with the geopolitical and economic centre of gravity shifting towards the Indo-Pacific. While Russia will remain the most acute direct threat to the United Kingdom, China's increasing power, stature, and assertiveness will have turned it into the most significant geopolitical factor on the global stage.[9] Second, this more multipolar world will be characterized by a growing contest to shape the international environment. In particular, democratic and autocratic States will be locked into systemic competition to shape global governance structures. Third, the pace of technological change will quicken, with advances in science

---

[4] Ibid. 8.
[5] Ibid.
[6] Ibid. 6.
[7] United Kingdom Government, *Global Britain in a Competitive Age: The Integrated Review of Security, Defence, Development and Foreign Policy* (Cabinet Office 2021).
[8] Ibid. 24.
[9] Ibid. 62–63.

INTRODUCTION   3

and technology becoming more critical to the functioning of economies and societies, to reshaping political systems and to driving cooperation and competition between States. Finally, the world will continue to face transnational challenges, such as poverty, instability, and migration driven by climate change and biodiversity loss, or the continued threats posed by terrorism and organized criminality. An update of the *Integrated Review* published in March 2023 notes that these trends have accelerated, leading to the growing prospect that the international security environment will deteriorate further in the near future.[10] Specifically, the update declares that systemic competition is now the 'dominant geopolitical trend and the main driver of the deteriorating security environment', fuelled by a growing convergence among authoritarian States that challenge 'the basic conditions for an open, stable and peaceful international order, working together to undermine the international system or remake it in their image'.[11]

The National Security Strategy of the United States and the updated *Integrated Review* of the United Kingdom tell a similar story: rivalry among democratic and authoritarian systems, in particular between the United States and a resurgent China, coupled with mutually reinforcing transnational challenges that are compounding wider global instability, are the main strategic challenges of our time.

Russia's war of aggression against Ukraine demonstrates that resort to force as an instrument of national power remains an option for States engaged in geopolitical competition. Conventional war has not disappeared. In fact, Russia's war poses a risk of wider escalation. Similarly, while China's leadership might prefer to achieve its strategic aims without engaging in direct military confrontation with the United States, neither small-scale incidents nor large-scale escalation, principally over Taiwan, can be ruled out. The risk of miscalculation and escalation also looms large in relation to other actors, such as Iran and North Korea. High-intensity warfare among major military powers cannot, therefore, be discounted.[12] Deterrence through force, and if deterrence fails, the ability to prevail in actual conflict, must therefore be an integral part of the posture adopted by democracies in an age of persistent competition.

However, absent wider escalation leading to direct military confrontation between the principal powers, geopolitical competition today mostly takes the form of contestation below the threshold of armed conflict, using instruments and methods short of open war to gain an advantage.[13] This form of competition

---

[10] United Kingdom Government, *Integrated Review Refresh 2023: Responding to a More Contested and Volatile World* (Cabinet Office 2023) 8.

[11] Ibid.

[12] See Colin S. Gray, *Another Bloody Century: Future Warfare* (Weidenfeld and Nicolson 2005).

[13] Patrick Porter, 'Advice for a Dark Age: Managing Great Power Competition' (2019) 42 The Washington Quarterly 7, 11.

4 INTRODUCTION

is characterized by several features. First, it extends across virtually all domains and comes in many different guises. Technological and social changes have rendered modern societies more interdependent and interconnected. These changes have also opened them up more readily to foreign interference.[14] Most functional and thematic areas of modern life, including the political sphere, culture, the economy, information, critical infrastructure, and cyberspace, are vulnerable to acts of disruption and subversion. Accordingly, in recent years, we have witnessed hostile actors operating across various domains to employ a broad range of measures against liberal democracies in pursuit of their strategic interests, including the use of diplomatic pressure, trade, proxies, tourism, economic espionage, military exercises, cyber operations, disinformation, direct investment, leveraging diasporas, exploiting social and political divisions, and fostering financial and other dependencies.[15]

Second, competition short of war varies in its severity and aggressiveness. Russia, China, and other actors engage in acts that may be described as *normal* competitive engagements, such as expanding their influence abroad or developing their military capabilities. Such activities may be harmful to the interests of liberal democracies, but they do not contradict their core principles and thus do not differ materially from the kind of measures they may resort to themselves. However, autocratic competitors also engage in acts that are *transgressive*, that is acts that violate established rules and expectations of conduct or which are otherwise incompatible with the values of open societies, such as serious human rights violations, coercive interference, or exorbitant territorial and other jurisdictional claims.[16] By adjusting the volume, nature, and pattern of their actions, strategic competitors are able to vary the pace of contestation. At the top end, they pursue goals that are decidedly hostile in nature, such as fanning social and political discord, undermining trust in democratic institutions and processes, and shaping the environment for potential future military engagements.

Third, the renewed intensity of geopolitical competition has blurred the line between war and peace.[17] Even though contestation on the whole remains below the threshold of open conflict, some of the actions, instruments, and methods involved do entail military capabilities and resort to violence. Examples include the Salisbury poisoning incident, which the United Kingdom declared to be an unlawful use of force by Russia in contravention of the United Nations Charter,[18]

---

[14] Mark Leonard, *The Age of Unpeace: How Connectivity Causes Conflict* (Bantam Press 2021).

[15] For a comprehensive list of tactics employed by the People's Republic of China, see Bonny Lin et al, *Competition in the Gray Zone: Countering China's Coercion against U.S. Allies and Partners in the Indo-Pacific* (RAND 2022) 135–38, table 8.1.

[16] This distinction is inspired by the one drawn between benign, normal, and transgressive activities in Christopher Paul et al, *A Guide to Extreme Competition with China* (RAND 2021) v–vi.

[17] We leave aside, for now, the question of how clear that line was to begin with.

[18] Theresa May, Prime Minister, 'Statement on the Salisbury Incident' (12 March 2018) <https://www.gov.uk/government/speeches/pm-commons-statement-on-salisbury-incid

and China's reliance on naval and paranaval assets to assert its claims in the South China Sea.[19] There is widespread concern that revisionist States are using measures short of war to achieve strategic outcomes typically pursued through military action and that such measures could be a prelude to war. Indeed, in Ukraine, the great powers are already engaged in indirect conflict through proxy warfare. Relations between them can therefore no longer be described as entirely peaceful, given the persistence, intensity, and hostile character of their rivalry. In an environment where anything can be 'weaponized' and everything has turned into some form of 'warfare',[20] a clear line between war and peace is difficult to draw.

2. The role and relevance of international law

The present age of geopolitical competition may be more intense and openly antagonistic, but it is not an era of lawlessness. On the contrary, international law remains centre stage.

Rules of international law serve as a normative framework within which strategic rivals compete with each other. The rules formulate binding expectations and standards of behaviour, distinguishing permissible forms of competition from impermissible ones. Legal institutions provide venues for States to assert opposing claims, while legal processes offer avenues for redress. Clearly, whether these rules, institutions, and processes are sufficiently robust to contain geopolitical competition within acceptable boundaries and to mitigate its adverse effects is a matter of ongoing concern. The challenges are formidable.

Many rules and principles of international law that were developed in the pre-digital era do not fit activities designed to exploit the increased interconnectedness of modern societies very well. Although there is broad agreement that international law applies in novel domains such as cyberspace,[21] there is continued disagreement over how exactly the relevant rules should apply. Faced with the prospect of significant harm, some States are extending

---

ent-response-14-march-2018> accessed 30 May 2023. See Stephen Lewis, 'Salisbury, Novichok and International Law on the Use of Force' (2018) 163 RUSI Journal 10.

[19] Andrew Sven Erickson and Ryan D. Martinson (eds), *China's Maritime Gray Zone Operations* (Naval Institute Press 2019).

[20] Mark Galeotti, *The Weaponisation of Everything: A Field Guide to the New Way of War* (Yale University Press 2022).

[21] E.g. Group of Governmental Experts on Advancing Responsible State Behaviour in Cyberspace in the Context of International Security, 'Report' (14 July 2021), UN Doc. A/76/135, para 69; Open-ended Working Group on Developments in the Field of Information and Telecommunications in the Context of International Security, 'Final Substantive Report' (10 March 2021), UN Doc. A/AC.290/2021/CRP.2, para 34.

6 INTRODUCTION

the established principles in new directions, for example, by suggesting that cyber operations causing 'widespread economic effects and destabilisation' may amount to the use of force in violation of Article 2(4) of the United Nations Charter.[22] Similarly, there is disagreement about what types of activities the principle of non-intervention prohibits, with mounting support to extend its scope to disruptive interference and to acts that deprive a State of its freedom of control, in other words its decision-making capacity, over matters falling within its reserved domain of domestic jurisdiction.[23]

At the top end of the spectrum, the prohibition of the use of force demands that strategic competition should be carried out through peaceful means. Russia's war of aggression against Ukraine has manifestly and gravely violated that prohibition.[24] In the eyes of many commentators, Russia's invasion presents one of the most serious challenges to the international order established after World War II, since it repudiates a norm at its very core: the prohibition of forcible annexation of foreign territory.[25] Others have questioned this assessment, arguing that Russian aggression cannot be distinguished decisively from Western violations, in particular the use of force against Iraq in 2003, since the level of lawlessness and the severity of the harm they have caused is comparable.[26] In any event, the rules governing the use of force were not in a good shape even before Russia's invasion. A substantial number of States have adopted expansive interpretations of the right of self-defence over the last two decades to justify the flexible use of force on a more limited scale, progressively undermining the prohibition to use force at the borderline between war and peace.[27]

---

[22] Norway, in United Nations General Assembly, 'Official Compendium of Voluntary National Contributions on the Subject of How International Law Applies to the Use of Information and Communications Technologies by States submitted by Participating Governmental Experts in the Group of Governmental Experts on Advancing Responsible State Behaviour in Cyberspace in the Context of International Security established pursuant to General Assembly Resolution 73/266' (13 July 2021), UN Doc. A/76/136, 70.

[23] E.g. Australia, in ibid. 5; United Kingdom Attorney General, 'International Law in Future Frontiers' (19 May 2022) <https://www.gov.uk/government/speeches/international-law-in-future-frontiers> accessed 30 May 2023.

[24] United Nations General Assembly, 'Resolution ES-11/1' (18 March 2022) ('*Deplores in the strongest terms* the aggression by the Russian Federation against Ukraine in violation of Article 2(4) of the Charter').

[25] Ingrid Brunk and Monica Hakimi, 'Russia, Ukraine, and the Future World Order' (2022) 116 American Journal of International Law 687.

[26] E.g. Alejandro Chehtman, 'Unpacking the Comparison between Ukraine and Iraq' (*CIL Dialogues*, 20 March 2023) <https://cil.nus.edu.sg/blogs/unpacking-the-comparison-between-ukraine-and-iraq/> accessed 30 May 2023; Srinivas Burra, 'Russian Invasion of Ukraine Is Not an Exception or Rupture but a Continuity' (*Cambridge Core Blog*, 22 February 2023) <https://www.cambridge.org/core/blog/2023/02/22/russian-invasion-of-ukraine-is-not-an-exception-or-rupture-but-a-continuity/> accessed 30 May 2023.

[27] E.g. see Christian Henderson, 'The 25 February 2021 Military Strikes and the "Armed Attack" Requirement of Self-Defence: from "*Sina qua Non*" to the Point of Vanishing?' (2022) 9 Journal on the Use of Force and International Law 55.

Overall, there is much uncertainty and normative drift in the international legal system, compounded by its underlying structural deficiencies, including its weak institutions and enforcement mechanisms. Yet the rules of international law serve not only as guardrails for geopolitical competition, however deficient and weak. They also embody substantive values and goals. These are important to both democratic and autocratic powers.

The hallmark of liberal democracies is a commitment to what is often described as a 'thick' or 'substantive' understanding of the rule of law. Not only should the exercise of public authority and social life more generally be governed by rules that are equally applicable to all, but such laws must carry the democratically expressed consent of the population and respect fundamental rights and freedoms. This commitment to the rule of law, and associated principles such as good governance, political pluralism, and human rights, is widely seen as the normative lifeblood which sustains the political vitality and moral strength of liberal democracies.

By contrast, such a thick understanding of the rule of law is an anathema to autocratic governments: a genuine commitment to respect democracy, political pluralism, and human rights, as these notions are understood and for the most part practiced in the West, is incompatible with regime survival. Russia and China consequently promote State-centric principles of international law at the expense of human rights. For example, their Declaration on the Promotion of International Law of 2016 champions the principles of sovereign equality and non-intervention in the internal or external affairs of States, without mentioning human rights once.[28] More recently, Russia and China have adopted a different approach by seeking to appropriate the meaning of 'democracy' in a joint statement issued on the eve of the full-scale invasion of Ukraine.[29] In a thinly veiled reference to the West, the statement expresses Russian and Chinese opposition to 'interference in the internal affairs of sovereign states under the pretext of protecting democracy and human rights'.[30] Declaring democracy to be 'a universal human value, rather than a privilege of a limited number of States', the text goes on to proclaim the freedom of each nation to 'choose such forms and methods of implementing democracy that would best suit its particular state, based on its social and political system, its historical background, traditions and unique cultural characteristics'.[31]

---

[28] Ministry of Foreign Affairs of the Russian Federation, 'The Declaration of the Russian Federation and the People's Republic of China on the Promotion of International Law' (25 June 2016) <https://www.fmprc.gov.cn/eng/wjdt_665385/2649_665393/201608/t20160801_679466.html> accessed 30 May 2023.

[29] President of Russia, 'Joint Statement of the Russian Federation and the People's Republic of China on the International Relations Entering a New Era and the Global Sustainable Development' (4 February 2022) <http://www.en.kremlin.ru/supplement/5770> accessed 30 May 2023.

[30] Ibid.

[31] Ibid.

8 INTRODUCTION

These examples underline that international law is not beyond the reach of geopolitical competition. It is not a set of rules that stands above the tumble of great power politics, attempting to constrain it with greater or lesser success. Rather, it is an integral part of that rivalry. States are invested in international law because it defines the terms of their competition. The rules of international law reflect value preferences and choices about political objectives. They provide principled justifications for policy action. They are a source of legitimacy and, equally, a means for delegitimizing competitors. Both the National Security Strategy of the United States and the *Integrated Review* of the United Kingdom recognize the need for democracies to proactively shape the future international order, including its rules, institutions, norms, and standards, in order to ensure that it reflects democratic values and is conducive to their interests, rather than those of autocratic regimes.[32] To adapt a famous line from Carl von Clausewitz,[33] law is a continuation of politics with other means. What this means is that international law is an instrument of geopolitical competition, a domain in which that competition takes place, and an object of strategic contestation all at the same time.[34]

We recall these points not because they have not been made before, but because they have certain implications worth spelling out. The position of the law in the contemporary strategic environment cannot be reduced to the simplistic image of law-observing status quo powers seeking to conserve the international order in its current form against an onslaught by revisionist lawbreakers. Support for the status quo and revisionism are relative notions. Neither is absolute, but a matter of degree and comparisons.[35] For example, while certain standards core to the identity of liberal democracies, such as respect for human rights, form part of the existing body of international law, other principles, such as a democratic form of government that is politically pluralist, subject to checks and balances, served by an independent media, and respects civil liberties, are not. Strengthening democracy around the world, which is one of the goals formulated in the National Security Strategy,[36] is not necessarily a status quo policy. Both democracies and autocracies defend the status quo in some areas and pursue revisionist objectives in others.

The binary image of status quo versus revisionist powers also ignores the fact that Western nations have stretched the boundaries of international legality

---

[32] E.g. see The White House (n 3) 8–9, 11, 32; United Kingdom Government (n 7) 12, 28, 35, 45.

[33] Carl von Clausewitz, *On War* (Princeton University Press 1976) 87.

[34] In more detail, see Aurel Sari, *Hybrid Threats and the Law: Building Legal Resilience*, Hybrid CoE Research Report 3 (The European Centre of Excellence for Countering Hybrid Threats 2021) 12–17.

[35] *Cf.* Michael J. Mazarr, *Mastering the Gray Zone: Understanding a Changing Era of Conflict* (Strategic Studies Institute and US Army War College 2015) 16–24.

[36] A goal set by The White House (n 3) 8.

INTRODUCTION 9

and, at times, overstepped them. Some of those breaches may be less severe than Russia's invasion of Ukraine and the justifications offered for them may chime more readily with universal values than those advanced by Moscow for its actions.[37] Nevertheless, Western transgressions fuel accusations of double standards, making it more difficult for democracies to build broad coalitions against autocratic regimes. This is not lost on the update to the United Kingdom's *Integrated Review*, it seems, which warns that systemic competition cannot be reduced to 'democracy versus autocracy' but is a more complex phenomenon that requires working with 'countries to protect our shared higher interest in an open and stable international order, accepting that we may not share all of the same values and national interests'.[38]

Accordingly, strategic competition in the legal domain is not a confrontation between those who favour rules and those who prefer a world without them. What is at stake is not a choice between a legal order and one without law, but the shape, content, and operation of the rules that make up that order. Portraying this as a fight for a rules-based international order is not overly helpful. This is so partly because it is open to question whether international order is really *based* on rules.[39] This overstates the importance of the law if it is meant to suggest that rules are the single most important source of order. More importantly for our purposes, the idea that autocratic regimes threaten the very survival of the international legal system, as has been suggested at times,[40] misrepresents the nature of the challenge: the risk that liberal democracies are facing is not a lawless world, but one in which key norms of coexistence are weakened and where the prevailing rules and institutions reflect authoritarian preferences and interests.

In sum, law is integral to geopolitical competition and matters because rules, strategic considerations, great power interests, and ordering are finely interwoven.

---

[37] The missile strikes by France, the United Kingdom, and the United States against chemical weapons facilities in Syria in April 2018 are a case in point. For an analysis suggesting that the incident was transformative in formulating or consolidating customary international law, see Michael P. Scharf, 'Striking a Grotian Moment: How the Syrian Airstrikes Changed International Law Relating to Humanitarian Intervention' (2019) 19 Chicago Journal of International Law 586. For a less enthusiastic assessment, see Agata Kleczkowska, 'The Illegality of Humanitarian Intervention: The Case of the UK's Legal Position Concerning the 2018 Strikes in Syria' (2020) 35 Utrecht Journal of International and European Law 35.

[38] United Kingdom Government (n 10) 9.

[39] Patrick Porter, *The False Promise of Liberal Order: Nostalgia, Delusion and the Rise of Trump* (Polity Press 2020) 83.

[40] Joseph R. Biden Jr., 'What America Will and Will Not Do in Ukraine', The New York Times (New York, 31 May 2022) <https://www.nytimes.com/2022/05/31/opinion/biden-ukraine-strategy.html> accessed 30 May 2023.

10 INTRODUCTION

3. Why hybrid threats and grey zone conflict?

In the West, hostile tactics below the threshold of war have been widely described with the help of two concepts: hybrid threats and grey zone conflict. The North Atlantic Treaty Organization (NATO) has defined hybrid threats as 'activities that aim to create ambiguity and blur the lines between peace, crisis, and conflict'[41] by employing 'a broad, complex, and adaptive combination of conventional and non-conventional means, and overt and covert military, paramilitary, and civilian measures [...] in a highly integrated design'.[42] Meanwhile, the grey zone has been described as 'a conceptual space between peace and war, occurring when actors purposefully use single or multiple elements of power to achieve political-security objectives with activities that are typically ambiguous or cloud attribution and exceed the threshold of ordinary competition, yet intentionally fall below the level of large-scale direct military conflict'.[43]

Both concepts draw attention to the fact that today, strategic competition is in large measure carried out below the threshold of conventional armed conflict and involves integrated action across multiple domains. Whereas the notion of hybrid threats emphasizes the complementary use of different instruments of statecraft, the grey zone concept underlines the ambiguous character of competition and its aggressive quality that nevertheless falls short of war. Beyond this, the meaning of neither concept is settled.

While the unsettled meaning of the hybrid threats and grey zone notions is one factor that explains their success in recent years,[44] it is also one of the main objections that has been directed against them. Both terms have been repeatedly criticized for being fundamentally vague and ambiguous. To some, this imprecision has rendered them 'catch-all' phrases without any distinct analytical value,[45] buzzwords 'that can mean almost anything',[46] as reflected in their inconsistent use in strategic discourse.[47] Others have gone further, suggesting that these terms should be eliminated from the strategic lexicon as they 'cause more harm

---

[41] Brussels Summit Declaration Issued by the Heads of State and Government participating in the meeting of the North Atlantic Council, 11 July 2018, para 21.

[42] Warsaw Summit Communiqué Issued by the Heads of State and Government participating in the meeting of the North Atlantic Council, 9 July 2016, para 72.

[43] Department of Defense Strategic Multi-Layer Assessment, 'Grey Zone Effort Update', September 2016.

[44] See Chiara Libiseller, ' "Hybrid Warfare" as an Academic Fashion' (2023) 46 Journal of Strategic Studies 858.

[45] Hew Strachan, *The Direction of War: Contemporary Strategy in Historical Perspective* (CUP 2013) 82.

[46] Ilmari Käihkö, 'The Evolution of Hybrid Warfare: Implications for Strategy and the Military Profession' (2021) 51 Parameters 115, 126.

[47] Silvie Janičatová and Petra Mlejnková, 'The Ambiguity of Hybrid Warfare: A Qualitative Content Analysis of the United Kingdom's Political–Military Discourse on Russia's Hostile Activities' (2021) 42 Contemporary Security Policy 312.

INTRODUCTION 11

than good and contribute to an increasingly dangerous distortion of the concepts of war, peace, and geopolitical competition'.[48]

These are powerful objections, but they should not be pressed too far. The criticisms are at their most compelling when directed against the use of hybrid threats and grey zone conflict as general theories of war and grand strategy. Their use for these purposes is unpersuasive, as neither hybrid threats nor grey zone conflict describe historically new phenomena,[49] just like hybrid warfare is not an accurate representation of the Russian way of war.[50] However, the criticisms lose much of their force when the two notions are employed in a more modest manner. This involves using them not as full-blown theories of contemporary conflict but as labels that help to describe and bring into sharper focus certain aspects of the changing character of war and geopolitical competition. The two concepts tell us something about the current strategic environment that is worth exploring on its own terms and for that reason they offer a useful analytical lens,[51] even if the tools for that analysis must be drawn from other theories and fields. Their utility thus lies in focusing the inquiry, rather than as replacements of existing strategic theory.[52]

Relying on the hybrid threats and grey zone conflict notions in this more modest manner allows us to engage with the challenges typically associated with these two concepts, while being mindful of their limitations. It is useful to draw two basic distinctions for these purposes.

First, it helps to differentiate between three different framings of hybridity: hybrid *war*, hybrid *warfare threats*, and hybrid *threats*.[53] Hybridity entered the mainstream debates in 2005 in the form of 'hybrid war', a phrase coined by James Mattis and Frank Hoffman, both of the US Marine Corps, to describe the shape of future warfare.[54] According to Mattis and Hoffman, future adversaries were likely to combine diverse forms of violence, including

[48] Donald J. Stoker and Craig Whiteside, 'Blurred Lines: Gray-Zone Conflict and Hybrid War—Two Failures of American Strategic Thinking' (2020) 73 Naval War College Review 13, 13.

[49] For historical background and parallels, see Williamson Murray and Peter R. Mansoor (eds), *Hybrid Warfare: Fighting Complex Opponents from the Ancient World to the Present* (CUP 2012).

[50] Bettina Renz, 'Russia and 'Hybrid Warfare'' (2016) 22 Contemporary Politics 283; Sandor Fabian, 'The Russian Hybrid Warfare Strategy—Neither Russian nor Strategy' (2019) 35 Defense and Security Analysis 308.

[51] Along similar lines, see Devid Betz, 'The Idea of Hybridity', in Ofer Fridman et al (eds), *Hybrid Conflicts and Information Warfare: New Labels, Old Politics* (Lynne Rienner 2019) 9, 24.

[52] *Cf.* Murat Caliskan, 'Hybrid Warfare through the Lens of Strategic Theory' (2019) 35 Defense and Security Analysis 40.

[53] For a more detailed intellectual history, see Ofer Fridman, *Russian "Hybrid Warfare": Resurgence and Politicization* (Hurst 2018).

[54] James N. Mattis and Frank G. Hoffman, 'Future Warfare: The Rise of Hybrid Wars' (2005) 131 Proceedings Magazine 18. For further discussion, see Frank G. Hoffman, *Conflict in the 21st Century: The Rise of Hybrid Warfare* (Potomac Institute for Policy Studies 2007); Frank G. Hoffman, 'Hybrid Threats: Reconceptualizing the Evolving Character of Modern Conflict' [2009] Strategic Forum 1.

12 INTRODUCTION

conventional warfighting, terrorism, insurgency, guerrilla tactics, and organized criminality, in order to offset the superior conventional capabilities of the United States. Mattis and Hoffman described this blend of different modalities of violence as 'hybrid war'.

In subsequent years, NATO embraced the idea of hybridity but did so by focusing on hybrid threats posed by adversaries 'with the ability to simultaneously employ conventional and non-conventional means adaptively in pursuit of their objectives'.[55] This extended the notion of hybridity beyond actual warfighting to cover situations of potential violence and the combined use of military and civilian instruments, as exemplified by Russia's annexation of Crimea. In response to Russia's actions, NATO leaders declared themselves ready at their Wales Summit in September 2014 to 'address the specific challenges posed by hybrid warfare threats, where a wide range of overt and covert military, paramilitary, and civilian measures are employed in a highly integrated design'.[56] Whereas 'hybrid warfare' in its original sense refers to a particular form of armed conflict, NATO's notion of 'hybrid warfare threats' describes the complementary use of military and civilian means in situations of actual conflict or near-conflict.

The third framing of hybridity as 'hybrid threats' is concerned with the synergistic use of non-violent means below the threshold of open hostilities.[57] Since all actors aspire to use the different instruments of statecraft at their disposal in a coherent and complementary manner, the hybrid threat construct relies heavily on its 'threat' element to distinguish the coherent conduct of policy by Western nations from the coherent conduct of policy by other actors. Accordingly, in recent years, the term 'hybrid threats' has been used primarily as a pejorative label to describe the activities undertaken by autocratic regimes to undermine or otherwise harm democratic nations, in particular by targeting their vulnerabilities and influencing their decision-making, within the wider context of geopolitical competition.[58]

Second, hybrid threats and grey zone conflict are both concerned with competition below the threshold of war. However, they address different aspects of the matter and are not synonymous:[59] hybrid threats focus on the malign activities

---

[55] Supreme Headquarters Allied Powers Europe and Allied Command Transformation, *Bi-SC Input to a New NATO Capstone Concept for the Military Contribution to Countering Hybrid Threats* (2010) 2–3.

[56] Wales Summit Declaration issued by the Heads of State and Government participating in the meeting of the North Atlantic Council, 5 September 2014, Press Release (2014) 120 (5 September 2014) para 13.

[57] European Commission & High Representative of the Union for Foreign Affairs and Security Policy, Joint Communication: Joint Framework on Countering Hybrid Threats - A European Union Response, JOIN(2016) 18 final (6 April 2016) 2.

[58] Andrew Mumford and Pascal Carlucci, 'Hybrid Warfare: The Continuation of Ambiguity by Other Means' (2023) 8 European Journal of International Security 192, 197.

[59] See European Centre of Excellence for Countering Hybrid Threats, 'Hybrid Threats as a Concept', <https://www.hybridcoe.fi/hybrid-threats-as-a-phenomenon/> accessed 30 May 2023.

and the instruments and tactics they employ, while the grey zone describes a space on the spectrum of conflict where such activities take place. Unlike the three different framings of hybridity, the idea of a grey zone divides the spectrum of conflict into three segments: peace, war, and the grey zone in-between that is neither peace nor war. The difficulty with this tripartite division is that it exchanges the blurred line between war and peace with two uncertain dividing lines: one between peace and the grey zone at the lower end and another one between the grey zone and war at the higher end. Rather than multiply the thresholds in this way, a more fruitful use of the grey zone notion is to conceptualize it as the liminal area on the spectrum of conflict where war and peace gradually blend into each other, with no sharp lines on either side. This approach holds on to the idea that war and peace are different conditions, but suggests that they are divided not by a single line, whether blurred or not, but by a wider zone of grey that combines both peaceful and warlike features at the same time.

Understood in this way, the notions of hybrid threats and grey zone conflict complement each other: hybrid threats refer to actions that combine a range of means and tactics across various domains to target national, societal, and institutional vulnerabilities to achieve incremental strategic gains by harming their targets in ways designed to remain below the level of open armed conflict, but which are more hostile in their character, intent, or objectives than acceptable forms of peaceful competition, and as such blend features that are both peaceful and warlike in a grey zone between war and peace.[60] Clearly, other forms of competitive engagements, from more benign interactions all the way to conventional or even nuclear war, remain available to States. However, hybrid threats and grey zone conflict are useful heuristic devices to shine the spotlight on what is one prominent manifestation of contemporary geopolitical rivalry.

4. The present volume

The purpose of this book is to assess the legal and ethical challenges that hybrid threats and grey zone conflict pose for liberal democracies. Three sets of questions arise in this respect.

The first set of questions revolves around the capacity and suitability of the existing rules and institutions of international law to regulate hybrid threats and grey zone conflicts. Although the use of military force remains a prominent feature of the contemporary security environment, hybrid and grey zone tactics are designed to achieve strategic gains by targeting an adversary without triggering

---

[60] See also Sean Monaghan, 'Countering Hybrid Warfare: Conceptual Foundations and Implications for Defence Forces' (MCDC Countering Hybrid Warfare Project 2019) 2–3.

14 INTRODUCTION

direct military confrontation. These tactics are thus characterized by hostile encounters that fall below the level of intensity of outright war, although they may be coercive in character and may entail military activity.[61] The ambiguous nature of hybrid and grey zone activities makes it difficult to determine whether the threshold between war and peace has been crossed. It also puts considerable strain on the principle of non-intervention, which forbids interference in the core sovereign functions of another State. It is often unclear whether malign interference, in particular in domains such as the cyber- and social media space, constitutes legally permissible competition or coercive intervention into such functions.[62] By operating at the dividing line between war and peace, and between lawful and unlawful competition, actors employing hybrid and grey zone tactics seek to exploit legal uncertainty to their own strategic advantage.

The second set of questions revolves around the role of law as an instrument, domain, and object of geopolitical contestation. Hybrid and grey zone actors rely on the law to further their strategic objectives. China, for example, has developed a multilayered strategy that combines legal and non-legal measures to expand its control over the South China Sea. The Russian government has used a multitude of legal tools to annex Crimea, support its full-scale invasion of Ukraine, and counter Western sanctions, in addition to leveraging international cooperation mechanisms, such as Europol, to silence opposition voices. Many of the legal tactics employed as part of a hybrid and grey zone campaign—such as taking advantage of gaps, thresholds and uncertainties in the law, evading accountability, advancing untenable legal arguments, abusing legal processes, circumventing binding commitments, and blatant violations of the applicable rules—are incompatible with the rule of law. Such tactics exploit and exacerbate the underlying weaknesses of the international legal order.

The third set of questions revolves around the ethical implications of the subject. In their efforts to counter hybrid and grey zone tactics, liberal democracies are confronted by several dilemmas. Their commitment to a thick understanding of the rule of law demands that they show greater restraint than their less scrupulous competitors and refrain from measures that would undermine the very values they seek to uphold. However, playing by the rules may impose a competitive penalty on liberal democracies and puts them at the mercy of the weak mechanisms of the international legal system. In key areas, such as the information and cyberdomain, the content and applicability of the relevant rules of international law are uncertain. Not only does this present hostile actors

---

[61] They may also continue after hostilities have broken out: *cf.* Tom Burt, 'Ongoing Russian Cyberattacks targeting Ukraine' (*Microsoft on the Issues*, 14 June 2023) <https://blogs.microsoft.com/on-the-issues/2023/06/14/russian-cyberattacks-ukraine-cadet-blizzard/> accessed 15 June 2023.

[62] E.g. Michael N. Schmitt, 'Virtual Disenfranchisement: Cyber Election Meddling in the Grey Zones of International Law' 19 Chicago Journal of International Law 30.

with opportunities to exploit, but it is also a source of disunity among liberal democracies. The challenges in applying conventional legal categories to grey zone activity underscore the need to consider basic liberal democratic ethical principles and how they might inform the development of legal concepts that more accurately reflect the underlying concerns raised by such activity. In addition, in their attempts to reduce their vulnerability to foreign interference, liberal democracies run the risk of undermining the freedoms and liberties that they seek to preserve against outside meddling. Democratic governments must therefore tread a fine line between doing what is necessary to prevail against their geopolitical competitors, but without sacrificing the values that distinguish them from autocratic regimes in the first place.

While many of the legal and ethical challenges that arise in this area have been discussed in academic and policy debates, they are seldom examined in a systematic manner. However, a systematic assessment is essential both for developing a better understanding of the field and for devising more effective policy responses to counter the adverse effects of hybrid and grey zone conflict on liberal democracies and on the international rule of law. This volume therefore brings together thinkers from various disciplines and backgrounds to explore some of the most pressing legal and ethical questions that hybrid threats and grey zone conflict pose. In doing so, the volume has two aims. The first is to provide readers with an understanding of the key concepts, trends and dynamics at work, thus addressing the overall picture. The second is to offer a detailed analysis of certain questions of particular interest, thereby providing depth and granularity.

The majority of the contributions to this volume were first presented at three events: a workshop on *Challenging the Grey Zone: The Changing Character of Warfare and the Application of International Law* hosted by The Judge Advocate General's Legal Center and School in Charlottesville, Virginia on 3–4 April 2019; a conference on *Legal Resilience in an Era of Hybrid Threats* convened by the Exeter Centre for International Law (ECIL) at the University of Exeter in the United Kingdom on 8–10 April 2019; and a workshop-style conference on *Hybrid Threats in the Grey Zone* held by the Center for Ethics and the Rule of Law (CERL) at the University of Pennsylvania on 5–7 December 2019.[63] The events highlighted a number of recurrent themes and questions, including the absence of a consensus on how best to define hybrid threats and grey zone conflict. To capture the richness and diversity of these discussions, the book does not impose a singular definition of these terms, beyond the general observations we offered earlier. Readers of the volume will therefore find a variety of approaches and positions expressed in these pages, not all of which share the same ground

---

[63] Respectively, see <https://www.penncerl.org/conferences/greyzone/>, <https://legalresilience. co.uk/> and <https://www.penncerl.org/conferences/hybridgreyzone/> accessed 30 May 2023.

16 INTRODUCTION

or point in the same direction. Nevertheless, the individual contributions share some common assumptions.

A prominent theme running through the chapters is the idea of grey zone and hybrid competition as a phenomenon that exploits the distinctive vulnerabilities of liberal democracies and of the international legal system. Activities of this nature are aimed at avoiding a clear legal characterization, which in turn renders a decisive response more difficult. This effect may be achieved via overt or covert means; the latter create uncertainty because of the importance of attribution in determining the appropriate legal characterization of an activity and the justified responses to it.

A second unifying theme is that the concepts of hybrid threats and grey zone conflict can be seen as lenses that focus our attention on key aspects of contemporary great power rivalry and its attendant legal challenges, including the instrumental use of law for the purposes of strategic competition. The notion of hybrid threats conveys the idea that hostile activities combine kinetic and non-kinetic measures across multiple domains. Hybrid threats thus span the entire spectrum of competitive interactions, ranging from non-forcible measures to armed coercion. The grey zone construct underscores that many of the tools and tactics used for these purposes exploit ambiguity, including uncertainty over the applicable law, and are both peaceful and warlike in character. Each concept thus highlights certain features of the current security environment, with corresponding advantages and limitations, in a complementary fashion. The book's elaboration of this idea provides a useful way of clarifying the common ground between the two concepts and the legal challenges they raise. It also contributes to greater conceptual 'interoperability' and dialogue between different scholarly and policy communities that have often employed one concept in preference over the other.

A third theme of the book is that gaining greater clarity about how conduct should be characterized in legal terms requires appreciation of the basic ethical concerns that are the basis for legal categories. In other words, what are the normative commitments that legal rules are meant to express, and how are they implicated in the terrain that the volume explores? The arena of armed conflict is governed by a well-developed set of rules that reflect relatively clear ethical principles, but there is much less consensus on the norms that should govern competition outside this arena. Several chapters in the volume reflect an effort to begin the process of providing guidance for the formulation of such norms.

Finally, the book adopts a critical approach and seeks to clarify what, if any, conceptual and other benefits the concept of hybrid threats and grey zone conflict offers to legal scholars and practitioners. The analytical utility of both concepts is subject to considerable disagreement, as we noted earlier, with some commentators embracing these notions and others rejecting them as unhelpful.

INTRODUCTION   17

The book brings together authors from both camps in order to avoid reifying the hybrid threat and grey zone concepts, and to subject them, and the debates they have generated in recent years, to critical analysis.

5. Synopsis

The book is divided into four parts. The first part brings together contributions that address the conceptual foundations and core assumptions of hybrid threats and grey zone conflict. To offer a guide to the concepts and terms used throughout this volume, *Christopher Marsh* explores the phenomenon of the grey zone, distinguishing it from the related but separate notions of political warfare and hybrid conflict. The chapter pays particular attention to how these concepts relate to each other, even overlap, and yet describe discrete phenomena in the field of international relations. Whereas the grey zone refers to a competitive space between peace and open conflict, political warfare denotes to the employment of all available means short of war to achieve national objectives, while hybrid war describes the combined use of regular and irregular modes of violence. Marsh argues that hybrid warfare and grey zone conflict are useful concepts, although greater clarity in their use would be a welcome development.

Continuing this discussion, *Melanie W. Sisson* takes another look at the grey zone but arrives at different conclusions. By treating grey zone activities as a systemic threat, the concept places behaviours that run counter to the practices and norms endorsed by the United States and its allies in opposition to global order. This framing reflects and perpetuates an overly simplistic worldview, one where nonconforming behaviours that are legal are considered ethically disreputable and where the positions of the United States and allied nations are portrayed as necessary defences against grey zone violations perpetrated by their geopolitical competitors. A review of responses to sub-threshold events reveals not only that grey zone activity in the conventional military domain is infrequent, but also that the United States has neither demonstrated a consistent intolerance for specific tactics nor reliably defended an identifiable set of principles and values. This suggests that the grey zone in military affairs is neither an analytically distinct category nor a phenomenon that requires new policy solutions.

Duncan MacIntosh addresses the role of ambiguity and uncertainty, two features widely associated with hybrid threats and grey zone conflict. Taking the work of Michael Mazarr as a point of departure, his chapter relies on decision-theoretic tools to discuss problems of choice under conditions of vagueness in grey zone confrontations. Whereas the Cold War was prosecuted on the logic of strategic rationality, specifically on the presumption that the superpowers would refrain from action that would leave everyone vastly worse off, MacIntosh argues

18 INTRODUCTION

that the central decision-theoretic problem of 'grey war' is whether it is rational to form and fulfil intentions the mutual fulfilling of which would leave both parties better off than had neither ever formed them. In other words, solving grey zone problems requires cooperatively solving the Prisoner's Dilemma. The chapter offers thirteen practical recommendations on how to go about this.

To provide a primer on the legal aspects of the subject, *Hitoshi Nasu* considers how existing international law contributes to the growth of hybrid threats as a strategic choice of hostile actors, causing law-abiding States to suffer disadvantages to the detriment of their security. Nasu argues that ability of hostile actors to employ hybrid tactics and exploit the grey zone does not derive primarily from the indeterminacy of the applicable rules of international law but from the structural problems of the international legal system. These problems create room for strategic exploitation, in particular in circumstances where three conditions are present: hostile actors targeting a law-compliant State, the use of non-State proxies for hostile purposes, and reliance on advanced technological capabilities and enablers.

Building on these points, *Tobias Vestner* focuses on the dividing line between war and peace. Recognizing that the difference between these two conditions is not clear-cut either in theory or in practice, he sets out to assess how international law conceptualizes war and peace and whether the relevant rules offer more suitable guidance for distinguishing one condition from the other. Vestner finds that due to its conceptualization and evolution, modern international law does not offer much clarity on the divide. Rather, it confuses the boundaries between war and peace and conflates the two concepts, leaving a relatively broad legal grey zone of normative permissibility. While this may be beneficial to the extent that it incentivizes great powers to resort to hybrid tactics and grey zone conflict, rather than to more destructive high-intensity and full-scale wars, the normative divide between war and peace is so indeterminate that these benefits cannot be taken for granted.

Looking below the dividing line between war and peace, *Ido Kilovaty* addresses the principle of non-intervention. By prohibiting States from coercively interfering with the affairs of other States, the principle distinguishes permissible forms of foreign intervention from impermissible ones and as such is one of the most relevant and promising general principles of international law for regulating grey zone engagements. However, Kilovaty argues that socio-technological changes affecting international relations, as manifested in cyberattacks, digital election interference, or deep fakes, have seriously challenged the efficacy, relevancy, and clarity of the principle on non-intervention. He warns that the two constitutive elements of the principle—the *domaine réservé* and coercion—are becoming increasingly irrelevant in today's world. Unless States do more to adapt non-intervention to emerging forms of interference enabled by cyberspace and new technologies, the principle may be on a path of becoming irrelevant in the coming decades.

The second part of the book is devoted to key arenas of hybrid and grey zone competition. *Beba Cibralic* opens this part with a chapter on information-based foreign influence. Liberal democracies are open political communities which place relatively few restrictions on the free flow of information. This is one of their strengths, but as Cibralic notes, it also renders them vulnerable to nefarious foreign influence. In her chapter, Cibralic provides a detailed overview of the analytical terrain for understanding information-based foreign influence and its epistemic consequences, distinguishing between what she calls different 'lines of effort', such as information campaigns, psychological operations, and reflexive control, before examining the concepts of propaganda, disinformation, narratives, and mediatization in greater detail. Cibralic argues that the cacophony of terms in use for understanding foreign influence can best be conceptualized by paying attention to the basic structure underpinning them.

Melissa K. Griffith concentrates on the closely related arena of cyberspace. She argues that States face a unique defence problem in this domain, insofar as their societies are increasingly dependent on cyberspace, yet the interconnected nature of this space enables hostile actors to exert influence at lower cost and with fewer logistical challenges than those associated with conventional and historical means. As a result of this 'critical interconnectedness', cyber operations are not just a core feature of geopolitical competition but are thriving in the messy middle between war and peace, straddling the lines between crime and statecraft and between espionage and attacks. Each of these three grey zones does not just blur conceptual or theoretical distinctions, but also complicates the policy decisions available to States. Griffith suggests that grey zone cyber operations therefore differ both from historical intelligence contests and from the more episodic, open military confrontations of interstate warfare, warning that the geopolitical implications of cyber operations below the threshold should not be overlooked or understated.

Orde F. Kittrie explores grey zone conflict in the legal domain, focusing on Chinese lawfare and its implications. As Kittrie explains, the People's Republic of China is currently the world's preeminent practitioner of sophisticated and systematic lawfare in the grey zone. For example, China is using lawfare in the maritime and aviation domains to extend its control over the South China Sea and as part of a struggle with the West to predetermine which side will dominate information technology during, or on the brink of, a future conflict. By comparison, the lawfare efforts of the United States and other democratic nations tend to be less diligent and less systematic. However, this is one difference that could be remedied with relative ease: if the United States and allied nations are to prevail in the current grey zone struggle against the People's Republic of China,

20 INTRODUCTION

they must adopt comprehensive and coordinated lawfare strategies and establish cross-departmental teams to implement these.

Joseph DeFranco, Diane DiEuliis, L. R. Bremseth, and *James Giordano* assess the potential of emerging technologies to cause disruptive effects in grey zone engagements. The use of emerging technologies can be the source of substantial problems, given that initially they may not be recognized as threats, and produce effects which, while potent, may not be easily attributable. In the light of other nations' activities in this domain, the authors suggest that the grey zone deployment of emerging technologies constitutes a clear, present, and viable future threat, compounded by the fact that hostile actors with access to such means may be guided by ethical standards and practices that do not comport with the ethical systems, principles, and restrictions of the United States and its allies. For these reasons, the authors believe that it will be increasingly important to analyse, quantify, and predict how competitors and adversaries may employ specific levelling and emerging technologies in both non-kinetic and kinetic ways. To assist with this task, they suggest expanding and improving the focus of the 'predictability horizon' to better perceive the future development and use of science and technology in grey zone engagements.

The chapter by *David Letts* addresses hybrid threats in the maritime domain. Much of the focus in this field has centred on the South China Sea, but as Letts observes, that region is not the only maritime space where vagueness and uncertainty in relation to the legal characterization of a particular activity have been present. The chapter therefore takes a wider approach and examines the nature of hybrid threats that are situated in the maritime grey zone, identifying the essential components of both maritime hybrid threats and maritime grey zone operations. Based on this analysis, the chapter reviews how the law of the sea deals with such threats and operations, using case studies to illustrate the issues at hand. Letts suggests that challenges in the maritime domain increasingly derive from strategically generated vagueness and ambiguity, designed to create legal uncertainty in relation to the nature of the threat and the response to it. This, he argues, harbours the potential for the emergence of new grey zone-specific legal norms in areas of law that have hitherto been considered as predominantly sound.

Continuing with geographical arenas of competition, *Camilla T. N. Sørensen* assesses China's evolving strategy in the Arctic. The strategic and geopolitical significance of the Arctic has grown in recent years as the region's natural resources are becoming more accessible and shorter sea routes between Europe and Asia are opening up. In recognition of this development, China seeks to establish its presence and influence in the region, knitting itself into the Arctic by establishing comprehensive relationships with Arctic States. While there is a tendency to treat all Chinese activities in the Arctic as hybrid threats or grey zone tactics, including a concern that China is taking advantage of the legal and institutional setup in the region, Sørensen argues that the risks and potential vulnerabilities related to a growing Chinese engagement should not be overblown. The Arctic, and China's priorities and presence in this region, are different from the South China Sea. Nonetheless, Sørensen suggests that there is reason to follow the evolving Chinese approach in the Arctic carefully, not least because Russia's weakened position following its full-scale invasion of Ukraine may present China with new opportunities.

Looking further afield, *Melissa de Zwart* argues that outer space has emerged as a unique environment for hybrid and grey zone operations. Outer space has grown from a domain accessible only to a small group of powers to a sphere that is vital to the commercial and military interests of most States. Interference with access to space assets has the potential to cause significant disruption, as those assets are now a key enabler of many elements of civilian life and military operations. Many features of outer space, including the inherently dual-use of space technology, the high level of secrecy, and the absence of a clear consensus on important questions regarding the use of space, are a source of tensions. De Zwart suggests that recent efforts to develop norms for responsible behaviours in outer space are a step in the right direction, yet the development of such norms itself provides a forum for further contestation among key actors and it appears idealistic to believe that they may lead to the creation of binding international law.

The third part of the volume consists of chapters assessing the instruments, tactics, and methods used in hybrid and grey zone competition. *Andrés B. Muñoz Mosquera* and *Nikoleta Chalanouli* set out to decode grey zone environments by providing an overview of the instruments and actors involved. The grey zone can be understood as a space where State and non-State actors engage in competitive activities aimed at weakening their adversaries across the entire diplomatic, informational, military, economic, financial, intelligence, and legal (DIMEFIL) spectrum. Given the breadth of this spectrum, grey zone approaches essentially use all tools of statecraft available to a given actor. This means that grey zone competition can take many different forms, though the aim to keep conflict below the threshold of hybrid or conventional war dictates what instruments and tactics are best suited for a specific situation and environment. The chapter discusses some of the relevant instruments in more detail, including media and information operations, lawfare, economic and financial levers, and cyber operations. Complicating matters is the fact that the edges of the grey zone are indistinct. Since grey zone activities may be coercive, rely on military means, and may be designed to shape the kinetic battlefield, they cannot always be clearly distinguished from hybrid and conventional forms of war. To gain a more nuanced understanding of how grey zone instruments are used in practice, it is useful to study individual actors, a point the chapter illustrates by comparing the

22 INTRODUCTION

approaches taken by China, Russia, Iran, and countries in the Middle East and North Africa region.

Approaching the subject from a wider perspective, *C. Anthony Pfaff* examines how the logic and grammar of grey zone activity shapes the norms that govern it. Whereas the logic of war is to remove an adversary's ability to choose to resist, the logic of grey zone conflict, as a form of competition short of war, is to compel an adversary to make choices that benefit the other party, without removing its ability to choose. Grey zone conflict thus places a limit on escalation, and actors in this zone prefer outcomes other than escalation into open armed conflict. The implication is that as long as escalation represents the worst outcome, the normative regime of the grey zone should continually facilitate escalation avoidance in the event of a crisis. However, what makes the grey zone a unique normative challenge is that the means employed by competitors challenge established norms. Pfaff explores this point in detail with reference to four specific instruments—the use of military force, non-State actors, cyber operations, and information operations—to determine in each case what norms would support an equilibrium and avoid escalation. While grey zone norms of this kind would not necessarily achieve peaceful relations, they should give adversaries reasons to prioritize limited objectives, non-violent means, and de-escalatory measures when crises arise.

Steven Wheatley examines the role and legal status of State lying in grey zone conflicts. Russia's various efforts to annex Ukrainian territory since 2014 provide one striking example of the utility of State lying to avoid the categorization of actions as clearly unlawful. Although presently international law does not prohibit State lying, there is a body of existing laws on insincere State utterances. Wheatley argues that we should extend this law to include lying by States in situations where States are coordinating plans of action, in other words when they are deciding how to act and react. Accordingly, where a State asserts the truth of some proposition, in circumstances where it is clear that the State expected to be believed, the addressee States would be entitled to act on the presumption that the State meant what it said. The rule would apply in grey zone conflicts where the State clearly intimated that it should be believed and that other States should rely on the utterance. In these circumstances, the State moves itself from a position of strategic interaction to good faith obligation.

On a related note, *Steven J. Barela* and *Samuli Haataja* discuss disinformation operations conducted across international borders, in particular operations involving election interference. Cross-border meddling in the internal affairs of States in the form of disinformation operations has become broad, deep, and precise. Barela and Haataja turn to the principle of non-intervention as the most relevant norm for determining the legality of such activities in hybrid and grey zone settings. Relying on the theoretical frameworks surrounding legitimacy and on information ethics, they develop a novel way to understand the concept of the *domaine réservé*, the domain which must be affected by coercion for the non-intervention principle to be violated. Based on this, they argue that the conferral and exercise of public power, and the operation of election processes as part of the proper functioning of the State as an information entity, should fall within this reserved domain. They also suggest that a broader approach to the element of coercion is required, one that considers the breadth, depth, and precision of hostile cyber operations.

Agata Kleczkowska reviews the rules of international law applicable to non-State actors. Non-State actors may engage in hybrid and grey zone conflict either independently in their own right or by acting on behalf of States. In the latter scenario, relying on non-State actors allows States to deploy a wider range of tactics than would otherwise be the case. As Kleczkowska explains, from a legal perspective, the involvement of non-State actors in hybrid and grey zone engagements falls within a grey zone of international law. This is so because few rules of international law are applicable specifically to non-State actors, while attributing their actions for the purposes of State responsibility is often impeded by the covert character of their cooperation with the patron State. The chapter argues that this lack of clarity is convenient for States, which have no real interest in equipping non-State actors with rights and obligations under international law. This is unlikely to change any time soon, meaning that the use of proxies will remain an attractive instrument of hybrid and grey zone competition.

Tyler Wentzell and *Barbara J. Falk* offer an assessment of the weaponization of dissent and civil society. They suggest that the sophistication and degree of Russian meddling overseas and in its near abroad is often overestimated, though this is not a new development. Russia has a long history of weaponizing dissent in the West, and the West has a long history of overestimating the extent and efficacy of Russia's interference. Indeed, taking a historical perspective reminds us that during the Cold War, the West also weaponized dissent, for example, by supporting the *Solidarność* (Solidarity) movement in Poland in the 1980s. By using intermediaries in this way, States trade deniability for control, making it difficult and at times impossible to determine who initiated such grey zone action. While apathy and inaction to foreign influence carry risks, seeing connections where none exist and overreacting does too. Wentzell and Falk suggest that in some of the historical examples they discuss, the States involved might have better countered foreign influence, both real and perceived, by strengthening civil society and pursuing reforms. The examples also suggest that perceptions of grey zone activity are often shaped by the moral assessments of an actor.

Finally, *Maegen Nix* and *Welton Chang* review the use of military and paramilitary means to develop a framework for assessing the military dimension of the grey zone. The absence of agreed standards for assessing military grey zone

24 INTRODUCTION

operations increases the probability that States will overlook triggers in the lead-up to conventional conflict. The lack of such standards also increases the risk of escalation to violent conflict, due to the absence of clear signalling of threatening intent. In their chapter, Nix and Chang distil and categorize the military activities of Russia, Iran, and the United States to provide an analytic framework that illuminates State use of military capabilities as part of grey zone operations. Their analysis shows that each of these three State leverages military assets, but also that significant differences exist in the methods employed and the objectives pursued. This furnishes important insights into future operational challenges, strengths, and weaknesses in global competition and puts into doubt the idea that the use of military instruments to conduct grey zone operations has to be small scale or surgical or has to have a narrow impact.

The fourth part of the volume focuses on the ethical, legal, and practical considerations that liberal democracies face in their efforts to counter hybrid and grey zone threats. To provide general context, *Edward Barrett* develops a rights-based framework consistent with liberal commitments to identify ethically permissible responses to hybrid and grey zone threats. Although the well-developed just war tradition may not seem applicable in the grey zone between war and peace, the tradition's core ethical principles can nevertheless offer guidance on what harm may be justified when responding to such threats. There are at least three grounds for justifying harm caused in defence against prior grey zone activities: attaining a lesser evil, consent by the harmed, and rights forfeiture. Barrett suggests that out of these three, a rights forfeiture justification is the most relevant. This stipulates that intentional defensive harm is justified only if an attacker has forfeited the rights affected by such harm through their wrongdoing and thereby becomes liable to suffer the defensive harm. The conditions for such liability are the same regardless of whether defensive harm is caused in response to lethal or to sub-lethal threats. However, given the international context, Barrett argues that harm in response to sub-lethal threats may be justified not just for narrow defensive ends but also for punitive reasons and against indirect participants.

Building on these points, *Michael A. Newton* argues that liberal democracies should engage in grey zone competition with renewed vigour to win at the 'strategic seams'. For Newton, the goal of international law should be to reinforce human dignity, global stability, and societal welfare. Hostile grey zone actors seek to neuter this overarching purpose of international law. The enemies of Western interests and institutions regularly appeal to accepted moral and legal norms to create barriers to the realization and defence of the values those norms are meant to safeguard. For example, China's salami slicing tactics in the South China Sea and its invocation of sovereignty mask efforts to undermine the sovereign rights of other States and stability in the Indo-Pacific region. In response, Newton calls on liberal democracies to be staunch defenders of the integrity of the law as applied in defence of human rights, freedoms, and international order. They should be proud and unafraid of their fellowship in preserving hopes for a free and peaceful world. Western States and their allies must also be more conscious of coordinating efforts and diplomacy in order to enhance deterrence and permit decisive action when necessary. This includes strengthening their legal interoperability. They may draw inspiration from the principles of war, for instance to preserve broad rights of individual and collective self-defence, and from other principles such as the 'clean hands doctrine', to prevent proponents of grey zone tactics benefitting from their misconduct.

Aurel Sari explores the utility of resilience thinking at the intersection between international law and contemporary security threats, asking how the notion of resilience may benefit liberal democracies in their efforts to address the legal challenges associated with hybrid threats and grey zone conflict. To answer this question, the chapter reviews the key features of resilience thinking and its reception in legal doctrine, arriving at a definition of legal resilience as the capacity of a legal system, first, to resist, recover from, and adapt to internal and external disturbances while maintaining its key features, and second, to contribute to the resilience of other natural or social systems. Understood in this way, Sari suggests that legal resilience can serve as an analytical tool and as a policy agenda for reinforcing the ability of legal systems to cope with the challenges posed by hybrid and grey zone tactics. For example, a legal resilience perspective can contribute to a better understanding of legal vulnerabilities. Most importantly, it provides an opportunity to develop and implement more robust legal policies by integrating legal considerations into other policy planning processes. The chapter argues that States and international organizations may realize these benefits by developing individual and collective legal resilience strategies, a new type of policy instrument.

Turning to the practical dimension of countering hostile activities, *Elizabeth Braw* writes on how liberal democracies may involve their civil society in defending against grey zone threats. Grey zone aggression is difficult to predict, which makes it challenging to design and implement measures that deter hostile actors through punishment. Consequently, deterrence by denial is even more important in this context than it is in defence against traditional military threats. Since civil society is a prominent target of hybrid and grey zone threats, the defence against such threats and deterrence signalling must likewise involve civil society. Braw suggests that such involvement can take place in several ways, for example, through voluntary citizen participation in schemes ranging from public-awareness campaigns to information-literacy courses and crisis-response training. However, to obtain society-wide benefits, such training must include participants' subsequent insertion into the command-and-control structure of

26   INTRODUCTION

a national crisis response. There is also considerable potential for involving the private sector in grey zone defence and deterrence, not least because it is in the interest of actors in the private sector to protect themselves against grey zone threats.

Mitt Regan and *Sarah Harrison* consider the challenges that liberal democracies face in providing security assistance to other States, specifically the difficulties that arise when cooperating with regimes that do not conform to liberal democratic principles. Providing security assistance to partner nations can extend donor State influence while avoiding direct intervention and confrontation with adversaries. As such, it has the potential to serve as an effective instrument of competition in the grey zone. However, liberal democracies encounter challenges in ensuring that security assistance effectively meets their security needs in ways that are consistent with liberal democratic values. Navigating these challenges requires that States be sensitive to the practical demands of enhancing partner State capabilities, and the values that may be in tension as they attempt to do so. Regan and Harrison offer a framework for identifying these challenges and appreciating the trade-offs that they may require, referring to the US experience to illustrate the difficulties involved.

Marlene Mazel shares a practitioners' perspective from Israel on the use of law for strategic purposes in national and international legal fora. Mazel notes that there has been an increase over the past two decades in the use of legal institutions and mechanisms to achieve tactical and strategic goals in what is often termed 'lawfare'. Reliance on legal strategies is becoming an integral part of conflict, leading Israel and other States to broaden their understanding and expertise in this arena. Against this background, the chapter describes some of the operational legal tools and strategies used against Israel and Israeli officials, and outlines some of the measures that the Israeli government has taken in response. To illustrate these points, it offers an account of the 31 May 2010 maritime incident as a case study and shares insights regarding how States and organizations can increase and strengthen their capacity and resilience in the legal domain. The experience of Israel and that of other States and organizations in this arena suggests that a failure to take heed of the growing practice of using legal tactics is unwise. If hostile actors treat law as a tool of strategic importance, democratic States must proactively respond, including by increasing national capacity.

Tiina Ferm writes on legal resilience from the perspective of a practitioner from Finland. Following Russia's aggression against Ukraine, the security environment of Finland has deteriorated dramatically. This required strengthening Finland's security and resilience on a fast schedule, including enhancing the country's preparedness to respond to hybrid threats. The chapter reviews the steps that Finland has taken to this end in the legal domain. Although security and the protection of fundamental rights should not be conflicting aims, certain

INTRODUCTION 27

forms of hybrid threats and malign influencing demand innovative solutions in a country governed by the rule of law such as Finland. Ferm explains this point by reviewing some of the most significant legislative amendments made in recent years, including to the Emergency Powers Act and the Border Guard Act. Resilience is at the heart of the Finnish approach to safeguarding functions vital to society, which includes ensuring the legality of the actions the security authorities may take in response to crises and emergency conditions, to preserve high levels of trust among the population.

Offering another perspective from practice, *Andrés B. Muñoz Mosquera, Jean Emmanuel Perrin, Panagiotis Sergis, Rodrigo Vázquez Benítez*, and *Borja Montes Toscano* explain the path to legal resilience taken by the Office of Legal Affairs at NATO's Allied Command Operations. The authors suggest that at its core, legal resilience is concerned with defending the rules-based international order against threats emanating from malign revisionists actors. To put this idea into practice, the Office developed its own terminology and processes centred around the notion of 'legal operations', defined broadly as the use of law as an instrument of power. Key to the conduct of legal operations in an alliance context is enhancing legal interoperability among member nations, which requires adopting the same, or at least mutually compatible, legal regimes and understandings. To further operationalization of the notion of legal operations, the Office of Legal Affairs developed a set of criteria to identify hostile legal actions, focusing on their intent, the instruments employed, and the impact on the target, all assessed with the help of a matrix. As the authors explain, the Office has also undertaken work on how legal information is collected with the aim of identifying hostile legal actions; the establishment of means for seeking legal information in certain clearly identified areas of interest; the inclusion of legal operations in the operational planning process; and the development of appropriate training programmes. The aim of these efforts is to enhance the ability of NATO and its Member States to defend themselves against hostile actions in the legal field, while respecting their own legal obligations and the international rule of law and thus, ultimately, to reinforce the rule of law in the face of hostile activities that disregard, debase, or abuse it.

I

WHAT ARE HYBRID THREATS AND GREY ZONE CONFLICT?

2
The Grey Zone and Hybrid Conflict
A Conceptual Introduction

Christopher Marsh

1. Introduction

According to the United Nations Charter, all signatories agree to refrain from the threat or use of force against the territorial integrity or political independence of any State. This is the famous Article 2(4) of the Charter that defines war as it is traditionally known. Violating a State's territorial integrity or political independence, therefore, is what war ostensibly looks like. If that is the case, some would argue that war is obsolescent or at least on the decline.[1] To be precise, the definition of war being used to identify a decline in war is that of 'an armed conflict between governments (in the case of international wars) or between a government and an at least somewhat organized domestic armed group (for civil wars) in which at least 1,000 people are killed each year as a direct consequence' of fighting.[2] But what about armed conflicts that do not meet the threshold of a thousand battlefield deaths per year? How are we to conceptualize of those conflicts, the so-called small wars?[3] And what about non-kinetic but malign activity by both State and non-State actors that seek to affect and impact other actors in the international system?

Enter, the 'grey zone', a concept that aims to define and describe the murky waters between war and not war (but not necessarily equating to peace). The grey zone is an environment in the greater global competitive space that is short of war but where tensions may be extremely high—and war may even be imminent

---

[1] John Mueller, *Retreat from Doomsday: The Obsolescence of Major War* (Basic Books 1989), and John Mueller, 'War Has Almost Ceased to Exist: An Assessment' (2009) 124 Political Science Quarterly 297. See also Nils Petter Gleditsch et al, 'The Decline of War' (2013) 15 International Studies Review 396.

[2] Mueller (2009) (n 1) 298. This definition, which is commonly used throughout the scholarship on war, comes from J. David Singer and Melvin Small, *The Wages of War 1816–1965: A Statistical Handbook* (Wiley 1972).

[3] Charles E. Callwell, *Small Wars: Their Principles and Practice* (Macmillan 1906). See also Christopher Daase and James W. Davis (eds), *Clausewitz on Small War* (OUP 2016); Sibylle Scheipers, 'Counterinsurgency or Irregular Warfare? Historiography and the Study of "Small Wars"' (2014) 25 Small Wars and Insurgencies 879.

Christopher Marsh, *The Grey Zone and Hybrid Conflict* In: *Hybrid Threats and Grey Zone Conflict*. Edited by: Mitt Regan and Aurel Sari, Oxford University Press. © Oxford University Press 2024. DOI: 10.1093/oso/9780197744772.003.0002

32 WHAT ARE HYBRID THREATS AND GREY ZONE CONFLICT?

but not yet quite triggered. It typically involves such non-kinetic activities as training separatists or resistance fighters, conducting 'active measures' (malign activities aimed at promoting disinformation), cyberattacks, and the like.[4] As Kapusta observes in what is probably the first scholarly attempt[5] to articulate the grey zone as a concept, 'adversaries can use ambiguity to avoid accountability for their actions'. In that same 2015 article in *Special Warfare*, moreover, Kapusta argued that irredentist States such as Russia 'typically choose to work in the grey zone precisely because they want to avoid full-scale war and its potential to trigger an overwhelming U.S. military response'.[6]

In this chapter, I seek to explore this phenomenon, including the concepts of political warfare and hybrid threats/conflict. In so doing, I pay particular attention to how these concepts relate to each other, overlap, and yet describe discrete phenomena in the competitive realm of international relations. This chapter begins with an attempt to identify the grey zone and then explore the Russian and Chinese use (or lack thereof) of such concepts. It then continues by seeking to define hybrid threats and distinguishing between the two concepts. Next, the concept of political warfare is explored as a possible replacement for the concept of the grey zone, though it is ultimately shown that the two terms are distinct and 'political warfare' as a term is problematic. Finally, the chapter offers a conclusion in which the author argues for greater clarity in the use of the terms yet believes that essentially the grey zone remains a useful concept and that hybrid conflicts are distinct from grey zone activities. This conclusion is offered to the reader as a guide for understanding concepts and terminology in subsequent chapters in this volume and elsewhere.

2. War and peace: the space in between

While the concept of the grey zone is seemingly quite useful, it is not without its weaknesses or detractors. For one, is there ever really peace in the international system? From drug wars and non-State actors trafficking in humans to the military application of information as an instrument of war, there is a vast expanse between 'peace' and 'war' that is far from pleasant and harmonious. One would do well to remember the words of former US President Ronald Reagan, who pointed out that 'peace is not absence of conflict', but rather 'it is the ability

---

[4] Thomas Rid, *Active Measures: The Secret History of Disinformation and Political Warfare* (Picador 2020). One would do well to read the seminal work on the subject: Richard H. Shultz and Roy Godson, *Dezinformatsia: Active Measures in Soviet Strategy* (Pergamon-Brassey's 1984).

[5] The first attempt to put in writing a description of the grey zone was a White Paper put out by the United States Special Operations Command (USSOCOM) J5, simply titled 'Grey Zone Paper', in 2015, prior to Philip Kapusta, 'The Gray Zone' (2015) 28 Special Warfare 23.

[6] Ibid. 23.

to handle conflict by peaceful means'.[7] This may be a very realist account of international relations and the human condition, but insofar as it helps explain the phenomenon at hand, it is a useful way of looking at things.

Additionally, human history is in many ways the history of conflict, with the ever-changing character of war (but not its nature, as Clausewitz pointed out),[8] evolving as the tools at our disposal lead to novel ways to kill each other. What value is the nuance between the terminology used if conflict is so prevalent throughout human civilization? In fact, such a distinction between war and peace and recognition of the competitive space in between is critical from the standpoint of international law and the web of international treaties that are in place to break this pattern of human history, as the many chapters in this volume illustrate.

As the United States and the West deal with 'strategic competitors', seeing the world through the lens of Great Power Competition, the grey zone retains great utility and helps explain the contemporary operational and strategic environments and the nature of contemporary conflict. The grey zone is a valuable conceptual tool that needs to be kept in the toolkit of concepts of military planners and analysts since it helps explain and articulate the contemporary global operating environment, particularly in Russia's near abroad, in the Russian War in Ukraine, and in the South China Sea and the Taiwan Strait.

Despite its recent entry into the lexicon of those who study war, the concept of the grey zone is not novel. In fact, it was the Cold War battleground in which the United States and the Soviet Union waged rival unconventional campaigns against each other. Calling it new neglects how the United States, Canada, and the rest of the North Atlantic Treaty Organization (NATO) previously organized to wage unconventional campaigns in the grey zone during the Cold War.[9] Nevertheless, the term itself is a recent creation and we are seeing frequent activities that meet this description.

Conventional and grey zone conflicts have similar ends. To paraphrase Clausewitz, in both cases the aim is to achieve political objectives by compelling an opponent to fulfil one's will.[10] While grey zone conflicts and conventional wars share similar ends, they achieve these ends via divergent ways and means. Specifically, grey zone conflicts tend to use multiple instruments of power. While this is often true of conventional conflicts as well, the relative weight of

---

[7] Ronald Reagan, 'Commencement Address', Eureka College (9 May 1982) <https://www.reaganfoundation.org/ronald-reagan/reagan-quotes-speeches/commencement-address-eureka-college/> accessed 11 March 2023.

[8] Carl von Clausewitz, *On War* (Michael Howard and Peter Paret trs, Princeton University Press 1976).

[9] David Oakley, 'Organizing for the "Grey Zone" Fight: Early Cold War Realities and the CIA's Directorate of Operations' (2019) 30 Small Wars and Insurgencies 62.

[10] von Clausewitz (n 8) 90.

the military instrument of power versus diplomatic, information, economic, financial, intelligence, and law enforcement (DIMEFIL) is reversed, with these latter instruments being utilized far more extensively than the military one in grey zone conflicts. Beyond favouring different instruments of power, grey zone conflicts seek to stay below the threshold of large-scale direct military conflict. This often involves efforts to increase ambiguity and obscure attribution.

Two additional clarifications warrant brief discussion. First, scholars have correctly recognized that the utility of the concept is severely diminished if grey zone conflict becomes a catchall for irregular warfare writ large.[11] Irregular warfare (IW) is the 'struggle among State and non-State actors for legitimacy and influence over the relevant population(s)',[12] and draws upon the special operations and conventional force missions of foreign internal defence (FID), counterinsurgency (COIN), counterterrorism (CT), unconventional warfare (UW), and stability operations to counter the IW activities of our adversaries.

IW techniques are often used in the grey zone, but the two terms are not synonymous. To this end, Michael J. Mazarr has attempted to bound the scope of grey zone conflict to clashes with limited aims that are moderately revisionist of the international order.[13] Second, belligerents adopting grey zone approaches do not do so because they are incapable of conventional conflict but because they perceive grey zone operations as a less costly and less risky way of achieving their desired ends. For example, in Ukraine in 2014, Russia tried to achieve its ends at lower cost and lower risk[14] through grey zone tactics and avoided a conventional invasion for many years before the 24 February 2022 full-scale invasion.[15]

As mentioned earlier, the grey zone is an environment in the greater global competitive space that is short of war but where tensions may be extremely high. It typically relies upon non-kinetic activities, such as training separatists, resistance fighters, and even cyber operations. As Kapusta observed in his *Special Warfare* article, 'Traditional war might be the dominant paradigm of warfare, but grey zone challenges are the norm.'[16] That is, when we think of what war looks like we tend to think of World War I and World War II—examples of large-scale, multi-domain military campaigns. But in fact, history is replete with many

---

[11] See, for example, Christopher Paul, 'Confessions of a Hybrid Warfare Skeptic', Small Wars Journal (3 March 2016) <https://smallwarsjournal.com/jrnl/art/confessions-of-a-hybrid-warfare-skeptic> accessed 11 March 2023.

[12] David Ucko and Tom Marks, *Redefining Irregular Warfare* (Modern War Institute at West Point 2022).

[13] Michael Mazarr, *Mastering the Grey Zone: Understanding a Changing Era of Conflict* (US Army War College Press 2016) 55.

[14] Christopher Marsh, 'Russian Risk, Hybrid Warfare, and the Gray Zone', in Bernd Horn (ed), *Risk: SOF Case Studies* (Canadian Special Operations Forces Command 2020) 317.

[15] On this point, see section 4.

[16] Kapusta (n 8) 22.

more examples of conflicts that simmer below this level of armed conflict (i.e. grey zone conflicts).

Many hoped that things would be different. After World War II, the states of the world came together to build institutions and treaty networks that would make that war truly a 'war to end all wars'. Such action was necessary with the advent and inevitable proliferation of nuclear weapons, which raised the lethality of war immeasurably. The result was the formation of the United Nations and in particular the inclusion of Article 2(4) of the UN Charter, which prohibits 'the threat or use of force against the territorial integrity or political independence of any State, or in any other manner inconsistent with the Purposes of the United Nations'.[17] This article attempted to give the world a 'red-line' that, once crossed, would trigger common-defence alliances to kick in, preventing aggression from succeeding, and hence deterring aggressive State actors from resorting to the use of force in the first place.

The results of these efforts have been mixed at best. As the late great military strategist Colin Gray put it in *Another Bloody Century*, the world is just as dangerous a place as it's ever been.[18] Trying to avoid 'another bloody century' has been the goal and strategic objective of the world's democratic states, led by the United States, Canada, and their NATO allies. Unfortunately, authoritarian states such as Russia and China have had other objectives on their agendas.

Very shortly after becoming the president of the United States in 2021, Joseph Biden and his national security team issued the Interim National Security Strategic Guidance (INSSG). The 2021 INSSG emphasized 'strategic competition', and added that 'strategic competition does not, and should not, preclude working with China when it is in our national interest to do so'. But as Bilms puts it, 'grey is here to stay' in the INSSG, meaning the grey zone will remain the main competitive space for as long as the United States maintains conventional overmatch, and for as long as America's adversaries seek to pursue incompatible interests, whether by triggering a war against the United States and NATO or not.[19]

Understanding the contemporary operating environment and the modes of engagement within it are critical to the West's maintaining its military primacy. Yet conflict has seemingly changed since the end of the Cold War, where two superpowers stood head-to-head in a stand-off only tempered by nuclear weapons and the amazing amount of destruction a nuclear strike would have

---

[17] Charter of the United Nations, 26 June 1945.

[18] Colin Gray, *Another Bloody Century: Future Warfare* (Phoenix 2005).

[19] Kevin Bilms, 'Grey Is Here to Stay: Principles from the Interim National Security Strategic Guidance on Competing in the Grey Zone' (Modern War Institute at West Point, 25 March 2021) <https://mwi.usma.edu/gray-is-here-to-stay-principles-from-the-interim-national-security-strategic-guidance-on-competing-in-the-gray-zone/> accessed 11 March 2023.

wrought should the two have ever come to blows directly. Of course, each side engaged in proxy wars, with the United States facing a resilient unconventional force in Vietnam and then the Soviet Union getting bogged down in Afghanistan. Some have argued that these unconventional wars have existed since warfare itself, with war among the great powers being a more modern manifestation of war.[20]

3. Is grey here to stay?

The concept of the grey zone to describe the competitive space between peace and all-out war is losing its popularity among many—particularly in the US Department of Defense, coming to be replaced by the phrase 'competition short of armed conflict'.[21] From such a view, in the contemporary global competitive space we are dealing with 'competitors' not 'adversaries', with the phrase drawing a cognitive line between competition and warfare where one does not exist. As Russian Chief of the General Staff Valery Gerasimov phrased it in a much-cited 2013 article, today 'wars are no longer declared and, having begun, proceed according to an unfamiliar template'.[22] This is not such a novel idea, actually. To realist international relations theorists (and practitioners), there never really is peace in the international system, only temporary cessations in fighting, which do not necessarily equate with peace. Conflict, therefore, is a permanent characteristic of the international system and the best we can hope for is to resolve conflicts short of large-scale war.

But today we are seeing intense conflict in which the belligerents are seeking to keep the level of violence below the level of armed conflict. Instead, States such as China use a multitude of activities and operations that must be considered bellicose but yet are designed to not trigger a military response, or in the case of NATO, a response under Article 5 of the North Atlantic Treaty. Russia, for its part, used the grey zone, active measures, and Soviet-era *maskirovka* ('camouflage', or deception operations) to persistently deny that it was preparing to invade Ukraine in the winter of 2022—persistently denying that its military buildup along its neighbour's border was a precursor to war all the way up until

---

[20] John Arquilla, 'Perils of the Gray Zone: Paradigms Lost, Paradoxes Regained' (2018) 7 PRISM 119.

[21] US Department of Defense, 'Joint Concept for Integrated Campaigning' (Department of Defense 2018).

[22] Valery Gerasimov, 'The Value of Science Is in the Foresight: New Challenges Demand Rethinking the Forms and Methods of Carrying Out Combat Operations' [2016] Military Review (January–February) 23, 24. Originally published as 'Tsennosti nauki v privedenie: Novyye vyzovy trebuyut pereosmysleniya form i sposobov vedeniya boyevykh deystviy', in *Voyenno-Promyshlennyy Kurier* (27 February 2013).

the day it did in fact invade—at which point it did not declare war but rather stated that Russian forces were engaged in a 'special military operation', as if that somehow changed the circumstances on the ground.

The concept of the grey zone is not without its weaknesses. But when it comes to certain geographical environments, such as Eastern Europe, the concept of the grey zone retains great utility. It could even be said that such States live in the grey zone. These are physical spaces where the competition is high and conflict may be playing itself out, if not imminent. While not necessarily a physical space per se, when it comes to Russia's near abroad and the hybrid warfare environment there, the concept seems to have a strong geographical dimension. This is a physical space over which Russia seeks a veto power, and appears to be using grey zone tactics to further its strategic objectives. For Russia, operating in the grey zone is also a way of mitigating risk. If Moscow can keep its actions—and those of its proxies—short of war, and engage in persistent denial, then the risk is low that they will be retaliated against or their actions even responded to. In short, operating in the grey zone is part of Russia's risk calculus.[23]

Grey zone conflict is best understood as an activity that is coercive and aggressive in nature, but that is deliberately designed to remain below the threshold of conventional military response and open interstate war. Grey zone approaches are said to be mostly the province of revisionist powers—those actors that seek to modify some aspect of the existing international order—and the goal is to reap gains, whether territorial or otherwise, that are normally associated with victory in war. Yet the West—particularly the United States—engages in covert and clandestine operations that are nearly indistinguishable from grey zone activities. What separates the two from each other? Simply the nature of the regime that is engaged in it or the objectives being sought?

Grey zone approaches are meant to achieve gains without escalating to overt warfare, without crossing established red-lines, and thus without exposing the practitioner to the penalties and risks that such escalation might bring.[24] Those risks are military responses by the West, which justifies its actions and resorting to military force based upon the international law of armed conflict.

Kapusta has argued that some level of aggression is a key determinant in shifting a challenge from the white zone of peacetime competition into the grey zone.[25] But in a world where cyber and other activities are hard to attribute to a specific malign actor, attributing aggression can be problematic. But this does not mean that the activity is not occurring in the grey zone. As a status quo power, the United States seeks to address disputes through diplomacy, but as a

---

[23] Marsh (n 14) 317.

[24] Hal Brands, 'Paradoxes of the Gray Zone' (*Foreign Policy Research Institute*, 5 February 2016) <https://www.fpri.org/article/2016/02/paradoxes-gray-zone/> accessed 21 December 2022

[25] Interview with the author, 1 November 2022, Tampa, Florida, USA.

realist power it has also always reserved the right to take military action to defend its interests, even acting upon that reservation despite multinational pressure to the contrary. Established laws, policies, authorities, and mechanisms are supposed to be used to arbitrate disagreements in peacetime.[26] But again, what of covert and clandestine operations? While perhaps conducted under the proper authorities according to US law, covert and clandestine operations may violate the international law of armed conflict and most certainly violate the sovereignty of the nation that is the target of covert and clandestine operations. But from an ethical perspective, they may still be the right thing to do. Since the West engages in covert activities, dare we say that it is also active in the grey zone?

4. Russian and Chinese operations in light of the grey zone

Mazarr writes that the defining features of grey zone conflict are that it is moderately but not radically revisionist in intent (in other words, its practitioners want to modify the international system rather than destroy it), that it is gradualist and coercive in nature, and that it is unconventional in the tools it employs.[27] And as I have argued previously, Russia chooses to operate in the grey zone as a way to mitigate risk.[28] The Russian military, however, does not use the term 'grey zone' at all and only uses the term 'hybrid warfare' in reference to US operations. Instead, they use the phrase 'indirect and asymmetric methods' and 'new generation warfare'.[29] Nevertheless, the environment the grey zone concept is meant to describe is certainly being identified by Russian military leaders. As Russian Chief of the General Staff Valery Gerasimov phrases it, 'In the twenty-first century we have seen a tendency toward blurring the lines between the states of war and peace. Wars are no longer declared and, having begun, proceed according to an unfamiliar template.'[30] Gerasimov—who penned these words prior to the Western concept of the grey zone being coined—is clearly identifying what the USSOCOM grey zone paper and Kapusta were intending to define as the grey zone.

Upon its invasion of Ukraine in February 2022, the threshold of 'actions below the level of armed conflict' was crossed—dramatically. Does this mean the concept of the grey zone is worthless or of no consequence? I would argue that quite

---

[26] Kapusta (n 8) 21.

[27] Mazarr (n 17). See also Michael Mazarr, 'Struggle in the Grey Zone and World Order' (*War on the Rocks*, 22 December 2015) <https://warontherocks.com/2015/12/struggle-in-the-gray-zone-and-world-order/> accessed 11 March 2023.

[28] Marsh (n 14).

[29] Charles Bartles, 'Russia's Indirect and Asymmetric Methods as a Response to the New Western Way of War' (2016) 2 Special Operations Journal 1.

[30] Gerasimov (n 22) 23.

the opposite is true. It appears that Russian military planners and even perhaps Putin himself used our belief in the grey zone against us, or at least tried to do so. Until January 2022, the West was not taking a Russian invasion of its neighbour very seriously. When the intelligence became too strong to deny the prospect of an imminent invasion any longer, Ukrainian President Volodymyr Zelenskyy came out publicly and—after thanking the United States for its help—declared that they rely upon their own intelligence, suggesting that they were hoping to not trigger the Kremlin into an invasion. Following the invasion and the massacre at Bucha, Zelenskyy suggested in a speech on 3 April that Ukraine lives 'in the grey zone', showing the impact that Western, and in particular American, military education and training have had on the Ukrainian defence and military establishment.

For its part, China also engages in grey zone activities, in this case in the South China Sea and in its interactions with the 'renegade province' of Taiwan. According to two scholars from the US Air Force's China Aerospace Studies Institute, this is a huge mistake. While Chinese President Xi Jinping believes in and likely mandates that the Chinese military use force in accordance with a concept Xi refers to as the 'peacetime employment of military force' (和平时期军事力量运用), Lee and Clay implore their readers to not use the term 'grey zone' in trying to understand Chinese actions short of military conflict.[31] The authors argue that the concept of the 'peacetime employment of military force' (which guides the People's Liberation Army to use force to prevent adversaries from reaching China's 'bottom line') is being used by Western defence analysts to explore what the West calls China's 'grey zone' operations—but that China does not have a 'grey zone' military strategy. If this brief chapter has accomplished anything, hopefully it is that the grey zone is not a strategy but a realm of operations below the threshold of large-scale conflict. As Lee and Clay argue in this very piece, there is a 'gap' on the Chinese use-of-force spectrum between small-scale skirmishes and something as large as a battle to retake Taiwan. What is that if not a grey zone? Again, I am not suggesting that China's strategy and operational concepts include a grey zone, but their activities—from maritime militias to island terraforming in the South China Sea certainly seem to be occurring in this 'non-existent' grey zone.

Coupled with persistent denial, the ambiguity of the grey zone gives Russia and China and their proxies the ability to act without provoking a direct and potentially overwhelming US military response, such as the West's arms supplies to Ukraine during the current Russian war there. The grey zone is a valuable

---

[31] Roderick Lee and Marcus Clay, 'Don't Call It a Gray Zone: China's Use-of-Force Spectrum' (*War on the Rocks*, 9 May 2022) <https://warontherocks.com/2022/05/dont-call-it-a-gray-zone-chinas-use-of-force-spectrum/> accessed 11 March 2023.

concept for describing Russian and Chinese military strategy and it is distinct from—though closely related to—the concept of political warfare.

5. The grey zone vs political warfare

While the grey zone refers to a competitive space between war and open conflict, as Votel et al point out, the methods for engaging adversaries in that environment have much in common with the political warfare that was predominant during the Cold War. As they define it, political warfare 'is played out in that space between diplomacy and open warfare, where traditional statecraft is inadequate or ineffective and large-scale conventional military options are not suitable or are deemed inappropriate for a variety of reasons'.[32] George Kennan, the State Department official widely accredited with coining the notion, defined political warfare as 'the employment of all the means at a nation's command, short of war, to achieve its national objectives', including overt measures such as white propaganda, political alliances, and economic programs, to 'such covert operations as clandestine support of "friendly" foreign elements, "black" psychological warfare, and even encouragement of underground resistance in hostile States'.[33] This is very much what the Russians refer to as support to 'colour revolutions', and they see US orchestration behind them whether it is there or not.

Other scholars, such as retired Lt Col Frank Hoffman, see the term as useless, if not outright misleading. As he states, words 'have meaning (or should), and I find the term imprecise—if not redundant—in one important sense: if all wars are political in their purpose (as the famous Prussian soldier-scholar Carl von Clausewitz insisted), what is different about this phenomenon?' Moreover, the term 'warfare' has been used by military scholars to address the 'physical conduct of war or the fighting and violent aspects of war. But there is no violence or lethal force in the kinds of political activity Kennan listed'. There is no 'warfare as we know it in these political and economic activities, which is why the term is an oxymoron'.[34]

Hoffman does not stop there, but points out that Kennan's definition of political warfare in its most simple form is 'the employment of all the means at a nation's command, short of war, to achieve its national objectives'. Directly relevant to our discussion here, Hoffman suggests that by limiting the concept of

---

[32] Joseph Votel et al, 'Unconventional Warfare in the Gray Zone' (2016) 80 Joint Force Quarterly 102.

[33] George Kennan, 'Policy Planning Staff Memorandum', US Department of State (4 May 1948) <https://history.state.gov/historicaldocuments/frus1945-50Intel/d269> accessed 11 March 2023.

[34] Frank Hoffman, 'On Not-So-New Warfare: Political Warfare vs Hybrid Threats' (*War on the Rocks*, 28 June 2014) <https://warontherocks.com/2014/07/on-not-so-new-warfare-political-warfare-vs-hybrid-threats/> accessed 11 March 2023.

political warfare to contexts 'short of war', by definition it cannot be warfare. Additionally, it remains unclear to Hoffman and the author whether or not the activities Kennan listed are things one does only short of war. Many of the activities cited by Kennan (propaganda, sanctions, subversion, etc) do not stop when a war officially begins. 'So', Hoffman concludes, 'both sides of this term are resistant to common understanding and the definition defies logic'.[35]

Putting aside the problems associated with 'political warfare' as a term, research does seem to indicate that something like this phenomenon exists. A recent study of political warfare by a group of scholars from RAND argues that the United States today faces a number of actors who employ a wide range of political, informational, military, and economic measures to influence, coerce, intimidate, or undermine US interests or those of friends and allies; many of these measures are often collectively referred to as 'political warfare'.[36] The study found that during the Cold War a range of practices across the diplomatic, informational, economic, and military (DIME) spectrum that fell short of conventional war but effectively advanced the actor's objectives were documented. Indeed, the team of researchers found that both State and non-State actors currently pursue their aims through a robust and diverse set of largely non-kinetic means, used to effectively destabilize, subvert, coerce, and co-opt adversaries. The team also found that modern political warfare has some unique characteristics. Non-State actors can conduct political warfare with unprecedented reach. Political warfare relies heavily on unattributed forces and means. The information arena is an increasingly important battleground, where perceptions of success can be determinative. Information warfare works in various ways by amplifying, obfuscating, and, at times, persuading. Compelling evidence supplied in a timely manner is the best antidote to disinformation. Political warfare often exploits shared ethnic or religious bonds or other internal seams. Finally, and most directly relevant to our discussion of grey zone conflicts, political warfare extends, rather than replaces, traditional conflict and can achieve effects at lower cost.[37] While this study and its findings are interesting and its argument has merit, a term that encompasses so many things is probably less useful than one that is more precise.

6. Hybrid warfare: War by many means

While the grey zone is a conceptual and possibly physical realm where malign activities take place, hybrid warfare is a method of war. Indeed, hybrid warfare can

---

[35] Ibid.

[36] Linda Robinson et al, *Modern Political Warfare: Current Practices and Possible Responses* (RAND Corporation 2018).

[37] Ibid.

occur in the grey zone but also outside it, in the realm of large-scale combat operations (LSCO). In short, hybrid warfare is a form of war that includes all means at a State's disposal—from covert operations all the way to nuclear weapons.

Prior to the debate about the existence of the grey zone, towards the mid to late 2000s, the development of the concept of hybrid threats and warfare was under way, with its proponents seeking to describe the integration and fusion of irregular and conventional tactics on a single battlefield or in a single theatre. This became known as 'hybrid warfare' and was best described by Frank Hoffman as when 'an adversary simultaneously and adaptively employs a fused mix of conventional weapons, irregular tactics, terrorism and criminal behavior in the battle space to obtain their political objectives'.[38]

This term that seeks to describe the behaviour of our adversaries employing complex and violent combinations is a construct initially developed by the US Marine Corps Combat Development Command, specifically by leading scholar-practitioners James Mattis and Frank Hoffman a decade ago before the popularity of the grey zone.[39] It was derived from historical analyses and references in foreign literature regarding a deliberate blending and blurring of modes of warfare. The term was even adopted in Service and Department of Defense documents including the 2006 and 2010 Quadrennial Defense Reviews. Former Secretary of Defense Robert Gates and leading military intellectuals like H. R. McMaster used this term to describe the complex and evolving character of conflict.

Former-NATO Secretary General Anders Fogh Rasmussen branded Russia's intervention in Ukraine in 2014 as an example of hybrid warfare, defining the operation as 'a combination of traditional military means and more sophisticated covert operations'.[40] To some, the concept of hybrid warfare has little utility and the environment it seeks to illuminate is better described by other terms such as 'irregular warfare'. But these are distinct terms and mean different things. One goal of this section is to provide conceptual clarity, such as that which exists for covert and clandestine operations. Though very similar, they are distinct and that distinction is critical.

As Arquilla phrases it in his analysis of the phenomenon, if 'we are to have a fresh definition for war in this era . . . let it be "hybrid warfare"'. As he continues, our adversaries 'see no gray zone "between war and peace." They see all as war. So

---

[38] Frank G. Hoffman, 'The Contemporary Spectrum of Conflict: Protracted, Gray Zone, Ambiguous, and Hybrid Modes of War', in Dakota L. Wood (ed), '2016 Index of U.S. Military Strength: Assessing America's Ability to Provide for the Common Defense' (The Heritage Foundation 2015) 25.

[39] Sean Monaghan, 'Countering Hybrid Warfare: So What for the Future Joint Force?' (2019) 8 PRISM 84.

[40] Anders Fogh Rasmussen, 'America, Europe and the Pacific', Speech at the Marines' Memorial Club Hotel in San Francisco (9 July 2014) <https://www.nato.int/cps/en/natohq/opinions_111659. htm> accessed 11 March 2023.

must we.'[41] Here I disagree with Professor Arquilla, for when it comes to Russia and its actions in Crimea and the Donbas beginning in 2014, and again in the build-up phase prior to Putin's 'special military operation' in 2022, Moscow does see a grey zone, and in fact they are using this approach to their advantage. If Moscow can stay short of being implicated in an all-out war, operating in the grey zone becomes a way of mitigating risk and can buy them time before a response. In the case of Ukraine in 2014, the former seemed to be the case, while in 2022 the situation seemed to more closely resemble the latter. Having witnessed the war in its many forms, from the use of small, hand-held drones all the way to sophisticated weaponry on the battlefield (and Ukrainian special operations forces conducting missions deep inside Russia proper) it is clear that the conflict is out of the grey zone and what we are witnessing is hybrid warfare.

This form of warfare is a blurring or blending of 'regular' and 'irregular' warfare, with non-State actors such as the PMC Wagner Group playing significant roles on or near the battlefield. These groups are engaged in activities that were once thought to be the exclusive preserve of states. And even states are increasingly turning to irregular strategies to blunt the impact of American power.[42] We are clearly witnessing an age of warfare where sporadic armed conflict is blurred together in time and space and being waged on several levels by a large array of national and subnational forces (and State and non-State actors).

To summarize, hybrid warfare describes a conflict 'in which States or non-State actors exploit all modes of war simultaneously by using advanced conventional weapons, irregular tactics, terrorism, and disruptive technologies or criminality to destabilize an existing order', and which blurs 'distinct categories of warfare across the spectrum, from active combat to civilian support'.[43] This definition, from 2009, still seems to this author to be a good description of the phenomenon of hybrid warfare more than a decade later.

7. Looking ahead: hybrid warfare and the grey zone

The purpose of this chapter was not to settle the debate once and for all on whether or not the grey zone exists and what the differences are between it and political warfare, hybrid threats, and hybrid warfare. Rather, the objective was much more modest: simply to explore the various ways in which the grey zone has been defined, to test the boundaries of those definitions, and to ultimately arrive at a useable set of definitions that can be used as a framework for the various

---

[41] Arquilla (n 20).

[42] Max Boot, *War Made New: Technology, Warfare, and the Course of History* (Gotham 2006).

[43] Robert Wilkie, 'Hybrid Warfare–Something Old, Not Something New' (2009) 23 Air and Space Power Journal 13.

studies in this edited volume. Hopefully, this modest objective has been achieved and we can have greater clarity in the use of the terms, viewing the grey zone as the space between war and not war and hybrid warfare as a multi-dimensional approach to warfare—including in outright LSCO. This conclusion is offered to the reader as a guide for understanding concepts and terminology in subsequent chapters in this volume and elsewhere.

3

Grey Zone Conflict and Military Affairs

Questioning the Premise

Melanie W. Sisson

> We have been handicapped however . . . by a national tendency
> to seek for a political cure-all, and by a reluctance to recognize
> the realities of international relations—the perpetual rhythm of
> struggle, in and out of war.
>
> George Kennan, 1948

1. Introduction

US foreign policy has an attachment to unhelpful binaries, with policymakers
and the public alike accustomed to thinking about international affairs as a
'good us' vs 'bad them' proposition, lived out under periods of peace and fought
out during periods of war. This is a contemporary and in many ways uniquely
American notion, created by the accident of geography, the nation's relative
youth, and a twentieth-century history that culminated in an extreme form of
US military dominance.

The latter condition, by enabling the United States to use force in ways and in
places remote enough to insulate the average American citizen not only from the
experience of military violence but also from the knowledge of it, has obfuscated
the reality that States are never really at peace, and only infrequently at war. Loud
oppositional narratives—freedom vs tyranny, good vs evil—together with in-
visible applications of force thus have fostered the idea that there is an international order that it is made righteous by liberal values and maintained through
American leadership.[1]

The perception that the United States has any meaningful control over the
course of international politics, however, is an illusion. States are constantly undertaking diplomatic, legal, and military manoeuvres to achieve their goals in

---

[1] Annita Lazar and Michelle M. Lazar, 'The Discourse of the New World Order: "Out-Casting" the
Double Face of Threat' (2004) 15 Discourse and Society 223.

Melanie W. Sisson, *Grey Zone Conflict and Military Affairs* In: *Hybrid Threats and Grey Zone Conflict*. Edited by: Mitt Regan
and Aurel Sari, Oxford University Press. © Oxford University Press 2024. DOI: 10.1093/oso/9780197744772.003.0003

46 WHAT ARE HYBRID THREATS AND GREY ZONE CONFLICT?

ways that challenge each other's interests, expectations, and standard operating assumptions, giving lie to the very idea of order, much less to the belief that it is the United States that imposes it. Where such challenges run counter to US preferences, they have come to be called grey zone activities, aggressions, or sub-threshold conflicts—all lexical variations on the theme applied by scholars, commentators, and practitioners of US defence policy to refer to behaviours that sometimes include the threat or the use of force, but neither are declared to be nor are intersubjectively recognizable as overt acts of war.[2]

Grey zone activities are not new, but the belief that they pose a systemic threat is recent. What used to be accepted as standard fare for States with conflictual interests—espionage, information operations (which technology has helped progress significantly from the days of leaflet-dropping and radio broadcasts), military coercion, proxy wars, and brinksmanship—now are treated as harbingers of a menacing disorder or, worse, a new order not of the choosing of the United States. This creates a dialectic that places the notion of global structure in opposition to behaviours that run counter to the practices and norms endorsed by the United States and its allies: those that conform are done in service of peace and stability, those that do not are dangerous efforts at subversion and replacement.[3] The contemporary framing of grey zone activities thus suggests that even when nonconforming behaviours are technically legal, they still are ethically disreputable, and de facto position US and partner actions as necessary defences against others' grey zone violations, and not as violations of their own.

There is irony in the fact that the grey zone reflects and perpetuates a black-and-white worldview in which those States with which America is not at war are satisfied with the status quo, and those States that are not satisfied with the status quo are seeking to 'undermine order, weaken [US] alliances and undercut [US] interests.'[4] Indeed, even where efforts have been made to relax this binary, it has been done in the lexicon of 'the continuum of conflict', a construct that does little to correct the idea that friends don't fight and that when others take action in ways that run counter to US interests, they undertake them *because* they run counter to US interests.[5] There is no acknowledgement, in other words,

---

[2] US Joint Chiefs of Staff, 'Statement of General Joseph L. Votel, US Army commander, United States Special Operations Command, before the House Armed Services Committee Subcommittee on Emerging Threats and Capabilities' (18 March 2015) <https://docs.house.gov/meetings/AS/AS26/20150318/103157/HMTG-114-AS26-Wstate-VotelUSAJ-20150318.pdf> accessed 25 February 2023.

[3] Michael J. Mazarr, *Mastering the Grey Zone: Understanding a Changing Era of Conflict* (US Army War College Press 2015).

[4] Frank G. Hoffman, 'Examining Complex Forms of Conflict: Grey Zone and Hybrid Challenges' (2018) 7 PRISM 30–47.

[5] Examples include, but are not limited to: Isaiah Wilson III and Scot Smitson, 'Solving America's Gray-Zone Puzzle' (2016) 46 Parameters 55; Kathleen Hicks et al, *By Other Means: Campaigning in the Grey Zone (Part 1)* (Center for Strategic and International Studies 2019); Antulio J. Echevarria II,

that all States, even those with which the United States has serious differences, are motivated by the affirmative pursuit of their own interests and not just by the desire to negate America's.

The artifice of the grey zone in US defence policy thus is to use legalism and moralism to avoid acknowledging two facts. First, that all States, including the United States, seek change in the world—else there would be no foreign policy. Second, that States should be expected to try to make those changes in the manner they judge most conducive to achieving their goals. Because war very infrequently is judged to be the manner most conducive, other modalities should be, and happily are, far more likely to obtain. Where the system's pervasive patterns of behaviour are adequate to those pursuits, States have no reason to break with them. When those patterns are perceived to impose constraints on strategy that are too costly or that produce suboptimal outcomes, however, States will find another way.

The means chosen can be straightforward affronts, they can be clever workarounds that exploit gaps and omissions, or they can be novel manipulations that take advantage of areas in which laws are silent and norms unformed or weak. In all cases, however, the essence of grey zone activity is to ask two questions: who cares enough about this particular limitation, standard, or norm to enforce it? And at what cost?

Much of the serious work done to date on the implications of grey zone activities for military affairs either sidesteps or misunderstands these questions. Some approaches treat the grey zone as though it were a domain or medium, and therefore seek to forward a unified defence 'concept to govern US strategy' and to prescribe policies that 'buttress US competitiveness' within it.[6] Other approaches do the opposite and focus on planning for specific scenarios, which renders them almost exclusively operational and tactical. Both tend to produce recommendations about how the US national security apparatus can better plan and organize to manage the grey zone, and for some this question is the primary focus of inquiry.[7] These frameworks all produce policy recommendations that

---

Operating in the Grey Zone: An Alternative Paradigm for US Military Strategy (US Army War College Press 2016); Benjamin Nguyen Jehle, *Grey Zone Challenges: Optimizing Organizational Structures and Improving Cognition for DoD and the Interagency* (School of Advanced Military Studies, US Army Command and General Staff College 2018); Hal Brands, 'Paradoxes of the Gray Zone' (*Foreign Policy Research Institute*, 5 February 2016) <https://www.fpri.org/article/2016/02/paradoxes-gray-zone/> accessed 25 February 2023.

[6] Hicks et al (n 5); Lyle J. Morris et al, *Gaining Competitive Advantage in the Gray Zone* (RAND 2019).

[7] Stacie L. Pettyjohn and Becca Wasser, *Competing in the Grey Zone: Russian Tactics and Western Responses* (RAND 2019); Hunter Stires, 'The South China Sea Needs a "COIN" Toss' (May 2019) 145 Proceedings <https://www.usni.org/magazines/proceedings/2019/may/south-china-sea-needs-coin-toss> accessed 25 February 2023.

address some combination of what a challenger is doing, how it is doing it, and how the US bureaucracy can reconfigure itself to better recognize and respond to it. They leave generally unaddressed the substance of the challenge itself: what pattern, practice, or principle is being contested through non-war military means and how important is it?

If the grey zone in military affairs is substantive analytically or practically, then examination of US responses to sub-threshold events should reveal which grey zone tactics the United States finds threatening and should illuminate the standards, principles, and norms policymakers believe must be defended. Although grey zone activities are often characterized as being 'deliberately designed to remain below the threshold of conventional military conflict' and 'to remain under key escalatory thresholds', after all, those designs sometimes fail.[8] Indeed, it is the fact of failures to avoid detection, attention, and reaction that makes grey zone activities a cause of concern in the first place.

Such a review, however, reveals not only that grey zone activity in the conventional military domain is infrequent but also that the United States has neither demonstrated a consistent intolerance for the use of specific tactics nor has reliably defended an identifiable set of principles and values. What the historical record instead makes clear is that post-Cold War US responses to grey zone activities in the military domain track very neatly with discrete strategic lines of effort: impeding Iraqi and North Korean nuclear proliferation, constraining Iran's influence in the Middle East, blunting Russia's ambitions in Europe, and ensuring access to and stability in East Asia.

This suggests that the grey zone in military affairs is not an analytically distinct category, and that neither is it a phenomenon that requires new policy solutions. The grievances of others, no matter how they are forwarded, are therefore better addressed for what they are: issues over which another actor has an instrumental or strategic conflict of interest with the United States.

Unless or until the United States chooses to resolve its disagreements—either through cooperation or through war—then it must be prepared to accept innovation in the ways in which other States seek to extend their claims, entrench their positions, change facts on the ground, or in other ways make progress towards achieving their aims. The work for the United States is not to eliminate these pathways but rather to make some of them more available and appealing than others. If it does so effectively, then sub-threshold events in the military domain will remain modest in number, and if it manages those that do arise skilfully, they will remain modest in risk, too.

---

[8] Brands (n 5); Michael J. Mazarr, 'Struggle in the Gray Zone and World Order' (*War on the Rocks*, 22 December 2015) <https://warontherocks.com/2015/12/struggle-in-the-gray-zone-and-world-order/> accessed 25 February 2023.

2. US military responses to grey zone challenges, 1991–2020

Logic would predict there to be a direct relationship between the importance of the interests under duress in a grey zone challenge and the severity of the US policy response, with less vital matters met with the softer set of tools of influence—diplomacy, for example, and perhaps a bit of economic coercion—and the most vital matters met with a military deployment. The lopsided nature of the post-Cold War international environment, however, might have suppressed and confounded these expectations.

In the first instance, the collapse of the Soviet Union meant that the United States enjoyed a truly remarkable advantage in military power, both unilaterally and via its alliance structures. By the end of 1991, the United States and the North Atlantic Treaty Organization (NATO) together accounted for 71.2 per cent of global defence spending. The United States was responsible for roughly 43 per cent of it and, with some minor fluctuations in the interim, maintained that proportion through 2011.[9] Even in 2018, when the US portion had declined to 36 per cent, the next largest contributor to the global total was China—at 14 per cent.[10]

The absence of anything even remotely resembling a peer competitor during this period might reasonably have reduced policymakers' perceptions of the ability of other States to challenge US global leadership in any meaningful way. This might have led the United States to be less bothered by the occurrence of defiant behaviours and therefore less likely to act in response to them. This same variable, however, might also distort the relationship between the value of the interests at stake and the selection of the military as a policy tool. The extent of the US military advantage, that is, might have decreased policymakers' sense of risk in dispatching the armed forces, thereby increasing the frequency with which they were inclined to do so.

Taken together, these cross-cutting dynamics suggest that the fact of a US military reaction to a sub-threshold challenge to its preferred principles and norms likely indicated that the challenge was believed to be important. It was not necessarily a reliable measure, however, of just how important policymakers believed it to be. For this, consistency of response is likely to be the more meaningful indicator. To what kind of challenges, then, to which standards and principles, by whom, and how often, did the United States react?

[9] SIPRI, 'Military Expenditure Database' <https://milex.sipri.org/sipri> accessed 25 February 2023
[10] SIPRI, 'Trends in World Military Expenditure, 2018' (April 2019) <https://sipri.org/sites/defa ult/files/2019-04/fs_1904_milex_2018_0.pdf> accessed 25 February 2023.

50 WHAT ARE HYBRID THREATS AND GREY ZONE CONFLICT?

2.1 1990–1999: democracy, stability, and the reluctant American policeman

Narratively, the 1990s started with rhetorical flourish (in sentiment if not in delivery) as President George H. W. Bush invited the world to understand the collapse of the Soviet Union as an opportunity for a 'new world order'. Undergirded by the steadying hand of the United States, this new order would propagate liberal ideals—sovereign self-determination, democracy, human rights, and economic exchange. Over the subsequent decade, however, the contours of international political life were discussed in far less evocative terms, focusing not on the global project of world order but rather on the extent and durability of US primacy.[11] These ideas may have been considered by many to be related, but they were not at the time understood to be the same.[12]

Although the size of the US defence budget and its overseas military presence declined over the course of the decade, the United States nonetheless retained an impressive distribution of forces in the Middle East, East Asia, and Europe, and its military transited the globe generally unmolested. Not surprisingly, direct affronts to US interests did not arise. Indirect challenges, however, did. Indeed, US policymakers regularly dispatched the armed forces in what were at the time referred to as 'military operations other than war' (MOOTW).[13] Many of these were for purposes of impeding the nuclearization of Iraq and North Korea, but the American military also imposed multiple variations of post-Gulf War no-fly zones in Iraq—emplaced to protect civilians against regime attacks and sequentially altered in response to the Iraqi military's limit-testing and incrementalism. The United States also twice sought to deter China from acting forcibly to resolve its ongoing dispute with Taiwan over the island's international political status, dispatching elements of the US armed forces in warning after Chinese military exercises and shows of force around the island.[14]

In addition to these activities, which had precedent and a long lineage in US national security policy, the United States also engaged its military in response to the behaviours of the governments of Haiti and Yugoslavia.[15] These deployments

---

[11] George H. W. Bush, 'Address to a Joint Session of Congress on the Persian Gulf Crisis and the Federal Budget Deficit', in *Speaking of Freedom: The Collected Speeches* (Scribner 2009) 127.

[12] Richard N. Haass, 'What to Do with American Primacy' (*Brookings*, 1 September 1999) <https://www.brookings.edu/articles/what-to-do-with-american-primacy/> accessed 25 February 2023.

[13] US Joint Chiefs of Staff, 'Joint Doctrine for Military Operations Other Than War', Joint Pub 3-07 (June 16, 1995) <https://www.bits.de/NRANEU/others/jp-doctrine/jp3_07.pdf> accessed 25 February 2023.

[14] Melanie W. Sisson et al, *Military Coercion and US Foreign Policy: The Use of Force Short of War* (Routledge 2020).

[15] The United States also deployed troops to Somalia. US involvement was initiated by the George H. W. Bush administration in an effort to counteract the compounding humanitarian consequences of famine and civil war. Over time, the US military effort evolved into an attempt at convincing

GREY ZONE CONFLICT AND MILITARY AFFAIRS   51

required additional explanation and public justification. For this, the administration of President William J. Clinton relied upon an appeal to principle coupled with attempts to connect abstract moral imperative to concrete risks of US inaction.

Responding in 1994 to the violent and non-democratic behaviours of the General Raoul Cedras junta in Haiti, Clinton managed simultaneously to express reluctance for the United States to 'be the world's policeman'—which is to say, the guarantor of international order—and also to hint at the need for the United States to retain its credibility as the primary defender of liberal values:

> Now the United States must protect our interests, to stop the brutal atrocities that threaten tens of thousands of Haitians, to secure our borders, and to preserve stability and promote democracy in our hemisphere and to uphold the reliability of the commitments we make. . . . More than 20 countries from around the globe, including . . . nations from as far away as Poland, which has so recently won its own freedom . . . have all agreed to join us because they think this problem in our neighborhood is important to their future interests and their security.[16]

Clinton advanced these themes to explain US intervention after the dissolution of Yugoslavia, which precipitated a period of pronounced violence that over time became an organized campaign of ethnic cleansing in which Bosnian Serbs, led by Slobodan Milosevic, expelled and murdered Bosnian Muslims. The United States, United Nations (UN), and NATO engaged incrementally over the course of years to stop the civil conflict, implementing and enforcing an arms embargo and a no-fly zone, creating and defending safe havens, and deploying peacekeeping forces. Elements of the Serb military consistently defied these measures—using what in today's terminology would be called grey zone tactics to work around the embargo, and to repeatedly test US and allied limits in the no-fly zone and on the ground—before Serb bombing of civilians within the Sarajevo safe area produced a forceful NATO response.[17]

In the aftermath of the subsequent three-week NATO bombing campaign, President Clinton again framed US participation as the product of a

---

leaders in Somalia to enact nationwide political reform. After eighteen US servicemembers were killed, the subsequent administration of William J. Clinton ended the deployment.

[16] William J. Clinton, 'Address to the Nation on Haiti', The American Presidency Project (15 September 1994) <https://www.presidency.ucsb.edu/documents/address-the-nation-haiti> accessed 25 February 2023.

[17] Ivo H. Daalder, 'Decision to Intervene: How the War in Bosnia Ended' (*Brookings*, 1 December 1998) <https://www.brookings.edu/articles/decision-to-intervene-how-the-war-in-bosnia-ended/> accessed 25 February 2023

52 WHAT ARE HYBRID THREATS AND GREY ZONE CONFLICT?

responsibility to do so, but still one that was not meant to imply stewardship of an international political order:

> As the Cold War gives way to the global village, our leadership is needed more than ever because problems that start beyond our borders can quickly become problems within them. . . . Just as surely as fascism and communism, these forces also threaten freedom and democracy, peace and prosperity. And they too demand American leadership. . . . Now that doesn't mean that we can solve every problem. . . . America cannot and must not be the world's policeman . . . but in this new era there are still times when America and America alone can and should make the difference for peace. The terrible war in Bosnia is such a case.[18]

When, in 1999, NATO once again decided to use force against Milosevic and his Bosnian Serb forces, Clinton reiterated both the moral and the practical imperative for US action. Despite occasional language about US values and credibility, however, the threat was framed very much as one of the possibility of wider war in Europe, akin to the prior world wars, and not as a means of preventing the degradation of US primacy or liberalism worldwide:

> Ending this tragedy is a moral imperative. It is also important to America's national interests. Take a look at this map. Kosovo is a small place, but it sits on a major fault line between Europe, Asia, and the Middle East. . . . All the ingredients for a major war are there. . . . Sarajevo, the capital of neighboring Bosnia, is where World War I began. World War II and the Holocaust engulfed this region. In both wars Europe was slow to recognize the dangers, and the United States waited even longer to enter the conflicts. Just imagine if leaders back then had acted wisely and early enough, how many lives could have been saved? How many Americans would not have had to die?[19]

By the close of the decade, the United States had engaged its military thirty-five times in efforts to forestall, halt, or reverse other governments' encroachments on democracy and human rights.[20] This was done, however, not from a sense of defensiveness against the rise of revisionist States or concern about the overall erosion of international order but rather from some combination of sincere

---

[18] William J. Clinton, 'Address to the Nation on Implementation of the Peace Agreement in Bosnia-Herzegovina', in Office of the Federal Register, *Public Papers of the Presidents of the United States: William J. Clinton, 1995 (Book II)* (US Government Printing Office 1997) 1784.

[19] William J. Clinton, 'Address to the Nation on Airstrikes Against Serbian Targets in the Federal Republic of Yugoslavia (Serbia and Montenegro)', in Office of the Federal Register, *Public Papers of the Presidents of the United States: William J. Clinton 1999 (Book I)* (US Government Printing Office 2001) 516.

[20] Sisson et al (n 14).

belief in the responsibility of the United States to propagate human rights and democracy, and concern that a failure to do so would degrade US credibility and increase the probability of another world war.

2.2 2000–2010: long wars and little else

US policymakers' perceptions of the international environment and of threats to US primacy changed immediately and dramatically on 11 September 2001, when Osama bin Laden's political terror organization, al Qaeda, hijacked airplanes and crashed them into symbolic sites in the United States. This backlash intensified both the 'good us' vs 'bad them' rhetoric of US foreign policy and the extent to which the military was used to implement it. But although the United States proceeded to do very many things with its military during the 2000s—including two decade-spanning wars in Afghanistan and in Iraq—very little of it qualifies as a response to grey zone activities. The majority of those that do qualify were continuations of pre-existing, long-term strategic lines of effort to conform the behaviours of Iraq, North Korea, and Iran to US preferences.

In pre-9/11 Iraq, this included continuing the last decade's pattern of forcibly rebuffing recurrent Iraqi challenges to the allied aircraft that were constantly patrolling what by then had become the longest no-fly zones in history.[21] Later in the decade, the military was used to remind North Korea of US limits three times, once when it tested a nuclear weapon and fired short-range missiles and twice when it acted aggressively against US ally South Korea—sinking a ship and firing on a populated island. The United States similarly reacted firmly to the Iranian military's detention of a contingent of British sailors in 2007, and twice during the decade objected to the combination of Iranian military drills and intransigence on its nuclear program, deploying forces to be sure Iran registered the complaint.

The United States also reacted once each to norm-challenging behaviours of China and Russia. In 2009, it responded to Chinese ships' reported harassment of a US submarine operating in the South China Sea, sending a missile-guided destroyer to escort it for the remainder of its transit. Although Russia got the attention of the United States in 2000 by deploying long-range bombers in northern territories abutting US and Canadian airspace in the Arctic, US policymakers did not react to the 2008 Russo-Georgian War as though it constituted a challenge either to the fact of US primacy or to the operative norms and standards

---

[21] The Associated Press, 'Iraq Flies Passengers Through No-Flight Zones', New York Times (New York 6 November 2000) <https://www.nytimes.com/2000/11/06/world/iraq-flies-passengers-through-no-flight-zones.html> accessed 25 February 2023.

54 WHAT ARE HYBRID THREATS AND GREY ZONE CONFLICT?

of political life that derived from it. Given that analysts at the time, and since, largely characterized the conflict as having been manufactured by Russia through the use of clandestine infiltration and agitation in order to achieve territorial control, this is a policy non-response that in hindsight looks both anaemic and benighted.[22]

2.3 2011–2020: old efforts, new rules, and freedom of navigation

By 2011, the war on terrorism had become a background condition, with Americans and policymakers still convinced that Islamic extremists hated liberal democracy but no longer convinced that al Qaeda or its progeny were an acute threat to American lives or livelihoods. In October, President Obama announced the withdrawal of the preponderance of US troops from Iraq, and by December they were gone.[23]

In Afghanistan, the war was ongoing, but the US engagement had begun its long, slow diminuendo. The success of a US raid to kill Osama bin Laden in 2011 was followed by drawdowns of US troops later that year and again in 2014, and although the United States remained active after the 2016 election of President Donald J. Trump, troop levels hovered at around nine thousand. Operations were largely air strikes and advise-and-assist missions in rural provinces.[24]

The closure and ebb of these war efforts either produced or simply coincided with a shifting of US attention to the civil wars in Libya and Syria. US military involvement in the former was consistent with efforts during the 1990s to prevent a State government from killing its own citizens using conventional weapons, the latter applied that commitment by upholding international laws banning the use of chemical weapons. US military operations with NATO in Libya were

[22] North American Aerospace Defense Command, 'NORAD Maintains Northern Vigilance' (9 September 2001) <https://www.norad.mil/Newsroom/Article/578022/norad-maintains-north ern-vigilance/#:~:text=NORAD%20conducted%20operation%20Northern%20Denial,Alaska%20 and%20one%20in%20Canada> accessed 25 February 2023; Michael Kofman, 'The August War, Ten Years On: A Retrospective on the Russo-Georgian War' (*War on the Rocks*, 17 August 2018) <https:// warontherocks.com/2018/08/the-august-war-ten-years-on-a-retrospective-on-the-russo-georg ian-war/> accessed 25 February 2023; Ben Smith, 'US Pondered Military Use in Georgia' (*Politico*, 3 October 2010) <https://www.politico.com/story/2010/02/us-pondered-military-use-in-georgia-032 487> accessed 25 February 2023.
[23] Matt Compton, 'President Obama Has Ended the War in Iraq', The White House (President Barack Obama) (21 October 2011) <https://obamawhitehouse.archives.gov/blog/2011/10/21/presid ent-obama-has-ended-war-iraq> accessed 25 February 2023; Tim Arango and Michael S. Schmidt, 'Last Convoy of American Troops Leaves Iraq', New York Times (New York 18 December 2011) <https://www.nytimes.com/2011/12/19/world/middleeast/last-convoy-of-american-troops-leaves-iraq.html> accessed 25 February 2023.
[24] Council on Foreign Relations, 'The US War in Afghanistan, 1999–2021' <https://www.cfr.org/ timeline/us-war-afghanistan> accessed 25 February 2023.

GREY ZONE CONFLICT AND MILITARY AFFAIRS   55

explained as an imperative of responding to the 'injustice' of the Moammar Qaddafi regime's brutal treatment of its citizens, with President Barack Obama arguing that failing to do so might endanger regional allies and partners, diminish the 'democratic values that we stand for', and render hollow 'the words of the international community'.[25]

Both the Obama and the subsequent Trump administrations' decisions to respond to Bashar al Assad's use of chemical weapons in the Syrian civil war relied on similar rhetorical themes, highlighting Assad's actions as crimes against humanity, as regionally destabilizing, and as constituting violations of international law that, if left unchecked, would erode other legal structures containing the worst weapons of war, including nuclear weapons.[26] To this extent, the United States was responding to overt violations of the principles of liberal order, even if it was not calling them such at the time.

The United States also continued to manage Iranian agitations with a firm hand. Early in the decade, Iranian activism—notably a military exercise accompanied by assertions of controlling the Strait of Hormuz—was met with a non-trivial US show of force, including the sailing of an aircraft carrier right through the Strait. During the middle years, the Iranian Navy's harassment of commercial ships and an attempt to evade inspections in compliance with a UN embargo on arms shipments to Houthi rebels operating in Yemen also were met with a US military response. In 2019, the United States again dispatched a carrier strike group to address what were described as 'credible threats' and 'provocation'—though to what and of what was not made entirely clear.[27] Repeated North Korean intransigence similarly was a feature of the 2010s; the United States used its armed forces to signal displeasure with North Korean nuclear and missile test activities eleven times.[28]

In marked contrast with its relative imperviousness to the incursion into Georgia in 2008, in 2014 the United States responded with some measure of both narrative and material vigour to Russia's wresting of the Crimea from its legitimate government in Ukraine. Within two months of the Russian action, elements

---

[25] Office of the Press Secretary, 'Remarks by the President on the Situation in Libya', The White House (President Barack Obama) (18 March 2011) <https://obamawhitehouse.archives.gov/the-press-office/2011/03/18/remarks-President-situation-libya> accessed 25 February 2023.

[26] Office of the Press Secretary, 'Remarks by the President in Address to the Nation on Syria', The White House (President Barack Obama) (10 September 2013) <https://obamawhitehouse.archives.gov/the-press-office/2013/09/10/remarks-president-address-nation-syria> accessed 25 February 2023; Office of the Press Secretary, 'Statement by President Trump on Syria', The White House (Donald J. Trump) (13 April 2018) <https://dod.defense.gov/Portals/1/features/2018/0418_syria/img/statement-by-president-trump-on-syria.pdf> accessed 25 February 2023.

[27] Julian Borger, 'US Deploys Aircraft Carrier and Bombers after "Credible Threat" from Iran', The Guardian (London 6 May 2019) <https://www.theguardian.com/world/2019/may/06/us-deploys-aircraft-carrier-and-bombers-after-troubling-indications-from-iran> accessed 25 February 2023.

[28] Sisson et al (n 14).

56 WHAT ARE HYBRID THREATS AND GREY ZONE CONFLICT?

of the US Army and Air Force deployed to conduct exercises in Poland, Latvia, Lithuania, and Estonia in OPERATION ATLANTIC RESOLVE.[29] Although the primary emphasis of the US response was to reinforce the NATO alliance, and specifically its deterrent posture vis-à-vis Russia, so too did President Obama make broader reference to the principles of sovereignty and national self-determination.[30]

In only one instance did the United States react to Chinese activity with the use of the military. In late March 2016, the Chinese People's Liberation Army Navy (PLAN) was discovered operating around the Scarborough Shoal, a chain of reefs and rocks in the Philippine exclusive economic zone (EEZ) in the South China Sea.[31] Concerned that the PLAN's activities presaged reclamation of the reef—a tactic the Chinese had used elsewhere to create land masses that extended both its claims to territorial waters and its military reach—the United States altered its annual exercises with the Philippine, Australian, and Japanese armed forces in ways designed to attract Beijing's attention. In BALIKATAN 2016, the United States increased the number and type of US assets scheduled to participate, and for the first time dispatched the Secretary of Defense—Ash Carter—to observe them.[32] In addition to lauding the exercise's beneficial effects on overall regional security, so too did Secretary Carter implicitly characterize China's actions as a challenge to international order by explicitly explaining the US response in those terms, stating that the United States 'will continue to stand up for our safety and freedom, for those of our friends and allies and for the values, principles and rule-based order that has benefitted so many for so long.'[33]

The Balikatan exercise was followed by a reduction in Chinese activity around the Scarborough Shoal and an increase in US activity in the waterways of East

---

[29] US European Command, 'Operation Atlantic Resolve Fact Sheet 2015' (June 2015) <https://www.europarl.europa.eu/meetdocs/2014_2019/documents/sede/dv/sede170615operationatlanticr esolve_/sede170615operationatlanticresolve_en.pdf> accessed 25 February 2023.

[30] Pat Towell and Aras D. Kazlauska, 'The European Deterrence Initiative: A Budgetary Overview', Congressional Research Service (8 August 2018) <https://www.everycrsreport.com/files/2018-08-08_IF10946_734833c14d577c4db921a3b9c4c64322889586c1.pdf> accessed 25 February 2023; Office of the Press Secretary, 'Press Conference with President Obama and Prime Minister Rutte of the Netherlands', The White House (President Barack Obama) (25 March 2014) <https://obamawhi tehouse.archives.gov/the-press-office/2014/03/25/press-conference-president-obama-and-prime-minister-rutte-netherlands> accessed 25 February 2023.

[31] David Brunnstrom and Andrea Shalal, 'Exclusive: US sees new Chinese activity around South China Sea Shoal', Reuters (18 March 2016) <https://www.reuters.com/article/us-southchinasea-china-scarborough-exclu-idUSKCN0WK01B> accessed 25 February 2023.

[32] Prashanth Parameswaran, 'US, Philippines Launch Wargames as China Issues Warning: Balikatan 2016 Kicks Off with Some Notable Firsts' (The Diplomat, 5 April 2016) <https://thed iplomat.com/2016/04/china-sounds-warning-as-us-philippines-launch-wargames/> accessed 25 February 2023.

[33] Terri Moon Cronk, 'Carter: Balikatan Exercise Demonstrates Close US, Philippines Relationship' (DoD News, 15 April 2016) <https://www.defense.gov/News/News-Stories/Arti cle/Article/722432/carter-balikatan-exercise-demonstrates-close-us-philippines-relationship/> accessed 25 February 2023.

and Southeast Asia. Under the auspices of Freedom of Navigation Operations (FONOPs), the US Navy proceeded to transit seas, straits, and skies for purposes of reinforcing the right to do so afforded to all States by international law. That the United States was doing so as part of a broader effort to uphold the rules-based order, however, did not find its first expression by the US Navy—which produces annual FONOPs reports that count and categorize these activities—until 2019.[34]

3. Neither grey nor a zone

The characteristics of US military activity during the post-Cold War period suggest either that the level of distress among national security analysts about grey zone behaviours is disproportionate to their actual occurrence or that this concern is not shared by policymakers. There are very few instances in which the primary US objection to the activities of others was on the basis of the means used rather than the ends sought and, in some cases, achieved. In Crimea in 2014, the United States was more concerned with Russia's intent and the war's outcome—territorial aggression culminating in annexation—than with the fact that Moscow used 'little green men' to achieve it. Similarly, China's land reclamation and island building engendered US ire not because of the techniques themselves but because they were employed for purposes of manufacturing economic claims and supporting military expansion.[35]

Neither do most instances in which the United States felt impelled to use demonstrations of force to demand conformity with its rules or preferences in the years between 1991 and 2020 reveal a clear and consistent commitment to particular principles, standards, or norms of State behaviour. Despite crises of democracy and conflicts that imperilled human rights, the United States did not undertake efforts in Africa to the extent or on the scale that it did in the Balkans and in the Middle East.[36] US inaction in response to the 1994 Rwandan genocide

---

[34] See US Department of Defense Annual Freedom of Navigation Reports: <https://policy.defe nse.gov/OUSDP-Offices/FON/> accessed 25 February 2023.

[35] Michael Kofman, 'Getting the Fait Accompli Problem Right in US Strategy' (*War on the Rocks,* 3 November 2020) <https://warontherocks.com/2020/11/getting-the-fait-accompli-problem-right-in-u-s-strategy/> accessed 25 February 2023; Richard W. Haass, 'Salami Tactics: Faits Accomplis and International Expansion in the Shadow of Major War' (2021) 5 Texas National Security Review 33; Robert Haddick, 'America Has No Answer to China's Salami-Slicing' (*War on the Rocks,* 6 February 2014) <https://warontherocks.com/2014/02/america-has-no-answer-to-chinas-salami-slicing/> accessed 25 February 2023.

[36] Daryl Glaser, 'Does Hypocrisy Matter? The Case of US Foreign Policy' (2006) 32 Review of International Studies 251.

58 WHAT ARE HYBRID THREATS AND GREY ZONE CONFLICT?

is a sobering counterpoint to the Clinton Administration's entreaties about the US stake in stopping brutal atrocities in Haiti and in the Balkans.[37]

US interest in land reclamation and the use of dangerous tactics to bolster claims in disputed waters also raised US hackles only variably. The Philippines, Malaysia, Taiwan, and Vietnam all have engaged in island building and have emplaced outposts on them, some military.[38] US objections largely have been mild—though in 2020 the US Navy did conduct a FONOPs to challenge an excessive Vietnamese claim—and these ostensibly grey-zone-qualifying activities seem not to be regarded as such by commentators and analysts.[39] The intensity of US attachment to the principle of territorial integrity similarly is rendered suspect by its own willingness to proceed with the 2003 invasion of Iraq without the approval—and even in the face of the disapproval—of the UN, the standard-bearer of the legal international order, and by its milquetoast response to Russia's bait-trap in Georgia in 2008.[40] Where the United States was comparatively stalwart was in its long-term efforts to constrain North Korean nuclearization, in its desire to limit the reach of the Iranian military, in its deterrent posture in Eastern Europe, in its readiness to warn China off from forcible action against Taiwan, and, increasingly, in its commitment to deterring harassment of ocean-going vessels operating in the world's seas.

To highlight these patterns in US defence policy is not to discount the reality that perceptions, concepts, and strategies evolve over time as the geopolitical

[37] Timothy Longman, 'What did the Clinton administration know about Rwanda?', The Washington Post (Washington, DC 6 April 2015) <https://www.washingtonpost.com/news/mon key-cage/wp/2015/04/06/what-did-the-clinton-administration-know-about-rwanda/> accessed 25 February 2023.

[38] Asia Maritime Transparency Initiative, 'Vietnam's Island Building: Double-Standard or Drop in the Bucket?' (CSIS, 11 May 2016) <https://amti.csis.org/vietnams-island-building/> accessed 25 February 2023; International Crisis Group, 'Vietnam Tacks Between Cooperation and Struggle in the South China Sea' (7 December 2021) <https://www.crisisgroup.org/asia/north-east-asia/china/ 318-vietnam-tacks-between-cooperation-and-struggle-south-china-sea#:~:text=Vietnam%20 is%20a%20major%20claimant,improve%20management%20of%20the%20disputes> accessed 25 February 2023; Bonnie S. Glaser, 'Why did China Build and Militarize Islands in the South China Sea, and Should the United States Care?', in Maria Adele Carrai et al (eds), The China Questions 2: Critical Insights into US-China Relations (Harvard University Press 2022) 231.

[39] Megan Eckstein, 'USS John S. McCain Conducts Second FONOP this Week, this Time off Vietnamese Island' (USNI News, 25 December 2020) <https://news.usni.org/2020/12/25/uss-john-s-mccain-conducts-second-fonop-this-week-this-time-off-vietnamese-islands> accessed 25 February 2023; US Department of Defense, 'Joint Press Conference by Secretary Carter and Minister of National Defense Thanh, in Hanoi, Vietnam' (1 June 2015) <https://www.defense.gov/News/ Transcripts/Transcript/Article/607052/> accessed 25 February 2023; BBC News, 'US calls for Land Reclamation "Halt" in South China Sea' (30 May 2015) <https://www.bbc.com/news/world-asia-32941829> accessed 25 February 2023.

[40] Ewen MacAskill and Julian Borger, 'Iraq War Was Illegal and Breached UN Charter, Says Annan', The Guardian (London 15 September 2004) <https://www.theguardian.com/world/2004/ sep/16/iraq.iraq> accessed 25 February 2023; Michael E. O'Hanlon, 'Why the War Wasn't Illegal' (Brookings, 26 September 2004) <https://www.brookings.edu/opinions/why-the-war-wasnt-illegal/> accessed 25 February 2023.

environment changes; it is very reasonable that the Clinton Administration's concerns in 1995 would be different to those of the Obama Administration in 2015. Neither is the purpose to levy any judgement about policy hypocrisy. It is, rather to assess how the grey zone operates as an analytical construct—to consider what value it adds to understanding the contemporary international political context, and whether it helps policymakers to navigate it.

What the record of US reactivity to others' perceived malfeasance reveals is that the grey zone's utility is limited by its inclusion criteria, which are only two: the action must be something other than a direct military assault on a US interest; and it must be undertaken by an actor that the United States has deemed an adversary. Grey zone challenges, that is, seem to be defined neither by the principle they place under duress nor by the tactic used, but rather by the nature of the relationship the agent of that tactic has with the United States. Unless or until the United States changes its positions on nuclear proliferation, Iranian influence in the Gulf, NATO, or its desire to retain its military and commercial footprint in Asia, then, it will continue to need to manage defiance and incrementalism in ways calibrated to the motives, interests, and values of the offender, not to the characteristics of the offence.

It is to be expected that States that find pursuit of their interests constrained by US preferences will continue to generate ever more novel means of pursuing them. Indeed, the United States and its partners and allies should continue to create conditions that encourage this kind of innovation. They should persist in using their armed forces to condition the international environment such that the most appealing grey zone tactics remain outside the military domain, and by tolerating both their use and, in many cases, their outcomes. It would be ahistorical and naive to suppose that dissatisfied States can be convinced away from their strategic goals, after all, and it is far better that they pursue them through diplomatic dissembling, economic coercion, and legal chicanery than through outright violence.

Tempering expectations about the analytical value of the grey zone in military affairs and suggesting that turning a blind eye to others' noncompliance can on occasion be preferable to uniformly countering it does not mean that policymakers do not need to concern themselves with the reasons, ways, and places in which States are testing limits and seeking to expand or dilute the boundaries of acceptable behaviour. To the contrary, the fact that States with interests that do not align neatly with US preferences are now greater in number; more varied in their political ideologies, systems, and cultures; and more economically and militarily capable than in decades prior means that there is a pressing need for the United States to be clear in defining its limits and disciplined in enforcing them.

Whether the United States is meaningfully aided in this by the idea of international order is an open question; it remains to be seen if order constitutes a fighting faith, even for the United States—much less for its alliance structure and beyond. If policymakers do determine that the idea of world order is the best strategy through which to secure vital interests, however, or even that the order itself is a vital interest, then the United States will need to become far more consistent in matching its actions to its rhetoric. Doing so does not require responsiveness to every breach, preparedness for every tactic or scenario, or an overarching grey zone strategy. What it does demand is a seriousness that the United States has not yet demonstrated about defining which principles of order are non-negotiable and inviolate; about reflecting those priorities in the distribution of its economic, diplomatic, and military capital; and about exercising vigilance and consistency in recognizing and responding quickly to attempts to degrade, diminish, or eliminate them.

4

We Have Met the Grey Zone and He Is Us

How Grey Zone Warfare Exploits Our Undecidedness about What Matters to Us

Duncan MacIntosh

1. Introduction

Grey zone attacks tend to paralyze response for two reasons. First, they present us with choice scenarios of inherently dilemmatic structure (e.g. Prisoners' Dilemmas and games of chicken), complicated by difficult conditions of choice, such as choice under risk or amid vagueness. Second, they exploit our uncertainty about how much we do or should care about the things under attack—each attack is small in effect, but their effects accumulate: how should we decide whether to treat a given attack as something meriting a serious response rather than a mere irritation to be ignored? This chapter brings standard decision-theoretic tools to bear on the issues, tools such as the maximization of expected utility principle and the precautionary principle. But it also develops three innovations. It shows that seeing it as possible to make choices not just of actions given our values but also choices of values themselves can extricate us from certain kinds of decisional paralysis. It shows how we can rationally regard ourselves as having bright decision lines even when nothing in the circumstance of choice has these lines in its structure. And it shows how certain conflict escalation risks from the former two strategies can be managed by both parties seeing that cooperation can yield a shareable surplus of goods, and that cooperation can be rational upon a rationally defensible change in their values so that each comes to derive utility from the success of both parties. This yields cooperative solutions to what amount to Prisoners' Dilemmas. The Cold War was prosecuted on the logic of strategic rationality and that part of game theory that is deterrence theory. We need a new logic from decision theorists for the games that constitute grey zone conflict.

In what follows, section 2 describes the character of grey zone conflicts, taking work by Michael Mazarr as a point of departure. Section 3 discusses problems of choice under conditions of vagueness in grey zone attacks. Section 3.1 distinguishes attacks not requiring response from attacks that may be

Duncan MacIntosh, *We Have Met the Grey Zone and He Is Us* In: *Hybrid Threats and Grey Zone Conflict.*
Edited by: Mitt Regan and Aurel Sari, Oxford University Press. © Oxford University Press 2024.
DOI: 10.1093/oso/9780197744772.003.0004

62   WHAT ARE HYBRID THREATS AND GREY ZONE CONFLICT?

misperceived as such, and discusses how to guard against and respond to the latter; 3.2 classes some attacks as having responses dictated by clear cost-benefit analyses; 3.3 discusses attacks requiring choice under conditions of vagueness proper; 3.3.1 covers sorites or true vagueness substructures; 3.3.2 covers structures in which it is appropriate to use the precautionary principle; 3.4 considers attacks exploiting intransitive preferences; section 4 looks at the problem of escalation resulting from both parties using the previous problem solutions; section 5 discusses impure coordination problems; section 6 looks at bargaining problems. Section 7 notices that, just as drawing lines to solve the problem of vagueness in choice can result in the escalation described in section 4, so can using similar solutions in resolving impure coordination problems and bargaining problems, with the result that parties find themselves in escalating games of chicken. Section 8 distinguishes zero-sum from win-win games, and total-conflict from partial-conflict scenarios, and offers general solutions to each. Section 9 summarizes the new roles for decision and game theorists in prosecuting the grey war in contrast to their role in the Cold War. Section 10 extracts thirteen pieces of specific advice from the overall analysis for how to ma-noeuvre in grey zone conflicts.

2. The character of grey zone conflict

Grey zone conflict is generally defined negatively as hostility between nation states that does not rise to the level of hot war prosecuted by their militaries.[1] It manages not to rise to that level by virtue of having one or more of the following features:

1. It involves aggressive actions insufficiently consequential to merit a mil-itary response, even though they have effects on whole nations and may therefore seem to be such that only State-level military agencies have the jurisdiction or ability to make response.
2. It uses the methods of anonymity and misrepresentation, and it is therefore difficult to know who to blame for the actions in question.[2]

---

[1] Richard Harknett, addressing the conference, 'Democracy in the Crosshairs: Cyber Interference, Dark Money and Foreign Influence' (Centre for Ethics and the Rule of Law, University of Pennsylvania Law School, November 2018), argued that grey zone conflict is the new norm, and that, unlike traditional conflict, which was fought with money, men, materiel, and kinetic warfare, it is more like a perpetual wrestling match, undertaken through cyberhacking, social media trol-ling, anonymous political influencing, trade wars, naming and shaming, law-fare (using nations' own laws against them by, for example, suing them), and so on. Each party seeks to influence the other by short-of-war techniques, sometimes called 'retorsion'.

[2] Someone's stealthing their action so that we can't attribute responsibility for it is sometimes a good thing. For if we could identify the perpetrator, we'd have to go through the trouble of making a response. In that pay-off structure, the secrecy of their action is almost a courtesy.

WE HAVE MET THE GREY ZONE 63

3. It uses non-kinetic methods or employs kinetic methods (bullets and blast) only marginally.
4. It uses techniques that, while they inflict some sort of harm, are not necessarily illegal.
5. It is not necessarily conducted by nation states but possibly occurs with their indulgence or protection, and it is therefore conducted by agents who have the shelter of uncooperative States against criminal prosecution even for actions that are illegal, while not rendering the sheltering nations sufficiently guilty of aggression as to be legally liable to a self-defensive State-level hot war response.
6. It is incremental and subtle by individual deed but may accumulate to large effect.
7. It is typically aimed at non-military targets (e.g. at businesses, informational infrastructures, the deliberative processes and mechanisms of a polity, or at individuals) while yet having effects on the fortunes of and relations between nations, and because its immediate targets are sub-national entities, ones who do not have the authority or power to respond, while yet not being extreme enough to justify State-level military response, it tends to go unpunished.
8. It involves actions response to which would in principle be possible from several agencies, but thereby in effect poses problems of divided agency, since the agencies must sort out which of them shall act, this complicated by the costs and pay-offs for the agencies involved, these in turn pitting the agencies against themselves and each other.
9. It is crafted precisely to be mild enough as not to evoke a squelching response, but harsh enough to advance the attacker's cause.

Discussion of grey zone conflicts is refreshingly free of group think, with three exceptions. First, it appears to be thought that grey zone attacks are a kind of enemy, much as terrorism is often thought of as an enemy. In fact, neither is an enemy. Terrorism, for example, is just the method of various enemies, namely, using violence against civilian populations for a political goal. That apart, the pretexts and solutions to 'the problem of terrorism' are as various as the specific grievances of the groups and individuals who resort to it around the world. Likewise, grey zone activity is not an enemy. It is just the method of some enemies, enemies again as various as the specific grievances of the groups and individuals who resort to it.

Second, because grey zone warfare is sometimes thought of as an enemy, it is thought that there should be a ministry of grey zone conflict, a whole-of-nation response to it, national preparedness to engage in it, and institutes for it. This conclusion is not wrong—the form of conflict does indeed need large study and

64 WHAT ARE HYBRID THREATS AND GREY ZONE CONFLICT?

large, distributed, and coordinated response. But the premise that grey zone assault is an enemy wrongly leads us to forget that there needs to be specific expertise in and response to, the various occasions of grey zone conflicts, which are many, and distinct. How to think of and respond to calculatedly incremental attacks is a worthy discipline. But the causes and cures of grey zone conflict between the United States and the oligarchs of Russia are likely to differ significantly from the causes and cures of such conflict with, say, China.

The most troubling group think idea, however, is this: that the careful studies of the facts of various conflicts (studies which I, too recommend) will by themselves dictate solutions. This is false. We find ourselves troubled by grey zone conflicts not just because of facts about the conflicts, but because of facts about us, in particular, facts to the effect that we haven't decided what to care about or how much to care about it in the conflicts at issue; and facts about the objectively dilemmatic nature of certain decision problems, these constituted of issues we face simply by being rational agents.

Many wise things have been written about grey zone conflict. A particularly good example is Michael Mazarr's essay, *Mastering the Gray Zone: Understanding a Changing Era of Conflict*.[3] Mazarr sees grey zone conflicts as caused by nations that he classes as incremental revisionists, nations that want to see changes in the world order without destroying that order, and that want to be partners in peace but with more influence in and more profit from that order. Mazaar's essay has five main recommendations, beginning with recognizing and encouraging processes in whose unfolding time is on our side. For example, in the conflict between Russia and the United States, the United States offers a superior ideology, polity, and economy, things that will probably prevail in the long run. Next, to help ensure this, the United States must strengthen the institutions and norms which the revisionists would undermine—protect the tools, institutions, and processes of deliberative democracy, for example, as well as the current global rules-based order. Third, the United States should recognize that not all conflicts need a military response; sometimes accommodation is fine. Next, we need to 'build forces, systems, technologies, concepts, and doctrines for a gradualist environment'. And finally, we need to 'punish selected revisionist acts and broadcast true red lines'—that is, we need to specify to prospective enemies what sorts of behaviours would elicit retaliatory punishments from us, and what those would be.

I generally endorse Mazarr's recommendations. But I anticipate and seek to resolve some conceptual issues in their implementation.

---

[3] Michael Mazarr, *Mastering the Gray Zone: Understanding a Changing Era of Conflict* (US Army War College Strategic Studies Institute 2015) 126–137.

WE HAVE MET THE GREY ZONE 65

Mazarr's first and second recommendations—that we should encourage and be patient in waiting for the effects of historical inevitabilities when they are on our side, and that we should strengthen the norms and institutions on which we rely, and which the revisionists would undermine—have difficulties: there will likely be grey in determining what counts as a significant threat to these norms and institutions, and what would be appropriate responses, which reprises the main problem. But, never mind; Mazarr is clearly right that the objectives he enumerates are important. However, the last three of Mazarr's recommendations are rife for trouble, each for the same reasons. Take the third, that sometimes we should meet challenge with accommodation rather than military resistance, and contrast it with the fifth, that we should punish selected revisionist acts and broadcast true red lines. These proposals specify not objectives but strategies; and we can't implement either strategy until we have decided what we care about and how much. And until then, we can't decide how to respond to incremental challenges, which means we wouldn't know how to go about implementing the fourth recommendation, that we should build the resources needed to help us contend with graduated challenges from revisionists.

Evidently Mazarr's recommendations face us with problems of choice under conditions of vagueness. I shall discuss such choice in detail. We will eventually see that attempts to solve these problems lead us into other types of problems familiar to decision theorists and game theorists, namely, impure coordination problems, bargaining problems, games of chicken, and Prisoners' Dilemmas.

3. Problems of choice under conditions of vagueness

An enemy steals a penny from me (or makes a minor land grab, or hacks my computer to get some business secret or some military secret, or trolls my delib-erative democratic venues with inflammatory posts, or is vaguely implicated in the death of a journalist, or finances the leadership of a discontented minority part of my population, attempting thereby to encourage a rebellion).[4] It's not worth the hassle to punish him. So he steals another penny. If I don't stop him, he'll eventually steal all my money. But each theft would be too much hassle to re-spond to. When should I respond? And how severely?[5] Maybe the problem isn't urgent after one penny. Maybe it is very urgent after 50 per cent of my pennies are

---

[4] This section develops ideas from Duncan MacIntosh, 'Intransitive Preferences, Vagueness, and the Structure of Procrastination', in Chrisoula Andreou and Mark D. White (eds), *The Thief of Time: Philosophical Essays on Procrastination* (OUP 2010) 68.

[5] This is sometimes called Camel's Nose warfare: your camel wants in your tent. He sticks his nose in. You don't trouble to shoo him away—what matters a camel's nose in a tent? So he sticks his whole head in . . . then a foot. . . .

stolen, if not before. What could decide to which penny theft I should respond seriously? And what could decide how many of my remaining pennies I should spend to protect those pennies? It may seem inherently vague where to draw the line; that is, it may not be obvious what further fact I could discover that would decide the matter. (It's difficult to say how many hairs you have to have on your head to count as not bald, and difficult not because we're missing some piece of factual information—this exemplifies so-called sorites problems.)

Mazarr makes a proposal which might seem to sidestep this problem, drawing on Thomas Schelling.[6] (I don't know whether Mazarr had this problem in mind when he made the proposal.) He expands on Schelling's suggestion that to stop a man who would kick a dog, you should provide escalating penalties for each step the man takes closer to the dog. I object that since each step is itself harmless and would cost you something to penalize it, you'll have difficulty motivating penalizing it. You won't be moved to do anything either until the last step, when it may be very difficult to stop the man, or after the kick, when it's too late. This illustrates a problem with Mazarr's suggestion that we should draw bright red lines to deter incremental aggression: what could motivate us to draw the line at one (sufficiently early) place rather than another?

Many people upon hearing about such issues favour mirroring—do whatever the other party does.[7] (If the man takes a step towards the dog, you take a threatening step towards the man.) This advice is a variant on tit-for-tat strategy, which says always offer peace first, but if you are then met with aggression, aggress back, and meet every aggression with one of your own, but meet olive branches with olive branches. The hope is to teach your enemy to be nice by penalizing nastiness and rewarding niceness. (If the man takes a step back from the dog, take a step back from the man.)

This strategy will induce niceness under some conditions, but not all (e.g. not where there are more inveterately nasty people than inveterately nice). And it has a disadvantage, one that is part of the explanation for why the strategy won't always work: you're going to take a hit at the outset if your enemy is bellicose enough. (The man gets a step on you towards the dog.) This may recommend you striking pre-emptively with a hit of your own if you suspect you are about to face a grey zone attack (you take a threatening step towards the man before he does anything), forcing the enemy to accept the first loss (he has lost ground on the matter of the dog).

But a further difficulty with mirroring is that it costs something to engage in a mirroring act, often more than the cost of just absorbing the hit you propose to

---

[6] Thomas Schelling, *The Strategy of Conflict* (Yale University Press 1960) 42.
[7] Thanks to Michael Watkins for discussion on this point.

WE HAVE MET THE GREY ZONE   67

counter. It is likewise costly to pre-empt, so it will be tempting to delay, hoping there will be no aggression after all.

The problem of how to deal with conflict structured by vagueness is really two problems. The first is how to see it as rational to decide to treat a point on a vague continuum as an inflection point, one arriving at which will trigger greater action. The second problem is how to see it as rational for the parties solving the first problem not to escalate into levels of conflict neither really wants.

Let us consider in more detail the first problem, that of choice in vagueness proper. There are several possible structures that grey zone attacks may exemplify, and we can see the problem by considering the structure that features difficult vagueness alongside some others that don't. This differential diagnosis will be useful in telling us how to respond to the various sorts of attack.

3.1 Structure 1: Attacks really not response-requiring vs attacks illusorily not response-requiring

I define structure 1 attack types as ones in which it may seem that each attack is trivial, that any number of such attacks would be tolerable, and that punishing any of them would be more costly than accepting them. In that event, arguably there is no problem; you needn't do anything, and indeed, you rationally shouldn't do anything. In fact, it may then be problematic to see these things as attacks; maybe any vestigial sense that one should respond needs philosophical therapy.[8] Perhaps some so-called grey-zone *conflicts* should really just be seen as acceptable forms of bargaining, or as some other acceptable sort of action.[9] It might be a mistake to represent moves in them as attacks, unjust harms, and so on. They are just pre-contractual manoeuvres, actions in a state of nature lacking the established norms needed for some action to count as wrong, bad, inappropriate. (Think of the conflict between capitalist and communist countries over ownership of intellectual property, or between countries with differing conceptions of fair competition and the role of government in subsidizing industries.) And our objecting to them merely shows that we should see the issues which source these manoeuvres as needing contracting. Until then, the actions are not assaults, free ridings, or any other form of legally recognized harm, for they are not yet illegal, not externalities to an extant deal. Or maybe they represent only borderline

---

[8] Although it's also possible that, while the actions in question are not significant attacks, it is significant that one would put up with them—symbolism may be in play, and that can matter. Maybe a foreign leader evidences in his smirk that he thinks our leader is a pawn. That's not an attack, but still, maybe we should do something about it, or, at the very least, take offence. Or do better next time we pick a leader.

[9] For example, as I write, the US Presidential administration of Joe Biden seeks to conceive jousting between the United States and China as competition, not conflict.

68 WHAT ARE HYBRID THREATS AND GREY ZONE CONFLICT?

infringements on such a deal, or actions that seem hard to classify; they are sort of infringements, sort of not. One country financing separatists in another country, as Russia did in the case of the Donbass region of Ukraine between 2014 and 2021, may be an example.[10]

On the other hand, there are scenarios that may have problematically led to the forgoing willingness to accept the so-called attacks. Suppose I've been drawn by steps to which I do not individually much object to a place I would have strongly protested at the outset: has anything bad happened? Maybe I've just been induced, by relatively unobjectionable means, to evolve in what I find acceptable. This would be fine if my basic values have remained unchanged and I've just discovered that I need to do different things to advance them, or discover that unexpected things count as satisfying them, or if I discover that they were premised on a factually false assumption. But in fact, it may be that I've in effect acquired so-called adaptive preferences, preferences for a lesser state of affairs that are acquired in stoical resignation upon recognition of the impossibility of attaining a better state.[11] (If I can't get Scotch, but beer is still available, I may come to prefer beer to Scotch.) And the rationality of forming adaptive preferences is contested. For it seems that unless I retain my current preference, I won't be motivated by it to advance it; so me undergoing adaptive preference change is the same as failing to advance my extant preferences and is therefore irrational. And even if I've come to desire a new situation and so am happy by the measure of desire satisfaction to be in it, arguably the acceptability of the situation should have been evaluated by my pre-change desires, which means my undergoing desire-revision was self-defeating. Telling me you're going to cut my arm off but not to worry, I'll get used to it, does not make me coming to desire to be one-armed rational.

But there is a way to think of rational agents on which acquiring adaptive preferences might be perfectly rational: imagine someone who most wants pleasant feelings, and who gets them by having other desires of theirs satisfied. So, what they want is as much desire satisfaction as they can get. And there are two ways to get it: alter their circumstance to bring about the ends they desire, or change their desires so that what they desire is what they can get in the circumstances. Either way, they will have the pleasant feeling of desire satisfaction. So, if the agent in question is like this, then perhaps their stance is

---

[10] The Russians might think that they have a right to protect their sphere of influence by meddling in another country, even though no one has intruded into their country. They experience NATO as standing too close. And Ukraine is used to Russians, and contains many Russian nationals and loyalists, so that there is some pretext for separatist impulses within Ukraine and some rationale for their support from Russia.

[11] For more on the distinction between rational and irrational changes in one's values, see Duncan MacIntosh, 'Preference-Revision and the Paradoxes of Instrumental Rationality' (1992) 22 Canadian Journal of Philosophy 503.

unproblematic. Their new preferences aren't really ones they have acquired simply because they can't get their old ones satisfied; rather, they are preferences they have adopted for instrumental reasons—as a way of advancing their desire to have preference satisfaction. They've changed their attitudes towards some possible ends as a means of attaining their most highly valued end.

There are, however, doubts about the coherence of such a psychology. For what is it to have a desire, other than to be moved to do what one believes would bring about what it is a desire for? So how could changing one's desires in these circumstances advance that cause? Meanwhile, if one also wants desire satisfaction in general, indifferently to having it by (a) changing the world to attain satisfaction of one's current desires, or (b) changing one's desires to have them fit what is available in the world, then how can one choose actions, especially where both options are available? Having a desire would seem to entrain the rationality of trying to change the world to fit it, but having a general desire for desire satisfaction would seem to entrain the rationality of not doing this, and instead simply renouncing the desire. And now one is hopelessly conflicted, and should therefore be paralyzed about which course to take.

There is more to say about the intelligibility of the forgoing moral psychology,[12] but let's move on to another scenario that may have led to me rationally finding both individual aggressions and their sum tolerable, even if irritating: my non-reaction to these steps may be rational on any measure due to facts about the concurrent or evolving contexts in which they occur. For example, maybe no step is worth punishing, nor any accumulation of steps. Perhaps, for example, in the meanwhile my wealth rises, so that, while each step costs me money, no step individually or cumulatively costs me more than the price of policing further steps. Or perhaps while each step is a harm, it is accompanied by benefits, and the latter would be disrupted by me policing the former. An example would be that, while Russia is harassing our democracy, it is also an ally against terrorism, and its rockets ferry supplies to our space station. In that event, perhaps Russia's harrying is just part of the price for the useful things. Indeed, perhaps we feel we in some sense owed some of the value to the party whom we would represent as thieving or aggressing, perhaps from some prior action of ours, or as a not unreasonable demand for influence in their sphere. As long as the value they give exceeds what they take, there is no irrationality in our non-response. Or maybe the cost to them of their aggressing is one we're happy to see them pay, so our non-reaction is a rope-a-dope play.

But what about this: suppose my enemy attacks me in some minor way, then eases off for a bit, then attacks in some further way, and so on. With this rhythm,

---

[12] Moral psychology is the study of what a mind must be like for its action choices to be subjectable to rational criticism.

perhaps they prevent me from having the experience of an accumulating grievance. Rather, I experience each event only as an isolated episode. Could my non-reactivity be rational? Or am I irrationally allowing to be used against me my psychological tendency not to connect dots interrupted by large gaps?

Relatedly, suppose my enemy regularly does things I find a little outrageous, constantly harassing me. But in so doing, they wear me down, lower my expectations about their good behaviour, and make me think they would stop only if I did something ridiculously escalating. Have I been rational? Have I been manipulated? Both?

Or what about this: my enemy continually harasses in a way that I begin to think is just in their nature, there's nothing to be done, one just has to accept it. So they have changed what I think my options are. Again, have I been rational? Have I been manipulated? Both?

Or this: my enemy continually harasses me in ways expensive to me but dangles the possibility of an immense assault if I retaliate. We see this in the conflict between Russia and Ukraine as I write (in March 2023): Russia's leader, Vladimir Putin, is nibbling away at Ukraine territory, induction suggests he'll keep doing this hoping to enlarge Russia to the size of the former Soviet Union, and he threatens NATO with nuclear weapons should it intervene. The odds of him using nuclear weapons are fantastically small given that this would entrain as much harm to him as to his enemies. But the mere chance of their use is experienced as deterring. Here arguably we have been threatened into using the disaster avoidance or precautionary principle as a decision principle, rather than the principle of maximizing expected utility. And this seems irrational on our part. For the effect is to make us care in lesser degree about our ethical values and assets, or at least to make us act as if we cared less about those things.

I should expand a bit on this: the precautionary principle says to choose the option that minimizes the possibility of the occurrence of the worst possible outcome. The expected utility principle says to choose the option that makes as high as possible the sum of the product of the probability and the utility of the possible outcomes of the actions open to you. The latter principle could justify you in doing an action that has a good probability of giving you a good outcome, but also a very small probability of a very bad outcome. Most decision theorists think the latter principle is the correct one to use whenever you know the desirability to you of each outcome your actions might produce, and the probability of its being produced given each possible action available to you. The principle best tells us how to balance risk and reward. Meanwhile, in such circumstances, the precautionary principle makes us excessively cautious. In the case of Russia and Ukraine, our focusing solely on making sure there is no chance of our triggering a nuclear attack prevents us from acting on other values (e.g. protecting the innocent from aggressors, supporting nascent democracies, and thinking it better to die than to live unfree). Surely these things are important enough that we should act to advance them even if this means a very small chance of a nuclear attack. But the threat of nuclear attack mesmerizes and makes us make choices reflexively against our values. Of course, it might be argued that the fact that it mesmerizes proves that we value not being victim of nuclear attack so much that, in order to avoid it, it is worth it to forgo advancing other things. But I suspect there is something more like a startle response in play here. You accidentally walk into a spider web, you panic, and you start doing spider web kung fu. But in fact you don't think spiders are a big deal, and you are now acting from reflex, not in a way that rationally expresses your values all things considered. Of course, a nuclear attack would be a big deal. But the horror of it, properly discounted by its extremely low probability of occurrence, is a much smaller deal.

Finally, I may be paralyzed by unresolved ambivalence about the morality or justice of my opponent's action. For example, Russia is currently trying to conquer Ukraine. Many in The West see this as a morally outrageous and gratuitous act of aggression. But (as we noted earlier) some say this is just Russia rightfully protecting its sphere, justifiably resisting NATO encroachment. And until we sort out which attitude is morally right, we won't know how to proceed.

In light of the forgoing discussions, we must distinguish between several sorts of cases:

1. My preferences are induced to change adaptively. Arguably this is irrational, and I should have resisted it by keeping in mind the preferences I began with, and continuing to focus on what actions would advance them.
2. My preferences remain the same but my estimate of the odds of any available action being able to advance them has gone down. The only risk of irrationality here is epistemic: I should ensure I haven't been fooled into thinking the situation intractable.
3. I just somehow have my will corroded so that, even though my values and my estimates of the odds of the actions open to me successfully advancing them remain the same, I just don't act. This is me being weak-willed, something generally thought irrational (although there is more to say case by case: e.g. it isn't necessarily irrational to fail to act because one is exhausted).
4. I'm lulled by the intermittency of the attacks into not seeing their cumulating effects. Here, I should have kept a tally and decided what to do in light of a full awareness of my losses as they increase.
5. I'm intimidated into making calculations by the precautionary principle rather than by the expected utility principle. Here I'm being irrational. I should remind myself of my priorities and my estimates of the probabilities of the possible consequences of the possible actions open to

72 WHAT ARE HYBRID THREATS AND GREY ZONE CONFLICT?

me, do an expected utility calculation, and act accordingly, choosing the action with the highest expected utility.

6. My ambivalence about which ethical lens to use in viewing a problem is being exploited to paralyze me. In this case, I should do moral arithmetic and proceed accordingly.[13]

3.2 Structure 2: Attacks retaliation to which is rationally dictated by clear cost-benefit analyses

In structure 2, each attack is trivial, but the attacks have accumulating negative effects, and at some known point, the cost of retaliating would be less than the cost of the accumulating negative effects. In that case you rationally must retaliate to the last acceptable attack—before then would be needlessly costly, after then, excessively costly.

3.3 Structure 3: Attacks requiring choices under conditions of vagueness

A third possibility: each attack represents an unpleasant but acceptable damage but also contributes to an accumulating damage that is unacceptable. In such situations there are two further possible sub-structures:

3.3.1 Sorites or true vagueness sub-structure

There is a zone in which the attacks would clearly not have accumulated to something worrisome, another zone in which they clearly would, and in between there is a zone where it's not clear what to say; moreover, the zones have vague borders—the transition between one and the next is not marked by a definite increment. Here, you need to pick a point within the clearly non-problematic zone to make serious responses. Until recently, the theory of rationality could not see doing this as rational, since for any point you pick there would be just as good reason for picking another, or, worse, there would be advantage to delaying until a later point. (You are given a bottle of wine and told that for each day you

---

[13] The West uses grey zone warfare, too. As I write, President Joe Biden is trying to 'boil the frog' in helping Ukraine against Russia. He is gradually ramping up the amount and quality of aid, being careful not to cross Russian red lines, but also stretching them. Interestingly, he is doing this by providing massive quantities of lethal weapons. But this is only a grey zone attack against Russia since it is legal to give weapons to countries that are merely defending themselves, and since the United States is not itself engaged in a hot war. Note that the responses to grey zone attacks I am proposing here can be used by our opponents, too. This will figure when we consider the problem of mutual escalation of conflict in section 4.

delay opening it, it gets better. No matter which day you pick to open it, there is always the argument that you should wait another day, because it will then be better. But if you follow that argument, you'll never open the wine, and so never benefit from the bottle.) Scenarios with these characteristics are in the family of so-called Sorites Problems. But as I have elsewhere argued, since regarding the fact that a delayed choice point will always be better as a reason to delay can be predicted to lead you to disaster (you never get to drink the wine), it is irrational to regard that as a reason to delay. So regarding it does not maximize one's expected utility. Instead, it maximizes to take the attitude that some arbitrary point within the good zone must be chosen, chosen by a symmetry-breaking technique, like flipping a coin, or throwing a dart at a representation of the continuum, then treating the point so chosen as the one at which to get serious.[14]

Chrisoula Andreou argues that such scenarios are counter-examples to the theory that, in each action, a rational agent would always make the choice that maximizes her expected utility. Instead, a rational agent would sometimes make the choice that is part of a course of action the taking of all parts of which would be maximizing in sum. This could result in an agent taking a non-maximizing action provided it was part of a maximizing total course. Not procrastinating retaliation indefinitely is a maximizing course, procrastinating indefinitely, non-maximizing. But to cease procrastinating, one must do a non-maximizing action, vis., take action now, even though it would be maximizing in that moment to delay yet again.[15]

I think the actions Andreou recommends are right, but not because of the rationale she offers. Rather, an agent can see that it is non-maximizing to procrastinate indefinitely, and unless she uses a symmetry-breaking technique like flipping a coin, and arbitrarily chooses a point to stop procrastinating, she'll never stop. So she uses the technique to pick a point because using it is maximizing, then she follows the technique because she committed to using it, a commitment I would portray as her coming to prefer to take the action that the technique dictated, which means that she's maximizing on her preferences even in following through on the outcome of the use of the technique—it has become more important to her to take the recommended action than to pursue further benefit as that was formerly defined by her previous preferences. Thus at no point is she failing to maximize action by action.

At any rate, in political situations where we face choice problems with this true vagueness structure, if we as a nation do not take the forgoing course of action, we are guilty of weakness of will.[16] After all, if we don't make an arbitrary

---

[14] See MacIntosh (n 4).

[15] Chrisoula Andreou, 'Temptation and Deliberation' (2016) 131 Philosophical Studies 583.

[16] See MacIntosh (n 4), for more, especially the introduction in which my analysis of procrastination as imprudent delay could be reframed as an analysis of irrational failures of response to grey zone conflict.

74 WHAT ARE HYBRID THREATS AND GREY ZONE CONFLICT?

choice on the continuum, we will never get to consume the good in question, which would be irrational. So now we must seek for the causes of our failing to do this. And so we might ask, drawing on the literature on weakness of will, how to cure ourselves of this tendency. The cures that have been proposed are diagnostic of the problem they are designed to cure—for example, creating scaffolds to our will, scaffolds in the form of plans (because we have none, and it is hard to implement a resolution without a specific plan), new laws (because the old don't direct us to respond in some specific way to the problem), the creation of institutions to deal with the problem (because all the current institutions think it is someone else's problem), clarifying lines of authority, subsuming multiple and competing authorities under one authority; divided authority is something many have complained about in America's response to grey zone attacks, and apparently this was a factor in the failure to prevent 9/11. No one knew who was supposed to prevent or respond to the catastrophe.

3.3.2 Precautionary principle sub-structures
The other possibility is that it is known that sooner or later a zone of disaster would be entered, but it is not known exactly when. In that case, the rule to follow is clearly the so-called precautionary principle, which says to minimize the maximum possible disaster and act immediately. For here, we lack the information required to operate the expected utility principle.

3.4 Structure 4: Attacks exploiting intransitive preferences

A fourth possible attack scenario is one in which each attack is unpleasant, responding to it would be even more unpleasant, and yet the attack contributes to accumulating effects that are increasingly unpleasant. Here, many decision theorists would think agents would be irrational if they did not act to prevent the very unpleasant outcomes.[17] But, as I have elsewhere argued,[18] since allowing each new outcome is preferred to acting to prevent it, the agent who does not prevent the attacks is not irrational. They just have value structures odd for being intransitive—the agent would rather not have had all these attacks, but would also rather not have done the things needed to not have them. That is, the agent prefers one attack to none (where they can only have none attacks if they deter the first attack, which they prefer not to do), they prefer two attacks to one (because, again, they don't want to go to the trouble of deterring the second attack),

---

[17] E.g. Chrisoula Andreou would say this were she to apply to this case the logic from her 'Environmental Damage and the Puzzle of the Self-Torturer' (2006) 34 Philosophy and Public Affairs 95.

[18] MacIntosh (n 4).

but they also prefer no attacks to two (or, for any number of attacks, n, greater than 0 attacks, they prefer 0 to n).[19] Perhaps this is rational behaviour; and perhaps intransitive preferences can afford a perfectly good rationale for not having to deter a sequence of grey zone attacks.[20]

On the other hand, some would argue that you are being 'money-pumped', and that you should object to this. The following is an illustrative case, and affords a definition of the concept: suppose that, given a choice between a brooch and watch, you'd pick the watch because it can tell time. Given a choice between a watch and a pen, you'd pick the pen because you can write with a pen. And given a choice between a pen and a brooch, you'd pick the brooch, because it's prettier than the pen. Further, you so prefer each option to the other that it would be worth a dollar to you to trade one for the other. Then you can be money-pumped: you'll keep offering another dollar to move from having one item to having another, in an endless circle of costly trades. How can you rationally escape being money-pumped? It might be suggested that you would need to recognize that your preference cycle is costing you, and that you would have to have transitive preferences about the cost. You'd then pick an arbitrary point to exit the cycle; for you'd realize that you care about having more money than less compared to having any of these objects. You have intransitive preferences ranging over these objects, but transitive preferences over money, always preferring more to less.

Unfortunately, all this does is present you as conflicted; it doesn't successfully justify its proposal about how you should resolve the conflict. You'd rather have more money than less, but also rather trade a dollar and the item you currently have for the next item offered to you. What should you do? It seems you have to give up part of your preference psychology. And yet, since your psychology is conflicted, it seems to give you no basis for choosing which part to give up.

It is not clear whether there can be creatures with intransitive preferences. But if there can, then if a country's population has transitive preferences, not

---

[19] For more on such scenarios, see MacIntosh (n 4) esp. 70–78. That passage covers Warren S. Quinn, 'The Puzzle of the Self-Torturer' (1990) 59 Philosophical Studies 79.

[20] Andreou (n 17) claims there are many real-world choice problems with this structure. E.g., you don't want to stop polluting, but you don't want the accumulating effects of polluting. You may now have intransitive preferences: for each moment at which you might stop polluting you can argue that one more polluting act won't make a difference and it would be a pain to stop, so you don't stop. But at some point, you've polluted so much that you'd love to go back to a point at which you haven't polluted too much, but you can't. So you prefer not stopping at each point but prefer stopping at some point to not stopping. That is, you have intransitive preferences. The same might be true of many Europeans on stopping Russia's invasion of Ukraine: it's a pain to fight them over Ukraine, so you don't. But if you don't fight them over something, you'll wind up in Russian-ruled hell. So, while there is no point at which you want to decisively fight the Russians, once they rule, you'll wish you'd picked a point to fight. You have intransitive preferences about Russian encroachment and the other things in your life. And perhaps the Russians are exploiting this fact about you. Are you irrational? See MacIntosh (n 4) for more on the structure of such scenarios.

76 WHAT ARE HYBRID THREATS AND GREY ZONE CONFLICT?

intransitive, they should not pick a leader with intransitive preferences, nor one with both transitive and intransitive preferences, for such leaders cannot rationally advance their population's goals.

4. The problem of escalation

Let us return to scenarios of the sort discussed in section 3.3.1. As we shall now see, there are really two problems with attacks that are grey zone attacks in virtue of implicating vagueness. The first problem is how to rationally justify picking a point in a vague continuum to decide to act, the problem we mooted in section 3.3.1. Applied to grey zone conflict, the solution is to create artificial bright lines the crossing of which by your enemy will make you retaliate. You would randomly pick one among the acceptable enforcement points in the spectrum, and one of the acceptable methods/costs. This is done by making a choice of values at the behest of the outcome of the use of a symmetry-breaking technique you have resolved to implement, vis., by coming to regard this increment as a difference in quality, not kind. You are choosing to be aggrieved, and are not aggrieved until you so choose. You don't discover that some harm to you is outrageous. Rather, you undertake to treat it as such. Note that, on this proposal, you are not just picking a moment at which to act, then acting. Rather, you are picking a point, deciding to place a certain value on that point, then acting from that value. The proposal is that you must undergo value change, and undergo it as part and parcel of action selection. You are to do action selection by means of value change selection. For without value change selection, you couldn't action select, because you'd have the usual reasons to backslide and delay, and so to renounce your choice of action.

An alternative way to construct a point at which you would act would be to pick an arbitrary deontic principle (a rule), which may amount to the same thing as just designating a level of welfare loss as intolerable.

So suppose you acquire deontic attitudes:[21] to return to the penny example, you come to regard the theft of some specific number of pennies as an outrage (for violating the rule, 'thou shalt not steal *this* outrageous amount'). Once you figure out what you count as an intolerable outrage, and what you're prepared to pay to correct it, you can manoeuvre. (Apparently it is a social fact about primates

---

[21] We used to have lots of these (e.g. 'better dead than red'). There was some advantage to having them: they made us resist all threats of communism, and left us free of grey zone confusions—any whiff of communism sent us into hysterics of retaliation. But there was also a disadvantage. For example, here, any whiff of communism sent us into hysterics of retaliation! The virtue of the principle is that it makes you resolute against communism, from which, therefore, the principle may save you. The downside is that it makes you expend resources on trivialities (in this case, on suppressing trivial wafts of communist thought unlikely to cumulate).

like us that we'll go to fantastically costly lengths to punish unjust violations of rules, even when the costs are vastly disproportionate to those inflicted on us by the rule violations.[22] The rationality of this is contested.[23])

On the other hand, if I come to regard your refusal to concede pennies as an outrage, and decide I'm prepared to expend resources to defeat your retaliation, our problem returns. (Perhaps I think you were never entitled to the pennies.) In fact, it returns multiplied; for now we each have a rationale for escalation. Thus, there is a danger that we have embarked on a game of chicken, like two teenagers racing towards each other in cars, each seeking to prove his superior bravery by forcing the other to veer off. The longer the game goes on, the greater the likelihood of death for both parties. And, obviously, converting the problem of choice under vagueness into a game of chicken carries with it new troubles: how are the participants to decide when to keep pushing and when to concede? The more we push, the more we risk disaster, but also the greater the chance that the other party will lose their nerve. So the second problem posed by grey zone conflicts characterized by vagueness is that if both parties avail themselves of the solution to the first problem, the problem of picking a point at which to dig in and act, each party will experience a reprising of that problem, this time, in the form of the question where to draw the line in escalation and decide that they are merely throwing good effort after bad.

The strategy of pushing relentlessly may work, if it tips the enemy into a space they don't want to go. But it may not. For if they are using grey zone techniques, since these are so cheap, probably there are further prices they are prepared to pay to attain their goal. This may issue in an escalated conflict. Such conflicts are still contests of wills, after all, and are won only when one party loses the will to continue.[24] The result then may be more expensive grey zone conflict.

Another possibility is to make the conflict non-grey by responding kinetically (blowing something up or shooting someone). This could work if the enemy was never prepared to engage in a shooting war. But such response is likely to be perceived by many parties as unjustly disproportionate. As I write, this is what has happened as Russia, feeling threatened by the possibility of Ukraine joining NATO, and so feeling victim of grey zone manoeuvring, attacked Ukraine in a hot war. Now most of the world is on Ukraine's side against perceived overreaction by Russia.[25] So radical escalation can be self-defeating. The lesson

---

[22] See Joseph Heath, *Following the Rules: Practical Reasoning and Deontic Constraint* (OUP 2008).

[23] See, for example, Jordan Howard Sobel, 'Must Constrained Maximizers Be Uncharitable?' (1996) 35 Dialogue: Canadian Philosophical Review 241.

[24] Brigadier General Ian Langford of Australia taught me this view of conflict and war.

[25] For more on this sort of scenario, see Duncan MacIntosh, 'The Sniper and the Psychopath: A Parable in Defense of the Weapons Industry', in Daniel Schoeni and Tobias Vestner (eds), *Ethical Dilemmas in the Global Defense Industry* (OUP 2023) 47.

78 WHAT ARE HYBRID THREATS AND GREY ZONE CONFLICT?

here will not much constrain liberal democracies, which are already resolved to manoeuvre justly in accord with international law and the laws of war, and so which would rather keep escalations to legal things, like sanctions. But the lesson should be cautionary to nations less committed to the rule-based international order.

We shall return to the possible consequences of using the strategies we've discussed in this section for dealing with conflicts featuring vagueness, but first, on to another sort of problem featuring in grey zone conflict.

5. Impure coordination problems

You and I would be better off making and keeping to a deal to split the profits from some possible joint enterprise than with no deal and each continuing in individual ventures giving each of us some meagre reward.[26] There are only two possible deals available. One profits me slightly more in some way not shareable (e.g. giving me more dignity, a reputation as a power broker, perception of my style of government or economy as superior), the other, you. Which deal should we agree on? And how should we decide? This logic often characterizes situations in which nation states are engaged in proxy warfare against each other by backing different parties in regional conflicts in parts of the world distant from both sponsoring countries. The conflicts are typically brutal civil wars, they are expensive for both sponsoring States, both would love to end the conflict, but each somewhat favours a somewhat different resolution. The same for the directly warring parties. Examples abound in the Middle East.

If there is such a conflict between you and me, it might be thought that any given impure coordination problem goes away to the degree that I decide to care less about the minor advantage to me of one of the deals, and more about the advantage of there being some deal rather than none.

On the other hand, the problem would equally disappear if you went that way. So maybe I should hold out for that. And now we are, again, in a game of chicken, with an incentive to escalate, but with a recognition that, unless at least one of us discovers a limit to this strategy, disaster awaits.[27]

On to one last form of problem featuring in grey zone conflict.

---

[26] This section develops ideas from Duncan MacIntosh, 'Buridan and the Circumstances of Justice (On the Implications of the Rational Unsolvability of Certain Co-ordination Problems)' (1992) 73 Pacific Philosophical Quarterly 150.

[27] Sometimes the only solution to be hoped for is one imposed by outside dictators with their own agenda. See ibid. See also Duncan MacIntosh, *Re-drawing the Boundaries of Sovereignty: Permissible and Obligatory Interventions in the Affairs of Sovereign Nations* (ms. Dalhousie University 2017).

6. Bargaining problems

You and I are aggressing against each other. Each of us gets some benefit from each of our aggressions. But each of us would be even better off if we both stopped. This is proposed. But I say I'll only stop if you let me have two free aggressions. Should you take the deal? Am I reasonable in demanding it? (The aggressions could be insults in a marital spat—'I just want to make a couple more points'. They could be small encroachments across a national border in a land grab, or hacks of the opponent's computers to steal business or military secrets.) What would a rational bargainer do?[28]

It might be thought that any bargaining problem I face goes away if I realize you won't agree to a deal that involves more pain to you than another possible deal, and won't keep to any deal that leaves you desiring revenge for pre-deal actions from me.[29]

On the other hand, the problem would equally well go away if you came to this realization. So maybe I should hold out for that. We are in an impure coordination problem again, the goods at stake that cannot be shared constituted of the requested additional aggressions. And we again find ourselves in a game of chicken, hoping the other concedes first.

7. Common structures to escalation-prone grey zone problems

We saw difficulties with the idea that vagueness-involving conflicts, impure coordination problems, and bargaining problems could be resolved by one or the other party becoming intransigent: if I decide I'll destroy you for any penny theft, for any solution to an impure coordination problem that doesn't favour me, for any solution to a bargaining problem that involves me conceding the right to inflict more pain to you, then maybe I can back you off to your second best choice. This is full commitment to see the game of chicken through to the possibly disastrous end. But my enemy has intransigence as a strategy available too. Of course, the United States is the most powerful country, so can't it prevail by intransigence? No. For it is not more powerful than all the other countries combined; brutal intransigence from it would only induce a coalition against it; the United States could find such intransigence suicidal in the form of courting nuclear threats from other nations; and in any case, the US deployment of great force

---

[28] This section develops ideas from Frederic Schick, *Having Reasons: An Essay on Rationality and Sociality* (Princeton University Press 1984).
[29] See David Gauthier, *Morals by Agreement* (OUP 1986).

80 WHAT ARE HYBRID THREATS AND GREY ZONE CONFLICT?

would have the self-defeating effect of destroying other goods, like international trade, on which the United States depends.

8. The general form of the solution to escalation-prone grey zone conflicts

In considering possible solutions to escalation problems, two important distinctions must be added to Mazarr's analysis of the competition between incremental revisionists whom he sees engaging in grey zone conflict: the distinctions between zero-sum and win-win games, and between total-conflict and partial-conflict games. In zero-sum games, one party can improve their position only if the other's position is worsened, while in win-win games, both can improve their situation if they coordinate. Relatedly, in total conflict scenarios, each party desires the non-satisfaction of the desires of the other party, so that, logically, neither can improve their position without the other's position being worsened; while in partial-conflict scenarios, both parties can improve their positions by cooperating in making and keeping to some agreement, but each party is incentivized by the prospect of even greater gain, and by the need for self-protection from the other party's seeking same, to defect from any such agreement. Zero-sum games aren't necessarily total conflicts. It's just that both parties want the same thing and they can't both have it, but the reason they want it isn't to frustrate the other party's wants. Likewise, win-win scenarios aren't the same as partial conflicts. For in win-win scenarios, neither party can improve its position unless both parties' positions get improved; while in partial conflicts there is a way for both parties' positions to be improved, but also the possibility of each improving its position even more at the other's expense.

In escalation scenarios in zero-sum games, there is little alternative to seeing the game of chicken to the end, increasing the costs of competition to the other in the form of the risk of disaster in the hopes that they will desist. We can see these as contests of wills in the sense that the parties are discovering who wants what is at stake more, and who has more resources to expend in seeking it. But there may still be resolution short of maximum escalation, for it often happens that one side can attract more allies to its cause, or more powerful allies, and so prevail. Or a third party will have its own stake in the conflict and try to create a solution by force or positive incentive. There can then arise a meta-conflict to the original conflict if another third party takes a conflicting position with the first. And so on.

Meanwhile, it is always worth investigating whether a situation really is zero sum. Russia and Ukraine both want Crimea. Well, why? For its seaport? Its resources? Surely these could be shared, or there could be lease or free trade arrangements. Surely these options would be better for both sides than grinding war. On the other hand, if the issue is national identity, or national pride, or anything else that involves relative standing, then hot war may seem inevitable. If two hockey players both want to make a million dollars a year, that could be arranged. If each wants to be uniquely the highest paid player, someone must accept less. But then, why does relative standing matter? Does it matter in itself, or only because it is a means to something else? Maybe Russia wants to rule Ukraine because it sees no other way to be secure. And maybe Ukraine wants to rule Ukraine because *it* sees no other way to be secure. But then maybe the rest of the world could provide security arrangements to each, and civilized relations could resume. (All of these ideas have been floated about the conflict.)

The lesson: people can think they are in an intractable situation requiring escalating violence when they are not. So an important tool in grey zone conflict is investigation into ways to see the situation as a win-win scenario or as merely a partial conflict. For example, while the parties may be in a zero-sum game about one sort of thing, they may be in a win-win or partial conflict about another—perhaps only one of us can put a church on that hill, but cooperating on mitigating climate change is more important. So, we are not all things considered in a zero-sum game.[30] Indeed, the kind of game the parties find themselves in can evolve with changes in their fortunes and attitudes. Thus, the value of decision-theoretic wisdom, political scholarship, diplomacy, and mediation—and, psychology: for by investigating the motivations behind conflict, there is the hope of arriving at genuine human needs, things it may be easier to satisfy than the imagined urgencies officially premising conflict. (What do leaders bent on conquest *really* need? What does the child in them need? And how can we give it without ruining the world?) And we may discover a win-win or partial conflict conception of the situation, the latter having the potential for a cooperative solution.

On, then, to partial conflicts. One might think that if two parties are engaging in grey zone belligerence, that is evidence that a cooperative solution cannot be had.[31] Quite possibly. Such solutions are available only where, given the parties' desires and circumstances, there is a surplus of shareable goods to be had from cooperation, if only each party could come to trust the other to do its part. That is, cooperation is possible only where there is not a total conflict, where each party derives welfare directly from the others' ill-fare.

Total conflict is rare. More commonly, each party benefits from a circumstance that can cause the ill-fare of the other, but neither party intrinsically delights in that ill-fare. Mazarr's analysis of grey zone conflict implies that it is not intractable in the way of total conflict—the parties merely want a greater share of goods. This may mean they are in a zero-sum game. But it doesn't follow

---

[30] Recall section 3.1 and Structure 1 scenarios, in which there is merely an illusory need to reply to attacks.

[31] Thanks to Jack Whitmer for this worry.

that they want each other to suffer—not unless that is a necessary means to a new sharing arrangement.

However, we need to know more about the specific grievance in any given grey zone conflict before we can generalize to solutions.[32] Some, for example, might be solvable by resource sharing. Others, only by the extraction of a pound of flesh in vengeance. Yet others might require only an apology. Or a promise of future non-belligerence.

A related concern is that some people just want power over others.[33] Think of Vladimir Putin and his desire to subordinate Ukraine. But even these conflicts may be only partial. Perhaps the party seeking power is prepared to offer the other party something it would accept in exchange for standing in the subordinated relationship, so that both are winners by the measure of their values. There is more to say here, of course. For example, if you offer to inflict less violence on me should I become subordinate to you, have we really made a trade in which we both benefit? Perhaps. Maybe you value being the boss more than I do. Maybe I value peace more than you do. So we trade. But let us move on now to cleaner cases of Prisoners' Dilemmas, ones requiring less cynicism to see as able to be solved by cooperation.

We saw that grey zone conflict can require cultivating intransigence as a defence from attacks, and that if both parties do this, they find themselves disastrously in escalating games of chicken. How are they to de-escalate? After all, each is such that, if it goes intransigent, and the other does not, then the first party wins by the measure of its current values and visions. Unfortunately, this is true of both of parties, so it cannot be relied upon as a unilateral strategy. Nor can the opposite strategy of being yielding. For if one party takes that strategy and the other party does not, the first loses.

Welcome to the Prisoner's Dilemma, that game-theoretic situation in which one party can do well only if the other does poorly, but where both can do fairly well by making and keeping agreements not to exploit each other, and instead to share the fruits of cooperative enterprises. (In chicken, maybe the drivers call off the game after each has shown enough bravery, thence to enjoy the cooperative surplus of long lives.)

To solve some grey zone problems, then, requires cooperatively solving the Prisoner's Dilemma. Can it be so solved?

In abstract Prisoners' Dilemmas, there is a pre-defined possible surplus of goods from the parties cooperating, and a pre-defined distribution of the goods to each party. The problem then becomes how the parties are to trust each other to do their parts in the solution. But in real world Prisoners' Dilemmas, because the conflict involves destructive actions, the magnitude of the surplus is greater the sooner

---

[32] Again, my thanks to Whitmer.
[33] Thanks to Jana Robinson for this point.

WE HAVE MET THE GREY ZONE   83

the conflict ends. This incentivizes speedy resolutions. However, the share of the surplus that will flow to each party must be bargained out. And each party can demand a greater share by threatening to destroy some of the surplus—that is the effect of a party prolonging the conflict. Fortunately, two factors push against extreme bargaining strategies. First, since the parties don't wish each other's destruction, only a greater share of goods, each has a stake in the other doing reasonably well—each will benefit from the other as a trading partner, for example, so each will want the others' economy to thrive well enough to be able to make purchases. Second, the parties see this as a grey zone conflict, so each wants to avoid hot war.[34]

These factors limit escalation inclinations, and inform what bargain for distributing the surplus is likely to be agreeable. But bargaining theory does not offer a consensus on what the exact distribution ought rationally to be. No matter; parties manage to muddle through.

After bargaining, how are the parties to trust each other to keep to the bargain? David Gauthier has a plausible proposal:[35] each party is rational in becoming such (i.e. in acquiring a disposition to the effect) that it will cooperate with the other in mutually beneficial peace provided the other is likewise disposed. The disposition's adoption of by either party would incentivize same by the other—for the promise of a share in the fruits of cooperation. And yet each is protected from vulnerability since action on the disposition is called for only if the disposition is detected in the other.

The problem now becomes an Assurance Game: how can each party assure the other that it will cooperate? Traditionally, this is thought possible only in so-called Iterated Prisoners' Dilemmas, situations in which the parties will interact repeatedly with agents who will know whether they have kept cooperative commitments, and so be incentivized to cooperate to preserve their reputation as cooperators, thence to induce cooperation from others with the aforementioned disposition.

But Gauthier thinks it possible to signal, by taking steps to be transparent, that one has acquired a reliable disposition to be cooperative, and so can be expected to cooperate even without the possibility of enforcement in later iterations.[36] Indeed, I have elsewhere suggested that one must come to value cooperation with other conditional cooperators as valuable for its own sake. Or one must become such that one's utility is partly conditional on that of the other party—we must each come to feel a stake in the desire satisfaction of the other.[37]

---

[34] My thanks to Aurel Sari for suggesting that this aversion to hot war finds a place in the analysis of grey zone conflict I've been offering.

[35] Gauthier (n 29).

[36] Ibid.

[37] This develops ideas in Duncan MacIntosh, 'Assuring, Threatening, a Fully Maximizing Theory of Practical Rationality, and the Practical Duties of Agents' (2013) 123 Ethics 625; that article proposes a variant on ideas originally proposed by Gauthier (n 29).

84 WHAT ARE HYBRID THREATS AND GREY ZONE CONFLICT?

Only in these ways would we have become inclined to refrain from exploiting other parties who have behaved trustingly towards us in non-iterated dilemmas, situations where it would be possible to escape punishment for breaking cooperative bargains.

Mutual intransigence is inherently escalating; mutual love, de-escalating. The resolution of the forgoing problems, then, requires all parties coming to have values and visions with the property that, if all parties adopt them, all will then be moved to act in ways that will improve the positions of everyone by complying with cooperative solutions to our Prisoners' Dilemmas.

9. The Cold War and the Grey War

While the central decision-theoretic problem of the Cold War was whether it was rational to form and fulfil intentions action on which would leave everyone vastly worse off, the problem of the 'grey war' is whether it is rational to form and fulfil intentions the mutual fulfilling of which would leave both parties better off than had neither ever formed them.[38] If we act as we commit to acting as part of threatening in the Deterrence Paradox game that defined the Cold War, everyone is dead. But if we act as we are to commit to acting in cooperative solutions to the Prisoner's Dilemma, everyone gets a share of the cooperative surplus. The Deterrence Paradox is necessarily a one-shot game— there will be no survivors for iterations. Grey War Prisoner's Dilemmas typically iterate, however, so the problem is easier to solve. In common with the solution to the Deterrence Paradox, the decisions that will cooperatively resolve the Prisoner's Dilemma will involve not just what actions to do but also what attitudes to have, in particular, concerning what things to care about and how much. Additionally, it will involve decisions about what degree of altruism to adopt towards the other parties in the conflict, and about what bargains to come to see as just.

10. Conclusion

This chapter's contribution to those decisions has been to make the following specific recommendations:

1. Eschew adaptive preferences.
2. Guard against enemies who posture as more intransigent than they really are.

---

[38] I here apply a distinction made in David Gauthier, 'Assure and Threaten' (1994) 104 Ethics 690.

WE HAVE MET THE GREY ZONE   85

3. Do not get worn down by repeated bad opponent action.
4. Do not be intimidated into using the precautionary principle instead of expected utility maximization.
5. Do moral analysis to decide whether one's opponent is morally right in its actions, this in order to avoid the paralysis that comes of being ambivalent on the matter.
6. Keep track of start-stop-start aggressions so as to see them as accumulating to ever greater harms.
7. Keep a tally of harms.
8. Avoid leaders who have intransitive preferences if you don't.
9. Where cost-benefit analysis doesn't afford natural bright lines as decision points for whether to counter grey zone attacks, use symmetry-breaking techniques to choose points in continua of harms as points to regard as egregious enough to merit response.
10. Adopt preferences whose adoption consists in coming to regard these points as serious wrongs, the responses, things desired intrinsically for their own sakes, this to avoid backsliding into further indecision.
11. Analyse conflicts to find out whether they are total or only partial, and zero sum or win-win.
12. In partial conflicts, defuse escalation by bargaining to solutions which recognize that the parties don't wish each other's destruction, that each prefers to avoid hot war, and that both have a stake in maximizing and sharing the cooperative surpluses from cooperative solutions to the Prisoners' Dilemmas that define these conflicts.
13. Come to place intrinsic value on compliance with these solutions, or on the welfare of the other party, provided the other party is doing likewise, in this way becoming a party who can be trusted not to avail of opportunities to exploit other parties in the resulting peace.

Acknowledgements

This chapter began as a paper for a conference entitled Challenging the Grey Zone: The Changing Character of Warfare and the Application of International Law, co-sponsored by the Centre for Ethics and the Rule of Law at the University of Pennsylvania Law School, The Middle East Centre, likewise at U. Penn, and The Judge Advocate General's Legal Centre and School in Charlottesville, Virginia, USA, April 2019. For useful discussion my thanks to Claire Finkelstein, Sheldon Wein, L.W., and students in my classes on the theory of rational decision. Thanks to Mitt Regan and Aurel Sari generally for their editorial work on the project; and to Sari particularly for some extremely helpful and insightful comments on the penultimate draft.

5

Legal Aspects of Grey Zone and Hybrid Threats

A Primer

Hitoshi Nasu

1. Introduction

Grey zone strategies and tactics are nothing new in the modern history of warfare.[1] With the rise of guerrilla tactics, irregular warfare bolstered de-colonization efforts in the 1950s to 1960s, which led to the relaxation of combatant qualification by setting out conditions on which guerrilla fighters could enjoy prisoner-of-war status.[2] The proliferation of insurgent movements generated low-intensity conflicts in different parts of the world in the 1980s, challenging the traditional notion of armed conflict in an inter-State context.[3] Hybrid threats involving a combination of the conventional mode of warfare with more diverse, irregular mode of hostilities capable of unleashing a high degree of destructive force have added complexities to twenty-first-century warfare. Such threats manifested in the Southern Lebanon War in 2006,[4] the seizure of Crimea by Russia in 2014,[5]

[1] William Murray and Peter Mansoor (eds), *Hybrid Warfare: Fighting Complex Opponents from the Ancient World to the Present* (CUP 2012); John P. Cann, 'Low-Intensity Conflict, Insurgency, Terrorism and Revolutionary War', in M. Hughes et al (eds), *Palgrave Advances in Modern Military History* (Palgrave Macmillan 2006) 107.

[2] Protocol Additional to the Geneva Conventions of 12 August 1949, and Relating to the Protection of Victims of International Armed Conflicts art. 44(3), 8 June 1977, 1125 UNTS 3. For details, see Georges Abi-Saab, 'Wars of National Liberation in the Geneva Conventions and Protocols' (1979-IV) 165 Recueil des Cours 353, 417–26; Frits Kalshoven, 'Reaffirmation and Development of International Humanitarian Law Applicable in Armed Conflicts: The Diplomatic Conference, Geneva, 1974–1977, Part I: Combatants and Civilians' (1977) 8 Netherlands Yearbook of International Law 107, 122–34.

[3] See e.g. Lewis B. Ware et al, *Low-Intensity Conflict in the Third World* (Air University Press 1988).

[4] See e.g. Frank G. Hoffman, *Conflict in the 21st Century: The Rise of Hybrid Warfare* (Potomac Institute for Policy Studies 2007) 35–42; Stephen D. Biddle and Jeffrey A. Friedman, *The 2006 Lebanon Campaign and the Future of Warfare: Implications for Army and Defense Policy* (US Army War College Strategic Studies Institute 2008).

[5] See e.g. András Rácz, *Russia's Hybrid War in Ukraine: Breaking the Enemy's Ability to Resist* (Finnish Institute of International Affairs 2015), ch. 4; Ines Gillich, 'Illegally Evading Attribution? Russia's Use of Unmarked Troops in Crimea and International Humanitarian Law' (2015) 48 Vanderbilt Journal of International Law 1191.

Hitoshi Nasu, *Legal Aspects of Grey Zone and Hybrid Threats* In: *Hybrid Threats and Grey Zone Conflict.*
Edited by: Mitt Regan and Aurel Sari, Oxford University Press. © Oxford University Press 2024.
DOI: 10.1093/oso/9780197744772.003.0005

88   WHAT ARE HYBRID THREATS AND GREY ZONE CONFLICT?

and the use of maritime militia by China for its assertive territorial and maritime claims in the South China Sea.[6]

These evolutions in military tactics and operational manoeuvre are important considerations for developing military doctrines and ensuring combat readiness. Yet the international legal order is not necessarily disrupted as long as international law affords States adequate means to adapt their behaviour and to regulate the conduct of hostilities accordingly. Normative problems instead arise if the hybridization of warfare is instrumental to or results from the uncertainty or inefficacy of the law itself. It is therefore imperative to ask—is legal uncertainty within the existing structure of international law truly responsible for a grey zone that enables hostile actors to operate below the threshold of open conflict by posing hybrid threats?

This chapter critically considers how the existing structure of international law contributes to the growth of hybrid threats as a strategic choice of hostile actors. To that end, this chapter first reviews the legal regimes of *jus ad bellum* and *jus in bello* as the current legal framework of warfare, with a particular focus on threshold legal questions under these regimes (section 2). The chapter will then identify critical flaws in the current legal framework of warfare due to misalignment of different legal thresholds (section 3). However, the strategic exploitability of this flaw has deeper roots in the structural problems of international law when three conditions for enabling recalcitrant States to operate in a grey zone by posing hybrid threats are present (section 4). The chapter concludes with an observation that hybrid threats are likely to remain a preferred mode of offensive operations that recalcitrant States engage against law-abiding States by exploiting flaws in the current legal system of warfare until international law itself is adapted to the new reality of international relations.

2. The current legal framework of warfare

In international relations, the use of violence is regulated in a series of dichotomous legal structures. These structures emerged largely from strategic considerations that prevailed at different times in history. But there are also normative reasons that reflect incongruous readiness on the part of sovereign States to subject themselves to the system of international law. A combination of these strategic considerations and normative clarification through jurisprudence

---

[6] See e.g.Andrew S. Erickson and Ryan D. Martinson, *China's Maritime Gray Zone Operations* (US Naval Institute 2023); Rob McLaughlin, 'The Law of the Sea and PRC Gray-Zone Operations in the South China Sea' (2022) 116 American Journal of International Law 821; James Kraska and Michael Monti, 'The Law of Naval Warfare and China's Maritime Militia' (2015) 91 International Law Studies 450.

developed by international adjudications has added complications to the dichotomous legal structures governing the use of violence in international relations.

2.1 The distinction between *jus ad bellum* and *jus in bello*

The idea of just war, distinguishing permissible wars from those fought without a just cause, has existed from the early times of human history. It has been advanced, espoused, and debated among priests, theologists, jurists, and scholars in different parts of the world.[7] With the emergence of positive international law, these ideas became discredited and abandoned in recognition of the sovereign's unrestricted freedom to pursue its self-preservation by means of self-help and in the exercise of the right of intervention against weaker States.[8] Nevertheless, States were generally inclined to avoid a declaration of war and sought a justifying cause for the use of force short of war.[9] With the modern efforts to prevent wars emerged the body of law that requires justification for the use of force in international relations (*jus ad bellum*).

Equally rooted in historical origins is the idea that war must be fought with restraint in accordance with the modern law and customs of war.[10] Francis Lieber codified these ideas and practices, which President Lincoln issued as General Order No 100 of 1863 as a field manual for the American Civil War.[11] The idea of humanizing warfare also motivated the Red Cross movement, with the adoption of the 1864 Geneva Convention and the subsequent development of the Geneva law for the protection of victims of war.[12] These initiatives inspired States to use

---

[7] See e.g. Yoram Dinstein, *War, Aggression and Self-Defence* (6th edn CUP 2017) 67–71; Thomas M. Franck, *Fairness in International Law and Institutions* (Clarendon Press 1995) 245–50; Arthur Nussbaum, *A Concise History of the Law of Nations* (Macmillan Press 1947) 1–114; Joachim von Elbe, 'The Evolution of the Concept of the Just War in International Law' (1939) 33 American Journal of International Law 665, 669–85.

[8] P. H. Winfield, 'The History of Intervention in International Law' [1922–23] British Year Book of International Law 130; Ellery C. Stowell, *Intervention in International Law* (John Byrne and Co. 1921) 317–55.

[9] See e.g. Albert E. Hindmarsh, *Force in Peace: Force Short of War in International Relations* (Harvard University Press 1933) 84–89; Ahmed M. Rifaat, *International Aggression* (Almqvist and Wiksell International 1979) 19–20; Ian Brownlie, *International Law and the Use of Force by States* (Clarendon Press 1963) 26–28.

[10] For diverse origins and practices in different parts of the world, see e.g. Samuel C. Duckett White, *The Laws of Yesterday's Wars* (Brill 2021); Leslie C. Green, 'The Law of War in Historical Perspective' (1998) 72 International Law Studies 39.

[11] General Order No 100: Instructions for the Government of Armies of the United States in the Field (24 April 1863).

[12] Convention for the Amelioration of the Condition of the Wounded in Armies in the Field (22 August 1864), 129 CTS 361; Geneva Convention for the Amelioration of the Condition of the Wounded and Sick in Armies in the Field (6 July 1906), 202 CTS 144; Geneva Convention Relative to the Treatment of Prisoners of War (27 July 1929), 118 LNTS 343; Geneva Convention for the Amelioration of the Condition of the Wounded and Sick in Armies in the Field (27 July 1929), 118 LNTS 303.

90 WHAT ARE HYBRID THREATS AND GREY ZONE CONFLICT?

international agreements as a means of prohibiting the use of inhumane weapons and restricting the methods of warfare,[13] which formed the basis for developing the law governing the conduct of hostilities (*jus in bello*).

These two strands of legal development did not merge even when the use of force in international relations was outlawed under Article 2(4) of the United Nations (UN) Charter in the aftermath of World War II.[14] Indeed, major codification efforts for the law of war took place soon after the UN's establishment, with the adoption of the four Geneva Conventions in 1949.[15] The dual structure created as a result has meant that there is an obligation to comply with *jus in bello* whether or not the use of force is justifiable under *jus ad bellum* and, as will be discussed in section 2.3, whether it is directed against another State in international armed conflict or against a non-State actor in non-international armed conflict. In other words, the legality or legitimacy of the use of force has no impact on the applicability of *jus in bello* to all the belligerent parties involved.[16] Resort to violence in international relations must be justified under both bodies of law. As will be discussed in section 3, there is a potential for discrepancy between these two legal regimes when the threshold for triggering the application of each legal regime is misaligned.

2.2 Use of force thresholds under *jus ad bellum*

The prohibition of the use or threat of force in international relations, as enshrined in Article 2(4) of the UN Charter, is central to the modern legal regime of the *jus ad bellum*. This principle is well established under customary international law,[17] prohibiting any use of force in international relations unless it

[13] Declaration (IV, 2) on the Use of Projectiles the Objects of Which is the Diffusion of Asphyxiating or Deleterious Gases, 29 July 1899, 187 CTS 453; Declaration (IV, 3) Concerning Expanding Bullets, 29 July 1899, 187 CTS 459; Regulations Respecting the Laws and Customs of War on Land art. 25, annexed to Convention (IV) Respecting the Laws and Customs of War on Land, 18 October 1907, 205 CTS 277; Convention (VIII) Relative to the Laying of Automatic Submarine Contact Mines, 18 October 1907, 205 CTS 331.

[14] Charter of the United Nations, 26 June 1945, 1 UNTS XVI art. 2(4).

[15] Geneva Convention for the Amelioration of the Condition of the Wounded and Sick in Armed Forces in the Field, 12 August 1949, 75 UNTS 31 (Geneva Convention I); Geneva Convention for the Amelioration of the Condition of Wounded, Sick and Shipwrecked Members of Armed Forces at Sea, 12 August 1949, 75 UNTS 85 (Geneva Convention II); Geneva Convention Relative to the Treatment of Prisoners of War, 12 August 1949, 75 UNTS 135 (Geneva Convention III); Geneva Convention Relative to the Protection of Civilian Persons in Time of War, 12 August 1949, 75 UNTS 287 (Geneva Convention IV).

[16] Bryan Peeler, *The Persistence of Reciprocity in International Humanitarian Law* (CUP 2019); Sean Watts, 'Reciprocity and the Law of War' (2009) 50 Harvard International Law Journal 365. For challenges in the context of non-international armed conflict, see Marco Sassòli and Yuval Shany, 'Should the Obligations of States and Armed Groups under International Humanitarian Law Really Be Equal?' (2011) 93 International Review of the Red Cross 425.

[17] *Military and Paramilitary Activities in and against Nicaragua (Nicaragua v. US) (Merits)* [1986] ICJ Rep. 14, paras 188–90.

LEGAL ASPECTS OF GREY ZONE AND HYBRID THREATS   91

is justifiable as an exercise of the right of self-defence or authorized by the UN Security Council. Although the use of force does not encompass mere political or economic coercion,[18] the precise parameters of what amounts to a use of force prohibited under this principle have been subject to debate.[19] The boundaries of the prohibition are becoming increasingly obscure due to the emergence of non-traditional means to cause disruptive effects, such as cyberattacks.[20]

The International Court of Justice has done little to help clarify the principle's boundary in its application to international disputes.[21] In *Costa Rica v. Nicaragua*, for example, the Court failed to pronounce that Nicaragua's military presence in a disputed territory was a breach of the principle; instead, it merely acknowledged that '[t]he fact that Nicaragua considered that its activities were taking place on its own territory does not exclude the possibility of characterizing them as an unlawful use of force'.[22] The Fact-Finding Commission in Georgia defined the prohibition of the use of force as covering 'all physical force which surpasses a minimum threshold of intensity',[23] which contributed to the view that small-scale or targeted forcible acts below a minimum threshold of intensity would not fall within the scope of the prohibition.[24] These developments have created legal ambiguity, which recalcitrant States may exploit by pursuing small-scale and targeted military operations to avoid concerted condemnation.

These problems are further compounded when the parameters of what amounts to a use of force are not aligned with those of armed attack as a threshold requirement for exercising the right of self-defence. As the International Court of Justice established in *Nicaragua v. US*, armed attacks are the 'most grave forms of the use of force' and must be distinguished from the use of force of a lesser

[18] Oliver Dörr and Albrecht Randelzhofer, 'Article 2(4)', in Bruno Simma et al (eds), *The Charter of the United Nations: A Commentary* (3rd edn OUP 2012) 200, 208–10.

[19] See e.g. Lianne J. M. Boer, ' "Echoes of Times Past": On the Paradoxical Nature of Article 2(4)' (2015) 20 Journal of Conflict and Security Law 5; John D. Becker, 'The Continuing Relevance of Article 2(4): A Consideration of the Status of the U.N. Charter's Limitations on the Use of Force' (2004) 32 Denver Journal of International Law and Policy 583; Belatchew Asrat, *Prohibition of Force under the UN Charter: A Study of Article 2(4)* (Iustus Förlag 1991) 35–46.

[20] See Michael N. Schmitt, 'Grey Zones in the International Law of Cyberspace' (2017) 42 Yale Journal of International Law Online.

[21] Claus Kreß, 'The International Court of Justice and the "Principle of Non-Use of Force"', in Marc Weller (ed), *The Oxford Handbook of the Use of Force in International Law* (OUP 2015) 561; John Norton Moore, 'Jus ad Bellum Before the International Court of Justice' (2012) 52 Virginia Journal of International Law 903.

[22] *Certain Activities Carried Out by Nicaragua in the Border Area (Costa Rica v. Nicaragua) and Construction of a Road in Costa Rica along the San Juan River (Nicaragua v. Costa Rica)* [2015] ICJ Rep. 665, para 97.

[23] Independent International Fact-Finding Mission on the Conflict of Georgia, 'Report' (September 2009) vol. II, 242.

[24] For discussion, see Tom Ruys, 'The Meaning of "Force" and the Boundaries of the Jus ad Bellum: Are "Minimum" Uses of Force Excluded from UN Charter Article 2(4)?' (2014) 108 American Journal of International Law 159; Mary E. O'Connell, 'The Prohibition on the Use of Force', in Nigel D. White and Christian Henderson (eds), *Research Handbook on International Conflict and Security Law* (Elgar 2013) 89, 102–07; Olivier Corten, *The Law against War* (Hart 2010) 50–92.

92   WHAT ARE HYBRID THREATS AND GREY ZONE CONFLICT?

degree of gravity, such as mere frontier incidents and logistical or other support for rebel activities.[25] Below this high-gravity threshold, response options for States are limited to diplomatic protests, retortion, and countermeasures without involving the use of force.[26] This threshold, set by the International Court of Justice in the development of its jurisprudence, again incentivizes recalcitrant States to engage in low-intensity conflict, depriving the target State of decisive opportunities to act in self-defence.

Recalcitrant States could further obfuscate the application of the *jus ad bellum* by using private militia groups as a proxy to engage in combat on their behalf. A State is only held responsible for acts of violence committed by non-State actors when their conduct is attributed to the State on the grounds that, for example, they are acting in complete dependence on the State as its de facto organ,[27] are exercising elements of governmental authority,[28] or are otherwise acting on the State's instruction or under its direction and control.[29] The victim State therefore cannot hold another State accountable for the use of force perpetrated by armed groups when they are operating autonomously with varying degrees of State support that fall below these thresholds.[30]

Similar constraints affect the victim State's ability to act in self-defence if, as the International Court of Justice held in its *Palestinian Wall* advisory opinion, the right of self-defence were to be recognized only in the case of armed attack by one State against another, but not in cases where an armed attack emanates from a non-State actor.[31] In *Nicaragua*, the Court conceded that the conduct of armed groups sent by and on behalf of a State into the territory of another State could amount to an armed attack,[32] but as discussed above, only when the scale

---

[25]   *Nicaragua* (n 17) paras 191 and 195.

[26]   Ibid. 127, para 249. See also International Law Commission, 'Draft Articles on Responsibility of States for Internationally Wrongful Acts, with Commentaries' (2001) II[2] Yearbook of the International Law Commission 31, 131–32.

[27]   Articles on Responsibility of States for Internationally Wrongful Acts, UN Doc. A/56/10 (2001) Annex, art. 4 (hereinafter ASR); *Nicaragua* (n 17) para 109; *Application of the Convention on the Prevention and Punishment of the Crime of Genocide (Bosnia and Herzegovina v. Serbia and Montenegro)* (Judgment) [2007] ICJ Rep. 43, paras 390–94.

[28]   ASR, art. 5. For various limiting factors of this attribution ground, see Jennifer Maddocks, 'Outsourcing of Governmental Functions in Contemporary Conflict: Rethinking the Issue of Attribution' (2019) 59 Virginia Journal of International Law 47.

[29]   ASR, art. 8; *Nicaragua* (n 17) paras 113–15; *Bosnian Genocide* (n 27) paras 396–406.

[30]   See Kilian Roithmaier, 'Holding States Responsible for Violations of International Humanitarian Law in Proxy Warfare: The Concept of State Complicity in Acts of Non-State Armed Groups' (2023) 14 European Journal of Legal Studies 140; Jennifer Maddocks, 'Russia, the Wagner Group, and the Issue of Attribution' (*Articles of War*, 28 April 2021) <https://lieber.westpoint.edu/russia-wagner-group-attribution/> accessed 11 March 2023.

[31]   *Legal Consequences of the Construction of a Wall in the Occupied Palestinian Territory* (Advisory Opinion) [2004] ICJ Rep. 135, para 139.

[32]   *Nicaragua* (n 17) para 195 (referring to UNGA Res. 3314 'Definition of Aggression' (13 December 1974) Annex, art. 3(g)).

and effect of their activities meet the high threshold of gravity.[33] However, due to non-State actors' greater ability to engage in hostilities, an increasing number of States have adopted an expansive view whereby the right to use force in self-defence may be exercised against non-State actors,[34] especially when the territorial State from which they are operating is unwilling or unable to prevent the armed attacks they launch.[35]

The advancement in modern technologies has increased the ease at which individuals, or a group of individuals, may commit acts of violence with a far greater destructive effect than ever before. A combination of the conventional mode of warfare involving regular armed forces with more diverse, irregular modes of hostilities capable of unleashing a high degree of destructive force, has added to the complexities of modern and future warfare.[36]

With the assistance of various technologically advanced means of warfare readily available to them, the greater role of non-State actors is changing the dynamics of modern warfare. While coordinating their operations through a web of de-centralized networks, non-State actors may emulate conventional armed forces in terms of the scale and effects of combat or complement a State's political and military apparatus in the form of a proxy war when their political or military objectives are closely aligned.[37] Such combination of traditional means of warfare and de-centralized operations, described as 'hybrid warfare', allows hostile actors to exploit legal misalignment within the existing structure of international law for a political or military advantage against their opponents.

2.3 Conflict classification for *jus in bello*

The legal regime that applies to the conduct of hostilities during an armed conflict is also based on a dual structure according to the classification of the conflict. In international armed conflict—the armed conflict between two or more States—the 1949 Geneva Conventions and, if applicable, 1977 Additional

---

[33] See Abdulqawi A. Yusuf, 'The Notion of "Armed Attack" in the Nicaragua Judgment and Its Influence on Subsequent Case Law' (2012) 25 Leiden Journal of International Law 461, 463–70.

[34] See various views expressed in the Arria-formula meeting convened at the UN Security Council, annexed to Letter dated 8 March 2021 from the Permanent Representative of Mexico to the United Nations addressed to the President of the Security Council, UN Doc. S/2021/247 (16 March 2021).

[35] See e.g. Jutta Brunnée and Stephen J. Toope, 'Self-Defence Against Non-State Actors: Are Powerful States Willing But Unable to Change International Law?' (2018) 67 International and Comparative Law Quarterly 263; Ashley S. Deeks, '"Unwilling or Unable": Toward a Normative Framework for Extraterritorial Self-Defense' (2012) 52 Virginia Journal of International Law 483.

[36] See James N. Mattis and Frank Hoffman, 'Future Warfare: The Rise of Hybrid Wars' (2005) 131 *US Naval Institute Proceedings Magazine* 18.

[37] See generally Assaf Moghadam, Vladimir Rauta, and Michel Wyss (eds), *Routledge Handbook of Proxy Wars* (Routledge 2023); Groh L. Tyrone, *Proxy War: The Least Bad Option* (Stanford University Press 2019).

94 WHAT ARE HYBRID THREATS AND GREY ZONE CONFLICT?

Protocol I, from which the primary body of customary international law derives, are set to 'apply to all cases of declared war or of any other armed conflict which may arise between two or more of the High Contracting Parties, even if the state of war is not recognized by one of them'.[38] On the other hand, the law applicable to non-international armed conflict—the armed conflict between a State and a non-State actor or between non-State actors—is limited to Article 3 common to the 1949 Geneva Conventions[39] and, if applicable, 1977 Additional Protocol II,[40] which are supplemented by a growing body of customary international law. The varied range of obligations applicable under these legal regimes is subject to different triggering thresholds.

An international armed conflict arises when 'one or more States have recourse to armed force against another State, regardless of the reasons for or the intensity of the confrontation'.[41] There is no minimum level of intensity required to qualify inter-State hostilities as an international armed conflict.[42] By contrast, a non-international armed conflict does not arise unless the armed group displays some degree of organization and engages in 'protracted armed violence' of a certain level of intensity against government authorities or other organized armed groups.[43] Below this threshold, the State must operate in a law enforcement paradigm under stricter legal constraints, including the obligation to protect various human rights.

[38] Common Article 2 to the Geneva Conventions I to IV.

[39] It reads, in part: 'In the case of armed conflict not of an international character occurring in the territory of one of the High Contracting Parties, each Party to the conflict shall be bound to apply, as a minimum, the following provisions: (1) Persons taking no active part in the hostilities, including members of armed forces who have laid down their arms and those placed "hors de combat" by sickness, wounds, detention, or any other cause, shall in all circumstances be treated humanely, without any adverse distinction founded on race, colour, religion or faith, sex, birth or wealth, or any other similar criteria. To this end, the following acts are and shall remain prohibited at any time and in any place whatsoever with respect to the above-mentioned persons: (a) violence to life and person, in particular murder of all kinds, mutilation, cruel treatment and torture; (b) taking of hostages; (c) outrages upon personal dignity, in particular humiliating and degrading treatment; (d) the passing of sentences and the carrying out of executions without previous judgment pronounced by a regularly constituted court, affording all the judicial guarantees which are recognized as indispensable by civilized peoples; (2) The wounded and sick shall be collected and cared for'.

[40] Protocol Additional to the Geneva Conventions of 12 August 1949 and Relating to the Protection of Victims of Non-International Armed Conflicts (Protocol II) (June 8, 1977) 1125 UNTS 609.

[41] Knut Dörmann et al (eds), *Commentary on the First Geneva Convention: Convention (I) for the Amelioration of the Condition of the Wounded and Sick in Armed Forces in the Field* (International Committee of the Red Cross 2016) paras 236–40.

[42] *Cf.* International Law Association Committee on the Use of Force, 'Final Report on the Meaning of Armed Conflict in International Law' (adopted at The Hague Conference, 2010) 32–33 (requiring belligerent parties to be engaged in fighting of some intensity). But see Dieter Fleck, 'Scope of Application of International Humanitarian Law', in Dieter Fleck (ed), *The Handbook of International Humanitarian Law* (4th edn OUP 2021) 50, 52.

[43] See generally Sandesh Sivakumaran, *The Law of Non-International Armed Conflict* (OUP 2012) ch. 1; Anthony Cullen, *The Concept of Non-International Armed Conflict in International Humanitarian Law* (CUP 2010).

LEGAL ASPECTS OF GREY ZONE AND HYBRID THREATS   95

The hostile party engaging in hybrid warfare could exploit these different triggering thresholds by deliberately repeating isolated and sporadic acts of violence so that the situation remains below the requisite threshold of intensity for non-international armed conflict. This room for exploitation can be narrowed by attributing the acts of an armed group to a State. Indeed, the International Criminal Tribunal for the Former Yugoslavia has established that the State may be held accountable for the conduct of a non-State armed group when it wields overall control over the group by equipping and financing them or by coordinating and helping in the general planning of their military activity.[44] Unlike attribution for the purposes of establishing the international responsibility of the State, there is no need to demonstrate that the State has issued instructions for the commission of specific acts contrary to international law.[45] As such, the State cannot deny its involvement in an international armed conflict when the surrogate armed groups, militia, or paramilitary units operate as de facto State organs,[46] or are otherwise acting on their behalf.[47] The State employing hybrid warfare could nonetheless exploit these legal thresholds by deliberately concealing the nature and level of assistance in directing the group of individuals to mount a hostile campaign against the foreign target.[48]

3. Hybrid threats at the intersection of *jus ad bellum* and *jus in bello*

The development of jurisprudence since the 1986 *Nicaragua* judgment goes some way to clarify threshold legal questions for the law of armed conflict—the hostile action either amounts to a use of force prohibited under international law or does not when it can be justified as a lawful exercise of sovereignty or in the exercise of the right of self-defence; the State is either engaging in an international

---

[44] Prosecutor v. Tadić (Appeals Chamber Judgment) ICTY-94-1-A (15 July 1999) para 131.

[45] Note, however, that with regard to 'individuals or groups not organised into military structures', the *Tadić* Tribunal considered it 'necessary to ascertain whether specific instructions concerning the commission of that particular act had been issued by that State to the individual or group in question; alternatively, it must be established whether the unlawful act had been publicly endorsed or approved ex post facto by the State at issue: Ibid. para 137.

[46] Ibid. para 144 ('private individuals acting within the framework of, or in connection with, armed forces, or in collusion with State authorities may be regarded as *de facto* State organs').

[47] See also Prosecutor v. Bosco Ntganda (Trial Chamber Judgment) ICC-01/04-02/06 (8 July 2019) para 128; Prosecutor v. Jean-Pierre Bemba Gombo (Trial Chamber III) ICC-01/05-01/08 (21 March 2016) para 130; Prosecutor v. Germain Katanga (Trial Chamber II) ICC-01/04-01/07 (7 March 2014) para 1178; Prosecutor v. Thomas Lubanga Dyilo (Trial Chamber I) ICC-01/04-01/06 (14 March 2012) para 541.

[48] It should be noted, however, that the ICTY also suggested that '[w]here the controlling State in question is an adjacent State with territorial ambitions on the State where the conflict is taking place, and the controlling State is attempting to achieve its territorial enlargement through the armed forces which it controls, it may be easier to establish the threshold': *Tadić* (n 44) para 140.

or non-international armed conflict or in a peacetime law enforcement operation. However, the different legal thresholds thus emerged under each regime are not well aligned to produce a coherent legal picture that falls squarely within the law of peace or the law of war.

For example, an armed incursion into the border area where sovereign title is contested may trigger a confrontation that is characterized as an international armed conflict between neighbouring States. As the Ethiopia-Eritrea Claims Commission confirmed, the law of armed conflict applies irrespective of the status of territory disputed between belligerent parties, and each party remains responsible for any damage unlawfully caused to persons or property no matter where the damage takes place.[49] However, the deployment of military forces in such a frontier incident alone, according to the International Court of Justice's judgment in *Nicaragua*, is insufficient to qualify as an armed attack that justifies the use of force by the other side of the border dispute as an exercise of the right of self-defence.[50] The defending State's response options are thus limited to non-forcible means, including countermeasures involving a breach of its international legal obligations towards the other party to the dispute, despite the fact that the situation itself is characterized as an international armed conflict.

The defending State may adopt the position that the right of self-defence can be exercised against any use of force by equating it as an armed attack irrespective of its scale or gravity.[51] This position is better aligned with the low threshold for the classification of an international armed conflict. The recalcitrant State can nevertheless create and exploit a legal grey zone by engaging non-State actors, such as militias and hackers. The situation may still be classified as an international armed conflict when the recalcitrant State does so by supporting or coordinating hostile activities. However, the recalcitrant State does not incur international responsibility for the activities carried out by the non-State actors unless there is evidence of direct control that meets the high threshold of attribution under the law of State responsibility as discussed above. The defending State would thus be unable to seek redress, as a breach of the principle prohibiting the use of force or a violation of its sovereignty, for the hostile activities engaged by armed groups with the support of the recalcitrant State but otherwise without any direction or control.[52] Its right to act in self-defence would also be denied

---

[49] Eritrea Ethiopia Claims Commission, *Partial Award: Central Front Ethiopia's Claim 2* (28 April 2004) paras 27–29.

[50] *Nicaragua* (n 17) para 195.

[51] As adopted by the United States: Office of the General Counsel, US Department of Defense, *Law of War Manual* (rev. edn, 2023)§ 1.11.5.2.

[52] For criticisms of such an arbitrary outcome, see Marko Milanovic, 'Special Rules of Attribution of Conduct in International Law' (2020) 96 International Law Studies 295, 317–31; Kubo Mačák, *Internationalized Armed Conflicts in International Law* (OUP 2018) 44–47.

unless the defending State is allowed to exercise the right of self-defence against non-State actors.

The legal characterization of the situation becomes even more tenuous when non-State actors engage in non-conventional modes of operation, acting as the recalcitrant State's surrogate armed groups without that State exercising any substantial degree of control over them. General appeals for mobilization would be insufficient to establish State responsibility for hostile activities or the State's involvement in an armed conflict. In the absence of any evidence suggesting State support by equipping, financing, or coordinating their hostile activity, the defending State has no choice but to treat hostile activities as criminal conduct and to take law enforcement action against them. Such a situation cannot be characterized as a non-international armed conflict unless and until hostile activities are conducted in a coordinated and organized manner and reach a high level of intensity. When the defending State escalates its response by taking military action within the recalcitrant State's territory, such action requires justification under the *jus ad bellum*.

The complex legal picture depicted above is the result of legal clarification through the development of jurisprudence. Each of these rules has been developed independently without a centralized process of law-making and has set a varying legal threshold based on its own rationale that stands to reason—for example, the right to use force in self-defence is reserved for the most grave forms of the use of force so that armed confrontation does not unnecessarily spiral out of control; the intensity of hostilities and the degree of control over non-State actors are set to low so that a greater number of people can enjoy the protective benefits of international humanitarian law. When jointed together, however, flaws emerge from the application of these legal regimes where nebulous threshold criteria are misaligned.

The 'low intensity of violence' threshold for classifying armed confrontation as an international armed conflict is not aligned with the 'armed attack' threshold as the requisite condition for military action in self-defence. The 'certain intensity of violence' threshold for a non-international armed conflict is not aligned with the parameters of what amounts to a use of force in international relations, as opposed to law enforcement action. The 'effective control' threshold for attributing the hostile conduct of non-State actors to the supporting State is not aligned with the 'overall control' threshold, according to which the supporting State becomes a party to the international armed conflict.

As the two legal regimes must be observed at the same time, the State may find itself in a situation where it is involved in an international armed conflict but unable to justify its forcible response to hostile activities under the *jus ad bellum*. In other situations, the State may consider itself constrained to take law enforcement action against hybrid threats when military action would have been justifiable had the threats been demonstrably emanating from the supporting State.

Flaws in the current legal framework of warfare thus manifest themselves at the intersection between the legal regime of the *jus ad bellum* that provides legal justifications for resorting to an armed force against external threats and the legal regime of the *jus in bello* that governs the conduct of hostilities in international or non-international armed conflict. The misalignment of nebulous threshold criteria under the two legal regimes creates a disparity between the hostile intent on the part of a recalcitrant State, the legal characterization of the situation, and the availability of legal justification for military action based on the perceived reality on the part of a defending State. However, this disparity alone is not entirely responsible for a legal grey zone that is vulnerable to exploitation in hybrid warfare. The strategic exploitability of this disparity cannot be fully appreciated without considering how these legal regimes apply in the sovereignty-based structure of international law.

4. Grey zone as the structural problem of international law

The ability of hostile actors to exploit a grey zone by employing hybrid tactics does not derive from the indeterminacy of the rules but represents structural problems of international law. The indeterminacy of rules is inherent in any system of legal regulation and, as such, is not in itself a problem in a legal system where judicial resolution is readily available for interpretive disputes.[53] Rather, problems lie with the sovereignty-based structure of international law, where the compliance with applicable rules depends primarily on their national implementation in good faith.[54] As a legal system built on the consent and practice among sovereign States its normative strength as a tool for international governance hinges upon the extent to which the relevant rules of international law are internalized in the domestic legal system and decision-making processes.

This fundamental premise on which international relations rest has the potential to create a space that malicious actors can exploit particularly against law-abiding nations. The misalignment of legal thresholds at the intersection of the *jus ad bellum* and the *jus in bello*, as discussed above, contributes to the exploitability of this legal system against the nations that abide by their legal commitments. Yet, in itself, misalignment is insufficient to create a grey zone that is vulnerable to exploitation in hybrid warfare. There are three conditions that enable recalcitrant States to operate in a grey zone by posing hybrid threats.

---

[53] Julia Black, *Rules and Regulators* (Clarendon Press 1997) 6–45.
[54] See generally Robert Kolb, *Good Faith in International Law* (Hart 2017).

First, the target State must have a well-developed legal system in which its international law obligations are systematically internalized. The ability to exploit flaws in the current legal framework of warfare is to a large extent attributed to the target State's commitment to and implementation of international law in good faith. When recalcitrant States take advantage of this commitment to the rule of law, law-compliant States face marked disadvantages in the range of tactical manoeuvres that may be available against hostile actors. The target State could be prevented from taking forcible measures against hybrid threats when, for example, the hostile activities are not perceived to be grave enough to constitute an armed attack or there are political and strategic concerns about the possible escalation of hostilities. Proactive military action to deter hybrid threats, when it involves attacks directed against the recalcitrant State, has the risk of legitimizing the latter's open involvement in the armed conflict as an exercise of the right of self-defence. The recalcitrant State may also count on the lack of readiness on the part of the adversary's allies to act in collective self-defence because of the haphazard process of collective decision-making especially where, as is the case with NATO,[55] the decision to invoke collective defence is contingent upon the consensus of all member States.

The defending State may instead decide to take law enforcement action to deal with malicious activities conducted by non-State actors. In that case, the ability to use lethal force as a means of apprehending offenders is restricted under the requirements of domestic law. This means that the defending State observing stricter limits on the use of force pursuant to law enforcement paradigms is more likely to be vulnerable to hybrid threats unless its domestic legislation allows for flexible escalation in the mode of operation as appropriate to the level and type of hostilities it faces. When operating in a law enforcement mode, defending forces may only resort to the minimum use of force that is proportionate to the threat involved and only to the extent reasonably necessary to halt the attack.[56] These domestic law constraints cause difficulties in responding effectively to coordinated attacks in an organized manner.

The second condition upon which a legal grey zone emerges for malicious exploitation is that the recalcitrant State engages militia groups to conduct hostile activities in peacetime, but with strategic goals that go beyond criminal activities. The objective of hybrid tactics is to achieve strategic goals by using a degree and form of force that is legally insufficient to permit the target State to respond

---

[55] Michael N. Schmitt, 'The North Atlantic Alliance and Collective Defense at 70: Confession and Response Revisited' (2019) 34 Emory International Law Review 85, 112; Aurel Sari, 'The Mutual Assistance Clauses of the North Atlantic and EU Treaties: The Challenge of Hybrid Threats' (2019) 10 Harvard National Security Journal 405, 415.

[56] Basic Principles on the Use of Force and Firearms by Law Enforcement Officials, adopted at the Eighth UN Congress on the Prevention of Crime and the Treatment of Offenders, 27 August—7 September 1990, UN Doc. A/CONF.144/28/Rev.1 (1991) 112–16.

effectively.[57] Such a strategy provides an incentive for the recalcitrant State to encourage its population to take part in hostilities in support of its national interest, but without clear evidence of control over their activities. To that end, the government may appeal to the strong sentiment of nationalism by way of motivating the self-organization and coordination of hostile activities directed against the target State.

Technological advances offer the third condition that helps self-organized militia engage in hostilities at various levels of intensity and in different domains such as maritime and cyberspace. As Frank Hoffman observes, hybrid warfare is not just a blend of regular and irregular warfare. Rather, the fusion of technologically advanced capabilities with fanatical and protracted fervour of irregular tactics lies at the core of this concept.[58] Technologically advanced capabilities readily available to both government and non-government sectors have increased the ability of individuals, or a group of individuals, to engage in various non-military forms of warfare in a way that surpasses the organizational, sectoral, or geographical boundaries that have been embedded in modern statecraft.

In addition, modern technologies, such as information technology and artificial intelligence-enabled deep fake technology, have provided clandestine actors with the ability to deny their involvement or to make it difficult to establish their involvement in hostile activities.[59] Plausible deniability that results therefrom makes hybrid warfare appealing as a 'tool of obfuscation', for example, to advance national interest over disputed territory or waters by forceful presence or incursion, without risking open conflict involving confrontation of military forces. The clandestine nature of militia activities thanks to these modern technologies defies the premise upon which States agree to implement international law in good faith.

The structural problems of international law, when these three conditions are present, pose challenges to the rules-based international order. Recalcitrant States enjoy the increased ability to engage in covert operations through surrogate armed groups in a non-conventional mode of hostilities to achieve their strategic goals. Defending States, on the other hand, find themselves constrained to act within the legal framework applicable to the type of situation as they perceive it. As this problem persists or even grows, Shane Reeves and Robert Barnsby have warned, States 'may begin to see this area of international law as more of an anachronistic nuisance than a legal imperative'.[60] When the law of

---

[57] Aurel Sari, 'Hybrid Warfare, Law, and the Fulda Gap' in Christopher M. Ford and Winston S. Williams (eds), *Complex Battlespaces* (OUP 2019) 161, 179–82.

[58] Frank G. Hoffman, 'Hybrid Warfare and Challenges' (2009) 52 Joint Force Quarterly 34, 37–38.

[59] Hitoshi Nasu, 'Deepfake Technology in the Age of Information Warfare' (*Articles of War*, 1 March 2022), available at https://lieber.westpoint.edu/deepfake-technology-age-information-warfare/.

[60] Shane R. Reeves and Robert E. Barnsby, 'The New Griffin of War: Hybrid International Armed Conflicts' (2013) Harvard International Review 16, 17.

armed conflict is seen as ineffectual, political and military incentives to comply with humanitarian obligations will also dissipate.

5. Conclusion

The modality of warfare has evolved and continues to change as various capabilities are developed, combined, and re-configured to enable armed forces, regular or irregular, to achieve their tactical and strategic goals. With the greater availability of technologically advanced capabilities, hybrid warfare is likely to remain a preferred mode of offensive operations for recalcitrant States that are prepared to operate at the edges of legality. It may be employed as a 'tool of obfuscation' to achieve fait accompli by taking over disputed territory or waters without risking open conflict involving confrontation of military forces. A grey zone could also be built over time to maintain persistent threats aiming at incremental revision to the existing international order by exploiting ambiguity and plausible deniability of the operation.

This chapter has demonstrated that the legal regime of the *jus ad bellum* that provides legal justifications for resorting to an armed force against external threats is misaligned with the legal regime of the *jus in bello* that governs the conduct of hostilities in international or non-international armed conflict. The disparity created as a result provides room for strategic exploitation (1) when a recalcitrant State takes advantage of the target State's internal compliance mechanisms for the good faith implementation of international law; (2) by engaging non-State actors to conduct hostile activities for strategic purposes; and (3) with technologically advanced capabilities that enable them to operate in a clandestine yet highly harmful manner at various levels of intensity and in different domains.

This analysis has demonstrated the vulnerability of international legal system when hybrid tactics are employed in a way that exploits flaws in the current legal framework of warfare which has been built through the development of jurisprudence. The malicious exploitation of this vulnerability has the potential to undermine the system of international law, as a tool to regulate State behaviour, premised on the national implementation of rules in good faith. There is therefore a good reason to regard grey zone situations created by hybrid threats as challenges to the rules-based international order. If hybrid threats continue to be posed or become widespread, international law will need to be adapted to the new reality of international relations in a way that reduces room for exploitation and allows for flexible escalation in the mode of operation as appropriate to the level and type of hostilities confronting the State.

6

The Divide between War and Peace

Tobias Vestner

'War is peace'.

George Orwell, *1984*

1. Introduction

War and peace reflect a dichotomy inherent in the desire of human beings to classify complex situations into simple and understandable concepts. Binary categories are straightforward and powerful: good and bad; right and wrong; new and old; black and white; normal and extraordinary. These categories provide clear divides that allow us quickly to grasp facts and orient action. In the divide between war and peace, the latter is an aspiration—the good and the ordinary—while the former is the situation to be avoided, the extraordinary that justifies special means, inflicts suffering, and demands sacrifice.

Yet reality is more nuanced than this dichotomy suggests. First and foremost, international politics is a permanent form of competition manifested in various scales of grey. States struggle for survival, power, and influence. Stability arises from the balance of power, international institutions, and transnationally shared values. While stability may result in the absence of war, this is not a given. Continuous preparation for war, engagement in alliances, support of proxy State and non-State actors, and conflicts at the peripheries of great powers' spheres of influence are all common features of a relatively stable international order. In addition, economic and financial competition and confrontation regarding ideals and forms of governance, such as fundamental rights and democracy, continue among States. Peace and stability may be a warlike situation for some and result in war for others.

As Clausewitz suggests with the statement that 'war is a continuation of politics by other means', war and peace are closely intertwined and interdependent in international politics. Accordingly, military strategists have thought and planned in dynamic scales between war and peace ever since. The famous Latin saying, '*Si vis pacem, para bellum*' ('if you want peace, prepare for war') suggests that wars can be prepared for and fought for the sake of peace, and a common phrase during World War I was that it was the 'war to end all wars'. More specifically, deterrence uses the projection of force to dissuade potential attackers and thereby prevent war. Military operations are categorized accordingly. The 2022 US Army Field Manual,[1] for instance, captures the idea of military operations spanning a continuum from peace to war, ranging from stability operations to large-scale combat operations. Certain military operations, such as counterinsurgency operations, are defined as 'full-spectrum operations', precisely because they cover the whole spectrum of conflict from peace to war.[2]

The reality of war and peace is indeed not clear-cut. The period after World War II was stable and did not result in war between the two great powers. Yet, because of their permanent confrontation, it was labelled the 'Cold War'. This term suggests that there was a state of war, but that it was a more nuanced affair than the binary opposition between war and peace suggests. Similarly, the era of 'Pax Americana' that followed brought global stability, yet also witnessed the emergence of the global war against terrorism, many intra-State conflicts, and a number of inter-State wars involving the hegemon, notably the war against Iraq in 2003.

In 2022, war broke out between Russia and Ukraine, leading to global repercussions and increased tensions between Russia and NATO allies, with the latter providing significant political and military support to Ukraine. The United States has also become more concerned by a rising and potentially revisionist China. So far, competition between the United States and its allies and Russia and China has not led to open war but rather a peace with indirect and limited direct military confrontation, leading to a debate as to whether the world would enter a 'Cold War 2.0'.[3] Hybrid threats, hybrid warfare, and grey zone conflict are core features of these trends and dynamics. Their very rationale is to take political, strategic, and military advantage of potentially blurred conceptual lines between war and peace.[4]

This raises the question of whether definitions of war and peace can inform a better understanding of modern competition, confrontation, and conflict, in particular of hybrid warfare and grey zone conflict. No common or widely accepted definitions of war and peace exist in the literature, however.

---

[1] US Department of the Army, *FM 3-0 Operations* (Headquarters, Department of the Army 2022).

[2] In such scenarios, armed forces perform many tasks beyond combat. Force is used on a continuum scale. See US Department of the Army, *FM 3-24, MCWP 3-33.5, Insurgencies and Countering Insurgencies* (Headquarters, Department of the Army 2014). The escalation of force is cited in sec. 1-25, paras 1–142.

[3] See e.g. Elliott Abrams, 'The New Cold War', National Review (3 March 2022) <https://www.nationalreview.com/magazine/2022/03/21/the-new-cold-war/> accessed 30 May 2023; Evan Osnos, 'Sliding toward a New Cold War', The New Yorker (26 February 2023) <https://www.newyorker.com/magazine/2023/03/06/sliding-toward-a-new-cold-war> accessed 30 May 2023.

[4] As noted by other chapters in this volume.

THE DIVIDE BETWEEN WAR AND PEACE   105

Clausewitz described war as an 'act of force to compel our enemy to do our will.'[5] Hobbes considered war as the known disposition to war to the extent that there is no assurance of the contrary: all other time would be peace.[6] More recent thinkers define war by the absence of peace.[7] Peace, on the other hand, can also be defined negatively, namely, as the absence of violence.[8] 'Positive peace', however, which is built on early Christianity's perception of peace in the form of tranquillity, has been invoked since the 1970s as an alternative understanding of peace—one characterized by justice, equality, and rights.[9] Similarly, the notion of 'quality peace' defines a different level of peace, essentially abandoning the divide between war and peace and instead defining peace as a continuum.[10]

While these conceptualizations are analytically useful, how international law treats the divide between war and peace allows us to assess how States have jointly conceptualized and continue to perceive war and peace in international relations. The respective rules under international law represent commonly agreed views on the subject with global validity. Moreover, they provide normative guidance on how States should behave in the context of war and peace. While international law thus aims to constrain State action,[11] it also serves to screen and provide information on how States intend to behave.[12] States may measure other States' actions as acceptable or unacceptable by comparing their actions with the standards provided by international law.[13] To this end, international law inherently relies on definitions, categories, and concepts, and intrinsically works towards giving them meaning according to States' views, agreements, and common language.[14] Hence, international law informs how States agree to treat war and peace as part of their mutual relations.

Accordingly, this chapter inquires how international law treats the divide between war and peace by tracing and analysing the relevant legal rules of *jus ad bellum* and *jus in bello*. Thereby, the chapter clarifies the divide's meaning as it

---

[5] Carl von Clausewitz, *On War* (Michael Howard and Peter Paret trs, Princeton University Press 1976) 75.

[6] Thomas Hobbes, *Leviathan* (1651) 82, cited in Stephen C. Neff, *War and the Law of Nations: A General History* (CUP 2005) 141, n 28.

[7] For an account of what war entails, see Larry May (ed), *War: Essays in Political Philosophy* (CUP 2008). For an overview of modern political theorists, see Irving Louis Horowitz, *The Idea of War and Peace: The Experience of Western Civilization* (3rd edn, Transaction 2007).

[8] For an overview of most definitions of peace, see Christian Davenport, Eric Melander, and Patrick M. Regan, *The Peace Continuum: What It Is and How to Study It* (OUP 2018) 36–47.

[9] See e.g. Johan Galtung, 'Violence, Peace, and Peace Research' (1969) 6 Journal of Peace Research 167.

[10] Davenport et al (n 8).

[11] Andrew Guzman, *How International Law Works: A Rational Choice Theory* (OUP 2008).

[12] Jana Von Stein, 'Do Treaties Constrain or Screen? Selection Bias and Treaty Compliance' (2005) 99 American Political Science Review 611.

[13] Jack L. Goldsmith and Eric A. Posner, *The Limits of International Law* (OUP 2005).

[14] Martti Koskenniemi, *From Apology to Utopia: The Structure of the Legal Argument* (CUP 2006).

is commonly agreed by States and manifested in related behaviour. It also offers insights into the respective legal challenges that are particularly relevant to hybrid threats, hybrid warfare, and grey zone conflict. The chapter finds that international law has evolved in such a way as to encapsulate war with different labels and legal concepts: war is prohibited under the banner of the use of force; war is fought in the name of international peace and security when authorized by the UN Security Council; war tends to be justified as self-defence; and the existence of war is determined by the relatively aleatory application of the law of armed conflict (LOAC)/international humanitarian law (IHL).

Hence, the chapter argues that due to its conceptualization and evolution, modern international law does not offer much clarity on the divide between war and peace. Rather, international law confuses the boundaries and conflates the concepts—implying certain parallels to what Orwell had termed 'war is peace'— to the extent that there is a relatively broad legal grey zone on the two notions. This results in analytical difficulties, but also a certain normative permissibility, which is particularly relevant in the context of hybrid threats, hybrid warfare, and grey zone conflict. The chapter concludes by identifying normative implications for the future of peace and war.

2. Peace became the norm

The divide between war and peace has been a central focus of moral and legal thinking regarding States' international relations and coexistence. Neff identifies four different eras of thinking on war and peace in international law.[15] Until the Middle Ages, there was a strong association between justice and war. This led to the development of the 'Just War Doctrine'. With natural law as the dominant legal framework, war was primarily perceived as a worldly means to enforce a godly order. In the words of Cicero: 'Wars, then, ought not to be undertaken except for this purpose, that we may live in peace, without injustice'.[16] Although conscious that peace was an ideal, early thinkers insisted that worldly action should follow this ideal. Hence, the need for a *casus belli* to resort to war, namely, an acceptable reason that would uphold larger community ideals. Christian political philosophers who perceived war as the means to combat evil further developed this, ultimately establishing criteria for a war to be just.[17]

---

[15] Neff (n 6) 3. The following draws on Neff's analysis of the four eras of thinking.

[16] Marcus Tullius Cicero, *On Duties*, 14–15, cited ibid. 13, n 2.

[17] These are generally: having just cause, being a last resort, being declared by a proper authority, possessing right intention, having a reasonable chance of success, and the end being proportional to the means used.

THE DIVIDE BETWEEN WAR AND PEACE   107

The law of nations emerged from the period of around 1600 to 1815 and overshadowed the Just War Doctrine. Grotius marked its creation with his treatise 'The Rights of War and Peace'.[18] States became the sole subjects of international law and the formalities of inter-State relations became central features of the international legal system. Law was perceived as the creation of humans, not nature, and so was war. Adopting a utilitarian view of international politics that culminated in a Hobbesian world view, war was perceived as a duelling form of State interaction. This was complemented by the development of standing armies that separated warfighters with a professional ethos from civilians. With due regard to form, formal requirements had to be observed for a war to be a 'perfect war', although 'imperfect wars' were still considered wars when they fulfilled objective requirements. Overall, the normative stance of natural law remained present throughout legal thinking in this period, but the functioning of international law became more formalistic and morally unloaded.

The nineteenth-century international legal system continued to develop in this direction. With legal positivism becoming the dominant paradigm, war was perceived as a clash of rival State interests and an accepted feature of international politics. International law now ignored moral perceptions of war. War was also no longer at the service of justice or community values, but simply a tool of State interest. Hence, war became an institution of international law with rules of an objective character. War and peace were now completely separate states of affairs with distinct rules governing State behaviour. Interestingly from the point of view of modern grey zone conflicts and hybrid threats, the nineteenth-century international legal system foresaw 'measures short of war', namely, interventions to promote the international community's general interests, reprisals as a self-help measure against prior wrongdoing, and emergency actions like self-defence. These were acts of war during the general state of peace that would not trigger the state of war. Like war, they were not illegal, but they were still regulated by international law.

The international legal system following World War I re-endorsed the medieval just-war outlook. The period of the League of Nations established a distinction between lawful and unlawful resort to war. War was first outlawed by the 1928 Kellogg-Briand Pact.[19] After World War II, States banned the threat and use of force in international relations by the UN Charter and established the UN collective security system to monitor and enforce this ban.[20] War was dismissed as

[18] Hugo Grotius, *The Rights of War and Peace* (Richard Tuck ed, Liberty Fund 2005).
[19] Oona A Hathaway and Scott J Shapiro, *The Internationalists: How a Radical Plan to Outlaw War Remade the World* (Simon and Schuster 2018).
[20] Nicholas Tsagourias and Nigel D White, *Collective Security: Theory, Law and Practice* (CUP 2013).

a concept under international law and peace was set as the norm in international politics. Similarly, the four Geneva Conventions (GCs) of 1949 did not give normative significance to war but were built on the rather technical notion of 'armed conflict'. It soon became clear, however, that war would remain a feature of international politics: since the adoption of the UN Charter, war in a colloquial, practical sense has never ceased to exist around the globe.

This leads to two sets of issues. First, if war is ruled out and has no proper normative significance, meaning that peace is the norm, then international law does not provide a straightforward distinction between war and peace. However, it is more complicated than this. A closer study of how international law labels and deals with warlike situations is necessary to identify the conceptualization and nuances of the war-peace divide. Second, if the norm is peace but the reality is often war, then there seems to be a disconnect between the normative state of affairs—'peace'—and the actual reality in many parts of the world—'war'. This has a particular significance in the context of hybrid threats, hybrid warfare, and grey zone conflict, because many argue that States take warlike actions below the thresholds of the prohibition on the use of force under *jus ad bellum* and armed conflicts under *jus in bello*, so essentially they take warlike actions during peacetime.[21] More generally, this suggests that the normative treatment of war and peace does not accurately reflect reality.

The following sections will address these issues in detail. They will show how international law has evolved to encapsulate war with different labels and legal concepts: war is prohibited under the banner of the use of force; war is fought in the name of international peace and security; war tends to be justified as self-defence; and the existence of war is determined by the application of LOAC/IHL. They will also show that there is no substantial disconnect between law and reality, because the law has adapted to State practice. Hence, the divide between war and peace in international law has evolved such that it mainly consists of a single legal grey zone that is relatively indeterminate. International law has thus become unclear and indeterminate regarding the divide between war and peace, with both analytical and normative consequences.

---

[21] Rosa Brooks, 'Rule of Law in the Gray Zone' (Modern War Institute, July 2, 2018) <https://mwi.usma.edu/rule-law-gray-zone/> accessed 30 May 2023; Williamson Murray and Peter R. Mansoor (eds), *Hybrid Warfare: Fighting Complex Opponents from the Ancient World to the Present* (CUP 2012); Scott H. Englund, 'A Dangerous Middle-Ground: Terrorists, Counter-Terrorists, and Gray-Zone Conflict' (2019) 5 Global Affairs 389; Steven Haines, 'War at Sea: Nineteenth-Century Laws for Twenty-First Century Wars?' (2016) 98 International Review of the Red Cross 419; Jeffrey Kahn, 'Hybrid Conflict and Prisoners of War: The Case of Ukraine' (2018) SMU Dedman School of Law Legal Studies Research Paper 381 <https://papers.ssrn.com/sol3/papers.cfm?abstract_id=3127020> accessed 30 May 2023; Aurel Sari, 'Legal Resilience in an Era of Grey Zone Conflicts and Hybrid Threats' (2020) 33 Cambridge Review of International Affairs 846.

THE DIVIDE BETWEEN WAR AND PEACE   109

3. A permeable ban of the use of force

The post-World War II international legal order proscribes war, and the general state of international affairs from a normative perspective should be peace. The UN Charter mentions 'war' once in its preamble: 'We the peoples of the United Nations determined to save succeeding generations from the scourge of war . . .'.[22] Apart from this fleeting mention and a few references to World War II, war is non-existent in the Charter. The UN's main purpose is formulated positively as 'to maintain international peace and security'.[23] In this spirit, the UN Charter does not outlaw 'war' but explicitly prohibits the 'threat or use of force' under its Article 2(4). Two exceptions remain, however, namely, UN Security Council action under the collective security system and the right to individual or collective self-defence. Both exceptions were narrowly drafted to allow to react to a breach of the prohibition of the use of force in order to re-establish peaceful coexistence.

Yet since 1945, State practice has undermined the strict prohibition of the use of force. It is empirically difficult to know when the prohibition has actually prevented States from using force, because only violations are apparent to observers outside decision-making processes. Nonetheless, given the manifold conflicts around the globe, it is hard to contend that the general state of affairs in international relations is peace. Glennon had already identified 680 violations of the prohibition on the use of force by 2010,[24] and since then States have continued to violate the prohibition.[25] Indeed, any use of force between States that reaches a certain threshold of gravity[26] without authorization by the UN Security Council is a breach of the UN Charter. Even when a State lawfully uses force in legitimate self-defence, the initial armed attack against this State would be a violation of Article 2(4).

---

[22] Charter of the United Nations (June 26, 1945) 1 UNTS XVI (UN Charter).

[23] Article 1(1), UN Charter.

[24] Michael J. Glennon, *The Fog of Law: Pragmatism, Security, and International Law* (Stanford University Press 2010) 228.

[25] For prominent examples, see Tom Ruys, Olivier Corten, and Alexandra Hofer (eds), *The Use of Force in International Law: A Case-Based Approach* (OUP 2018).

[26] See, for example, *Corfu Channel Case (United Kingdom v Albania)* (Merits) [1949] ICJ Rep. 4, 35, and *Fisheries Jurisdiction Case (Spain v Canada)* (Jurisdiction) [1998] ICJ Rep. 432, 466, para 84, where the Court seems to affirm that the 'minimum use of force' does not fall within the scope of Article 2(4); however, see also the *Nicaragua* case regarding 'less-grave forms' of the use of force that are violations of the UN Charter: *Military and Paramilitary Activities in and against Nicaragua (Nicaragua v United States of America)* (Merits) [1986] ICJ Rep. 14, para 191. For a comprehensive analyses of this issue, see Olivier Corten, 'What Do "Use of Force" and "Threat of Force" Mean?' in Olivier Corten, *The Law Against War: The Prohibition on the Use of Force in Contemporary International Law* (2nd edn, Hart 2021); Tom Ruys, 'The Meaning of "Force" and the Boundaries of the Jus ad Bellum: Are "Minimal" Uses of Force Excluded from UN Charter Article 2(4)?' (2014) 108 American Journal of International Law 159.

110 WHAT ARE HYBRID THREATS AND GREY ZONE CONFLICT?

Already in 1970, Franck diagnosed the death of Article 2(4) of the UN Charter because of its inability to prevent States from using military force in international affairs.[27] The seeming irrelevance of the Charter law has also led scholars to ask the editor of the Oxford Commentary on the UN Charter why he would bother to continue working on it.[28] Indeed, it appears that States no longer believe in the system of the Charter because the collective security guarantees they have received in exchange for renouncing their individual and collective rights to resort to force tend not to work.[29] States continue to invest in their individual capacities to ensure their national security, which suggests that they do not fully rely on the protection offered by the prohibition of the use of force. Even if States routinely emphasize the value of Article 2(4), their actions are not so different from a situation where the provision did not exist.[30] The rules of behaviour embedded in the Charter can therefore be perceived as aspirational norms.[31]

Indeed, if a rule is breached by a significant number of States a significant number of times over a significant period of time, it can hardly be described as a constraining norm of international law. Seen from this perspective, Article 2(4) has fallen into desuetude due to a 'thick' contrary practice of States.[32] Alternatively, one could argue that the prohibition lacks precision and that therefore States often do not violate the prohibition. If so, given that the international law system is consent-based (meaning that States are free to act how they please as long as they do so without violating their legal obligations), disputes over its application are likely to be decided in favour of the State proposing to act.[33] This indeed leads to the same conclusion, namely, that Article 2(4) does not effectively ban States from using force against each other. Thus, it can be concluded that 'this decaying de jure catechism is overly schematized and scholastic, disconnected from State behaviour, and unrealistic in its aspirations for State conduct'.[34]

The debate on a customary rule prohibiting the use of force between States further illustrates the limits of the norm. Those who argue that the customary

---

[27] Thomas M. Frank, 'Who Killed Article 2(4)? or: Changing Norms Governing the Use of Force by States' (1970) 64 American Journal of International Law 809, 809–10.

[28] Bruno Simma et al (eds), *The Charter of the United Nations: A Commentary* (3rd edn, OUP 2012) Vol 1, Preface.

[29] Jean Combacau, 'The Exception of Self-Defence in the U.N. Practice', in Antonio Cassese (ed), *The Current Legal Regulation of the Use of Force* (Martinus Nijhoff 1986) 32.

[30] Ibid. 30.

[31] Richard Anderson Falk, *Revitalizing International Law* (Iowa State University Press 1989) 96.

[32] This was recently pointed out in the context of the war between Russia and Ukraine. See Claus Kreß, *The Ukraine War and the Prohibition of the Use of Force in International Law* (Torkel Opsahl Academic EPublisher 2022) para 4; Nico Krisch, 'After Hegemony: The Law on the Use of Force and the Ukraine Crisis' (*EJIL Talk*, March 2, 2022) <https://www.ejiltalk.org/after-hegemony-the-law-on-the-use-of-force-and-the-ukraine-crisis> accessed 30 May 2023.

[33] Michael J. Glennon, *Limits of Law, Prerogatives of Power: Interventionism after Kosovo* (Palgrave Macmillan 2001) 63–64.

[34] Mary Ellen O'Connell, Christian J Tams, and Dire Tladi, *Self-Defence against Non-State Actors* (CUP 2019) 19.

THE DIVIDE BETWEEN WAR AND PEACE   111

rule is identical to Article 2(4) struggle to make the case because States have used military force against each other both before and after the UN Charter. In addition, the reactions of other States were often ambiguous and inadequate.[35] Those who argue that the customary norm is different from Article 2(4) also face the difficulty of proving a coherent *opinio juris* among States.

Scholarly work on the prohibition of the use of force under the banner of '*jus contra bellum*' leads to the same conclusion. A conservative view of the prohibition, namely, that the UN Charter's prohibition is well defined, implies that States' repeated violations are all too obvious.[36] The same is true for a normative reading of the prohibition, namely, an interpretation that focuses more on what the law should be rather than what it is in practice.[37] Interestingly, Gray, in her rigorous analysis of international law on the use of force, rarely spells out that State actions would represent violations of Article 2(4). Thus, she tends to avoid taking a position on the viability of the prohibition—yet she does explicitly recognize that the rule is under stress.[38]

More recently, Russia's manifest violation of the prohibition of the use of force against Ukraine in 2022 provoked strong condemnations by the international community, including by the UN General Assembly.[39] Western States also strongly reacted both rhetorically and with concrete measures, such as sanctions and the provision of military assistance to Ukraine. These reactions uphold and may strengthen the prohibition in the long run because they confirm States' attachment to the prohibition.[40] Nonetheless, resolute reactions as in this case tend to be the exception in international affairs. Many violations of the prohibition tend to be tolerated, or at least to provoke little reaction.

The consequence of these developments regarding the prohibition of the use of force is that peace as the norm according to the black letter of the UN Charter does not reflect reality. As such, although it may be beneficial to have an aspirational norm to indicate how States should behave, the norm does not help to provide clarity on situations, because it has been violated too often to represent the actual standard of behaviour. Indeed, there is a disconnect between what States

---

[35] Christine Gray, *International Law and the Use of Force* (4th edn, Oxford University Press 2018) 28, citing Gaetano Arangio-Ruiz, *The UN Declaration on Friendly Relations and the System of Sources of International Law: With an Appendix on the Concept of International Law and the Theory of International Organisation* (Sijthoff and Noordhoff 1979).

[36] Raphaël van Steenberghe, 'The Law against War or Jus contra Bellum: A New Terminology for a Conservative View on the Use of Force?' (2011) 24 Leiden Journal of International Law 747.

[37] See Robert Kolb, *International Law on the Maintenance of Peace: Jus Contra Bellum* (Edward Elgar 2018).

[38] Gray (n 35) Introduction.

[39] See e.g. UN General Assembly Resolution ES-11/1 (March 2, 2022) UN Doc. A/RES/ES-11/1.

[40] Juliette François-Blouin, 'Implications for International Security Law', in Thomas Greminger and Tobias Vestner (eds), *The Russia-Ukraine War's Implications for Global Security: A First Multi-issue Analysis* (Geneva Centre for Security Policy 2022).

112 WHAT ARE HYBRID THREATS AND GREY ZONE CONFLICT?

have agreed on and portray as the norm and their actual standard of behaviour. The delimitation of proper behaviour has thus become indeterminate. Therefore, the prohibition is not particularly useful for identifying the divide between war and peace. Moreover, the repeated violation of the prohibition suggests that it is permeable. Thus, the norm that there is 'peace' is not particularly constraining but rather relatively permissive for States. This means that the norm that there is peace tends to be confusing and poorly delimited. This also suggests that the prohibition is too loose to provide proper legal boundaries for assessing and guiding hybrid threats and military action in grey zone conflicts.

4. War with—and in—the name of peace

In line with treating the normal State of international affairs as peace, the UN collective security system does not foresee war as a general status. The Charter only foresees wars as exceptions, but does not call these exceptions 'war'. According to Article 39 of the Charter, the Security Council 'shall determine the existence of any threat to the peace, breach of the peace, or act of aggression'. Any following measures based on Articles 41 and 42 of the Charter shall intend to 'maintain or restore international peace and security'. The closest concept to war is thus an 'act of aggression', which is a narrowly defined action.[41] A 'breach of the peace' means that the peace is undermined, although there is no associated definition of what this situation would be other than not peace.

The notion of peace under Article 39 of the UN Charter has therefore been defined in a negative way as the absence of conflict. This serves the purpose of allowing the Security Council to react to a conflict. It has then been applied more extensively to encompass a set of political, social, and economic circumstances obstructing the rise of future conflicts,[42] which serve to promote general conditions for conflict prevention. Yet Security Council action only focuses on 'international peace and security', not 'war'. Any Council reaction is conceptualized as a measure to ensure international peace and security, even if this involves the use of military force over a long period of time. Indeed, any such action can be considered a form of law enforcement in response to the violation of the prohibition of the use of force and other values agreed by UN member States, rather than war between equal parties.[43]

---

[41] UN General Assembly Resolution 3314 (XXIX), 'Definition of Aggression' (14 December 1974) UN Doc. A/RES/3314 (XXIX).

[42] Benedetto Conforti and Carlo Focarelli, *The Law and Practice of the United Nations* (4th edn, Brill 2010) 206.

[43] See e.g. Jean d'Aspremont, 'The Collective Security System and the Enforcement of International Law', in Marc Weller (ed), *The Oxford Handbook of the Use of Force in International Law* (OUP 2015) 129.

THE DIVIDE BETWEEN WAR AND PEACE   113

In practice, the Security Council only uses a 'threat to peace' as the qualifier for its action.[44] Chapter VII resolutions are usually adopted after and on the basis of the qualification of a situation as a 'threat to peace and security' by the Security Council. Alternatively, the Council has adopted resolutions under Chapter VII by referring back to resolutions where it had already made such a determination. In a few cases, the Security Council has omitted to qualify the situation as such because of the disagreement over the scope of its own powers.[45]

The Security Council's qualification of situations as a 'threat to peace', however, is so broad and diverse that it does not provide much indication as to what could constitute war or a warlike situation. From a temporal perspective, the notion of threat implies that a conflict has arisen or is likely to arise (albeit limited to situations with a concrete and acute risk of conflict in a particular case).[46] Yet the category is subject to extensive interpretation. In 1992, for instance, the Security Council issued a statement affirming that the 'non-military sources of instability in the economic, social, humanitarian and ecological fields have become threats to peace and security'.[47] The 2004 High-level Panel Report also stated that the Security Council is fully empowered under Chapter VII to address the full range of security threats with which States are concerned.[48]

The material scope of the notion of a threat to peace is also very wide. While inter-State conflicts are considered the model case of a threat to peace, the notion has been broadened to encompass States' internal situations. Internal crises with implications for regional or global stability have thus been qualified as threats to peace.[49] The Security Council subsequently did the same regarding purely internal conflicts without any direct international or transboundary ramifications.[50] The violation of human rights (first and foremost the targeting of civilians[51] and the widespread suffering of the civilian population in armed conflicts[52]), the proliferation of arms, and terrorism have also been qualified as threats to peace.[53] Thus, although States tend not to perceive the designation of a particular situation as a 'threat to peace' as being at the unrestricted discretion

---

[44] Simma et al (n 28) 1293.

[45] E.g. UN Security Council Resolution 1160 (31 March 1998) UN Doc. S/RES/1160; UN Security Council Resolution 1970 (26 January 2011) UN Doc. S/RES/1970.

[46] Simma et al (n 28) 1291.

[47] UN Security Council Presidential Note (31 January 1992) UN Doc. S/23500, 3.

[48] High-level Panel on Threats, Challenges and Change, 'A More Secure World: Our Shared Responsibility' (United Nations 2004).

[49] E.g. Palestine in 1948; South Africa in the 1970s and 1980s; Sierra Leone, Liberia, and Somalia in the 1990s and 2000s; Indonesia in 1948; Congo in 1961; Yugoslavia in 1991; and Somalia in 1992.

[50] Simma et al (n 28) 1279, 1282–83.

[51] UN Security Council Resolution 1296 (19 April 2000) UN Doc. S/RES/1296; see also, e.g. UN Security Council Verbatim Record (11 November 2009) UN Doc. S/PV.6216.

[52] See, e.g., United Nations General Assembly Resolution 2675 (XXV) (December 9 December, 1970) UN Doc. A/RES/2675 (XXV).

[53] Simma et al (n 28) 1281–82.

of the Security Council, it is hard to argue that this is a well-defined legal concept. In addition, there are only very rudimentary legal limits on the Security Council's discretionary powers,[54] and the Council is mainly a political organ that uses its institutional and legal prerogatives in line with its permanent members' preferences.[55]

The consequence of the UN Security Council's practice is that situations that could easily be qualified as war are not, but only qualified as a—somewhat benign—'threat to peace'. The same applies to the use of military force authorized or mandated by the Security Council in reaction to such threats, which is not called 'war'. The reactions are fought with and in the name of peace: they are called 'all necessary means' to 'establish and maintain international peace and security'. While this may be helpful for ensuring an aspirational discourse on world peace and may indicate that the reaction should be limited, this confounds the reason and rationale for intervention with the actual actions and factual situation, namely warfighting and war. It certainly does not help to clarify the difference between situations of war and peace.

The war between Russia and Ukraine has not led to a paradigm shift in this regard. The Security Council has not classified the war between Russia and Ukraine due to Russia's ability to veto such a resolution. The UN General Assembly has called it an 'act of aggression',[56] although it does not talk of 'war' in its resolutions; the UN Secretary-General, the European Union, and others have used this term, however.[57] As such, the practice of the UN Security Council, even if based on the Charter's categories for taking action, is not particularly informative on the divide between war and peace but rather adds to the confusion characterizing these concepts. This means that it also does not elucidate the nuances of the divide in the context of hybrid warfare and grey zone conflict. Even if the Security Council were to determine that certain hybrid threats or actions would constitute a threat to peace, for instance, this would not clarify much, because this category is not well defined and consistently applied in practice. Such a determination would simply indicate that the Security Council

---

[54] Erika de Wet, *The Chapter VII Powers of the United Nations Security Council* (Hart 2004).

[55] Erik Voeten, 'The Political Origins of the UN Security Council's Ability to Legitimize the Use of Force' (2005) 59 International Organization 527; Adam Roberts and Dominik Zaum, *Selective Security: War and the United Nations Security Council since 1945* (Routledge 2008).

[56] See e.g. UN General Assembly Resolution ES-11/1 (n 39); UN General Assembly Resolution ES-11/2 (24 March 2022) UN Doc. A/RES/ES-11/2.

[57] See, e.g., 'Secretary-General's Remarks on Russian Decision on Annexation of Ukrainian Territory' (29 September 2022) <https://www.un.org/sg/en/content/sg/speeches/2022-09-29/secretary-generals-remarks-russian-decision-annexation-of-ukrainian-territory%C2%A0> accessed 30 May 2023; European Parliament, 'Russia's Escalation of Its War of Aggression against Ukraine', P9_TA(2022)0353 (6 October 2022); North Atlantic Treaty Organization, 'Statement by NATO Heads of State and Government' (24 March 2022) <https://www.nato.int/cps/en/natohq/official_texts_193719.htm> accessed 30 May 2023.

THE DIVIDE BETWEEN WAR AND PEACE   115

perceives the act seriously enough to consider reacting to it due to the risk of leading to war or insecurity.

5. Self-defence as a catch-all justification

Since the UN Charter does not foresee war as general state of affairs and the Security Council reacts to war and warlike situations in the name of peace, the question then becomes if and under what conditions States recognize war as a situation that is distinct from peace as per international law. In the past, States formally declared war to alter their official relations with opponents and other States and to change the general status of affairs and related rules of behaviour. This practice has fallen into desuetude.[58] Yet States tend to officially admit and declare their use of force as representing a warlike action when they justify their violence as self-defence. This is comparable to States' previous 'declarations of war', but with the exception that the status of peace does not formally change to the status of war. This also appears to be analogous to States renaming 'ministries of war' as 'ministries of defence'.

Originally intended as a temporary remedy for States to defend themselves against an armed attack until the UN Security Council takes action, self-defence has become the most prominent justification for using military force against States and non-State actors. Indeed, the concept has been so widely used that it has become the legal justification per se for any use of force.[59] Such a broad application in conjunction with the general difficulty of establishing the facts underlying the justification makes the legal concept relatively indeterminate and permissive. Hence, rather than being the right that justifies an exceptional action, it is the most prominent legal label for modern warfighting. Yet, different from formal declarations of war, which established a clear divide between war and other situations of violence, such as measures short of war, self-defence is not only invoked in the context of high-intensity conflicts but also for military actions limited in time, scope, and intensity. A prominent example is the

---

[58] Tanisha M Fazal, 'Why States No Longer Declare War' (2012) 21 Security Studies 557.

[59] Andrea Bianchi, 'The International Regulation of the Use of Force: The Politics of Interpretive Method' (2009) 22 Leiden Journal of International Law 651, 670 ; Gray (n 35), 121; Tom Ruys, 'Armed Attack' and Article 51 of the UN Charter (CUP 2011) 53–54; Terry D. Gill and Kinga Tibori-Szabó, 'Twelve Key Questions on Self-Defense against Non-State Actors' (2019) 95 International Law Studies 467, 482; Russell Buchan, 'Non-forcible Measures and the Law of Self-defence' (2023) 72(1) International & Comparative Law Quarterly 1, 2. Yet, for the argument that the baseline probability of claiming the right remains low, see Atsushi Tago, 'Why Do States Formally Invoke the Right of Individual Self Defense? Legal-, Diplomatic- and Aid-politics to Motivate States to Respect International Law' (2013) 30(2) Conflict Management and Peace Science 161.

116 WHAT ARE HYBRID THREATS AND GREY ZONE CONFLICT?

targeted US strike to kill Qasem Soleimani, an Iranian military commander in 2021.[60]

The right to use force in collective or individual self-defence against unlawful attacks finds its legal basis in Article 51 of the UN Charter. The provision does not indicate either the precise meaning or a definition of the right to self-defence but is drafted in strict terms.[61] Major disputes exist as to what amounts to an armed attack and the temporal scope of the right's invocation.[62] State practice suggests that the resort to defensive force is associated with a State reacting to another State's use of force in preservation of the former's territorial domain and physical existence. Many affirm that a parallel and broader notion of self-defence exists under customary law that the adoption of the Charter has left untouched,[63] according to which a State may resort to self-defence when the necessity to react is 'instant, overwhelming and leaving no choice of means'.[64] In addition, measures taken in the exercise of self-defence must not be unreasonable or excessive, but rather limited by necessity and proportionality.[65] The International Court of Justice (ICJ) affirmed that only 'the most grave forms of the use of force' constitute an armed attack, and that 'less grave forms' are excluded.[66] This does not, however, offer much clarity for assessing what amounts to an armed attack in practice.

At the outset, Article 51 was generally perceived as not allowing anticipatory self-defence,[67] albeit self-defence under customary law is also deemed to allow defensive force in instances of imminent or actual dangers to the physical integrity of the State in question.[68] After the terrorist attacks of 11 September 2001

[60] Christian Henderson, 'The 25 February 2021 Military Strikes and the "Armed Attack" Requirement of Self-Defence: from "Sina qua Non" to the Point of Vanishing?' (2022) 9 Journal on the Use of Force and International Law 55.

[61] Derek W. Bowett, Self-defense in International Law (Lawbook Exchange 2014) 187; see also Jan Klabbers, International Law (2nd edn, CUP 2017) 209; Hans Kelsen, The Law of the United Nations: A Critical Analysis of Its Fundamental Problems (Stevens and Sons 1950) 269, 797–98.

[62] Malcolm N. Shaw, International Law (8th edn, CUP 2017) 861.

[63] Bowett (n 61) 184, 188; see also Institut de Droit International, 'Present Problems of the Use of Armed Force in International Law, Resolution 10A' (2007) <https://www.idi-iil.org/app/uploads/2017/06/2007_san_02_en.pdf> accessed 30 May 2023; and HL Deb (21 April 2004) vol 660, cols 370-1; the ICJ confirmed that Article 51 does not subsume or supervene customary international law. Therefore, they constitute two different sources of law that continue to exist alongside the others. See Nicaragua (n 26) 94.

[64] 'Letter from Webster to Lord Ashburton (6 August 1842)', in H. Miller (ed), Treaties and Other International Acts of the United States of America (US Government Printing Office 1934) Vol 4, 454–55.

[65] The ICJ affirmed that (1) the necessity of the responsive action with respect to the threat or actual attack and (2) the proportionality therewith are two cumulative conditions necessary for the right to self-defence to be lawfully exercised. See Oil Platforms (Islamic Republic of Iran v United States of America) (Merits) (2003) ICJ Rep. 161, para 43.

[66] Nicaragua (n 26) 101; Oil Platforms (n 65) 187.

[67] For an analysis of such arguments and proposed counterarguments, see Ian Brownlie, International Law and the Use of Force by States (Clarendon Press 1981) 276–78.

[68] Ibid. 252; Leland M. Goodrich and Edvard Hambro, Charter of the United Nations: Commentary and Documents (World Peace Foundation 1946) 301.

THE DIVIDE BETWEEN WAR AND PEACE   117

(the so-called 9/11 attacks), however, the United States expanded the temporal scope of application to include the notion of 'pre-emptive self-defence'. This concept refers to the use of force to halt a particular tangible course of action that the potential victim State perceives will shortly evolve into an armed attack against itself. This requires having good reasons to believe that the attack is likely, is near at hand, and, in case of its materialization, will result in significant harm.[69] A broader understanding of self-defence, so-called 'preventive self-defence', refers to the use of force to halt a serious future threat of an armed attack without clarity about when or where that attack may occur. The use of force may also be viewed as preventive when it purports to respond to a State's or group's threatening behaviour in the absence of credible evidence that the State or group has the capacity and intent to attack.[70]

Another tendency regarding the expansive use of Article 51 concerns the invocation of the right to self-defence against non-State actors. State practice has followed two different approaches. Some claim that acting in self-defence in response to an attack by non-State actors may find support in the wording of Article 51 because it does not define the perpetrator of the armed attack and therefore non-State actors can qualify as such.[71] Others argue that using force against non-State actors does not fall under the scope of Article 2(4) of the Charter because it only prohibits the use of force against other States. Therefore, self-defence against non-State actors would not require a justification under Article 51.[72] The ICJ cases on the *Corfu Channel, Tehran Hostages, Military and Paramilitary Activities in and against Nicaragua,* and *DR Congo v. Uganda* established an inter-State reading of Article 51 by consistently resorting to the notion of attribution to link a non-State armed group's attack to the State allegedly supporting it.[73] Yet arguably, the ICJ left open the question as to whether a State is entitled under Article 51 to react in self-defence against an attack launched by

---

[69] Ashley Deeks, 'Taming the Doctrine of Pre-Emption', in Weller (n 43) 661, 662–63.

[70] Ibid. 663.

[71] Klabbers (n 61) 213; Yoram Dinstein, *War, Aggression and Self-defence* (6th edn, CUP 2017) 241; Sean D. Murphy, 'Terrorism and the Concept of "Armed Attack" in Article 51 of the UN Charter' (2002) 43 Harvard International Law Journal 41, 50; Separate Opinion of Judge Higgins, in *Legal Consequences of the Construction of a Wall* (Advisory Opinion) (2004) ICJ Rep. 136, 215; for a counterargument, see André De Hoogh, 'Restrictivist Reasoning on the Ratione Personae Dimension of Armed Attacks in the Post 9/11 World' (2016) 29 Leiden Journal of International Law 19, 22.

[72] Jörg Kammerhofer, *Uncertainty in International Law: A Kelsenian Perspective* (Routledge 2011) 38–39.

[73] *Corfu Channel* (n 26) 22; see also UN General Assembly Resolution 2625 (XXV), 'Declaration on Principles of International Law concerning Friendly Relations and Cooperation among States in Accordance with the Charter of the United Nations' (24 October 1970) UN Doc. A/RES/2625 (XXV); *United States Diplomatic and Consular Staff in Tehran* (*United States of America v Iran*) (Judgment) (1980) ICJ Rep. 3, 35; *Nicaragua, supra* n. 26; *Armed Activities on the Territory of the Congo* (*Democratic Republic of the Congo v Uganda*) (Merits) (2005) ICJ Rep. 168.

118   WHAT ARE HYBRID THREATS AND GREY ZONE CONFLICT?

an armed group operating from abroad without this attack being linked to any State (an unattributable armed attack).[74]

The 9/11 terrorist attacks were a turning point, because practice thereafter departed from the ICJ jurisprudence on attribution, which some consider to have altered customary law.[75] With Operation Enduring Freedom, the United States responded in self-defence under Article 51 to the attacks perpetrated by Al-Qaeda in New York and Washington, DC, although they were not attributable to the then de facto Taliban government according to the traditional criterion of effective control upheld by the ICJ.[76] Although this line of reasoning had been contested in the past, the international community accepted it.[77] After 9/11, Western States' interpretation and application of Article 51 of the Charter further expanded.[78] To justify their action in self-defence, including when fighting against the Islamic State of Iraq and the Levant (ISIL; also known as Islamic State of Iraq and Syria, ISIS; and Daesh) after 2014, States have often referred to the unwillingness or inability of the territorial State to suppress the extra-territorial threat posed by the non-State actor operating therefrom.[79] States not directly involved supported—or at least did not condemn—this justification, but the 'unwilling or unable' doctrine remains debated.[80]

[74] For the conclusions drawn by commentators from this gap, see e.g. Kimberley N Trapp, 'Can Non-State Actors Mount an Armed Attack?' in Weller (n 43) 679, 689; Michael Byers, 'Terrorism, the Use of Force, and International Law after 11 September' (2002) 51 International and Comparative Law Quarterly 401, 409–10.

[75] Carsten Stahn, 'International Law at a Crossroads? The Impact of September 11' (2002) 62 Zeitschrift für ausländisches öffentliches Recht und Völkerrecht 183, 216, 227; see also Anne-Marie Slaughter and William Burke-White, 'An International Constitutional Moment' (2002) 43 Harvard International Law Journal 1, 20.

[76] The criterion of effective control is confirmed in the International Law Commission's, 'Draft Articles on Responsibility of States for Internationally Wrongful Acts', in [2001] Yearbook of the International Law Commission Vol II(2), 26.

[77] Shaw (n 62) 865; Trapp (n 74) 694. See the UN Security Council condemnation of Israel's attack on the Palestinian Liberation Organization headquarters in Tunisia in 1985 and the concern expressed by a number of governments with respect to the territorial integrity of Sudan and Afghanistan after the US attack; see Byers (n 74) 407; Antonio Cassese, 'The International Community's Legal Response to Terrorism' (1989) 38 International and Comparative Law Quarterly 589, 598–99.

[78] Olivia Flash, 'The Legality of the Air Strikes against ISIL in Syria: New Insights on the Extraterritorial Use of Force Against Non-state Actors' (2016) 3 Journal on the Use of Force and International Law 37, 56.

[79] With respect to the US attack on Afghanistan in 2001, President Bush affirmed that the Taliban regime was 'sponsoring and sheltering and supplying terrorists'. See George W. Bush, 'Address to a Joint Session of Congress and the American People' (White House, 20 September 2001) <https:// georgewbush-whitehouse.archives.gov/news/releases/2001/09/20010920-8.html> accessed 30 May 2023; more recently with respect to the intervention against ISIL/ISIS in Syria, see Flash (n 78) 57 ff; for the underlying theory, see Ashley S. Deeks, ' "Unwilling or Unable": Toward a Normative Framework for Extra-Territorial Self-Defense' (2012) 52 Virginia Journal of International Law 483.

[80] Kevin Jon Heller, 'Ashley Deeks' Problematic Defense of the "Unwilling or Unable" Test' (Opinio Juris, 15 December 2011) <http://opiniojuris.org/2011/12/15/ashley-deeks-failure-to-defend-the-unwilling-or-unable-test/> accessed 30 May 2023; Dawood I. Ahmed, 'Defending Weak States against the "Unwilling or Unable" Doctrine of Self-Defense' (2013) 9 Journal of International Law and International Relations 1, 23; Flash (n 78) 54.

THE DIVIDE BETWEEN WAR AND PEACE   119

This leads to the conclusion that States tend to invoke the right to self-defence for a large variety of unilateral uses of military force. Although not all invocations of the right are accepted by other States, the long-standing practice of broad and repeated invocation suggests that the parameters of the right are vast. This is reflected in the doctrinal debates notably regarding the definition of an armed attack, anticipatory self-defence, and the right to act in self-defence against non-State actors.[81] As a consequence, self-defence has become an agile catch-all justification for using force in international relations. States' use of the concept of self-defence when attacking other States suggests that it is even turned on its head: instead of reacting to a wrongful act, it is used like the right to act in contradiction to the prohibition of the use of force under Article 2(4) of the UN Charter. As a result, this prohibition is further undermined.

Moreover, these normative developments blur the divide between war and peace. States invoke self-defence when using force similarly to how they declared war in the past. The justification of self-defence thus indicates that there is war, warlike situations, or acts of war. Contrary to declarations of war, this does not transform the formal state of affairs into war, however. More importantly, states invoke the concept for such a broad spectrum of military force that it has become too loosely delimited to serve as an indicator for the categorization of specific situations. The divide between peace and war as relating to states' use of force for self-defence is thus blurred, offering little analytical clarity and normative guidance. This notably applies to coercive measures forming part of hybrid threats and grey zone conflict.

6. The subjectivity of armed conflict

Since *jus ad bellum* does not provide much clarity on the divide between war and peace, *jus in bello* (LOAC, IHL) may serve for identifying the divide's underlying elements, criteria, and conditions. Just as its name suggests, this branch of law deals with the occurrence of 'armed conflicts'. While it is often called 'international humanitarian law', in particular in diplomatic contexts and by humanitarian organizations,[82] militaries prefer the term 'law of armed conflict'. The US military, as a notable exception, continues to call this the 'law of war'.[83] This

---

[81] Efforts to clarify these debates had mitigated results so far. See e.g. Elizabeth Wilmshurst, 'The Chatham House Principles of International Law on the Use of Force in Self-Defence' (2006) 55 International and Comparative Law Quarterly 963.

[82] For an analysis of the emergence of the term IHL, see Amanda Alexander, 'A Short History of International Humanitarian Law' (2015) 26 European Journal of International Law 109.

[83] US Department of Defense, *Law of War Manual* (updated edn, December 2016).

120 WHAT ARE HYBRID THREATS AND GREY ZONE CONFLICT?

suggests that the US armed forces perceive situations in which this branch of law applies as war, or at least as circumstances that deserve a legal framework tailored to war.

Like the UN Charter, the GCs and their Additional Protocols (APs) generally do not use 'war' as a legal concept. The major exception is that formal 'declarations of war' or the recognition of belligerency can trigger the application of LOAC as per common Article 2 of the GCs. States tend not to declare wars anymore, however, and it is widely considered that this is not necessary for LOAC to apply in international armed conflicts (IACs).[84] The GCs and APs also rarely use the term 'war'. The concept of 'prisoners of war', 'customs of war', 'operations of war', and 'time of war' are notable exceptions.[85] Because LOAC builds on the legal concept of 'armed conflict' but without defining the term, one must assess how it applies in order to understand which situations States perceive as armed conflicts.[86]

Common Article 2 of the GCs provides for the material scope of LOAC applicability to IAC, namely, declared wars and 'any other armed conflict which may arise between two or more of the High Contracting Parties, even if the state of war is not recognized by one of them'.[87] This reflects a shift from a purely formalistic approach (declared wars) to one where the existence of an IAC depends on objective legal criteria.[88] The International Criminal Tribunal for the former Yugoslavia (ICTY) specified in the *Tadić* case that the mere 'resort to armed force between states' would qualify as an IAC[89] (the so-called first shot theory).[90] Any other criterion related to the length of the conflict, the intensity of the violence, or a denial of the state of war would generally be irrelevant.[91] While some, including the International Committee of the Red Cross (ICRC), go further and consider that the mere capture of a soldier of the enemy's forces is enough to

---

[84] International Committee of the Red Cross, *Commentary on the First Geneva Convention* (CUP 2016) paras 194, 206; Marco Sassòli, *International Humanitarian Law: Rules, Controversies, and Solutions to Problems Arising in Warfare* (Edward Elgar 2019) 172 ff.

[85] See e.g. Article 44, Convention for the Amelioration of the Condition of the Wounded and Sick in Armed Forces in the Field (12 August 1949) 75 UNTS 135 (Geneva Convention I); Article 144, Convention relative to the Protection of Civilian Persons in Time of War (12 August 1949) 75 UNTS 287 (Geneva Convention IV).

[86] For a broad analysis, see Terry D. Gill, 'Rethinking the Scope of Application of International Humanitarian Law and Its Place in the International Legal System' (2022) 60 Military Law and the Law of War Review 58.

[87] Article 2, common to the four Geneva Conventions.

[88] International Committee of the Red Cross (n 84) paras 192–94, 201; Sassòli (n 84) 168; *Prosecutor v. Akayesu* (Judgment) ICTR-96-4-T, T Ch I (2 September 1998) para 624.

[89] *Prosecutor v. Tadić* (Decision on the Defence Motion for Interlocutory Appeal on Jurisdiction) ICTY-94-1-AR72 (2 October 1995) para 70.

[90] Dieter Fleck, 'Scope of Application of International Humanitarian Law', in Dieter Fleck (ed), *The Handbook of International Humanitarian Law* (4th edn, OUP 2021) 52.

[91] See International Committee of the Red Cross (n 84) paras 236 ff.

THE DIVIDE BETWEEN WAR AND PEACE   121

trigger the classification of a situation as an IAC,[92] others argue that a certain degree of intensity must be met.[93]

For an IAC to exist, an act of violence attributable to and approved by a State must be directed against someone or something representing another non-consenting State. An act *ultra vires* or a mistake is not sufficient.[94] Yet it remains controversial whether the targeting of an armed group within another State without consent could qualify as an attack against that State itself, or, by contrast, whether the conflict should only qualify as a non-international armed conflict (NIAC), which is the US position. An IAC also occurs in instances of military occupation (with or without armed resistance),[95] which arises when one State exercises effective control over the territory of another State without that State's consent.[96] The required level of control by the occupying power remains debated, however. One view is that the degree of control should resemble the degree usually exercised by a government on its own territory for the Hague Regulation to apply and that the mere invasion of the territory of another State would be enough for the fourth GC's provisions on occupation to apply.[97] Another view is that GC IV is applicable as soon as a person or object it regulates falls under the control of the occupying power.[98]

With regard to NIACs, since common Article 3 to the GCs does not provide any practical criterion for when a NIAC comes into existence, the ICTY specified that the relevant test should focus on two aspects,[99] namely, (1) whether the confrontation between the governmental armed forces and the armed group is of a 'protracted nature'; and (2) whether the parties to the conflict are sufficiently organized (particularly the armed group, because States' armed forces

---

[92] International Committee of the Red Cross (n 84) para 238, referring to state practice; see also Marian Nash, *Cumulative Digest of United States Practice in International Law, 1981–1988* (Office of the Legal Adviser, Department of State 1995) vol 3, 3456; Jean S. Pictet (ed), *Commentary on the Third Geneva Convention* (International Committee of the Red Cross 1960) 23, cited in Sassòli (n 84) 170.

[93] International Law Association, Use of Force Committee, 'Final Report on the Meaning of Armed Conflict in International Law' (International Law Association, The Hague, 2010) 2.

[94] International Committee of the Red Cross (n 84) para 241; Sassòli (n 84) 171.

[95] Article 2, common to the four Geneva Conventions.

[96] Annex to Convention (IV) Respecting the Laws and Customs of War on Land and its Annex: Regulations concerning the Laws and Customs of War on Land (Hague Regulations) (18 October 1907) 205 CTS 277.

[97] Jean S. Pictet (ed), *Commentary on the Fourth Geneva Convention* (International Committee of the Red Cross 1958) 60.

[98] For a debate on the topic, see Marten Zwanenburg, Michael Bothe, and Marco Sassòli, 'Is the Law of Occupation Applicable to the Invasion Phase?' (2012) 94 International Review of the Red Cross 29; see also Tristan Ferraro (ed), *Occupation and Other Forms of Administration of Foreign Territory: Expert Meeting* (International Committee of the Red Cross 2012) 24.

[99] *Tadić* (n 89) para 70; also confirmed in *Prosecutor v. Tadić* (Opinion and Judgment) ICTY-94-1-T (7 May 1997) para 562 and subsequent jurisprudence. See *Prosecutor v. Limaj and Others* (Judgment) ICTY-03-66-T (30 November 2005) para 84; *Prosecutor v. Boškoski and Tarčulovski* (Judgment) ICTY-04-82-T (10 July 2008) para 175; see also e.g. *Akayesu* (n 88) paras 619–20, and *Prosecutor v. Rutaganda* (Judgment and Sentence) ICTR-96-3-T (6 December 1999) paras 91–92.

122 WHAT ARE HYBRID THREATS AND GREY ZONE CONFLICT?

are presumed to be so).[100] The criterion of organization demands a command structure, the capacity to sustain military operations, a certain level of hierarchy and discipline within the group, and the ability to implement the basic LOAC obligations.[101] This determination is made on a case-by-case basis and grounded on factual considerations. Yet it is often difficult to determine whether a group can be considered a party to the conflict and to qualify the situation of violence as an NIAC.[102] The element of protracted violence has been subsequently reinterpreted as requiring a certain level of intensity rather than a minimum duration of the confrontation in line with AP II's requirements for application.[103] The ICTY has also summarized a non-exhaustive list of intensity indicators.[104]

LOAC applicability also ends based on the factual conditions for an armed conflict. LOAC of IAC ceases to apply with the general close of military operations, except for those provisions regulating prisoners of war and persons in the power of the enemy or whose liberty has been restricted for reasons related to the conflict that continue to apply until their final release or repatriation.[105] The ICTY has considered that the relevant criterion to determine when LOAC ceases to apply in IACs is the 'general conclusion of peace'.[106] The law of occupation ceases to apply when the occupying power loses control over the foreign territory or when the occupied State consents to the occupier's military presence in the occupied territory. While most agree that the law of NIACs continues to apply until the end of the conflict even when the criteria for its existence (intensity and organization) are no longer met during confrontations,[107] some contend the

[100] International Committee of the Red Cross (n 84) para 429.

[101] International Committee of the Red Cross, 'International Humanitarian Law and the Challenges of Contemporary Armed Conflicts: Report' (International Committee of the Red Cross 2003) 19.

[102] International Committee of the Red Cross, 'International Humanitarian Law and the Challenges of Contemporary Armed Conflicts' (2007) 89 International Review of the Red Cross 719, 743.

[103] Articles 1 and 2, Protocol Additional to the Geneva Conventions of 12 August 1949, and relating to the Protection of Victims of Non-International Armed Conflicts (8 June 1977) 1125 UNTS 609 (Additional Protocol II); see on this issue Stuart Casey-Maslen and Steven Haines, *Hague Law Interpreted* (Hart 2018) ch. 2.

[104] Sassòli (n 84) 181. These are the number, duration, and intensity of individual confrontations; the type of weapons and other military equipment used; the number and calibre of munitions fired; the number of persons and type of forces participating in the fighting; the number of casualties; the extent of material destruction; and the number of civilians fleeing combat zones. The involvement of the UN Security Council may also be a reflection of the intensity of a conflict. See *Prosecutor v. Haradinaj and Others* (Judgment) ICTY-04-84-T (3 April 2008) para 49.

[105] Article 6(2), 6(3), 6(4), Geneva Convention IV Article 3(b), Protocol Additional to the Geneva Conventions of 12 August 1949, and relating to the Protection of Victims of International Armed Conflicts (8 June 1977) 1125 UNTS 3 (Additional Protocol I); Article 5, Geneva Convention I; Article 5(1), Convention relative to the Treatment of Prisoners of War (12 August 1949) 75 UNTS 135 (Geneva Convention III); Article 2(2), Additional Protocol II.

[106] *Tadić* (n 89) para 70; Sassòli (n 84) 191.

[107] Sassòli (n 84) 192; *Haradinaj* (n 104) para 100.

opposite.[108] In this vein, an assessment of modern wars has revealed that current international law provides insufficient guidance to ascertain the end of many armed conflicts as a factual, normative, and legal matter.[109]

The LOAC's geographical scope of application is highly controversial, particularly because the GCs and APs do not contain explicit provisions on this issue. With respect to IACs, it is generally accepted that LOAC applies to the whole territory of the States involved in the conflict[110] and is not limited to the actual theatre of hostilities,[111] although some consider it to be applicable even outside the territory of the parties to the conflict to the extent that there are belligerent activities with a sufficient nexus with the conflict.[112] Regarding NIACs, the ICTY made it clear that LOAC applies to 'the whole territory under the control of a party, whether or not actual combat takes place there'.[113] The case is less clear regarding NIACs with extra-territorial elements, namely, when a State joins an NIAC occurring in the territory of another State with the latter's consent to fight a non-State armed group. While some consider that LOAC applicability is limited to the territory of the State where the actual conflict is taking place,[114] others argue that it applies also throughout the entire territory of the States involved extra-territorially.[115] This was potentially the case for European States involved in the conflict in Syria to fight ISIL/ISIS, for instance.

In addition, it has been suggested that the geographical scope of application of a NIAC may also extend to adjacent non-belligerent countries when the conflict or elements thereof spill over to them.[116] According to some, in such cases, LOAC would continue to apply as a spill-over effect even when in the neighbouring State the criteria for a NIAC (intensity and organization) are not met; a structural link between sporadic extra-territorial outbreaks of violence and the main

---

[108] Marko Milanovic, 'End of IHL Application: Overview and Challenges' (Scope of Application of International Humanitarian Law, Bruges, 2012) 87 <https://www.coleurope.eu/sites/default/files/uploads/page/collegium_43_webversie.pdf> accessed 30 May 2023; see also Derek Jinks, 'The Temporal Scope of Application of International Humanitarian Law in Contemporary Conflicts' (Background Paper prepared for the Informal High-Level Expert Meeting on the Reaffirmation and Development of International Humanitarian Law, Cambridge, 2003) 3 <https://www.hpcrresearch.org/sites/default/files/publications/Session3.pdf> accessed 30 May 2023.

[109] Dustin A. Lewis, Gabriella Blum, and Naz K. Modirzadeh, 'Indefinite War: Unsettled International Law on the End of Armed Conflict' (Harvard Law School Program on International Law and Armed Conflict 2017).

[110] International Committee of the Red Cross, 'International Humanitarian Law and the Challenges of Contemporary Armed Conflicts: Report' (International Committee of the Red Cross 2015) 13.

[111] See also *Tadić* (n 89) para 70.

[112] Sassòli (n 84) 187, 190.

[113] *Tadić* (n 89) paras 69–70.

[114] International Committee of the Red Cross (n 84) para 471, n 193.

[115] International Committee of the Red Cross (n 110) 14.

[116] International Committee of the Red Cross (n 84) para 474.

conflict would be sufficient.[117] State practice tends to support this.[118] Yet, taken to its extreme, such a view can imply the acceptance of the notion of a 'global battlefield' according to which LOAC is applicable without territorial limitations as long as an action has a nexus with an ongoing conflict fought elsewhere.[119] Although this approach represents the minority's view and practice, it does reflect US practice.[120] It has been central to the concept of the 'war on terror'[121] and plays a role regarding certain States' use of drones across the globe.[122]

The consequence of these normative developments and controversies is that *jus in bello*—the branch of international law applicable to armed conflicts—does not clearly indicate when an armed conflict exists and when a State or other actors are involved in such a conflict. Although the respective rules contain objective criteria and their core meaning is well accepted among States, the rules' delimitation has become vague due to extensive interpretation and State practice. This is well reflected in the doctrinal debates.[123] Efforts to classify situations of violence in an objective manner, such as by the Rule of Law in Armed Conflicts project,[124] have produced clarity but do not necessarily reflect States' perceptions. This suggests that even a substitute for 'war' as a state of affairs—'armed conflict'—tends to be so blurringly used that it does not provide clarity to assess the difference between war and peace. LOAC does indeed govern warfighting activities (called 'conduct of hostilities'), but its inconsistent application has the consequence that the legal qualification of a situation as armed conflict does not objectively explain or delimit any given situation compared to others. Rather, it is a legal framework that States apply in a relatively aleatory—or perhaps even subjective—manner.

In this context, States tend to avoid qualifying tensions and military confrontation with other States as armed conflicts to not escalate the tensions and crises.

---

[117] Marko Milanovic and Vidan Hadzi-Vidanovic, 'A Taxonomy of Armed Conflict', in Nigel D White and Christian Henderson (eds), *Research Handbook on International Conflict and Security Law* (Edward Elgar 2012) 33.

[118] International Committee of the Red Cross (n 84) para 474, n 198; further examples of conflicts that have spilled over into the territory of another state are given in Marko Milanovic, 'The Applicability of the Conventions to "Transnational" and "Mixed' Conflicts"', in Andrew Clapham, Paola Gaeta, and Marco Sassòli (eds), *The 1949 Geneva Conventions: A Commentary* (OUP 2015) paras 52, 56, 58.

[119] Sassòli (n 84) 189.

[120] International Committee of the Red Cross (n 110) 15.

[121] US President Obama rejected the term 'war on terror' in 2009, but asserted that the United States was at war with Al-Qaeda.

[122] Sassòli (n 84) 189; see International Committee of the Red Cross (n 84) para 482, n 212; see more on the debate on the war on terror and the geographic scope of the LOAC in International Committee of the Red Cross (n 110) 18.

[123] For further reading, see Elizabeth Wilmshurst (ed), *International Law and the Classification of Conflicts* (OUP 2012) 531.

[124] Geneva Academy, 'Rule of Law in Armed Conflicts' (*Rulac*) <https://www.rulac.org/> accessed 30 May 2023.

THE DIVIDE BETWEEN WAR AND PEACE 125

States also tend to not acknowledge officially the existence of NIACs so as not to recognize opponents as serious forces of opposition while downplaying their domestic political problems. The result is that war and peace can hardly be distinguished by States' application of LOAC. This also means that LOAC does not clearly circumscribe its application regarding hybrid threats, hybrid warfare, and grey zone conflict.

7. Implications and outlook

In his book *1984*, George Orwell wrote: 'War is peace'. These words are part of the official motto of the fictional nation of Oceania. They are also an expression of doublethink, which is the ability to hold two opposing ideas in one's mind simultaneously. An example of this is that Oceania's Ministry of Peace oversees war. This allows Oceania's citizens to live with constant contradictions in their lives and keeps them in a mental grey zone. As a result, they accept their fate and fully rely on and accept the dictates of the ruling elite. Accordingly, there is no divide between war and peace in Oceania. War equals peace and vice versa.

The normative treatment of the divide between war and peace is not doublethink as in *1984*. Yet, there are certain parallels. The international legal system does not contain 'war' as a consequential legal status, concept, or category. Rather, the general state of affairs is peace—even when the reality is war among and within multiple States. War or warlike actions are also conducted in the name of peace when the UN Security Council authorizes all necessary means to establish and maintain international peace and security. In addition, States tend to use the only exception to the prohibition of the use of force—self-defence—as a malleable justification for using military force and waging wars. Furthermore, State practice and interpretations regarding the application of *jus in bello*, which governs their conduct in war and warlike situations that are termed 'armed conflict', remain inconsistent and debated.

The result is that international law does not provide a clear divide between war and peace. While the core meaning of the respective rules remains rather undisputed, States' extensive interpretations and practice blur their precise delimitation and legal consequences. Peace and war also seem to be conflated to the extent that the normative treatment of the divide does not allow to distinguish one from the other and that there is a tension between the normative state of affairs ('peace') and the actual realities ('war'). Thus, the divide between war and peace is blurred. More specifically, the absence of clear delimitations by international law makes the divide a legal grey zone.

The consequence of this is that the normative framework on war and peace is more permissive than the black letter rules notably in the UN Charter suggest.

126 WHAT ARE HYBRID THREATS AND GREY ZONE CONFLICT?

This means that States have a relatively broad range of manoeuvre for resorting to military force and war. Distinguishing between legal and illegal actions and reacting to the latter is also rendered difficult. The Russian attack on Ukraine in 2022 is a notable exception where Russia did not seem to give particular attention to its legal justifications, which was identifiable as a flagrant violation of the prohibition of the use of force, and which led to rapid and strong reactions by the international community. This remains the exception, however, notably when great powers resort to force.

The legal grey zone regarding war and peace also results in the respective international rules not clearly regulating hybrid threats, hybrid warfare, and grey zone conflicts. This does not mean that these situations are not regulated by international law. Yet, since the rules and their application are not clearly delimited, States can take advantage of this by conducting military and other actions in the legal grey zone without fearing legal consequences. This finding is different from the more common assumption that States conduct hybrid activities below the thresholds of application of the given rules to avoid these rules' consequences. This can be positive to the extent that the legal grey zone is confined enough to draw States—notably great powers—away from resorting to high-intensity and full-scale wars in flagrant violation of the rules, and towards resorting to hybrid tactics and grey zone conflict due to the benefits of the legal grey zone. This chapter's analysis suggests, however, that the normative divide of war and peace is so indeterminate that this may not be the case. There is the risk that States may conclude that the divide is so blurred under international law that they can get away with practically anything.

This leads to the future of peace and war from a normative perspective. Based on this chapter's analysis, there are several avenues to be explored when reflecting on how to strengthen international law's ability to foster peace and prevent war. A fundamental point is that international law establishes peace as the general state of international affairs, but multiple realities around the globe represent war. How can this tension be alleviated? Should the norms be strengthened, and if so, how? Or should the expectations be lowered so that the norms more closely reflect reality? Would a more accurate and less normative discourse on war and peace foster or undermine existing international law? Another central point is the blurred normative divide between war and peace. How can this divide be sharpened? Or should the indeterminacy of certain rules be tolerated because it avoids clear violations and normative revisionism by States?

Several options derive from these questions. To strengthen and clarify the normative framework, States should increasingly condemn expansive interpretations and violations, notably regarding the prohibition of the use of force and the right to self-defence. Similarly, the use of judicial mechanisms, such as the ICJ and arbitration tribunals, can bring clarity. Similarly, stronger language from the UN Security Council, such as naming situations as 'war' and classifying situations as a 'breach of the peace' or even an 'act of aggression' rather than only as a 'threat to peace' would allow the legal terms to better reflect reality. Judging political leaders for the crime of aggression can also contribute to clarifying and strengthening the normative framework on war and peace. More prominently communicating that a situation qualifies as an armed conflict can also foster the application of *jus in bello* and align the normative treatment with the actual reality. This notably concerns hybrid threats, hybrid warfare, and grey zone conflict where hostile actions are specifically conducted in this legal grey zone between war and peace.

Alternatively, there is also the possibility to continue not to talk of 'war', but to focus on 'peace' in the normative realm. This may help to keep the ideal alive and expectations high. In this vein, similar to the notion of 'quality peace', which essentially abandons the divide between war and peace, but defines peace as a continuum, respect for international human rights law can be used as the normative indicator of levels of peace. This would be an approach that focuses on human security rather than the status of relations between States and would work independently of whether there is war or not. Such an approach would notably require the international community to further push the universal application of and respect for international human rights law—even during armed conflicts and particularly for hybrid threats, hybrid warfare, and grey zone conflict.

Ultimately, the essential point of the dichotomy between war and peace is a reminder of the need for analytical clarity and consequential action: peace is the aspiration, the good, and should be the ordinary; war should be the extraordinary to be avoided. Further research, debate, and action should prevent the normative treatment of the divide between war and peace from becoming doublethink where 'war is peace'. War is not peace, and peace is not war.

7

Rethinking Coercion in Cyberspace

Ido Kilovaty

1. Introduction

Among international law's most fundamental, yet obscure aspects of international law is non-intervention.[1] Non-intervention, deriving its rationale from the principle of territorial sovereignty,[2] sovereign equality,[3] and political independence[4] prohibits States from coercively interfering in the domestic or foreign affairs of other States. Non-intervention is now part and parcel of customary international law.[5] As the then-Permanent Court of International Justice iterated: 'the first and foremost restriction imposed by international law upon a State . . . [is that] it may not exercise its power in any form in the territory of another State'.[6] The same conception of non-intervention appears in many other judicial decisions and legal instrument as well.[7]

---

[1] *Case Concerning Military and Paramilitary Activities in and against Nicaragua (Nicaragua v. USA)* (Merits) (1986) ICJ Rep. 14, para 202 ('the Court considers that it is part and parcel of customary international law').

[2] Michael Schmitt and Sean Watts, 'Beyond State-Centrism: International Law and Non-State Actors in Cyberspace' (2016) 21 Journal of Conflict and Security Law 595, 600 ('The prohibition of intervention by a State into the internal or external affairs of other States derives directly from the principle of sovereignty.')

[3] E.g. Article 2(1) ('The Organization is based on the principle of the sovereign equality of all its Members'.) and Article 2(7) ('Nothing contained in the present Charter shall authorize the United Nations to intervene in matters which are essentially within the domestic jurisdiction of any State or shall require the Members to submit such matters to settlement under the present Charter; but this principle shall not prejudice the application of enforcement measures under Chapter VII'.) of the United Nations Charter.

[4] R. Y. Jennings and A. Watts, *Oppenheim's International Law* (9th edn, Longman 1992) 430–49.

[5] See Dissenting Opinion of Judge Jennings, *Nicaragua* (n 1) 534 ('there can be no doubt that the principle of non-intervention is an autonomous principle of customary law; indeed, it is much older than any of the multilateral Treaty regimes in question').

[6] *S.S. Lotus (France v. Turkey)* (1927) PCIJ Series A, No 10, 18.

[7] *Corfu Channel Case (Albania v. UK)* (Merits) (1949) ICJ Rep. 4, 35 (April 9); *Nicaragua* (n 1) paras 202, 205, and 251; Armed Activities on the Territory of the Congo (Democratic Republic of the Congo v. Uganda), (Judgment) (2005) ICJ Rep. 168, paras 161–65; United Nations General Assembly Resolution 2625 (XXV), 'Declaration on Principles of International Law Concerning Friendly Relations and Co-operation among States in Accordance with the Charter of the United Nations' (24 October 1970) (Friendly Relations Declaration), para 3.

Ido Kilovaty, *Rethinking Coercion in Cyberspace* In: *Hybrid Threats and Grey Zone Conflict*. Edited by: Mitt Regan and Aurel Sari, Oxford University Press. © Oxford University Press 2024. DOI: 10.1093/oso/9780197744772.003.0007

However, socio-technological change affecting international relations, such as cyberattacks,[8] digital election interference,[9] deep fakes,[10] and the growing role of social media platforms has seriously challenged the efficacy, relevancy, and clarity of the principle on non-intervention. Primarily, the two constitutive elements of non-intervention—*domaine réservé* and coercion—are becoming increasingly irrelevant in today's world.

Perhaps this irrelevancy is best exemplified by the activities constituting the Russian interference in the 2016 US election. Some activities in which Russia was involved, such as hacking voter rolls, may be in clear violation of the principle. However, other acts of interference which are just as detrimental to the political process pose more of a challenge to the principle. Are disinformation campaigns on social media in violation of the principle? Is it wrongful to use political bots to sway public opinion on the eve of a presidential election? What about doxing of a political organization such as the Democratic National Committee?[11] Are deep fakes 'coercive' and therefore unlawful?

This grey zone of non-intervention exists notwithstanding the fact that the prohibition on intervention is sprinkled throughout international law—in both treaties and custom. It has gained wide acceptance in the international community and has been reaffirmed multiple times in different international contexts. Nonetheless, States have done little to clarify the contents of the norm,[12] setting non-intervention on a path of becoming irrelevant in the coming decades, unless States do more to adapt non-intervention to emerging forms of interference enabled by cyberspace and new technologies. This contribution seeks to explore this emerging grey zone with respect to non-intervention.

This grey zone comes from the contours of non-intervention's two constitutive elements: *domaine réservé* and coercion. Cyberspace as a medium of interference, emerging technologies, and new platforms of communications are currently challenging these two elements. The purpose of this chapter is to argue that these global trends pose the greatest threat to the survival of the prohibition on non-intervention.

---

[8] See e.g. Oona Hathaway et al, 'The Law of Cyber-Attack' (2012) 100 California Law Review 817.

[9] See e.g. Nicholas Tsagourias, 'Electoral Cyber Interference, Self-Determination and the Principle of Non-Intervention' (*EJIL:Talk!*, 26 August 2019) <https://www.ejiltalk.org/electoral-cyber-interference-self-determination-and-the-principle-of-non-intervention-in-cyberspace/> accessed 25 February 2023.

[10] See e.g. Robert Chesney and Danielle Citron, 'Deepfakes and the New Disinformation War' (*Foreign Affairs*, 11 December 2018) <https://www.foreignaffairs.com/articles/world/2018-12-11/deepfakes-and-new-disinformation-war> accessed 25 February 2023.

[11] Michael Schmitt, 'Grey Zones in the International Law of Cyberspace' (2017) 42 Yale Journal of International Law Online 1, 2 ('It is unclear whether facilitating the release of actual emails—as distinct from, for example, using cyber means to alter election returns—amounts to coercion as a matter of law').

[12] Sean Watts, 'International Law and Proposed U.S. Response to the D.N.C Hack' (*Just Security*, 14 October 2016) <https://www.justsecurity.org/33558/international-law-proposed-u-s-responses-d-n-c-hack/> accessed 25 February 2023 ('Although the prohibition of intervention is longstanding, States have not done much to clarify precisely where this threshold of coercion lies').

To be clear, this chapter is not about 'cyberspace and non-intervention', a topic which has been explored extensively in scholarship. The chapter makes a larger point with regard to emerging technologies, cyberspace, and non-intervention, which is that the foundations of non-intervention are untenable given this global transformation. Some of the ambiguities surrounding non-intervention in general are further exacerbated in this technological context. The purpose of this chapter is to look at the elements of non-intervention through a socio-technological lens.

This chapter proceeds in three sections. In section 2, it will lay out the common understanding of non-intervention, primarily the content of the two constitutive elements–*domaine réservé* and coercion. In section 3, the chapter will lay out the aspects of socio-technological change which have transformed the world as we know it. This part will look at how the norm on non-intervention is severely challenged by socio-technological change. In section 4, the chapter will explore the future of non-intervention–its trajectories and challenges moving forward. Section 5 concludes this chapter.

2. Non-intervention

The modern conception of the principle of non-intervention is understood to contain two constitutive elements. These two elements transform an act of mere interference,[13] which is not illegal under international law, to an act of intervention, which is unlawful under international law.[14] Both elements are required in order to hold a State accountable for a violation of non-intervention. For example, Article 2(4) of the UN Charter[15] is a specific example of an unlawful intervention through the use of military force; however, the principle of non-intervention applies primarily to acts below the threshold of force.[16] An act of

---

[13] By 'interference' I mean 'activities that disturb the territorial State's ability to perform the functions as it wishes', although, interference by itself is currently not illegal under international law, unless it is coercive and targets the *domaine réservé*. See M. N. Schmitt, '"Virtual" Disenfranchisement: Cyber Election Meddling in the Grey Zones of International Law' (2018) 19 Chicago Journal of International Law 30, 45.

[14] Jennings and Watts (n 4), 432 ('the interference must be forcible or dictatorial, or otherwise coercive, in effect depriving the State intervened against of control over the matter in question. Interference pure and simple is not intervention').

[15] Article 2(4) of the UN Charter reads 'All Members shall refrain in their international relations from the threat or use of force against the territorial integrity or political independence of any State, or in any other manner inconsistent with the Purposes of the United Nations'.

[16] Duncan Hollis, 'Russia and the DNC Hack: What Future for a Duty of Non-Intervention?' (*Opinio Juris*, 25 July 2016) <http://opiniojuris.org/2016/07/25/russia-and-the-dnc-hack-a-violat ion-of-the-duty-of-non-intervention/> accessed 25 February 2023 ('customary international law has long recognized a 'duty of non-intervention that applies to State behavior in cases falling short of the use of force').

132 WHAT ARE HYBRID THREATS AND GREY ZONE CONFLICT?

unlawful intervention must, first, be directed at certain sovereign prerogatives, namely the *domaine réservé*,[17] and; second, it must be *coercive*.[18] This section considers the content of these two elements in the following two sub-sections.

2.1 Domaine réservé

In order to be wrongful, an act of interference must target a specific subset of protected State prerogatives. These prerogatives constitute the activities which are so deeply entrenched in the State's sovereignty and political independence that no outside interference with them is permissible. While the notion seems straightforward, it is often unclear what contents this concept holds.[19]

The International Court of Justice (ICJ) in its *Nicaragua* decision, has provided some guidance on the contents of *domaine réservé*. In that case, the Court concluded that the financial support and training provided by the United States to an opposition armed group within Nicaragua was a 'clear breach of the principle of non-intervention'.[20] The Court explained:

> a prohibited intervention must accordingly be one bearing on matters in which each State is permitted, by the principle of State sovereignty, to decide freely. One of these is the choice of a political, economic, social and cultural system, and the formulation of foreign policy. Intervention is wrongful when it uses methods of coercion in regard to such choices, which must remain free ones.[21]

Michael Schmitt, while exploring grey zones in international law, attempted to draw the line between matters under the sole discretion of the State and those that are not.[22] Schmitt provides that 'elections fall within the *domaine réservé*' while 'commercial activities typically do not'.[23] Intuitively, if a State engaged

---

[17] Jens David Ohlin, 'Did Russian Cyber Interference in the 2016 Election Violate International Law?' (2017) 95 Texas Law Review 1579, 1587 (a State's domaine reserve refers to 'its exclusive power to regulate its internal affairs without outside interference').

[18] *Nicaragua* (n 1), para 205 ('Intervention is wrongful when it uses methods of coercion in regard to such choices, which must remain free ones. The element of coercion, (. . .) defines, and indeed forms the very essence of, prohibited intervention').

[19] Ohlin (n 17) 1588; Schmitt (n 13) 45 ('The inherently governmental function concept lacks granularity, although some cases are clear. On the one hand, purely commercial activities, even if engaged in by State-owned enterprises, do not qualify, for they obviously are not within the exclusive purview of a State. On the other hand, law enforcement and defense of the State from external attack are inherently governmental in character. . . . Between these extremes lies a great deal of uncertainty').

[20] *Nicaragua* (n 1) para 242.

[21] Ibid.

[22] Schmitt (n 11) 7.

[23] Ibid.

in an act of interference 'intended to afford business advantages to its national companies', it would not run afoul of the principle on non-intervention.

While these two extremes are uncontroversial, Schmitt acknowledges that there may be a grey zone in the context of online communications.[24] States typically regulate online communications to a certain degree, yet this is not within the sole discretion of the regulating State.

Would an interference with online communications constitute an act against the *domaine réservé*? The answer, to many, is in the negative. But what about the *should* question? *Should* it be unlawful to interfere with online communication or political discourse on social media platforms? International law has not been able to address this timely question, particularly given the growing role of private speech platforms, namely social media, which have become the new public squares. Is the notion of *domaine réservé* still relevant in a world where social media platforms have transformed online communications and political campaigning?

2.2 Coercion

Coercion is a *sine qua non* in the context of non-intervention. The ICJ in *Nicaragua* exemplified the important and centrality of coercion to the norm of non-intervention, where it held that 'intervention is wrongful when it uses methods of coercion'[25] and that coercion is 'the very essence'[26] of intervention.

While the ICJ did not use the term 'coercion' in its *Corfu Channel* case, it rejected the argument that there is a 'right of intervention' recognized by international law, by noting that it views 'the alleged right of intervention as the manifestation of a policy of force, such as has, in the past, given rise to the most serious abuses'.[27]

In addition, the 1970 Declaration on Friendly Relations provides that:

> No state may use or encourage the use of economic, political or any other type of measures to coerce another State in order to obtain from it the subordination of the exercise of its sovereign rights and to secure from it advantages of any kind.[28]

---

[24] Ibid.
[25] *Nicaragua* (n 1) para. 205.
[26] Ibid.
[27] *Corfu Channel* (n 7) 35.
[28] Friendly Relations Declaration, para 3.

134   WHAT ARE HYBRID THREATS AND GREY ZONE CONFLICT?

Non-intervention and the coercion requirement carry to the cyberspace context as well. The *Tallinn Manual 2.0 on the International Law Applicable to Cyber Operations* provides that 'States may not intervene, including by cyber means, in the internal or external affairs of another State'[29] and subsequently clarifies that in order to be wrongful under international law, such intervention 'must be coercive in nature'.[30]

According to this widely accepted view, there can be no unlawful intervention without coercion. Any act of interference falling below the threshold of coercion is not unlawful under international law. But what does coercion actually mean? The relevant instruments on non-intervention do not provide a clear answer, which may signify that non-intervention suffers from a serious gap.[31] After all, if there is no intervention without coercion, and there is no robust theory on what coercion is, then the legitimacy of the principle dissipates.

Oppenheim, however, provides some useful guidance on coercion, by asserting that to qualify as prohibited intervention, 'interference must be *forcible or dictatorial, or otherwise coercive; in effect depriving the State intervened against of control over the matter in question*'.[32] In other words, an act of coercion exists when the victim State is *forced* to do something by an external State actor, or when it is faced with an ultimatum—do X (or refrain from doing X), or else.[33] Schmitt, similarly, defines an act of coercion as an action 'intended to cause the State to do something, such as take a decision that it would otherwise not take, or not to engage in an activity in which it would otherwise engage'.[34]

Coercion, therefore, is an action that deprives the State of its sovereign will. It is an action that seeks 'to force a policy change in the target State'.[35] A State loses its independence when its sovereignty is forcefully delegated by an external State actor. But sovereign will and independence may still be undermined even if something other than the *domaine réservé* is targeted, or when interference is not designed to be *coercive*. Consider for example a foreign State government that is engaged in microtargeting users on social media with disinformation, leading to a certain outcome in the victim State. This is a grey zone with respect to coercion that will be elaborated on in the following section.

---

[29] Michael N. Schmitt (ed.), *Tallinn Manual 2.0 on the International Law Applicable to Cyber Operations* (CUP 2017) Rule 66.

[30] Ibid.

[31] Ohlin (n 17) 1581 ('there is little in international law that outlines a complete theory of coercion').

[32] Jennings and Watts (n 4) 430–49.

[33] Ido Kilovaty, 'The Elephant in the Room: Coercion' (2019) 113 *American Journal of International Law Unbound* 87, 89.

[34] Schmitt (n 13) 51.

[35] Maziar Jamnejad and Michael Wood, 'The Principle of Non-Intervention' (2009) 22 Leiden Journal of International Law 345, 348.

3. Grey zones in non-intervention: cyberspace and emerging technologies

The gap in international law with respect to non-intervention is partially due to the rapid evolution of technology vis-à-vis the international legal systems.[36] In other words, the principle of non-intervention 'fail[s] to keep pace with technological advancements that render territorial limits irrelevant'.[37] It is not only technology that has made significant advancements in recent decades, but also the non-State actors involved in this space, who are increasingly powerful. The implication is that States do not need coercive tools to unduly and substantially influence internal or external affairs of another State,[38] and they do not need to target their operations directly against State functions.

These shifting notions of what constitutes non-intervention are not in themselves unprecedented. During the nineteenth century, international law afforded States protection only for their territorial integrity. Not until the twentieth century did the scope of non-intervention expand to protect political independence.[39] Yet again, non-intervention is at a crossroads, where socio-technological change calls for a reconsideration of non-intervention's scope.

To understand how non-intervention is currently challenged, it is necessary to explain what constitutes socio-technological change, as the term is used in this chapter. By socio-technological change I mean three distinct, yet interrelated, phenomena: *power diffusion and parity in the information age, new tools of interference,* and *democratization of power.*

3.1 Power diffusion and parity in the information age

Power diffusion and parity in the information age pertains to the increasingly substantial role of tech companies, primarily social media platforms in global politics. The reach, influence, and vulnerability of these platforms are unprecedented, and therefore pose a danger to State who may be affected by the discourse taking place on them.

---

[36] See generally Ryan Jenkins, 'Is Stuxnet Physical? Does It Matter?' (2013) 12 Journal of Military Ethics 68, 69.

[37] Simon Chesterman, 'Secret Intelligence' (2019) Max Planck Encyclopedia of Public International Law para 23.

[38] See Hollis (n 16) ('looking at the DNC hack, there's little evidence that Russia is trying to coerce any particular result. Indeed, it's not even clear that the goal of the hack was to support Trump's candidacy').

[39] Johannn-Christoph Woltag, *Cyber Warfare: Military Cross-Border Computer Network Operations Under International Law* 116 (Intersentia 2014).

136 WHAT ARE HYBRID THREATS AND GREY ZONE CONFLICT?

According to Joseph Nye, the problem is not necessarily that non-State entities become more powerful, but that 'in today's global information age . . . more things are occurring outside the control of even the most powerful States'.[40] This means that interfering with these platforms, as has been done by State actors many times in recent years, could effectively interfere with the domestic or foreign affairs of a State.

This growing power of global social media platform raises another concern—that of parity. Parity asks the question of whether these online platforms are on a par with States.[41] The answer is affirmative. Tech companies are becoming powerful in their own unique way, which challenges the notions of power and coercion that we typically associate with States. Tech companies and online platforms do not have territories, armies, or recognition as sovereign States, but their emerging power represents a new type of sovereignty—digital rather than Westphalian. Due to how interconnected States and online platforms are, it comes as no surprise that States are also vulnerable to exploitation, manipulation, disinformation, and microtargeting online.

The diffusion of power and parity in the information age illustrates that what constitutes (and what should constitute) *domaine réservé* is ambiguous in light of these developments.

3.2 New tools of interference

New tools of interference have to do with the growing array of means and methods of interference, primarily enabled by emerging technologies and the global reach of the internet. It is related to *power diffusion and parity in the information age* in the sense that the impact of these tools is amplified when they are used on the internet.

In the past, interference could be achieved through many means, including 'grandfather-style methods: scatter leaflets, throw around some printed materials, manipulate the radio or television. . . . But, all of a sudden, new means have appeared'.[42] There is a wide variety of new technological means of interference. Some examples include (1) online manipulation enabled by microtargeting and psychographic profiling, (2) political bots/trolls spreading

---

[40] Joseph Nye, 'Power Shifts', *Time* (New York, 9 May 2011).

[41] See Ido Kilovaty, 'Privatized Cybersecurity Law' (2020) 10 UC Irvine Law Review 1181, 1215; compare with Kristen Eichensehr, 'Digital Switzerlands' (2019) 167 University of Pennsylvania Law Review 665, 685–96.

[42] Evan Osnos, David Remnick, and Joshua Yaffa, 'Trump, Putin, and the New Cold War' (*The New Yorker*, 24 February 2017) <https://www.newyorker.com/magazine/2017/03/06/trump-putin-and-the-new-cold-war> accessed 25 February 2023.

disinformation and propaganda, (3) political doxing, and (4) deep-fake videos using the likeness of political figures. As technology moves forward, more tools become available.

What is troubling about these new tools is that non-intervention is not ready to address State actors who use them to interfere in the internal or external affairs of another State. The element of *coercion* requires an act that is forcible or dictatorial, or one that deprives the victim State of its sovereign will. Most of these tools are non-coercive by definition, though, they may still deprive the State of its independence and ability to make decisions freely.

3.3 Democratization of power

Democratization of power is the result of the coupling of *diffusion of power* with *new tools of interference*. The crux of *democratization of power* is that the internet is widely available and easy to navigate, and the new tools of interference are also widely available and (relatively) easy to master. The result is that non-State actors are becoming more capable of undermining the *domaine réservé* of States.

Some examples of these non-State actors include (1) hacking groups– Cozy Bear,[43] Fancy Bear,[44] and others; (2) political consulting firms, such as Cambridge Analytica,[45] and; (3) data analytics companies, like Palantir.[46] All of these actors, as well as many others, hold the means to interfere in the internal and external affairs of nation states. Non-intervention presupposes an intervention by a State actor, but this presupposition is untenable in today's socio-technological reality.

To be clear, socio-technological change is not the only challenge to non-intervention, yet it is the most significant one. In one context, three out of four challenges to the non-intervention norms were associated with cyber-space and emerging technologies: election interference, disinformation, and cyberthreats.[47]

---

[43] Crowdstrike, 'Who Is Cozy Bear (APT29)?' (19 September 2016) <https://www.crowdstrike.com/blog/who-is-cozy-bear/> accessed 25 February 2023.

[44] Crowdstrike, 'Who Is Fancy Bear (APT28)?' (12 February 2019), <https://www.crowdstrike.com/blog/who-is-fancy-bear/> accessed 25 February 2023.

[45] See Ido Kilovaty, 'Legally Cognizable Manipulation' (2019) 34 *Berkeley Technology Law Journal* 457, 473–76.

[46] See e.g. Peter Waldman, Lizette Chapman, and Jordan Robertson, 'Palantir Knows Everything about You' (*Bloomberg*, 19 April 2018) <https://www.bloomberg.com/features/2018-palantir-peter-thiel/?leadSource=uverify%20wall> accessed 25 February 2023.

[47] Denitsa Raynova, 'Towards a Common Understanding of the Nonintervention Principle', European Leadership Network (October 2017).

3.4 Non-intervention, socio-technological change, and the flaw of analogical reasoning

According to a view held by many States, international organizations, and commentators, international law applies to cyberspace and emerging technologies.[48] In line with this approach, there is nothing inherently different about cyberspace and emerging technologies that would pose a barrier to the applicability of well-established international law norms and principles, non-intervention included. As a consensus of experts at the UN Group of Governmental Experts on Developments in the Field of Information and Telecommunications process concluded: 'State sovereignty and international norms and principles that flow from sovereignty apply to the conduct by States of ICT-related activities and to their jurisdiction over ICT infrastructure within their territory'.[49]

But this analogical approach is exactly what contributes to the massive grey zones surrounding the norm on non-intervention. Applying principles, the logic of which is anchored in territorial and physical concepts, cannot work well in the digital and socio-technological contexts. Analogical reasoning permeates many areas of law and technology, for an obvious reason: if technology X is no different than preceding technology/method Y, then the same law that applied to Y should apply to X. But analogical reasoning is flawed in this context. While X and Y are very much alike, there are many critical differences between those two that would call for a re-evaluation of the law.

The flaw of analogical reasoning is very much apparent in the socio-technological context and non-intervention. While it makes sense to say that non-intervention applies today as it applied in the past, this approach does not lead to best results.[50] Rebecca Crootof writes that analogies are misleading when technologies are 'fundamentally different'[51] and that analogies are constraining because 'they restrict our ability to think imaginatively about a new technology'.[52]

---

[48] Harold Koh, 'International Law in Cyberspace' (2012) 54 Harvard International Law Journal 1, 2–3 ('Question 1: Do established principles of international law apply in cyberspace? Answer 1: Yes, international law principles do apply in cyberspace.').

[49] Group of Governmental Experts on Developments in the Field of Information and Telecommunications in the Context of International Security, 'Report' (22 July 2015) UN Doc. A/70/174, para 15.

[50] Luke Milligan, 'Analogy Breakers: A Reality Check on Emerging Technologies' (2011) 80 Mississippi Law Journal 1319, 1322 ('While analogical reasoning is particularly attractive to judges confronting technologies that were not likely foreseen at the time of the drafting of relevant legislation or precedent, the use of analogical reasoning to mediate old rules and emerging technologies has led to mixed results').

[51] Rebecca Crootof, 'Autonomous Weapon Systems and the Limits of Analogy' (2018) 9 Harvard National Security Journal 51, 79.

[52] Ibid. 80.

Forcing the norm on non-intervention on today's socio-technological landscape is like forcing a square peg in a round hole.

Below are examples of this analogical failure—namely the grey zones arising from the application of the norm on non-intervention as is to this new socio-technological context.

3.4.1 *Domaine réservé* is difficult to delineate

The concept of *domaine réservé* assumes that protected State prerogatives, such as domestic and foreign affairs, can be neatly labelled and distinguished from activity, usually that which is not in the sole discretion of a State, which is not protected from foreign interference. This assumption is increasingly becoming indefensible given the trends of socio-technological change.

For once, the ever-blurring line between State and non-State is making the distinction between the protected and unprotected nearly impossible. But it is not only the distinction between State and non-State that complicates the analysis but rather the increasing power of non-State actors, such as social media platforms, political consulting firms, data analytics companies, and hacking groups. Given that non-intervention requires State action, and often a State target, these non-State groups need to be under a certain degree of control by a State actor in order for non-intervention to be relevant.[53]

This grey zone creates a very appealing opportunity for States considering influence or interference operations. As exemplified by the Russian interference in 2016, States do not need to direct their operations at purely State targets or prerogatives to interfere with a domestic political process. They can achieve the same goal by leveraging the reach and scale of social media platforms, microtargeting methods, and manipulation techniques.

Indeed, Pavel Zolotarev, retired Russian general, strengthened this conclusion by saying that 'we had come to the conclusion, having analysed the actions of Western countries in the post-Soviet space—first of all the United States—that manipulation in the information sphere is a very effective tool'.[54] In other words, to make a State pursue a policy that it otherwise would not,[55] States can design their operations to take advantage of the internet, its widespread reach, and the ability to manipulate its users.

---

[53] Schmitt (n 13) 48 (actions of non-State actors need to be attributable to a State 'through instructions [by a State] to, or [State] control over, non-State actors such as IT companies, hacker groups, or terrorist organizations'). Also see Article 8, International Law Commission, Draft Articles on Responsibility of States for Internationally Wrongful Acts (24 October 2001) UN Doc. A/56/10.

[54] Osnos et al. (n 42).

[55] See Philip Kunig, 'Prohibition of Intervention' (2008) Max Planck Encyclopedia of Public International Law para 1 (intervention 'aims to impose certain conduct of consequences on a sovereign State').

140 WHAT ARE HYBRID THREATS AND GREY ZONE CONFLICT?

On this point, Brian Eagan similarly identified 'the very design of the Internet'[56] as an enabler of 'encroachment on other sovereign jurisdictions'.[57] According to Eagan, some of the difficult questions presented with respect to international law and cyberspace 'ultimately will be resolved through the practice and *opinio juris* of States'.[58] Cyberspace is therefore creating a grey zone for non-intervention by design.

This challenge is further exacerbated by technological innovation that would allow States to use even more sophisticated methods to interfere with a domestic process without targeting any *domaine réservé* targets. For example, deep-fake technology represents the new threat to democracy globally.[59] Deep fakes are fabricated videos or audios, utilizing machine-learning algorithms 'to insert faces and voices into video and audio recordings of actual people'[60] with the purpose of creating 're-alistic impersonations . . . making it appear that someone said or did something'.[61]

The introduction of deep-fake technology challenges the basic tenets of non-intervention. Among the harms identified by Bobby Chesney and Danielle Citron in their article on deep-fake technology are distortion of democratic discourse, manipulation of elections, undermining diplomacy, jeopardizing national security, and more.[62] It is clear that deep-fake technology may further decrease certainty in what constitutes *domaine réservé* and coercion, in particular as it is inching towards influencing the 2020 election.[63]

3.4.2 Coercion is an outdated standard

Interference becomes wrongful when it targets the *domaine réservé* using coercive methods. Coercion is the mischief that international law seeks to condemn, because it follows the logic that coercion is the sole method by which sovereign will can be subordinated.[64] If a State 'complies freely'[65] or 'the pressure is such that could reasonably be resisted',[66] then there is no subordination of sovereign will.[67] What follows is that acts that are not coercive, are by definition outside

---

[56] Brian J. Egan, Legal Adviser, US Department of State, 'Remarks at Berkeley Law School on International Law and Stability in Cyberspace' (10 November 2016) <https://2009-2017.state.gov/s/l/releases/remarks/264303.htm> accessed 25 February 2023.

[57] Ibid.

[58] Ibid.

[59] See e.g. Bobby Chesney and Danielle Citron, 'Deep Fakes: A Looming Challenge for Privacy, Democracy, and National Security' (2019) 107 California Law Review 1753.

[60] Ibid. 1758.

[61] Ibid. 1758.

[62] Ibid. Part II.B.2.

[63] Yvette Clarke, 'Deepfakes Will Influence the 2020 Election—And Our Economy, and Our Prison System' (*Quartz*, 2019) <https://qz.com/1660737/deepfakes-will-influence-the-2020-election>.

[64] Jamnejad and Wood (n 35) 348.

[65] Ibid.

[66] Ibid.

[67] Ibid.

the scope of non-intervention. The caveat is that there is a lot between volitional compliance and coercion, which creates a grey zone with regard to the standard of coercion. As ICJ Judge Rosalyn Higgins observed, 'not all maximally invasive acts are unlawful, and not all minimally invasive acts are lawful'.[68]

Non-intervention is a norm that emerged in an era where coercion was almost exclusively the method of effective intervention. Coercion puts an ultimatum in front of the victim State: *do X (or refrain from doing X), or else*. There are very good reasons why coercion is wrongful under international law, but delimiting non-intervention only to acts that are coercive misses an important point, which is that interference in this day and age may use new technological methods that can be extremely harmful and detrimental to sovereignty, self-determination, political independence, and democracy even in the absence of coercion. This gap is particularly important if non-intervention is to retain its de-escalatory nature of ensuring 'that nations live in peace with one another'[69] since interventions 'threaten international peace and security'.[70]

Yuval Shany and Dan Efrony recently performed eleven case studies on cyber operations to identify whether the rules contained in the *Tallinn Manual 2.0 on the International Law Applicable to Cyber Operations* had any effect on State practice and *opinio juris*.[71] While their conclusions are outside the scope of this chapter, their case studies illustrate an important, and often overlooked, lesson about coercion. That lesson is that coercion, as widely understood until now, is absent from all eleven case studies identified by Shany and Efrony, meaning that the norm of non-intervention, in its current narrow understanding, is almost irrelevant in a world where States increasingly resort to cyber operations as a method of interference.

Steven Barela has asserted that the release of the compromised Democratic National Committee (DNC) emails constituted coercion, because of its delegitimizing effect.[72] Barela argues that this form of election meddling and manipulation constitutes in itself an act of coercion.[73] While this is a persuasive

---

[68] Rosalyn Higgins, 'Intervention and International Law', in Hedley Bull (ed), *Intervention in World Politics* (Clarendon Press 1984) 30.

[69] Friendly Relations Declaration.

[70] Ibid.

[71] Dan Efrony and Yuval Shany, 'A Rule Book on the Shelf? Tallinn Manual 2.0 on Cyberoperations and Subsequent State Practice' (2018) 112 American Journal of International Law 583.

[72] Steven Barela, 'Cross-Border Cyber Ops to Erode Legitimacy: An Act of Coercion' (*Just Security*, January 12, 2017) <https://www.justsecurity.org/36212/cross-border-cyber-ops-erodelegitimacy-act-coercion> accessed 25 February 2023

[73] Ibid. (Barela argues that foreign actors meddling in election processes, with the intention of delegitimizing them, are committing an act of coercion because 'the disruption of a free and fair election strikes at a sine qua non for the State'. Barela asks whether 'disseminating true material can be considered coercion'). Ibid. (He answers that the Russian hack of the DNC could be considered coercive because releasing the hacked, authentic material was intended to manipulate 'public opinion on the eve of elections').

142 WHAT ARE HYBRID THREATS AND GREY ZONE CONFLICT?

argument, it does not go far enough. Coercion cannot contain the diversity of threats posed by new technologies. A new standard, therefore, is required. It well may be that severe manipulation of protected domestic and foreign affairs could become such a standard.

This does not to mean that we ought to discard coercion altogether, but rather that the norm of non-intervention, if it is to remain relevant, needs to recognize a more nuanced standard that would apply to these new methods of interference. This would require an assessment by the international community of which non-coercive forms of interference would significantly jeopardize the domestic and foreign affairs of a State as to make them wrongful under international law. In other words, the international community should be asking the same question as Quincy Wright: 'When does proper influence become illegal intervention'?[74]

On that note, the then UK Attorney General illustrated in his speech that cyber operations may violate the principle of non-intervention in a variety of ways, some of which are not per se *coercive*, as the concept is used in international law currently.[75] Some examples include cyber operations that 'cause hospital computer systems to cease functioning, prevent a State from managing its domestic economy, cause energy supply chains to stop functioning, and disrupt a State's ability to hold democratic elections'.[76] This reading affords coercion the broadest possible reading, which is useful in tackling the disruptive nature of novel cyber operations.

Some questions that may need further consideration in light of coercion's irrelevancy to today's methods of interference are the following: Is State-sponsored manipulation online wrongful? Would a State be in violation of non-intervention if it were to use political bots in violation of terms of service of social media platforms? Can interference through disruption be considered a prohibited intervention?

McDougal and Feliciano's consequentiality approach to coercion may have some significant utility for the future of non-intervention. They suggest looking at coercion beyond degree of coercion, and consider elements such as 'the importance and number of values affected, the extent to which such values are affected, and the number of participants whose values are so affected'.[77] Given the

---

[74] Quincy Wright, 'Espionage and the Doctrine of Non-Intervention in Internal Affairs', in Roland J. Stanger (ed), *Essays on Espionage and International Law* (Ohio State University Press 1962) 3, 4–5. Also see Schmitt (n 11) 8 ('Coercion is accordingly more than mere influence. It involves undertaking measures that deprive the target State of choice').

[75] Russell Buchan and Joe Devanny, 'Clarifying Responsible Cyber Power: Developing Views in the U.K. Regarding Non-intervention and Peacetime Cyber Operations' (*Lawfare*, 13 October 2022) <https://www.lawfareblog.com/clarifying-responsible-cyber-power-developing-views-uk-regarding-non-intervention-and-peacetime> accessed 25 February 2023.

[76] Ibid.

[77] Myres McDougal and Florentino Feliciano, 'International Coercion and World Public Order: The General Principles of the Law of War', in Myres S. McDougal, *Studies in the World Public Order* (Yale University Press 1987) 237, 251.

RETHINKING COERCION IN CYBERSPACE   143

substantial technological shifts globally, it may be helpful to look at coercion from the consequentiality angle, looking at the *effects* rather than the *tools and methods*.

These questions are particularly pressing given how States are already using methods of manipulation to interfere with domestic political processes.[78] The use of sophisticated manipulation techniques, usually with the help of machine learning to enhance microtargeting ability, is a major obstacle for non-intervention.[79] Manipulation through social media in way that impairs voters' ability to autonomously reflect and rationalize individual choices may sidestep the stringent coercion requirement. For example, the Russian interference in the 2016 US presidential election and the UK referendum on the secession from the European Union (Brexit)[80] through social media herald the future of online political manipulation which does not reach the level of coercion.[81] Indeed, the Internet Research Agency spent $2 million to promote Trump and denigrate Clinton through advertisement on social media platforms—Facebook, Twitter, and Instagram.[82]

The inability of non-intervention to apply to online manipulation stems largely from a conflation of propaganda and manipulation. Propaganda, as a method of interference, is usually not illegal under international law.[83] Propaganda may become somewhat problematic if 'the audiences' choice of alternatives [is] severely restricted as a result of the use of the instruments'.[84] But manipulation is qualitatively worse. Manipulation employs sophisticated techniques to undermine the autonomy and agency of individuals by exploiting their human

---

[78] Max Boot and Max Bergmann, 'Defending America from Foreign Election Interference' (*Council on Foreign Relations*, 6 March 2019) <https://www.cfr.org/report/defending-america-fore ign-election-interference> accessed 25 February 2023 ('Russia is continuing to try to 'wreak havoc over our elections' ... Other States and even non-State actors will also likely seek to emulate this model').

[79] Natasha Singer, 'Weaponized Ad Technology': Facebook's Moneymakers Gets a Critical Eye' *The New York Times* (New York, 16 August 2018) <https://www.nytimes.com/2018/08/16/technol ogy/facebook-microtargeting-advertising.html> accessed 25 February 2023.

[80] Patrick Wintour, 'Russian Bid to Influence Brexit Vote Detailed in New US Senate Report' *The Guardian* (London, 10 January 2018) <https://www.theguardian.com/world/2018/jan/10/russian-influence-brexit-vote-detailed-us-senate-report> accessed 25 February 2023.

[81] Craig Timberg, 'Russia Used Mainstream Media to Manipulate American Voters' *Washington Post* (Washington, 15 February 2018) <https://www.washingtonpost.com/business/technology/rus sia-used-mainstream-media-to-manipulate-american-voters/2018/02/15/85f7914e-11a7-11e8-9065-e55346f6de81_story.html> accessed 25 February 2023.

[82] Oliver Carroll, 'St. Petersburg 'Troll Farm' Had 90 Dedicated Staff Working to Influence US Election Campaign' The Independent (London, 17 October 2017) <https://www.independent.co.uk/ news/world/europe/russia-us-election-donald-trump-st-petersburg-troll-farm-hillary-clinton-a8005276.html> accessed 25 February 2023.

[83] Schmitt (n 13) 46 ('engaging in election propaganda does not amount to interference, at least as a matter of law. This conclusion is supported by the extensive State practice of engaging in both truthful and untruthful propaganda during foreign elections').

[84] Bhagevatula Murty, *Propaganda and World Public Order: The Legal Regulation of the Ideological Instrument of Coercion* (Martinus Nijhoff 1968), 1.

vulnerabilities.[85] This is further bolstered by technological tools like machine learning, enabling this manipulation to take place at scale.[86] Manipulation is propaganda on steroids. Schmitt agrees that 'manipulation of voters' ability to assess the messages in coming to their own decision tipped the scales and therefore constituted unlawful interference'.[87]

While there isn't a widely agreed-upon definition of manipulation, in the context of non-intervention, a definition focused on the democratic process is helpful. One way to define manipulation is as a 'set of tactics involving the collection and dissemination of information in order to influence or disrupt democratic decision-making'.[88]

Regardless of the definition of manipulation employed, it differs from persuasion in a variety of ways.[89] First and foremost, manipulation does not engage with rational capacities.[90] Some would also add that manipulation is hidden, in the sense that it influences and individual without the individual ever being aware of the influence.[91] The wrongfulness of manipulation is therefore in it bypassing any rational capacities of decision-making.

Manipulation does not necessarily use lies to bypass the rational capacities of the target. Though, on lying, scholars like Steven Wheatley argue that lying is the equivalent of coercion.[92] Therefore, if interference is manipulative in the sense that it deceives the targets, it leaves the targets with no choice but to act upon the false information provided by the manipulator. For example, this type of coercion is achieved through 'lying to the electorate with the intention of deceiving them into thinking and then voting differently'.[93]

[85] See Kilovaty (n 45) 471 ('manipulation exploits weaknesses and vulnerabilities of the subject based on data available about her. Manipulators learn these weaknesses and vulnerabilities by using advanced algorithms to analyze thousands of different data points and create a certain personality profile').

[86] Vyacheslav Polonski, 'How Artificial Intelligence Conquered Democracy', *The Independent* (London, 15 August 2017) <https://www.independent.co.uk/news/long_reads/artificial-intellige nce-democracy-elections-trump-brexit-clinton-a7883911.html> accessed 25 February 2023 ('This highly sophisticated micro-targeting operation relied on big data and machine learning to influence people's emotions. Different voters received different messages based on predictions about their susceptibility to different arguments').

[87] Schmitt (n 13) 47.

[88] Daniel Arnaudo et al, 'Combating Information Manipulation: A Playbook for Elections and Beyond', International Republican Institute (28 September 2021) <https://www.iri.org/resour ces/combating-information-manipulation-a-playbook-for-elections-and-beyond/> accessed 25 February 2023.

[89] Robert Noggle, 'The Ethics of Manipulation', Stanford Encyclopedia of Philosophy (2022), <https://plato.stanford.edu/entries/ethics-manipulation/> accessed 25 February 2023.

[90] Ibid.

[91] See Daniel Susser, Beate Roessler, and Helen Nissenbaum, 'Online Manipulation: Hidden Influences in a Digital World' (2019) 4 Georgetown Law Technology Review 1, 4.

[92] Steven Wheatley, 'Cyber and Influence Operations Targeting Elections: Back to the Principle of Non-Intervention' (2020) (*EJIL Talk!*, 26 October 2020) <https://www.ejiltalk.org/cyber-and-influence-operations-targeting-elections-back-to-the-principle-of-non-intervention/> accessed 25 February 2023.

[93] Ibid.

The *Tallinn Manual 2.0* does not mention manipulation per se, but it does offer a distinction between coercion and 'persuasion, criticism, public diplomacy, propaganda, retribution, mere maliciousness, and the like',[94] suggesting that the latter are not in violation of non-intervention because they are not coercive. This list, however, does not include manipulation, which may not be coercive per se but inherently includes more than State A having mere influence over State B. Although the *Tallinn Manual* gives a few relatively easy scenarios that do not reach the level of unlawful intervention, a few experts claimed context and consequences of an act are required to determine whether a violation occurred.[95] This disagreement is present in one example from the *Tallinn Manual*: State A leaks the domestic intelligence records of State B to create a political crisis within the victim State B,[96] with the result that State B adopts a policy that it would not have adopted otherwise. Drafters were split on whether State B's action was caused directly by the leak and was therefore coerced.[97] Without explicit coercion, it is debatable whether intervention occurred, which raises a host of issues for the future of non-intervention.

The difficulty with coercion as a standard for non-intervention is further exemplified in a divide between the *Tallinn Manual 2.0* experts with respect to cyber operation designed to hack electronic ballots and whether the victim's knowledge of the operation is required for non-intervention to be invoked.[98] The majority of *Tallinn Manual's* experts believed this to be an act of prohibited intervention regardless of knowledge. However, a few experts argued that it would only qualify as prohibited intervention if the victim State knows of such a cyber operation.[99]

This minority view is impractical in the cyber context since victim States would rarely be aware in real time that their or their citizens' decisions are being affected by manipulation, disruption, or disinformation. Such lack of knowledge should not preclude the wrongfulness of the initial intervening cyber operation. Even Michael Schmitt subsequently admitted that the ambiguity on this question 'represents a troubling threat to the democratic process'.[100] This hypothetical demonstrates the difficulty of applying coercion to a manipulation of election integrity. It is not a coercive act (do X, or else) but rather an act that deprives either the victim State or its citizens of a free choice.

---

[94] Schmitt (n 29) 318.
[95] Ibid. 319.
[96] Ibid.
[97] Ibid. 320.
[98] Ibid. 320–321.
[99] Ibid.
[100] Schmitt (n 13) 67.

3.4.3 Sowing distrust in political processes and institutions

A major trend in transnational interference is for intervening States to focus on swaying public opinion, sowing distrust in institutions, and political doxing. These objectives were largely exemplified by the Russian interference in the 2016 US presidential election. As the report issues by the Office of the Director of National Intelligence (ODNI Report) provided:

> Russian President Vladimir Putin ordered an influence campaign in 2016 aimed at the U.S. presidential election. Russia's goals were to undermine public faith in the U.S. democratic process, denigrate Secretary Clinton, and harm her electability and potential presidency. We further assess Putin and the Russian Government developed a clear preference for President-elect Trump.[101]

The ODNI Report portrays a troubling picture—States have no interest anymore in coercing each other to pursue a policy or a choice that they otherwise would not. Interference operations can be far more successful if it were to discredit opponents and target the public faith in political (usually democratic) institutions and processes. This is clearly a grey zone where non-intervention does not provide any more clarity on.

Schmitt agrees that the assertion that 'exfiltration of data and its weaponization through release at critical points in the election' constitutes intervention is 'somewhat supportable'.[102] This suggests that at there may be some nuance with doxing and swaying public opinion through the weaponization of information that may qualify the operation as unlawful intervention.

Indeed, as former President Obama was responding to Russia's interference in the 2016 presidential election, the White House identified that 'Russia's cyber activities were intended to influence the election, erode faith in U.S. democratic institutions, sow doubt about the integrity of our electoral process, and undermine confidence in the institutions of the U.S. government'.[103]

The texts of different instruments support the assertion that some propaganda may cross the line from legitimate speech to interference. For example, the 1976 Declaration on Non-Interference expressed concern about 'organized campaigns of vilification and intimidation' and 'subversion and defamation'. The 1981 Declaration on the Inadmissibility of Intervention and Interference goes

---

[101] Office of the Director of National Intelligence, 'Assessing Russian Activities and Intentions in Recent US Elections', Ica 2017-01d (6 January 2017) <https://www.intelligence.senate.gov/publicati ons/assessing-russian-activities-and-intentions-recent-us-elections> accessed 25 February 2023.

[102] Schmitt (n 13) 47.

[103] The White House, 'Fact Sheet: Actions in Response to Russian Malicious Cyber Activity and Harassment' (29 December 2016) <https://obamawhitehouse.archives.gov/the-press-office/2016/12/ 29/fact-sheet-actions-response-russian-malicious-cyber-activity-and> accessed 25 February 2023.

even further, by calling States to 'abstain from any defamatory campaign, vilification or hostile propaganda'.[104] While propaganda per se is not in violation of non-intervention, the concern expressed by both declarations illustrates that the integrity of political institutions and processes was of importance to the drafters.

Does massively swaying public opinion constitute unlawful intervention? What about making the public distrust its own institutions? These activities and their effect may be an important test for the norm of non-intervention.

3.4.4 The causal nexus problem

The problem with today's interference techniques may also be framed in terms of causation. While many of the past acts of interference had a direct causal link between the act and the coercive outcome, technological landscape at present may allow perpetrators to design their interference acts in a way that obfuscates this direct causal link.

For example, by employing Twitter tolls/bots, State A is able to lead to a certain coercive outcome in State B without necessarily targeting State B with any *direct* coercive act targeting its *domaine réservé*. As such, the coercive outcome from the use of political bots will only take place much later in time, in a manner that disassociates this bot network from the eventual outcome. While it is clear that Russia's extensive bot network on social media and other interfering acts had a significant impact on the discourse during the presidential election of 2016, it is still unclear to what degree it affected the outcome of the election.[105]

The Report on the Investigation into Russian Interference in the 2016 Presidential Election ('Mueller Report') identified the use of bot networks to amplify propaganda, disinformation, and manipulation campaigns online.[106] The same bot network was also the subject of the Special Counsel's Office indictment against thirteen Russian individuals involved in the disinformation campaigns on the eve of the 2016 presidential election.[107]

---

[104] UN General Assembly Resolution, 'Declaration on the Inadmissibility of Intervention and Interference in the Internal Affairs of States' (9 December 1981) UN Doc. A/RES/36/103, para 2(j).

[105] Philip Bump, 'Actually, The Mueller Report Showed That Russia Did Affect the Vote', *Washington Post* (Washington, 19 April 2019) <https://www.washingtonpost.com/politics/2019/04/19/actually-mueller-report-showed-that-russia-did-affect-vote/> accessed 25 February 2023.

[106] See Robert S. Mueller, 'Report on the Investigation into Russian Interference in the 2016 Presidential Election', Vol I (March 2019) 26 <https://www.justice.gov/archives/sco/file/1373816/download> accessed 25 February 2023 ('the IRA [Internet Research Agency] operated a network of automated Twitter accounts (commonly referred to as a bot network) that enabled the IRA to amplify existing content on Twitter').

[107] Department of Justice, 'Grand Jury Indicts Thirteen Russian Individuals and Three Russian Companies for Scheme to Interfere in the United States Political System' (16 February 2018) <https://www.justice.gov/opa/pr/grand-jury-indicts-thirteen-russian-individuals-and-three-russian-companies-scheme-interfere> accessed 25 February 2023 ('To hide the Russian origin of their activities, the defendants allegedly purchased space on computer servers located within the United States in order to set up a virtual private network. The defendants allegedly used that infrastructure to

148   WHAT ARE HYBRID THREATS AND GREY ZONE CONFLICT?

This problem overlaps with the difficulty of distinguishing State and non-State actors, as well as protected and unprotected domestic and foreign affairs. The difficulty of attribution certainly plays a major role here as well.[108] The emerging power of social media platforms is a double-edged sword, because it also makes liberal democracies immensely vulnerable if these platforms were to be misused by foreign governments.

4. Trajectory and challenges moving forward

The preceding section identifies some of non-intervention's grey zones in the socio-technological change context. But what is the trajectory of intervention in an era where non-intervention cannot keep up with socio-technological change?

This section identifies four trajectories and challenges moving forward. First, the grey zones identified in the previous section will likely be exploited by States seeking to evade accountability. Second, non-intervention and its two elements may simply become outdated and irrelevant. Third, it may prove difficult for new customary international law to emerge, in light of the non-transparent State practice. And fourth, an alternative standard for wrongful intervention is needed. It is unclear what such a standard could be. This chapter suggests disruption or manipulation as alternative standards in the aforementioned socio-technological context.

4.1 Exploitation of the grey zones

If non-intervention is incapable of addressing diffusion of power in the information age, new tools of interference, and the democratization of power, then States will likely seek ways to exploit these grey zones in ways that benefit them. States will increasingly push the limits of what is considered permissible under international law, which might incrementally turn non-intervention into a dead letter.

Schmitt, in his article on grey zones in international law, acknowledges that Russian operations and annexation of the Crimean Peninsula, as well as support of insurgent forces in eastern Ukraine and the hacking of the DNC demonstrate Russia's strategy of exploiting grey zones of international law.[109] By exploiting

establish hundreds of accounts on social media networks such as Facebook, Instagram, and Twitter, making it appear that the accounts were controlled by persons within the United States').

[108] See Hollis (n 16) ('Ironically, the potential for a false flag means that a State caught red-handed can always invoke plausible deniability and suggest that they are themselves a victim as some other, unknown super-sophisticated actor is trying to frame them').
[109] Schmitt (n 11) 1.

this grey zone, Russia frustrated 'the ability of U.S. officials to characterize it as unlawful and thereby have the grounds for fashioning a robust response'.[110]

Other States might take note of this strategy and utilize the same techniques. This exploitation of grey zones makes it difficult for the victim State to make a definitive determination that international law has been violated in the first place, which profoundly limits its ability to respond through countermeasures and seek reparations. This may open the door to further exploitation.[111]

4.2 Outdated standards for unlawfulness

The emergence of new technologies of influence and diffusion of power is leading to the irrelevancy of non-intervention's two elements—*domaine réservé* and coercion.

Internet users consume news, communicate with each other, and engage with representatives and political groups on social media. Social media platforms have truly transformed how individuals participate in the public square. This development amplifies the harm associated with abuse of this new socio-technological reality. The former Estonian president made a critical point on this amplification, particularly from the perspective of liberal and speech-friendly regimes that bear the consequences of such exploitation: 'Liberal democracies with a free press and free and fair elections are at an asymmetric disadvantage because they can be interfered with–the tools of their democratic and free speech can be used against them'.[112] Non-intervention in its current form simply cannot respond to this threat.

Indeed, cyber-dependent nations are vulnerable to manipulation, disruption, or attacks on their infrastructure, which could shut down political, economic, and social activities.[113] Acts of interference that use sophisticated technology can similarly undermine the political and economic stability of the victim State.

---

[110] Schmitt (n 13) 50.

[111] Schmitt (n 11) 2 ('By acting within legal grey zones, Russia makes it difficult for other States to definitively name and shame the country as having committed an internationally wrongful act').

[112] Ibid. 3.

[113] Paul Cornish, 'Deterrence and the Ethics of Cyber Conflict', in Mariarosaria Taddeo and Ludovica Glorioso (eds), *Ethics and Policies For Cyber Operations* (Springer 2017) 1, 4 ('[I]t is becoming increasingly difficult to imagine what life was like without social media, email, smartphones, broadband and so on'.); see also Christopher Joyner and Catherine Lotrionte, 'Information Warfare as International Coercion: Elements of a Legal Framework' (2001) 12 European Journal of International Law 825, 826 n.2 ('Stocks are purchased on-line. Applications for employment are made on-line. Work is done online. University degrees are earned on-line. Airplane tickets are bought on-line. Communications with friends occur on-line. People even register to vote on-line. The benefits of computer-based Internet system are enormous. Vast amounts of information are literally at the fingertips, facilitating research on virtually every topic imaginable. Financial and other business transactions can be executed almost instantaneously. Electronic mail, Internet websites and

150 WHAT ARE HYBRID THREATS AND GREY ZONE CONFLICT?

This is not to say that the freedom of speech ought to be curbed or restricted to meet the risks arising from new technologies (maybe some would argue that it should), but rather that influence and coercion take a new form in this socio-technological reality, which requires careful consideration of the conflicting values and the standards of non-intervention from now onward.

4.3 The non-transparency problem

The norm of non-intervention needs alternative elements and standards that account for the unique characteristics of today's interferences. This can be achieved either through emerging customary international law or a new treaty. Assuming that a new treaty is not currently on the international community's agenda, customary international law has a primary role in amending the content of the norm on non-intervention.

The socio-technological reality may undermine the ability of customary international law to develop at all. Primarily, the lack of transparency, involvement of private actors such as social media platforms, and State interest in maintaining obscurity may stifle the progression of customary international law on the issue.

Efrony and Shany identify three separate strategies adopted by States which may hinder such development: *optionality, parallel tracks*, and *gradation in law enforcement*,[114] all of which suggest that there is a serious transparency issue with respect to cyberspace and new technologies of interference. The emergence of new standards and elements of non-intervention may be hindered by the transparency challenge identified by Efrony and Shany.

The building blocks of a new norm of customary international law include information about the occurrence of an act of interference, the method used, direct and indirect consequences, and the response (or lack thereof) of the victim State. But in the technological context, it is difficult to access such evidence due to the secrecy that States maintain by default in that space. The optionality and parallel tracks strategies identified by Efrony and Shany are emblematic of this evidentiary challenge.

The covert nature of interference operations has become the norm since States have come to believe that publicity or transparency 'might expose their vulnerabilities, adversely affect their offensive or defensive capabilities, and weaken their power of deterrence'.[115] Brian Egan acknowledged this difficulty

computer bulletin boards allow instantaneous communications quickly and easily with virtually an unlimited number of persons or groups').

[114] Efrony and Shany (n 71) 648–52.
[115] Ibid.

in a speech given at Berkeley in which he highlighted the need for 'increased transparency ... to clarify how the international law on non-intervention applies to States' activities in cyberspace'.[116] Schmitt, reacting to Egan, seems to support the need for more transparency on the part of States operating in cyberspace.[117] Secrecy, however, remains the norm. How will the norm on non-intervention be revised then?

Until more public information and evidence become available, identifying a new customary international legal standard for cyberintervention may prove difficult to impossible. Schmitt believes that this will likely increase the role and weight of *opinio juris* serving as an 'interpretive function, rather than a law-creating one' in the absence of public State practice.[118] This is a persuasive outlook, since the norm on non-intervention already exists, and all that is required is a consistent and uniform consensus in the international community that States now follow new standards with respect to non-intervention as a matter of law. In addition, States still have some incentive to be transparent about their practices, because those States whose practices with respect to new technologies of influence are transparent may benefit from the ability to control and steer the development of customary international law toward a desirable direction, or at the very least, convince States to come out of their shadowy practices with respect to new technologies and cyberspace.[119]

4.4 In search of a new standard for intervention: disruption? manipulation?

The ambiguities surrounding non-intervention call for a new standard. Assuming that we can overcome the difficulties presented in this section, what should this standard be?

Previously, I have argued that we are entering an era of disruption.[120] Coercion is still an important threshold for the wrongfulness of intervention, but disruption is becoming far more commonplace to be ignored by non-intervention.[121]

---

[116] Egan (n 56).

[117] Michael Schmitt, 'US Transparency Regarding International Law in Cyberspace' (*Just Security*, 15 November 2016) <https://www.justsecurity.org/34465/transparency-international-law-cybersp ace/> accessed 25 February 2023.

[118] Schmitt (n 11) 20 ('it will likely be left to States to address grey zones through State practice and expressions of opinio juris. However, because most State practice in cyberspace is classified, the bulk of the heavy lifting will likely have to be accomplished by opinio juris').

[119] Kilovaty (n 33) 90.

[120] Ido Kilovaty, 'Doxfare: Politically Motivated Leaks and the Future of the Norm on Non-Intervention in the Era of Weaponized Information' (2018) 9 Harvard National Security Journal 146, 169.

[121] See e.g. William Mattessich, 'Digital Destruction: Applying the Principle of Non-Intervention to Distributed Denial of Service Attacks Manifesting No Physical Damage' (2016) 54 Columbia

152 WHAT ARE HYBRID THREATS AND GREY ZONE CONFLICT?

As such, an act of interference that significantly disrupts a political process in another State therefore should constitute an act of unlawful intervention.[122] The severity and magnitude thresholds of such disruption may need to be determined before disruption is to become an alternative standard to coercion, but McDougal and Feliciano's consequentiality approach may serve as a starting point.

Manipulation may also constitute an alternative standard to coercion. Emerging technologies allow States to engage in interference that is not coercive by nature, but one that manipulates political, economic, and social processes to a degree that deprives the victim State of its sovereign will and freedom of choice.

Manipulation is not a new phenomenon, but recent technological advancements, the availability of data, and the global nature of the Internet give manipulation a far more menacing form than ever before.[123] As Roberto Gonzales put it: '[s]ince we are never totally free of outside influence, what gives us (part) authorship over our own actions is that we regard our own reasons for acting as authoritative. Manipulation thwarts that'.[124] Manipulation can undermine sovereign will directly, but also indirectly where it reaches a critical mass of the population, which may then force the State to make a certain decision that it otherwise would not pursue.

The same threshold question comes up with respect to manipulation as well. At what point does manipulation become illegitimate? What sorts of tools are more susceptible to being considered illegal?

Manipulation allows the interfering State to influence the subconscious of the victim State or misinform its citizens to a degree that they demand policy change from their own State. Is this really any different than coercion? I argue that the outcome would be no different, though the difference is in the means: coercion is forceful, manipulation is subtle, but wrongfulness should attach to both.

5. Conclusion

Socio-technological change is transforming not only society itself but also the way in which States conduct their foreign affairs and influence operations. While applying existing norms and principles may be intuitive, such an approach does not always yield positive results. Non-intervention is an example of a norm that is unable to address the vast, global, and unprecedented socio-technological

---

Journal of Transnational Law 873 (applying the norm on non-intervention to distributed denial of service attacks).

[122] Kilovaty (n 120) 169.
[123] See Kilovaty (n 45) 472–76.
[124] Susser et al (n 91).

change, namely, *diffusion of power and parity in the information age, new tools of interference,* and *democratization of power.* This chapter identifies the grey zones arising from such change, while also hypothesizing the trajectories and challenges for non-intervention moving forward. Unless non-intervention adapts to this socio-technological reality, it will become a dead letter in international law in the years to come.

II
ARENAS OF HYBRID AND GREY ZONE COMPETITION

8

A Topography of Information-Based Foreign Influence

Beba Cibralic

1. Introduction

In Anton Chekov's 'Kashtanka', an inebriated Luka Alexandrovich, one of the story's central characters, spews out a bunch of religious expressions, mixing Russian with Old Church Slavonic without realizing it. He thinks he understands the Old Church Slavonic, he has the impression of knowing, the feeling of knowing, but he does not really know what the Old Church Slavonic means. It's not entirely incomprehensible to him—after all, he's heard the expressions in Church since he was a child, and there's a similarity between Old Church Slavonic and Russian—but it's not comprehensible either.

And so it is too with the cacophony of terms—'propaganda', 'information campaigns', 'information operations', 'disinformation'—used to frame and discuss foreign influence. Our familiarity with the terms gives us the impression that we know what they entail when, in reality, we experience the feeling or impression of knowing. Our situation is not too dissimilar to that of Luka Alexandrovich. Unfortunately for us, when the terms bleed into each other, they can lack the precision to be useful.

This chapter provides an opinionated lexicon that captures the core concepts in the discourse on foreign influence—a topography of the landscape, even. The overarching aim is to provide conceptual clarity in a domain where we often use language in vague ways.

Given the bloating in the foreign influence genre—and the fact that 'campaign', 'operation', and 'effort' appear in various terms—I use the umbrella term 'line of effort' (borrowed from military lingo) to refer to a more general category encompassing the specific terms. Section 2 begins by outlining the structure of a line of effort and providing a bird's-eye view of prominent types. Because of the ways in which foreign influence can undermine epistemic security, this study focuses on the concepts concerned with knowledge and truth. To that end, I limit myself to influence involving information, rather than influence involving coercive diplomacy, economic threats or sanctions, blackmail, or military force.

Beba Cibralic, *A Topography of Information-Based Foreign Influence* In: *Hybrid Threats and Grey Zone Conflict*. Edited by: Mitt Regan and Aurel Sari, Oxford University Press. © Oxford University Press 2024.
DOI: 10.1093/oso/9780197744772.003.0008

While the other activities are undoubtedly important, they are sufficiently different to warrant a separate study.

Sections 3 to 6 examine four concepts—often conflated or confused with one another—critical to understanding the epistemic impacts of influence: propaganda, disinformation, narratives, and mediatization. No explanation of such fraught terms is ever neutral or merely descriptive; what follows is my assessment of how best to conceptualize them for analytical purposes.

2. Lines of Effort

A line of effort is a cluster of activities orchestrated for a particular effect. While there is variation, a line of effort generally has the following structure: an *agent* (an individual, group, State, etc.) in some *context* (environment, country, period of time, etc.) targets an *audience* (an individual, group, State, etc.) using *instruments* (a technique, tool, medium, information, etc.) for the sake of some desired *end* (sway public opinion, change behaviour, disrupt an election, etc.).

Consider the following illustrative example: when Russia invaded Ukraine at the beginning of 2022, Ukraine's Ministry of Digital Transformation organized an 'Internet Army': a group of volunteers to help Ukraine's cause in the cyber and information realm. In April 2022, the Internet Army began discouraging Western companies continuing to do business in Russia. It targeted American and European companies, such as Johnson & Johnson, McDonald's, and Nestlé, with the aim of pressuring those companies to halt their operations in Russia. While no company admitted to succumbing to the pressure, several targeted companies withdrew or scaled back operations in Russia. It was a strong campaign (perhaps almost as effective as the July 2022 Vogue appearance by Ukraine's President Volodymyr Zelenskyy and First Lady Olena Zolenska).

Using the skeletal structure just articulated, we can break down the example as follows: an agent (an arm of the Ukrainian government) in some context (Ukraine is in an armed conflict with Russia) targets an audience (Western companies) using instruments (the Internet Army, social media, public pressure) for the sake of some desired end (discouraging Western companies from doing business in Russia).

We can make a number of generalizations about lines of effort with respect to intentionality, agency, veracity, and scope. All lines of effort are used intentionally or towards some purpose(s). It would be implausible to suggest that an actor drives a line of effort unintentionally, accidentally, or unknowingly (although it is sensical, and indeed common, for the actor(s) waging the campaign to co-opt others into unknowingly contributing). These intentions may not be known to the target of the line of effort or to other audiences, but there is some intentional

A TOPOGRAPHY OF INFORMATION-BASED FOREIGN INFLUENCE   159

force behind the line of effort. Ascertaining intentions in international relations is notoriously difficult, and misunderstandings abound. Intentions may sometimes be known, but it is more likely they are guessed at or inferred.

The term 'influencing agent' need not denote an individual. Typically, it is organizations—States, agencies, or bureaucracies within States (the military, intelligence agencies, etc.), companies, political groups, and so on—that engage in a line of effort, not individuals. There are exceptions, of course. One can imagine a highly influential person waging an information campaign.

Within each line of effort, the information used may be true or false, accurate or inaccurate, non-misleading or misleading. A line of effort is not defined by the veracity of the information. Often, a line of effort contains a range of different kinds of information—some true and some false. In all cases, the way in which the information is presented is supposed to have some specific effect: to change minds, induce scepticism, deceive, convince, and so on.

Finally, lines of effort tend to be discrete. While it is conceivable that a line of effort becomes totalizing, most are delineated. When a particular line of effort balloons beyond the established conceptual space, it makes less sense to refer to it as a line of effort.

There are different kinds of lines of effort. Let's begin with influence operations. A frequently cited 2009 RAND study defines influence operations as 'the coordinated, integrated, and synchronized application of national diplomatic, informational, military, economic, and other capabilities in peacetime, crisis, conflict, and post-conflict to foster attitudes, behaviours, or decisions by foreign target audiences'.[1] The audience can be an individual, group, military organizations, subgroups of a population, or mass publics.[2] The RAND definition is not the only one. Herbert Lin and Jackie Kerr put forth another prominent definition. According to Lin and Kerr, influence operations unfold 'across three dimensions: a physical dimension comprised of people, places and things; an informational or virtual dimension, where data is collected, processed, stored, and disseminated; and a cognitive or emotional dimension that reflects the minds and emotions of those who transmit, receive and respond to the physical acts and information encountered in the other two dimensions'.[3] While it has its merits,

---

[1] Eric Larson et al, *Foundations of Effective Influence Operations: A Framework for Enhancing Army Capabilities* (RAND 2009) 2.

[2] Ibid. In the definition, RAND also specifies that the purpose of influence operations is to 'further U.S. interests and objectives', but we can imagine that an influence operation conducted by the Russian Federation would be furthering Russian interests and objectives. This holds for all States, except perhaps in cases where a State conducts an influence operation to (1) further its own interests as well as the interests of an ally, or (2) only further the interests of an ally.

[3] Herbert Lin and Jackie Kerr, 'On Cyber-Enabled Information/Influence Warfare and Manipulation', Center for International Security and Cooperation (2017) 5 <https://fsi-live.s3.us-west-1.amazonaws.com/s3fs-public/cyber-enabled_influence_warfare-ssrn-v1.pdf> accessed 25 February 2023.

160 ARENAS OF HYBRID AND GREY ZONE COMPETITION

the Lin and Kerr definition is more confusing because the boundaries between the three dimensions do not seem to track the categories listed in the dimensions. Data processing and storage involve physical space, not just virtual space, and people—who Lin and Kerr place in physical space—exist not only in the physical dimension, but in the informational and emotional dimensions as well.

A related concept is 'information campaign'. Information campaigns are coordinated communicative activities that aim to reach large groups of people typically through mass media.[4] For example, the United Nations Refugee Agency has a page describing how information campaigns should be planned, implemented, and monitored.[5] A government sponsoring a domestic anti-smoking campaign is another useful example.

There is often confusion about the distinction between influence operations and information campaigns. Like information campaigns, influence operations have a cognitive or emotional dimension: actor A tries to shape what or how actor B thinks.

The RAND definition suggests a few distinctions between the two that prove useful. First, influence operations may involve information, but they are not limited to the information domain. The use of economic capabilities, for example, also fits under the umbrella of an influence operation. Second, influence operations are conducted by States: the targeting State A wages a campaign against the targeted State B. Information campaigns, meanwhile, need not be conducted by States.

Psychological operations are a twin concept to influence operations. Often called PSYOPS—and, for a brief period of time, referred to as 'Military Information Support Operations', or MISO[6]—these are planned operations that convey select information to foreign audiences with the proxy aim of influencing their emotions, motives, and objective reasoning for the ultimate goal of shaping the behaviour of foreign governments, organizations, groups, and individuals.[7] PSYOPS can involve misleading speech, but they also include other kinds of activities.[8] According to the US Army's official recruitment page, PSYOP

---

[4] Caroline Jack, 'Lexicon of Lies: Terms for Problematic Information', Data and Society Research Institute (2017) 4 <https://datasociety.net/wp-content/uploads/2017/08/DataAndSociety_Lexico nofLies.pdf> accessed 25 February 2023.

[5] United Nations High Commissioner for Refugees, 'Information Campaigns—Guidance on Registration and Identity Management' <https://www.unhcr.org/registration-guidance/chapter4/ information-campaigns/> accessed 25 February 2023.

[6] Meghann Myers, 'The Army's Psychological Operations Community Is Getting Its Name Back', Army Times (6 November 2017). <https://www.armytimes.com/news/your-army/2017/ 11/06/the-armys-psychological-operations-community-is-getting-its-name-back/> accessed 25 February 2023.

[7] Chairman of the Joint Chiefs of Staff, 'Joint Publication 3-13.2: Psychological Operations' (7 January 2010) <https://irp.fas.org/doddir/dod/jp3-13-2.pdf> accessed 25 February 2023.

[8] RAND, 'Psychological Warfare' <https://www.rand.org/topics/psychological-warfare.html> accessed 25 February 2023.

A TOPOGRAPHY OF INFORMATION-BASED FOREIGN INFLUENCE   161

soldiers specialize in 'unconventional capabilities, cultural expertise, language proficiency, military deception and advanced communications techniques' encompassing all forms of 'media'.[9]

Sometimes, two distinct lines of effort go by the same name. The clearest example of this is the term 'information operations'. This is a military term that refers to the integrated employment, during military operations, of information-related capabilities for the purpose of influencing, corrupting, disrupting, or usurping the enemy's informational capacities while protecting friendly forces.[10] As Christopher Paul emphasizes, 'information operations as formally described and practiced is a planning, coordinating, and integrating function. It is a staff function, done by a staff officer'.[11]

In 2017, Facebook released a report on disinformation in which it used the term 'information operations' to mean 'actions taken by organized actors (governments or non-State actors) to distort domestic or foreign political sentiment, most frequently to achieve a strategic and/or geopolitical outcome'. As Paul notes, Facebook's definition is inconsistent with formal Department of Defence usage. This has created some confusion in public discussions about what an information operation entails. What Facebook has described is closer to an influence operation, as conventionally understood. Given that the term 'information operations' is 'beset by ambiguity', Paul suggests that it's time to abandon it.

Over the last six years, a number of anachronistic categories from the Cold War era have risen in prominence to describe contemporary lines of effort. 'Reflexive control' is perhaps the richest concept from this era. As Ido Kilovaty explains, reflexive control involves one State A identifying and seeking to exploit the weaknesses of a competitor State B; the goal is for A to influence B's decision-making in a manner that is advantageous to A. To accomplish this, A can 'study the moral, psychological, and personal factors of the target so that those factors can be mimicked or manipulated so as to shape [B's] perceptions and disconnect them from reality'.[12] One effective manner of engaging in reflexive control

---

[9] Ibid.

[10] Chairman of the Joint Chiefs of Staff, 'Joint Publication 3-13: Information Operations' (20 November 2014) <https://defenseinnovationmarketplace.dtic.mil/wp-content/uploads/2018/02/12102012_io1.pdf> accessed 25 February 2023.

[11] Christopher Paul, 'Is It Time to Abandon the Term Information Operations?' (RAND, 13 March 2019) <https://www.rand.org/blog/2019/03/is-it-time-to-abandon-the-term-information-operations.html> accessed 25 February 2023. The relative importance of information operations depends on the kind of military engagement needed. Dell Dailey (who was then head of the State Department's counterterrorism operations) claimed that 'Since Al-Qaeda and other terrorists' center of gravity lies in the information domain, it is there that we must engage it' (cited by Susan Carruthers, *The Media at War* (2nd edn, Macmillan 2011) 201). We can imagine other contexts in which information plays a less significant role.

[12] Ido Kilovaty, 'Doxfare: Politically Motivated Leaks and the Future of the Norm on Non-Intervention in the Era of Weaponized Information' (2011) 9 Harvard National Security Journal 146, 159.

is by creating an informational context, through propaganda, disinformation campaigns, and so on, that shapes the target's decision-making.

Reflexive control draws attention to two aspects of foreign influence that, while present in other lines of effort, are not as prominently featured. The first aspect is using information not just to shape what someone thinks or believes but to create a particular epistemic environment. The second aspect is targeting decision-making, not merely belief formation, values, or attitudes. Both elements featured prominently in the case of Russian interference in the 2016 US presidential election.[13] Philosopher Regina Rini gives an illustrative example she calls 'weaponized scepticism', which refers to foreign influence against democratic states not intended to deceive, but rather to undermine the democratic value of testimony and corrode trust in the democratic system.[14]

Another concept that has risen in popularity is 'social engineering'. The term 'social engineering' is increasingly employed to describe the constellation of activities used by various actors to engage in influence. Robert W. Gehl and Sean T. Lawson broadly define social engineering as getting a group of people to act in a way that it would not normally. The authors explain that early practitioners of social engineering mostly operated through newspapers, radio, and movies. However, social engineering is now a mixture of interpersonal actions and mass personal influence, the latter of which relies on the use of social media.[15] As with influence operations, social engineering is not limited to information and communication-based activities.[16] Both reflexive control and social

---

[13] For a deeper exploration of reflexive control, see Thomas Rid, *Active Measures* (Profile Book 2020).

[14] In Rini's words, 'the goal is to induce skepticism. By flooding the channels of public discourse with falsehood, then allowing citizens to know that this has happened, anti-democrats make it reasonable for us to trust no one, least of all our co-citizens' (Rini, 'Weaponized Skepticism', 2).

[15] Robert Gehl and Sean Lawson, *Social Engineering* (MIT Press 2022). In the book, Gehl and Lawson identify the following four strategies as the dominant kinds of social engineering. *Trashing:* this involves examining an individual's or company's old, discarded emails. The Russian hacking organization, Fancy Bear, was trashing when it went through 2016 presidential nominee Hillary Clinton's old emails. *Pretexting:* this strategy is executed in order to make a target act without thinking. Russia has used pretexting on a massive scale since 2016 by putting out content that supports both conservative and progressive worldviews to generate a reaction from a target audience. *Bullshitting:* this entails using a mixture of deception, accuracy, and friendliness to help create and control an online community. Bots and trolls frequently use a mixture of false and true information to create this community while encouraging emotional reactions. *Penetration:* this strategy includes getting control over the supposedly irrational 'Others' who control networks. Of relevance is the number of times a piece of propaganda or misinformation is viewed across multiple platforms. Note that there are different ways to define the terms described here. Indeed, the way in which Gehl and Lawson define 'bullshitting' is not identical to the definition popularized by Harry Frankfurt in 'On Bullshit' (1986). Moreover, Gehl and Lawson's definition of pretexting is not the dominant one. More commonly, pretexting is understood as a method of creating a scenario in which a person divulges information they would not otherwise divulge. Consider a tabloid journalist, person X, calling a hospital and pretending to be a celebrity patient in the hospital, person Y, in order to learn more about person Y's condition. The journalist's actions are an example of pretexting.

[16] Outside the context of foreign influence, the term 'social engineering' often refers to government policies aiming to reshape society in a way that technocrats favour; for example, by direct

A TOPOGRAPHY OF INFORMATION-BASED FOREIGN INFLUENCE   163

engineering are concerned with the complex interplay between an audience's epistemic environment and a speaker's ability to subvert or manipulate that environment.

Not only have scholars resurrected or appropriated terms to capture kinds of lines of effort, they have also created new ones that help us make sense of the phenomenon. One particularly helpful conceptualization is 'foreign influence efforts' (FIEs). Diego Martin, Jacob Shapiro, and Michelle Nedashkovskaya, researchers who study trends in online foreign influence, define FIEs as follows: (1) they are coordinated campaigns by one State to impact one or more specific aspects of politics in another State, (2) through media channels, including social media, by (3) producing content designed to appear indigenous to the target State.[17] Put differently, FIEs are *foreign* (i.e. an attempt by State A to project content in State B); *deceptive* (i.e. masquerading as organic to country B); and *political* (i.e. they have a clearly defined political objective). Martin et al emphasized that FIEs are distinct from traditional propaganda, which the authors understand to be 'political information provided by country X about country Y in ways which do not seek to mask its origin' that may be 'true or false',[18] and local political activity, which may include disinformation.[19] The authors also contrast FIEs with traditional information operations; while FIEs may be coordinated with other traditional efforts, they are specifically designed to disguise the origin of the content. Speaker-identity deception is a key feature of FIEs.

With this more defined landscape in mind, I turn to a deeper examination of the core concepts necessary to understand the epistemic impacts of lines of effort, beginning with propaganda.

3. Propaganda

The best way to understand propaganda is to focus on the mechanism by which it operates: what characterizes propaganda is not speaker identity or the content of information, but *how* a speaker spreads a message. This section provides a brief sketch of the different ways of conceptualizing propaganda and shows that many

---

regulation or indirect incentives such as tax credits for desired behaviour. China's 'One Child Policy' is often called a form of social engineering. This meaning of social engineering dates back more than a century and concerns more than influencing what people believe. In the context of cybersecurity and information security, the usage of 'social engineering' is quite different from this definition; here, it instead refers to using forms of psychological influence to obtain confidential information.

[17] Diego Martin et al, 'Recent Trends in Online Foreign Influence Efforts' (2019) 18 Journal of Information Warfare 15, 16.
[18] Ibid.
[19] Ibid.

164 ARENAS OF HYBRID AND GREY ZONE COMPETITION

of these definitions are unstable and overlapping. This examination will allow us to see why a mechanism-centred view of propaganda is best.

Edward Bernays, a pioneer in the field of public relations, explained that the word 'propaganda' was coined by the Catholic Church in 1622, in connection with its missionary efforts and battle against Protestantism: 'propaganda fide' means 'propagation of the faith'.[20] In the Church's early usage of the term, there was no negative connotation. By the start of the twentieth century, 'propaganda' was a neutral descriptor for public relations techniques. Bernays defines it as 'a consistent, enduring effort to create or shape events to influence the relations of the public to an enterprise, idea or group'.[21] Fascinatingly, Bernays attributes the improved status of those working in propaganda to the success of the 'Allied campaign to celebrate (or sell) Democracy'.[22] This early definition of propaganda parallels the dominant contemporary definition of information campaign.[23]

Later in the twentieth century, a more pejorative definition of propaganda became dominant: propaganda as the manipulation of the rational will to close off debate.[24] This is the classical definition that many of us are most familiar with. On Jason Stanley's reading, propaganda of the classical sort functions not simply by closing off rational debate by appeal to emotion—after all, emotions can be rational and track reasons—but by *manipulating* the rational will.[25] Manipulation plays a critical role in this version.[26] This is not, of course, the only conceptualization of propaganda from this period. Walter Lippmann explains propaganda as consisting of the use of symbols that assemble emotions after they have been detached from their ideas. This art, writes Lippmann, is what helps create one general will out of a multitude of general wills.[27] Propaganda enables leaders and

---

[20] Edward Bernays, Propaganda (new edn, IG Publishing 2004), 147–48.

[21] Ibid. 52.

[22] Ibid. 12. As Bernays explains on the same page:

> [World War I] improved the status of those working in the fields of public persuasion. Formerly, the lords of industry and commerce had often seen the advertising agent as a charlatan, associated with the tawdry bunkum used to peddle patent medicines and cigarettes, and trying to sell a service that any boss with half a brain could surely manage on his own ... The great Allied campaign to celebrate (or sell) Democracy, etc., was a venture so successful, and, it seemed, so noble, that it suddenly legitimised such propagandists who, once the war had ended, went right to work messaging or exciting various publics on behalf of entities like General Motors, Procter and Gamble, John D. Rockefeller, General Electric.

[23] There are other interesting parallels between definitions of propaganda and information campaigns in the literature. On Jason Stanley's account of propaganda, an anti-smoking campaign would count as a kind of propaganda. An acceptable kind of propaganda, to be sure, but propaganda nonetheless. See Jason Stanley, *How Propaganda Works* (Princeton University Press 2016) 58–60, for an explanation of the kinds of 'supporting propaganda' Stanley takes to be acceptable in democracies.

[24] Ibid. 48.

[25] Ibid. 48.

[26] Manipulation is, generally speaking, a kind of influence over someone's beliefs, desires, and behaviours without their conscious awareness definitions.

[27] There is, Lippmann adds, no Hegelian mystery.

A TOPOGRAPHY OF INFORMATION-BASED FOREIGN INFLUENCE 165

politicians to take action: '[s]ince the general opinions of large numbers of persons are almost certain to be a vague and confusing medley, action cannot be taken until these opinions have been factored down, canalized, compressed and made uniform'.[28] On Lippmann's version, the mechanism by which propaganda operates is not manipulation.

Other definitions abound. Frequently, propaganda simply means the voice of the State or State-sponsored media. On this definition, propaganda is characterized by speaker identity (i.e. the State) and not by mechanism. Consider the following usage. Before 2013, broadcasts like Voice of America, Radio Free Europe, and other programs produced by the Broadcasting Board of Governors could not be aired in the United States. This is because of a so-called anti-propaganda law known as the Smith-Mundt Act which, thanks to amendments made by Arkansas Senator J. William Fulbright in the 1970s as well as Nebraska Senator Edward Zorniksy in the mid-1980s, prevented American taxpayers from funding propaganda targeting American audiences.[29] On this usage of the term, propaganda means State-sponsored media with the aim of influencing foreign audiences.

No single conceptualization of propaganda dominates academic scholarship today. Echoing the early definition of propaganda that Bernays articulated, many scholars have acknowledged that the conceptual boundaries between propaganda and other forms of media, like advertising and publicity, are often unclear.[30] That is not to say, of course, that the early definition has had a renaissance; scholars continue to use the term in varied ways, with some revising the definition of propaganda to accommodate information communications technologies.[31] A number of these new concepts focus on how propaganda works and not on how propaganda can be distinguished from other types of communication with respect to scale, kind, and permissibility.[32] Stanley himself

---

[28] Walter Lippmann, *The Phantom Public* (Harcourt, Brace 1925) 45.

[29] John Hudson, 'U.S. Repeals Propaganda Ban, Spreads Government-Made News to Americans' (Foreign Policy, 14 July 2013) <https://foreignpolicy.com/2013/07/14/u-s-repeals-propaganda-ban-spreads-government-made-news-to-americans/> accessed 25 February 2023.=

[30] Claire Wardle, 'Information Disorder: The Essential Glossary' (Shorenstein Center on Media, Politics and Public Policy, July 2018) <https://firstdraftnews.org/wp-content/uploads/2018/07/infoDisorder_glossary.pdf> accessed 25 February 2023.

[31] Alicia Wanless and James Pamment, 'How Do You Define a Problem Like Influence?' (2019) 18 Journal of Information Warfare 1, 5–6. In their literature review, Wanless and Pamment give the following examples: Benkler, Faris, and Roberts coined the concept of 'network propaganda' as 'the ways in which the architecture of a media ecosystem makes it more or less susceptible to disseminating persuasive messaging'; Wooley and Howard's 'computational propaganda' considers 'the assemblage of social media platforms, autonomous agents, and big data tasked with the manipulation of public opinion'; and Wanless and Berk proposed 'participatory propaganda' as a model that reflects the propagandist's ability to not just persuade a target audience to the propagandist's benefit but also to co-opt them into engaging, adapting, and spreading propaganda themselves through tools such as social media, which is their take on Jowett and O'Donnell's earlier definition.

[32] Ibid. 6.

166 ARENAS OF HYBRID AND GREY ZONE COMPETITION

eschews the classical definition in favour of his own account of propaganda, which explains the difference between kinds of propaganda, the relationship between propaganda and demagoguery, and the particular role propaganda plays in liberal democracies.[33]

These unstable definitions do us no favours. Propaganda is most useful as a concept when its definition is narrow and the phenomenon it seeks to capture is tractable. For this reason, the classical definition, which focuses on mechanism, is best for analytical purposes. Using this version, we are able to draw important distinctions between propaganda and related phenomena. First, propaganda is not equivalent to State-sponsored media; State-sponsored media might include propaganda, but it need not. Propaganda might also be used by non-State actors. Second, not all information campaigns involve propaganda; those that do not manipulate do not constitute propaganda. This delineation of what is and is not propaganda does not resolve all issues of clarity, as scholars may still understand the mechanism differently. It is, however, an improvement on current usage.

4. Disinformation

Disinformation is distinct from propaganda and ought not be a catch-all term for epistemic malaise, as it has sometimes been used. As I'll argue in this section, the best way to understand disinformation is to limit it to the intentional spread of false, inaccurate, or misleading information. This does not mean that we should not analyse the consequences of disinformation, which may include epistemic, political, and social harm. It does, however, mean that we should separate the consequences from the concept itself.

Since Russia's meddling in the 2016 US presidential election, scholars and policymakers have been acutely aware that disinformation and fake news can be used by States to undermine democratic decision-making. Disinformation is not, however, a new concept. In the 1950s, the Soviet Union used active measures, techniques to undermine and disrupt the policies of opposition governments. One such technique was 'dezinformatsiya', the dissemination of false or misleading information to the media in targeted States.[34] There's evidence to suggest that the English word 'disinformation' can be traced back to the Russian word 'dezinformatsiya'.[35]

---

[33] For more, see Stanley (n 23).
[34] Jack (n 4) 10.
[35] Aristedes Mahairas and Mikhail Dvilyanski, 'Disinformation–Дезинформация (Dezinformatsiya)' (2018) 3 The Cyber Defense Review 21. Some historical case studies of disinformation, however, are not a dominant part of the conversation, although perhaps they ought to be. Bennett and Livingston give a jarring example:

A TOPOGRAPHY OF INFORMATION-BASED FOREIGN INFLUENCE   167

Today, there is ample inconsistency in how disinformation is defined.[36] For example, not all researchers accept that information must be false to qualify as disinformation, or that there is a distinction between misinformation and disinformation.[37]

Some scholars believe that we best represent the relationships between these different ways of spreading false or misleading information when we consider them all within the category of 'fake news'. In a popular taxonomy of the phenomenon, Claire Wardle suggests that fake news comes in seven distinct types of mis/disinformation in the information ecosystem. These seven types sit on a scale that loosely tracks, according to Wardle, the intention to deceive from most likely to least likely: fabricated content ('New content [that] is 100% false, designed to deceive and do harm'), manipulated content ('When genuine information or imagery is manipulated to deceive'), imposter content ('When genuine sources are impersonated'), false context ('When genuine content is shared with false contextual information'), misleading content ('Misleading use of information to frame an issue or individual'), false connection (such as headlines that do not support the content), and satire/parody.[38]

Most usefully, misinformation is defined as information that is unintentionally false, inaccurate, or misleading information, and disinformation is information that is deliberately false, inaccurate, or misleading. Disinformers may vary in their intentions and motivations for creating disinformation. They are united as a group—and separated from misinformers—by the fact that they intentionally spread false, inaccurate, or misleading information.

> Racial dog whistles became all the more pronounced by the time Reagan's vice president ran for the presidency himself in 1988. George H. W. Bush's campaign manager Lee Atwater teamed up with Floyd Brown to make one of the most outrageous political commercials in US campaign history. The [William R.] Horton advert claimed Democratic candidate Governor Michael Dukakis had allowed a brutal killer out on a weekend furlough. While temporarily free, Horton raped a woman. If the same advert were produced by the Russian Internet Research Agency today, it would be labeled disinformation.

See W. Lance Bennett and Steven Livingston, *The Disinformation Age: Politics, Technology, and Disruptive Communication in the United States* (CUP 2020) 19–20. This example is striking because it reminds us that what is included and excluded in scholarship, in our conceptual analysis, often depends on the context we work and live in. For more, see Julie Posetti and Alice Matthews, 'A Short Guide to the History of "Fake News" and Disinformation' [2018] International Center for Journalists <https://www.icfj.org/sites/default/files/2018-07/A%20Short%20Guide%20to%20History%20of%20Fake%20News%20and%20Disinformation_ICFJ%20Final.pdf> accessed 25 February 2023.

[36] Wanless and Pamment (n 31) 1.

[37] Ibid. 4. For competing accounts in analytic philosophy, see the writings of Regina Rini, Alex Gelfert, Don Fallis, and Pepp et al.

[38] See Claire Wardle, 'Information Disorder: The Essential Glossary' (Shorenstein Center on Media, Politics and Public Policy, July 2018) <https://firstdraftnews.org/wp-content/uploads/2018/07/infoDisorder_glossary.pdf.> accessed 25 February 2023.

168 ARENAS OF HYBRID AND GREY ZONE COMPETITION

For theoretical purposes, marking the distinction between misinformation and disinformation is useful. That is, intentions may be relevant for helping us understand and differentiate between different activities. For practical purposes, however, whether intentions matter will depend on context. In some cases, ascertaining intent is not possible or too difficult in practice. Caroline Jack explains how professional standards shape the manner in which someone evaluates intent. Journalists and researchers face reputational damage and legal repercussions when they misrepresent a speaker's intent, and they avoid making claims about a speaker's intent unless there is verifiable proof of an intent to deceive.[39] In cases where there is ambiguity, journalists and others may opt for labelling something as misinformation rather than disinformation.[40]

In the mis/disinformation literature, epistemic unreliability is often combined with political disruptiveness, which can lead to conceptual confusion. For example, the definition of disinformation provided by W. Lance Bennett and Steven Livingston takes this form: 'we define disinformation as intentional falsehoods or distortions, often spread as news, to advance political goals such as discrediting opponents, disrupting policy debates, influencing voters, inflaming existing social conflicts, or creating a general backdrop of confusion and informational paralysis'.[41] Similarly, in the European Commission's final report of the High Level Expert Group on Fake News and Online Disinformation, disinformation includes all forms of false, inaccurate, or misleading information designed, presented, and promoted to intentionally cause public harm or for profit.[42] In the case of these two definitions, disinformation is characterized not only by intentionality but by a specific set of intentions deemed nefarious because of their political impacts. This definition of disinformation is confusingly narrow. One can imagine someone intentionally sharing false, inaccurate, or misleading information for purposes other than the ones specified in this list. What this narrower definition captures is a subset of disinformers who are nefarious actors, which may be useful for analytical purposes but ought not to be confused with a general definition of disinformation.

---

[39] Caroline Jack, 'Lexicon of Lies: Terms for Problematic Information' [2017] Data and Society Research Institute 1–20, 4. <https://datasociety.net/wp-content/uploads/2017/08/DataAndSociety_LexiconofLies.pdf> accessed 25 February 2023.

[40] Ibid. 4. There are two adjacent points worth highlighting. First, there is an imbalance of power. As Jack explains, 'actors who distribute deceptive or misleading content can do so without facing major threats to their own credibility, while posing potential legal and reputational threats to those who report on or critique them'. Second, the other advantage that the deceivers have is this: they are prepared to lie about the journalists and their work, but the journalists cannot lie back. This asymmetry gives actors who are willing to lie a valuable advantage over institutions bound, either legally or reputationally, to telling the truth.

[41] Bennett and Livingston (n 35) 3.

[42] European Commission, 'A Multi-Dimensional Approach to Disinformation: Report of the Independent High Level Group on Fake News and Online Disinformation' (Publications Office of the European Union, 2018), 11.

A TOPOGRAPHY OF INFORMATION-BASED FOREIGN INFLUENCE   169

Just as confusingly, 'disinformation' is sometimes used as a term to cover broader phenomena such as widespread scepticism or conspiracy theories. Russell Muirhead and Nancy Rosenblum offer a compelling account of one such example. The authors argue that 'fake news', as it is used in contemporary parlance, is 'something new' that 'goes beyond the claim of a deliberate misinformation campaign, of misleading reports and malicious fakery'.[43] Muirhead and Rosenblum suggest this is the case because 'the charge is not simply a label applied to news coverage that is erroneous or deceptive or biased. Fake news is an accusation of conspiracy. It is meant to convey that the mainstream news media are secretly colluding to defeat Trump and to disempower his supporters'.[44]

According to Muirhead and Rosenblum, individuals who, like former US President Donald Trump, publicly label institutions like the *New York Times* and *Washington Post* 'fake news' go beyond rejecting expert judgement and existing facts; they reject the reliability of the institution to produce knowledge. This delegitimization process threatens democracy by 'eroding not just trust in institutions but their meaning, value, and authority'.[45] Muirhead and Rosenblum are right to suggest that the way in which the term 'fake news' is applied to mainstream media, where the target is an institution and not just a piece of journalism, is conceptually distinct from the term 'disinformation'. Indeed, referring to mainstream media as 'fake news' has powerful epistemic consequences. Narrowly, it positions us to believe that the media are biased against Trump; broadly, it says something about how truth is hooked onto news. This charge of conspiracy, when effective, can lead to pervasive scepticism and renders it difficult, if not impossible, for a democracy to operate with a well of shared knowledge.

Hannah Arendt's distinction between the traditional lie and the modern lie offers a helpful framing for differentiating disinformation from this kind of conspiracy. In 'Truth and Politics', Arendt distinguishes between two types of lies: the traditional lie and the modern (or, totalitarian) lie. Both the traditional and the modern lie have as their basis the alteration of 'factual data'.[46] There are, however, two core differences between the traditional and the modern lie. The first is the all-encompassing scope of the modern lie. Traditional lies concern 'only particulars'; they tear 'a hole in the fabric of factuality' but do not change the whole context.[47] Modern lies 'are so big that they require a complete rearrangement of the whole factual texture—the making of another reality, as it were,

---

[43] Nancy L. Rosenblum and Russell Muirhead, *A Lot of People Are Saying: The New Conspiracism and the Assault on Democracy* (Princeton University Press 2019), 14.
[44] Ibid. 113.
[45] Ibid. 14.
[46] Hannah Arendt, 'Truth and Politics', in *Between Past and Future: Eight Exercises in Political Thought* (Viking Press 1968) 227–64, 253.
[47] Ibid. 253.

into which they fit without seam, crack, or fissure'.[48] On a grand scale, there is not much that 'prevents these new stories, images, and non-facts from becoming an adequate substitute and factuality'.[49] While traditional lies could be more easily spotted when one had an understanding of the whole context, modern lies changed that whole context. The second crucial difference is that while the traditional lie was 'directed at the enemy and was meant to deceive him . . . [those who lied] were not likely to fall victim to their own falsehoods; they could deceive others without deceiving themselves'.[50] Not so for the modern political lie. There is a 'completeness and potential finality, which were unknown to former times', that characterize the modern lie; the lies constitute the 'making of another reality'.[51] For Arendt, this 'organized lying' is one of the main elements of totalitarian movements.

Disinformation is best thought of, more narrowly, as the traditional lie; it can tear a hole in reality. But disinformation is less helpfully understood as the modern lie; phenomena like fake-news-as-conspiracy are better examples. Some narratives, as we will see in the next section, are also good candidates for the modern lie.

5. Narratives

Narratives are often described as campaigns or constructs used for a particular end. I posit that we need a broader understanding, one that encompasses history and social memory. Doing so allows us to see the complex relationship between truth and politics, reveals that narratives are not truth-tracking in the way that disinformation campaigns are, and shows that narratives and propaganda, often conflated, operate by different mechanisms.

In *LikeWar*, Singer and Brooking write that '[n]arratives are the building blocks that explain both how humans see the world and how they exist in large groups. They provide the lens through which we perceive ourselves, others, and the environment around us'.[52] The authors go on to explain how ISIL/Daesh created and maintained its narrative in a not dissimilar way to that done by reality stars like the Kardashians. While Singer and Brooking are right to introduce narratives as relevant concepts for understanding influence, they are wrong to characterize narratives as simply spun tales and built stories. This implies that

---

[48] Ibid. 253.
[49] Ibid. 253.
[50] Ibid. 253.
[51] Ibid. 249.
[52] Peter Warren Singer and Emerson T. Brooking, *LikeWar: The Weaponization of Social Media* (Houghton Mifflin Harcourt 2018) 157.

narratives are always artificial, and obfuscates the role that self-perception and historical memory—at the individual, group, and State levels—all play in the development of narratives.

Narratives are overarching interpretations of the present, past, and future in which particular facts come to make sense—and, in a way, make sense by confirming the central story. Narratives can be described as interpretations of history, but they need not be limited to this. Certain religious narratives, for example, are concerned with future-oriented elements (the end of the world) and come to play an important role in how believers think about their reality (the promise of heaven). A narrative can be helpfully compared to a hermeneutic circle, whereby a textual whole is interpreted by looking at its parts, but the parts are interpreted by looking at the whole.

Another useful conceptualization of narratives is that they are overarching structures that give meaning to particular factual claims. Believing a narrative can be described as 'being in a picture'—it is as if you were existing within a set structure that makes you feel as if what you saw were the world in its entirety.[53]

This is not to say that narratives or hermeneutic circles are always closed and impermeable to change. Narratives can both be open and subject to revision. Some facts may not confirm the narrative and still be accepted as fact; this, in turn, forces a critical moment of questioning, allowing understanding to grow rather than remain fixed. The narrative then changes. How this works in reality is less neat than what's been described here, and a variety of factors need to be in place for this to happen. Consider, for example, which conditions needed to be in place in the United States in the summer of 2020 for dominant views on policing to be challenged across mass media and popular culture.

Various examples from international relations illustrate the importance of narratives. China espouses a well-rehearsed narrative of what its role is on the world stage. On the surface, China's approach to foreign policy is direct and clear. Put succinctly: China seeks global partnerships based on the pillars of tolerance, equality, and peace; China respects international law and wants to uphold the norms of sovereignty and territorial integrity; and China is willing to work with all States, irrespective of institutional and ideological differences.

On this narrative, China is an anti-hegemonic leader that is committed not only to its own peaceful development but to the development of other economically insecure countries.[54] Moreover, China is guided by a combination

---

[53] I borrow this phrase from Benjamin Lipscomb who, in his book *The Women Are Up to Something* (OUP 2021), describes how Elizabeth Anscombe, Philippa Foot, Mary Midgley, and Iris Murdoch challenged the dominant picture of how the world is, developed and defended by thinkers like A. J. Ayer and Richard Hare.

[54] See Samuel Kim, *China and The World: Chinese Foreign Policy Faces the New Millennium* (Perseus 1998),for an early articulation of this view.

172 ARENAS OF HYBRID AND GREY ZONE COMPETITION

of pragmatism coupled with respect for the international order, its institutions, and the sovereignty of all States. Similar rhetoric can be observed in official government policy pronouncements and the speeches of leading Party figures. President Xi Jinping articulated this narrative in a speech in Germany in 2014:

> The Chinese nation is a peace-loving nation. . . . In ancient times, the following axioms were already popular in China: 'A warlike State, however big it may be, will eventually perish'. 'Peace is of paramount importance'. 'Seek harmony without uniformity'. 'Replace weapons of war with gifts of jade and silk'. 'Bring prosperity to the nation and security to the people'. 'Foster friendship with neighbours'. 'Achieve universal peace'. These axioms have been passed down in China from generation to generation.[55]

Another narrative that deeply informs China's perception of its own foreign policy is the 'Century of Humiliation'. This refers to the period between 1839 and 1949 when China was subject to Western and Japanese imperialism.[56] According to this narrative, land loss and other concessions during this time frame are not the new status quo; instead, a unified China is understood as the status quo, and division is understood as an interregnum before reunification. Within this frame, the 'return' of Hong Kong from the United Kingdom and Macau from Portugal are successful examples of progress towards a unified China, and Taiwan is still a work-in-progress whose absence leaves China fractured.[57]

But this is not the narrative that dominates discussion of China in the United States. Since 2017, Americans across the political spectrum have viewed China as an aggressor, in part because of China's disagreement with the United States and allies over freedom of navigation (FON) and overflight in the South China Sea, its territorial dispute with Japan regarding the Senkaku/Diaoyu Islands, and the continuing standoff with South Korea and the United States over the deployment of the Terminal High Altitude Area Defense (THAAD). Moreover, with increased reports from Xinjiang emerging in 2018 and 2019, China has been accused of genocide. This is not the first time China's human rights abuses have been in the public eye—the Tiananmen Square massacre and the 2008 Beijing Olympics put a spotlight on the Chinese government's human rights violations—but it is the first time the charge of genocide has been made.

---

[55] Xi Jinping, 'Speech by H.E. Xi Jinping President of the People's Republic of China' (28 March 2014) <https://www.fmprc.gov.cn/mfa_eng/wjdt_665385/zyjh_665391/201404/t20140421_678152.html> accessed 25 February 2023.

[56] Alison Adcock Kaufman, 'The "Century of Humiliation", Then and Now: Chinese Perceptions of the International Order' (2010) 25 Pacific Focus 1.

[57] Ibid.

The United States has competing narratives about the role it plays on the world stage. One dominant narrative concerns the Pax Americana. On this telling, the Pax Americana established a secure and stable international order. This new global system, the infrastructure of which was constructed following World War II, has uniquely served and advanced the interests of the world, and not, according to this narrative, just the interests of American hegemony. As Henry Kissinger wrote, when the United States took the 'torch of international leadership' following World War I, it added an important new quest for world order: the spread of liberty and democracy.[58] The Pax Americana was sustained through the promotion of the Washington consensus: observing common rules and norms, embracing liberal economic systems, forswearing territorial conquest, respecting national sovereignty, and adopting participatory and democratic systems of governance.

This is not, however, the only version of this story. The Iran-Contra Scandal, the illegal bombings of Cambodia,[59] the Vietnam war, the 2003 invasion of Iraq, and the US support of despotic regimes provide ample fodder for challenging the Pax Americana narrative. Indeed, in an open society in which freedom of expression is protected robustly, narratives are debated and challenged; the fiercest criticism of the United States often comes from Americans holding their government to account.[60]

Narratives are central to the influence debate because in constituting and propagating them, agents can shape the social reality of those they influence. They can paint or colour or redraw the picture in ways that give them power

[58] Henry Kissinger, *World Order* (Penguin 2014) 7.
[59] Notably, Kissinger was an architect of these.
[60] In more recent years, there has been ample disagreement over the rules-based order narrative. According to the United States and allies, the rules-based order is a patchwork of norms of cooperation and goodwill that protect important interests and freedoms. The description of the international system as a 'rules-based order' is sometimes used to describe the global system as it exists (and warn against States trying to challenge the system—e.g. 'China is going to challenge the liberal order'), and other times is held as a regulative ideal of what the system ought to be and thus what it in practice approximates or approaches, despite its imperfections. Both Russia and China believe that the Anglo-American narrative of the 'rules-based order' only serves Western interests and protects the military supremacy of the United States and its allies. Both countries call for focus on international law—in particular, a respect for State sovereignty—and are quick to point out when Western States do not follow international law. (This is not to imply that Russia and China respect international law; both States frequently break it.) Interestingly, Russia's attitude is shaped not just by the political advantageousness of pushing against the United States but by another specific narrative that dominates. For Russia's political class, there is one standard narrative of the West's betrayal after the Soviet Union was dismantled. The story goes as follows: the United States did not let Russia join the North Atlantic Treaty Organization (NATO), nor did it disband NATO. In fact, NATO was expanded in the 1990s. Meanwhile, Russia withdrew its troops from the Eastern bloc, disbanded the Warsaw Pact, and closed its military bases in Cuba and Vietnam as promised, reflecting Russia's goodwill. The United States did not reciprocate in the way that Russia was led to believe it would. This narrative of Western betrayal continues to inform Russian foreign policy and, to some extent, serve as a justification (at least in the eyes of key foreign policy decision makers) for Russia's invasion of Ukraine and increased aggression in Europe.

over those who identify with being in the picture. Being able to create or propagate a captivating narrative is a powerful means of engaging in influence. Note, too, that we do not have full control of the narratives that we live within, and are ourselves constrained by what we can come to know because of where we sit and who we are.

The relationship between narratives and truth is difficult to ascertain in broad strokes. Are large-scale narratives like these national mythologies even candidates for being 'true' or 'false'? They may include factual claims, but in their large structure they are interpretations of national history, not factual claims. Indeed, one's interpretation of the facts depends on one's situatedness within a particular narrative. One might reasonably assess China's foreign policy proclamation that China 'seeks global partnerships based on the pillars of tolerance, equality, and peace' is misleading on the grounds that, in reality, China often seeks global partnerships through the Belt and Road Initiative that are unequal and significantly disadvantageous to parties other than China. And yet one can easily imagine a response from a Chinese party member situated within the narrative: by 'tolerance' we mean not conditioning our willingness to do business with partners on liberal reforms or other changes in their internal governance; by 'equality' we mean that we bargain reciprocally; and by 'peace' we mean no military pressure on our partners.

Narratives can, however, be built on points that track reality to differing degrees. Not all narratives are equal, and it is far from clear whether they each deserve attention and their day in the court of public opinion. When certain narratives are built on false factual statements that are ballooned onto a gigantic scale, we have reason to worry. Narratives that are unmoored from reality are uncannily similar to Arendt's 'modern lie' and may be more dangerous than the 'traditional lie'.

6. Mediatization

In the context of foreign influence, much is made of the weaponization of social media. But using social media as a tool is only one feature of a broader phenomenon: the way in which media shapes how we can influence and be influenced. I'll explain why social media does in fact matter greatly, and then explain why mediatization, as a concept, is the right focus for analytical inquiry.

Let's begin with social media, whose power is illustrated in a story Singer and Brooking tell of ISIL/Daesh's surprisingly victorious invasion of Mosul. Armed with 1,500 fighters, second-hand AK-47s, pickup trucks, and their social media accounts, ISIL/Daesh was somehow able to ignite enough fear that thirty thousand defenders of Mosul retreated, leaving much of their equipment for ISIL/

A TOPOGRAPHY OF INFORMATION-BASED FOREIGN INFLUENCE 175

Daesh to claim. How do we make sense of this event? ISIL/Daesh had successfully weaponized social media by broadcasting their invasion; the hashtag 'AllEyesonISIS' went viral. As Singer and Brooking explain, what played out on social media changed the dynamics on the ground.[61]

But there is another way, arguably deeper and more accurate, of understanding the 'weaponization of social media' and related phenomena. It is not merely the use of social media for political or military ends, but a kind of mediatization.[62]

'Mediatization' refers to the process whereby social and cultural institutions and modes of interaction are changed as a consequence of the growth of the media's influence.[63] It affects all domains of life, from the seemingly trivial to the indisputably important.[64] In the context of warfare, mediatization refers to the process by which warfare is 'embedded in and penetrated by media, such that to plan, wage, legitimize, assuage, historicize, remember, and to imagine war requires attention to that media and its uses'.[65] To say that war and conflict are not merely mediated is to suggest that they are reliant on media. 'Mediation' refers to the act of communication by means of a medium in a specific social context.[66]

One prominent example comes from the US military's media strategy. The US military has been operating one of the world's most innovative media strategies for decades.[67]

---

[61] Daesh/ISIL and authoritarian regimes are not the only ones capable of social media influence. In 'Troops, Trolls and Troublemakers: A Global Inventory of Organized Social Media Manipulation', Samantha Bradshaw and Philip N. Howard share that authoritarian regimes are not the best at organized social media manipulation, and that the earliest reports of government involvement in nudging public opinion involve democracies. See Samantha Bradshaw and Phillip N. Howard, 'Troops, Trolls and Troublemakers: A Global Inventory of Organized Social Media Manipulation', Computational Propaganda Research Project (2017) <https://ora.ox.ac.uk/objects/uuid:cef7e8d9-27bf-4ea5-9fd6-855209b3e1f6/download_file?file_format=application%2Fpdf&safe_filename=Troops-Trolls-and-Troublemakers.pdf&type_of_work=Report> accessed 25 February 2023.

[62] 'Media' refers to various vehicles for mass communication, from broadcasting to the internet. Social media is not the only relevant platform today, although it has drawn ample scholarly attention in recent years, in no small part because of the perceived role disinformation on social media seemed to play in the outcome of the 2016 US presidential election. The internet has not replaced other traditional media; cable TV and radio remain information staples in contemporary American society. There is also significant research that suggests that TV networks like Fox News are just as, if not more, responsible for the spread of disinformation than social media platforms like Facebook. See, for example, Yonchai Benklar's writings on network propaganda (in particular, Yonchai Benklar, Robert Faris, and Hal Roberts, *Network Propaganda* (OUP 2018)).

[63] Ibid. 4. It is distinct from concepts like agenda-setting, priming, and framing, which, while relevant to the study of political communications, is outside our scope. For more, see Dietram A. Scheufele and David Tewksbury, 'Framing, Agenda Setting, and Priming: The Evolution of Three Media Effects Models' (2017) 57 Journal of Communication 9.

[64] For a compelling read, see, for example, Neal Gabler, *Life: The Movie: How Entertainment Conquered Reality* (Vintage Books 2000).

[65] Andrew Hoskins and Ben O'Loughlin, 'Arrested War: The Third Phase of Mediatization' (2015) 18 Information, Communication and Society 1320.

[66] Frank Esser and Jesper Strömbäck, 'Mediatization of Politics: Towards a Theoretical Framework', in *Mediatization of Politics*, edited by Frank Esser and Jesper Strömbäck, 3–4 (Palgrave Macmillan 2014).

[67] Sebastian Kaempf, 'The Ethics of Soft War on Today's Mediatized Battlespaces', in *Soft War: The Ethics of Unarmed Conflict*, edited by Michael Gross and Tamar Meisels, 104, 107. (CUP 2017).

176 ARENAS OF HYBRID AND GREY ZONE COMPETITION

Drawing from Susan L. Carruthers' seminal work, *The Media at War*, Sebastian Kaempf explains how and why this 'soda-straw-view' media strategy—that is, showing only a limited view of content in an intentionally structured way—has been so effective. Since the Vietnam War, the Pentagon has limited the media's access to the battlefield: no American body bags are shown, the sight of collateral damage is frequently omitted, and footage of the war itself is limited to a 'very narrow, technical level', thus obscuring the 'overall operational . . . [and] strategic dimensions' of how the war is unfolding.[68] Consider this example from the Second Gulf War:

> During the 2003 Iraq war, reporters for the first time were embedded with front line troops, providing unprecedented live television footage of the war. And yet, as detailed research has shown, 70 percent of this footage focused on the lives of individual U.S. soldiers (creating an emotional bond for the home front with 'our' soldiers), 20 percent of the overall coverage focused on the personal experience of the embedded journalist him/herself (who, dressed half-civilian, half soldier, served as a bridge between the home and battlefront), and only the remaining 10 percent of the reporting was on the actual war-fighting . . . which— because it was shown from the perspective of U.S. forces—painted U.S. soldiers not as aggressors but as beleaguered victims.[69]

This example demonstrates the kind of influence media can have not just in determining the scope of our knowledge, but how we react to information, what we take to be news and newsworthiness, and, ultimately, which kinds of perspectives and people we are sympathetic to. This power to influence is in part why controversies arise when journalists make mistakes in reporting or failing to meet the appropriate epistemic standards.[70] More strongly, mediatization plays a direct role in the success of a conflict, particularly those involving counterinsurgencies, because success requires winning support from the local population.[71]

The media, and news in particular, has always been important to warfare. BBC founder Lord John Reith described news as the 'shock troops of propaganda'.[72]

---

[68] Ibid. 107, 110.

[69] Ibid. 110.

[70] For a discussion on how choice of media (podcast vs. print) determines which epistemic norms are appropriate for foreign policy reporting, see Beba Cibralic, ' "Caliphate" and the Problem of Testimony' (Social Epistemology Review and Reply Collective, 29 December 2020) <https://social-epistemology.com/2020/12/29/caliphate-and-the-problem-of-testimony-beba-cibralic/> accessed 25 February 2023.

[71] Laurie R. Blank, 'Media Warfare, Propaganda and the Law of War', in Gross and Miesels (n 67) 88, 92.

[72] Carruthers (n 11) 72.

A TOPOGRAPHY OF INFORMATION-BASED FOREIGN INFLUENCE   177

Similarly, Goebbels wrote in 1942 that '[n]ews policy is a weapon of war; its purpose is to wage war and not to give information'.[73] Carruthers goes on to explain that both the Axis and Allied powers competed to dominate the news cycle by either suppressing information that was unfavourable or releasing what was advantageous as quickly as possible.[74] What might be striking to a modern audience is that liberal democracies, including the United Kingdom, engaged in censorship during the war: 'the Naval censor later recalled that Churchill at the Admiralty would "hold on to a bit of bad news for a time on the chance of getting a bit of good news to publish as an offset"'.[75]

Our discussion of warfare enables us to see the relevance of mediatization to foreign influence. As the discussion in section 5, 'Narratives', exemplifies, the media contributes to the construction of implicit and explicit narratives. Warfare, for example, might seem as a fundamentally material domain of human activity, but it is suffused with efforts to generate narratives that prevail against those of adversaries. So too in contexts outside an armed conflict: the media contributes to the construction of implicit and explicit narratives that can help influence other States.[76]

What remains critical for our purposes is the recognition that mediatization, properly construed, does not fit neatly within the confines of a single campaign, a single line of effort. The processes by which media shapes us and our social world are also the processes by which foreign actors can engage in influence.

---

[73] Ibid. 72.

[74] Ibid. 73.

[75] Quoted by Lasswell, 1927, in Carruthers (n 11) 52. There are many other examples we can point to. Consider two more. American coffins: From 2003 to 2009, the Bush administration banned photography of coffins returning to the United States with the bodies of soldiers killed in action (ibid. 8). Drawing on work by Alexievich 1992, Susan Carruthers writes that this prohibition uncannily echoes 'the Kremlin's insistence that dead soldiers returning from Afghanistan during its war there from 1979 to 1988 be sealed in zinc coffins, bolted shut to prevent images of Red Army fatalities gaining public currency' (ibid.). British media during Guerra de las Malvinas/The Falklands war: Communication in Britain around the Falklands war was deeply shaped by the Ministry of Defence's information policies. Permanent Under Secretary of the Ministry of Defence 'laid down guidelines for editors as to what they could not cover, while officers and crews were briefed on what was discussable with their journalist shipmates. Eight topics were deemed inadmissible: speculation about possible future action; plans for operations; operational capabilities and readiness of individual units; details about military techniques and tactics; logistical information; intelligence about Argentine forces; equipment capabilities and defects; and communications' (Harris, 1983, 26, referenced by Carruthers (n 11) 121). While the official position is that no censorship was practiced, Carruthers writes that journalists who adopted 'a more dispassionate or critical tone found their stories delayed for days in transit or referred to the MOD in London for further 'fact checking'. In this way, bad news turned into old news, and hence no news at all' (ibid. 122).

[76] It would be overly simple to suggest that States can always influence media in direct ways. Moreover, the kinds of mediatization that impact us today go well beyond direct State intervention. For example, the global spread of Rupert Murdoch's media empire goes beyond the State level yet powerfully shapes politics and national narratives. It represents a kind of supranational political influence.

7. Conclusion

In this chapter, I have attempted to provide a detailed overview of the analytical terrain for understanding information-based foreign influence and its epistemic consequences. In brief, the arguments I have made are as follows. Firstly, the cacophony of terms we use for understanding foreign influence can best be conceptualized by paying attention to the basic structure underpinning a line of effort. Secondly, propaganda is best defined by the mechanism by which it operates, and is not merely State-sponsored media. Thirdly, disinformation ought not be defined by its consequences but by veracity of information and intentions, nor should it be confused with other kinds of conspiracies. Fourthly, narratives are not truth-tracking in the same way as disinformation, although they—like disinformation—may lead to pervasive scepticism, or Arendt's 'big lie'. Fifthly, mediatization is a broader and more complex phenomenon than discussions on the weaponization of social media typically account for, and merits more attention.

9

In Pursuit of Geopolitical Advantage

Hacking Below the Threshold of War

Melissa K. Griffith

1. Introduction

An ever-increasing number of States have begun to formally recognize grey zone competition (sometimes referred to as, or evoked alongside, hybrid threats) as a pressing national security challenge. Yet, while we know a great deal about the dynamics of conflict and war, we know far less about the dynamics of geostrategic competition that occurs in the grey zone, remaining below the threshold of military confrontation or warfare. It is here that geopolitical competition between States takes on unique features in cyberspace and poses unique policy challenges.

While cyber operations can, have, and will continue to be used alongside kinetic means in periods of armed conflict (it would be naïve to think that in times of war, the fifth domain would simply be ignored by cyber-capable countries),[1] much of the activity observed to date has occurred outside this context and without triggering open military confrontation. Importantly, these grey zone operations differ in meaningful ways from their historical predecessors. An environment of (1) critical interconnectedness, (2) featuring pervasive malicious activity at scale in pursuit of geopolitical advantage, and (3) operational flexibility (born from persistence in systems and the modular nature of tools at hackers' disposal) sets grey zone cyber operations apart from both historical intelligence contests as well as the more episodic, open military confrontations of interstate warfare.

As a result, not only are cyber operations a core feature of grey zone competition or conflict more broadly, but by simultaneously thriving in the grey zone and the ability to be impactful (including potentially strategically) from the grey zone, they are redefining how we conceptualize the importance of and the array

---

[1] For a detailed examination of the ways in which offensive cyber operations can be incorporated into and contribute to the overall military effort, see Daniel Moore, *Offensive Cyber Operations: Understanding Intangible Warfare* (Hurst 2022). Moore focuses his attention on the spectre of cyber-warfare (a subset of what he refers to as intangible warfare).

Melissa K. Griffith, *In Pursuit of Geopolitical Advantage* In: *Hybrid Threats and Grey Zone Conflict*. Edited by: Mitt Regan and Aurel Sari, Oxford University Press. © Oxford University Press 2024. DOI: 10.1093/oso/9780197744772.003.0009

of defensive policies the United States and partner countries must deploy in the face of sustained competition below the threshold of war.

This chapter will proceed in four parts. In section 2, I provide a brief introduction to cyberspace and an overview of the unique defence problem States face in this domain: critical interconnectedness. It is the dual dynamics of dependence on and the globally interconnectivity of cyberspace that underpins how and why States hack. Section 3 introduces how cyber operations not only exist in but are thriving below the threshold. This messy middle between war and peace, however, is not the only grey zone of note in cyberspace. Cyber operations can also straddle the line between (1) crime and statecraft and (2) espionage and attacks. Each of these three grey zones not just blurs academic conceptual or theoretical distinctions but complicates the policy decisions available to States, ranging from the technical/tactical to the strategic. Third, in section 4, I analyse the character of geostrategic competition in cyberspace with a specific focus toward the variety of strategic, operational, and tactical purposes hacking can serve, both as discrete operations and as sustained campaigns comprising a series of operations. Notably, the scale and scope of cyber operations set them apart from their historical predecessors in important ways. Fourth, and given that the prior two sections each ends with a discussion of 'key takeaways', in section 5 I briefly summarize the role cyber operations are playing in redefining the importance of grey zone competition more broadly.

2. From cyberspace to cyber operations: the problem of critical interconnectedness

Before diving into the unique contours of the grey zone challenges posed by cyber operations, it is first necessary to define the threat space itself. What is cyberspace and why have hackers been able to leverage it for an array of tactical, operational, and strategic purposes? The defence problem now facing States, which I refer to as critical interconnectedness, is the product of two overlapping but distinct dynamics: their dependence on and the global interconnectivity of cyberspace. The former dynamic stems from the activity occurring on or through cyberspace while the latter is a feature of the terrain itself.

States, particularly advanced industrial economies, are increasingly dependent on cyberspace. Today, cyberspace—a globalized and interwoven network of networks and devices '(and the users behind them) through which information is stored, shared, and communicated online'[2]—is central to how

---

[2] P. W. Singer and Allan Friedman, *Cybersecurity and Cyberwar: What Everyone Needs to Know* (OUP 2013) 13.

economies compete; individuals and communities communicate; and States provide security for their populations. It underpins the likes of our electricity grids, healthcare systems, communications networks, and banking and financial services, as well as the ways our militaries fight and our intelligence community gathers intelligence. As an increasing number of activities move onto this deeply interconnected digital terrain, they become susceptible to cyber operations targeting the confidentiality of the data traversing these networks as well as the integrity and availability of both the data and the systems themselves.

Moreover, the globalized nature of these networks enables actors to leverage that dependence to carry out operations in ways that would not have been possible in conventional domain(s). Namely, it is interconnectedness that enables actors to spy, disrupt, destroy, defray, and exert influence at a distance while avoiding an array of familiar logistical challenges and costs associated with conventional and historical means.

Notably, critical interconnectedness—both States' dependence on and the interconnectivity of cyberspace—is only likely to get worse. Unlike the domains of air, land, and sea, cyberspace is simultaneously a manmade terrain and a domain through which human activity traverses. This domain of conflict and State competition is built, maintained, and advanced by humans, many if not most of whom are currently sitting within industry rather than government. And it is actively growing.

As early as 1993, Bruce Sterling recognized this evolving nature of the terrain, colourfully describing the growth of the internet—a core backbone and component of cyberspace—as follows: '[t]he headless, anarchic, million-limbed internet is spreading like bread-mold'.[3] The growth of the internet can perhaps be most viscerally expressed through the ongoing transition from IPv4 to IPv6. IP, which stands for internet protocol, is a set of rules that govern the communication of data over the internet. IP addresses, the phone numbers of the internet, are unique numerical labels assigned to every device connected. These addresses allow data to be transmitted from one device to another. IPv4, with its 32-bit IP addresses, supported about 4.3 billion unique addresses (or connected devices) globally. A number that seemed, at least initially, to far exceed potential future demand. However, with the exponential growth of the internet and the increasing number of devices requiring IP addresses, 4.3 billion is proving to be insufficient. In contrast, IPv6, with its 128-bit IP addresses, can support approximately the same number of connected devices as scientists estimate there are grains of sand on planet Earth (7.5 sextillion to be exact).[4]

---

[3] Bruce Sterling, 'A Short History of the Internet', *The Magazine of Fantasy and Science Fiction* (February 1993) 4.

[4] Robert Krulwich, 'Which Is Greater, The Number of Sand Grains on Earth or Stars in the Sky?' (*NPR*, 17 September 2012) <https://www.npr.org/sections/krulwich/2012/09/17/161096233/which-is-greater-the-number-of-sand-grains-on-earth-or-stars-in-the-sky> accessed 15 February 2023.

182 ARENAS OF HYBRID AND GREY ZONE COMPETITION

Looking beyond the internet, mobile telecommunications networks, which today provide access to and leverage the internet in their daily operations, paint a similar picture. The development and deployment of 5G, the 'fifth generation' of mobile network technology, heralds significant increases to bandwidth and the number of connections while decreasing latency. In plain English, 5G, and subsequently 6G, promises faster connections and larger capacity than 4G networks allowed.[5] As a result, telecommunications networks can support an ever-increasing number of interconnections between devices and networks. As their utility grows, so do the array of promised use cases, including other critical infrastructure sectors. Take, for example, the internet of things (IoT)—an ecosystem of connected devices from baby cameras to agricultural sensors. The explosive growth of IoT devices simultaneously both increases the potential attack surface and introduces specific software vulnerabilities of their own.[6] As leading cybersecurity firms such as Symantec, along with a myriad of others, have pointed out on numerous occasions, "security" is not a word that gets associated with this category of devices'.[7] As potentially one of the most important networks of the twenty-first century and a component part of cyberspace, 5G is the very definition of high levels of dependency on a deeply interconnected ecosystem.

Notably, awareness of this new venue, or domain, of competition has only increased over the past thirty or so years. Cyber operations, leveraging critical interconnectedness, have become an ever increasing and sophisticated part of statecraft as '[h]ackers wiretap, spy, alter, sabotage, disrupt, attack, manipulate, interfere, expose, steal, and destabilize' for strategic and tactical gain.[8] To date, most of them do so from below the threshold of war.

3. Thriving in the grey zones

Before turning our attention to how cyber operations are both thriving in and shifting the art of the possible for State competition from within the grey zone, it is first necessary to define the core theme underpinning this edited volume as it relates to operations occurring in and through cyberspace.

The term 'grey zone' has been increasingly evoked—as both a growing phenomenon in the twenty-first century and a particularly challenging defence

---

[5] Melissa K. Griffith, '5G and Security: There Is More to Worry about than Huawei' (The Woodrow Wilson International Center for Scholars' Science and Technology Innovation Program (STIP), November 2019).

[6] Lorenzo Pupillo et al, 'Task Force Report on Strengthening the EU's Cyber Defence Capabilities' (The Centre for European Policy Studies, 26 November 2018).

[7] Mario Ballano Barcena and Candid Wueest, 'Insecurity in the Internet of Things' (*Symantec*, 12 March 2015).

[8] Ben Buchanan, *The Hacker and the State* (Harvard University Press 2020) 7.

problem—while simultaneously remaining loosely or underdefined. This is un-surprising given that the term emerged out of an area of ambiguity and uncertainty in international relations. Beyond sitting in the messy middle between war and peace, what is the grey zone? How is it distinct from previous forms of State competition? And how have cyber operations found themselves as one of the central animating features of grey zone competition?

Notably, in the context of cyber operations (historical and contemporary), the 'grey zone' encompasses a broader set of concerns including, but not limited to, activity short of war. This includes operations straddling the line between (a) crime and statecraft and (b) espionage and attacks. Each of these three grey zones blurs not just academic conceptual or theoretical distinctions but legal, institutional, and jurisdictional distinctions as well. This in turn complicates the policy decisions available to States, ranging from the technical/tactical to the strategic.

3.1 Between war and peace

The term 'grey zone' is most frequently used to evoke competition below the threshold of armed conflict but above the range of activity associated with (though perhaps more accurately understood as activity perceived to be more or less tolerable during) periods of peace. Here, alongside an array of other tools at States' disposal, cyber operations continue to thrive.

Whilst the focus of increasing policy and academic attention, State competition below the threshold of war is not new. Even in periods of relative peace—defined largely for their absence of significant armed conflicts—States compete for advantage using a variety of tools at their disposal. After all, as the old intelligence adage goes, there are friendly nations but no friendly intelligence services. Peace is not without competition. This trend persists even as competition gives way to conflict. Take the Cold War, as one such example. While the Cold War was primarily characterized by political, economic, and military competition between the United States and the Soviet Union, it did involve several situations and dynamics that could be considered to have taken place in a grey zone, ranging from covert actions to propaganda and, depending on one's definition of grey zone, proxy wars. The Cold War also had a rich history of intelligence collection: including Signals Intelligence (SIGINT), Human Intelligence (HUMINT), Geospatial Intelligence (GEOINT), Measurement and Signature Intelligence (MASINT), Imagery Intelligence (IMINT), and Open-Source Intelligence (OSINT).

Are cyber operations, like their historical predecessors and contemporary counterparts, deployed below the threshold of war? At present, the academic

184 ARENAS OF HYBRID AND GREY ZONE COMPETITION

consensus is a resounding yes. The vast majority of cyber operations are conducted below the threshold of armed conflict, serving as a new venue for covert action, influence, and intelligence collection as States strive to achieve strategic outcomes.[9] Here, cyber operations are best understood as a new tool in a State's toolkit, one wielded in an age old game—seeking geopolitical advantage.

What was initially a suite of activity that could be waved off by its fiercest critics as largely theoretical, has increasingly become realized. The vast majority of cyber operations are not just located below the threshold. They are thriving there. In 2016 alone, often referenced as a critical turning point, we witnessed incidents spanning numerous critical sectors globally: communication (Deutsche Telecom and Yahoo), democratic institutions (the US Democratic National Committee and the Philippines Commission on Elections), energy (the power grid in Ukraine), financial services (the Central Bank of Bangladesh and Tesco Bank), healthcare (the Australian Red Cross and National Health Service Hospitals in the United Kingdom), information technology (IT) services (domain name provider Dyn), and security (the FBI and Homeland Security in the United States).[10]

The impressive range of cyber operations does not end with the breadth of targets. Their goals are equally as diverse. States and State-affiliated actors have utilized cyber operations for a wide range of purposes including

- espionage (e.g. US intelligence gathering efforts to ascertain the goals, concerns, and negotiating positions of key UN Security Council members regarding potential sanctions on Iran in 2010);[11]
- to disrupt essential services (e.g. Russian hackers targeting the Ukrainian power grid in 2015 resulting in blackouts around the country);[12]

---

[9] For a sampling of scholarship animating the ongoing debate over how to best describe cyber operations outside the context of war, refer to John Arquilla and David Ronfeldt, 'Cyberwar Is Coming!' (1993) 12 Comparative Strategy 141; Richard A. Clarke and Robert Knake, *Cyber War: The Next Threat to National Security and What to Do About It* (Harper Collins 2011); Nazli Choucri, *Cyberpolitics in International Relations* (MIT Press 2012); Timothy Junio, *A Theory of Information Warfare* (PhD dissertation, University of Pennsylvania 2013); Sean Lawson, 'Beyond Cyber-Doom: Assessing the Limits of Hypothetical Scenarios in the Framing of Cyber-Threats' (2013) 10 Journal of Information Technology and Politics 86; Thomas Rid, *Cyber War Will Not Take Place* (OUP 2013); Jon R. Lindsay and Lucas Kello, 'Correspondence: A Cyber Disagreement' (2014) 39 International Security 181;George Perkovich and Ariel E. Levite, eds., *Understanding Cyber Conflict: Fourteen Analogies* (Georgetown University Press 2017).
[10] European Political Strategy Centre, 'Building an Effective European Cyber Shield: Taking EU Cooperation to the Next Level' (European Commission 2017).
[11] Buchanan (n 8) 13–15.
[12] Walters Riley, 'Russian Hackers Shut Down Ukraine's Power Grid' (*Newsweek*, 14 January 2016) <https://www.newsweek.com/russian-hackers-shut-ukraine-power-grid-415751> accessed 15 February 2023.

IN PURSUIT OF GEOPOLITICAL ADVANTAGE   185

- to inflict physical damage (e.g. Stuxnet, a destructive computer worm designed to undermine the Iranian nuclear program by secretly setting Iran's nuclear centrifuges to dangerously high speeds in 2010);[13] and
- to destabilize countries (e.g. Russian interference in the 2016 and 2020 US and 2017 French elections).[14]

All of these examples demonstrate a growing trend. Cyber operations are increasingly being leveraged by States as a tool of statecraft. Importantly, use of this tool is not limited to specific regime types—though the specific character and purpose of these operations does differ in notable ways across States. The latter will come into focus in later sections of this chapter.

Why hack below the threshold? Hacking short of, and in the absence of, armed conflict brings with it several benefits. It allows States to play into the bureaucratic seams of their target countries and legal—both domestic and international— ambiguities. In winter of 2019, one senior US intelligence official remarked over coffee that the degree to which the United States can compete effectively in this new domain will hinge around Americans' ability to minimize their own seams while effectively identifying and playing into those of their adversaries.

Cyber operations also offer States an opportunity to compete for advantage in a manner that simultaneously challenges historical defence approaches[15] while also avoiding the potentially catastrophic consequences of warfighting. Grey zone operations targeting the United States puts the latter in stark relief. Even from the vantage of a near-peer adversary, seeking advantages through war would be deeply costly (with victory uncertain) both in light of US military resources and the consequences of any sustained war between two resource-rich, heavily populated, and nuclear States. Theresa Whelan, former US Principal Deputy Assistant Secretary of Defense for Homeland Defense and Global Security (HD&GS), explicitly articulated this concern in 2019, arguing that

---

[13] Kim Zetter, 'An Unprecedented Look at Stuxnet, the World's First Digital Weapon' (*Wired*, 3 November 2014) <https://www.wired.com/2014/11/countdown-to-zero-day-stuxnet/> accessed 15 February 2023.

[14] Thomas Rid, 'How Russia Pulled Off the Biggest Election Hack in U.S. History' (*Esquire*, 20 October 2016) <https://www.esquire.com/news-politics/a49791/russian-dnc-emails-hacked/> accessed 15 February 2023; Matt Laslo, 'Russia Is Going to Up Its Game for the 2020 Elections' (*Wired*, 31 July 2019) <https://www.wired.com/story/russia-2020-election-security-mark-warner/> accessed 15 February 2023; and Megha Mohan 'Macron Leaks: the Anatomy of a Hack' (BBC, 9 May 2017) <https://www.bbc.com/news/blogs-trending-39845105> accessed 15 February 2023.

[15] Significant attention, for example, has been paid to the limitations of deterrence. For scholarship focused on deterrence refer to Will Goodman, 'Cyber Deterrence: Tougher in Theory than in Practice?' (2010) 4 Strategic Studies Quarterly 102; Clorinda Trujillo, 'The Limits of Cyberspace Deterrence' (2014) 75 Joint Force Quarterly 43; Thomas Rid and Ben Buchanan, 'Attributing Cyber Attacks' (2015) 38 Journal of Strategic Studies 4; Martin Libicki, 'Would Deterrence in Cyberspace Work Even with Attribution?' (Georgetown Journal of International Affairs, 21 April 2015); Joseph S. Nye Jr, 'Deterrence and Dissuasion in Cyberspace' (2016) 41 International Security 44.

'[t]he gray zone is a pretty busy place these days because our adversaries see it as the space where they can achieve their national objectives without triggering full-scale combat with us'.[16] Operations don't fall into the grey zone by accident. They are calibrated to land there, to take full advantage of the ambiguities and advantages of the space.

If we take seriously the concern at the heart of the aforementioned Stuxnet operation—setting back the Iranian nuclear program while simultaneously attempting to avoid further destabilizing the region—the decision to leverage cyber operations can be viewed as a direct substitute for a riskier kinetic action. Israel has, after all, repeatedly demonstrated both the capability and the willingness to target Iran's nuclear and ballistic missile programs.[17] In contrast to drone strikes, Stuxnet leveraged digital tools to quietly compromise enrichment efforts by manipulating the speed and pressure of Iranian centrifuges while simultaneously manipulating the Human Machine Interfaces (the digital representation of those systems on a computer screen) so that the centrifuges appeared to be operating normally.

Uncovered in 2010, this act of cyber sabotage is one of the first examples of a cyber operation generating physical effects in the real world (physically damaging centrifuges). It is also an example of an operation that went out of its way to limit potential collateral damage outside the Natanz facility by designing the worm to affect only particular kinds of industrial control systems and limiting payload delivery to systems that met specific criteria. In its very design, the teams behind Stuxnet took seriously the risk of collateral damage unique to cyberspace born from global interconnectivity. Given both its advanced design and the kinetic capabilities of the States Stuxnet has subsequently been attributed to, it presents itself as a calibrated substitute for other, and possibly escalatory, kinetic tools at both the United States and Israel's disposal.

Moreover, though it can sometimes be easy to abstract away from this fact, the line between war and not-war is as much a political decision as it is the result of some intrinsic bright line detailing a specific threshold of violence. The extent to which cyber operations fall below the threshold is shaped as much by the decisions undertaken by States not to escalate, or cross the Rubicon, with their responses as it is the calibrated actions of hackers. This is not a particularly

---

[16] Terri Moon Cronk, 'Adversaries Pose Unconventional Threats in "Gray Zone," DOD Official Says' (US Department of Defense, 16 October 2019) <https://www.defense.gov/News/News-Stories/Article/Article/1990408/adversaries-pose-unconventional-threats-in-gray-zone-dod-official-says/> accessed 15 February 2023.

[17] Most recently, Israel has used drone strikes to set back Iran's nuclear and ballistic missile programs. Siladitya Ray, 'Israel Reportedly Carries Out Drone Strikes on Iranian Factory on Eve of Blinken's Middle East Tour' (*Forbes*, 29 January 2023) <https://www.forbes.com/sites/siladityaray/2023/01/29/israel-reportedly-carries-out-drone-strikes-on-iranian-factory-on-eve-of-blinkens-middle-east-tour/?sh=a30189173eaa> accessed 15 February 2023.

novel observation. Yet this recognition, that it is not just the hackers but the defenders that determine whether cyber operations will cross thresholds, is all too often strikingly absent from discussions of why cyber operations have, to date, remained contained to the grey zone rather than serving as the catalyst for escalation.[18]

In what context do cyber operations occur? While cyber operations can be, and have been, leveraged in the context of armed conflict, the vast majority of activity has been intentionally situated below the threshold. It is this grey zone activity that, therefore, represents the vast majority of observed cases to date. This is not to say that cyber operations would not be leveraged in times of war, Daniel Moore details the dynamics of this threat environment in impressive detail in his book *Offensive Cyber Operations*.[19] Rather, a significant, and perceived to be impactful, portion of hacking sits below the threshold.

This is not the only grey zone that cyber operations skirt, however. This subset of activity is further complicated by two additional areas of ambiguity—each grey zones in their own right.

3.2 Between crime and statecraft

In addition to the context in which operations can occur—above or below the threshold of armed conflict—cyber operations have also blurred the line between crime and statecraft.

While crime and statecraft are often conceived of and treated as distinct categories of cyber activity, there is important empirical overlap between the two. States can carry out criminal endeavours for geopolitical purposes: such as undermining the global financial system, funding weapons programs, stealing intellectual property from industry competitors, or holding infrastructure or organizations for ransom.

One of the most prolific and notable examples of this trend can be found in North Korean operations targeting international financial institutions. At first glance, the specific operational goals of the Lazarus group's numerous heists appear to be financial. And they are. Each operation also, however, serves a broader geopolitical purpose. These heists are an important avenue through which North Korea has sought to circumvent global sanctions in order to fund its nuclear and

---

[18] Herbert Lin, 'Escalation Dynamics and Conflict Termination in Cyberspace' (2012) 6 Strategic Studies Quarterly 46; James D Fielder, 'Bandwidth Cascades: Escalation and Pathogen Models for Cyber Conflict Diffusion' (*Small Wars Journal*, 19 June 2013) <https://smallwarsjournal.com/jrnl/art/bandwidth-cascades-escalation-and-pathogen-models-for-cyber-conflict-diffusion> accessed 15 February 2023; Erica Borghard and Shawn Lonergan, 'Cyber Operations as Imperfect Tools of Escalation' (2019) 13 Strategic Studies Quarterly 122.

[19] Moore (n 1).

188 ARENAS OF HYBRID AND GREY ZONE COMPETITION

missile programs. These programs are not cheap. To put them into context, the Korean institute for Defense Analysis in Seoul estimated that North Korea spent over $620 million on missile tests in the first half of 2022 alone.[20] In wake of international sanctions, there is a clear need for funds. Cyber operations provide one, and a potentially more lucrative, solution than other means at their disposal. For example, a recent stream of North Korean hacking efforts specifically targeted cryptocurrency exchanges. This low hanging fruit represented a sharp increase in short-term earning potential. In the first five months of 2022, North Korean hackers netted more than $840 million by stealing crypto assets from exchanges around the globe. That figure is estimated by some to be approximately $200 million more than the spoils North Korean hackers secured in all of 2021.[21] However, it is worth noting, the subsequent nosedive in cryptocurrency markets has starkly limited North Korea's ability to cash in on those specific spoils. Crypto assets have proven to be volatile, even for thieves.

Another prominent example of this dynamic can be found in prolific industrial espionage and intellectual property (IP) theft undertaken by Chinese threat actors. Notably, and similarly to North Korea, these cyber operations are part of a broader trend. In their 2020 report on the global challenges of protecting intellectual property, the European Union soundly pointed the finger at China, ranking them as 'Europe's 'priority 1' worst offender, thanks to the scale and persistence of its policies, practices and negligence'.[22] A 2022 Carnegie Endowment for International Peace report succinctly summarized that 'technology is both target and enabler of Beijing's systemic trade abuses'.[23] As of April 2022, the *Financial Times* reported that '[a]bout 80 per cent of all economic espionage prosecutions brought by the US Department of Justice allege conduct that would benefit the Chinese State' and that '[o]ne 2017 estimate put the cost to the US of stolen trade secrets, pirated software and counterfeiting by China at between $225bn and $600bn a year'.[24] One of those prosecutions included two Chinese nationals: Zhu Hua and Zhang Shilong. In 2018, the US Department of Justice charged both with 'conspiracy to commit computer intrusions, conspiracy to

---

[20] Josh Smith, 'Crypto Crash Threatens North Korea's Stolen Funds as It Ramps Up Weapons Tests' (*Reuters*, 29 June 2022) <https://www.reuters.com/technology/crypto-crash-threatens-north-kor eas-stolen-funds-it-ramps-up-weapons-tests-2022-06-28/> accessed 15 February 2023.

[21] William Pesek 'Crypto Hitting "Mother of All Economic Crises" Threatens North Korea' (*Forbes*, 9 December 2022) <https://www.forbes.com/sites/williampesek/2022/12/09/crypto-hitting-mot her-of-all-economic-crises-threatens-north-korea/?sh=1af4403153af> accessed 15 February 2023.

[22] Miriam Rozen, 'EU Chides China and Others for IP Breaches—Again', *Financial Times* (London, 18 June 2020) <https://www.ft.com/content/0d48a5dc-9362-11ea-899a-f62a20d54625> accessed 15 February 2023

[23] Jon Bateman, 'Countering Unfair Chinese Economic Practices and Intellectual Property', Carnegie Endowment for International Peace (25 April 2022).

[24] 'America Is Struggling to Counter China's Intellectual Property Theft', *Financial Times* (London, 18 April 2022) <https://www.ft.com/content/1d13ab71-bffd-4d63-a0bf-9e9bdfc33c39> accessed 15 February 2023

commit wire fraud, and aggravated identity theft'.[25] Both Hua and Shilong were members of APT10, a 'hacking group who acted in association with the Tianjin State Security Bureau and engaged in global computer intrusions for more than a decade, continuing into 2018, including thefts from Managed Service Providers and more than 45 technology companies'.[26]

The blurred line between criminally motivated and geopolitically motivated hacks do not end with North Korean or Chinese operations. The explosion of ransomware-as-a-service has widened the conversation to include Russia. The concerns are threefold. First, there is a strong overlap between ransomware groups and Russian ransomware groups. Chainalysis, an American blockchain analysis firm, found that as of 2021, 74 per cent of ransomware cryptocurrency payments went to groups 'highly likely to be affiliated with Russia'.[27] Second, Russia appears to have been providing a safe harbour for ransomware groups as long as they did not hit Russian targets. Notably, Darkside, the group responsible for the 2021 Colonial Pipeline ransomware attack, built in a failsafe to ensure just that. How? Countless malware strains used by ransomware groups will check for the presence of Cyrillic languages on the target system. If they're detected, the malware will exit rather than install.[28] Third, some of these ransomware groups appear to be politically aligned with the Russian State. Most notably, Conti stated their support for Russia's 2022 invasion of Ukraine only to fall victim to a series of leaks in retribution by some of their customers who had previously been leveraging their services.[29] Unlike the North Korean and Chinese cases discussed above, however, the link between the criminal activities of ransomware groups and the geopolitical motivations of the Russian State are less direct and explicit in nature.

A second trendline emerges when we widen the aperture from crimes committed for geostrategic purposes to groups that carry out both criminal and geostrategically motivated operations. Here APT41—also known as Double Dragon, Barium, Winnti, Wicked Panda, and Wicked Spider, to name a few— is an apt example. Although a particularly prolific Chinese intelligence asset,

---

[25] Department of Justice Office of Public Affairs, 'Two Chinese Hackers Associated With the Ministry of State Security Charged with Global Computer Intrusion Campaigns Targeting Intellectual Property and Confidential Business Information' (20 December 2018) <https://www.just ice.gov/opa/pr/two-chinese-hackers-associated-ministry-state-security-charged-global-computer-intrusion> accessed 15 February 2023.

[26] Ibid.

[27] Joe Tidy, '70% of Ransomware Revenue Goes to Russia-linked Hackers' (BBC, 14 February 2022) <https://www.bbc.com/news/technology-60378009> accessed 15 February 2023.

[28] 'Try This One Weird Trick Russian Hackers Hate', *KrebsonSecurity*, 17 May 2021, https://kreb sonsecurity.com/2021/05/try-this-one-weird-trick-russian-hackers-hate/> accessed 15 February 2023

[29] Corin Faife, 'A Ransomware Group Paid the Price for Backing Russia', *The Verge*, 28 February 2022, https://www.theverge.com/2022/2/28/22955246/conti-ransomware-russia-ukraine-chat-logs-leaked> accessed 15 February 2023

APT41 also has a history of carrying out financially motivated crimes on the side. As detailed in a 2019 report, FireEye demonstrated 'with high confidence that APT41 is a Chinese State-sponsored espionage group that is also conducting financially motivated activity for personal gain'.[30] Their divergent missions complicate the attribution process, or rather the responsibility models, States and industry might undertake in an effort to shine a light on and ultimately mitigate APT41's operations.[31] On the one hand, there is an array of financially motivated intrusions ranging from ransomware to virtual currency manipulation. On the other, there are an array of State-backed cyber espionage operations targeting 'the healthcare, high-tech, and telecommunications sectors' and, previously, 'theft of intellectual property'.[32]

In theory and in practice, distinguishing between crime and statecraft can be important. These distinctions aid in the delineation of key authorities and responsibilities domestically and internationally. They map onto how States perceive operations and who they seek to hold accountable. Additionally, not all criminal behaviour can or should rise to the level of a 'national security imperative'. Operations that purposefully, or otherwise, straddle the divide between crime and statecraft complicate all three.

3.3 Between espionage and attacks

Finally, cyber operations can also present another form of ambiguity and uncertainty around their purpose. While operational goals focusing on compromising the confidentiality of data (espionage) versus those seeking to degrade, deny, destroy, or disrupt (attacks) are conceptually distinct, delineating between them can be far messier in practice.

Notably, while Ben Buchanan has written extensively on how a dilemma of interpretation complicates how targets interpret malicious cyber activity upon discovery within their systems[33]—access for espionage purposes and access that lays the groundwork for an attack can be difficult to distinguish in practice—the concern articulated here is far greater. These types of operations may be difficult to distinguish. Yet, equally important, persistence in a network provides

---

[30] Nalani Frasier et al, 'APT41: A Dual Espionage and Cyber Crime Operation', *FireEye*, 7 August 2019.

[31] For a discussion of the difference between attribution—hands on keyboard—versus responsibility, read Jason Healey, 'The Spectrum of National Responsibility for Cyberattacks' (Fall/Winter 2011) 18 The Brown Journal of World Affairs 57–70.

[32] Nalani Frasier et al (n 30).

[33] Ben Buchanan, *The Cybersecurity Dilemma: Hacking, Trust and Fear Between Nations* (OUP 2017).

strategic and operational flexibility for malicious actors in the future. Espionage is merely one form of access. Access can also include establishing the groundwork for a subsequent disruptive or destructive operation (operational preparation of the environment) or simply for the purpose of maintaining persistence in networks for as long as possible to allow for the possibility of a variety of operations in the future (holding an adversary at risk). All of these goals—espionage, operational preparation of the environment, and holding an adversary at risk—encourage sustained footholds in networks for as long as possible. All three can be difficult to distinguish from each other both from a technical and a geopolitical vantage.

Moreover, access achieved for one set of goals can be leveraged for new goals as intentions and priorities of States change over time. Depending on the type of persistence (or access) established, pivoting from espionage to attack may be easier or harder, but not impossible. For example, in the immediate aftermath of SolarWinds—a persistent, Russian cyber espionage operation that compromised a significant number of US government and corporate networks—immediate speculation over the intent of the operators emerged. Espionage? An attack thwarted early in its lifecycle? Or perhaps espionage that could later shift to support a new set of mission permeators if events warranted it? Notably, Sergio Caltagirone, vice president of threat intelligence at Dragos, specifically identified these concerns—long-term, persistence in networks, and systems shifting from access to attack—in initial remarks in the wake of SolarWinds.[34] He argued that it was important not to quickly jump to the conclusion of 'espionage' because, importantly, persistence in Industrial Control System (ICS) networks has routinely been leveraged for both espionage and attacks.[35]

This operational flexibility, born from persistence in systems and the modular nature of tools at hackers' disposal, both introduces a third grey zone of particular concern for the cybersecurity community and complicates below-the-threshold concerns. It results in a dilemma of interpretation, but also the ability of States to hold potential future adversaries at risk and leverage footholds as goals and geopolitical contexts evolve over time. Notably, these geopolitical contexts include, but are not limited to, crossing the threshold into periods of armed conflict.[36]

---

[34] 'Dragos Webinar Solar Winds Compromise and ICS/OT Networks' (*Dragos*, 23 December 2020) <https://www.youtube.com/watch?v=yZmaMX7hfek> accessed 15 February 2023.

[35] Melissa K. Griffith, 'In the Wake of SolarWinds, the U.S. Must Grapple With the Future and Not Just the Past' (*Lawfare*, 26 April 2021) <https://www.lawfareblog.com/wake-solarwinds-us-must-grapple-future-and-not-just-past> accessed 15 February 2023.

[36] Russia's ongoing invasion of Ukraine serves as a recent example of operational footholds and cadences shifting as geopolitical contexts evolve.

192 ARENAS OF HYBRID AND GREY ZONE COMPETITION

3.4 Key takeaways

Importantly, while much of the focus of grey zone debates evoke 'below-the-threshold' concerns, there are a series of grey zones that cyber operations fall into which complicate both academic understanding and policy responses. These include debates over 'in what contexts', 'by which actors', and 'for what purposes' has cyberspace become a domain of competition.

Moreover, as I have previously argued in detail, cyber operations fall into these grey zones, in part, as a matter of choice, rather than due solely to some intrinsic feature of the domain itself. After all, the cybersecurity dynamics present are 'informed as much by geopolitics and adversary preferences as they are by the technical and operational realities of cyberspace'.[37] Take the third category of grey zones as an example. Actors' preferences shape operational decisions aided by the flexibility of technical footholds. In contrast, the responses of those being hacked are complicated by a 'dilemma of interpretation' born from the technical challenge of distinguishing between various goals, all of which can present similarly but may be interpreted differently as the geopolitical context shifts over time.

4. Impactful from below the threshold

In practice, cyber operations below the threshold of war—from espionage to attacks—can serve a variety of strategic, operational, and tactical purposes. Often at the same time.

Intelligence collection, whether for espionage or counterintelligence purposes, is not new. Nor is the relationship between cybersecurity and intelligence activities particularly surprising given that, as Michael Warner—former CIA historian and current NSA and US Cyber Command historian—has succinctly demonstrated, '[c]yber technologies and techniques in some respects originated in the intelligence profession'.[38] Importantly, cyber operations, and cybersecurity, emerged in and evolved from the motivations behind and tools leveraged by State's competing below the threshold. A fact that also underpins, in part, Thomas Rid's now well-known argument that cyber operations are best understood as sophisticated versions of 'three activities that are as old as warfare itself: subversion, espionage, and sabotage'.[39]

---

[37] Griffith (n 35).
[38] George Perkovitch and Ariel E. Levite (eds), *Understanding Cyber Conflict: 14 Analogies* (Georgetown University Press 2017) 17.
[39] Rid (n 9).

However, to present cyber-enabled intelligence collection as simply a continuation of historical trends would overlook an important and consequential distinction. While there are core similarities between cyber operations and other forms of competition below the threshold, there are also critical differences. These include an evolution of the means (hacking) and the ends (ranging from operational goals like intelligence gathering to strategic goals that seek to enhance or degrade sources of national power). Additionally, the unique scale and scope (the number and diversity of the possible targets) of cyber-enabled operations sets them apart from their historical predecessors.[40] As does their utility, given the potential scale and scope over time, for pursuing not just tactical advantages—diplomatically, economically, or militarily—but strategic advantages.

As we study the 'who' and 'how' behind cyber operations, we cannot afford to lose sight of the 'why'. Cyberspace has simultaneously (a) transformed 'the art of the possible' and (b) facilitated and incentivized the proliferation of cumulative, sustained operations in concert (campaigns) seeking geopolitical advantage below the threshold of armed conflict.

4.1 Putting cyber-enabled espionage operations in context

Cyber-enabled espionage operations benefit heavily from the character of cyberspace itself. Its billions of networked devices and their users around the world enables far greater possible scale and scope of data collection than its historical espionage predecessors. As early as the 1990s, Moonlight Maze[41] (the codename US authorities gave a series of Russian hacks considered to be among the first examples of State-sponsored cyber espionage), gained access to and exfiltrated data pertaining to 'a variety of sensitive US projects, including weapons-guidance systems and naval intelligence codes'.[42] How much data? If investigators had printed out all the files and then stacked them, they estimated that the stack

---

[40] For examples, refer to Michael Warner, 'The Character of Cyber Conflict', in 'Policy Roundtable: Cyber Conflict as an Intelligence Contest', edited by Robert Chesney and Max Smeets (*Texas National Security Review*, 17 September 2020) <https://tnsr.org/roundtable/policy-roundtable-cyber-confl ict-as-an-intelligence-contest/> accessed 15 February 2023; Michael P. Fischerkeller and Richard J. Harknett, 'Cyber Persistence, Intelligence Contests, and Strategic Competition', in ibid.; Richard J. Harknett and Max Smeets, 'Cyber Campaigns and Strategic Outcomes' (2022) 45 Journal of Strategic Studies 534; Michael P. Fischerkeller, Emily O. Goldman, and Richard J. Harknett, *Cyber Persistence Theory: Redefining National Security in Cyberspace* (OUP 2022).

[41] Juan Andres Guerrero-Saade et al, 'Penquin's Moonlit Maze: The Dawn of Nation-State Digital Espionage' (*Kaspersky Lab*, 3 April 2017) <https://securelist.com/penquins-moonlit-maze/77883/> accessed 15 February 2023.

[42] Kim Zetter, 'New Evidence Links a 20-Year-Old Hack on the US Government to a Modern Attack Group' (*Vice*, 3 April 2017) <https://www.vice.com/en/article/vvk83b/moonlight-maze-turla-link> accessed 15 February 2023.

194 ARENAS OF HYBRID AND GREY ZONE COMPETITION

would have been taller than the Washington Monument.[43] A staggering image, and yet, the scale of Moonlight Maze is dwarfed by more recent operations.

As hackers gain more real-world experience and sophistication over time and cyberspace becomes increasingly critical and interconnected, this trend has only accelerated. Fast forward to 2019/2020 when Russian hackers leveraged SolarWinds' Orion platform (used to manage IT systems), to gain access to US government and corporate networks. Though hardly a household name, SolarWinds had approximately thirty-three thousand Orion customers globally. It was this broad consumer base that allowed hackers to gain footholds across a wide range of organizations (approximately eighteen thousand in total). Ultimately, after gaining these initial footholds, hackers paired down their targets, electing to only maintain access to and actively exploit closer to a hundred organizations' networks. These included US government departments such as Homeland Security, State, Commerce, Energy, and Treasury as well as private companies such as FireEye, Microsoft, Intel, and Deloitte. Despite this narrowing, as I argued in a 2021 *Lawfare* piece, the 'number of organizations simultaneously exploited—while smaller than the initial footholds would have allowed—is still quite high in comparison to the scale and scope achievable through non-cyber-enabled intelligence collection'.[44] SolarWinds, with its scale, sophistication, and quiet persistence in networks, is meaningfully distinct from historical spying given the scale (number) and scope (diversity) of targets it simultaneously accessed and then exploited.

Even more recently, somewhere between thirty thousand and sixty thousand organizations were compromised in the 2021 Chinese Microsoft Exchange Server hacks.[45] The initial operation was attributed to Hafnium, an advanced persistent threat (APT) group (also referred to as APT40).[46] The malware was discovered on more than two thousand machines in the United Kingdom alone.[47] After first becoming aware of four vulnerabilities being actively exploited in January, Microsoft released multiple security updates for affected servers in the first week of March (notably ahead of their monthly update cycle).[48] Later that same month,

---

[43] Eric Lipton, David E. Sanger, and Scott Shane, 'The Perfect Weapon: How Russian Cyberpower Invaded the U.S', *The New York Times* (New York, 13 December 2016) <https://www.nytimes.com/2016/12/13/us/politics/russia-hack-election-dnc.html> accessed 15 February 2023.

[44] Griffith (n 35).

[45] Charlie Osborne, 'Everything You Need to Know about the Microsoft Exchange Server Hack' (*ZDNET*, 19 April 2021) <https://www.zdnet.com/article/everything-you-need-to-know-about-microsoft-exchange-server-hack/> accessed 15 February 2023

[46] Danny Palmer, 'Microsoft Exchange Server zero-day attacks: Malicious Software Found on 2,300 Machines in the UK' (*ZDNET*, 15 March 2021) <https://www.zdnet.com/article/microsoft-exchange-server-zero-day-attacks-malicious-software-found-on-2300-machines-in-uk/> accessed 15 February 2023.

[47] Ibid.

[48] For one discussion of why this release occurred earlier than expected refer to Charlie Osborne, 'Microsoft Investigates Potential Ties between Partner Security Firm, Exchange Server Attack Code

Palo Alto Networks estimated that there were at least 125,000 unpatched servers worldwide.[49] That number appeared, and expectedly so, to be steadily dropping with Microsoft estimating that at least 82,000 servers remained unpatched a few days later.[50] The size of these numbers would be concerning in and of themselves, but they are even more so when you consider the array of malicious actors, including ransomware crews, that began to target compromised systems in the wake of the initial Chinese State-sponsored hackers. That scale, and scale at speed, was keenly felt by security professionals and governments alike. Amidst remediation efforts that March, Antti Laatikainen, a senior cybersecurity consultant at F-Secure, remarked that '[t]ens of thousands of servers have been hacked around the world', noting that '[t]hey're being hacked faster than we can count'.[51]

When it comes to the unique scale and scope that cyberspace lends to espionage efforts, quantity takes on a quality of its own. As does the reality that State operations can be co-opted, accompanied, and/or obfuscated by a range of non-State activity. In these two regards, cyber-enabled cyber espionage operations differ significantly from their historical predecessors.

4.2 Keeping an eye on the ends and not just the means behind espionage

More is not always better, but when more is coupled with suites of digital tools to aid in the parsing and analysis of that data as well as significant domestic bureaucratic and political backing, the actions States are then empowered with have the potential to be exceedingly impactful. In fact, the grave damage that can be wrought from cyber espionage operations is found not just in what was accessed but in how that information will be leveraged.[52] Intelligence collection, of any scale or scope, is rarely an end in and of itself. In practice, like the parent category of cyber operations, cyber-enabled espionage serves a variety of strategic,

---

Leak' (*ZDNET*, 15 March 2021) <https://www.zdnet.com/article/microsoft-investigates-potential-tie-between-partner-firm-and-potential-exchange-bug-leak/> accessed 15 February 2023.

[49] Unit 42, 'Remediation Steps for the Microsoft Exchange Server Vulnerabilities' (*Palo Alto Networks*, 9 March 2021) <https://unit42.paloaltonetworks.com/remediation-steps-for-the-micros oft-exchange-server-vulnerabilities/> accessed 15 February 2023.

[50] Microsoft Security Team, 'Protecting On-Premises Exchange Servers against Recent Attacks' (Microsoft, 12 March 2021) <https://www.microsoft.com/en-us/security/blog/2021/03/12/protect ing-on-premises-exchange-servers-against-recent-attacks/> accessed 15 February 2023.

[51] Jason Sattler, 'Significant Attacks on Microsoft Exchange ProxyLogon Detected' (*F-Secure*, 19 March 2021) <https://blog.f-secure.com/microsoft-exchange-proxylogon/> accessed 15 February 2023.

[52] Griffith (n 35).

196 ARENAS OF HYBRID AND GREY ZONE COMPETITION

operational, and tactical purposes. States losing sight of those purposes do so at their own peril.

4.2.1 In support of a diversity of goals

How then, can cyber-enabled intelligence operations leverage this scale to enhance or degrade national sources of power? What benefits can these operations and campaigns yield beyond the strategic?

The following are four broad categories of impact—ranging from the strategic to the tactical.

First, intelligence collection serves as important input into diplomatic, economic, and military planning. As Warner argued in response to efforts by Rovner and others to contrast military methods with intelligence methods, '[i]ntelligence methods do not contrast with military methods--the methods of intelligence *are* military methods'.[53] I would extend this argument a step further. Though 'modern intelligence grew up in military establishments, which still provide the bulk of global intelligence resources', intelligence methods are also deployed in service of economic and diplomatic goals alongside military goals.

Assessments of the impacts stemming from other cyber-enabled espionage activity should include this range of potential use cases. For example, a State may seek to leverage information gathered on the negotiating strategies and voting preferences of other UN Security Council members before an important vote to inform their approach to negotiations. This use case is not merely theoretical. Buchanan, in his 2019 book *the Hacker and the State,* detailed how the National Security Agency (NSA) obtained the necessary legal authorization to expand its data collection efforts in the lead up to a key vote in 2010. They leveraged that access to quickly build 'a picture of what key Security Council members were saying in their internal debates. The analysists then rushed that information to [Secretary of State Condoleezza] Rice and others, who used it to guide their negotiating strategy'.[54] The result? A resolution for tougher sanctions on Iran for its ongoing nuclear program passed by a vote of twelve to two. In isolation, any one such effort can provide important tactical diplomatic advantages. In aggregate, far more so.

Negotiating strategies for a key UN vote is merely one example amongst many. Access to the State Department's Bureau of European and Eurasian Affairs' emails in the wake of SolarWinds could help inform Russian strategy and efforts in the region—ranging from diplomatic efforts to future military campaigns. Espionage can assist with ongoing or future operations through actionable

[53] Warner (n 40).
[54] Buchanan (n 8) 13–15.

intelligence such as reconnaissance on a subsequent target or insight into another State's defensive cybersecurity capabilities and crisis management plans. Yet, all too often these knock-on effects are inadequately understood and/or addressed, either because victims have (a) poor visibility into the intent behind an operation or (b) the 'why' behind hacks is overshadowed by detailed examinations and rehashing the 'how'.

Second, counterintelligence operations can degrade another State's cyber capabilities, offensive or otherwise. This can begin with the theft of a country's hacking techniques and tools. If these capabilities and/or tradecraft are then leaked publicly, as was the case with both the Shadow Brokers[55] and Vault 7[56] hack-and-leak operations that targeted the NSA and the Central Intelligence Agency (CIA), respectively, degrading the target's capabilities is coupled with the added bonus of global proliferation. EternalBlue, an NSA exploit leaked by the Shadow Brokers in 2017, was subsequently leveraged by both North Korean hackers to power WannaCry and Russian hackers to power NotPeya.[57]

Neither the degradation of capabilities nor proliferation concerns are limited to State capabilities, however. As previously noted, one notable feature of the SolarWinds operation was that it targeted leading cybersecurity companies.[58] Though it is important to note that their red team tools may not be as damaging in the wild as CIA or NSA tools, gaining access was one observable objective of the hack. Moreover, given that these particular tools were developed to help these companies' customers cultivate more robust defences, accessing them offered hackers a more robust understanding of one aspect of how companies like FireEye secure its customers.[59] As a consequence, targeting cybersecurity companies could serve several functions at once—ranging from degradation of capabilities to tactical and operational decisions now undertaken with a more keen knowledge of private-sector security capabilities.

---

[55] David. E. Sanger, 'Shadow Brokers Leak Raises Alarming Questions: Was the NSA Hacked?' *The New York Times* (New York, 16 August 2016) <https://www.nytimes.com/2016/08/17/us/shadow-brokers-leak-raises-alarming-question-was-the-nsa-hacked.html> accessed 15 February 2023.

[56] Jeff Stone, 'A Researcher Made an Elite Hacking Tool out of the Info in the Vault 7 leak' (*CyberScoop*, 27 February 2019) <https://cyberscoop.com/vault-7-operation-overwatch-cia-hacking-tools-rsa-conference/> accessed 15 February 2023.

[57] Lily Hay Newman, 'The Leaked NSA Spy Tool That Hacked the World' (*Wired*, 7 March 2018) <https://www.wired.com/story/eternalblue-leaked-nsa-spy-tool-hacked-world/#:~:text=Though%20their%20methods%20and%20objectives,line%20of%20reliable%20hacker%20favorites> accessed 15 February 2023; Alex Hern, 'WannaCry, Petya, NotPetya: How Ransomware Hit the Big Time in 2017', *The Guardian* (London, 30 December 2017) <https://www.theguardian.com/technology/2017/dec/30/wannacry-petya-notpetya-ransomware> accessed 15 February 2023.

[58] Griffith (n 35).

[59] FireEye, 'Unauthorized Access of FireEye Red Team Tools' (*Mandiant*, 8 December 2020) <https://www.mandiant.com/resources/blog/unauthorized-access-of-fireeye-red-team-tools> accessed 15 February 2023.

198 ARENAS OF HYBRID AND GREY ZONE COMPETITION

Notably, degradation is a goal that is mirrored in covert (cyber) action focused on the destruction, defraying, and degrading of systems. Here, Stuxnet—with its focus on limiting nuclear proliferation—is an illustrative example.

Third, espionage, particularly intellectual property theft, can be a mechanism for enhancing or building military advantage as well as generating wealth. For example, John Carlin and Ben Buchanan, in *Dawn of the Code War* and *Hacker and the State,* respectively, detail how China leveraged information gathered through hacking to build its Y-20 plane, an eerie copy of the US Air Force's C-17, as well as exfiltrate and leverage detailed information on the F-22 and F-35.[60] Notably, Chinese hacking extends far beyond military planes into (a) other weapons systems and platforms and (b) operational and logistical plans. As Buchanan emphasized, even with limited visibility into Chinese espionage operations for the specific purpose of gaining military advantages, ample evidence of an 'extensive Chinese hacking campaign that reaches into nearly every part of the American military enterprise' now exists in the public domain.[61]

Moreover, Chinese intellectual property theft has not been limited solely to explicit military purposes. As previously noted, it has extended into industrial espionage and intellectual property theft as well. This reality has not gone unnoticed. In a 2011 statement to the US House Permanent Select Committee on Intelligence, US Representative Mike Rogers characterized Chinese economic espionage as reaching an 'an intolerable level', likening it to a 'scourge' and 'piracy'.[62] Chinese economic espionage also caught the ire of the Director of the FBI, Christopher Wray. In a 2020 speech to the Hudson Institute in Washington, DC, Wray pointed to what he saw as China's twin goals of surpassing the United States economically and technologically while highlighting the critical role that cyber operations have played in efforts to realize those goals. He went on to leverage the language of campaigns, arguing that '[t]he Chinese government is engaged in a broad, diverse campaign of theft'. Specifically, that Chinese espionage efforts, taken cumulatively, represent 'one of the largest transfers of wealth in human history'.[63]

Data gathered from cyber operations can be also used to bolster national programs focused on the development and deployment of geostrategically significant technologies, ranging from semiconductors to Artificial Intelligence

---

[60] John Carlin, *Dawn of the Code War: America's Battle Against Russia, China, and the Rising Global Cyber Threat* (PublicAffairs 2018) 273–74; Buchanan (n 8) 98–103.

[61] Buchanan (n 8) 102.

[62] Mike Rogers, 'Statement to the U.S. House, Permanent Select Committee on Intelligence', Open Hearing: Cyber Threats and Ongoing Efforts to Protect the Nation (4 October 2011) 2 <https://irp.fas.org/congress/2011_hr/100411rogers.pdf> accessed 15 February 2023.

[63] Russell Flannery, 'China Theft of U.S. Information, IP One of Largest Wealth Transfers in History: FBI Chief' (*Forbes,* 7 July 2020) <https://www.forbes.com/sites/russellflannery/2020/07/07/china-theft-of-us-information-ip-one-of-largest-wealth-transfers-in-history-fbi-chief/?sh=52e15bf04440> accessed 15 February 2023.

(AI).[64] In a 2021 Wilson Center publication focused on the intersection between cybersecurity and artificial intelligence (AI), Meg King and I highlighted one example of this dynamic. Specifically, how data gathered from cyber operations can potentially be funnelled into a country's domestic AI program. Why? 'Cyber espionage operations are uniquely suited for gathering large amounts of data across a diversity of targets', which is significant in this context because 'data plays a vital role in the training, validating, and testing of AI systems'.[65] Access to data will, though only in part, determine the success of China's AI ambitions. Notably, as first reported by NPR, part of the motivation behind the Microsoft Exchange hack may have been to collect data to power the growth and capabilities of China's AI systems.[66] Semiconductors are also, if not more so, essential to China's AI ambitions (providing the computational power in the compute, data, and algorithms triad underpinning machine learning).[67] They are also foundational to a suite of technologies far beyond machine learning.[68] Yet, here too, China has sought to leverage cyber operations to their advantage. For example, technical examinations of Operation Skeleton Key revealed that it appeared to be 'aimed at stealing as much intellectual property as possible, including source code, software development kits, and chip design' from at least seven Taiwanese chip firms from 2018 to 2020 alone.[69]

Fourth, and finally, though the dedicated focus of another chapter in this edited volume, it is worth briefly noting that cyber espionage operations have also historically been leveraged in the course of influence (or information) operations, specifically hack-and-leak efforts. Examples vary in terms of targets and perpetrators, including the US 2016[70] and French 2017[71] elections as well as what

---

[64] For an example of cyber espionage operations targeting the semiconductor industry, refer to Andy Greenberg, 'Chinese Hackers Have Pillaged Taiwan's Semiconductor Industry' (*Wired*, 6 August 2020) <https://www.wired.com/story/chinese-hackers-taiwan-semiconductor-industry-skeleton-key/> accessed 15 February 2023.

[65] Meg King and Melissa K. Griffith, 'Cybersecurity and AI: Three Security Concerns to Watch' (Wilson Center, 19 October 2021) <https://www.wilsoncenter.org/blog-post/cybersecurity-and-ai-three-security-concerns-watch> accessed 15 February 2023.

[66] Ibid.

[67] Melissa K. Griffith and Donald F. McLellan, 'AI, Semiconductors, and the Importance of Technology Education for Policymakers' (Wilson Center, 31 May 2022) <https://www.wilsoncenter. org/blog-post/ai-semiconductors-and-importance-technology-education-policymakers> accessed 15 February 2023.

[68] Melissa K. Griffith and Sophie Goguichvili, 'The U.S. Needs a Sustained, Comprehensive, and Cohesive Semiconductor National Security Effort' (Wilson Center, 23 March 2021) <https://www. wilsoncenter.org/blog-post/us-needs-sustained-comprehensive-and-cohesive-semiconductor-national-security-effort> accessed 15 February 2023.

[69] Andy Greenberg, 'Chinese Hackers Have Pillaged Taiwan's Semiconductor Industry' (*Wired*, 6 August 2020) <https://www.wired.com/story/chinese-hackers-taiwan-semiconductor-industry-skeleton-key/> accessed 15 February 2023.

[70] Rid (n 14).

[71] Mohan (n 14).

200 ARENAS OF HYBRID AND GREY ZONE COMPETITION

Buchanan described as the ongoing 'tit-for-tat hack-and-leak operations' between the United Arab Emirates and Qatar[72].

4.2.2 From operation to campaign

While the reach and diversity of cyber operations can be staggering, their scale and scope becomes even more concerning when understood not as discrete events, but in combination with other operations to comprise long-running campaigns. The importance of campaigns is not merely semantic. The significance of this conceptual shift—portions of which can be found across cybersecurity industry, academic, and policy work—is threefold: first, it points to sustained State and State-affiliated efforts, at scale, across time; second, it highlights the geopolitical context within which these operations occur; and third, it draws attention to cumulative effects, namely, 'death by a thousand cuts',[73] which have the potential to generate far broader advantages than any one discrete operation could achieve.

What distinguishes an operation from a campaign? The former are a discrete set of coordinated actions directed at a computer or network. Depictions of their lifecycle—such as Buchanan's Intrusion Model, Lockheed Martin's Kill Chain, and Mandiant's Attack Lifecycle—detail, step by step, how hackers hack. Operational examinations of hacks primarily focus on how malicious actors compromised the confidentially, integrity, or availability of data and systems, often honing in on concepts such as target reconnaissance, initial entry, command and control, establishing footholds, pivoting, lateral movement, persistence, and actions on objective.[74] In contrast, leveraging one of the clearest definitions to date, campaigns are a series of coordinated operations, the explicit purpose of which is to 'achieve a cumulative outcome leading to strategic advantage'.[75] Here the focus is not on how hackers gain access to networks or the specific goal of each operation (e.g. espionage or disruption of service), but rather how, in tandem, these operations pursue strategic advantages (e.g. enhancing or degrading sources of relative national power).

The aforementioned Microsoft Exchange hacks are an example of a cyber operation. The hundreds, if not thousands, of companies targeted by Chinese cyber

---

[72] Buchanan (n 8) 316.

[73] For an example, see James Scott and Drew Spaniel, *China Espionage Dynasty: Economic Death by a Thousand Cuts* (Institute for Critical Infrastructure Technology 2016).

[74] Buchanan (n 33); Eric Hutchins, Michael Cloppert, and Rohan Amin, 'Intelligence-Driven Computer Network Defense Informed by Analysis of Adversary Campaigns and Intrusion Kill Chains' (Lockheed Martin 2010) <https://www.lockheedmartin.com/content/dam/lockheed-martin/rms/documents/cyber/LM-White-Paper-Intel-Driven-Defense.pdf> accessed 15 February 2023; Matt Monte, *Network Attacks and Exploitation: A Framework* (Wiley 2015); Mandiant, 'Targeted Attack Lifecycle' <https://www.mandiant.com/resources/insights/targeted-attack-lifecycle> accessed 15 February 2023.

[75] Harknett and Smeets (n 40) 541.

operators seeking to illicitly acquire US intellectual property are an example of a long-standing and cohesive campaign.

It is worth noting that while there is widespread agreement that cyber operations differ in important ways from their historical sub-threshold predecessors, how consequential these differences are remains an active area of debate.[76] Here, I find myself in the company of the likes of Michael Fischerkeller, Emily Goldman, Richard Harknett, Max Smeets, and Michael Warner who share the view that strategic outcomes stemming from cyber operations are possible short of war.[77] However, there is a similarly robust but contrasting school of thought—anchored by the works of Erik Gartzke, Martin Libicki, Joshua Rovner, and others—which views the impacts of cyber operations in a far more limited manner.[78] They do so for a diversity of reasons, which include but are not limited to cyber operations' imperfect coercive utility and their core similarities to historical intelligence activities (namely, deception). This ongoing debate heavily hinges off what is considered 'value' in general and 'strategic value' in particular. While I agree with Gartzke, for example, that cyber operations are unlikely to be the final arbiter of competition in an anarchical world, Smeets aptly hit the nail on the head when he observed that '[i]f one uses 'final arbitration' as a criterion for analysis, almost no capability would pass the test'.[79]

Notably, the recognition that cyber operations can and have strategic consequences while deliberately situating themselves short of war is not limited to academic scholarship. It has been mirrored in US government policy and doctrine as well. General Paul Nakasone, Director of the NSA and Commander of Cyber Command, explicitly emphasized the potential for strategic value, arguing that adversaries have and continue to leverage the grey zone in order to gain 'strategic advantage through competition without triggering armed conflict'.[80] This concern also animates the 2018 shift from the Department of Defense and Cyber

---

[76] An excellent primer on the contours of this ongoing debate can be found at Chesney and Smeets (n 40).

[77] Richard J. Harknett and Michael P. Fischerkeller, 'Engagement, Agreed Competition, Cyberspace Interaction Dynamics, and Escalation' (2019) Special Issue: Cyber Defense Review 267; Michael Warner, 'A Matter of Trust: Covert Action Reconsidered' (2019) 63 Studies in Intelligence 33; Warner (n 40); Harknett and Smeets (n 40); Fischerkeller et al. (n 40).

[78] Erik Gartzke, 'The Myth of Cyberwar: Bringing War in Cyberspace Back Down to Earth' (2013) 38 International Security 41; Erik Gartzke and Jon R. Lindsay, 'Weaving Tangled Webs: Offense, Defense, and Deception in Cyberspace' (2015) 24 Security Studies 316; Joshua Rovner, 'Cyber War as an Intelligence Contest' (War on the Rocks, 16 September 2019) <https://warontherocks.com/2019/09/cyber-war-as-an-intelligence-contest/> accessed 15 February 2023; Jon Lindsay, 'Military Organizations, Intelligence Operations, and Information Technology', in Chesney and Smeets (n 40); David V. Gioe, Michael S. Goodman, and Tim Stevens, 'Intelligence in the Cyber Era: Evolution or Revolution?' (2020) 135 Political Science Quarterly 191.

[79] Max Smeets, 'The Strategic Promise of Offensive Cyber Operations' (2018) 12 Strategic Studies Quarterly 93

[80] Paul M. Nakasone, 'A Cyber Force for Persistent Operations' (2019) 92 Joint Force Quarterly 10, 11.

202 ARENAS OF HYBRID AND GREY ZONE COMPETITION

Command towards a strategy of defend forward and persistent engagement[81]—at the heart of which lies a concern around adversaries persistently shaping the environment to their advantage, which cumulatively has the potential to lend itself not just to tactical and operational advantages but to strategic as well.

Campaigns have also been featured in cybersecurity industry and academic reporting. Mandiant, in their groundbreaking 2013 APT1 report, detailed a 'multi-year, enterprise-scale computer espionage campaign' by 'China's 2nd Bureau of the People's Liberation Army (PLA) General Staff Department's (GSD) 3rd Department (Military Cover Designator 61398)'.[82] The report analysed intrusions against nearly 150 victims over seven years. In fact, it was the unique 'scale and impact of APT1's operations' which, alongside a perceived lack of public attribution to the Chinese government to date, ultimately 'compelled [them] to write' their report.[83] Mandiant went on to further emphasize the scale and scope by acknowledging that 'no one entity can understand the entire complex picture that many years of intense cyber espionage by a single group creates'.

Importantly APT1 was just one of China's cyber espionage units. In the very title of the report (*APT1: Exposing One of China's Cyber Espionage Units*), they also explicitly called attention to the broader context of Chinese cyber operations, namely, that APT1 is just one unit. In 2016, Adam Segal identified approximately twenty Chinese cyber espionage units that 'go after political and military intelligence, as well information that will bolster China's economic competitiveness'.[84] In 2022, Harknett and Smeets went on to link campaigns to strategic outcomes by examining how a diversity of Chinese units have sought to affect sources of national power.[85]

Visibility and reporting across industry and government paints a stark picture. China has leveraged the 'art of the possible'—the scale and scope enabled by the terrain, cyberspace, itself—to carry out hacks at scale with the intent to achieve strategic advantage.[86] While cyber campaigns are not the sole domain of any one set of hackers. the unique expansiveness and persistence of Chinese hacking groups targeting the United States and Europe—in large part—fuelled the growth of the vibrant private cybersecurity industry we see today and has sparked an important shift from operation to campaign when assessing impact.

Focusing solely on discrete operations can obscure the broader strategic intent, and potential impact, of cyber activity both to date and in the future. This

---

[81] US Department of Defense, 'Cyber Strategy' (2018) <https://media.defense.gov/2018/Sep/18/2002041658/-1/-1/1/CYBER_STRATEGY_SUMMARY_FINAL.PDF> accessed 15 February 2023.

[82] 'APT1: Exposing One of China's Cyber Espionage Units', *Mandiant*, 2013.

[83] Ibid. 2.

[84] Adam Segal, *Hacked World Order: How Nations Fight, Trade, Maneuver, and Manipulate in the Digital Age* (PublicAffairs 2016) 114.

[85] Harknett and Smeets (n 40) 535.

[86] Ibid. 540.

is not to say that any single operation is not impactful or that it does not provide important advantages. Rather, operations do not occur in a vacuum. As such, focusing our assessments of 'impact' solely on operational goals systematically underestimated their strategic potential.

Put simply, while it can be tempting to conceive of hacking solely as a series of episodic (if long-running) operations, strategic competition in cyberspace is also taking place over a series of cumulative campaigns by States. Examining each hack in isolation risks overlooking both the geopolitical motivations behind, the sheer scale and scope of activity, and the array of potential impacts occurring below the threshold of armed conflict.

4.2.3 From intent to impact

Importantly, intent and impact are not synonyms. There are a series of intervening variables that shape effectiveness both in general and in any given target.[87] These include innovation dynamics, which differ across industries and technologies; the often-difficult process of successfully jumping from blueprints to functioning replicants; the expertise, tools, and vast capacity needed to not only vacuum up large volumes of data but to parse through, decrypt, and piece together data at scale; and the ability to effectively target and then subsequently integrate intelligence gains into broader planning processes.

Has China's recent rise hinged off a sustained series of cyber espionage campaigns? They have clearly created and sustained an expansive set of efforts consistent with their geopolitical goals. It is clear, through both their behaviour and rhetoric, that China believes these efforts to be worth the cost. While measuring the exact degree of impact on innovation and competitiveness across a diversity of geostrategically important technologies is more challenging to parse out, China's sustained focus alone is particularly concerning when the operations and campaigns in question are that of a geostrategic rival and near-peer competitor.

4.3 Looking beyond espionage: cyberattacks to degrade, disrupt, destroy, and deny

Cyber operations in the grey zone extend beyond those targeting the confidentiality of data. Although we have not witnessed a cyber Pearl Harbor, cyber 9/11,

---

[87] For examples of scholarship delving into the degree to which intent has translated into impact, refer to on Jon Lindsay, 'The Impact of China on Cybersecurity: Fiction and Friction' (2014) 39 International Security 7; Andrea Gilli and Mauro Gilli, 'Why China Has Not Caught Up Yet: Military-Technological Superiority and the Limits of Imitation, Reverse Engineering, and Cyber Espionage' (2019) 43 International Security 141; Harknett and Smeets (n 40).

or the civilization-ending cyberwar that animated some of the early imaginings, advanced industrial economies remain heavily dependent on cyberspace. That dependence makes cyberspace a tried and tested tool through which malicious actors can degrade, disrupt, destroy, or deny the critical day-to-day functioning of society and the State. Notably, these cyber attacks, like the exploitation seen in intelligence-gathering activities, benefit in important ways from the scale and scope of cyberspace. They can also be seen not just as one of operations, but within the context of extended cyber campaigns.

Take, for example, the scale and scope of NotPetya. In 2017, the Russian hacker group known as Sandworm leveraged the hijacked update servers of Linkos Group—a small, family-run Ukrainian software business—to establish a hidden back door into thousands of PCs. Sandworm used this back door to release a piece of destructive malware that was designed to spread automatically, rapidly, and indiscriminately.[88] Notably, it is the indiscriminate spread that has dominated much of the discussion. Due to the interconnectivity of cyberspace, NotPetya was responsible for more than $10 billion in total global damages accompanied by a wave of screens rapidly turning black across Ukraine in a matter of minutes and around the world in a matter of hours.[89] Among its victims were the Danish shipping company Maersk, pharmaceutical giant Merck, FedEx's European subsidiary TNT Express, French construction company Saint-Gobain, and, further demonstrating the interconnected nature of cyberspace, the Russian oil company Rosneft.

Potential for expansive scale and scope does not necessitate operations of unprecedented scale and scope. In cyberspace, deliberately constrained and targeted destructive operations, such as Stuxnet, exist alongside operations of incredible scale, either by design or mistake. Yet, it is in the deeply discriminate nature of Stuxnet that one clue to its origin lies. Neither the United States nor Israel has claimed credit for Stuxnet, though States rarely if ever do in cyberspace even in the face of significant evidence. However, in addition to evidence gleaned from leaked documents and digital forensics, Richard Clark (a former White House Cybersecurity Coordinator) has argued that the design of the operation itself points a strong finger, in part, at the United States. '[I]t very much had the feel to it of having been written by or governed by a team of Washington lawyers'. Why? '[They] want to make sure that they very much limit the effects of the action. So that there's no collateral damage'.[90] Stuxnet

---

[88] Andy Greenberg, 'The Untold Story of NotPetya, the Most Devastating Cyberattack in History' (*Wired*, 22 August 2018) <https://www.wired.com/story/notpetya-cyberattack-ukraine-russia-code-crashed-the-world/> accessed 15 February 2023

[89] Ibid.

[90] Ron Rosenbaum, 'Richard Clarke on Who Was Behind the Stuxnet Attack' (*Smithsonian Magazine*, April 2012) <https://www.smithsonianmag.com/history/richard-clarke-on-who-was-behind-the-stuxnet-attack-160630516/> accessed 15 February 2023.

leveraged the critical interconnectedness of cyberspace to target over a hundred centrifuges simultaneously. Unlike NotPetya, however, which spread indiscriminately, it did not, by design, seek to impact machines with the same or similar industrial control systems that it encountered 'in the wild' outside of Natanz. Both operations demonstrated significant potential scale and scope. The degree to which leveraging that scale and scope was desirable (and deliberately architected around), however, differed between the sets of actors responsible.

Moreover, similar to cyber-enabled espionage, the power of scale is not limited to discrete operations. The aforementioned North Korean attacks provide an apt example of a cumulative campaign seeking financial gain. Largely secluded from the liberal international world order, North Korea has sought its strategic objectives through a series of State-sanctioned criminal activities described by Bruce Bechtol as 'the first government-run highly sophisticated set of criminal financial networks in existence since Nazi Germany'.[91] In this broader geopolitical context, an array of cyber operations has made its way into their toolkit.

The North Korean campaign has featured three avenues for theft:

(1) duping financial institutions' computer systems into (a) transferring funds (featured in their SWIFT bank heists) or (b) withdrawing funds (ATM cashouts);

(2) extorting money by encrypting data, rendering it unusable, until the victim pays for a decryption key (i.e. ransomware); and

(3) as the pantheon of financial institution evolved, targeting cryptocurrency exchanges worldwide.[92]

Taken together, this campaign across financial institutions globally speaks to a trifecta of goals: undermining trust in global financial institutions, of which North Korea is largely excluded; funding its nuclear and missile programs; and circumventing global sanctions to bolster its domestic economy. In the process, according to the US Office of the Director of National Intelligence's 2021 Annual

---

[91] Bruce Bechtol, 'North Korean Illicit Activities and Sanctions: A National Security Dilemma' (2018) 51 Cornell International Law Journal 62.

[92] Saher Naumaan, 'Lazarus on the Rise: Insights from Swift Bank Attacks' (*Besides Belfast 2018*, 27 September 2018) <https://www.youtube.com/watch?v=_kzFNQySEMw> accessed 15 February 2023; Sergei Shevchenko, 'Two Bytes to $951m' (*BAE Systems*, 25 April 2016) <https://www.baesystems.com/en/cybersecurity/two-bytes-to-951m> accessed 15 February 2023; Sergei Shevchenko and Adrian Nish, 'Cyber Heist Attribution' (*BAE Systems*, 13 May 2016) <https://baesystemsai.blogspot.com/2016/05/cyber-heist-attribution.html> accessed 15 February 2023; Carly Page, 'North Korean Hackers Are Targeting Blockchain Companies with Malicious Crypto-Stealing Apps' (*TechCrunch*, 19 April 2022) <https://tcrn.ch/3MahRzI> accessed 15 February 2023; Cybersecurity and Infrastructure Security Agency, 'North Korean State-Sponsored Cyber Actors Use Maui Ransomware to Target the Healthcare and Public Health Sector', CISA Alert (AA22-187A) (6 July 2022) <https://www.cisa.gov/news-events/cybersecurity-advisories/aa22-187a> accessed 15 February 2023.

Threat Assessment, North Korea has potentially stolen hundreds of millions of dollars through its sustained criminal campaign.[93]

4.4 Key takeaways

Cyber operations in the grey zone can serve a variety of strategic, operational, and tactical purposes. Characterizing activity in cyberspace short of war as simply an evolution of historical intelligence contests overlooks important ways in which cyber operations differ from these predecessors, namely, their scale and scope. Notably, cyberspace has simultaneously (a) transformed 'the art of the possible' and (b) facilitated and incentivized the proliferation of cumulative, sustained operations in concert (i.e. campaigns). As a result, not only are cyber operations thriving in the grey zone, they are also impactful—geopolitically impactful—from below the threshold.

5. Concluding thoughts

Grey zone cyber operations differ meaningfully from both historical intelligence contests as well as the more episodic, open military confrontations of interstate warfare. Yet, the geopolitical implications of cyber operations below the threshold should not be overlooked or understated. Notably, these operations, both individually and when embedded into campaigns, benefit significantly from increased scale and scope when compared to their historical intelligence predecessors. They can and have served a variety of geopolitical functions—from the tactical to the strategic—often at the same time. As we study the 'who' and 'how' behind cyber operations, we cannot afford to lose sight of the 'why'.

---

[93] US Office of the Director of National Intelligence, '2021 Annual Threat Assessment' (13 April 2021) <https://www.dni.gov/index.php/newsroom/reports-publications/reports-publications-2021/item/2204-2021-annual-threat-assessment-of-the-u-s-intelligence-community> accessed 15 February 2023.

10

Lawfare, China, and the Grey Zone

Orde F. Kittrie

1. Introduction

Sun Tzu, the preeminent ancient Chinese military strategist and author of *The Art of War*, wrote that 'defeating the enemy without fighting is the pinnacle of excellence'.[1] Consistent with his adage, the People's Republic of China (PRC) today is waging sophisticated and systematic lawfare, deftly using law as a weapon to achieve warfighting objectives without needing to fire a shot.

The stakes are high. For example, as this chapter will describe, the PRC is currently using grey zone lawfare in the maritime and aviation domains to take control of the South China Sea.

In addition, the PRC and the West are using lawfare in a struggle to predetermine which side would dominate the information technology domain during, or on the brink of, a future kinetic conflict. The chapter will delineate both this struggle and its enormous stakes. For example, if the United States and its allies fail now to stop the PRC from dominating their telecommunications networks, China could someday be in position to shut down the West's critical electrical and other infrastructure without bombing a single power plant. In addition, the PRC is developing the means to revolutionize the brink and conduct of any future kinetic conflict through the hyper-personalization of war, in which it would deploy financial, health, and other personalized data about Western troops to blackmail, distract, and demoralize individual Western warfighters and their families.

This examination of PRC grey zone lawfare comes at a time of increasing tension between the PRC on the one hand and its Asian neighbours, the United States, and the NATO alliance on the other. In February 2022, days before Russia invaded Ukraine, Chinese leader Xi Jinping and Russian President Vladimir Putin declared that their partnership now had 'no limits' and committed to cooperate in opposing 'certain States' attempts to impose their own 'democratic standards' on other countries' and in shaping a new international order more

---

[1] Sun Tzu, *The Art of War* (J. J. L. Duyvendak tr, Wordsworth 1998).

Orde F. Kittrie, *Lawfare, China, and the Grey Zone* In: *Hybrid Threats and Grey Zone Conflict.* Edited by: Mitt Regan and Aurel Sari, Oxford University Press. © Oxford University Press 2024. DOI: 10.1093/oso/9780197744772.003.0010

conducive to their own authoritarian regimes.[2] Since the war began, China has undercut Western sanctions by increasing its own trade with Russia, including the export of semiconductors Moscow desperately needs to resupply its military.[3]

Over the course of 2022, the PRC escalated its rhetoric and menacing military actions towards Taiwan.[4] This included massive military exercises practicing a blockade of the island.[5] President Joe Biden responded by declaring on four separate occasions that the United States will defend Taiwan militarily in the event it is attacked by China.[6] This represents a change to the traditional US policy of ambiguity as to how it would respond to such an attack.[7] It comes at a time when US officials reportedly fear that an attack by the PRC is becoming more likely.[8]

In response to the PRC's escalating rhetoric and actions, the North Atlantic Treaty Organization (NATO), the preeminent military alliance of liberal democracies, has for the first time developed a comprehensive China strategy. In its new 'Strategic Concept', issued in June 2022, NATO declared that the PRC 'strives to subvert the rules-based international order' and asserted that the PRC's 'stated ambitions and coercive policies challenge our interests, security and values'.[9]

NATO heads of State and government committed to work together 'to address the systemic challenges posed by the PRC to Euro-Atlantic security'.[10] As if to underscore these concerns, the June 2022 NATO summit included, for the first time, the leaders of four Asia-Pacific countries: Australia, Japan, New Zealand, and South Korea.[11] NATO has, at the same time, developed a sophisticated initiative to address lawfare (which NATO refers to as 'legal operations').[12]

The PRC's current lawfare reflects both Sun Tzu's famous adage and also the assertion of a modern Chinese military text, the *Science of Military Strategy*, that 'war is not only a military struggle, but also a comprehensive contest on

---

[2] US-China Economic Security and Review Commission, '2022 Report to Congress' (November 2022) <https://www.uscc.gov/sites/default/files/2022-11/2022_Annual_Report_to_Congress.pdf> accessed 5 March 2023.

[3] Ibid.

[4] Ibid.

[5] Ibid.

[6] Kevin Liptak, 'Biden's Past Promises for US to Defend Taiwan under Microscope in Meeting with China's Xi' (*CNN*, 14 November 2022) <https://www.cnn.com/2022/11/13/politics/joe-biden-taiwan/index.html> accessed 5 March 2023

[7] Ibid.

[8] Ibid.

[9] North Atlantic Treaty Organization, 'Strategic Concept' (29 June 2022) <https://www.nato.int/nato_static_fl2014/assets/pdf/2022/6/pdf/290622-strategic-concept.pdf> accessed 5 March 2023.

[10] Ibid.

[11] Amy Qin and Austin Ramzy, 'Labeled a "Challenge" by NATO, China Signals Its Own Hard-Line Worldview', New York Times (New York, 1 July 2022), <https://www.nytimes.com/2022/07/01/world/asia/china-nato.html> accessed 5 March 2023

[12] See, e.g., Rodrigo Vazquez Benitez, Kristian W. Murray, and Pavel Kriz, 'Legal Operations: The Use of Law as an Instrument of Power in the Context of Hybrid Threats and Strategic Competition' [2021] Army Lawyer, Issue 5, 51.

fronts of politics, economy, diplomacy, and law'.[13] Meanwhile, the PRC's evident willingness to challenge the current rules-based international order reflects the words of Wang Xiangsui, a People's Liberation Army (PLA) colonel and co-author of the influential book *Unrestricted Warfare*, who wrote, 'War has rules, but those rules are set by the West . . . so do we need to fight according to your rules? No'.[14]

The PRC is the world's current preeminent practitioner of sophisticated and systematic lawfare in the grey zone. The PRC's embrace of lawfare is particularly notable—and worrying—because the PRC is the leading rival of the United States for global dominance and will continue to be so for the foreseeable future. Since the United States is a far more law-oriented society, with a higher proportion of its best minds entering the legal field, and has pre-eminently shaped the current rules-based international order, one might expect it to be the world's dominant lawfare power. But its lawfare efforts tend to be far less diligent and systematic than those of the PRC. Unlike the PRC, and now NATO, the United States has no lawfare strategy or doctrine.

The second section of this chapter will provide some context, including an overview of why law is becoming an increasingly powerful weapon of war.[15] The third section will provide an overview of China's lawfare doctrine. The fourth section will address China's long-standing use of maritime and other access-denial lawfare against the United States and its allies. The fifth section will address both sides' efforts to use lawfare to shape the future of information technologies. In doing so, the fifth section will describe the critical role that civilian information technologies are likely to play during a period of heightened tensions just short of, or in, any future kinetic conflict between China and the West. The sixth section will address the PRC's grey zone use of its trade regulatory authorities to pursue military policy objectives.

2. Lawfare's increase in power and prevalence

The term 'lawfare' was introduced into the legal and international relations literature by Charles J. Dunlap, Jr. in 2001, when he was a colonel in the US Air

---

[13] US Department of Defense, 'Annual Report to Congress: Military Power of the People's Republic of China 2007' (2007) 13 <https://apps.dtic.mil/sti/pdfs/ADA528060.pdf> accessed 5 March 2023.

[14] John Pomfret, 'China Ponders New Rules of "Unrestricted War"' Washington Post (Washington, DC, 8 August 1999) <https://www.washingtonpost.com/archive/politics/1999/08/08/china-ponders-new-rules-of-unrestricted-war/ad255e11-9670-4580-a0ff-7f7befb76f3e/> accessed 5 March 2023.

[15] In addressing these topics, this chapter draws heavily on several previous works by the author, including Orde F. Kittrie, *Lawfare: Law as a Weapon of War* (OUP 2016) and Orde F. Kittrie, 'Lawfare and US National Security' (2011) 43 Case Western Reserve Journal of International Law 393.

Force Judge Advocate General's Corps.[16] Dunlap ultimately defined 'lawfare' as 'the strategy of using—or misusing—law as a substitute for traditional military means to achieve a warfighting objective'.[17]

In my 2016 book *Lawfare: Law as a Weapon of War*, I refined Dunlap's definition to focus on both effect and intention. I suggested that in order to qualify as lawfare, an action must meet the following two tests:

(1) the actor uses law to create the same or similar effects as those traditionally sought from conventional kinetic military action—including impacting the key armed force decision-making and capabilities of the target; and
(2) one of the actor's motivations is to weaken or destroy an adversary against which the lawfare is being deployed.[18]

I suggested in my book that the increasing power and prevalence of law as a weapon of war is largely the result of four factors. These factors, which have retained their pre-eminence, include the increased number and reach of international laws and tribunals, the rise of influential non-governmental organizations focused on law of armed conflict and related issues, the information technology revolution, and the advance of globalization and thus economic interdependence. These factors provide important context for the rise and power of PRC lawfare.

2.1 Increased number and reach of international laws and tribunals

Governments worldwide have entered into more than forty-five thousand bilateral treaties and eight thousand multilateral treaties since World War II.[19] In addition, several globally focused tribunals applying international law have been created in recent decades, including the World Trade Organization (WTO) dispute settlement provisions (1995), the International Tribunal for the Law of the Sea (1996), and the International Criminal Court (2002). The maritime lawfare

---

[16] Charles J. Dunlap, Jr., 'Law and Military Interventions: Preserving Humanitarian Values in 21st Conflicts' (Humanitarian Challenges in Military Intervention Conference, Carr Center for Human Rights Policy, 29 November 2001) <http://people.duke.edu/~pfeaver/dunlap.pdf> accessed 5 March 2023.

[17] Charles J. Dunlap, Jr., 'Lawfare Today . . . and Tomorrow' (2011) 87 International Law Studies 315.

[18] Kittrie, *Lawfare: Law as a Weapon of War* (n 15).

[19] Thomas J. Miles and Eric A. Posner, 'Which States Enter into Treaties, and Why?' (John M. Olin Program in Law and Economics Working Paper No. 420, 2008) <https://chicagounbound.uchicago.edu/law_and_economics/623/> accessed 5 March 2023.

discussed later in this chapter centres on disputes related to the UN Convention on the Law of the Sea (UNCLOS), which entered into force in 1994.

2.1.1 The rise of NGOs focused on law of armed conflict and human rights law

Human rights non-governmental organizations (NGOs) such as Amnesty International (AI) and Human Rights Watch play a key role in documenting, and drawing Western attention to, alleged violations of human rights law and the law of armed conflict. Their reports and accusations have come to carry considerable weight with countries that are responsive to public opinion and care about their international image.

Human rights NGOs have far less impact on autocratic countries like China and Russia, and on terrorist groups such as Hamas and Hezbollah, that place relatively low priority on their publics' opinions and on how their law of armed conflict and human rights compliance records are perceived internationally. This contributes to such autocratic countries and terrorist groups engaging in 'compliance-leverage disparity lawfare', a type of lawfare which is designed to gain advantage from the greater leverage that international law and its processes exert over the United States and other democracies.

This chapter will describe how the PRC regularly engages in compliance-leverage disparity lawfare against the United States and its allies. Such behaviour is consistent with the PRC military's *Basics of International Law for Modern Soldiers*, which states: 'We should not feel completely bound by specific articles and stipulations detrimental to the defence of our national interests. We should therefore always apply international laws flexibly in the defence of our national interests and dignity, appealing to those aspects beneficial to our country while evading those detrimental to our interests'.[20]

2.1.2 The information technology revolution

The vast increase in online data availability has enabled governmental and even non-governmental lawfare practitioners located anywhere on earth to quickly find and deploy many types of information at the level of detail and timeliness necessary to wage lawfare. These include commercial satellite imagery, ship-tracking websites, corporate annual reports, trade press articles, foreign press articles, international agreements, local laws, and national laws from around the world.

---

[20] Zhao Peiying (ed), *Basics of International Law for Modern Soldiers* (1996) 3, quoted in Jonathan G. Odom, 'A China in the Bull Shop? Comparing the Rhetoric of a Rising China with the Reality of the International Law of the Sea' (2012) 17 Ocean and Coastal Law Journal 201, 222.

212 ARENAS OF HYBRID AND GREY ZONE COMPETITION

At the same time, personal and other digital communications technology and the proliferation of online media outlets have enabled governments, NGOs, and even individuals to in some cases record and disseminate remarkable evidence of war crimes and other violations of international law. For example, researchers collecting evidence in Bucha and other war crimes scenes which Ukraine recaptured from Russia produced detailed dossiers linking particular perpetrators to specific crimes.[21]

However, the information technology revolution has, with limited exceptions,[22] been less useful thus far in identifying perpetrators in areas such as Xinjiang to which access has been closed off by authoritarian regimes. Indeed, information technology has in the case of the PRC thus far played a greater role in perpetrating oppression than in documenting human rights abuses.[23]

Both China and the United States recognize that control over information technology services, and the data that they generate, would likely be an important weapon on the brink of or in a future hot conflict between them. As a result, a struggle over such control is a major aspect of the current grey zone lawfare between them.

2.1.3 Globalization and economic interdependence

The final major reason for the increasing power and prevalence of lawfare is the advance of globalization, which has vastly increased governments' non-kinetic leverage over other countries and their companies by intensifying international economic interdependence. Since 1970, national economies have become much more dependent on trade, with the share of trade as a percentage of worldwide gross domestic product (GDP) increasing from 25 per cent in 1970 to 57 per cent in 2021.[24] The share of trade as a percentage of China's GDP has increased particularly sharply, from 5 per cent in 1970 to 37 per cent in 2021.[25] Meanwhile, the share of trade as a percentage of US GDP has increased from 11 per cent in 1970 to 25 per cent in 2021.[26]

---

[21] Yousur Al-Hlou et al, 'Caught on Camera, Traced by Phone: The Russian Military Unit that Killed Dozens in Bucha', *The New York Times* (New York, 22 December 2022) <https://www.nytimes.com/2022/12/22/video/russia-ukraine-bucha-massacre-takeaways.html> accessed 5 March 2023.

[22] See e.g. Scilla Alecci, 'UK, US and Germany say Xinjiang Police Files Offer "Shocking" New Evidence of China's Human Rights Abuses' (*International Consortium of Investigative Journalists*, 24 May 2022) <https://www.icij.org/investigations/china-cables/uk-us-and-germany-say-xinjiang-police-files-offer-shocking-new-evidence-of-chinas-human-rights-abuses/> accessed 5 March 2023.

[23] See e.g. Steven Feldstein, 'China's High-Tech Surveillance Drives Oppression of Uyghurs' (*Bulletin of the Atomic Scientists*, 27 October 2022) <https://thebulletin.org/2022/10/chinas-high-tech-surveillance-drives-oppression-of-uyghurs/> accessed 5 March 2023

[24] World Bank, 'Trade (% of GDP)' <https://data.worldbank.org/indicator/NE.TRD.GNFS.ZS> accessed 5 March 2023.

[25] World Bank, 'Trade (% of GDP)—China' <https://data.worldbank.org/indicator/NE.TRD.GNFS.ZS?locations=CN> accessed 5 March 2023

[26] World Bank, 'Trade (% of GDP)—United States <https://data.worldbank.org/indicator/NE.TRD.GNFS.ZS?locations=US> accessed 5 March 2023

As a result of the rise in trade, many nations (including China and the United States) have an increased reliance on international commerce, and many companies are subject to significant leverage in jurisdictions beyond where they are headquartered. For example, the PRC owned some $934 billion in US Treasury securities as of September 2022[27] and also had vast leverage over many major US companies, including those with investments in China and those that are heavily dependent on the Chinese market. At the same time, the US government has regulatory leverage over, for example, the many major Chinese companies that have come to be listed on US stock exchanges (there were 262 Chinese companies listed on the three largest US exchanges as of September 2022).[28] None of this existed in Mao's day.

US grey zone lawfare has regularly leveraged transnational economic interdependence, especially since the US Treasury Department first began its sophisticated use of international economic lawfare about fifteen years ago.[29] During 2022, the United States used economic lawfare as a remarkably effective grey zone tool to degrade Russia's ability to resupply its kinetic invasion of Ukraine. In a report issued in October 2022, the US State Department detailed how the use of export controls and sanctions to restrict Russia's access to advanced technology had 'degraded the Russian weapons industry's ability to produce and stockpile weapons to replace those that have been destroyed in the war'.[30]

For example, US-led financial sanctions 'immobilized about $300 billion worth of Russian Central Bank assets, limiting the central bank's ability to aid the war effort and mitigate sanctions impacts'.[31] In addition, US-led restrictions on the export to Russia of various foreign components, including especially semiconductors, 'nearly ceased' the production of 'Russian hypersonic ballistic missile[s];' 'stalled' production of Russia's 'next-generation airborne early warning and control military aircraft'; and 'shut down' Russian plants 'producing surface-to-air missiles'.[32]

While this and other recent lawfare initiatives of the US Treasury and Commerce departments have been remarkably impactful, the United States—unlike the PRC, NATO, and Israel[33]—has yet to adopt a comprehensive and

---

[27] 'Foreign Holdings of Treasuries Drop to Lowest Since May 2021' (*Reuters*, 16 November 2022) <https://www.reuters.com/business/finance/update-foreign-holdings-treasuries-drop-lowest-since-may-2021-data-2022-11-16/> accessed 5 March 2023.

[28] US-China Economic Security and Review Commission, 'Chinese Companies Listed on Major US Stock Exchanges' (30 September 2022) <https://www.uscc.gov/sites/default/files/2022-09/Chinese_Companies_Listed_on_US_Stock_Exchanges.pdf> accessed 5 March 2023.

[29] See e.g. Kittrie (n 15) 311–28.

[30] 'The Impact of Sanctions and Export Controls on the Russian Federation', US Department of State, 20 October 2022, <https://www.state.gov/the-impact-of-sanctions-and-export-controls-on-the-russian-federation/> accessed 5 March 2023.

[31] Ibid.

[32] Ibid.

[33] See e.g. Kittrie, *Lawfare: Law as a Weapon of War* (n 15).

214   ARENAS OF HYBRID AND GREY ZONE COMPETITION

coordinated lawfare strategy, doctrine, or mechanism. Such a strategy, doctrine, and mechanism would enable the United States to make even more effective use of lawfare.

3. China's lawfare doctrine

Unlike the US government, the PRC has explicitly adopted lawfare (the synonymous term in Chinese is '*falu zhan*' or 'legal warfare') as a key element of its strategic doctrine. In 2003, the Chinese Communist Party Central Committee and the Chinese Central Military Commission approved the concept of 'Three Warfares', highlighting in their doctrine the following non-kinetic tools:

> *Psychological Warfare:* the use of propaganda, deception, threats, and coercion to affect the enemy's ability to understand and make decisions
> *Media Warfare:* the dissemination of information to influence public opinion and gain support from domestic and international audiences for China's military actions
> *Legal Warfare:* the use of international and domestic laws to gain international support and manage possible political repercussions of China's military actions.[34]

Since this decision, several PRC military texts have been dedicated entirely to *falu zhan*.[35] In addition, important conceptual context for the PRC's use of legal warfare is provided by a treatise titled *Unrestricted Warfare*, which was written by two PLA colonels, Qiao Liang and Wang Xiangsui, and published by the PLA in 1999. The treatise suggests various tactics—including legal warfare—that developing States, China in particular, might use to offset their military inferiority vis-à-vis the United States.[36] Liang was subsequently promoted to major general and rose to deputy secretary of the PRC's National Security Policy Committee.[37]

---

[34] US Department of Defense, 'Annual Report to Congress: Military Power of the People's Republic of China 2008' (2008) 19; Central Military Commission, 'People's Liberation Army of China Regulation on Political Work', Article 14(18) (December 2003), cited in Paul A. Stempel, 'Reading Lawfare in Chinese: The Meaning of the Term 'Falu Zhan ("Lawfare") in Chinese Military Literature' (July 2011) (unpublished article).

[35] Stempel (n 34). Stempel notes that when the Chinese government printed a translated version of an article titled 'Lawfare: A Decisive Element of 21st-Century Conflicts?' by Major General Charles Dunlap, the former Deputy Judge Advocate General of the US Air Force who coined the term 'lawfare', the PRC's translators used the term *falu zhan* where Dunlap used the term 'lawfare'.

[36] Qiao Liang and Wang Xiangsui, *Unrestricted Warfare* (Pan American 2002).

[37] See e.g. US-China Perception Monitor, 'The Inaugural Carter Center—Global Times Foundation Forum for Young Chinese and American Scholars' (2014), Qiao Liang biographical paragraph <http://www.uscnpm.org/papers> accessed 5 March 2023.

LAWFARE, CHINA, AND THE GREY ZONE 215

In 2008, the US State Department's International Security Advisory Board noted that China was engaged in the previously referenced, non-kinetic 'Three Warfares' even as the United States and the PRC existed nominally in a state of peace:

> It is essential that the United States better understand and effectively respond to China's comprehensive approach to strategic rivalry, as reflected in its official concept of 'Three Warfares'. If not actively countered, Beijing's ongoing combination of Psychological Warfare (propaganda, deception, and coercion), Media Warfare (manipulation of public opinion domestically and internationally), and Legal Warfare (use of 'legal regimes' to handicap the opponent in fields favorable to him) can precondition key areas of strategic competition in its favor.[38]

The PRC's use of lawfare is consistent with the doctrines of the Chinese Communist Party Chairman Mao Zedong, as well as those of Sun Tzu. Unlike many Western strategists, Mao also tended to think of the clash of arms as just one element, and not necessarily the most important element, of conflict.

China's vigorous use of lawfare is rooted in the uniquely instrumental role law has played, and continues to play, in historical and contemporary Chinese culture.[39] In pre-Communist imperial China, law served as a tool of authority, not a constraint upon it.[40] Following the Communist revolution of 1949, China adopted the Marxist view that law serves as an instrument of politics (rather than, for example, a check on politics and an autonomous, objective arbiter of justice).[41]

Consistent with Sun Tzu's emphasis on winning without fighting, PRC strategists have emphasized that legal warfare should begin, and is exceptionally valuable, 'before the outbreak of physical hostilities'.[42] Today, China is actively engaged in lawfare in the maritime, aviation, space, information technology, and trade domains.

PRC lawfare today is aimed at both gaining current advantage and tilting future kinetic battlegrounds to China's benefit. This chapter's next section will illustrate this by describing how the PRC deploys lawfare arguments, in the maritime

---

[38] International Security Advisory Board, 'China's Strategic Modernization: Report from the ISAB Task Force' (US Department of State 2008) <https://nuke.fas.org/guide/china/ISAB2008.pdf> accessed 5 March 2023.

[39] Robert Strausz-Hupé et al, *Protracted Conflict: A Challenging Study of Communist Strategy* (Harper 1959).

[40] See e.g. Dean Cheng, 'Winning without Fighting: Chinese Legal Warfare' (Heritage Foundation, 18 May 2012) <https://www.heritage.org/asia/report/winning-without-fighting-chinese-legal-warfare> accessed 5 March 2023.

[41] Eric W. Orts, 'The Rule of Law in China' (2001) 34 Vanderbilt Journal of Transnational Law 43.

[42] Cheng (n 40).

and aviation domains, in order to promote Beijing's access control strategy both by creating current facts on the ground (e.g., turning disputed reefs into airbases) and by promoting future international legitimacy for China's expanding claims of sovereignty rights.

4. PRC grey zone lawfare in the maritime and aviation domains

The PRC has been engaged in a sophisticated maritime and aviation lawfare strategy for over a dozen years. In 2009, James Kraska and Brian Wilson, two senior US Navy attorneys, warned that 'China has begun to engage in a resourceful legal warfare, or "lawfare" strategy to deny access to its coastal seas to warships and aircraft of the United States, Japan, and other countries in the region.'[43] In Kraska and Wilson's description, the PRC was endeavouring to use 'international law as an instrument to deter adversaries prior to combat . . . [including by shifting the law of the sea] away from long-accepted norms of freedom of navigation and toward interpretations of increased coastal State sovereign authority.'[44]

In the years since, the PRC has continued to work to change international law, so as to push US and other ships and aircraft farther away from China's coastline, in order to provide its military more breathing room in a potential future kinetic conflict. This lawfare has focused in large part on the South China Sea.

The South China Sea encompasses an area of around 1.4 million square miles[45] (1.5 times larger than the Mediterranean Sea).[46] According to various estimates, some $3 to $5 trillion per year in trade, more than one fifth of the world's total, transits through the South China Sea.[47] The Sea also reportedly contains approximately 11 billion barrels of oil and 190 trillion cubic feet of natural gas in proved and probable reserves.[48] That equals approximately 3 per cent

---

[43] James Kraska and Brian Wilson, 'China Wages Maritime Lawfare' (*Foreign Policy*, 12 March 2009) <http://foreignpolicy.com/2009/03/12/china-wages-maritime-lawfare/> accessed 5 March 2023.

[44] Ibid.

[45] 'South China Sea', Encyclopedia Britannica <https://www.britannica.com/place/South-China-Sea/Economic-aspects> accessed 5 March 2023

[46] 'Mediterranean Sea', Encyclopedia Britannica, https://www.britannica.com/place/Mediterranean-Sea> accessed 5 March 2023.

[47] Jim Gomez and Aaron Favila, 'US Admiral Says China Fully Militarized Isles' (*Associated Press*, 21 March 2022) <https://apnews.com/article/business-china-beijing-xi-jinping-south-china-sea-d229070bc2373be1ca515390960a6e6c> accessed 5 March 2023; Sean M. Holt, 'Five Countries, Other than China, Most Dependent on the South China Sea' (*CNBC*, 17 November 2022) <https://www.cnbc.com/2022/11/18/five-countries-other-than-china-most-dependent-on-the-south-china-sea.html> accessed 5 March 2023.

[48] US Energy Information Administration, 'South China Sea' <https://www.eia.gov/international/analysis/regions-of-interest/South_China_Sea> accessed 5 March 2023.

of global proven natural gas reserves.[49] The Sea is surrounded by Brunei, China, Indonesia, Malaysia, the Philippines, Singapore, Taiwan, and Vietnam.[50]

The PRC has for decades claimed sovereignty or some form of exclusive jurisdiction over most of the South China Sea.[51] It has done so by asserting a variety of claims which have long been rejected—as inconsistent with international law—by the United States, numerous States, and an arbitral tribunal.[52]

The PRC's claims were for many years expressed through its circulation of maps featuring a 'nine-dashed-line' asserting control over the vast majority of the South China Sea. In a 2009 submission to the UN Secretary General, the PRC stated 'China has indisputable sovereignty over the islands in the South China Sea and the adjacent waters, and enjoys sovereign rights and jurisdiction over the relevant waters as well as the seabed and subsoil thereof (see attached map)'.[53]

The most authoritative refutation of these PRC claims was issued in 2016, by an arbitral tribunal convened in accordance with UNCLOS, the multilateral treaty governing maritime sovereignty.[54] The PRC is a party to UNCLOS.[55] Ruling on a claim brought against the PRC by the Philippines, the tribunal issued a unanimous decision ruling in favour of the Philippines on nearly every count.[56] Under the terms of UNCLOS, the tribunal decision is final and binding on the PRC.[57] Yet the PRC has refused to abide by the arbitral decision, declaring it 'null and void'.[58]

Since 2016, the PRC has shifted to making claims based on its purported sovereignty over four 'island groups' in the South China Sea.[59] This includes claims not only to the actual islands but also to ostensibly related maritime features that are either fully submerged or below water at high tide.[60] The four-island group

[49] British Petroleum, 'Statistical Review of World Energy: 2021' <https://www.bp.com/content/dam/bp/business-sites/en/global/corporate/pdfs/energy-economics/statistical-review/bp-stats-review-2021-natural-gas.pdf> accessed 5 March 2023

[50] US Department of State, 'People's Republic of China: Maritime Claims in the South China Sea' (January 2022) 3 <https://www.state.gov/wp-content/uploads/2022/01/LIS150-SCS.pdf> accessed 5 March 2023.

[51] Ibid. 1.

[52] *South China Sea Arbitration (The Republic of Philippines v. The People's Republic of China)*, Award, PCA Case No. 2013-19 (July 12, 2016).

[53] US Department of State, 'China: Maritime Claims in the South China Sea' (5 December 2014) <https://www.state.gov/wp-content/uploads/2019/10/LIS-143.pdf> accessed 5 March 2023.

[54] *South China Sea Arbitration* (n 52).

[55] Ibid.

[56] Ibid.

[57] Permanent Court of Arbitration, 'South China Sea Arbitration (*The Republic of Philippines v. The People's Republic of China*)', Press Release (12 July 2016) <https://pcacases.com/web/sendAttach/1801> accessed 5 March 2023. While the United States is not a party to UNCLOS, it considers the relevant provisions of UNCLOS to 'reflect customary international law binding on all states. See US Department of State (n 53) 5.

[58] Congressional Research Service, 'China Primer: South Sea Disputes' (19 December 2022) <https://crsreports.congress.gov/product/pdf/IF/IF10607> accessed 5 March 2023.

[59] US Department of State (n 50) 2, 5.

[60] Ibid.

218 ARENAS OF HYBRID AND GREY ZONE COMPETITION

claim depends on many of the same mischaracterizations of the law of the sea, and has much the same practical effect of vastly expanding China's purported maritime seas, as did the nine-dash-line.

UNCLOS provides that each State is entitled to a 12-nautical-mile territorial sea over which it enjoys sovereignty, as well as a 200-nautical-mile exclusive economic zone (EEZ) in which it enjoys the sole right to exploitation of natural resources.[61] UNCLOS specifies that foreign States have freedom of navigation and overflight within EEZs.[62]

The 12- and 200-nautical-mile lines are measured not just from a State's mainland but also from any islands which are part of the State. For these purposes, UNCLOS defines an island as 'a naturally formed area of land, surrounded by water, which is above water at high tide', excluding '[r]ocks which cannot sustain human habitation or economic life of their own'.[63] Each such island generates its own 12-nautical mile-territorial sea and 200-nautical-mile EEZ.[64] A rock which is above water at high tide but not capable of sustaining habitation or economic life generates only a territorial sea.[65]

Whether a feature meets the criteria of being above water at high tide, or sustaining human habitation or economic life of its own, must be assessed based on its natural state.[66] Human activity cannot transform a low-tide or submerged feature or a rock into an island that is fully entitled to maritime zones.[67] UNCLOS specifically provides that '[a]rtificial islands, installations and structures do not possess the status of islands'.[68]

Beijing has continued to both express, and act pursuant to, its alternative interpretation of these and other provisions of the law of the sea. For example, the PRC falsely claims 'sovereignty' over more than one hundred features in the South China Sea that are submerged below the surface at high tide.[69] The PRC uses such claims to extend its territorial sea and EEZ claims.[70]

The PRC is also engaged in construction designed to turn some submerged reefs and mere rocks into inhabited islands. For example, the PRC occupies and has built artificial islands on Mischief Reef and Subi Reef, which it appeared to use as a basis for its maritime sovereignty claims. The 2016 tribunal confirmed that both reefs are submerged at high tide in their natural conditions, which

---

[61] UN Convention on the Law of the Sea (10 December 1982) 1833 UNTS 3 (UNCLOS).
[62] UNCLOS, Arts. 58 and 87.
[63] Ibid. Art. 121.
[64] Ibid.
[65] Congressional Research Service (n 58).
[66] US Department of State (n 50) 6.
[67] Ibid. 6–7.
[68] UNCLOS, Art. 60.
[69] US Department of State (n 50) 1.
[70] Ibid.

LAWFARE, CHINA, AND THE GREY ZONE   219

means they are not entitled to territorial seas.[71] 'As time goes on', said Professor Ingrid Wuerth, 'it may become harder and harder to document which features were 'rocks', which were 'islands' and which were neither prior to construction—and these determinations may be essential to resolving contested maritime claims in the region'.[72]

As of spring 2022, the PRC had not only turned both Mischief Reef and Subi Reef into artificial islands but also placed on them multi-story buildings, airstrips, fighter jets, seaports, and missile systems.[73] PRC military officials were also repeatedly (and contrary to international law) ordering US Navy planes flying nearby to exit what the PRC officials claimed was China's territory.[74]

In addition to claiming (and seeking to enforce) 12-nautical-mile territorial seas around artificial islands, the PRC also falsely asserted that it can regulate passage on the seas, and also overflight within the airspace, in its EEZ. For example, PRC officials have repeatedly complained about foreign military vessels transiting the Taiwan Strait even though the strait, 70 miles wide at its narrowest, goes well beyond China's 12-nautical-mile territorial sea.[75]

Raul Pedrozo, a professor of military law at the US Naval War College, referred to China's 'untenable position that foreign military activities in the EEZ are subject to coastal notice and consent' as part of 'China's ongoing lawfare strategy to misstate or misapply international legal norms to accommodate its anti-access strategy'.[76] China has used this inaccurate interpretation of EEZ law to justify the interception and harassment of US and other nations' ships operating within its EEZ, and of US and other nations' aircraft flying above its EEZ.[77]

Nor is China's maritime coercion exclusive to its regular armed forces. The People's Armed Forces Maritime Militia (PAFMM) is a naval militia force organized at the local level which, according to a US Defense Department report, 'plays a major role in coercive activities to achieve China's political goals without fighting, part of broader PRC military doctrine stating confrontational operations short of war can be an effective means of accomplishing political objectives'.[78] PAFMM includes nearly two hundred thousand fishing

---

[71] *South China Sea Arbitration* (n 52) 174.
[72] Ingrid Wuerth, 'US Policy on the South China Sea' (*Lawfare*, 26 March 2015) <https://www.lawfareblog.com/us-policy-south-china-sea> accessed 5 March 2023
[73] Gomez and Favila (n 47).
[74] Ibid.
[75] Lynn Kuok, 'Narrowing the Differences between China and the US Over the Taiwan Strait' (*International Institute for Strategic Studies*, 13 July 2022) <https://www.iiss.org/blogs/analysis/2022/07/narrowing-the-differences-between-china-and-the-us-over-the-taiwan-strait> accessed 5 March 2023.
[76] Raul Pedrozo, 'The Building of China's Great Wall at Sea' (2012) 17 Ocean and Coastal Law Journal 253, 284.
[77] M. Taylor Fravel and Charles L. Glaser, 'How Much Risk Should the United States Run in the South China Sea?' (2022) 47 International Security 88.
[78] US Department of Defense, 'Annual Report to Congress: Military and Security Developments Involving the People's Republic of China 2018' (16 May 2018) 72 <https://media.defense.gov/

220 ARENAS OF HYBRID AND GREY ZONE COMPETITION

vessels,[79] often indistinguishable from regular fishing vessels,[80] which train with the PRC Navy and Coast Guard and take direction from PRC authorities.[81]

Ostensibly private Chinese 'cargo ships and fishing vessels are used as government proxies to interfere with US ships'.[82] On occasion they are dispatched en masse to 'intimidate and ram fishing or law enforcement boats from other countries'.[83] Using fishing vessels in this manner 'provides the Chinese government with some level of plausible deniability', making it more challenging to hold the PRC accountable, although from a practical perspective 'the pattern of behavior is easily ascribable to the Chinese government'.[84]

China's continued actions pursuant to its inaccurate interpretations of the law of the sea appear to be aimed at changing customary international law. Customary international law can be nullified or even changed through State practice undertaken in conjunction with an assertion that such practice is consistent with international law.[85]

In the law of the sea context, customary international law can, over time, be affected by maritime operations, diplomatic statements, domestic implementing legislation, and the writings of legal scholars, as well as statements and judgements from international organizations and tribunals.[86] Supplementing its maritime operations, China's EEZ lawfare strategy includes 'declaratory statements incorporated into China's UNCLOS ratification depositary instrument', domestic legislation formally claiming security interests in its EEZ, development of supportive legal scholarship, and a strategic communications campaign.[87]

For the PRC, however, such lawfare activities as turning reefs into islands are not necessarily designed to create an argument that would win before the International Court of Justice the next year. Sometimes, the activity is apparently designed in part to create a legal or legal-sounding argument that can create a narrative today that will 'persuade the Chinese people that their government's

2018/Aug/16/2001955282/-1/-1/1/2018-CHINA-MILITARY-POWER-REPORT.PDF> accessed 5 March 2023

[79] James Kraska and Michael Monti, 'The Law of Naval Warfare and China's Maritime Militia' (2015) 91 International Law Studies 450, 452.

[80] Ibid.

[81] US Department of Defense (n 78.

[82] Pedrozo (n 76) 284.

[83] Ian Urbina, 'How China's Massive Fishing Fleet Is Transforming the World's Oceans' (*Slate*, 2 September 2020) <https://slate.com/news-and-politics/2020/09/beijing-fishing-fleet-subsidies-north-korea.html> accessed 5 March 2023.

[84] Robert T. Kline, 'The Pen and the Sword: The People's Republic of China's Effort to Redefine the Exclusive Economic Zone through Maritime Lawfare and Military Enforcement' (2013) 216 Military Law Review 122.

[85] See e.g. Statute of the International Court of Justice (26 June 1945), 33 UNTS 933, Art. 38.

[86] Robert C. De Tolve, 'At What Cost? America's UNCLOS Allergy in the Time of "Lawfare"' (2012) 61 Naval Law Review 1.

[87] Ibid.

actions are justified'.[88] The activity may also, or instead, be designed to plant the seed of arguments that will grow in strength as the PRC causes customary international law to evolve and/or as neighbours, intimidated by the PRC's military might, acquiesce to its claims. Thus, from the perspective of the United States, Australia, and their allies, it is essential to contest such claims early and forcefully lest they gain momentum and set the stage for a future fait accompli.

Demonstrating continuing control over a specific body of water or island is 'vitally important to claims of sovereignty' over it under theories of historic title, customary international law, and UNCLOS.[89] The extent to which other States accept or contest a historic claim is a key criteria for establishing the claim.[90] Since inaction may be viewed as acquiescence to the claim, China benefits legally from creating or bolstering a claim by creating a new island or other facts, and then militarily dissuading other States from contesting the claim.[91]

This strategy for obtaining sovereignty over South China Sea islands and waters is, as one US Navy legal expert put it, 'slowly proving effective . . . if successful, China will have achieved through the use of lawfare what it traditionally would have had to achieve almost solely through military force'.[92] As Professor Douglas Guilfoyle, a leading Australian maritime law expert put it in October 2022, China is successfully 'advancing a series of legal, historical, and security arguments in favor of what seems to be a new regional maritime order, one centred on rules generated in Beijing'.[93]

5. US-China grey zone lawfare in the information technology domain

Both China and the United States recognize that control over information technology services, and the data they generate, is currently a principal cold war battlefield and would likely be an important weapon on the brink of or in a future hot conflict between them. As a result, a struggle over such control is a major aspect of the current grey zone lawfare between Beijing and Washington. The information technology battle is being fought in lawfare domains including the following: theft of intellectual property, the content of international law in

[88] Peter Dutton, 'China's Maritime Disputes in the East and South China Seas, Testimony of Peter Dutton' (2014) 67 Naval War College Review 7.
[89] Kline (n 84).
[90] Ibid.
[91] Ibid.
[92] Ibid.
[93] Douglas Guilfoyle, 'AUKUS and the International Rules-Based Order in the Maritime Domain' (*Security and Defense Plus*, 25 October 2022) <https://www.unsw.adfa.edu.au/security-defence-plus-aukus-and-international-rules-based-order-maritime-domain> accessed 5 March 2023.

222 ARENAS OF HYBRID AND GREY ZONE COMPETITION

the cyber arena, control over Americans' private information, and whose tele-communications pipelines supply the world.

5.1 Theft of intellectual property

The stakes of this battle are extremely high. Even now, in peacetime, '[t]he theft of intellectual property by the People's Republic of China costs America as much as $500 billion per year', according to William Evanina, director of the US government's National Counterintelligence and Security Center.[94]

The PRC's intellectual property theft is aimed in part at strengthening its weapons systems. According to a US Defense Department report, the PRC leverages 'State-sponsored industrial and technical espionage' in part to 'increase the level of technologies and expertise available to support military research, development, and acquisition'.[95] According to Daniel Coats (when he was US Director of National Intelligence) and numerous press reports,[96] the PRC has stolen designs and other data for the US Air Force's F-35 and F-22 aircraft programs.[97] In 2019, Secretary of Defense Mark Esper warned that China is perpetrating 'the greatest intellectual property theft in human history'.[98]

The other principal aim of the PRC's theft of intellectual property is to bolster its commercial enterprises. FBI director Christopher Wray and MI5 Director General Ken McCallum addressed this issue in a July 2022 joint address to business leaders in London. McCallum noted that the event was the first time the heads of the FBI and MI5 had ever shared a public platform, and explained that they were 'doing so to send the clearest signal we can on a massive shared challenge: China'.[99]

---

[94] Naveed Jamali and Tom O'Connor, 'US, China's Cold War is Raging in Cyberspace, Where Intellectual Property is a Costly Front' (*Newsweek*, 16 September 2020) <https://www.newsweek.com/us-chinas-cold-war-raging-cyberspace-where-intellectual-property-costly-front-1532133> accessed 5 March 2023.

[95] US Department of Defense, 'Military and Security Developments Involving the People's Republic of China, Annual Report to Congress 2020' (2020) xi <https://media.defense.gov/2020/Sep/01/2002488689/-1/-1/1/2020-DOD-CHINA-MILITARY-POWER-REPORT-FINAL.PDF> accessed 5 March 2023.

[96] See e.g. Eli Fuhrman, 'How China Stole the Designs for the F-35 Stealth Fighter' (*1945*, 15 July 2021) <https://www.19fortyfive.com/2021/07/how-china-stole-the-designs-for-the-f-35-stealth-fighter/> accessed 5 March 2023.

[97] Daniel R. Coats, 'Worldwide Threat Assessment of the US Intelligence Community' (11 May 2017) <https://www.dni.gov/files/documents/Newsroom/Testimonies/SSCI%20Unclassified%20SFR%20-%20Final.pdf> accessed 5 March 2023.

[98] Ellen Ioanes, 'China Steals US Designs for New Weapons, and It's Getting Away with 'The Greatest Intellectual Property Theft in Human History' (*Business Insider*, 24 September 2019) https://www.businessinsider.com/esper-warning-china-intellectual-property-theft-greatest-in-history-2019-9> accessed 5 March 2023.

[99] MI5, 'Joint Adress by MI5 and FBI Heads' (6 July 2022) <https://www.mi5.gov.uk/news/speech-by-mi5-and-fbi> accessed 5 March 2023.

In his speech at the event, FBI director Christopher Wray described the PRC's motivation as follows: 'The Chinese government is set on stealing your technology—whatever it is that makes your industry tick—and using it to undercut your business and dominate your market. And they're set on using every tool at their disposal to do it'.[100]

Wray described one such tool as the PRC's 'lavishly resourced hacking program that's bigger than that of every other major country combined'.[101] Wray explained that '[t]he Chinese Government sees cyber as the pathway to cheat and steal on a massive scale'.[102]

But Wray emphasized that 'in addition to traditional and cyber-enabled thievery, there are even more insidious tactics they'll use to essentially walk through your front door—and then rob you'.[103] The PRC does this, he said, 'by making investments and creating partnerships that position their proxies to steal valuable technology'.[104]

Wray described how the PRC frequently does this by evading Western laws and leveraging PRC laws. He explained that the PRC 'uses elaborate shell games to disguise its efforts' from Western governments' investment-screening programs like the Committee on Foreign Investment in the United States.[105] Wray also noted the PRC's efforts to change US laws, including 'when the Chinese Embassy warned US companies that, if they want to keep doing business in China, they need to fight bills in our Congress that China doesn't like'.[106]

The PRC leverages its own laws in several ways, explained Wray. For example, the PRC requires that Western companies doing business in China 'partner with Chinese businesses, partners that often turn into competitors'.[107]

In addition, Wray warned his audience of Western businesses that the PRC is 'legislating and regulating their way into your IP and your data'.[108] For example, a 2017 Chinese law requires particular Western companies to store their data in China, where the PRC government 'has easier access to it'.[109] The PRC's access is eased by another 2017 law that forces Chinese organizations and individuals 'to assist in Chinese intelligence operations' and a series of 2021 laws that gives the PRC 'access to and control of' data collected in China.[110]

---

[100] Federal Bureau of Investigation, 'Director's Remarks to Business Leaders in London' (6 July 2022) <https://www.fbi.gov/news/speeches/directors-remarks-to-business-leaders-in-london-070622> accessed 5 March 2023.
[101] Ibid.
[102] Ibid.
[103] Ibid.
[104] Ibid.
[105] Ibid.
[106] Ibid.
[107] Ibid.
[108] Ibid.
[109] Ibid.
[110] Ibid.

224 ARENAS OF HYBRID AND GREY ZONE COMPETITION

Wray hinted at the difficulty that the United States and its allies have in fighting back against the PRC's no-holds-barred tactics, stating that in 'targeting countries around the world that value the rule of law . . . Beijing may think our adherence to the rule of law is a weakness'.[111] While he insisted 'they're wrong', he did not explain in what way they're wrong or provide an explanation as to how the US government can turn the tables on the PRC.[112]

5.2 Battle over the content of international law in the cyber arena

In its 2022 annual report to Congress, the US-China Economic Security Review Commission declared that 'China enjoys an asymmetric advantage over the United States in cyberspace due to the CCP's unwillingness to play by the same rules'.[113] The Commission explained that the two countries 'diverge sharply on the norms that should guide responsible State behavior in cyberspace during peacetime'.[114]

One example the Commission provided was 'China's perpetration of cyberespionage for illegitimate economic advantage'.[115] While such cyberespionage is apparently not prohibited by international law,[116] the United States has declared that it will 'help build an international environment that recognizes such acts as unlawful and impermissible',[117] a stance supported by the G-20.[118] The PRC's persistence in undertaking such espionage violates the 2015 political agreement of President Barack Obama and President Xi Jinping that 'neither country's government will conduct or knowingly support cyber-enabled theft of intellectual property, including trade secrets or other confidential business information, with the intent of providing competitive advantages to companies or commercial sectors'.[119]

---

[111] Ibid.

[112] Ibid.

[113] US-China Economic Security and Review Commission (n 2) 418.

[114] Ibid.

[115] Ibid.

[116] NATO Cooperative Cyber Defence Centre of Excellence, 'Cyber Law Toolkit: Economic cyber espionage' <https://cyberlaw.ccdcoe.org/wiki/Scenario_09:_Economic_cyber_espionage#cite_note-66> accessed 5 March 2023.

[117] The White House, 'International Strategy for Cyberspace' (May 2011) <https://obamawhitehouse.archives.gov/sites/default/files/rss_viewer/international_strategy_for_cyberspace.pdf> accessed 5 March 2023.

[118] G20 Leaders' Communique, Antalya Summit (2015) <https://www.consilium.europa.eu/media/23729/g20-antalya-leaders-summit-communique.pdf> accessed 5 March 2023.

[119] The White House, 'Fact Sheet: President Xi Jinping's State Visit to the United States' (25 September 2015) <https://obamawhitehouse.archives.gov/the-press-office/2015/09/25/fact-sheet-president-xi-jinpings-state-visit-united-states> accessed 5 March 2023.

LAWFARE, CHINA, AND THE GREY ZONE   225

The Commission also described how the United States and China 'differ substantially in their interpretations of certain provisions [of international law] that would be relevant to cyber operations in a military context'.[120] For example, China disagrees with the US view that malicious cyber activities may constitute a use of force that triggers the target country's right under international law to 'defend itself through proportionate offensive operations, cyber or otherwise'.[121]

5.3 Battle over control of Americans' private information

The hyper-personalization of war, in which militaries collect and deploy electronic dossiers on individual members of their opponents' militaries, has been predicted by experts including Maj. Gen. Charles J. Dunlap, Jr., USAF (Ret)., who separately introduced the term 'lawfare' into the legal and international relations literature.[122] Both the collection and the deployment of such dossiers could leverage other developing technologies including drones and facial recognition software.[123] Swarms of drones equipped with facial recognition software could 'roam battlefields looking for very specific members of an enemy's force', with the goal of either killing or communicating with them.[124]

It would not be surprising to see the PRC use such dossiers to wage lawfare against, or otherwise threaten, particular US or allied commanders. PRC analysis of the second Iraq War noted with great interest that the US-led coalition contacted Iraqi generals directly to warn them of prosecution if they followed any orders by Saddam Hussein to use weapons of mass destruction.[125]

Personal information could also be used to wreak havoc on the home front of targeted warfighters. An adversary could distract and demoralize the warfighter by emptying their bank accounts, hacking and publishing their medical records or messaging accounts, or sending them false messages from their families.[126] An adversary could also hack into the bank, medical, school, social media, or other accounts of the warfighters' spouses, children, or other relatives and issue very precise threats to them.[127] Something similar has already occurred,

---

[120] US-China Economic Security and Review Commission (n 2) 461.
[121] Ibid.
[122] Charles J. Dunlap Jr., 'The Hyper-Personalization of War: Cyber, Big Data, and the Changing Face of Conflict' (2014) 15 Georgetown Journal of International Affairs 108–18 <https://scholarship.law.duke.edu/faculty_scholarship/3381/> accessed 5 March 2023.
[123] Ibid. 110–11.
[124] Ibid. 111.
[125] Dean Cheng, 'Winning without Fighting: Chinese Legal Warfare' (*Heritage Foundation*, 18 May 2012) <http://www.heritage.org/research/reports/2012/05/winning-without-fighting-chinese-legal-warfare> accessed 5 March 2023.
[126] Dunlap (n 122).
[127] Ibid. 112, 115.

when Muslim extremists in Denmark 'tried to intimidate families of Danish soldiers in Afghanistan' by contacting them directly, hacking email accounts, and 'intercepting cell phone calls between soldiers in Afghanistan and their families'.[128]

Such hyper-personalized warfare could cause the warfighter to become anxious about the safety of their loved ones and make it extremely difficult for them to focus on their warfighting duties.[129] As such, it would be consistent with 'psychological warfare', which the PRC adopted alongside 'legal warfare' as a key element of its strategic doctrine.

The strong possibility that hyper-personalization will drastically change future armed conflicts underscores the importance of control over Americans' private information. One example of the battle over such control is the US government effort to restrict access to TikTok.[130] TikTok has approximately one hundred million monthly active users in the United States, fifty million of whom use it daily.[131] FBI Director Wray warned in December 2022 that control over TikTok provides the PRC with the ability to collect user data which 'can be used for traditional espionage operations' and with the ability to conduct 'malicious cyber activity' through 'access to the software' on millions of Americans' devices.[132]

In contrast, the Chinese internet is far more restricted, by what is sometimes dubbed 'the Great Firewall of China'. The PRC blocks foreign social media platforms including Facebook, Instagram, and Twitter; leading Western news sources including the *New York Times* and *Wall Street Journal*; entertainment and media sites including Netflix and YouTube; search engines including Google; and messaging apps including Signal and WhatsApp.[133] The PRC also rigorously censors communications on domestic social media.[134]

The PRC has already acquired massive amounts of Americans' personal information by hacking into databases. Attorney General William Barr attributed

---

[128] Ibid. 113.

[129] Ibid. 115.

[130] David Ingram, 'Biden Signs Tik Tok Ban for Government Devices' (*NBC News*, 30 December 2022) <https://www.nbcnews.com/tech/tech-news/tiktok-ban-biden-government-college-state-federal-security-privacy-rcna63724> accessed 5 March 2023.

[131] Alex Sherman, 'TikTok reveals detailed user numbers for the first time' (*CNBC*, 24 August 2020) <https://www.cnbc.com/2020/08/24/tiktok-reveals-us-global-user-growth-numbers-for-first-time.html> accessed 5 March 2023.

[132] Christopher Wray, '2022 Josh Rosenblatt Memorial Talk' (2 December 2022, University of Michigan) <https://fordschool.umich.edu/sites/default/files/2022-12/2022-12-02%20Christopher%20Wray_%202022%20Josh%20Rosenthal%20Memorial%20talk%20%28Audio%20ENG%29.txt> accessed 5 March 2023.

[133] See e.g. Junaid Ahmed, 'The Complete List of Blocked Websites in China' (*Security Gladiators*, 8 November 2022) <https://securitygladiators.com/censorship/blocked-websites-china/> accessed 5 March 2023.

[134] Gu Ting, 'China Steps Up Social Media Censorship, 'Upgrades' Great Firewall Ahead of Congress' (*Radio Free Asia*, 7 October 2022) <https://www.rfa.org/english/news/china/ccp-censorship-10072022135730.html> accessed 5 March 2023.

to the PRC the 2015 hack of the US Office of Personnel Management which stole the personnel records of practically every US federal civilian employee, including not just Social Security numbers but also the security clearance forms known as SF-86s, which contain very detailed and sensitive information.[135] Barr also attributed to the PRC the 2017 hack of Equifax which stole the personal credit and other information of 147 million people, roughly the entire adult population of the United States.[136] In addition, he attributed to the PRC the 2015 hack of Anthem, which stole the insurance information of nearly eighty million Americans.[137]

As a result of such hacks, Chinese intelligence has amassed a 'database more detailed than any nation has ever possessed about one of its adversaries'.[138] The value of this database includes 'identif[ying] potential weaknesses—through background checks, credit scores, and health records—of intelligence targets China may someday hope to recruit' or otherwise influence.[139]

A third method by which the PRC has attempted to acquire Americans' personal data has been through the purchase of US companies. For example, in 2020 the US government's Committee on Foreign Investment in the United States blocked a Chinese entity from buying a fertility clinic in San Diego, which contains the home port of the US Pacific Fleet.[140]

John Demers, head of the Justice Department's National Security Division, expressed concern that fertility clinic data, 'among the most intimate information about you', could be used by the PRC to coerce Americans.[141] He also speculated that such data could be used to develop 'some kind of biological weapon', noting that 'if you had all of the data of a population you might be able to see what the population is most vulnerable to and then develop something that's taking advantage of that vulnerability'.[142]

Notwithstanding these concerns, at least one other US fertility clinic has reportedly already been successfully purchased by entities connected to the Chinese Communist Party.[143] If Washington is going to more successfully counter the PRC's efforts to collect and deploy electronic dossiers of individual

---

[135] Garrett M. Graff, 'China's Hacking Spree Will Have a Decades-Long Fallout' (*Wired*, 11 February 2020) <https://www.wired.com/story/china-equifax-anthem-marriott-opm-hacks-data/> accessed 5 March 2023.

[136] Ibid.

[137] Ibid.

[138] Ibid.

[139] Ibid.

[140] Eamon Javers, 'US Blocked Chinese Purchase of San Diego Fertility Clinic Over Medical Data Security Concerns' (*CNBC*, 16 October 2020) https://www.cnbc.com/2020/10/16/trump-administration-blocked-chinese-purchase-of-us-fertility-clinic.html> accessed 5 March 2023.

[141] Ibid.

[142] Ibid.

[143] Ibid.

5.4 Battle over whose telecommunications pipelines supply the world

The high value of personal information makes it essential to control the major telecommunications pipelines that transmit it. The grey zone lawfare battle over control of such pipelines includes efforts to set the technical standards which govern such pipelines. It also includes efforts to promote or retard the use of Huawei and other Chinese-made telecommunications equipment.

Technical standards are essential to the interoperability of telecommunications platforms. In 2021, the PRC released a fifteen-year plan, sometimes referred to as China Standards 2035, laying out China's strategy for setting the global standards for the next generation of technologies in fields including telecommunications and artificial intelligence.[144] China's technical advantage over other countries in 5G reportedly gives the PRC important leverage in standards discussions.[145]

The PRC's technical standards strategy is working to 'stack the digital deck in China's favor', according to a 2021 report by Daniel Russel, who previously served as President Obama's National Security Council Senior Director for Asian Affairs.[146] Russel's report outlines how the PRC has been achieving this objective.

For example, the PRC is working diligently to increase its influence within international standards development organizations (ISDOs), including by vigorously lobbying for key positions in these organizations.[147] The PRC's 'top-down, State-centric approach towards technical standards setting' contrasts sharply with the US government's 'longstanding hands-off approach, [which leaves] standard setting to the private sector and experts'.[148]

---

[144] Xinhua News Agency, 'The Chinese Communist Party Central Committee and the State Council Publish the 'National Standardization Development Outline' (Georgetown University Center for Security and Emerging Technology, 19 November 2021) <https://cset.georgetown.edu/publication/the-chinese-communist-party-central-committee-and-the-state-council-publish-the-national-standardization-development-outline/> accessed 5 March 2023.

[145] Helen Toner, 'Will China Set Global Tech Standards?' (ChinaFile, 22 March 2022) <https://www.chinafile.com/conversation/will-china-set-global-tech-standards> accessed 5 March 2023

[146] Daniel R. Russel and Blake H. Berger, 'Stacking the Deck: China's Influence in International Technology Standards Setting' (Asia Society Policy Institute, 2021) <https://asiasociety.org/sites/defa ult/files/2021-11/ASPI_StacktheDeckreport_final.pdf> accessed 5 March 2023.

[147] Ibid. 18.

[148] Daniel R. Russel and Blake Berger, 'Will China Set Global Tech Standards?' (ChinaFile, 22 March 2022) <https://www.chinafile.com/conversation/will-china-set-global-tech-standards> accessed 5 March 2023

LAWFARE, CHINA, AND THE GREY ZONE   229

Beijing's involvement raises concerns that it will advocate for standards that 'ease greater surveillance or censorship through network infrastructure or protocols', no matter where the equipment is manufactured.[149] US Secretary of Commerce Gina Raimondo warned in November 2022 that China often 'packs' important international standard-setting bodies with 'government and business representatives who work together to push the country's authoritarian standards and values'.[150]

In addition, once Chinese standards are adopted, that 'creates a path dependency that locks other countries into using Chinese vendors'.[151] The use of Chinese vendors then provides 'access to immense quantities of data that are useful to both Chinese companies and government agencies'.[152] As a result, '[n]umerous US government officials have raised concerns about how the adoption of Chinese standards could cause potential compromises to national and personal security'.[153]

In addition to the grey zone lawfare battle over international telecommunications standards, the United States is also using lawfare to attempt to prevent Chinese companies, namely, Huawei and ZTE, from dominating the world's telecommunications network equipment. Huawei and ZTE are among the world's four largest makers of such equipment, along with the Finnish firm Nokia and the Swedish firm Ericsson.[154] Huawei is estimated to have the largest share of the global market, with about 30 per cent.[155]

The US government has repeatedly used law as a weapon to restrict Huawei's presence in the United States and limit its presence in global networks. For example, in 2017 and 2018, Congress prohibited various US government agencies from using or obtaining Huawei equipment or services.[156] In November 2021, the Federal Communications Commission effectively barred both Huawei and ZTE from selling new equipment in the United States.[157] In 2020, the Commerce

---

[149] Graham Webster, 'Will China Set Global Tech Standards?' (*ChinaFile*, 22 March 2022) <https://www.chinafile.com/conversation/will-china-set-global-tech-standards> accessed 5 March 2023.

[150] US Department of Commerce, 'Remarks by US Secretary of Commerce Gina Raimondo on the US Competitiveness and the China Challenge' (30 November 2022) <https://www.commerce.gov/news/speeches/2022/11/remarks-us-secretary-commerce-gina-raimondo-us-competitiveness-and-china> accessed 5 March 2023.

[151] Russel and Berger (n 146) 7.

[152] Ibid. 7.

[153] Russel and Berger (n 148).

[154] Jill C. Gallagher, 'US Restrictions on Huawei Technologies: National Security, Foreign Policy, and Economic Interests', Congressional Research Service (5 January 2022), 5, <https://crsreports.congress.gov/product/pdf/R/R47012> accessed 5 March 2023.

[155] Ibid.

[156] Ibid. 12–15.

[157] Reuters, 'US Bans Huawei, ZTE Equipment Sales Amid Chinese Spying Fears' (*CNN*, 26 November 2022) <https://www.cnn.com/2022/11/26/us/us-washington-huawei-zte-ban-security-risk-intl-hnk/index.html> accessed 5 March 2023.

230   ARENAS OF HYBRID AND GREY ZONE COMPETITION

Department limited Huawei's access to foreign-produced semiconductors made with US technologies.[158] In 2019 and 2020, the Justice Department charged Huawei with financial fraud, sanctions violations, racketeering, and conspiracy to steal trade secrets.[159]

Meanwhile, the US government has also been pressuring its allies to ban Huawei. For example, the UK[160] and Canadian[161] governments reportedly banned Huawei from their 5G telecoms network at least partly in response to US pressure. The UK's official reason for the ban was reportedly that US sanctions on Huawei would render the Chinese company's technology unreliable.[162]

Australia was the first country to ban Huawei products from its 5G network. It did so in 2018, after Mike Burgess, director-general of the Australian government's Signals Directorate, determined that Huawei products would not only risk PRC 'interception of telephone calls'.[163] Burgess identified an even greater risk: that much of Australia's critical infrastructure would come to be dependent on 5G and Beijing would be able to order Huawei to shut it off.[164]

Huawei has insisted that it would not comply with an order from the PRC government. The Australian prime minister who decided to bar Huawei, Malcolm Turnbull, did not believe the company. 'Huawei says, 'Oh no, we would refuse'. That's laughable', said Turnbull, asserting Huawei 'would have no option but to comply',[165] including because of the PRC's 2017 law that requires all Chinese persons and companies to cooperate with the government on any national security matter.[166]

Such a shutdown, Burgess concluded, would mean, 'The sewerage pump stops working. Clean water doesn't come to you . . . the public transport network doesn't work'.[167] In other words, the PRC would be able to bring Australia to its knees without firing a shot.

---

[158] Gallagher (n 154) 27.

[159] Ibid. 1–2.

[160] Alexander Smith, 'After Months of US Pressure, U.K. Bans China's Huawei from Its 5G Network' (*NBC News*, 14 July 2020) <https://www.nbcnews.com/news/world/after-months-u-s-pressure-u-k-bans-china-s-n1233752> accessed 5 March 2023.

[161] Andy Blatchford, 'Canada Joins Five Eyes in Ban on Huawei and ZTE' (*Politico*, 19 May 2022) <https://www.politico.com/news/2022/05/19/canada-five-eyes-ban-huawei-zte-00033920> accessed 5 March 2023.

[162] Smith (n 160).

[163] Peter Hartcher, 'Huawei? No Way! Why Australia Banned the World's Biggest Telecoms Firm', Sydney Morning Herald (Syndey, 11 May 2021) <https://www.smh.com.au/national/huawei-no-way-why-australia-banned-the-world-s-biggest-telecoms-firm-20210503-p57oc9.html> accessed 5 March 2023.

[164] Ibid.

[165] Ibid.

[166] Ibid.

[167] Ibid.

6. PRC grey zone lawfare using its trade authorities

In recent years, the PRC has accelerated deployment of its trade authorities to pursue military policy objectives. In contrast with the United States, China's coercive measures have typically not been formally announced (presumably in part as a way to circumvent potential WTO objections).

One such incident occurred in September 2010, after a Chinese boat, fishing in waters controlled by Japan but claimed by the PRC, collided with two Japanese Coast Guard ships.[168] Japan detained the Chinese boat's captain and refused at first to release him, saying his case was being handled by Japan's courts.[169] The PRC government then blocked exports to Japan of rare earth minerals, which are critical to Japan's manufacturing sector and largely supplied by China.[170] The PRC reportedly did so by quietly advising Chinese companies to halt rare earth exports and quietly ordering PRC customs officials to discretely block any such exports.[171] Publicly, PRC officials denied having imposed an embargo, while asserting that all of China's rare earth exporters 'simultaneously decided to halt shipments because of their personal feelings towards Japan'.[172]

Had there been a public announcement of a government-mandated export ban, Japan could have filed an immediate complaint with the WTO, alleging a violation of free trade laws.[173] However, the PRC's quiet blocking of such exports, combined with a public denial that it was taking such a step, put pressure on Japan without incurring legal consequences. A few days later, Japan released the Chinese captain.[174] When China lost a WTO ruling in 2014 in relation to its formal restrictions on rare earth exports, the ruling did not address the PRC's informal embargo on Japan, nor prevent a future such informal embargo.[175]

The PRC took a similar WTO-evading approach to South Korea in 2017. Following Seoul's installation of a US Terminal High Altitude Area Defense (THAAD) battery, China imposed unannounced economic sanctions on South

---

[168] Keith Bradsher, 'Amid Tension, China Blocks Vital Exports to Japan', *The New York Times* (New York, 22 September 2010) <http://www.nytimes.com/2010/09/23/business/global/23rare.html?pagewanted=all> accessed 5 March 2023.

[169] Bloomberg News, 'China Denies Japan Rare-Earth Ban Amid Diplomatic Row' (*Bloomberg*, 23 September 2010) <https://www.bloomberg.com/news/articles/2010-09-23/china-denies-japan-rare-earth-ban-amid-diplomatic-row-update1-> accessed 5 March 2023.

[170] Bradsher (n 168).

[171] Ibid.

[172] Paul Krugman, 'Rare and Foolish', *The New York Times* (New York, 17 October 2010) <http://www.nytimes.com/2010/10/18/opinion/18krugman.html> accessed 5 March 2023.

[173] Bradsher (n 168).

[174] AFP, 'China Blocked Exports of Rare Earth Metals to Japan, Traders Claim' (*The Telegraph*, 24 September 2010) <http://www.telegraph.co.uk/finance/china-business/8022484/China-blocked-exports-of-rare-earth-metals-to-Japan-traders-claim.html> accessed 5 March 2023.

[175] WTO Dispute Settlement, *China—Measures Related to the Exportation of Rare Earths, Tungsten and Molybdenum*, Dispute DS431 (29 August 2014).

232 ARENAS OF HYBRID AND GREY ZONE COMPETITION

Korean tourism, retail, and entertainment firms.[176] While the PRC never specifically linked the sanctions to the THAAD deployment, the message was clearly and painfully received.[177] A drastic decrease in Chinese tourism to South Korea cost the latter's economy an estimated $6.5 billion in lost revenue.[178] The billions in lost revenue contrast notably with the smaller ($800 million) cost of the THAAD battery.[179]

Such measures posed a greater economic risk to South Korea than to China; 26 per cent of South Korea's exports go to China,[180] and China provides 24 per cent of South Korea's imports.[181] In contrast, South Korea receives 4.5 per cent of China's exports,[182] and provides 8.8 per cent of China's imports.[183]

During the 2022 South Korean election, when one leading presidential candidate proposed that South Korea field a second THAAD battery to protect against North Korean missiles, the other responded by warning that doing so was a 'really dangerous act' that would 'ruin our economy' by provoking China.[184]

The PRC's use of its trade authorities to achieve military objectives has not been limited to its Asian neighbours. For example, in 2021, the PRC used these authorities in response to Lithuania's invitation to Taiwan to open a 'Taiwan Representative Office' in Vilnius.[185] Lithuania's invitation ran counter to the PRC's efforts to isolate Taiwan, potentially in preparation for kinetic action against the island.

Chinese customs responded by simply (and without a formal announcement) deleting Lithuania from its list of origin countries, making it impossible to file customs forms for cargoes to or from Lithuania.[186] When this failed to alter Lithuania's behaviour, the PRC first warned multinationals that they would be

[176] Christine Kim and Ben Blanchard, 'China, South Korea Agree to Mend Ties After THAAD Standoff' (*Reuters*, 30 October 2017) <https://www.reuters.com/article/us-northkorea-missiles/china-south-korea-agree-to-mend-ties-after-thaad-standoff-idUSKBN1D003G> accessed 5 March 2023.

[177] Ibid.

[178] Ibid.

[179] David Choi, 'South Korean Presidential Candidates Spar Over Need for More THAAD Missile Defense' (*Stars and Stripes*, 4 February 2022) <https://www.stripes.com/theaters/asia_pacific/2022-02-04/south-korea-thaad-missile-defense-battery-presidential-candidates-4623125.html> accessed 5 March 2023.

[180] Trading Economics, 'South Korea Exports by Country' <https://tradingeconomics.com/south-korea/exports-by-country> accessed 5 March 2023.

[181] Trading Economics, 'South Korea Imports by Country' <https://tradingeconomics.com/south-korea/imports-by-country> accessed 5 March 2023.

[182] Trading Economics, 'China Exports by Country' <https://tradingeconomics.com/china/exports-by-country> accessed 5 March 2023.

[183] Trading Economics, 'China Imports by Country' <https://tradingeconomics.com/china/imports-by-country> accessed 5 March 2023.

[184] Choi (n 179).

[185] Andrius Sytas, 'Lithuania Says Chinese Customs Is Blocking Its Exports' (*Reuters*, 3 December 2021) <https://www.reuters.com/article/china-lithuania-trade/lithuania-says-chinese-customs-is-blocking-its-exports-idUSKBN2II0Y7> accessed 5 March 2023

[186] Ibid.

subjected to secondary sanctions if they did not sever their ties with Lithuania, and then blocked from clearing PRC customs the cargoes of at least one German firm that sources from Lithuania.[187]

The PRC's coercive use of its trade authorities has also included Australia. In October and November 2020, the PRC took an unannounced series of purportedly technical actions restricting its trade with Australia.[188] This included delaying shipments of perishables such as fruit and live lobster, and verbally telling importers to avoid the import of several other Australian products due to possible delays clearing customs.[189] As a result of China's unofficial ban of Australian coal, several vessels laden with that product remained stuck off the coast of China for some six months.[190] The PRC reportedly issued no formal notice of the bans.[191]

Such measures pose a greater economic risk to Australia than China; 42 per cent of Australia's exports go to China,[192] making it Australia's largest market by far, and 29 per cent of Australia's imports come from China, making it Australia's largest source by far.[193] In contrast, 2 per cent of China's exports go to Australia, ranking it fourteenth,[194] and 6.7 per cent of China's imports come from Australia, ranking it fourth.[195]

That November, the PRC issued a public list of fourteen complaints about Australian government security policy, which Beijing said had 'poisoned' bilateral relations.[196] Many of the grievances were essentially complaints about Australian lawfare or interference with PRC lawfare. They included Australia: rejecting

---

[187] Matthew Reynolds and Matthew P. Goodman, 'China's Economic Coercion: Lessons from Lithuania' (*CSIS*, 6 May 2022) <https://www.csis.org/analysis/chinas-economic-coercion-lessons-lithuania> accessed 5 March 2023.

[188] Su-Lin Tan, 'China-Australia Relations: What's Happened Over the Past Year, and What's the Outlook?', South China Morning Post (20 April 2021) <https://www.scmp.com/economy/china-economy/article/3130109/china-australia-relations-whats-happened-over-past-year-and?module=inlineandpgtype=article> accessed 5 March 2023.

[189] Su-Lin Tan, 'What Happened Over the First Year of the China-Australia Trade Dispute?', South China Morning Post (28 October 2020) <https://www.scmp.com/economy/china-economy/article/3107228/china-australia-relations-what-has-happened-over-last-six?module=inlineandpgtype=article> accessed 5 March 2023.

[190] Su-Lin Tan (n 188).

[191] Su-Lin Tan (n 189).

[192] Trading Economics, 'Australia Exports by Country' <https://tradingeconomics.com/australia/exports-by-country> accessed 5 March 2023.

[193] Trading Economics, 'Australia Imports by Country' <https://tradingeconomics.com/australia/imports-by-country> accessed 5 March 2023.

[194] Trading Economics, 'China Exports by Country' <https://tradingeconomics.com/china/exports-by-country> accessed 5 March 2023.

[195] Trading Economics, 'China Imports by Country' <https://tradingeconomics.com/china/imports-by-country> accessed 5 March 2023.

[196] Jonathan Kearsley, Eryk Bagshaw, and Anthony Galloway, 'If You Make China the Enemy, China Will Be the Enemy': Beijing's Fresh Threat to Australia', Sydney Morning Herald (Sydney, 18 November 2020) <https://www.smh.com.au/world/asia/if-you-make-china-the-enemy-china-will-be-the-enemy-beijing-s-fresh-threat-to-australia-20201118-p56fqs.html> accessed 5 March 2023.

several Chinese investments on national security grounds; banning Huawei and ZTE from its 5G network; making a 'statement on the South China Sea to the United Nations;' and 'interfer[ing] in China's Xinjiang, Hong Kong and Taiwan affairs'.[197]

7. Conclusion

The PRC's grey zone lawfare has thus far been remarkably successful in achieving its objectives without firing a shot. Beijing's successes have leveraged several differences between the PRC on the one hand and the United States and its liberal democratic allies on the other hand. While it may not be possible to mitigate the PRC's leveraging of all of the differences, others could be more effectively managed by the West.

One difference is the greater leverage that law and its processes exert over the United States and its liberal democratic allies. This leverage results from a difference in ideology (with the PRC taking an exceptionally instrumental view of law), the lack of judicial or other independent checks and balances within the PRC government, and the relatively minimal influence over the PRC of NGOs, independent media, and other private-sector actors.

A second difference is the PRC's greater ability (including pursuant to its 2017 law) and willingness to use purportedly private-sector Chinese companies, individuals, and boats as proxies. This includes large companies such as Huawei as well as individual fishing vessels in the South China Sea. The West can, and should, respond by developing more effective means of countering the PRC's use of proxies to advance lawfare and other national policies behind a veil of 'plausible deniability'.

A third, somewhat related, difference is the PRC's particular ability, as an authoritarian regime, to take government actions without transparency. As a result, the PRC, unlike liberal democracies, can readily benefit from particular grey zone lawfare steps (such as blocking trade) without being held accountable for them under international law.

A fourth difference is the West's general hesitancy to regulate the internet and other telecommunications platforms that are available to Western audiences (especially compared with the 'great firewall of China' which strictly controls the Chinese internet). A fifth difference is that many of China's neighbours are more reliant on trade with the PRC than vice versa.

A sixth difference, which would be the easiest to remedy, is the US lack of a sophisticated and systematic, whole-of-government lawfare strategy and

---

[197] Ibid.

mechanism. If the United States is to win its current grey zone struggle against the PRC, and be fully prepared for a future kinetic war against China, it must promptly both adopt a comprehensive and coordinated lawfare strategy and create an interagency team to implement it.

The objectives should include both enhancing the US lawfare arsenal in general and better understanding and more effectively countering PRC lawfare. Implementation could enhance US lawfare by collecting and drawing lessons from case studies of US and allied lawfare successes and failures; by systematically identifying or developing US and allied points of lawfare leverage over the PRC; and by enhancing coordination and synergies amongst lawfare practitioners in the US government, allied governments, and the private sector. The initiative could more effectively counter PRC lawfare by improving the US's currently non-systematic monitoring of PRC lawfare; identifying and preparing for PRC next steps in current lawfare arenas; and identifying and preparing for PRC lawfare in new arenas.

11

Emerging Bio-Technologies for Disruptive Effects in Grey Zone Engagements

Joseph DeFranco, Diane DiEuliis, L. R. Bremseth, and James Giordano

'The supreme art of war is to subdue the enemy without fighting'.

Sun Tzu

1. Grey zone engagements

Considerable and expanding aspects of political and military actions directed at adversely impacting, if not defeating, an opponent often involve clandestine operations that can be articulated across a spectrum. These operations are frequently augmented by supporting missions that range from overt warfare to far more subtle engagements that do not meet current criteria for explicit acts of war. Routinely, the United States, its allies, and a number of its adversaries have employed clandestine tactics and operations across kinetic and non-kinetic (i.e. grey zone) domains. Arguably, the execution of clandestine kinetic operations is employed more readily, as these collective activities often occur after the initiation of conflict (i.e. 'Right of Bang'), and their effects may be observed and/or measured to various degrees. Given that clandestine grey zone activities are less visible, they may be particularly effective because often they are unrecognized and occur 'Left of Bang'. Other nations, especially adversaries, understand the relative economy of force that non-kinetic engagements enable, and increasingly are focused upon developing and articulating advanced methods for their operations.

Much has been written about the fog of war.[1] Grey zone engagements can create unique uncertainties prior to and/or outside of traditional warfare, precisely because they have qualitatively and quantitatively 'fuzzy boundaries'[2] as

---

[1] For example, W. A. Owens, *Lifting the Fog of War* (Johns Hopkins University Press 2000).
[2] A fuzzy boundary exists within a fuzzy set and describes a concept or condition in which the application can vary according to context or circumstances. See S. Haack *Deviant Logic, Fuzzy Logic: Beyond the Formalism* (University of Chicago Press 1996).

Joseph DeFranco, Diane DiEuliis, L. R. Bremseth, and James Giordano, *Emerging Bio-Technologies for Disruptive Effects in Grey Zone Engagements* In: *Hybrid Threats and Grey Zone Conflict.* Edited by: Mitt Regan and Aurel Sari, Oxford University Press. © Oxford University Press 2024. DOI: 10.1093/oso/9780197744772.003.0011

238 ARENAS OF HYBRID AND GREY ZONE COMPETITION

blatant acts of aggression. The intentionally induced ambiguity of grey zone engagements can establish plus-sum advantages for the executor(s), and zero-sum dilemmas for the target(s). For example, a limited-scale grey zone action, which exerts demonstrably significant effects but does not meet defined criteria for an act of war, places the targeted recipient(s) at a disadvantage: First, in that the criteria for response (and proportionality) are vague and therefore any response could be seen as questionable; and second, in that if the targeted recipient(s) responds with bellicose actions, there is considerable likelihood that they may be viewed as (or provoked to be) the aggressor(s), and therefore susceptible to some form of retribution that may be regarded as sanctionable.

Grey zone engagements often utilize non-military means to expand the effect-space beyond the conventional battlefield. The Department of Defense and Joint Staff do not have a well agreed-upon lexicon to define and to express the full spectrum of current and potential activities that constitute grey zone engagements.[3] It is unfamiliar—and can be politically uncomfortable—to use non-military terms and means to describe these engagements. And as previously noted, it can be politically difficult, if not precarious, to militarily define and respond to grey zone activities.

2. Disruptive effects

Grey zone engagements are best employed to incur disruptive effects in and across various dimensions (e.g. biological, psychological, and social) that can lead to intermediate- to long-term destructive manifestations (in a number of possible domains, ranging from the economic to the geopolitical). The latent disruptive and destructive effects should be framed and regarded as 'Grand Strategy' approaches that evoke outcomes in a 'long engagement/long war' context, rather than merely in more short-term tactical situations.[4]

Thus, grey zone operations should be regarded as tools of mass disruption, designed to sustain compounding results that can evoke both direct and indirect de-stabilizing effects. These effects can occur and spread (1) from the cellular (e.g. affecting physiological function of a targeted individual) to the socio-political

---

[3] James Andrew Lewis, 'Technological Competition and China' (Center for Strategic and International Studies, 30 November 2018) <https://www.csis.org/analysis/technological-competit ion-and-china> accessed 25 February 2023; L. Ferdinando, 'DoD Must Be More Agile In Technology Development, Official Says' (*DoD News*, 18 April 2018) <https://dod.defense.gov/News/Article/Arti cle/1497393/> accessed 25 February 2023; S. Maucione, 'DoD 2020 Budget Puts Heavy Emphasis on Development of Emerging Technologies' (*Federal News Radio*, March 13, 2019) <https://federalnews network.com/defense-main/2019/03/dod-2020-budget-puts-heavy-emphasis-on-development-of-emerging-technologies/amp/> accessed 25 February 2023.

[4] Zachary S. Davis and Michael Nacht (eds), *Strategic Latency: Red, White, and Blue; Managing the National and International Security Consequences of Disruptive Technologies* (Lawrence Livermore National Laboratory 2018).

scales (e.g. to manifest effects in response to threats, burdens and harms incurred by individual and/or groups), and (2) from the personal (e.g. affecting a specific individual or particular group of e.g. individuals) to the public dimensions in effect and outcome (e.g. by incurring broad-scale reactions and responses to key grey zone events).[5]

As noted in the Worldwide Threat Assessment of the US Intelligence Community, '[r]apid advances in biotechnology, including gene editing, synthetic biology, and neuroscience, are likely to present new economic, military, ethical, and regulatory challenges worldwide as governments struggle to keep pace'.[6] It is important to recognize various nations' dedicated enterprises in developing methods of grey zone operations (e.g. China and Russia), and that such endeavours may not comport with ethical systems, principles, and restrictions of the United States and its allies.[7] These differing ethical standards and practices, if and when coupled to states' highly centralized abilities to coordinate and synchronize activity of the so-called triple helix of government, academia, and the commercial sector, can create synergistic force-multiplying effects to mobilize resources and services that can be non-kinetically engaged.[8]

3. Technologies as enabling tools in grey zone engagements

Nation states, virtual nations, and state- and non-state actors' abilities to exert change are enhanced both by (1) radical levelling technologies (RLTs)—extant technologies that can be employed in novel ways to exert disruptive effects in certain contingencies (e.g. changes in social economic markets, vulnerabilities, and volatilities); and (2) emerging technologies (i.e. as threats, ETT) that can be utilized for their novel properties and capabilities to exercise multi-focal and multi-scalar disruptions to produce transformative and de-stabilizing effects in support of grey zone engagements. Emerging technologies can be particularly problematic given that they are new and may not be viewed or defined as threats,

[5] J. Giordano, 'Battlescape Brain: Engaging Neuroscience in Defense Operations' (2017) 3 HDIAC 13.

[6] Daniel R. Coats, 'Worldwide Threat Assessment of the US Intelligence Community to the Senate Select Committee on Intelligence' (29 January 2019) <https://www.intelligence.senate.gov/sites/default/files/documents/os-dcoats-012919.pdf> accessed 25 February 2023.

[7] Celeste Chen, Jacob Andriola, and James Giordano, 'Biotechnology, Commercial Veiling, and Implications for Strategic Latency: The Exemplar of Neuroscience and Neurotechnology Research and Development in China', in Davis and Nacht (n 4) 12; Guillermo Palchik, Celeste Chen, and James Giordano, 'Monkey Business? Development, Influence, and Ethics of Potentially Dual-Use Brain Science on the World Stage' (2018) 11 Neuroethics 111.

[8] Henry Etzkowitz and Loet Leydesdorff, 'The Dynamics of Innovation: From National Systems and "Mode 2" to a Triple Helix of University-Industry-Government Relations' (2000) 29 Research Policy 109.

240 ARENAS OF HYBRID AND GREY ZONE COMPETITION

and can evoke effects which, while potent, may not be easily recognizable or attributable to the technology or the actor(s).

To date, the threat of existing radiological, nuclear, and (high yield) explosive technologies has been and remains generally well surveilled and controlled. However, new and convergent innovations in the chemical, biological, cybersciences, and engineering fields are yielding tools and methods that at present are not completely or effectively addressed by the Biological Toxin and Weapons Convention (BTWC) or Chemical Weapons Convention (CWC).[9]

Our ongoing work is focused primarily upon the brain sciences.[10] As recently noted in the 'Worldwide Threat Assessment of the US Intelligence Community to the Senate Select Committee on Intelligence',[11] the neurosciences and technologies (neuroS/T) entail and obtain new technologies that can be applied to affect chemical and biological systems in both kinetic (e.g. chemical and biological 'warfare' that may sidestep definition—and governance—by the BTWC and/or CWC), or non-kinetic, grey zone ways (which fall outside of, and, therefore, are not explicitly constrained by the scope and auspices of the BTWC, CWC, or code(s) of conventional warfare).[12]

At present, neuroscience and technology (neuroS/T) is being used in military contexts:

- for diagnostics and treatments of medical conditions;
- to create human-machine networks for optimizing particular types and dimensions of operational performance of military and intelligence personnel; and
- to develop non-lethal and lethal weapons.

[9] J. Snow, 'Dealing with Virtual Nations: Operating at Speed in Technology Influenced Environments' (TRADOC Mad Scientists' meeting, National Intelligence University, Washington, DC, 27 August 2018); Daniel Gerstein and James Giordano, 'Re-Thinking the Biological and Toxin Weapons Convention?' (2017) 15 Health Security 638.

[10] See James Giordano and Rachel Wurzman, 'Neurotechnology as Weapons in National Intelligence and Defense' (2011) 2 Synesis 138; James Giordano (ed), *Neurotechnology in National Security and Defense: Technical Considerations, Neuroethical Concerns* (CRC Press 2015); Joseph DeFranco, Diane DiEuliis, and James Giordano, 'Rethinking Neuroweapons: Emerging Capabilities in Neuroscience and Neurotechnology' (2019) 8 PRISM 49; Joseph DeFranco, Maureen Rhemann, and James Giordano, 'The Emerging Neurobioeconomy: Implications for National Security' (2020) 18 Health Security 267.

[11] Coats (n 6).

[12] Diane DiEuliis and James Giordano, 'Why Gene Editors Like CRISPR/Cas May Be a Game-Changer for Neuroweapons' (2017) 15 Health Security 296; James Giordano, 'Weaponizing the Brain: Neuroscience Advancements Spark Debate' (2017) 6 National Defense 17; Christine Aicardi et al, 'Opinion on Responsible Dual Use from the Human Brain Project' (December 2018) <https://www.humanbrainproject.eu/en/follow-hbp/news/opinion-on-responsible-dual-use-from-the-human-brain-project/> accessed 25 February 2023; Chris Forsythe and James Giordano, 'On the Need for Neurotechnology in the National Intelligence and Defense Agenda: Scope and Trajectory' (2011) 2 Synesis 5; Malcolm Dando, *The Chemical and Biological Nonproliferation Regime after the Covid-19 Pandemic* (Palgrave Macmillan 2023).

DISRUPTIVE EFFECTS IN GREY ZONE ENGAGEMENTS   241

In the main, it is the latter two types of application that foster the most concerns. For example, a variety of pharmacological agents (e.g. stimulants, including amphetamine derivatives; eugeroics, such as modafinil; and nootropics, such as the racetams), and brain-machine interfaces (such as EEG-based neurofeedback, transcranial magnetic and electrical stimulation, and brain-computer interfaces) can be employed to modulate activity within identified neurological networks operative in cognitive and motor processes and functions to facilitate and/or optimize key performance elements instrumental to the training and capabilities of warfighters and intelligence operators.[13]

As well, neuroS/T can be weaponized to target neurological substrates and mechanisms that affect physiology, cognition, emotions, and behaviours. Such 'neuroweapons' include drugs to degrade physiologic and cognitive functions, and/or to alter emotional states to affect the desire or capacity for aggression and combat; organic toxins that can induce neuromuscular paralysis and death; microbial agents (e.g. bacteria and viruses, inclusive of 'bio-hacked', genetically modified organisms) that can incur various levels of morbidity—or mortality, and a number of technologies that can be used to alter sensory, perceptual, cognitive, and motoric functions. Moreover, recent developments in bioscience have enabled novel capability RLT and ETT that fortify and expand their potential utility and use in both kinetic and grey zone operations. Such developments include the following.

3.1 Gene editing

Apropos current events, the use of gene editing technologies and techniques to modify existing microorganisms,[14] and/or selectively alter human susceptibility to disease,[15] reveal the ongoing and iterative multinational interest in and weaponizable use(s) of emerging biotechnologies as instruments to produce 'precision pathologies' and incur 'immaculate destruction' of selected targets.[16] The advent of CRISPR/Cas-based gene editing methods, which can be used to quickly alter the molecular sequence of genetic material, and in these ways rapidly and easily modify components, systems and/or entire organisms have enabled a somewhat more facile approach and has re-enthused interest and

---

[13] For more information, see Giordano and Wurzman (n 10); Giordano (n 10).

[14] Diane DiEuliis and James Giordano, 'Gene editing using CRISPR/Cas9: Implications for Dual-Use and Biosecurity' (2017) 15 Protein and Cell 1.

[15] See e.g. Julia Belluz 'Is the CRISPR Baby Controversy the Start of a Terrifying New Chapter in Gene Editing?' (*Vox*, 22 January 2019) <https://www.vox.com/science-and-health/2018/11/30/18119589/crispr-technology-he-jiankui> accessed 25 February 2023.

[16] For a more in-depth review, see Joseph DeFranco et al, 'Emerging Technologies for Disruptive Effects in Non-kinetics Engagements' (2019) 6 *HDIAC* 48.

capabilities rendered by such techniques. Thousands of guide RNA sequences are broadly available, which can be used to direct genetic editing to modify the structural and functional components of proteins, cells, tissues, and whole biological entities, and these tools foster new research uses in a variety of health and scientific disciplines.[17] Pairing this new capability to target and study genetic material with other ETs (e.g. neuroscience) could engender the development of potentially hazardous genetic modifications.

Of course, gene editing has limitations. Designing genetically active molecules that can target and affect the DNA in the nucleus of a cell can be arduous. Constructing molecules that are permeable to natural barriers (the blood-brain barrier, cell membranes, etc.) can be difficult if they are large or chemically inapt. In some cases, these constraints can be overcome both by using ETs or other/ older gene editing techniques, and as CRISPR/Cas systems continue to increase in utility. For example, the Cas12 RNA-guided nuclease effector is a smaller and, in some cases, more functional version of Cas9 which increases the efficacy of CRISPR systems.

Indeed, older/other gene editing techniques may be used in conjunction with CRISPR/Cas systems to enable more precise genetic targeting. Many constraints of older techniques have been de-limited through the use of new(er) methods like transcription activator-like effector (TALE) and CRISPR/Cas gene modifying approaches that were developed for their simplicity and effectiveness within bacteria.

CRISPR/Cas nucleases can be easily programmed to target a DNA segment of interest by pairing them with guide RNA. Currently, CRISPR/Cas-systems are widely recognized as a superior gene editing technology. But like any molecular technique, CRISPR/Cas-based methods can be unsuccessful in vivo for numerous reasons. For instance, modifying genetic material can invoke cellular defence mechanisms to repair altered genes (sometimes rendering the modification null) or induce apoptosis (i.e. cell death). Additionally, limited cellular uptake of CRISPR can constrain effects and outcomes. These restrictions have been overcome in recent studies that have inhibited DNA damage caused by CRISPR/Cas9, or have used gene delivery vectors to enhance uptake and optimize results.

Extant unknowns of genomics, proteomics, and neuroscience can both limit CRISPR utility and/or lead to a host of unanticipated (but not necessarily unusable) effects that can be leveraged to influence public health and national security. For example, controlling (if not suppressing) off-target effects (i.e. 'side effects') is necessary for a successful gene editing system. However, while off-target mutations may be a problem for therapeutics or the enhancement of

---

[17] DiEuliis and Giordano (n 12).

organisms, such off-target manifestations might not be problematic (or in some cases may be desirable) when using gene editing technology to design a weapon to induce broad-ranging effects. To be sure, if intended objectives of morbidity or lethality were obtained, it is likely that other (non-morbid or non-lethal) off-target effects would be viewed as less important or disregarded altogether. Further, the use of a combinatory approach (i.e. examining all gene editing systems and/or technologies for their utility) may increase the ease of genetically modifying benign microbes and proteins to be pathogenic, and altering extant pathogens so as to make them more dangerous. These methods could be used to engineer bioagents that evade detection or attribution.

3.2 Biodata

CRISPR may also be used to perform rapid, comprehensive screens of specific genes and the phenotypes (i.e. structures and functions) they produce.[18] This information could be utilized to reveal ways that certain individuals and/or groups could be specifically targeted. We have referred to these various categories of information as 'biodata', noting that emerging technologies such as CRISPR, taken with multi-modal information from other forms of assessment (e.g. neuroimaging, biomarkers) have broadened the scope of potential variables that may be identified, accessed, assessed, and, perhaps, ultimately affected.[19] The 'digitization of biology' (i.e. information about the genetic code, translated proteins, and/ or related metadata) is an unexploited quarry of opportunity for any actor who wishes to specifically target an organism. There are concerns about breaches of individual privacy and how such biodata might be interpreted and used to incur certain biases in the ways that individuals or groups are viewed and/or treated. But the risk and threat of physical harms that could be incurred through access to such information must now also be considered.

In this light, biodata may be of even greater concern if and when neuropsychiatrically relevant. Such information could be used to identify individual and group susceptibilities and vulnerabilities to particular agents and effects, which may be instrumental in gene-edited production of novel and more precise microbes, toxins, antigens, or drugs. Moreover, (neuro)biodata can be manipulated to change individual and group medical records in ways that can influence the tenor and scope of clinical care, if not social, legal, and political regard.

---

[18] Katia Tarasava et al, 'CRISPR-Enabled Tools for Engineering Microbial Genomes and Phenotypes' (2018) 13 Biotechnology Journal 1.

[19] Diane DiEuliis, Charles D. Lutes, and James Giordano, 'Biodata Risks and Synthetic Biology: A Critical Juncture' (2018) 9 Journal of Bioterrorism and Biodefense 1.

244 ARENAS OF HYBRID AND GREY ZONE COMPETITION

3.3 Nanoengineering

Nanotechnology is a relatively new science that examines and engineers particles and devices at an atomic or molecular level (1–100 nm). Nanoscience and engineering have been, and are increasingly, viewed for their viability to create neurotoxic/neuropathologic agents.[20] A recent review has raised concerns about incomplete effectiveness of protective barriers against the penetrance of nanomaterials to the brain, and this may afford an opportunity for vectoring these substances to the cerebral space to exert a variety of uses.[21] Specifically, attention was focused upon the potential of nanomaterials to induce neuroinflammation, oxidative stress, and neuronal cell death and to alter production of various neuroactive chemicals and affect network properties of the brain.

Such evidence shows that nanoparticles can access the central nervous system via a number of routes. Uptake of nanoparticles through the nasal cavity can directly reach the brain through the olfactory tract, and because neurons have the capability to assimilate nanoparticles, the effect can spread throughout the brain. Pulmonary intake involves nanoparticles first crossing the lung-blood barrier, and subsequently the blood-brain barrier, to affect the nervous system. Translocation of nanoparticles from the gut and/or skin to the brain have also been documented, but the efficiency and potency of those routes are less understood.[22]

Current applications of nanotechnology include (1) the insertion of nanodevices to remotely control organisms; (2) creation of nanocarriers/ capsules which could be used to transport molecules (carrying chemicals, proteins, or DNA/RNA) across membranes and the blood-brain barrier to target specific tissues or organs; and (3) development of novel neurological molecules that are less (or not) susceptible to current countermeasures and/or therapeutics. Nanomaterials can also be employed to enhance other ETTs. As stated earlier, natural barriers can inhibit or reduce the penetrance and action of CRISPR molecules in the brain, and nanocarriers have been developed to increase the assimilation of CRISPR molecules into targeted cells. Thus, although still under-exploited for its kinetic and non-kinetic, grey zone potential, nanotechnology is being explored for its dual or direct military use by a number of nations—including the United States.[23]

---

[20] Giordano (n 10); DeFranco et al (n 10).

[21] Anna Bencsik, Philippe Lestaevel, and Irina Guseva Canu, 'Nano-and Neurotoxicology: An Emerging discipline' (2018) 160 Progress in Neurobiology 45.

[22] Ibid.

[23] For more information on nanoengineering programs, see Hitoshi Nasu and Robert McLaughlin (eds), *New Technologies and the Law of Armed Conflict* (T. M. C. Asser Press 2014); and references cited in DeFranco et al (n 14).

3.4 Current conventions, and the dilemma of control

Obviously, research, production, and stockpiling of defined neuro-microbiologicals, and select chemicals and toxins are constrained and/or proscribed by the extant BTWC and CWC. However, other neurobiological substances (e.g. pharmaceutical formulations of neurotropic drugs, organic neurotoxins, and bio-regulators) and neurotechnologies (e.g. neuromodulatory devices) developed and utilized as medical products might not be, and these are readily and commercially available.[24] As noted in a 2008 report of the National Research Council of the National Academies of Sciences entitled Emerging Cognitive Neuroscience and Related Technologies, products intended for the health market can be, and often are, studied and developed for possible employment in military applications (e.g. to optimize or degrade aspects of human performance).[25] In the United States, any such activity in federally funded programs would be subject to oversight in accordance with dual-use research of concerns (DURC) policies (of 2012 and 2014), reflecting the general tenor of the BTWC and CWC to date.[26]

But while such oversight and regulation constrain dual-use neuroS/T research in participatory states, it may provide opportunities for non-participatory countries and/or non-state actors to make in-roads in such enterprises to achieve a new balance of power.[27] NeuroS/T is an international endeavour, and a number of nations are engaged in dedicated programs of neuroS/T research with defence applications that may exert global strategic influence. Moreover, neuroS/T R/D need not be illicit; exemptions for health and routine experimental use may foster a grey zone within which investigations for viability and employment as weapons may be undertaken.

The dedication of private and/or governmentally supported industrial efforts to neuroS/T R/D could also enable and (at least be argued to) justify postures and protocols of diminished transparency, as commercial interests can be shielded as means to protect proprietary interests and intellectual property. Under such veils, dual-use agendas can be fostered and developed. An additional concern is that neurobiological and neurochemical substances and certain neurotechnologies can be obtained and/or developed (i.e. 'bio-hacked') with relative ease by individual non-State actors who may be supported by state-endorsed venture capital, and who may operate without regard for regulations

---

[24] James Giordano, 'The Neuroweapons Threat' (2016) 72 Bulletin of the Atomic Scientists 1.

[25] Jonathan D. Moreno, *Mind Wars: Brain Science and the Military in the 21st Century* (Bellevue Literary Press 2012).

[26] See National Institute of Health Office of Science Policy <https://osp.od.nih.gov/policies/biosafety-and-biosecurity-policy/> accessed 25 February 2023.

[27] Forsythe and Giordano (n 12).

defined by the current BTWC, thereby creating further opportunistic windows for influence.

Indubitably, there are novel risks associated with misuse of the information and capabilities conferred by RLTs and ETT. It should be presumed that access to such information and tools by bad actors is high, as many databases are openly shared, and those that are not shared have been, or may be, vulnerable to being hacked.[28] Access to this information and capability increasingly enables grey zone engagements, thereby fortifying the need to identify, meet, assess, and counter novel threats. Exemplary of such enterprise is the development and growth of a relatively new discipline, 'cyber biosecurity', which focuses upon evaluation, mitigation, and prevention of unwanted surveillance, intrusions, and malicious action(s) within cyber systems of the biomedical sciences.[29] However, for cyber biosecurity—or any program of coordinated assessment, mitigation, and prevention—to exert a sustained and iterative effect, it must exist within and be synergized by a larger infrastructure of dedicated effort.

4. Towards address, mitigation, and prevention

Without philosophical understanding of and technical insight to the ways that grey zone engagements entail and affect civilian, political, and military domains, coordinated assessment and response to any such engagement(s) becomes procedurally complicated and politically difficult. Therefore, we propose and advocate increasingly dedicated efforts to enable sustained, successful surveillance, assessment, mitigation, and prevention of development and use of RLTs and ETT in national security. As we have claimed, we believe that it will be increasingly important to analyse, quantify, and predict how particular RLTs and ETTs can, and likely will be, employed by foreign competitors and adversaries in both non-kinetic and kinetic ways. Currently, the models used by the United States and its allies tend to favour a somewhat limited timescale and linear pattern of S/T development. And, if/when more extensive timescales are used, linear modelling and limited analysis of the scope of effects can constrain accuracy and reliability of predictions.

Current research and progress in S/T is assuming a more exponential increase, which reflects contemporary competitors' more long-term visions, if not aspirations. Thus, we feel that it is nearsighted to solely focus on five- to ten-year developments. Yet, it may be that the lenses currently used for more far-sighted

---

[28] DiEuliis et al (n 19).

[29] Jean Peccoud et al, 'Cyberbiosecurity: From Naive Trust to Risk Awareness' (2018) 36 Trends in Biotechnology 4.

views tend to be restricted in scope. This is problematic because such models can fail to recognize and appreciate the ways that both short- and long-term enterprises may be used to evoke strategically latent, multi-focal, disruptive effects to establish balances of power in the future.

To this point, we advocate expanding and improving the focus of the 'predictability horizon' to better perceive three vistas of future S/T development and use; these are the: (1) vista of probability (present to five years); (2) vista of possibility (six to fifteen years); and (3) vista of potentiality (sixteen to thirty years). We assert that in light of current trends in global S/T research and development, it is important to examine what is probable, and from such probabilities, what is possible thereafter. Identification and depiction of possibilities (and the multidimensional factors that would be necessary for their actualization) enables a more salient view to better gauge the potentialities that could be realized sixteen to thirty years into the future.

Of course, more proximate developments are easier to define and predict. Moving farther into the future, extant and emerging technologies can foster a greater variety of uses and effects. The potential uses and influences of S/T are more difficult to accurately model due to (1) diverse socio-political and economic pushing and pulling forces (in society and science), and (2) the contingencies of socio-culture and political variables that establish 'fertile' grounds for viable uses of S/T. Using a solely inductive (i.e. advancing) approach to S/T analysis and prediction may be inadequate. Rather, we recommend combining inductive methods with deductive (i.e. retrospective) analytics that are aimed at identifying potential uses and values of S/T (and the multi-varied factors required for its articulation) in the sixteen- to thirty-year future time frame, and working backwards to address and model what possibilities and probabilities would be necessary to allow such long-term occurrences. We refer to this (deductive-inductive) approach as integrative S/T intelligence (InS/TINT) that engages temporal and socio-cultural trends, contingencies, and necessities to define, analyse, model, and predict strategically latent S/T developments, uses, and effects on the global stage.

Such an enterprise requires (1) ongoing assessment of current S/T, research trends, and implicitly and/or explicitly stated long-term goals of competitors and/or possible adversaries; (2) multinational cooperation to monitor the development of S/T that could be weaponized; and (3) establishing more acute, improved perspectives of non-kinetic engagements and the viable roles that S/T can play in leveraging their effects. Toward these goals, the United States and its allies must recognize and assess both the explicit/overt and more tacit aspects of research and use activities of several countries that already have enterprises dedicated to dual- and/or direct-use of S/T in warfare, intelligence, and national security (WINS) operations. This will mandate deeper surveillance of international S/T research and agendas to accurately evaluate both near- and longer-term activities, progress, and trajectories. Surveillance should focus on (1) university and research sites; (2) the extent and directions of private and public support in S/T; (3) efforts towards recruitment of researchers; (4) S/T commercialization; (5) current/future military postures; and (6) current/future market space occupation and leveraging potential.

As we have previously described, this will demand conjoined efforts from multiple national resources (that are beyond a whole-of-government approach) We posit that implementing these goals will require coordinated focal activities to (1) increase awareness of radical leveraging and emerging technologies that can be utilized as grey zone threats; (2) quantify the likelihood and extent of threat(s) posed; (3) counter identified threats; and (4) prevent or delay adversarial development of future threats Towards this end, we opine the need for a whole-of-nation approach to mobilize the organizations, resources, and personnel required to meet other nations' synergistic triple helix capabilities to develop and non-kinetically engage RLTs and ETT.

Utilizing this approach will necessitate establishment of:

- A network of offices to coordinate academic and governmental research centers to study and to evaluate current and near-future grey zone threats.
- Methods to qualitatively and quantitatively identify threats and the potential timeline and extent of their development.
- A variety of means for protecting the United States and allied interests from these emerging threats. ·
- Computational approaches to create and to support analytic assessments of threats across a wide range of emerging technologies that may be leveraged and afford purchase in grey zone engagements.

5. Conclusion

In light of other nations' activities in this domain, we view grey zone deployment of emerging technologies as a clear, present, and viable threat. In this light, we opine that the type of program that we have proposed is crucial. Critical to such a program is development of guidelines that liberal democracies could employ towards ethical use of current and emerging biotechnologies that would guide both responses to their utilization by adversaries, as well as their own (offensive) uses, in particular settings, and under specific conditions.[30]

---

[30] James Giordano, Chris Forsythe, and James Olds, 'Neuroscience, Neurotechnology and National Security: The Need for Preparedness and an Ethics of Responsible Action' (2010) 1 American Journal of Bioethics-Neuroscience 35.

Dedication and sustainability of programs of this sort will require ongoing domestic funding and participation and support of like-minded, multinational allies. But we perceive such effort and commitment to be worthwhile, important, and necessary, as the threat of emerging technologies is clear—both at present and for the future. As we have stated in the past, and reiterate here, it is not a question of if such methods will be utilized, but rather when, to what extent, and by which group(s). Moreover, and perhaps more importantly, the question is if the United States and its allies will be prepared for these threats when—or before—they are rendered.

Authors' Note

The opinions expressed in this piece are those of the authors, and do not necessarily reflect those of the US Department of Defense, US Special Operations Command. and/or the organizations with which the authors are involved. This chapter was adapted, with permission, from the authors' publications: Joseph DeFranco et al, 'Emerging Technologies for Disruptive Effects in Non-kinetics Engagements' (2019) 6 HDIAC 48; and J. DeFranco, D. DiEuliis, L. R. Bremseth, J. J. Snow, and J. Giordano, 'Emerging Technologies for Disruptive Effects in Non-Kinetic Engagements' (2019) 6 HDIAC Currents 49–54; and J. Giordano, 'Battlescape Brain: Engaging Neuroscience in Defense Operations' (2017) 3 HDIAC 13. Support for this work was provided in part by J-5 Donovan Group, USSOCOM (JD, JGCSCI (LRB; JG), and Georgetown University Medical Center (JG).

12

The Maritime Domain

David Letts

1. Introduction

In recent years, the maritime domain has been subject to a number of activities in different regions throughout the world that have been characterized as being 'hybrid threats' occurring in the maritime 'grey zone'. Much of the focus on these hybrid threats has centred on activities that have occurred in the South China Sea, but that region is not the only maritime space where vagueness and uncertainty in relation to the legal characterization of a particular activity has been present. The purpose of conducting these activities is to deliberately introduce lack of legal clarity regarding the manner in which the activity can be validly assessed, with the result that choosing an appropriate response becomes operationally, politically, and legally challenging.

The aim of this chapter is to examine the nature of hybrid threats that are situated in the maritime grey zone and assess the legal dimensions of the consequences that arise from this type of activity. The chapter will concentrate on actions taken by States, rather than non-State actors, and begin by examining some of the key concepts and issues related to both hybrid threats and grey zone activity through the lens of what has been termed 'political warfare'. The next part of the chapter will attempt, as far as possible, to define the essential components of maritime hybrid threats and then undertake a similar appraisal for the maritime grey zone and operations that occur in that zone. In order to inform this analysis, the chapter will also look at a number of examples that are often cited as representing either hybrid threats or maritime grey zone operations or both. After dealing with definitional aspects, the chapter will assess how the law of the sea deals with hybrid threats and maritime grey zone activity, again using case studies to illustrate the issues. The final parts of the chapter will consider elements of the actions of powerful States that have used hybridity and grey zone operations to achieve their aims, provide some observations regarding whether there is a unique element about the maritime domain that makes it particularly susceptible to these types of activities, and consider whether new solutions and responses might be needed to counter the impact of these activities. A short conclusion will complete the chapter.

David Letts, *The Maritime Domain* In: *Hybrid Threats and Grey Zone Conflict.* Edited by: Mitt Regan and Aurel Sari, Oxford University Press. © Oxford University Press 2024. DOI: 10.1093/oso/9780197744772.003.0012

2. Political warfare, hybrid threats and the grey zone–some introductory thoughts

Understanding what the term 'political warfare' means can be confusing. There is some support for the idea that political warfare includes grey zone operations or hybrid threats as well as information warfare and subversion.[1] The aim of these operations is to achieve strategic effects without using kinetic force. In such cases, the overarching purpose of political warfare is to shield the real or dominant purpose of an activity, so that any response options that are being considered by the affected State become obscured and difficult to determine. A key means of achieving this purpose is to use obfuscation and imprecise characterization of both the activity itself and the legal classification that should be allocated to it.

In relation to maritime activity, the types of threats and operations that can be classified as political warfare that have occurred in maritime regions include, for example, States asserting they have sovereignty over certain maritime features (or sovereign rights) in circumstances where the validity of such claims is clearly contested, the involvement of a range of vessels in activities that have an unclear or questionable legal basis, and the employment of a variety of de-centralized warfare or quasi-military operations that exploit an opponent's weakness. Further discussion of these examples will occur later in this chapter.

Of course, political warfare is not confined to the maritime domain; nor is the ability to undertake activities that can be categorized as being elements of political warfare confined to States, as the capabilities of non-State actors are also rising in this regard. Recognition that these activities pose challenges to existing norms of international behaviour has also occurred. For example, the Chief of the Australian Defence Force, General Angus Campbell, raised the need for vigilance in dealing with modern threats to order and stability during a speech in June 2019 when he stated that a 'new, modernised version of political warfare may have already begun'.[2] General Campbell identified activities such as 'information campaigns, cyber operations and theft of intellectual property, coercion and propaganda'[3] as being the key indicators of political warfare, and these types of activity are also some of the essential elements of hybrid threats and grey zone

---

[1] Compare the different approaches of one author to this issue. See T. Paterson, 'The "Grey Zone": Political Warfare Is Back' (*Lowy Interpreter*, 3 September 2019) <https://www.lowyinstit ute.org/the-interpreter/grey-zone-political-warfare-back> accessed on 25 February 2023 and T. Paterson and L. Hanley (2020) 'Political Warfare in the Digital Age: Cyber Subversion, Information Operations and 'Deep Fakes' (2020) 74 Australian Journal of International Affairs 439.

[2] B. Nicholson, 'ADF Chief: West faces a New Threat from 'Political Warfare' (*ASPI Strategist*, 14 June 2019) <https://www.aspistrategist.org.au/adf-chief-west-faces-a-new-threat-from-political-warfare/> accessed on 25 February 2023.

[3] Ibid.

operations. Similarly, a few years earlier General Joseph Dunford, who was the US Chairman of the Joint Chiefs of Staff at the time, noted that:

> It's clear that adapting to the evolving character of war in the 21st century is going to require significant changes to our planning, our organization, and our command and control constructs . . . and we're already—to be honest with you, we're already behind. We're already behind in adapting to the changing character of war today, in so many ways.[4]

The concept of political warfare is not a new invention, even though its characteristics might have significantly evolved with the advances in technology that have occurred in the late twentieth and early twenty-first centuries. In fact, the notion that a State might use 'all the means at a nation's command, short of war, to achieve its national objectives'[5] has been recognized since at least 1948 when George Kennan produced his well-known memorandum for the US Department of State: *The Inauguration of Organized Political Warfare.*[6] Kennan's memorandum identified that political warfare can be 'both covert and overt . . . [and] . . . range from such overt actions as political alliances, economic measures (as ERP), and "white" propaganda to such covert operations as clandestine support of "friendly" foreign elements, "black" psychological warfare and even encouragement of underground resistance in hostile states'.[7]

If it is accepted that the term 'political warfare' represents an overarching concept that covers both hybridity and grey zone activity, it can be further postulated that the two constituent terms are really the areas that have been at the forefront of recent concerns regarding the new wave of threats being faced by States. Looking at just the grey zone, there is ample evidence of how concerned States are about the impact and effect of grey zone activities as well as the number of such activities that are occurring globally. For example, on 2 July 2020, the Australian Government released the *2020 Defence Strategic Update*[8] and this document makes numerous references to the threats that arise from an expansion of grey zone activities in the Indo-Pacific region, and sets out a series of

---

[4] General Joseph Dunford's remarks at the National Defense University graduation, Washington, DC (10 June 2016) <https://www.jcs.mil/Media/Speeches/Article/797847/gen-dunfords-remarks-at-the-national-defense-university-graduation/> accessed on 25 February 2023.

[5] US Department of State, Policy Planning Staff, 'The Inauguration of Organized Political Warfare' Memorandum of April 30, 1948, in *Foreign Relations of the United States, 1945–1950: Emergence of the Intelligence Establishment*, edited by C. Thomas Thorne Jr. and D. S. Patterson (US Government Printing Office 1996) 668.

[6] Ibid.

[7] Ibid.

[8] Australian Government Department of Defence, '2020 Defence Strategic Update' (2020) <https://www.defence.gov.au/about/strategic-planning/2020-defence-strategic-update > accessed on 13 November 2023.

responses that the Australian government will take in mitigation. In relation to the types of grey zone activities that have been conducted, the *Update* contends that these have been both 'military and non-military forms of assertiveness and coercion aimed at achieving strategic goals without provoking conflict'.[9] The *Update* further notes that grey zone activities are being 'integrated into statecraft and are being applied in ways that challenge sovereignty and habits of cooperation . . . [including] . . . challenges to the long established and mutually beneficial security partnerships that Australia has with many countries, including in the Indo-Pacific'.[10] These concerns have been heightened in 2022 as a result of the arrangements that have been made between the governments of Solomon Islands and China for security cooperation.

It would be disingenuous not to recognize that the use of terms that encompass 'hybrid' war/threat and 'grey zone' activities or operations are not without criticism. In fact, in one recent publication the authors have argued 'that the adoption of [these] two prominent and fashionable theoretical terms and their various iterations . . . is an example of an American failure to think clearly about political, military and strategic issues and their vitally important connections'.[11] The same authors conclude their analysis by suggesting that the terms 'hybrid war' and the 'grey zone' will soon follow other 'buzzwords' 'into oblivion' and that the present use of these terms 'is not merely unhelpful, it is dangerous'.[12] While the conclusion reached by these two authors has some attraction in terms of simplifying the categorization of ill-defined concepts, it is likely that the continued use of terms that encompass 'hybrid' concepts and refer to the 'grey zone' is unlikely to cease.

For completeness, there is one further topic that will be briefly addressed in this preliminary section of the chapter: 'lawfare'. Major General (ret'd) Charles Dunlap is widely attributed with being responsible for bringing the concept of lawfare into regular use among academic, government/military and media commentators in recent times. Dunlap himself advised that the 'term lawfare has existed for some time, but its modern usage first appeared in a paper . . . [he] . . . wrote for Harvard's Kennedy School in 2001'.[13] Writing years later in 2017, Dunlap makes the point that the definition of lawfare has evolved

---

[9] Ibid. 5. The 'Update' at 12 provides examples of grey zone activities that include: the use of paramilitary forces, militarization of disputed features, exploiting influence, interference operations and the coercive use of trade and economic levers.

[10] Ibid. 12

[11] D. Stoker and C. Whiteside, 'Blurred Lines: Gray-Zone Conflict and Hybrid War–Two Failures of American Strategic Thinking' (2020) 73 Naval War College Review 4.

[12] Ibid. 29

[13] C. Dunlap, 'Lawfare 101: A Primer' (2017) 97 Military Review 8, 9 referring to C. Dunlap, 'Law and Military Interventions: Preserving Humanitarian values in 21st Century Conflicts' (paper presented at Humanitarian Challenges in Military Intervention Conference, Washington, DC, 29 November 2001).

over time but he posits that lawfare is 'best understood as the use of law as a means of accomplishing what might otherwise require the use of traditional military force'.[14] Lawfare can be used to achieve both positive and negative outcomes for a State and in fact Dunlap ascribes ideological neutrality to the term, by noting that 'it is a weapon that can be used for good and evil, depending upon who is wielding it and for what reasons'.[15]

Criticism of using the term 'lawfare' has also occurred, with Aurel Sari recently writing that 'the concept suffers from several limitations'[16] including not being confined to situations of war, imprecision in terms of standards to be applied, and openness to abuse through discrediting 'perfectly routine legal claims by tarnishing them with the brush of illegitimacy'.[17] An argument could be made that many elements of China's 'Position Paper'[18] regarding jurisdiction of the Arbitral Tribunal in the South China Sea Arbitration[19] is an example of the latter. There may be some validity to these criticisms, but it is also true to note that the elements of lawfare that are most often cited have a solid position alongside both hybridity and grey zone activity.[20]

So, on that basis, the next part of the chapter will seek to provide some definitional assistance in order to obtain an understanding of what constitutes a hybrid threat as well as the grey zone when interpreted in the context of the maritime domain.

3. Maritime hybrid threats: some definitional issues

The concepts of 'hybrid threat' and 'hybrid warfare' encompass 'the use of nonconventional methods, such as cyber warfare, as part of a multi-domain warfighting approach to disrupt and disable an opponent's actions without

---

[14] Dunlap, 'Lawfare 101: A Primer' (n 13) 9.

[15] Ibid.

[16] Aurel Sari, 'Legal Resilience in an Era of Grey Zone Conflicts and Hybrid Threats' (2020) 33 Cambridge Review of International Affairs 846, 852.

[17] Ibid.

[18] Ministry of Foreign Affairs, the People's Republic of China, 'Position Paper of the Government of the People's Republic of China on the Matter of Jurisdiction in the South China Sea Arbitration Initiated by the Republic of the Philippines' (7 December 2014) <https://www.fmprc.gov.cn/mfa_eng/zxxx_662805/t1217147.shtml> accessed on 25 February 2023.

[19] *In the Matter of an Arbitration before An Arbitral Tribunal Constituted under Annex VII to the 1982 United Nations Convention on the Law of the Sea between The Republic of the Philippines and the People's Republic of China*, PCA Case no. 2013-19, Award on Jurisdiction and Admissibility (29 October 2015); *In the Matter of an Arbitration before an Arbitral Tribunal Constituted under Annex VII to the 1982 United Nations Convention on the Law of the Sea between The Republic of the Philippines and the People's Republic of China*, PCA Case no. 2013-19, Award (12 July 2016) (hereafter SCS Arbitration).

[20] See generally the examples provided in Dunlap, 'Law and Military Interventions' (n 13) 4–6.

256 ARENAS OF HYBRID AND GREY ZONE COMPETITION

engaging in open hostilities'.[21] It has been suggested that achieving consensus in relation to the definition of hybrid warfare is not yet possible as the 'definition is flexible at best and tailored to suit the actor's wider purposes'.[22] In this sense, hybrid warfare has been described as '. . . an emerging, but ill-defined notion in conflict studies . . . [that] . . . refers to the use of unconventional methods as part of a multi-domain warfighting approach'.[23] The lack of consensus on any agreed definition of what is meant by 'hybrid' provides assistance to those who employ this methodology to hide the true legal nature of the actions they are taking.

Despite whatever concerns may exist regarding whether or not a settled definition can be found, some common elements that describe 'hybridity' do exist, including the use of conventional and unconventional forces, irregular tactics, subversion, coercion, foreign interference, and potential linkages to criminal activities. Another characteristic is that while hybrid measures are intended to be provocative and can also encompass an escalating dimension, they are still primarily 'designed to be non-kinetic and non-lethal . . . and they do not necessitate or justify a warlike response'.[24] The overall aim of hybrid threats and activity is to deceive an opponent through a simultaneous combination of conventional and unconventional operations anywhere along the conflict continuum.

Hybrid threats can emanate from distinctly overt action by States, covert activities that are undertaken by State agencies which are not easily characterized as being attributable to a State, as well as activities that are conducted by non-State actors. Importantly, as noted above, hybrid threats can be found to exist throughout the entire spectrum of conflict, regardless of any concerns regarding whether or not there is any general acceptance of what now constitutes that 'spectrum'.[25] This means that hybrid threats could arise from a range of non-kinetic operations that fall well short of meeting the threshold for armed conflict all the way through to operations that can be categorized as comprising conventional warfare. If looked at in this way, hybrid threats can be viewed as occupying a

---

[21] S. Bachmann, A. Dowse, and H. Gunneriusson, 'Competition Short of War–How Russia's Hybrid and Grey-Zone Warfare Are a Blueprint for China's Global Power Ambitions' (2019) 1 Australian Journal of Defence and Strategic Studies 41.

[22] Ibid. 43. See also E. Buchanan, 'Hybrid Warfare: Australia's (Not So) New Normal' (*ASPI Strategist*, 9 May 2019) <https://www.aspistrategist.org.au/hybrid-warfare-australias-not-so-new-normal/> accessed on 25 February 2023, where it is argued that the term 'hybrid warfare sounds very postmodern, but it's nothing new'.

[23] A. Dowse and S. D. Bachmann, 'Explainer: What Is "Hybrid Warfare" and What Is Meant by the "Grey Zone"?' (*The Conversation*, 17 June 2019) <https://theconversation.com/explainer-what-is-hybrid-warfare-and-what-is-meant-by-the-grey-zone-118841> accessed on 25 February 2023.

[24] Paterson (n 1).

[25] See generally the discussion in F. G. Hoffman, 'Examining Complex Forms of Conflict: Gray Zone and Hybrid Challenges' (2018) 7 PRISM 30, esp. 31, where Hoffman posits that the US security community 'lacks' a 'well-understood taxonomy describing the elements that constitute the "continuum of conflict"'. Compare Hoffman's criticism with the detailed analysis of conflict classification, including case studies, in E. Wilmshurst (ed), International Law and the Classification of Conflicts (OUP 2012)

continuing position across the full spectrum of conflict that simply changes its nature depending upon where on the spectrum any given activity actually falls. An example of the use of hybrid measures that often appears in the media is the approach taken by Russia towards the Ukraine prior to the commencement of hostilities in February 2022. It has been assessed that Russia has used 'a combination of activities, including disinformation, economic manipulation, use of proxies and insurgencies, diplomatic pressure and military actions'[26] to achieve desired outcomes. It is possible that the failure of these activities to achieve their desired aim contributed to the much more direct action that has occurred since February 2022.

Following this approach, it can be asserted that maritime hybrid threats include a range of activities situated along the spectrum of conflict that are designed to exploit the vulnerabilities of accepted norms of international law so that an advantage can be obtained against an opponent in the maritime domain. An example that is often cited in the maritime domain is the actions that China has taken in the South China Sea, where the adoption of a hybrid strategy to gain control over a number of maritime features over the past decade has resulted in what is essentially a *fait accompli* being achieved by China in terms of the occupation of some key artificial installations. However, definitional confusion has the potential to arise in relation to the use of this example as these same Chinese actions have also been described as being part of the grey zone,[27] so clarification of this point, using the same example, will occur in the following section.

4. Defining the maritime grey zone

A threshold question to consider is whether a maritime grey zone can ever actually exist. If a legal positivist view is adopted, then scope for recognition of any grey zone is reduced—if not actually eliminated altogether. Although perhaps this view is rather simplistic, it has some attraction in the sense that the grey zone, or at least grey zone warfare, is really a legal classification and threshold issue that must have an end point where a decision on classification is made. If that approach is adopted, then once the applicable threshold for armed conflict has been reached, regardless of whether it is an international[28] or non-international

---

[26] Dowse and Bachmann (n 23).

[27] Australian Government Department of Defence (n 8), 12.

[28] Common Article 2 of the four Geneva Conventions of 1949: Geneva Convention for the Amelioration of the Condition of the Wounded and Sick in Armed Forces in the Field (12 August 1949) 75 UNTS 31; Geneva Convention for the Amelioration of the Condition of Wounded, Sick and Shipwrecked Members of Armed Forces at Sea (12 August 1949) 75 UNTS 85; Geneva Convention Relative to the Treatment of Prisoners of War (12 August 1949) 75 UNTS 135; Geneva Convention Relative to the Protection of Civilian Persons in Time of War (12 August 1949) 75 UNTS 287.

258 ARENAS OF HYBRID AND GREY ZONE COMPETITION

armed conflict,[29] then any pretence at the existence of a grey zone will disappear. Conversely, if the applicable threshold is not reached, then the situation will be characterized as one where methods of response that fall short of those that can be legitimately used during armed conflict will need to be employed.

The great difficulty in adopting a positivist approach, and claiming that classification is simply a matter of reaching a decision, is that there is no general agreement on *whose* decision has the ultimate authority in terms of conflict classification. The most common approach to answering this question is to accept that States will be the ultimate decision makers regarding whether or not any given situation has reached the required threshold for the laws of armed conflict to apply, although courts and tribunals also have a role in assisting with the interpretation of such situations.[30] The final observation to be made on the issue of *who* can decide on conflict classification is to note that the United Nations Security Council may play a role in this regard if the wording of a particular UN Security Council Resolution is sufficiently clear on the point. A relatively recent example where this occurred is provided by UNSCR 2098 (2013) which referred, inter alia, to 'recurring cycles of conflict and persistent violence by armed groups' as being part of the justification behind authorizing the deployment of the "Intervention Brigade" to 'carry out targeted offensive operations . . . in strict compliance with international law, including international humanitarian law'.[31] The Resolution, in effect, determined that an armed conflict existed in the Democratic Republic of the Congo and authorized the use of military force, in accordance with international humanitarian law, to 'neutralize' the armed groups that were operating in opposition to the government.

Another preliminary observation regarding the grey zone relates to trying to obtain some precision around the use of the term 'grey zone' itself, and in particular to clarify its application to maritime activities. One way in which 'grey zone' could be used is to describe an *activity* that takes place in the maritime domain that is below the threshold at which it could be considered that the law of armed conflict applies.[32] Such an activity might nevertheless represent a clear intention

---

[29] Common Article 3 of the four Geneva Conventions of 1949.

[30] See generally C. Dwyer and T. McCormack, 'Conflict Characterisation', in R. *Routledge Handbook on the Law of Armed Conflict*, edited by Liivoja and T. McCormack, 50–70 (Routledge 2016); see also S. Vite, 'Typology of Armed Conflicts in International Humanitarian Law: Legal Concepts and Actual Situations' (2009) 91 International Review of the Red Cross 69. For an assessment of the role played by courts and tribunals in the maritime domain, see R. McLaughlin and D. Stephens, 'International Humanitarian Law in the Maritime Context: Conflict Characterization in Judicial and Quasi-Judicial Contexts', in *Applying International Humanitarian Law in Judicial and Quasi-Judicial Bodies: International and Domestic Aspects*, edited by D. Jinks et al (T.M.C. Asser Press 2014) 103; *Case Concerning Military and Paramilitary Activities in and against Nicaragua (Nicaragua v. USA)* (Merits) (1986) ICJ Rep. 14, paras. 216–220.

[31] UN Security Council Resolution 2098 (28 March 2013), paras. 9 and 12(b)

[32] It was noted earlier that this approach has recently been adopted by the Australian Government Department of Defence (n 8).

on the part of a State to obtain territorial or political advantage at the expense of another State (or States).

Examples that are often cited as maritime grey zone activities include the use of vessels that are not immediately recognizable as State vessels, such as fishing vessels, to achieve political aims of a State as well as using such vessels to undertake quasi-law enforcement activities. These types of activities have a consequential impact on intervention for law enforcement purposes and the use of appropriate levels of force as well as between the use of force and any situation that could be considered an armed attack which might trigger the application of the law of armed conflict. Similarly, the continued use of coercive tactics by vessels that may seem to be operating outside the direction or control of State authorities is another way in which grey zone activities might occur. Claims of sovereignty over territory, maritime features, maritime zones, and/or claims regarding the existence of sovereign rights over certain maritime zones can all be an underlying aspect of a maritime grey zone campaign.

These 'grey' activities can be situated anywhere along the spectrum of possible conflict with uncertainty arising as to whether or not they fall on one side or the other of a particular legal threshold. For example, some of these 'grey' activities would fall outside the scope of armed conflict, and therefore below the threshold at which a State might feel compelled to respond with military force, while other activities would be categorized as falling above the threshold and therefore a military response could be warranted and legally justified. This uncertainty is no doubt one of the major attractions of such activities for some States.

The term 'maritime grey zone' can also be used to refer to the *area* of uncertainty within which a particular activity falls. It is within this *area* that exploitation of uncertainty about whether or not a particular activity is, or is not, above or below one of the variety of legal thresholds that form the basis for characterization of such activities takes place.[33] The grey zone, understood in this way, has been described as 'a metaphorical state of being between war and peace, where an aggressor aims to reap either political or territorial gains associated with overt military action without crossing the threshold of open warfare with a powerful adversary'.[34]

In either case, the primary purpose of States (and non-State actors) using the maritime grey zone to describe either an *activity* or an *area* is to obscure the true character of whatever behaviour is taking place in that location, and as a result create legal uncertainty regarding what responses can justifiably be made in relation to that behaviour.

---

[33] See H. Nasu, 'Challenges of Hybrid Warfare to the Implementation of International Humanitarian Law in the Asia-Pacific', in *Asia-Pacific Perspectives on International Humanitarian Law*, edited by S. Linton, T. McCormack, and S. Sivakumaran (Cambridge University Press 2019) 224.

[34] A. Singh, *Deciphering Grey-Zone Operations in Maritime-Asia* (ORF 2018) 2

One result of this uncertainty is that the achievement of kinetic effects through the deployment of military weapons systems are usually peripheral notions in the grey zone, as the overwhelming emphasis is placed on operations that do not involve the use of lethal force but nevertheless include 'a well worked out chain of maritime power elements up to and including the presence of combat forces'.[35]

In summary, the term 'grey zone' has been used to describe two distinct concepts. First, the discrete *activities* employed by a number of States whereby indirect actions have been the way in which they have sought to obtain an advantage over other States without the need to use the more traditional means and methods of warfare.[36] Second, to describe a legal grey zone or *area* that arises from the uncertainty regarding threshold and conflict classification that flows from certain types of activities, including those that can be characterized as hybrid threats. Further complications arise from the argument put forward by Cormac and Aldrich that 'the rapidly proliferating literature on "grey", "hybrid", and "non-liner warfare" is confused and references a bewildering range of military, political, and economic developments associated with the changing nature of war over several decades'.[37]

5. The intersection between hybrid threats and the grey zone

Earlier in this chapter, we mentioned the example of Chinese action in the South China Sea to take control of certain maritime features and construct artificial islands upon them. The key methods adopted by China to achieve its goals involved a combination of hybrid threats and activities that included:[38]

- the use of ostensibly civil platforms such as fishing vessels and other non-military craft to pursue sovereign objectives regarding disputed maritime features in the South China Sea through 'intimidating acts';
- development of an organized and professional maritime militia that was regularly deployed to the area around the disputed maritime features;
- construction of artificial islands, with subsequent militarization of the facilities that were built on the artificial islands;

---

[35] Robbin Laird, 'China's Maritime Gray Zone Operations' (26 March 2019) <https://defense.info/book-review/2019/03/chinas-maritime-gray-zone-operations/> accessed on 25 February 2023.

[36] See generally the discussion by the Australian Government Department of Defence (n 8), regarding the grey zone and response options at pages 12, 14, 25, 27, and 30.

[37] R. Cormac and R. J. Aldrich, 'Grey Is the New Black: Covert Action and Implausible Deniability' (2018) 94 International Affairs 477.

[38] A. Chorn and M. Sato, 'Maritime Gray Zone Tactics: The Argument for Reviewing the 1951 U.S.–Philippines Mutual Defense Treaty' (*CSIS New Perspectives in Foreign Policy*, 1 October 2019) 4–5.

THE MARITIME DOMAIN   261

- interference with vessel passage and navigation in the vicinity of the maritime features occupied by China;
- cyber activities, disinformation campaigns, and the use of economic measures that have resulted in spiralling debt levels for the recipients of economic aid.

The actions taken by China in each of the above examples raises the prospect of a hybrid threat where boundaries are pushed, but only to a level where it is likely that a military response to that threat will not occur. In this way the hybrid threat remains in the maritime grey zone so that while coercion is clearly being experienced, there is difficulty trying to determine what type of response, if any, should be taken. The end result has really been a strategic victory to China in circumstances where the legality of Chinese action is clearly in doubt.

6. Can the 1982 UN Convention on the Law of the Sea Adequately Deal with Hybridity and the Maritime Grey Zone?

The next part of this chapter will examine if there are solutions contained in the *1982 United Nations Convention on the Law of the Sea*[39] that can address some of the problems posed by hybrid threats and grey zone activity. The LOSC emerged from the Third United Nations Conference on the Law of the Sea and was negotiated over a period of nearly a decade from late 1973 until the final session of the Conference concluded at Montego Bay, Jamaica, in December 1982. Conceptually, the LOSC was constructed as a 'package deal' that requires States party to accept the Convention in its entirety with only very limited scope for any deviation or reservation from the 320 Articles, 9 Annexes and subsequent Implementing Agreement relating to Part XI of the Convention. In essence, the LOSC is supposed to provide a 'one-stop-shop' for dealing with the major elements of ocean governance including the use and extent of maritime spaces, and for providing a dispute resolution system that would ensure that issues that arose between parties could be satisfactorily resolved.

It has been noted that when negotiating the LOSC there was a 'strong desire that the Convention allow for flexibility of practice in order to ensure durability over time . . .'[40] and '[T]he concept of the package pervaded all work on

---

[39]   UN Convention on the Law of the Sea (10 December 1982) 1833 UNTS 397 (hereafter LOSC).

[40]   United Nations Office for Ocean Affairs and the Law of the Sea, *The Law of the Sea: Official Texts of the United Nations Convention on the Law of the Sea of 10 December 1982, and of the Agreement Relating to the Implementation of Part XI of the United Nations Convention on the Law of the Sea of 10 December 1982, with Index and Excerpts from the Final Act of the Third United Nations Conference on the Law of the Sea*, UN Publication E.97.V.10 (1997), 1.

262 ARENAS OF HYBRID AND GREY ZONE COMPETITION

the elaboration of the Convention . . . [and] . . . permeates the law of the sea as it exists today'.[41] This history of the LOSC, while undoubtedly a critical element of the Convention's structure, is also potentially a weakness as the very flexibility that the LOSC necessarily provides also has the potential to exacerbate the ability of States to hide behind its veneer and thereby conduct maritime grey zone operations.

Accordingly, it is appropriate to examine some recent maritime incidents to determine if certain States have taken advantage of the ambiguity that is said to exist in some parts of the LOSC to further their own national interests in a manner that was never contemplated when the LOSC was negotiated.

6.1 A comparison: 'the military activities exception'

One example of how differences in LOSC interpretation arise can be obtained from comparing the two different conclusions that were reached recently when the nature of 'military activities' was considered by the Arbitral Tribunal in the South China Sea Arbitration and by the International Tribunal for the Law of the Sea (ITLOS) in the dispute between the Ukraine and Russia. In both cases, a dispute had been brought before a tribunal constituted under the LOSC and in each case the nature of an exception from the jurisdiction of the relevant tribunal under LOSC Article 298(1)(b) needed to be resolved.

6.2 The South China Sea Arbitration

In the case of the South China Sea Arbitration, one of the issues that the Arbitral Tribunal considered was the nature of the activity that had occurred between Chinese vessels and Philippine military forces stationed on the vessel *Sierra Madre* which is permanently aground on Second Thomas Shoal.[42] It is not necessary to go into detail regarding the nature of the interaction between the Chinese and the Philippines in the vicinity of Second Thomas Shoal other than to note that the issue the Philippines complained about primarily concerned interference by China with resupply activities involving personnel stationed on the *Sierra Madre*.[43]

After assessing the information available to it the Tribunal found

---

[41] Ibid. 2.

[42] SCS Arbitration, paras. 1110–62.

[43] The 'Factual Background' to the incidents at Second Thomas Shoal can be located at SCS Arbitration, paras. 1112–27.

THE MARITIME DOMAIN   263

that the essential facts at Second Thomas Shoal concern the deployment of a detachment of the Philippines' armed forces that is engaged in a stand-off with a combination of ships from China's Navy and from China's Coast Guard and other government agencies. In connection with this stand-off, Chinese Government vessels have attempted to prevent the resupply and rotation of the Philippine troops on at least two occasions. Although, as far as the Tribunal is aware, these vessels were not military vessels, China's military vessels have been reported to have been in the vicinity. In the Tribunal's view, this represents a quintessentially military situation, involving the military forces of one side and a combination of military and paramilitary forces on the other, arrayed in opposition to one another. As these facts fall well within the exception, the Tribunal does not consider it necessary to explore the outer bounds of what would or would not constitute military activities for the purposes of Article 298(1)(b).

It was on this basis that the Tribunal decided that it did not have any jurisdiction to consider the Philippines' submission in relation to events that had occurred at Second Thomas Shoal due to the declaration made by China pursuant to LOSC Article 298(1)(b).

6.3 ITLOS and the Kerch Strait

In somewhat similar circumstances, ITLOS came to a completely different conclusion in relation to the nature of the activities involving Russian vessels and Ukrainian vessels in the Kerch Strait in November 2018.[44] Upon ratification of the LOSC, both Russia and Ukraine lodged declarations under LOSC Article 298 exempting disputes concerning military activities from the Convention's dispute resolution processes.[45] The brief facts of this incident are that three Ukrainian naval vessels were fired upon by Russian Coast Guard vessels, acting together with a Russian naval vessel and military aircraft, and the Ukrainian vessels and their crews (all military personnel) were subsequently detained by Russian authorities.[46] The Ukrainian vessels were attempting to sail from a port in the Black Sea, through the Kerch Strait, to a port in the Sea of Azov. In deciding if it had jurisdiction to deal with Ukraine's request for 'Provisional Measures', ITLOS

[44] International Tribunal for the Law of the Sea, *Case concerning the detention of three Ukrainian naval vessels (Ukraine v. Russian Federation), Provisional Measures*, Order (May 15, 2019) (hereafter 'ITLOS Decision').
[45] Ibid. paras. 46–50.
[46] Ibid. paras. 30–32. See also J. Kraska, 'Did ITLOS Just Kill the Military Activities Exemption in Article 298' (*EJIL:Talk!*, 27 May 2019) <https://www.ejiltalk.org/did-itlos-just-kill-the-military-act ivities-exemption-in-article-298/> accessed on 25 February 2023.

264 ARENAS OF HYBRID AND GREY ZONE COMPETITION

was required to consider the nature of the 'military activities exemption' under LOSC Article 298(1)(b) in circumstances where the activities of the Russian authorities could be characterized as being either 'law enforcement' or 'military'.

The Tribunal stated that

> the distinction between military and law enforcement activities cannot be based solely on whether naval vessels or law enforcement vessels are employed in the activities in question. This may be a relevant factor but the traditional distinction between naval vessels and law enforcement vessels in terms of their roles has become considerably blurred.[47]

The Tribunal considered that as well as the nature of the vessels, the characterization of the activity should be assessed by looking at the nature of the activity and the circumstances in which it takes place. After assessing the facts before it, and although the activities involved Ukrainian military vessels and Russian Coast Guard vessels with other military platforms in the proximity, ITLOS decided that it did have jurisdiction to proceed with the application for provisional measures, and that the military activities exception did not apply.[48]

Comparison of the reasoning applied in the SCS Arbitration and the ITLOS Decision provides little certainty for the future. The relatively broad understanding of military activities that emerged from the SCS Arbitration, and which resulted in the Arbitral Tribunal finding that it did not have jurisdiction to deal with incidents that had occurred at Second Thomas Shoal, is now at odds with the more restrictive reasoning applied by ITLOS in its Decision whereby that Tribunal found that it did have jurisdiction to deal with Ukraine's application. Such uncertainty is precisely the environment in which the maritime grey zone flourishes and can only add to the uncertainty that States feel while trying to deal with a wide variety of hybrid maritime threats.

The incident in the Kerch Strait provides a further illustration of how States can use the maritime grey zone to create uncertainty regarding their actions. Russia claimed that its actions in seizing the Ukrainian vessels and crews were 'military activities' for the purpose of arguing that ITLOS had no jurisdiction to hear the case before it.[49] However, Russia also relied on its internal Code of Criminal Procedure to justify the seizure and detention of the vessels and crews[50] a position which would seem to contradict Russia's position in relation to the applicability of LOSC Article 298.[51] The final point to note regarding the Kerch

[47] ITLOS Decision, para. 64.
[48] Ibid. paras. 74–77.
[49] Ibid. para. 8.
[50] Ibid. para 32.
[51] The Dissenting Opinion of Judge Kolodkin in the ITLOS Decision would seem to support this view.

Strait incident is that after ITLOS granted Ukraine's request for provisional measures on 25 May 2019, the crews and vessels were finally returned to Ukraine in September and November 2019, respectively.[52]

7. Hybrid threats, the maritime grey zone, and the 'shroud of legitimacy'

There is an overarching theme that has been followed throughout this chapter: hybrid threats that occur in the maritime grey zone are deliberately masked by a shroud of legitimacy that is typically used by powerful States to disguise legally questionable actions that are designed to thwart the legitimate rights or interests of weaker States. This section of the chapter will examine a number of recent cases or incidents that demonstrate how States have used the ambiguity that pervades hybrid threats and the grey zone to push their agendas.

The first example arises from the South China Sea Arbitration, despite the non-appearance of China during the Tribunal's hearings, and it relates to the persistent Chinese assertion that its '9 dash line' claim in the South China Sea sits outside the parameters of the LOSC and is valid on other (largely unspecified) grounds.[53] This opaqueness is designed to slowly erode what might be termed contemporary or orthodox LOSC interpretations, or at least create uncertainty, and over time permit the insertion of an interpretation that is much more favourable to the position that China is seeking to have recognized. A persistent multi-pronged campaign sits behind these efforts, by using a combination of official statements, academic writings and news reports to, in effect, create an enduring narrative that will, over time, be accepted as being legally valid. This type of hybrid threat is ostensibly at the lower end of the scale, as there is no immediate and direct threat arising. However, when viewed in the context of the other activities being undertaken by China in the South China Sea, the continued 9-dash line claim by China can be seen as part of an overall, complex and long-term strategy that seeks to alter existing legal frameworks to the ultimate advantage of China and the detriment of others with direct, or indirect, interests.

Closely related to the 9-dash line claim is the increase in naval presence in the region by warships and military aircraft from a number of States—most notably the United States. The freedom of navigation activities of the US Navy, including so-called 'operational assertions' by warships, have been described as 'a form of

---

[52] BBC News, 'Russia Returns Ukrainian Boats Seized Off Crimea' (18 November 2019) <https://www.bbc.com/news/world-europe-50458521> accessed on 25 February 2023.
[53] SCS Arbitration, paras. 169–278.

maritime grey zone operation . . .'[54] insofar as these operations are conducted in a manner that is not anticipated to result in a military response to the presence of the vessels in contested waters. However, the resumption of transits through contested waters by the USN has not been without criticism due to the conflicting messages that have been sent following some transits by USN vessels, such as USS Lassen in 2015.[55] Passage by US vessels has been continually contested by China, as was the transit near the Paracel Islands by the United Kingdom vessel HMS Albion in August/September 2018 where both China and the United Kingdom insisted that their interpretation of the legality of the action was correct.[56] In a follow-up to HMS Albion's transit, calls have been made for a 'more systematic approach to the region, and to China's defiance of legal norms'.[57] Australian military aircraft and warships have also been subjected to increasingly provocative Chinese challenges in the Indo-Pacific region, including the use of lasers and chaff to interfere with flight operations.[58]

While the above examples relate to situations where States have used the grey zone to induce uncertainty, one recent example from the US Navy demonstrates that steps can be taken to remove doubt regarding the characterization of activity as well. This example can be found in the recent action taken by the US Navy to change the ship classification of Expeditionary Sea Base class ships from USNS auxiliary ships to USN warships. This change occurred so that any doubt regarding whether the vessels, and those personnel operating from the platforms, had an entitlement to fully engage in naval warfare—including offensive belligerent acts—was removed. In August 2019, a memorandum was sent from the Chief of Naval Operations to the Secretary of the Navy requesting the change and approval was swiftly given.[59] In taking these steps, the US Navy acted precipitously to ensure that lingering 'grey' questions were resolved.

---

[54] J. Goldrick, 'Grey Zone Operations and the Maritime Domain' (*ASPI Special Report*, 11 October 2018) <https://www.aspi.org.au/report/grey-zone-operations-and-maritime-domain> accessed on 25 February 2023.

[55] See R. Pedrozo and J. Kraska, 'Can't Anybody Play This Game? US FON Operations and the Law of the Sea' (*Lawfare*, 17 November 2015) <https://www.lawfareblog.com/cant-anybody-play-game-us-fon-operations-and-law-sea> accessed on 25 February 2023.

[56] BBC News 'British Navy's HMS Albion Warned over South China Sea "Provocation"' (6 September 2018) <https://www.bbc.com/news/uk-45433153> accessed on 25 February 2023.

[57] J. Hemmings, 'Charting Britain's Moves in the South China Sea' (*RUSI Commentary*, 6 February 2019) <https://rusi.org/explore-our-research/publications/commentary/charting-britains-moves-south-china-sea> accessed on 13 November 2023.

[58] T. Wilkins, 'By Accident or Design—or Designed Accident? China's Unsafe Air Intercepts' (*ASPI Interpreter*, 1 July 2022) <https://www.aspistrategist.org.au/by-accident-or-design-or-desig ned-accident-chinas-unsafe-air-intercepts/> accessed on 25 February 2023.

[59] Action Memo from Chief of Naval Operations to Secretary of the Navy dated 23 August 2019 (copy on file with author).

8. The unique nature of the maritime domain

A question can be asked as to whether the unique characteristics of the maritime domain have contributed to 'grey zone operations' taking place at a greater pace and frequency than is the case in other environments. Certainly, there are a wide range of examples and situations where maritime grey zone operations have taken place, including in the Persian (or Arabian) Gulf, the Black Sea and the Sea of Azov and, perhaps most notably, the South China Sea. For example, one way in which some States are reportedly taking advantage of the maritime grey zone is by vessels 'going dark' and turning off their automated identification system (AIS) in order to evade detection while conducting operations that are contrary to a sanction regime.[60] Such an activity would simply not be possible in the terrestrial sphere as the requirement for an AIS-like capability does not exist in this sense.

A related question arises in terms of assessing whether there are special aspects of certain maritime regions, such as the exclusive economic zone (EEZ) that result in an easier application of indirect operational methods that have the overall objective of advancing a particular State's interests at the expense of other States, but in a manner that is not easily challenged. The reason for singling out the EEZ is that this is a region where coastal States have sovereign rights, but not sovereignty, over the water column and seabed. Also, the EEZ can extend up to 200nm from the coast which means that many States can have difficulty seeking to enforce their rights in this zone due to the vast nature of the maritime area involved.

Closer to the coastline, there are many examples of States trying to enforce restrictions on the passage of military vessels in the territorial sea, such as seeking prior notification or permission, where such restrictions are simply not provided for in the LOSC. A number of these States have included their view of the legality of seeking to limit warship passage by making declarations when they ratified (or signed) the LOSC, despite the text of the Convention being quite clear that such declarations are not in conformity with the LOSC.[61]

9. New solutions and responses

The question then arises as to whether new solutions and responses are needed to adequately deal with the manner in which maritime grey zone incidents

---

[60] See R. Pedrozo, 'DPRK Maritime Sanction Enforcement' (2020) 96 International Law Studies 116.

[61] Examples of States that have made declarations that purport to limit warship passage by requiring prior notification or permission include Bangladesh, China, Croatia, Egypt, Iran (upon signature), Malta, Montenegro, and Oman: <https://treaties.un.org/Pages/ViewDetailsIII.aspx?src=TREATYandmtdsg_no=XXI-6andchapter=21andTemp=mtdsg3andclang=_en> accessed on 25 February 2023

have been used by States to further their objectives. One such response is that attributed to then-Chief of Naval Operations Admiral John Richardson in early 2019 when he reportedly 'made it very clear' to his Chinese counterpart that the United States would regard its maritime militia in the same way as it does the Chinese navy.[62] The Chinese maritime militia, known as the People's Armed Forces Maritime Militia (PAFMM) has been described as an 'organised group of patriotic fishermen recruited from China's coastal regions'[63] that are routinely deployed to the South China Sea and often supported by Chinese Coast Guard vessels. The PAFMM have been used extensively by China in harassment and interference operations that constitute hybrid threats, including the incident involving USNS Impeccable in 2009.[64] The clear inference from Admiral Richardson's comment is that the US Navy will not consider there is any grey zone surrounding the characterization of Chinese maritime militia vessels and would therefore be able to respond to threats emanating from those vessels with legal clarity.

Could other responses be warranted in relation to hybrid threats and grey zone activity? One possibility is that amendment to the LOSC could be sought in order to clarify those aspects of the Convention that are the source of difference between States and thereby eliminate these issues. However, there are several impediments to such a course of action, not least of which is the fact that the United States is not party to the LOSC, coupled with the fact that there has been a marked unwillingness on the part of States-party to the LOSC to interfere with the Convention by attempting to convene a fourth UN Conference. States seem to be content to live with whatever shortfalls are considered to exist with the Convention, rather than risk the unknown consequences of seeking changes to the current LOSC.

The other complicating issue is that notwithstanding the absence of the United States from the LOSC, there has also been the recent behaviour of Russia and China whereby these States have refused to accept the dispute resolution mechanisms that are an integral aspect of the LOSC. In the *Arctic Sunrise* case[65] the Russian Federation refused to appear before ITLOS and this was repeated in the dispute with Ukraine that has been previously discussed. As noted, China

---

[62] Ryan Pickrell, 'China's South China Sea Strategy Takes a Hit as the US Navy Threatens to Get Tough on Beijing's Sea Forces' (*Business Insider*, 29 April 2019) <https://www.businessinsider.com.au/us-navy-tough-on-china-paramilitary-fishing-fleet-gray-zone-tactics-2019-4?r=USandIR=T> accessed on 25 February 2023.

[63] A. Patalano, 'When Strategy Is 'Hybrid' and Not 'Grey': Reviewing Chinese Military and Constabulary Coercion at Sea' (2018) 31 The Pacific Review 822.

[64] For details of this incident, see Goldrick (n 54) 15–16.

[65] International Tribunal for the Law of the Sea, *The Arctic Sunrise Case (Kingdom of the Netherlands v. Russian Federation), Provisional Measures*, Order (22 November 2013) <https://www.itlos.org/fileadmin/itlos/documents/cases/case_no.22/published/C22_Order_221113.pdf> accessed on 25 February 2023.

adopted a similar policy of non-appearance in the SCS Arbitration. These actions by Russia and China are a worrying aspect of behaviour by powerful States against weaker States where selected interpretations of the law have been used to justify the stance that each State has taken. The potential for this behaviour to be repeated in the future must be assessed as being high.

10. Conclusion

This chapter has attempted to address whether the notion that grey zone operations pose a threat in the maritime domain is valid. It might be thought that such threats that arise in the maritime domain should be easily resolved by reference to existing instruments of international law, especially the LOSC; however, this has not proved possible. In fact, the very reason why a number of States have undertaken maritime activities that do not have legal clarity is that the appropriate response by 'affected' States is difficult to determine.

The case studies that have been addressed in this chapter fit within the environs of the maritime grey zone as they have all occurred in a manner that sits below the threshold at which the law applicable to international armed conflict would apply. However, many of these incidents have sought to provoke a reaction from the 'victim' State, and in some cases may have then been used to 'justify' the manner in which the 'aggressor' State has behaved.

The decision to use tactics and procedures that are subject to differing legal interpretations is not a new phenomenon, but the impact is now more pervasive given the leveraging effect of technology, the capacities of States to interfere with other States in abstract ways, and an increasing reliance on multilateralism in responses. The risk that arises is a challenge to a range of long-standing, fundamental legal concepts that have an important role to play in ensuring that the maritime domain remains an area where commerce and maritime activity can be freely undertaken within the bounds of international law. Increasingly, challenges in the maritime domain are being felt from strategically generated vagueness and ambiguity that is designed to create legal uncertainty in relation to both the nature of the threat and the response to it. This can ultimately lead to less certainty and predictability regarding the applicable legal regime, or threshold, to be applied as well as the potential for the emergence of new grey zone-specific legal 'norms' in areas of law that have hitherto been considered as predominantly sound.

The potential solution lies with actions from States that will manage and mitigate the risks, while acknowledging that it is unlikely that the trend towards hybridity and operations that are conducted in the maritime grey zone will disappear any time soon.

Authors' Note

This chapter has been prepared following a 'Grey Zone' workshop at the University of Pennsylvania on December 6–7, 2019. While the author was unable to attend the workshop, a preliminary chapter was presented at that workshop and the author is grateful for the subsequent feedback from the organizers and a number of participants.

13

The Evolving Chinese Strategy in the Arctic

Entering the Grey Zone?

Camilla T. N. Sørensen

1. Introduction

In recent years, great power competition has increasingly framed developments in the Arctic. The promise of Arctic sea routes shortening the travel distance between Europe and Asia, the increasingly accessible mineral and energy resources in the region, and the changing conditions for research activities as well as military operations make the great powers—the United States, Russia, and China—assign growing geo-economic and geo-strategic importance to the Arctic.[1] Not being an Arctic State, China faces challenges in establishing its presence and influence in the region, especially in the context of intensifying great power competition and outright hostility with the United States and growing mistrust towards China among several of the other Arctic States. China is focused on knitting itself into the Arctic by establishing strong comprehensive relationships with Arctic States, building especially on cooperation in research, resource extraction, and infrastructure development. However, increasingly, this Chinese strategy is encountering resistance, in particular due to an overall more cautious approach in both the United States and Europe towards cooperation with China.[2] This forces Beijing to rethink its Arctic engagement, prompting warnings from both Western academic and political circles that Chinese grey zone tactics known from its conduct in the South China Sea may also emerge in the Arctic.[3]

---

[1] Rebbecca Pincus, 'Three-Way Power Dynamics in the Arctic' (2020) 14 Strategic Studies Quarterly 40.

[2] E.g. Camilla T. N. Sørensen, 'Intensifying Great Power Politics Play into the Arctic—Implications for China's Arctic Strategy?' [2019] Arctic Yearbook <https://arcticyearbook.com/arctic-yearbook/2019/2019-scholarly-papers/323-intensifying-u-s-china-security-dilemma-dynamics-play-out-in-the-arctic-implications-for-china-s-arctic-strategy> accessed 15 March 2023.

[3] E.g. Stehanie Pezard et al, *China's Strategy and Activities in the Arctic. Implications for North American and Transatlantic Security* (RAND Corporation 2022) 45–62; Matthew Revels, 'Combating the Gray Zone: Enhancing America's Arctic Force Posture' (*Georgetown Security Studies Review*, 11

Camilla T. N. Sørensen, *The Evolving Chinese Strategy in the Arctic* In: *Hybrid Threats and Grey Zone Conflict*. Edited by: Mitt Regan and Aurel Sari, Oxford University Press. © Oxford University Press 2024.
DOI: 10.1093/oso/9780197744772.003.0013

There is a growing tendency to categorize all Chinese activities in the Arctic as grey zone tactics or hybrid threat activities. This tendency is fuelled by the low transparency of the Chinese system, characterized by complex relations and overlaps between the party-State, the military, universities, State-owned national and provincial companies, private companies, and other Chinese entities.[4] Furthermore, such increasingly widespread preoccupation with Chinese grey zone activities in the Arctic relates to a growing emphasis in Washington, but also increasingly in the other Arctic capitals such as Copenhagen, Oslo, and Helsinki, on the dual-use challenge, namely, the potential parallel civilian and military use of Chinese facilities and capabilities in the Arctic.[5] The concern is that the Chinese are actually taking advantage of the legal and institutional setup in the region and their cooperation with Arctic States and stakeholders, for example, in the field of research, to gradually increase their 'below the threshold' presence and activities, which then over time are to be used for military purposes.[6]

While it is crucial to think through and pre-empt risks and potential vulnerabilities related to a growing Chinese engagement in the Arctic, these should not be over-blown. The Arctic, and China's priorities and presence in this region, is very different from the South China Sea.[7] Furthermore, the legal and institutional framework of the Arctic has developed in agreement and with support from regional States.[8] The Arctic Council is the leading high-level intergovernmental forum in the region and consists of the so-called Arctic-8, which are the eight States with territories within the Arctic—that is the United States, Russia, Canada, Norway, Kingdom of Denmark, Iceland, Sweden, and Finland. Consequently, the Arctic is not an unregulated space in which China is easily able to insert itself. The tendency to conflate Chinese activities in the South China Sea

November 2022) <https://georgetownsecuritystudiesreview.org/2022/11/11/combating-the-gray-zone-enhancing-americas-arctic-force-posture/> accessed 15 March 2023.

[4] Anne-Marie Brady terms this 'the party-state-military-market nexus': see Anne-Marie Brady, *China as a Polar Great Power* (CUP 2017), 114–36.
[5] E.g. The White House, 'National Strategy for the Arctic Region' (October 2022) 6 <https://www.whitehouse.gov/wp-content/uploads/2022/10/National-Strategy-for-the-Arctic-Region.pdf> accessed 15 March 2023.
[6] E.g. Anne-Mary Brady, 'Facing Up to China's Military Interests in the Arctic' (*China Brief*, 10 December 2019) <https://jamestown.org/program/facing-up-to-chinas-military-interests-in-the-arctic/> accessed 15 March 2023; David Auerswald, 'China's multifaceted Arctic Strategy' (*War on the Rocks*, 24 May 2019) <https://warontherocks.com/2019/05/chinas-multifaceted-arctic-strategy/> accessed 15 March 2023.
[7] Elizabeth Buchanan and Bec Starting, 'Why the Arctic Is Not the 'Next' South China Sea' (*War on the Rocks*, 5 November 2020) <https://warontherocks.com/2020/11/why-the-arctic-is-not-the-next-south-china-sea/> accessed 15 March 2023.
[8] As underlined in a recent RAND report, there is, in contrast to the South China Sea, no Arctic State that has sought to dominate the entire region and there are no major disputes over territorial waters or exclusive economic zones among the Arctic States. See Benjamin J. Sacks et al, *Exploring Gaps in Arctic Governance: Identifying Potential Sources of Conflict and Mitigating Measures* (RAND Corporation, 2021) 3.

and the Arctic is not grounded in careful analysis. It rather reflects the general growing focus on, as well as the mounting concerns about, the implications of a stronger and more assertive China and how intensifying US-China great-power competition increasingly sets the overall frame for international economics, politics, and security.

This chapter examines the evolving Chinese strategy in the Arctic, focusing especially on whether we see Chinese grey zone tactics aimed at taking advantage of the legal gaps, thresholds, and uncertainties in Arctic governance to gradually push for a change in the Arctic governance regime allowing more influence for non-Arctic States such as China. It finds that there are various Chinese efforts to challenge the privileges of the Arctic States in Arctic governance and gradually influence or shape Arctic governance. However, these Chinese efforts have so far been limited, offering little support to warnings about Chinese lawfare activities in the Arctic.[9] There is nonetheless reason to continue to carefully follow the evolving Chinese approach to the Arctic. This is especially the case following the full-scale Russian invasion of Ukraine in February 2022 that potentially presents China with new opportunities. A more isolated and weakened Russia increasingly dependent on China is forced to compromise regarding its resistance towards allowing non-Arctic States into the region, including into Arctic governance. Consequently, the Russian bargaining position in relation to China— including concerning the Arctic—weakens, and with the Arctic Council on pause following the Russian invasion of Ukraine, there is more room for China to push for non-Arctic-specific governance.[10]

Section 2 of the chapter contextualizes and examines the interests driving China's strategic prioritization of the Arctic. The third section looks at the evolving Chinese approach to or tactics for establishing Chinese presence and influence in a more challenging Arctic context. Key in this section is to examine whether there are growing Chinese grey zone undertakings. Consequently, this is used in section 4 as a departure point for discussing the new strategic

---

[9] E.g. Auerswald (n 6); Brady (n 6). Lawfare or legal warfare is included as one of 'Three Warfares' employed by the Chinese Communist Party (CCP) with the others being public opinion warfare and psychological warfare. The aim of legal warfare is to shape the legal context in building the legal justification for actions. *Cf.* Peter Mattis, 'China's Three Warfares in Perspective' (*War on the Rocks*, 30 January 2018) <https://warontherocks.com/2018/01/chinas-three-warfares-perspective/> accessed 15 March 2023. Another helpful definition highlights States' gradual or instrumental approach to law and defines lawfare as States regularly employing law and legal arguments to pursue their own strategic objectives outside the context of active hostilities. See Aurel Sari, 'Legal Resilience in an Area of Grey Zone Conflicts and Hybrid Threats' (2020) 33 Cambridge Review of International Affairs 852.

[10] In March 2022, the seven Western Arctic States—the United States, Canada, Norway, Kingdom of Denmark, Finland, Sweden and Iceland—decided to pause the Arctic Council following the Russian invasion of Ukraine. See Pavel Devyatkin, 'Can Cooperation Be Restored?' [2022] Arctic Yearbook <https://arcticyearbook.com/arctic-yearbook/2022/2022-briefing-notes/443-can-coop eration-be-restored> accessed 15 March 2023.

274 ARENAS OF HYBRID AND GREY ZONE COMPETITION

opportunities potentially opening for China to establish its presence and influence in the Arctic following the Russian invasion of Ukraine.

2. China's interests in the Arctic

In January 2018, Beijing published its first ever white paper on Arctic policy, laying out its expanding range of interests and highlighting the ways that China as a 'near-Arctic State' aims to contribute to developments in the region.[11] The publication of the white paper underlines how Beijing assigns priority to the establishment of Chinese presence and influence in the Arctic. Together with the deep seabed and outer space, the polar regions, that is the Arctic and the Antarctic, are identified in Chinese strategic considerations and plans as 'new strategic frontiers'.[12] These new strategic frontiers are characterized as the most challenging areas to operate in and extract resources from. Therefore, the expectation is that the great power that manages this first—that is, develops and masters the necessary innovative knowledge and new technologies, for example, in terms of building satellite receiver stations, offshore platforms, cables and pipelines, and deep seaports under polar conditions—stands to gain crucial strategic advantages, guaranteeing it a dominant position in the great power competition of the twenty-first century.[13]

Ensuring access to the Arctic is thus assessed as essential in Beijing both in order to ensure that Chinese researchers, engineers, and other experts get the opportunity to acquire critical resources, advance their knowledge, and improve their technological capabilities and solutions, and to ensure Chinese influence over the evolving regulations and governance regimes in these frontiers.[14] The

---

[11] State Council Information Office of the People's Republic of China, 'China's Arctic Policy' (26 January 2018) <https://www.chinadailyasia.com/articles/188/159/234/1516941033919.html> accessed 15 March 2023.

[12] E.g. 'The Draft National Security Law will increase Security in Space and Other New Areas' [国家安全法草案拟增加太空等新型领域的安全维任务] *Xinhua* (24 June 2015), http://www.chinanews.com/gn/2015/06-24/7363693.shtml> accessed 15 March 2023. The National Security Law from 2015 directs attention towards 'new strategic frontiers', declaring that '[t]he State adheres to the peaceful exploration and use of outer space, the international seabed region, and the polar regions, enhances the ability of safe access, scientific investigation, development and utilization, strengthens international cooperation and safeguards our activities in outer space, the international seabed region and the polar regions'. See Chinese Ministry of Defence, National Security Law of the People's Republic of China (2015), Article 32 (in Chinese) <http://www.mod.gov.cn/regulatory/2016-02/19/content_4621258_3.htm> accessed 15 March 2023.

[13] Camilla T. N. Sørensen, 'The Ice Dragon: Chinese Interests in the Arctic' (European Centre of Excellence for Countering Hybrid Threats, 5 November 2019) <https://www.hybridcoe.fi/publications/hybrid-coe-strategic-analysis-19-the-ice-dragon-chinese-interests-in-the-arctic/> accessed 15 March 2023.

[14] Carla Freeman, 'An Uncommon Approach to the Global Commons: Interpreting China's Divergent Positions on Maritime and Outer Space Governance' (2022) 241 China Quarterly 1.

Chinese 'Made in China 2025' strategy identifies key sectors or industries such as robotics, space technology, artificial intelligence, the next generation of communication and information technology such as 5G networks, and maritime technology and capabilities. Within these key sectors or industries, China aims to take the lead in developing new technologies and knowledge, and in setting global standards through targeted investments, acquisitions, and research and development.[15] Setting global standards is also one of the main drivers behind the 'Belt and Road Initiative' (BRI), which since June 2017 has included the Arctic sea routes under the heading of the 'Polar Silk Road'. There is thus a significant Arctic dimension to the 'Made in China 2025' strategy and the BRI. The Arctic therefore links up with the ongoing restructuring and upgrading of the Chinese economy as well as China's broader and long-term geo-economic and geo-strategic visions and plans.[16]

There are three specific, but interrelated, drivers behind China's strategic prioritization of the Arctic over the last decade. The first is strengthening China's Arctic research capacity and knowledge. Climate change, happening faster in the polar regions than anywhere else, has a direct impact inside China, causing extreme weather patterns and negatively affecting China's agriculture and economy. There is therefore an aspiration to better understand the changing Arctic climate to be able to predict and prepare for the implications as well as in order to gradually establish China as a valuable partner for the Arctic States.[17] The content and focus of China's research agenda in the Arctic have, however, been changing and broadening in the recent decade. This relates to how the domestic focus of establishing China as a leading power within innovative knowledge and new technology has been further intertwined and thus emphasized with the intensifying great power competition with the United States. Similar to the United States, China also gives strong priority to reducing its dependencies and thus increasing its self-reliance, especially within strategic resources and key technologies.[18] As mentioned earlier, China puts emphasis on the Arctic as

---

[15] Elsa B. Kania, 'Made in China 2025, Explained' (*The Diplomat*, Arlington, VA, 1 February 2019) <https://thediplomat.com/2019/02/made-in-china-2025-explained/> accessed 15 March 2023.

[16] Camilla T. N. Sørensen and Christopher Weidacher Hsiung, 'The Role of Technology in China's Arctic Engagement: A Means as well as an End in Itself' [2021] Arctic Yearbook <https://arcticyearbook.com/arctic-yearbook/2021/2021-scholarly-papers/383-the-role-of-technology-in-china-s-arctic-engagement-a-means-as-well-as-an-end-in-itself> accessed 15 March 2023.

[17] Chinese Arctic scholars often highlight that their contribution to the development of polar-related science and technology is also a way to establish China as an important polar nation. E.g. Lulu Zhang et al, 'Reforming China's Polar Science and Technology System' (2019) 44 Interdisciplinary Science Reviews 392. See also Rasmus Bertelsen, Li Xing and Mette Højris Gregersen, 'Chinese Arctic Science Diplomacy: An Instrument for Achieving the Chinese Dream?' in *Global Challenges in the Arctic Region: Sovereignty, Environment and Geopolitical Balance*, edited by Elena Conde and Sara Iglesias Sánchez (Taylor and Francis 2016) 442.

[18] E.g. Bates Gill, 'China's Quest for Greater Technological Self-Reliance' (*Asia Society Essay*, 21 March 2021) <https://asiasociety.org/australia/chinas-quest-greater-technological-self-reliance> accessed 15 March 2023.

a new strategic frontier in this regard. In recent years, China has begun to conduct increasingly sophisticated scientific experiments as part of its Arctic research expeditions.[19] It provides Arctic-specific knowledge and experience, but it also gives Chinese researchers, engineers, and other experts opportunities to try out and further develop their overall innovative knowledge and technological capabilities under harsh and challenging conditions. This is a crucial point that underlines how China's effort to establish itself as an Arctic stakeholder is persistent and serves long-term goals. It is a priority linking up with the domestic agenda and therefore there is continuous encouragement in various official documents for an expansion of China's Arctic research activities and capacity. The knowledge and technology developed have both or parallel civilian and military use and thus play into Beijing's 'military-civilian fusion' (MCF) strategy and the priority of developing a world-class Chinese military.[20]

The second specific driver behind China's strategic prioritization of the Arctic over the last decade is the objective to ensure Chinese access to Arctic resources considered necessary for securing and diversifying China's supply. This covers a broad range of resources, such as oil, gas, and rare earth minerals, which the Arctic region holds in large amounts that are now becoming more accessible. Furthermore, China, which already possesses one of the world's largest distant-water fishing fleets, is increasingly interested in ensuring access to Arctic fishing grounds.[21] The third specific driver is to promote and secure favourable access to the Arctic sea routes, which besides their crucial importance for extracting Arctic resources are considered attractive alternatives to the longer and strategically vulnerable routes through the Strait of Malacca and the Suez Canal. The general assessment is that the Arctic sea routes will not be commercially viable in the near future, but the Chinese leadership and companies, particularly the State-owned shipping company COSCO, seem to have a more optimistic outlook. As early as 2016, COSCO announced plans to launch a regular service through the Arctic to Europe by way of the Northern Sea Route. In line with these plans, it has been testing the Arctic sea routes and designing and building new ships that are

---

[19] Ryan D. Martinson, 'The Role of the Arctic in Chinese Naval Strategy' (*China Brief*, 20 December 2019) <https://jamestown.org/program/the-role-of-the-arctic-in-chinese-naval-strategy/> accessed 15 March 2023.

[20] The focus of the MCF strategy is to increase integration between China's civil research and commercial sectors and its military, law enforcement, and defence industrial sectors. See Elsa B. Kania, 'In Military-Civil Fusion, China Is Learning Lessons from the United States and Starting to Innovate' (*The Strategy Bridge*, 27 August 2019) <https://thestrategybridge.org/the-bridge/2019/8/27/in-military-civil-fusion-china-is-learning-lessons-from-the-united-states-and-starting-to-innovate> accessed 15 March 2023; Taylor M. Fravel, 'China's "World-Class Military" Ambitions: Origins and Implications' (2020) 43 Washington Quarterly 85.

[21] William G. Dwyer, 'China's Strategic Interests in the Arctic' (2016) 2 Army War College Review 8.

better suited to the conditions in the region.[22] Especially the Transpolar Passage, or the Central Passage, cutting straight across the North Pole, seems to attract growing Chinese interest. It is not only the shortest of the three Arctic sea routes, but its attractiveness from a Chinese perspective is also that, unlike the Northern Sea Route and the Northwest Passage, it runs mostly through international waters, where all States have freedom of navigation, and hence Chinese ships would not have to follow the specific regulations of the relevant Arctic State, most relevant Russia in relation to the Northern Sea Route.[23]

3. The tactics of establishing Chinese presence and influence in the Arctic

Beijing has until recently aimed to ensure its presence and influence in the Arctic by establishing strong and comprehensive relationships with all of the Arctic States and stakeholders, and by gradually increasing China's engagement in Arctic governance. The main Chinese tactic has been to offer benefits, such as specific knowledge or investments, to Arctic States and stakeholders, who then develop their own interests in keeping China engaged in the region and in further developing their relations with Chinese stakeholders. In other words, China has sought to knit itself into the region on multiple levels through bilateral and multilateral agreements and engagements in the fields of research, infrastructure, and resource extraction, for example.[24] The challenge for China has been to strike the right balance between pro-activeness and reassurance in order not to heighten concern among the Arctic States about an overly assertive Chinese approach in the region. The degree of success for Beijing varies depending on the State in question, but generally speaking, China's initiatives and behaviour are increasingly approached with scepticism from the Western Arctic States, that is

---

[22] Malte Humpert, 'Chinese Shipping Company COSCO to Send Record Number of Ships Through Arctic' (*High North News*, 13 June 2019) <https://www.highnorthnews.com/en/chinese-shipping-company-cosco-send-record-number-ships-through-arctic> accessed 15 March 2023.

[23] *Cf.* Mia Benneth, 'The Arctic Shipping Route, No One Is Talking Abort' (*The Maritime Executive*, 5 August 2019) <https://www.maritime-executive.com/editorials/the-arctic-shipping-route-no-one-s-talking-about?__ac_lkid=3e7-cc58-1ee8-9f6d17170d5ecfa> accessed 15 March 2023, who notes that few States, except China, are preparing for an ice-free Arctic Ocean and that China could be trying to establish a first-mover advantage in the Transpolar Passage. Such an analysis finds support in China's eleventh Arctic expedition conducted in the autumn of 2020, which exclusively operated in international waters. The eleventh Arctic expedition was China's first Arctic expedition with the domestically built polar icebreaker Xuelong 2. See Feng Shuang, 'China's Polar Icebreaker Heading Home from Arctic Expedition' *Xinhua* (Beijing, 17 September 2020) <http://www.ecns.cn/news/2020-09-17/detail-ihaaeqyp8471195.shtml> accessed 15 March 2023.

[24] Camilla T. N. Sørensen, 'China Is in the Arctic to Stay as a Great Power: How China's Increasingly Confident, Proactive and Sophisticated Arctic Diplomacy Plays into Kingdom of Denmark Tensions' [2018] Arctic Yearbook <https://arcticyearbook.com/arctic-yearbook/2018/china-the-arctic> accessed 15 March 2023.

the Arctic-8 minus Russia, that share growing unease about a stronger and more assertive China.[25] Such growing unease often has very little to do with the Arctic, but reflects a generally more sceptical and cautious approach to cooperation with China on a range of issues. Consequently, there is a complex mix of crosscutting global and regional security dynamics that increasingly play out in the Arctic making it more difficult for China to manoeuvre in the region. More and more issues are securitized with the growing concerns about dual-use application restricting cooperation with China (e.g. in relation to research and technology).

As mentioned in the previous section, China has in recent years begun to conduct increasingly sophisticated scientific experiments as part of its Arctic research expeditions. For instance, during China's ninth Arctic expedition in 2018, Chinese researchers deployed unmanned observational equipment such as an indigenously produced autonomous underwater glider for deep-sea environment observation. According to a research report, activities such as these have greatly enhanced China's ability to observe and monitor the Arctic environment.[26] Moreover, Chinese researchers successfully launched China's first polar observation satellite, BNU-1, in September 2019. It is set to monitor sea ice drift and ice shelf collapse with the expectation that it will greatly improve China's remote sensing capability and promote the safe usage of the Arctic sea routes.[27] Since 2004, Beijing has had a research station on Svalbard. In addition, China has recently opened the Aurora Observatory in Iceland.[28] China has also been working with Finland on jointly developing the China-Finland Arctic Monitoring and Research Centre between China's Institute of Remote Sensing and Digital Earth and Finland's Arctic Space Centre. The main objective is to collect, process, and share satellite data to support environmental monitoring, climate research, and Arctic navigation.[29]

Establishing such research stations and facilities in the Arctic plays into the rollout of China's BeiDou-2 navigation satellite system, China's space science program and more accurate weather forecasting methods. Beijing has long aimed at developing its own global navigation satellite capacity to limit any

---

[25] Oscar Almén and Christopher Weidacher Hsiung, 'China's Economic Influence in the Arctic Region: The Nordic and Russian Cases' (Swedish Defence Research Agency, 2022) 32–33.

[26] Wei Zexun et al, 'Overview of the 9th Chinese National Arctic Research Expedition' (2020) 13 Atmospheric and Oceanic Science Letters 1.

[27] Brady (n 6). The domestically built Chinese polar icebreaker Xuelong 2 is equipped with oceanographic survey and monitoring apparatus allowing for advanced research in polar oceanography, biodiversity, atmospheric and environmental conditions. See Zhao Lei, 'Icebreaker, Satellite and Stations Bridge Polar Research Gap' *China Daily* (Beijing, 30 September 2019) <https://www.chinadaily.com.cn/a/201909/30/WS5d9178efa310cf3e3556e5cf.html> accessed 15 March 2023.

[28] E.g. Nong Hong, *China's Role in the Arctic. Observing and Being Observed* (Routledge 2020) 207.

[29] Ibid. See also Chinese Academy of Social Science, 'China and Finland sign a cooperation agreement on Arctic Space Observation Joint Research Center' [中芬签订北极空间观测联合研究中心合作协议] (17 April 2018) <http://www.radi.cas.cn/dtxw/rdxw/201804/t20180417_4997963.html> accessed 15 March 2023.

dependency and vulnerabilities connected with relying on the American GPS system. In 2020, China completed its navigation satellite structure with a total of thirty-five satellites placed in three different types of orbit.[30] China operates a remote satellite ground station in Kiruna, Sweden, as part of its global navigation satellite capacity. In recent years, China has conducted several experimental probes in the Arctic to test its communication capabilities. For example, in a 2019 evaluation, China assessed a number of technologies, including Very High Frequency (VHF) radio connectivity, medium-frequency Navtex systems, and the DSC system, as part of the Global Maritime Distress Safety System.[31] These facilities, systems, and programs evidently have a dual-use character.

A concern, especially in the United States, is that China is also gradually building up an explicitly military presence in the Arctic. As the 2019 report on China's military power published by the US Department of Defense warned, 'Civilian research could support a strengthened Chinese military presence in the Arctic Ocean, which could include deploying submarines to the region as a deterrent against nuclear attacks'.[32] Although such development over time cannot be ruled out, there is currently no evidence of an actual Chinese military presence in the region.[33] However, it is highly likely that the Chinese military is seeking to gain more knowledge and experience of Arctic or rather polar-specific operations, which ties in with the Chinese view on the polar regions as new strategic frontiers.[34]

The evolving Chinese research agenda in the Arctic with the obvious dual-use dimension underlines the challenge of categorizing Chinese activities in the region. There is no doubt that there is a presence of various Chinese entities reflecting the above-mentioned complex relations and overlaps between the party-State, the military, universities, State-owned national and provincial companies, private companies, and other Chinese entities. On the other hand, there does not seem to be overall political control and coordination between the many Chinese stakeholders. There are incentives and guidelines from Beijing, such as the ones presented in the white paper on Arctic policy from January 2018, but these are

[30] Andrew Jones, 'China to Complete Its Answer to GPS with Beidou Navigation Satellite launches in March, May' (*SpaceNews*, 28 February 2020) <https://spacenews.com/china-to-complete-its-answer-to-gps-with-beidou-navigation-satellite-launches-in-march-may/> accessed 15 March 2023.

[31] Malte Humpert, 'China Looking to Expand Satellite Coverage in Arctic—Experts Warn of Military Purpose' (*High North News*, 4 September 2019) <https://www.highnorthnews.com/en/china-looking-expand-satellite-coverage-arctic-experts-warn-military-purpose> accessed 15 March 2023.

[32] US Department of Defense, 'Annual Report to Congress. Military and Security Developments Involving the People's Republic of China 2019' (2 May 2019) 114.

[33] See also Hilde-Gunn Bye, 'Chinese Activity Increases in the High North: No Sign of Military Presence, Says IFS Researcher' (*High North News*, 28 May 2020) <https://www.highnorthnews.com/en/chinese-activity-increases-high-north-no-sign-military-presence-says-ifs-researcher> accessed 15 March 2023.

[34] Martinson (n 19).

280　ARENAS OF HYBRID AND GREY ZONE COMPETITION

general and broad. It still seems that many Chinese companies, including State-owned ones, are driven by market concerns and potential profit rather than by political directives.[35] Hence, there are several cases of Chinese companies pulling out of Arctic engagements due to deteriorating market conditions or an unfavourable business outlook.[36]

Regarding the warnings of Chinese lawfare activities in the Arctic alluded to earlier, the prevailing concern in both Western academic and political circles is that Beijing is increasingly challenging and questioning Arctic governance, namely, the legitimacy and effectiveness of the existing legal and institutional frameworks in the region, in order to promote frameworks that would give non-Arctic States such as China greater influence.[37] Arguably, Beijing could seek to do this directly, using its role as an observer at the Arctic Council and the various working groups, for example, to obstruct from within by questioning the competence of the Arctic Council. It could also pursue its objectives indirectly by supporting other groups that have similar interests, such as Arctic Indigenous people or groups that also want a bigger say.[38] There is a lively debate on the attractiveness of such tactics in China, and Chinese Arctic scholars often question the Arctic governance scheme and call for revisions.

In China, the Arctic governance regime is generally seen as interim and unsettled with opportunities for non-Arctic great powers such as China to shape its further development and the institutionalization of rules and regulations in the region.[39] Such Chinese ambition is also visible in the white paper on

[35] Almén and Hsiung (n 25), 27–29.

[36] E.g. the decision of the Chinese energy company CNOOC in January 2018 to withdraw from the Dreki oil exploration project in the waters off Iceland in the wake of the collapse of global oil and gas prices after 2014. See Marc Lanteigne, 'Stumbling Block: China-Iceland Oil Exploration Reaches an Impasse' (*Over the Circle*, 24 January 2018) <https://overthecircle.com/2018/01/24/stumbling-block-china-iceland-oil-exploration-reaches-an-impasse/> accessed 15 March 2023.

[37] E.g. Rebecca Pincus and Walter Berbrick, 'Gray Zones in Blue Arctic: Grappling with China's Growing Influence' (*War on Rocks*, 24 October 2018) <https://warontherocks.com/2018/10/gray-zones-in-a-blue-arctic-grappling-with-chinas-growing-influence/> accessed 15 March 2023; Rush Doshi, Alexis Dale-Huang, and Gaoqi Zhang, 'Northern Expedition: China's Arctic Activities and Ambitions' (Brookings Institution 2021).

[38] On China's (discursive) support for Arctic Indigenous peoples, see e.g. Mia Benneth, 'At Arctic Circle Forum, China Shows Arctic Geopolitics Are above Mike Pompeo's Pay Grade' (*Eye on the Arctic*, 13 May 2019) <https://www.rcinet.ca/eye-on-the-arctic/2019/05/13/china-arctic-geopolit ics-environment-arctic-circle-forum-conference/> accessed 15 March 2023. Since 2016, China has actively engaged with Japan and South Korea in the so-called Trilateral High-Level Dialogue on the Arctic. All three hold observer status in the Arctic Council but share an ambition to play a greater role in Arctic affairs and being accepted as an Arctic stakeholder. See Marc Lanteigne, 'Three to Get Ready: Northeast Asian Neighbours Discuss Joint Arctic Policies' (*Over the Circle*, 9 June 2018) <https://overthecircle.com/2018/06/09/three-to-get-ready-northeast-asian-neighbours-discuss-joint-arctic-policies/> accessed 15 March 2023.

[39] E.g. Pan Yixuan, 'Global Governance needed for Arctic Affairs', *China Daily* (Beijing, 10 May 2019) <http://global.chinadaily.com.cn/a/201905/10/WS5cd4b107a3104842260bad41.html> accessed 15 March 2023; Zhang Yao, 'Ice Silk Road Framework Welcomed by Countries, Set New Direction for Arctic Cooperation', *Global Times* (Beijing, 7 April 2019) <http://www.globaltimes. cn/content/1144928.shtml> accessed 15 March 2023; Li Shiyue, Zhang Yiming, and Li Zhenfu,

THE EVOLVING CHINESE STRATEGY IN THE ARCTIC 281

Arctic policy, where it is highlighted how the Arctic should not be regarded as a demarcated region, referring specifically to how climate change in the region has global implications and international impacts. It is therefore not up to the Arctic States alone to establish the rules and norms for the future development of and access to the region and its resources. Non-Arctic States like China have a role to play and legal rights to engage in Arctic research, navigation, overflight, and a series of economic activities such as resource extraction, fishing, and laying cables and pipelines. The paper refers specifically to China's legal rights as a signatory to the Spitsbergen Treaty and the United Nations Convention on the Law of the Sea (UNCLOS).[40]

These are cautious efforts to challenge the privileges of the Arctic States in Arctic governance and gradually influence or shape Arctic governance, building the justification for a stronger Chinese role and influence. Furthermore, it reflects Chinese promotion of non-Arctic-specific governance to the region linking up with how the Chinese describe the Arctic as a global common.[41] Still, there is no strong empirical support that Chinese Arctic officials have been pushing an assertive line, either in bilateral relations or in Arctic Council settings.[42] An exception can be found in the Chinese position with regard to the Spitsbergen Treaty, and specifically the degree to which Norway, whose sovereignty over the Arctic archipelago is formally recognized with the treaty, is obliged to treat nationals and companies from States that are party to the treaty in the same way as Norwegian nationals and companies.[43] During an exchange at the Svalbard Science Forum in 2019, Chinese representatives openly challenged Norwegian claims, arguing for greater scientific leeway, and the Chinese Arctic and Antarctic

---

'Research on the Arctic Multilateral Governance Mechanism under the Framework of the Greater Arctic' [大北极框架下的北极地区多边治理机制研究] (2017) Arctic Affairs [北极表题] 71–76.

[40] State Council Information Office (n 11).

[41] Freeman (n 14).

[42] It is also worth noting that China is not alone in questioning and challenging the control and privileges of the Arctic States, as France has presented similar arguments, for example. See e.g. Siri Gulliksen and Amund Trellevik, 'France Compares the Arctic to the Middle East, Claims Region Belongs to No-One' (*High North News*, 1 October 2019) <https://www.highnorthnews.com/en/fra nce-compares-arctic-middle-east-claims-region-belongs-no-one> accessed 15 March 2023.

[43] Most Chinese Arctic scholars promote an adjustable or evolutionary approach, as opposed to Norway, which follows a stricter interpretation approach. Furthermore, they often point out how Norwegian sovereignty on Svalbard is limited due to the principle of non-discrimination, stating that signatory States such as China are entitled to the right of residence on Svalbard and the right to fish, hunt, or undertake any kind of maritime, industrial, mining, or trade-related activity. E.g. Qin Tianbao, 'Dispute over the Applicable Scope of the Svalbard Treaty' (2015) 8 Journal of East Asia and International Law 162; Liu Huirong and Zhang Xinyuan, 'Research on the Legal Application of Svalbard Waters – From the perspective of the United Nations Convention on the Law of the Sea' [斯瓦尔巴群岛海域的法律适用问题研究—以《联合 国海洋法公约》为视角] (2006) 6 Journal of Ocean University of China [中国海洋大学学报] 4; Lu Fanghua, 'An Analysis of the Nature of Norway's Jurisdiction in Svalbard from the Perspective of the Spitsbergen Treaty' [挪威对斯瓦尔巴德群岛管辖权的性质辨析] (North China Institute of Science and Technology, 2019) 12.

282 ARENAS OF HYBRID AND GREY ZONE COMPETITION

Administration has similarly questioned the Norwegian position.[44] Judging from the debate among Norwegian scholars and journalists, the Chinese have become bolder not only in demanding unhindered access to the archipelago, but also in claiming the right to manage their own station without being hindered or restricted by the Norwegians.[45]

Despite the lively critical debate among Chinese Arctic scholars, and indications of a bolder approach regarding Svalbard, Chinese lawfare behaviour in the Arctic is thus far rather low-profile compared to the Antarctic, where Beijing has been more prone to challenge the Antarctic Treaty System (ATS), causing growing concern and criticism.[46] Nevertheless, there is little doubt that Beijing sees the Arctic governance system as evolving, not fixed, and that Beijing aims at gaining influence on how it evolves.[47] A last example of negotiations related to Arctic governance, where China has been more outspoken in actively seeking to shape and influence the outcome, were those held in 2018 on the Central Arctic Ocean Fisheries Agreement (CAOFA), a binding fishing moratorium. The negotiations exposed a divide between China, which sought a four-year moratorium, and several of the Arctic States, which sought thirty years. A sixteen-year moratorium was eventually established, and the CAOFA is due to expire in 2034.[48]

Following the above-mentioned Chinese emphasis on the Arctic as global commons, it is interesting to note how a broad and flexible range of Chinese narratives has developed, often combining regional and global arguments.[49] The white paper on Arctic policy contains both.[50] According to the regional argument, the Arctic States and Indigenous peoples' organizations have an

[44] Mari Rian Hanger, 'Kina med krass kritikk av norsk forskningsstrategi for Svalbard' (*Universitetsavisa.no*, 16 January 2019) <https://www.universitetsavisa.no/forskning/2019/01/16/Kina-med-krass-kritikk-av-norsk-forskningsstrategi-for-Svalbard-18378967.ece> accessed 15 March 2023.

[45] E.g. Torbjørn Pedersen, 'Et dristigere Kina er i ferd med å bli et Svalbard-problem', *Aftenposten* (Olso, 25 March 2019) <https://www.aftenposten.no/meninger/debatt/i/0nVQ3M/et-dristigere-kina-er-i-ferd-med-aa-bli-et-svalbard-problem-torbjoern> accessed 15 March 2023.

[46] Bergin and Press describe China as 'an active, vocal and at a times disruptive, unconstructive, presence in ATS meetings, underlining a growing diplomatic assertiveness in Antarctic affairs'. See Anthony Bergin and Tony Press, 'Eyes Wide Open: Managing the Australia-China Antarctic Relationship' (Australian Strategic Policy Institute, April 2020) <https://www.aspi.org.au/report/eyes-wide-open-managing-australia-china-antarctic-relationship> accessed 15 March 2023.

[47] As stated in the White Paper on Arctic policy: 'China is committed to improving and complementing the Arctic governance regime'. See State Council Information Office (n 11).

[48] *Cf.* Liu Nengyu, 'How Has China Shaped Arctic Fisheries Governance?' *The Diplomat* (Arlington, VA, 18 June 2018) <https://thediplomat.com/2018/06/how-has-china-shaped-arctic-fisheries-governance/> accessed 15 March 2023

[49] *Cf.* Mia M. Bennett, 'How China Sees the Arctic: Reading between Extraregional and Intraregional Narratives' (2015) 20 *Geopolitics* 645; Patrik Andersson, 'The Arctic as a "Strategic" and "Important" Chinese Foreign Policy Interest: Exploring the Role of Labels and Hierarchies of China's Arctic Discourses' (2021) Journal of Current Chinese Affairs 1.

[50] State Council Information Office (n 11).

inherent right to make regional decisions due to their geographical location in the region. The global argument, on the other hand, describes the Arctic as an open and globalized space (i.e. global commons) where non-Arctic States and stakeholders influence and are influenced by developments and dynamics in the region. Consequently, non-Arctic States and stakeholders should be included in decision-making in the Arctic. This is also because their involvement is necessary for developing solutions to regional issues.[51] In other words, the global argument highlights forces and activities that cross boundaries and demonstrate the unavoidable interconnectedness of the Arctic and other regions.[52] For example, the Chinese State-owned shipping company COSCO has argued that access to the Northern Sea Route could provide substantial fuel savings for the benefit of the global climate, thus justifying free access to the region based on global concerns.[53] Related to the global argument is the Chinese emphasis, also present in the white paper, on how China in following international rules and treaties has certain rights and interests in the Arctic.[54] Along the same lines, Chinese Arctic scholar Li Zhenfu has introduced the concept of 'the Greater Arctic' [大北极], which comprises not only the eight Arctic States, but forty-five other States connected to the region by different economic and logistical ties.[55] Applying both regional and global arguments gives Beijing discursive flexibility that allows it to cater to several audiences, including groups such as environmental non-governmental organizations (NGOs) and non-Arctic States and entities that further more global narratives.[56]

Summing up, there are indications of a more confident and assertive Chinese approach in the Arctic, including to Arctic governance, which in Beijing's perspective is temporary and requires adjustments in order to more effectively deal with the changing Arctic and its importance to, and influence on, Arctic as well as non-Arctic States. There has not been any outright Chinese questioning of the existing legal and institutional setup in the Arctic. However, there are hints of careful Chinese efforts to challenge the privileges of the Arctic States and gradually increase China's influence on how Arctic governance further evolves.

---

[51] Bennett (n 49) 657–58; Brady (n 4) 35. See also Chinese Ministry of Foreign Affairs, 'Chinese Ministry of Foreign Affairs, 'Keynote Speech by Vice Foreign Minister Zhang Ming at the China Country Session of the Third Arctic Circle Assembly' (17 October 2015) <http://www.fmprc.gov.cn/mfa_eng/wjbxw/t1306858.shtml> accessed 15 March 2023.

[52] Guo Peiqing et al, *Research on the International Issues of the Arctic Route* [北极航道的国际问题研究] (Ocean Press 2009) 320; Brady (n 4) 220–25 and 243.

[53] Bennett (n 49).

[54] State Council Information Office (n 11).

[55] Li Zhenfu, 'Pan-Northeastern Asia in the Perspective of the Greater Arctic' [大北极视角下的反东北亚] (2016) 8 China Ship Survey [中国船检] 26–28.

[56] Bennett (n 49).

4. New opportunities for China in the Arctic?

Is China going to take advantage of a weakened Russia in the Arctic? There are reasons to expect so, not only related to reaching attractive deals on gas and oil from the Russian Arctic, but also on some of the more long-term Chinese interests in establishing its presence and influence in the Arctic. Already before the Russian invasion of Ukraine in February 2022, there were signs of how the changing balance of power between Russia and China is playing out in the Arctic. The region has been an area of growing Russian and Chinese cooperation over the last decade, and the Russia-China joint statement from February 2022 declares that: 'The sides agreed to continue consistently intensifying practical cooperation for the sustainable development of the Arctic'.[57] This is the first time that the Arctic is mentioned in a Russia-China joint statement and it arguably indicates how a weakened Russia that is increasingly dependent on China is forced to compromise regarding its resistance towards allowing non-Arctic States into the region, including into Arctic governance. Previously, Moscow has been a keen supporter of maintaining Arctic governance solely for Arctic States. For example, Moscow was hesitant to include non-Arctic States, including China, into the Arctic Council as observers in 2013 and only agreed to this after strong reassurances that the privileges of the Arctic States would be upheld and that the non-Arctic States would respect the existing Arctic governance structure.[58] Now, the Russian bargaining position has weakened and there arguably is more room for China to push for non-Arctic-specific governance. As argued above,[59] China clearly has an ambition to increase its role and influence in Arctic governance and has started to give clear hints at how it prefers non-Arctic-specific governance: Arctic governance is thus not for Arctic States alone.

With the weakened Russian bargaining position and the leading Arctic governance forum, the Arctic Council, on pause following the Russian invasion of Ukraine, there are new openings for Beijing to push its agenda. Beijing could start to encourage an open or an international alternative to the Arctic Council with more ammunition as the paralysis of the Arctic Council supports longstanding Chinese critique of the Arctic governance regime being inefficient and insufficient. So far, there have not been any Chinese moves in this direction, but the longer the Arctic Council is on pause, the more room it arguably provides for Beijing to mobilize support and gain traction among other non-Arctic States and

---

[57] President of Russia, 'Joint Statement of the Russian Federation and the People's Republic of China on the International Relations Entering a New Era and the Global Sustainable Development' (4 February 2022), <en.kremlin.ru/supplement/5770> accessed 15 March 2023.
[58] E.g. Camilla T. N. Sørensen and Ekaterina Klimenko, 'Emerging Chinese-Russian Cooperation in the Arctic: Possibilities and Constraints' (SIPRI 2017) 37–39 <https://www.sipri.org/sites/default/files/2017-06/emerging-chinese-russian-cooperation-arctic.pdf> accessed 15 March 2023.
[59] See section 3.

even Arctic Indigenous people or groups for its global narrative and arguments about the Arctic as global commons. It is also possible that in order to demonstrate the inadequacy of Arctic governance and to promote global inclusiveness, Beijing will strengthen and expand its participation in international multilateral regimes, actively seeking to shape their decisions and decision-making processes while promoting their stronger say on Arctic matters in areas such as energy, shipping, and environmental protection.[60] If uniform regulations and governing authority in the various UN agencies gain more ground in the region, the Arctic Council and the broader Arctic governance regime risk being gradually undermined and made redundant.

With the likely NATO-membership to Finland and Sweden, the Arctic Council is going to consist of seven NATO members and Russia, and therefore it is also possible that Russia starts seeing its own interests in a push for a new or drastically changed Arctic governance regime potentially providing China with an opening to insert itself more decisively.[61] Such Russian reaction could be further encouraged if the other seven Arctic States on their side increase cooperation, for instance in the form of an Arctic-7 Arctic Council.[62] It is interesting to note how the Chinese special envoy to the Arctic, Feng Gao, in October 2022 stressed that China will not support an Arctic Council without Russia. More specifically, he emphasized that if the seven Western Arctic States move ahead without Russia, the Arctic Council will still be there, but it will be a different institution and it will not be supported by China.[63] It is rare for China to engage in such clear messaging on issues of Arctic governance.

Consequently, by combining legal and non-legal arguments and measures, various routes are open to China to exploit and take advantage of the legal gaps, thresholds, and uncertainties in Arctic governance to its own strategic advantage. The space for China to do so has expanded with a weakened Russia and the frozen Arctic Council. As China continues to enhance its economic, political, and military power vis-à-vis Russia's stalling economy, weakening political influence and failing military, it is likely to further increase Chinese confidence

---

[60] Already today, Arctic fishing regulation is dominated by the UN Food and Agriculture Organization (FAO), Arctic shipping is subject to International Maritime Organization (IMO) norms and regulations; and extensions of coastal states' continental shelves require the advice of the UN Commission on the Limits of the Continental Shelf (UNCLOS). See Pezard et al (n 3) 25.

[61] Ibid. viii; Jeremy Greenwood and Shuxian Luo, 'Could the Arctic Be a Wedge Between Russia and China?' (*War on the Rocks*, 4 April 2022) <https://warontherocks.com/2022/04/could-the-arctic-be-a-wedge-between-russia-and-china/> accessed 15 March 2023.

[62] Trine Johassen, 'The Arctic Council: The Arctic 7 Resume Limited Work without Russia' (*High North News*, 8 June 2022) <https://www.highnorthnews.com/en/arctic-council-arctic-7-resume-limited-work-without-russia> accessed 15 March 2023.

[63] Trine Johassen, 'China: Will Not Acknowledge Arctic Council without Russia' (*High North News*, 15 October 2022) <https://www.highnorthnews.com/en/china-will-not-acknowledge-arctic-council-without-russia> accessed 15 March 2023.

286 ARENAS OF HYBRID AND GREY ZONE COMPETITION

and a sense of entitlement also in the Arctic. The concern among the Western Arctic States should be that if China first succeeds with Russia's more or less passive acceptance to establish an alternative governance mechanism or a stronger Chinese presence and activities, including military, then these advances will not be easy to reverse. On the contrary, they would contribute to a gradual change of the status quo in the region to China's strategic advantage.

5. Conclusion

Establishing presence and influence in the Arctic is a persistent Chinese priority that ties in with China's ability to succeed in the ongoing restructuring and upgrading of the Chinese economy. It also plays into China's broader and long-term geo-economic and geo-strategic visions and plans. The debate on China's evolving strategy in the Arctic and on whether to frame the Chinese Arctic and broader polar engagement as grey zone activities is likely to intensify in the coming years. As Arctic politics and security become increasingly intertwined with great-power politics, specifically the NATO-Russia conflict and the US-China great-power competition, many challenges and implications are evolving for the Arctic States, for Arctic governance, and for specific policy areas with relevance to the Arctic. The changing Chinese engagement brings new vulnerabilities calling for more focus among Arctic States and stakeholders on the identification and management of risks. It requires building knowledge and intelligence on China within the Arctic States, including on Chinese politics and economic statecraft, in order to be able to carefully analyse the instruments, techniques, and means applied by each Chinese activity and to assess the potential vulnerabilities engendered.[64] Such a thorough analysis is also the only starting point for designing useful legal and institutional mechanisms or frameworks to deter and defend.

The focus of this chapter has especially been on examining whether we see Chinese grey zone tactics aimed at taking advantage of the legal gaps, thresholds, and uncertainties in Arctic governance to gradually push for a change in the Arctic governance regime allowing more influence for non-Arctic States such

---

[64] *Cf.* the so-called Bjarnason-report conducted for the Nordic foreign ministries and aimed at developing recommendations on how the Nordic countries—Denmark, Iceland, Norway, Sweden, and Finland—should jointly address, among other challenges, increased Chinese involvement in the Arctic. A specific recommendation here is that the Nordic countries should develop a common Nordic analysis, policy, and approach to Chinese involvement in the Arctic and pursue it within relevant regional networks to which they are all parties. See Björn Bjarnason, 'Nordic Foreign and Security Policy 2020: Climate Change, Hybrid and Cyber Threats and Challenges to the Multilateral, Rules-Based World Order. Nordic Foreign and Security Policy 2020 Proposal' (1 July 2020) 12 <https://www.regjeringen.no/globalassets/departementene/ud/vedlegg/europapolitikk/norden/nordicreport_2020.pdf> accessed 15 March 2023.

as China. This has especially become a relevant issue following the Russian invasion of Ukraine in February 2022, which has weakened the Russian bargaining position in relation to China and put the Arctic Council on halt opening new opportunities for China to push for non-Arctic-specific governance. The analysis points to various Chinese efforts to challenge the privileges of the Arctic States in Arctic governance and gradually influence or shape Arctic governance. However, these Chinese efforts have so far been limited, giving little support to warnings about Chinese lawfare activities in the Arctic. There are nonetheless reasons to continue to carefully follow the evolving Chinese strategy in the Arctic. As argued, the Chinese will continue to cautiously promote changes in the Arctic governance regime but remain under the threshold of eliciting a strong opposing response.

The Chinese leadership headed by Xi Jinping increasingly emphasizes the need to proactively shape an international environment conducive to its stated goal of national rejuvenation, where China regains great power status, respect, and influence. In the eyes of Xi Jinping, global governance is 'unjust and improper' with many governance deficits.[65] His call for a stronger and more confident promotion of 'Chinese solutions' and 'Chinese wisdom' is also highly likely to play into the evolving Chinese engagement in the Arctic.

---

[65] Xinhua, 'Xi Stresses Urgency to Reform Global Governance' (13 October 2015) <www.china. org.cn/china/2015-10/13/content_36805468.htm> accessed 15 March 2023; Bates Gill, *Daring to Struggle. China's Global Ambitions under Xi Jinping* (OUP 2022) 135–61.

14

Hybrid and Grey Zone Operations in Outer Space

Melissa de Zwart

1. Introduction: The Starlink/China Space Station incident

On 3 December 2021, China submitted a Note Verbale to the United Nations Committee on the Peaceful Uses of Outer Space (UNCOPUOS) alleging that two Starlink satellites, launched by US company SpaceX, had created 'dangers to the life and health of astronauts aboard the China Space Station'.[1] It was claimed that the China Space Station had to implement two preventative collision avoidance manoeuvres on 1 July and 21 October 2021, respectively. This claim was interesting, not so much for the assertion of the need to undertake collision avoidance procedures, but rather for the manner in which the note 'referred' the Secretary-General of the UN to Article V of the Outer Space Treaty, which provides that:

> States Parties to the Treaty shall immediately inform the other States Parties to the Treaty or the Secretary-General of the United Nations of any phenomena they discover in outer space . . . which could constitute a danger to the life or health of astronauts.[2]

The Note is expressed as a notification under Article V of two 'close encounters' between the China Space Station and Starlink satellites. In the first instance, it is claimed that the China Space Station took an evasive manoeuvre to avoid a potential collision with a Starlink satellite which moved to an orbit close to the space station, and in the second case it claimed that the satellite was 'continuously maneuvering, the maneuver strategy was unknown and orbital errors were hard to be assessed' and this was deemed to be a collision risk.[3] The note

---

[1] United Nations Committee on the Peaceful Uses of Outer Space, 'Note Verbale dated 3 December 2021 from the Permanent Mission of China to the United Nations (Vienna) addressed to the Secretary-General' (6 December 2021), UN Doc. A/AC.105/1262.

[2] Treaty on Principles Governing the Activities of States in the Exploration and Use of Outer Space, including the Moon and Other Celestial Bodies (27 January 1967), 610 UNTS 205 (Outer Space Treaty).

[3] Ibid.

Melissa de Zwart, *Hybrid and Grey Zone Operations in Outer Space* In: *Hybrid Threats and Grey Zone Conflict*. Edited by: Mitt Regan and Aurel Sari, Oxford University Press. © Oxford University Press 2024.
DOI: 10.1093/oso/9780197744772.003.0014

290 ARENAS OF HYBRID AND GREY ZONE COMPETITION

identified the dates and identifiers of the Starlink spacecraft and requested the Secretary-General to circulate this information to all parties to the Outer Space Treaty and bring to the attention of those parties the obligations under Article VI of that Treaty that:

> States Parties to the Treaty shall bear international responsibility for na-
> tional activities in outer space, including the moon and other celestial bodies,
> whether such activities are carried on by governmental agencies or by non-
> governmental entities, and for assuring that national activities are carried out
> in conformity with the provisions set forth in the present Treaty.[4]

The Note did not make any explicit claim regarding a violation of the Outer Space Treaty. It is noted that in any event UNCOPUOS would have no power to mediate such a claim. Neither did the claim refer to the more directly relevant provision of the OST, Article IX.[5] Article IX sets out the obligation for States to 'conduct all their activities in outer space . . . with due regard to the corresponding interests of all other States Parties to the Treaty', as well as the requirement to identify any incident of 'harmful interference' and undertake international consultations before proceeding with such an activity.[6] It is arguable that by evoking the specific language of Article V, China was attempting to place the crewed China Space Station in a superior position in terms of right of way in space, whilst calling out a commercial US operator for allegedly erratic and unpredictable behaviour.[7] If so, this heralds a new international platform for virtue signalling in the space power context. It was clearly intended as a global reminder that no matter how diverse and successful the activities of SpaceX are, the US government remains responsible for those actions.

The United States responded to the Chinese Note with its own Note Verbale in January 2022, with a statement explicitly affirming its commitment to international cooperation and upholding obligations under the Outer Space Treaty as well as rejecting any risk of collision.[8] It responded directly to the claims that the China Space Station was at risk of collision with Starlink satellites, stating that the US Space Command did not estimate a significant probability of collision between the China Space Station and the identified Starlink satellites. It confirmed that if it had identified a significant probability of collision, the United States would have provided a close approach notification to the Chinese point of

---

[4] Ibid.
[5] Michelle Hanlon and Josh Smith, 'China Says Elon Musk's Starlink Is 'Phenomenal', but What Is the Real Message?' (*The Space Review*, 3 January 2022) <https://thespacereview.com/article/4306/1> accessed 30 August 2022.
[6] Outer Space Treaty.
[7] Hanlon and Smith (n 5).
[8] UN Committee on the Peaceful Uses of Outer Space (n 1).

contact for the Space Station. It also noted that there was no evidence of any contact having been made or attempted by China with the United States regarding concerns with respect to those particular satellites.

The US Note went beyond merely refuting the Chinese claims. The United States also took the opportunity of this exchange to reinforce international awareness of its own good practices and adherence with global norms with respect to outer space. It expressed the view that 'adherence by all nations to the Treaty's principles' constitutes 'the fundamental foundation for nations' conduct in outer space' and 'urged all nations to uphold' their own commitments under the Outer Space Treaty. Beyond the terms of the Outer Space Treaty and reinforcing its commitment to 'sustainable, rules-based activities in outer space', the US Note affirmed that the United States had supported the adoption of the (non-binding) 'Guidelines for the Long-term sustainability of outer space activities' in UNCOPUOS[9] and urged all nations to abide by and implement the specific guidelines applicable to collision avoidance. The Note reiterated key applicable elements of those Guidelines, including provision of updated contact information and sharing information on space objects and orbital events; promoting the collection, sharing, and dissemination of space debris monitoring information; and performing conjunction assessment during all orbital phases of controlled flight.

This restatement of the Guidelines is followed with a description of the role played by US Space Command in providing warning with respect to potential hazards and the sharing of space situational awareness. It outlined the process observed for provision of information, including in this specific instance to the government of China, regarding collision avoidance manoeuvres where a potential collision hazard is identified.[10]

China followed up with a further public statement, that it was open to creating more formal lines of communication with the United States regarding space safety.[11] At a press conference in February 2022, Zhao Lijian, spokesperson for China's Ministry of Foreign Affairs, again reiterated the claims of

---

[9] Annex II: 'Guidelines for the Long-Term Sustainability of Outer Space Activities' to United Nations General Assembly, 'Report of the Committee on the Peaceful Uses of Outer Space, Sixty-second Session (12–21 June 2019)' (2019) UN Doc. A/74/20, 50.

[10] The US Space Surveillance Network, currently operated by US Space Command but previously provided by the US Air Force, has provided conjunction analysis and warning notifications for decades. There is now a growing recognition of the need for greater involvement and cooperation with commercial providers in offering detection and tracking of space objects Eric Tegler, 'The Commercial Satellite Industry Is Increasing Awareness in Space But It's Not Changing Behavior Yet' (*Forbes*, 17 December 2021) <https://www.forbes.com/sites/erictegler/2021/12/17/the-commercial-satellite-industry-is-increasing-awareness-in-space-but-its-not-changing-behavior-yet/?sh=723ae 24d3a23> accessed 30 August 2022.

[11] Jeff Foust, 'China Proposes Formal Lines of Communication with US on Space Safety' (*SpaceNews*, 15 February 2022) <https://spacenews.com/china-proposes-formal-lines-of-communication-with-u-s-on-space-safety/> accessed 30 August 2022.

close approaches by the Starlink satellites and the risk this posed to the Chinese astronauts. He also claimed that the note was filed with the UN both to satisfy China's international obligation under Article V and after failing to get a response from the United States after multiple attempts to contact them via email.[12] After calling out the United States for 'not showing a responsible attitude as a space power', he then expressed China's hope that 'all countries will respect the international system in outer space based on international law and jointly safeguard the life and safety of astronauts and the safe and stable operation of space facilities in orbit'.[13]

This incident not only highlights the potential for the increasing commercial uses of space to create tension between states, it also illustrates key exemplars of the space domain which make is particularly susceptible to grey zone operations. Whilst, the exchange of notes to the UNCOPUOS is an unusual mechanism for identifying a potential dispute it reflects the state of stalemate that has developed in the various UN channels dedicated to treaty development with respect to outer space. China made no attempt to negotiate or seek a resolution to its complaint. Rather it simply used this platform to publicly criticize the actions of a US private space company and to remind the international community of its own adherence to international space law. The United States responded in kind with an assertion of its own good space behaviours. In terms of addressing the specific incident, it is unlikely that the specific details of the two proximity events will be further clarified. Neither State has released details of the precise distances involved and the Chinese spokesperson explicitly stated that the United States was in 'no position to unilaterally set a threshold of emergency collision criteria'.[14] It has also been observed that there are no clear and transparent rules regarding the threshold distance for collision avoidance.[15]

The proliferation of satellites in Low Earth Orbit is attracting extensive global interest, including from China which has plans for its own constellation of thirteen thousand satellites.[16] Whilst multiple companies race to deploy constellations of thousands of satellites, there is growing concern regarding the

---

[12] Ministry of Foreign Affairs of the People's Republic of China, 'Foreign Ministry Spokesperson Zhao Lijian's Regular Press Conference on February 10, 2022' (10 February 2022) <https://www.fmprc.gov.cn/mfa_eng/xwfw_665399/s2510_665401/2511_665403/202202/t20220210_10640952.html> accessed 30 August 2022.

[13] Ibid.

[14] Ibid.

[15] Theresa Hitchens, 'US rejects Charge that Starlink Satellites Endangered China's Space Station' (*Breaking Defense*, 3 February 2022) <https://breakingdefense.com/2022/02/us-rejects-charge-that-starlink-satellites-endangered-chinas-space-station/,> accessed 30 August 2022.

[16] Andrew Jones, 'China's Megaconstellation Project establishes Satellite Cluster in Chongqing' (*Space News*, 12 January 2022) <https://spacenews.com/chinas-megaconstellation-project-establishes-satellite-cluster-in-chongqing/> accessed 31 August 2022.

hazards potentially created by these constellations to the crowded space environment, the creation of space debris, and view of the night sky.[17]

In the context of increased access to and use of outer space for commercial and strategic purposes, there is an intricate dance being performed by various space actors, to simultaneously claim its own responsible behaviours and to denounce the reckless actions of others. It is very likely that the spat between China and United States, via the proxy of SpaceX, is far from over.

This chapter argues that space has become a unique environment for grey zone operations. As space has grown from a domain accessible only to a small group of space powers to a vital sphere of commercial and military operations, with more than ninety-seven states and organizations with assets in space, and many more dependent upon access to and use of those assets, there is increasing scope for tension.[18] This tension is exacerbated by the statement by various actors that space is now a 'warfighting domain'.[19]

This chapter will begin by identifying key attributes of space operations which make it susceptible to grey zone operations. Space is a key enabler of many elements of the daily operations of military and civilian society. Any interference with access to space assets has the capacity to cause significant disruption. Those effects are likely to be both asymmetric and unpredictable.

The next section provides an overview of the relevant international space law, followed by an analysis of the Artemis Accords process, which embraces a new approach to setting standards for cooperation in space. This process has the capacity to both build and fracture current partnerships in space.

The following section identifies the key threat to the continued use of the space domain, destructive anti-satellite (ASAT) tests, which leads on to the discussion of the push for the development of norms of responsible behaviour in order to avoid the continuation of destructive behaviours in space.

The final section will discuss these developments in the context of how we can better identify and manage these grey zone threats to ensure continued access to space, concluding that the current UN Open Ended Working Group on Responsible Behaviours is a step in the right direction but will still provide gaps for different standards and interpretation, leaving space susceptible to rising tension.

---

[17] Melissa de Zwart and Joel Lisk, 'Low Earth Orbit, Satellite Constellations and Regulation' (*Flinders University*, 28 July 2022) <https://apo.org.au/node/318785> accessed 30 August 2022.

[18] United Nations Office for Outer Space Affairs, 'Online Index of Objects Launched into Outer Space' <https://www.unoosa.org/oosa/osoindex/search-ng.jspx?lf_id=> accessed 30 August 2022.

[19] US Space Force, *Spacepower: Doctrine for Space Forces* (Space Capstone Publication, June 2020) <https://www.spaceforce.mil/Portals/1/Space%20Capstone%20Publication_10%20Aug%202020. pdf> accessed 30 August 2022; Everett C. Dolman 'Space Is a Warfighting Domain' (2022) 1 Aether: A Journal of Strategic Airpower and Spacepower 82.

294 ARENAS OF HYBRID AND GREY ZONE COMPETITION

2. Space and hybrid operations

Space exemplifies the conditions which give rise to both hybrid threats and grey zone operations. Space has now been recognized in many jurisdictions as a domain, alongside land, sea, air, and cyber.[20] This recognition, however, reflects many of the legal and practical complexities that also exist in recognizing cyber as a separate domain. In this section, the key defining elements of grey zone operations as applied to the space domain will be identified.

Space technology is *inherently dual use*, in the sense that it may be used for both civilian and military purposes. In many instances, technology created originally for military purposes has commercial applications and use that far outstrip those origins. For example, Global Navigation Satellite Strategy (GNSS) technology now underpins countless civilian applications, including banking, internet, navigation, and applications. The 'Day Without Space' exercise conducted by various governments reveals the *profound impact upon civilians* created by disruption of access to satellite services.[21]

The use of space is frequently characterized by *a desire to ensure freedom of one's own actions and operations whilst delegitimizing or restricting those of their opponents.*[22] This strategy can be seen in the drafting and calibration of the Outer Space Treaty. The Outer Space Treaty may be best understood as an arms control treaty, forged during the Cold War to ensure that neither of the spacefaring nations at that time was able to place a weapon of mass destruction in orbit around the Earth, the possibility for nuclear catastrophe already acknowledged as a likely outcome of this scenario.[23]

This is exacerbated by the *high level of secrecy* that is associated with the space domain. The perpetuation of a belief that powers in space are characterized by asymmetry of assets and interests, increases the tension and risk of conflict in space. This asymmetry poses particular challenges to the effectiveness of non-binding norms in this area and creates difficulties even for allies working together in this domain.[24]

---

[20] For example, NATO declared space to be an operational domain in 2019. See NATO, 'NATO's overarching Space Policy' (17 January 2022) <https://www.nato.int/cps/en/natohq/official_texts_190862.htm?selectedLocale=en> accessed 30 August 2022.

[21] See e.g. German Aerospace Center (DLR), 'A New Animation Shows "A Day without Space"' (11 June 2021) <https://www.dlr.de/content/en/articles/news/2021/02/20210611_a-new-animation-shows-a-day-without-space.html> accessed 30 August 2022.

[22] Aurel Sari, 'Legal Resilience in an Era of Grey Zone Conflicts and Hybrid Threats' (2020) 33 Cambridge Review of International Affairs 846, 856; Aurel Sari, 'Hybrid Warfare, Law and the Fulda Gap', in *Complex Battlespaces: The Law of Armed Conflict and the Dynamics of Modern Warfare*, edited by Christopher M. Ford and Winston S. Williams (OUP 2019) 161, 186–87.

[23] Melissa de Zwart 'Outer Space', in *New Technologies and the Law in War and Peace*, edited by William H. Boothby (CUP 2019) 338.

[24] Sean Carberry, 'Over-Classification, Lack of Standards Stymies Allied Space Forces (Updated)' (*National Defense*, 24 June 2022) <https://www.nationaldefensemagazine.org/articles/2022/6/24/over-classification-lack-of-standards-stymies-allied-space-forces> accessed 31 August 2022.

There is an *absence of a clear consensus* on important issues regarding use of the space domain in key areas such as resource extraction and utilization, which is used by adversaries to exploit the gaps. There is no clearer example of this than the narratives used around destructive ASAT tests. There are no explicit laws which prohibit the conduct of a destructive ASAT test. Only four countries have conducted such a test; however, their contribution to a growing debris field is significant. A further example is the conduct of Rendezvous and Proximity Operations, which involve close approaches to the satellite of another state, without consent or explanation.[25] These gaps in the law are both corrosive to norms and leave scope for the rules themselves to become highly politicized.[26] Braw's suggestion that 'gray-zone aggression could be called geopolitical gaslighting' seems particularly apt in this context of these operations undertaken far from the Earth's surface where there could be multiple explanations for the behaviours and limited data against which motivations and intent can be measured.[27]

Space is the domain of international law. However, despite there being five international space treaties and multiple other international instruments, it lacks clarity of interpretation and application. This lack of clarity regarding the applicable rules in space provides scope for conflict at the level of the appropriate interpretation. As Sari has observed, with respect to the continued assertion of various states that they are compliant with international law, where others are not, has the capacity to *weaken the respect for the law*.[28]

In recent years, a remarkable and innovative New Space industry has developed and there is now a significant reliance upon commercial space providers to conduct activities previously only undertaken by states, for example, delivering crew and cargo to the International Space Station.[29] The importance and role of the commercial space sector in a security context is unclear. Whilst many commentators suggest that the growing commercial space sector will impose a burden on defence assets, expecting protection from strategic threats, it is also proposed that commercial assets may provide resilience and continuity in the

---

[25] For example, the close approach by the Russian Luch satellite to the space assets of various states and commercial operators, Brian Weeden and Victoria Samson (eds), 'Global Counterspace Capabilities: An Open Sources Assessment', Secure World Foundation (April 2020); Jana Robinson, 'Prominent Security Risks Stemming from Space Hybrid Operations', in *War and Peace in Outer Space*, edited by Cassandra Steer and Matthew Hersch (OUP 2021) 229.

[26] See Sari, chapter 24, in this volume.

[27] Elisabeth Braw, *The Defender's Dilemma: Identifying and Deterring Gray-Zone Aggression* (American Enterprise Institute 2022) 29.

[28] Sari, 'Legal Resilience' (n 22) 857.

[29] Matt Weinzierl and Mehak Sarang, 'The Commercial Space Age Is Here: Private Space Travel Is Just the Beginning' (*Harvard Business Review*, 12 February 2021) <https://hbr.org/2021/02/the-commercial-space-age-is-here> accessed 31 August 2022.

event of degradation or attack on military assets and, further, may provide additional capability.[30]

The physical attributes of space are unique, but bear some similarities to the sea in terms of ambiguity of operations and difficulty of monitoring behaviours. In this context, *attribution also becomes complicated*, not the least of which due to the immense distances and the operation and speed of orbit. Space is of course global in effect. The ambiguity of attribution and the opacity of operations in the space domain is an opportunity for states to deny or delegitimize any military or political responses to their behaviour.[31] There is little understanding regarding the nature and consequences of hostility in space. As Grego notes, the unevenness of reliance on space assets and the fact that attacks on space assets may be seen as less harmful for terrestrial operations and human life, may lead to a preference for attacks on a satellite.[32] Further, the uneven distribution of reliance upon space, and hence consequences of the threat of loss of that capability result in lack of consensus of the value of preventing such an attack: 'there is little shared sense of what the proper response to a military space activity is and where the escalation thresholds or 'red lines' lie'.[33]

The United States has historically relied upon its technological advantage in the space domain, developing more advanced space technology and deploying more space assets. Currently, the United States has more military space capability than any of its rivals. However, this technological superiority can also serve as a greater risk, making it more vulnerable to lack of access to the space domain. This *asymmetry* therefore poses a unique risk situation and has also stalled the development of further laws in this area. Further, this technological superiority is no longer assured, with China and other states rapidly acquiring space expertise and assets.[34]

All these attributes create unique vulnerabilities for hybrid operations and may act as a deterrent to further beneficial uses of space. They also have the capacity to promote competition at the expense of cooperation in the space domain. The issues were recognized at the outset of the space race and the next

[30] James Clay Moltz, 'The Changing Dynamics of Twenty-First-Century Space Power' (2019) 12 Journal of Strategic Security 15, 37.

[31] Braw (n 27) 135, citing Erik Reichborn-Kjennerud and Patrick Cullen, 'What Is Hybrid Warfare?' (Norwegian Institute of International Affairs, January 2016) <https://nupi.brage.unit.no/nupi-xmlui/bitstream/handle/11250/2380867/NUPI_Policy_Brief_1_Reichborn_Kjennerud_Cullen.pdf> accessed 31 August 2022.

[32] Laura Grego, 'Outer Space and Crisis Risk', in Steer and Hersch (n 25) 277.

[33] Ibid. 277.

[34] John Olson et al, 'State of the Space Industrial Base 2022' (August 2022) <https://assets.ctfassets.net/3nanhbfkr0pc/6L5409bpVlnVyu2H5FOFnc/7595c4909616df92372a1d31be609625/State_of_the_Space_Industrial_Base_2022_Report.pdf> accessed 29 August 2022; Jacqueline Feldscher, 'China Could Overtake US in Space without "Urgent Action" Warns New Pentagon Report' (*Defense One*, 24 August 2022) <https://www.defenseone.com/technology/2022/08/china-could-overtake-us-space-without-urgent-action-report/376261/> accessed 29 August 2022.

3. The evolution of international space law

Since the dawn of the space age, space has been characterized by a desire to ensure freedom of one's own actions whilst seeking to impose limits on those of one's rivals. This approach characterizes the very essence of international space law.

The first GA Resolution on the use of outer space was adopted on 14 November 1957.[35] The use of the phrase 'exclusively for peaceful purposes' was to be repeated in many subsequent resolutions, declarations, and the treaties that followed. The UN Committee on the Peaceful Uses of Outer Space was established as an ad hoc committee in 1958 and as a permanent committee in 1959.[36] UNCOPUOS deals specifically with matters related to the peaceful uses of outer space, with matters relating to military uses of space referred to the UN Conference on Disarmament. As with other issues in the space domain, the fragmentation of issues across different bodies and committees has created issues in terms of establishing a clear understanding and a single authoritative forum for dealing with disputes and misunderstandings.

Given the Cold War context of the early years of space exploration, and the nature of space technology itself, the early focus of space-related treaty making is best understood as an effort towards arms control.[37] The first specific reference to outer space in a multilateral treaty was in the Partial Test Ban Treaty in 1963, providing that each Party undertook 'to prohibit, to prevent, and not to carry out any nuclear weapon test explosion . . . in the atmosphere . . . including outer space'.[38] The United States and USSR each announced compliance with this prohibition by refraining from placing any weapons of mass destruction (WMD) or nuclear weapons in outer space. UNGA Resolution 1884 further called upon States to 'refrain from placing in orbit around the earth any objects carrying nuclear weapons or any other kinds of weapons of mass destruction, installing such weapons on celestial bodies, or stationing such weapons in outer space' or 'causing, encouraging or in any way participating' in such activities.[39]

---

[35] UN General Assembly Resolution 1148 (XII) (14 November 1957).
[36] UN General Assembly Resolution 1348 (XIII) (13 December 1958) and UN General Assembly Resolution 1472 (XIV) (12 December 1959).
[37] P. J. Blount, 'Renovating Space: The Future of International Space Law' (2011) 40 Denver Journal of International Law and Policy 515, 516–18; Joanne Irene Gabrynowicz, 'Space Law: Its Cold War Origins and Challenges in the Era of Globalization' (2004) 37 Suffolk University Law Review 1041, 1041–47.
[38] Treaty Banning Nuclear Weapon Tests in the Atmosphere, in Outer Space and under Water (5 August 1963) 480 UNTS 43 (Partial Test Ban Treaty), Article I.
[39] UN General Assembly Resolution 1884 (XVIII) (17 October 1963).

The Treaty on Principles Governing the Activities of States in the Exploration and Use of Outer Space, including the Moon and Other Celestial Bodies is the foundational treaty of international space law. As of 2022, the Outer Space Treaty has 112 ratifications and 23 signatories.[40] The Outer Space Treaty, forged in the context of race for space supremacy of the 1960s, a race which saw the US technological advantage run second to Soviet firsts on a number of key occasions, adopts much of the language of the proceeding UN Resolutions. The provisions of the Outer Space Treaty focus on transparency, balance, and ensuring freedom of access to space. For example, Article I of the Outer Space Treaty provides that:

> The exploration and use of outer space, including the Moon and other celestial bodies, shall be carried out for the benefit and in the interests of all countries, irrespective of their degree of economic or scientific development, and shall be the province of all mankind.[41]

This aspirational language draws upon UNGA Resolution 1962 (XVIII) which expressed the intention 'that the exploration and use of outer space shall be carried on for the benefit of mankind and for the benefit of States irrespective of their degree of economic or scientific development'.[42]

Article III of the Outer Space Treaty provides:

> States Parties to the Treaty shall carry on activities in the exploration and use of outer space, including the Moon and other celestial bodies, in accordance with international law, including the Charter of the United Nations, in the interest of maintaining international peace and security and promoting international cooperation and understanding.[43]

This language also adapts the wording of UNGA Resolution 1962 (XVIII) which stated that

> the principles of freedom, exploration and use of outer space shall be carried on for the benefit and the interest of all mankind whereby outer space and the

---

[40] UN Committee on the Peaceful Uses of Outer Space, 'Status of International Agreements relating to Activities in Outer Space as at 1 January 2022' (2022), UN Doc. A/AC.105/C.2/2022/CRP.10.

[41] Outer Space Treaty, Art. I.

[42] UN General Assembly Resolution 1962 (XVIII), 'Declaration of Legal Principles Governing the Activities of States in the Exploration and Use of Outer Space' (13 December 1963). See further Stephen Hobe, 'Article I', in *Cologne Commentary on Space Law Volume 1: Outer Space Treaty*, edited by Stephen Hobe, Bernhard Schmidt-Tedd, and Kai-Uwe Schrogl (Carl Heymanns 2009) 29.

[43] Outer Space Treaty, Art. III.

celestial bodies shall be free for exploration and use by all states on the basis of equality and in accordance with international law.[44]

The use of language mandating freedom, cooperation, and equality in the exploration of space in these instruments belies the secrecy and competition with which space activities were being undertaken during this time. Despite expressions of the desirability of space for the benefit of all, states were engaging in highly classified activities developing all aspects of their space programs, including military uses, and even weaponry. It is worth noting Articles X and XII, each of which express some element of cooperation, including observation.

Article IV of the Outer Space Treaty is the key provision dealing with military uses of outer space. It provides:

> States Parties to the Treaty undertake not to place in orbit around the earth any objects carrying nuclear weapons or any other kinds of weapons of mass destruction, install such weapons on celestial bodies, or station such weapons in outer space in any other manner.
>
> The moon and other celestial bodies shall be used by all States Parties to the Treaty exclusively for peaceful purposes. The establishment of military bases, installations and fortifications, the testing of any type of weapons and the conduct of military manoeuvres on celestial bodies shall be forbidden. The use of military personnel for scientific research or for any other peaceful purposes shall not be prohibited. The use of any equipment or facility necessary for peaceful exploration of the moon and other celestial bodies shall also not be prohibited.[45]

This Article reaffirms the 1963 Treaty regarding prohibition of the placement of WMD in orbit, on celestial bodies or in outer space. It then goes further to require that the Moon and other celestial bodies shall be used 'exclusively for peaceful purposes'. The 'establishment of military bases, installations, and fortifications; the testing of any types of weapons; and the conduct of military manoeuvres on any celestial body is expressly forbidden. This wording leaves open the placement of weapons or military establishments in space. As Koplow has observed, it is arguable that in agreeing to restrict such activities the space-faring states were only banning activities that they 'either could not accommodate or had no interest in attempting, while preserving their full freedom to conduct any of

[44] UN General Assembly Resolution 1962 (XVIII).
[45] Outer Space Treaty, Art. IV.

300 ARENAS OF HYBRID AND GREY ZONE COMPETITION

the deployments, tests, and constructions they might someday find militarily valuable'.[46]

An area of significant debate is the extent to which the Outer Space Treaty was intended to apply to non-State commercial space activity. As noted above,[47] Article VI requires States to 'bear international responsibility for national activities in outer space . . . whether such activities are carried on by governmental agencies or by non-governmental entities'. Further, States are required to undertake 'authorization and continuing supervision' of the activities of non-governmental entities. This Article imposes responsibility upon States for the space activities of private operators and obliges States to ensure compliance of those operators with the obligations of the Outer Space Treaty. This Article derives from a compromise between the views of the USSR that no private activities should be permitted in space and the US view that private enterprise should be allowed to flourish in space as elsewhere.[48] There remains a lack of consensus regarding what is encompassed within the concept of 'national activities' and hence the scope of the obligation under this Article. Various interpretations may be applied to the concept of 'national activities in outer space' which look to concepts of nationality, attribution with respect to activities undertaken, and concepts of jurisdiction under international law.[49]

Article VII provides that:

> Each State Party to the Treaty that launches or procures the launching of an object into outer space, including the moon and other celestial bodies, and each State Party from whose territory or facility an object is launched, is internationally liable for damage to another State Party to the Treaty or to its natural or juridical persons by such object or its component parts on the Earth, in air or in outer space, including the moon and other celestial bodies.[50]

Article VIII deals with 'jurisdiction and control' of space objects, confirming that the State Party 'on whose registry an object launched into outer space is carried shall retain jurisdiction and control over such object, and over any personnel

---

[46] David Koplow, 'Deterrence as the MacGuffin: The Case for Arms Control in Outer Space' (2019) 10 Journal of National Security Law and Policy 293, 328.

[47] See n 4 and accompanying text.

[48] Frans von der Dunk, 'The Origins of Authorisation: Article VI of the Outer Space Treaty and International Space Law', in National Space Legislation in Europe: Issues of Authorisation of Private Space Activities in the Light of Developments in European Space Cooperation, edited by Frans von der Dunk (Martinus Nijhoff 2011) 3, 3–4.

[49] Christian Robison 'Changing Responsibility for a Changing Environment: Revaluating the Traditional Interpretation of Article VI of the Outer Space Treaty in Light of Private Industry' (2020) 5 University of Bologna Law Review 1, 12–15.

[50] See also Convention on International Liability for Damage Caused by Space Objects (29 March 1972), 961 UNTS 188 (Space Liability Convention).

thereof, while in outer space or on a celestial body'. Further, ownership of 'objects launched into outer space, including objects landed or constructed on a celestial body, and of their component parts, is not affected by their presence in outer space or on a celestial body or by their return to the Earth' and such objects (and their component parts) shall be returned to that State. This provision has profound effects on the legal arrangements regarding removal of space debris.

Article IX articulates key concepts of 'due regard' and 'harmful interference', as well as addressing contamination of the space or Earth environment by exploration activities:

> In the exploration and use of outer space, including the moon and other celestial bodies, States Parties to the Treaty shall be guided by the principle of co-operation and mutual assistance and shall conduct all their activities in outer space, including the moon and other celestial bodies, with due regard to the corresponding interests of all other States Parties to the Treaty. States Parties to the Treaty shall pursue studies of outer space, including the moon and other celestial bodies, and conduct exploration of them so as to avoid their harmful contamination and also adverse changes in the environment of the Earth resulting from the introduction of extraterrestrial matter and, where necessary, shall adopt appropriate measures for this purpose. If a State Party to the Treaty has reason to believe that an activity or experiment planned by it or its nationals in outer space, including the moon and other celestial bodies, would cause potentially harmful interference with activities of other States Parties in the peaceful exploration and use of outer space, including the moon and other celestial bodies, it shall undertake appropriate international consultations before proceeding with any such activity or experiment. A State Party to the Treaty which has reason to believe that an activity or experiment planned by another State Party in outer space, including the moon and other celestial bodies, would cause potentially harmful interference with activities in the peaceful exploration and use of outer space, including the moon and other celestial bodies, may request consultation concerning the activity or experiment.

It is worth noting the other articles which express some element of cooperation, including observation,[51] notification,[52] and visitation.[53]

A further four space treaties were developed by the UN: the Rescue and Return Agreement;[54] the Liability Convention;[55] the Registration

---

[51] Outer Space Treaty, Art. X.
[52] Ibid. Art. XI.
[53] Ibid. Art. XII.
[54] Agreement on the Rescue of Astronauts, the Return of Astronauts and the Return of Objects Launched into Outer Space (22 April 1968), 672 UNTS 119.
[55] Space Liability Convention.

302 ARENAS OF HYBRID AND GREY ZONE COMPETITION

Convention;[56] and the Moon Agreement.[57] The last of these treaties has received little adoption, with only eighteen ratifications and four signatures. The United States has explicitly stated that the Moon Agreement does not reflect customary international law and that it does not consider the Moon Agreement to be 'an effective or necessary instrument to guide nation states regarding the promotion of commercial participation in the long-term exploration, scientific discovery, and use of the Moon, Mars, or other celestial bodies.'[58]

Further to this, recognizing the crucial role performed by certain satellites in nuclear deterrence, the United States and USSR determined that attacks on early warning and crisis communication satellites should be avoided.[59] They also recognized the specific role played by satellites as protected 'national technical means' of verification of Treaty compliance.[60]

The growing recognition of the increasing threat posed by the proliferation of space debris to continued access to space, especially to prized orbits and management of the radiofrequency spectrum prompted UNCOPUOS to establish a Working Group on the Long Term Sustainability of Outer Space Activities, which produced a set of voluntary, non-binding guidelines encouraging the adoption of national regulatory frameworks, the supervision of national space activities, promotion and sharing of space debris monitoring information, and the investigation of measures to manage space debris, as noted by the United States in its response to the Chinese Note Verbale.[61]

Despite this work of UNCOPUOS on space sustainability and some other measures discussed below, it seemed that after the failure of the Moon Agreement to garner signatories, States had exhausted the extent of their agreement on principles applicable to the use of outer space. Despite this, the development of space technology continued rapidly and even witnessed international collaboration on projects such as the International Space Station. It has also witnessed the increase in activities which pose a threat to the safety of the space domain, such as destructive ASAT tests, and activities which stretch and challenge the provisions of the UN Space Treaties, such as proposals for the construction of long-term habitations on the Moon and resource extraction and use.

---

[56] Convention on Registration of Objects Launched into Outer Space (14 January 1975), 1023 UNTS 15.

[57] Agreement Governing the Activities of States on the Moon and Other Celestial Bodies (18 December 1979), 1363 UNTS 3.

[58] Executive Office of the President, Executive Order 13914, 'Encouraging International Support for the Recovery and Use of Space Resources' (6 April 2020), 85 Fed. Reg. 20381, 20381–82.

[59] Grego (n 32), 273–74.

[60] Interim Agreement between the United States of America and the Union of Soviet Socialist Republics on Certain Measures with Respect to the Limitation of Strategic Offensive Arms (26 May 1972), 944 UNTS 3 (SALT I); Treaty between the United States of America and the Union of Soviet Socialist Republics on the Limitation of Anti-Ballistic Missile Systems (26 May 1972), 944 UNTS 13.

[61] See n 9.

The next section will consider the efforts by the United States, through NASA's Artemis Accords, to develop new frameworks and consensus for these activities.

4. The Artemis Accords

The Artemis Accords were released by NASA as a set of high-level principles on 15 May 2020.[62] The release of the Accords followed growing speculation in early 2020 that the Trump Administration was developing a 'legal blueprint for mining on the moon'.[63] This speculation had been fuelled by an Executive Order which stated:

> Americans should have the right to engage in commercial exploration, recovery, and use of resources in outer space, consistent with applicable law. Outer space is a legally and physically unique domain of human activity, and the United States does not view it as a global commons. Accordingly, it shall be the policy of the United States to encourage international support for the public and private recovery and use of resources in outer space, consistent with applicable law.[64]

The Executive Order reaffirmed the principles which had been set out in the US Commercial Space Launch Competitiveness Act 2015. Title IV of that Act, 'Space Resource Exploration and Utilization', provided for: '1. recognition of the rights of a US citizen "engaged in commercial recovery of . . . a space resource" to that resource; 2. a mandate for the implementation of a domestic US regime requiring authorization and supervision of resource extraction and recovery activities; and 3. the promotion and facilitation of US commercial space resources exploration and extraction; in accordance with US obligations under international law'.[65] Acknowledging that such activities would require the involvement of commercial operators, the Executive Order foreshadowed the need for some alternative road rules for the commercial use of space, setting the stage for the development of the Artemis Accords, which operate as an agency-to-agency agreement rather than a multilateral treaty between states.

[62] Eric Berger, 'NASA Creates Artemis Accords in Effort to Extend Its Values to the Moon: "We Don't Want to Only Carry Astronauts to the Moon, We Want to Carry Our Values"' (*Ars Technica*, 16 May 2020) <https://arstechnica.com/science/2020/05/nasa-creates-artemis-accords-in-effort-to-ext end-its-values-to-the-moon/> accessed 31 August 2022.

[63] Joey Roulette, 'Trump Administration Drafting Artemis Accords Pact for Space Mining' (*Reuters World News*, 6 May 2020) <https://www.reuters.com/article/uk-space-exploration-moon-mining-exclusi-idUKKBN22H2S1> accessed 31 August 2022.

[64] Executive Order 13914 (n 57).

[65] Frans von der Dunk, 'Asteroid Mining: International and National Legal Aspects' (2017) 26 Michigan State International Law Review 83.

304 ARENAS OF HYBRID AND GREY ZONE COMPETITION

The Artemis Accords are articulated as a series of principles that must be agreed to by the relevant space agency of a state that wants to participate in the Artemis program. Each national space agency joins NASA in the Artemis program by executing the Artemis Accords agreement.[66] The use of contractual agreements to determine the rules of the joint venture clearly builds upon the success of the International Space Station Intergovernmental Agreement.[67] The original signatories to the Artemis Accords were the United States, Australia, Canada, Italy, Japan, Luxembourg, United Arab Emirates, and United Kingdom. There are now twenty-nine Artemis Accords signatories as of September 2023.[68] Whilst initially indicating that it was open to participation in the Artemis Accords,[69] Russia subsequently declared the Artemis Gateway (which built in part on the existing collaboration in the International Space Station) is too 'US-centric'.[70] NASA remains legally prohibited from collaboration with any Chinese entity using government funding under the Wolf Amendment. Russia and China are developing their own International Lunar Research Station which will involve robotic and human missions, as well as resource extraction, communication, energy and other scientific activities.[71] The planning of two missions to the Moon within the same time frame has the potential to create further international tension, with competition for the 'best' landing site and resources available on the Moon.

The Artemis Accords consist of ten foundation principles, which may be developed further in the specific terms of a bilateral agreement. It has been observed that these principles fall roughly into two extremes: existing norms that are conform broadly to the equivalent provisions of the UN Space Treaties, with the notable exception of the Moon Agreement, and those that extend well

[66] NASA, 'The Artemis Accords: Principles for Cooperation in the Civil Exploration and Use of the Moon, Mars, Comets and Asteroids for Peaceful Purposes' (13 October 2020) <https://www.nasa.gov/specials/artemis-accords/img/Artemis-Accords-signed-13Oct2020.pdf> accessed 31 August 2022.

[67] Agreement among the Government of Canada, Governments of Member States of the European Space Agency, the Government of Japan, the Government of the Russian Federation, and the Government of the United States of America concerning Cooperation on the Civil Inter International Space Station (29 January 1998) .

[68] US Department of State, 'United States Welcomes Germany's Signing of the Artemis Accords' (15 September 15 2023) <https://www.state.gov/united-states-welcomes-germanys-signing-of-the-artemis-accords/> accessed 2 November 2023.

[69] John Sheldon, 'Lunapolitics: Russia's Roscosmos Signals Openness to US-proposed Artemis Accords' (*SpaceWatch.global,* May 2020) <https://spacewatch.global/2020/05/lunapolitics-russias-roscosmos-signals-openness-to-us-proposed-artemis-accords/ (accessed 31 August 2022).

[70] Jeff Foust, 'Russia skeptical about participating in lunar Gateway' (*Space News*, October 12, 2020) <https://spacenews.com/russia-skeptical-about-participating-in-lunar-gateway/> accessed 31 August 2022.

[71] Andrew Jones, 'China, Russia reveal roadmap for international moon base' (*Space News*, June 16, 2021) <https://spacenews.com/china-russia-reveal-roadmap-for-international-moon-base/> accessed 31 August 2022.

beyond the scope of existing international space law and attempt to establish new norms of behaviour.[72]

The provisions which may be described as broad reaffirmations of fundamental space law principles are:

Section 3: Peaceful Purposes: This section requires signatories to affirm that the activities under the Accords shall be 'exclusively' for peaceful purposes and in accordance with relevant international law'. The concept of peaceful purposes appears four times in the Outer Space Treaty, most notably in Article IV. Whilst the exact scope of the concept remains open to conjecture, it is accepted as a fundamental tenet of international space law and its presence in the Artemis Accords is uncontroversial. Similarly, the requirement to conduct activities in accordance with international law is a fundamental provision of Article III of the Outer Space Treaty.

Section 4: Transparency: This section requires 'transparency in the broad dissemination of information regarding their national space policies and space exploration plans' and the sharing of scientific information resulting from activities conducted pursuant to the Accords with the public and international scientific community on a good-faith basis and consistent with Article XI of the Outer Space Treaty. Clear communication about space activities is recognized as vital to the safe use of space for peaceful purposes, although the details regarding how that communication should occur remain opaque.

Section 6: Emergency Assistance: Article V OST requires parties to render assistance to 'astronauts' and the Rescue and Return Agreement prescribes obligations regarding rendering assistance to 'personnel of a spacecraft' who are in distress. The effect of this section is to reinforce these obligations by requiring signatories to 'commit to taking all reasonable efforts to render necessary assistance to personnel in outer space who are in distress, and acknowledge their obligations under the Rescue and Return Agreement'. With increased activities in outer space, involving both government and private actors, it is not clear that all personnel operating in the space environment would satisfy the traditional concept of 'astronaut'. Private space operators, including SpaceX, Blue Origin and Virgin Galactic all use the term 'astronaut'; however, they also make use of terms such as 'commercial crew' and 'passengers'. By referring to all 'personnel

---

[72] Melissa de Zwart, 'To the Moon and Beyond: The Artemis Accords and the Evolution of Space Law', in *Commercial and Military Uses of Outer Space*, edited by Melissa de Zwart and Stacey Henderson (Springer 2021) 65; Melissa de Zwart, 'The Impact of the Artemis Accords on Resource Extraction', in *In-Space Manufacturing and Resources*, edited by Volker Hessel et al (Wiley 2022) 351; Jeff Foust, 'What's in a Name when It Comes to an "Accord"?' (*The Space Review*, 13 July 2020) <https://www.thespacereview.com/article/3987/1> accessed 31 August 2022; Christopher Johnson, 'The Space Law Context of the Artemis Accords (Part 2)' (*Space Watch Global*, 28 May 2020) <https://spacewatch.global/2020/05/spacewatchgl-feature-the-space-law-context-of-the-artemis-accords-part-2/> accessed 31 August 2022.

in outer space who are in distress', this provision seeks to extend its effect beyond any technical definition of astronauts or personnel of a spacecraft, and avoids the semantic complexity of whether an individual satisfies various domestic and other rules regarding qualification as an astronaut.[73]

Section 7: Registration of Space Objects: The Registration Convention requires the launching state of a space object to register that object and, where there are two or more launching states, to determine which of them shall register that object. This section explicitly requires parties to the Accords to determine the appropriate means and state of registration for any project conducted pursuant to the Accords.

Section 8: Release of Scientific Data: A fundamental concept as outlined in Article I of the Outer Space Treaty is the encouragement of international cooperation. As noted above,[74] the UN Space Treaties also contain numerous mentions of visits to facilities, observation, consultations, and provision of certain information to the UN and other States. Whilst this section asserts that the signatories 'are committed to the open sharing of scientific data' and 'plan to make the scientific results obtained from the cooperative activities under these Accords available to the public and the international scientific community' in a timely manner, the Accords will require signatories to 'coordinate with each other in advance regarding the public release of information that relates to the other Signatories' activities under these Accords in order to provide appropriate protection for any proprietary and/or export-controlled information'. Notably the commitment to share scientific data openly is not intended to apply to private sector operations unless being conducted on behalf of an Agency.

The principles which extend beyond the concepts contained within the UN Space Treaties include:

Section 5: Interoperability: Successful collaboration between multiple parties, including agencies and commercial operators will require participants to use current interoperability standards for space-based infrastructure, as well as to establish standards where they do not currently exist or are inadequate. Russia has indicated that, despite the fact that it will not be participating in the Lunar Gateway project, it wants to ensure that standard interfaces are used so Russian spacecraft may dock with the Gateway.[75]

Section 9: Preserving Outer Space Heritage: The preservation of the Apollo Moon Landing site has attracted significant interest in recent years.[76] This

---

[73] Frans von der Dunk and Gerardine Goh, 'Article V', in Hobe, Schmidt-Tedd, and Schrogl (n 42) 94.

[74] See section 3.

[75] Foust (n 69).

[76] NASA, 'NASA's recommendation to space-faring entities: How to protect and preserve the historic and scientific value of US Government Lunar Artifacts' (11 July 2011), <https://www.nasa.gov/directorates/heo/library/reports/lunar-artifacts.html> accessed 31 August 2022.

section commits signatories to 'preserve outer space heritage' including 'historically significant human or robotic landing sites, artifacts, spacecraft, and other evidence of activity on celestial bodies in accordance with mutually developed standards and practices'. Further, signatories agree to contribute to multilateral efforts to preserve space heritage. This provision raises two issues: the matter of who determines whether a site is of heritage value and the consequence of placing limits on access to the site identified for other users and whether this may amount to a de facto appropriation of the relevant area in breach of Article II of the Outer Space Treaty.[77]

Section 10: Space Resources: Stating that the 'utilization of space resources can benefit humankind by providing critical support for safe and sustainable operations' this section affirms that such extraction and utilization 'should be executed in such a manner that complies with the Outer Space Treaty and in support of safe and sustainable space activities'. Reflecting the current state of international debate on the legality of resource extraction, the section continues: 'the extraction of space resources does not inherently constitute national appropriation under Article II of the Outer Space Treaty', and that 'contracts and other legal instruments' relating to space resources should be consistent with that Treaty'. This provision deliberately seeks to promote and advance the development of rules and norms regarding the extraction and use of space resources. Whilst not being developed within the COPUOS process, the section obliges signatories 'to use their experience under the Accords to contribute to multilateral efforts to further develop international practices and rules applicable to the extraction and utilization of space resources, including through ongoing efforts at the COPUOS'. It is noted that there are other projects which address the lack of rules in this area, including the Hague International Space Resources Governance Working Group which has developed and adopted a set of guiding principles in the Building Blocks for the Development on an International Framework on Space Resource Activities.[78]

Section 11: Deconfliction of Space Activities: The key provision of the Outer Space Treaty dealing with the management of competing uses of outer space is Article IX, which articulates concepts of 'due regard' and 'harmful interference'. This section requires signatories to acknowledge and reaffirm their commitment to these provisions, in particular, of the Outer Space Treaty and to act in accordance with the requirements with respect to these concepts under Article

---

[77] Outer Space Treaty, Art. II ('Outer space, including the moon and other celestial bodies, is not subject to national appropriation by claim of sovereignty, by means of use or occupation, or by any other means').

[78] The Hague Space Resources Working Group, 'Building Blocks for the Development of an International Legal Framework on Space Resources Activities' (November 2019) <https://www.uni versiteitleiden.nl/binaries/content/assets/rechtsgeleerdheid/instituut-voor-publiekrecht/lucht--en-ruimterecht/space-resources/bb-thissrwg--cover.pdf> accessed 31 August 2022.

308   ARENAS OF HYBRID AND GREY ZONE COMPETITION

IX. Signatories also affirm their commitment to the United Nations Guidelines for the Long-term Sustainability of Outer Space Activities. Critically, this section states that signatories will 'contribute to multilateral efforts to further develop international practices, criteria, and rules applicable to the definition and determination of safety zones and harmful interference'. The concept of 'safety zones' whilst being one well-recognized in aviation law, is not currently recognized in space law, despite there being a 200km 'keep out' zone in place around the ISS. In this context a 'safety zone' is defined as an 'area in which nominal operations of a relevant activity or an anomalous event could reasonably cause harmful interference'. This provision represents an attempt to ensure that competing uses of a celestial body, such as the surface of the Moon, for resource extraction activities, may be conducted with some degree of mutual co-operation and understanding. It goes beyond applying those principles to members of the Artemis Accords and actively obliges signatories to work towards development of international norms recognizing and applying such zones. This is one of the provisions of the Accords likely to be contested by non-Artemis states. As Johnson observes, safety zones will have to be articulated carefully to partners, and to the international community, in a way that stresses that Artemis activities are not asserting property rights over the boundaries of such zones. Instead, they should be explained as 'the physical manifestation of due regard amongst Artemis partners'.[79] This, however, leaves open the issue of recognition of these zones by non-Artemis actors and further, the potential for the creation of competing systems of safety zones. It can be anticipated that this will be an area for grey zone tension as is the subject of the next section of the chapter, destructive ASAT tests.

The Artemis Accords therefore provide both a shield and a target in the context of grey zone activities. They seek to assert and promote certain positions with respect to uses of space, but their very articulation of course provides scope for manipulation of those positions by competing space powers.

5. Destructive ASAT tests

Four states have been identified as having conducted destructive ASAT tests.[80] Research done by Secure World Foundation establishes that more than fifty ASAT tests were conducted by the United States and USSR between 1959 and 1995, of which a 'dozen weapons hit satellites, creating more than 1200 pieces of

---

[79] Christopher Johnson, 'The Space Law Context of the Artemis Accords (Part 2)' (*Space Watch Global*, 28 May 2020) <https://spacewatch.global/2020/05/spacewatchgl-feature-the-space-law-context-of-the-artemis-accords-part-2/> accessed 31 August 2022.
[80] Weeden and Samson (n 25).

HYBRID AND GREY ZONE OPERATIONS IN OUTER SPACE   309

trackable orbital debris'.[81] Since 2005, a further five destructive tests have been conducted by United States, Russia, China, and India.[82]

China destroyed its own FengYun 1C weather satellite in 2007, which created more than two thousand pieces of trackable debris. This destructive test was part of an ongoing sequence of Chinese ASAT tests, none of which resulted in the creation of debris, but which clearly demonstrated the potential and ability to do so.[83] The United States destroyed a malfunctioning reconnaissance satellite in February 2008, as part of operation Burnt Frost. The United States continues to assert that this action was not an ASAT test but rather an action necessary to prevent the satellite's remaining stock of toxic hydrazine fuel from creating a hazard if it survived atmospheric re-entry. It further asserted that the destruction was undertaken in such a way as to minimize the creation of debris. However, in reality the destruction created 174 pieces of debris tracked by the Space Surveillance Network which took over eighteen months to re-enter the atmosphere. There was significant public messaging about the need for the destruction of the potential hazard, but this has not been verified.[84]

In March 2019, India declared itself a 'space power' upon the destruction of its own satellite in a project named 'Mission Shakti'.[85] After a prior unsuccessful test in February 2019, India announced on 27 March 2019 that it had destroyed its own fridge-sized satellite in Low Earth Orbit (LEO) with a kinetic weapon. Prior to this test, the Indian space program, operated through the Indian Space Research Organisation (ISRO) had publicly declared that it was not involved in any military space activity. However, Mission Shakti involved the deliberate destruction of its own asset, which had apparently been launched expressly for this purpose. In a carefully worded statement, Indian Prime Minister Modi declared that this test was a further success of the Indian space program and one which 'will make India stronger, even more secure and will further peace and harmony'.[86] This deliberate choice of language is intended to control the discourse

---

[81] Brian Weeden and Victoria Samson, 'It's Time for a Global Ban on Destructive Antisatellite Testing' (*Scientific American*, 14 January 2022) <https://www.scientificamerican.com/article/its-time-for-a-global-ban-on-destructive-antisatellite-testing/> accessed 31 August 2022.

[82] Ibid.

[83] Brian Weeden, 'Chinese, American, and Russian Anti-Satellite Testing in Space', Secure World Foundation (17 March 2014) <https://swfound.org/media/167224/through_a_glass_darkly_ma rch2014.pdf> accessed 30 August 2022.

[84] Ibid.

[85] George Dvorsky, 'India Declares Itself a 'Space Power' after Shooting Down Its Own Satellite' (*Gizmodo*, 28 March 2019) <https://www.gizmodo.com.au/2019/03/india-declares-itself-a-space-power-after-shooting-down-its-own-satellite/> accessed 30 August 2022.

[86] Eric Berger, 'India Shoots Down a Weather Satellite, Declares Itself a 'Space Power'" (*Ars Technica*, 28 March 2019) <https://arstechnica.com/science/2019/03/india-shoots-down-a-weat her-satellite-declares-itself-a-space-power/> accessed 30 August 2022; Narendra Modi, Twitter (27 March 2019) ('#MissionShakti is special for 2 reasons: India is only the 4th country to acquire such a specialised and modern capability. Entire effort is indigenous. India stands tall as a space power! It

surrounding the test, specifically to affirm India's assertion of its adherence to the concept of space as a peaceful domain, ironically through the demonstrated success of a destructive act.

The Official FAQ released by the Indian Foreign Ministry asserted that in conducting the test India was 'not in violation of any international law or Treaty to which it is a Party or any national obligation'.[87] The statement focused on the allegedly responsible manner in which the test had been conducted rather than the destructive outcome of the test itself. It declared that the test was 'done in the lower atmosphere to ensure that there is no space debris. Whatever debris that is generated will decay and fall back onto the earth within weeks'. The FAQ noted that whilst the 'test was done to verify that India has the capability to safeguard our space assets' and that it is 'the Government's responsibility to defend the country's interests in outer space':

India has no intention of entering into an arms race in outer space. We have always maintained that space must be used only for peaceful purposes. We are against the weaponization of Outer Space and support international efforts to reinforce the safety and security of space based assets.

Further, the FAQ affirmed that:

India believes that Outer space is the common heritage of humankind and it is the responsibility of all space-faring nations to preserve and promote the benefits flowing from advances made in space technology and its applications for all.

Crucially, the FAQ also affirmed that India is a member of 'all the major international treaties relating to Outer Space' (including participation in UNCOPUOS) and 'already implements a number of Transparency and Confidence Building Measures (TCBMs)'. It asserts that, whilst India supported UNGA resolution 69/ 32 on No First Placement of Weapons on Outer Space, there is a need for substantive legal measures to prevent an arms race in outer space. It also affirms India's support for the 'consideration of the issue of Prevention of an Arms Race

---

will make India stronger, even more secure and will further peace and harmony') <https://twitter. com/narendramodi/status/1110801488559759360> accessed 31 August 2022.

[87] Ministry of External Affairs, Government of India, 'Frequently Asked Questions on Mission Shakti, India's Anti-Satellite Missile test conducted on 27 March, 2019' (27 March 2019) <https:// www.mea.gov.in/press-releases.htm?dtl/31179/Frequently_Asked_Questions_on_Mission_Shakti_ Indias_AntiSatellite_Missile_test_conducted_on_27_March_2019> accessed 30 August 2022.

HYBRID AND GREY ZONE OPERATIONS IN OUTER SPACE 311

in Outer Space (PAROS) in the Conference on Disarmament where it has been on the agenda since 1982'.

Much of the public focus on the Mission Shakti destruction was on the claims that the test was undertaken responsibly and would produce minimal debris. There were, however, a few comments regarding the risk it posed to the space environment, specifically in LEO. NASA Administrator Jim Bridenstine denounced the test as a 'terrible, terrible thing' and noted the risk to the safety of the International Space Station.[88] The German delegation at UNCOPUOS made a Statement on Space Debris in direct response to the Mission Shakti test, calling for a 'legally binding prohibition of the intentional destruction of space objects resulting in the generation of long-lasting debris, including in situations of armed conflict'.[89]

In 2021, Russia conducted a destructive ASAT test on one of its own satellites, COSMOS 1408, a defunct spy satellite, generating a field of debris that forced the International Space Station (ISS) crew to take shelter in their Soyuz and SpaceX Dragon capsules. The destruction of the COSMOS 1408 generated more than 1,500 pieces of trackable debris and likely thousands more that are too small to be tracked. Russia's space agency, ROCOSMOS, dismissed concerns regarding the debris field, tweeting: 'The orbit of the object, which forced the crew today to move into spacecraft according to standard procedures, has moved away from the ISS orbit. The station is in the green zone.'[90]

The action generated widespread international condemnation, including from the US Space Command, US State Department and NASA, attracting claims of hypocrisy from Russia.[91] Despite this, no state has adopted the official position that destructive ASAT tests are prohibited under the UN space treaties.[92] However, in April 2022 the United States announced a moratorium on ASAT testing, undertaking not to conduct destructive direct-ascent anti-satellite missile testing.[93] Whether this position will be adopted by other states remains

[88] Jeff Foust, 'NASA Warns Indian Anti-Satellite Test Increased Debris Risk to ISS' (*Space News*, 2 April 2019) <https://spacenews.com/nasa-warns-indian-anti-satellite-test-increased-debris-risk-to-iss/> accessed 30 August 2022.

[89] Permanent Mission of the Federal Republic of Germany to the Office of the United Nations and to the other International Organizations, 'Statement on Space Debris at the 58th session of the UN Space Legal Subcommittee, Vienna, 1–12 April 2019' <https://wien-io.diplo.de/iow-en/news/statement-debris/2208724> accessed 30 August 2022.

[90] Roscosmos, Twitter (16 November 2021) <https://twitter.com/roscosmos/status/14602562 20124782595?lang=en> accessed 31 August 2022.

[91] Michael Sheetz, 'Russia Calls U.S. "Hypocritical" for Condemning Anti-Satellite Weapons Test' (*CNBC*, 16 November 2021) <https://www.cnbc.com/2021/11/16/russia-us-hypocritical-for-con demning-anti-satellite-asat-weapon-test.html> accessed 31 August 2022.

[92] Douglas Ligor 'Reduce Friction in Space by Amending the 1967 Outer Space Treaty' (*War on the Rocks*, 26 August 2022) https://warontherocks.com/2022/08/stabilize-friction-points-in-space-by-amending-the-1967-outer-space-treaty/> accessed 29 August 2022.

[93] The White House, 'Remarks by Vice President Harris on the Ongoing Work to Establish Norms in Space' (18 April 2022) <https://www.whitehouse.gov/briefing-room/speeches-remarks/2022/ 04/18/remarks-by-vice-president-harris-on-the-ongoing-work-to-establish-norms-in-space/>

312 ARENAS OF HYBRID AND GREY ZONE COMPETITION

to be seen, but it provides a signal that the United States sees this as an emerging 'red line' of international behaviour.

Clearly, these ASAT tests in terms of both the tests themselves and the surrounding communications exemplify grey zone activities, actions that send signals and provoke a sense of heightened tension, whilst being cloaked in ambivalent, at best, and misleading, at worst, narratives.

The next section will address recent steps to develop norms of responsible behaviours in space.

6. The development of norms of responsible behaviour

Despite the fact that the Prevention of an Arms Race in Outer Space (PAROS) has been the subject of an annual resolution of the UNGA and a standing item on the agenda of the Conference on Disarmament (CD) since 1982 'no significant action has been undertaken multilaterally on space security for decades'.[94] The UN has supported Transparency and Confidence Building Measures since 2005. The UN Group of Governmental Experts (GGE) formed in 2011, issued its Final Report on 'Transparency and Confidence Building Measures in Outer Space Activities', which was presented to the UNGA in December 2013.[95] However, contrary to initial optimism, its recommendations have largely been ignored. A further GGE initiative on the prevention of an arms race in outer space concluded with little fanfare in 2019.[96]

Other initiatives have included the European Code of Conduct for Activities in Outer Space, formally proposed in December 2008, and the Draft Treaty on the Prevention of the Placement of Weapons in Outer Space, the Threat of Use of Force Against Outer Space Objects, formally tabled by Russia and China in 2008 in the CD and revised in 2014. These proposals have reached an impasse, as Russia and China have insisted that the CD is the appropriate forum for the negotiation of an arms control treaty. The CD is deadlocked over its program of work, so no progress can be made in that venue. Further, the United States

---

accessed 31 August 2022; Ankit Panda and Benjamin Silverstein, 'The U.S. Moratorium on Anti-Satellite Missile Tests Is a Welcome Shift in Space Policy' (Carnegie Endowment for International Peace, April 20, 2022) <https://carnegieendowment.org/2022/04/20/u.s.-moratorium-on-anti-satellite-missile-tests-is-welcome-shift-in-space-policy-pub-86943> accessed 31 August 2022.

[94] Paul Meyer, 'Dark Forces Awaken: The Prospects for Cooperative Space Security' (2016) 23 The Nonproliferation Review 495, 496.
[95] UN General Assembly, 'Report of the Group of Governmental Experts on Transparency and Confidence Building Measures in Outer Space Activities' (July 29, 2013), UN Doc. A/68/189.
[96] UN Office for Disarmament, 'Group of Governmental Exerts on Further Effective Measures for the Prevention of an Arms Race in Outer Space' <https://www.un.org/disarmament/topics/outerspace/paros-gge/> accessed 31 August 2022.

has disagreements regarding the definitions and wording of that draft. In addition, there is disagreement over approach: the United States and others believe that these issues are better dealt with by political and non-binding instruments, with Russia, China, and others, asserting the need for a binding treaty.[97] The European Code of Conduct also appears to have stalled with no clear champion to take it forward.[98]

Fundamentally, there remains a lack of consensus regarding the appropriate mechanism to progress agreement on the responsible uses of outer space. As has become very evident, the continued destruction of satellites and creation of space debris will render space unusable. Further, the deployment of large constellations of satellites will compete for space in LEO. As noted, the return of humans to the Moon is likely to occur in this decade, and this involves plans for resource extraction. All of these developments are likely to contribute to rising tension. Further, it is clear that all of the gaps, uncertainties, and lack of clear definitions create the scope for misunderstandings. This is precisely the environment within which grey zone tactics may be deployed, to exploit the gaps and between knowledge and uncertainty.[99]

In December 2021, the UN General Assembly passed the UK-sponsored resolution 'Reducing Space Threats through Norms, Rules and Principles of Responsible Behaviour'.[100] This resolution convened an open-ended working group to consider current and future threats to space systems and 'actions, activities and omissions that could be considered irresponsible' and to 'make recommendations on possible norms, rules and principles of responsible behaviour relating to threats by States to space systems'. These recommendations are also to include how such norms would 'contribute to the negotiation of legally binding instruments, including on the prevention of an arms race in outer space'.

The Open-Ended Working Group met twice in 2022 and 2023 and will report back to the General Assembly.

This is a positive step forward for space security, despite the complexities created by the Russian invasion of Ukraine. However, it remains at this stage a non-binding process, which may trip over the same hurdles encountered by other initiatives. As Koplow has summarized with respect to the application of arms control in the space context, there are several issues which create complexity.[101]

---

[97] Paul Meyer, 'Diplomacy: The Missing Ingredient in Space Security', in Steer and Hersch (n 25) 287.

[98] Ibid. 292.

[99] Jim Malachowski, 'Don't Gamble on the Next Space Race: Win in the Orbital Gray Zone Now' (*Space Force Journal*, 31 January 2021) <https://spaceforcejournal.org/dont-gamble-on-the-next-space-race-win-in-the-orbital-gray-zone-now/> accessed 31 August 2022.

[100] UN General Assembly Resolution 76/231, 'Reducing Space Threats through Norms, Rules and Principles of Responsible Behaviours' (24 December 2021), UN Doc. A/RES/76/231.

[101] Koplow (n 46) 334–35.

314 ARENAS OF HYBRID AND GREY ZONE COMPETITION

These include the dual-use nature of most space technology, which makes it almost impossible to define the capability or hardware that is to be prohibited or regulated. For example, robotic arms designed to remove space debris may also be used to damage another satellite. Also related to lack of transparency of capability, states have claimed that in some instances destruction of a space asset is necessary to avoid greater harm. The issue of verification remains especially complex with assets placed in remote launch locations or orbits, creating the need for strong frameworks for data sharing with respect to space situational awareness.[102] Finally, in the event that a violation is identified, what is the appropriate and adequate response? Of course, the success of any such norms would require acceptance and modelling by all spacefaring states, as well as those with counterspace technology.

Other initiatives include unilateral initiatives such as the US Department of Defense Tenets of Responsible Behavior in Space.[103] The document commences with the statement that the Department of Defense 'has been a leader in space operations since the dawn of the space age'. Noting the 'increased risk of collisions, as well as of miscalculations or misunderstandings' with the growing congestion of space, it states that, unless otherwise directed, space operations will be conducted in accordance with the stated Tenets of Responsible Behaviour, including:

- Operating in, from, to, and through space with due regard to others and in a professional manner;
- Limiting the generation of long-lived space debris;
- Avoidance of the creation of harmful interference;
- Maintenance of safe separation and safe trajectory; and
- Communication and notifications to enhance the safety and stability of the domain.

Again, a unilateral and non-binding declaration has limited effect on the actions of others. However, in the domain of space, it has already been noted that much of the grey zone activity derives precisely from the adoption of public statements and overt articulations of position. In an area where actions take place so far away and motivations are frequently obscured and difficult to verify, expressed positions such as these do play an important role.

---

[102] Michael Gleason, 'No Haven for Misbehavin': A Framework for Verifying Space Norms' (Centre for Space Policy and Strategy 29 March 2022) < https://csps.aerospace.org/papers/no-haven-misbehavin-framework-verifying-space-norms> accessed 31 August 2022.

[103] US Department of Defense, 'Tenets of Responsible Behavior in Space' (7 July 2021) <https://media.defense.gov/2021/Jul/23/2002809598/-1/-1/0/TENETS-OF-RESPONSIBLE-BEHAVIOR-IN-SPACE.PDF> accessed 31 August 2022.

7. Responses to grey zone threats

Space is an increasingly important strategic domain. It remains to be seen how far initiatives such as the Artemis Accords and the Open Ended Working Group can go in terms of furthering the recognition and implementation of norms of responsible behaviour that will enable the use of space to flourish for commercial and government actors. Beyond this, it appears idealistic that such norms may then lead to the creation of further binding international law. A realistic checklist may include the following as action items:

- Continue to foster and contribute to the development of international space law and norms that mandate responsible behaviour and prohibit the creation of debris.
- Ensure that international laws and norms support the development of a vibrant commercial space industry and that such laws and norms are reflected in national domestic space laws.
- Support an open forum for the discussion and clarification of international space laws.
- Develop technology-sharing arrangements that foster the growth of interoperable space technologies and support commercial engagement.
- Promote cooperation in space through projects such as Artemis and other space exercises and projects.[104]

It remains to be seen whether the development of norms will promote or deter grey zone activity. The norm-building process itself provides a forum for further competition over which space power best exemplifies the values of international space law and upholds those rules with the most integrity. However, it is clear that there is a pressing need to get the rules clear in the near future, before the presence of humans in orbit and on the Moon leads to conflict.

---

[104] This list draws in part on concepts identified in Moltz (n 30) 89–90.

III

INSTRUMENTS, TACTICS, AND METHODS IN THE GREY ZONE

15

Decoding Grey Zone Environments

Andrés B. Muñoz Mosquera and Nikoleta Chalanouli

1. Introduction

The notion of 'grey zone' refers to an environment that exists in between peace and war, a sphere in which revisionist actors pose hybrid threats in order to achieve objectives that otherwise would require major political, military, or economic efforts. Chinese pressure on South Pacific maritime boundaries and Iranian support to Hezbollah in Lebanon offer examples of grey zone competition that exploit the lower and upper thresholds of the conflict continuum. Brands proposes the following definition of the notion:

> [G]ray zone conflict is best understood as activity that is coercive and aggressive in nature, but that is deliberately designed to remain below the threshold of conventional military conflict and open interstate war. Gray zone approaches are mostly the province of revisionist powers—those actors that seek to modify some aspect of the existing international environment—and the goal is to reap gains, whether territorial or otherwise, that are normally associated with victory in war. Yet gray zone approaches are meant to achieve those gains *without* escalating to overt warfare, *without* crossing established red-lines, and thus *without* exposing the practitioner to the penalties and risks that such escalation might bring.[1]

As Schadlow points out, '[t]he space between war and peace is not an empty one'.[2] Rather, it is filled with ongoing competitive activities by State and non-State actors, aimed at weakening the position of their adversaries across the entire diplomatic, informational, military, economic, financial, intelligence, and

---

[1] Hal Brands, 'Paradoxes of the Gray Zone' (Foreign Policy Research Institute February 5, 2016) <https://www.fpri.org/article/2016/02/paradoxes-gray-zone/> accessed 21 December 2022.

[2] Nadia Schadlow, 'Peace and War: The Space Between' (*War on the Rocks*, 18 August 2014) <https://www.warontherocks.com/2014/08/peace-and-war-the-space-between/> accessed 21 December 2022.

Andrés B. Muñoz Mosquera and Nikoleta Chalanouli, *Decoding Grey Zone Environments* In: *Hybrid Threats and Grey Zone Conflict*. Edited by: Mitt Regan and Aurel Sari, Oxford University Press. © Oxford University Press 2024. DOI: 10.1093/oso/9780197744772.003.0015

320   INSTRUMENTS, TACTICS, AND METHODS IN THE GREY ZONE

legal (DIMEFIL) spectrum.[3] This is not a novel development: in one way or another, grey zone competition has taken place throughout the course of human history. In essence, it simply involves the holistic use of all available means to affect others' weaknesses. Jordan thus suggests that one of the elements that defines grey zone conflict is the intentional, multidimensional, and integrated use of the different instruments of power.[4] The space in between peace and war is thus multilayered and to a degree fluid. It straddles across multiple domains and demands a 360-degree view of all the spheres where the clash between the actors' political, military, economic, social, infrastructure, and information (PMESII) components[5] can take place.[6]

Today, grey zone activities undermine the legitimacy of democratic institutions, disrupt social cohesion, and risk wearing down societies and their way of life. Identifying grey zone activities and the threats they pose is key to developing resilience. This requires investment in preparedness to ensure that law-abiding actors benefit from the capacity to adapt in the face of grey zone threats and, if necessary, to recover from their effects. These capacities, as well as the means to exercise them, are instrumental for developing a coherent strategic response at the national and international level and therefore also for the adoption of credible deterrence and defence postures. To this end, it is imperative to formulate a comprehensive grey zone doctrine that would permit planners to provide efficient and effective tools for decision makers both nationally and internationally.

Starting from the idea of 'threats', the second section of this chapter reflects on what the grey zone is, its nature and characteristics, and why this concept should be considered in conjunction with that of hybrid warfare, although the chapter does not develop the latter. The third section explores some of the key instruments of grey zone competition, while the fourth focuses on selected grey zone aggressors in order to illustrate the practical dimension of the subject. Based on this, the chapter identifies some additional lessons and implications of grey zone competition, before offering some concluding observations.

---

[3] Cale Horne, Stephen Shellman, and Brandon Stewart, 'Nickel and DIMEing the Adversary: Does It Work or PMESII Them Off?' (International Studies Association Annual Convention, San Francisco 2008).

[4] Javier Jordán, 'El conflicto internacional en la zona gris: una propuesta teórica desde la perspectiva del realismo ofensivo' (2018) 48 Revista Española de Ciencia Política 129, 132.

[5] US Joint Chiefs of Staff, *Joint Publication 2-0: Joint Intelligence* (US Government Printing Office 2007) I-25.

[6] Andrés B. Muñoz Mosquera and Abraham Muñoz Bravo, 'The Legal Domain: A Need for Hybrid Warfare Environments' (2017) 2 NATO Legal . . . matters! A Newsletter of the NATO Legal Community 1, 8.

2. Grey zone and hybrid warfare: manifestations of hybrid threats

2.1 Introducing the grey zone

Grey zone environments, which are not new, occupy the temporal and physical space between a paradisiac state of peace and a state of war, whether hybrid or conventional. As underlined by Chambers,[7] hostile activities taking place in this zone are designed to maintain deniability and thereby impede the responses of the actors and institutions they target. Ambiguity is thus one of the defining characteristic of grey zone environments and one that is more important in this context than it is in open warfare.[8]

Grey zone threats are prevalent today for three reasons. The first reason is related to the economy of force. International actors that do not have access to conventional military capabilities, or not in such abundant supply as to defeat more capable powers, may resort to grey zone tactics as an alternative way of harming their adversaries. Second, the general prohibition against the use of force in international law severely limits the range of situations in which open recourse to violence may be justified, thus creating an incentive to avoid crossing this threshold in a clear and unambiguous manner. Third, new technologies are providing new instruments for exerting power and influence, for example, by enabling international actors to reach critical masses of internal and external audiences and to avoid easy attribution of their activities, both at minimum monetary and reputational cost.

Grey zone environments and competitive engagements may differ substantial from one case to the next, depending on the actors involved and the historical, political, social, and geographical circumstances of their confrontation. Nevertheless, it is also true that all grey zone encounters share a degree of coerciveness, even aggressiveness. Although remaining below the threshold of open hostilities, this coerciveness entails a combination of political, economic, informational, psychological, and military pressure to achieve war-like objectives

---

[7] John Chambers, 'Countering Gray-Zone Hybrid Threats—An Analysis of Russia's "New Generation Warfare" and Implications for the US Army' (Modern Warfare Institute 18 October 2016) 14–17 <https://mwi.usma.edu/wp-content/uploads/2016/10/Countering-Gray-Zone-Hybrid-Threats.pdf> accessed 21 December 2022.

[8] See also Brands (n 1), who pointed out that 'gray zone challenges are thus inherently ambiguous in nature. They feature unconventional tactics, from cyberattacks, to propaganda and political warfare, to economic coercion and sabotage, to sponsorship of armed proxy fighters, to creeping military expansionism. Those tactics, in turn, are frequently shrouded in *misinformation* and deception, and are often conducted in ways that are meant to make proper *attribution* of the responsible party difficult to nail down. Gray zone challenges, in other words, are *ambiguous* and usually *incremental aggression*. They represent that coercion that is, to varying degrees, disguised; they eat away at the status quo one nibble at a time' (emphasis added).

during peace.[9] To take one example from China: Chinese air force colonels Qiao Liang and Wang Xiangsui writing in *Unrestricted Warfare* (1998) have argued that military options will no longer be adequate and that alternative methods of coercion are gaining in importance, including in the sphere of international diplomacy, the economy, cyberspace, law, and the information space.[10]

Various international actors, including States and non-State actors,[11] resort to grey zone tactics in order to assert their strategic interests whilst minimizing the risk of triggering robust countermeasures. Revisionist or 'dissatisfied' States such as Russia and China aim to shape the international legal order in their own image, for instance, in the context of maritime claims, while the governing regimes of rogue States such as Iran and North Korea retain their grip on power through coercion, suppression of human rights, and the repression of democratic principles, coupled with a chronic inability to engage constructively with the outside world.[12] These actors operate in the grey zone to achieve their goals without using kinetic means, a point highlighted in the US National Defense Strategy of 2018.[13]

The view that grey zone competition and the related notion of hybrid warfare are elusive concepts, or that they may even be unnecessary and unhelpful, is not uncommon. Even though they are not free from difficulties, these concepts nevertheless point towards real challenges in the contemporary security environment. Conventional strategies and doctrine do not adequately account for the risks posed by grey zone conflict and thus do not offer appropriate means and ways to counter them.[14] The same is true for hybrid warfare, which is a form

---

[9] Katerina Oskarsson, 'The Effectiveness of DIMEFIL Instruments of Power in the Gray Zone' (2017) 1 OPEN Publications, Allied Command Transformation 1, 7.

[10] Andrés B. Muñoz Mosquera and Nikoleta Chalanouli, 'China, an Active Practitioner of Legal Warfare' (*Lawfire*, 2 February 2020) <https://sites.duke.edu/lawfire/2020/02/02/guest-post-andres-munoz-mosqueras-and-nikoleta-chalanoulis-essay-china-an-active-practitioner-of-legal-warfare/#_ftn1>, accessed 8 February 2023.

[11] Non-State actors may be used as proxies to carry out militarized intimidation or control territory to exert influence or achieve specific security or political outcomes. See Melissa Dalton et al, *By other Means: U.S. Priorities in the Gray Zone (Part II)* (Center for Strategic and International Studies 2019) 2.

[12] Anthony Lake, *Confronting Backlash States* (1994) 73 Foreign Affairs 45, 46.

[13] US Department of Defense, 'Summary of the 2018 National Defense Strategy of the United States of America: Sharpening the American Military's Competitive Edge' (Department of Defense 2018) ('both revisionist powers and rogue regimes are competing across all dimensions of power. They have increased efforts short of armed conflict by expanding coercion to new fronts, violating principles of sovereignty, exploiting ambiguity, and deliberately blurring the lines between civil and military goals').

[14] On risk, see Nathan P. Freier et al, *Outplayed: Regaining Strategic Initiative in the Gray Zone* (US Army War College Press 2016) 27–29 ('gray zone challenges grip U.S. and partner decision-making and persistently put strategy development and implementation squarely on the horns of a seemingly intractable dilemma. In some instances, senior US and allied leaders perceive that active and assertive responses to gray zone competition and conflict hazard undesirable escalation, excessive cost; and uncertain, indeterminate, or unfavorable outcomes. Thus, they perceive an *inherent "risk of action"*. On the other hand, *marginal, ineffectual, or non-existent responses to gray zone*

of warfare characterized by the complementary use of diverse levers of power to alter the existing political, religious, or territorial status quo, among others.[15] The inadequacy of conventional strategies and doctrine in meeting these challenges is precisely what makes the notions of grey zone competition and hybrid warfare conceptually and practically useful for developing a better understanding of contemporary security challenges. Grey zone is perspective-dependent, which is to say that the notion hands an advantage to those who rely on it to decode risks and adversarial behaviour and who incorporate it into their planning to obtain their objectives across the DIMEFIL.

With these conceptual and practical benefits in mind, it is worth recalling Mazarr's description of the grey zone as a series of actions with revisionist intent. Actors dissatisfied with the status quo, which they are intent to modify to their advantage, lead this 'alteneu'[16] endeavour. To reduce the risk of escalation, they

> [a]re employing sequences of gradual steps to secure strategic leverage. The efforts remain below thresholds that would generate a powerful U.S. or international response, but nonetheless are forceful and deliberate, calculated to gain measurable traction over time. In one important sense, they are classic "salami-slicing" strategies, fortified with a range of emerging gray area or unconventional techniques. They maneuver in the ambiguous no-man's-land between peace and war, reflecting the sort of aggressive, persistent, determined campaigns characteristic of warfare but without the overt use of military force.[17]

Despite the prevalence of grey zone tactics, evidently not every aspect of strategic competition or every instance of coercive confrontation on the international stage amounts to grey zone conflict. To avoid overextending the concept, it is useful to complement these more theoretical considerations with practical examples, as we do in section 4, and by distinguishing grey zone competition from situations of hybrid warfare. Doing so underlines that grey zone competition is a planned, subtle, and gradual campaign, designed to keep conflict within

---

challenges can engender the opposite—some significant "risk of inaction." Here choosing not to act— likely because of the perceived risks engendered—leads to equally unpalatable outcomes. The United States, for example, potentially *vacates or leaves vulnerable core interests to the predations of hostile forces*; U.S. decision-makers hoping but not knowing for sure whether opponents will seize on the opportunities inaction presents. In this regard, *gray zone competition and conflict may represent the most uncomfortable and vexing decision space possible for U.S. leadership'*) (emphasis added).

[15] See Muñoz Mosquera and Muñoz Bravo (n 6) 7–8.
[16] Meaning 'oldnew'.
[17] M. Mazarr, *Mastering the Gray Zone: Understanding a Changing Era of Conflict* (United States Army War College Press 2015) 3–4.

324 INSTRUMENTS, TACTICS, AND METHODS IN THE GREY ZONE

bearable limits without crossing red lines that may lead to open warfare, whilst still obtaining strategic gains in DIMEFIL, including territorial expansion.

2.2 Grey zone and hybrid warfare

Identifying the features that separate grey zone conflict from hybrid warfare[18] is not an easy task. The two notions are not incompatible and in fact are sometimes treated as synonymous. They seem to occupy the same operational environment and one may lead to the other. They may be understood as subsets of hybrid threats, a broader notion that covers the entire spectrum of conflict, from competition below the threshold of war at one end to large-scale hostilities at the other end. Nevertheless, grey zone conflict and hybrid warfare are distinct ideas. While grey zone competition is coercive and even aggressive in nature, it is deliberately designed to remain below the threshold of conventional military conflict and open interstate war.[19] By contrast, hybrid warfare entails the use of force, including methods of conventional war. Accordingly, the key feature that distinguishes grey zone activities from hybrid warfare is that the latter involves open resort to armed force and thus, from a legal perspective, engages the relevant rules of international law governing the use of force.[20] As Mazarr explains:

> [G]ray zone strategies pursue political objectives through calculated and integrated campaigns . . . In spirit and execution, they are more like military campaigns . . . but they employ mostly non-military or non-kinetic tools. They strive to remain under key escalatory thresholds. And, finally, they are willing to edge gradually toward their objectives rather than making an all-out grab. This definition distinguishes the gray zone both from asymmetric violence like

---

[18] Frank G. Hoffman, 'Conflict in the 21st Century: The Rise of Hybrid Wars' (Potomac Institute for Policy Studies 2007)('[H]ybrid warfare can be characterized as a comprehensive strategy based on a broad, complex, adaptive and often highly integrated combination of conventional and unconventional means. It uses overt and covert activities, which can include military, paramilitary, irregular and civilian actors, targeted to achieve (geo)political and -strategic objectives. Hybrid warfare is directed at an adversary's vulnerabilities, focused on complicating decision making and conducted across the full spectrum (which can encompass diplomatic, political, information, military, economic, financial, intelligence and legal activity) whilst creating ambiguity and deniability. Hybrid strategies can be applied by both state and non-state actors'). See also United Kingdom Ministry of Defence, 'Written Evidence submitted to Defence Committee' (1 March 2016) para. 15, <https://data. parliament.uk/writtenevidence/committeeevidence.svc/evidencedocument/defence-committee/ russia-implications-for-uk-defence-and-security/written/28854.pdf>, accessed 21 December 2022.

[19] Brands (n 1).

[20] Josep Baqués, 'Towards a Definition of the "Gray Zone" Concept' (Instituto Español de Estudios Estratégicos 2017) <www.ieee.es/en/Galerias/fichero/docs_investig/2017/DIEEEINV02-2017_ Concepto_GrayZona_JosepBaques_ENGLISH.pdf>, accessed 21 December 2022.

terrorism and insurgency, and from hybrid campaigns that combine classic military operations with asymmetric techniques, as in Lebanon in 2006.[21]

Understood in this way, in principle, grey zone competition and hybrid warfare exclude each other. An actor faced with grey zone competition is, by definition, not in a hybrid warfare situation, given that grey zone activities do not include forms of armed confrontation. What complicates such seemingly clear delineations, however, is that grey zone activities may consist of military exercises, border violations, or other non-consensual intrusions into sovereign territory, airspace or territorial waters, international sanctions and embargoes, retorsions such as closing embassies, or withdrawals from international agreements and organizations. Depending on the context, at least some of these acts may be coercive in nature, designed to constrain the choices or decision-making capability of the State targeted by these measures. Some of these acts may even involve the limited use of force, without, however, reaching the legal threshold of an armed conflict, the level of an armed attack within the meaning of Article 51 of the Charter of the United Nations,[22] and hence Article 5 of the North Atlantic Treaty, or the definition of aggression set out in the United Nations General Assembly Resolution 3314 (XXIX).[23]

Nevertheless, even though grey zone competition stops short of situations of armed conflict, at the top end, it may involve the hostile use of special operations, military exercises, the training and arming of proxies, intelligence collection, surveillance and reconnaissance through military means, or paramilitary activities such as intensive coast-guard operations. This means that the border between the grey zone and hybrid warfare is indistinct.[24] It also means that the armed forces have a role to play in countering grey zone competition. While they may not be the lead agency, the military may assist and support the civilian authorities by deploying specialized capabilities. These include intelligence collection and surveillance, mobility, and the various capabilities associated with special operations. However, the armed forces and the defence sector may also make a broader and at times more indirect contribution, for example, through training partners, defence industry cooperation, joint exercises, collective air policing, reassurance, and deterrence or by exercising the freedom of navigation. Counter-grey zone activities thus need

---

[21] M. Mazarr, 'Struggle in the Gray Zone and World Order' (*War on the Rocks*, 22 December 2015) <www.warontherocks.com/2015/12/struggle-in-the-gray-zone-and-world-order/>, accessed 21 December 2022.

[22] Charter of the United Nations (26 June 1945), 1 UNTS XVI.

[23] UN General Assembly Resolution 3314 (XXIX), Definition of Aggression (14 December 1974).

[24] Baqués (n 20).

to combine conventional and unconventional military operations with wider, cross-departmental activities.[25]

3. Grey zone tools uncoded

Grey zone approaches use all available tools that could affect the adversary's DIMEFIL. However, as uncertainty and ambiguity are the key factors exploited by an opponent in order to keep its activities sub-threshold and to avoid triggering a hybrid or a conventional war, this also dictates what instruments are best suited for a specific grey zone situation or environment. We discuss some of the relevant tools in this section. Although the list is far from exhaustive, it illustrates the nature and diversity of the different instruments available to hostile actors. Many of the measures in question are aimed against the society of a State targeted by grey zone competition. The general public and its individual members thus become both direct and indirect targets of hostile action, prompting some to suggest that in effect the entire population of a targeted State may be 'used as an immense human shield'.[26]

3.1 Media and information operations

The media is a key tool for an effective grey zone strategy, whether in the form of the classical pamphlet or state-of-the-art social media. Tactics in the information domain include not only the simple dissemination of 'fake news' to mislead or influence, which today is very much in the spotlight,[27] but also the piling of fake news upon other fake news in order to create a news-confusion environment. Such measures are typically designed to exploit existing political frustrations and divisions within targeted societies. More sophisticated information operations may aim to advance a particular narrative based on a detailed understanding of the vulnerabilities of another nation. Examples include the US presidential election of 2016, which was targeted by a series of cyber influence operations aimed at influencing voters ahead of the polls. However, even sophisticated information operations are not guaranteed success, but may be countered with the help of proactive and holistic strategic communications campaigns.

---

[25] See HM Government, 'National Security Capability Review' (Cabinet Office 2018) 10–11.
[26] Baqués (n 20) 10.
[27] French Parliament voted to pass a law against the 'fake news', allowing courts to determine whether reports published during election periods are credible or should be taken down. Other nations, such as Singapore, have adopted or are considering empowering the relevant authorities to disrupt the spread of fake news.

3.2 Lawfare

Lawfare involves the use of law as a weapon or as an instrument to influence another party. While lawfare may be designed to achieve effects in other spheres, such as in the information domain, lawfare operations are conducted in the legal domain,[28] where they often exploit asymmetries in the regulatory environment or in the opposing parties' commitment to the rule of law. As one of us has written elsewhere, in such asymmetric environments, law-abiding actors

> need to use Lawfare affirmatively to ensure that public international law is being applied within its full remit. Such 'preemptive' Zeusian Lawfare will give the political and military leadership the necessary room to fine-tune the planning and conduct of military operations reflecting on anticipated Lawfare by the opponent. Lawfare counteraction has extreme limitations in terms of time, space and applicable procedures. Law-abiding actors will be confronted with short-lead time for political decision-making and military planning based on incomplete intelligence and open-source information, an incommensurate broadness of the battlespace—tangible and virtual, and the 'dictates' of compliance with the rule of law: to follow democratic procedures and be subject to court review and public opinion scrutiny. Moreover, law-abiding actors will also confront both international organizations to which they belong and which have been 'infected', by Hadesian Lawfare and international tribunals used by non-law-abiders who know the non-intuitive nature of international humanitarian law. This requires a comprehensive legal approach and broader legal interoperability, which includes the use of affirmative Lawfare in an offensive and defensive manner.[29]

In addition, it is important to underline that lawfare is not concerned solely with questions of legality in a narrow, technical sense but also with questions of legitimacy. As Baqués points out, in the context of grey zone competition, 'the ability of the parties to stay (or appear to stay) within the bounds of legality is fundamental, as well as the ability to highlight irregularities (from that same legal point of view) in the adversary's behavior'.[30]

---

[28] On the legal domain, see Muñoz Mosquera and Muñoz Bravo (n 6) 9–10. See also Aurel Sari, 'Hybrid Warfare, Law and The Fulda Gap', in *Complex Battlespaces: The Law of Armed Conflict and the Dynamics of Modern Warfare*, edited by Winston Williams and Christopher M. Ford (OUP 2018) 182–84.

[29] Andres B. Muñoz Mosquera and Sascha Dov Bachmann, 'Lawfare in Hybrid Wars: The 21st Century Lawfare' (2016) 7 Journal of International Humanitarian Legal Studies 63, 86.

[30] Baqués (n 20).

328 INSTRUMENTS, TACTICS, AND METHODS IN THE GREY ZONE

3.3 Economic guerrilla

Economic and financial levers offer another set of opportunities for harming an adversary in a grey zone environment. For example, economic dependencies may be created or exploited to erode the cohesion of an alliance, as Russia attempted to do in relation to Greece in 2015.[31] Such tactics may take the form of providing credits and subsidies, buying infrastructure,[32] or granting access to sources of energy.[33] Economic and financial measures are often supported by media and information operations, as well as the manipulation of law or reliance on proxies or other 'agents', including non-governmental organizations, which thus become knowing or unwitting conduits of grey zone effects. To counter such measures, developing and maintaining economic cohesion among partners is of critical importance. For example, the support provided by the EU to Greece has created a degree of deterrence to discourage third parties from exploiting economic and financial vulnerabilities.

3.4 Cyber operations

Grey zone activities conducted in cyber space include a very broad range of measures, such as the use of cyber means to disseminate or obtain information or to disrupt everyday activities and sectors, such as banking, healthcare, education, public administration, the justice system, critical infrastructure, and the emergency services. Cyber activities may also be aimed at military capabilities, including critical command systems, intelligence, or weapons systems. Successful cyberattacks may also generate effects in other spheres, for example, by portraying governments unable to defend against them as weak and unreliable in the eyes of their own population. Given their relatively low cost and potential effects, malign cyber operations are 'low hanging fruits' for grey zone actors. The large-scale cyberattacks that affected Estonian government sites,

---

[31] Mark Rice-Oxley, 'Greek Prime Minister Reaches Out to Vladimir Putin for Help in Financial Crisis', *The Guardian* (London, 19 June 2015) <https://www.theguardian.com/world/2015/jun/19/greek-prime-minister-vladimir-putin-help-financial-crisis> accessed 21 December 2022 ('Putin has met Tsipras on several occasions this spring as the debt crisis has intensified, leading to suggestions that Moscow might be prepared to step in where Brussels fears to tread in order to bolster its influence in southeastern Europe. The two countries announced a deal earlier in the day to route a pipeline through Greece that would carry Russian gas to Europe. Greece can expect transit payments—but not until the project is completed in 2019. Putin's aides indicated that Moscow would consider lending Greece money if required, though no formal request had yet been submitted').

[32] George Georgiopoulos, 'China's Cosco Acquires 51 Percent Stake in Greece's Piraeus Port', Reuters (10 August 2016) <https://www.reuters.com/article/greece-privatisation-port/chinas-cosco-acquires-51-pct-stake-in-greeces-piraeus-port-idUSL8N1AR252> accessed 21 December 2022.

[33] Rice-Oxley (n 31).

banks, the media ,and political parties in 2007, disrupting ordinary activities in the country on a wide scale, offer a clear example.

Countering hostile cyber operations conduct as part of grey zone campaigns requires a range of different measures both nationally and internationally. Recognizing this, NATO leaders emphasized the role of the Alliance 'in facilitating co-operation on cyber defense including through multinational projects, education, training, and exercises and information exchange, in support of national cyber defence efforts' and pledged to ensure that NATO as a whole would be 'cyber aware, cyber trained, cyber secure and cyber enabled'.[34] Given the continued uncertainty as to how existing rules of international law, such as the principle of non-intervention, apply in this context, some commentators have called for the formulation of a new legal framework, the *jus extra bellum*, against which national security claims and actions in cyberspace may be assessed and which might facilitate reaching consensus on regulating particularly egregious cyber activities that all parties agree should be prohibited.[35]

3.5 Challenging the territorial status quo

Some revisionist actors challenge established international standards governing aerial and maritime spaces, including by contesting the applicable legal regimes and thus control over specific areas, such as territorial waters, islands, or the exclusive economic zone. A good example is the dispute over the Sea of Azov and the incident in the Kerch Strait,[36] which involved a confrontation between Ukraine and Russia in the legal domain on matters relating to the law of the sea. It is submitted that '[a]ll future counter grey zone actions—especially those focused on sophisticated, high-end revisionist threats—should focus on deliberate dislocation of adversary and competitor concepts of operation or courses of action'.[37]

4. Grey zone actors: putting theory into practice

The present section takes a closer look at a set of prominent grey zone actors. Among them, China may be considered a grey zone 'purist', with some analysts of

---

[34] North Atlantic Treaty Organization, 'Cyber Defence Pledge', Press Release (2016) 124 (8 July 2016) <www.nato.int/cps/en/natohq/official_texts_133177.htm>, accessed 21 December 2022.

[35] Michael Jefferson Adams, '*Jus Extra Bellum*: Reconstructing the Ordinary, Realistic Conditions of Peace' (2014) 5 Harvard National Security Journal 377.

[36] See James Kraska, 'The Kerch Strait Incident: Law of the Sea or Law of Naval Warfare?' (EJIL:Talk!, 3 December 2018) <www.ejiltalk.org/the-kerch-strait-incident-law-of-the-sea-or-law-of-naval-warfare>, accessed 21 December 2022.

[37] Freier (n 14) 87.

330 INSTRUMENTS, TACTICS, AND METHODS IN THE GREY ZONE

the Chinese People's Liberation Army (PLA) predicting that future wars will be marked by 'three non-warfares': non-contact, non-linear, and non-symmetric.[38] Russia, by contrast, seems more disposed towards moving from grey zone activities to hybrid warfare and back, whilst not being averse to crossing the line into conventional war, as it did in Georgia and Ukraine, and potentially reverting back to hybrid warfare and grey zone competition. Actors in Iran and the Middle East and North Africa (MENA) region are less nuanced and gradual in their approaches and assessing their posture from a grey zone perspective is not always straightforward.

4.1 China

China may be regarded as the most 'purist' among the various grey zone actors, as it typically pre-conditions key areas of strategic competition by preparing the legal domain and by creating fait accompli to shape the environment in its favour. These techniques are used by China to assert its interests and control, project power, and achieve information superiority in order to gain and maintain off-battlefield supremacy.[39] After two decades of continuous economic growth, China clearly feels confident to challenge the influence of the United States in its immediate sphere of interest, in particular the South and East China Seas, in key geographical regions further afield and also in industries of strategic importance. China's approach reflects its doctrine of the 'three warfares' endorsed by the Central Committee of the Communist Party of China: psychological warfare, media warfare, and legal warfare. More specifically, in 2003, the Central Military Commission recognized '[t]hat in the modern information age nuclear weapons have proven essentially unusable and kinetic force is the preferred option in ever decreasing scenarios'.[40] In line with this idea, China's grey zone activities incorporate '[p]olitical, military, and commercial instruments . . . military and paramilitary forces, government agencies, and State-owned enterprises as weapons'.[41] The combined use of these different instruments, including paramilitary intimidation and lawfare, is illustrated particularly clearly by China's use of law enforcement assets 'to warn off and bully competitor oil companies and finishing fleets' in the South China Sea.[42]

---

[38] See Frank G. Hoffman, 'Examining Complex Forms of Conflict Gray Zone and Hybrid Challenges' (2018) 7 PRISM 31, 33.

[39] See Muñoz Mosquera and Nikoleta Chalanouli (n 10).

[40] Stephan Halper, 'China: The Three Warfares' (University of Cambridge, May 2013) 11 <https://cryptome.org/2014/06/prc-three-wars.pdf> accessed 10 February 2023.

[41] Freier (n 14) 33.

[42] Ibid. 38.

China does not hide that it is a revisionist power. China aspires to territorial control by creating land artificially in the South China Sea in the Spratly Island chain.[43] However, as Mazarr notes, building islands 'is merely one of the most obvious of many actions, ranging from propaganda to economic coercion and swarming fleets of fishing vessels, that China has been taking to solidify its assertion of territorial and resource rights throughout the region'.[44] China works gradually, ensuring that deliberate and 'aggressive' actions do not cross red lines and thresholds in a blatant manner, thus getting other powers and competitors accustomed to new facts on the ground and changing the status quo step by step. China's maritime claims illustrate this grey zone 'salami-slicing' strategy. China challenges the established legal order of the sea by claiming exorbitant law enforcement powers and authorities to protect its sovereign rights and interests in its exclusive economic zone. In addition, China has asserted rights, jurisdiction, and control over the resources and maritime features that fall within a vast stretch of water delimited by a self-declared nine-dash line.[45] In arbitral proceedings brought by the Philippines, a tribunal established under the dispute settlement mechanism of the United Nations Convention on the Law of the Sea held that China's claim to historic rights within the nine-dash line was incompatible with the Convention.[46] Other recent examples from other domains include the cancellation by the Chinese authorities of Western journalists' credentials and the adoption of new rules for foreign media outlets operating in China.[47]

4.2. Russia

Russia's geopolitical goals include maintaining its position as a nuclear power, retaining a prominent role in the international community, and preserving its hegemon role in its near abroad. Regarding the latter, Russian leaders entertain revisionist intentions in relation to the geographical sphere of the former Soviet Union and have used various combinations of traditional and non-traditional

---

[43] Neil Connor, 'China Triggers New Storm over Military Build-up on Artificial Islands', *The Telegraph* (London, 9 January 2018), <www.telegraph.co.uk/news/2018/01/09/diplomatic-protests-china-shows-militarised-artificial-islands/>, accessed 21 December 2022.

[44] Mazarr (n 17) 1.

[45] See further discussion in Robert Beckman, 'The UN Convention of the Law of the Sea and the Maritime Disputes in the South China Sea' (2013) 107 American Journal of International Law 142, 157.

[46] *South China Sea Arbitration* (*Philippines v. China*), Award, PCA Case No. 2013-19 (12 July 2016) para. 261.

[47] Marc Tracy, Edward Wong, and Lara Jakes, 'China announces that It Will Expel American Journalists', *The New York Times* (New York, 17 March 2020) <https://www.nytimes.com/2020/03/17/business/media/china-expels-american-journalists.html> accessed 21 December 2022.

332 INSTRUMENTS, TACTICS, AND METHODS IN THE GREY ZONE

instruments across the DIMEFIL spectrum against the West in pursuit of these aims. In fact, Russia has proven masterly capable of exploiting Western weaknesses. Specifically, it has combined the gradual and measured application of Russian instruments of power against the vulnerabilities of Western nations with ongoing threats of force, illustrated by the exercises Zapad-2017 (West-2017) and Vostok-2018 (East-2018),[48] and flagrant acts of aggression against its neighbours. Russia thus complements non-kinetic with kinetic measures in an effort to restore the status quo ante of 1991.

This combination puts Western alliances and organizations on the back foot and at continuous risk, including risks borne from inaction and the lack of political cohesion. Thus, in their early stages, Russia's actions against Georgia and Ukraine 'remained well below the West's vague threshold of unambiguous provocation and have also occurred in the shadow of Russia's latent destructive and disruptive military potential.'[49]

In addition, lawfare is a key component of the Russian approach to grey zone competition, hybrid warfare situations, and conventional warfare. Russia's legal model for the annexation of Crimea and the Donbas was well planned in advance.[50] Another example of the deliberate nature of the Russian resort to lawfare is its use in the Arctic and Eastern Ukraine, where lawfare was employed for the preparation of the battlefield and for building legitimacy of the occupation of Ukraine.[51] Internally, in May 2015, Russian President Vladimir Putin passed a

---

[48] Agence France-Presse in Chita, 'Russia Begins Its Largest Ever Military Exercise with 300,000 Soldiers', *The Guardian* (London, 11 September 2018) <www.theguardian.com/world/2018/sep/11/russia-largest-ever-military-exercise-300000-soldiers-china>, accessed 21 December 2022.

[49] Freier (n 14) 41.

[50] The various elements of this model are described by Muñoz Mosquera and Bachmann (n 29) 85, to include (1) the modification of internal laws to affect external territories: bill amendment on the incorporation of territories of neighbouring States providing for the annexation of regions of neighbouring States following popular local referenda (February–March 2014); (b) citizenship: citizen law amendment using residency claims dating back to USSR and Russian Empire to grant current Russian citizenship (April 2014); (c) passports: the practice of giving away Russian passports to claim the presence of Russian citizens in neighbouring regions (Abkhazia, South Ossetia, Crimea); (d) the misuse of the United Nations Security Council: attempts to use the UN Security Council to sanction potential Russian opening of 'humanitarian corridors'; (e) the use of 'fake' internal legal proceedings: the sentencing of Ukrainian officials *in absentia* by Russian courts; and (f) the misleading use of the term 'peacekeeping': vigorous propaganda fabricating a legal case to justify the sending of Russian 'peacekeeping forces' into Eastern Ukraine to prevent 'a humanitarian catastrophe' or a 'genocide' against Russian speakers.

[51] Sascha Dov Bachmann and Andres B. Muñoz Mosquera, 'Northward Ho! How Russian Lawfare Is Conquering the Arctic' (The Fletcher Forum of World Affairs 9 March 2017) <https://www.fletcherforum.org/home/2017/3/8/northward-ho-how-russian-lawfare-is-conquering-the-arctic> accessed 21 December 2022 ('The regulations passed by Russian legislators to create and finance these resources must be considered "time bomb" lawfare, as any action by NATO members to confront Russian activities will be considered an interference in Russian internal affairs and perhaps as a breach of international·law. The precariousness of the Arctic legal framework prepares the ground for a repeat of a pre-Crimean occupation by Russian utilizing lawfare in order to claim increased 'sovereignty rights').

DECODING GREY ZONE ENVIRONMENTS   333

law that enables the Russian authorities to adopt legal sanctions against foreign non-governmental organizations or firms designated as 'undesirable' on national security grounds.[52] On March 2020, the Russian President also signed a Decree which added Crimea to the list of border territories where foreign citizens and enterprises, or stateless persons, are forbidden to own land.[53] Legal measures thus play a consistent and substantial role in enabling, facilitating, and justifying Russia's activities in other domains.

4.3 Iran

Iran's main goal is to counter the influence of the United States and Saudi Arabia in the region. As a revisionist power, it seeks to exploit the United States and its allies' weaknesses by generating hybrid threats and fostering regional instability. It also poses threats further afield by expanding its network of relationships and interests worldwide, including in Western and Latin American nations. Iran relies prominently on proxies, one of the staple tools of grey zone competition. Iran's influence over Hezbollah provides it with the ability to shape events in Lebanon, which in turn permits it to foster instability affecting Israel, thus making it a key actor in the region. It is also necessary to mention Iran's nuclear program. The pursuit of nuclear capabilities makes Iran an actor of global significance on a matter that has succeeded to split the West and thus very much forms a part of its grey zone approach. Finally, the instability in Yemen and the military involvement of Saudi Arabia shows how Iran has gradually moved from grey zone to hybrid warfare, and eventually to conventional war. As a result of this multi-pronged approach, the West suffers the consequences of Iran's grey zone activities, while regional actors are entangled by Iran's hybrid warfare and, in the case of Yemen, conventional war. Not unlike the case of China, Iranian grey zone activities also have a strong maritime dimension. While the focus of these activities is mostly on the Ormuz strait, Iran has developed a maritime grey zone projection capability through proxies, namely, Hezbollah in Lebanon and Gaza and Ansar Allah Houthis in Yemen.[54]

---

[52] BBC News, 'Russia's Putin Signs Law against "undesirable" NGOs' (24 May 2015) <https://www.bbc.com/news/world-europe-32860526> accessed 21 December 2022.

[53] US Mission to the Organization for Security and Cooperation in Europe, 'Ongoing Violations of International Law and Defiance of OSCE Principles and Commitments by the Russian Federation in Ukraine' (2 April 2020) <https://osce.usmission.gov/on-russias-ongoing-aggression-against-ukraine-and-illegal-occupation-of-crimea-5/> accessed 21 December 2022.

[54] Javier Jordán, 'Estrategias de Irán en la Zona Gris del Conflicto: Su Dimensión Marítima' (2018) 275 Revista General de Marina 723, 730–38.

4.4 The MENA region

Actors operating in the MENA region differ in several respects from the three State actors considered so far and are discussed here mainly by way of contrast. The MENA region has been endemically cursed with failed governments and administrations as well as continuous competition over access to fossil energy resources. This has made the region a fertile source of hybrid threats posed by States and non-State actors. However, these threats mostly take the form of hybrid warfare and preparation for conventional war. Sophisticated grey zone campaigns, such as those that are designed to take effect over the time by applying pressure and altering the status quo gradually, are less prevalent.

Yet, there are exceptions. The Isla Perejil (Leila or Tura) incident of 2002 provides an example of grey zone action by actors in the MENA region. On 11 July 2002, Moroccan gendarmerie occupied the island which belongs to Spain but is claimed by Morocco and otherwise has no particular strategic value. Moroccan marines replaced the gendarmerie and a naval patrol was deployed. To complement its use of paramilitary and military power, Morocco took extensive diplomatic measures, courting support from the Arab League, the African Union, and France; engaged in an information campaign; leveraged ongoing negotiations on fisheries with the EU; and resorted to legal means, including by disputing the legal status of the island and claiming the need to combat human and drug trafficking as a justification for its actions. Morocco's multilayered approach demonstrated creativity, ambiguity and synchronization—all archetypical characteristics of grey zone campaigns. Spain eventually countered these measures and evicted the Moroccan marines by deploying its own troops and succeeded, with the United States acting as a mediator, to restore the status quo ante.[55]

5. Lessons of the grey zone

Based on our overview of the instruments of grey zone competition and assessment of key actors operating in this sphere, we can identify certain additional features and implications of the grey zone. This helps to further sharpen the contours of the concept and provides some lessons for responding to hostile grey zone campaigns.

---

[55] Javier Jordán, 'Una Reinterpretación de la Crisis del Islote Perejil desde la Perspectiva de la Amenaza Híbrida' (2018) 274 Revista General de Marina 941, 946–49.

5.1 The limits of revisionism

Grey zone actors seek to modify the status quo to their advantage, rather than destroy it altogether.[56] Their actions may not be compatible with basic principles of international law and they may actively seek to change some aspects of the international legal system and order. However, they do not intend to wreck that system, but mould it into a shape more convenient to their interests and one that satisfies their geopolitical frustrations.

5.2 Grey zone and the law

While continued compliance with the applicable rules of international law may seem to put States and organizations targeted by grey zone actions at a disadvantage, respect for the rule of law in the face of illegality is also source of strength. Hostile actors circumventing and abusing the law not only expose themselves to international condemnation, thereby putting their reputation at risk, but in doing so also offer a justification and rationale for appropriate countermeasures, for instance, in the form of sanctions and embargoes. Moreover, countering lawfare and other malign legal activities requires measures in the legal domain, including strengthening legal interoperability and cooperation, which in turn demands respect for the rule of law.[57]

5.3 What goes around, comes around

Grey zone campaigns are designed to weaken, divide, and distract their targets. This is not a one-way street, however. While the political values and legal principles that define liberal democracies rule out the use of certain instruments and methods, they still leave room for a wide range of measures that can impose costs on hostile actors exploiting the grey zone, all across the DIMEFIL.

5.4 Avoiding the risk of inaction

Grey zone competition poses challenges for traditional forms of deterrence and defence. Both deterrence and defence obey the logic of action and reaction, in

---

[56] For further detail, see Adam Elkus, '50 Shades of Gray: Why the Gray Wars Concept Lacks Strategic Sense' (*War on the Rocks*, 15 December 2015) <www.warontherocks.com/2015/12/50-shades-of-gray-why-the-gray-wars-concept-lacks-strategic-sense/>, accessed 21 December 2022.

[57] Andrés B. Muñoz Mosquera, Sascha Dov Bachmann, and J. Abraham Muñoz Bravo, 'Hybrid Warfare and the Legal Domain' (2019) 31 Terrorism and Political Violence 98, 102.

that they involve measures aimed at avoiding a particular threat or mitigating and reversing its effects once it has materialized. In this sense, deterrence and defence are threat-driven. However, the ambiguity and strategic gradualism that are the hallmark of grey zone campaigns dull the threat perception and alarm systems of the target. It makes it difficult to determine what developments require a response and what that response should be, precisely because these features of grey zone activity are designed to avoid clear thresholds and red lines that would trigger pre-established response procedures. Awareness and understanding of the real threats are therefore imperative.

5.5 Piercing the veil of ambiguity

Uncertainty and ambiguity are critical enablers of grey zone approaches. They impede an accurate assessment of the situation and thus may severely hinder the adoption of appropriate countermeasures. Dissipating this uncertainty and ambiguity is key to avoid suffering incremental costs and to prevent the gradual attainment of the objectives pursued by grey zone aggressors. Thus, Brands argues that it is necessary to pierce ambiguity since it is

[c]entral to denying gray zone belligerents the benefits of no attribution, exposing the nature and illegitimacy of their actions, and raising the various costs . . . As just one example, consider how it was firm evidence of Russian-backed separatists' responsibility for the tragic downing of MH-17 over Ukraine that cleared the way for the imposition of harsher international sanctions against Moscow.[58]

6. Conclusion

The grey zone concept is best understood as a particular manifestation of hybrid threats: it refers to the space in between peace and war that is marked by competitive engagements that are more antagonistic than ordinary peaceful relations, but which remain below the threshold of open violence. The instruments and methods of grey zone competition are varied. The overall aim of actors operating in this space is to destabilize their adversaries. A wide range of tools across the DIMEFIL spectrum may serve this purpose, which means that grey zone competition may take many different forms. Complicating matters is the fact that the edges of the zone are indistinct. This is so partly because grey zone activities

---

[58] Brands (n 1).

may be coercive and rely on military means, potentially involving limited uses of force, and partly because they may be designed to shape the battlefield, thus leading to hybrid or conventional forms of war.

Amongst the various actors resorting to grey zone competition, China may be seen as its most purist proponent, while Russia is far more willing to move from the grey zone into hybrid warfare situations and even open military conflict, as it did in Ukraine in 2022. By contrast, while Iran in many respects can be described as a grey zone actor, applying the concept to actors in the MENA region highlights the limitations of this tactic and also of the analytical power of the concept.

Countering the hybrid threats faced by liberal democracies with any chance of success requires a proper understanding and appreciation of the key features of grey zone engagements, their main instruments and tactics, and the objectives and modus operandi of the State and non-State adversaries operating in this space. The concept thus helps to make sense of a more multipolar security environment, which in turn is a precondition for developing appropriate response options to hybrid threats, including by adopting a credible deterrence and robust defence posture.

Authors' Note

This text was drafted in a personal capacity. The views and opinions of the authors expressed herein should therefore not be interpreted as stating or reflecting those of their respective employers, universities, associations, and organizations of which they are members.

16

Coercing Well

The Logic, Grammar, and Norms of the Grey Zone

C. Anthony Pfaff

1. Introduction

Kathleen Hicks describes the 'grey zone' as a 'contested arena' between war and peace where actors pursue their ends by employing means that are 'somewhere between routine statecraft and open warfare'.[1] It is the undifferentiated application of non-violent—'white'—and violent—'black'—means for limited ends that make this space 'grey'. While this space has always existed between State actors in competition, technology and increased connectivity afford both State and non-State actors more grey space in which to compete.

The spread of cyber technologies and increasing global connectivity, for example, have enabled a range of coercive, if non-violent, measures by exposing new vulnerabilities. Targets for these kinds of attacks include critical infrastructure and services as well as publics who are subjected to information operations intended to undermine government legitimacy and paralyze decision-making. These changes enable the pursuit of higher stakes at lower costs, allowing peer competitors to gain critical advantage while avoiding war and weaker actors to take on global powers and succeed.

Moreover, these means challenge current international norms because in some cases they do not seem to apply and in others they seem to proscribe an effective response. Without some kind of intervention, international actors might drift towards the kind of lawlessness that characterized the international order in eras prior to World War II. Moreover, because of the low barrier for use of some of these means, the 'great power competition' of the pre-war era could be replaced by competition among a variety of international actors, which will expose publics to a cacophony of disruptions from which there may be little room to escape.

---

[1] Lindsey R. Sheppard et al, 'By Other Means: U.S. Priorities in the Gray Zone (Part I)' (Centre for Strategic and International Studies 2019) 2.

C. Anthony Pfaff, *Coercing Well* In: *Hybrid Threats and Grey Zone Conflict.* Edited by: Mitt Regan and Aurel Sari, Oxford University Press. © Oxford University Press 2024. DOI: 10.1093/oso/9780197744772.003.0016

340 INSTRUMENTS, TACTICS, AND METHODS IN THE GREY ZONE

Such a drift, however, is not inevitable. It may not even be likely. Where old norms erode or simply disappear, new ones often take their place. For example, normative regimes based on honour eventually gave way to ones based on rights as the introduction of ranged weapons and mass mobilization made the kind of personal combat that honour governed obsolete.[2] This chapter will examine how the norms of an international order based on providing alternatives to escalation might evolve in response to coercive measures that threaten to make that order obsolete as well.

So while the future need not be moral chaos, it is still the case that international actors—both State and non-State—will have to make decisions about the kinds of norms that will guide their behaviour. While those choices will be informed by prior moral commitments, they will also be shaped by the practical necessities associated with realizing the interests in conflict. Norms that render an activity self-defeating are rarely sustainable unless actors have the ability to avoid that activity. Generally, that is not the case with international conflict and competition.

To understand what norms *should* govern the grey zone, this chapter will examine how the logic and grammar of grey zone activity shape the norms that govern it. Specifically, it will look at how international actors compete under conditions where escalation avoidance limits the measures they would rationally employ. However, in placing this limit, they also encourage proliferation of means that not only impose costs but also impact the kinds of choices actors can make as well as their ability to choose in the first place.

2. Logic and grammar of the grey zone

Where logic reflects the purpose of an activity, grammar comprises the rules by which that activity functions. In language, grammars help speakers make sense of what they *should* say given what they *want* to mean. It also helps them make sense of what other speakers say to them. In linking war to politics, the Prussian General Carl von Clausewitz observed that war was 'merely another kind of writing and language for political thoughts'.[3]

Failing to align the two, Clausewitz further argued, is much like a person who is not conversant in a language and thus sometimes says something he does not

---

[2] Michael Walzer, *Just and Unjust Wars: A Moral Argument with Historical Illustrations* (4th edn, Basic Books 2006) 16. Andrew Seth Myer argues a similar evolution occurred during the Warring States period in ancient China. Andrew Seth Myer, *The Dao of the Military: Liu An's Art of War* (Columbia University Press 2012) 7–12.

[3] Carl von Clausewitz, *On War* (Michael Howard and Peter Paret tr., Princeton University Press 1976) 605. First published 1833.

THE LOGIC, GRAMMAR, AND NORMS OF THE GREY ZONE   341

intend. In fact, he viewed war as 'merely another kind of writing and language for political thoughts'.[4] One can extend the metaphor by adding that in addition to aligning logic with grammar, one *should* further align both with the norms of good conversation. It is one thing to be intelligible; it is another to be fluent. The latter, arguably, is preferable to the former.

To assess the connection between logic, grammar, and norms for the grey zone, one needs to be more precise about what exactly it is. Put simply, 'grey zone' is one of many terms used to describe the current state of international competition below the threshold of war, which includes 'hybrid warfare', 'irregular warfare', and 'active measures' to name a few.[5] Whatever the right word to describe this competitive space is, and what distinguishes it from war, as the Center for Strategic and International Studies (CSIS) 'Gray Zone Project' puts it, the growing reliance on indirect, non-military tools to achieve political objectives without risking escalation.[6] Of course, military force can play a role in the grey zone, as the project recognizes; however, as an alternative to war, the grey zone places restrictions on measures that risk escalation to war. Failure to observe those restrictions likely means one is either no longer in the grey zone or soon about to leave.

If the grey zone is an alternative to war, there is no reason to believe that strategies, tactics, and means prescribed by war's grammar will be effective in the grey zone, or at least not in the same way. There is, in fact, some evidence to think this is true. According to the Militarized Compellent Threats dataset, from 1918 to 2001, stronger powers were successful in threatening weaker powers only 41.4 per cent of the time.[7] This disparity suggests superior military capabilities will not achieve the same results in the grey zone that they do in war.

Why that is the case is not necessarily obvious. For Clausewitz, the logic of war is the logic of imposing one's will on an enemy to achieve a political objective.[8] One eliminates enemies' capacity to resist by eliminating their combat capability faster than they can eliminate one's own. Thus, the grammar of war is expressed by strategies of annihilation and attrition aimed at destroying as much enemy military capability as possible.[9] Because both war and coercion serve political ends, it would appear on the surface that they share a similar logic. If so, then the stronger actor would be the one who can best annihilate and attrite and so should

---

[4] Ibid. 607.

[5] David McFarland, *Understanding Hybrid Warfare: Navigating the Smoke and Mirrors of International Security* (McFarland 2021) 8.

[6] Center for Strategic and International Studies, 'Gray Zone Project' <https://www.csis.org/programs/gray-zone-project> accessed 29 August 2022.

[7] Todd S. Sechser, 'Militarized Compellent Threats, 1918–2001' (2011) 28 Conflict Management and Peace Science 377.

[8] Clausewitz (n 3) 75.

[9] C. Anthony Pfaff, *Resolving Ethical Challenges in an Era of Persistent Conflict* (Strategic Studies Institute 2011) 9.

generally prevail against weaker ones. However, the emphasis on limiting escalation affects the choices not only that actors can make, but that they *should* make to be successful. One way to understand the difference is that in war, imposing one's will entails eliminating an enemy's ability to *choose* to resist. Of course, enemies can choose to surrender before their ability to resist is taken away; however, should they not, the point of war is to then continue to force the issue.

In the grey zone, whether due to ability or interest, adversaries retain their ability to choose. Thus, rather than to take choice away, the point of grey zone activities is to get the adversary to make choices that are more advantageous to one's own interests. It is this limit on escalation that accounts for much of the differences between the logic and grammar of war and that of the grey zone. Whether actors impose those limits because they assess they would lose a war or it would be too costly to fight even if they won, what is important for this analysis is that for both actors, escalation to war is their worst outcome. When that preference changes, they are, again, likely no longer in the grey zone.

The most obvious difference between warfighting and coercing lies in the kinds of objectives one can pursue to achieve success. As political scientist Patricia Sullivan argues, there is a difference between 'brute force' objectives and 'compliance' objectives. Brute force objectives, like the seizure of territory or elimination of industrial capacity, are achieved through the destruction of those military forces used in their defence. The formula for victory is simple to state, even if difficult to achieve. One wins wars by destroying enemy military capacity, which reduces the enemy's ability to resist. Once the enemy is no longer capable of resisting, one can then impose one's will. In this context, achieving the military objective is closely linked, if not identical, to achieving the political one.

On the other hand, compliance objectives, like deterring cyberattacks or compelling the removal of military forces from a contested area, depend on changing adversaries' minds about what is in their interests.[10] In this case, there is no necessary connection or causal effect between what actors do and whether those objectives are achieved. This disconnect arises because the emphasis on changing minds gives adversaries the initiative since they get to decide what kind of threat or punishment they will endure.[11]

US operations in Iraq in both 1991 and 2003 aptly illustrate this difference. In 1991, the US-led coalition successfully imposed its will by forcing Saddam Hussein to give up control of Kuwait. However, in the subsequent 'peace', the same coalition was not able to compel Saddam to permit inspectors from the International Atomic Energy Agency to have access to sites where he was thought

---

[10] Patricia Sullivan, 'War Aims and War Outcomes: Why Powerful States Lose Limited Wars' (2007) 51 Journal of Conflict Resolution 504.

[11] Tony Pfaff, *Resolving Ethical Challenges in an Era of Persistent Conflict* (Strategic Studies Institute 2011) 9–15.

THE LOGIC, GRAMMAR, AND NORMS OF THE GREY ZONE 343

to be developing nuclear weapons.[12] In 2003, a new US-led coalition again imposed its will (in part because Saddam did not provide that access) and forced him from power. However, it was not able to convince Iraq's various factions to accept the new order it tried to impose and eventually withdrew without having met all of its political objectives.[13]

In this view, war and coercion are not so much on different sides of a threshold or ends of a spectrum but different ways of going about realizing strategic interests and objectives. This difference does not mean kinetic operations—where an actor employs physical violence—cannot play a role in coercion or that non-military measures cannot be effective in war. However, what this difference does entail is that all kinetic operations are not the same. Those intended to take, seize, or otherwise remove the enemy's choice would be examples of brute force. Those intended to encourage an opponent to make certain choices would be examples of 'coercive force', at least as the term is used here. With this understanding of what the grey zone is, I will next discuss how it works.

2.1 The logic and grammar of coercion

With this understanding of what the grey zone is, I will next use the concepts of logic, grammar, and norms to discuss the nature of activities in this zone and the possibilities for arriving at norms to govern them. Cold War Scholar Thomas J. Schelling described the difference between warfighting and coercion as the difference between 'the power to hurt and the power to seize'.[14] He saw strategic competition as a kind of bargaining, but one where gains for one side reflected a loss for the other. Under such conditions there are a range of outcomes that are better for both sides than no agreement, but because any one of those outcomes still represents a better deal for one than the other, reaching an agreement can be difficult, if not impossible.

As Schelling further pointed out, actors concede when they believe their opponent will not do so and their own concession will yield a better outcome than continued resistance. This dynamic incentivizes actors to bargain in order to raise the other's satisfaction with one's preferred outcome. This bargaining can be explicit, where adversaries negotiate directly or tacit, where each adversary

---

[12] Sarah Graham-Brown and Chris Toensing, 'A Backgrounder on Inspections and Sanctions', in *The Iraq War Reader: History, Documents, Opinions*, edited by Micah L. Sifry and Christopher Cerf, 165–73 (Simon and Schuster 2003).

[13] Ali A. Allawi, *The Occupation of Iraq: Winning the War, Losing the Peace* (Yale University Press 2007) 458–60. Anthony S. Cordesman, 'Iraq after the US Withdrawal' (Center for Strategic and International Studies 2 July 2012) <https://www.csis.org/analysis/iraq-after-us-withdrawal> accessed 14 September 2022.

[14] Thomas C. Schelling, *Arms and Influence* (Yale University Press 2008) 5.

344 INSTRUMENTS, TACTICS, AND METHODS IN THE GREY ZONE

observes and interprets the actions of the other, aware the other is doing the same.[15] The logic behind this bargaining is to incentivize cooperation rather than simply eliminate resistance. Doing so depends not simply on imposing costs; rather, it depends on placing adversaries in positions where they must act, *and* their most rational option is the one most beneficial to one's own cause. The next thing to discuss then is what it takes to place adversaries in those kinds of positions.

2.2 Credibility and capability

Effective coercion depends on a threat that is both credible and capable. Credibility is a function of an adversary believing that it is rational for one to act on a particular threat.[16] If an adversary believes that one's cost of employing a deterrent measure, for example, is less than the cost of conceding to its challenge, one's threat is credible. Credibility, however, is not sufficient to deter an adversary from acting. One's threat must also be capable. Capable threats are those that not only impose a cost on prospective challengers but also leave those challengers worse off than if they had not acted.[17] So, for measures to be effective, adversaries need to believe it is *rational* for one to defend a particular interest with means adequate to make it *irrational* for an adversary to challenge in the first place.

2.3 Calibrating demands

Even when one has what appears to be a credible and capable threat, coercion can still fail. Intuitively, the stronger the actor, the higher the cost they can impose on an opponent and thus the more likely an opponent will choose not to bear those costs and concede. Unfortunately, that intuition seems to have little application in real-world interactions. As noted above, the relationship between strength and coercive success is anything but direct.

When making demands, coercive success depends on the value of the demand, the probability the coercer would win if the interaction resulted in conflict, and the cost to either actor for engaging in military conflict.[18] The reasoning here is relatively straightforward. If the value of the demand is high for the coercing

---

[15] Thomas C. Schelling, *The Strategy of Conflict* (Harvard University Press 1980) 21–22.

[16] Frank C. Zagare and D. Marc Kilgour, *Perfect Deterrence* (CUP 2000) 66–67.

[17] Ibid. 82.

[18] Todd S. Sechser, 'A Bargaining Theory of Coercion', in *Coercion: The Power to Hurt in International Politics,* edited by Kelly M. Greenhill and Peter Krause (OUP 2018) 63.

THE LOGIC, GRAMMAR, AND NORMS OF THE GREY ZONE   345

actor, then conceding is likely to impose a correspondingly high cost on the target of that demand, especially in the zero-sum bargaining contexts Schelling described. Counterintuitively, lowering the demand may not increase chances of success, even where targets are weaker, especially if there is the expectation of future demands.

Given a credible and capable threat it is always rational to concede in a single iteration interaction. However, in what Robert J. Art and Kelly M. Greenhill call the 'capability-intention dilemma', capability can be undermined if the target believes its adversary will continue to make demands. In fact, weaker actors are incentivized to resist in order to cause stronger coercers to moderate their demands.[19] This dynamic can significantly increase the perceived cost of cooperation, making it less likely the target of coercion will concede. This dynamic could account for the high number of coercive failures for stronger actors mentioned above.

Coercion is much more likely to succeed where targets of coercion believe (1) the coercer prefers conflict to concession and (2) their escalation or resistance will fail. Thus, if the value of the demand is equal to or less than the probability of the coercer winning plus the cost to the target for conceding, the coercion should succeed.[20] The possibility of future iterations, however, does offer coercers an opportunity to assess their opponents, especially their sensitivity to the human and financial costs of war.[21] Coercers can do this by making high demands and threatening high costs without regard to whether imposing those costs are actually in their interests. Such 'separating strategies' require the coercer to calibrate the demand so that strong opponents refuse while weak ones concede.[22] While doing so encourages the coercer to open with higher demands, and thus risk a greater chance for failure, it can lead to bigger payoffs in subsequent interactions. Moreover, very strong actors may be incentivized to take bigger risks since they can better afford failure.

Thus, counter-intuitively, the stronger the coercing actor, the more likely coercive failure. Moreover, the more resolved the target of coercion, the more likely coercive success. In the former case, stronger actors are more likely to risk failure up front to obtain higher payoffs in future iterations. In the latter's case, more resolved targets incentivize coercers to better calibrate their demands, offering something more acceptable to the target than if it were not resolved.[23]

[19] Robert J. Art and Kelly M. Greenhill, 'Coercion: An Analytical Overview', in Greenhill and Krause (n 18) 3; Sechser (n 18) 69–70.
[20] Sechser (n 18) 63.
[21] Todd S. Sechser, 'Reputations and Signaling in Coercive Bargaining' (2016) 62 Journal of Conflict Resolution 321.
[22] Ibid.
[23] Sechser (n 18) 73.

2.4 Strategies of coercion

Employing credible and capable threats as well as calibrating demands specifies how actors can bargain in this context. Given the emphasis on cooperation, actors will need to be able to impose costs as well as provide inducements. To impose costs, actors can certainly use force or, to lower the risk of escalation, non-violent means such as cyber and information operations or economic sanctions. They can raise the stakes regarding a particular conflict of interest to signal resolve or lower them to encourage cooperation. They can also alter the value of the status quo to impact adversaries' thresholds for action. As they engage in this range of activities, escalation management becomes critical, unless war is no longer the worst outcome. How these measures are used successfully determine—in part at least—the grammar of coercion.

2.5 Raising the stakes

Classical theories of coercion, like Schelling's, generally recommend threatening the highest costs possible to ensure an adversary cooperates to maintain a *status quo*, usually described in terms of a balance of power. Doing so may make sense among nuclear-armed actors who can literally impose the highest stakes imaginable: annihilation. However, as the Cold War illustrated, while the threat of annihilation may have prevented the United States and Soviet Union from direct armed conflict, it displaced their confrontations to proxies where the stakes were lower—from a superpower perspective, at least—often leading to quagmires like Vietnam for the United States and Afghanistan for Russia.[24]

Stakes, in this context, are a function of both the value of the interest and the likelihood of conflict. Thus, the higher the stakes the more tempting it is to bear the cost of acting or any subsequent escalation. Under such conditions, actors may feel an urgency to act because they want the advantages associated with seizing the initiative and are willing to bear whatever costs they incur. As RAND's Michael Mazarr pointed out, 'when a potential aggressor sees an urgent need to act', deterrence usually fails.[25] The normative implication here is that one should avoid raising the stakes under these conditions unless escalation, and likely war, are more in one's interest than the status quo.

---

[24] Andreas Krieg and Jean-Marc Rickli, *Surrogate Warfare: The Transformation of War in the Twenty-First Century* (Georgetown University Press 2019) 20.

[25] Colin Clark, 'What Are the Best Ways to Shield Taiwan from a Hungry China' (*Breaking Defense*, 29 July 2021) <https://breakingdefense.com/2021/07/best-ways-to-shield-taiwan-from-a-hungry-china/> accessed 14 March 2022.

This dynamic is again evident in the NATO confrontation with Russia over Ukraine. In the run-up to the crisis, Russia clearly had a greater stake in resolving the Ukraine crisis in its favour than NATO.[26] However, Russia arguably made a mistake in its 17 December 2021 ultimatum, in which it essentially demanded NATO accept a Russian sphere of influence in Eastern Europe, including over NATO members.[27] By doing so, Russia not only raised the stakes, giving NATO more reason to resist, but also foreshadowed future iterations, making it more rational for NATO to bear higher costs and take greater risks than the alliance was previously willing.

2.6 Valuing the status quo

Survival of the status quo depends on how highly valued it is. Even if actors do not prefer it relative to their own alternatives, it may still be preferable than the consequences of challenging it. This may seem like an obvious point; however, as Frank C. Zagare points out, it is largely ignored in classical deterrence theory, which dismisses the importance of diplomatic initiatives to stability.[28] For example, in 2016, Jin Canrong, a close advisor to Chinese President Xi Jinping, detailed a strategy that intertwined US and Chinese interests and also established a set of alternatives to the global presence of the United States, like the Belt and Road Initiative, to eventually displace US influence, regionally and globally.[29]

By cooperating with the United States on some interests and challenging the United States on others, China is in a better position to exercise influence than it could have been if did not cooperate at all. The normative implication here is where preservation of the status quo is one's preferred outcome, one should find ways to increase its value for others—including adversaries—as well. Where survival of the status quo is not preferable, it makes more sense to prioritize establishing a more attractive one rather than simply imposing costs to punish its defenders.

---

[26] Ian Bremmer, 'Russia Cares More about Ukraine than U.S. Does' (*GZERO*, 24 January 2022) <https://www.gzeromedia.com/quick-take/russia-cares-more-about-ukraine-than-the-us-does> accessed 14 September 2022.

[27] Andrew Roth, 'Russia Issues List of Demands It Says Must Be Met to Lower Tensions in Europe', *The Guardian* (London, 17 December 2021) <https://www.theguardian.com/world/2021/dec/17/russia-issues-list-demands-tensions-europe-ukraine-nato> accessed 14 September 2022.

[28] Frank C. Zagare, *Game Theory, Diplomatic History, and Security Studies* (OUP 2019) 141–42.

[29] Manyin Li, 'What China Really Wants: A New World Order' (*National Review*, 7 March 2021) <https://www.nationalreview.com/2021/03/what-china-really-wants-a-new-world-order/> accessed 14 September 2022.

348 INSTRUMENTS, TACTICS, AND METHODS IN THE GREY ZONE

2.7 Managing escalation

As noted earlier, the threshold that differentiates the grey zone from war is the limit the former places on escalation. Put another way, actors in the grey zone are identified by preferring any outcome other than escalation to armed conflict. When that preference is asymmetric—one actor prefers conflict while the other does not—it is likely the latter will concede to the former. In such cases, it is not clear that the logic of the grey zone applied.

Escalatory spirals can occur when mutual fear and vulnerability lead actors to increase their advantage in a way that reinforces similar fears in another actor, often escalating to war. For example, Germany's expansion of its fleet in the early 1900s initiated an arms race with Britain, whose leaders were unsure of German intentions.[30] Should a crisis occur under these conditions, escalation is almost certain; especially where actor's worst outcome is concession. Even under these conditions, however, there are opportunities to limit the escalation and consequently the scope of the conflict. This limit can be expressed in a number of ways, including irregular operations, use of proxies, or a compromise such as a negotiated or brokered settlement.[31] The normative implication here is that as long as escalation represents one's worst outcome, one should continually identify off ramps in the event of a crisis.

A crisis occurs when actors have interests in conflict that are exclusive: realizing one entails not realizing the other. For example, Russia's demand that that NATO commit to limiting ties to Ukraine arguably did not conflict with any NATO interest, assuming expansion does not count as an interest. Demanding that NATO forces withdraw from countries that were not members prior to 1997, as the Russians did in December 2021, would compromise the alliance's ability to defend its members, arguably a vital NATO interest.[32]

In a crisis, a relationship can go in one of three directions: war, capitulation, or compromise. Cooperation, whether in the form of capitulation or compromise depends on how each actor values the interest, how likely they think they can achieve it through escalation, and how burdensome the cost of compromise. Essentially, compromise must be less costly than imposing one's will on an adversary, which typically involves an escalation to war.[33] This is essentially the same

---

[30] Andrew Kydd, 'Game Theory and the Spiral Model' (1997) 49 World Politics 371.

[31] Zagare (n 28) 85.

[32] Russian Foreign Ministry, 'Agreement on Measures to ensure the Security of the Russian Federation and Member States of the North Atlantic Treaty Organization' (17 December 2021) <https://mid.ru/ru/foreign_policy/rso/nato/1790803/?lang=en&clear_cache=Y> accessed 12 October 2022.

[33] Bruce Bueno De Mesquita and David Lalman, *War and Reason: Domestic and International Imperatives* (Yale University Press 1992) 103.

THE LOGIC, GRAMMAR, AND NORMS OF THE GREY ZONE   349

dynamic as making a demand or giving an ultimatum, the difference being a demand or ultimatum need not reflect a conflict of interest.

Even where both actors prefer conflict, there is still a rational path to limit it. That path depends, however, on actors' ability to signal resolve while at the same time signalling an openness to a limited resolution. Timing here is obviously important—as well as a barrier—to resolution as the first one to soften may encourage stronger resistance and thus be forced to concede. This dynamic creates an obvious incentive to escalate; however, where both sides prefer not to escalate but also do not wish to give up any gains, the possibility for a limited settlement exists. The normative implication here is to facilitate conditions for such a settlement, actors should consider more measured, in-kind responses that demonstrate resolve to escalate but the willingness to compromise.[34]

More to the point, actors can influence their opponents' preferences by providing alternatives to escalation that these opponents can rationally take up. Thus, effective escalation management requires at least three things: (1) a credible and capable threat; (2) an 'off ramp' to give an opponent a less costly but rational option to continued escalation; and (3) the ability to communicate both options to adversaries in ways they will both understand and trust. This third point provides another normative implication. The lesson from single-iteration prisoner dilemmas is that because sides cannot communicate and coordinate, neither can realize the better outcome described by mutual cooperation. Thus ensuring such an ability to communicate and coordinate exists even with one's adversary should be an imperative.

Thus, in the grey zone, pushing an adversary too hard invites escalation; however, conceding too much can invite more challenges, possibly forcing one to choose between escalation or loss of a vital interest. Neither outcome is generally desirable. Thus in the normative space the grey zone carves out, actors should generally prefer limited outcomes or even some concession to escalation unless the interest at stake is too vital or indivisible to compromise. To avoid or limit the costs of concession, one should avoid raising the stakes regarding a conflict of interest unless their adversary's response is neither credible—they would be worse off if they employ it—nor capable—one would not be if they did.

To avoid challenges to the status quo, actors should also find ways to raise its value for the adversary, even if there is no outcome where one or more competing actors would prefer it to an alternative. Moreover, one should also avoid raising the value of the status quo to the extent it is no longer worth defending, otherwise one may find oneself in the role of challenger. When challenging a status quo, one has a greater chance of success if one pursues a strategy where, in addition to imposing costs, one also finds ways to make it attractive enough that the value of

---

[34] Zagare (n 28) 91–93.

350 INSTRUMENTS, TACTICS, AND METHODS IN THE GREY ZONE

defending it falls below an adversary's threshold for acting. Of course, observing these norms will not necessarily prevent escalation. Thus, actors should identify escalation off ramps as well as acceptable limited outcomes. To facilitate escalation avoidance, actors should also ensure there are ways to communicate and coordinate with adversaries.

This characterization of grey zone norms is not intended to be comprehensive; however, it does illustrate where egoistic actors in competition might find space to cooperate. While these norms are essentially practical, they also reflect moral sentiments such as valuing peace over war, preservation over destruction, while upholding an obligation to defend, protect, and promote well-being. Thus, while they account for self-interest, they are not wholly determined by it. This point suggests that it will be difficult to disentangle their application from one's ethical obligations. How those obligations manifest themselves will depend as much on the means employed as it will on the objectives sought.

3. Grey zone norms

The norms, such as escalation avoidance, willingness to compromise, and raising an adversary's value of the status quo, of course, apply to coercion in general. What makes the grey zone a unique normative challenge, however, is how the means used challenge the established norms that would otherwise normally govern them. It is important to note that means employed in the grey zone, like cyber and information operations, have application in other contexts, including war. Moreover, means associated with warfighting or more traditional 'Great Power Competition' of past eras, like military force and economic sanctions, can have an effect in grey zone. The following discussion will focus on those means for which in the normative environment of the grey zone, either there are few rules to govern them or the rules that are there render their application ineffective.

3.1 The evolution of norms

Analysing the evolution of norms first requires an understanding of the actors the norms will govern. Because of the emphasis on interactions as the unit of analysis, one must further consider how these actors form preferences and how those preferences interact.[35] This analysis treats actors as both egoistic and

---

[35] David A. Lake and Robert Powell (eds), *Strategic Choice and International Relations* (Princeton University Press 1999) 4.

rational. They are egoistic in that they prioritize their interests over others' and rational in that they seek to maximize their utility however they define it.[36] This simple notion of rationality, of course, says nothing about *how* they define utility. Thus, non-rational influences from psychology, culture, history, personal interest, and domestic politics can affect how actors value certain outcomes in ways that are difficult to discern or predict.[37] For example, Russian Prime Minister Vladimir Putin's desire for a legacy as the man who restored Russia to its Cold War or imperial 'greatness' may not be rational from the perspective of Russian interests or even his own; however, one can still count his actions as rational relative to that desire.[38]

At their most basic, norms express a standard against which one can judge or appraise actions.[39] In international relations, Gary Goertz points out that norms are connected to behaviour and choice and help explain regularity, predictability, and order. International norms can be formal or informal. They can evolve or they can be imposed. However they are constituted or arise, normative structures form 'regimes' that express standards of international behaviour given a particular focus. For example, the 'sovereignty regime' is the structure of norms that specify how States should exercise sovereignty as well as what rights, permissions, and obligations they have as a result of that exercise.[40]

While Goetz argues that norms are not necessarily connected to expectations—one can express a standard without an expectation anyone will uphold it—expectations do help explain a norm's effectiveness. From a game-theoretic perspective, norms can be understood as strategies that reflect actors' expectations of how others will behave in specific situations. To the extent that best strategy applies to all actors in a given situation, that strategy represents a Nash Equilibrium, which is actor's best strategy given the expected strategy of other players. When that best strategy applies to all actors, it becomes normative as it is the strategy actors *should* select.[41]

While such equilibria may be normative, they are not necessarily norms. As Cristina Bicchieri points out in *The Grammar of Society*, Nash equilibria may identify patterns of behaviour but to the extent they simply reflect self-interest,

---

[36] Zagare (n 28) 10.

[37] Janice Gross Stein, 'Deterring Terrorism, not Terrorists', in *Deterring Terrorism: Theory and Practice*, edited by Alex Wilner and Andreas Wenger (Stanford University Press 2012) 46, 52–54; Daniel Kahneman and Amos Tversky, 'Conflict Resolution: A Cognitive Perspective', in *Barriers to Conflict Resolution*, edited by Kenneth Arrow et al (W. W. Norton and Co. 1995) 45.

[38] Kimberly Marten, 'President's Putin's Rationality in Russia's Invasion of Ukraine' (*PONARS Eurasia*, 9 March 2022) <https://www.ponarseurasia.org/president-putins-rationality-and-escalation-in-russias-invasion-of-ukraine/> accessed 9 March 2022.

[39] David Copp, *Morality, Normativity, and Society* (OUP 1995) 19–20.

[40] Gary Goertz, *International Norms and Decision Making: A Punctuated Equilibrium Model* (Rowman and Littlefield 2003) 13–21.

[41] Ibid. 62–63.

352 INSTRUMENTS, TACTICS, AND METHODS IN THE GREY ZONE

they do not identify norms. As she puts it, norms, specifically social norms, identify those conditions where one *should* cooperate even if it does involve some—short-term at least—material cost. In fact, she argues, when actors start with a preference for cooperation and the expectation others involved share that preference, mixed-motive games, where actors rationally cooperate or compete depending on what other actors would rationally choose, transform into coordination games, where actors do best when they choose the same strategy.[42]

This transformation occurs because in mixed-motive games, like the 'prisoner dilemma', actors may be motivated to cooperate or defect depending on the other's choices. Thus, their preferences in order from best to worst are (1) defect when the other cooperates; (2) cooperate when the other cooperates; (3) defect when the other defects; and (4) cooperate when the other defects. This ordering occurs despite the fact that the second-best outcome (mutual cooperation) offers both actors a higher payoff. The reason for that 'paradoxical' outcome is that if actors expect the other to cooperate, they should defect, to obtain their best outcome. If actors expect the other to defect, they should also defect, to avoid their worst outcome.[43] Knowing that the other actor sees the situation the same way, the only rational choice for either is to defect.

However, the presence of a shared norm places a premium on cooperation, which makes mutual cooperation the first preference for both actors. Where mutual cooperation is both actors' preferred outcome, actors reach equilibrium by coordinating the specifics of those outcomes.[44] For example, in order to achieve an agreement on nuclear arms control, US President Richard Nixon and Soviet Premier Leonid Brezhnev originally agreed to a 'Principle of Agreement' that was essentially an agreement to agree, but little else. What that did, however, was commit them to cooperate to work out the details, even though doing so came at some cost.[45] In effect, they established a shared norm for cooperation that transformed subsequent negotiations from a mixed-motive interaction to one of coordination. If enough other countries agree to something as well, it becomes customary international law, even if not everyone agrees to it.

Of course, a single instance of coordination is not enough to establish a norm. However, over time, repeated cooperation can at least set the expectation that cooperation will preferred in the future. As Robert Axelrod famously pointed out in *The Evolution of Cooperation*, when the interaction is iterated actors have the opportunity to impose costs for defection, then cooperation becomes the rational choice as long as the other does the same.[46] Robert Keohane, in *After*

---

[42] Cristina Bicchieri, *The Grammar of Society* (CUP 2006) 2–3, 25–26.
[43] Zagare (n 28) 9.
[44] Bicchieri (n 42) 26.
[45] Geoffrey Brennan et al, *Explaining Norms* (OUP 2013) 96–97.
[46] Robert Axelrod, *The Evolution of Cooperation* (Basic Books 1984) 13.

THE LOGIC, GRAMMAR, AND NORMS OF THE GREY ZONE   353

Hegemony, argued that this kind of iterative 'tit-for-tat' interactions could account for the acceptance of moral norms on the basis of self-interest.[47]

Pursuing the dominant—rational—strategy even repeatedly, however, is not sufficient to establish a norm. As mentioned earlier, norms do more than specify self-interest. They also bundle cultural, social, and other values into preferences that create conditions where actors might *want* to cooperate despite there being some material cost. So, making the transformation from self-interested practice to normative behaviour is not inevitable. This is where expectations play an important role. Multiple iterations of cooperation can create an expectation that others will abide a norm as well as believe that others expect that of them as well, independent of the particular circumstances of any particular iteration. When that happens, mutual cooperation replaces mutual defection as the rationally preferable choice. The fact that others may not choose cooperation in a given interaction does not necessarily change the norm or the expectation. Neither does whether the violation is sanctioned, though sanctions certainly can play a role in maintaining the norm. Because these expectations can hold independent of the actions of others, holding the norm remains rational, even if there is some cost.[48]

This setting aside of self-interest does not entail self-interest plays no role. As Keohane also points out, upholding norms is a way of signalling cooperation, which has its own benefits.[49] The point here, however, is to identify conditions where actors in competition would abide by a norm, even if violating it conferred an advantage. For example, in the St Petersburg Declaration of 1868, State actors agreed to a norm banning low-calibre soft-lead munitions because of a concern regarding unnecessary suffering, despite the fact those munitions could be useful against wooden supply wagons, which was their original intended purpose.[50] Thus, they set aside an advantage that was not norm violating in order to avoid an outcome that was.

This account of norms is, of course, not exhaustive. Moral norms, for example, apply independent of self-interest. Descriptive norms, likes those that apply to fashion and etiquette, may exist even when a significant number of relevant actors violate them.[51] Casual Friday, for example, only has meaning where there are workplace norms for more formal dress. Of course, if no one upheld a norm, one

---

[47] Robert Keohane, *After Hegemony: Cooperation and Discord in the World Political Economy* (Princeton University Press 2005) 127.

[48] Cristina Bicchieri, *The Grammar of Society: The Nature and Dynamics of Social Norms* (OUP 2019) 26.

[49] Keohane (n 47) 127.

[50] Adam Roberts and Richard Guelff (eds), *Documents on the Laws of War* (2nd edn, Clarendon Press 1989) 29–33.

[51] Bicchieri (n 48) 20–21, 29–31.

would reasonably ask whether it is a norm. Thus, thresholds, as will be discussed later, matter when understanding how norms arise and are sustained.

In this view, international norms are like social norms in that they are contingent and conditional. They are contingent on actors being in a particular situation and conditional on the expectations other will conform. Thus, they exist when a sufficient number of actors believe they exist, they pertain in particular types of situations, and others will act on them.[52] They arise and are sustained based on the preferences international actors have regarding the outcomes of those interactions. Put another way, rational actors in competition will generally mutually cooperate or mutually defect. Rarely will they risk cooperation if there is not some reason to trust the other will as well. Either way, when such interactions iterate, they establish expectations for behaviour, which over time become normative. To the extent they cooperate, they establish an obligation; to the extent they defect, they establish a permission.

The contingent and conditional nature of international norms do not preclude connection to broader ethical sensibilities that hold independent of interest. The most obvious connection lies in the activity itself: governments have a prima facie obligation to protect their citizens and promote their interests and well-being by virtue of the social contract.[53] Thus when confronted with an adversary, competition becomes a moral imperative. So, international norms differ somewhat from social norms because in an important way, the interests of others are baked in.

Moreover, how one competes can often be informed by prior moral commitments and concerns even if they do not override self-interest. The delegates at St Petersburg arguably agreed to its provisions because they shared a commitment to avoid unnecessary suffering. Similar commitments will inform the norms of competition. As philosophers Michael Gross and Tamar Meisels point out, the tools of competition, which include grey zone means such as cyber and information operations, raise the same questions regarding 'necessity, last resort, and the chance of success' that warfighting norms do.[54] However, in the normative space carved out in the grey zone, these commitments may inform, but will likely underdetermine, normative practice. Thus, to understand how actors will fill those gaps one also needs an account of how normative equilibria propagate. Simply because something is rational from an ideal perspective for actors involved does not entail that those actors will perceive that or, even if they do, act on it.

---

[52] Ibid. 11.

[53] Walzer (n 2) 54.

[54] Michael L. Gross and Tamar Meisels, 'Soft War: The Ethics of Unarmed Conflict', in *Soft War: The Ethics of Unarmed Conflict*, edited by Michael L. Gross and Tamar Meisels (CUP 2017) 3.

3.2 Military force

Military forces can have a coercive effect whether or not they resort to violence. Writing in the late 1970s, Barry M. Blechman and Stephen S. Kaplan found that factors that determined how well these forces influenced other actors included the size and character of the armed forces, their operations and deployments, military assistance, and the conduct of discrete operations.[55] They found that the Navy was used most to signal resolve, because ships are relatively easy to move in an out of a crisis area and were generally less disruptive than ground-based forces. The Army, on the other hand, was used the least largely due to the difficulty in moving significant forces but also because the forward presence of Army forces in places like Europe and Korea already had a sufficient deterrent effect and thus required fewer operations to reinforce it. As a result, when ground forces were required for discrete operations, Marines were used more often, in part because of their close association with Navy and their emphasis on quick reaction, limited operations, and flexible utilization. Finally, they analysed the impact of land-based aircraft, which included fixed-wing and helicopters from all services. In general, transport aircraft were used more often in political operations than in combat or patrol aircraft.[56]

Interestingly, however, they found increased uses of kinetic operations did not coincide with increased favourable outcomes. Rather, land-based combat aircraft were associated with the highest rate of favourable outcomes, in part at least because their use was not latent in the way naval and ground forces can be. They had a similar finding between land-based and amphibious ground forces, where the former had a higher rate of favourable outcomes than the latter, though when used together that rate significantly increased. Overall, they found that political operations involving military force were successful in 75 per cent of cases over the short term, but less than half over the long term. For example, the use of B-52s in 1973 over Laos—with which the United States was technically not at war—assured US allies giving them more confidence and resolve to continue fighting as well as compelling its adversaries—North Vietnam and the Pathet Lao—to cease fighting. However, fighting renewed and the Pathet Lao eventually took over Laos.[57]

3.3 Normative implications

The obvious concern with the use of force is that it invites more force in response. The result is often increasing escalation until at least one side is no longer able

---

[55] Barry M. Blechman and Stephen S. Kaplan, *Force without War* (Brookings 1978) 5–14, 85.
[56] Ibid. 38–46.
[57] Ibid. 88–102.

to respond or has left the grey zone and gone to war. To avoid such escalation, in fact, international law does not permit an armed response to just any use of force. Article 51 of the UN Charter, for example, permits the use of force only in response to an armed attack. While the Charter itself says little about what constitutes an armed attack, subsequent legal analysis suggests that it must produce 'serious consequences' such as 'territorial incursions, human casualties, or considerable destruction of property'.[58] Moreover, any armed response must be limited by what is necessary to avert an imminent or ongoing attack or bring it to an end.[59]

Thus, the killing of Islamic Republican Guard Corps Qods Force Commander Qassem Soleimani, for example, was viewed by many as illegal. The United States justified the attack based on Soleimani's role in orchestrating attacks against bases that housed US troops, claiming self-defence. However, the UN special rapporteur on extrajudicial killings faulted the strikes because they were not in response to an imminent attack and thus not self-defence. Moreover, the rapporteur pointed out that the attack was also conducted inside Iraq without consent of the Iraqi government. Thus, as precedent, it threatened to widen not just the conflict but general permissions to target soldiers everywhere.[60]

However, as former Deputy Judge Advocate for the US Air Force, Major General (ret) Charles Dunlap argues, findings like these ignore the reality of how Iran prosecuted its conflict through the use of proxies and its own irregular forces. As he points out, imminence does not need to depend on knowing where and when an attack it will take place. Rather, it can also depend on a pattern of continuing armed activity, the scale of the attack, and the alternatives the United States may have for self-defence given the 'modern-day capabilities, techniques, and technological innovations of terrorist organizations'.[61] The same concern could be true of State adversaries as well.

In fact, in his critique of the US decision to abandon its containment of Saddam Hussein in favour of war in 2003, Just War theorist Michael Walzer places some of the blame on the fact that there really is not an ethical theory governing the use of force below the threshold of war. As he argued, without such norms, war itself may seem morally preferable to ongoing, but ethically ambiguous, uses of force

---

[58] Yoram Dinstein, *War, Aggression and Self-Defense* (4th edn, CUP 2005) 193.

[59] Elizabeth Wilmshurst, 'Principles of International Law on the Use of Force by States in Self-Defence' (1 October 2005) <https://www.chathamhouse.org/2005/10/principles-international-law-use-force-states-self-defence> accessed 4 September 2022.

[60] Special Rapporteur on Extrajudicial, Summary or Arbitrary Executions, 'Report' (29 June 2020), UN Doc. A/HRC/44/38, 15 <https://www.ohchr.org/EN/HRBodies/HRC/RegularSessions/Session44/Documents/A_HRC_44_38_AUV.docx> accessed 4 September 2022.

[61] Charles Dunlap, 'The Killing of General Soleimani Was Lawful Self-Defense, Not Assassination' (*Lawfire*, 3 January 2020) <https://sites.duke.edu/lawfire/2020/01/03/the-killing-of-general-soleimani-was-lawful-self-defense-not-assassination/> accessed 14 September 2022.

THE LOGIC, GRAMMAR, AND NORMS OF THE GREY ZONE   357

aimed at constraining adversaries' ability to threaten. Thus, arguments about *jus ad bellum* need to be extended to *jus ad vim* that may be more permissive regarding when force is permitted but more restrictive in the objectives and means considered.[62]

In balancing the use of force with the need to avoid escalation, Daniel Brunstetter argues balance may be found between the norms of law enforcement, which emphasize limited force and human rights, and the norms of war, which enable greater latitude regarding the use of force, but that deny due process and places innocents at risk.[63] Which model one is permitted to use depends on effective governance and a monopoly on the use of force. Where those conditions exist, one should prioritize means that reflect a peacetime standard of human rights and where the use of force is clearly linked to its proposed effect. Where those conditions do not exist, one may risk collateral harm but to the extent possible resist 'depressing' the peacetime human rights standard.[64] These requirements further entail that discrimination and proportionality in *jus in vi* will have to meet higher standards than its *jus in bello* counterparts, regardless of the conditions under which such operations occur.[65] Given the grey zone emphasis on limiting escalation, this analysis suggests that emphasis should be placed on codifying *jus ad vim* conditions into international law.

Provocative, but non-violent posturing, moving, or changing the disposition of military forces will remain permissible. They allow adversaries a way of signalling that the other should take seriously. While such measures could set conditions for escalation, it will be the one who resorts to violence first who would generally be in violation. Exceptions, as will be discussed in the following sections, may be made when that violence is in response to non-kinetic but extremely disruptive means such as cyber and information operations. Even then, such violence should be limited and designed to avoid the harm and limit the escalation those non-kinetic measures threaten.

While self-defence will also be permitted, as noted above, current international law may place excessive restrictions, making self-defence as a norm unsustainable. For example, if one assumes the standard for imminence employed by the UN special rapporteur, then it seems the United States in Iraq is placed in a difficult situation where it must (1) withdraw its forces; (2) endure attacks

---

[62] Walzer (n 2) xiv–xvii.

[63] David Brunstetter and Megan Braun, 'From Jus ad Bellum to Jus ad Vim: Recalibrating Our Understanding of the Moral Use of Force' (2013) 27 Ethics and International Affairs 87, 97–98.

[64] Daniel R. Brunstetter, 'The Purview of State-Sponsored Violence: Law Enforcement, Just War, and the Ethics of Limited Force', in *The Ethics of War and Peace Revisited: Moral Challenges in an Era of Contested and Fragmented Sovereignty*, edited by Daniel R. Brunstetter and Jean Vincent Holeindre (Georgetown University Press 2018) 235.

[65] Brunstetter and Braun (n 63) 96–101.

without responding; or (3) engage in reprisals to compel Iran to cease sponsoring attacks. Given that the first two are equivalent to cooperating while the other defects—generally the worst outcome for an actor—they do not likely represent a stable equilibrium for the United States. The third option, however, is the equivalent of mutual defection, which, as described above, is a stable equilibrium. So, absent loosening some of the restrictions on self-defence, armed reprisals as normative may be the only equilibrium left.

At this point, norms associated with warfighting may overlap in the grey zone. When, as described above, limited attacks aimed at disrupting or deterring future attacks are the only alternative to concession, restraint seems arbitrary. As Walzer argues, 'Reprisal is a practice carried over from the war convention to the world of 'peacetime', because it provides an appropriately limited form of military action. It is better to defend the limits than to try to abolish the practice'.[66] These restrictions are found in the intent behind the reprisal as well as the object and means. In war, reprisals are permitted only to compel an adversary to conform to the law. They must be proportionate to the original violation and directed only at those involved.[67] Violent reprisals against individuals or groups not involved with the original violation are not permitted.

It is worth noting that these norms of reprisal described above roughly describe how Iran is employing force against the United States and its partners. In response to US sanctions that reduced Iran's oil exports, for example, Iran responded with attacks on oil tankers, pipelines, and Saudi Arabia's refinery at Abqaiq. Moreover, this pattern is not isolated. After the United Kingdom seized an Iranian oil tanker, violating international sanctions, the Iranians seized a British one.[68] In each case, the use of force was in response to some harm and clearly observed limits both in regard to what was targeted and how. In the case of the Abqaiq attack, Iran's Houthi proxies used more than twenty Iranian-made drones and missiles to attack the refinery. While Saudi Arabia's oil production was cut in half, there were no reported casualties.[69]

While it may make sense to permit limited armed reprisals, the grey zone offers non-violent alternatives that may prove just as, if not more so, effective. Cyber technologies, for example, open up a range of possible measures that may be more effective than more traditional political, military, or economic ones in

[66] Walzer (n 2) 221.
[67] Ibid. 207.
[68] Thomas S. Warrick, 'If the US Launches Cyberattacks on Iran, Retaliation Could Be a Surprise' (*Fifth Domain*, 31 January 2020) <https://www.fifthdomain.com/thought-leadership/2020/01/30/if-the-us-launches-cyberattacks-on-iran-retaliation-could-be-a-surprise/> accessed 14 September 2022.
[69] Frederick Kagan, 'Attribution, Intent, and Response in the Abqaiq Attack' (American Enterprise Institute, October 2019) 4 <https://www.criticalthreats.org/wp-content/uploads/2019/10/RPT-Kagan_Attribution-Intent-and-Response-3.pdf> accessed 7 September 2022.

affecting State behaviour. In fact, an important challenge to current norms is the fact that non-violent measures, like cyber operations, can be so disruptive actors will be compelled to consider using force in response. The difficulty is, of course, is that there is little precedent for establishing what sorts of cyber operations would be appropriate and which ones would not. It just is difficult to determine the ethics of an act when its effects are poorly understood. The *Tallinn Manual*, for example, argues that cyber operations that result in physical destruction or harm could be treated as a 'use of armed force' under international law; however, it says little new about non-violent, disruptive effects such operations can have.[70]

Moreover, to be effective, it may be necessary to loosen restrictions on targeting non-responsible actors because a cyberattack directed at a government or military leader may not be possible or effective. However, it is then worth asking, what would be better: a discriminate and proportionate kinetic strike against military targets that kills at least some military personnel or an indiscriminate, disproportionate cyber operation, such as the one conducted by the Russians against Estonia in 2007, that significantly disrupts civil life. Setting aside the efficacy question, permitting the less discriminate, non-lethal option may make more moral and ethical sense. Of course, extremely disruptive cyber operations can lead to physical harms, as Iran appeared to do to Turkey in 2015, when it shut down a power plant in Istanbul in response to Turkey's support for Saudi Arabia that left millions without power.[71] Under such conditions it is not clear what counts as proportionate.

3.4 Non-State actors

In the grey zone, non-State actors primarily play two roles. First, as discussed above, they can act as proxies for State actors, enabling them to impose costs on adversaries while limiting costs to themselves as well as the risk of escalation. Second, they can be actors in their own right, as the events of 9/11 clearly demonstrated. The difficulty for State actors who must confront them is that non-State actors do not generally respond to coercive measures the way State actors might.

One reason is that violent non-State actors are often more resilient to coercive measures than State actors because they are often in a better position to avoid

---

[70] Michael N. Schmitt (ed), *Tallinn Manual 2.0: On the International Law Applicable to Cyber Operations* (CUP 2017) 341–42.
[71] Micah Halpern, 'Iran Flexes Its Power by Transporting Turkey to the Stone Age', *Observer* (London, 22 April 2015) <http://observer.com/2015/04/iran-flexes-its-power-by-transporting-turkey-to-the-stone-ages/> accessed 14 September 2022.

360 INSTRUMENTS, TACTICS, AND METHODS IN THE GREY ZONE

or absorb costs State actors may want to impose. Unlike State actors who are anchored in a territory and, generally at least, prefer survival even at the expense of an ideal, the same cannot be said of non-State actors. Many operate globally, in secret, and will often make significant sacrifices before altering their behaviour in a way they perceive undermines their ideal. Thus, as Jeffrey W. Knopf notes, it is not simply that the fanaticism often associated with these groups increases the costs they are willing to bear. Rather, their ability to operate in the shadows means they have no 'return address' to direct any response.[72] Without a return address, it is unclear how State actors can impose costs necessary for coercion to work.

Moreover, as Alex Wilner and Andreas Wenger observe, if coercion is a bargaining tactic to change adversary behaviour, then it only works when one gives adversaries an alternative they can accept. However, if one's policy towards violent non-State actors is one of annihilation, they will not likely believe provisions one offers for their continued existence. As Wilner and Wenger point out, 'If al-Qaeda rightly assumes that the United States is seeking its eventual annihilation, it will have little reason to believe that an alternative deterrent relationship, in which it is allowed to survive, is ever possible'.[73] Of course, finding space where the target of terrorist attacks can 'tolerate' a terrorist is nonsensical at best. So, the reality may just be that there are few alternatives to deter terrorist attacks. The best one may do is disrupt attacks in planning or underway or degrade terrorist capabilities.

These points suggest that coercive strategies that rely simply on imposing costs, even if they are carefully calibrated, are likely to fail.[74] One only need to consider that the US cruise missile attacks in 1998 on al Qaeda targets in Sudan and Afghanistan as punishment intended to compel the group to stop attacking US citizens and territory, successfully destroyed their targets but, as evidenced by the events of September 11, 2001, were clearly ineffective.[75]

As ongoing operations against al Qaeda, ISIS, and their global affiliates suggest, targeted killings may be effective at disrupting specific operations but are not effective in compelling terrorists to abandon indiscriminate violent attacks. Charles Kirchofer, in analysing the Israeli experience during the Second Intifada, suggests coercive effects can be realized when senior leadership is effectively targeted. He argues that Israel's targeted killing of Hamas leadership forced them to choose between continuing operations and losing their current leadership,

---

[72] Jeffrey W. Knopf, 'The Fourth Wave in Deterrent Research', in *Deterring Terrorism: Theory and Practice*, edited by Alex Wilner and Andreas Wenger (Stanford University Press 2012) 21.

[73] Alex Wilner and Andreas Wenger, 'Linking Deterrence to Terrorism', in Wilner and Wenger (n 72) 4.

[74] Frank Harvey and Alex Wilner, 'Counter-coercion, the Power of Failure, and the Practical Limits of Deterring Terrorism', in Wilner and Wenger (n 72) 98.

[75] Gregory F. Treverton, *Framing Compellent Strategies* (RAND 2000) 29.

THE LOGIC, GRAMMAR, AND NORMS OF THE GREY ZONE   361

many of whom had played a role in the group's founding, or ceasing operations at least until their vulnerability could be addressed.

He further argues that the lull in operations at the end of 2003 was the result of a deliberate decision by Hamas to cease operations within Israel's pre-1967 borders in exchange for a halt to Israel's targeted killings of Hamas leadership. That ended when, after a series of tit-for-tat exchanges, Israel killed the Hamas leader responsible for the original cease-fire negotiations. After that, Hamas escalated rapidly as they saw the exchanges as proportional responses, but the killing of the negotiator as 'breaking of the rules'. So, coercion does appear to have limits absent a positive incentive, such as observing limits on escalation and renewing targeting of senior leaders.[76]

But this problem rests on the assumption that violent non-State actors are unitary organizations. Rather, as Knopf also points out, it is better to think of them as 'systems', comprised of multiple actors, with varying relationships with the organization as well as varying vulnerabilities. So, while one may not be able to deter, for example, suicide bombers—or the leaders who sent them—one may be able to deter actors associated with financing, logistics, intelligence, and so on.[77]

Moreover, even within a terrorist group's core membership, not all actors have the same interests. Organization leaders, for example, have to care about the long-term viability and success of the organization whereas other members may undertake suicide missions and have no concerns at all. Thus, terrorist leaders may be incentivized to refrain from certain operations if they are convinced that they will fail or, even if successful, not have the intended impact. This point suggests that a defensive posture intended to decrease the likelihood of operational success and an offensive posture to increase risk to specific members of the terrorist network could act as deterrent threats if one could signal that the threat exists and is significant enough to achieve effects the group's leadership would not prefer. Furthermore, if one can also de-link terrorist operations from terrorist objectives by portraying the terrorist cause as illegitimate, one may also be able to deter at least certain kinds of operations.[78]

The bottom line here is that deterring violent non-State actors depends on denying them the ability to either operate or benefit from the political effect of their operations. In other words, if the population is not terrorized, then terrorists cannot achieve their political goals. Doing so would not likely place terrorist leaders in positions where they would not stop trying, but it would give them reasons to avoid risk when doing so. If one can target senior leadership directly, one may get an agreement—even if tacit—to curtail operations. However,

---

[76] Charles Kirchofer, 'Targeted Killings and Compellence: Lessons from the Campaign in the Second Intifada' (2016) 10 Perspectives on Terrorism 15.

[77] Knopf (n 72) 23.

[78] Ibid. 25–27.

362 INSTRUMENTS, TACTICS, AND METHODS IN THE GREY ZONE

for such deterrence to be sustainable, one will likely have to accept the existence of the organization and avoid targeting senior leaders as long as they hold to their side of the bargain.

3.5 Normative implications

The challenge of non-State actors lies in their relationship with State actors. To the extent they operate on behalf of a State, like Iran's proxies in Iraq, they can allow the State actor to impose costs while avoiding accountability, especially in the context of international law. Currently, standards for holding sponsors liable for their proxies is high, often requiring 'effective' or 'overall' control where an organ of the sponsoring State directs proxy activity or proxy forces are integrated into the sponsoring States' armed forces or security services.[79]

Precedents include the International Court of Justice finding against the United States in *US v Nicaragua* which held that even though the United States provided Contra rebels material support and even a manual that advised attacking civilian targets, the United States did not have effective control, and thus was not liable because no organ of the State directed the Contras to do so. Enforcing a higher standard of overall control, the International Criminal Tribunal for the former Yugoslavia held that because Serbian forces drew personnel from the Yugoslav Army, and were paid by the Yugoslav Army, they were effectively part of the Yugoslav Army.[80] Given these precedents, it would be difficult for the United States to hold Iran responsible for its proxies in international court. Moreover, it has so far been impossible for the United States to hold them responsible in Iraq's courts because the government simply is not strong enough to challenge them.[81]

Where violent non-State actors, like al Qaeda, operate within a State boundary but without State sponsorship, two additional concerns arise. The first regards State sovereignty. While ideally, States where terrorist groups operate would cooperate with other States' counter-terror operations, that may not always be in their interests or within their capabilities, as is the case with Iraq. Where they cooperate, the normative challenge is resolved: State actors should respect the other's sovereignty and find ways to cooperate. Where they do not, State actors have to consider whether to violate the sovereignty of the harbouring State.

---

[79] Oona A. Hathaway et al, 'Ensuring Responsibility: Common Article 1 and State Responsibility' (2017) 95 Texas Law Review 539.

[80] Ibid. 554–58.

[81] Federico Manfredi Firmian, 'Curbing Militia Power in Iraq' (London School of Economics, 1 January 2022) <https://blogs.lse.ac.uk/mec/2022/01/01/curbing-militia-power-in-iraq/> accessed 14 September 2022.

THE LOGIC, GRAMMAR, AND NORMS OF THE GREY ZONE   363

Here, mutual defection would constitute the harbouring State failing to co-operate and the target State violating the harbouring State's sovereignty. Given, as Walzer points out, the right to sovereignty entails the responsibility to control what is going on within one's borders, it makes little sense to hold sovereignty as a barrier to acting against the violent non-State actor. This point does suggest that any action—kinetic or otherwise—should only be directed at the violent non-State actor to the extent possible unless it is clear the harbouring State is sponsoring those groups. Then it may make sense to permit the use of military force in accordance with the *jus ad vim* norms described above.

The second concern is collateral harms. Even where States cooperate with counter-terror operations, terrorist groups may be able to operate in areas where the State has little control. This was arguably the case with Pakistan, where Islamic terrorist groups opposing US and Afghan forces in Afghanistan were able to establish havens, which contributed to their ability to eventually drive the United States out and overthrow the Afghan government.[82] Under these conditions, as discussed above, States are likely permitted to engage violent non-State actors; however, it is not clear how much collateral harm should be tolerated. In fact, as mentioned earlier, Brown University's 'Costs of War Project' estimates approximately 387,000 civilians have been killed during the last two decades of US counter-terror and counter-insurgent operations. In comparison, terrorist groups killed more than 320,000 persons in the period between 2006 and 2020.[83]

While it is impossible to calculate how many persons counter-terror operations have saved, the parity of these numbers suggests that the connection between the use of military force and the disruption and degradation of terrorist operations is not very clear. However, the lethality these numbers reflect suggests a vicious circle where States feel pressure to punish terrorist actors and these actors feel pressure to respond in kind. When those counter-terror operations impose collateral harm on civilians belonging to a cooperating State, that incentivizes that State to withdraw its cooperation. That is clearly what happened in Iraq, where US strikes mentioned above sparked widespread, violent protests and resulted in Parliament's recommendation to force US combat troops to leave Iraq.[84]

This dynamic suggests equilibrium may be found where State actors conducting counter-terror operations do so in accordance with the *jus ad vim*

---

[82] Clayton Thomas, 'U.S. Military Withdrawal and Taliban Takeover in Afghanistan: Frequently Asked Questions', Congressional Research Service (17 September 2021) <https://crsreports.congr ess.gov/product/pdf/R/R46879> accessed 14 September 2022.

[83] Statista, 'Number of Fatalities Due to Terrorist Attacks Worldwide between 2006 and 2020' (5 August 2022) <https://www.statista.com/statistics/202871/number-of-fatalities-by-terrorist-atta cks-worldwide/> accessed 8 September 2022.

[84] Eric Levenson et al, 'Iraqi Parliament Votes for Plan to End US troop Presence in Iraq after Soleimani Killing' (CNN, 5 January 2020) <https://www.cnn.com/2020/01/05/world/soleimani-us-iran-attack/index.html> accessed 14 September 2022.

364 INSTRUMENTS, TACTICS, AND METHODS IN THE GREY ZONE

model described above, prioritizing law-enforcement standards over military ones, especially when pursuing enablers who, by virtue of their role, do not represent an immediate threat. Where collateral harm is unavoidable, State actors should only loosen peacetime human rights standards when there is a clear connection between the proposed strike and the disruption of terrorist operations or degradation of terrorist capabilities. An exception to the above might be when terrorist groups occupy and govern territory as Daesh did in 2014 in Iraq and Syria.[85] By occupying and governing territory, these groups become non-State actors in name only, and are able to mobilize internal resources to continue operations. In such cases, it is not clear one is in the grey zone anymore and that the warfighting model applies.

3.6 Cyber operations

Cyber operations allow actors to disrupt adversaries' networked systems while bypassing their military capabilities. Effective targets could be military or civilian and typically include critical infrastructure, communications systems, and other systems that are vulnerable to malware and whose destruction or degradation would cause significant disruption either to specific military operations or to civil society. Israel's cyberattack that disrupted Syria's air defence systems as it planes struck a possible nuclear facility is an example of the former.[86] Russia's previously mentioned massive denial of service attacks against Estonia in 2007, when it had the statue commemorating Russian soldiers in World War II, is an example of the latter.[87]

Of course, systems need not be networked to be vulnerable as the introduction of the Stuxnet virus into Iran's nuclear centrifuge demonstrated.[88] Because cyber means are typically low cost and generally unattributable, they would appear an ideal means of coercion, especially for weaker powers, including non-State actors, who want to impose costs without risking escalation. Unfortunately for those actors, in practice the efficacy of coercive cyber operations has so far been limited. One limitation is that cyber means can only be used once. There are two reasons this is the case. First, once a cyber means is employed, it can be

[85] William Theo Oosterveld and Willem Bloem, 'The Rise and Fall of ISIS: From Evitability and Inevitability' Hague Center for Strategic Studies (1 January 2017) <https://www.jstor.org/stable/resr ep12613?seq=4#metadata_info_tab_contents> accessed 14 September 2022.

[86] Sharon Weinberger, 'How Israel Spoofed Syria's Air Defense System' (*Wired*, 4 October 2007) <https://www.wired.com/2007/10/how-israel-spoo/> accessed 8 September 2022.

[87] Damien McGuiness, 'How a Cyberattack Transformed Estonia' (BBC News, 27 April 2017) <https://www.bbc.com/news/39655415> accessed 14 September 2022.

[88] Josh Fruhlinger, 'Stuxnet Explained: The First Known Cyberweapon' (*CSO*, 31 August 2022) <https://www.csoonline.com/article/3218104/stuxnet-explained-the-first-known-cyberweapon. html> accessed 8 September 2022.

THE LOGIC, GRAMMAR, AND NORMS OF THE GREY ZONE   365

detected and eliminated. So, one would have to develop an entirely new means to re-infect the same system. Second, cyber targets tend to be unique so one often has to develop unique malware for the different kinds of systems one wants to target.[89]

Thus, it should not be surprising that, by themselves at least, cyber means are not generally effective at coercing State behaviour. In fact, according to a study by Brandon Valeriano, Benjamin Jensen, and Ryan C. Maness, of 192 coercive cyber operations surveyed only 5.7 per cent were successful.[90] Even highly publicized ones often cited as reasons to fear cyber operations often failed to achieve desired results. The Russian cyber operation directed at Estonia, for example, did not get the statue reinstated. What it did do was force Estonians to improve their defences to the point the attacks were no longer effective. Additionally, Iranian cyber operations that shut down a power plant in Istanbul for three days in 2015 in retaliation for Ankara's support for Saudi Arabian operations against Houthi rebels in Yemen did not change Ankara's position.[91] The list goes on.

The point here is not that sufficiently massive cyber operations disrupting US infrastructure, for example, would not place coercive pressure on the United States. But such instances are not simply rare; they have not happened yet. There are two reasons, in addition to the ones cited above, that help account for the ineffectiveness of cyber operations. First, is the persistent nature of cyber operations entailing aggressing actors constantly losing access while defending actors are constantly afforded the opportunity to improve their defences. When actors activate malware, they make it easier for defenders not only to locate it and delete it but also to identify the vulnerabilities that allowed the infection in the first place.[92] Thus, if actors remain reasonably vigilant, their networked systems will become more resilient over time imposing higher costs and lower payoffs for aggressors.

Second, part of what makes cyber operations attractive—non-attribution— also limits their efficacy. As Thomas Rid famously observed in the introduction to *Cyber War Will Not Take Place,* an act of war must be instrumental, political, and at least potentially violent.[93] While cyber operations can certainly be violent and instrumental, they can only be political when they are attributed. As Rid points out, 'A violent act and its larger political intention must also be attributed

---

[89] Erica D. Borghard and Shawn W. Lonergran, 'The Logic of Coercion in Cyberspace' (2017) 26 Security Studies 470.
[90] Brandon Valeriano, Benjamin Jensen, and Ryan C. Maness, *Cyber Strategy: The Evolving Character of Power and Coercion* (OUP 2018) 17.
[91] Micah Halpern, 'Iran Flexes Its Power by Transporting Turkey to the Stone Age', *Observer* (London, 22 April 2015) <http://observer.com/2015/04/iran-flexes-its-power-by-transporting-turkey-to-the-stone-ages/> accessed 8 September 2022.
[92] Dorothy E. Denning and Bradley J. Strawser, 'Active Cyber Defense: Applying Air Defense to the Cyber Domain', in *Understanding Cyber Conflict: 14 Analogies,* edited by George Perkovich and Areil E. Levite (Georgetown University Press 2017) 193, 196.
[93] Thomas Rid, *Cyber War Will Not Take Place* (OUP 2013) xv.

to one side at some point during the confrontation.[94] Adversaries cannot be expected to change their behaviour if they do not know who is attacking them and why. Moreover, there is also often 'no agreed upon language' that enables actors to make sense of the operations' intent.[95] For example, there was a series of tit-for-tat cyber operations conducted by Iran and Israel against each in 2020 that appeared to be more a learning exercise regarding capabilities and redlines than directed at any particular behaviour.[96]

That point does not mean that unattributed cyber operations do not have utility. However, they are generally only effective in combination with non-cyber efforts as well.[97] For example, the Stuxnet virus that is often credited with convincing the Iranians to negotiate the Joint Comprehensive Plan of Action (JCPOA) would not have worked had it not been for diplomatic initiatives and economic inducements along with the threat of military action should the Iranians proceed with developing nuclear weapons.[98]

3.7 Normative implications

First, it is important to note that all cyber operations are not normatively equal. The unattributable nature of cyber operations makes them ideal for activities like espionage. However, cyber-enabled espionage is no more morally concerning than non-cyber-enabled espionage. This point does not mean there should not be norms regarding who States can collect on and for what, but those seem to apply independent of the grey zone. However, given that international actors benefit by not holding others to these norms, it is unlikely that one will see any shared restrictions on cyber espionage evolving into customary international law any time soon.

Where cyber operations do raise normative concerns is when they cause some level of physical destruction. As mentioned above, the *Tallinn Manual*, which was created in the aftermath of the cyberattacks on Estonia, argues that cyber operations that result in some kind of physical destruction may count as 'armed force', which, by implication, could permit a proportionate kinetic response.[99] However, most cyberattacks, even ones utilized to coerce, would be covered by that point. As Clair Sullivan observes, for example, restrictions on cyber as

---

[94] Ibid. 2.

[95] Borghard and Lonergran (n 89) 455–57.

[96] J. D. Work and Richard Harknett, 'Troubled Vision: Understanding recent Israeli–Iranian Offensive Cyber Exchanges' (Atlantic Council, 22 July 2020) <https://www.atlanticcouncil.org/in-depth-research-reports/issue-brief/troubled-vision-understanding-israeli-iranian-offensive-cyber-exchanges/> accessed 14 September 2022.

[97] Borghard and Lonegran (n 89) 474; Valeriano (n 90) 39.

[98] Valeriano (n 90) 106.

[99] Schmitt (n 70) 339.

THE LOGIC, GRAMMAR, AND NORMS OF THE GREY ZONE 367

armed force would not apply to the reported North Korean hack of Sony to coerce them into not releasing the movie *The Interview*.[100]

This last point raises concerns regarding how much disruption would be permissible. The ransomware that shut down the Colonial Pipeline in June 2021, for example, caused fuel shortages all across the east coast of the United States until the company paid the ransom.[101] While it was a criminal act intended to extort funds rather than to coerce State behaviour, it is not hard to imagine attacks by a State actor against a number of distributors that creates shortages severe enough to significantly affect the economy, including causing inflation and job loss.

This point implies another rational constraint on disruptive cyber operations. To the extent the disruption that actors suffer exceeds the benefit they gain by being connected to the internet and World Wide Web, actors are more likely to sever or limit that connection to reduce their vulnerability. If nothing else, actors will be incentivized to improve their defences or reduce their exposure, thus limiting the disruption adversaries can cause. Thus, too much disruption is not only self-defeating over the long-term but it could also limit access States seek to conduct less disruptive intelligence operations.

Likely with these considerations in mind, State actors, even adversarial ones, have begun cooperating regarding cyber norms. In October 2021, for example, the United States and Russia jointly submitted a resolution to the UN General Assembly that endorsed the findings of the UN's Open-Ended Working Group and Group of Governmental Experts in the Field of Information and Telecommunications in the Context of International Security.[102] Among other things, the resolution endorsed an 'open, secure, stable, accessible, and peaceful information and technology environment', while acknowledging that specific norms would need to develop over time.[103]

It is an open question whether this endorsement can serve as a framing agreement that sets conditions for cooperation the same way Nixon and Brezhnev's arms control framing agreement did; however, the chances of that increase if both sides prioritize it. It does seem an equilibrium exists where continued defection decreases the utility of internet for both civilian and security purposes, making it rational to observe some kind of restraint.

---

[100] Claire Sullivan, 'The Sony Hack and the Role of International Law' (2017) 8 Journal of National Security Law and Policy 437, 449–50.

[101] William Turton and Kartikay Mehrota, 'Hackers Breached Colonial Pipeline Using Compromised Password' (*Bloomberg*, 4 June 2021) <https://www.bloomberg.com/news/articles/2021-06-04/hackers-breached-colonial-pipeline-using-compromised-password> accessed 8 September 2022.

[102] UN General Assembly Resolution 76/19, 'Developments in the Field of Information and Telecommunications in the Context of International Security, and Advancing Responsible State Behavior in the Use of Information and Communications Technologies' (8 December 2021).

[103] UN General Assembly Resolution 75/240, 'Developments in the Field of Information and Telecommunications in the Context of International Security' (31 December 2020).

368 INSTRUMENTS, TACTICS, AND METHODS IN THE GREY ZONE

3.8 Information operations

Information operations can play a significant role in shaping actors' choices not only by misleading them but also by eroding the political will necessary to act. Russian information operations aimed at dividing NATO and sowing distrust among populations in Europe are cases in point.[104] Of course, information operations are not new. Tom Rid, in *Active Measures: The Secret History of Disinformation and Political Warfare*, estimates that during the Cold War there were more than ten thousand disinformation operations on both sides.[105] What makes information operations in the grey zone different is how technologies permit much more sophisticated, precise, and *convincing* efforts that are capable of deceiving decision makers and undermining the internal cohesion of States and alliances.

Technology has not just sped up information operations; it has enabled broader, more effective targeting of whole societies. Trolls use social media to undermine public confidence in governing institutions, spear phishing frequently leaks critical information often embroiling political parties, businesses, and mid-level officials in distracting scandals, and sophisticated fake photographs and news stories can create tremendous confusion in times of crisis. Information operations now is a whole-of-society endeavour, in which civilians may be knowingly or unknowingly functioning as proxies on behalf of a government.[106]

One of the more confounding aspects of current information operations is their *precision*. Global connectivity and data collection allow actors to connect not just with groups but often with individuals. In the pre-internet world, advertisers used demographics to broadcast information to the masses hoping to hit the desired target audience. Now adversaries can target individuals based on those individual's digital behaviour and patterns. Moreover, they can use that information to shape narratives in their favour. For example, Russians were reportedly able to target specific actors in the Democratic National Committee during the 2016 election, stealing emails and other information, which they then released to portray Hillary Clinton's campaign as corrupt and ineffective.[107]

---

[104] G. H. Karlsen, 'Divide and Rule: Ten Lessons about Russian Political Influence Activities in Europe' (2019) 5 Palgrave Communications 1.

[105] Thomas Rid, *Active Measures: The Secret History of Disinformation and Political Warfare* (Farrar, Straus, and Giroux 2020) 5.

[106] Catherine A. Theohary, 'Information Warfare: Issues for Congress', Congressional Research Service (5 March 2018) 1 <https://sgp.fas.org/crs/natsec/R45142.pdf> accessed 14 September 2022.

[107] Ellen Nakashima and Shane Harris, 'How the Russians hacked the DNC and passed its emails to Wikileaks', *The Washington Post* (Washington, DC, 13 July 2018) <https://www.washingtonpost.com/world/national-security/how-the-russians-hacked-the-dnc-and-passed-its-emails-to-wikileaks/2018/07/13/af19a828-86c3-11e8-8553-a3ce89036c78_story.html> accessed 25 August 2021.

Information operations can target both decision makers and the populations they represent simultaneously. In targeting both, information operations can deny decision makers critical information they need to make informed decisions while at the same time undermining the political will they need to act. Perhaps more importantly, information operations are making it challenging to understand opponents' real motives due to their ability to conceal their role and intentions in these activities. As a result, they not only set conditions for indecision but also inject uncertainty regarding adversary goals and the costs they are willing to bear to achieve them.

As described above, information operations' primary utility seems to be in disrupting actors' ability to respond to an adversary's provocation. Russian information operations during their recent invasion of Ukraine have been characterized by acts defacing government websites to make it appear vulnerable, undermining popular morale by faking news the government had surrendered, and sowing distrust between Ukraine and NATO members.[108] These kinds of operations will not compel Ukraine to surrender; however, they could undermine the population's will to fight and NATO's ability to provide support. Thus, like cyber operations, information operations generally find their greatest utility when coupled with other kinds of efforts directed at the same or similar objectives.

3.9 Normative challenge

Like cyber operations, information operations raise questions regarding who would be a legitimate target and what counts as legitimate means. Given the point of coercion is to affect the decisions of international actors, those who make decisions on behalf of those actors would generally be legitimate targets. These could include civilian government leaders, members of the legislature, and certainly the military.

It is less clear if members of the general population would also count, even though popular opinion can influence what governments can do. However, the precedent the Just War Tradition establishes is that a mere connection to military capability does not entail one is a legitimate target. There is a difference between what soldiers need to fight and what they need to live.[109] Thus, farmers, even farmers who grow food for the military, would not be legitimate targets

---

[108] Alden Wahlstrom et al, 'The IO Offensive: Information Operations Surrounding the Russian Invasion of Ukraine' (*Mandiant,* 19 May 2022) <https://www.mandiant.com/resources/blog/information-operations-surrounding-ukraine> accessed 7 September 2022.

[109] Walzer (n 2) 146.

because food is a basic necessity required independent of warfighting. While the modes of information operations, like the internet and social media, are not basic necessities (yet), their use is ubiquitous enough to daily civil life to make their exploitation indiscriminate, if not impermissible.

To the extent such operations are indiscriminate it stands that there should be a prima facie prohibition against them. However, the logic of coercion would suggest that to the extent such operations can prevent an adversary from escalating, they should be permitted. For example, if Ukraine can convince Russian soldiers not to fight or the Russia population to protest the war, then it seems self-defeating, if not irresponsible, to prohibit such operations. Another possible justification for indiscriminate information operations would be a reprisal. Unlike the use of force, information operations generally produce little physical harm, so, like certain cyber operations, they may be preferable as a response to an adversary's illegal act, especially if the alternative is violence.

The next thing to consider is the extent to which deception would be permitted. Actors can deceive in a number of ways including falsifying one's identity, creating fake sources and evidence, and simply lying. These techniques are ubiquitous in the information sphere.[110] However, one feature of deceptive operations is that once they are discovered, they cease to be effective. Over time, the exposure of multiple deceptions would, rationally if not actually, encourage governments and publics to be more discerning and resilient. For example, Russian disinformation targeting the 2020 US elections appeared much less successful than those they conducted in 2016 because social media sites learned to identify and eliminate false actors and individuals learned to be more sceptical regarding the content on these platforms.[111] Moreover, their continued use has diminished Russian credibility overall, though their use of high-volume multivolume venues and rapid, continuous, and repetitive messaging Russia is able to achieve some effects despite lacking credibility.[112]

Given these considerations, an equilibrium would likely place few restrictions on targeting decision makers; however, it would also limit indiscriminate attacks to those operations intended to avoid escalation, encourage de-escalation, or act as a reprisal. It would also likely place few limits on deception when targeting decision makers; however, their decreasing utility suggests that they should be avoided and that governments should engage in education programs designed to inoculate their populations against such operations.

---

[110] Christopher Paul and Miriam Matthews, 'The Russian 'Firehose of Falsehood' Propaganda Model: Why it Might Work and Options to Counter It' (RAND 2016) <https://www.rand.org/pubs/perspectives/PE198.html> accessed 7 September 2022.

[111] Josh A. Goldstein and Shelby Grossman, 'How Disinformation Evolved in 2020' (Brookings, 4 January 2021) <https://www.brookings.edu/techstream/how-disinformation-evolved-in-2020/> accessed 7 September 2022.

[112] Paul and Matthews (n 110).

4. Conclusion

It should be clear from this analysis that grey zone norms differ from those of warfighting in important ways. First, unlike Just War Theory, which condemns at least one side as the aggressor, grey zone norms accept that all actors have a right—for lack of a better word—to compete. Certainly, actors in competition can choose causes which are morally questionable. This analysis, for example, would call into question objectives that are inherently escalatory, such as forced integration of Taiwan by the Chinese government. It would not, however, have much to say about a desire to integrate Taiwan peacefully. Of course, there may be moral reasons—such as the authoritarian and rights-violating nature of the Chinese government—to object to integration under any conditions. However, settling that question falls outside the grey zone.

Another key difference is the role loss plays in shaping permissions. In war, the imminent possibility of catastrophic defeat could justify a 'supreme emergency' where one is allowed to set aside restrictions like discrimination and proportionality if by doing so one can avoid that defeat.[113] By its very nature, losses in the grey zone are generally not catastrophic in the way defeat in war is. In fact, as discussed above, they can be a part of a deliberate strategy to better calibrate future demands. So, while a Nazi victory in Europe may have justified some indiscriminate bombing by the British, as Walzer argues,[114] Iranian success at driving US forces out of Iraq, for example, would not likely justify an indiscriminate cyber operation that significantly disrupted civil life in Iran. Part of the reason is that in the grey zone competition does not really end and there is always another round.

Another difference lies in their purpose. The purpose of Just War Theory, and by extension the law of armed conflict and international humanitarian law it informs, is to prevent war and failing that, limit the destruction caused by war. Competition, however, is unavoidable in a way war is not. So, it makes little sense to devise an ethic of it that prevents it. So more than simply limiting the destructive aspects of international competition, a better normative regime would promote its constructive aspects as well. Cold War scholar Herman Kahn described this kind of competition 'agonistic', from the Greek word for 'struggle', which entails even committed adversaries observing norms that allow them to manage, and even benefit from, competition while minimizing the potential for costly escalation.[115]

Employing the same term, Belgian political theorist Chantal Mouffe describes 'agonistic relationships' as ones where opponents view each other 'not as an enemy to be destroyed, but as an adversary whose existence is legitimate and

---

[113] Walzer (n 2) 268.
[114] Ibid.
[115] Herman Kahn, *On Escalation: Metaphors and Scenarios* (Praeger 1965) 18.

must be tolerated'.[116] That toleration does not entail capitulation. It just entails accepting certain 'rules of the game' that not only constrain destructive acts but channel competitive behaviour in positive directions.[117] The space race is a good example. Not only did the technology developed provide global benefit, so far, at least, negative impacts have been limited and space remains largely unmilitarized. There are more current precedents. For example, despite alarmist claims that Russia is militarizing the Arctic to support a rush for resources, it has generally been cooperative with its Arctic neighbours and a constructive member on the Arctic Council.[118] Moreover, it has so far willingly settled its territorial disputes in accordance with international law, like the UN Convention on the Law of the Sea as it did with Norway in 2010.[119]

Whether agonism will displace antagonism as normative of international competition remains to be seen. For every example of constructive competition there are often several more examples of destructive ones. Russia's cooperation in the Arctic certainly did not serve as a basis for cooperation in Ukraine, where it chose instead to escalate to war. However, by regarding grey zone norms as equilibria where actors *should* cooperate, even if it means giving up some short-term advantage, actors can identify not only ways to avoid an escalatory crisis but also ways out of one even while taking the advantage the grey zone confers for pursuing one's interests.

In some ways, this conception of grey zone norms bears some resemblance to John Rawls's 'reflective equilibrium', where actors abstract themselves from their personal circumstances to determine how to fairly distribute social goods. For example, one might rationally agree to some income redistribution if one did not know if one were going to be rich or poor.[120] In the view described here, however, actors are not required to disregard the interests they actually have. Rather, they are simply encouraged to put themselves 'in the shoes' of their competitors when evaluating how they pursue those interests. Doing so will not necessarily achieve peaceful relations, but it should give actors reason to prioritize limited objectives, non-violent means, and de-escalatory measures when crises arise.

---

[116] Chantal Mouffe, *The Return of the Political* (Verso 2020) 4–5.

[117] Ibid. 4. See also Chantal Mouffe, 'An Agonistic Approach to the Future of Europe' (2012) 43 New Literary History 633.

[118] Thomas Grove, 'Russia Moves to Outmuscle U.S. in Arctic' *Wall Street Journal* (New York, 25 May 2021) <https://www.wsj.com/articles/russian-military-seeks-to-outmuscle-u-s-in-arctic-1162 1935002> accessed 1 June 2021.

[119] Luke Harding, 'Russia and Norway Resolve Arctic Dispute', *The Guardian* (London, 15 September 2010) <https://www.theguardian.com/world/2010/sep/15/russia-norway-arctic-border-dispute> accessed 1 June 2021.

[120] John Rawls, *A Theory of Justice* (Belknap Press 1971) 18–22, 46–53.

17
Lying in the Grey Zone

Steven Wheatley

1. Introduction

This chapter examines the role and legal status of State lying in grey zone conflicts. The focus is on the problem of States lying to other States in their inter-State communications (the work does not consider the status of official policies of deception, concealment, disinformation, or propaganda campaigns).

The work begins by examining the utility of State lying in grey zone conflicts, looking at the example of Russia's 2014 annexation of Crimea, where it appears that Russia 'lied' about its relationship with the 'little green men'. There is presently no international law prohibition on State lying (no *lex lata*). There is, however, a body of existing laws on insincere State utterances which hold the State to its word, even when the State does not mean what it says. The contention here is that we should extend this law on insincere State utterances to include lying by States (the *lex ferenda*). Because the existing laws are explained by the principle of good faith, the proposed prohibition on State lying would only apply when States were coordinating plans of action, creating problems for its application in grey zone conflicts. The chapter looks to resolve some of these difficulties, before concluding with a summary of the argument.

2. Lying in the grey zone

The notion of 'grey zone' competition between States has gained currency in writings and policy debates.[1] For scholars on defence and war studies, grey zone conflicts are those that sit between war and peace.[2] Whilst there is no agreed definition, three elements are common in descriptions of grey zone actions: (1) grey zone actions pursue strategic political objectives; (2) grey zone actions fall short of the threshold that might trigger a military response; and (3) grey zone

---

[1] See e.g. Melissa Dalton et al, *By other Means: Adapting to Compete in the Gray Zone (Part II)* (Center for Strategic and International Studies 2019).
[2] Donald Stoker and Craig Whiteside, 'Blurred Lines: Gray-Zone Conflict and Hybrid War—Two Failures of American Strategic Thinking' (2020) 73 Naval War College Review 1, 7.

Steven Wheatley, *Lying in the Grey Zone* In: *Hybrid Threats and Grey Zone Conflict*. Edited by: Mitt Regan and Aurel Sari, Oxford University Press. © Oxford University Press 2024. DOI: 10.1093/oso/9780197744772.003.0017

374 INSTRUMENTS, TACTICS, AND METHODS IN THE GREY ZONE

actions are not easily characterized as violations of international law.[3] Grey zone actions include, then, those which exploit uncertainty as to whether impugned State behaviour is wrongful as a matter of international law, or not.[4] Aurel Sari explains the point this way:

> [T]he grey zone concept focuses on the competitive space within which [States] conduct their activities. By definition, this space is marked by ambiguity about the nature of the conflict and the legal status of the parties, which in turn generates uncertainty about the applicable law.[5]

Russia's efforts to annex Ukrainian territory in 2014 and 2022 provide one example of the utility of the grey zone tactic of State lying to avoid the categorization of actions as clearly 'unlawful'.

In 2014, Russia appears to have pursued its strategic objective of annexing Ukrainian territory through grey zone actions.[6] The bare facts can be summarized as follows: groups of armed men whose uniforms lacked any clear identifying marks (hence they were dubbed 'little green men') surrounded the airports and occupied the Crimean parliament and raised a Russian flag; the Crimean parliament voted to join the Russian Federation; this decision was confirmed in a controversial referendum; President Putin then signed a law formally integrating Crimea into Russia.[7] The United Kingdom government characterized Russian actions in the following way:

> Russia deployed military troops to the Crimean peninsula, which the Kremlin had decided to take by force. Russia then tried to give its actions a veneer of legitimacy with a sham referendum. . . . In Crimea, Russia violated the first principle of international law—that countries may not acquire territory or change borders by force.[8]

---

[3] See Michael J. Mazarr, *Mastering the Gray Zone: Understanding a Changing Era of Conflict* (US Army War College Press 2015) 58; Michael C. McCarthy et al, *Deterring Russia in the Gray Zone* (US Army War College Press 2019) 5; and Lyle J. Morris et al, *Gaining Competitive Advantage in the Gray Zone* (RAND 2019) 8–9.

[4] Rosa Brooks, 'Rule of Law in the Gray Zone' (Modern War Institute, July 2, 2018) <https://mwi.usma.edu/rule-law-gray-zone/>, accessed 9 March 2023.

[5] Aurel Sari, 'Legal Resilience in an Era of Grey Zone Conflicts and Hybrid Threats' (2020) 33 Cambridge Review of International Affairs 846, 855.

[6] Geraint Hughes, 'War in the Grey Zone: Historical Reflections and Contemporary Implications' (2020) 62 Survival 131, 132.

[7] See generally 'The Crisis in Crimea and Eastern Ukraine', *Encyclopaedia Britannica* <https://www.britannica.com/place/Ukraine/The-crisis-in-Crimea-and-eastern-Ukraine>, accessed 7 March 2023.

[8] Neil Bush, 'Seventh Anniversary of Russia's illegal Annexation of Crimea: UK Statement' (4 March 2021) <https://www.gov.uk/government/speeches/seven-years-of-illegal-occupation-of-crimea-by-the-russian-federation-uk-statement>, accessed 7 March 2023.

The main argument supporting this illegality thesis was that the deployment of Russian special forces (*Spetsnaz*) during the annexation was a violation of the international law prohibition on the use of force.[9] Russia denied that its military forces were involved,[10] claiming that the heavily armed men who occupied the airports and parliament were local self-defence units.[11] The law here is straightforward:[12] If the 'little green men' were Russian special forces, Russia was responsible for a serious violation of international law;[13] If they were local self-defence units, the relevant legal issue was Crimea's right to self-determination.[14] To avoid legal condemnation, it appears Russia 'lied' about its relationship with the little green men. When asked whether Russian special forces had been operating on Ukrainian territory, Russian President Vladimir Putin later explained, 'The Russian Army was always there'.[15]

By lying about its operations in Ukraine in 2014, Russia appears to have created enough uncertainty about the facts and its legal responsibility for 'the little green men' to realize its strategic objective of annexing the Ukrainian territory of Crimea—with limited international condemnation, certainly as judged by the response of the General Assembly. GA Res. 68/262 simply affirms, in rather oblique terms, the 'territorial integrity of Ukraine', calls on 'all States' to refrain from attempts to modify Ukraine's borders through the use of force, and urges 'all parties to pursue immediately the peaceful resolution of the situation'. The resolution does not mention Russia by name.[16]

---

[9] Lauri Mälksoo. 'The Annexation of Crimea and Balance of Power in International Law' (2019) 30 European Journal of International Law 303, 305.

[10] For Russia's justification of the annexation (including a denial of 'Russian intervention in Crimea, some sort of aggression'), see President of Russia, 'Address by President of the Russian Federation' (18 March 2014) <http://en.kremlin.ru/events/president/news/20603>, accessed 8 March 2023.

[11] See Vitaly Shevchenko, ' "Little green men" or "Russian invaders"?' (BBC News, 11 March 2014) <https://www.bbc.co.uk/news/world-europe-26532154> accessed 8 March 2023.

[12] See generally Shane R. Reeves and David Wallace, 'The Combatant Status of the "Little Green Men" and Other Participants in the Ukraine Conflict' (2015) 91 International Law Studies 361.

[13] States are responsible for the actions of their own military forces. See International Law Commission, 'Draft Articles on Responsibility of States for Internationally Wrongful Acts, with Commentaries' (2001) II(2) Yearbook of the International Law Commission 31, Art. 4. States are also responsible for the actions of non-State actors acting under their immediate direction and control (ibid. Art. 8).

[14] See, on this point, Roy Allison, 'Russian "Deniable" Intervention in Ukraine: How and Why Russia Broke the Rules' (2014) 90 International Affairs 1255, 1259–60; also Thomas D. Grant, 'Annexation of Crimea' (2015) 109 American Journal of International Law 68.

[15] See Carl Schreck, 'From "Not Us" to "Why Hide It?": How Russia Denied Its Crimea Invasion, Then Admitted It' (Radio Free Europe, 26 February 2019) <https://www.rferl.org/a/from-not-us-to-why-hide-it-how-russia-denied-its-crimea-invasion-then-admitted-it/29791806.html>, accessed 9 March 2023.

[16] UN General Assembly Resolution 68/262, 'Territorial Integrity of Ukraine' (1 April 2012) paras. 1–3.

376 INSTRUMENTS, TACTICS, AND METHODS IN THE GREY ZONE

The muted reaction in 2014 can be contrasted with the General Assembly's response in 2022, when Russia pursued its objective of annexing Ukrainian territory through inter-State war and dubious referendums.[17] GA Res. ES-11/4 expressly condemns Russia, declaring:

> [T]he unlawful actions of the Russian Federation with regard to the illegal so-called referendums [in the] Donetsk, Kherson, Luhansk and Zaporizhzhia regions of Ukraine[,] have no validity under international law and do not form the basis for any alteration of the status of these regions of Ukraine.[18]

These differing responses by the UN General Assembly in 2014 and 2022 highlight the potential benefits of the grey zone tactic of State lying to avoid condemnation of State actions as unambiguously 'unlawful'.

3. On lying

According to *The Stanford Encyclopedia of Philosophy*, the most widely accepted definition of a lie is by the philosopher, Arnold Isenberg: 'A lie is a statement made by one who does not believe it with the intention that someone else shall be led to believe it'.[19]

The same understanding can be seen in an influential definition provided by the international lawyer, Hugo Grotius.[20] In his analysis of 'What Is Lawful in War', where he considers whether lying to the enemy is permitted as an exception to the general prohibition on lying,[21] Grotius defines lying as

> the propagation of a truth, which any one believes to be false, in him amounts to a lie. There must be in the use of the words therefore an intention to deceive, in order to constitute a falsehood in the proper and common acceptation.[22]

Both these definitions share the same three elements: (1) there must be a statement of claimed fact; (2) the speaker does not believe that the claimed fact is

---

[17] Pjotr Sauer and Luke Harding, 'Putin Annexes Four Regions of Ukraine in Major Escalation of Russia's War', *The Guardian* (London, 20 September 2022).

[18] UN General Assembly Resolution ES-11/4, Territorial Integrity of Ukraine: Defending the Principles of the Charter of the United Nations' (13 October 2022) para. 3.

[19] Arnold Isenberg, 'Deontology and the Ethics of Lying' (1964) 24 Philosophy and Phenomenological Research 463, 466, referred to by James Edwin Mahon, 'The Definition of Lying and Deception', in *The Stanford Encyclopedia of Philosophy*, edited by Edward N. Zalta (2016) para. 1.

[20] See generally ibid. esp para. 2.3.

[21] Hugo Grotius, *The Rights of War and Peace, including the Law of Nature and of Nations* [1625] (A. C. Campbell tr, Walter Dunne 1901), Book III, Ch I, § XVII.

[22] Ibid. Book III, Ch I, § X.

true; (3) the speaker intends that the addressee does believe that the claimed fact is true.

First, there must be a written or spoken statement of claimed fact.[23] Lies take the form of assertives (i.e. statements of claimed facts about the world) which can be categorized as being true or false.[24] Thus, the act of lying must be distinguished from the act of dissembling, where the truth is hidden in a misleading statement, which is not literally untrue.[25] Hugo Grotius quotes, with approval, the Roman scholar Cicero's view that the skill of dissimulation 'is absolutely necessary for statesmen to possess'.[26] A good example of the difference can be seen in the response given by US President Jimmy Carter's chief of staff, in 1980, at the time of the Tehran Hostage Rescue Mission. When asked by the Iranian Foreign Minister whether Carter would 'do anything rash, like attack Iran', Hamilton Jordan replied 'Don't worry. He won't. President Carter is not a militaristic man'.[27] The first part of the response was a lie, a denial of military action, while military action was underway. The second is an example of dissembling, because, whilst it implies that Carter is not planning military action, Jordan does not say this is the case.

Second, the speaker does not believe that the statement of claimed fact is true. Lying is not the same as asserting something which is not in fact true. A person lies when they assert the truth of some proposition which they themselves do not believe to be true.[28]

Third, for an utterance to be categorized as a lie, the speaker must intend that the addressee believe that the claimed fact is true. There must be an intention to deceive—but the addressee does not have to be deceived. Consider the following example. The president of State A says, 'We have successfully developed our own nuclear weapons capacity', with the aim of deterring an attack by State B. Now suppose that the president was lying. Here, the intention is not only to deter State B but also to deceive State B. But State A only deceives State B if State B believes State A has developed nuclear weapons. But whether State B believes the statement, or not, the president is still lying. One either lies, or one does not. Lying, as the legal philosopher, Neil MacCormick observes, 'is not . . . a success-word'.[29]

---

[23] See, on this point, Mahon (n 19) para. 1.1 ('[L]ying requires that a person make a statement').

[24] Allan Beever, *Law's Reality: A Philosophy of Law* (Edward Elgar 2021) 52.

[25] Grotius (n 21) Book II, Ch I, § XI (A lie 'cannot be understood, but in a sense different from the real meaning of the speaker.').

[26] Ibid. Book II, Ch I, § VII.

[27] Tung Yin, 'National Security Lies' (2018) 55 Houston Law Review 729, 736–37.

[28] J. L. Austin, *How to Do Things with Words* (Clarendon Press 1962) 41 ('insincerity . . . is an essential element in lying as distinct from merely saying what is in fact false').

[29] Neil MacCormick, 'What Is Wrong with Deceit?' (1983) 10 Sydney Law Review 5, 9.

4. The law on state lying (*lex lata* and *lex ferenda*)

In the absence of agreement on an international treaty on State lying, the most likely source of a regulative rule would be customary international law.[30] There are, though, only a few examples of state practice from which we might identify a regulative rule on State lying, with the major work on lying in international relations concluding that, whilst 'lying is sometimes a useful instrument of state-craft[,] it is not commonplace'.[31] One instance is the 1960 U-2 incident, when the United States claimed that a downed spy plane was on a weather research mission. Soviet leader, Nikita Khrushchev later announced the capture of the pilot, Gary Powers, explaining that the USSR had kept this secret, 'because if we had given out the whole story, the Americans would have thought up still another fable'.[32] Soviet Foreign Minister Andrei Gromyko then opened a debate in the UN Security Council by saying that, after its first 'lying version', the United States had admitted its responsibility for violating Soviet air space.[33] Reflecting on the legal implications of the U-2 incident, Quincy Wright concluded that 'In time of peace, there is a presumption that governments will not attempt to mislead other governments on questions of fact by express statement'.[34]

The problem for any claim that there is a prohibition on State lying under customary international law is the limited evidence of state practice and absence of evidence (which I could find) that States consider that State lying is, or should be, prohibited as a matter of international law (the *opinio juris* element). Indeed, there are instances similar to the U2 incident, when States did not complain about seemingly insincere State utterances. Take the 2023 example of the United States shooting down a Chinese balloon over US airspace. China claimed it was 'a civilian airship used for research, mainly meteorological, purposes'.[35] The US rejected this, reporting the balloon's equipment 'was clearly for intelligence surveillance'.[36] The US Senate Majority Leader said, 'I think the Chinese were caught

---

[30] The Statute of the International Court of Justice lists in Article 38(1)(b), as one of the sources of international law, 'international custom, as evidence of a general practice accepted as law'.

[31] John J. Mearsheimer, *Why Leaders Lie: The Truth about Lying in International Politics* (OUP 2011) 13.

[32] Yin (n 27) 761.

[33] Quincy Wright, 'Legal Aspects of the U-2 Incident' (1960) 54 American Journal of International Law 836, 840.

[34] Ibid. 852.

[35] People's Republic of China Ministry of Foreign Affairs, 'Foreign Ministry Spokesperson's Remarks on the Unintended Entry of a Chinese Unmanned Airship into US Airspace Due to Force Majeure' (3 February 2023) <https://www.fmprc.gov.cn/mfa_eng/xwfw_665399/s2510_665401/2535_665405/202302/t20230203_11019484.html> accessed 7 March 2023.

[36] Julian Borger, 'Chinese Balloon Was "Clearly" for Spying, Says US', *The Guardian* (London, 9 February 2023) <https://www.theguardian.com/us-news/2023/feb/09/chinese-balloon-spying-state-department> accessed 7 March 2023.

lying',[37] but the US government complained only that the presence of a People's Republic of China (PRC) surveillance balloon in US airspace was a violation of US sovereignty and international law.[38]

As well as accounts of the positive law in force (the *lex lata*), international lawyers can make arguments about what the law should be (the *lex ferenda*).[39] *Lex ferenda* arguments take one of two forms: either the proposed rule is said to be more just or equitable than the existing law or the proposed rule would tidy up the existing law, by filling lacunae or eliminating anomalies.[40]

Lex ferenda arguments often make the case that the proposed rule would be more in line with the demands of morality than the old law. In moral theory, lying is often seen as presumptively wrong.[41] The two most common explanations for this are that lying undermines the right of the other person to make their own decisions, based on a proper understanding of the facts,[42] and that lying involves a breach of trust, because the speaker invites the other person to believe in the truth of the expressed proposition.[43] But there are conflicting moral arguments, inspired by utilitarian considerations, which require us to ask whether, on balance, a particular lie does more harm than good.[44] Following Niccolò Machiavelli, who noted that 'experience shows that in our times the rulers who have done great things are those who have set little store by keeping their word',[45] these utilitarian considerations are often applied to lies uttered by political leaders.[46] John Mearsheimer's *Why Leaders Lie* examines the subject of State lying from this 'Machiavellian' perspective, concluding that, whilst lying is sometimes useful, it is not commonplace, not least because of the natural scepticism that States have about the claims of other States, with Mearsheimer making the point that 'Lying is only effective when the potential victim thinks that the liar is probably telling the truth'.[47]

---

[37] Ed Pilkington, 'Schumer Says Chinese "Humiliated" after Three Flying Objects Shot Down' *The Guardian* (London, 12 February 2023) <https://www.theguardian.com/us-news/2023/feb/12/schumer-chinese-humiliated-flying-objects-shot-down> accessed 7 March 2023.

[38] US Department of State, 'Secretary Blinken's Call with People's Republic of China (PRC) CCP Central Foreign Affairs Office Director Wang Yi' (3 February 2023) <https://www.state.gov/secretary-blinkens-call-with-peoples-republic-of-china-prc-ccp-central-foreign-affairs-office-director-wang-yi/> accessed 7 March 2023.

[39] Aaron X. Fellmeth and Maurice Horwitz, *Guide to Latin in International Law* (OUP 2009).

[40] Hugh Thirlway, 'Reflections on Lex Ferenda' (2001) 32 Netherlands Yearbook of International Law 3, 10.

[41] J. A. Barnes, *A Pack of Lies: Towards a Sociology of Lying* (CUP 1994) 136.

[42] Grotius (n 21) Book III, Ch I, § XI.

[43] Charles Fried, *Right and Wrong* (Harvard University Press 1978) 67.

[44] Alasdair Macintyre, 'Truthfulness, Lies, and Moral Philosophers: What Can We Learn from Mill and Kant?' 16 Tanner Lectures on Human Values (Princeton University Press 1994) 306, 325.

[45] Niccolò Machiavelli, *The Prince* [1513] (Quentin Skinner and Russell Price eds, Cambridge University Press 1988) ch. 18, 61.

[46] Michael Walzer, 'The Problem of Dirty Hands' (1973) 2 Philosophy and Public Affairs 160, 180.

[47] Mearsheimer (n 31) 29–30.

380   INSTRUMENTS, TACTICS, AND METHODS IN THE GREY ZONE

Lex ferenda arguments can also look to tidy up the existing law, by filling gaps or eliminating anomalies. The argument in this chapter sits within this category of *lex ferenda* writings, looking to tidy up the existing laws on insincere State utterances by recognizing that State lying should be seen as legally wrongful when States are coordinating their plans of actions in good faith. The argument is necessarily normative, because the International Court of Justice has made clear that, whilst the principle of good faith can explain the need for a primary, regulative rule, it cannot create that rule.[48]

The inspiration for the argument developed in this chapter lies in the disagreement between the philosophers of language Ludwig Wittgenstein and John Searle on the status of lying. Wittgenstein argued that 'Lying is a language-game that needs to be learned like any other one'.[49] In other words, we must learn how to lie (i.e. to appear to have a good reason for saying something that we don't believe). Searle disagreed, saying: 'I think Wittgenstein was wrong[,] because lying consists in violating one of the regulative rules [of language use], and any regulative rule at all contains within it the notion of a violation'.[50]

Searle's point is that speaking a language is a rule-governed practise that depends on speakers complying with certain rules of language use. One of these rules is that the speaker should mean what they say—a point that applies whether they are making a promise[51] or asserting some fact about the world.[52] Lying violates the rules of language use because the speaker is not sincere when they assert some proposition about the world.[53] This point is significant, because, whilst there is no international law on State lying, there are established laws on insincere State utterances.

5. The existing law of insincere State utterances

The law on insincere State utterances is a collection of international law rules which holds the State to its word when the State does not mean what it says. We see this in the law on unilateral declarations, in the law of treaties, and in the doctrine of estoppel.

---

[48] *Border and Transborder Armed Actions (Nicaragua v. Honduras)* (1988) ICJ Rep. 69 para. 94.

[49] Ludwig Wittgenstein, *Philosophical Investigations* (4th edn, M. S. Hacker and Joachim Schulte eds, Wiley-Blackwell 2009) 96.

[50] John R. Searle, 'The Logical Status of Fictional Discourse' (1975) 6 New Literary History 319, 326.

[51] John R. Searle, *Speech Acts: An Essay in the Philosophy of Language* (CUP 1969) 63.

[52] Ibid. 66.

[53] J. L. Austin explains the point this way: 'the unhappiness here is . . . exactly the same as the unhappiness infecting "I promise ..." when I do not intend [to carry out my promise]. [T]o say "I promise," without intending, is parallel to saying "it is the case" without believing'. Austin (n 28) 50.

LYING IN THE GREY ZONE 381

Under the law on unilateral declarations, an insincere promise is still a promise. We see this in the *Nuclear Tests* case. During the late 1960s and early 1970s, France conducted a series of atmospheric tests of nuclear weapons in French Polynesia. On 25 July 1974, French President Valéry Giscard d'Estaing said, 'I had myself made it clear that this round of atmospheric [nuclear] tests would be the last'.[54] The president was speaking for France. By this utterance, he made public the country's intention to cease all atmospheric nuclear tests at the end of the 1974 series. By making a promise with the intention of being legally bound, France changed its legal position, and was 'thenceforth legally required to follow a course of conduct consistent with the declaration'.[55] The sincerity of the promise was irrelevant,[56] with the ICJ explaining the point this way: 'Once the Court has found that a State has entered into a commitment concerning its future conduct it is not the Court's function to contemplate that it will not comply with it'.[57]

Even if the president did not mean what he said (if, for example, France was contemplating more tests), Giscard d'Estaing would still have made a promise, one that could be kept or broken—as New Zealand claimed in the 1990s, when France recommenced underground nuclear testing in the South Pacific.[58]

In the *Nuclear Tests* case, the International Court of Justice explained the existence of the law on unilateral declarations by reference to the principle of good faith: 'Just as the very rule of *pacta sunt servanda* in the law of treaties is based on good faith, so also is the binding character of an international obligation assumed by unilateral declaration'.[59]

In the law of treaties, an insincere agreement still binds both parties. The standard example here is the 1938 Munich Agreement, when Adolf Hitler promised to resolve future disputes in Europe by peaceful means, in return for the annexation of the Sudetenland in Czechoslovakia. A 1963 report by the International Law Commission makes the following point:

It might be true that Germany had negotiated at Munich *without any intention of complying with the agreement* concluded; but the agreement had not been

[54] *Nuclear Tests (New Zealand v. France)* (1974) ICJ Rep. 257 para. 37.
[55] Ibid. para. 43.
[56] As Thomas Franck noted at the time: 'A spokesman for state policy—like the President [...]—must be taken to intend the natural consequences of his words'. See Thomas M. Franck, 'Word Made Law: The Decision of the ICJ in the *Nuclear Test* Cases' (1975) 69 American Journal of International Law 612, 616.
[57] *Nuclear Tests* (n 54) para. 60.
[58] See *Request for an Examination of the Situation in Accordance with Paragraph 63 of the Court's Judgment of 20 December 1974 in the Nuclear Tests (New Zealand v. France)* (1995) ICJ Rep. 288 para. 62.
[59] *Nuclear Tests* (n 54) para. 46.

382 INSTRUMENTS, TACTICS, AND METHODS IN THE GREY ZONE

vitiated by fraud: the proof of that was precisely that Germany by its subsequent actions had *broken the agreement*, which was legally valid.[60]

There is nothing legally wrongful about a State agreeing to do something which it has no intention of doing. There is only an internationally wrongful act when the State fails to perform the promised action (the State can always change its mind and keep its word). Any international agreement, even an insincere agreement, where the States parties *manifest* an intention to be legally bound, binds the parties, as a matter of international law, and must be performed by them in good faith (*pacta sunt servanda*).[61]

In the law on unilateral declarations and the law of treaties, the internationally wrongful act is the failure by the State to keep to its word. This failure can be the result of the (in)actions of any State official.

The doctrine of estoppel is different because, here, only certain State officials can bind the State to a stated position of fact, and only certain State officials can repudiate that stated position of fact. The internationally wrongful act is the second, inconsistent speech action by someone speaking for the State. The point is significant for any proposed law on State lying because it shows that some internationally wrongful acts can only be committed by those high-ranking officials whose utterances count as the utterances of the State.

Under the doctrine of estoppel, the State is bound by its words, even if the State does not mean what it says. The ICJ has confirmed that the concept of estoppel follows from the principle of good faith.[62] The doctrine is neatly explained by the International Court of Justice in its 1990 *Land, Island and Maritime Frontier Dispute* judgment: Estoppel concerns 'a statement or representation made by one party to another and reliance upon it by that other party to his detriment or to the advantage of the party making it'.[63] There are four component elements in any claim of estoppel. First, there must be an assertion of claimed fact by someone entitled to speak for the State on the matter in question.[64] Second, there must be

---

[60] International Law Commission, '678th Meeting' (1963-I) Yearbook of the International Law Commission 27, 31 (emphasis added).

[61] Vienna Convention on the Law of Treaties (23 May 1969) Art. 26, 1155 UNTS 331.

[62] *Delimitation of the Maritime Boundary in the Gulf of Maine Area (Canada v United States of America)* (1984) ICJ Rep. 246 para. 130.

[63] *Land, Island and Maritime Frontier Dispute ((El Salvador/Honduras: Nicaragua intervening)* (1990) ICJ Rep. 92 para. 63. See also *North Sea Continental Shelf (Federal Republic of Germany/ Netherlands)* (1969) ICJ Rep. 3 para. 30.

[64] See Kaijun Pan, 'A Re-Examination of Estoppel in International Jurisprudence' (2017) 16 Chinese Journal of International Law 751, para. 30. Those people authorized to bind the State to a position 'include heads of State, heads of Government and ministers for foreign affairs and other persons representing the State in specified areas'. Other officials can speak for the State, but only when it appears clear to the other party that they are speaking for the State. See Hugh Thirlway, 'Law and Procedure of the International Court of Justice 1960–1989: Part One' (1990) 61 British Yearbook of International Law 1, 37. ('[T]he constitutional niceties of the position of a given official are less important than the impression produced *ab extra* as to his competence to speak for the State'.)

reliance on the asserted position of fact by the State addressed by the utterance.[65] This is evidenced by the addressee State acting differently, or not acting when it would otherwise have acted.[66] Third, there must then be an inconsistent assertion of fact—again by someone entitled to speak for the State on the matter in question.[67] Finally, the change in position must have resulted in a detriment to the addressee State,[68] including by way of a relative detriment through an advantage gained by the first State.[69]

Under the doctrine of estoppel, the internationally wrongful act is the second, inconsistent speech act by someone speaking for the State.[70] It does not matter that both assertions might be true; nor does it matter if the first utterance is mistaken, and the second utterance is true.[71] Nor does it matter if the first utterance was a lie, and the second utterance was the truth, with Derek Bowett explaining that 'the principle of good faith requires that the party adhere to its statement whether it be true or not'.[72] Hugh Thirlway explains the point by quoting the Red Queen, in Lewis Carroll's *Through the Looking Glass*: 'When you've once said a thing, that fixes it, and you must take the consequences'.[73]

6. Good faith in the coordination of plans of action

The requirement for international law rules on unilateral declarations, treaties, and estoppel is explained by the principle of good faith.[74] In *Nuclear Tests*, the International Court of Justice explained the point in the following way:

Other officials do not ordinarily speak for the State, even when speaking in an official capacity. Thus, in *Delimitation of the Maritime Boundary in the Gulf of Maine Area* (n 62) para. 139, the ICJ confirmed that Canada could not 'rely on the contents of a letter from an official of the Bureau of Land Management of the Department of the Interior . . . as though it were an official declaration of the United States Government on that country's international maritime boundaries'.

[65] D. W. Bowett, 'Estoppel before International Tribunals and Its Relation to Acquiescence' (1957) 33 British Yearbook of International Law 176, 185–86.

[66] *Sovereignty over Pedra Branca/Pulau Batu Puteh, Middle Rocks and South Ledge (Malaysia/Singapore)* (2008) ICJ Rep. 12 para. 228.

[67] Bowett (n 65) 201.

[68] *Land and Maritime Boundary between Cameroon and Nigeria (Cameroon v. Nigeria: Equatorial Guinea intervening)*, Preliminary Objections (1998) ICJ Rep. 275 para. 57.

[69] Dissenting Opinion of Sir Percy Spender, *Temple of Preah Vihear (Cambodia v. Thailand)* (1962) ICJ Rep. 6, 101, at 143–44.

[70] See Thomas Cottier and Jörg Paul Müller, 'Estoppel' (2007) Max Planck Encyclopedia of Public International Law paras 1 and 5.

[71] Separate Opinion of Sir Gerald Fitzmaurice, *Temple of Preah Vihear* (n 69) 52, 63.

[72] Bowett (n 65) 184.

[73] Quoted by Hugh Thirlway, 'The Law and Procedure of the International Court of Justice 1960–1989: Supplement, 2005: Parts One and Two' (2005) 76 British Yearbook of International Law 1, 19.

[74] The principle of good faith can be found in Article 2(2) of the Charter of the United Nations and General Assembly Resolution 2625 (XXV), 'Declaration on Principles of International Law

One of the basic principles governing the creation and performance of legal obligations, whatever their source, is the principle of good faith. Trust and confidence are inherent in international co-operation, in particular in an age when this co-operation in many fields is becoming increasingly essential.[75]

The principle of good faith holds the State to its words when States move from strategic interactions to good faith cooperation. States act strategically when they act in their own interests, for their own reasons, making it difficult for other States to predict likely actions and reactions. The situation can be characterized as a type of inter-State 'Prisoner's Dilemma', whereby States make calculated decisions without knowing how other States will respond.[76] These uncertainties can, though, be mitigated using the speech actions of promising (the doctrine of unilateral declarations), agreeing (law of treaties), or asserting (doctrine of estoppel).[77] Indeed, one of the basic functions of international law is to reduce uncertainty and unpredictability by holding States to the voluntary commitments represented by their speech actions.[78] By promising or agreeing or asserting, States manifest a commitment to move from strategic interactions to good faith cooperation. But to actually reduce uncertainty and unpredictability, the State must mean what it says when it makes a promise or an agreement or asserts some claimed fact about the world. This then allows States 'to avoid anticipating each time all the possible avenues of conduct and result, and to concentrate on the expectable and legitimate behaviour'.[79]

---

concerning Friendly Relations and Co-operation among States in accordance with the Charter of the United Nations' (24 October 1970).

[75] *Nuclear Tests* (n 54) para. 46.

[76] See e.g.S. Plous, 'The Nuclear Arms Race: Prisoner's Dilemma or Perceptual Dilemma?' (1993) 30 Journal of Peace Research 163. The classic Prisoner's Dilemma can be explained as follows: Asa and Bea commit a crime. The police suspect them but have no evidence. Both are brought to the police station and kept in separate interrogation rooms. Asa and Bea are then offered a 'deal'. If they confess, they will be sentenced to two years in prison. If they do not confess, they will be sentenced to five years, if convicted. The only evidence will be the confessions. If both stay silent, both walk free; but if Asa stays silent and Bea confesses, then Bea gets two years, whilst Asa gets five years in jail. So, what is Asa to do? Here, Asa and Bea are interacting strategically, each trying to figure what the other will do—based on their understanding of human nature, and the character of the other person. See generally Steven Kuhn, 'Prisoner's Dilemma', in *The Stanford Encyclopedia of Philosophy*, edited by Edward N. Zalta (2019).

[77] For individuals, the uncertainties involved in the Prisoner's Dilemma can be mitigated using the prior speech actions of promising ('I will never talk to the police'), agreeing ('We both agree to stay silent'), or asserting ('I will never speak to the police, I am not a grass'). See generally on the way speech actions allow for the coordination of individual plans of action, Jürgen Habermas, *The Theory of Communicative Action, Volume 1: The Reason and the Rationalization of Society* (Thomas McCarthy tr, Beacon Press 1984) 307–08.

[78] See, Henner Gött, *The Law of Interactions Between International Organizations* (Springer 2020) 157 (and references cited).

[79] Robert Kolb, *Good Faith in International Law* (Bloomsbury 2017) 24.

The principle of good faith holds the State to its words, even when the State does not mean what it says. We saw this in the law on unilateral declarations, where an insincere promise is still a promise; in the law of treaties, where an insincere agreement still binds both parties; and in the doctrine of estoppel, where the State is bound by its words, even if the State does not mean what it says.

The reason for this is straightforward. The principle of good faith allows States to coordinate their plans of actions by voluntarily moving from strategic interactions to good faith cooperation through the speech actions of promising or agreeing or asserting. Good faith means that the addressee State is entitled to rely on the promise, agreement, or assertion when deciding for itself what to do next. The sincerity of the utterance cannot be a relevant factor because only the State making the utterance knows whether the utterance is sincere, or not. The addressee State cannot know, because (to the hearer) an insincere promise takes the form of a sincere promise, an insincere agreement takes the form of a sincere agreement, and an insincere statement of fact takes the form of a sincere statement of believed fact. This is why the principle of good faith holds the State to its words, even when the utterance is not sincere. Kolb explains the point this way: '[G]ood faith protects the legitimate expectations of another subject generated through a deliberate conduct, *whatever the true intentions* or will of the acting subject'.[80]

A State moves from a position of strategic interaction to good faith cooperation through voluntary speech actions—by making a unilateral declaration, concluding a treaty, or asserting the truth of some proposition. This then entitles the addressee State to place confidence in the ordinary meaning of the words used, to trust that the State was sincere in making the promise or agreement, or to trust that it believed in the veracity of the asserted fact. Simply put, the addressee State is entitled to rely on the ordinary implications of the words used when deciding what to do next, on the understanding that the State making the utterance meant what it said.

7. State lying

The argument here is that we should extend the established laws on insincere State utterances, explained by the principle of good faith, to cover State lying. This point was made already by Emer de Vattel, in his 1797 work, *The Law of Nations*, when he argued that 'good faith consists not only in the observance of our promises, but also in not deceiving on such occasions as lay us under any sort of obligation to speak the truth'.[81] Under the proposed law on State lying, there

---

[80] Ibid. 23 (emphasis added).
[81] Emer de Vattel, *The Law of Nations* (Liberty Fund 2008) para. 177.

386 INSTRUMENTS, TACTICS, AND METHODS IN THE GREY ZONE

would be an internationally wrongful act when (1) someone speaking for the State claimed that some fact was true; (2) the State did not believe in the truth of the expressed proposition; and (3) the State intended to deceive the audience targeted by the utterance.[82]

The first element in State lying is that someone speaking for the State asserts the truth of some proposition. The problem is that States cannot speak, meaning that some flesh-and-blood person must speak for the State and assert the truth of some proposition. The question is: Who can speak for the State? Under international law, we can differentiate between the utterances of persons speaking for the State; and utterances which can be attributed to the State.[83] Take the example of lies told by a low-ranking public official to incite genocide. These lies are attributable to the State, which would be responsible for a violation of international law.[84] But low-ranking public officials cannot make promises or agreements that bind the State; nor can they commit the State to an asserted position of fact under the doctrine of estoppel—a point confirmed by the ICJ in *Gulf of Maine*, when it concluded that an official of the US Bureau of Land Management did not speak for the United States.[85]

So, who speaks for the State for the purposes of asserting the truth of some proposition under the proposed rule on State lying?

Under the established rules on insincere State utterances, explained by the principle of good faith, only the utterances of certain high-ranking government officials, that is, those *speaking for* the State, can move the State from a position of strategic interaction to a position of good faith cooperation. We see this, for example, in the doctrine of estoppel, where only the utterances by high-ranking government officials count as assertions of claimed fact by the State (thereby binding the State to that position).[86] The objective of the principle of good faith is to reduce uncertainty and unpredictability by holding States to their voluntary commitments. But to actually reduce uncertainty and unpredictability, the State must be taken to mean what it says. This is why the principle of good faith holds the State to its words, even when the utterance is not sincere—more specifically, the principle holds those entitled to speak for the State to their words when States move from strategic interactions to good faith cooperation, so that the addressee State can rely on those words when deciding what to do next.

[82] This is a straightforward application of the generally accepted definition of lying to the concept of 'State lying'. See nn 19 and 22 (and accompanying text).

[83] See Draft Articles on State Responsibility (n 13) Art. 4(1) ('The conduct of any State organ shall be considered an act of that State').

[84] See Antonio Cassese, 'On the Use of Criminal Law Notions in Determining State Responsibility for Genocide' 5 (2007) Journal of International Criminal Justice 875, 878.

[85] Pan (n 64). As previously noted, this point is significant because it demonstrates the possibility that only the utterances of certain officials can result in the finding of an internationally wrongful act (recall, it is the second, inconsistent speech action which is the internationally wrongful act).

[86] Ibid.

LYING IN THE GREY ZONE   387

Because only certain people can speak for the State when States are coordinating plans of action, only certain people can lie for the State for the purposes of the proposed law on State lying. The proposed law would be an extension of the existing body of laws on insincere State utterances, explained by the principle of good faith. When States move from strategic interactions to good faith cooperation, those speaking for the State (heads of State, heads of Government, and foreign ministers, etc.) would be expected to mean what they say when asserting some claimed fact about the world. Other States would be entitled to rely on these utterances when deciding what to do next. The same point does not apply in relation to low-ranking government officials. Consider, for example, a situation in which the president of State A wrongly claims that 'State B has nuclear weapons'—similar to the claim that President Putin made to justify the invasion of Ukraine.[87] States can legitimately complain if it transpires the president was lying, because they should be able to rely on the sincerity of the assertions of heads of State when deciding what to do next. But the same considerations do not apply in relation to the utterances of low-ranking officials, who do not speak for the State. So, if the same lie was uttered by an low-ranking government official, this would not count as an utterance by the State.[88] The utterance would be attributable to the State, but low-ranking government officials do not speak for the State, and they cannot lie for the State for the purposes of the proposed law on State lying. The necessary consequence is that only claimed statements of fact made by high-ranking government officials—heads of State, heads of Government, foreign ministers (and their spokespersons), and so on—count as utterances by the State for the purposes of the proposed law on State lying.

The second element in State lying is that 'the State' does not 'believe' in the truth of the expressed proposition.[89] There are two ways we can understand this requirement. Either the relevant belief must be attributable to those high-ranking government officials authorized to voluntarily limit the State's freedom of action; or the relevant belief can be the belief of any State official. Consider the following: Russell is a spy employed by State A. He reports to his superiors that he has seen evidence that State B is developing nuclear weapons. State A's foreign

---

[87] See President of Russia, 'Address by the President of the Russian Federation' (24 February 2022) <http://en.kremlin.ru/events/president/news/67843> accessed 9 March 2023. *Cf.* Laurence Norman, 'Ukraine Isn't Working on Nuclear Weapons, U.N. Official Says, in Rebuke to Russia', *Wall Street Journal* (New York, 2 March 2022).

[88] See, for example, 'Russia, without Evidence, says Ukraine Making Nuclear "Dirty Bomb"' (Reuters, 6 March 2022) <https://www.reuters.com/world/europe/russia-without-evidence-says-ukraine-making-nuclear-dirty-bomb-2022-03-06/> accessed 9 March 2023 ('an unnamed source [in the Russian government said] that Ukraine was close to building a plutonium-based 'dirty bomb' nuclear weapon, although the source cited no evidence'.)

[89] International law has no problem talking about the 'beliefs' of States. We see this, for example, in the identification of customary international law, which requires 'evidence of a belief' by States that a practice is accepted as law: *North Sea Continental Shelf* (n 63) para. 77.

388 INSTRUMENTS, TACTICS, AND METHODS IN THE GREY ZONE

minister then tells a meeting of the UN Security Council they have evidence State B is developing nuclear weapons. Now suppose Russell was lying. Lying involves saying something that you do not believe to be true. State A's Foreign Minister believes that State B is developing nuclear weapons, so they are not lying.[90] But, 'What does *State A believe* to be true?' Either State A is deemed to 'believe' everything that every State official (including Russell) believes (or does not believe), or State A's beliefs can only be established by those high-ranking government officials, like the foreign minister, with the authority to coordinate plans of action with other States.

Again, the logic of the international law principle of good faith shows that the relevant beliefs must be the beliefs of those high-ranking government officials with the authority to voluntarily limit the State's freedom of action. The principle of good faith holds the State to its words, when States move from strategic interactions to good faith cooperation. Specifically, the principle holds those entitled to speak for the State to their words, so that the addressee State can rely on those words when deciding what to do next. Lying involves the speaker saying something they do not believe to be true. State beliefs are manifested in any utterance which can be framed in terms that 'We believe that X is true'—for example, 'We believe that State B is developing nuclear weapons'. The addressee State is entitled to proceed on the understanding that those speaking for the State believed in the truth of the expressed proposition—whilst recognizing that those speaking for the State might, in fact, be mistaken. The addressee State is not entitled to proceed on the understanding that every State official believed that the proposition was true. So, when State A's Foreign Minister informs the UN Security Council that 'State B is developing nuclear weapons', State A does not lie because the foreign minister believes the statement to be true—even though Russell, a low-ranking State agent, does not believe that the statement is true.

The final element in State lying is the intention to deceive. State lying occurs when someone speaking for the State asserts the truth of some proposition which the State does not believe—and the assertion is made with the intention of deceiving another State into believing that the expressed proposition is true. There are only two reasons why a State would assert the truth of some proposition: Either the State is looking to inform the other State, or it is trying to deceive

---

[90] We see the problem in US Secretary of State Colin Powell's assertion to the other States on the UN Security Council, in 2003, that, 'Saddam Hussein and his regime are concealing their efforts to produce more weapons of mass destruction'. Powell claimed that 'every statement I make today is backed up by sources, solid sources . . . . What we're giving you are facts and conclusions based on solid intelligence': U.S. Secretary of State Colin Powell Addresses the UN Security Council <https://georgewbush-whitehouse.archives.gov/news/releases/2003/02/20030205-1.html> accessed 1 October 2021. The evidence is that Powell believed what he was saying, claiming to have been misled by 'some people in the intelligence community who knew at that time that [the intelligence] sources were not good, and shouldn't be relied upon'. David Zarefsky, 'Making the Case for War: Colin Powell at the United Nations' (2007) 10 Rhetoric and Public Affairs 275, 298.

LYING IN THE GREY ZONE 389

the other State. We cannot know whether the State had the intention of informing or deceiving, but there are things we do know: we do know the available evidence in the public domain;[91] we do know what reasonable conclusions (i.e. beliefs) can be drawn from that evidence; we do know what the State said; and we do know the affect (or the likely affect) on the addressee, if the utterance is believed. Based on what we know, we can construct a narrative to explain,[92] 'What motive (i.e. intention) might the State have for asserting the truth of the proposition?' There are only two possibilities: Either the State had the intention of informing (even if it turns out to have been mistaken), or the State had the intention of deceiving the other State by lying. Where there is a clear disconnect between what the State knew (or is deemed to have known) and what the State said, we can conclude that the State was intending to deceive the addressee State. This is particularly the case when it appears that the State was trying to influence the addressee State, to gain some relative advantage.

8. Between competition and coordination: fifty shades of grey

One of the basic functions of international law is to allow States to move from strategic interaction to good faith cooperation and the coordination of plans of action using speech actions. States interact strategically when they act, and react, for their own reasons, in their own interests. States move from strategic interactions to good faith cooperation through the speech actions of promising (law on unilateral declarations), agreeing (law of treaties), or asserting (doctrine of estoppel). The principle of good faith holds the State to its words, even if the State did not mean what it said when promising or agreeing or asserting. This is reflected in the established laws on insincere State utterances, which allow the addressee State to treat the utterance as if it was sincere when deciding what to do next.

The proposed law on State lying (the *lex ferenda*) would, necessarily, only apply when States moved from strategic interactions to good faith co-operation. The requirement for the proposed law is explained by the principle of good faith, which holds those speaking for the State to their words when States voluntarily move to good faith cooperation. When States are interacting strategically, for their own reasons, in their own interests, there would, consequently, be no legal prohibition on State lying under the proposed law. Lying about the activities of

[91] See *United States Diplomatic and Consular Staff in Tehran* (*United States of America v. Iran*) (1980) ICJ Rep. 3, para. 12.
[92] On this point, see *Corfu Channel* (*United Kingdom of Great Britain and Northern Ireland v. Albania*) (1949) ICJ Rep. 4, 18.

390 INSTRUMENTS, TACTICS, AND METHODS IN THE GREY ZONE

spy planes or spy balloons would not, for example, be an internationally wrongful act. On the other hand, lying when States are looking to coordinate their plans of action would be an internationally wrongful act. A global pandemic is one situation when States properly look to coordinate their plans of action.[93] Lying about the scale of an outbreak would, then, be an internationally wrongful act—for example, when US President Donald Trump accused China of under-reporting its number of Covid cases.[94]

The grey zone sits between strategic competition and good faith cooperation. A report by the US State Department's International Security Advisory Board explained: '[Grey zone actions] occupy a space between normal diplomacy . . . and open military conflict [making] deliberate use of instruments of violence, terrorism, and dissembling.[95]

The problem is that this dividing line, between strategic competition and good faith cooperation, is not always clear. Indeed, we might say there are fifty shades of grey between cooperation and competition, from allies falling out (e.g. when the US was accused of spying on German Chancellor Angela Merkel),[96] to talk of a 'special chemistry' between strategic enemies looking to collaborate (e.g. the 2018 summit between Donald Trump and North Korea's Kim Jong Un).[97]

Under the law proposed here, State lying would be internationally wrongful when States moved from strategic interactions to good faith cooperation. States manifest an intention to move to good faith cooperation through the speech actions of promising (unilateral declarations), agreeing (law of treaties), or asserting (doctrine of estoppel and proposed law on State lying). There is no obligation for States to move from strategic interactions to good faith cooperation. Each State enjoys sovereign freedom of action—the so-called Lotus principle, which provides that anything not explicitly prohibited by international law is impliedly permitted.[98] The State voluntarily puts itself in a position of good faith cooperation by intimating that it means what it says by holding itself out as being sincere when promising or agreeing or asserting some claimed fact about the

---

[93] See World Health Assembly Resolution WHA73.1, 'COVID-19 Response' (19 May 2020), para 1, which calls for 'the intensification of cooperation and collaboration'.

[94] 'Trump Says China's Coronavirus Numbers Seem "on the Light Side"' (Reuters, 2 April 2020) <https://www.reuters.com/article/uk-health-coronavirus-trump-china-idAFKBN21K0AE> accessed 7 May 2022.

[95] See e.g. International Security Advisory Board, 'Report on Gray Zone Conflict' (2017) 2.

[96] 'NSA Spying Row: Denmark Accused of Helping US Spy on European Officials' (BBC News, 31 May 2021) <https://www.bbc.co.uk/news/world-europe-57302806> accessed 7 May 2022.

[97] Jeong-Ho Lee, 'North Korea Says Trump's "Empty Promise" Dashes Hopes for Deal' (*Bloomberg*, 12 June 2020) <https://www.bloomberg.com/news/articles/2020-06-12/north-korea-says-it-sees-no-benefit-from-engaging-with-trump> accessed 7 May 2022.

[98] See An Hertogen, 'Letting *Lotus* Bloom' (2015) 26 European Journal of International Law 901, 902 (and references cited). The 'Lotus' principle is named after the *Case of the SS 'Lotus' (France v. Turkey)*, PCIJ, Ser. A, No. 10, 18.

world. In these circumstances, it is reasonable for the addressee State to rely on the sincerity of the utterance.

State lying in the grey zone would be legally wrongful where the State intimated that it was telling the truth and the other State could reasonably rely on the veracity of the expressed proposition. A State puts itself in a position of good faith cooperation by intimating that it means what it says by holding itself out as being sincere—including when asserting some claimed fact about the world. There is no middle ground—no shades of grey. States can try and hide in the grey zone, but international lawyers live in a black and white world in which behaviour is either lawful or unlawful.

State lying occurs when someone speaking for the State asserts the truth of some proposition that the State does not believe, with the intention of deceiving the addressee State, in circumstances where the State intimates that it means what it says—and that other States can reasonably rely on the utterance when deciding what to do next. The prohibition would not apply in times of war; it would apply in circumstances of normal diplomacy; its application in the grey zone would depend on the circumstances: If the State clearly intimated that it meant what it said (i.e. that it should be believed, and that the addressee State should rely on the utterance when deciding what to do), and it was reasonable, in the circumstances, for the addressee State to rely on the utterance, this would be an internationally wrongful act if it transpired the State was lying.

9. Conclusion

This chapter has made the case that States should recognize a new regulative rule prohibiting State lying when States move from strategic interactions to the good faith coordination of their future plans of action. The proposed rule would tidy up the existing law on insincere State utterances, following the logic of the established legal principle that States are taken to mean what they say when coordinating plans of action in good faith. State lying would be legally wrongful when States were coordinating plans of actions—but not in cases of strategic competition (paradigmatically, not in times of war). Where a State asserted the truth of some proposition, in circumstances where it is clear it expected to be believed, the addressee States would be entitled to proceed on the basis the other State meant what it said when deciding how to act and react.

State lying presents an existential threat to the international law system.[99] The authority of the international law system—its capacity to regulate effectively

---

[99] The dangers of lying by domestic politicians are well recognized in democratic States, as it destroys the basis of trust which make political deliberations possible. See e.g. Sissela Bok, *Lying: Moral Choice in Public and Private Life* (Vintage 1999).

States behaviours—depends on its ability to translate the speech actions of States into legally binding norms of behaviour. Insincere utterances undermine the very possibility of State cooperation using speech actions—hence the existence of the body of laws on insincere State utterances. Hugo Grotius recognized these dangers in the seventeenth century when he observed that successful communication depends on the speaker meaning what they say because the very purpose of communication is the development of mutual understanding. Lying undermines this possibility of mutual understanding, violating the right of the addressee to make their own decisions based on a proper understanding of the facts. He explains the point this way: 'The rights here spoken of are peculiarly connected with this subject. They imply that liberty of judgement, which men are understood, by a kind of tacit agreement, to owe to each other in their mutual intercourse'.[100]

This work has made the case for a new regulative rule in the form that 'Those speaking for the State must not lie to other States when States are coordinating plans of action'. The rule would apply in conditions of normal diplomacy but not in times of war. The rule would apply in grey zone conflicts where the State clearly intimated that it should be believed, and that other States should rely on the utterance. In these circumstances, the State moves itself from a position of strategic interaction to good faith obligation (there is no obligation to do this, States can always dissemble or stay silent). If it turns out that the State did not believe in the truth of the expressed proposition, and that it intended to deceive the addressee State, this would be an internationally wrongful act and the addressee State would have legitimate grounds for complaint if it transpired the State was lying in the grey zone.

Acknowledgement

My thanks to Allan Beever, Duncan Macintosh, and Aurel Sari for their comments on previous versions of the paper.

[100] Grotius (n 21) Book III, Ch I, § XI.

18

Rethinking the International Law of Interference in the Digital Age

Steven J. Barela and Samuli Haataja

1. Introduction

If the invention of one-to-many communications gave rise to propaganda machines in the twentieth century,[1] what has the digital era opened with many-to-many (peer-to-peer) communications?[2] One result is that rapid advancements in information and communication technologies (ICTs) have increased the capacity for intervention across borders with disinformation operations, election meddling, or public influence campaigns. Alarmingly, the global community has witnessed a dramatic rise in such activities and the targeted societies have found themselves destabilized, and sometimes nearly paralyzed, as citizens' views of facts and events become intensely contested.[3] The intelligence community in the United States has identified foreign manoeuvres taking place during the 2016 and 2020 presidential elections,[4] and similar actions have been reportedly carried out in the run-up to voting in the United Kingdom,[5]

---

[1] Philip M. Taylor, *Munitions of the Mind: A History of Propaganda* (Manchester University Press 2003); David Holbrook Culbert, David Welch, and Nicholas J. Cull, *Propaganda and Mass Persuasion: A Historical Encyclopedia, 1500 to the Present* (ABC Clio 2003); Robert Edwin Herzstein, *The War that Hitler Won: The Most Infamous Propaganda Campaign in History* (G. P. Putnam's Sons 1978).

[2] Cherilyn Ireton and Julie Posetti (eds), *Journalism, 'Fake News' and Disinformation* (UNESCO 2018).

[3] Steven J. Barela and Jérôme Duberry, 'Understanding Disinformation Operations in the Twenty-First Century', in *Defending Democracies: Combating Foreign Election Interference in a Digital Age*, edited by Duncan B. Hollis and Jens D. Ohlin (OUP 2021).

[4] For the 2016 election, see US Intelligence Community, 'Assessing Russian Activities and Intentions in Recent U.S. Elections' (6 January 2017); and Robert S. Mueller, 'Report on the Investigation Into Russian Interference in the 2016 Presidential Election (Volume 1)' (US Department of Justice, March 2019) 36–40 (hereinafter Mueller Report Vol. I). For the 2020 election, see National Intelligence Council, 'Foreign Threats to the 2020 US Federal Elections' Intelligence Community Assessment (10 March 2021) <https://www.dni.gov/files/ODNI/documents/assessme nts/ICA-declass-16MAR21.pdf> accessed 11 March 2023 (hereinafter US Intel Report on 2020 Election).

[5] United Kingdom House of Commons Digital, Culture Media and Sport Committee, 'Disinformation and "Fake News": Final Report', Session 2017–19 (14 February 2019) ch. 6. See also the UK intelligence report outlining the shortcomings of government investigations into Russian

---

Steven J. Barela and Samuli Haataja, *Rethinking the International Law of Interference in the Digital Age* In: *Hybrid Threats and Grey Zone Conflict*. Edited by: Mitt Regan and Aurel Sari, Oxford University Press. © Oxford University Press 2024. DOI: 10.1093/oso/9780197744772.003.0018

394 INSTRUMENTS, TACTICS, AND METHODS IN THE GREY ZONE

France,[6] Germany,[7] Spain,[8] Italy,[9] and Mexico.[10] Moreover, Eastern Europe finds itself under consistent assault of disinformation operations,[11] and the World Health Organization alerted us to an 'infodemic' accompanying the COVID-19 pandemic.[12]

Not only has this activity been disruptive to open societies, but it has also been a shock to the international system as cross-border meddling in internal affairs has become broad, deep, and precise. Such wide interference has put the besieged States on their heels and searching for recourse to what would fall into the categories of hybrid warfare or grey zone conflict. Consequently, we believe it is beneficial to turn towards international law with a perspective on legal resilience and an operational mindset in order to clarify what has been an exploited legal ambiguity.[13] As some States seek to take advantage of an uncertainty created by technological developments, the legal status of certain actors, and the applicable laws, it is necessary to put forward sound interpretations of law that allow States to protect their sovereign interests while still providing constraints against the abuse of responsive measures.

meddling: Intelligence and Security Committee of Parliament, 'Russia' (21 July 2020) <https://isc.independent.gov.uk/wp-content/uploads/2021/03/CCS207_CCS0221966010-001_Russia-Report-v02-Web_Accessible.pdf> accessed 11 March 2023.

[6] Iris Boyer and Théophile Lenoir, 'ÉLECTIONS 2022: L'écosystème d'information sous pression. Rapport du Groupe de veille numérique à l'intégrité électorale' (Institute for Strategic Dialogue 2022) <https://www.isdglobal.org/isd-publications/elections-2022-the-french-information-ecosystem-put-to-the-test/> accessed 11 March 2023; Bakamo, 'Patterns of Dis-information in the 2017 French Presidential Election' (Bakamo 2017) <https://www.bakamosocial.com/frenchelection/>, French Election Social Media Landscape (2017) accessed 11 March 2023.

[7] Raquel Miguel, 'The Battle against Disinformation in the Upcoming Federal Election in Germany: Actors, Initiatives and Tools' (EU Disinfo Lab, 24 September 2021) <https://www.disinfo.eu/publications/the-battle-against-disinformation-in-the-upcoming-federal-election-in-germany-actors-initiatives-and-tools/> accessed 11 March 2023.

[8] Javier Lesaca, 'Los zombis de la desinformación', El País (Madrid, 11 November 2017) <https://elpais.com/politica/2017/11/12/actualidad/1510498943_521481.html> accessed 11 March 2023; David Alandete, 'La trama rusa empleó redes chavistas para agravar la crisis catalana', El País (Madrid, 11 November 2017) <https://elpais.com/politica/2017/11/10/actualidad/1510341089_316043.html> accessed 11 March 2023; Javier Lesaca, 'Why did Russian Social Media Swarm the Digital Conversation about Catalan Independence?', Washington Post (Washington DC, 22 November 2017) <https://www.washingtonpost.com/news/monkey-cage/wp/2017/11/22/why-did-russian-social-media-swarm-the-digital-conversation-about-catalan-independence/?utm_term=.93e3893e11ff> accessed 11 March 2023.

[9] David Alandete and Daniel Verdú, 'How Russian Networks worked to Boost the Far Right in Italy', El País (Madrid, 1 March 2018) <https://elpais.com/elpais/2018/03/01/inenglish/1519922107_909331.html> accessed 11 March 2023.

[10] David Alire Garcia and Noe Torres, 'Russia Meddling in Mexican Election: White House aide McMaster', Reuters (7 January 2018) <https://www.reuters.com/article/us-mexico-russia-usa-idUSKBN1EW0UD> accessed 11 March 2023.

[11] See generally European Union East StratCom Task Force <https://euvsdisinfo.eu/>.

[12] Matt Richtel, 'W.H.O. Fights a Pandemic Besides Coronavirus: An "Infodemic"', New York Times (New York, 6 February 2020) <https://www.nytimes.com/2020/02/06/health/coronavirus-mis information-social-media.html> accessed 11 March 2023.

[13] See Muñoz Mosquera et al, chapter 29, in this volume.

LAW OF INTERFERENCE IN THE DIGITAL AGE 395

Although there are a variety actions that are manifesting this tension within the international system, our chapter focuses specifically on fragments of falsehood widely spread by design using ICTs. That is, we discuss disinformation operations conducted across international borders, termed in this chapter as 'disinfo-ops'. By employing a theory of legal resilience to analyse and confront this tactic meant to unsettle adversaries, our intention is to offer an avenue to adapt to the new threat, while strengthening both national resilience and the international legal system itself.

In this chapter, we will present what we believe to be the most applicable route for determining the legality of the novel cyber influence activities in section 2: the principle of non-intervention. We will then present a proposal for understanding this rule of international law with axiological content for the *domaine réservé* and empirical content for the definition of 'coercion' (and point to research routes that are now opening on this front) in section 3. We will then conclude our work in section 4.

2. The naturally applicable law: non-intervention

The principle of non-intervention arguably sits at the centre of the Westphalian system with each sovereign nation free to operate within its own realm without outside interference. In this sense, it can also be said that the concept undergirds the entire international legal order. For this reason, we believe it is all the more important that the prohibition of intervention be clearly understood as technology drastically changes the capacities for meddling across borders.

2.1 Some historical understanding

At this point, a variety of scholars have analysed the legal contours of *disinfo-ops* and delineated which portions of international law are implicated. These include possible violations of sovereignty, intervention, self-determination, and the requirement to exercise due diligence over non-State actors conducting cross-border cyber operations within a State's territory.[14] Providing an overall view,

---

[14] See e.g. Michael Schmitt, '"Virtual" Disenfranchisement: Cyber Election Meddling in the Grey Zones of International Law' (2018) 19 Chicago Journal of International Law 30; Jens D. Ohlin, 'Did Russian Cyber-Interference in the 2016 Election Violate International Law?' (2017) 95 Texas Law Review 1579; Jens D. Ohlin, *Election Interference International Law and the Future of Democracy* (CUP 2020); Barrie Sander, 'Democracy under the Influence: Paradigms of State Responsibility for Cyber Influence Operations on Elections' (2019) 18 Chinese Journal of International Law 1; Nicholas Tsagourias, 'Electoral Cyber Interference, Self-Determination and the Principle of Non-Intervention in Cyberspace', in *Governing Cyberspace: Behaviour, Power and Diplomacy*, edited by Dennis Broeders and Bibi van den Berg (Rowman and Littlefield 2020), 45; Przemysław Roguski, 'Violations

Michael Schmitt, Director of the Tallinn Manual Process, has concluded that certain States are exploiting the grey zones found in the law with an aim to 'avoid consensus condemnation of their cyber operations as violations of binding international legal norms'.[15]

Though there are various possibilities and challenges to take into consideration, we believe the principle of non-intervention is a properly fitting category of international law to analyse the legality of such operations—even if the norm needs to be developed in new circumstances.[16] While non-military incursions into another State are less explicitly prohibited in treaty law, customary law forbids the lesser forms of intervention. Understandably, a great deal of attention has been on acts that might qualify as uses of 'force' or as 'armed attacks', since these are often the most destructive to a State and its interests; these are also the explicit terms used in the UN Charter to outlaw armed intrusions from abroad.[17] Yet at issue here is action taken below those thresholds that are implicit in Article 2(1) of the UN Charter based on the sovereign equality of States.[18]

While intervention has already been singled out as a 'truly Protean concept',[19] this should be coupled with the fact that the wide expansion of ICTs across the globe has created a capacity for intervention that is vastly different in kind and scope from anything that has come before. We are not considering propaganda pamphlets dropped from an airplane, but rather instruments of influence that can now be individually tailored, deployed much more broadly, and then

of Territorial Sovereignty in Cyberspace', in *Governing Cyberspace: Behaviour, Power and Diplomacy*, edited by Dennis Broeders and Bibi van den Berg (Rowman & Littlefield 2020), 65; Harriet Moynihan, 'The Application of International Law to State Cyberattacks: Sovereignty and Non-intervention' (Royal Institute of International Affairs, December 2019) <https://www.chathamhouse.org/2019/12/application-international-law-state-cyberattacks> accessed 11 March 2023; Sean Watts and Theodore Richard, 'Baseline Territorial Sovereignty and Cyberspace' (2018) 22 Lewis and Clark Law Review 771; Antonio Coco and Talita de Souza Dias, ' "Cyber Due Diligence": A Patchwork of Protective Obligations in International Law' (2021) 32 European Journal of International Law 771; Eric Talbot Jensen and Sean Watts, 'A Cyber Duty of Due Diligence: Gentle Civilizer or Crude Destabilizer?' (2017) 95 Texas Law Review 1555; and Michael Schmitt, 'In Defense of Due Diligence in Cyberspace' (2015) 125 Yale Law Journal Forum 68.

[15] Schmitt, 'In Defense of Due Diligence' (n 14) 66.

[16] Steven J. Barela, 'Cross-Border Cyber Ops to Erode Legitimacy: An Act of Coercion' (*Just Security*, 12 January 2017) <https://www.justsecurity.org/36212/cross-border-cyber-ops-erode-legitimacy-act-coercion/> accessed 11 March 2023; Steven J. Barela, 'Bots, Trolls and *Dezinformatsiya*: The Continuing Russian Campaign to Divide the Democratic Party in the USA' (*E-International Relations*, 27 September 2017) <https://www.e-ir.info/2017/09/27/the-continuing-russian-campaign-to-divide-the-democratic-party-in-the-usa/> accessed 11 March 2023; Steven J. Barela, 'Zero Shades of Grey: Russian-Ops Violate International Law' (*Just Security*, 29 March 2018) <https://www.justsecurity.org/54340/shades-grey-russian-ops-violate-international-law/> accessed 11 March 2023; Steven J. Barela, 'Disobeying Trump: "Context and Consequences" of Russian Ops' (*Just Security*, 27 September 2018) <https://www.justsecurity.org/60883/disobeying-trump-context-consequences-russian-ops/> accessed 11 March 2023.

[17] Charter of the United Nations (June 26, 1945), 1 UNTS XVI, Articles 2(4) and 51, respectively.

[18] Ibid. See also Moynihan (n 14); Watts and Richard (n 14).

[19] Jan H. W. Verzijl, *International Law in Historical Perspective*, Vol. I (A.W. Sijthoff 1968) 236.

delivered in a nearly continuous fashion.[20] Though a great deal of discussion has occurred over how globalization illustrates an expansion of inter-State interests, legal arguments have been consistently put forward for a sacrosanct domain that belongs to each State.

The United Nations General Assembly (UNGA) has passed over thirty-five resolutions addressing the unlawfulness of interference and intervention, with most activity on this matter taking place in the 1960s through to the 1980s.[21] Yet few of these resolutions are authoritative and they have at times been passed on divided votes. The most significant of these international soft-law instruments would be those passed with a substantial majority: the 1965 Declaration on the Inadmissibility of Intervention,[22] the 1970 Declaration on the Principles of Friendly Relations (adopted without a vote signalling consensus),[23] and the 1981 Declaration on the Inadmissibility of Intervention and Interference.[24]

The most relevant jurisprudence for understanding the law on this point is the International Court of Justice (ICJ) *Nicaragua* decision of 1986, which outlined that an unlawful intervention occurs when an action that can be attributed to a State, first, affects the internal or external affairs of another State and, second, is coercive in nature.[25] As with all wrongful acts on this level, it must be attributable to a State, which can become quite difficult with ICTs. Nonetheless there are two matters that are specific to this rule. First, we must clearly establish what is the protected matter being targeted—a fundamental right derived from sovereignty often termed today the *domaine réservé*. Second, as the term 'coercion' is undefined in international law,[26] we aim to move beyond its conventional meaning to

---

[20] See Barela and Duberry (n 3).

[21] Maziar Jamnejad and Michael Wood, 'The Principle of Non-Intervention' (2009) 22 Leiden Journal of International Law 345, 349–51; Chimène I. Keitner, 'Foreign Election Interference and International Law', in Hollis and Ohlin (n 3) 179.

[22] UNGA, 'Declaration on the Inadmissibility of Intervention in the Domestic Affairs of States and the Protection of their Independence and Sovereignty', UN Doc. A/2131 (XX) (21 December 1965); passed with 109 to 0, with one abstention. It is worth noting that the International Court of Justice in its *Nicaragua* decision (n 25) held that the United States had its own particular history on the vote related to this resolution: 'It is true that the United States, while it voted in favour of General Assembly resolution 21 3 1 (XX), also declared at the time of its adoption in the First Committee that it considered the declaration in that resolution to be "only a statement of political intention and not a formulation of law"' (Official Records of the General Assembly, Twentieth Session, First Committee, A/C. 1 /SR. 1423, p. 436).

[23] UNGA, 'Declaration on Principles of International Law concerning Friendly Relations and Cooperation among States in accordance with the Charter of the United Nations', UN Doc. A/RES/ 2625 (XXV) (24 October 1970).

[24] UNGA, 'Declaration on the Inadmissibility of Intervention and Interference in the Internal Affairs of States', UN Doc. A/Res/36/103 (9 December 1981); passed 120 for, 22 against, and 6 abstentions.

[25] International Court of Justice, *Case Concerning Military and Paramilitary Activities in and Against Nicaragua (Nicaragua v. United States of America) (Merits)* [1986] ICJ Rep. 14, para. 205.

[26] Jamnejad and Wood (n 21).

398 INSTRUMENTS, TACTICS, AND METHODS IN THE GREY ZONE

embrace broader interpretations needed in this context and provide parameters for measurement and normative content.[27] Each of these points of law is essential to circumscribe the right to respond to an unlawful action when there is no outside enforcement mechanism in the international realm.

At the same time, it is important that we do not shy away from the fact that interference across borders has been profuse. This can be seen clearly in the fact that the case law just mentioned on *Nicaragua* arises from a US intrusion. In fact, one scholar has tallied the United States and the USSR/Russia have engaged in partisan electoral meddling 117 times between 1946 and 2000.[28] Hence major players in some of the cross-border cyber interference under discussion today have a deep history on this count.

Moreover, the United States, one of today's victims, has itself reached across international frontiers numerous times to meddle in the democratic affairs of other States. For instance, we can point to the actions carried out by the United States in Iran in 1953,[29] Guatemala in 1954,[30] and Chile in 1973.[31] This can be particularly relevant since progress on this issue has been early and explicit within the region of the Americas. Not only was the 'good-neighbour policy' promoted by US President Franklin Roosevelt and followed by the 1933 Montevideo Convention on the Rights and Duties of States,[32] the Organization of the American States was the first regional organization to enter a provision in its constitution to proscribe intervention within the hemisphere.[33]

---

[27] For an excellent overview of applying this principle in cyberspace, and persuasive argumentation on redefining 'coercion' in this context, see Sean Watts, 'Low-Intensity Cyber Operations and the Principle of Non-Intervention', in *Cyber War: Law and Ethics for Virtual Conflicts*, edited by Jens Ohlin, Kevin Govern, and Claire Finkelstein, 249–70 (OUP 2015).

[28] Dov H. Levin, 'Partisan Electoral Interventions by the Great Powers: Introducing the PEIG Dataset' (2019) 36 Conflict Management and Peace Science 88. See also Dov Levin, 'Should We Worry about Partisan Electoral Interventions? The Nature, History, and Known Effects of Foreign Interference in Elections', in Hollis and Ohlin (n 3) 19.

[29] Stephen Kinzer, *All the Shah's Men: An American Coup and the Roots of Middle East Terror* (John Wiley and Sons 2003).

[30] David M. Barrett, 'Sterilizing a "Red Infection": Congress, the CIA, and Guatemala, 1954' (Promo66 Liceo Guatemala, 27 June 2007) <http://promo66.blogspot.com/2007/06/sterilizing-red-infection.html> accessed 11 March 2023.

[31] Kristian Gustafson, *Hostile Intent: U.S. Covert Operations in Chile, 1964–1974* (Potomac Books 2007).

[32] Montevideo Convention on the Rights and Duties of States (26 December 1933), 165 LNTS 19 (Article 8: 'No state has the right to intervene in the internal or external affairs of another'). Chairman of the US delegation and Secretary of State, Cordell Hull, declared: 'Every observing person must by this time thoroughly understand that under the Roosevelt administration the United States Government is as much opposed as any other government to interference with the freedom, the sovereignty, or other internal affairs or processes of the governments of other nations'.

[33] Charter of the Organisation of American States (30 April 1948), Art. 15: 'No State or group of States has the right to intervene, directly or indirectly, for any reason whatever, in the internal or external affairs of any other State. The foregoing principle prohibits *not only armed force but also any other form of interference* or attempted threat against the personality of the State or against its political, economic and cultural elements' (emphasis added).

Nevertheless, as some might take issue with a former culprit now claiming itself to be a victim, the ICJ also broached this point:

> It is not to be expected that in the practice of States the application of the rules in question should have been perfect, in the sense that States should have refrained, with complete consistency, from the use of force or from intervention in each other's internal affairs. The Court does not consider that, for a rule to be established as customary, the corresponding practice must be in absolutely rigorous conformity with the rule.[34]

Put another way, illicit actions are not excused by other illicit practice.

2.2 Advancements in the cyber context

Agreement among States has been slow on the applicable international law pertaining to cyberspace. There has been work at the United Nations by the Group of Governmental Experts (GGE) on Developments in the Field of Information and Telecommunications in the Context of International Security. Only a tiny step was taken in its 2013 report concluding that 'international law and in particular the UN Charter, is applicable'.[35] Since that time, its work has become more substantial. Specifically, the 2015 report by the GGE set forth that States have jurisdiction over infrastructure that is located within their territory, that they cannot use proxies to commit internationally wrongful acts, and should work to ensure non-State actors do not use their territory to do so. Of most significance here, the government experts were also able to agree that 'States must observe, among other principles of international law, State sovereignty, sovereign equality, [...] and non-intervention in the internal affairs of other States'.[36]

This was reiterated in the 2021 report by the GGE and in the 2021 report from the UN Open-Ended Working Group (OEWG) on responsible State behaviour in cyberspace.[37] Through these processes, States have expressed their general agreement that international law applies in cyberspace but there continues to be debate about the specifics. In this context, many States have outlined their

---

[34] *Nicaragua* (n 25) para. 186.

[35] Group of Governmental Experts on Developments in the Field of Information and Telecommunications in the Context of International Security, UN Doc. A/68/98 (24 June 2013).

[36] Group of Governmental Experts on Developments in the Field of Information and Telecommunications in the Context of International Security, UN Doc. A/70/174 (22 July 2015).

[37] Group of Governmental Experts on Advancing Responsible State Behaviour in Cyberspace in the Context of International Security, UN Doc. A/76/135 (14 July 2021); United Nations Open-Ended Working Group an Developments in the Field of Information and Telecommunications in the Context of International Security, 'Final Substantive Report' (10 March 2021).

400 INSTRUMENTS, TACTICS, AND METHODS IN THE GREY ZONE

official views on how the law applies; however, this process has become a site for contestation.[38]

Also of import to our analysis, the Tallinn Manual Project offers valuable interpretations by a team of global experts on how international law applies to cyber operations.[39] As it relates to State sovereignty, the *Tallinn Manual 2.0* provides that this principle indeed applies in cyberspace,[40] and that States 'must not conduct cyber operations that violate the sovereignty of another State'.[41] As for the non-intervention principle, Rule 66 stipulates that States 'may not intervene, including by cyber means, in the internal or external affairs of another State'.[42] In the commentary to Rule 66, the *Tallinn Manual* experts reaffirmed the position adopted by the ICJ in the *Nicaragua* case that, to amount to a prohibited intervention, any act must be coercive in nature and it must affect the internal or external affairs of the target State.[43] The requirement for coercion is a key factor differentiating violations of sovereignty with violations of the non-intervention principle.[44] As to what constitutes a State's internal affairs, the experts highlighted that 'the choice of both the political system and its organisation' are clearly within the internal affairs of a State as they 'lie at the heart of sovereignty'.[45] A specific example given by the experts in relation to Rule 66 is where one State uses cyber means to 'alter electronic ballots and thereby manipulate an election'.[46] A number of States have also adopted the position that a prohibited intervention occurs where a cyber operation is coercive and affects a State's internal or external affairs.[47] As an example, where cyber means are used to manipulate election results, many States would consider this an unlawful intervention.[48]

---

[38] See 'Official Compendium of Voluntary National Contributions on the Subject of how International Law applies to the Use of Information and Communications Technologies by States submitted by Participating Governmental Experts in the Group of Governmental Experts on Advancing Responsible State Behaviour in Cyberspace in the Context of International Security established pursuant to General Assembly resolution 73/266', UN Doc A/76/136* (13 July 2021) (hereinafter Official Compendium).

[39] Michael Schmitt (ed), *Tallinn Manual on the International Law Applicable to Cyber Warfare* (CUP 2013) (hereinafter *Tallinn 1.0*).

[40] Michael Schmitt (ed.), *Tallinn Manual 2.0 on the International Law Applicable to Cyber Operations* (CUP 2017) (hereinafter *Tallinn 2.0*) Rule 1, 11.

[41] Ibid. Rule 4, 17.

[42] Ibid. 312.

[43] Ibid. 314.

[44] Ibid. 24.

[45] Ibid. 315.

[46] Ibid. 313.

[47] Official Compendium (n 38).

[48] See Jeremy Wright, 'Cyber and International Law in the 21st Century' (Attorney General's Office, 23 May 2018) <https://www.gov.uk/government/speeches/cyber-and-international-law-in-the-21st-century> accessed 11 March 2023; Brian Egan, 'Remarks on International Law and Stability in Cyberspace' (US Department of State, 10 November 2016) <https://2009-2017.state.gov/s/l/releases/remarks/264303.htm> accessed 11 March 2023; Australian Government, 'Australia's International Cyber Engagement Strategy (2019 International Law Supplement)' (2019) 5 <https://www.internationalcybertech.gov.au/sites/default/files/2020-11/2019%20Legal%20Supplment_0.PDF> accessed 11 March 2023.

Of the two elements needed for an unlawful intervention, coercion has been particularly problematic and subject to debate (see section 3.2).[49] The Tallinn Manual experts defined coercion as 'an affirmative act designed to deprive another State of its freedom of choice, that is, to force that State to act in an involuntary manner or involuntarily refrain from acting in a particular way'.[50] The experts distinguished coercion from other forms of pressures, such as 'persuasion, criticism, public diplomacy, propaganda . . . retribution, mere maliciousness, and the like'.[51] They noted that 'unlike coercion, such activities merely involve either influencing (as distinct from factually compelling) the voluntary actions of the target State, or seek no action on the part of the target State at all'.[52] According to the experts, to amount to coercion, the act in question 'must have the potential for compelling the target State to engage in an action that it would otherwise not take (or refrain from taking an action it would otherwise take)'.[53]

Since the publication of the *Tallinn Manual* in 2017, a number of States have adopted broader approaches to coercion than the narrow approach adopted by the *Tallinn Manual* experts. For example, according to Australia, coercion involves means that 'effectively deprive the State of the ability to control, decide upon or govern matters of an inherently sovereign nature'.[54] Germany maintains that coercion involves situations where a State's internal processes relating to its *domaine réservé* are 'significantly influenced or thwarted' and the victim State's 'will is manifestly bent' by the conduct.[55] The UK also maintains that a broader approach to coercion is needed than the one adopted by the *Tallinn Manual*, and suggests that in some cases this could include 'disruptive cyber behaviours' even where it is not possible to point to specific conduct they were compelled to carry out or prevented from engaging in.[56]

With this abridged presentation of the applicable law in place, we will now turn to the particulars that need development to advance an operational mindset.

---

[49] See Ido Kilovaty, 'The Elephant in the Room: Coercion' (2019) 113 AJIL Unbound 87.

[50] *Tallinn 2.0* (n 40) 317, citing Robert Y. Jennings and Arthur Watts (eds), *Oppenheim's International Law, Volume 1, Peace* (9th edn, Longman 1992) 430–31.

[51] *Tallinn 2.0* (n 40) 318.

[52] Ibid. 318–19.

[53] Ibid. 319.

[54] Australian Government, 'Australia's Position on how International Law applies to State Conduct in Cyberspace' (2020) <https://www.internationalcybertech.gov.au/our-work/annexes/annex-b> accessed 11 March 2023.

[55] Federal Government of Germany, 'On the Application of International Law in Cyberspace' (March 2021) 6 <https://www.auswaertiges-amt.de/blob/2446304/32e7b2498e10b74fb17204c54665b df0/on-the-application-of-international-law-in-cyberspace-data.pdf> accessed 11 March 2023.

[56] Suella Braverman, 'International Law in Future Frontiers' (Attorney General's Office, 19 May 2022) <https://www.gov.uk/government/speeches/international-law-in-future-frontiers> accessed 11 March 2023.

3. A proposal for legal resilience

When it comes to attributing an act in cyberspace to a State, there will be multiple important issues regarding evidence and State responsibility.[57] Nevertheless, in this work we will set aside the technical issue of attribution for two reasons. First, States have due diligence obligations if unlawful activity is emanating from their territory.[58] Second, attribution has been determined with some specificity in certain circumstances which can be instructive for further pursuits.[59] For our purposes, setting this issue aside will allow us to focus explicitly on the so-called *domaine réservé* that must be subject to coercion for a violation of the non-intervention principle to occur.

3.1 The *domaine réservé*: incorporating axiological content

The concept of *domaine réservé* (reserved domain) has traditionally referred to matters that fall within the domestic or internal affairs of a State. Namely, matters that are not regulated by international law and are only within the domestic competence or jurisdiction of States.[60] Sometimes it is distinguished from the broader State functions that States have the authority to exercise.[61] The concept is

---

[57] Nicholas Tsagourias and Michael Farrell, 'Cyber Attribution: Technical and Legal Approaches and Challenges' (2020) 31 European Journal of International Law 941; Kristen Eichensehr, 'The Law & Politics of Cyberattack Attribution' (2020) 67 UCLA Law Review 520; International Law Commission, 'Draft Articles on Responsibility of States for Internationally Wrongful Acts', UN Doc. A/56/10, 24 October 2001.

[58] See generally Coco and Dias (n 14); Jensen and Watts (n 14); Schmitt, 'In Defense of Due Diligence' (n 14). Although unresolved as a binding rule, the UN GGE 2021 Report (n 37) discussed the norm of due diligence at 10, §§ 29–30. The report adopted many of the same criteria found in the *Tallinn Manual 2.0* on the issue, at chs. 6 and 7.

[59] See e.g. US Select Committee on Intelligence, US Senate, 'Russian Active Measures Campaigns and Interference in the 2016 US Election. Volume 1: Russian Efforts against Election Infrastructure' (116th Cong. 2019–20, 1st Sess., Report 116-XX); US Select Committee on Intelligence, US Senate, 'Russian Active Measures Campaigns and Interference in the 2016 US Election. Volume 2: Russia's Use of Social Media' (116th Cong. 2019–20, 1st Sess., Report 116-XX). For granular detail on Russian persons and organizations see (Mueller) Indictments, *US v. Internet Research Agency* et al, No. 1:18-cr-32-DLF, 2018 WL 914777 (D.D.C. 16 February 2018); *US v. Viktor Borisovich Netyksho et al*, No. 1:18-cr-215-ABJ (D.D.C. 13 July 2018); *US v. Elena Alekseevna Khusyaynova*, No. 1:18-MJ-464 (E.D. Va. 28 September 2018).

[60] Katja Ziegler, 'Domaine Réservé', in *Max Planck Encyclopaedia of Public International Law* (OUP 2013) para. 1.

[61] The *Tallinn Manual*, for example, distinguishes a State's 'inherently governmental functions' (relevant for a sovereignty violation) from the concept of *domaine réservé* (relevant to the non-intervention principle). *Tallinn 2.0* (n 40) 24. Relatedly, there remains a debate over whether sovereignty is a primary rule or simply a principle that has no binding effect. Though a growing number of States have confirmed its status as an obligatory rule (see e.g. Austria, Bolivia, China, Czech Republic, Finland, France, Germany, Guatemala, Guyana, Iran, Netherlands, New Zealand, Republic of Korea, and Switzerland), the United Kingdom has remained an intransigent outlier on the question since a speech made in 2018. Wright (n 48). See also Michael Schmitt, 'The Sixth United Nations GGE and

generally traced to the advisory opinion of the Permanent Court of International Justice (PCIJ) in 1923 on *Nationality Decrees Issued in Tunis and Morocco*.[62] This decision involved a dispute between France and Great Britain about whether or not issuing nationality decrees was, under international law, solely a matter within the domestic jurisdiction of States.[63] The PCIJ maintained that the concept of matters that are 'solely within the domestic jurisdiction'—that is, a State's reserved domain—refers to those that 'are not, in principle, regulated by international law' and for which 'each State is sole judge'.[64] The Court maintained that this is a question which 'depends upon the development of international relations'.[65] Such a formulation has given rise to the understanding that the *domaine réservé* can be said to be both a 'relative' and 'dynamic' concept that adjusts itself to interpretation and practice.[66] Since that judgement of the PCIJ was handed down, given increased interdependence among States and the development and expansion of international law into many policy areas, there has been a noticeable reduction in what is considered to relate solely to the reserved domain of a State, and where international law now governs.

Various examples demonstrate how the purely domestic arena has shrunken over time: jurisdiction and treatment of the property of foreign nationals in one's own territory (regulated by bilateral investment treaties), absolute discretion on admission of foreign nationals (modified by asylum and refugee law), nationality (constrained by laws on statelessness), or even the structure of a State's political system (now arguably shaped by the principle of self-determination).[67] More generally, it can also be said that the development of international human rights law has encroached upon matters that had been previously left entirely to the *domaine réservé*. Yet there are practical explanations for this shift. There has been an objective growth in the interdependence of States, an emergence of additional actors and subjects of international law, along with the proliferation of treaties and mechanisms of enforcement. Finally, there has also been progressive regional and international integration.[68]

Historically, the concept of *domaine réservé* has not been associated as closely with the non-intervention principle as it has become within the cyber context.[69]

International Law in Cyberspace' (*Just Security*, 10 June 2021) <https://www.justsecurity.org/76864/the-sixth-united-nations-gge-and-international-law-in-cyberspace/> accessed 11 March 2023.

[62] *Nationality Decrees Issued in Tunis and Morocco*, Advisory Opinion, (7 February 1923), 1923 PCIJ Series B No. 4.

[63] Ibid. 21.

[64] Ibid. 24.

[65] Ibid.

[66] Ziegler (n 60) para. 2.

[67] Ibid. para. 5.

[68] Ibid. para. 6–26.

[69] William Ossoff, 'Hacking the Domaine Réservé: The Rule of Non-Intervention and Political Interference in Cyberspace' (2021) 62 Harvard International Law Journal 295, 298–308.

404 INSTRUMENTS, TACTICS, AND METHODS IN THE GREY ZONE

Here it has become a shorthand to refer to matters that must not be subject to coercion. While the ICJ did not use the specific term in *Nicaragua*, increasingly the phrase is used to capture what the ICJ referred to there as 'matters in which each State is permitted, by the principle of State sovereignty, to decide freely' and the examples of 'choice of a political, economic, social and cultural system, and the formulation of foreign policy' that it provided.[70] This is evident, for example, in the *Tallinn Manual* where the commentary to Rule 66 mainly focuses on the concept of *domaine réservé* and how it must be affected by coercion.[71] A number of States have also adopted a similar approach in the cyber context. For example, we have seen statements demonstrating this trend from Estonia,[72] Germany,[73] Norway,[74] Switzerland,[75] New Zealand,[76] and Canada.[77] Outside of general categories that are included within the concept of *domaine réservé*, a number of States have also specifically mentioned elections to fall within its scope.[78]

As such, while the scope of the concept of *domaine réservé* has declined with the growth and development of international law, in the cyber context it has become a shorthand to capture what the target of the coercive cyber activity must be for the activity to constitute a violation of the non-intervention principle. However, beyond the ICJ's categories and examples such as national elections that many States have provided as falling with the scope of the *domaine réservé*, there continues to be uncertainty about the concept in terms of whether it is a fixed list of sovereign functions or something that morphs when international law governs an area.[79]

In order to provide more shape to this core space for all States, we suggest looking to the concepts of *legitimacy* and *information ethics*. Each of these concepts offers an axiological view on essential parts of every society, and we believe they should inform the international law regarding *disinfo-ops*.[80]

---

[70] *Nicaragua* (n 25) para. 205.

[71] *Tallinn 2.0* (n 40) 314–16. See also Watts (n 27) 263–65.

[72] See 'Estonia', in Official Compendium (n 38) 25.

[73] The Federal Government of Germany (n 55) 5.

[74] See 'Norway', in Official Compendium (n 38) 68–69.

[75] See 'Switzerland', in Official Compendium (n 38) 87.

[76] New Zealand Foreign Affairs and Trade, 'The Application of International Law to State Activity in Cyberspace' (1 December 2020) 2 <https://dpmc.govt.nz/publications/application-international-law-state-activity-cyberspace> accessed 11 March 2023.

[77] Government of Canada, 'International Law applicable in cyberspace' (April 22, 2022) <https://www.international.gc.ca/world-monde/issues_development-enjeux_developpement/peace_security-paix_securite/cyberspace_law-cyberespace_droit.aspx?lang=eng> accessed 11 March 2023.

[78] These include Australia, Estonia, Germany, Netherlands, and Norway. See Official Compendium (n 38) 5, 25, 34, 57, 69, respectively.

[79] Watts (n 27) 264–65. For a cogent exploration of the manner in which cyberspace puts extraordinary pressure on the concept of legal jurisdiction, see Duncan Hollis, 'Re-Thinking the Boundaries of Law in Cyberspace: A Duty to Hack?)', in Ohlin et al (n 27) 129.

[80] Others have drawn on the right to self-determination. See Ohlin (n 14); Tsagourias (n 14). Our focus, however, is on developing a deeper account of the concept of *domaine réservé* in today's information societies and does not refute whether an additional violation of international law might also be an applicable rubric.

LAW OF INTERFERENCE IN THE DIGITAL AGE   405

For the law to be resilient, our contention is that it should be rooted in sound philosophical concepts that cross disciplinary boundaries (i.e. an interdisciplinary endeavour that seeks to sow richness and coherence).[81] Otherwise, legal authorizations that rest on shaky grounds can be seen as nothing more than efforts of expediency and in the end weaken the international rule-based system, or even jeopardize a State's own authority in the eyes of its citizens. Hence, this proposal represents a conscious integration of philosophy and international law in the hope of providing a stabilizing interpretation of the existing constraints for both culprits and victims of such wrongful acts. Of course, this amalgamation is certainly not novel, as the consummate scholar Martin Wight has described the four hundred years of international theory leading up to the surge of its study in the twentieth century as a partition 'between philosophically minded international lawyers and internationally minded political philosophers'.[82]

3.1.1 Legitimate authority

For any State to function, a legitimate authority must be established; this is a sine qua non for all societies. Administration officials, civil servants, and citizens must know who has the *right to command* and by consequence who holds the *duty to obey*. Without such a basic understanding, individuals cannot act in concert (i.e. move together as a unit and exert power).[83] In a democracy, free and fair elections lay in place this elemental cornerstone of conferring legitimacy upon an authority and thus represent an acutely fragile and precious interest that should be protected by the law of non-intervention. For those who have investigated legitimacy as a target in contemporary asymmetrical conflict,[84] cross-border disinformation operations using ICTs certainly appear directed at this indispensable element of the State. As a result, we argue here that distorting the facts surrounding an election can amount to a destabilizing blow to the *domaine réservé*.

---

[81] See e.g. Allen F Repko and Rick Szostak, *Interdisciplinary Research: Process and Theory* (3rd edn, SAGE 2016); Didier Wernli and Frédéric Darbellay, 'Interdisciplinarity and the 21st century University' (November 2016) <https://www.leru.org/files/Interdisciplinarity-and-the-21st-Century-Research-Intensive-University-Full-paper.pdf> accessed 11 March 2023; Robert Frodeman, Julie Thompson Klein, and Roberto Carlos Dos Santos Pacheco (eds), *The Oxford Handbook of Interdisciplinarity* (OUP 2017); Mark Juergensmeyer et al, *The Oxford Handbook of Global Studies* (OUP 2018).

[82] Martin Wight, *International Theory: The Three Traditions* (Holmes and Meier 1992) 3.

[83] See the cogent work that separates the concept of power from violence by distinguishing coerced obedience, Hannah Arendt, 'On Violence', in *Crises of the Republic* (Harcourt, Brace & World 1970) 103.

[84] Steven J. Barela, *International Law, New Diplomacy and Counterterrorism: An Interdisciplinary Study of Legitimacy* (Routledge 2014); Steven J. Barela, *Legitimacy and Drones: Investigating the Legality, Morality and Efficacy of UCAVs* (Ashgate 2015). See also the military doctrine of General David Petraeus which put forward 'Legitimacy Is the Main Objective', in US Department of Defense, Army Field Manual (FM 3-24), 'Counterinsurgency' (15 December 2006) 1–16.

406 INSTRUMENTS, TACTICS, AND METHODS IN THE GREY ZONE

The basic structure of legitimacy acting as the foundation of a functioning society was notably articulated by sociologist Max Weber in his 'Politics as a Vocation' speech:

> Like the political institutions historically preceding it, the state is a relation of men dominating men, a relation supported by means of legitimate (i.e. considered to be legitimate) violence. If the state is to exist, the dominated must obey the authority claimed by the powers that be. When and why do men obey? Upon what inner justifications and upon what external means does this domination rest?[85]

This, of course, is an expansion upon the well-known phrasing that Weber offered as a definition of the State which has come to dominate a great deal political thought: 'a human community that (successfully) claims the *monopoly of the legitimate use of physical force* within a given territory'.[86] We suggest that while there has been great attention on the point of physical force in Weber's definition, much less has been placed on the uncoerced obedience that is garnered by a legitimate authority. Democracies depend heavily upon this element of compliance without compulsion to execute their internal matters.

This is neither the place to explore the three typologies presented by Weber nor to respond to why he suggests individuals choose to obey these forms of authority.[87] It will suffice to focus here on the fact that Weber has pointed out that '[t]oday the most usual basis of legitimacy is the belief in legality, the readiness to conform with rules which are formally correct and have been imposed by accepted procedure'.[88] After advancing 'legality' as a dominant form of legitimate authority, Weber goes on to present it as rational grounds 'resting on a belief in the "legality" of patterns of normative rules and the right of those elevated to authority under such rules to issue commands'.[89] It is not only Weber who put this formal legal validity forward as an important pillar of legitimacy; it is a finding shared by many scholars of the subject.[90]

---

[85] Also known for being a philosopher, jurist, and political economist. Max Weber, 'Politics as a Vocation', in *From Max Weber: Essays on Sociology*, edited by H. H. Gerth and translated by C. Wright Mills (OUP 1946) para. 6. This speech was delivered at Munich University in January 1919, but not published until October of that year.

[86] Ibid. para. 4 (emphasis in the original).

[87] Ibid. Weber suggested there is (1) '"traditional" domination exercised by the patriarch and the patrimonial prince of yore' (para. 8); (2) 'authority of the extraordinary and personal *gift of grace* (charisma)' (para. 9); and (3) 'domination by virtue of "legality," by virtue of the belief in the validity of legal statute and functional "competence" based on rationally created *rules*' (para. 10).

[88] Max Weber, *The Theory of Social and Economic Organization* (A. M. Henderson and Talcott Parsons trs, Free Press 1947) 131.

[89] Ibid. 328.

[90] See e.g. Jürgen Habermas, *Legitimation Crisis* (Thomas McCarthy tr, Heinemann Educational Books 1976); David Beetham, *The Legitimation of Power* (Palgrave McMillian,1991); Deborah Cook, 'Legitimacy and Political Violence: A Habermasian Perspective', (2003) 30 Social Justice 108; Martha

Partly because of its inherently interdisciplinary nature, there is precious little in the literature about how to measure the augmentation, stability, or erosion of legitimacy. Developing tools for assessing, or even discussing, the effects of mucking up the process for establishing authority would be enormously valuable. Nevertheless, even though the status of legitimacy can be abstract and nebulous, there are sufficient ways to talk about and analyse this complex subject for our purposes.

For example, the Italian historian Guglielmo Ferrero's work on the *Principles of Power* from 1942 is enlightening.[91] He succinctly explained that a government is 'legitimate if the power is *conferred* and *exercised* according to principles and rules accepted without discussion by those who must *obey*'.[92] In other words, legitimacy can be examined through three key questions:

1. How is power **granted?**
2. How is it **employed?**
3. Does **obedience** flow naturally?

Irregularities in the process for bestowing command are perhaps the most obvious and should raise warning flags when foreign powers are involved in meddling within this space of internal matters.[93] Breaking and distorting information flows related to an election and candidates can compromise the entire process and its results. Regardless of whether a *disinfo-op* has a direct impact on the results of the election and can be concluded with certainty (an almost impossible standard), disruption in the habitual confidence citizens have in an anointed leader, accompanying policies or the process itself is a veritable danger.

As one straightforward example of the first two components of legitimacy laid out by Ferrero, one can look to the investigation of Robert Mueller who was named as Special Counsel for the US Department of Justice to conduct a 'full and thorough investigation of the Russian government's efforts to interfere in the 2016 presidential election'.[94] The final report is telling for our purposes, as it is divided into two volumes that reflect the concerns we aim to illuminate about the

---

Crenshaw, *Terrorism, Legitimacy, and Power: The Consequences of Political Violence* (Wesleyan University Press 1983).

[91] Guglielmo Ferrero, *The Principles of Power* (G.P. Putnam's Sons 1942).

[92] Ibid. 135 (emphasis added). For a similar framing of how to gauge and discuss legitimacy, see generally Beetham (n 90).

[93] In this context it is appropriate to reiterate the fact that the U.S. has done this precise type of internal damage to other democracies (n 29–31 and accompanying text).

[94] Rod Rosenstein, Office of the Deputy Attorney General, 'Appointment of Special Counsel to Investigate Russian Interference with the 2016 Presidential Election and Related Matters', Order No. 3915-2017 (May 17, 2017) <https://www.nytimes.com/interactive/2017/05/17/us/politics/docum ent-Robert-Mueller-Special-Counsel-Russia.html> accessed 11 March 2023.

408 INSTRUMENTS, TACTICS, AND METHODS IN THE GREY ZONE

targeting of legitimacy. That is, the subject matter of report precisely captures the first two queries put forward by Ferrero on how legitimate power is 'conferred' and 'exercised'.

The most pertinent conclusion in the first volume of the Mueller Report for our purposes is that '[t]he Russian government interfered in the 2016 presidential election in sweeping and systematic fashion'.[95] The report catalogues numerous actions carried out by Russia: 'active measures' through social media accounts on Facebook and Twitter including botnet activities, operations involving political rallies, targeting and recruiting US persons, GRU (Russian Chief Intelligence Office) hacking the Clinton Campaign, and a dissemination of the hacked materials by DCLeaks, Guccifer 2.0, and finally WikiLeaks; GRU officers' attempts to access computer networks of State and local government entities and Russian government links to and contacts with the Trump campaign. Although it took until 2019 for these details to be revealed, an intelligence services report was made public in January 2017 before President Trump took office, exposing the broadlines of the foreign meddling.[96] Put simply, and in Ferrero's terms, power was *not* bestowed 'according to principles and rules accepted without discussion'. A heated debate was provoked.

Secondly, it cannot be overlooked that interference in an electoral process can lead to concerns with how power is exercised by a newly installed government. Law enforcement and intelligence agencies would need to, and with full legal authority, examine the nature and extent to which an outside government has intruded into matters related to an election.[97] Since such investigation could erode the perceived legitimacy of an established government, there could also be great temptation for an authority to curb, short-circuit, or obstruct justice from proceeding. To wit, if an authority exercises power in such a case to protect the legitimacy gained through the electoral process, or to cover up illegality, it would be inextricably tangled with the initial cross-border operation.

The Mueller Report is once again instructive on this issue, since the entire second volume delves into how power was employed in relation to the interference. It concluded: 'Our investigation found multiple acts by the President that were capable of exerting undue influence over law enforcement investigations,

---

[95] Mueller Report Vol. I (n 4) 1.

[96] US Intelligence Community, 'Assessing Russian Activities' (n 4). See also Barela, 'Cross-Border Cyber Ops to Erode Legitimacy' (n 16).

[97] This is precisely what we saw with the Mueller inquiry: David Kris, 'Why the FBI's Investigation Into the President Was Unavoidable' (*Lawfare*, 12 January 2019) <https://www.lawfareblog.com/why-fbis-investigation-president-was-unavoidable> accessed 11 March 2023; See also Marty Lederman, 'Why It's a Mistake to Be a-Waitin' "the" Mueller Report (and Why You Should Instead Focus on Two Other Reports)' (*Just Security*, 18 March 2019) <https://www.justsecurity.org/63275/why-its-a-mistake-to-be-a-waitin-the-mueller-report-and-why-you-should-instead-focus-on-two-other-reports/> accessed 11 March 2023.

including the Russian-interference and obstruction investigations'.[98] There were eleven specific acts investigated and detailed in the report, ranging from efforts to remove the Special Counsel, redefine and limit his remit, reverse the recusal of the Attorney General, and direct and indirect contact with witnesses to influence testimony.[99] The exercise of power was clearly not accepted without discussion.

Because it was found that there were both statutory and constitutional defences for the application of obstruction-of-justice statutes,[100] a great strain was created within the government. This pressure is perhaps best exemplified in the less than clear conclusion presented in the final paragraph of the Mueller report,

> The evidence we obtained about the President's actions and intent presents difficult issues that would need to be resolved if we were making a traditional prosecutorial judgment. At the same time, if we had confidence after a thorough investigation of the facts that the President clearly did not commit obstruction of justice, we would so state. Based on the facts and the applicable legal standards, we are unable to reach that judgment. Accordingly, while this report does not conclude that the President committed a crime, it also does not exonerate him.[101]

It is our view that this difficult-to-decipher conclusion actually provides clarity for our purposes. We suggest that this vividly illuminates the tension created by a *disinfo-op* into a democracy with a constitutional separation of powers.[102] Such an operation creates a nearly unresolvable stress on a strictly internal matter.

As for the third question regarding the natural flow of obedience, this is an element that can only be assessed over time and would be an indication that doubts are harboured about the legitimacy of an authority. There are a host of forms that relevant noncompliance can take (e.g. cabinet ministers or military resignations, mass demonstrations, strikes, or mass civil disobedience).[103] As a

---

[98] Robert S. Mueller, 'Report on the Investigation into Russian Interference in the 2016 Presidential Election (Volume 2)' (US Department of Justice, March 2019) 157.

[99] Ibid.

[100] Ibid. 159–81.

[101] Ibid. 182.

[102] Ibid. 171–77.

[103] See generally Beetham (n 90) 117–60. One particularly dramatic instance has been explored and detailed by the historian Ferrero (n 91). He notes that while there is a seeming impossibility that the refusal to obey a government would become widespread, the events of the French Revolution offer a window onto such an episode: 'On July 14, 1789, the Bastille was stormed and taken in a tremendous rising of the people, under circumstances familiar to everyone. It is less familiar that this victorious uprising was followed, for the first time in history, by the event which we held, not without reason, to be impossible: All over France, for six weeks, as soon as the news from Paris was heard, all the people—peasants, workers, lower middle classes, officials, upper-classes—as at a signal after secret agreement, refused to obey'. Ferrero (n 91) 82–83.

result, one gauge to measure if this pull has been diminished is to watch for unauthorized acts that flout the will of the leader. Such an occurrence would represent an erosion of legitimacy that creates a precariousness and volatility and could even deeply threaten a State's internal stability. Nevertheless, even without a dramatic collapse, a persistent deficit of obedience would upset the functioning of government and endanger its ability to act quickly and decisively. In normal times, this would be frustrating. But at moments of crisis, an inert government is a dangerous hamstring—something that could be seen as an advantage for a foreign adversary.

Again, the circumstances of the victorious president in the US 2016 election are edifying. For instance, the Trump administration never fully filled all positions of government and experienced unprecedented turnover—92 per cent at the end of his term.[104] Journalists also covered a relentless torrent of leaks during his time in office which would indicate a weakened pull towards compliance with the president's authority.[105] Furthermore, credible reporting spotlighted the much more severe issues of disobedience and defiance, such as Gen. Mattis's avoidance of an order to kill Syrian President Bashar al-Assad after a chemical attack on civilians in April 2017[106] and removal of documents to be signed from the president's desk.[107] Even if the public would become rather numb to reporting on such actions, they were described by one commentator as a 'soft coup' in 2018 well before the events of 6 January 2021.[108] Moreover, it was described in a notorious op-ed from inside the Trump executive branch, 'officials in his own administration are working diligently from within to frustrate parts of his agenda and his worst inclinations'.[109] Such a persistent deficit in obedience upsets the functioning of government and endangers its ability to act quickly and decisively.

Specialists of legitimacy also point out that it is a mistake to think about the concept in binary terms. There will always be different levels of agreement and conformity throughout the life of any government. We must use a discerning eye

---

[104] Kathryn Dunn Tenpas, 'Turnover on the President's "A Team"', (Brookings Institute, January 2021) <https://www.brookings.edu/research/tracking-turnover-in-the-trump-administration/> accessed 11 March 2023. See also 'Tracking How Many Key Positions Trump Has Filled So Far', *Washington Post* <https://www.washingtonpost.com/graphics/politics/trump-administration-appointee-tracker/database/> accessed 11 March 2023.

[105] See e.g. Johnathan Swan, 'White House Leakers Leak about Leaking', *Axios* (13 May 2018); for insider account of dysfunction and duplicity see also Cliff Sims, *Team of Vipers: My 500 Extraordinary Days in the Trump White House* (Thomas Dunne Books 2019).

[106] Bob Woodward, *Fear: Trump in the White House* (Simon & Schuster 2018) 146–49.

[107] Ibid. 17–19, 23, 158, 265.

[108] David A Graham, 'We're Watching an Antidemocratic Coup Unfold' *The Atlantic* (Washington, DC, 5 September 2018) <https://www.theatlantic.com/politics/archive/2018/09/trump-mattis-kelly-new-york-times/569416/> accessed 11 March 2023.

[109] Op-ed by Anonymous, 'I Am Part of the Resistance Inside the Trump Administration', *New York Times* (New York, 5 September 2018).

LAW OF INTERFERENCE IN THE DIGITAL AGE   411

and qualified pronouncements when speaking about legitimacy. As it has been explained by one scholar, 'Legitimacy may be eroded, contested or incomplete; and judgements about it are usually judgements of degree, rather than all-or-nothing.'[110] Hence it would be incorrect to declare that this dynamic has been disrupted only when there is a clear collapse of legitimacy, or a complete breakdown of the internal order. Erosion of confidence in the process can result in differing degrees of a 'legitimacy deficit', or 'delegitimation'.[111] Regardless of the level of dysfunction sown, the delicate and vital dynamic of legitimacy is clearly a matter of internal concern.

There is, of course, a great deal of work to be done on exploring the legal significance of foreign powers working with internal forces to erode the legitimacy of a governing system.[112] Moreover, the 'Big Lie' about a stolen election in 2020 that was followed by a failed insurrection and continued efforts to promote this false narrative opens a great deal of terrain for future research.[113] It is within this context that we contend that taking aim at the legitimacy of elevating an authority presents potentially grave consequences and must be taken into consideration for the law of non-intervention. In the simplest terms, it is our contention that the sine qua non for all societies of a legitimate authority should be interpreted as part of the *domaine réservé*.

3.1.2 Information ethics

For the study of *disinfo-ops*, we also believe attention should be placed on integrating 'information ethics' with international law. To do so, we will explore the notion that damaging or distorting data within the 'infosphere' related to an election and candidates can represent a part of the *domaine réservé*, since

---

[110] Beetham (n 90) 20.

[111] Ibid. 209. Of course, recognition and respect from other States can have an impact on how citizens see their own government.

[112] The investigation of coordination or 'collusion' by Special Counsel Mueller was important on this point, especially when considering the difficulty of arriving at a dispositive legal criminal conclusion, Mueller Report Vol. I (n 4). Nevertheless, it is relevant that just after the disrupted US election in 2016, actions were authorized against Russia by President Obama. The statement released illuminates our point: 'Russia's cyber activities were intended to influence the election, *erode faith* in U.S. democratic institutions, *sow doubt* about the integrity of our electoral process, and *undermine confidence* in the institutions of the U.S. government'. Beyond affecting the outcome, our italicized portions indicate that the Obama administration concluded that this foreign actor wished to target the legal procedure for how a democracy confers power. See The White House, Office of the Press Secretary, 'FACT SHEET: Actions in Response to Russian Malicious Cyber Activity and Harassment' (29 December 2016) <https://obamawhitehouse.archives.gov/the-press-office/2016/12/29/fact-sheet-actions-response-russian-malicious-cyber-activity-and> accessed 11 March 2023. In the 2020 election, intelligence reporting concluded: 'A key element of Moscow's strategy this election cycle was its use of proxies linked to Russian intelligence to push influence narratives [. . .] including some close to former President Trump and his administration'. See, National Intelligence Council, 'Foreign Threats to the 2020 US Federal Elections' (n 4) i.

[113] Until a final report is issued, see Select Committee to Investigate the January 6th Attack on the United States Capitol, <https://january6th.house.gov/> accessed 11 March 2023.

412 INSTRUMENTS, TACTICS, AND METHODS IN THE GREY ZONE

democracies are built on the assumption that citizens can access truthful reports and make an informed decision to elevate someone to authority or meaningfully participate in determining what is best for the society.

At the very same time, it is essential to understand that we are not arguing that such action amounts to 'material damage'. To do so would open the door to the possibility that such an unlawful act crosses the threshold into the use of force. While some have argued that deleting data or otherwise rendering it useless should be interpreted as such, our argument here should not be misattributed to the same category. The purposeful and widespread distortions related to an election or candidates referred to here are suggested to be an act that occurs below the threshold of force and relates specifically to the inviolable space unique to the State itself.[114]

For this discussion, we begin with Luciano Floridi.[115] His 'information ethics' is best described as a form of environmental ethics that extends its ethical concern beyond the physical environment to also digital environments and entities which collectively constitute the 'infosphere'. It adopts an informational ontology as a minimum common denominator so that all entities can be viewed from a similar perspective in terms of their information structures and hence as 'information entities'.[116] This means that 'not only all persons, their cultivation, wellbeing, and social interactions, not only animals, plants, and their proper natural life, but also anything that exists, from paintings and books to stars and stones' can be viewed as information entities that collectively constitute the infosphere.[117] Further, information ethics adopts the view that everything, by virtue of its existence, should have a basic degree of moral value. This is the principle of ontological equality.[118]

---

[114] However, on how this theoretical perspective can be used to view the harm in non-material cyberattacks as a form of violence that should be considered within the use of force framework, see Samuli Haataja, *Cyber Attacks and International Law on the Use of Force: the Turn to Information Ethics* (Routledge 2019).

[115] See Luciano Floridi, 'Information Ethics: On the Philosophical Foundation of Computer Ethics' (1999) 1 Ethics and Information Technology 33; Luciano Floridi, *The Ethics of Information* (OUP 2013). On information ethics and cyber warfare, see Mariarosaria Taddeo, 'Information Warfare: A Philosophical Perspective' (2012) 25 Philosophy and Technology 105; Mariarosaria Taddeo, 'Just Information Warfare' (2016) 35 Topoi 213; Ugo Pagallo, 'Cyber Force and the Role of Sovereign States in Informational Warfare' (2015) 28 Philosophy and Technology 407; Massimo Durante, 'Violence, Just Cyber War and Information' (2015) 28 Philosophy and Technology 369. See also Massimo Durante, 'Re-designing the Role of Law in the Information Society: Mediating between the Real and the Virtual' (2010) 2(3) European Journal of Legal Studies 19; Massimo Durante, 'Dealing with Legal Conflicts in the Information Society. An Informational Understanding of Balancing Competing Interests' (2013) 26 Philosophy and Technology 437; Ugo Pagallo, 'The Realignment of the Sources of the Law and their Meaning in an Information Society' (2015) 28 Philosophy and Technology 57.

[116] Luciano Floridi, 'Information Ethics, its Nature and Scope' (2006) 36(3) Computers and Society 21, 33.

[117] Luciano Floridi, *Information: A Very Short Introduction* (OUP 2010) 113.

[118] Floridi, 'Information Ethics' (n 115) 44.

LAW OF INTERFERENCE IN THE DIGITAL AGE   413

As a result of the ontological equality principle, every information entity, 'simply for the fact of being what it is, enjoys a minimal, initial, overridable, equal right to exist and develop in a way which is appropriate to its nature'.[119] In this context, being or existence is seen as inherently good whereas entropy is regarded as evil. Floridi adopts a very particular definition of entropy that is different to the use of the term in thermodynamics, for example. In his use of the term, it essentially refers to any degradation of being, such as the destruction or corruption of information entities.[120]

To guide the behaviour of responsible and caring agents within the infosphere, information ethics provides basic rules that aim to respect and promote the well-being of the entire infosphere.[121] Information ethics therefore provides an environmental approach to thinking about what is good for the infosphere and offers an approach that advocates respect for both the material and non-material world.[122]

Elsewhere, one of the authors of this chapter (Haataja) draws on information ethics and Floridi's work to conceptualize the State in informational terms as an information system, and the harm that cyber operations can cause to States in terms of entropy.[123] We draw on this here, but focus on how thinking about the State in terms of its information structures can help better understand the impact that *disinfo-ops*, as inherently informational operations, can have on the proper internal operation of States with democratic systems of government in particular.

When viewed as an information entity on a conceptual level, the State can be seen as a non-static and continuously changing entity. Vast amounts of data are communicated, stored, and processed by this entity given the nature and extent of global information infrastructures and information flows which enable everything from internet and other communications to global finance flows in and out of States globally.[124] Similarly, within society, more and more individuals use ICTs and an increasing number of devices are embedded with ICTs.[125] Consequently,

---

[119] Floridi, *Information* (n 117) 113.

[120] Floridi, *Ethics of Information* (n 115) 67.

[121] Ibid. 71. These rules are: (0) entropy ought not to be caused in the infosphere (null law); (1) entropy ought to be prevented in the infosphere; (2) entropy ought to be removed from the infosphere; and (3) the flourishing of informational entities as well as of the whole infosphere ought to be promoted by preserving, cultivating and enriching their well-being.

[122] Luciano Floridi, 'Information Ethics: An Environmental Approach to the Digital Divide' (2002) 9 Philosophy in the Contemporary World 39, 42.

[123] Haataja (n 114). See also Samuli Haataja, 'The 2007 Cyber Attacks against Estonia and International Law on the Use of Force: An Informational Approach' (2017) 9 Law, Innovation and Technology 159; Samuli Haataja and Afshin Akhtar-Khavari, 'Stuxnet and International Law on the Use of Force: An Informational Approach' (2018) 7 Cambridge International Law Journal 99.

[124] See also Fleur Johns, 'Data Territories: Changing Architectures of Association in International Law' (2016) 47 Netherlands Yearbook of International Law 107.

[125] For statistics on the trajectory of the number of smart devices and users of those devices globally, see CISCO, 'Cisco Annual Internet Report (2018–2023) White Paper' <https://www.cisco.com/

414 INSTRUMENTS, TACTICS, AND METHODS IN THE GREY ZONE

the informational substance of the State as a dynamic or non-static entity continuously changes; however, its form or pattern as an information entity persists.

The pattern of this entity is evident in its systematic features. Like a 'multiagent system' constituted by its components, the State is an information system capable of interaction, it has a degree of autonomy, it is adaptable, and it has an inherent purpose towards which it gears its functions.[126] It is situated not only in the physical world (within its territory), but also in the virtual world of cyberspace in which it increasingly interacts with other entities. As a result, it has both physical and virtual properties—a presence within its territorial boundaries and a virtual presence that transcends territory. This is illustrated, for example, by the idea that State sovereignty is considered not only to extend to the jurisdiction over the physical ICT infrastructure within its territory but also to the conduct of States' 'ICT-related activities'[127] in cyberspace where they can engage and interact with other entities.

The form or pattern of the State in turn is evident in its structural configuration. The State's informational structures—the organisational structures of its institutions, typically seen in the structural separation of powers between legislative, executive, and judicial institutions—configure its structure as an entity. These structures are 'bound together by a system of communication',[128] both internally within and between these structures, and externally between its institutions and those of other State entities.[129] The exact configuration of these

---

c/en/us/solutions/collateral/executive-perspectives/annual-internet-report/white-paper-c11-741490.html> accessed 11 March 2023.

[126] These features are based on Floridi's description of the state as a multiagent system or 'MAS'. He maintains that it is teleological, interactive, autonomous, and adaptable. Luciano Floridi, *The Fourth Revolution* (OUP 2014) 180–81. Alexander Wendt, in considering states as persons, discusses their similarity to organisms. Many of these features are similar to those attributed to states as 'multiagent systems' by Floridi. Wendt maintains that much like organisms: (1) states are individual as they each have a 'distinct system with its own history'; (2) states are organised; (3) states are homeostatic as they actively resist their own degradation (which is achieved through a spatial and political closure of the boundary between the domestic and international realms, and the internal structure of the state 'that channels the behaviour of their members toward the goal of state survival'); (4) states are autonomous as 'their behaviour is determined partly independent of their environment'; (5) however, unlike organisms they are incapable of reproduction. Alexander Wendt, 'The State as Person in International Theory' (2004) 30 Review of International Studies 289, 307–09.

[127] UN Group of Governmental Experts on Developments in the Field of Information and Telecommunications in the Context of International Security (n 35) 8.

[128] Norbert Wiener, *Cybernetics: or Control and Communication in the Animal and the Machine* (Technology Press 1948) 33, cited in Terrell Ward Bynum, 'Norbert Wiener and the Rise of Information Ethics', in *Information Technology and Moral Philosophy*, edited by Jeroen Van Den Hoven and John Weckert (CUP 2008) 12.

[129] Similarly, Anne-Marie Slaughter, for example, argues that states have become 'disaggregated' into networks of actors, making up what she describes as a 'world of governments, with all the different institutions that perform the basic functions of governments—legislation, adjudication, implementation—interacting both with each other domestically and also with their foreign and *supra*national counterparts'. Anne-Marie Slaughter, *A New World Order* (Princeton University Press 2005) 5.

LAW OF INTERFERENCE IN THE DIGITAL AGE   415

structures may change among States (i.e. the core configuration of power within the State, such as the degree or extent to which legislative, executive, and judicial powers are separated). The structural configuration may also change over time (transforming States from constitutional monarchies to independent republics, for example), and they can be embedded with different value systems (from secular liberal democracies to religious autocracies). However, the basic structure of these entities (i.e. their form or pattern) persists, despite continuous changes to their informational substance.[130]

Viewed as an information entity, the State is a complex information system: a dynamic entity constituted by various sub-systems and configured by the protocols under which it operates. With increasing amounts of information flowing in and out of it, and more and more entities becoming connected to the infosphere, the State becomes increasingly complex over time. The primary purpose of this entity is to care for and protect the well-being of its region of the infosphere.[131]

Against this conceptual account of the State, the democratic election process can now be considered to better appreciate how *disinfo-ops* can be used to undermine this process and interfere with matters within a State's *domaine réservé*. As mentioned, democracies are based on the assumption that citizens can make an informed decision to elevate someone to a position of authority, and elections are an integral aspect of this process. This process involves a range of entities and interactions operating within the informational environment related to the elections in question. In this process, individuals eligible to vote are able to input their vote into the voting system, a system which in itself involves various entities and processes operating in a particular way. For example, in the United States, the 2002 Help America Vote Act defines a 'voting system' as 'the total combination of mechanical, electromechanical, or electronic equipment (including the software, firmware, and documentation required to program, control, and support the equipment)' used to define ballots, cast and count votes, report or display election results, and maintain and produce an audit trail.[132] Here the voting system is a combination of mechanical and digital, human and artificial processes that operate as part of the broader election process within a democratic system of government. Democratic States rely on these systems and processes to operate properly and confer legitimacy.

---

[130] Bynum, writing about Norbert Wiener's 'cybernetic account of human nature', maintains that for Wiener, 'a person consists of a complex pattern of information embodied in matter and energy. Although the *substance* changes, the *form* must persist if the person is to flourish or even exist. Thus, a human being is an "information object", a dynamic form, or pattern persisting in an ever-changing flow of matter and energy'. Bynum (n 128) 12 (emphasis in original).

[131] The notion of an entity's 'region of the infosphere' is drawn from Floridi's informational analysis of business. See Floridi, *Ethics of Information* (n 115) 289–90.

[132] Help America Vote Act of 2002, 42 USC 15481 § 301 (2002).

416 INSTRUMENTS, TACTICS, AND METHODS IN THE GREY ZONE

While there are multiple vectors through which the proper functioning of the election process can be compromised,[133] *disinfo-ops* target a particular aspect of this process. When deciding how to vote, normally individuals make this decision based on information available within the infosphere. Most democratic systems of government are premised to some degree on a right of freedom of speech—the ability of the members of the polity to freely communicate their views and interpretations of information with others. Similarly, where information is introduced into this ecosystem (whether through advertising or the media) there are laws in place regulating the content and delivery of this information. Therefore, normally the information flows among these entities (whether individuals or public- and private-sector organizations) are regulated to promote a healthy informational environment and foster the ability of individuals to make informed decisions when they vote.

Disinfo-ops, however, involve the intentional introduction of a form of pollution into this environment that is aimed at undermining the decision-making process of individual voters. As will be seen in the following section, these hostile information flows can be targeted directly at individuals based on their values and preferences using social media data and algorithms. They can also involve doxing—the widespread release of real of stolen documents—such as the leaking of private emails that seek to undermine the election campaign of a specific candidate. While this form of dissemination of information can occur normally through, for example, the media (whether domestic or foreign), it becomes particularly problematic where the true source of the information is 'spoofed' to give the appearance it is coming from a seemingly legitimate source, such as a real individual expressing their views online.[134] This deliberately hinders the ability of individuals to evaluate the source of the information and undermines their properly informed decision-making process. Consequently, even if it can be questionable whether such acts do 'material damage', it is much less uncertain that this is taking place within the *domaine réservé* of a State.

3.2 Coercion: incorporating empirical content

Although it is not a language that is repeated in *Tallinn 2.0*, the first manual released in 2013 zeroed in on the specific issue of election interference, 'the

---

[133] For example, Russia's actions during the US election involved spear-phishing, a form of cognitive hacking aimed at obtaining human user credentials in order to obtain access to data in computer systems and networks, and this information was then released at strategic points in time into the public domain in order to influence the views (and ultimately decision-making process) of voters.

[134] Schmitt also notes that the messaging activities by Russian trolls which involved the impersonation of Americans sought to convey a message to the US electorate in a way that made it appear it was coming from Americans (opposed to Russians). He concludes that 'this manipulation of voters' ability to assess the messages in coming to their own decision tipped the scales and therefore constituted unlawful interference'. See Schmitt, '"Virtual" Disenfranchisement' (n 14) 46–47.

LAW OF INTERFERENCE IN THE DIGITAL AGE 417

decisive test remains coercion. Thus, it is clear that not every form of political or economic interference violates the non-intervention principle'.[135] Even so, some examples of electoral coercion are identified by the team of experts: 'Cases in point are the manipulation by cyber means of elections or of public opinion on the eve of elections, as when online news services are altered in favour of a particular party, *false news* is spread, or the online services of one party are shut off'.[136] Thus, even before 'fake news' became a common political refrain and tool, it was already seen as a threat that could rise to the level of coercion.

Yet to initiate this part of the discussion, it is useful to underscore the fact that 'international law provides no conclusive definition of the term'.[137] Conventionally understood, it can be taken as a form of compelling another actor to do our will.[138] We recognize this definition as the standard approach and it is reasonably understood in this manner within the *lex lata*. At the same time, we believe that there is room—and in the context of legal resilience under new circumstances, a pressing need—to interpret the term progressively.[139] One jurist who has lucidly explained the problem that arises with this particular idiom is Tom Farer:

[135] *Tallinn 1.0* (n 39) 45.
[136] Ibid. (emphasis added).
[137] Schmitt, ' "Virtual" Disenfranchisement' (n 14) 49. Elsewhere Schmitt presented the Russian strategy as intentionally working within grey zones of the law and labelled it 'asymmetrical lawfare'. He also expressed his opinion on our question of coercion in the 2016 U.S. election: 'The opposing, and slightly sounder, view is that the cyber operations manipulated the process of elections and therefore caused them to unfold in a way that they otherwise would not have. In this sense, they were coercive'. Michael Schmitt, 'Grey Zones in the International Law of Cyberspace' (2017) 42 Yale Journal of International Law Online 1, 8. Others have also expounded upon 'coercion' in this context. For instance, Jens Ohlin argues that a distinction should be made since the incident was 'corrosive to the proper functioning of a democracy . . . [yet] it is unclear whether it should count as coercive'. Ohlin (n 14) 1592. Duncan Hollis suggests the incident is problematized by 'the absence of coercion'. He proposed that though the 'timed dumps' of information through Wikileaks may have involved coercion, he notes how in this context 'it is not clear what the threatened consequences were, let alone who its targets were'. Similarly, in relation to Russia's activities through social media, he argues that these 'efforts are even harder to label as coercion since, at best, all they did was impact people's opinions, which may or may not have impacted some number of subsequent votes'. See Duncan B Hollis, 'The Influence of War: the War for Influence' (2018) 32 Temple International and Comparative Law Journal 31, 40–41. Ido Kilovaty claims that the incident did not involve a form of coercion captured by existing interpretations. Though he does suggest that when such doxing 'significantly disrupts' internal matters that are at the sole discretion of that State, 'this disruption should serve as a sufficient substitute for coercion'. See Ido Kilovaty, 'Doxfare: Politically Motivated Leaks and the Future of the Norm on Non-Intervention in the Era of Weaponized Information' (2018) 9 Harvard National Security Journal 146, 169–172.
[138] For more elaborate formulations, see the Declaration on Friendly Relations (n 23): 'No State may use or encourage the use of economic political or any other type of measures to coerce another State in order to obtain from it the subordination of the exercise of its sovereign rights and to secure from it advantages of any kind'; and *Tallinn 2.0*: 'an affirmative act designed to deprive another State of its freedom of choice, that is, to force that State to act in an involuntary manner or involuntarily refrain from acting in a particular way'. *Tallinn 2.0* (n 40) 317.
[139] For one expression of the need to keep eyes open to a novel situation, see Rosalyn Higgins, 'Intervention and International Law', in *Themes and Theories*, edited by Rosalyn Higgins (OUP 2009) 272 ('Rules are really only the accumulated body of past decisions, which, while an essential starting point, tell us little about variables and still less about changing circumstances').

418   INSTRUMENTS, TACTICS, AND METHODS IN THE GREY ZONE

> The nub of the matter is that the word 'coercion' has no normative signifi-
> cance; there is nothing illegal about coercion. Coercion is normal in all human
> relationships, including those between lovers. It's part of life. So is cooperation.
> Indeed, every human relationship is some mixture of coercion and coopera-
> tion. So to say that a particular relationship is coercive is to say nothing at all
> about its legitimacy.[140]

As a result of this ambiguity, our suggestion is to infuse the term of coercion
with empirical content to provide a standard of measurability to a norm that
can act as gatekeeper for the authorization of self-help. In other words, while
our primary aim in the preceding passages was to add axiological substance
to the understanding of the *domaine réservé*, here our goal is to continue with
sound interdisciplinarity and affix the term of 'coercion' with an empirical
meaning that is open to testing and verifiability. As we are only beginning to
fully grasp the changes brought to our societies with the wide introduction of
ICTs, it is necessary to gather and collate empirical data to shine a light on the
scope and accuracy of today's operations. At the very same time, it is necessary
to be attentive to the fact that broadening the definition of this term could open
the door to unmerited or arbitrary actions in a self-administered international
system.

To pave the legal path for this proposal we turn to Sean Watts, who in 2015
explored the challenges of low-intensity cyber operations[141] and drew attention to the pre-cyber work by McDougal and Feliciano proposing that coercion
should be determined by 'consequentiality'.[142] To translate this model to today's
world of ICTs, Watts suggested that 'McDougal and Feliciano's dimensions of coercion might consider the *nature of State interests* affected by a cyber operation,
the *scale* of effects the operation produces in the target State, and the *reach* in
terms of number of actors involuntarily affected by the cyber operation in question'.[143] In this formulation, coercion is understood as more than simply forcing
a desired outcome from another State. The significance of the interests that have
been targeted is relevant, along with the expanse of the operation—both in scale
and reach.

---

[140] Tom Farer, 'Political and Economic Coercion in Contemporary International Law' (1985) 79
American Journal of International Law 405, 406.

[141] Watts (n 27.

[142] Myres McDougal and Florentino Feliciano, 'International Coercion and World Public
Order: The General Principles of the Law of War' (1958) 67 Yale Law Journal 771, 782–83. For further
discussions beyond Watts on developing this opening in the cyber context, see Barela, 'Cross-Border
Cyber Ops to Erode Legitimacy' (n 16) and Kilovaty (n 137). Kilovaty suggested that 'doxfare' should
be interpreted as coercive when it causes 'disruption', yet this criterion lacks verifiable constraints that
can help avoid abuse.

[143] Watts (n 27) 257 (emphasis added).

LAW OF INTERFERENCE IN THE DIGITAL AGE   419

It is also the case that a minority of the *Tallinn Manual* authors, in fact, argued that 'it is impossible to prejudge whether an act constitutes intervention without knowing its specific *context and consequences*'.[144] Instead, these authors adopted the view that we must know and use these parameters to determine if 'a particular act that would not normally qualify as coercive could raise it to that level'.[145] Consistent with this view, we argue that a more holistic approach is necessary when it comes to influence operations targeting an electorate in cyberspace.

Specifically, it is our view that consideration should be given to the *breadth*, *depth*, and *precision* of a cyber operation to determine whether it should rise to the level of coerciveness necessary to constitute a violation of the non-intervention principle. However, what has become disturbingly obvious is that there is an essential lack of empirical knowledge when it comes to online influence operations; we are not able to measure their scale, reach, and accuracy in targeting.[146] As a result, we aim to highlight the problem and the need for concentrated empirical study that can help guide our interpretations of the law in these changed circumstances.

There has been little stopping the large-scale creation of false profiles on social media platforms that can interact under the cover of anonymity. This means that it is relatively easy to launch a legion of forged actors (i.e. bots and trolls) to execute an expansive influence operation in cyberspace. Moreover, the massive collection and analysis of personal data and an ability to tailor and micro-target messaging has created a capacity for communication never known before.[147] Of great import, the precise degree to which this is happening has been impossible to quantify because social media companies have been unwilling to grant independent access to outsiders to protect trade secrets and the privacy of users.[148] Researchers have built creative methods for data collection such as employing the time-consuming process of scraping data using application programming interfaces (APIs) created by the social media companies; despite valuable

---

[144] *Tallinn 2.0* (n 40) 319 (our italics).

[145] Ibid.

[146] See e.g. Irene V Pasquetto et al, 'Tackling Misinformation: What Researchers Could Do with Social Media Data' (2020) 1 Harvard Kennedy School Misinformation Review 1.

[147] See generally Barela and Duberry (n 3).

[148] Joshua Tucker et al, 'Social Media, Political Polarization, and Political Disinformation: A Review of the Scientific Literature' (Hewlett Foundation, March 2018) <https://www.hewlett.org/wp-content/uploads/2018/03/Social-Media-Political-Polarization-and-Political-Disinformation-Literature-Review.pdf> accessed 11 March 2023. Furthermore, tech companies in the United States are also not responsible for content posted by users (Communications Decency Act, 47 U.S.C. § 230(c)(1): 'No provider or user of an interactive computer service shall be treated as the publisher or speaker of any information provided by another information content provider'.).

420 INSTRUMENTS, TACTICS, AND METHODS IN THE GREY ZONE

outcomes shining a light on tech companies' false public claims, the data can be expunged leaving no way to duplicate results.[149]

The Cambridge Analytica debacle raised important questions on this front, as a research data scientist was found to have harvested the personal data from up to 87 million Facebook profiles.[150] What is more, the leak of tens of thousands of internal Facebook documents has shown that the company collects, retains, and studies their own massive troves of data—and that the findings have exhibited negative impacts on societies.[151] As a result of this monopoly, Facebook and other social media companies currently decide unilaterally what can be investigated about their companies and if/how they are being used by foreign actors.

Fundamentally, we do not have amassed numbers on the extent to which foreign campaigns have been operating on social media platforms because tech companies have refused access to outside researchers. The dim result for both scientific study and threat assessment is best captured in the US Senate Select Committee on Intelligence (SSCI) report in 2019:

> While the Committee findings describe a substantial amount of Russian activity on social media platforms, the full scope of this activity remains unknown to the Committee, the social media companies, and the broader U.S. Government.[152]

Pressure has been gathering over the previous years to address this problem as the number of government actors, civil society organizations, and researchers

---

[149] See e.g. Craig Timberg, 'Russian Propaganda May Have Been Shared Hundreds of Millions of Times, New Research Says', *Washington Post* (Washington, DC, 5 October 2017) <https://www.washingtonpost.com/business/technology/2017/10/30/4509587e-bd84-11e7-97d9-bdab5a0ab381_story.html> accessed 11 March 2023; Craig Timberg and Elizabeth Dwoskin, 'Facebook Takes Down Data and Thousands of Posts, Obscuring Reach of Russian Disinformation', *Washington Post* (Washington, DC, 12 October 2017) <https://www.washingtonpost.com/news/the-switch/wp/2017/10/12/facebook-takes-down-data-and-thousands-of-posts-obscuring-reach-of-russian-disinformation/> accessed 11 March 2023. For detailed social science analysis see Jonathan Albright <https://medium.com/@d1gi> accessed 11 March 2023. See also Jeff Horwitz, 'Facebook Seeks Shutdown of NYU Research Project into Political Ad Targeting' *Wall Street Journal* (New York, 23 October 2020) <https://www.wsj.com/articles/facebook-seeks-shutdown-of-nyu-research-project-into-political-ad-targeting-11603488533> accessed 11 March 2023.
[150] Carole Cadwalladr, 'The Cambridge Analytica Files: "I Made Steve Bannon's Psychological Warfare Tool": Meet the Data War Whistleblower' *The Guardian* (London, 18 March 2018) <https://www.theguardian.com/news/2018/mar/17/data-war-whistleblower-christopher-wylie-faceook-nix-bannon-trump> accessed 11 March 2023; Matthew Rosenberg, Nicholas Confessore, and Carole Cadwalladr, 'How Trump Consultants Exploited the Facebook Data of Millions', *New York Times* (New York, 17 March 2018) <https://www.nytimes.com/2018/03/17/us/politics/cambridge-analytica-trump-campaign.html> accessed 11 March 2023.
[151] Jeff Horwitz, 'The Facebook Files' *Wall Street Journal* (New York, October 1, 2021) <https://www.wsj.com/articles/the-facebook-files-11631713039> accessed 11 March 2023.
[152] US Senate Select Committee on Intelligence, 'Volume 2: Russia's Use of Social Media with Additional Views' (n 59) 4 (emphasis added).

LAW OF INTERFERENCE IN THE DIGITAL AGE   421

clamouring for access has been rising.[153] This pressure has brought important changes and we can expect steadily increasing access and research in the coming years.

As a starting place, Twitter began releasing datasets in 2018 that it determined to be foreign or domestic State-backed entities aiming to influence elections and other civic conversations.[154] That same year, a project was launched by *Social Science One*—incubated at Harvard's Institute for Quantitative Social Science— built on an agreement with Facebook allowing researchers to access one petabyte (one million gigabytes) of data to study 'the effects of social media on democracy and elections'.[155] After many delays and pressure, the first Facebook datasets were finally delivered in 2020.[156] However, the company admitted in 2021 to handing over incomplete datasets with roughly half of US Facebook users excluded,[157] and experts have expressed serious concerns about the propriety of the project: 'My opinion is that Facebook is working with researchers mainly to gain positive news coverage'.[158]

Nevertheless, landmark change is arriving. The European Parliament adopted the Digital Services Act (DSA), and the final text was approved by the Council of the European Union (EU) in October 2022.[159] This act overhauls EU law

[153] See e.g. US Senate Select Committee on Intelligence, 'New Reports Shed Light on Internet Research Agency's Social Media Tactics' (17 December 2018) <https://www.intelligence.senate. gov/press/new-reports-shed-light-internet-research-agency%E2%80%99s-social-media-tactics> accessed 11 March 2023. See also a group of nearly fifty academics contributing to a paper detailing the gains that could be made with such data, Pasquetto et al (n 146); Mathias Vermeulen, 'The Keys to the Kingdom: Overcoming GDPR Concerns to Unlock Access to Platform Data for Independent Researchers' Data and Democracy, A Knight First Amendment Institute and Law and Political Economy Project (July 2021) <https://knightcolumbia.org/content/the-keys-to-the-kingdom> accessed 11 March 2023; CyberPeace Institute, 'Playing with Lives: Cyberattacks on Healthcare Are Attacks on People' (2021) <https://cyberpeaceinstitute.org/report/teaser/index.html> accessed 11 March 2023.

[154] See Twitter, Information Operations <https://transparency.twitter.com/en/reports/informat ion-operations.html> accessed 11 March 2023.

[155] See Social Science One: Building Industry-Academic Partnerships <https://socialscience.one/> accessed 11 March 2023.

[156] Social Science One, Co-Chairs and European Advisory Committee, 'Public Statement' (11 December 2019) <https://socialscience.one/blog/public-statement-european-advisory-committee- social-science-one> accessed 11 March 2023; Social Science One, 'Unprecedented Facebook URLs Dataset now Available for Academic Research through Social Science One' (13 February 2020) <https://socialscience.one/blog/unprecedented-facebook-urls-dataset-now-available-research-thro ugh-social-science-one> accessed 11 March 2023.

[157] Craig Timberg, 'Facebook Made Big Mistake in Data It Provided to Researchers, Undermining Academic Work', *Washington Post* (Washington, DC, 10 September 2021) <https://www.washing tonpost.com/technology/2021/09/10/facebook-error-data-social-scientists/> accessed 11 March 2023.

[158] Simon Hegelich, 'Facebook Needs to Share More with Researchers' *Nature* 579 (24 March 2020) <https://www.nature.com/articles/d41586-020-00828-5> accessed 11 March 2023.

[159] Regulation (EU) 2022/2065 of the European Parliament and of the Council of 19 October 2022 on a Single Market For Digital Services and amending Directive 2000/31/EC (Digital Services Act) [2022] OJ L 277/1.

regarding digital service providers' legal responsibility for the content their users post and obligations for content moderation. This major set of regulations has many facets to make powerful tech platforms accountable and more transparent, and could affect users all over the world as it enters into force.[160] As a starting point for our purposes, the legislation requires transparency measures for the algorithms that construct the core architecture facilitating the amplification and spreading of harmful disinformation. This provision will offer a view behind the curtain for the first time.

Most pertinently, the DSA provides a framework for compelling data access.[161] Article 40 of the DSA forces 'very large online platforms or very large online search engines' (those with at least forty-five million active monthly users in the EU, including Facebook, Twitter, Google, Instagram, and TikTok) to make data that 'contributes to the detection, identification and understanding of systemic risks' available to 'vetted researchers'.[162] There is much to be fleshed out in the application of this provision. For example, there is the important question of how data will be shared while complying with the General Data Protection Regulation (GDPR) as platforms have at times invoked this legislation to prevent data-sharing with researchers.[163] However, this was overcome with a technical solution for the *Social Science One* project,[164] and various proposals have already been put forward to address this valid concern.[165] Solutions can be found for extremely important privacy-compliant access.

---

[160] For a series of articles fleshing out various aspects of the DSA, see Algorithm Watch, 'A Guide to the Digital Services Act, the EU's New Law to Rein in Big Tech' (21 September 2022) <https://algorithmwatch.org/en/dsa-explained/> accessed 11 March 2023.

[161] Steven J. Barela, 'Dawning Digital Data Access via New EU Law' (*Just Security*, 20 October 2022) <https://www.justsecurity.org/83622/dawning-digital-data-access-via-new-eu-law/> accessed 11 March 2023.

[162] Digital Services Act (n 159) Art. 40(1)(4)(8).

[163] Facebook, 'Response to European Digital Media Observatory Call for Comments: The GDPR and Sharing Data for Independent Social Scientific Research' (21 December 2021) <https://about.fb.com/wp-content/uploads/2020/12/Facebook-Response-to-EDMO-Request-for-Submissions.pdf> accessed 11 March 2023.

[164] An agreement was made to apply 'differential privacy' to the datasets in order to prevent reidentification of individuals represented in the data through an introduction of adding calibrated 'noise'. Georgina Evans and Gary King, 'Statistically Valid Inferences from Differentially Private Data Releases, with Application to the Facebook URLs Dataset' (2022) Political Analysis 1, <https://tinyurl.com/yc5mx3sw> accessed 11 March 2023.

[165] Vermeulen (n 153) has keenly suggested developing a code of conduct to facilitate the sharing of data that conforms to the law, and this idea has been further developed by the European Digital Media Observatory, 'Report of the European Digital Media Observatory's Working Group on Platform-to-Researcher Data Access' (May 31, 2022) <https://edmo.eu/wp-content/uploads/2022/02/Report-of-the-European-Digital-Media-Observatorys-Working-Group-on-Platform-to-Researcher-Data-Access-2022.pdf> accessed 11 March 2023; see also Lidia Dutkiewicz, 'From the DSA to Media Data Space: the possible solutions for the access to platforms' data to tackle disinformation', European Law Blog: News and Comments on EU Law (19 October 2021) <https://europeanlawblog.eu/2021/10/19/from-the-dsa-to-media-data-space-the-possible-solutions-for-the-access-to-platforms-data-to-tackle-disinformation/> accessed 11 March 2023.

Greater understanding is coming for identifying *disinfo-ops* (attribution); identifying who is engaging with disinformation and why; detecting how platforms enable, facilitate, or amplify disinformation (algorithms); and an ability to test the effectiveness of interventions by platforms to counter disinformation.[166] Furthermore, this first opening surely portends a further unlocking of datasets. As one-piece of evidence, in the US Senate, there is a bipartisan proposal for legislation gaining ground to also provide researchers with access to social media data.[167]

There is an important awakening to the gravity of this problem and the need for researched solutions to understand the scope and reach of cross-border operations. It is important for international lawyers to be aware of and ready to capitalize on this extremely important aperture. We believe the data access can be harnessed to answer empirical questions related to the breadth, depth, and precision of *disinfo-ops* and thus provide a much less ambiguous and measurable definition of 'coercion'.

4. Conclusion

In this chapter we have built on an idea aptly captured by Michael Schmitt: '[u]ntil States exercise their prerogative to develop new norms and interpret existing ones in the context of cyber operations, those States that are not committed to a rule-based international order will enjoy an asymmetrical advantage over those that are dedicated to compliance with the law'.[168] With this in mind, we have proposed an interdisciplinary roadmap that draws on the theoretical frameworks surrounding legitimacy and information ethics to consider the non-intervention principle as it applies to *disinfo-ops* involving election interference. Through these frameworks, we offered a novel way to understand the concept of the *domaine réservé*, that is, the domain which must be affected by coercion for the non-intervention principle to be violated. We have fleshed out how the legitimacy of the conferral and exercise of power, and the operation of the election process as part of the proper operation of the State as an information entity, fall within this domain and why it is so critical for interpretations of the law to

---

[166] Vermeulen (n 153); Pasquetto et al (n 146).

[167] Senator Chris Coons, 'Coons, Portman, Klobuchar announce legislation to ensure transparency at social media platforms: Bipartisan proposal would provide researchers and the public with access to previously undisclosed data' (9 December 2021) <https://www.coons.senate.gov/news/press-releases/coons-portman-klobuchar-announce-legislation-to-ensure-transparency-at-social-media-platforms> accessed 11 March 2023.

[168] See Schmitt, '"Virtual" Disenfranchisement' (n 14) 67. See also Jamnejad and Wood (n 21) 346 ('Just as the reach of international law is constantly changing, so too is the line between what is, and what is not, prohibited under the non-intervention principle').

include these ideas in the digital age. Finally, we demonstrated how a broader approach to the element of coercion is required—one that considers the breadth, depth, and precision of a cyber operation—and how improved access to data from social media companies will aid in quantifying the impact of these operations in the future.

Novel capacities made available by ICTs endanger core interests of individual States, and the international legal order itself. Progress is needed.

19

Trapped in the Grey Zone

International Law Applicable to Non-State Actors

Agata Kleczkowska

1. Introduction

The term 'hybrid warfare' not only describes actions which combine different techniques and tools of combat but also denotes the involvement of States and non-State actors (NSAs) in hostile activities.[1] This latter mode of operation is well established. It has been used, inter alia, by Russia during the armed conflict in Georgia, Chechnya, and Ukraine;[2] by the United States, Turkey, and Russia in Syria;[3] by Sudan in Darfur;[4] or by Serbia during the armed conflict in Balkans in the 1990s.[5]

NSAs may act both independently or in cooperation with States. NSAs which are independent of States include individuals, secessionist movements, insurgents, religious associations, terrorist organizations, and transnational corporations. They often possess their own resources and structure and may pursue their political, military, economic, or social goals in defiance of the States in whose territory they operate. Their capabilities differ from those at the disposal of States. In hybrid warfare, this may confer a significant advantage on NSAs, as States are often ill-equipped to defend themselves against unconventional or non-military methods typically employed by such actors.

---

[1] Magnus Normark, 'How States Use non-State Actors: A *Modus Operandi* for Covert State Subversion and Malign Networks' (European Centre of Excellence for Countering Hybrid Threats 2019) 2; Erik Reichborn-Kjennerud and Patrick Cullen, 'MCDC Countering Hybrid Warfare Project: Understanding Hybrid Warfare' (Multinational Capability Development Campaign 2017) 4.

[2] Mark Galeotti, 'Hybrid, Ambiguous, and Non-linear? How New Is Russia's 'New Way of War'?' (2016) 27 Small Wars and Insurgencies 282, 285–86, 295–96; International Institute for Strategic Studies, *The Military Balance 2015* (Routledge 2015) 5.

[3] Vladimir Rauta, 'A Structural-Relational Analysis of Party Dynamics in Proxy Wars' (2018) 32 International Relations 1, 10.

[4] International Criminal Court, 'Public Redacted Version of the Prosecutor's Application under Article 58', Case No. ICC-02/05, Doc. No. ICC-02/05-157-AnxA (July 14, 2008), paras. 288–92, 300, 303, 305, 307, and 310.

[5] See the description of employment of armed groups by Serbia in Croatia and Bosnia and Hercegovina: *Prosecutor v. Jovica Stanišić and Franko Simatović* (Indictment), Case No. IT-03-69 (May 1, 2003), paras. 3–7.

Agata Kleczkowska, *Trapped in the Grey Zone* In: *Hybrid Threats and Grey Zone Conflict.* Edited by: Mitt Regan and Aurel Sari, Oxford University Press. © Oxford University Press 2024. DOI: 10.1093/oso/9780197744772.003.0019

426   INSTRUMENTS, TACTICS, AND METHODS IN THE GREY ZONE

Where States and NSAs cooperate, States may use the special capabilities of NSAs to deploy a wider range of tactics either on the battlefield or as part of geopolitical competition below the threshold of hostilities.[6] In other words, States gain an opportunity 'to deploy entities in the target country with certain skillsets suitable for specific activities',[7] such as in the investment market or in cyberspace.

One way to describe the role of NSAs that cooperate with States is with reference to the term 'proxy'. There is no legal definition of a 'proxy', even though both in legal doctrine and in the field of international relations there have been several attempts to develop a definition of the term. The word dates back to the Latin word *procurare*, meaning 'to take care of' or 'to watch over'.[8] Accordingly, the term 'proxy' refers to an external actor,[9] State, or NSA that executes actions delegated to it by a patron State.[10] To put it differently, instead of acting through its own organs and officials, States commission proxies with certain tasks that their regular agents are either unable to carry out themselves or which they prefers their regular agents not to be directly involved in.[11] Thus, proxies act in the interests of the patron State.[12] At the same time, the patron State provides assistance to a proxy, for example, in the form of armaments, training, financial support, intelligence, or logistical assistance. Patron States may exercise varying levels of control over their proxies. A particular proxy may be dependent on the

---

[6] Reichborn-Kjennerud and Cullen (n 1) 1–2 and 4; Frank G. Hoffman, 'Hybrid Warfare and Challenges' (2009) 52 Joint Forces Quarterly 34, 36.

[7] Normark (n 1) 3–4. See the Airiston Helmi case, a real-estate company owned by a Russian entrepreneur, which purchased land in Finland, including islands, lots, and buildings along strategically important maritime routes and military areas around Turku. Properties were often equipped with advanced monitoring systems, satellite communications, a helipad, and their own water transport. See Urve Eslas, 'Under Moscow's Shadow' (*CEPA*, 18 October 2018) <https://cepa.org/under-mosc ows-shadow/> accessed 15 August 2022; Piotr Szymański, 'Finland: Suspicious Russian Properties' (Centre for Eastern Studies, 7 November 2018) <https://www.osw.waw.pl/en/publikacje/analyses/ 2018-11-07/finland-suspicious-russian-properties> accessed 15 August 2022).

[8] Jean Baptiste Gardin Dumesnil, *Latin Synonyms, with Their Different Significations: And Examples Taken from the Best Latin Authors* (J. M. Gosset tr, Whittaker, 3rd edn, 1825) 445.

[9] Rauta distinguishes between auxiliary forces, proxies, affiliated forces, and surrogate forces. He describes proxies as armed groups not forming part of regular forces but fighting for and on behalf of States; moreover, 'they operate by entirely replacing the regular forces on the battlefield'. See Vladimir Rauta, 'Towards a Typology of non-State Actors in 'Hybrid Warfare': Proxy, Auxiliary, Surrogate and Affiliated Forces' (2019) 33 Cambridge Review of International Affairs 1, 7–14.

[10] For the purposes of this chapter, the term 'proxy' will refer to an NSA. Instead of 'patron State', some scholars use the term 'beneficiary', see Rauta (n 3) 8, or 'State sponsor', see Filip Bryjka, 'Operational Control over Non-State Proxies' (2020) 31 Security and Defence Quarterly 1, 10.

[11] Rauta (n 9) 7.

[12] American Bar Association, Center for Human Rights & Rule of Law Initiative, 'Report: The Legal Framework Regulating Proxy Warfare' (December 2019) 3; Christopher Lamb, 'The Nature of Proxy Warfare', in *The Future of Conflict in the 1980s*, edited by William J. Taylor Jr. and Steven A. Maaranen (Lexington Books 1982) 169, 169; Andrew Mumford, 'Proxy Warfare and the Future of Conflict' (2013) 158 RUSI Journal 40, 40. See also Bryjka (n 10) 6; Bertil Dunér, 'Proxy Intervention in Civil Wars' (1981) 18 Journal of Peace Research 353, 353.

assistance of a State, but it may also possess a greater degree of independence and for this reason not fall under the full control of its patron.[13]

From a legal perspective, much of the activity of NSAs, either as independent actors or as proxies, remains in the grey zone of international law. The majority of international legal norms is applicable only to States but not to NSAs, while the attribution of responsibility for proxies' actions to States is often hindered by the covert character of their cooperation with the patron State.[14] This is also one of the reasons why NSAs' actions fit perfectly into the framework of hybrid warfare: States targeted by proxies may not even realize that they are under some kind of attack sponsored by a hostile State until a late stage, at which point the hostile State may have already achieved its objectives and may continue to deny its involvement to avoid legal responsibility for the attack.[15]

The thesis advanced in this chapter is that the unclear status of NSAs is convenient for States, and since it is for States to decide what status NSAs should enjoy in the international legal system, they have no interest in equipping NSAs with rights and obligations under international law. Doing so would have serious consequences for States: on the one hand, States could be forced to allow NSAs to take part in decision and law-making processes, such as participating in treaty negotiations and seeing their practice and *opinio juris* count towards the formation of customary law. On the other hand, States could no longer hide behind the NSAs' actions to pursue some covert activities. Even if States decided to boost the status of NSAs under international law to make NSAs directly responsible for their own acts, such a change would not guarantee that patron States could evade all responsibility for relying on proxies, as they may still incur responsibility for wrongful acts committed by their own agents and organs in the context of their cooperation with NSAs. Moreover, even if NSAs gained legal status under international law, they may still be unable to provide adequate reparations for breaches of international law they commit, for instance, due to the lack of adequate financial resources. In that case, those victimized by the NSA conduct will most likely look for reparations from the patron State. Summing up, even though States' inertia allows NSAs to continue to act in the grey zone of international law, this vagueness is also used by States to their benefit, which apparently outweighs the option of settling the status of NSAs under international law.

---

[13] Bryjka (n 10) 4–5; American Bar Association (n 12) 6; Lamb (n 12) 170. When during armed conflicts regular and irregular forces strategically cooperate with each other, such conflicts are sometimes labelled as compound wars. See Hoffman (n 6) 36; Sascha Dov Bachmann and Andrés B. Muñoz Mosquera, 'Lawfare and Hybrid Warfare: How Russia Is Using the Law as a Weapon' (2015) 102 Amicus Curiae 25.

[14] Normark (n 1) 3.

[15] Lamb (n 12) 173; American Bar Association (n 12) 5–6. See also Normark (n 1) 3; Sabine C. Carey, Michael P. Colaresi, and Neil J. Mitchell, 'Governments, Informal Links to Militias, and Accountability' (2015) 59 Journal of Conflict Resolution 850, 851–52 and 856.

428 INSTRUMENTS, TACTICS, AND METHODS IN THE GREY ZONE

The present chapter is divided into two parts: the first part discusses the legal framework applicable to NSAs acting independently from States. It focuses on three categories of NSAs—individuals, armed non-State actors, and transnational corporations—to demonstrate that their rights and obligations under international law are limited and that the scope of these rights and obligations is determined by States. The second part focuses on States' responsibility for the actions of their proxies. It discusses the options of attributing the proxies' actions to States on the basis of the rules of State responsibility and examines certain treaties, by way of example, which impose duties on States with regard to the conduct of proxies. It concludes that due to the ambiguities in the rules of attribution of responsibility, as well as imprecise treaty norms, States may evade responsibility for their proxies' actions.

2. Non-State actors which operate independently from States

The term 'non-State actor', if understood to refer to all actors that are not States, covers a very broad range of entities, starting from intergovernmental and non-governmental organizations, through to religious associations and ending up with individuals. Since the focus of this chapter is on hybrid warfare and those non-public actors which exploit the grey zones of international law, the analysis is limited to individuals, armed non-State actors (ANSAs), and corporations.

The responsibility of States for the acts of NSAs[16] and the responsibility of NSAs for their own acts[17] have been topics of interest in legal doctrine for quite some time now. Despite the fact that international law largely remains State-centric, certain other actors also enjoy a limited international legal personality or at least are subject to some international legal norms. However, as NSAs do not form a homogenous group, it is necessary to discuss how international law regulates their activities by distinguishing different types of NSAs from one another.

2.1 Individuals

Before the development of human rights law, international law addressed the legal situation only of certain groups of individuals, such as diplomatic envoys, or under certain conditions, like individuals caught up in an international armed

[16] E.g. Lassa Oppenheim, *International Law: A Treatise*, Vol. 1 (Longmans, Green and Co 1905) 211–214.

[17] E.g. Hersch Lauterpacht, *International Law and Human Rights* (Stevens and Sons 1950) 29–47.

INTERNATIONAL LAW APPLICABLE TO NON-STATE ACTORS   429

conflict. Today, scholars are in general agreement that individuals possess some degree of limited legal personality in international law.[18] First of all, international law confers some substantive rights on individuals, especially in the field of human rights and international humanitarian law (IHL). Secondly, international law grants individuals some procedural rights and capacities, such as standing to file a complaint before international bodies, for instance, in the complaint system based on the European Convention on Human Rights.[19] Finally, individuals have some obligations under international law and may be held directly responsible on the grounds of international law for committing certain crimes, such as genocide, crimes against humanity, war crimes, or aggression. Even though individuals are usually tried for these violations of international law before domestic courts, under some circumstances they may be brought to justice before international courts, such as the International Criminal Court, as well.[20]

This brief account demonstrates that States decide the scope of rights and obligations of individuals under international law, since it is States that conclude human rights treaties, determine the scope of jurisdiction of international courts, or establish the right of petition under various accountability mechanisms. More importantly from the perspective of this chapter, States are primarily responsible for enforcing the law, including international law, against individuals, and only in extreme cases of the most serious crimes, and under certain conditions, do they hand over jurisdiction to try individuals to international bodies. Thus, ultimately it is for States to recognize and penalize acts that individuals may commit in the context of hybrid warfare.

2.2 Armed non-State actors

Another category of NSAs which often operates in the grey zones of international law is ANSAs. This collective name refers to rebels, insurgents, national liberation movements, terrorist organizations, and similar armed groups.

The status of ANSAs under international law too has attracted considerable attention in legal debate and scholarship in recent years, though no consensus has emerged on the matter.[21] Some scholars

---

[18] See Kate Parlett, *The Individual in the International Legal System: Continuity and Change in International Law* (CUP 2011) 37; Gerhard Hafner, 'The Emancipation of the Individual from the State under International Law' (2011) 358 Recueil des Cours 263, 321–52 and 369–436.

[19] Convention for the Protection of Human Rights and Fundamental Freedoms (4 November 1950), 213 UNTS 221, Art. 34.

[20] Rome Statute of the International Criminal Court (17 July 1998), 2187 UNTS 3, Art. 25(1).

[21] This interest is confirmed, inter alia, by the variety of definitions of ANSAs that have been created in the doctrine of international law. E.g. see Anthea Roberts and Sandesh Sivakumaran, 'Lawmaking by Nonstate Actors: Engaging Armed Groups in the Creation of International Humanitarian Law'

430 INSTRUMENTS, TACTICS, AND METHODS IN THE GREY ZONE

claim[22] that ANSAs possess 'aspects' of international legal personality,[23] limited international personality under Common Article 3 of the Geneva Conventions,[24] 'functional' international legal personality,[25] or international legal personality only with regard to 'fundamental human rights obligations'.[26] Moreover, there are views that ANSAs are subject to rights and responsibilities under IHL as parties to an armed conflict,[27] including the rules set out in Common Article 3 of the Geneva Conventions and their Second Additional Protocol.[28] However, many

(2012) 37 Yale LJ 107, 126; Annyssa Bellal and Stuart Casey-Maslen, 'Enhancing Compliance with International Law by Armed Non-State Actors' (2011) 3 Goettingen Journal of International Law 175, 176; Konstantinos Mastorodimos, *Armed Non-State Actors in International Humanitarian and Human Rights Law: Foundations and Framework of Obligations, and Rules on Accountability* (Ashgate 2016) 159; International Law Association, 'Non-State Actors', *Final Report, Johannesburg Conference* (2016) 4 <http://www.ila-hq.org/download.cfm/docid/2B7FD370-5D20-41BD-994C08779F5F2 582> accessed 15 August 2022.

[22] The opposite view is taken inter alia by Anton O. Petrov, 'Non-State Actors and Law of Armed Conflict Revisited: Enforcing International Law through Domestic Engagement' (2014) 19 Journal of Conflict and Security Law 279, 281; Marco Pedrazzi, 'The Status of Organized Armed Groups in Contemporary Armed Conflicts', in *Non-State Actors and International Humanitarian Law— Organized Armed Groups: A Challenge for the 21st Century*, edited by Marco Odello and Gian Luca Beruto (Franco Angeli 2010) 69.

[23] International Law Association (n 22) 14.

[24] Liesbeth Zegveld, *Accountability of Armed Opposition Groups in International Law* (Cambridge University Press 2002) 57.

[25] Veronika Bilková, 'Establishing Direct Responsibility of Armed Opposition Groups for Violations of International Humanitarian Law?' in *Responsibilities of the Non-State Actor in Armed Conflict and the Market Place: Theoretical Considerations and Empirical Findings*, edited by Noemi Gal-Or, Math Noortmann, and Cedric Ryngaert (Brill Nijhoff 2015) 265, 277; Marco Sassòli, 'Taking Armed Groups Seriously: Ways to Improve their Compliance with International Humanitarian Law' (2010) 1 International Humanitarian Legal Studies 5, 13.

[26] Tilman Rodenhauser, 'Human Rights Obligations of Non-State Armed Groups in Other Situations of Violence: The Syria Example' (2012) 3 Journal of International Humanitarian Studies 263, 274.

[27] See Republic of Columbia, Constitutional Court, Ruling No. C-225/95, Re: File No.L.A.T.-040 (18 May 1995), para. 17 <https://casebook.icrc.org/case-study/colombia-constitutional-conformity-protocol-ii> accessed 15 August 2022. See also Sandesh Sivakumaran, 'Binding Armed Opposition Groups' 2006 (55) International and Comparative Law Quarterly 369, 390.

[28] Jean-Marie Henckaerts and Louise Doswald-Beck, *Customary International Humanitarian Law* (Cambridge University Press 2005) 299, 497–98; Zegveld (n 24) 10; Anne Peters, *Beyond Human Rights: The Legal Status of the Individual in International Law* (Cambridge University Press 2016) 223–24; Stephane Ojeda, 'The Kampala Convention on Internally Displaced Persons: Some International Humanitarian Law Aspects' (2010) 29 Refugee Survey Quarterly 58, 65; Ezequiel Heffes, 'Generating Respect for International Humanitarian Law: The Establishment of Courts by Organized Non-State Armed Groups in Light of the Principle of Equality of Belligerents' (2005) 18 Yearbook of International Humanitarian Law 181, 183; Sivakumaran (n 27) 372; Ezequiel Heffes and Brian E. Frenkel, 'The International Responsibility of Non-State Armed Groups: In Search of the Applicable Rules' (2017) 8 Goettingen Journal of International Law 39, 41; Jann K. Kleffner, 'The Applicability of International Humanitarian Law to Organized Armed Groups' (2011) 93 International Review of the Red Cross 443, 449; Annyssa Bellal and Stuart Casey-Maslen, 'Rules of Engagement: Protecting Civilians through Dialogue with Non-State Actors' (Geneva Academy of International Humanitarian Law and Swiss Federal Department of Foreign Affairs, 2011) 24 <https://www.geneva-academy.ch/joomlatools-files/docman-files/Research%20documents/Rules-of-Engagement-EN.pdf> accessed 15 August 2022; Noam Lubell, *Extraterritorial Use of Force against Non-State Actors* (OUP 2010) 18.

questions remain unresolved. On what exact grounds are ANSAs supposed to be bound by international law? Does the applicability of international law require their consent? Can ANSAs be bound by international law on the grounds of customary law?

At the present stage of international law, the answer to these questions is negative. Most legal acts that ANSAs accept as binding upon them in the context of armed conflict are simply of a political character[29] or are drafted in connection with the specific circumstances of an armed conflict that an ANSA participates in and are therefore inapplicable outside the context of that conflict.

Furthermore, where legally binding instruments refer to the situation of ANSAs, they typically do not confer any duties on them, but rather oblige States to prevent ANSAs from undertaking certain actions. One example is Article 4 of the Optional Protocol to the Convention on the Rights of the Child on the involvement of children in armed conflict,[30] which 'reflects the traditional view that only States have obligations under international human rights law and can become parties to treaties, whereas the behaviour of non-State entities is to be regulated by domestic law'.[31] Article 4(1) of the Optional Protocol states that 'Armed groups that are distinct from the armed forces of a State should not, under any circumstances, recruit or use in hostilities persons under the age of 18 years'. Importantly, Article 4(1) uses the term 'should not' to highlight that the Optional Protocol does not infer any legal obligations on armed groups.[32] Article 4(2) clarifies who is the addressee of duties expressed in Article 4(1): 'States Parties shall take all feasible measures to prevent such recruitment and use, including the adoption of legal measures necessary to prohibit and criminalize

---

[29] Most of declarations submitted by ANSAs include general referral to humanitarian law, and not specific legal norms. E.g. see Geneva Call, 'What We Do' <https://www.genevacall.org/what-we-do/> accessed 8 March 2023). Although some ANSAs issue declarations or sign commitments which refer to the Geneva Conventions and Additional Protocols, a careful reading of these documents demonstrates that they are not binding under international law. E.g. see the letter from the Algerian National Liberation Front to the Committee of the Red Cross: Front de Libération Nationale/ Armée de Liberation Nationale, 'Lettre du Comité de Libération de l'Afrique du Nord au Comité International de la Croix-Rouge' <http://theirwords.org/media/transfer/doc/sc_dz_fln_aln_1956_03-ad93ce79b5a926e49501e3d304a82b73.pdf> accessed 8 March 2023. In this correspondence, the delegation of the Front indicated that since the beginning of the conflict with France, the French side had been violating the Third Geneva Convention relative to the Treatment of Prisoners of War. Thus, the Front itself declared that it is 'ready to apply' the provisions of this Convention in relation to all French soldiers captivated by the Front on the grounds of Article 2(3) of the Convention, but on the condition of the reciprocity of its application by the French side.

[30] Optional Protocol to the Convention on the Rights of the Child on the Involvement of Children in Armed Conflict (12 February 2022), 2173 UNTS 222.

[31] UNICEF, 'Guide to the Optional Protocol on the Involvement of Children in Armed Conflict' (December 2003) 17 <https://www.refworld.org/docid/49997b01c.html> accessed 8 March 2023.

[32] Ibid.; Andrew Clapham, 'The Rights and Responsibilities of Armed Non-State Actors: The Legal Landscape & Issues Surrounding Engagement' (1 February 2010) 25 <https://repository.graduateinstitute.ch/record/16583/files/SSRN-id1569636.pdf> accessed 15 August 2022.

432 INSTRUMENTS, TACTICS, AND METHODS IN THE GREY ZONE

such practices'.[33] 'All feasible measures' include also the adoption of domestic legislation.

Finally, while some commentators portray customary international law as a collection of basic rules of mankind that bind any actor,[34] as a formal source of international law, custom binds only subjects of international law but not ANSAs.

The only realistic ground for binding ANSAs with norms of international law seems to be the principle of legislative jurisdiction, which presupposes that ANSAs are bound by international law because the members of ANSAs are under the jurisdiction of a State which in turn is bound by rules of international law and is obliged to ensure respect for these rules by every person under its jurisdiction.[35] However, the principle of legislative jurisdiction makes it possible only to assign responsibility to the *members* of an ANSA, not to the ANSA as such, and also implies that any responsibility of members of ANSAs arises under domestic law and before domestic enforcement organs. Thus, this principle does not give rise to direct international responsibility of ANSAs.

Finally, one should also discuss the special situation of the insurrectional movements. An example of insurgents using hybrid tactics may be Mujahideen fighting against Soviet forces in Afghanistan during the USSR intervention (1979–89). The Mujahideen fighters were mostly local men, not professional soldiers, though they benefitted from the support of the United States.[36] Paradoxically, their irregular nature was their biggest strength, as the Soviet army was not prepared for counter-insurgency operations and the tactics employed by the Mujahideen, such as ambushes, blocking enemy lines of communication, sieges, raids, and urban combat.[37]

The situation of insurrectional movements which succeed in establishing a new State or government, or those ANSAs which managed to gain effective control over territory, constitutes an exception to the rule that international law does not regulate the responsibility of ANSAs. Under Article 10 of the Articles on Responsibility of States for Internationally Wrongful Acts,

---

[33] Moreover, to highlight that the Optional Protocol does not confer any legal status on armed groups, Article 4(3) declares that: 'The application of the present article shall not affect the legal status of any party to an armed conflict'.

[34] J. J. Paust, 'Nonstate Actor Participation in International Law and the Pretense of Exclusion' (2011) 51 Virginia Journal of International Law 977, 977–83, 998–99.

[35] Jann K. Kleffner, 'The Applicability of International Humanitarian Law to Organized Armed Groups' (2011) 93 International Review of the Red Cross 443, 445; Sivakumaran (n 27) 381.

[36] Gary Anderson, 'Counter-Hybrid Warfare: Winning in the Gray Zone' (*Small Wars Journal*, 12 February 2018) <https://smallwarsjournal.com/jrnl/art/counter-hybrid-warfare-winning-gray-zone> accessed 8 March 2023.

[37] C. J. Dick, 'Mujahideen Tactics in the Soviet-Afghan War' (Conflict Studies Research Centre, January 2002) 6–9, <https://edocs.nps.edu/AR/org/CSRC/csrc_jan_02.pdf> accessed 8 March 2023.

INTERNATIONAL LAW APPLICABLE TO NON-STATE ACTORS   433

1. The conduct of an insurrectional movement which becomes the new Government of a State shall be considered an act of that State under international law.
2. The conduct of a movement, insurrectional or other, which succeeds in establishing a new State in part of the territory of a pre-existing State or in a territory under its administration shall be considered an act of the new State under international law.[38]

The basis for the attribution, in this case, is the continuity between an insurrectional movement and a new government or a State formed by the movement.[39] Thus, in contrast to other ANSAs, insurrectional movements which manage to acquire State-like functions[40] have international rights and obligations, and consequently may be held responsible for violating applicable rules of international law.[41]

It has already been mentioned that some authors point out the special significance of Article 3 of the Geneva Conventions,[42] which states as follows: 'In the case of armed conflict not of an international character occurring in the territory of one of the High Contracting Parties, each Party to the conflict shall be bound to apply, as a minimum, the following provisions (. . .).'

Thus, it is posited that ANSAs, being a party to the conflict, are obliged to comply at least with the duties stemming from Article 3. However, one should bear in mind the purpose of this rule. During the preparatory works on the Geneva Conventions, only insurgents were considered possibly bound by Article 3, but even in their case 'doubt was expressed as to whether insurgents could be legally bound by a Convention which they had not themselves signed. But if the responsible authority at their head exercises effective sovereignty, it is bound by the very fact that it claims to represent the country, or part of the country.'[43] It

---

[38] International Law Commission, 'Draft Articles on Responsibility of States for Internationally Wrongful Acts, with Commentaries' (2001) II(2) Yearbook of the International Law Commission 31.

[39] Articles on State Responsibility, Art. 10.

[40] See Hans Kelsen, *Principles of International Law* (Reinhart and Company 1952) 161, 292; Math Noortmann, 'Non-State Actors in International Law', in *Non-State Actors in International Relations*, edited by Bas Arts, Math Noortmann, and Bob Reinalda (Ashgate 2001) 67. *Cf.* Sivakumaran (n 27) 380; Tilman Rodenhäuser, 'Human Rights Obligations of Non-State Armed Groups in Other Situations of Violence: The Syria Example' (2012) 3 International Humanitarian Legal Studies 263, 265.

[41] Gauthier de Beco, 'Compliance with International Humanitarian Law by Non-State Actors' (2005) 3 Humanitäres Völkerrecht 190, 198.

[42] E.g. see Geneva Convention Relative to the Treatment of Prisoners of War (12 August 1949), 75 UNTS 135 (Geneva Convention III). See also Sandesh Sivakumaran, *The Law of Non-International Armed Conflict* (OUP 2012) 236–37; Lindsay Moir, *The Law of Internal Armed Conflict* (CUP 2002) 52–53; Jean-Marie Henckaerts, 'Study on Customary International Humanitarian Law: A Contribution to the Understanding and Respect for the Rule of Law in Armed Conflict' (2005) 87 (857) International Review of the Red Cross 175, 196.

[43] Jean Pictet (ed), *Commentary on the I Geneva Convention for the Amelioration of the Condition of Wounded and Sick in Armed Forces in the Field* (International Committee of the Red Cross 1952) 51.

clearly follows from this that the only ANSAs that are bound by Common Article 3 are those which have managed to gain effective control over a territory and can claim to represent the State.

To sum up, apart from insurrectional movements and those ANSAs which exercise effective control over territory, ANSAs are not directly bound by rules of international law. As a result, they also cannot be held directly responsible for violations of international law. The only options for accountability are either to bring to justice members of such armed groups in an individual capacity or to attribute wrongful conduct carried out by the group or its members to a State by invoking the principle of State responsibility, as discussed in more detail in the second part of this chapter.

2.3 Transnational corporations

When it comes to transnational corporations, the idea of their international legal personality derives primarily from international investment law. It is based principally on the Convention on the Settlement of Investment Disputes between States and Nationals, which confers direct standing on investors, including transnational corporations, in international adjudication.[44] However, this international legal personality of transnational corporations is highly questionable outside the legal regime of international investment law. While transnational corporations are certainly bound by certain international rules, including international human rights law and IHL, on the grounds of the domestic law of States which have jurisdiction over them, they cannot be held directly responsible under international law as they lack international legal personality.

2.4 Conclusions

Among NSAs, the situation of individuals and insurrectional movements is special as they possess some rights and obligations directly under international law. In contrast, the majority of the rules of international law, including the most

---

The most recent version of the commentary on Article 3 does not mention this conclusion of the preparatory works. Instead, it enumerates different grounds on which ANSAs may be bound by Article 3. See International Committee of the Red Cross, *Commentary on the First Geneva Convention* (CUP 2016) para. 508.

[44] Convention on the Settlement of Investment Disputes between States and Nationals of other States (11 September 1964), 575 UNTS 159, Art. 25. See Christian Walter, 'Subjects of International Law', *The Max Planck Encyclopedia of International Law* paras. 19–20 <http://opil.ouplaw.com> accessed 15 August 2022.

fundamental ones deriving from human rights law and IHL, are not applicable to armed groups and transnational corporations. Ultimately, States remain responsible for enforcing compliance with international law by NSAs through the mechanisms of domestic law. Thus, unless the State's domestic legal system, under the jurisdiction of which a specific NSA falls, prohibits or penalizes certain violations of international law, NSAs may not be held responsible for such breaches.

3. The responsibility of proxies under international law

While the legal status of NSAs under international law does not differ depending on whether they act independently or as proxies for a State, there is one crucial difference between these two situations: depending on the level of control exercised by a patron State over an NSA acting as its proxy, it may be possible to attribute the NSAs actions to the patron State.

3.1 Responsibility of proxies vs States' control over proxies

As a matter of general principle, States are responsible for their own acts. The conduct of private persons or entities is not attributable to the State under international law, unless a sufficiently close connection exists between the State and the private party, such as an NSA.[45] This is the case, for instance, where the NSA has committed a wrongful act on the instructions of, or under the direction or control of a State, as may happen in the case of a proxy-patron State relationship.[46] This principle is expressed in Article 8 of the Articles on Responsibility of States for Internationally Wrongful Acts in the following terms:

> The conduct of a person or group of persons shall be considered an act of a State under international law if the person or group of persons is in fact acting on the instructions of, or under the direction or control of, that State in carrying out the conduct.[47]

---

[45] Articles on State Responsibility, 47.
[46] Obviously, the patron State may not overtly admit to its relationship with the proxy. The term 'plausible deniability' is often employed in this context. See Rory Cormac and Richard J. Aldrich, 'Grey Is the New Black: Covert Action and Implausible Deniability' (2018) 94 International Affairs 477, 479–81, 485, and 490.
[47] Articles on State Responsibility.

436   INSTRUMENTS, TACTICS, AND METHODS IN THE GREY ZONE

In order to attribute a proxy's conduct to a State, there must be a direct link between the two. This requirement is based on the International Court of Justice (ICJ) judgement in the case of *Military and Paramilitary Activities in and Against Nicaragua*,[48] where the ICJ stated that:

> United States participation, even if preponderant or decisive, in the financing, organizing, training, supplying and equipping of the contras, the selection of its military or paramilitary targets, and the planning of the whole of its operation, is still insufficient in itself, on the basis of the evidence in the possession of the Court, for the purpose of attributing to the United States the acts committed by the contras in the course of their military or paramilitary operations in Nicaragua. [...] even the general control by the respondent State over a force with a high degree of dependency on it, would not in themselves mean, without further evidence, that the United States directed or enforced the perpetration of the acts contrary to human rights and humanitarian law alleged by the applicant State. Such acts could well be committed by members of the contras without the control of the United States. For this conduct to give rise to legal responsibility of the United States, it would in principle have to be proved that that State had effective control of the military or paramilitary operations in the course of which the alleged violations were committed.[49]

Thus, according to the ICJ, the level of control exercised by the United States over specific acts committed by *contras* was not sufficient to attribute the responsibility for their actions to the United States.[50]

The effective control test thus sets the threshold for attribution on the basis of an agency relationship very high.[51] To meet that threshold, a State must give instructions to its proxy concerning each specific wrongful act or exercise effective control over each such act; general instructions and general control with regard to the overall conduct of a proxy are not sufficient for attributing its actions

---

[48] *Cf.* International Law Commission, 'Report of the International Law Commission on the Work of its Fiftieth Session (20 April–12 June 1998, 27 July–14 August 1998)' (2004) UN Doc. A/53/10, para. 394; American Bar Association (n 12) 14.

[49] *Military and Paramilitary Activities in and against Nicaragua (Nicaragua v United States of America)* (Merits) [1986] ICJ Rep. 14, para. 115.

[50] American Bar Association (n 12) 14–15.

[51] That was also the conclusion reached by Judge Al-Khasawneh in his dissenting opinion in the case of *Application of the Convention on the Prevention and Punishment of the Crime of Genocide (Bosnia and Herzegovina v. Serbia and Montenegro)* (Merits) [2007] ICJ Rep. 43, although he made it in a different context: since the United States and the *contras* shared the same objective, that is overthrowing of the Nicaraguan government, 'to require both control over the non-State actors and the specific operations in the context of which international crimes were committed is too high a threshold'. See *Dissenting Opinion of Vice-President Al-Khasawneh* [2007] ICJ Rep. 241, para. 39. The point also applies to proxies that wish to remain independent, but at the same time are ready to cooperate with the State which has the same objectives.

INTERNATIONAL LAW APPLICABLE TO NON-STATE ACTORS 437

to a State.[52] That is also why the ICJ ruled that the massacres in the Srebrenica area cannot be attributed to the Federal Republic of Yugoslavia (FRY) since 'the decision to kill the adult male population of the Muslim community in Srebrenica was taken by some members of the VRS [Army of the Republika Srpska] Main Staff, but without instructions from or effective control by the FRY'.[53]

However, the International Criminal Tribunal for the former Yugoslavia (ICTY) expressed a different view on the attribution of NSAs' acts to States, presenting the so-called 'overall control test' in the case of *Prosecutor v. Duško Tadić*:

> In order to attribute the acts of a military or paramilitary group to a State, it must be proved that the State wields overall control over the group, not only by equipping and financing the group, but also by coordinating or helping in the general planning of its military activity. Only then can the State be held internationally accountable for any misconduct of the group. However, it is not necessary that, in addition, the State should also issue, either to the head or to members of the group, instructions for the commission of specific acts contrary to international law.[54]

Moreover, referring to the effective control test, the ICTY noted that:

> This requirement, however, does not go so far as to include the issuing of specific orders by the State, or its direction of each individual operation. Under international law it is by no means necessary that the controlling authorities should plan all the operations of the units dependent on them, choose their targets, or give specific instructions concerning the conduct of military operations and any alleged violations of international humanitarian law.[55]

It follows from this quotation that the ICTY did not negate the effective control test. Rather, it limited the relevance of the effective control test to situations when the controlling State is not the territorial State where the NSA is active, or when the controlling State is the territorial State but there is turmoil, civil strife and the State authority is weakened.[56]

The ICJ did not share the ICTY's position, but distinguished between the two tests in the case of the *Application of the Convention on the Prevention and Punishment of the Crime of Genocide*. According to the ICJ, the effective control

---

[52] *Genocide Case* (n 51) para. 400.
[53] Ibid. para. 413.
[54] *Prosecutor v. Duško Tadić*, Appeals Chamber, Judgment, IT-94-1-A (15 July 1999), para. 131.
[55] Ibid. para. 137.
[56] Ibid. paras. 138–39.

438 INSTRUMENTS, TACTICS, AND METHODS IN THE GREY ZONE

test is the appropriate standard for attributing an NSA's actions to a State. This is so because the overall control test is both 'unsuitable' and 'unpersuasive', as it broadens 'the scope of State responsibility well beyond the fundamental principle governing the law of international responsibility: a State is responsible only for its own conduct'.[57] The ICJ's view has been shared by the majority of the doctrine of international law,[58] even though some expert bodies, like the International Committee of the Red Cross (ICRC), claim that the overall control test may also be used to attribute the responsibility of an NSA to a State. According to the 2016 ICRC Commentary to Article 2 of the Geneva Conventions:

> Relying on the effective control test, on the other hand, might require reclassifying the conflict with every operation, which would be unworkable. Furthermore, the test that is used must avoid a situation where some acts are governed by the law of international armed conflict but cannot be attributed to a State.[59]

The overall control test, even if applicable only to cases when attribution is crucial for the determination of the status of an armed conflict, can still have substantial practical consequences. For instance, evidence was gathered that Russia exercises overall control over its proxies in Donetsk and Luhansk, which in turn allowed for the recognition of an international armed conflict (IAC) in Ukraine and activated the relevant IHL rules, which are applicable only during IAC.[60]

This brief analysis illustrated some of the key points in the debate concerning the proper attribution test. Although this debate might look like nothing more than an intellectual exercise, it has very practical consequences, as the attribution test determines who is responsible for violations of international law. However, the unsettled position of the law leaves multiple questions unanswered: How far do the effective and overall control tests differ? Are there situations when attribution is possible under one test but impossible under the other? Who should decide which test is the appropriate one?[61]

---

[57] *Genocide Case* (n 51) paras. 404–406.

[58] E.g. see Stefan Talmon, 'The Responsibility of Outside Powers for Acts of Secessionist Entities' (2009) 58 International and Comparative Law Quarterly 493, 517; Marko Milanovic, 'State Responsibility for Genocide' (2006) 17 European Journal of International Law 553, 577–81, and 584–85; Michael N. Schmitt and Liis Vihul, 'Proxy Wars in Cyberspace: The Evolving International Law of Attribution' (2014) 1 Fletcher Security Review 54, 64; American Bar Association (n 12) 15.

[59] Geneva Convention for the Amelioration of the Condition of the Wounded and Sick in Armed Forces in the Field (12 August 1949), 75 UNTS 31 (Geneva Convention I). See International Committee of the Red Cross (n 43) para. 271.

[60] Marco Sassòli, 'Application of IHL by and to Proxies: The "Republics" of Donetsk and Luhansk' (*Articles of War*, 3 March 2022) <https://lieber.westpoint.edu/application-ihl-proxies-donetsk-luhansk/> accessed 15 August 2022.

[61] Ryan Goodman, 'Legal Limits on Military Assistance to Proxy Forces: Pathways for State and Official Responsibility' (*Just Security*, 14 May 2018) <https://www.justsecurity.org/56272/

INTERNATIONAL LAW APPLICABLE TO NON-STATE ACTORS   439

Until these problems are sufficiently addressed, States will be able to use the grey zone existing in the sphere of rules of international responsibility to hide behind proxy actions. If a State sends its armed forces to fight in an armed conflict or entrusts a certain operation, for instance, in cyberspace, to one of its organs, it is clear that it will bear responsibility for its actions. Clearly, to avoid this outcome, it is convenient for a State to delegate these tasks to proxies if by so doing the State's responsibility for the same violations may never be established.[62]

A good illustration of how States use this grey zone of international law is Russia's reliance on proxies in its military operations against Ukraine, in particular the so-called Wagner Group that has been active in Ukraine since 2014. The Wagner Group is often described by State officials and the media as a 'private military organization',[63] but in fact, it is 'a network of business and groups of mercenaries that have been linked by overlaps in ownership and logistic networks'.[64] The terms 'private' and 'business' could suggest that it acts independently from Russian authorities, but it is no secret that the Group assists Russia in Kremlin-backed operations.[65] However, despite many allegations, it remains unclear what the exact links between the Russian authorities and the Wagner Group are.[66] On the one hand, the direct connection between the Wagner Group and Russian State organs is proven by the fact that the Group recruited detainees from Russian prisons, promising them amnesties after six months' service in the organization.[67] On the other hand, Yevgeniy Prigozhin, known as a leader

---

legal-limits-military-assistance-proxy-forces-pathways-state-official-responsibility/> accessed 15 August 2022.

[62] Oona A Hathaway et al, 'Ensuring Responsibility: Common Article 1 and State Responsibility for Non-State Actors' (2017) 95 Texas Law Review 539, 563; Articles on State Responsibility, 48–49.

[63] E.g. see Nathan Luna and Leah Vredenbregt, 'What to Know about the Wagner Group, a "Brutal" Russian Military Group Fighting in Ukraine', *ABC News* (2 February 2023) <https://abcn ews.go.com/International/International/wagner-group-brutal-russian-military-group-fighting-ukraine/story?id=96665326> accessed 8 March 2023. The research for this chapter was completed in March 2023.

[64] Amy Mackinnon, 'Russia's Wagner Group Doesn't Actually Exist' (*Foreign Policy*, 6 July 2021) <https://foreignpolicy.com/2021/07/06/what-is-wagner-group-russia-mercenaries-military-contractor/> accessed 8 March 2023.

[65] US Department of the Treasury, 'Treasury Sanctions Russian Proxy Wagner Group as a Transnational Criminal Organization' (26 January 2023) <https://home.treasury.gov/news/press-releases/jy1220> accessed 8 March 2023.

[66] E.g. see Stanislav Miroshnychenko, 'Wagner Group: Why They Are Not Mercenaries, and Russia Is Equally Responsible for Them Like for Its Regular Armed Forces' (Media Initiative for Human Rights, 4 January 2023) <https://mipl.org.ua/en/wagner-group-why-they-are-not-merc enaries-and-russia-is-equally-responsible-for-them-like-for-its-regular-armed-forces/> accessed 8 March 2023.

[67] 'Wagner Chief Frees Prisoners Who Fought in Ukraine for Russia' (*Aljazeera*, 5 January 2023) <https://www.aljazeera.com/news/2023/1/5/russian-ex-prisoners-released-from-ukrainian-frontl ine> accessed 8 March 2023.

440 INSTRUMENTS, TACTICS, AND METHODS IN THE GREY ZONE

of the Group, has repeatedly expressed vocal criticism over the war efforts of the Russian Ministry of Defence.[68] As the Wagner Group reportedly committed serious crimes[69] and operates not only in Ukraine but also in Syria, Libya, the Central African Republic, and Mali,[70] the question of the legal attribution of its actions to Russia may be a critical problem for the organ adjudicating atrocities committed not only during the armed conflict in Ukraine but also in other parts of the world.

3.2 States' responsibility for proxy actions on the grounds of treaties

The overall control test and the effective control test allow attributing the conduct of NSAs to States. In addition, States have also entered into specific commitments under certain treaties that oblige them to prevent proxies from carrying out certain actions or to refrain from engaging with proxies. Two significant examples of such treaties are the Geneva Conventions of 1949 and the Arms Trade Treaty.

3.2.1 Article 1 of the Geneva Conventions

Article 1 common to the Geneva Conventions states that: 'The High Contracting Parties undertake to respect and to ensure respect for the present Convention in all circumstances'.[71] This provision is today considered to be 'of cardinal importance for the promotion of "elementary considerations of humanity"'.[72] The

---

[68] Ellen Nakashima, John Hudson, and Paul Sonne, 'Mercenary Chief Vented to Putin over Ukraine War Bungling' *The Washington Post* (Washington, DC, 25 October 2022) <https://www.washingtonpost.com/national-security/2022/10/25/putin-insider-prigozhin-blasts-russian-generals-ukraine/> accessed 8 March 2023.

[69] Lorenzo Tondo et al, 'Alleged Wagner Group Fighters Accused of Murdering Civilians in Ukraine' *The Guardian* (London, 25 May 2022) <https://www.theguardian.com/world/2022/may/25/wagner-group-fighters-accused-murdering-civilians-ukraine-war-crimes-belarus> accessed 8 March 2023.

[70] 'What is Russia's Wagner Group of Mercenaries in Ukraine?' *BBC News* (23 January 2023) <https://www.bbc.com/news/world-60947877> accessed 8 March 2023.

[71] This obligation was reaffirmed in, inter alia, *Nicaragua* (n 49) para. 220; *Legal Consequences of the Construction of a Wall in the Occupied Palestinian Territory* (Advisory Opinion) [2004] ICJ Rep. 136, paras. 158–59; *Armed Activities on the Territory of the Congo (Democratic Republic of the Congo v. Uganda)* (Merits) [2005] ICJ Rep. 168, paras. 211 and 345; United Nations Security Council Resolution 681 (20 December 1990) UN Doc. S/RES/681, para. 5. See also Protocol Additional to the Geneva Conventions of 12 August 1949, and relating to the Protection of Victims of International Armed Conflicts (Protocol I) (8 June 1977), 1125 UNTS 609, Art. 1(1). It is important to note that the obligation to 'respect and ensure respect' is also established in Article 38(1) of the Convention on the Rights of the Child (20 November 1989), 1577 UNTS 3 with regard to IHL rules relevant to the protection of children during armed conflict. Thus, the remarks made in this section also refer to that provision.

[72] Laurence Boisson De Chazournes and Luigi Condorelli, 'Common Article 1 of the Geneva Conventions Revisited: Protecting Collective Interests' (2000) 82 International Review of the Red Cross 67, 85. For more statements about this obligation, see two documents submitted during the

INTERNATIONAL LAW APPLICABLE TO NON-STATE ACTORS 441

obligation 'to respect' means that a State must take affirmative action to ensure that all its organs, as well as private persons and entities acting on its behalf, comply with the Conventions' norms.[73] This also includes NSAs, but only those whose operations can be attributed to a State.[74]

The fact that the duty 'to ensure respect' applies to all State parties, regardless of whether they are also parties to an armed conflict or not,[75] and comprises both positive and negative obligations,[76] significantly reduces the ability of States to rely on proxies as a way to evade their obligations under international humanitarian law. Thus, even if the attribution of a proxy operation to a State is impossible, and a State cannot be labelled a party to an armed conflict, it is still obliged to ensure that a proxy complies with the Geneva Conventions to the extent that it exercises some degree of control over that proxy.

When it comes to positive obligations, States 'must do everything reasonably in their power to prevent and bring (. . .) violations [of Geneva Conventions] to an end'.[77] That may include such duties as providing legal advisers to assist in the adoption and implementation of proper national legislation, including penal codes; training legal advisers within the armed forces; teaching IHL as part of military training; exerting diplomatic pressure in case of violations of IHL, and even taking retorsions.[78] For example, this means that regardless of the possibility of attributing to Russia the actions of its proxies, Russia is still obliged to ensure that groups such as the 'Kadyrovtsy'[79]—Chechen fighters named after their leader Ramzan Kadyrov, accused of the most flagrant crimes, including atrocities committed in Bucha—are trained to comply IHL and to investigate any alleged violations and penalize infringements.

---

proceeding in *Legal Consequences of the Construction of a Wall in the Occupied Palestinian Territory* (n 71): *Legal Memorandum submitted by the Arab Republic of Egypt* (28 January 2004) 35; and *Written Statement of the Hashemite Kingdom of Jordan* (30 January 2004), para. 5.80 <https://www.icj-cij.org/public/files/case-related/131/1559.pdf>.

[73] International Committee of the Red Cross (n 43) para. 144.

[74] Hathaway et al. (n 62) 567.

[75] International Committee of the Red Cross (n 43) para. 153; *Legal Consequences of the Construction of a Wall* (n 71) para. 158. For arguments supporting opposite view, see *Separate Opinion of Judge Kooijmans* [2004] ICJ Rep. 219, paras. 46–49.

[76] To similar effect, see the Convention against Torture and Other Cruel, Inhuman or Degrading Treatment or Punishment (10 December 1984), 1465 UNTS 85, Art. 2(1) of which states as follows: 'Each State Party shall take effective legislative, administrative, judicial or other measures to prevent acts of torture in any territory under its jurisdiction'. See also Articles 4–5 of the Convention.

[77] International Committee of the Red Cross (n 43) para. 154.

[78] Umesh Palwankar, 'Measures Available to States for Fulfilling Their Obligation to Ensure Respect for International Humanitarian Law' (1994) 34 International Review of the Red Cross 9, 11–14.

[79] Mansur Mirovalev, 'The Real Role of pro-Russian Chechens in Ukraine' *Aljazeera* (18 August 2022) <https://www.aljazeera.com/news/2022/8/18/the-real-role-of-pro-russian-chechens-in-ukraine> 8 March 2023.

442 INSTRUMENTS, TACTICS, AND METHODS IN THE GREY ZONE

Pursuant to their negative obligations, States 'may neither encourage, nor aid or assist in violations of the Conventions by Parties to a conflict'.[80] For instance, if a certain operation that a proxy is about to execute may foreseeably violate the Conventions, the patron State is obliged to refrain from cooperating with the proxy in the commission of those actions. Also, it must refrain from transferring weapons, financial support, or any other material assistance if it has knowledge that such support will be used to commit violations of the Conventions.[81] For example, if the United States suspects that the military support it provides for pro-governmental fighters in Yemen is used to violate IHL, it should halt any such assistance.[82]

In addition, Article 1 obliges States to 'respect and ensure respect' 'in all circumstances', which means that this duty is binding not only during an armed conflict, whether international or non-international,[83] but also in peacetime.[84]

3.2.2 Arms Trade Treaty

The provision of arms by a patron State to a proxy can have a number of negative consequences, including sparking a conflict or increasing its duration and intensity. Moreover, weapons may easily end up in the hands of unintended recipients.[85] For this reason, it is important to refer to the regulations of the Arms Trade Treaty. In a section of its preamble entitled 'Principles', the Treaty acknowledges the importance of:

> Respecting and ensuring respect for international humanitarian law in accordance with, inter alia, the Geneva Conventions of 1949, and respecting and ensuring respect for human rights in accordance with, inter alia, the Charter of the United Nations and the Universal Declaration of Human Rights.[86]

Furthermore, pursuant to Article 6 of the Treaty, States may not authorize the transfer of conventional arms covered by Articles 2(1), 3, or 4,[87] if the transfer

---

[80] International Committee of the Red Cross (n 43) para. 154. See also J.-M. Henckaerts and L. Doswald-Beck (eds), *Customary International Humanitarian Law*, Volume I: Rules (CUP 2005), Rule 144; American Bar Association (n 12) 15.

[81] International Committee of the Red Cross (n 43) paras. 160–62.

[82] Oona A. Hathaway et al, 'Common Article 1 and the U.S. Duty to Ensure Respect for the Geneva Conventions in Yemen' (*Just Security*, 26 April 2018) <https://www.justsecurity.org/55415/common-article-1-u-s-duty-ensure-respect-geneva-conventions-yemen/> 8 March 2023.

[83] Boisson De Chazournes and Condorelli (n 72) 68–69.

[84] International Committee of the Red Cross (n 43) para. 145. That includes, inter alia, the obligation to disseminate knowledge about IHL and to adopt proper domestic regulations in order to ensure compliance with IHL. See Boisson De Chazournes and Condorelli (n 72) 71.

[85] American Bar Association (n 12) 6. For instance, antiaircraft missiles provided by the United States in 1989 to the mujahideen in Afghanistan were later found in Bosnia, Iran, Kashmir, Tunisia, and Palestine.

[86] Arms Trade Treaty (2 April 2013), 3013 UNTS 269.

[87] Article 2(1): 'This Treaty shall apply to all conventional arms within the following categories: (a) Battle tanks; (b) Armoured combat vehicles; (c) Large-calibre artillery systems; (d) Combat aircraft;

would violate their obligations under measures adopted by the UN Security Council acting under Chapter VII of the Charter of the United Nations, in particular arms embargoes. Such transfers are also prohibited if they would breach States' relevant international obligations under agreements to which they are parties, especially those relating to the transfer of, or illicit trafficking in, conventional arms.[88] More importantly, this prohibition refers also to a situation when a State 'has knowledge at the time of authorization that the arms or items would be used in the commission of genocide, crimes against humanity, grave breaches of the Geneva Conventions of 1949, attacks directed against civilian objects or civilians protected as such, or other war crimes as defined by international agreements to which it is a Party'.[89] However, even if the export is not prohibited under Article 6, prior to its authorization, a State is obliged to assess the potential that the conventional arms or items would, inter alia, contribute to or undermine peace and security; could be used to commit or facilitate a serious violation of IHL or of international human rights law; or an act constituting an offence under international conventions or protocols relating to terrorism.[90]

All these provisions are applicable to weapons provided by States to proxies. Thus, States would be in breach of the Treaty if the weapons they provided to proxies would violate UN embargoes, contravene IHL rules or human rights, or would contribute to the commission of an international crime or an act of terrorism. An example of such a breach of the Treaty may be the export of arms by several States, including the United States, the UK, Bulgaria, and Serbia,[91] to Saudi Arabia and the United Arab Emirates which use these imported weapons to equip their proxies in Yemen, despite accusations of serious violations of IHL.[92] Another case concerns Central and East European States, namely, Bosnia and Hercegovina, Bulgaria, Croatia, Czech Republic, Montenegro, Slovakia, Serbia, and Romania,[93] exporting their arms to Saudi Arabia, Jordan, the United

---

(e) Attack helicopters; (f) Warships; (g) Missiles and missile launchers; and (h) Small arms and light weapons'. Article 3: 'Each State Party shall establish and maintain a national control system to regulate the export of ammunition/munitions fired, launched or delivered by the conventional arms covered under Article 2 (1), and shall apply the provisions of Article 6 and Article 7 prior to authorizing the export of such ammunition/munitions'. Article 4: 'Each State Party shall establish and maintain a national control system to regulate the export of parts and components where the export is in a form that provides the capability to assemble the conventional arms covered under Article 2 (1) and shall apply the provisions of Article 6 and Article 7 prior to authorizing the export of such parts and components'.

[88] Arms Trade Treaty, Arts. 6 (1), 6(2).
[89] Ibid. Art. 6(3).
[90] Ibid. Art. 7(1).
[91] The UK, Bulgaria, and Serbia are parties to the Arms Trade Treaty.
[92] Amnesty International, 'Arms Control' <https://www.amnesty.org/en/what-we-do/arms-control/> accessed 8 March 2023; Amnesty International, 'When Arms Go Astray' <https://arms-uae.amnesty.org/en/> accessed 8 March 2023.
[93] All these States are parties to the Arms Trade Treaty.

Arab Emirates, and Turkey, key arms markets for Syria and Yemen. Weapons and ammunition sold by these States have been used, inter alia, by the Free Syrian Army, Ansar al-Sham, the Islamic State, factions fighting for Bashar-al-Assad, and Sunni forces in Yemen.[94]

Each State Party to the Arms Trade Treaty should establish and maintain a national control system, including a national control list, which it must provide to the Secretariat.[95] States are also obliged to 'maintain national records, pursuant to its national laws and regulations, of its issuance of export authorizations or its actual exports of the conventional arms'.[96] In addition, States are also under a reporting obligation, whereby they must provide to the Secretariat information about both measures undertaken in order to implement the Treaty, as well as concerning authorized or actual exports and imports of conventional arms.[97]

The Arms Trade Treaty is by no means flawless. The criteria prohibiting export under Article 7 are too vague and potentially subject to abusive interpretation; the Treaty does not prohibit training, transport, and providing surveillance equipment; it does not cover weapons technology; and it refers only to the sale of arms, leaving aside loans, leases, aid, or gifts of weapons.[98] There is no sanctions mechanism in case of non-compliance with the reporting obligation or in case of doubts concerning the credibility of the submitted report. It is highly doubtful whether the provisions of the Treaty have attained a customary status, while the Treaty itself has not attained universal participation. Currently, 111 States are parties to the Treaty, excluding the United States, Russia and South Korea, three of the eight biggest arms exporters in the world.[99]

Overall, the adoption of the Arms Trade Treaty is certainly a positive step forward in the worldwide control of the export and import of conventional arms. Yet, given both its material scope and lack of universal participation, the Treaty has not completely eliminated the provision of weapons by States to proxies in situations where the latter may use these arms discriminately and in violation of basic humanitarian rules.

---

[94] Ivan Angelovski, Miranda Patrucic, and Lawrence Marzouk, 'Revealed: The £1bn of Weapons flowing from Europe to Middle East' *The Guardian* (London, 27 July 2016) <https://www.theguard ian.com/world/2016/jul/27/weapons-flowing-eastern-europe-middle-east-revealed-arms-trade-syria> accessed 8 March 2023. Under Article 11(1) of the Arms Trade Treaty, each State Party is obliged to take measures to prevent the diversion of the conventional arms it transfers.

[95] Arms Trade Treaty, Arts. 5(2), 5(4). The Secretariat's task is to assist States Parties in the effective implementation of the Treaty (Art. 18).

[96] Arms Trade Treaty, Art. 12(1).

[97] Ibid. Art. 13.

[98] Ghazala Yasmin Jalil, 'Arms Trade Treaty: A Critical Analysis' (2016) 36 Strategic Studies 78, 87–90.

[99] Katharina Buchholz, 'The World's Biggest Arms Exporters' (*Statista* 14 March 2022) <https://www.statista.com/chart/18417/global-weapons-exports/> accessed 15 August 2022.

4. Conclusions

The aim of this chapter has been to review the international legal norms applicable to NSAs. To this end, the chapter distinguished between NSAs which act independently and those which act as proxies. As the category of NSAs is not homogeneous, it was necessary to differentiate between different actors. The first part of the chapter focused on three types of actors: individuals, ANSAs, and transnational corporations. The second part of the chapter turned to the status of proxies, demonstrating how the level of control over proxies influences the potential responsibility of States.

The analysis has shown that NSAs, both those acting independently and those acting as proxies, operate in the grey zones of international law: there are few rules that are applicable to them directly. By contrast, States are subject to various obligations not to employ or support proxy forces to carry out acts that they themselves are barred from undertaking by international law. In addition, States may also be held accountable for the wrongful conduct of proxies, provided that their relationship is sufficiently close to justify the attribution of that conduct to the State. However, both of these avenues of accountability suffer from substantial flaws and shortcomings: on the one hand, treaties which bind States, such as the Arms Trade Treaty, do not form a comprehensive system and lack effective enforcement mechanisms. On the other hand, rules of attribution are vague and require precise knowledge of the relationship between States and proxies, which often is lacking.

The biggest beneficiaries, as well as creators, of this grey zone are States. They are also the only actors able to change the law, but at the same time the ones that abuse the status of NSAs to escape accountability. The use of non-State entities seems to be too valuable and attractive in pursuing hybrid warfare, so it is unlikely that the current state of affairs will change any time soon.

What about States which are targeted by hybrid warfare and the NSAs' activities? They have two options: if members of NSAs may be subject to the jurisdiction of the targeted State or the jurisdiction of international courts or other accountability mechanisms are engaged, enforcement action may be taken against the members of proxy NSAs under domestic law or possibly international criminal law. Alternatively, the targeted State may seek to invoke the responsibility of the patron State. In that case, it would have to present sufficient evidence to establish that the proxies were acting on behalf of the patron State, so that their conduct is attributable to that State in line with the rules of State responsibility.

20

From Red Scare to Red Scare, Grey Zone to Grey Zone

Weaponizing Dissent and Civil Society

Tyler Wentzell and Barbara J. Falk

1. Introduction

Not long after the Arab Spring, Russian General Valeryi Gerasimov, the Chief of the General Staff, penned an article in *Military Industrial Kurier*, titled 'The Value of Science in the Foresight'.[1] Gerasimov noted that modern conflicts were no longer characterized by a clear binary between war and peace. Most conflicts would occur right at the threshold of these two states of being, where countries had to carefully manage their actions to advance their interests without leading to undue escalation. In these kinds of conflicts, Gerasimov reasoned, non-military means would likely prove more decisive than bald firepower. Information operations would precede combat, and special operations forces would complement opposition forces already in a given territory. Working together, these forces would establish a 'permanently operating front' throughout the enemy State. The overt commitment of military force—'often under the guise of peacekeeping and crisis regulation'—would take place primarily to achieve 'final success in the conflict'.[2]

Gerasimov's article was not an articulation of a future Russian campaign plan, and certainly not one of doctrine.[3] Nonetheless, the idea of the 'Gerasimov

---

[1] Valery Gerasimov, 'The Value of Science Is in the Foresight: New Challenges Demand Rethinking the Forms and Methods of Carrying out Combat Operations', *Military-Industrial Kurier* (27 February 2013), tr. Robert Coalson (2016) 96 Military Review 23.

[2] Gerasimov's article was subsequently translated and explained on Russia expert Mark Galeotti's blog, *In Moscow's Shadows,* after which it became famous. Mark Galeotti, 'The 'Gerasimov Doctrine' and Russian Non-Linear War' (*In Moscow's Shadows: Analysis and Assessment of Russian Crime and Security,* June 2014) <https://inmoscowsshadows.wordpress.com/2014/07/06/the-gerasimov-doctr ine-and-russian-non-linear-war/> accessed 21 August 2022.

[3] Galeotti subsequently wrote that in calling Gerasimov's article the 'Gerasimov Doctrine', he sought only to produce a snappy title. He repudiated the term in a proviso on his blog, explaining:

> (a) Gerasimov didn't invent this; if any CoGS deserves the 'credit' it would be his predecessor Makarov, but even so it is really an evolutionary, not revolutionary process; and (b) it's not a

448 INSTRUMENTS, TACTICS, AND METHODS IN THE GREY ZONE

Doctrine' stuck and became something of a bogeyman in Western perceptions of Russian activities and intentions. Despite frequent missteps in Russian intelligence fieldcraft and military operations, the sophistication and degree of Russian meddling overseas and in its near abroad is often overestimated. A clear example of this was the widespread belief in significant and direct Russian influence in the 2016 US presidential campaign. While the publicly acknowledged interference should not be discounted, its extent and efficacy proved to be wildly overestimated.[4] Similarly, the Russian invasion of Ukraine was not preceded (as widely expected) by sophisticated political, cyber, and economic attacks paralyzing Ukraine and isolating it from its allies. This chapter argues that none of this is new. Russia has a long history of weaponizing dissent in the West, and the West has a long history of overestimating its extent and efficacy. Moreover, during the Cold War, the West also weaponized dissent, literally and figuratively, in grey zone activities in Eastern Europe. This chapter takes a historical approach to this phenomenon. Looking at specific examples from the Red Scare in Canada from 1919 until 1949, through to CIA operation QRHELPFUL to support the independent trade union and social movement *Solidarność* (Solidarity) in Poland in the 1980s. Indeed, given the role played by the CIA and pro-democracy organizations such as the National Endowment for Democracy, not without reason does Russian President Vladimir Putin voice continued suspicions about Western support for 'colour revolutions' aimed at unseating authoritarian rulers in the name of pro-Western democracy.

2. Grey zone(s)

The term 'grey zone' has multiple meanings which, we contend, are less distinctive that one might think upon initial examination. In particular, we examine the term as it was used in the late Cold War among dissident communities in Central and Eastern Europe as well as its current conceptual elasticity to discuss operations and activities below the legal threshold of war.

> doctrine, which is in the Russian lexicon a truly foundational set of beliefs as to what kinds of war the country will be fighting in the future and how it will win them—this is more an observation about a particular aspect of particular kinds of wars in the 21stC, there is certainly no expectation that this is *the* Russian way of war. So stop it, please!

Ibid. See also Mark Galeotti, 'The Mythical "Gerasimov Doctrine" and the Language of Threat' (2019) 7 Critical Studies on Security 157.

[4] See Robert S. Mueller III, 'The Mueller Report Presented with Related Materials by *The Washington Post*: Introduction and Analysis by Rosalind S. Helderman and Matt Zapotosky (Scribner 2019), esp. Volume I, 72–214; Linda Greenhouse, 'The Impeachment Question', The New York Review of Books (27 June 2019) 18–22.

In the late 1980s, after Mikhail Gorbachev initiated both *perestroika* and *glasnost* in the Soviet Union, it became increasingly clear that the Kremlin would be less and less likely to intervene militarily or politically to prop up increasingly unpopular and moribund communist governments within the Eastern Bloc. Aside from Poland, where an estimated ten million joined Solidarity at its height, dissident movements following the 1968 crushing of the Prague Spring by Soviet tanks and those of four other States providing 'fraternal assistance', largely consisted of small, dedicated communities ranging from Helsinki Watch groups to nationally specific organizations such as Charter 77 in Czechoslovakia and issue-specific groups such as the environmentalist group Danube Circle (*Duna Kör*) in Hungary. As a group, these activists, or 'dissidents', were willing to risk regime public shaming, social ostracization, loss of profession and income, restriction of educational opportunities for children, trumped up charges for crimes against the State, political trials, and imprisonment.[5] However, by the late 1980s, a series of proximate and longer-term events and causes loosened public fear, and among those most active below the surface were those in the 'grey zone'.

In 1990, Czech dissident Jiřina Šiklová published 'The "Grey Zone" and The Future of Dissent in Czechoslovakia'—published after the fall of the Berlin Wall in November 1990 but penned beforehand.[6] She argued that critical to successfully challenging the regime are those in the intelligentsia, 'professionally erudite' who worked inside State socialist structures, many of whom 'perceived the errors of the socialist system early on' and did not 'have to buttress their careers by means of a party card or by taking on political functions'.[7] Those in the grey zone were not politically active or publicly demonstrative in support of dissident aims and ideas, yet they were strategically valuable given their expertise and experience. Their human capital translated easily into administerial and technocratic know-how often lacking among the dissidents, many of whom had long been expelled from careers or were non-conformists at heart. 'Grey' also implied an uncertain status, those never entirely clean, compromised from a strictly moral point of view, conditioned as they were by the vicissitudes of compromise and cooperation. The grey zone was numerically much larger than the dissident

---

[5] On dissident/dissidence in Central and Eastern Europe see Kacper Szulecki, *Dissidence in Communist Central Europe: Human Rights and the Emergence of New Transnational Actors* (Palgrave Macmillan 2019); Barbara J. Falk, 'Resistance and Dissent in Eastern and Central Europe: An Emerging Historiography' (2011) 25 East European Politics and Societies 318.

[6] Jiřina Šiklová, 'The 'Grey Zone' and The Future of Dissent in Czechoslovakia' (1990) 57 Social Research 347. She acknowledges borrowing the term from Rudolf Prokop, Ladislav Sádecký, and Karel Bina, 'České dějepisectví včera, dnes a zítra' (1988) 22 Historické studie 113. After 1968, Šiklová was ousted from her position at Charles University and worked as a janitor, researcher, and social worker and was a Charter 77 signatory—but unofficially functioned as an important clandestine courier in getting *samizdat* texts into the hands of those who could transport them to the West for wider distribution (for which she was imprisoned).

[7] Šiklová (n 6) 350.

450 INSTRUMENTS, TACTICS, AND METHODS IN THE GREY ZONE

ghetto—and existed, in Šiklová's estimation, in every social, professional, or interest group. They escaped easy definition first by their invisibility and second by a lack of a program or set of core beliefs: 'they and their children generally slip through the various checks and screening processes, obtain a decent education, an acceptable job classification, a decent (if not exorbitant) measure of professional success'.[8] The communist establishment was keenly aware of the dangers of an expanding grey zone, and why the regime doubled down periodically on 'purges, screenings, interrogations, consolidated employee data files, party card exchanges, etc'.[9] Being in the grey zone meant being potentially radicalized, one short action or stand from outright dissent.

In the post-Cold War, post-2014 Russian annexation of Crimea, the 'grey zone' has taken on specific security and military connotations. In 2016, the US Department of Defense defined the grey zone as 'a conceptual space between peace and war'.[10] As the editors of this volume emphasize, multiple elements of State power are used to advance or secure objectives with may be more or less political or military in nature. Moreover, activities in the 'grey zone' are ambiguous enough to complicate attribution and enhance plausible deniability. Legally, the goal is to remain below the threshold of war. Practically, such activities keep conflict short of large-scale kinetic involvement. Indeed, as Elizabeth Braw argues, 'Gray-zone warfare does not involve persistent use of military force, while hybrid warfare does'.[11] Further, she asserts that 'today's and tomorrow's wars have a much stronger component of gray-zone aggression and a much smaller component of conventional war than do traditional wars'.[12]

Given this expansive view, the tent of grey zone activities is broad, including the funding or direction of foreign or domestic civil society organizations; political and economic espionage and infiltration; the use of mainstream, alternative, and social media to undermine the adversary (with an almost endless array of tactics); promotion or funding of protest, civil unrest, or direct political challenges to a regime; the infiltration of academia; the purposeful use of 'willing dupes' in all facets of public life alongside or in addition to bribery and corruption of officials in the targeted State; cyber threats and attacks; economic leverage especially with respect to energy or food supplies in uneven dependency relationships or stake in or control of critical security infrastructure; and finally all forms of lawfare.[13] For purposes of our discussion, civil society organizations

---

[8] Ibid. 353.

[9] Ibid. 354.

[10] Department of Defense Strategic Multi-Layer Assessment, 'Gray Zone Effort Update' (September 2016).

[11] Elisabeth Braw, *The Defender's Dilemma: Identifying and Deterring Grey Zone Aggression* (American Enterprise Institute 2022) 11.

[12] Ibid. 11.

[13] Almost anything short of territorial violation or armed attack can be considered within the grey zone. Many grey zone definitions exist alongside or overlap with the 'hybrid' side of hybrid

include non-governmental organizations, transnational organizations, but also charitable organizations, religious orders and denominations, lobby groups, and economic associations. In defining lawfare (itself an elastic concept), we draw from the influential Lawfare website, which describes a 'nebulous zone in which actions taken or contemplated to protect the nation interact with the nation's laws and institutions' and 'the use of law as a weapon of conflict'.[14] There is an obvious definitional conundrum here—the definition has become so elastic that anything security related that is also State challenging or undermining can be considered a grey zone threat or activity.

However, we are also interested in connecting the past with the present. Common to the grey zone as used by Central and East European dissidence and contemporary authors and research organizations is a sense of liminality. A grey zone is a transitional space, a difficult-to-fix location that is both unsettling (in terms of potentially containing or promoting the possibility of threat) as well as theoretical and kinetic no-man's land, outside the regular time/space continuum and binary of peace/war. The liminality of the grey zone is also evident by its enigmatic nature, where proof of status is elusive, and deniability is easier. The grey zone is the realm of the uncanny, where one needs extra perception and focus to determine what is really going on. Attribution is challenging and deniability is often the norm.

3. Red Scares

The 1917 Bolshevik Revolution fundamentally changed the nature of Karl Marx's spectre of communism haunting Europe. Communists, anarchists, and other left-wing revolutionaries had long caused fear among State security services in Europe and elsewhere, but such radical groups tended to be small and disorganized. State-backing gave the movement leadership and resources. These resources were scant at first—given the demands of suing for peace with Germany, winning the raging civil war, and reforming the State apparatus—but

---

warfare definitions. See especially the discussions of hybrid threats offered by various research reports published online by the NATO Strategic Communications Centre of Excellence in Riga, Latvia, as well as the European Centre of Excellence for Countering Hybrid Threats in Helsinki, Finland. Particularly helpful are the research reports 'Hybrid Threats: A Strategic Communications Perspective' at <https://stratcomcoe.org/publications/hybrid-threats-a-strategic-communications-perspective/79> accessed 20 February 2023 as well as Hybrid CoE's discussion of hybrid threats as a concept at <https://www.hybridcoe.fi/hybrid-threats-as-a-phenomenon/> accessed 21 August 2022.

[14] Lawfare, 'About Lawfare: A Brief History of the Term and the Site' <https://www.lawfareb log.com/about-lawfare-brief-history-term-and-site> accessed 21 August 2022. The Lawfare Blog authors draw from a range of sources, from People's Liberation Army strategy on unrestricted warfare through to the work of Charles Dunlap.

452   INSTRUMENTS, TACTICS, AND METHODS IN THE GREY ZONE

the creation of the Third or Communist International (Comintern) in March 1919 was cause for alarm. General strikes, the June 1919 bombing campaign in the United States, and the creation of Moscow-aligned Communist Parties around the world seemed to signal that a robust plot against democracy and capitalism was afoot. While this initial period (1917–20) is often termed the 'First' Red Scare with the post- World War II discovery of Soviet spying and the ensuing McCarthyite witch hunt (1947–57) being the 'Second', this chapter sets aside the distinction as there is more that connects the two events than separates them.[15]

In Canada, the crisis seemed to run deep. Some historians have begun to style the period of 1918–25 as the 'Workers' Revolt', a period that saw increased militancy in strike action.[16] The Winnipeg General Strike, which shut down the city from 15 May–25 June 1919, is the most famous, but there were lesser-known general strikes that year in Victoria, British Columbia; Calgary and Edmonton, Alberta; Brandon, Manitoba; Toronto, Ontario; and Amherst, Nova Scotia. Local authorities called upon the militia to quell unrest by force at least eight times between the Armistice and 1921 and held them in high readiness on several other occasions. Although such military call-outs soon decreased in frequency, the deployments to the Cape Breton coalfields in 1923 and 1925 were the largest domestic operations since the 1885 Northwest Rebellion.[17] Some of these groups drew inspiration from events in the Soviet Union, but they were not fuelled by 'Moscow gold'.[18]

While much of the outward signs of this dissent had mostly quieted by 1925, the policing struggle to keep the 'Red Menace' in check continued. The Royal Canadian Mounted Police (RCMP) Security Service actively monitored the

[15] In the literature, the first 'Red Scare' occurred after World War I, with the second 'Red Scare' occurring after World War II. However, anticommunism in both Canada and the United States was much more of a continuum, beginning with Western fears and responses to the Russian Revolution in 1917. In the United States, see Christopher M. Finan, *From the Palmer Raids to the Patriot Act: A History of the Fight for Free Speech in America* (Beacon Press 2007); Larry Ceplair, *Anti-Communism in 20th Century America: A Critical History* (ABC-CLIO 2011); Ellen Schrecker, *Many Are The Crimes: McCarthyism in America* (Princeton University Press 1998); and M. J. Heale, *American Anticommunism: Combating the Enemy Within, 1830–1970* (Johns Hopkins University Press 1990). In Canada, see David MacKenzie, *Canada's Red Scare* (Canadian Historical Association 2001). Reg Whitaker and Gary Marcuse eschew the language of the 'Red Scare' in favour of 'Cold War conservatism', but what they both document and analyse is the era of the second 'Red Scare': see Reg Whitaker and Gary Marcuse, *Cold War Canada: The Making of a National Insecurity State 1945–1957* (University of Toronto Press 1994).

[16] Gregory S. Kealey, '1919: The Canadian Labour Revolt' (1984) 13 Labour/Le Travail 11; Craig Heron, *The Workers' Revolt in Canada, 1917–1925* (University of Toronto Press 1998).

[17] Don Macgillivray, 'Military Aid to the Civil Power: The Cape Breton Experience in the 1920s' (1974) 32 Acadiensis 45; Craig Heron, *Working in Steel: The Early Years in Canada, 1883–1935* (University of Toronto Press, 2008) 155–57.

[18] On the question of how funding from the USSR was used to support the Communist Party of the United States of America (CPUSA) and communist parties more generally—referred to as 'Moscow gold'—see Tuomas Savonen, *Minnesota, Moscow, Manhattan: Gus Hall's Life and Political Line Until the Late 1950s* (Finnish Society of Arts and Letters 2020), esp. 237–55; Andrew Campbell, 'Moscow's Gold: Soviet Financing of Global Subversion' (1999) 40 National Observer 19.

FROM RED SCARE TO RED SCARE, GREY ZONE TO GREY ZONE   453

comings and goings of Communist Party of Canada (CPC) officials, infiltrated undercover officers, hired informants, read their mail, and attended and reported on their public meetings. The Toronto Police established a Red Squad in 1929, and other municipalities soon followed. Municipal officials denied the CPC licenses for public halls, prohibited speaking in languages the police officers could not understand (the first use of tear gas in Canada was to disperse a commemoration of Lenin in a hall when a speaker spoke in Yiddish in contravention of a police order), and dispersed meetings by force when they congregated in parks, streetcorners, and other public spaces.[19] In 1931, eight leaders of the CPC and related organizations were arrested and charged under Section 98 of the *Criminal Code.* Their conviction rendered the CPC an illegal organization. Thereafter, it was illegal to be a member of the party, attend a meeting, or distribute and/or possess its literature. The party went underground and otherwise operated through front organizations.[20] With the party illegal, and its leaders imprisoned, one would presume that whatever power the CPC had would quickly dissipate. However, as the following example illustrates, the perceived influence of the communist movement went well beyond its real power.

On 15 October 1932, the *Toronto Daily Star* printed an exclusive interview with Karl Radek, an important Bolshevik leader in the 1917 revolution who had recently returned to prominence following a spat with Josef Stalin.[21] Radek told reporter Pierre Van Paassen that, 'capitalism is doomed, a blind man can see that'. Soviet propaganda abroad, he said, had done nothing more than raise the class-consciousness of the workers, pointing out the contradictions inherent in a capitalist system. He continued,

> Certain countries lock up Communists and think that they have blocked the path to the social revolution therewith. Others torture them with a fiendishness that surpasses credibility. All in the same of civilization and decency and order and Christian principles, of course. But the crisis goes on and deepens day by day. . . . We do not need to make propaganda. Your own government is the best propagandist for socialism that can be imagined.[22]

---

[19] Lita-Rose Betcherman, *The Little Band: The Clashes between the Communists and the Political and Legal Establishment in Canada, 1928–1932* (Deneau Publishers 1982) 14–28

[20] Dennis Molinaro, *An Exceptional Law: Section 98 and the Emergency State, 1919–1936* (University of Toronto Press for the Osgoode Society for Canadian Legal History 2017); Dennis Molinaro, 'Section 98: The Trial of Rex v. Buck et al and the "State of Exception" in Canada, 1919–36', in *Canadian State Trials Volume IV: Security, Dissent, and the Limits of Toleration in War and Peace, 1914–39,* edited by Barry Wright, Eric Tucker and Susan Binnie (University of Toronto Press for the Osgoode Society for Canadian Legal History 2015).

[21] Pierre Van Paassen, 'Bloodshed and Revolution Foreseen by Moscow Editor', *Toronto Daily Star* (Toronto, 15 October 1932).

[22] Ibid.

454 INSTRUMENTS, TACTICS, AND METHODS IN THE GREY ZONE

Fascism, Radek claimed, would naturally flow from the capitalist system as it tried to reassert its power, but this would inevitably lead to a crisis, 'then one crisis will follow the other with ever more intensity. Revolutions will break out spontaneously. There will be rivers and oceans of blood. Far worse than Russia ever saw in 1917. Because the capitalists abroad will not surrender as easily as the Russian nobility did fifteen years ago'.[23]

Radek's comments were not articulations of policy, nor were they threats or admissions of Soviet conduct. They were, however, very representative of Comintern and national CPC materials in the English-speaking world: the revolution was inevitable because capitalism's collapse was inevitable. The communist system would be there to pick up the pieces. Yet many saw remarks like these as only thinly veiled threats, and constructed links between such words and events where no direct connection existed. This was made plain in the 1932 Kingston Penitentiary riot.

The first of two major riots erupted at the Kingston Penitentiary—the residence of the eight imprisoned CPC leaders—only two days after publication of Radek's remarks. The warden twice called upon the local military garrison for armed assistance. Guards deployed tear gas against the prisoners and fired rifles and shotguns seemingly at random to quiet the prisoners. Less random were the three rifle bullets and ten buckshot pellets fired into CPC leader Tim Buck's cell.[24]

Assumptions were made. The shots fired at Tim Buck were styled as a failed political assassination in the pages of the left-wing press. Meanwhile, security services assumed the uprising was part of a larger plot. On 21 October, in a rare interview, Superintendent of Penitentiaries D. M. Ormond, a recently retired militia brigadier, told reporters, 'Read the papers. Read what was said in Moscow the other day, [referring to Van Passen's interview with Radek] that disturbances would shortly break out all over the world. Read what has been happening in London, England, read what has been happening across Canada'.[25] Ormond believed that the uprising had been meant to coincide with an attack by armed communists from outside the facility (which was, in part, why he retained soldiers to assist the guards for weeks after the violence subsided), and when prisoners violently rioted at the Saint Vincent de Paul Penitentiary in Quebec, he assumed that there was a broader conspiracy in play.[26] At the request of the Minister of Justice (Ormond's immediate supervisor), the military sent

[23] Ibid.
[24] Joseph Archambault, *Royal Commission to Investigate the Penal System of Canada* (Patenaude 1938) 81–97; Tim Buck, *Yours in the Struggle: Reminiscences of Tim Buck* (New Canada Publication 1977) 221.
[25] Frederick Griffin, 'Cell Fixtures Destroyed by 500 Snarling Convicts' *Toronto Daily Star* (Toronto, 21 October 1932).
[26] 'Tear Gas Quiets Week-End Unrest, Kingston Reports' *The Globe* (24 October 1932); 'Story of Arms Cache "Poppycock"—Ormond' *Toronto Daily Star* (25 October 1932).

FROM RED SCARE TO RED SCARE, GREY ZONE TO GREY ZONE 455

a platoon of soldiers to Prince Albert, Saskatchewan—Canada's most isolated penitentiary—in anticipation of an uprising that never came.[27]

Ormond's final report on the disturbances omit any reference to a communist conspiracy, presumably because he never found any evidence to support his assumptions.[28] His assumption, based on conjecture and not on hard facts, drove operational decisions in Kingston, induced a wholly unnecessary military deployment to Prince Albert (apart from the Kingston deployment, this was the only such operation since 1925), and surely obscured analysis as to the actual causes of the unrest. This obfuscation led to a delay in necessary reforms, to a political debacle that contributed to a change in government in 1935, and ultimately to a Royal Commission in 1938 that concluded that the Kingston Penitentiary uprising, as well as even more violent events at Saint Vincent de Paul, were principally the result of poor living conditions. It also determined that the CPC leaders in Kingston had only played a marginal role in organizing the strike that led to the riot, and that there was no discernible connection to Moscow.[29]

Mackenzie King's Liberals defeated Prime Minister R. B. Bennett's Conservatives in a landslide in 1935. King fulfilled his election promise of repealing Section 98 of the *Criminal Code*, making the CPC legal again. The period of illegality had not weakened the movement; in fact, it had grown in membership, in part due to the publicity and sympathy created by the ban. But the experience of operating mostly underground had created new networks and skills that they used almost immediately in the most significant and tangible example of CPC influence in the interwar period apart from labour organizing: the recruiting, organizing, deploying, and supporting of Canadian volunteers to fight in the Spanish Civil War.[30]

Notwithstanding any one individual's personal motivations for going to Spain, the fact remains that most of the volunteers were members of the CPC or the Young Communist League, that the network that got them to Spain was operated by the CPC and European affiliates, and that Soviet intelligence agents and Red Army officers played important roles within the International Brigades.[31]

---

[27] 'Government Sends Troops Here' *Prince Albert Daily Herald* (9 November1932); Princess Patricia's Canadian Light Infantry (PPCLI) Archives, PPCLI Regimental Orders, November 12, 1932.

[28] LAC, Department of Justice, Drafts and Final Report, 1932 Disturbance at Kingston Pen, by Brigadier D.M. Ormond, access to information request A-2018-01015 (hereafter Ormond Draft Report).

[29] Archambault (n 24).

[30] See Tyler Wentzell, 'Canada's Foreign Enlistment Act and the Spanish Civil War' (2017) 80 Labour/Le Travail 213.

[31] Michael Petrou, *Renegades: Canadians in the Spanish Civil War* (UBC Press 2008), 24; Wentzell (n 30) 213–17; Richard Baxell, *British Volunteers in the Spanish Civil War: The British Battalion in the International Brigades, 1936-1939* (Routledge 2004) 12–15; Daniel Kowalsky, 'Operation X: Soviet Russia and the Spanish Civil War' (2014) 91 Bulletin of Spanish Studies 159; Fridrikh Igorevich Firsov et al, *Secret Cables of the Comintern, 1933-1943* (Yale University Press 2014) 85–110.

456   INSTRUMENTS, TACTICS, AND METHODS IN THE GREY ZONE

At the time, the RCMP had significant knowledge regarding the CPC's role in organizing the volunteers based on its investigations following an order in council in July 1937 that rendered the endeavour illegal—Inspector Tony Zaneth (who had cut his teeth working undercover during the Winnipeg General Strike) acquired the relevant ships manifests from White Star Lines, corroborated with passport information and surveillance of known recruiting offices. However, the RCMP had almost no information on the actions of the volunteers in Spain or the role played by Soviet officers there. With few exceptions, they were dependent on newspaper reporting and scant information provided by the British consulate in Valencia.[32]

The RCMP knew, for example, that the first 'Canadian' volunteer was not actually Canadian at all. Emil Kleber, the commander of the first International Brigade that defended Madrid in November 1936, had publicly claimed to be an Austrian-born naturalized Canadian. An investigation discovered that Kleber was not Canadian, but the RCMP did not know who he was, and certainly had no evidence that he was Soviet intelligence officer Manfred Stern.[33] Similarly, they knew that Red Army officers were in Spain based on newspaper reporting but had no independent means of gathering useful information. With the opening of archives in the 1990s, we now know that some Red Army officers held important command appointments, such as 'General Walter' as commander of the 35th Division, the higher headquarters of the XVth Brigade which contained most of the American, British, and Canadian volunteers. Walter's real name was Karol Swierczewski, and he was a serving Red Army officer.[34] And while other Red Army officers at the brigade and battalion-level exclusively worked as mentors, there were exceptions. For instance, from 9–17 March 1938, Red Army officer Nicolay Monselinzef (nicknamed 'Maxim') was appointed acting commander of the XVth Brigade.[35] Reports by the Canadian and British battalion commanders make it clear that they received and accepted the commands of both Maxim and his assistant, Red Army officer Ivan Nikoliavitch.[36] The RCMP feared that

[32] For example, the Communist Party press only became aware that one of its members, Edward Cecil-Smith, had been appointed the commander of the Mackenzie-Papineau Battalion after it had been reported in the pages of the *New York Times,* based on an interview with a returned volunteer in New York City.

[33] Manfred Braun, *A Comintern Agent in China, 1932–1939* (Hearst 1982) 26; Boris Volodarsky, *Stalin's Agent: The Life and Death of Alexander Orlov* (OUP 2015) 228–29. For examples of Canadian newspaper coverage, see 'Grimmest Battle of the War' *Toronto Daily Star* (28 November 1936); Frederick Griffin, 'Valencia's Vivid Sky' *Toronto Daily Star* (1 December 1936); 'Kleber Not Citizen, Records Show', *Toronto Daily Star* (12 February 1937).

[34] Antony Beevor, *The Battle for Spain: The Spanish Civil War, 1936–1939* (Penguin Books 2006) 196–97.

[35] Russian State Archive of Socio-Political History, Fond 545, Opis 3, Delo 475, The Withdrawal of Aragon (April 1938).

[36] Cecil-Smith's full report is held at Library and Archives Canada (LAC), MG30 E173, Makenzie-Papineau Battalion Collection, Cecil-Smith Papers, 1–2. It is reproduced in part in William Beeching, *Canadian Volunteers: Spain, 1936–1939* (Canadian Plains Research Centre, 1989). See also the report

FROM RED SCARE TO RED SCARE, GREY ZONE TO GREY ZONE   457

the returned volunteers would provide a cadre of hardened revolutionaries and monitored many of them for the rest of their lives. No such threats materialized, although Russian intelligence made good use of Canadian passports seized in Spain to assist in emplacing agents in the United States and Mexico.[37]

The early years of World War II saw a series of rapid changes in Western perceptions of the Soviet Union. After years of framing Nazism as the greatest threat to humanity, the Soviet Union entered its Non-Aggression Pact and told Communist Parties around the world to keep their homelands out of the war. Delays in determining and communicating ensuing policy led to tremendous embarrassment for Communist Parties which initially rallied for a united defence of Poland against the Nazi invaders, only to declare their desire for peaceful coexistence with Germany just days later. CPC leaders went into hiding in the still-neutral United States, while party members in Canada were interned as an illegal organization for its anti-war stance.[38] When Germany invaded the Soviet Union in June 1941, the CPC reversed its policy on the war and its members (now operating under the brand of the Labour-Progressive Party, or LPP) were let out of internment camps and even permitted to join the Canadian military. Fred Rose, an LPP leader in Montreal, was elected as a Member of Parliament. In Moscow, the Soviet Union dissolved the Comintern—an act meant to show that it was no longer interested in interfering in the internal affairs of its war-time allies.

The defection of Soviet cypher clerk Igor Gouzenko to Canadian authorities marked a new chapter in Western perceptions of the Soviet Union. State security services had long suspected the presence of Soviet spies hiding within the communist movement but had failed to uncover them using traditional policing techniques. Of those later convicted, only Fred Rose and Sam Carr, two long-time functionaries of the CPC and later LPP, had been subjects of police investigations. The others, despite all but one having a connection to the LPP, likely would not have been discovered at all but for Gouzenko 'coming in from the cold'.[39] Furthermore, although some of these agents had successfully offered up information regarding diplomatic communications and nuclear secrets,

---

filed by British Battalion commander, Sam Wild: RGASPI, Fond 545, Opis 3, Delo 497, report by Sam Wild, 28 April 1938, 1–2.

[37] Myron Momryk, 'Ignacy Witczak's Passport, Soviet Espionage and the Origins of the Cold War in Canada' (2011) 68 Polish American Studies 67; Steve Hewitt, ' "Strangely Easy to Obtain": Canadian Passport Security, 1933–73' (2008) 23 Intelligence and National Security 381.

[38] Reg Whitaker, 'Official Repression of Communism during World War II' (1986) 17 Labour/Le Travail 135; Buck (n 24) 290–99.

[39] Regarding the investigation, see Reg Whittaker's 'The Gouzenko Affair: From Star Chamber to the Court Room', in *Canadian State Trials Volume 5: World War, Cold War, and Challenges to Sovereignty, 1939–1990*, edited by Barry Wright, Susan Binnie, and Eric Tucker (University of Toronto Press 2022) 125.

458 INSTRUMENTS, TACTICS, AND METHODS IN THE GREY ZONE

including providing samples of isotopes, most of the information acquired through this network was shockingly mundane. For instance, Edward Mazerall, the first defendant tried for conspiracy to breach the *Official Secrets Act*, provided information on radio sets for which he was sentenced to four years in prison. The reports in question were scheduled for publication in trade journals and, his supervisor testified, would have been provided to Soviet officials if they had simply requested them through the proper channels.[40]

The immediate investigation of Gouzenko's documents led to eleven convictions, ten in Canadian courts.[41] While the secretive investigation employed draconian methods, the public trials were rather dull and uncontroversial compared to the public spectacle around the American Hollywood Ten, Alger Hiss, Julius and Ethel Rosenberg, or the British Cambridge Five. Subsequent revelations may prove otherwise, but Soviet espionage does not appear to have been particularly successful in gaining much influence in Canada outside the communist movement itself. The closest exception might have been Herbert Norman, a successful Canadian diplomat by the 1950s who was labelled a communist in testimony before the Internal Security Sub-committee of the US Senate's Judiciary Committee. He surely had some contacts with the movement in his youth, but there was no evidence he maintained such associations by the 1950s and there is certainly no meaningful evidence of espionage. Nonetheless, the resulting hounding and looming end of his successful career played no small part in his suicide. As historian Jack Granatstein commented, 'Herbert Norman was evidently damned if he did admit to being a 1930s communist and, as unfortunately became his fate, damned if he lied in a vain attempt to protect himself. Norman was a Canadian victim of the dark, dirty decades of the 1930s and 1950s'.[42]

With the benefit of hindsight, security officials clearly overestimated the degree of Soviet penetration and influence in Canada. On the surface, they could observe the direct influence of the Soviet Union on Canadians through sponsored visits, training programs, publications, the CPC, and Canadian-Soviet friendship societies.[43] With only slightly more effort, they could see that some

---

[40] 'Gave Lunan Two Reports, Got No Money—Mazerall', *Toronto Daily Star* (20 May 1946); 'Data Available to Russia Officially, Defence Claims', *Toronto Daily Star* (21 May 1946); *Rex v. Mazerall,* [1946] O.R. 762 (ON CA).

[41] For more on the disclosures arising from the criminal trials, see Barbara J. Falk and Tyler Wentzell, 'The Enemy Within: Review and Comparison of Early Cold War Canadian and American Spy Trials', in Wright et al (n 39) 177.

[42] J. L. Granatstein and David Stafford, *Spy Wars: Espionage and Canada from Gouzenko to Glasnost* (Key Porter Books Limited 1990) 103.

[43] Regarding Soviet friendship societies in Canada and elsewhere, see Jennifer Anderson, *Propaganda and Persuasion: The Cold War and the Canadian-Soviet Friendship Society* (University of Manitoba Press 2017); Rachel Appelbaum, *Empire of Friends: Soviet Power and Socialist Internationalism in Cold War Czechoslovakia* (Cornell University Press 2019) 19–49. Regarding

Canadians were willing to risk life and liberty to advance Soviet interests, and that there was *some* Soviet penetration of the government—surely, they thought, there was more if they kept digging. But they had trouble distinguishing between affinity for the Soviet State and desire for socialist/liberal reforms, which sometimes obscured their understanding of causation. While some Canadians desired a Soviet-style revolution, many more simply saw the Soviet network as a useful means to pursuing the liberal changes they desired. In their zeal, police often destroyed lives and reputations, eroding their moral legitimacy, and obscuring their vision. A 'carrot and stick' approach—of more limited policing of dissent while actively pursuing social change—might have more ably mollified dissenters.

4. Solidarity and otherwise meddling in Eastern Europe

During the Cold War, Western powers supported independent organizations and movements of dissent in fledgling civil societies in Central and Eastern Europe—part of an effort to hold communist governments to account to their legal obligations under the Helsinki Accords, but politically an effort to 'bore from within'. Ironically, this was the same strategy that Western governments accused communist parties of doing within democracies, supported ideologically and/or financially by the Soviet Union, as the Canadian and American Red Scares illustrate. In Central and Eastern Europe, the activism and support sometimes occurred in the 'grey zone' and was seen positively. In liberal democracies, such action was considered dangerous and destabilizing 'Fifth Column' types of activities.

Poland is the example par excellence of Western 'grey zone' activity targeting a crucial Eastern Bloc State—characterized as domestic interference, espionage, and worse by the Soviet Union, but styled as heroic and far-sighted support to a free and independent self-governing trade union and social movement that, in Cold War triumphalist lore, hastened communism's collapse domestically and regionally. Moreover, Poland is an important case to examine because only in recent years has the full story of the grey zone fully emerged due to the diligent work of archivists and historians from Europe and the United States.

Solidarność, or Solidarity, was born out of a decade of Polish economic crisis, a history of labour unrest on the Baltic Coast, and a catalytic wave of industrial strikes throughout Poland in the summer of 1980. The fulcrum of activism was the Lenin shipyard in Gdánsk, where local committees sought to create 'free'

Canadian travelers to the Soviet Union in the interwar period, see Kirk Niergarth's unpublished manuscript, *Canadian Communists*.

460   INSTRUMENTS, TACTICS, AND METHODS IN THE GREY ZONE

trade unions (not the Leninist transmission belt unions which were effectively
an organizational adjunct of the party-State), formed common cause with aggrieved workers, and together skilfully broadened demands to include not only
material and economic improvement but also political concessions.[44] Largely
Warsaw-based intellectuals, many already well practiced in open and public dissent, played a critical role, using their networks and skills to promote international coverage. Having initially brought the country to a standstill, Solidarity
managed to do what no other social movement or dissident group did during the
decades of communist rule: establish itself as a broad-based, geographically, and
politically diverse movement that, at its high point in 1981, encompassed fully
one third of Poles, approximately nine million members (and about one third
of those were also party members).[45] From the signing of the Gdánsk Accord
on 30 August 1980, through to the imposition of martial law on 13 December
1981, Solidarity effectively built the real and virtual infrastructure of both an
informal and extra-party opposition, not designed to overthrow communism
but to provide for self-organization, widen the aperture of independent civil society, and literally change the discourse and change expectations of what might
be politically possible.[46] Consolidation of gains, an extraordinarily open (and
fractious) National Congress in September 1981, global attention and support

[44] As Robert Brier argues, dissident activists were influential in convincing strikers to frame
demands within emerging human rights discourse, including the right to strike as part of freedom
of association, consonant with rights already guaranteed by international treaties to which Poland
was signatory (e.g. the Helsinki Final Act) and the Polish constitution. See Robert Brier, *Poland's
Solidarity Movement and the Global Politics of Human Rights* (CUP 2021) 36–37.
[45] Solidarity was both encouraged and romanticized in the West, drawing support from across
the political spectrum, from Reaganite policy wonks to leftist intellectuals interested in social
movements and the goal of democratizing socialism. See, for example, the range of analyses in the
first decade after Solidarity's creation: Stan Persky, *At the Lenin Shipyard* (New Star Books 1981);
Alain Touraine et al, *Solidarity: The Analysis of a Social Movement 1980–1981* (CUP 1983); Henrik
Flakierski, 'Solidarity and Egalitarianism' (1983) 25 Canadian Slavonic Papers 380; David Ost,
Solidarity and the Politics of Anti-Politics (Temple University Press 1990); Roman Laba, *The Roots
of Solidarity: A Political Sociology of Poland's Working Class Democratization* (Princeton University
Press 1991).
[46] For analyses of how events unfolded and how they were contemporaneously interpreted by
political scientists and contemporary historians, see especially Timothy Garton Ash, *The Polish
Revolution: Solidarity 1980–1982* (J. Cape 1983); Jane Leftwich Curry (ed), *Dissent in Eastern Europe*
(Praeger 1983); Jadwiga Staniszkis, *Poland's Self-Limiting Revolution* (Princeton University Press
1984); and David Ost, *Solidarity and the Politics of Anti-Politics* (Temple University Press 1990). For
scholarship that situates Solidarity in the broader literature of Central and East European dissent and
dissidence and assess its role in the collapse of communism, see, inter alia, Vladimir Tismaneanu,
Reinventing Politics: Eastern Europe from Stalin to Havel (Free Press 1992); Padraic Kenney, *A
Carnival of Revolution: Central Europe 1989* (Princeton University Press 2002); Barbara J. Falk, *The
Dilemmas of Dissidence in East-Central Europe: Citizen Intellectuals and Philosopher Kings* (Central
European University Press 2003); Mark Kramer, 'The Collapse of East European Communism and
the Repercussions within the Soviet Union: Part 1' (2003) 5 Journal of Cold War Studies 178 and
Mark Kramer, 'The Collapse of East European Communism and the Repercussions within the Soviet
Union: Part 2' (2004) 6 Journal of Cold War Studies 3; Constantine Pleshakov, *There Is No Freedom
without Bread! 1989 and the Civil War That Brought Down Communism* (Farrar, Straus and Giroux
2009); James Mark et al, *1989: A Global History of Eastern Europe* (CUP 2019).

from Western States, and increasing economic instability all coalesced to strike fear and concern in the minds of not only Polish communist leaders but also in the Soviet Union and in the hardline leaderships of East Germany and Czechoslovakia. While initially considering the imposition of martial law as a 'lesser of two evils' in the spring of 1981—the other being a Soviet-engineered invasion as had crushed the Prague Spring in 1968—the tough choice was made by General Wojciech Jaruzelski the day before the operation. As the 1980s progressed, economic decline continued, Polish indebtedness soared, pressure from Western governments continued, Gorbachev came to power, eventually signalling a willingness to let East European governments go their own way, and all the while Solidarity continued successfully underground, operating illegally at home amidst grey zone admiration if not assistance as well as overt and covert support from a variety of Western sources—and it is this grey zone operation that is the focus here.

In the last decade, taking advantage of newly declassified sources, access to archives, as well as biographies, memoirs, and oral histories of key leaders and interlocutors, more nuanced and detailed analyses of Western support for Solidarity have emerged. Retired CIA historian Benjamin B. Fischer published the first semi-scholarly account in 2012 but was hindered in his analysis because he could not refer to classified material and thus relied on extant popular and journalistic accounts.[47] At that time, estimates of CIA funds to support of Solidarity ranged from $10 million to $50 million USD.[48]

In 2018, almost three decades after the fall of communism, Seth G. Jones penned a popular narrative history of the CIA covert operation, codenamed QRHELPFUL. Under the personal direction of CIA Director William Casey, and based on a presidential finding signed by on 4 November 1982, QRHELPFUL was set up to 'provide money, nonlethal equipment to moderate Polish opposition

---

[47] Benjamin B. Fischer, 'Solidarity, the CIA and Western Technology' (2012) 25 International Journal of Intelligence and Counter Intelligence 427. Aside from his later role as CIA historian, Fischer was also involved in QRHELPFUL, working for Dick Malzahn, chief of the Soviet-East Europe group in the International Activities Division (IAD). Malzahn chaired a CIA study group on Soviet 'active measures' (*aktivynyye meropriatia*): influence operations involving front groups, covert broadcasting, disinformation campaigns and deliberate assassinations. See also Thomas Rid, *Active Measures: The Secret History of Disinformation and Political Warfare* (Farrar, Straus and Giroux 2020).

[48] Earlier discussions of CIA support to Solidarity can be found in the sources cited by Fischer, e.g. Andrzej Paczkowski, 'Playground of the Superpowers, Poland 1980–1989: A View from Inside', in *The Last Decade of the Cold War: From Conflict Escalation to Conflict Transformation*, edited by Olav Njolstad (Frank Cass 2004) 321; Robert M. Gates, *From the Shadows: The Ultimate Insider's Story of Five Presidents and How They Won the Cold War*' (Simon and Schuster 1996); Carl Bernstein and Mario Politi, *His Holiness: Pope John Paul II and the Hidden History of Our Time* (Doubleday 1996); Peter Schweitzer, *Victory: The Reagan Administration's Secret Strategy That Hastened the Collapse of the Soviet Union* (Atlantic Monthly Press 1994). American non-scholarly sources have tended to proceed in a Cold War 'triumphalist' vein that privileges the US role in 'winning' the Cold War.

462 INSTRUMENTS, TACTICS, AND METHODS IN THE GREY ZONE

groups through surrogate third parties, hiding the U.S. government's hand'.[49] The CIA was 'also authorized to conduct clandestine radio broadcasting'.[50]

Jones documents how CIA station assets in France, West Germany, Italy, Norway, and Sweden used 'ratlines'—clandestine channels to funnel material, people, and most importantly money into Poland, often 'suspending the normal rules of tradecraft'.[51] Especially during martial law, photocopiers, fax machines, walkie-talkies, videocassette recorders, portable radio transmitters, radio parts (to construct listening devices), and personal computers were smuggled across Poland's relatively porous border. Given Poland's endemic economic instability, the country was in constant need of goods and assistance from the West, and, aside from outright smuggling, legitimate cargo provided shipment opportunities. Jones asserts that the CIA spent 'roughly 20 million' on the program overall—the 'single largest source of external aid to Solidarity'.[52]

Jones builds on the seminal work of Gregory F. Domber, who examines and analyses all forms of American support for Solidarity, as well as the impact of 'American actions and policies on the shape, timing, and outcome of Poland's revolution [in 1989]'.[53] While not ignoring the role of the CIA, Domber situates the Agency's role in a larger story of American assistance, from the congressionally funded Radio Free Europe operating out of Munich, through to the efforts of the American Federation of Labor (AFL-CIO), the Committee to Support Solidarity (CSS), Catholic Relief Services, the NED, congressional efforts, and official and unofficial diplomatic efforts especially out of the US embassy in Warsaw. The role of particular leaders and Solidarity 'champions'—from President Ronald Reagan and Pope John Paul II through to AFL-CIO President Lane Kirkland, as well as many lesser known but pivotal Americans and émigré Poles, such as Tom Kahn who worked for the AFL-CIO, and Eric Chenoweth, Irene Lasota, Jakub Karpiński, Mirosław Chojecki, and Piotr Naimski who together were among the

---

[49] Seth G. Jones, *A Covert Action: Reagan, the CIA, and the Cold War Struggle in Poland* (W. W. Norton 2018) 139. While Jones had access to many more sources than Fischer was willing to cite or Domber had access to, including materials from the Mitrokhin archive, he regularly cites from interviews with those involved using code names to hide identities, or maddeningly lists 'author interviews with multiple sources'— acceptable practice for journalistic accounts, far less so for historical scholarship.

[50] Ibid. 139. Jones points out that earlier scholarship, notably Gregory F. Domber, *Empowering Revolution: America, Poland, and the End of the Cold War* (University of North Carolina Press 2014), erroneously concluded there was no presidential finding. In fact, there had to have been to authorize both action and expenditures.

[51] Jones (n 49) 164. The overseas hub of activity was Paris, where much earlier a covert operation (QRBERETTA) was initiated to fund the influential Polish émigré journal, *Kultura*. In short, QRHELPFUl was not the Agency's first Polish rodeo.

[52] Jones (n 49) 304–05. Jones states the next largest funders were the National Endowment for Democracy (NED) (approximately $9 million between 1984 and 1989) and the AFL-CIO (approximately $250,000 through the Polish Workers Aid Fund).

[53] Domber (n 50).

FROM RED SCARE TO RED SCARE, GREY ZONE TO GREY ZONE 463

founders of the New York-based Committee in Support of Solidarity (CSS).[54] Agency and leadership matter as much as organizational and financial aid.[55]

Sanctions following the imposition of martial law had an impact, especially insofar as Poland's ability to reschedule loans through the Paris Club was hindered. But this did not mean the United States created Solidarity or singlehandedly kept it going. Domber rightly concludes that 'Solidarność was an essentially spontaneous reaction in which thousands and then millions of Polish workers decided to act out against decades of political repression and economic oppression' and that the 'roots of Solidarność are found in *indigenous institutions* like the Workers' Defence Committee (KOR) and a history of strikes and riots, particularly events on the Baltic Coast in 1970, not in any foreign pronouncement'.[56] But money and materiel mattered profoundly. In the 1988 wave of strikes, an important precursor to Solidarity's re-legalization and eventually the 1989 Roundtable Talks and subsequent elections, financial assistance was provided for those who lost jobs or suffered regime repercussions. Moreover, support was directed specifically to *moderate* voices, all dedicated to negotiated change and nonviolence—those, somewhat ironically, who hailed from the liberal and left side of the Polish non- or anti-communist political spectrum, and not nationalist or radically anti-communist groups more likely to promote radical overthrow, operate underground rather than openly, preferring conspiracy and infiltration.[57]

Fischer, Jones, and Domber agree that the all the funds, CIA and otherwise, were a relative bargain, and remarkable given American willingness and strategic necessity to preserve the relative autonomy of the Polish opposition—so much so that much of the leadership and certainly the rank and file were unaware of CIA provenance. Fischer in particular contrasts the CIA program with the $5 billion directed to the Muhajideen in Afghanistan, and the Polish operation generated tangible and lasting results with significantly less post-Cold War blowback. Comparing *all* Polish assistance to *just* the cost of smuggling Stinger missiles and attendant technology to the Muhajideen in Afghanistan following the Soviet invasion yields the obvious conclusion that the Polish operation was by far the more successful of the two.

---

[54] On both Tom Kahn's efforts as well as the pivotal role played by the CSS, see Domber (n 50) 27, 70–74, 110–18. Domber elaborates how personalities and efforts overlapped and supported one another, not just in the United States but also including émigré publishers such as Jerzy Giedroyc in Paris, philosopher Leszek Kołakowski at Oxford, and personnel at Radio Free Europe in Munich to name a few.

[55] Domber concludes the NED provided approximately $10 million (not the $9 million estimated by Jones) to support the opposition in Poland through various grantee organizations, see Domber (n 50) 267.

[56] Domber (n 50) 261. On earlier opposition movements as important precursors to Solidarity, see Falk (n 46) and Michael H. Bernhard, *The Origins of Democratization in Poland* (Columbia University Press 1993).

[57] Domber (n 50) 270–74.

464   INSTRUMENTS, TACTICS, AND METHODS IN THE GREY ZONE

CIA and civil society efforts operated in the grey zone, well below the legal threshold of war, and were designed not to attract too much Soviet ire and provide plausible deniability. Solidarity as a case indicates the depth and breadth of Western 'grey zone' operations in the Soviet sphere of influence in a critical satellite State, Poland. Yet Solidarity is relevant also to arguments that what make contemporary grey zone operations so destabilizing today are the multiple access points provided by the internet generally and social media specifically. How can this be so, given the pre-internet universe of the 1980s?

Piotr Wciślik challenges our understanding of social media as coetaneous with the internet, suggesting that the term applies to samizdat, tamizdat, and underground publishing in Poland.[58] Building on Tom Standage's earlier definition of social media as 'two-way, conversational environments in which information passes horizontally from one person to another along social networks, rather than being delivered vertically from an impersonal central source', Wciślik argues that such communication is social *because* it is decentralized and information flows person to person rather than from the centre to an unknown periphery.[59] The provision of technology and materiel was a huge force multiplier, effectively providing the infrastructure necessary for social media understood in this sense. Second, unlike later internet-driven social media-fuelled movements, the Polish underground had already built up socially embedded and sustainable networks of trust and were thus more resilient. Such connections were both forged and maintained through long publishing cycles. Third, the lessons of this kind of successful social movement building ought to be learned. As Zeynep Tufekci's work illustrates, weak social ties and the speed associated with online organizing can certainly assist in generating huge crowds into public spaces, such as Tahrir Square in Cairo in 2011, but movements lacking historical infrastructure, strong social ties, which require *time* rather than *speed*, have a more difficult time consolidating gains or even establishing a stable presence.[60] Capacity building, as occurred in Poland, was

---

[58] Samizdat, from the Russian word to 'self-publish', has come to mean all forms of underground/unofficial publishing not sanctioned by the communist party/state. Tamizdat referred to texts published in exile (by Western published or by émigré in East European languages) that were then smuggled across the Iron Curtain. See especially H. Gordon Skilling, *Samizdat and an Independent Society in Central and Eastern Europe* (Macmillan 1989); Frederike Kind-Kovács and Jessie Labov (eds), *Samizdat, Tamizdat and beyond: Transnational Media during and after Socialism* (Berghahn 2013), Ann Komaromi, *Soviet Samizdat: Imagining a New Society* (Northern Illinois University Press 2022).

[59] Tom Standage, quoted in Piotr Wciślik, *Dissident Legacies of Samizdat Social Media Activism: Unlicensed Print Culture in Poland 1976–1990* (Routledge 2021), 25–26. For Wciślik's full argument on unlicensed print culture in Poland as 'samizdat social media' see ibid., esp. ch. 1, 23–40. On the resilience and impact of such media in generating what he calls 'prefigurative politics', see ibid. ch. 6, '117–41.

[60] Zeynep Tufekci, *Twitter and Tear Gas: The Power and Fragility of Networked Protest* (Yale University Press 2017).

crucial.[61]

As with the Canadian example, the benefit of hindsight with respect to Solidarity, demonstrates how Western actors and agencies, acting clandestinely and openly, within both government and civil society, via multiple lines of effort, effectively operated in a grey zone below the threshold of conflict. Although the fall of communism in either Poland specifically or the region broadly was hardly historically inevitable, such efforts were cumulatively critical to the scope and nature of regime change. Moreover, the Polish case is arguably the first example of the 'revolutions from below' which came to be both described and derided as 'coloured' revolutions by President Vladimir Putin today. Not without reason was the Kremlin paranoid then and now—correctly, as it turns out in the Polish case, given that the United States was supporting Solidarity with more than just rhetoric from the White House. Moreover, American efforts were designed to avoid earlier Cold War failures, such as 1956 in Hungary where incitement of rebellion occurred with no follow-through, and simultaneously evade any kind of nuclear showdown, as the Soviets had done during the 1962 Cuban Missile Crisis.[62] Moreover, while it may appear that adversarial activities in contemporary grey zones—both in terms of activities are locations—are 'new' given the advent of internet, Wciślik convincingly argues that the samizdat sphere of unlicensed print culture *was* an early form of social media, albeit without the same depth and speed.

5. Conclusion

More than three decades after the collapse of communism, civil society has become a battle space yet again, this time amplified through social media algorithms and deliberate efforts of mis/disinformation on the part of State-based adversaries or through their intermediaries. Effectively, civil society has been 'weaponized'—again demonstrating the porousness of borders and the horizontalization and verticalization of law, politics, and conflict. Still, observers should consider civil society's long history a strength rather than a weakness. The protection of independent space separate from the economy and the State can serve as a bulwark against 'grey zone' hybrid threats. This is essential given that the 'grey zone' no longer refers to the liminal space between an authoritarian State and complicit and quiescent society but also to a zone of vulnerability and style of attack. Moreover, this 'grey zone' allows adversaries that operate in the

---

[61] Tufekci draws upon the work of Amartya Sen's capability approach to theories of development as well as Martha Nussbaum's capability theory of justice. See Tufekci (n 60) 191–92.

[62] Domber (n 50) 256.

space of legally opaque plausible deniability, comfortably below the standard threshold of an 'attack'.

The 'grey zone', therefore, is simultaneously indicative of a 'location' and an 'activity' or connoting a set of activities, both a noun and a verb. It is a contested space in civil society between the State and the individual, an area where States seek to hold influence and authoritarian States seek to reduce and control. However, it is also a range of hostile or at least competitive activities that fall below the threshold of clearly attributable armed conflict. These activities may be centrally controlled and coordinated by actors close to the State security apparatus and following a defined strategy, or they might be almost random occurrences perpetrated by rogue agents, sympathizers, 'fellow travellers', or members of a diaspora population. It is often difficult to tell from the outside, and that is usually the point.

Conventional warfare permits the drawing of clear lines between centralized decision makers in a State security apparatus, the actors who carry them out, and the outcomes of those actions. Unfortunately, the grey zone does not lend itself to these clean lines. As the examples provided show, even the passage of time and opening of archives will not necessarily disclose the origin of a specific action, to say nothing of the resulting outcomes. By using intermediaries, States trade deniability for control—creating a problem for historians and security practitioners alike. Both face the reality that sometimes we know but cannot prove who initiated an action, that we do not know (yet) who initiated an action, or even that we *cannot know* who initiated an action—either because the chain of causation is especially disparate or because the sources either do not exist or are essentially inaccessible.

With such incomplete information, observers are often confronted with an old problem: correlation does not imply causation. If a given outcome aligns with a perceived strategic goal, it is all too easy to infer that the actor who induced it is a mere proxy, acting upon the tug of puppet strings that we cannot see. Apathy and inaction carry risk, but so do seeing connections where they do not exist, as well as the overestimation of foreign influence and overreaction to it. In many cases described, States might have better countered foreign influence (real or perceived) by strengthening civil society and pursuing reforms. Seeing a communist conspiracy as the cause of penitentiary unrest, for instance, hampered necessary reform, eroded the credibility of the Canadian State in the eyes of many progressive actors, and fuelled support for the very communist movement that the State sought to marginalize. Moreover, Canadian authorities long overestimated the degree to which the Soviet Union had penetrated the Canadian State and the degree of control exercised by Moscow over the Communist Party of Canada. Still, they were entirely correct that there was meddling and espionage, albeit mostly ineffective.[63]

---

[63] John Manley, 'Moscow Rules? "Red" Unionism and "Class against Class" in Britain, Canada, and the United States, 1928–1935' (2005) 56 Labour/Le Travailleur 9.

Furthermore, as the Solidarity example clearly illustrates, perceptions of grey zone activity are often shaped by moral assessments of an actor. A standard Western view might be: Solidarity was a peaceful and democratic movement (a moral actor) that harmed an evil empire. Therefore, its role in the collapse of the Soviet Union was simply the inevitable result of progress— allegations by Putin and others of Western conspiracies within Solidarity, Georgia's Rose Revolution, or Ukraine's Orange Revolution are mere paranoia amongst people on the wrong side of history. In fact, moral and immoral actors alike can be propped up, manipulated, or otherwise influenced. The fact that Solidarity received quiet foreign support does not erode its moral standing, legitimacy, or agency. Conversely, our assessment of the (im)morality of a given actor should not colour how we assess its agency, ultimate intentions, impact, or success.

21

A Grey Zone Analytic Framework for Military Operations

Maegen Nix and Welton Chang

1. Introduction

This chapter seeks to systematically define the military (conventional and paramilitary) dimension of the grey zone.[1] The lack of an agreed upon foundation from which to assess and understand how military grey zone operations (GZO) relate to and are executed as a part of politics increases the probability that States will overlook triggers in the lead-up to conventional conflict. Ambiguity also increases the risk of escalation to violent conflict due to the absence of clear signalling of threatening intent. In this chapter, we distil and categorize the military grey zone activities and organizations of Russia, Iran, and the United States and provide an analytic framework that illuminates State behaviour across political systems. The perspective furnishes insight into future operational challenges, strengths, and weaknesses in global competition. It illuminates differing relationships between the military and the State, and the extent to which political values affect the scope of military operations in the grey zone.

2. Military operations in the grey zone

Military operations conducted in support of a State's political goals are essential to global competition and may be carried out by State, State-supported and non-State actors. Military capabilities provide political authorities with unique instruments that can be performed in combination with diplomatic and economic ensembles, weaving harmonic or dissonant arrangements of national power. The grey zone operations that are described in this chapter represent a

---

[1] Paramilitary forces are separate from conventional armed forces but may exhibit similarities in 'organization, equipment, training, or mission'. Irregular forces, on the other hand, can join in paramilitary or conventional military operations but lack the same level of organization, equipment, and so on. A guerrilla force, for example, is considered an irregular force. See Joint Chiefs of Staff, 'Counterinsurgency Operations', JP 3-24 (25 April 2018), GL-5.

Maegen Nix and Welton Chang, *A Grey Zone Analytic Framework for Military Operations* In: *Hybrid Threats and Grey Zone Conflict*. Edited by: Mitt Regan and Aurel Sari, Oxford University Press. © Oxford University Press 2024. DOI: 10.1093/oso/9780197744772.003.0021

Figure 21.1. The Conflict Continuum

defined arena of State behaviour within the geopolitical competitive field and focus principally on the practice of military and paramilitary forces.

To be effective, a GZO analytic methodology must offer a holistic definition, provide for analysis of comparative political systems, and explore a variety of conflict attributes. Here we present conflict as a continuum overlaid upon the backdrop of competitive international relations. It represents a heuristic within which GZO are bound (see figure 21.1).[2] According to this continuum, 'peace' lies on one side of the spectrum; it may be secure and unthreatened or alternatively stable and able to mitigate threats. Peace may also be positive or negative. In the latter case, if government security forces require a large presence and leverage martial law to keep the peace, then it would be viewed a 'negative' peace.

Stable peace transitions to 'instability' when a political authority, whether authoritarian or democratic, has trouble mitigating threats, resulting in overt displays of conflict (both violent and non-violent). Next along the continuum is 'crisis'; this occurs when a political authority is unable to mitigate threats to stability so that conflict escalates and impacts a higher portion of the populace. The final phase of the conflict continuum is 'war', defined as attributable, institutionalized armed conflict. 'Institutionalized armed conflict' generally marks the upper threshold between GZO and non-GZO (war) with possible exceptions. For example, if armed conflict is of very short duration and/or at very low intensities, then it may not reach the level of 'war'. This occurred with the 2010 sinking of the ROKS Cheonan, a South Korean vessel sunk by a torpedo launched from a North Korean mini submarine. Although the single incident caused a crisis, it was not intended to (and did not) escalate to wide-scale armed conflict between the two Koreas and was not a GZO.

GZO are thus bound by thresholds within the conflict continuum. They are absent from secure and uncontested peace and external to ubiquitous, internationally sanctioned, legal, and rule-following State competition. GZO are generally found between the thresholds of stable peace and institutionalized armed

---

[2] This 'Conflict Continuum' should not be confused with the US Department of Defense Joint Doctrine Note (JDN) 1-19 that introduces the 'Competition Continuum' and discusses its perspective regarding campaigning through cooperation, CBAC, and armed conflict. See US Department of Defense, 'Competition Continuum', Joint Doctrine Note 1-19 (2019) <https://www.jcs.mil/Portals/36/Documents/Doctrine/jdn_jg/jdn1_19.pdf> accessed 25 February 2023.

A GREY ZONE ANALYTIC FRAMEWORK FOR MILITARY OPERATIONS   471

conflict. They are carried out through a deliberate, cohesive campaign that involves multiple lines of effort (LOE), drawing from a combination of illicit diplomatic, informational, military, economic, financial, and legal mechanisms (DIMEFIL). Activities within the grey zone often evade competitor institutional awareness and target or influence civilian populations, purposefully, going around State officials or recognized patterns of international law or protocol. In violation of conventional norms, GZO frequently trespass other's State sovereignty. Political objectives for GZO campaigns may relate to achieving outcomes that necessitate the violation (or dramatic reinterpretation) of international norms.[3]

With respect to operational attributes, GZO often involve incessant disinformation, denials of involvement, and short periods of intense military combat. They include a strong information component that is crucial to overall campaign success. GZO can leverage remotely commanded State proxies that provide ambiguity and plausible deniability for the State implementing the GZO campaign. And finally, GZO prioritize indirect actions to achieve objectives, eschewing sustained military intervention. They rely on military combat and intense violence as a last resort (e.g. whenever more indirect measures are failing to achieve desired political effects).

GZO generally do not involve independent non-State actors (although some would argue that ISIS is an exception); civil wars and strife without third-party involvement; a formal declaration of war; a significant and sustained amount of traditional combat; two countries with repeated violent incidents (e.g. along their border); and a single incident of a punitive nature (i.e. devoid of a coherent campaign). Examples of conflict that do not constitute grey zone activity include decisive periods during later stages of the 2014 Eastern Ukraine crisis that involved significant Russian forces engaged in sustained (days, weeks) traditional combat operations; the Russian invasion of Ukraine in 2022; the Russia-Georgia war in 2008 that primarily involved traditional combat operations; the India-Pakistan standoff in Kashmir; terrorism perpetrated by Al Qaeda against the United States; narco-wars in Columbia and Mexico; and civil wars or violent tribal rivalries in Africa where major powers are not involved.

It should be noted that the 'grey zone operations' colloquialism was created and is predominantly used by liberal democracies, not unlike the Cold War phrase 'the free world'. GZ methods support a logical and advantageous political strategy that falls outside of the way most Western countries would prefer to engage in international relations, in no small part because behaving in such a manner contradicts stated democratic social norms and ideals outside of war.

---

[3] Many thanks to Christina Houfek and Dr. Summer Agan on their thoughts and comments on GZ doctrine.

472 INSTRUMENTS, TACTICS, AND METHODS IN THE GREY ZONE

China and Russia consider GZO part of ubiquitous political warfare and competition between States. Because of existing normative variations between national actors, GZ actions are carried out in vastly different ways by competing institutions. The following section further explores the attributes that generally characterize the breadth of GZO.

3. Unpacking GZO attributes, a suggested taxonomy and conceptual framework

George Kennan defined political warfare at the beginning of the Cold War. It is the sum of all coordinated indirect actions toward a national objective (i.e. employment of all means at a nation's command short of war to accomplish strategic goals). In the case of the Cold War, it was imperative that the two superpowers compete through political warfare in ways that would not initiate a major war between them. In order to avoid nuclear escalation, the United States and Russia drove conflict into third-party geographic regions, attempting to increase their spheres of political influence. In some cases, military and paramilitary engagement stayed within the bounds of what we call the grey zone, where units mobilized to achieve strategic effects. The Bay of Pigs in 1961 is one example. In other cases, engagement transitioned to institutional armed conflict where conventional military forces deployed as part of institutionalized armed conflict (e.g. the Vietnam War and the Korean War).

Unsurprisingly, political warfare falls in a similar (but not completely overlapping) region of the conflict continuum as GZO, particularly with respect to the use of illicit activities.[4] GZO should be considered a large part of political warfare with new expressions and motivations in the digital and information age. While political ideology reigned supreme during the Cold War, pitting democracy against communism, the fight today is more concerned with a delineation between open democratic societies and authoritarian political systems that afford little personal liberty of speech, thought, and action. There is also a good deal of economic hegemony at play, a race for natural resources and wealth.

Even though the drivers of political warfare have not changed over time, GZO tactics are dramatically different, making their methods and effects seem like something new. Moreover, authoritarian goals are uniquely served by emerging technology. The impact of cyber and information operations, for example, is swifter ('going viral') and further reaching than anything possible during Cold War influence engagements. The agency that individual citizens have today to

---

[4] Political warfare includes 'above'- and 'below'-board behaviours, not just illicit activity or subversion, for example.

A GREY ZONE ANALYTIC FRAMEWORK FOR MILITARY OPERATIONS 473

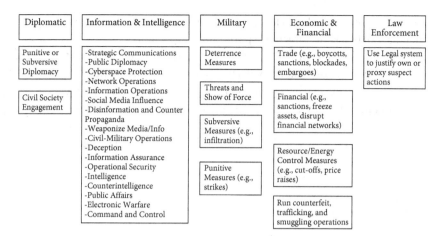

Figure 21.2. GZO Measures Taxonomy

access the information environment transforms open societies in wondrous ways at the same time it makes them vulnerable to misinformation and deceit, unable to know for sure the truth of any message or its originating composer. Certainly, the market of ideas and the liberty of free speech has become a target of manipulation by entities hoping to weaken civic unity within democracies.[5]

Figure 21.2 shows a conceptual framework and taxonomy for GZO.[6] The depicted measures of national power or LOE constitute GZO DIMEFIL sources. GZ activities that fall within a given category may be taken independently or, more likely, executed in concert with other measures to achieve political objectives. Combinations might include multiple actions (by a military, paramilitary, or proxy) within one LOE or across measures. For example, in the military LOE for GZO, one can think in terms of deterrence measures, a show of force or threats, subversive measures, and punitive measures. A military punitive strike based on information from a paramilitary infiltration could be used within the

---

[5] They may also result from funded proxy organizations and companies for hire.
[6] Based on the GZO definition presented in this chapter, informational and intelligence measures almost always accompany grey zone tactics. They frequently pair with military measures and the capability list in figure 21.2 draws heavily from military doctrine. The US Defense Department, for example, lists the following measures as information related capabilities (IRCs): Intelligence, Command and Control, Cyberspace Ops, Military Information Support Ops, Civil Military Operations, Space Operations, Electromagnetic Spectrum Operations, Strategic Communications, Operational Security (OPSEC) and Information Assurance, Physical Security, Special Technical Operations, Network Engagement, Physical Attack, and Military Deception. Because GZO are also utilized by nondemocratic regimes, however, additional measures are included based on observed behaviour that will be described later in the chapter. See Joint Chiefs of Staff, 'Information Operations', Joint Publication 3-13 (20 November 2014) <https://irp.fas.org/doddir/dod/jp3_13.pdf> accessed 25 February 2023.

474 INSTRUMENTS, TACTICS, AND METHODS IN THE GREY ZONE

GZ to assassinate a political leader. A military punitive strike could also support an unlawful blockade, targeting a port or shipping channel.

Note that outside of GZO, DIMEFIL efforts are generally more distinct with respect to actors and agency. Diplomatic efforts are made by official diplomatic professionals through established communications channels. In the United States, this would include civil and foreign service members from the Department of State. Law Enforcement measures would be serviced by the Federal Bureau of Investigation (FBI) or other federal civilian legal employees. Finally, economic and financial measures would likewise be made by connected executive or legislative means and personnel, particularly since Congress has the power to set budgets and authorize spending.

The Information and Intelligence LOE is different because many of its associated actions can be conducted by organizations across all measures within and outside GZO. It is no surprise that information is essential and ubiquitous to all decision-making processes. To use the United States again as an exemplar, the Department of the Defense (DoD), the FBI, the Central Intelligence Agency (CIA), the Department of State, and the Department of the Treasury house their own internal organizational units that serve as part of the intelligence community. Collected information and intelligence drive their internal decision-making processes and operations.

The heuristic taxonomy in figure 21.2 focuses on activities that reasonably fall within GZO. With respect to diplomatic measures, nation State actions that fall below the GZ threshold include forming alliances and coalitions; signing treaties and conducting diplomatic negotiations; operating embassies; formally recognizing the establishment of other States; and reducing or resolving conflict through political and diplomatic channels. These activities are not listed within figure 21.2. Only punitive, illicit, or subversive activities apply.

Grey zone behaviours in the diplomatic measures category include breaking diplomatic relations; support to peaceful protests or demonstrations by opposition groups; bribes to local politicians and other leaders; and the orchestration of coordinated corruption. Diplomatic activities that may or may not be in the GZ depend on circumstances and include the formation of political opposition in a foreign country; leading and inciting violent protest and demonstrations by opposition groups; or causing a change in political or military leadership via coups, assassinations, and other violence. These latter behaviours support declared institutionalized conflict above the GZ as well. They are often perceived as escalatory measures that might in and of themselves cross the GZ threshold during a given conflict—or be used in wartime.

With respect to informational and intelligence elements of national power, there are a variety of behaviours that fall above and below the GZ. Those that lie below the threshold include public affairs and participation in international

A GREY ZONE ANALYTIC FRAMEWORK FOR MILITARY OPERATIONS   475

conferences and forums. They also include intelligence and open-source collection to better understand environmental threats, the practice of counterintelligence, and operational security to deny the undesirable information collection, as well as investment in communication resources such as the Voice of America.

Information measures that are punitive but legal or hidden and illegal (though not an act of war) fall squarely in the GZ. Examples include the use of social media to recruit potential agents; the use of information campaigns for mass political or ideological manipulation; mass propaganda or misinformation to create tensions within a nation or between other nations; theft of intellectual property; the use of cyberattacks to gather intelligence; the release of stolen digital property; and the conduct of large-scale deception operations, including the injection of false information into foreign decision-making. Withstanding institutionalized armed conflict, GZ behaviour includes cyber manoeuvre to degrade nation State systems and infrastructure, cyber-enabled information warfare, and election influence or tampering.

Akin to the breakdown of diplomatic or informational and intelligence elements of national power, the enumeration of activities within each category begins to bring more fidelity to the breadth and scale of behaviour within the GZ. It lends structure to analysis and highlights trends in behaviour and strategy, creating opportunities to counter or respond. For example, in many instances, informational measures and economic measures share equities with military measures. US Navy SEALs or military boarding teams from Navy vessels might board foreign merchant ships in support of Maritime Interception Operations (MIO) to search for contraband during sanctioned embargoes. Military forces, primarily the Marine Corps, conduct counterintelligence functions and force protection responsibilities for American embassies around the world. Military medical, veterinary, and response units administer health care and deliver aid or resources such as communications and energy after natural disasters or emergencies.

High-risk military activities that are circumstantially GZO because they could be considered acts of war include leading armed groups such as insurgent forces against a host government; supporting large-scale violence through proxies; or secretly entering and seizing control of key facilities or sabotaging infrastructure within another nation (e.g. airports, media outlets, rail stations, or government buildings). Military GZO short of war include the threat of invasion or potential nuclear escalation; infiltrating operators into another country; deliberate violations of territorial air or maritime space; organizing or leading foreign protest and demonstrations; conducting electronic and cyberattack; developing proxies for future use; and amassing forces along a border as a show of force. Routine training, exercises, doctrinal development, organizational development, and partner engagements fall below the GZ threshold. The use of weapons

476 INSTRUMENTS, TACTICS, AND METHODS IN THE GREY ZONE

of mass destruction, an overt military invasion, sustained military strikes within another country, and engagement in traditional sustained combat operations are reserved for institutionalized armed conflict.

The previous sections of this chapter defined GZO and introduced a systemic view of grey zone measures, providing an analytic framework for comparative operational lines of effort across different State actors. In doing so, we see the fluidity of the manoeuvre space, particularly when military institutions can engage under the rubric of, or in combination with, other measures. The following sections will leverage the provided taxonomy and delve into comparative examples that focus on how Russia, Iran, and the United States use military and paramilitary forces within the GZ.

4. Russia: military and paramilitary GZO

Only a few Russian conflicts in the post-Cold War era are primarily or fundamentally limited to the grey zone. Virtually all of them, however, have utilized GZO at some point. Since the fall of the Berlin Wall, Russian operations have ranged from grey zone conflict (e.g. Estonia 2007, France 2017, South Korea 2018, and the United States 2016) to traditional military conflict (e.g. the 2008 Russo-Georgian 5-Day War and the 2022 invasion of Ukraine). Cases in between include hybrid conflicts (Lithuania 1991, Chechnya 1994–2000, and E. Ukraine in the summer of 2014) that involved significant GZO that then transitioned into traditional combat operations for long periods of time.

Russia's military measures enable many of the nation's GZO objectives. Furthermore, numerous non-military measures would be unfeasible without hidden support from their military or paramilitary forces. Regular military units are used to demonstrate shows of force, to include significant offensive cyber capabilities. Cyberattacks, for example, have been used against Ukraine, Estonia, Georgia, Poland, Romania, the United States, France, Germany, and the United Kingdom. Additionally, regular military units occasionally deploy for limited interventions as needed in support of the rebel groups Russia backs. Around the first and second Chechen Wars, regular forces were used repeatedly to level Grozny over time, target and terrorize the civilian population, as well as to conventionally counter Chechnya's resistance force.[7]

Russian paramilitary forces include organizations such as its 'little green men' (often SPETSNAZ); components of the Federal Security Service (FSB),

[7] Maegen Nix and Shana Marshall, 'The Chechen Revolution: 1991–2002', in *Casebook on Insurgency and Revolutionary Warfare, Vol II 1962–2009*, edited by Paul J. Tompkins Jr. and Chuck Crossett (US Special Operations Command 2012) 233.

A GREY ZONE ANALYTIC FRAMEWORK FOR MILITARY OPERATIONS 477

the Foreign Intelligence Service (SVR), and the military's Main Intelligence Directorate (GRU); the Private Military Company (PMC) Wagner Group; and 'Cossack, Chechen, Serbian and Russian paramilitary volunteers'.[8] While cyber espionage and sabotage capabilities, are often outsourced to Russian-aligned cyber threat groups, and Russian-aligned cybercrime groups, they are similarly performed by the FSB's Centre 16 and Centre 18, the SVR, the GRU's 85th Main Special Service Centre (GTsSS), and the GRU's Main Centre for Special Technologies (GTsST).[9] Whether cyber-related or boots on-the-ground, these forces are more involved in destabilizing activities, to include support to resistance. In general, out-of-uniform actions conducted by Russian paramilitary organizations provide the government deniability of its participation in GZO.

Russia's military LOE supports desired influence, destabilization, and coercion-related objectives. Its military activities related to coercion are as likely to resemble the behaviour of criminal organizations (like the Russian mafia) as those associated with traditional military operations. Common characteristics include the extensive use of proxies for direct civil engagement; repeated denials of Russian military or paramilitary involvement; extensive use of information warfare and intelligence measures; and the leveraging of local populations to provide support to Russian-backed rebels or separatists (with that support gained either by winning narratives, creating political parties, or from acts of coercion). Russia's support to resistance actors is foundational to its conceptualization of GZO and deserves deeper analysis.

Resistance actors are individuals, networks, or groups engaging in opposition to political authorities or structures.[10] Conventionally, resistance encompasses actors outside the legal political system, but Russia's focus on Western societies, which protect a broad range of political opposition, has complicated this emphasis. Here, resistance actors also encompass those operating within the legal political system but are nevertheless challenging the predominant liberal paradigm of Western society.

Russian support to resistance actors occurs on a spectrum that ranges from non-lethal aid to lethal aid. Non-lethal aid is aid provided to a resistance actor that is not specifically designed to inflict physical harm on an adversary. Non-lethal aid may include training, food rations, medical supplies, and communications

---

[8] US Special Operations Command, 'Little Green Men': A Primer on Modern Russian Unconventional Warfare, Ukraine 2013–2014' (2015) <https://www.soc.mil/ARIS/books/pdf/14-02984_LittleGreenMen-UNCLASS-hi-res.pdf> accessed 25 February 2023

[9] Cybersecurity and Infrastructure Security Agency, 'Russian State-Sponsored and Criminal Cyber Threats to Critical Infrastructure', CISA Alert (AA22-110A) (9 May 2022) <https://www.cisa.gov/news-events/cybersecurity-advisories/aa22-110a> accessed 25 February 2023.

[10] Summer Agan (ed), *Assessing Revolutionary and Insurgent Strategies: The Science of Resistance* (US Special Operations Command 2019) <https://www.soc.mil/ARIS/books/pdf/science-resistance.pdf> accessed 25 February 2023.

equipment, among other types of aid.[11] Russia's non-lethal aid in support of resistance actors includes provision of financial resources, assistance with the development of ideological platforms, information preparation of the environment in support of resistance actors' objectives, as well as moral and political support in the international forum. Lethal aid includes resourcing resistance actors with weapons, weapons systems, materiel, and other force enablers intended to inflict harm on an adversary. The provision of lethal aid to a resistance actor, including transitions to lethal aid from non-lethal aid, signifies a concomitant shift in resource intensity and visibility where lethal aid requires more training, requires State oversight, and generates higher visibility.[12]

Developing and then leveraging resistance actors is beneficial to the Kremlin as it allows Russia to destabilize the political systems of its adversaries while maintaining deniability.[13] Resistance actors are also effective as local actors and require fewer resources to engage adversaries.[14] Strategically, Russia directs its support to resistance actors across Europe, not just at specific European nations. Western democratic societies, with strong legal protections for political opposition, are rich playing fields for Russia's GZO ambitions. This illuminates how liberal democracies can be especially vulnerable to certain types of GZO. Of the 252 parties represented in Europe's parliaments, at least 30 of them are hardcore anti-Western and support pro-Russian platforms with an additional 31 labelled moderate on those same issues. The Austrian Freedom Party (FPÖ) and Italy's Lega Nord, for example, have signed pacts of cooperation with Putin's party, United Russia.[15] This section analyses Russia's range of support to resistance actors, the variety of institutional actors involved, and examples of Russia's support to resistance actors within Europe.

There are numerous institutional actors within the Russian State and broader society that influence, oversee, or execute resistance support operations. The four primary classes of actors include Russian intelligence actors (that often have paramilitary components), Russian military actors, Russian ideological freelance

---

[11] Bulent Kilic, 'What Exactly Is Non-Lethal Aid?' (*Foreign Policy*, 2 August 2012) <https://foreignpolicy.com/2012/08/02/what-exactly-is-non-lethal-aid/> accessed 25 February 2023.

[12] The information on the presence of Russian military units in Donbas is gathered by informnapalm.org, a volunteer, crowd-sourced intelligence-gathering organization operating in Ukraine. Inform Napalm, 'Russian Military Intervention in Ukraine: Overview, Evidence and Map' (17 September 2016) <https://informnapalm.org/en/russian-military-intervention-ukraine-overview-evidence-map/> accessed 25 February 2023.

[13] Many thanks to Dr. Summer Agan for her thoughts and comments on this section.

[14] Amos C. Fox and Andrew J. Rossow, 'Making Sense of Russian Hybrid Warfare: A Brief Assessment of the Russo-Ukrainian War', *The Land Warfare Series*, No. 112 (March 2017) <https://www.ausa.org/sites/default/files/publications/LWP-112-Making-Sense-of-Russian-Hybrid-Warfare-A-Brief-Assessment-of-the-Russo-Ukrainian-War.pdf> accessed 25 February 2023.

[15] Gustav Gressel, 'Fellow Travelers: Russia, Anti-Westernism, and Europe's Political Parties' (European Council on Foreign Relations, July 2017) <http://www.ecfr.eu/page/-/ECFR225_-_FELLOW_TRAVELLERS1.pdf> accessed 25 February 2023.

A GREY ZONE ANALYTIC FRAMEWORK FOR MILITARY OPERATIONS   479

actors, and mercenary/paramilitary actors. The decentralized approach to GZO resistance support means that some efforts are coordinated across Europe while others are not.[16] President Putin is the final source of authority while also occasionally an active player in GZO resistance support.[17]

The primary intelligence actors involved in GZO resistance support include the Federal Security Service (FSB), the Foreign Intelligence Service, and the Main Intelligence Directorate (GRU).[18] Military actors are likewise spread across numerous institutions. There were an estimated eighty-nine Russian military, law enforcement, and other security force units operating in or around Donbas in 2014–2016.[19] Russian ideological freelance actors, which support Russian strategic objectives, have few overt ties to Putin or the Kremlin, and are backed by wealthy Russian businessmen with ties to Putin's regime.[20] The final class of actors, paramilitary mercenaries, include organized criminal networks and violent non-State actors with varying degrees of training who are witting and unwitting agents of Russia's GZO.[21] The private military company, Wagner Group, which has ties to powerful oligarchs close to Putin, is also believed to be involved in the Kremlin's violent GZO where attribution is undesirable.[22]

Russian support to resistance actors in Europe and nearby regions includes support for actors with varying legality, tactical dispositions, and ideological orientations. Russia's pragmatic ideology allows the State to support resistance actors with anti-capitalist, leftist liberal ideologies (Occupy Wall Street) or far-right social conservatives (Hungary's Jobbik) with minor linguistic changes.[23] Within NATO, Russia has supported legal and illegal resistance actors, including some that exhibit a tactical disposition towards violence. Outside of NATO, Russia has supported actors engaged in violent activities, including Serbian nationalists charged with planning an unsuccessful plot to assassinate the prime

---

[16] Mark Galeotti, 'Controlling Chaos: How Russia Manages its Political War in Europe' (European Council on Foreign Relations, August 2017) <http://www.ecfr.eu/publications/summary/controlling_chaos_how_russia_manages_its_political_war_in_Europe> accessed 25 February 2023.

[17] Ibid.

[18] Andrei Soldatov, 'Putin's Secret Services: How the Kremlin Corralled the FSB' (*Foreign Affairs*, 31 May 2018) <https://www.foreignaffairs.com/articles/russia-fsu/2018-05-31/putins-secret-servi ces?cid=nlc-fa_fatoday-20180531> accessed 25 February 2023.

[19] See Inform Napalm (n 12).

[20] Andrew Higgins, 'Foot Soldiers in a Shadowy Battle between Russian and the West', *The New York Times* (New York, 28 May 2017) <https://www.nytimes.com/2017/05/28/world/europe/ slovakia-czech-republic-hungary-poland-russia-agitation.html> accessed 25 February 2023.

[21] Ibid.; Robert Verkaik, 'The Truth behind McMafia: London Is the Jurisdiction of Choice' for Russia's Gangs' (*iNews*, 5 January 2018) <https://inews.co.uk/news/world/russian-crime-london-mcmafia/> accessed 25 February 2023; Adrian Chen, 'The Agency', *The New York Times Magazine* (New York, 2 June 2015) <https://www.nytimes.com/2015/06/07/magazine/the-agency.html> accessed 25 February 2023.

[22] Josh K. Elliott, 'Expendables: How Shadowy Mercenaries Cash in on Russia's Wars' (*Global News*, 7 August 2018) <https://globalnews.ca/news/4370181/russian-mercenary-army-wagner/> accessed 25 February 2023.

[23] Galeotti (n 16).

minister of Montenegro to foil the country's attempts to accede to NATO.[24] In Hungary, Russia has supported the illegal paramilitary group the Hungarian National Front (MNA) with military training through the GRU. The MNA's ideology is predominantly far-right nationalist with anti-Semitic and anti-Roma propaganda that fuels the group's claims to defend the Hungarian homeland.[25] Similarly in the Czech Republic, the paramilitary group the National Home Guard (NHG) has Russian connections. The NHG relies on information provided in Russian media outlets to support its narrative of insecure borders, anti-NATO propaganda, and the necessity of supporting an armed home guard to protect Czechs from outsider threats.[26]

Russia's provision of non-lethal and lethal aid to resistance actors is a crucial component of its GZ campaigns in the near abroad and farther afield in Europe. Although Russia's lethal aid to Ukrainian separatists has generated a great deal of attention, less research has been dedicated to gaining a better understanding of Russia GZO in Europe. The Kremlin's ideological flexibility and the diverse institutional actors involved in support to resistance have helped Russia expand its influence in the region while maintaining plausible deniability and non-attribution for its actions. Countering GZO in this context is particularly challenging as Russia supports legal political opposition groups that operate in Western conventional political systems. Moreover, Russia's support to resistance actors with the capacity for armed violence, and ideological motivations for the use of violence, indicates that Russia is preparing for the possibility of leveraging this capability in future GZO even within NATO boundaries.

5. Iran: military and paramilitary GZO

Similar to Russian GZO, Iran leverages military and paramilitary capabilities within its contested regional environment while also engaging in conflict above the threshold for war (e.g. Iraq, Syria, and Yemen). Regarding conventional capabilities, Tehran's military forces comprise naval, ground, air, and cyber

---

[24] Ben Farmer, 'Russia Plotted to Overthrow Montenegro's Government by Assassinating Prime Minister Milo Djukanovic Last Year, According to Senior Whitehall Sources', *The Telegraph* (London, 19 February 2017) <https://www.telegraph.co.uk/news/2017/02/18/russias-deadly-plot-overthrow-montenegros-government-assassinating/> accessed 25 February 2023.

[25] Attila Juhász et al, 'The Truth Today Is What Putin Says It Is: The Activity of Pro-Russian Extremist Groups in Hungary' (*Political Capital*, August 2017) <http://www.politicalcapital.hu/pc-admin/source/documents/PC_NED_country_study_HU_20170428.pdf> accessed 25 February 2023.

[26] Petra Vejvodová, Jakub Janda, and Veronika Víchová, 'The Russian Connections of Far-Right Paramilitary Organizations in the Czech Republic' (*Political Capital*, April 2017) <http://www.politicalcapital.hu/pc-admin/source/documents/PC_NED_country_study_CZ_20170428.pdf> accessed 25 February 2023.

A GREY ZONE ANALYTIC FRAMEWORK FOR MILITARY OPERATIONS   481

components. These units typically engage in regional patrols, shows of force, and intelligence, surveillance, and reconnaissance activities. Conventional programs also pursue nuclear and ballistic missile capabilities, as well as limited space-based initiatives.[27] During the spring of 2016, Iran overtly 'deployed a small number of ground forces from the regular military to Syria-the first such deployment outside Iran since the 1980–88 Iran-Iraq War.[28] Its cyber forces generally outsource GZO to proxies and trusted intermediaries loyal to the regime while denying direct involvement.[29]

While Iran's use of paramilitary and proxy forces continues to expand globally (e.g. Venezuela and Columbia), it concentrates most of its resources across the Middle East, spanning territory from Lebanon to Bahrain, Iraq, Syria, and Afghanistan. Iran's paramilitary umbrella includes three organizations. First, the Islamic Revolutionary Guards Corps-Quds Force (IRGC-QF) conducts foreign engagement to expand Iran's theocracy and political foundation.[30] We will look most intensely at this organization's activity in the GZ as it plays the strongest diplomatic and strategic role. The IRGC-QF is credited with orchestrating attacks against US and Western targets (e.g. the Jewish Community Center in Buenos Aires in 1994, the 1996 Khobar Towers bombing in Saudi Arabia, and numerous attacks during the Iraq and Afghanistan wars).[31] Second, Iran's Department 400 (the Misaq Unit) is a kinetic-focused paramilitary component.[32] And third, the 'national militia', or the Basij, conducts heavy internal security.

The missions associated with Iran's military GZO measures are almost exclusively led by the State's principal paramilitary organization. The QF connects to the State's political integrity more directly than the paramilitary components within Russia, the United States, or China. China's power, for example, is distributed across the political party as well as the conventional military. Russia's centre of gravity is also outside of paramilitary and irregular assets. Regardless, numerous GZ actions are the same across States. For example, Iranian and Russian

---

[27] US Department of Defense, 'Fiscal Year 2014 Report on Military Power of Iran' (January 2015) <https://fas.org/man/eprint/dod-iran-2014.pdf> accessed 25 February 2023.

[28] US Department of Defense, 'Fiscal Year 2016 Report on the Military Power of Iran' (January 2017) <https://fas.org/man/eprint/dod_iran_2016.pdf> accessed 25 February 2023.

[29] Dorothy Denning, 'How Iran's Military Outsources Its Cyberwarfare Forces' (*Navy Times*, January 2020) <https://www.navytimes.com/news/your-navy/2020/01/23/explainer-how-irans-military-outsources-its-cyberwarfare-forces/> accessed 25 February 2023; David Sanger, 'Obama Ordered Wave of Cyberattacks against Iran', *The New York Times* (New York, 1 June 2012) <https://www.nytimes.com/2012/06/01/world/middleeast/obama-ordered-wave-of-cyberattacks-against-iran.html?pagewanted=all&_r=0> accessed 25 February 2023.

[30] Defense Intelligence Agency, 'Unclassified Report on Military Power of Iran' (April 2010) <https://man.fas.org/eprint/dod_iran_2010.pdf> accessed 25 February 2023.

[31] Stratfor, 'Iran: Quds Force in Venezuela' (2010) <https://worldview.stratfor.com/article/iran-quds-force-venezuela> accessed 25 February 2023.

[32] On Department 400, see e.g. Anthony H. Cordesman, *The Gulf Military Balance: Vol. 1: The Conventional and Asymmetric Dimensions* (Rowman and Littlefield 2014) 149.

482   INSTRUMENTS, TACTICS, AND METHODS IN THE GREY ZONE

paramilitary units develop proxies, grow militias,[33] and partner with terrorist organizations.[34] They lead manoeuvre elements to gain military objectives[35] and hand over key installations to local militias and paramilitaries. Furthermore, they deny their own involvement, engage in information warfare, and manipulate local populations to provide support.

Iran's paramilitary also serves a broader mission than Russia's military and paramilitary units. They provide outreach for public and social services, to include religious training and indoctrination, that engages local populations and transcends traditional nonlethal aid. They hold formal State diplomatic positions that establish interstate relationships and global basing opportunities. Certain leaders within the QF serve as foreign ambassadors and partner with political organizations in countries like Afghanistan, Lebanon, and Venezuela. And finally, the QF lead Iran's battlefield operations and intelligence collection—to include leadership of the State's Syrian and Yemeni engagement.[36] China and Russia have such large conventional capabilities that their paramilitary units would not overpower traditional service leadership.

QF leaders licitly and illicitly fund their GZO, to include public and social services, often outside of State financial support.[37] They depend upon illicit finance such as counterfeiting,[38] heroin production and trafficking,[39] and weapons

[33] The IRGC-QF directly supports 'Hezbollah and other militias in Syria, including perhaps 8,000 to 12,000 Shi'a foreign fighters from countries like Afghanistan, Yemen, and Iraq'. See Seth G. Jones and Maxwell B. Markusen, 'The Escalating Conflict with Hezbollah in Syria' (Center for Strategic and International Studies, June 2018) <https://csis-website-prod.s3.amazonaws.com/s3fs-public/publication/180620_JonesMarkusen_EscalatingConflict_FINAL.pdf> accessed 25 February 2023.

[34] Relationships with Columbian and Mexican drug cartels provide QF and Hezbollah with opportunities to 'leverage transportation, money laundering, arms trafficking, corruption, human trafficking and smuggling infrastructures, as well as other organized crime and terrorist groups around the world'. See Alma Keshavarz, 'A Review of Iran's Revolutionary Guards and Qods Force: Growing Global Presence, Links to Cartels, and Mounting Sophistication' (Small Wars Journal, 23 December 2015) <https://smallwarsjournal.com/jrnl/art/a-review-of-iran%E2%80%99s-revolutionary-guards-and-qods-force-growing-global-presence-links-to-car> accessed 25 February 2023.

[35] These range from missile attacks to assassinations. For example, in 2011, Masour Arbabsiar attempted to assassinate the Saudi Ambassador to the United States in Washington, DC. See Keshavarz (n 34).

[36] US Department of Defense (n 28).

[37] Stratfor, 'Iran: Quds Force in Venezuela' (2010) <https://worldview.stratfor.com/article/iran-quds-force-venezuela> accessed 25 February 2023 ('IRGC-QF members usually are stationed in foreign embassies, charities and religious or cultural institutions as intelligence officers to develop ties with the Shiite diaspora and other potential allies. The U.S. military even has labeled incoming and outgoing Iranian ambassadors to Iraq as IRGC-QF members').

[38] QF led a large-scale scheme to counterfeit Yemeni bank notes worth hundreds of millions of dollars to support regional destabilizing activities. See US Department of the Treasury, 'Treasury Designates Large-Scale IRGC-QF Counterfeiting Ring' (20 November 2017) <https://home.treasury.gov/news/press-releases/sm0219> accessed 25 February 2023.

[39] US Department of the Treasury, 'Treasury Designates Iranian Qods Force General Overseeing Afghan Heroin Trafficking Through Iran' (7 March 2012) <https://home.treasury.gov/news/press-releases/tg1444> accessed 25 February 2023.

A GREY ZONE ANALYTIC FRAMEWORK FOR MILITARY OPERATIONS   483

trafficking.[40] Across these activities, QF provide medical care to supporters and distribute funds to families of 'martyrs' as well as imprisoned HAMAS fighters.[41] The QF also engage in financial and economic activities, concurrently running a handful of engineering and construction front companies (e.g. Mahan Air).[42]

A prime example of QF dominion over State strategy can be seen in Iran's partnership with Syria. Iranian forces, led by former QF commander Qasem Soleimani, provided Syria conventional and unconventional military aid and intelligence during the events leading up to 2012 and beyond. According to both US government reports and Iranian official statements, Tehran helped create a 50,000 strong Syrian paramilitary group known as Jaysh al-Shabi (the People's Army) to aid Syrian government forces.[43] Iran's GZO, in combination with support from Hezbollah, shaped Syrian strategies that played out during the Syrian Civil War. Illicit assistance in the face of restrictive international sanctions made the provided loans, oil, and military support fall into the GZ. QF also brought paramilitary fighters from Iraq, Afghanistan and Pakistan, 'some of whom received training from Hezbollah proxy operatives in bases in Iran and Syria'.[44]

Thus far, this chapter has described the grey zone as an operating environment in which specified types of State behaviour come into play. Both Russia and Iran engage heavily in GZ campaigns and use their militaries and paramilitaries in combination with other GZ measures. Neither political elite experiences domestic institutional resistance to the ways in which their forces manipulate the

---

[40] In 2018, a Taliban Deputy Shadow Governor for Herat Province, Afghanistan, accepted weapons and military aid from the QF after vising an Iranian training camp for the Taliban. One use for the funding was to it to the fighters' families. See US Department of the Treasury, 'Treasury and the Terrorist Financing Targeting Center Partners Sanction Taliban Facilitators and their Iranian Supporters' (23 October 2018) <https://home.treasury.gov/news/featured-stories/treasury-and-the-terrorist-financing-targeting-center-partners-sanction> accessed 25 February 2023.

[41] As of 2017, the Izz-Al-Din Al-Qassam Brigades worked through Awad to distribute funds to the families of 'martyrs' in the West Bank. US Department of the Treasury, 'Treasury Targets Facilitators Moving Millions to HAMAS in Gaza' (29 August 2019) <https://home.treasury.gov/news/press-relea ses/sm761> accessed 25 February 2023.

[42] Defense Intelligence Agency, 'Unclassified Report on Military Power of Iran' (April 2010) <https://man.fas.org/eprint/dod_iran_2010.pdf> accessed 25 February 2023; US Department of the Treasury, 'Iran-Related Civil Aviation Industry Advisory: Deceptive Practices by Iran with respect to the Civil Aviation Industry' (23 July 2019) <https://www.treasury.gov/resource-center/sancti ons/Programs/Documents/20190723_iran_advisory_aviation.pdf> accessed 25 February 2023.

[43] Iran Pulse, 'Head of Ammar Strategic Base: Syria Is Iran's 35th Province; If We Lose Syria We Cannot Keep Tehran' (14 February 2013) <https://iranpulse.al-monitor.com/index.php/2013/02/ 1346/head-of-ammar-strategic-base-syria-is-irans-35th-province-if-we-lose-syria-we-cannot-keep-tehran/> accessed 25 February 2023; US Department of the Treasury, 'Treasury Sanctions Al-Nusrah Front Leadership in Syria and Militias Supporting the Asad Regime' (11 December 2012) <https://home.treasury.gov/news/press-releases/tg1797> accessed 25 February 2023; Karim Sadjadpour, 'Iran's Unwavering Support to Assad's Syria', *CTC Sentinel*, August 2013. <https:// ctc.westpoint.edu/wp-content/uploads/2013/08/CTCSentinel-Vol6Iss88.pdf> accessed 25 February 2023.

[44] Miriam Berger, 'Qasem Soleimani Helped Shaped Brutality of the Syrian War', *The Washington Post* (Washington, DC, 3 January 2020) <https://www.washingtonpost.com/world/2020/01/03/ qasem-soleimani-helped-shape-brutality-syrian-war/> accessed 25 February 2023.

484 INSTRUMENTS, TACTICS, AND METHODS IN THE GREY ZONE

state of the conflict continuum in competing nations. Their governments purposefully target civilians and life-sustaining critical infrastructure of other countries to gain strategic political ends. Similar tactics against civilian populations are also used during institutionalized armed conflict, so the cultural differences that divide national tactics and policies doesn't exist solely within the grey zone arena.

In the next section, we turn to look at how the United States operates within, and often in parallel to, the GZ. Iran is an Islamic Republic in which a standing theocracy controls the rule of law. Iranian politicians are subordinate to an Islamic cleric, or Supreme Leader, who controls the nation's foreign policy and armed forces. Comparatively, Russia is a strict autocracy even though its constitution supposes independent executive, legislative, and judicial institutions. The political elite in both countries maintain tight control over their domestic media outlets and restrict the political rights and civil liberties afforded by Western liberal institutions. In the United States at present, political power is diffuse and the executive branch experiences significant legislative oversight when it comes to the military and foreign policy.

6. United States: military and paramilitary GZO

United States military and paramilitary GZO resemble Russian and Iranian activity in the grey zone, particularly during certain periods of its history. Based on warfighting lessons learned during World War II, the National Security Act of 1947 established the modern US military as well as the Central Intelligence Agency (CIA). In 1949, the Central Intelligence Agency Act allowed 'the CIA to secretly fund intelligence operations and develop personnel procedures outside standard U.S. government practices'.[45] Although the post-war legislation created the House and Senate Armed Services Committees (HASC/SASC), it supplied minimal provisions for fiscal, operational, or statutory oversight over intelligence and paramilitary operations. Still responding to the surprise attack on Pearl Harbor, subsequent intelligence requirements necessary to run a large-scale world war, and the beginning burden of the Cold War, institutional intentions regarding GZO oversight and military measures held fewer behavioural restrictions and mores.

A prime example of an American military and paramilitary collaboration that tested the boundaries of the grey zone is the Bay of Pigs, which began in 1960

---

[45] Central Intelligence Agency, 'Legacy—History of the CIA' (2022) <https://www.cia.gov/legacy/cia-history> accessed 25 February 2023 ('By 1953, the Agency was an established element of the U.S. government. Its contributions in the areas of political action and paramilitary warfare were recognized and respected').

during President Eisenhower's administration and culminated in 1961 during the Kennedy administration. Fearful that Cuba's turn to communism and its relationship with the Soviet Union would cut off US interests in the region, the CIA planned to train and equip Cuban exiles to invade their homeland and overthrow Fidel Castro. Army Special Forces and the Air Force secretly trained recruits on weapons tactics, guerrilla operations, paratrooping, and aviation. The CIA painted and disguised old World War II bombers for an ill-conceived punitive strike on Cuban military assets. Shortly after the first strike, Cuba called an emergency session of the United Nations where the unwitting US Ambassador insisted the attacks were made by Castro's own defecting air force. Photos and information of the plane, however, revealed foul play and thus altered the second phase of the strike meant to accompany the principal amphibious assault. After additional shortcomings, US Naval assets were unable to evacuate the retreating landing party, two were hit by Cuban rockets, and much of the landing force was taken prisoner.

Despite the strategic and tactical failure, the Bay of Pigs did not mark a turning point in US foreign policy toward non-intervention. On the contrary, President Kennedy stated in a speech on 20 April 1961, 'Any unilateral American intervention, in the absence of an external attack upon ourselves or an ally, would have been contrary to our traditions and to our internal obligations. But let the record show that our restraint is not inexhaustible'.[46] He went on to urge solidarity between the United States and Latin America, using the lessons learned in Cuba as an opportunity to, 'reexamine and reorient our forces of all kinds' in order 'to intensify our efforts for a struggle in many ways more difficult than war'. Sixty years ago, in a perceived existential Cold War environment, military and paramilitary intervention in the political affairs of other nations was considered necessary.

US military GZO continued throughout the Cold War (e.g. Grenada/ Operation Urgent Fury 1983, Nicaragua 1980s, Afghanistan mujahedeen support 1980s, Iran/Desert One 1980, and the Iran-Contra Affair 1985). It was a time when the executive branch enjoyed and exercised more independent military and paramilitary power than today's current presidents, whether due to differences in appetite, cultural norms, or legislative limitations. Congress, however, soon began greater efforts to fetter presidential autonomy during the late 1970s and early 1980s. The House and Senate Permanent Select Committees on Intelligence stood up in 1977 and the Intelligence Oversight Act of 1980 passed. The Goldwater-Nichols Act of 1986 saw initial reform to many processes and the Casey Accords were signed. Specifically, these accords 'grew out of the furor

---

[46] John F. Kennedy, 'Address before the American Society of Newspaper Editors' (20 April 1961) <https://www.jfklibrary.org/archives/other-resources/john-f-kennedy-speeches/american-society-of-newspaper-editors-19610420> accessed 25 February 2023.

486 INSTRUMENTS, TACTICS, AND METHODS IN THE GREY ZONE

in Congress in 1984 after the disclosure that the C.I.A. had helped organize the mining of harbors in Nicaragua on behalf of the contras'.[47]

Based on the standing Intelligence Oversight Act, President Reagan should have notified Congressional Intelligence committees 'when he authorized a covert foreign military or intelligence operation'. Therefore, following a substantive review concluding in the summer of 1986, then CIA Director Casey signed an amended accord in which he 'promised to notify the Senate panel of any covert action approved by the president in which 'significant military equipment actually is to be supplied for the first time in an ongoing operation'. Since that executive concession, the relationships between the CIA, the armed forces, and their respective oversight committees have continued to have ups and downs based on domestic and international events and crises. For example, the end of the Cold War, the events of 9/11, the War on Terrorism, and today's rising tide of State competition have impacted decision-making and views on the use of violence as a tool of foreign policy. So too do fears of foreign election tampering, critical infrastructure manipulation and cyberattacks, IP theft, and diminishing natural resources.

As such, there are four strong examples of recent American GZO. First, in 2015 the United States ended a four-year, $1 billion CIA program and a three-year $500 million Department of Defense program to arm and train Syrian rebels against a Russian-backed Syrian government.[48] Proponents of the program suggested that the scope of GZO determined by its rules of engagement were extremely limited. Others argued that US political goals were untenable and operational limitations prevented the escalation of the campaign into institutionalized armed conflict between Russia and the United States. Regardless of the subjective commentary, this example illustrates certain contemporary bounds of US military and paramilitary GZ activity.

A second example of GZ operations involves American counterterrorism activities. This includes the drone strikes that killed al Qaeda leader Ayman al-Zawahiri in July 2022 in Kabul, Afghanistan and Iranian General Qassem Soleimani in January 2020 at the Baghdad international airport. It also includes the compound infiltration and shooting of Osama bin Laden in Abbottabad, Afghanistan in May 2011. These types of activities may be carried out by either the paramilitary elements of the CIA and/or special forces components of the US military. They are GZO even though the United States takes responsibility for

[47] Fox Butterfield, 'Casey Said to Have Failed to Follow Arms Rule', *The New York Times* (New York, 3 April 1987) <https://www.nytimes.com/1987/04/03/world/casey-said-to-have-failed-to-follow-arms-rule.html> accessed 25 February 2023.

[48] Mark Mazzetti, Adam Goldman, and Michael Schmidt, 'Behind the Sudden Death of a $1 Billion Secret C.I.A. War in Syria', *The New York Times* (New York, 2 August 2017) <https://www.nytimes.com/2017/08/02/world/middleeast/cia-syria-rebel-arm-train-trump.html> accessed 25 February 2023.

A GREY ZONE ANALYTIC FRAMEWORK FOR MILITARY OPERATIONS   487

the actions. This is because such actions enter the sovereign territory of another State.[49] At the same time, in comparison to Russian and Iranian GZO, significant planning goes into these evolutions with the intent to minimize the loss of life to civilians.[50]

The third example regards US activity in support of Taiwan's democracy, also known as the Republic of China (ROC).[51] Even though United States does not officially recognize Taiwan as an independent State, it provides significant military aid and joint training to the territory claimed by the People's Republic of China (PRC). Consecutive administrations approved billions of dollars in weapons aid to counter potential blockades or invading forces from the mainland. While not officially encouraging independence, US arms sales of offensive weapons to be used against China and its support joint exercises promote Taiwanese combat readiness and constitute GZ activities that could escalate to war.

One final example of US military GZO includes the evolving use of cyber capabilities against perceived global threats. Most of this activity falls into the military's traditional advise and assist role. US Cyber Command sends hunt forward teams comprised of civilian and military personnel to foreign countries in order to help them prevent, deter, and respond to cyberattacks. Working with countries such as Estonia, Croatia, Lithuania, Montenegro, North Macedonia, and Ukraine, these teams work with equivalent counterparts to defend friendly networks, often against Russian-supported cyber proxies (e.g. Conti, Killnet, and UNC1151). US cyber operations enter the grey zone because the networks and pathways of virtual activity are global in nature; they aren't confined to the physical borders of State territories.

US cyber operations are tightly controlled and monitored by oversight and do not target competitor civilian infrastructure. In 2018, the Trump administration confirmed a cyberattack against Russia's Internet Research Agency in response to election interference. Also, when the press announced that the US conducted retaliatory cyberattacks against Iran in 2019, the noted targets were specifically

---

[49] Between 2010 and 2013, 'Islamabad's records showed that about 2,200 deaths had been caused by drone strikes and a further 600 people had suffered serious injuries'. See Owen Bowcott, 'US drone strikes in Pakistan "carried out without government's consent"', *The Guardian* (London, March 15, 2013) <https://www.theguardian.com/world/2013/mar/15/us-drone-strikes-pakistan> accessed 25 February 2023.

[50] Charlie Savage, 'White House Tightens Rules on Counterterrorism Drone Strikes', *The New York Times* (New York, October 7, 2022) <https://www.nytimes.com/2022/10/07/us/politics/drone-stri kes-biden-trump.html> accessed 25 February 2023 ('President Biden signed a classified policy limiting counterterrorism drone strikes outside conventional war zones, tightening rules that President Donald J. Trump had loosened').

[51] Edward Wong and John Ismay, 'U.S. Aims to Turn Taiwan Into Giant Weapons Depot', *The New York Times* (New York, 5 October 2022) <https://www.nytimes.com/2022/10/05/us/politics/tai wan-biden-weapons-china.html> accessed 25 February 2023.

488 INSTRUMENTS, TACTICS, AND METHODS IN THE GREY ZONE

focused on weapons systems connected to rockets and rocket launchers.[52] Where Russian and Iranian cyber GZO attacks indiscriminately degrade and target public and private critical infrastructure and systems (e.g. Colonial Pipeline and Solar Winds), the United States strictly adheres to rules of engagement that minimize civilian collateral damage and unknown second- and third-order effects.

Table 21.1 explicitly itemizes US military and paramilitary measures within the grey zone since the end of World War II and compares it to the behaviours noted in the other two case studies. The United States has grown much more restrictive on intervening in other States over time. But for purposes of understanding the realm of possibility, it is important to open the time aperture and identify the fact that a democracy's GZ behaviour depends upon its circumstances. Variables include the executive leadership, public political support for foreign policy, and perceived political or existential security threats.

7. Comparative GZO

This chapter defined the military (conventional and paramilitary) dimension of the grey zone between stable peace and institutionalized armed conflict. It introduced how Russian, Iranian and American GZ military organizations behave across information and intelligence, economic and financial, and military measures. Each State leverages military assets in ways that establish a baseline of behaviour for comparative institutions. Similarities and differences highlight strengths and weaknesses associated with each State actor. Comparisons also show us how military GZO might evolve over time.

All three States exhibit varying levels of capacity to intervene in the political processes of other nations. For example, Iran effects strong and persistent conventional military and paramilitary GZO in its regional sphere of influence and leverages paramilitary illicit networks globally. Knowing that conventional military activity will draw the attention and intrusion of the international community, Iran relies heavily on the actions and leadership of its primary paramilitary actor the IRGC-QF, more so than Russia or the United States. This is because the QF is often responsible for GZO and non-GZO activity in war, economics, and diplomacy. The nature of Iran's regional geography, State alliances, and transnational illicit networks binds its behaviour to depend upon military GZO to carry out significant foreign policy initiatives from Lebanon, Iraq, and Syria to Yemen and Afghanistan. When it runs military GZ campaigns in and against countries

---

[52] David Sanger, 'Obama Ordered Wave of Cyberattacks Against Iran', *The New York Times* (New York, 1 June 2012) <https://www.nytimes.com/2012/06/01/world/middleeast/obama-orde red-wave-of-cyberattacks-against-iran.html?pagewanted=all&_r=0> accessed 25 February 2023.

Table 21.1. US Examples of GZ Military and Paramilitary Activities

GZ Military and/or Paramilitary Activity	Russia	Iran	US
Recruit, train, fund, equip, and use proxies in various roles from nonviolent anti-government activities to differing levels/scale of violence	X	X	X
Recruit, train, fund, equip, and use proxies to support illicit trade and finance	X	X	X
Run counterfeit rings and drug/weapons smuggling operations to generate operating income	X	X	O
Insert/infiltrate own agents into country	X	X	X
Develop and use agents from within country (e.g. to lead insurgents)	X	X	X
Organize and lead foreign protests, demonstrations, and political parties	X	X	O
Bribe, intimidate, blackmail, kidnap, and coerce local politicians and other leaders—including police and military	X	X	O
Lead armed groups/militias (e.g. insurgent forces) including skirmishes with opposition forces	X	X	X
Employ human shields to block/immobilize adversary military units	X	X	O
Seize installations (e.g. airports, rails, government, and media)	X	X	X
Conduct EW/cyberattacks (e.g. cyber sabotage and cyber-enabled info warfare; use social media to amplify messages and mobilize people, use ubiquitous sensing/high-tech reconnaissance such as UAS to dominate information environment over opposition	X	X	X
Conduct psychological operations/coercion	X	X	X
Conduct large-scale deception/denial operations	X	X	X
Execute regime change in military and/or political leadership (e.g. coups and assassinations)	X	X	X
Amass forces on the border as a show of force	X	X	X
Conduct large-scale exercises (e.g. that relate to intervening in current crises)	X	X	X
Conduct deliberate incursions of air and maritime space	X	X	X
Perform discrete acts of violence at key moments (e.g. direct kinetic actions, sniping, bombing, and ramming)	X	X	X
Threaten invasion by words and actions (i.e. force posturing)	X	X	X
Threaten potential nuclear escalation	X	X	O
Provide lethal and nonlethal aid	X	X	X
Use relief columns of 'humanitarian assistance' (e.g. to resupply paramilitary forces)	X	X	O
Provide public and social services	O	X	X
Indoctrinate and radicalize sympathetic populations (religious, diaspora, ethnic)	X	X	O

490 INSTRUMENTS, TACTICS, AND METHODS IN THE GREY ZONE

like the United States, Iran maintains plausible deniability and secrecy. This includes methodologies associated with terrorism, transnational criminality, as well as cyber and information operations that degrade democratic processes, increase domestic political tensions, and target critical civilian infrastructure for attack.

Although Russia's GZO do not dominate the Kremlin's overall foreign policy engagement, its conventional military and paramilitary GZ capabilities are uniquely intertwined with its practice of escalation towards conventional military institutional armed conflict. While Iranian international relations depend on paramilitary networks and infrequently commit conventional forces in war, Russian GZO are used more fluidly across the conflict continuum. For example, Russia uses military and paramilitary GZO to prepare the operational environment for conventional engagement, particularly along its periphery and perceived sphere of influence. Associated actions include the development of partnered political candidates or a resistance movement's political elite. It may include information operations that radicalize elements of a populace or exacerbate tensions within another country. Russia also uses military, paramilitary, and proxy GZO, like cyberattacks on critical infrastructure or disinformation campaigns, in retaliation for perceived political slights or against regional political policies it does not like. Further afield, in the United States and in Western democracies, Russia uses GZO in sustained engagement to destabilize and perturb its competitors. Given the constant and expansive use of military GZO in the Russian toolset, certainly those that cross over with information and intelligence measures, the capabilities of its GZ units are more accomplished and effective than its conventional non-GZ forces.

Of the three State use cases, the United States currently employs military GZO least of all. The institutional hurdles for military operations in the GZ domain or reciprocating in kind behaviour are extremely laborious and culturally suspect. This reflects liberal democratic institutional arrangements and political norms that constrain use of the military in GZO more than in non-liberal democratic States. This is not to say that the United States eschews military conventional conflict or intervention to carry out foreign policy (e.g. Iraq and Afghanistan). Rather, the American default tends towards non-GZO engagement with the military element of national power often leading diplomatic and economic measures. Three areas of exception include GZO actions that support counterterrorism and countering weapons of mass destruction (WMD), State and non-State allies engaged in conflict against near peer or authoritarian regimes, and cyber operations.

Even in these examples, however, GZO are extremely limited and controlled to prevent impacts outside of precise military targets. Where Russian tactics actively focus on impacting civilian populations, US GZO attempt to limit civilian

A GREY ZONE ANALYTIC FRAMEWORK FOR MILITARY OPERATIONS 491

casualties. And although there once was historic precedent during the Cold War, it would be extremely unusual in today's environment for US forces to foment resistance against another State or to plot the downfall of a competing regime. It is much more likely—even routine—for US military forces to train, advise, and assist partner nation militaries to stand up to threatening GZO or conventional operations as a preventative measure. Such training might even include how to partner and operate as a resistance force in the face of an invading nation. As with institutional arrangements, these constraints reflect liberal democratic values that limit the scope of acceptable military GZO compared to non-democratic States.

Although mostly contained in a training atmosphere, the United States maintains the proficiency for GZ intervention operations even though it seldom supports standing campaigns. If provoked or given cause, it could escalate military GZO to previous Cold War levels of activity. While States like Russia, China, and Iran intensify persistent GZO against the American public, for example, there could come a tipping point when the cyber-physical threat is perceived to be cumulatively existential or when the narrative of the demise of democracy at the hands of controlling and vilified autocracies gains domestic traction. The acknowledgement of a grievous external threat by both political parties and strong leadership to confront cyber- and information attacks, could rally the nation enough to change its standing policy on limited military and paramilitary use in the GZ.

Conversely, the effects of Russian and Iranian information operations, to include the polarization and radicalization of the US electorate and political parties, could become more egregious over time. In combination, Russia could find a sympathetic political leader with the aspiration of emulating excessive executive control over the political system. Russian military and paramilitary units could help mobilize demonstrations and rallies in support of this pro-Russian figure, enough to overturn election results and spur legitimate changes in voting laws across the nation. The cost of this competitive and outsourced GZ approach, coupled with its return on investment, would yield far superior outcomes for Russia than traditional conventional military conflict between peers. The latter strategy is inordinately expensive and difficult to pull off. In addition, because the world invests so much in military capabilities, it is easier and even natural to further develop military led GZ capabilities (whether native or proxy) in situations short of full-scale war.

8. Conclusion

This chapter distilled and categorized military activities to provide an analytic framework that illuminates State use of military capabilities as part of GZO across comparative political systems, thereby gaining insight into future operational challenges, strengths, and weaknesses. As military GZO operations evolve in response to emerging technologies and tactics, without standards of practice that reliably signal threat intent, use of GZO could lead to unintended escalations more frequently than anticipated. The use of proxies enables plausible deniability of campaigns against civilian critical infrastructure such as banking, health care, communications infrastructure, food supplies, and energy. One example is the unrestrained manner that the Russian and Assad regimes fought within Syria: using WMD against civilians, intentionally targeting civilian critical infrastructure like hospitals and schools, or committing what some critics labelled genocide.[53] Most recently, there was enough ambiguity around the suspected sabotage of the Nord Stream pipeline that the responsible (likely State military forces) parties have not been held accountable.[54] The idea that use of militaries to conduct GZO have to be small-scale, be surgical, or have narrow impact is greatly tested by just these two examples. By developing a holistic, taxonomic approach to understanding GZO, we believe that more analytic attention will be paid to an understudied aspect of GZO.

[53] Keenan Kassar, 'What's Happening in Syria is Genocide', *The Washington Post* (Washington, D.C., 11 March 2020) <https://www.washingtonpost.com/opinions/2020/03/11/whats-happening-syria-is-genocide/> accessed 25 February 2023.

[54] Joanna Plucinska, 'Nord Stream Gas "Sabotage": Who's Being Blamed and Why?' (*Reuters*, 6 October 2022) <https://www.reuters.com/world/europe/qa-nord-stream-gas-sabotage-whos-being-blamed-why-2022-09-30/> accessed 25 February 2023.

IV

COUNTERING HYBRID AND GREY ZONE THREATS: HOW CAN LIBERAL DEMOCRACIES RESPOND?

22

An Ethical Framework for Assessing Grey Zone Responses

Edward Barrett

1. Introduction

In the late 1700s, philosopher Immanuel Kant wrongly predicted that the increasing destructiveness of war would encourage States to seek peace through global governance. Although destructiveness has soared, States have not significantly mitigated their sovereignty.[1] Instead and increasingly, they are maximizing their relative power by continuously harming adversaries through a combination of lethal and especially sublethal actions that avoid and even redefine the threshold of 'cause for war'—a line legally associated with the UN Charter Article 51 notion of 'armed attack'.[2]

Presaged by the 'unrestricted warfare' strategy outlined by two People's Liberation Army colonels in 1999, this phenomenon is now widely recognized as consisting of 'hybrid threats' that are employed in ways that create a 'grey zone'.[3] This zone has been defined as 'a conceptual space between peace and war, occurring when actors purposefully use multiple elements of power to achieve political-security objectives with activities that are ambiguous or cloud attribution and exceed the threshold of ordinary competition, yet fall below the level of large-scale direct military conflict, and threaten US and allied interests by challenging, undermining, or violating international customs, norms, or laws'.[4] This competitive approach describes, for example, the Russian operations to annex the ethnically mixed Crimea, which employed ambiguously uniformed special

---

[1] See Immanuel Kant, 'Idea for a Universal History with a Cosmopolitan Purpose' and 'Perpetual Peace: A Philosophical Sketch', in *Political Writings* (H. B. Nisbet and Hans Reiss eds, Cambridge University Press 1991). I am interpreting his project to require sovereignty compromises but not world government.

[2] On threshold stretching, see Ben Connable, Jason H. Campbell, and Dan Madden, *Stretching and Exploiting Thresholds for High-Order War: How Russian, China and Iran Are Eroding American Influence Using Time-Tested Measures Short of War* (RAND 2016).

[3] See Qiao Liang and Wang Xiangsui, *Unrestricted Warfare* (PLA Literature and Arts Publishing House 1999).

[4] George Popp and Sarah Canna, *The Characterization and Conditions of the Gray Zone* (NSI 2016).

Edward Barrett, *An Ethical Framework for Assessing Grey Zone Responses* In: *Hybrid Threats and Grey Zone Conflict*. Edited by: Mitt Regan and Aurel Sari, Oxford University Press. © Oxford University Press 2024.
DOI: 10.1093/oso/9780197744772.003.0022

496 COUNTERING HYBRID AND GREY ZONE THREATS

forces, political manipulation, information operations, and relatively low levels of threatened and actual violence.

Such measures are hardly new. States have always used low-level lethal and/ or sublethal means to weaken others economically, militarily, culturally, socially, and politically. But technological developments such as computers and the internet have magnified the regularity and effectiveness of especially sublethal means, particularly against open societies that are increasingly dependent on these technologies. In addition to fiscal pathologies and social cleavages, liberal democracies are now constantly beset with denial-of-service attacks, the theft of intellectual property and weapons plans, the distribution of socially destabilizing information, and attempts to manipulate elections.

This chapter uses a rights-based framework consistent with liberal commitments to identify ethically permissible responses to such threats.[5] Although the well-developed Just War tradition may seem inapplicable to responding in a grey zone between peace and war, the tradition's undergirding ethical principles about justified harm can guide such responses to unjustified lethal or sublethal harm.[6] Section 2 outlines these principles; the third and fourth sections apply them to, respectively, unjustified lethal and sublethal grey zone attacks; the fifth section applies relevant principles to fictitious and real cases; and the conclusion briefly underscores the importance of jurisprudence for determining ethically appropriate responses.

2. Justified defensive harm

In liberal theory, moral agents normally possess a dignity or moral worth that renders the preconditions to their flourishing—their rights—inviolable.[7] Accordingly, they are permitted to defend themselves from rights violations. However, any intentional defensive harm against unjustified harm must itself be justified. There are at least three possible justifications for intentional defensive harm: attaining a lesser evil, consent by the harmed, and rights forfeiture.

Lesser evil justifications that involve intentional harm to rights-bearers are typically invalid, as illustrated by the famous 'Bridge' version of the trolley problem, where an innocent is used as a means of defending others. Some

---

[5] To simplify the analysis, we'll for now assume that attribution is not a problem. The attribution issue will be raised in an example later.

[6] For the purposes of this chapter, the *ad bellum* criteria are right intention, proper authority, just cause, last resort, reasonable chance of success, and broad proportionality, and the *in bello* criteria are discrimination, necessity and broad proportionality.

[7] I am assuming a foundationalist perspective on human rights. For an analysis of foundationalist and anti-foundationalist arguments, see John Tasioulas, 'Towards a Philosophy of Human Rights' (2012) 65 Current Legal Problems 1.

exceptions seem legitimate, of course. For example, consider a 'Sophie's Choice' case: if smothering a crying baby were necessary to save five other innocents from being discovered and murdered, one could argue that this necessary evil would be permitted, as the baby will be unjustly killed anyway. Bernard Williams's 'Jim and the Indians' case is similar: if Jim's choice is between shooting one innocent to save nineteen or watching all twenty be murdered, then the former—while tragic—seems permissible. Another class of situations involve intentionally violating rights in order to secure weightier ones, for example, damaging and using another's vacant house in order save oneself from a deadly blizzard. In all of these exceptional cases, a 'necessary and lesser evil justification' seems valid. However, these exceptions are unlikely to apply to most responses to unjustified grey zone attacks.

Similarly, consent—actual or hypothetical—cannot justify such responses. Obviously, wrongdoers do not actually consent to intentional defensive harm. But Michael Skerker has offered a hypothetical consent-based defence of the moral equality of combatants that could be applied to the conduct of grey zone operations.[8] He asserts that in the absence of just and effective global governance, States have the duty to provide collective goods such as security; and in order to 'protect any political entity over time', affected parties would hypothetically consent to a 'security standard' requiring all minimally just States' combatants to use the most rights-respecting of available norms and tactics that will reliably, effectively, proportionately, and efficiently win wars.[9] However, for our purpose of discerning justified responses to unjustified grey zone attacks, this framework possesses several problems. First, the security standard doesn't address crucial issues captured by *jus ad bellum* criteria, especially just cause. Second, it provides no definitions of 'minimally just' or 'rights-respecting'. Third, rights, instead of serving as a constraint on pursuing good consequences for one's group, need to be respected only inasmuch as the proportionate attainment of good consequences allows. Fourth, and highlighting a problem with all hypothetical consent justifications, which specify actors and their available information: it's not clear that long-standing and nonaggressive liberal States would consent to such reciprocal permissions. Finally, any standards generated by a hypothetical consent heuristic must be justified in another way.

Given the universality of rights, harmful grey zone responses instead require a rights forfeiture justification, which stipulates that any intentional defensive harm is justified only if the attacker has forfeited the rights affected by such harm—life, bodily integrity, freedom, property, reputation, and so on— through his wrongdoing and thus become liable to the harm. Agreeing with Jeff

[8] Michael Skerker, *The Moral Status of Combatants: A New Theory of Just War* (Routledge 2020).
[9] Ibid. 129–32, 183.

498 COUNTERING HYBRID AND GREY ZONE THREATS

McMahan's arguments, I will assume that liability is instrumental: 'For a person to be liable to harm on grounds of defence, harming him must have a defensive effect'.[10]

Liability is a function of at least four conditions: effectiveness, necessity, culpability, and narrow proportionality. First and apropos of the instrumental nature of liability, wrongdoers are liable to defensive harm only when it will be effective. Effectiveness is 'internal' to liability because a wrongdoer's basic worth and potentialities require that any diminution to the preconditions to their flourishing result in the defence of actual or potential victims. Second and related, wrongdoers are liable to defensive harm only when it is necessary. Necessity is also internal to liability because a wrongdoer's basic worth and potentialities require that any defensive harm be not only effective but also necessary for defence.[11] If passive defences would be effective, harm is unjustified. Third, while the relevance of culpability to liability is contested, I will assume that only culpable wrongdoing—done freely, and with knowledge or vincible ignorance of the relevant facts and norms—compromise a wrongdoer's dignity and subsequent rights.[12] A harmful response to an 'innocent threat' or 'innocent aggressor' would be morally excused due to the responder's inability to know that the agent was not culpable, but would not be justified on rights forfeiture grounds.[13] While defensively harming an innocent might be all things considered justified by a special obligation (to oneself, for example) or as a necessary/lesser evil, these two considerations are unlikely to apply to assessments of responses to grey zone attacks. Fourth, and especially important for our analysis, wrongdoers are liable only to defensive harm that is narrowly proportionate. The harm done to the wrongdoer must be commensurate with the importance of the rights being defended. A good explication of this principle is Jonathan Quong's 'stringency account' of proportionate responses. In his words: 'The stringency of a right depends on the severity of the harm that will befall the right-holder if the right is infringed or violated'.[14] Framed differently and as mentioned earlier, the wrongdoer must have forfeited the rights that such harm would otherwise violate.

---

[10] Jeff McMahan, 'The Limits of Self-Defense', in *The Ethics of Self-Defense*, Christian Coons and Michael Weber (Oxford University Press 2016).

[11] For an excellent analysis of whether effectiveness and necessity are internal to liability, see Helen Frowe, *Defensive Killing* (OUP 2014), ch. 4.

[12] On the contested relationship between culpability and liability, see e.g. David Rodin, *War and Self-Defense* (OUP 2005), and Jeff McMahan, *Killing in War* (OUP 2009).

[13] While defensively harming an innocent might be all things considered justified by a special obligation or as a necessary/lesser evil, these two considerations are unlikely to apply to assessments of responses to grey zone attacks.

[14] Jonathan Quong, 'Proportionality, Liability, and Defensive Harm' (2015) 43 Philosophy and Public Affairs 144.

3. Lethal responses in the grey zone

These four liability preconditions generate key Just War criteria concerned with intentional lethal defensive harm: reasonable chance of success, last resort and just cause *ad bellum*; and discrimination and necessity *in bello*.[15] Because of the narrow proportionality requirement, only grave harm—such as loss of life and life-supporting property—establishes a just cause.[16] The principle of double effect generates the criteria associated with unintended harm (i.e. collateral damage): wide proportionality *ad bellum* and *in bello*.[17] In other words, except for legitimate authority and right intention, all the criteria are generated by the principles of rights forfeiture and double effect.

Given that grey zone operations 'fall below the level of large-scale direct military conflict', are these traditional just war criteria applicable? In the preface of the 2006 edition of *Just and Unjust Wars*, Michael Walzer suggested that a separate framework called '*jus ad vim*' ('justice before force') be developed to morally assess violent 'measures short of war'.[18] Inspired by Walzer, several scholars have sought to defend the need for, and to construct, such a framework.[19] Daniel Brunstetter and Megan Braun argue that the traditional *ad bellum* criteria fail to account for at least four distinct ethical requirements of relatively low-scale lethal defensive harm. First, principles such as just cause, reasonable chance of success, and last resort must be 'continually reassessed in advance of each use of force'.[20] Second, in order to avoid large-scale war, a principle not included in *ad bellum* must continually be applied: probability of escalation. Measures short of war that will likely escalate into war 'are not justifiable, and must be subject to the stricter

---

[15] For the sake of simplicity, I will not treat the impact of culpability on just cause or discrimination.

[16] For Rodin, proportionate goods also include non-lethal harms such as mutilation and rape, which profoundly and permanently undermine bodily and psychological health, and grave infringements of liberty such as enslavement and wrongful lifetime incarceration. See Rodin (n. 12) 43–48.

[17] The principle of double effect prohibits unnecessary side effect harm, thus creating a second *in bello* necessity requirement. As noted, a response is narrowly proportionate when the harm done to the wrongdoer is commensurate with the importance of the rights being defended. A response is widely proportionate when the harm done to those who are not liable to be harmed is not excessive in relation to the response's good effects. See Jeff McMahan, 'Liability, Proportionality, and the Number of Aggressors', in *The Ethics of War: Essays*, edited by Saba Bazargan and Samuel C. Rickless (Oxford University Press 2017).

[18] Michael Walzer, *Just and Unjust Wars: A Moral Argument with Historical Illustrations* (Basic Books 2006) xv–xvi.

[19] See Daniel Brunstetter and Megan Braun, 'From *Jus ad Bellum* to *Jus ad Vim*: Recalibrating Our Understanding of the Moral Use of Force' (2013) 27 Ethics and International Affairs 87; Daniel Brunstetter and Megan Braun, 'Rethinking the Criterion for Assessing CIA-Targeted Killings: Drones, Proportionality and *Jus ad Vim*' (2013) 12 Journal of Military Ethics 304; and Brandt S. Ford, '*Jus ad vim* and the Just Use of Lethal Force-Short-of-War', in *Routledge Handbook of Ethics and War*, edited by Fritz Allhoff, Nicholas Evans, and Adam Henschke (Routledge, 2013) 63.

[20] Brunstetter and Braun, 'Rethinking the Criterion for Assessing CIA-Targeted Killings' (n 19) 306.

jus ad bellum regime'.[21] Third, because the threat justifying a lethal response is less grave than that of full-scale war, collateral damage is less justifiable.[22] Fourth, for the same reason, wide proportionality calculations must be 'concerned not only with the loss of civilian life but also the more subtle harms including property destruction, post-traumatic stress disorder and social disruption'.[23]

While correctly highlighting these ethical requirements, Brunstetter and Braun fail to recognize two facts that make an *ad vim* framework unnecessary. First, as argued by Helen Frowe, the ethical requirements cited by Brunstetter and Braun are not unique to measures short of war.[24] The legitimate and rightly motivated authorizers of large-scale violence also must continually reassess just cause, chance of success, necessity, and proportionality, and defensive violence must cease if any of these requirements cease to exist. Second, properly understood and applied, the *ad bellum* criteria incorporate all of the concerns allegedly addressed only by an *ad vim* framework. For example, the *ad bellum* proportionality criterion accounts for escalation and the two collateral damage issues raised by Brunstetter and Braun.[25]

That said, *ad vim* advocates have raised issues often overlooked by Just War theorists, especially the need to reassess pre-conflict judgments during the conflict. The categorization of criteria as pertaining to *ad bellum* versus *in bello* exists in order to emphasize the moral issues most relevant to the respective decision makers (political vs military) at those junctures, and can be misinterpreted as establishing a strict distinction between the criteria's applicability. But ultimately, Frowe is correct: the traditional Just War criteria provide adequate ethical guidance for using intentional lethal defensive harm against unjustified threats in the grey zone.

4. Sublethal responses in the grey zone

The distinction between the principles relevant to lethal versus sublethal responses should not be overdrawn. The principles of rights forfeiture and double effect determine permissible defensive responses to all unjustified harm. Defensive responses must be narrowly proportionate, effective, and necessary, and unavoidable side effect harm to innocents must be widely proportionate.[26]

---

[21] Brunstetter and Braun, 'From *Jus ad Bellum* to *Jus ad Vim*' (n 19) 99.

[22] Brunstetter and Braun, 'Rethinking the Criterion for Assessing CIA-Targeted Killings' (n 19) 318.

[23] Ibid. 319.

[24] Helen Frowe, 'On the Redundancy of Jus ad Vim: A Response to Daniel Brunstetter and Megan Braun' (2016) 30 Ethics and International Affairs 120.

[25] Ibid. 121–23.

[26] In response to my suggestion of a wide proportionality constraint on sublethal collateral damage, some argued that such a restriction would be tantamount to saying that someone

ETHICAL FRAMEWORK FOR ASSESSING GREY ZONE RESPONSES   501

Ultimately, narrow proportionality determines what type of response is justified—lethal or sublethal. When you add considerations of effectiveness, necessity, and wide proportionality, you get a spectrum of justified responses that range from large-scale lethal to small-scale sublethal.

The narrow proportionality principle sharply differentiates justified responses to lethal versus sublethal harm. While murderers and unjust combatants are liable to lethal defensive harm, agents of sublethal harm normally are not.[27] In cases of sublethal attacks, because the unjustified harms involved are not life-threatening, the wrongdoer retains the right to life and is not liable to be defensively killed. By analogy, killing a pickpocket, even if doing so were effective and necessary for defence against theft, would be unjustified. In the face of constant sublethal attacks, this narrow proportionality-driven constraint can be emotionally frustrating and politically destabilizing. However, this constraint also creates two possibilities with defensive ramifications that do not obtain for lethal defensive harms: inflicting not only defensive harm, but also punitive harm that is effective and necessary for specific deterrence; and targeting indirect participants. Let's briefly discuss each of these.

4.1 Punitive harm

The justified ends of harm are defence and punishment.[28] Examples of punitive harm are the capital punishment of safely imprisoned criminals, austere incarceration conditions, and non-compensatory fines. The traditional justifications for punitive harm are retributive and consequentialist. Retributivists argue that harming wrongdoers is justified because they deserve it; their suffering is good in itself. Consequentialists justify punitive harm as an effective and necessary means to attaining rights-related benefits, namely, the specific deterrence of a perpetrator from engaging in future wrongdoing, the reform of the perpetrator, and the general deterrence of other would-be wrongdoers.

Retributive and consequentialist justifications for punitive harms are fraught with controversies that I cannot hope to definitively adjudicate in this piece.

---

contemplating opening up a new business to benefit consumers could only do so if the foreseen but unintentional harm to potential competitors were proportionate. However, participants in the business context consensually enter a competitive game in which other businesses might undercut them. They have no right of noncompetition, but only a right that their competitors observe the norms of market ethics: no coercion, force, or fraud and compliance with the law and the general ethical norms of the society in which they conduct business.

[27] In rare cases, such as cyber intrusions that seek to cause low-level harm as part of an existentially threatening campaign, anticipatory lethal responses might be justified.

[28] I would include recovery as an *ex post facto* form of defence.

502 COUNTERING HYBRID AND GREY ZONE THREATS

Instead, I'll offer conclusions that are restrictive and resonate in liberal societies. First and with apologies to Kant, human rights require that punishment serve a purpose, thus ruling out desert-based retributive punishments.[29] Second and echoing Kant, human rights and their forfeiture require that even wrongdoers not be used as an example-setting means of preventing possible wrongful acts by unspecified others, which rules out consequentialist punishments for reasons of general deterrence and public order. One could argue that a wrongdoer could forfeit their right to not be punished in order to deter others if they were somehow responsible for a wrong that another specific person might commit. But even if their degree of responsibility could be accurately assigned, their punishment would be preventive, and thus subject to the same epistemically related moral hazards that bedevil preventive war: are we certain that wrongdoing will happen, and that our defensive/punitive measures will be effective?[30] Alternatively, one could argue that the right to not be punished in order to deter others could be overridden by the utility of general deterrence, but I suspect that this utility would be difficult to prove, or insufficient to override the right. However and importantly, general deterrence can be a side effect of permissible defensive and punitive harm.[31]

Third, the remaining and legitimate consequentialist purposes of punishment are specific deterrence and reform. Because lethal punitive harm cannot accomplish these purposes, capital punishment (*qua* punishment) and punitive war are impermissible. But sublethal harm can deter and reform wrongdoers, and therefore may be used both defensively and punitively if narrowly proportionate, effective, and necessary.

For example, consider the increasingly common case of recurring cyber theft targeting banks. In a domestic context, many would accept that incarcerating a cyber thief is justifiable as a defensive measure. But we could also argue that punitive harms that impose hard treatment might be justifiable as well. Although my justificatory scheme rules out retribution and general deterrence as grounds for punishment, the specific deterrence and reform of the wrongdoer would remain

---

[29] Retributivism has been defended as a means of emphasizing the validity of a society's morality—a way of 'planting the flag of moral truth'. However, this is a consequentialist general deterrence argument, and therefore problematic from my perspective. Alternatively, retributivism has been defended as a means of securing a victim's right to 'expressively defeat' the indignity. See David Luban, 'War as Punishment' (2012) 39 Philosophy and Public Affairs 299. Luban's piece is a seminal treatment of the historical shift away from punitive war, however. While he defends retributivism, he argues that because of human psychology and the lack of an impartial third party, punitive war in practice is revengeful and unjust because it over-harms (sourcing Suarez).

[30] I'll later say more about these moral hazards.

[31] For an important duty (to the victim)-based justification of punishing the guilty for the purpose of general deterrence, see Victor Tadros, *The Ends of Harm: The Moral Foundations of Criminal Law* (OUP 2011). For an effective critique of Tadros's arguments, see Kimberly Kessler Ferzan, 'Rethinking *The Ends of Harm*' (2013) Law and Philosophy 177.

valid consequentialist grounds for punishments, and allow such punishments as an extremely austere standard of living and non-compensatory fines. Of course, a cyber thief's liability to these harms would require that they be not only narrowly proportionate but also effective and necessary. And if justified punitive measures eventually effectively deter or reform the domestic cyber thief, both punitive and defensive harms would become unnecessary, and the now non-liable thief should be freed.[32] Over time, precisely because of justified sublethal punitive harm, our cyber thief would become non-liable to any harm, defensive or punitive.

That's the domestic context. However, in an international one, morally justified defensive responses to sublethal harm can be—as I mentioned—frustrating. Incarceration of the cyber terrorist might be impossible because of a host State's non-cooperation and the inability to capture the wrongdoer through an otherwise permissible intervention. Passive defences might prove ineffective. And the sublethal defensive countermeasures to which the wrongdoers are liable might not sufficiently degrade their harmful capabilities. However, because narrowly proportionate responses in these cases are sublethal, additional and proportionate punitive harm would be permissible if effective and necessary for the relevant purposes.[33] Given that the impossibility of incarceration when dealing with foreign aggressors would make reform unlikely, the purpose of such punitive harm would be specific deterrence. Accordingly, punitive measures would not seek to degrade capabilities but instead seek to alleviate malevolent intentions by degrading the wrongdoer's standard of living—especially personal property and reputation. And if effective, such measures would have a defensive effect, and render further harms unnecessary.[34]

4.2 Targeting indirect participants

The second possibility created by the narrow proportionality limitation is the targeting of those who are indirectly participating in unjustified harm. Some have argued that culpable indirect participants in unjustified lethal harm—such as civilian financiers or munitions factory workers of an aggressor State—are morally liable to lethal defensive harm.[35] (Although someone who holds this

---

[32] Ultimately, given the reference to a liability standard, I am construing justified sublethal punitive harm as largely defensive (i.e. the purposes of specific deterrence and reform are the protection of society).

[33] It must be emphasized that tit-for-tat responses may be unethical. Countermeasures and punitive responses must themselves be justified.

[34] In this case, specific deterrence is ultimately defence through different means.

[35] See e.g. Helen Frowe, 'Non-Combatant Liability in War' (unpublished paper) <https://www.helenfrowe.com/uploads/8/1/6/0/8160867/10._frowe_-_non-combatant_liability.pdf>, accessed 10 December 2022.

504 COUNTERING HYBRID AND GREY ZONE THREATS

position might also argue that there are reasons for legally protecting indirect participants from targeting.) My intuitions run in the other direction, especially when the participant's role is causally distant and/or partial. Perhaps the culpable driver of an assassin is lethally targetable, but the financiers of a collective murderous enterprise are not. Traditionally, the ethics and law of war have rightly drawn a bright line around civilians, who are at worst only indirectly responsible for unjustified lethal harms and thus are not liable to be killed.

However, indirect participants in unjustified lethal or sublethal attacks may be liable to defensive and punitive sublethal harms that are narrowly proportionate, effective, and necessary—a difference that comports with criminal law. Therefore, non-cooperative political leaders of the territory where a wrongdoer resides, as well as civilian accomplices such as financiers, surely would be liable to substantial defensive and punitive sublethal harms. The combination of these countermeasures and punishments might be enough to reduce the harm, and even coerce States to cooperate and accomplices to desist.

5. Grey zone cases

5.1 Emergency dispatcher attack

While municipalities' '911' emergency communications centres have been saving lives for decades, budget shortfalls have required deep cuts to personnel and an increased reliance on computer-aided dispatch (CAD) systems, which allow dispatchers to immediately map caller locations and rapidly locate and notify the closest emergency responders. Without CAD systems, average response times would increase from ten minutes to thirty minutes. Studies have estimated that for medical emergencies, this response delay would increase mortality rates by 25 per cent. Additional costs would include increased suffering and health care costs and property loss and decreased productivity.

Would a series of cyberattacks on these systems that resulted in response delays and several otherwise-avoidable deaths justify a lethal response? Given the unjustified loss of life, a lethal response would be narrowly proportionate and thus permissible if the other *ad bellum* and *in bello* criteria were met. However, as argued in our analysis of low-scale lethal attacks, even if a lethal strike would be defensively effective and necessary, the wide proportionality requirement to achieve a net benefit would certainly limit the response—especially if escalation were likely.

Assuming that a defensive use of force is permissible, perpetrator attribution adds a second challenge, especially to grey zone attacks involving cyberspace. Technical aspects of computers and the internet can undermine certainty

ETHICAL FRAMEWORK FOR ASSESSING GREY ZONE RESPONSES   505

about a wrongdoer's location, equipment, personal identity, and/or institutional affiliation—and can even implicate innocent parties. In the CAD system case, circumstantial evidence—motive, means, and opportunity—points to many parties, not just China and Russia. Especially when responding lethally (as uneasiness with the domestic capital punishment attests), probability is not enough; near certainty is required.[36] Since circumstantial evidence does not adequately establish certainty and may be all that is available in cyberattack cases, passive defences against, and denial-based deterrence of, future incidents may the only legitimate responses.[37]

5.2 Logic bombs in electrical grids

Long-standing fears of cyberattacks on electrical grids became a reality with the CrashOverride attack on Ukraine in 2016. CrashOverride was a malicious piece of software (malware) hiding in a computer that was part of the Supervisory Control and Data Acquisition (SCADA) network allowing operators to monitor and control Kiev's electrical infrastructure. At a preprogrammed time, the logic bomb automatically activated and popped circuit breakers at substations, creating winter darkness in western Kiev. Although technicians were able to detach the breakers from the computer and restore power in just over an hour, the malware's capabilities, reusability, and lack of fingerprints raised alarms among infrastructure security experts.

What would be a morally permissible response to the discovery of malware in the electrical grid SCADA systems of nearly every urban area from Boston to Washington that—in addition to tripping circuit breakers—could destroy electrical generators and thus cause a mass casualty event? Is the mere installation of such malware an act of war, even if the malware's launcher component contains no activation time? At first glance, planting inert logic bombs across the East Coast electrical grid seems less troubling than the *Emergency Dispatcher Attack* and Ukraine 2016 cases, given that the harms in these cases were actual. But the potential harms in this new case are massive and even existential. Especially if there were widespread destruction of generators in winter, thousands could perish from cold, starvation, and violence. And a loss of nuclear warning and command and control systems would render the United States vulnerable to a nuclear attack.

---

[36] For a utilitarian defence of responding when only 90 per cent certain, see Randall Dipert, 'The Ethics of Cyberwarfare' (2010) 9 Journal of Military Ethics 384. Although I disagree with this suggestion, Dipert's article was the first on cyberwarfare ethics and remains definitive.
[37] States might publicly inflate their attribution capabilities in order to maximize deterrence.

506 COUNTERING HYBRID AND GREY ZONE THREATS

However, despite these extraordinary stakes, nothing harmful has happened yet, and any harmful response would thus have to satisfy the demanding requirements of preventive anticipatory defence. One could argue that wrongdoers forfeit rights and incur liability when actively preparing to harm, which is why conspiracy is a crime. But because active preparation is difficult to verify internationally, imminent aggression (i.e. mobilized forces on one's border) traditionally has been considered the valid indicator of liability. Unfortunately, and unlike nuclear attacks, there is no way to know when logic bomb attacks are imminent (unless they are preprogrammed and one is privy to the activation time). Therefore, when imminence is unknowable, certainty about active preparation to cause grave harm would justify anticipatory self-defensive measures—if the other *ad bellum* criteria, including last resort, were met.[38] But caution is in order: this form of anticipatory defence is morally hazardous for epistemic and bureaucratic reasons. Obtaining certainty about active preparation is notoriously difficult, as is creating organizations where intelligence analysts' assessments are correctly interpreted and available. These two problems highlight the importance of passive defences in an era of difficult-to-deter and stealthy threats.

Assuming that anticipatory defence was justified, let's also assume that the malware installations are traced to hackers thought to be affiliated with the Russian military's 'GRU' intelligence agency, but that Russian government collusion with the hackers cannot be verified. Could the United States justify a strike against non-State actors within Russian borders? Stated differently: at what point does an attacked State's right to defend itself trump the sovereignty of a State that is the geographic source, but not the cause, of a lethal attack? Although sovereignty is a legal concept, its ethical foundation is the right of individuals to associate for political purposes and the duty of others to not interfere. However, sovereignty is also accompanied by responsibilities, internal and external. Just as States that harm their own citizens can lose their right to non-interference, creating a permission or even obligation to intervene, States that are unwilling to protect other States' citizens from threats emanating from or traversing their jurisdictions, or that are unable to do so and refuse necessary assistance, also lose their right of non-intervention.

Finally, what if a fully autonomous system could detect and thwart an imminent attack by State or non-State actors on critical infrastructure, eliminating the need for morally hazardous forms of anticipatory defence? While automated passive defences would be ethically unproblematic, automated cyber countermeasures that strike network targets inside another State should not be

---

[38] In many cases, simply removing the infected computers from the grid would eliminate the threat.

ETHICAL FRAMEWORK FOR ASSESSING GREY ZONE RESPONSES   507

used prior to an existing conflict. While operationally advantageous, such systems should not be allowed to subvert the ethical requirement that legitimate political authorities decide whether to initiate conflict.

5.3 A thousand cuts

The economic costs of cybercrime and cyber espionage by foreign actors include the loss of commercial intellectual property; direct financial loss; lost negotiating strategies; cyber security costs; opportunity costs, such as additional spending to offset losses of military technology and jobs; and reduced real wages and employment. For years, these costs have been tolerable, resembling those of car crashes and pilferage—approximately 1 per cent of GDP and one-third of a per cent in employment.[39]

However, let's assume that the evidence and costs of malicious cyber activity have skyrocketed over a few years. A Chinese iPhone clone—'cPhone'—has reduced Apple's share of the global smartphone market from 15 per cent to 7 per cent, requiring layoffs of twenty thousand employees. Cybercrime and cyber espionage are now estimated to annually shave 5 per cent off the GDP, accounting for a GDP that is contracting by 1 per cent annually. Unemployment has jumped from 4 per cent to 12 per cent, wages have fallen, and an already-underfunded entitlement system is facing new pressures. On the other hand, assume that China's GDP is growing 10 per cent annually, and its defence spending has increased from 2 per cent to 4 per cent. When the U.S. and Chinese defence budgets are compared using purchasing power parity (PPP), and given that only two thirds of US forces are relevant to deterrence and warfighting in the Pacific, regional stability is questionable. There are rumours that Japan is consulting with Israel about nuclear deterrence forces. We'll also assume that the harm is reliably attributed to 'Unit 61398' of the Chinese military's cyber forces and that unit's non-State clients in mainland China, that the Chinese deny wrongdoing, and that our passive defences and deterrence by denial are increasingly ineffective.

What kind of response would be justified? As previously argued, persons forfeit their right to life and therefore become liable to lethal force only when culpably employing, or planning to employ, means known to be capable of murdering or destroying/stealing life-sustaining property. So on the one hand, culpably attempting or planning to cause low-level harm as part of an existentially threatening campaign would create a liability to lethal kinetic or cyber

---

[39] For an overview of these costs, see James Andrew Lewis and Stewart Baker, *The Economic Impact of Cybercrime and Cyber Espionage* (Center for Strategic and International Studies 2013). Worth noting: the level of this theft-based harm is disputed, in part because companies are reticent to report it.

508 COUNTERING HYBRID AND GREY ZONE THREATS

force. However, in these cases, uses of force would be preventive, and thus subject to the moral concerns about anticipatory self-defence that were just raised.

On the other hand, constant cyber intrusions that combine to merely reduce living standards do not justify lethal responses, which would be disproportionate. But consistent with the analysis in the third part of this chapter, sublethal harm may be used both defensively and punitively if proportionate, effective, and necessary; and the targets of these responses could be both direct and indirect participants.

5.4 Election manipulation

What if two years after a close but undisputed presidential election, and during a successful administration led by a president with a 65 per cent approval rating (as high as Eisenhower's in 1955), it was discovered that the president did not actually win the election? Instead, the firm that provided cybersecurity software to every electronic voting machine was infiltrated by Russian hackers. Malware was dispersed through a software update just prior to the election, and enough votes were shifted from the vehemently anti-Russia candidate to change the winner of both the popular vote and electoral college. Would this level of election interference constitute an act of war?

Determining a proportionate response to a cyberattack that changes the result of a presidential election requires clarity about what rights have been violated. Because violence was neither a cause nor an effect of the 'regime change', one could argue that the perpetrators would not be liable to a lethal response. The only possible harm seems to be in publicly disclosing the interference, which could result in domestic and/or international strife. However, any strife would be rooted in the widespread violation of important voting rights. One can argue that like other rights, the right to participate in the selection of one's political leaders is a precondition to human flourishing. A well-designed democracy is regarded as the most reliable means of protecting basic human rights, and political participation helps cultivate important virtues. And although the cyberattack disenfranchised only a relatively small percentage of voters and resulted in an ethically legitimate regime, it also could undermine confidence and participation in politics, and eventually lead to an erosion of other social and political rights. This danger accounts for the severity of punishments for even small-scale voter fraud, which is a felony.

But for ethically sound reasons, voter fraud is not a capital crime. As pointed out throughout this chapter, responses must be narrowly proportionate; the severity of the rights violation determines the harm permitted in response. It is possible that voter fraud could intentionally install a tyrannical regime, in which case the fraudsters and tyrants might be liable to lethal defensive force. But in

ETHICAL FRAMEWORK FOR ASSESSING GREY ZONE RESPONSES   509

most cases, including the one suggested here, the stealing of votes is not life threatening, and therefore justifies only a sublethal response. However, sublethal responses to serious election interference may be defensive and punitive, and target direct and indirect participants.

Finally, what if the election interference were initially undetected, unattributed, or covered up, and its perpetrators finally were known twenty years later? Assuming that no additional attacks of the same sort have occurred, any sublethal response at that late point could not be justified as a defensive act. Additionally, as it would be difficult to argue that the perpetrators need to be deterred anymore, punishment for the purpose of specific deterrence seems unjustified. But even if defensive and punitive harm are prohibited, the perpetrators would owe compensation for damages and could be coercively punished for refusing to compensate, and State actors who protect them could be punished for doing so.

5.5 Vaccine lies

A final and real case involves COVID-19 vaccines. In many ways, the US response to the virus was relatively lacklustre. Compared to Taiwan and South Korea, testing, tracing, and quarantine efforts were poor; and compliance with distance and mask protocols was mixed. But the United States excelled in one respect: vaccine discovery, production, and distribution. Its companies— Moderna, Pfizer, and Johnson & Johnson—produced the first, safest, and most effective vaccines, and by mid-May 2020, the United States was near the top in doses administered per one hundred people.[40]

Predictably, hackers and intelligence agencies from Russia and China attempted to steal vaccine research, production, and distribution information, but were mostly unsuccessful.[41] However, these organizations were more successful in spreading disinformation about the vaccines' costs, safety, and efficacy. Leveraging preexisting vaccine scepticism and using a variety of media, these States amplified existing critiques and created new ones in order to increase the market share of Russian and Chinese vaccines (Sputnik X and Sinovac), exacerbate US social divisions, and reduce the US vaccination rate.[42]

---

[40] Henrik Pettersson et al, 'Tracking COVID Vaccinations Worldwide' (*CNN*, 2 December 2022) <https://edition.cnn.com/interactive/2021/health/global-covid-vaccinations/> accessed 28 February 2023.

[41] Gordon Corera, 'Coronavirus: Hackers Targeted Covid Vaccine Supply "Cold Chain"' (*BBC*, 3 December 2020) <https://www.bbc.co.uk/news/technology-55165552> accessed 28 February 2023.

[42] Michael R. Gordon and Dustin Volz, 'Russian Disinformation Campaign Aims to Undermine Confidence in Pfizer, Other Covid-19 Vaccines, U.S. Officials Say', *Wall Street Journal* (New York, 7 March 2021) <https://www.wsj.com/articles/russian-disinformation-campaign-aims-to-undermine-confidence-in-pfizer-other-covid-19-vaccines-u-s-officials-say-11615129200> accessed 28

The effects of vaccine rate reductions on COVID cases and deaths could be serious, especially if they prevented herd immunity. A study by the Imperial College London estimated deaths rates in highly sceptical countries such as France would be 8.7 times higher than the rate in places with ideal vaccination rates of 98 per cent, while rates in moderately sceptical Germany and low hesitancy UK would be 4.5 and 1.3 times higher, respectively. Overall, modest levels of hesitancy could add 236 deaths per million people over a two-year period.[43]

Might vaccine disinformation warrant a lethal response? Given the additional deaths resulting from vaccine scepticism, there seems to be just cause for a lethal response. However, assuming reliable attribution, at least three facets of the situation militate against responding lethally. First, because there are so many possible causes of one's opinions, establishing a causal link between the disinformation and scepticism would be difficult. Second, even if a link can be established, the degree of causation is likely be low, in turn reducing the harm to which the perpetrator would be liable. Especially in cases where wrongdoers are merely amplifying existing critiques among already sceptical individuals, the culpability for additional deaths would be extremely low.

Third, even if we assume that disinformation was solely created by a perpetrator and heavily influenced a recipient who was not already sceptical, the recipient would bear at least some of the responsibility for their erroneous viewpoint. Unlike coercion, manipulation does not override the will. And adults in a free society have opportunities to inform themselves. Unless manipulators have somehow eliminated the possibility of accessing alternative viewpoints, those who are manipulated are to some degree culpable for their ignorance, again reducing the wrongdoer's liability.

6. Conclusion

While this piece sought to construct a sort of 'unified theory' of the ethics of grey zone operations, I will conclude with some notes and cautions that indicate the work that remains.

February 2023; Simon Shuster, 'Meet the Russian "Information Warrior" Seeking to Discredit COVID-19 Vaccines' (*Time*, 21 March 2021) <https://time.com/5948017/news-front-covid-19-information-war/> accessed 28 February 2023; Robin Emmott, 'Russia, China Sow Disinformation to Undermine Trust in Western Vaccines: EU' (*Reuters*, 28 April 2021) <https://www.reuters.com/world/china/russia-china-sow-disinformation-undermine-trust-western-vaccines-eu-report-says-2021-04-28/> accessed 28 February 2023.

[43] Todd Gillespie, 'Vaccine Skepticism Risks Increasing Covid Mortality Ninefold' (*Bloomberg*, 25 March 2021) <https://www.bloomberg.com/news/articles/2021-03-25/vaccine-skepticism-could-increase-covid-mortality-up-to-ninefold> accessed 28 February 2023.

First, having expanded the purpose (punishment) and recipients (indirect participants) of justified harm, it would be wise to add a cautionary note that is often directed toward lethal 'targeted killing' operations but applies to any level of harm. While due process might not require courts or uniforms, extraordinary care must accompany the identification and treatment of liable individuals, and appropriately transparent institutional structures must be created to ensure such care. Second, although sublethal collateral damage is preferable to lethal, it must not be ignored. Non-participants are not liable to any form of harm, and any collateral damage to them therefore must be widely proportionate.

Third, because punishments must fit crimes, more ethical thought is required on what constitutes narrowly proportionate punitive harm to direct and indirect participants in international contexts. And finally, assuming we have identified punitive harm that is narrowly proportionate, the experience embedded in statutes, case law, and law enforcement should be the source of judgements about effectiveness vis-à-vis deterring criminals. We cannot determine which punitive measures are ethically permissible without this experience.

23

Winning at the Strategic Seams

Michael A. Newton

1. Introduction

International law exists to preserve order and predictability among States and international institutions. It should not become a wedge that widens teleological cracks in the foundation of the shared system. At the same time, liberal democracies must confront the reality that in 'an increasingly specialized legal environment, few institutions are left to speak the language of general international law, with the aim of regulating, at a universal level, relationships that cannot be reduced to the realization of special interests and that go further than technical coordination'.[1] Western nations must remain committed to persistent defence of human dignity, self-determination, and personal freedoms. By extension, democracies provide the diplomatic and technical authority that reinforces the resilience of the modern legal architecture developed to preserve and enhance those values. Grey zone conflicts represent an existential threat to this model.

Western States must reaffirm their vision of the global order. International law in the real world must remain practicable and effective[2] because 'rules that are incompatible with the survival of sovereign nations' and which unduly impede effective military and political action 'risk being ignored and, thereby, not preventing any harm from occurring'.[3] To adapt the common military parlance, the first principles of order that bind liberal democracies should serve as the rally points around which States unite without hesitation in defence of those values. We must revert to first principles as the signposts for the way forward even as the uncertainties of the modern milieu multiply. As a logical corollary, States must

---

[1] International Law Commission, 'Report of the Study Group of the International Law Commission, finalized by Mr. Martti Koskenniemi Fragmentation of International Law: Difficulties Arising from the Diversification and Expansion of International Law' (13 April 2006), UN Doc. A/CN.4/L.682 and Add.1, para. 502.

[2] *Case of N.D. and N.T. v. Spain*, App Nos 8675/15 and 8697/15 (ECHR, 13 February 2020) para. 171.

[3] On the need to construct enforceable rules of IHL, see Janina Dill and Henry Shue, 'Limiting the Killing in War: Military Necessity and the St. Petersburg Assumption' (2012) 26 Ethics and International Affairs 311.

Michael A. Newton, *Winning at the Strategic Seams* In: *Hybrid Threats and Grey Zone Conflict*. Edited by: Mitt Regan and Aurel Sari, Oxford University Press. © Oxford University Press 2024. DOI: 10.1093/oso/9780197744772.003.0023

514 COUNTERING HYBRID AND GREY ZONE THREATS

be vigilant to ensure that international norms serve as bulwarks against forms of grey zone warfare that undermine human dignity, comity between States, sustainable peace accompanied by commerce that lifts lives, and fundamental freedoms that permit people to enjoy those fruits. The terminological familiarity of international law concepts often results in overly formulaic applications in practice.

The concept of 'grey zone warfare' describes a persistent and growing threat to the survival of the rule-based international order. The demonstrable gap between internationally accepted articulations of international norms and their perceived utility need not be inevitable. Lawyers, philosophers, and Just War scholars have long debated the proper relationship between *jus ad bellum* principles warranting the resort to force and the *jus in bello* utility of the proportionality principle. *Lex lata* remains firm that each legal context functions as distinct and independent body of law.[4] *Jus in bello* empowers warfighters yet imposes restraints over the conduct of armed conflicts. Grey zone opponents seek to create strategic and operational paralysis by exploiting the seams between differing legal paradigms. The explosion of legal mechanisms in the modern era of fragmentation adds to the malaise of indecision and seeming inadequacy when evaluating viable responsive measures. This chapter describes the subtle but undeniable role of *jus post bellum* considerations linking otherwise disparate invocations of international law. *Jus post bellum* thinking provides useful analytical continuity that can become a load-bearing pillar for effective responsive actions.

The shared premise that drives grey zone warfare is that Western interests and institutions are no longer suited to the modern world. We need to remember Dean Acheson's observation at the signing ceremony to the North Atlantic Treaty that 'strength and courage will accrue . . . to all peoples of the world community who seek for themselves, and for others equally, freedom and peace'. To paraphrase Roman Emperor Marcus Aurelius, liberal democracies need to stop talking about their shared norms and recommit themselves to defending those norms with vigour in the real world.[5] In other words, we must recommit ourselves to decisive action rather than whining in the face of adversity. The challenges are real and growing. As only one example, Vladimir Putin discussed the poisoning of Sergei Skripal[6] by noting that 'the liberal idea' has 'outlived its

---

[4] Serena K. Sharma, 'Reconsidering the Jus ad Bellum/Jus in Bello Distinction', in *Jus Post Bellum: Towards a Law of Transition from Conflict to Peace*, edited by Carsten Stahn and Jan Kleffner (TMC Asser 2008) 9.

[5] Marcus Aurelius, *Meditations* (Martin Hammond tr, Penguin 2014) ('No more roundabout discussion of what makes a good man. Be one!') Book Ten, para. 16.

[6] Readers will recall that he was a former Russian military intelligence officer who acted as a double agent for the UK's intelligence services during the 1990s who was poisoned in Salisbury, UK.

purpose'.[7] Putin has postulated that liberal democracies are 'obsolete' because they 'come into conflict with the interests of the overwhelming majority of the population'.[8] This is an Alice in Wonderland narrative whereby tyrants cause genocide, aggression, and grievous suffering based on the façade that they seek to eradicate those evils.

Leadership, courage, and larger vision provide the elements needed to counter insidious grey zone threats to Western interests and institutions. Section 2 of this chapter explains my conception of the strategic seams currently exploited by adaptive adversaries. Liberal democracies must accept the truism that legal norms are in contestation and constant ferment. Section 3 then describes the necessity for legal integration as a tangible defence against grey zone disorder. Logically, then, Western States must avoid efforts to equate a dualist narrative between the rule of law and the onset of conflict. They must embrace the competition from malignant actors in order to sustain the vigour of shared norms and institutions.

Section 4 addresses an oft-repeated misunderstanding of the relationship between the rule of law and the onset of competition between States. States cannot permit Cicero's context of specific argument as an advocate during a famous trial ('silent enim leges inter arma') to become a warped pretext for conducting grey zone conflicts. Grey zone warfare is not binary because classic conceptions of peacetime versus conflict are inapplicable. Section 5 postulates the utility of classic Principles of War. They are time-tested tenets to guide decision-making in the face of instabilities and provocations. Because peace is the proper object of kinetic warfare, the Principles of War provide a ready-made template for unified action in the face of persistent grey zone tactics. Finally, section 6 suggests that the reinvigorating the Clean Hands doctrine in international law would help Western nations and those that support the liberal international order triumph in the face of instabilities.

2. The struggle for law

Grey zone warfare seeks to neuter the overarching purposes of international law. Opponents appeal to accepted moral and legal norms as a barrier to effective defence of those values. Through this paradox, the enemies of Western interests and institutions seek to erode the law through such hijacking.[9] The International

---

[7] Lionel Barber, Henry Foy, and Alex Barker, 'Vladimir Putin says Liberalism Has "Become Obsolete"', *Financial Times* (London, 27 June 2019) <https://www.ft.com/content/670039ec-98f3-11e9-9573-ee5cbb98ed36> accessed 7 February 2023.

[8] Ibid.

[9] In the first century of its existence (between 632 and 732), Islam permanently conquered, Arabized, and Islamized nearly three quarters of Christendom, thereby permanently severing it.

516 COUNTERING HYBRID AND GREY ZONE THREATS

Law Commission Fragmentation Report conceded that 'normative conflict is endemic to international law. Because of the spontaneous, decentralized and non-hierarchical nature of international law-making—law-making by custom and by treaty—lawyers have always had to deal with heterogeneous materials at different levels of generality and with different normative force'.[10] This reality represents the legal and strategic avenue of approach for enemies who seek to sow mistrust and friction amongst erstwhile allies. The resultant indecision and legal imprecision provide an open pathway for adversaries seeking to undermine the values that bind liberal democracies. Just as the North Atlantic Treaty Organization (NATO) would never have condoned abandoning the defence of the Fulda Gap in the face of numerically superior Warsaw Pact forces, we should not permit Western values to be sundered through grey zone contestation.

Though the rise of illiberal States presents varied challenges to international order, the struggle for law is embedded in the very fibre of the modern system. Prior to signing the North Atlantic Treaty on the afternoon of April 4, 1949, President Truman spoke to the foreign ministers present in the auditorium. 'In this pact', he said, 'we hope to create a shield against aggression and the fear of aggression—a bulwark which will permit us to get on with the real business of government and society, the business of achieving a fuller and happier life for all our citizens'.[11] Representing the United Kingdom, Ernest Bevin noted that the signers represented countries with 'spiritual affinities' and peoples 'who do not glorify war' but do not 'shrink from it in the face of aggression'. He solemnly pledged that '[s]peaking for the British people, I can assure you that they have agreed to make their contribution for the pool of peace'.

The parameters of modern international law remain susceptible to contextual argumentation. Russian disinformation efforts in Georgia, Ukraine, Moldova, and Western States highlight domestic divisions and debates seeking to sow destabilization. Information warfare becomes an asymmetric tool in the grey zone that spreads on social media and other platforms and seeks to corrode the capacity of States to respond to security threats. Similarly, opponents of Western values seek to supplant the role of the judiciary as the appropriate branch for dispute resolution. Aharon Barak, of the Israeli Supreme Court, summarized one

---

Europe came to be known as 'the West' because it was literally the remaining and westernmost appendage of Christendom *not* to be swallowed up by Islam. See Raymond Ibrahim, *Sword and Scimitar* (De Capo Press 2018).

[10] International Law Commission (n 2) para. 486.
[11] Article 5 of the North Atlantic Treaty (4 April 1949), 34 UNTS 244 reads: 'The Parties agree that an armed attack against one or more of them in Europe or North America shall be considered an attack against them all and consequently they agree that, if such an armed attack occurs, each of them ... will assist the Party or Parties so attacked by taking [...] such action as it deems necessary, including the use of armed force, to restore and maintain the security of the North Atlantic area'.

salient aspect the legitimate role of the judiciary that dictatorial States seek to displace (speaking about the proportionality principle applicable during *jus in bello, jus ad bellum* debates, and human rights jurisprudence) as follows:

> [T]he question is not what I would decide in a given circumstance, but rather whether the decision that the military commander made is a decision that a reasonable military commander was permitted to make. . . . Who decides about proportionality? Is it a military decision to be left to the reasonable application of the military, or a legal decision within the discretion of the judges? . . . Proportionality is not a standard of precision; at times there are a number of ways to fulfill its conditions . . . a zone of proportionality is created; it is the borders of that zone that the court guards.[12]

Invocation of international norms by parties who seek to erode those self-same standards helps atrophy robust norms into extensions of asymmetric combat power by artificially crippling combatant capabilities. Sovereignty becomes the Chinese tool of choice to undermine the sovereign prerogatives and sovereign equality of nations within its perceived sphere of domination. As one recent writer noted, 'there is no war or peace—only war *and* peace. Those who grasp this will conquer, like China, and those who don't will speak Chinese'.[13] As only one example, China's salami-slicing tactics in the South China Sea and its frequent invocation of core concepts of sovereignty mask efforts to undermine stability in the Indo-Pacific region. Indeed, even after an agreement with the Philippines purporting to improve maritime relations, the Chinese coast guard vessel continues to harass Filipino fishing vessels within the Philippines' exclusive economic zone (EEZ). China has subjected the Philippines to various other forms of economic and political aggression, including parking a massive fleet of maritime militia vessels in the EEZ.

China invoked law of the sea rules as a pretext for undermining the sovereign rights of other States that accrue from that same set of norms.[14] This conduct is unjustifiable and illegal under current international norms yet does not create sufficient threat to warrant escalation into kinetic conflict as an unqualified 'attack' that would generate an unqualified and uncontroversial right of individual or collective self-defence. Conversely, China copied the grey zone tactic of delegitimizing judicial interventions on behalf of shared international norms. China was well within its sovereign rights to take reservations to the UN Convention on the Law of the Sea that prevented compulsory jurisdiction

---

[12] Michael Newton and Larry May, *Proportionality in International Law* (OUP 2014) 179.

[13] Sean McFate, *The New Rules of War* (William Morrow 2019) 73–74.

[14] Rob McLaughlin, 'The Law of the Sea and PRC Gray-Zone Operations in the South China Sea' (2022) 116 American Journal of International Law 821.

518 COUNTERING HYBRID AND GREY ZONE THREATS

over disputes related to the area in both the Law of the Sea Tribunal and the International Court of Justice.[15] The Chinese government ignored its explicit assurances that the disputed islands in the South China Sea would not be militarized. However, in July 2016, the Permanent Court of Arbitration held that China's claim to all waters within its self-proclaimed nine-dash line were without merit.[16] Thus the PCA ruling found that Beijing's activities within the Philippines' two-hundred-nautical-mile EEZ, such as illegal fishing and environmentally ruinous artificial island construction, infringed on Manila's sovereign rights. The Chinese government views the South China Sea decision as being 'illegal, null and void'.[17] Similar to the Russian presence in the Sahel region and in Syria, Chinese diplomats invoke international norms of peace and security, even as they wield grey zone tactics to undermine international comity along with peace and security in fact. Thus, the force of otherwise binding international law is delegitimized, even as its proponents use the grey zone to undermine sovereign self-defence and regional unity.

International law and the aging institutional structures created after World War II may be on the verge of irrelevance due to these stresses. Indecision by States seeking to uphold human rights and international order signals indifference to those values. Diplomats must remain diligent to guard the foundational pillars that support modern international law and regional relations. We must

---

[15] China promulgated the following diplomatic demarches:

Declaration:

1. In accordance with the provisions of the United Nations Convention on the Law of the Sea, the People's Republic of China shall enjoy sovereign rights and jurisdiction over an exclusive economic zone of 200 nautical miles and the continental shelf.
2. The People's Republic of China will effect, through consultations, the delimitation of boundary of the maritime jurisdiction with the States with coasts opposite or adjacent to China respectively on the basis of international law and in accordance with the equitable principle.
3. The People's Republic of China reaffirms its sovereignty over all its archipelagoes and islands as listed in article 2 of the Law of the People's Republic of China on the Territorial Sea and Contiguous Zone which was promulgated on 25 February 1992.
4. The People's Republic of China reaffirms that the provisions of the United Nations Convention on the Law of the Sea concerning innocent passage through the territorial sea shall not prejudice the right of a coastal State to request, in accordance with its laws and regulations, a foreign State to obtain advance approval from or give prior notification to the coastal State for the passage of its warships through the territorial sea of the coastal State. 25 August 2006

Declaration under Article 298:

The Government of the People's Republic of China does not accept any of the procedures provided for in Section 2 of Part XV of the Convention with respect to all the categories of disputes referred to in paragraph 1 (a) (b) and (c) of Article 298 of the Convention.

[16] *South China Sea Arbitration (The Republic of Philippines v. The People's Republic of China)*, Award, PCA Case No. 2013-19 (July 12, 2016) paras. 169–278.

[17] Chinese Ministry of Foreign Affairs, 'Foreign Ministry Spokesperson Wang Wenbin's Regular Press Conference on July 13, 2022' (13 July 2022) <https://www.fmprc.gov.cn/mfa_eng/xwfw_665 399/s2510_665401/202207/t20220713_10719475.html> accessed 7 February 2023.

be clear-eyed and resolute regarding the optimal end state for current grey zone conflicts. Western allies along with all other States that believe that international law serves an important expressive value in clarifying the desired relationships between States and international organizations should confront these challenges without equivocation.

Sustaining the rule-based international order is the sine qua non of authentic deterrence. Lack of will paired with lack of capacity leads to inadequacy which threatens international stability. Phrased another way, proponents of grey zone tactics seek to shape a world with enervated global norms that serves their narrow sovereign interests. International consensus regarding the kind of world that best balances the rights and duties of all States is difficult to achieve and is not self-sustaining. From that perspective, *jus post bellum* considerations serve as important connecting tendons that buttress international order in the face of unconventional and persistent challenges. Developing a strategy to combat another strategy is nothing more than marketing. The following section will address the imperative for legal integration as a cornerstone of effective action to counter grey zone challenges.

3. Strategic seams and the concept of legal integration

NATO rests upon the bedrock commitment of sovereign partners to contribute military power in pursuit of a shared but pragmatic goal, *to wit*: international equilibrium in defence of democratic States founded on the rule of law. The creation of NATO was a watershed event in the history of Western civilization derived from the common heritage of the victorious World War II allies. Hugo Grotius anticipated this interconnected but independent set of doctrines based on the realization that justice is best described as pursuit of 'the common good'.[18] The State Department Introduction to the Treaty text observed that the treaty 'has its roots in the common heritage and civilization of the peoples living on both shores of the North Atlantic Ocean', and specifically commends the 'common, ingrained faith in the dignity and worth of the individual, in the principles of democracy, and in the rule of law'.[19] Confronting challenges in the grey zone requires similar determination to preserve the role of law while shaping it to serve larger interests of States that share common values.

NATO's southern and eastern flanks represent persistent sources of conflict. The Warsaw Communiqué noted 'an arc of insecurity and instability

---

[18] Hugo Grotius, *The Law of War and Peace* (first published 1625, Francis W. Kelsey tr, Oxford Clarendon Press 1925) Vol. 1, ch. 1, sec. VIII.

[19] Department of State Publication 3497, General Foreign Policy Series 10, June 1949.

520 COUNTERING HYBRID AND GREY ZONE THREATS

along NATO's periphery and beyond'. The second paragraph of the Brussels Declaration summarized the current challenges as follows:

> We face a dangerous, unpredictable, and fluid security environment, with enduring challenges and threats from all strategic directions; from state and non-state actors; from military forces; and from terrorist, cyber, and hybrid attacks. Russia's aggressive actions, including the threat and use of force to attain political goals, challenge the Alliance and are undermining Euro-Atlantic security and the rules-based international order. . . . We face hybrid challenges, including disinformation campaigns and malicious cyber activities. The proliferation of weapons of mass destruction and advanced missile technology also continues to threaten the security of our nations. In light of all this, our unity and solidarity are stronger than ever; we will take all necessary steps to ensure our collective defence.[20]

The modern system of international law is neither self-sustaining nor self-correcting. The concept of legal interoperability is modelled after the broader concept of force interoperability, which NATO defines as '[t]he ability of the forces of two or more nations to train, exercise and operate effectively together in the execution of assigned missions and tasks'.[21]

Legal interoperability, by extension, is an essential aspect of shared military and diplomatic power because it permits allies to overcome barriers posed by differing legal frameworks applicable to (or shared obligations interpreted differently by) each nation.[22] Hence, it is an essential feature of effective deterrence. As one NATO expert opined, '[l]egal interoperability is understood here as the ability of the forces of two or more nations to operate effectively together in the execution of assigned missions and tasks and with full respect for their legal obligations, notwithstanding the fact that nations concerned have varying legal obligations and varying interpretations of these obligations'.[23] Another adviser with NATO legal experience emphasized 'the ability to have a generally shared single common body of law—as it allows for a critical analysis to focus, compare

---

[20] North Atlantic Treaty Organization, 'Brussels Summit Declaration Issued by the Heads of State and Government Participating in the Meeting of the North Atlantic Council in Brussels 11-12 July 2018' (11 July 2018) <https://www.nato.int/cps/en/natohq/official_texts_156624.htm> accessed 7 February 2023.

[21] NATO Standardisation Office, 'NATO Glossary of Terms and Definitions', AAP-06 (2014).

[22] International Committee of the Red Cross, 'International Humanitarian Law and the Challenges of Contemporary Armed Conflicts' (2011) 32 (highlighting that '[a]n important practical challenge is to ensure that peace operations are conducted taking into consideration the different levels of ratification of IHL instruments and the different interpretations of those treaties and of customary IHL by troop contributing States').

[23] M. Zwanenburg, 'International Humanitarian Law Interoperability in Multinational Operations' (2013) 95 International Review of the Red Cross 681, 681–84.

WINNING AT THE STRATEGIC SEAMS 521

and identify potential areas of legal divergences and strains and, in turn, assess, for the operational commander, the impact these divergences may have on operational interoperability'.[24] The advent of grey zone conflicts challenges these aspirations.

Legal interoperability is an important counterbalance against shifting political dynamics of coalition decision-making. Indeed, the absence of legal homogeneity between coalition partners often requires such improvisation. By way of illustration, US delegates to the negotiations leading up to the 1997 Ottawa Landmines Convention[25] sought to preserve defensive obligations deterring high-intensity armed conflict while advancing the shared goal to prevent loss of innocent life caused by unrecovered landmines.

Commenting on the binary choice required by the text, President Clinton remarked:

One of the biggest disappointments I've had as President, a bitter disappointment for me, is that I could not sign in good conscience the treaty banning land mines, because we have done more since I've been President to get rid of land mines than any country in the world by far.[26]

Similar to the Rome Statute,[27] the Ottawa Convention does not allow reservations. Its broad prohibitions are inflexible in adjusting to the larger need to deter a numerically superior enemy from crossing an international border clearly marked by high fences, guard towers, and emplaced minefields between barbed wire fences. The United States refrained from acceding to the Ottawa Convention, and other treaties, not because of visceral distrust of multilateral instruments but because delegates adopted treaty provisions that undermine legitimate and shared security equities. This is well within the prerogatives of any sovereign state. We must seek cohesion among allies during grey zone challenges.

In the real world, declarations and understandings of NATO States enhance the prospects for unhesitating collective self-defence, notwithstanding divergent treaty duties vis-à-vis the United States. Canada entered the following understanding (substantively identical to those promulgated by Poland and the United Kingdom):

---

[24] K. Abbott, 'A Brief Overview of Legal Interoperability Challenges for NATO Arising from the Interrelationship between IHL and IHRL in Light of the European Convention on Human Rights' (2014) 96 International Review of the Red Cross 107.

[25] Convention on the Prohibition of the Use, Stockpiling, Production and Transfer of Anti-Personnel Mines and on their Destruction (1 March 1999), 2056 UNTS 211.

[26] White House, 'Clinton Remarks on Comprehensive Test Ban Treaty' (6 October 1999).

[27] Rome Statute of the International Criminal Court (1 July 2002), 2187 UNTS 90, Article 120.

It is the understanding of the Government of Canada that, in the context of operations, exercises or other military activity sanctioned by the United Nations or otherwise conducted in accordance with international law, the mere participation by the Canadian Forces, or individual Canadians, in operations, exercises or other military activity conducted in combination with the armed forces of States not party to the Convention which engage in activity prohibited under the Convention would not, by itself, be considered to be assistance, encouragement or inducement in accordance with the meaning of those terms in article 1, paragraph 1 (c).[28]

If NATO seeks to deter hostile military advances by massed conventional forces invading from its periphery, only the United States will be legally permitted to employ mines on the national borders to prevent aggression. If American landmines represented the most effective deterrent to aggression committed against Poland or the Baltic States, neither the North Atlantic Council nor the most starry-eyed internationalist would rightfully register opposition. These legal efforts reflect the central conception of military and political structures premised on order and the achievement of organized authority orchestrated to accomplish shared objectives. Grey zone challenges do not confront NATO or other alliances with the clear-cut applicability of established self-defence prerogatives. However, shared security interests and the legal framework that binds States are nevertheless actively undermined. Hence, Western States and their allies must be all the more conscious of coordinating efforts and diplomacy in order to enhance deterrence and permit decisive action when necessary.

4. Cicero's prescriptions for grey zone conflicts

Hugo Grotius quoted the Roman philosopher Cicero for the proposition that 'there is no medium between war and peace'.[29] In the modern era, disagreements over the form and function of legal norms within the grey zone undermine swift action by sovereigns with shared interests. Grotius presaged sharp intellectual cleavages that led to distinctive bodies of law known as the Law of War versus

---

[28] Canada, 'Understanding' (3 December 1997) <https://treaties.un.org/Pages/ViewDetails.aspx?src=TREATYandmtdsg_no=XXVI-5andchapter=26andclang=_en> accessed 7 February 2023. The United Kingdom 'Declaration' (31 July 1998), ibid., reads as follows: 'It is the understanding of the Government of the United Kingdom that the mere participation in the planning or execution of operations, exercises or other military activity by the United Kingdom's Armed Forces, or individual United Kingdom nationals, conducted in combination with the armed forces of States not party to the [said Convention], which engage in activity prohibited under that Convention, is not, by itself, assistance, encouragement or inducement for the purposes of Article 1, paragraph (c) of the Convention'.

[29] Grotius (n 18).

WINNING AT THE STRATEGIC SEAMS   523

Law of Peace.[30] Objective manifestations marked this archaic demarcation such as 'a declaration of war, followed by a breach of diplomatic relations and active hostilities'.[31] Modern international law long ago eroded that binary division. For example, bland statements that *lex specialis* requires full subordination of other bodies of law to *jus in bello* norms during conflicts do not align with state practice. Neither do they eliminate debates and indecisiveness among allies faced with grey zone challenges.[32]

For example, indecision over the applicability of accepted norms during cyber operations divides States because of the inherent complexity between articulations of self-defence conducted under *jus ad bellum* standards and malleable assessments for assessing proportionate (and hence lawful) responses under human rights law or the law of retorsion or of state responsibility.[33] Legal indeterminacy creates debate among like-minded States that grants unwarranted latitude to actors with malign motives. Cicero's voice echoes some two thousand years later to aid States grappling with the complexities of grey zone challenges.

Cicero understood that 'the only excuse for going to war is that we may live in peace unharmed'.[34] Liberal democracies must embrace their overarching commitment to engage grey zone challenges with the goal of building more sustainable peace built on their shared values. Departing from the modern *jus post bellum* framework in kind but not design, Cicero qualified the treatment of the vanquished enemy to varying degrees because he knew that gracious peace was 'a sound basis for the building of an empire'.[35] Ulysses S. Grant intuited the same premise when he permitted vanquished Confederates to retain their horses and personal sidearms to prevent 'unnecessary humiliation' while forbidding celebratory cannon fire because 'we did not want to exult in their downfall'.[36] In like manner, the utility of various coalition tactics must depend upon the necessity for resort to conflict in the first place.[37] *Jus ad bellum* echoes this premise by

---

[30] The very title of Hugo Grotius's classic work framed the issue in precisely this manner because that was the intellectual and philosophical fissure that he sought to explicate.

[31] Leslie Green, 'Armed Conflict, War and Self Defense', in *Essays on the Modern Law of War* (Transnational 2nd edn 1999) 75. The law of neutrality was also a central feature of this regime.

[32] Michael A. Newton, 'The DoD Law of War Manual as Applied to Coalition Command and Control', in *The United States Department of Defense Law of War Manual: Commentary and Critique*, edited by Michael A. Newton (CUP 2018) 360.

[33] Group of Government Experts on Advancing Responsible State Behaviour in Cyberspace in the Context of International Security, 'Report' (14 July 2021), UN Doc. A/76/135.

[34] Marcus Tullius Cicero, 'On Moral Duties (De Officiis)', in *Ethical Writings of Cicero* (Andrew P. Peabody tr, Little, Brown 1885) I, 35.

[35] Roland H. Bainton, *Christian Attitudes toward War and Peace: A Historical Survey and Critical Re-evaluation* (Abingdon 1960) 41.

[36] Ulysses S. Grant, *Memoirs and Selected Letters 1839–1865* (Library of America 1990) 739–44.

[37] Richard Tuck, *The Rights of War and Peace: Political Thought and the International Order from Kant to Grotius* (OUP 1999) 20–21 (describing the inherent limitations of a war conducted for what Cicero termed 'glory' as opposed to wars fought for national survival).

524   COUNTERING HYBRID AND GREY ZONE THREATS

virtue of the truism that law cannot favour the aggressor in form or application if it is to remain viable in a healthy international system.

By the same token, Cicero was clear that law must serve larger interests of self-defence without regard to formalist constraints. His oft-repeated maxim that 'silent enim leges inter armes'[38] is often incorrectly attributed to mean 'in times of war, the law falls silent'.[39] When applied to the domain of conflict, Clausewitz famously dismissed legal constraints by suggesting that 'war is an act of force, and there is no logical limit in the application of force ... Attached to force are certain self-imposed, imperceptible limitations hardly worth mentioning, known as international law and custom, but they scarcely weaken it'.[40]

Cicero was not arguing that extra-legal methods are appropriate during *in extremis* situations based on utilitarian necessity.[41] In historical fact, Cicero was arguing as defence counsel for close friend Milo, who had been set upon while travelling by armed brigands under the leadership of a political foe. On trial for the murder of Clodius, Cicero argued that his client enjoyed a right of self-defence that superseded other potentially applicable constraints.[42] Relying on this theory of self-defence under circumstances that rendered the killing understandable and even laudable, the relevant portion of Cicero's oration follows:

> There is therefore a law, gentlemen, not one written down anywhere but a natural law, not one that we have learned, inherited, and read, but one that we have seized, imbibed, and extracted from nature herself, a law for which we were not taught, but made, which we know not from instruction but from intuition, the law which states that, if any attempt is made upon our lives, if we encounter violence and weapons, whether of brigands or enemies, then every method of saving ourselves is morally justifiable. When swords are drawn the laws fall silent.[43]

[38] Marcus Tullius Cicero, *Pro Milone* (Thomas J. Keeline ed., CUP 2021) IV, xi.

[39] William H. Rehnquist, 'Dwight D. Opperman Lecture: Remarks of the Chief Justice of the United States' (1999) 47 Drake Law Review 201, 205–08 ('Here we have an illustration of an old maxim of Roman law—Inter Arma Silent Leges—which loosely translated means that in time of war the laws are silent ... perhaps we can accept the proposition that though the laws are not silent in wartime, they speak with a muted voice').

[40] Carl von Clausewitz, *On War* (Michael Howard and Peter Paret tr., Princeton University Press 1976) 75, 77. First published 1833.

[41] See e.g. *Smith v. Shaw* (N.Y. 1815) 12 Johns. 257, 261 (arguing that in times of war necessity and the public good may justify certain acts in accordance with Cicero's maxim)

[42] Mark Edward Clark and James S. Ruebel, 'Philosophy and Rhetoric in Cicero's "Pro Milone"' (1985) 128 Rheinisches Museum für Philologie 57, 65 ('The notion of justifiable self-defense was of course thoroughly accepted at Rome long before the advent of Stoicism, but the two ideologies converge conveniently here; somewhat later on, Cicero appeals again to this doctrine, in terms which ring increasingly Stoic.').

[43] Marcus Tullius Cicero, 'For Milo', in *Cicero: Defence Speeches* (D. H. Berry tr, OUP 2008) 10–11.

The takeaway with respect to grey zone conflicts is plain. Liberal democracies must be staunch defenders of the integrity of the law as applied in defence of human rights, freedoms, and international order. Of course international law applies, but it does so in modified form and with an entirely different set of normative benchmarks. Liberal democracies must be proactive in shaping norms and expectations and protect larger interests. Liberal democracies should shape legal norms that preserve human dignity and protect the right to life within the context of both *jus ad bellum* and *jus in bello*, all the while under the shadow of the need to create an enduring peace.

Grotius recognized this truism in the Prolegomena to his classic work by noting that '[i]f "laws are silent among arms", this is true only of civil laws and of laws relating to the judiciary and the practices of peacetime, and not of the other laws which are perpetual and appropriate to all circumstances'. This understanding empowers the role of international law as a good faith instrument to oppose lawless invocations of convenience during grey zone conflicts. Phrased with slightly more precision, international law balances military and political expediency and larger alliance interests (such as ensuring strategic or tactical victory, preserving the lives of friendly forces and innocent citizens, and bringing the conflict to its optimal and swiftest conclusion) against countervailing uncertainty presented by persistent opponents. Liberal democracies must invoke appropriate legal norms to prevent their usurpation by actors who would use anarchy and uncertainty to harm freedom-loving individuals and cultures.

5. Returning to first principles—principles of war

Grey zone adversaries seek to hide behind the principles of international law as subterfuge for waging conflict and achieving their strategic objectives. Emer Vattel recognized the irony of this tactic in his 1758 classic:

> Pretexts are at least a homage which unjust men pay to justice. He who screens himself with them shows that he still retains some sense of shame. He does not openly trample on what is most sacred in human society; he tacitly acknowledges that a flagrant injustice merits the indignation of all mankind.[44]

Yielding to the pressures of uncertainty or shirking from recurrent challenges in the grey zone would cede the figurative battlefield to those who suppress human liberty. Like high-intensity kinetic conflict, political and military structures

---

[44] Emer de Vattel, *The Law of Nations* (Béla Kapossy and Richard Whatmore eds, Liberty Fund Inc. 2008) 487. First published 1758.

526   COUNTERING HYBRID AND GREY ZONE THREATS

around the world are premised on order and the achievement of organized authority orchestrated to accomplish the goals of conflict. It cannot be forgotten that the principle of Objective emerged as the first of the universally recognized Principles of War around 1800.[45] The law itself should be a fulcrum to balance competing goals and ameliorate strains within a coalition conducting grey zone conflict.

Warfare is not an exact science or an exercise in engineering. Napoleon was correct that during conflicts, the moral is to material as three to one.[46] Liberal democracies should be unashamed to advocate for their values and core interests. They cannot suppress tyranny through a mechanical or pro forma exercises of hollow rhetoric. The overarching 'Objectives' (styled *jus post bellum*) of any war provide the template for evaluating military and legal efficacy as well as the very modalities for justifying and waging the conflict. Liberal democracies must contend for their values in the face of grey zone competitions.

Even as they embrace the challenges ahead, like-minded allies would be well served to revisit the foundational Principles of Warfare as adapted to the challenges of modern grey zone conflicts. I do not seek to oversimplify but to expand the boundaries of strategic imagination. As noted, the Principles of War crystallized as conventional military doctrine at the beginning of the nineteenth century. The accepted principles are Objective, Offensive, Mass, Economy of Force, Manoeuvre, Unity of Command, Security, Surprise, and Simplicity. They are studied by historians, tacticians, military experts, and students around the world who seek to understand the art of warfare. Their application and implications indicate military success or failure. Victory or defeat hangs on the diligence and daring of combatants and diplomats. Famous battles and campaigns become understandable against the backdrop of these time-tested tenets. The Principles of War serve as a predicative model in many instances such as, inter alia, Hannibal's tactics at Cannae, or the genius of Napoleon at Austerlitz, MacArthur at Inchon, the decision to split forces against superior enemy forces at Chancellorsville, the famous left hook during the First Gulf War, and so many other battles and campaigns. History shows that the Principles of War also predict the pathway to ignominy for those who simply ignore their power. In the same light, liberal democracies cannot concede that the proper role of law impedes effective responses during grey zone hostilities. International law exists to serve consensus values and is never static. Hence, politicians and strategists would be well served to contemplate adaptation of these core considerations into the modern grey zone context.

---

[45] John Whiteclay Chambers II (ed), *The Oxford Companion to American Military History* (OUP 1999) 557.

[46] This truism helps explain the increasing importance of information warfare as a necessary adjunct to warfighting, strategy, and logistics in the modern era of interconnected communications.

WINNING AT THE STRATEGIC SEAMS   527

For example, given that the domain of doubt creates paralysis and uncertainty, liberal democracies should be vigilant in clarifying the contours of international law to preserve broad rights of individual and collective self-defence. This is the principle of Offensive (sometimes termed 'retaining the tactical and strategic initiative'). Clarity of purpose is the vital element in shaping effective multinational coalitions (which helps provide literal Mass on a kinetic battlefield and diplomatic Mass in the form of unified opposition to grey zone tactics among allies). The use of information to retain the offensive and generate Mass using the Simplicity of an understandable narrative is at the heart of the Chinese concept of 'Three Warfares'.[47] Because clarity of purpose binds free nations together, they must be clear about their fidelity to shared objectives by standing for sovereignty and legitimate self-defence balanced against respect for human rights and international comity. The core *jus cogens* prohibition against waging aggressive war merely serves as the floor for this shared vision of international cooperation and overall welfare (exemplifying Objective, Offensive, Mass, Unity of Command).

In the modern era of interconnected communications, information becomes a vital weapon in the arsenal of democracy.[48] The truth has salience and power. Though he could never have imagined the internet or an globally interconnected network of near instantaneous information, Lt. Gen. Sir Ian Hamilton was completely correct with his observation that '[O]n the actual day of battle naked truths may be picked up for the asking; by the following morning they have already begun to get into their uniforms'.[49] In a more modern context directed against the tyranny of the USSR, Nobel Laureate Aleksandr Solzhenitsyn argued that lies were the most vulnerable point of oppression. He argued that violence 'has nothing to cover itself with but lies, and lies can only persist through violence. And it is not every day and not on every shoulder that violence brings down its heavy hand: It demands of us only a submission to lies, a daily participation in deceit—and this suffices as our fealty'.[50]

Grey zone conflicts can be conceived as the propagation of inaccurate portrayals of law to extort law-abiding States and undermine actual respect for law in defence of human values and basic freedoms. Western values serve as covalent bonds to preserve freedoms, human liberty, and international peace and security. Solzhenitsyn was correct in advocating that individual citizens and the democracies that serve them must 'break out of the imaginary encirclement of our inertness, the easiest way for us and the most devastating for the lies. For

---

[47] Peter Mattis, 'China's "Three Warfares" in Perspective' (*War on the Rocks*, 30 January 2018) <https://warontherocks.com/2018/01/chinas-three-warfares-perspective/> accessed 7 February 2023.

[48] As reflected in several other chapters of this work.

[49] Ian Hamilton, *A Staff Officer's Scrap Book: Volume 1* (Edward Arnold, 1905) v.

[50] Aleksandr Solzhenitsyn, 'Live Not by Lies!', in *The Solzhenitsyn Reader: New and Essential Writings 1947-2005* (Edward W. Ericson Jr. and Daniel Mahoney eds, ISI Books 2006) 556, 557–58.

when people renounce lies, lies simply cease to exist. Like parasites, they can only survive when attached to a person.[51] In light of the fact that repressive governments exploit Twitter, Facebook, YouTube, and so on, to target their own populations and those of democratic countries, Western allies must actively co-operate to prevent attempts to divide the populations of democratic nations with the attendant goal of weakening their governments from the inside.[52]

Space does not permit full explication of these themes. Free States have the *erga omnes* obligation to defend freedom and human dignity. In doing so, they preserve their core values and the very basis of their existence as viable state ac-tors in the international domain. The fight does not belong to any single nation or any single coalition. This is Economy of Force. Every nation has differing strengths, domestic legal authorities, and varying constituencies. Democracies should not strive to take identical steps in the same manner. They must marshal their particular talents to oppose the proponents of grey zone stratagems.

6. Reinvigorating the Clean Hands doctrine as a baseline

At a basic level, the Clean Hands doctrine precludes a tribunal from accepting a claimant's contention when the claimant itself has been involved in an illegality related to the basis of the dispute. There is a divide among scholars and jurists re-garding the existence of the Clean Hands doctrine in public international law.[53] On a broader scale, proponents of grey zone tactics and misappropriation of in-ternational law rights and duties should not be permitted to benefit from their misconduct.

Widespread application of the clean hands doctrine stands in a state of limbo at present. Some tribunals have applied the doctrine, while others have recognized but not applied the concept, and others have denied its existence as an international norm. Other tribunals, like the ICJ, have declined to take a po-sition on the existence of the clean hands doctrine.[54] As noted in the *Guyana/*

---

[51] Ibid.

[52] Price Floyd, 'We Missed Social Media's Dark Side. Let's Be Smarter about the Metaverse' (Defense One, 14 February 2023) <https://www.defenseone.com/ideas/2023/02/we-missed-social-medias-dark-side-lets-be-smarter-about-metaverse/382964/> accessed 7 February 2023.

[53] 'Diplomatic Protection', 56th session, (2004) 1 Yearbook of the International Law Commission 4, para. 35 (Brownlie), UN Doc. A/CN.4/SER.A/2004; 'State Responsibility', 52nd session, (2000) 1 Yearbook of the International Law Commission 218, para. 17 (Crawford), UN Doc. A/CN.4/SER.A/2000; 'State Responsibility', 51st session (1999) 2 Yearbook of the International Law Commission 85, paras. 411–15, UN Doc. A/CN.4/SER.A/1999/Add.1 (Pt 2) (discussion of clean hands in the ILC's report on State responsibility). See also 'Report of the International Law Commission', 57th session, 2005, UN Doc. A/60/10, 110 (Special Rapporteur on Diplomatic Protection, John Dugard).

[54] *Certain Iranian Assets (Islamic Republic of Iran v. United States of America), Preliminary Objections,* Judgment (2019) ICJ Rep. 2019, para. 122.

Suriname arbitration, '[n]o generally accepted definition of the clean hands doctrine has been elaborated in international law'.[55] Furthermore, the 2014 *Yukos* arbitration reached the conclusion that 'unclean hands' does not exist as a general principle of international law'.[56] Despite these assertions, the jurisprudence suggests that certain manifestations of the clean hands doctrine do exist under international law.

According to the principle of *nullus commodum capere de sua injuria propria* (no advantage [may be] gained from one's own wrong), a claimant is barred from claiming restitution when its own illegal actions were the sole cause of the alleged violation committed by the respondent. *Nullus commodum capere de sua injuria propria* applies where one party to a dispute invokes another party's responsibility that was brought about by the first party's illegality.[57] During grey zone conflicts where one party warps international norms to suit its own malevolent goals, international coalitions should stand united in opposing such manipulation of law. Even if a clear-cut case of *nullus commodum capere de sua injuria propria* cannot be argued, or simply in the alternative, the related concept of *ex delicto non oritur actio* may be applicable. While similar to *nullus commodum capere de sua injuria propria*, this principle emphasizes the fact that the claimant's illegality creates a right to which the claimant seeks recognition, rather than forcing the action of the second party. Under this principle, 'an unlawful act cannot serve as the basis of an action in law'.[58]

Judge Anzilotti explained the latter application in the *Eastern Greenland* case. The Norwegian government gave its unilateral assurance to Denmark that the Danes may impose 'sovereignty over the whole of Greenland . . . with no difficulties on the part of Norway'.[59] Norway was precluded from obtaining a declaratory judgment regarding the validity of its occupation under this principle due to its unlawful contradiction of its earlier promise to Denmark.[60] In practice, a more robust invocation of the Clean Hands doctrine would prevent grey zone efforts from relying on illegal actions as a fulcrum for achieving otherwise existing rights. Western States and their allies would thus be liberated from artificial

---

[55] Award in the Arbitration regarding the Delimitation of the Maritime Boundary between Guyana and Suriname (September 17, 2007) 30 Reports of International Arbitral Awards 1, para. 418.

[56] Permanent Court of Arbitration, *Yukos Universal Ltd (Isle of Man) v. The Russian Federation*, PCA Case No. AA227, 18 July 2014, para. 1363. See also Dominic Liew Jr., 'Finding Clarity amidst Confusion: Cleaning up the Clean Hands Doctrine in International Investment Law' (2020) 32 Singapore Academy of Law Journal 643 ('[T]here is presently no universally accepted definition of the clean hands doctrine in public international law').

[57] Ori Pomson and Yonaton Horowitz, 'Humanitarian Intervention and the Clean Hands Doctrine in International Law' (2015) 48 Israel Law Review 219, 233.

[58] Legal Status of Eastern Greenland (1933) PCIJ Rep (Ser A/B, No 53), Dissenting Opinion of Judge Anzilotti, 95.

[59] Ibid. 36.

[60] Ibid. Dissenting Opinion of Judge Anzilotti, 94.

530   COUNTERING HYBRID AND GREY ZONE THREATS

constraints imposed by unclear legal boundaries. Grey zone warfare would become a much less desirable tactic and hence less effective if law-abiding States were entitled to revert to something of the Lotus era standard from a century ago by which their responses to grey zone challenges were entitled to deference absent an express and consensual prohibition drawn from a precise rule of international law. This would sharpen debate over the specific contours of applicable international law and demonstrate the wrongfulness of the grey zone aggressor.

A more recent application of the *ex delicto non oritur actio* principle is found in a report and recommendations of the UN Compensation Commission (UNCC) when it was faced with the question of whether to provide compensation to claimants for work carried out in violation of the trade embargo against Iraq during the First Gulf War.[61] The UNCC considered this principle in denying compensation to private parties that violated the embargo, despite their rights having been violated.[62] Therefore, this is an accepted principle of international law in pleadings before international dispute-settlement mechanisms. However, its application relies on the claim itself resulting from an unlawful act. The Syrian government's actions to undertake atrocity crimes created the evidence of those crimes. Russian aggression into Ukraine generated its own acts of illegal annexation. The principle of *ex delicto non oritur actio* prohibits recognition of property interests derived from illegal predicate actions.

Another argument in favour of the Clean Hands doctrine in international law is tied to the notions of equity and good faith, which courts have found are general principles of international law.[63] Generally, the principle of good faith prohibits a party from benefitting from their wrongful conduct.[64] This general definition finds support through international tribunals and scholars alike.[65] Though jurisprudence provides a basis to argue the Clean Hands doctrine exists as matter of international law, it must be noted that the international court decisions which form a basis for this conclusion may have low precedential value.[66] Litigants arguing the existence of clean hands rely on several separate opinions or dissents to argue for the existence of the Clean Hands doctrine in international law, but

[61] United Nations Security Council Resolution 687 (8 April 1991), UN Doc. S/RES/687, para. 18.

[62] United Nations Compensation Commission Governing Council, 'Report and Recommendations Made by the Panel of Commissioners Concerning the First Instalment of "E2" Claims' (3 July 1998), UN Doc. S/AC.26/1998/7, para. 172.

[63] Aleksandr Shapovalov, 'Should a Requirement of Clean Hands Be a Prerequisite to the Exercise of Diplomatic Protection: Human Rights Implications of the International Law Commission's Debate', (2005) 20 American University International Law Review 829, 839 n. 33

[64] Robert Kolb, 'Principles as Sources of International Law (With Special Reference to Good Faith)' (2006) 53 Netherlands International Law Review 1.

[65] Steven Reinhold, 'Good Faith in International Law' (2013) 2 UCL Journal of Law and Jurisprudence 40, 46; Michael Akehurst, 'Equity and General Principles of Law' (1976) 25 International and Comparative Law Quarterly 801.

[66] Liew (n 56).

WINNING AT THE STRATEGIC SEAMS   531

because these opinions are from single judges or from dissenting opinions, some courts and scholars have not found these opinions to be persuasive.[67]

Viewed as an extension of good faith as a substantive rule of international law, it can be argued the Clean Hands doctrine exists as a specific application of the principle of good faith. Alternatively, if good faith is viewed as a principle to guide decision-making instead of a substantive rule, the principle of good faith may be used to explain the purpose behind the Clean Hands doctrine. Liberal democracies should strive to develop a consensus regarding the contours of the doctrine as applicable to the impermissible actions of grey zone adversaries. From the perspective of States rebutting efforts to undermine the larger fabric of international law, liberal democracies should be vigilant in reinforcing its core tenets rather than permitting incremental but persistent encroachments.

7. Conclusion

The goals of international law are complicated and often controversial. Treaty provisions often represent suboptimal compromises that embed ambiguities designed to placate domestic constituencies. At the same time, no aspect of the integrated legal system is static. We cannot allow the prevailing narratives to be overtaken by those who would seek to undermine our alliances and undermine our common values—those that seek to divide us and corrode the foundations of human freedom the world over. Despite its fragmented nature, and often divided discourse, the goal of international law should be to reinforce human dignity, global stability, and societal welfare. Any state or action that threatens this over-arching purpose must be met with the condemnation and consensus opposition of free nations.

These purposes could result in what might be termed a relativist/escalatory objection. Vigorous pursuit of Western interests will, by definition, clarify the divides between legal and policy positions of other States and alliances. The very nature of international law requires this competition for norms. Law-abiding States should welcome countervailing efforts to resist their vision by promotion

---

[67] For the decisions commonly relied on, see *Legal Status of Eastern Greenland (1933)* PCIJ Rep Series A/B No 53, 308 (Dissenting opinion of Judge Anzilotti); *The Diversion of Water from the Meuse (Netherlands v. Belgium)* (1937) PCIJ Rep Series A/B No 70 (Hudson Separate Opinion; Anzilotti Dissenting Opinion); *United States Diplomatic and Consular Staff in Tehran (United States of America v. Iran)*, Judgment (1980) ICJ Rep. 3, 51–52 (Dissenting Opinion of Judge Morozov); *Military and Paramilitary Activities in and against Nicaragua (Nicaragua v United States)*, Merits, Judgment (1986) ICJ Rep. 14, 336–37 and 392–93 (Dissenting Opinion of Judge Schwebel); *Legality of Use of Force (Yugoslavia v Belgium)*, Provisional Measures, Order of 2 June 1999 (1999) ICJ Rep. 124, 184–85 (Dissenting Opinion of Vice-President Weeramantry); *Arrest Warrant of 11 April 2000 (Democratic Republic of the Congo v. Belgium)*, Judgment (2002) ICJ Rep. 3, 159–61 (Dissenting Opinion of Judge ad hoc Van den Wyngaert).

532 COUNTERING HYBRID AND GREY ZONE THREATS

of alternative visions. If, indeed, the purpose of international law is to enhance shared norms and values, then little is gained by festering and inconclusive debates over the actual normative meaning of law. Full-throated invocation of international legal norms to combat grey zone threats may well suffice to manage those challenges. However, agreement on the binding force of norms is the necessary predicate to decisive coalition action in sovereign self-defence when warranted.

Writing in the *ABA Journal* in 1948, Justice Robert Jackson presaged this modern reality by reflecting on his experiences as the Chief Prosecutor at the International Military Tribunal:

> We men of the law, in all lands, should be aware lest political differences lead us to exaggerate the differences in our legal philosophies and functions. Many political differences are as superficial to the real structure of society as cosmetics are to the anatomy of the individual. It is matters affecting the anatomy of society that lawyers chiefly deal with—and it is anatomy that societies like individuals differ least. Everywhere, in the aftermath of war, the legal profession is trying to repair the legal anatomy of shattered social bodies; everywhere they are struggling against anarchy.[68]

That sentiment rings doubly true for liberal democracies faced with intractable grey zone conflicts. International law should promote larger communal interests and human freedoms. In like manner, the American Declaration of Independence was a clarion call to freedom in the face of perceived persecution. As he signed the document, delegate Stephen Hopkins acknowledged his palsy but reminded observers that though 'my hand shakes my heart stands firm'.[69] Nations should be proud and unafraid of their fellowship in preserving hopes for a free and peaceful world. Resisting grey zone efforts to erode human dignity and institutional integrity requires adaptive techniques and legal interpretations, firm resolve, and resilient defence.

Acknowledgements

The author is deeply appreciative to the friends who have helped shape these thoughts. Any errors, omissions, or oversights are solely attributable to the author and are his responsibility.

---

[68] Honorable Robert Jackson, 'Lawyers Today: The Legal Profession in a World of Paradox' (1947) 33 American Bar Association Journal 24, 89.

[69] Robert G. Ferris and Richard E. Morris, *The Signers of the Declaration of Independence* (National Park Service 1973) 79–81.

24

Legal Resilience

Just a Warm and Fuzzy Concept?

Aurel Sari

1. Introduction

In modern usage, the term 'resilience' refers to the 'action or an act of rebounding or springing back' or 'the power of resuming an original shape or position after compression, bending' and the like.[1] In its literal meaning, the term describes the property of an object or material to resume its initial shape once certain forces it has been subjected to are relaxed. The resilience of a blade of grass, for example, refers to its ability to bend in the wind and return to an upright position without breaking. Figuratively, the term is often applied to individuals, groups, and social relationships to refer to their capacity to recover from the 'effects of a misfortune, shock or illness'[2] or to describe their robustness and adaptability under duress.[3]

Resilience has become a popular idea across many disciplines.[4] No doubt it owes part of its success to the fact that it is a 'stretchy and a pervasive concept'.[5] The term is capable of carrying diverse meanings and it is used differently from one context to another.[6] Another reason for its popularity is the fact that the notion comes with positive connotations: clearly, resilience is a good thing to have. Whatever its

---

[1] "resilience, n.", *Oxford English Dictionary Online* (OUP February 2018).

[2] Ibid.

[3] Peter Rogers, 'The Etymology and Genealogy of a Contested Concept', in *The Routledge Handbook of International Resilience*, edited by David Chandler and Jon Coaffee (Routledge 2014) 13, 14.

[4] E.g. Steven M. Southwick et al, 'Resilience Definitions, Theory, and Challenges: Interdisciplinary Perspectives' (2014) 5 European Journal of Psychotraumatology 25338; Ran Bhamra, Samir Dani, and Kevin Burnard, 'Resilience: The Concept, A Literature Review and Future Directions' (2011) 49 International Journal of Production Research 5375.

[5] Sandra Walklate, Ross McGarry, and Gabe Mythen, 'Searching for Resilience: A Conceptual Excavation' (2014) 40 Armed Forces and Society 408, 410; Frans Osinga, 'Organizing for Insecurity and Chaos: Resilience and Modern Military Theory', in *Netherlands Annual Review of Military Studies 2016: Organizing for Safety and Security in Military Organizations*, edited by Robert Beeres et al (T.M.C. Asser Press 2016) 43.

[6] Rogers (n 3) 19. See also Fridolin Simon Brand and Kurt Jax, 'Focusing the Meaning(s) of Resilience: Resilience as a Descriptive Concept and a Boundary Object' (2007) 12 Ecology and Society Article 23.

Aurel Sari, *Legal Resilience* In: *Hybrid Threats and Grey Zone Conflict.* Edited by: Mitt Regan and Aurel Sari, Oxford University Press. © Oxford University Press 2024. DOI: 10.1093/oso/9780197744772.003.0024

534 COUNTERING HYBRID AND GREY ZONE THREATS

exact meaning, it is surely better to be resilient than not to be. In short, resilience is a warm and fuzzy concept: a notion that lacks a single definition, but one that is widely understood to refer to a goal or quality worth pursuing.[7]

The purpose of this chapter is to explore the utility of resilience thinking at the intersection between international law and contemporary security threats. Specifically, it asks what benefits, if any, the notion of resilience may offer for addressing the legal challenges associated with grey zone conflict and hybrid threats.

This turn to resilience has not escaped criticism. Helmut Aust, for example, has suggested that appeals to resilience 'entail a tendency to securitize responses to hybrid threats' and that this risks giving up what defines 'free and open societies'.[8] Aust is of course right to note that the language of resilience places legal questions within the broader strategic context and in this sense securitizes the law. However, the close relationship between law and security—or law and politics more generally—is not the product of resilience thinking, but the fact that law is both an instrument of and a constraint on politics. The real issue, therefore, is not whether appeals to resilience securitize the law, but what kind of political values and security objectives they promote. Here, Aust is correct to warn about the dangers of over-reach: the risk that open societies may curtail some of the very freedoms that they seek to protect against malign interference. However, such over-reach is not inevitable, as long as we guard against it. Nor does the risk of over-reach diminish the reality of authoritarian interference and the need to protect liberal values and institutions against it.

With these points in mind, section 2 of the chapter reviews the key features of resilience thinking and its reception in legal doctrine to formulate a definition of 'legal resilience'. Section 3 explores the utility of legal resilience in the context of grey zone conflict and hybrid threats, suggesting that the notion offers certain analytical and normative benefits that are worth pursuing. To realize these benefits, section 4 calls on open societies and institutions to develop 'legal resilience strategies' to serve as conceptual and policy frameworks to resist, recover from, and adapt to disturbances in the legal domain in a more comprehensive and systematic fashion. Section 5 offers some concluding thoughts.

2. Resilience and the law

The origins of contemporary resilience thinking are often traced to the field of ecology, in particular to the work that Canadian ecologist Crawford Holling

---

[7] Chris Zebrowski describes resilience as an 'emergent security value': see Chris Zebrowski, *The Value of Resilience: Securing Life in the Twenty-first Century* (Routledge 2017) 107–09.

[8] Helmut Philipp Aust, 'Hybrid Warfare and the Turn to Resilience: Back to the Cold War?' (2020) 3 Humanitäres Völkerrecht 293, 309.

published in the early 1970s.[9] In fact, Holling was not the first to use the term. Understood generically as the capacity to bounce back from adversity, the concept has cropped up in other disciplines long before it became popular in the field of ecology.[10] Nevertheless, Holling's work has been particularly influential and offers a convenient point of departure for our purposes.

2.1 Resilience thinking

Traditional models of ecological systems were based on the assumption that natural systems exposed to external disturbances, such as human intervention, would return to a pre-existing stable equilibrium once the disruption had passed.[11] Holling questioned these assumptions in a seminal paper published in 1973.[12] In his view, the traditional equilibrium-centred view was too static and led to inappropriate and even counter-productive practices in natural resource management. Holling distinguished between stability, defined as the 'ability of a system to return to an equilibrium state after a temporary disturbance', and resilience, the 'measure of the persistence of systems and of their ability to absorb change and disturbance and still maintain the same relationships between populations or state variables'.[13] Ecological systems could thus display low stability, for instance, by experiencing wild fluctuations in their population size, but nevertheless be highly resilient. Conversely, other ecosystems could be stable over time but enjoy low resilience and thus suffer a sudden and potentially catastrophic collapse due to their inability to tolerate even a limited degree of further disturbance.[14]

Other authors often employed resilience in a narrow sense to describe the speed at which natural systems return to their original equilibrium following a perturbation.[15] In response, Holling distinguished between two definitions of resilience which emphasize different aspects of stability.[16] *Engineering*

[9] E.g. Jeremy Walker and Melinda Cooper, 'Genealogies of Resilience: From Systems Ecology to the Political Economy of Crisis Adaptation' (2011) 42 Security Dialogue 143.

[10] E.g. Nicholas Garmezy used the concept in the field of psychology to explore how children were able to develop normal functions in high-risk environments: Nicholas Garmezy, 'Vulnerability Research and the Issue of Primary Prevention' (1971) 41 American Journal of Orthopsychiatry 101. See Philippe Bourbeau, *On Resilience: Genealogy, Logics, and World Politics* (CUP 2018) 3–8.

[11] Lance H. Gunderson and Craig R. Allen, 'Why Resilience? Why Now?', in *Foundations of Ecological Resilience*, edited by Lance H. Gunderson, Craig R. Allen, and C. S. Holling (Island Press 2010) xiii, xiv–xv.

[12] C. S. Holling, 'Resilience and Stability of Ecological Systems' (1973) 4 Annual Review of Ecology and Systematics 1.

[13] Ibid. 14. See also C. S. Holling, 'The Resilience of Terrestrial Ecosystems: Local Surprise and Global Change', in *Sustainable Development of the Biosphere*, edited by William C. Clark and R. E. Munn (CUP 1996) 292, 296–97.

[14] Holling (n 12) 6–10.

[15] E.g. Stuart L. Pimm, 'The Complexity and Stability of Ecosystems' (1984) 307 Nature 321, 322.

[16] C. S. Holling, 'Engineering Resilience versus Ecological Resilience', in *Engineering within Ecological Constraints*, edited by Peter C. Schulze (National Academy Press 1996) 31.

resilience focuses on a system's efficiency, constancy, and predictability.[17] These are attributes encountered primarily in the physical sciences and engineering—hence the name. They represent the more traditional definition of resilience concerned with stability near an equilibrium state. In essence, engineering resilience is about elasticity. It describes a system's ability to resist disturbance and its capacity to return to its state of origin. *Ecological resilience*, by contrast, focuses on persistence, change, and unpredictability.[18] These attributes reflect the preoccupations of biologists and recognize that external disturbances may be uneven and erratic. Ecological resilience is concerned with conditions far removed from a system's original equilibrium, which may lead that system to flip into a different regime or stable state, rather than return to its original position. Here, resilience describes the amount of disturbance that a system can absorb before changing its essential functions and other core features.

Holling argued that it is important to distinguish between these two forms of resilience because they encourage different strategies for managing complexity, disturbance, and change.[19] Whereas engineering resilience emphasizes maintaining *efficiency of function* and thus seeks to guarantee that a system continues to perform its essential tasks without a drop in performance, ecological resilience focuses on maintaining *existence of function* by seeking to ensure that a system retains its essential characteristics.[20] Put differently, engineering resilience resists change, whereas ecological resilience mitigates its effects. Unlike engineering resilience, ecological resilience thus emphasizes a system's ability to adapt.[21]

Inspired by Holling's distinction, adaptability has emerged as a prominent theme in the literature on socio-ecological resilience.[22] Whereas classic ecological models viewed human action as an external driver of change, socio-ecological approaches treat humans and nature as interdependent systems.[23] Since human societies typically benefit from the capacity to reorganize themselves and modify their environment in response to outside pressure, proponents of a socio-ecological perspective put adaptability at the heart of resilience. Adaptability has been defined for these purposes as 'the capacity of actors in a system to influence resilience'.[24] The adaptive capacity of a system refers to its own ability 'to

---

[17] Ibid. 33.

[18] Ibid.

[19] Ibid.

[20] C. S. Holling and Lance H. Gunderson, 'Resilience and Adaptive Cycles', in *Panarchy: Understanding Transformations in Human and Natural Systems,* edited by Lance H. Gunderson and C. S. Holling (Island Press 2002) 25, 28.

[21] Ibid. 32.

[22] E.g. Eric Desjardins et al, 'Promoting Resilience' (2015) 90 Quarterly Review of Biology 147.

[23] W. Neil Adger, 'Social and Ecological Resilience: Are they Related?' (2000) 24 Progress in Human Geography 347.

[24] Brian Walker et al, 'Resilience, Adaptability and Transformability in Social–Ecological Systems' (2004) 9 Ecology and Society Article 5.

learn, combine experience and knowledge, adjust its responses to changing external drivers and internal processes, and continue developing within the current stability domain';[25] in short, its ability to grow more resilient. This emphasis on adaptability has been incorporated into more recent definitions of resilience. Authors working in this area thus define resilience as 'the capacity of a system to absorb disturbance and reorganize while undergoing change so as to retain essentially the same function, structure, identity, and feedbacks'.[26]

The notion of socio-ecological resilience has also initiated a growing interest in adapting institutions. Applying a resilience perspective to institutions— understood broadly as 'rules of the game' that arise from formal and informal norms and rules and organizational structures[27]—directs our attention to the qualities and features that enable institutions to adapt, so as to be better prepared for dealing with surprises and uncertain futures. The quest for adapting institutions is concerned with the 'capacity of people, as part of social–ecological systems, from local groups and private actors to the State, to international organizations, to deal with complexity, uncertainty and the interplay between gradual and rapid change'.[28]

The work on adapting institutions creates a bridge between socio-ecological understandings of resilience and its use in the social sciences.[29] In the field of international relations,[30] regime theorists have equated resilience with regime robustness to refer 'to the "staying power" of international institutions in the face of exogenous challenges and to the extent to which prior institutional choices constrain collective decisions and behaviour in later periods'.[31] Institutions that

[25] Carl Folke et al, 'Resilience Thinking: Integrating Resilience, Adaptability and Transformability' (2010) 15 Ecology and Society Article 20. See also Marten Scheffer, *Critical Transitions in Nature and Society* (Princeton University Press 2009) 103; Carl Folke, Johan Colding, and Fikret Berkes, 'Synthesis: Building Resilience and Adaptive Capacity in Social–Ecological Systems', in *Navigating Social-Ecological Systems: Building Resilience for Complexity and Change*, edited by Carl Folke, Fikret Berkes, and Johan Colding (CUP 2003) 352.

[26] Carl Folke et al., 'Regime Shifts, Resilience, and Biodiversity in Ecosystem Management' (2004) 35 Annual Review of Ecology, Evolution, and Systematics 557, 558.

[27] Emily Boyd and Carl Folke, 'Adapting Institutions, Adaptive Governance and Complexity: An Introduction', in *Adapting Institutions: Governance, Complexity, and Social-Ecological Resilience*, edited by Emily Boyd and Carl Folke (CUP 2012) 1, 3.

[28] Emily Boyd and Carl Folke, 'Conclusions: Adapting Institutions and Resilience', in Boyd and Folke (n 27) 264, 274–75. See also Reinette Biggs, Maja Schlüter, and Michael L. Schoon, 'An Introduction to the Resilience Approach and Principles to Sustain Ecosystem Services in Social-Ecological Systems', in *Principles for Building Resilience: Sustaining Ecosystem Services in Social-Ecological Systems*, edited by Reinette Biggs, Maja Schlüter, and Michael L. Schoon (CUP 2015) 1, 7ff.

[29] For an overview of the use of resilience in the social sciences, see Katrina Brown, 'Global Environmental Change I: A Social Turn for Resilience?' (2014) 38 Progress in Human Geography 107.

[30] On the different strands of resilience thinking in international relations, see Philippe Bourbeau, 'Resilience and International Politics: Premises, Debates, Agenda' (2015) 17 International Studies Review 374, 376–80.

[31] Andreas Hasenclever, Peter Mayer, and Volker Rittberger, *Theories of International Regimes* (CUP 1997) 2.

give way under external pressure, either by suffering a fundamental shift in their normative content or by experiencing a dramatic drop in norm compliance among their members, are thought to lack resilience.[32] Change is thus portrayed as a negative development, whilst resilience is understood positively as resistance to change. This essentially reflects the values associated with what Holling called engineering resilience. Others have taken a broader approach, borrowing insights from socio-ecological notions of resilience. Philippe Bourbeau, for example, has defined resilience as 'the process of patterned adjustments adopted by a society or an individual in the face of endogenous or exogenous shocks'.[33] This definition emphasizes adaptation, viewing it as a dynamic process. In doing so, it avoids assumptions about the existence of social equilibria and instead suggests that disturbances and adaptation are context-dependent and socially construed.

2.2 The reception of resilience in legal scholarship

Resilience thinking has also made inroads into legal scholarship. An in-depth review of the legal literature published in the period between 1985 and 2013 suggests that growing numbers of scholars are relying on the concept.[34] Even a passing glance at more recent publications confirms that this trend continues. In legal writing, the meaning and usage of resilience is inspired mostly by ecological understandings of the term. Accordingly, the distinction drawn between engineering and ecological resilience is widely accepted and repeated.[35] Similarly, resilience is discussed mostly in connection with uncertainty, complexity, and change.[36] However, despite its growing popularity, the reception of resilience thinking in legal scholarship has been uneven. In some fields, resilience has become a popular idea, whereas in others it has not made much of an impression at all. Broadly speaking, legal scholarship on resilience falls into three groups.

First, resilience has proven fashionable with legal experts working on environmental matters. This should not come as a surprise, given the thematic

---

[32] Ibid.

[33] Philippe Bourbeau, 'Resiliencism: Premises and Promises in Securitisation Research' (2013) 1 Resilience 3, 10.

[34] Tracy-Lynn Humby, 'Law and Resilience: Mapping the Literature' (2014) 4 Seattle Journal of Environmental Law 85.

[35] E.g. Jonathan Rosenbloom, 'Fifty Shades of Gray Infrastructure: Land Use and the Failure to Create Resilient Cities' (2018) 93 Washington Law Review 317, 340–344; Thomas D. Barton, 'Re-Designing Law and Lawyering for the Information Age' (2016) 30 Notre Dame Journal of Law, Ethics and Public Policy 1, 16.

[36] E.g. Robin Kundis Craig, 'Learning to Think about Complex Environmental Systems in Environmental and Natural Resource Law and Legal Scholarship: A Twenty-Year Retrospective' (2012) 24 Fordham Environmental Law Review 87, 92.

overlap between environmental law and ecology. A substantial part of this literature explores how more adaptive regulatory mechanisms may promote ecological resilience,[37] including in areas such as energy policy,[38] water management,[39] climate change,[40] and the conservation of biodiversity.[41] Other authors have explored the extent to which the existing rules of international environmental law have absorbed resilience as a normative principle.[42] One prominent concern in this field, often voiced by authors from the United States, is that old-fashioned views of nature still dominate the law. Instead of encouraging adaptive and flexible natural resource governance, environmental and administrative law thus promote rigid conservation practices which are widely regarded as sub-optimal and as an obstacle to enhancing ecosystem resilience.[43]

A second strand of legal scholarship has explored how law may contribute to the resilience of systems other than the natural environment. As in the literature on environmental matters,[44] this body of writing treats legal rules and regimes as instruments which may enhance the resilience of other social systems. For example, law has been identified as a critical component of disaster management.[45] Law confers binding force on disaster management plans, distributes risk across society, allocates resources, provides a framework for monitoring performance, and sustains specialized decision-making mechanisms. Law therefore plays a vital role in enabling effective disaster management, from risk assessment to emergency intervention and recovery. Other studies have focused

[37] E.g. Ahjond S. Garmestani and Craig R. Allen (eds), *Social-Ecological Resilience and Law* (Columbia University Press 2014); Mary Jane Angelo, 'Stumbling Toward Success: A Story of Adaptive Law and Ecological Resilience' (2008) 87 Nebraska Law Review 950.

[38] Andrew Long, 'Complexity in Global Energy-Environment Governance' (2014) 15 Minnesota Journal of Law, Science and Technology 1055.

[39] Andrea M. Keesen and Helena E. M. W. van Rijswick, 'Adaptation to Climate Change in European Water Law and Policy' (2012) 8 Utrecht Law Review 38.

[40] Joseph Wenta, Jan McDonald, and Jeffrey S. McGee, 'Enhancing Resilience and Justice in Climate Adaptation Laws' (2018) Transnational Environmental Law 1.

[41] Jan McDonald, Phillipa C. McCormack, and Anita Foerster, 'Promoting Resilience to Climate Change in Australian Conservation Law: The Case of Biodiversity Offsets' (2016) 39 University of New South Wales Law Journal 1612.

[42] Lia Helena de Lima Demange, 'The Principle of Resilience' (2012) 30 Pace Environmental Law Review 695.

[43] E.g. Jonathan H. Adler, 'Dynamic Environmentalism and Adaptive Management: Legal Obstacles and Opportunities' (2015) 11 Journal of Law, Economics and Policy 133; Hannah E. Birge et al, 'Social-Ecological Resilience and Law in the Platte River Basin' (2014) 51 Idaho Law Review 229; Fred Bosselman, 'What Lawmakers Can Learn from Large-Scale Ecology' (2002) 17 Journal of Land Use and Environmental Law 207; Alyson C. Flournoy, 'Preserving Dynamic Systems: Wetlands, Ecology and Law' (1996) 7 Duke Environmental Law and Policy Forum 105.

[44] *Cf.* Ahjond S. Garmestani, Craig R. Allen, and Melinda H. Benson, 'Can Law Foster Social-Ecological Resilience?' (2013) 18 Ecology and Society Article 37.

[45] See Alexia Herwig and Marta Simoncini (eds), *Law and the Management of Disasters: The Challenge of Resilience* (Routledge 2017).

on the contribution that regulatory action makes to enhancing the resilience of the banking sector,[46] the electricity grid,[47] data privacy,[48] international financial systems,[49] and critical infrastructure.[50] Some of this work suggests that resilience principles extend to the law itself, for example, requiring adaptive forms of regulation in fields such as information and communication technology.[51]

The third strand of legal scholarship is concerned with the resilience of the law itself. Save for a handful of exceptions,[52] most of the writing falling into this category invokes the notion of resilience in an uncritical way, seemingly unaware of the debates that are raging over its meaning in other disciplines. It thus ends up employing the term in its narrow, engineering sense to describe the resistance of specific legal rules and regimes to internal or external shocks. Examples include publications invoking resilience with reference to the common law as a regulatory framework for policing powers,[53] the constitutional foundations of the European Union,[54] governance based on political conventions,[55] the Paris Agreement on climate change,[56] national constitutions,[57] and the legal basis of European banking agencies.[58]

Only a small number of authors have explored how resilience theory, as developed in the socio-ecological literature, maps onto the law more generally.

---

[46] Gregory J. Lyons, Jeremy Hill, and Edite Ligere, 'Basel Bank Resilience and Liquidity Proposals Confirm the Global Paradigm Shift toward Increased Financial Regulatory Oversight' (2010) 127 Banking Law Journal 226.

[47] Jonathan Schneider and Jonathan Trotta, 'What We Talk about When We Talk about Resilience' (2018) 39 Energy Law Journal 353.

[48] Janine S. Hiller and Jordan M. Blanke, 'Smart Cities, Big Data, and the Resilience of Privacy' (2016) 68 Hastings Law Journal 309.

[49] Douglas W. Arner, 'Adaptation and Resilience in Global Financial Regulation' (2010) 89 North Carolina Law Review 1579.

[50] Marta Simoncini and Alessandro Lazari, 'Principles and Policies of Resilience in European Critical Infrastructures: Cases from the Sectors of Gas and Air Transport' (2016) Legal Issues of Economic Integration 41.

[51] Pierre De Vries, 'The Resilience Principles: A Framework for New ICT Governance' (2011) 9 Journal on Telecommunications and High Technology Law 137.

[52] E.g. Tatiana Borisova, 'The Institutional Resilience of Russian Law through 1905–1917 Revolutions' (2017) 5 Russian Law Journal 108.

[53] John Burchill, 'A Horse Gallops down a Street: Policing and the Resilience of the Common Law' (2018) 41 Manitoba Law Journal 161.

[54] Christina Eckes, 'International Sanctions against Individuals: A Test Case for the Resilience of the European Union's Constitutional Foundations' (2009) 15 European Public Law 351.

[55] K. D. Ewing, 'The Resilience of the Political Constitution' (2013) 14 German Law Journal 2111.

[56] Rafael Leal-Arcas and Antonio Morelli, 'The Resilience of the Paris Agreement: Negotiating and Implementing the Climate Regime' (2018) 31 Georgetown Environmental Law Review 1.

[57] Xenophon Contiades and Alkmene Fotiadou, 'On Resilience of Constitutions: What Makes Constitutions Resistant to External Shocks' (2015) 9 Vienna Journal on International Constitutional Law 3.

[58] Niamh Moloney, 'European Banking Union: Assessing Its risks and resilience' (2014) Common Market Law Review 1609, 1644ff.

Among these, J. B. Ruhl has set out to identify what design principles make legal systems more resilient and adaptive,[59] leading him to formulate several key insights. First, according to Ruhl, the resilience of a legal system says nothing about the desirability of its substantive content.[60] Bad law may be resilient just as much as good law. Resilience therefore should not be treated as a self-evident value in the field of law. Second, the use of law as an instrument to render other social systems more resilient must be distinguished from the resilience of the legal system itself.[61] Accordingly, there are two sides to legal resilience: resilience *through* law and resilience *of* law. Third, Ruhl suggests that any legal system has many potential equilibrium states at many different scales.[62] In other words, different components and layers of a legal system may display different degrees of resilience. Fourth, no agreed method exists for quantifying and measuring the resilience of a legal system.[63] Finally, the adaptive capacity of a legal system, that is, its ability to reorganize in response to external drivers, includes the ability to switch between different resilience strategies (e.g. between engineering and ecological forms of resilience).[64]

Other work in this field suggests that the design features which render law more resilient and adaptable are not uniform across different legal systems. The objectives, content, procedures, institutions, and vulnerabilities of legal regimes are simply too diverse for there to be a single, universally applicable recipe to enhance their resilience and adaptability. For example, Craig Anthony Arnold and Lance H. Gunderson suggest that environmental law could increase its adaptive capacity by adopting a polycentric and multimodal structure, favouring flexible standards and discretionary decision-making and embracing iterative processes with feedback loops among multiple participants.[65] These features may well enhance environmental law's ability to foster ecological resilience, but it would be a stretch to assume that the same mix of features would necessarily render other legal regimes, for instance, international human rights law, more resilient and adaptive.

---

[59] J. B. Ruhl, 'General Design Principles for Resilience and Adaptive Capacity in Legal Systems—With Applications to Climate Change Adaptation and Resiliency in Legal Systems' (2010) 89 North Carolina Law Review 1373.

[60] Ibid. 1382.

[61] Ibid.

[62] Ibid. 1384.

[63] Ibid. 1385.

[64] Ibid. 1392.

[65] Craig Anthony (Tony) Arnold and Lance H. Gunderson, 'Adaptive Law and Resilience' (2013) 43 Environmental Law Reporter 10426. See also Daniel A. DeCaro et al, 'Legal and Institutional Foundations of Adaptive Environmental Governance' (2017) 22 Ecology and Society Article 32.

3. Legal resilience, grey zone conflict and hybrid threats

Based on the foregoing, we may define legal resilience as the capacity of a legal system, first, to resist, recover from, and adapt to internal and external disturbances whilst maintaining its key features and, second, to contribute to the resilience of other natural or social systems. This dual definition reflects the distinction drawn between the two aspects of legal resilience identified earlier—resilience of the law itself and resilience mediated through law. The definition describes legal resilience as a capacity rather than a process. Law may be more or less resilient. Resilience is therefore a property of legal systems, whilst efforts to maintain or increase this property are best seen as an ongoing process.

For the purposes of this definition, legal systems are understood in a broad sense as a set of functionally, thematically, or hierarchically related rules, procedures, and institutions. The notion of a legal system thus may refer to a specific legal regime or branch of law, the legal order of a State, the internal law of an international organization, or the international legal system as a whole. Alternatively, it may also refer to rules, procedures, and institutions that are connected more loosely by functional or thematic ties, but without forming a distinct legal regime or branch of law, such as the law of disaster management or the law of military operations. Finally, the definition recognizes that engineering and ecological resilience entail different coping strategies. It therefore describes legal resilience as the capacity to resist, recover from, and adapt to disturbance, whether that disturbance originates from within the law or stems from extra-legal sources. Such disturbances will have exceeded a legal system's capacity to cope if the system is unable to sustain the core features that make up its identity (e.g. its substantive content, structure, or function). These features are referred to as a legal system's persistence criteria.[66]

It is important to underline that legal resilience so defined merely describes a property that legal systems may possess to varying degrees. Legal resilience is not a theory of the relationship between law and other social systems, a blueprint for strengthening the rule of law or an off-the-shelf strategy for countering contemporary security threats, including those posed by grey zone conflict, hybrid threats, and hybrid warfare. Instead, legal resilience is best understood as a perspective—a conceptual framework and mindset—for thinking about the law's ability to withstand shocks and to deal with pressure for change in a diverse range of contexts.[67]

---

[66] See D. Gabbay and J. M. Moravcsik, 'Sameness and Individuation' (1973) 70 The Journal of Philosophy 513, 517.

[67] Cf. Brian H. Walker and David Salt, *Resilience Thinking: Sustaining Ecosystems and People in a Changing World* (Island Press 2006) 1–14. See also Theo Brinkel, 'The Resilient Mind-Set and Deterrence', in *Netherlands Annual Review of Military Studies (Winning without Killing: The Strategic*

3.1 An analytical benefit?

What, then, does legal resilience offer in the present context? The first benefit of adopting a legal resilience perspective is analytical. Legal resilience shines a spotlight on the capacity of the law to cope with the disturbances caused by grey zone and hybrid threats. This focuses our attention, first, on the law's vulnerabilities and coping mechanisms and, second, on what support law may lend to other systems in addressing their own vulnerabilities and strengthening their respective coping mechanisms. However, some care is required, as adopting a legal resilience perspective raises methodological dilemmas.[68]

Resilience is a theory about systems. The identity of the system is therefore critical to any resilience analysis.[69] However, in the field of law, system boundaries are not always easy to demarcate. Law is predominantly structured along functional, thematic, and hierarchical lines and operates on multiple scales, including the individual, communal, regional, national, transnational, and global.[70] Most functional regimes, such as consumer law, span several jurisdictions and have national, regional, and international dimensions.[71] To complicate matters, legal questions often cut across multiple legal regimes and orders. This was recognized by the Parliamentary Assembly of the Council of Europe when it suggested that the use of non-forcible measures by hybrid adversaries 'should be examined in the light of domestic criminal law and, if necessary and depending on the situation, relevant international legal instruments covering specific policy areas (such as the law of the sea or norms on combating cybercrime, terrorism, hate speech or money laundering)'.[72]

Due to the multiscale and cross-cutting nature of law, it is easy to end up with a framework of analysis that is either over- or under-inclusive. The analytical framework will be over-inclusive if the disturbance caused by a hybrid act manifests itself on a significantly lower scale or in a significantly narrower

---

and Operational Utility of Non-Kinetic Capabilities in Crises), edited by Paul A. L. Ducheine and Frans P. B. Osinga (T. M. C. Asser 2017) 19.

[68] See also Lennart Olsson et al, 'A Social Science Perspective on Resilience', in *The Routledge Handbook of International Resilience*, edited by David Chandler and Jon Coaffee (Routledge 2014) 49; Debra J. Davidson, 'The Applicability of the Concept of Resilience to Social Systems: Some Sources of Optimism and Nagging Doubts' (2010) 23 Society and Natural Resources 1135.

[69] Richard A. Barnes, 'The Capacity of Property Rights to Accommodate Social-Ecological Resilience' (2013) 18 Ecology and Society Article 6

[70] Cf. Sandra Walklate, Ross McGarry, and Gabe Mythen, 'Searching for Resilience: A Conceptual Excavation' (2014) 40 Armed Forces and Society 408.

[71] See Hans W. Micklitz and Mateja Durovic, *Internationalization of Consumer Law: A Game Changer* (Springer 2017); Geraint G. Howells et al, *Handbook of Research on International Consumer Law* (Edward Elgar 2010).

[72] Parliamentary Assembly of the Council of Europe Resolution 2217, 'Legal challenges related to hybrid war and human rights obligations' (26 April 2018), para. 7.

544   COUNTERING HYBRID AND GREY ZONE THREATS

thematic area than the legal system studied. For example, international law has relatively little to say about non-coercive interference by one State in the public discourse of another State. Hence international law would not constitute a sufficient reference point in this instance. By contrast, the analytical framework will be under-inclusive if the disturbance occurs at a significantly higher scale or in a wholly different thematic area than the legal system selected. For example, the use of chemical weapons may have no impact on the resilience of Dutch election law, but obviously this is the wrong framework for analysis. These points suggest that a disturbance-driven, rather than a system-driven, analysis often may be more appropriate. This involves relying on the grey zone activity or hybrid threat to define the boundaries of the legal system to be assessed: if the threat engages multiple jurisdictions and legal regimes, then legal resilience is a matter of their collective capacity to resist, recover from, and adapt to that threat.

The notion of an original stable state constitutes another source of difficulty. One of the core principles of ecological resilience is that natural systems may have more than one equilibrium and therefore may flip between different stable states.[73] Ruhl suggests that legal systems may have multiple equilibrium states too.[74] However, the idea of a legal equilibrium is problematic. Examples can be found where a legal system may be said to have flipped from one stable configuration to another as a result of shocks. In the past, the absolute doctrine of State immunity comprehensively barred national courts from exercising their jurisdiction over foreign States.[75] This doctrine came under increasing pressure during the twentieth century as governments began to engage in commercial transactions on a wide scale. A growing number of States abandoned the old rule, thereby paving the way for the emergence of a more restrictive doctrine of State immunity.[76] This episode in the development of the law of State immunity may be re-told as a legal system losing its resilience in the face of sustained disturbance, eventually flipping over into a new stable state.[77]

However, the idea of an equilibrium becomes less compelling when legal change is gradual and evolutionary in nature, rather than abrupt and radical. For example, there can be no doubt that the growth of human rights law has weakened the State-centric features of international law,[78] but this has not

---

[73] Holling (n 12).

[74] Ruhl (n 59) 1384.

[75] *The Parlement Belge* [1880] 5 PD 197 (Court of Appeal); *The Cristina* [1938] AC 485 (House of Lords), 490.

[76] See Hazel Fox and Philippa Webb, *The Law of State Immunity* (3rd edn, OUP 2015) 25–49; Xiaodong Yang, *State Immunity in International Law* (CUP 2012) 6–32.

[77] Indeed, resilience theory may offer an explanation for the evolution of other rules of customary international law too. *Cf. Case Concerning Military and Paramilitary Activities in and against Nicaragua (Nicaragua v. USA)*, (Merits) (1986) ICJ Rep. 14, para. 207.

[78] See Menno T. Kamminga and Martin Scheinin (eds), *The Impact of Human Rights Law on General International Law* (OUP 2009).

involved any obvious 'flip' from one equilibrium to another. Indeed, it is more credible to describe the impact of human rights on general international law as a process of gradual adaptation rather than as a sudden switch into a new configuration brought about by disturbances that exceeded the State-centric model's resilience. Yet even where change is abrupt, the historical reference point is critical. The post-1989 transition of former communist societies into open-market economies exposed their legal systems to immense shocks. The transformation of socialist legal systems therefore may be interpreted as a sign of their insufficient resilience. However, to the extent that this transformation involved a return to earlier legal traditions, it may also be interpreted as proof of pre-socialist law's resilience.[79]

Selecting a legal system's persistence criteria has significant methodological implications too. In her analysis of Russian law, Tatiana Borisova argues that the traditional equilibrium of the Russian legal system rested on the relationship between the sovereign, the people and a class of legal intermediaries.[80] Although the 1905 and 1917 revolutions upset this equilibrium, Borisova suggests that Russian law nevertheless proved highly resilient, as the Soviet authorities quickly rediscovered its value as an instrument of State power. This argument locates the Russian legal system's resilience in its continuing utility as an instrument of social control, despite the fact that its substantive content, processes, and institutions proved far less resilient to the dramatic changes set in motion by the October Revolution.[81]

3.2 A normative dimension?

What these examples and caveats demonstrate is that legal resilience is very much in the eye of the beholder. It is far from obvious how key elements of the concept—including the notion of a legal system, stable equilibria, disturbance, and persistence criteria—should be applied in concrete cases. Adopting a legal resilience perspective thus involves a series of methodological choices. These choices not only frame the analysis, but also shape its outcome, depending on whether changes in the law are seen as transitions from one stable state to another or as successful adaptations. This is not to suggest that legal resilience analysis is erratic, but to stress that it is contingent on the observer's vantage point. For example, seen from a Soviet perspective, the post-communist transformation of

---

[79] *Cf.* David Stark, 'On Resilience' (2014) 3 Social Sciences 60, 62.
[80] Borisova (n 52).
[81] E.g. Becky L. Glass and Margaret K. Stolee, 'Family Law in Soviet Russia, 1917–1945' (1987) 49 Journal of Marriage and Family 893.

546 COUNTERING HYBRID AND GREY ZONE THREATS

socialist legal systems illustrates their lack of resilience, whereas from a post-Soviet perspective, the same transformation may demonstrate the long-term resilience of alternative legal traditions. The Soviet and post-Soviet perspectives are clearly incompatible, but their respective assessments of the law's resilience may both be correct within the confines of their own methodological horizons. It is not that resilience theory leads to inconsistent results, but that it tells multiple stories, depending on the analytical reference points chosen by the narrator.

The message to take away in the present context is that the methodological choices which inform the legal resilience perspective involve the exercise of political judgement. The hostile instrumentalization of the law by grey zone and hybrid adversaries, as described throughout this volume, poses a challenge to the national interests of the targeted States. However, whether or not the instrumentalization of law is hostile is a matter of perception: measures that one State may regard as valuable acts of statecraft another State may deem to be detrimental to its interests. The same holds true for legal resilience: whether legal stability is celebrated as a sign of law's resilience or condemned as its failure to adapt, and conversely, whether legal change is hailed as a legal system's successful adaptation or lamented as its lack of resilience, depends on whether stability and change are perceived as positive or as negative developments.[82]

Legal resilience therefore is not solely an analytical concept, but also a normative one.[83] As David Alexander has observed, one person's resilience may be another's vulnerability.[84] Entering into judgements about the value of legal resilience seems unavoidable.[85] As we noted earlier, ecologists criticize environmental law as maladaptive because it has been slow to incorporate socio-ecological insights. Yet environmental law's failure to adapt is a sign of its remarkable resistance to change, in other words its resilience. Accordingly, when ecologists denounce the law as maladaptive, they do so on the basis of a value

---

[82] For example, the People's Republic of China maintains its 'unequivocal and consistent' support for the absolute doctrine of State immunity. However, acting in the spirit of 'consultation, compromise and cooperation', it has supported the adoption of the UN Convention on State Immunity, which reflects the restrictive doctrine, partly because China believes that the Convention 'would assist in balancing and regulating the practices of states, and will have positive impacts on protecting the harmony and stability of international relations'. See *Democratic Republic of the Congo and Others v. FG Hemisphere Associates LLC (Final appeal nos. 5, 6 and 7 OF 2010 (Civil)*, Hong Kong Court of Final Appeal (8 June 2011), paras. 44 and 46. From the Chinese perspective, the Convention is an instrument for adapting the law in the interests of stability and legal certainty. It should be noted, however, that China has not ratified the Convention and has not abandoned its support for the absolute doctrine of immunity.

[83] Henrik Thorén and Lennart Olsson, 'Is Resilience a Normative Concept?' (2018) 6 Resilience 112. See also Barnes (n 69); Brand and Jax (n 6).

[84] D. E. Alexander, 'Resilience and Disaster Risk Reduction: An Etymological Journey' (2013) 13 Natural Hazards and Earth System Sciences 2707, 2714. See also Simin Davoudi, 'Resilience: A Bridging Concept or a Dead End?' (2012) 13 Planning Theory and Practice 299, 305–306.

[85] See also Andrea M. Keesse et al, 'The Concept of Resilience from a Normative Perspective: Examples from Dutch Adaptation Strategies' (2013) 18 Ecology and Society.

judgement as to what aims the law should pursue. This, in turn, leads them to see legal change as desirable and legal stability as unappealing.

This normative dimension represents the second benefit of adopting a legal resilience perspective. In essence, legal resilience is a status quo strategy. For States that seek to safeguard the current configuration of the international legal order and their own position within it, legal resilience is a goal worth pursuing. A legal resilience perspective encourages such States to reinforce the capacity of relevant domestic and international rules, processes, and institutions to withstand the challenges posed by grey zone and hybrid adversaries and to make systematic use of relevant legal instruments as a means to strengthen their national resilience against such threats. Adopting a legal resilience perspective thus provides national authorities and international organizations with a framework for setting and pursuing legal policy goals.

More specifically, for liberal democracies, legal resilience essentially entails a program of defending liberal values in international law against encroachments and subversion by illiberal forces, including by authoritarian regimes.[86] The distinction drawn between different modalities of resilience, in particular between resistance and adaptation strategies, harbours some useful lessons in this regard. Clearly, there is a need to resist serious threats to the international rule of law both by reaffirming basic norms and by imposing costs on those who transgress them. Liberal democracies have thus rightly spearheaded the international response to Russia's war of aggression against Ukraine.[87] However, doing so under the banner of upholding the 'rules-based international order' against the forces of revisionism is at best misleading and at worst counter-productive.[88] It is misleading because it glosses over the fact that the political West can hardly be described as the defender of the legal status quo without qualifications, given that it has pushed and at times overstepped the boundaries of international law in areas such as the rules governing the use of force. Nor is it credible to suggest that the machinations of authoritarian States, serious though they are, threaten the very existence of the international legal system. Indeed, framing the response to Russia's war of aggression as a fight for the survival of the rules-based international order as a whole is potentially counter-productive precisely because the hyperbole and selectiveness of this framing lends credence to the charges of hypocrisy that Russian diplomats and their allies so frequently hurl against the

---

[86] Cf. Vincent Charles Keating and Amelie Theussen, 'Cum Haereticis Fides Non Servanda: International Law's Resilience in a Pluralistic World?', in *Rebooting Global International Society: Change, Contestation and Resilience*, edited by Trine Flockhart and Zachary Paikin (Palgrave Macmillan 2022) 215, 231.

[87] David L. Sloss and Laura A. Dickinson, 'The Russia-Ukraine War and the Seeds of a New Liberal Plurilateral Order' (2022) 116 American Journal of International Law 798, 799–802.

[88] E.g. Sergei V. Lavrov, 'On Law, Rights and Rules' (2021) 19 Russia in Global Affairs 228.

West,[89] and because the implicit assumption that liberal and democratic values enjoy universal validity does not resonate with governments that in fact are not fully committed to these values. A more nuanced approach is needed to uphold international law in general and liberal gains in particular: in addition to resistance, there is also a place for adaptation and, at times, accommodation in the interest of building broad coalitions against the most severe threats. Framing this endeavour as a Manichean struggle of status quo powers against revisionists, a struggle between rule-followers and rule-breakers, suggests that what is at issue is a choice between *stasis* and change, whereas in reality it is about the direction of change and adaptation.

4. Putting legal resilience into practice: legal resilience strategies

While a legal resilience perspective can be applied to individual rules and institutions, its main benefit lies at the level of systems, where it provides a conceptual framework to help think through the modalities for resisting, recovering from, and adapting to disturbances in the legal domain in a more comprehensive and systematic fashion. To realize this benefit, liberal democracies should develop legal resilience strategies. Inspired by national security strategies adopted by many States, the purpose of legal resilience strategies is to formulate a comprehensive and forward-looking policy to counter the challenges arising in the legal domain, including those associated with grey zone conflict and hybrid threats. Whilst they may vary in length and detail, typically, legal resilience strategies should identify the legal concerns posed by grey zone and hybrid threats, offer a vision for countering them, set specific policy objectives, and establish appropriate ways and means for achieving these. Due to the cross-cutting nature of their subject matter, legal resilience strategies should be designed as top-level policy documents and developed through inter-departmental processes at the senior level. They should be treated as an opportunity to engage diverse expert communities and stakeholders in the formulation of legal policy and to integrate the latter into other strategic planning processes and policies, as an integral part of a nation's grand strategy.

By definition, individual legal resilience strategies will be shaped by the position and interests of the nations and institutions developing them. Nevertheless, certain elements and guidelines are of general applicability.

---

[89] Cf. Vincent Charles Keating and Amelie Theussen, '*Cum Haereticis Fides Non Servanda*: International Law's Resilience in a Pluralistic World?', in *Rebooting Global International Society: Change, Contestation and Resilience* (Palgrave Macmillan 2022) 215, 231.

4.1 Understanding and awareness

Hostile actors exploit legal vulnerabilities. The first task in developing a legal resilience strategy, therefore, is to identify the relevant legal vulnerabilities.[90] This involves three steps. First, it calls for ascertaining the objectives that hostile actors seek to achieve through the use of legal means, together with their intent, legal capabilities, and the legal tactics they employ to achieve those objectives. The goal is to build up as clear and detailed a picture as possible about the way in which adversaries utilize the law and legal arguments to their advantage. The second step involves determining which legal systems should be covered by the legal resilience strategy. It is advisable to select relevant legal orders and to combine this with a disturbance-driven approach, as suggested earlier. For States, legal orders of interest will include their own domestic legal system, the internal law of any international organizations of which they are members, the domestic legal system of allies, as well as the international legal order. Further relevant legal systems should be selected with reference to relevant grey zone and hybrid threats. Although the exposure of States and international organizations to such threats will vary, tactics of interest are likely to include hostile information operations and strategic communication; election interference; support for organized protest movements, separatists, and extremist groups; strategic leaks; economic leverage; the exercise of influence through cultural and social organizations; industrial espionage; foreign aid and humanitarian assistance; energy dependence; and cyber operations. A legal resilience strategy should map the legal questions and systems engaged by these activities and identify how adversaries utilize and exploit the law to carry them out. The final step is to assess the risks that the vulnerabilities so identified present and to prioritize them based on their gravity. This may be done with the help of a matrix that groups legal vulnerabilities into different categories. The outcome could be recorded in a separate document, a legal vulnerabilities register, that is kept under continuous review in the light of the evolution of the threat landscape.

4.2 Legal preparedness: addressing legal vulnerabilities

Legal preparedness is concerned with mitigating known legal vulnerabilities and building capacity to deal with unexpected ones. Some of the vulnerabilities identified as part of a legal resilience strategy may be addressed through domestic legislation. For example, the law of the United Kingdom prohibits any

---

[90] E.g. see Joseph R. Biden Jr., 'President Biden: What America Will and Will Not Do in Ukraine', *The New York Times* (New York, 31 May 2022) <https://www.nytimes.com/2022/05/31/opinion/biden-ukraine-strategy.html> accessed 25 February 2023.

550 COUNTERING HYBRID AND GREY ZONE THREATS

person from carrying on the business of 'consultant lobbying' unless they are registered for that purpose.[91] However, consultant lobbying is defined as a commercial activity and therefore does not cover the conduct of foreign officials or government employees.[92] Calls have been made for the law to be changed so as to compel such persons to register their activities.[93] Similar rules exist elsewhere. The Foreign Agents Registration Act of the United States requires persons acting on behalf of foreign powers in a political or quasi-political capacity to disclose their relationship and information about their activities.[94] Adopting similar legislation in the United Kingdom would subject political activities carried out on behalf of foreign entities to greater transparency and thus remedy a potential legal vulnerability. As this case illustrates, many grey zone and hybrid threats are best addressed through domestic law. This is so because a wide range of unfriendly and hostile measures, such as support for political extremists, acts of industrial espionage, or strategic leaks, do not infringe international law, or at least do not do so manifestly. National legislation therefore offers a more appropriate regulatory and enforcement framework to counter these threats.[95]

However, other known vulnerabilities may not be addressed quite so easily. For example, as long as hostile State and non-State actors employ a comprehensive array of violent and non-violent tactics, the legal thresholds governing the use of force will remain a critical flashpoint. States subject to hybrid campaigns cannot revise these thresholds unilaterally by legislative fiat to reduce their exposure to hostile manipulation. Instead, the competent authorities must be prepared to continuously monitor acts of hybrid warfare, such as unconventional military operations,[96] to determine whether they have crossed the relevant thresholds and to be ready to respond accordingly. This demands a detailed understanding of the legal environment, but it also requires appropriate mechanisms and resources to gather, assess, and act upon relevant information. Similarly, adversaries should be expected to mask their own illicit operations by donning the mantle of 'plausible deniability'.[97] Accordingly, before covert malign

[91] Transparency of Lobbying, Non-party Campaigning and Trade Union Administration Act 2014, 2014 c. 4, sec. 1.

[92] Office of the Registrar of Consultant Lobbyists, *Guidance on the Requirements for Registration* (London, 2015) 13.

[93] Deborah Haynes, 'Call for Law to Curb "Creeping Influence" from Hostile Foreign Powers' (*Sky News*, 2 February 2019) <https://news.sky.com/story/call-for-law-to-curb-creeping-influence-from-hostile-foreign-powers-11635716> accessed 25 February 2023.

[94] 22 U.S.C. ch. 11.

[95] *Cf.* Tiina Ferm, chapter 28, in this volume.

[96] See Michael N. Schmitt and Andru E. Wall, 'The International Law of Unconventional Statecraft' (2014) 5 Harvard National Security Journal 349.

[97] E.g. Shane R. Reeves and David Wallace, 'The Combatant Status of the Little Green Men and Other Participants in the Ukraine Conflict' (2015) 91 International Law Studies 361. Cf. Rory Cormac and Richard J. Aldrich, 'Grey is the New Black: Covert Action and Implausible Deniability' (2018) 94 International Affairs 477.

activities can be countered through legal action, they must be attributed to the adversary behind them. This is a matter of compelling intelligence, evidence, and public presentation and thus calls for close collaboration among different branches of government.

The dynamic nature of grey zone and hybrid threats further underscores the need for building capacity. Not all legal vulnerabilities are known or identified as such in advance. In fact, experience demonstrates that competition in the legal sphere can be fast-paced and unpredictable. Before the Salisbury poisoning incident,[98] few would have anticipated that the Chemical Weapons Convention would become the subject of a legal scuffle between the United Kingdom and Russia. Even where legal flashpoints can be predicted, the exact circumstances that may trigger a standoff in the legal sphere can seldom be foretold with absolute certainty. For instance, bearing in mind Crimea's geographical position, it should not have come as a surprise that Russia and Ukraine became engaged in a dispute involving the law of the sea. Yet neither the timing of the Kerch Strait incident nor the way it has played out could have been forecast by most observers.[99]

Faced with such uncertainty regarding the nature and timing of the legal challenges posed by hybrid threats, any legal resilience strategy must make provision for dealing with legal contingencies, understood for these purposes as unforeseen developments requiring a critical legal input or posing a challenge to core legal interests. In doing so, inspiration may be drawn from the principles of civil emergency management.[100] The response to legal contingencies may be divided into three phases: a preparation phase which involves the establishment of appropriate response mechanisms, the allocation of responsibilities between stakeholders, the preparation of contingency plans, and regular training and exercising; a response phase which involves coordinated action to mitigate the immediate risks and prevent further damage or escalation; and a recovery phase which involves longer-term measures to restore the status quo ante, reduce vulnerabilities, adapt in the light of lessons learned, and take other appropriate measures to limit an adversary's capacity to gain an advantage from the instrumentalization of the law.

---

[98] See Mark Urban, *The Skripal Files: Putin, Poison and the New Spy War* (Macmillan 2019).

[99] See James Kraska, 'The Kerch Strait Incident: Law of the Sea or Law of Naval Warfare?' (*EJIL:Talk*, 3 December 2018) <https://www.ejiltalk.org/the-kerch-strait-incident-law-of-the-sea-or-law-of-naval-warfare/> accessed 25 February 2023.

[100] Cf. Cabinet Office, 'Responding to Emergencies: The UK Central Government Response Concept of Operations' (19 April 2013) <https://assets.publishing.service.gov.uk/government/uploads/system/uploads/attachment_data/file/192425/CONOPs_incl_revised_chapter_24_Apr-13.pdf> accessed 25 February 2023.

4.3 Legal preparedness: contributing to societal resilience

Legal preparedness is also concerned with the role that law plays in enabling and supporting policy action in other fields. Law provides a basis for a wide range of diplomatic, economic, military, financial, and other activities aimed at countering hybrid threats and hybrid actors.[101] For law-abiding States and rules-based organizations, it is critical that executive action is underpinned by appropriate legal authorizations. However, law also enables competent authorities to set policy goals and impose obligations on third parties with a binding effect. For example, in 2008, the Council of the European Union adopted a directive on the identification and designation of European critical infrastructures.[102] It directs each member State to identify European critical infrastructures and to ensure that their operators have suitable security plans in place to ensure their protection against major threats. In 2016, the European Parliament and the Council adopted Directive (EU) 2016/1148 aimed at achieving a high common level of security of network and information systems within the European Union.[103] Amongst other things, the Directive requires all member States to adopt a national strategy on the security of network and information systems and to ensure that operators of essential services take appropriate and proportionate technical and organizational measures to manage the risks posed to the security of such systems. To give effect to their obligations, the member States have adopted national implementing legislation.[104] While the imposition of higher standards has been welcomed, concerns remain that the resulting regulatory landscape remains too fragmented.[105] Indeed, similar fears have been expressed in other sectors.[106]

Adopting a legal resilience perspective should encourage relevant authorities to consider the role that law plays in this area in a more systematic and holistic manner. Accordingly, legal resilience strategies may serve as a tool for assessing law's contribution to resilience across different social sectors. This involves mapping how existing regulatory frameworks support the resilience objectives

---

[101] E.g. Zebrowski (n 7) 109ff.

[102] Council of the European Union, 'Directive 2008/114/EC on the identification and designation of European critical infrastructures and the assessment of the need to improve their protection' (8 December 2008([2008] OJ L 345/75. Generally see Marjolein B. A. van Asselt, Ellen Vos, and Isabelle Wildhaber, 'Some Reflections on EU Governance of Critical Infrastructure Risks' (2017) 6 European Journal of Risk Regulation 185.

[103] European Parliament and Council of the European Union, 'Directive (EU) 2016/1148 concerning measures for a high common level of security of network and information systems across the Union' (6 July 2016) [2016] OJ L 194/1.

[104] E.g. The Network and Information Systems Regulations 2018, No. 506 (United Kingdom).

[105] House of Lords and House of Commons Joint Committee on the National Security Strategy, *Cyber Security of the UK's Critical National Infrastructure*, Third Report of Session 2017–19 (12 November 2018), 21.

[106] E.g. Graeme T. Laurie and Kathryn G. Hunter, 'Mapping, Assessing and Improving Legal Preparedness for Pandemic Flu in the United Kingdom' (2009) 10 Medical Law International 101.

pursued in key policy areas, assessing the performance of these legal frameworks against common criteria, such as their comprehensiveness, effectiveness, and robustness, and identifying shortcomings in the law. NATO, for example, has identified seven baseline requirements for civil preparedness: assured continuity of government and critical government services; resilient energy supplies; ability to deal effectively with uncontrolled movement of people; resilient food and water resources; ability to deal with mass casualties; resilient civil communications systems; and resilient civil transportation systems.[107] For NATO and its member States, an Allied legal resilience strategy could serve as a useful tool through which to map and assess the legal dimension of these seven baseline requirements. In addition to this analytical benefit, adopting a legal resilience perspective may inform the design and reform of relevant regulatory frameworks so as to improve their ability to promote societal resilience.[108]

4.4 Resistance and adaptation

Legal resilience strategies should articulate an overall vision and roadmap for countering the legal challenges posed by grey zone and hybrid threats. This requires the competent authorities to consider what forms of resilience to promote. As noted earlier, engineering resilience focuses on static responses to disturbance, emphasizing the capacity to resist and recover from shocks. By contrast, ecological resilience favours dynamic responses which mitigate the effects of disturbance through adaptation. Both forms of resilience have a role to play in the legal sphere.

The resilience of legal systems turns in no small measure on their ability to command continued compliance with their rules. Amongst other things, resilience is about resistance to violations of the law. A legal resilience strategy must therefore address how hostile actors may be encouraged or compelled to honour their obligations and deterred from violating them. At the same time, legal resilience strategies must also consider how to respond to breaches of the law and to recover from their effects. Collective self-defence and sanctions mechanisms, such as Article 5 of the North Atlantic Treaty and Article 215 of the Treaty on

---

[107] North Atlantic Treaty Organization, 'Commitment to Enhance Resilience, Issued by the Heads of State and Government participating in the meeting of the North Atlantic Council in Warsaw, 8–9 July 2016', Press Release (2016) 118 (8 July 2016). See Lorenz Meyer-Minnemann, 'Resilience and Alliance Security: The Warsaw Commitment to Enhance Resilience', in *Forward Resilience: Protecting Society in an Interconnected World*, edited by Daniel S. Hamilton (Center for Transatlantic Relations, Paul H. Nitze School of Advanced International Studies 2016) 91.

[108] Cf. Jakub Harašta, 'Legally Critical: Defining Critical Infrastructure in an Interconnected World' (2018) 21 International Journal of Critical Infrastructure Protection 47, 53. See also Barbara A. Cosens et al, 'The Role of Law in Adaptive Governance' (2017) 22 Ecology and Society 1–30.

554   COUNTERING HYBRID AND GREY ZONE THREATS

the Functioning of the European Union, offer examples of arrangements for responding to third-party violations. From a legal resilience perspective, the question to ask is whether these frameworks are efficient and whether dedicated arrangements should be adopted in other areas, for instance in the cyber or information domain. However, increasing the capacity for resistance and recovery is not sufficient. As James Crawford warns, any legal system will only survive 'if it has the capacity to change and develop over time'.[109] Compliance is difficult to secure if the law is perceived as illegitimate or unworkable. This brings into play ecological notions of resilience and the need for adaptation. To the extent that powers wedded to the status quo are unable to resist demands for change, they will need to accommodate revisionist actors by showing a willingness to adapt the international system. This requires careful thought about the right combination of resistance and adaptation. Russia's war of aggression against Ukraine illustrates the dilemma: at what point, if any, should Kyiv and its allies switch from a strategy of resistance to a strategy of adaptation and in relation to which specific questions?

These considerations point to the value of more detailed studies on the evolutionary trends of the international legal order.[110] Some years ago, the Hague Institute for the Internationalisation of Law suggested that the international legal system may evolve in four possible directions, depending on how the two main drivers of change, the progressive internationalization of law and the growth of private governance regimes, were to interact.[111] States and international organizations should engage with such forecasts as part of their legal resilience strategies, as this would assist them in formulating what future legal order they wish to promote and what legal future(s) they seek to avoid. In fact, at this level of generalization, it may well be appropriate and useful to apply the notion of legal equilibrium states and consider what factors may induce a legal order to flip from one stable state, such as a more centralized international order, into a different one, for example, a more fragmented, chaotic and pluralist world.[112]

4.5 Inter-operability, cooperation and bridging

Due to the multilayered and cross-cutting nature of the law, the cause of legal resilience can seldom be advanced through unilateral measures. In most cases, countering the legal challenges posed by grey zone and hybrid threats demands

---

[109] James Crawford, 'The Current Political Discourse Concerning International Law' (2018) 81 Modern Law Review 1, 22.

[110] See Aurel Sari and Agnieszka Jachec-Neale, 'International Law in 2050', Exeter Centre for International Law (2018).

[111] Hague Institute for the Internationalisation of Law, *Law Scenarios to 2030* (The Hague, 2012).

[112] *Cf.* Ibid. 13.

concerted action by several actors at multiple levels. This is obvious in the case of collective measures taken at the international level, such as economic sanctions. However, even at the domestic level, effective resistance, recovery from, and adaptation to grey zone and hybrid threats typically requires coordination and cooperation among various stakeholders. The protection of critical infrastructure illustrates the point. Legal resilience strategies must therefore provide the impetus for cooperation among relevant public and private actors across different sectors and throughout the local, regional, national, and international levels.

In fact, since legal resilience is not a purely legal endeavour, it is imperative that legal resilience strategies foster closer cooperation among relevant expert communities, for example, between legal experts and strategic communication specialists. Proponents of resilience thinking often underline its inter-disciplinary nature and its potential to serve as a bridging concept that can stimulate dialogue and collaboration among disciplines.[113] Simply put, adopting a legal resilience perspective highlights—for the benefit of policymakers—that societal resilience has a legal dimension and that law has a resilience aspect. Legal resilience strategies should therefore seek to complement resilience thinking and strategies in other fields, for example, the resilience policies developed within the European Union[114] and NATO,[115] and vice versa.

5. Conclusion

As J. B. Ruhl has cautioned, resilience theory offers 'nothing in the way of strategies legal scholars have not already covered'.[116] Indeed, it would be a

---

[113] E.g. Katrina Brown, *Resilience, Development and Global Change* (Routledge 2016), 69–99; Simone A. Beichler et al, 'The Role played by Social-Ecological Resilience as a Method of Integration in Interdisciplinary Research' (2014) 19 Ecology and Society Article 4.

[114] E.g. European Commission and High Representative of the Union for Foreign Affairs and Security Policy, 'Joint Communication: A Strategic Approach to Resilience in the EU's External Action' (7 June 2017) JOIN(2017) 21 final; European Commission and High Representative of the Union for Foreign Affairs and Security Policy, 'Joint Communication: Joint Framework on Countering Hybrid Threats: A European Union Response' (6 April 2016), JOIN(2016) 18 final, 5–15; Council of the European Union, 'Council Conclusions on EU Approach to Resilience', 3241st Foreign Affairs Council Meeting (28 May 2013).

[115] Commitment to Enhance Resilience (n 98). See also Wolf-Diether Roepke and Hasit Thankey, 'Resilience: The First Line of Defence' (*NATO Review*, 27 February 2019 <https://www.nato.int/docu/review/2019/Also-in-2019/resilience-the-first-line-of-defence/EN/index.htm> accessed 25 February 2023; Guillaume Lasconjarias, *Deterrence through Resilience: NATO, the Nations and the Challenges of Being Prepared* (NATO Defense College 2017); Daniel S. Hamilton, 'Going Beyond Static Understandings: Resilience Must be Shared, and It Must Be Projected Forward', in *Critical Infrastructure Protection Against Hybrid Warfare Security Related Challenges*, edited by Alessandro Niglia (IOS Press 2016) 23; Jamie Shea, 'Resilience: A Core Element of Collective Defence' (*NATO Review*, 30 March 2016) <https://www.nato.int/docu/review/2016/also-in-2016/nato-defence-cyber-resilience/en/index.htm> accessed 25 February 2023.

[116] Ruhl (n 59) 1403.

mistake to turn to resilience and expect a ready-made master plan for countering the legal effects of grey zone conflict and hybrid threats. In the present context, the benefits of adopting a resilience perspective lie elsewhere.

Legal resilience offers a framework for assessing and enhancing the capacity of legal systems to manage the challenges posed by adversaries resorting to grey zone and hybrid tactics. It is both an analytical tool and a policy agenda. A legal resilience perspective helps to better understand the legal dimension of grey zone and hybrid threats, in particular, the vulnerabilities of affected legal systems, their respective coping mechanisms, and the dual role that law plays in this area both as an object and as a medium of resilience. At the same time, a legal resilience perspective also contributes to greater legal preparedness in countering the hostile instrumentalization of the law and in addressing the vulnerabilities of other social systems exposed to such threats. Perhaps most importantly, a legal resilience perspective provides an opportunity to develop and implement more robust legal policies by integrating legal considerations into other policy planning processes and give more concrete and nuanced meaning to broad strategic objectives such as upholding the rules-based international order. Nor should the deterrent effect of legal resilience be overlooked: not only do tackling legal vulnerabilities deny their utility to adversaries, but greater legal preparedness also imposes additional costs on hostile actors. As this chapter has suggested, States and international organizations may realize these benefits by developing individual and collective legal resilience strategies, a new type of policy instrument setting out a detailed program for countering the legal challenges posed by grey zone and hybrid threats.

25

How to Involve Civil Society in Grey Zone Defence

Elisabeth Braw

1. Introduction

In April 2022, Swedish National Television launched a new reality-television series. In the past two or so decades, reality-TV established has itself as a constant audience favourite, and shows in Europe, North America, and beyond now feature every conceivable iteration of dating shows and talent-spotting. But Swedish National Television's new show featured a more cutting-edge subject: national security. *Societal Collapse* focuses on precisely that: prospective national crises ranging from solar flares to crippling ransomware attacks. In each episode, a group of politicians, agency heads, generals, editors-in-chief, and others in charge of the daily functioning of a modern society are tasked with wargaming a sudden crisis. It is excellent entertainment and a superb way of educating the public about emerging national-security threats. That makes *Societal Collapse* a pioneer in addressing today's deteriorating geopolitical environment. Proliferating and morphing grey zone aggression, which targets civil society, means that it is no longer enough for governments to try to defend their countries against this aggression using only the government apparatus. In an era of proliferating threats in the grey zone between war and peace, everyone has a role to play.

Societal Collapse was conceived by Felix Herngren, who is not a crisis manager but an actor and director. (He is also one of the show's two co-hosts.) Herngren, Swedish National Television explained in a press release announcing *Societal Collapse*, wanted to create a show that 'in a compelling and educational manner illustrates how Sweden functions—is supposed to function in a major crisis'.[1] Seated next to one another in the television studio, and with the two co-hosts presenting the scenario and interjections, the leaders have to decide how

---

[1] 'Samhällskollaps testar Sveriges krisberedskap', *OM OSS* (20 April 2022) <https://omoss.svt.se/arkiv/bloggarkiv/2022-04-20-samhallskollaps-testar-sveriges-krisberedskap.html> accessed 25 February 2023.

Elisabeth Braw, *How to Involve Civil Society in Grey Zone Defence* In: *Hybrid Threats and Grey Zone Conflict.* Edited by: Mitt Regan and Aurel Sari, Oxford University Press. © Oxford University Press 2024.
DOI: 10.1093/oso/9780197744772.003.0025

to steer the country through any given crisis in real time. Doing so turns out to be far less straightforward than expected, and the show does not even include the public, whose actions and reactions to the unfolding events are a crucial factor in governments' success in containing any given crisis. Even without the participation of the public, this makes *Societal Collapse* entertaining—and educational—television.

2. Grey zone aggression: targeting civil society

In addition to being compelling television entertainment, *Societal Collapse* should be seen as a pioneering national-security effort. For at least the past three–four years, grey zone aggression has been vigorously discussed, not just in academic circles but especially in the circles of policymakers and business leaders. Grey zone aggression, in my definition, is the use of hostile acts outside the realm of armed conflict to weaken a rival country, entity, or alliance[2], and it is discussed so vigorously because it is not an abstract threat but a menace that harms the functioning of liberal democracies on a daily basis. In my book *The Defender's Dilemma*, I catalogued a range of current tools of grey zone aggression, including subversive business practices, gradual border alternation, and coercion using the target country's companies and citizens.[3] Indeed, grey zone aggression is characterized by its focus on civil society and the functioning of modern societies. This aggression is also made easier by the fact that liberal democracies are free and open societies and suffer from what I call 'the convenience trap'[4]: the more convenient life in these countries becomes, the more opportunities there are for hostile States and their proxies to harm such countries by attacking one or more aspects of the convenient life.

Indeed, grey zone aggression will continue to evolve in a way that military aggression does not. While armed forces have a limited range of ways in which they can harm the target country—and they are, of course, also bound by the Geneva Conventions—the grey zone between war and peace is wide open for innovation. The aggressor can, and will, thus keep exploiting liberal democracies' vulnerabilities. These vulnerabilities are exacerbated by the fact that liberal democracies are intimately linked to other countries, including increasingly hostile ones such as China, through globalization. As discussed in detail in *The Defender's Dilemma*, this constantly morphing nature of the aggression—and the

---

[2] Elisabeth Braw, *The Defender's Dilemma* (AEI Press 2022) ch. 1.
[3] Ibid.
[4] Elisabeth Braw, 'Briefing Paper: The Case for Joint Military-Industry Greyzone Exercises' (Royal United Services Institute, 28 September 2020) <https://static.rusi.org/20200928_braw_greyzone_ex ercises_web.pdf> accessed 25 February 2023.

HOW TO INVOLVE CIVIL SOCIETY IN GREY ZONE DEFENCE 559

fact that it takes place below the threshold of armed military violence—makes it extremely difficult for targeted countries to signal deterrence by punishment. They simply cannot know what they are seeking to deter by punishment and, if it is an activity that is serious enough to punish only in accumulation, when the level of unacceptability has been reached.

All this makes societal resilience absolutely crucial in defence against grey zone aggression. Indeed, societal resilience is a crucial component of grey zone deterrence by denial, because, by signalling that their civil societies can absorb blows caused by grey zone aggression, Western governments can change a prospective attacker's cost-benefit calculus. To be sure, deterrence by denial is less powerful than deterrence by punishment. Apart from deterrence by denial signalled through the presence of armed forces—which are of little use in grey zone deterrence—the space deterrence by denial could occupy is, however, also glaringly empty.

This may be because, over the past three decades, 'Western countries'[5] have been so dominated by maximization of individual pursuits that governments are wary of asking their citizens to contribute to any collective undertaking, especially one connected to negative or frightening situations. It is, for example, worth noting that, following the end of the Cold War, virtually all European countries that had military service suspended it: Germany, France, Italy, and Sweden were among the countries that suspended conscription for men during post-Cold War period's first couple of decades.

Over the past several years, military service has been resurrected in some countries, including Sweden and Lithuania, though on a selective basis and thus not comprising every young man and indeed not every young woman.[6] Yet the growth of grey zone aggression and the decline of traditional warfare, Russia's invasion of Ukraine notwithstanding, means that Western countries need new and additional capabilities in order to signal to prospective attackers that aggression would not be worth their while. Western countries need to be able to demonstrate to grey zone aggressors that their societies are able to withstand harm caused by grey zone aggression, whatever form that aggression may take, and swiftly bounce back from any harm. This is particularly important because grey zone aggression directly targets civil society in a way that kinetic aggression does not.

In fact, while past centuries saw countries' battle for territory as the main currency of global power, territory may no longer be the main way in which

---

[5] I use the term as synonymous with liberal democracies.

[6] For further details, see Elisabeth Braw, 'Competitive National Service: How the Scandinavian Model Can Be Adapted by the UK' (Royal United Services Institut, 23 October 2019) <https://rusi.org/explore-our-research/publications/occasional-papers/competitive-national-service-how-scandinavian-model-can-be-adapted-uk> accessed 25 February 2023.

560 COUNTERING HYBRID AND GREY ZONE THREATS

a country increases its power. China undoubtedly holds territorial designs on Taiwan, but its ambitions concerning other liberal democracies are focused primarily on weakening their global power and acquiring their best technology and their most promising companies. In *Made in China 2025*, its strategic plan for economic superpower status, Beijing lists the technology areas in which it aims to gain superiority: new information technology; high-end numerically controlled machine tools and robots; aerospace equipment; ocean engineering equipment and high-end vessels; high-end rail transportation equipment; energy-saving cars and new energy cars; electrical equipment; farming machines; new materials, such as polymers; and biomedicine and high-end medical equipment.[7] *Made in China 2025* thus explicitly lists the sectors in which Beijing will try to exploit Western science and technology and innovation, to Western countries' detriment and China's advantage. This is different from regular innovation strategies in that Beijing does not grant Western companies and scientists the same access to China as it expects Western countries to offer its representatives. The strategy should help them better understand which sectors are particularly vulnerable to subversive investments and takeovers, and to legal and illegal acquisition of intellectual property.

Increasingly, China also harms Western companies in response to statements or actions by the governments of the companies' home countries.[8] Norwegian fishermen have been targeted as proxies for their home governments, as have Swedish companies including Ericsson, a wide swath of Lithuanian industry, Taiwanese farmers, and Australian winemakers. When Russia invaded Ukraine, Western governments imposed crippling sanctions on Russian strategic sectors. This prompted France's finance minister, Bruno le Maire, to explain that the West had declared 'economic war' on Russia,[9] a statement that unintentionally provided the Kremlin with an opportunity to target Western companies on the basis that they were part of the economic war. It did not take long for government

---

[7] James McBride and Andrew Chatzky, 'Is "Made in China 2025" a Threat to Global Trade?' Council on Foreign Relations (13 May 2019) <https://www.cfr.org/backgrounder/made-china-2025-threat-global-trade> accessed 25 February 2023.

[8] See e.g. Elisabeth Braw, 'Why Corporate Apologies to Beijing Backfire', *The Wall Street Journal* (New York, 24 July 2022) <https://www.wsj.com/articles/why-corporate-apologies-to-beijing-backfire-taiwan-china-ccp-beijing-consumers-dior-boycott-uyghurs-11658689342> accessed 25 February 2023; and Elisabeth Braw, 'How Do You Stop Beijing from Bullying? Take Away Its Prada Bags', *The Wall Street Journal* (New York, 10 August 2021) <https://www.wsj.com/articles/ericcson-beijing-australia-sweden-denmark-5g-national-security-trade-luxury-goods-zte-huawei-11628631680> accessed 25 February 2023. The grey zone practice of targeting companies as proxies for their home governments is further discussed in Braw (n 2), which also discusses other forms of grey zone aggression.

[9] Richard Lough, 'French Minister Declares Economic 'War' on Russia, and Then Beats a Retreat' (*Reuters*, 1 March 2022) <https://www.reuters.com/world/france-declares-economic-war-against-russia-2022-03-01/> accessed 25 February 2023.

officials to suggest that Russia would seize the assets of Western companies leaving Russia.[10] This later came to pass.

Russia has for years specialized in disseminating disinformation in Western countries and thus undermining civil discourse and ultimately democracy. Its multi-pronged attack on the 2016 US election campaign is well known and does not need to be further analysed here.

Iran and North Korea, in turn, continue to engage in cyber aggression to which civilian infrastructure is particularly vulnerable. In 2014, North Korean hackers, acting on behalf of the country's regime, hacked Sony Pictures, an apparent retaliation after the studio released a comedy, *The Interview*, that ridiculed North Korean leader Kim Jong Un. The hackers first stole vast amounts of information from Sony's network, which they then sent to journalists. This resulted in a flurry of stories that were highly embarrassing to Sony. The hackers also deleted corporate data, then issued threats against movie theatres, which they said would be attacked if Sony did not cancel the release of *The Interview*.[11] Sony responded by pulling the release, only to be persuaded by the Obama administration not to give in to threats. In a connected scheme, the same hackers stole $75 million from a Slovenian cryptocurrency company and $11.8 million of digital currency from a New York financial services company.[12]

As with Western companies losing intellectual property to Chinese competitors, and Western citizens unprepared for Russian disinformation campaigns, North Korean trio's victims were poorly equipped to defend themselves because they had not been considering themselves part of national security. When Colonial Pipeline was hit by a ransomware attack in May 2021, US East Coast drivers, in turn, demonstrated how the public can unwittingly aid grey zone aggression simply by being unprepared. In response to the attack, Colonial temporarily suspended its operations. This was a measure designed to limit the damage the attack could cause. The public, however, reacted in a manner that makes sense on an individual basis but cripples society: they filled up on gasoline. As a result, the incident wreaked havoc on the US East Coast as gas stations ran out of fuel.[13] The chaotic response by the US public signalled to hostile actors that it is relatively easy and inexpensive to disrupt daily life in America.

---

[10] 'Russia Moves towards Nationalizing Assets of Firms That Leave—Ruling Party' (*Reuters*, 9 March 2022) <https://www.reuters.com/business/russia-approves-first-step-towards-nationalising-assets-firms-that-leave-ruling-2022-03-09/> accessed 25 February 2023.

[11] See Emily St. James and Timothy B. Lee, 'The 2014 Sony Hacks, Explained' (*Vox*, 3 June 2015) <https://www.vox.com/2015/1/20/18089084/sony-hack-north-korea> accessed 25 February 2023; and 'Three North Koreans Indicted in Sony Hack' (*Voice of America*, 17 February 2021) <https://www.voanews.com/a/economy-business_three-north-koreans-indicted-sony-hack/6202175.html> accessed 25 February 2023.

[12] 'Three North Koreans Indicted' (n 11).

[13] 'Panic Buying and Hoarding Add to Long Lines and Outages at Gas Stations as Colonial Pipeline Shutdown Drags on' (*CBS News*, 12 May 2021) <https://www.cbsnews.com/news/gas-prices-colonial-pipeline-shutdown-panic-buying-hoarding-long-lines-outages/> accessed 25 February 2023.

562 COUNTERING HYBRID AND GREY ZONE THREATS

Today no Western country has whole-of-society grey zone defence. Sweden's Cold War total defence was an extremely comprehensive system involving all parts of society, but it was largely disbanded in the 1990s and was, at any rate, set up for defence against a territorial invasion, not grey zone aggression.[14] Indeed, China, Russia, Iran, North Korea, and any other countries wishing to imitate their strategy of increasing power through grey zone aggression are encouraged in this behaviour by Western responses to current grey zone aggression. Indeed, it is logical that China, Russia, Iran, and North Korea continue to use grey zone aggression against Western and other countries, especially since it incurs little cost in blood or treasure, can cause considerable harm, and often offers plausible deniability. While grey zone aggression is a favoured tool by such powerful countries, it could also become a dirty weapon favoured by smaller and poorer countries. Belarus's weaponization of migration in the fall of 2021, which was designed to harm the European Union, is a good example of such grey zone use.

Defence against grey zone aggression is, of course, particularly difficult because the aggression can appear anywhere, it can feature any virtually any means, and it is difficult to detect because in low intensity the activity can often resembles non-hostile activities in the globalized world. While acquisitions of cutting-edge Western technology companies by companies in another Western country are simply part of the globalized economy, systematic Chinese acquisitions of such companies should raise red flags.

When does something that could also be a legitimate activity constitute grey zone aggression? What about activities that are unethical but not illegal? What about illegal acts that do not constitute aggression of a magnitude that would on every occasion warrant retaliation by the targeted country's government? Because grey zone aggression is such a novel tool of all-round aggression, because it can be disguised as regular interaction in the globalized world, and because it is constantly morphing, in the first instance Western governments need to address three issues:

- Which activities constitute grey zone aggression? This list would need to be continuously updated.
- In the case of activities that are not illegal, above which threshold or quantity do they constitute grey zone aggression?
- Above which threshold do governments have a responsibility to retaliate? Governments should clearly avoid escalation, which means the retaliation needs to be horizontal and in the grey zone. For the threat of retaliation to be a form effective deterrence it must, of course, be communicated to the adversary.

---

[14] For more information about Sweden's total defence, see Braw (n 2) ch. 9.

A more comprehensive task, however, follows these definitions: building societal resilience. Societal resilience is indispensable in defence against grey zone aggression in two ways: it can help absorb the blow of such aggression, and this societal ability to absorb the blow can—must—be used in governments' deterrence signalling. Societal resilience is, in fact, the most important part in deterrence-by-denial of grey zone aggression. Given that hostile States closely monitor liberal democracies including their civic life, governments clearly should not signal deterrence by denial through societal resilience if they have not built the resilience, as the aggressor would not believe their deterrence signalling.

3. Declining civic participation

Even though there are obvious differences between Western societies, most governments are reluctant to ask the public to contribute to society in any ways that citizens are not already accustomed to. Given that few people would enjoy hearing that the government expects them to do more for society, this is perhaps understandable.

At the same time, societies are fragmenting. The trend towards less civic engagement in the United States was painstakingly documented by Robert Putnam in *Bowling Alone: The Collapse and Revival of American Community*.[15] Between the 1950s and the book's publication, Americans' interaction with one another had plummeted, and even in the quarter-century prior to *Bowling Alone,* Americans' attendance of club meetings had dropped by 58 per cent.[16] Other Western countries, too, have experienced a decline in civic participation; indeed, this trend has been accelerated since the arrival of social media, which disincentivizes in-person interaction (by incentivizing digital exchanges) and encourages aggressive behaviour towards users who hold opinions different from one's own. Social media's role in fuelling phenomena such as the anti-vaxxer movement, the anti-5G movement, and, of course, the January 6 assault on the Capitol is well-known. It is in no way surprising that societies where ever-fewer people interact with one another on a regular basis—on civic issues ranging from volunteering to bowling and choral singing—fragment, with people ending up interacting with an ever-smaller range of people. The working-from-home trend accelerated by the COVID pandemic is likely to further reduce societal interaction with a wider range of people.

---

[15] Robert D. Putnam, *Bowling Alone: The Collapse and Revival of American Community* (Simon and Schuster, 2000).

[16] Robert D. Putnam, 'Research' <http://bowlingalone.com/?page_id=7> accessed 25 February 2023.

564 COUNTERING HYBRID AND GREY ZONE THREATS

Tragically for the cohesion of societies, the interaction that is increasing is often based on shared political concerns that may have been fuelled by anger—and false information—spread via social media. Far-right and far-left activists have, for example, found common cause in the anti-vaxxer movement[17], but far from being a sign of friendships beyond traditional enclaves the anti-vaxxer movement is united only in its anger over COVID-19 vaccination policies. Declining civic participation, the resulting societal fragmentation, and the space this provides for misinformation and disinformation risk making liberal countries extremely hard to govern. This is extremely concerning on its own, but it also presents an obvious opportunity for the West's adversaries to further weaken Western societies.

Even though there is no comprehensive study of Western citizens' attitudes to the current divisions within their societies, it stands to reason that a majority or sizeable minority would prefer less fragmentation and discord. Furthermore, the fewest residents of any Western country would like to see its essential services regularly disrupted and its economy weakened. Grey zone aggression is dramatically demonstrating why societal resilience is needed, and because living in comfort depends on grey zone aggression being curtailed, it is in citizens' and companies' interest to be part of the effort. That makes it easier for policymakers to invite them to be part of such an effort, which can take place in a range of different ways.

4. How to involve society

'I would say to the House, as I said to those who have joined this government: "I have nothing to offer but blood, toil, tears and sweat"', newly appointed Prime Minister Winston Churchill told the UK House of Commons on 13 May 1940.[18] His new government went to work, building an extraordinary whole-of-society effort that would see people of both genders and many ages—including the teenage Princess Elizabeth—take on roles supporting the defence of the country. Air raid wardens, for example, were volunteers who guided fellow residents to shelters as soon as air-raid alarm sounded. They were also the first ones leaving the shelter after the alarm indicated the bombing raid was over, making sure that it was safe for others to emerge, too, and they provided first aid to anyone injured.[19] Princess Elizabeth participated in the government's Dig for Victory

---

[17] Francis Russell, 'Pox Populi: Anti-Vaxx, Anti-Politics' (2022) 59 Journal of Sociology 699 <https://doi.org/10.1177/14407833221101660> accessed 25 February 2023.

[18] Winston Churchill, HC Deb, 13 May 1940, vol 360, c1502.

[19] 'ARP Wardens' (May 2020) <https://royalarmouries.org/wp-content/uploads/2020/05/ARP-Warden-Worksheet.pdf.> accessed 25 February 2023.

campaign, which encouraged people to use all available land to grow vegetables and thus reduce the country's food shortage. Upon turning 18, the future monarch volunteered as an automotive mechanic in the Auxiliary Territorial Service (ATS), the women's branch of the British Army.[20]

This massive effort—which was replicated, in various ways, in countries ranging from Finland to the United States—helped keep societies going even as a significant percentage of men were serving in the armed forces and even as many of the countries were being savaged by invading forces. Today, governments do not need to ask their countries' populations to contribute in any ways remotely resembling World War II efforts, though Emmanuel Macron struck a tone reminiscent of World War II appeals in a speech in August 2022. 'I am thinking of our people, who will need great fortitude to face the coming times, to overcome uncertainty, adversity, and sometimes the easy way out, and, united, to accept the pay the price of our freedom and our values. The ghosts of revanchism, flagrant violations of State sovereignty, intolerable contempt for entire peoples, and imperialist motivations are resurfacing from the past to force themselves on the daily life of our Europe, our neighbours, our friends', the French President told residents of Bormes-les-Mimosas at an event celebration the seventy-eighth anniversary of the village's liberation from Nazi occupation.[21]

Citizen involvement could begin at a basic level: through public awareness campaigns. A good example is the leaflet *If Crisis or War Comes*, published by the Swedish Civil Contingencies Agency (MSB) in May 2018 and sent by post to every household in the country.[22] The leaflet, an updated version of the Cold War leaflet *If War Comes*, features easy-to-understand information—presented in short sentences and with plenty of illustrations—about the threats facing Sweden, how to know whether a contingency or a piece information could stem from a hostile actor, how to prepare for disruption to vital services and what to do should such disruptions or other contingencies come to pass.[23]

---

[20] 'A Princess at War: Queen Elizabeth II During World War II' (National World War II Museum, 22 March 2021) https://www.nationalww2museum.org/war/articles/queen-elizabeth-ii-during-world-war-ii> accessed 25 February 2023.

[21] Sofia Fischer, 'French President Emmanuel Macron Doubles Down on Pessimism', *Le Monde* (Paris, 20 August 2022) https://www.lemonde.fr/en/politics/article/2022/08/20/french-president-emmanuel-macron-doubles-down-on-pessimism_5994164_5.html> accessed 25 February 2023.

[22] Elisabeth Braw, 'Swedes Are Expected to Prepare for Emergencies. Coronavirus Shows Why Britons Should Be Too', *The Guardian* (London, 13 March 2020) <https://www.theguardian.com/p/ded5a?CMP=gu_com> accessed 25 February 2023.

[23] For the Swedish version, see Swedish Civil Contingencies Agency, 'Om krisen eller kriget kommer' (2018) <https://www.msb.se/sv/publikationer/om-krisen-eller-kriget-kommer> accessed 25 February 2023. The leaflet is also available in English and other languages at <https://www.msb.se/sv/rad-till-privatpersoner/broschyren-om-krisen-eller-kriget-kommer> accessed 25 February 2023, and as an audiobook in Swedish and English.

566 COUNTERING HYBRID AND GREY ZONE THREATS

'An emergency can result in society not functioning in the way we are used to', the leaflet warns and goes on to list a number of services that may suddenly be affected:

- The heating stops working.
- It becomes difficult to prepare and store food.
- The shops may run out of food and other goods.
- There is no water coming from the taps or the toilet.
- It is not possible to fill up your car.
- Payment cards and cash machines are not working.
- Mobile networks and the internet are not working'.[24]

When the leaflet was published, many perceived such advice as alarmist, especially officials and citizens in countries lacking the whole-of-society approach to national security that had served Sweden so well during the Cold War. Less than two years later, the COVID-19 pandemic struck China and the rest of the world, causing the very kind of mayhem the MSB had warned of. While water and energy kept flowing, supplies of food and other crucial goods suddenly became scarce as panic-stricken citizenries responded to the pandemic by stockpiling. Such panic reactions and resulting shortages could have been avoided if people had been educated in an MSB manner before the pandemic struck.

Indeed, given that crises short of war will increasingly afflict countries, public education will become an indispensable tool. At the time of writing, numerous countries are suffering from energy shortages, one of the outcomes from Russia's invasion of Ukraine, and they are also suffering from water shortages or flash floods caused by climate change. Citizen crisis education already exists in earthquake-prone cities and regions including Tokyo and San Francisco. 'Actual emergencies look more like people coming together than cities falling apart. SF72 is about prompting San Franciscans to get connected before an emergency—so we can be that much better off when something happens', San Francisco's emergency-hub website, SF72, advises San Franciscans.[25] The website also explains how to prepare for an earthquake, which involves always having indispensable supplies such as bottled water at home and maintaining a list of whom to contact after an earthquake and how to reach them. The website also provides instructions of what to do during an earthquake. The awareness that

---

[24] Swedish Civil Contingencies Agency, 'If Crisis or War Comes' (2018) <https://rib.msb.se/filer/pdf/28706.pdf> accessed 25 February 2023.

[25] 'Home', SF72 <https://www.sf72.org/home> accessed 25 February 2023.

an earthquake may strike and cause massive destruction does not seem to deter people from wanting to live in these cities.[26]

The education could also take place through infotainment and entertainment. Swedish National Television's *Societal Collapse* could be replicated and adapted. Adaptation options could include inviting members of the public to participate in the show or in individual segments. Such members of the public could be personally invited—an engineer with a water utility, say, or a top-achieving boy scout or girl scout.[27] Alternatively, they could be selected through an open call in the way done by reality-TV shows. Despite having been made as purely commercial ventures, the Hollywood production *Contagion*—starring Matt Damon, Kate Winslet, Jude Law, Gwyneth Paltrow, and Laurence Fishburne—and the enormously successful Norwegian television drama *Occupied* features storylines that can be defined as grey zone aggression. Through them, audiences around the world became aware, years ago, that a pandemic could strike and that Russia could take measures to harm energy supply in Europe. Today Western governments could maintain a regular exchange with their respective countries' entertainment industry about emerging national-security threats. This should clearly be done on an unclassified basis and with no quid pro quo or other demands on the filmmakers. Considering the increasing threats against Western societies and their grip on the public's attention it would, however, be in the entertainment industry's interest to participate in such a dialogue.

Courses form a more ambitious way of educating the public and should be the next layer in the societal-participation pyramid. One area where citizen education would bring immediate benefit both to individual citizens and to wider society is information literacy. Even though Western societies today feature enormous amounts of information, citizens have no training in verifying it. This educational gap, which spans all income groups, educational levels, and generations, has already done serious harm to Western democracies. The January 6 storming of the Capitol belongs to this category, as do the anti-vaxxer protests and attacks on vaccination sides; the anti-facemask movement; the attacks on 5G towers, which are prompted by the conviction that 5G spreads COVID-19; and many other hostile actions committed by residents of Western democracies against their countries' own institutions and infrastructure. Indeed, the

---

[26] 'All-Transactions House Price Index for San Francisco-San Mateo-Redwood City, CA (MSAD)' (*FRED*, 31 May 2022) <https://fred.stlouisfed.org/series/ATNHPIUS41884Q> accessed 25 February 2023; and Hiroyasu Oda, 'Tokyo Property Prices Near Bubble-Era Levels' (*Nikkei Asia*, 19 February 2019) <https://asia.nikkei.com/Business/Markets/Property/Tokyo-property-prices-near-bubble-era-levels> accessed 25 February 2023.

[27] Elisabeth Braw, 'Let's All Get Involved in Wargaming the Next Emergency', *The Times* (London, 25 July 2022) <https://www.thetimes.co.uk/article/lets-all-get-involved-in-wargaming-the-next-emergency-n6cb2n6lg> accessed 25 February 2023.

568   COUNTERING HYBRID AND GREY ZONE THREATS

massive challenge facing Western information-based economies is that citizens are surrounded by information without the ability to assess the information's accuracy.

This is a fundamental problem that information-literacy courses could help solve. The courses would teach participants how to verify information and would be funded by national or State governments, depending on the country. The specific course content, in turn, would be designed by a committee of respected information professionals such as librarians. Public libraries, which in most Western countries are present even in the smallest communities, also remain a largely trusted institution, with librarians largely seen as unpolitical experts focused on the acquisition of knowledge.[28] A country's information-literacy course would be developed and continuously updated—to reflect emerging forms of misinformation, disinformation, and delivery—by the syllabus committee, and would be taught by librarians at the countries' public libraries.

The case for information-literacy courses is strengthened by August 2022 findings by researchers at the University of Cambridge and other universities as well as Jigsaw (Google). After showing ordinary citizens instructional videos, the researchers found that 'these videos improve manipulation technique recognition, boost confidence in spotting these techniques, increase people's ability to discern trustworthy from untrustworthy content, and improve the quality of their sharing decisions.'[29]

Information-literacy courses could be offered in several ways, for example, over five evenings during one week or as a one day-long course taught on a Saturday, and would conclude with a test. For school-age children, the curriculum could either be integrated into the existing school curriculum, as they are in Finland, or offered as an after-school course, again over five evenings one week or on a Saturday. Passing the test would give each participant an information-literacy certificate. While the government could clearly not demand that every citizen take the course, holding an information-literacy certificate would be an asset on people's résumés. Indeed, given the harm misinformation and disinformation are already causing to Western societies, employers may begin requiring job applicants to be information-literate. In the absence of information-literacy courses, employers clearly cannot expect applicants to hold formal information-literacy qualifications, but they may begin administering information-literacy tests. Being information-literate would, of course, also be highly beneficial for the individual citizen, and having a critical mass of information-literate citizens

---

[28] The fact that librarians' image is changing in the United States—with both the left and the right attacking libraries over their book-stocking choices—ought to be a source of major concern.

[29] Jon Roozenbeek et al, 'Psychological Inoculation Improves Resilience against Misinformation on Social Media' (2022) 8 Science Advances Article eabo6254 <https://www.science.org/doi/10.1126/sciadv.abo6254?cookieSet=1> accessed 25 February 2023.

would be crucial as Western countries try to defend themselves against disinformation campaigns.

Since teenagers are both heavily exposed to disinformation and misinformation and are extremely agile learners, national and State governments—perhaps in association with journalist associations, news-media associations, or both—could also launch disinformation-detection competitions for teenagers. Like all citizens, journalists today battle enormous amounts of false information, some of it spread or amplified by hostile States, and are unable to detect or source every falsehood. Governments could fund disinformation-detection competitions, which would be administered by journalist and news-media associations and would see teenagers invited to investigate a set amount of information, verify it, and detect and trace falsehoods. Because teenagers may think differently than journalists, it is likely they would make discoveries that elude journalists. In addition, the competitions would raise teenagers' awareness of the presence of misinformation and disinformation in the information they consume. This is especially important as new social-media platforms, especially TikTok, increasingly dominate teenagers' news intake.

Open houses hosted by news organizations would present another opportunity. The idea, first introduced by me in a 2014 report[30], would see news organizations host regular open houses where members of the public would be able to observe the making of a newspaper or a radio or television news program. Just like British and other parliamentarians host weekly open houses that any constituent can attend, news organizations could host open houses at their headquarters, at local offices, and at pop-up offices around the country. Ordinary citizens, who could be invited through lotteries or sign-up lists, would spend a day or half a day observing the organization's journalists at work; sit in on news conferences; and perhaps advise the journalists regarding happenings in their community and events they consider newsworthy. This would give such members of the public, and by extension their friends and acquaintances, a better understanding of how journalism works, and it would help dismantle some of the misunderstandings of journalism that often create distrust among the wider population. Conversely, regular interactions with regular members of the public would help journalists better understand their priorities and concerns. Open houses would thus help bridge the divide between journalists and the public, an important step given that news media enjoys dangerously little trust in today's societies. The 2022 Edelman Trust Barometer, for example, found that that news media is trusted by

---

[30] Elisabeth Braw, 'Working Paper: Citizen Alienation and the Political and Media Elite' (University of Oxford Reuters Institute for the Study of Journalism, August 2014) <https://reutersinstitute.politics.ox.ac.uk/sites/default/files/2018-01/Citizen%20alienation%20and%20the%20political%20and%20media%20elite.pdf> accessed 25 February 2023.

570 COUNTERING HYBRID AND GREY ZONE THREATS

50 per cent of the population in the twenty-eight countries surveyed.[31] Business, non-governmental organizations (NGOs), and the government all enjoy more trust, Edelman found.

There is also enormous opportunity for other forms of training and education. Over past generations, male teenagers have often been called up for military service. Military skills are, however, of little use against grey zone aggression. Yet, today as in the past, teenagers and people in their twenties form an enormous and untapped source of societal engagement and expertise. At the moment, however, there are extremely few opportunities for them to be trained in emergency preparedness and emergency response. A new Latvian national-security curriculum is seeing teenagers learn about the threats facing the country and practical training in emergency response,[32] and in the 2017 presidential election campaign, Emmanuel Macron promised to introduce universal national service (SNU) in France.[33] The scheme as devised by Macron would focus on national cohesion and new national security challenges, but its implementation has struggled, partly due to the fact that it is unclear who should be ultimately responsible for national security in a wider sense.

There is a strong case for training teenagers in national security, and especially for offering crisis preparedness and crisis response training on a voluntary basis. Typically, teenagers are physically stronger than other adults, they learn more quickly, and they are easier to assemble as they are accustomed to group learning. There is also evidence that a critical mass of teenagers would be willing to participate. In Germany, nearly 43,000 people—mostly eighteen-year-olds did the 'Voluntary Social Year' in 2021–22, a period of service of mostly twelve months in care institutions such as hospitals.[34] Even more impressively, in Britain and other countries nearly half a million young people participated in the Duke of Edinburgh Award between April 2021 and March 2022, through which they did nearly 2.2 million hours of community service. The initiative, launched by Prince Philip, Duke of Edinburgh, in 1956, invites teenagers to participate in

---

[31] 'The Trust 10' (Edelman, 2022) <https://www.edelman.com/sites/g/files/aatuss191/files/2022-01/Trust%2022_Top10.pdf> accessed 25 February 2023.

[32] More about the Latvian curriculum in Elisabeth Braw, 'The Case for National Resilience Training for Teenagers' (Royal United Services Institute, 2 March 2020) <https://static.rusi.org/rusi_pub_174_2019_12_resilience_braw_final.pdf> accessed 25 February 2023.

[33] Alison Hird, 'France's Macron Urges Armed Forces to Get Behind National Service' (RFI, 14 July 2022) <https://www.rfi.fr/en/france/20220714-france-s-macron-urges-armed-forces-to-get-behind-national-service> accessed 25 February 2023.

[34] Bundesministerium für Familie, Senioren, Frauen und Jugend, 'Freiwilliges Soziales Jahr' <https://www.daten.bmfsfj.de/daten/daten/freiwilliges-soziales-jahr--137090>. In addition, some forty thousand Germans volunteer with the Federal Volunteer Service, which unlike the Voluntary Social Year involves only a part-time commitment, and of course in other volunteer organizations such as the THW, a disaster-response federal agency based on the participation of some eighty thousand volunteers.

HOW TO INVOLVE CIVIL SOCIETY IN GREY ZONE DEFENCE 571

the fields of volunteering, physical, skills, and expedition.[35] During the COVID-19 pandemic's worst months in 2020, 330,000 young Britons helped people in their communities as part of the Duke of Edinburgh Award: sewing PPE (personal protective equipment), delivering food to needy neighbours, and performing virtual concerts for people in nursing homes.[36] In many other countries, teenagers are active as boy scouts and girl scouts.

Countries could build on this existing engagement by offering crisis-response training to older teenagers, administered by the Red Cross, national civil-contingencies agencies, or similar organizations. The training would feature crisis preparedness and especially crisis response skills including first aid, and would conclude with crisis-response certification. Importantly, graduates would be added to national databases of crisis responders so that emergency and social agencies could reach them in case of need. Even without such command-and-control system, the trained crisis responders could clearly be useful in their communities, but adding them and their contact details to a national structure would guarantee efficient use of the training.[37] Organizing teenager participation in crisis response would also signal to a country's adversaries that instead of being a liability in a crisis, teenagers are a resource that will help keep society functioning during a crisis and thus reduce the effect of any grey zone aggression the adversary may be planning.

The curricula for such training should be written by government-appointed committees of experts to ensure that the training addressed national-security needs, and the training would be government-funded. The delivery of the training, in turn, could be carried out by organizations such as the Red Cross, civil-contingencies agencies, or a combination of the two. The training would be continued through refresher courses, with which the participants could keep their crisis-responder certification current. The content of the courses and refresher courses would also be updated to reflect current risks to society, both man-made and nature-made ones. The former category will continue to grow as a result of geopolitical confrontation, while the latter will continue to grow as a result of climate change.[38]

People of all ages could be trained in crisis response in a similar way. Courses could be designed for people in employment and people between jobs and in retirement, many of whom would welcome the opportunity to join a highly

---

[35] The Duke of Edinburgh's Award, 'History' <https://www.dofe.org/about/#history_div> accessed 25 February 2023. See also Elisabeth Braw, 'We Need an Army of Teenage Volunteers for the Next Crises', *The Times* (London, 23 August 2022) <https://www.thetimes.co.uk/article/we-need-an-army-of-teenage-volunteers-for-the-next-crises-8263pztm2> accessed 25 February 2023.

[36] The Duke of Edinburgh's Award (n 36).

[37] For further details, see Braw (n 2) ch. 9.

[38] For further details, see Braw (n 31).

meaningful activity that would also provide interaction with fellow citizens. Indeed, many retirees possess skills—including ones that can be refreshed—that are extremely beneficial to society during crises. In addition, many of them know how to operate complex equipment manually, a skill that has become rare as machinery has become digitized but which is crucial in case of cyberattacks.[39]

In recent months and years, many Western countries have seen calls for a return to mandatory military service for men and the expansion of mandatory military service to women. Most recently, during the 2022 general election campaign, Sweden's Liberal Party proposed a return to mandatory military service.[40] Universal conscription is often seen as a catch-all remedy: it enhances national security and it sees all young men—and today potentially all young women—perform a period of community service. Yet apart from a few front-line States facing Russia, Western armed forces only need a limited number of highly specialized soldiers.

Although military service does not provide defence against grey zone aggression, it is worth highlighting the selective military service of the kind perfected by Norway. The Norwegian system was introduced in 2001 after it became clear that the armed forces no longer needed the services of all able-bodied young men. Instead, the armed forces only selected as many conscripts as they needed, a figure that settled around seven to eight thousand per year, out of annual birth male cohorts of around thirty thousand. That made military service an asset on young people's resumes, and admission became competitive. The competitiveness further increased in 2016, when military service was expanded to women. With around sixty thousand young men and women assessed for the same number of places each year, admission became twice as competitive. In 2021 the armed forces selected 9,888 young Norwegians for military service, of whom 34.5 per cent were women.[41] Denmark has a similar model, and Sweden and Lithuania have also adapted versions of it.[42]

Following the Norwegian model, governments could introduce competitive national-service schemes that would allow not just the armed forces but also other parts of the governments to select—on the basis of competition—participants in

---

[39] See e.g. Elisabeth Braw, 'Older Workers Are a Secret Weapon against Cyber Attacks', *Financial Times* (London, 5 July 2021) <https://www.ft.com/content/c4ea6fb3-6262-4426-9503-05391f0e5 23a> accessed 25 February 2023. For further details about training for working-age and retired adults, see Braw (n 2) ch. 10.

[40] 'L vill att alla ska göra värnplikt' (*Sveriges Radio*, 24 August 2022) <https://sverigesradio.se/arti kel/l-vill-att-alla-ska-gora-varnplikt> accessed 25 February 2023.

[41] Norwegian Armed Forces, 'Forsvaret i tall' (29 April 2022) <https://www.forsvaret.no/om-forsvaret/forsvaret-i-tall> accessed 25 February 2023.

[42] For more details, see Elisabeth Braw, 'Competitive National Service: How the Scandinavian Model Can Be Adapted by the UK' (Royal United Services Institute, 23October 2019) <https://rusi. org/explore-our-research/publications/occasional-papers/competitive-national-service-how-scand inavian-model-can-be-adapted-uk> accessed 25 February 2023.

national-service programs. Because they are relatively modest in size, Western governments already struggle to respond to emergencies of different kinds. Indeed, it can be argued that what is needed in a national emergency is not an omnipresent government but an empowered citizenry with the skills needed to keep society operating even in case of a severe crisis, both through individual efforts and through participation in ones led by public authorities. Like all the other schemes discussed, the selective national-service scheme would do just that. After completing their service in the program, which could range between six and twelve months, the participants would enter a standing reserve that could be called up on case of emergencies.[43] While participation would be voluntary, having been selected for such a highly competitive scheme would be an asset on young people's CVs of the same calibre as having been admitted to a prestigious university. Moreover, since the selection would be based on aptitude rather than school background or traditional test scores, the program would offer equal opportunity of admission to people of all backgrounds.

The other part of civil society that should be involved in defence against grey zone aggression is, of course, the private sector. As we have seen, Western companies can be both direct and indirect targets of grey zone aggression. Cyber aggression has indisputably become a constant occurrence, with much of it attributed to hostile States. Not even extremely powerful technology companies like Google can hit back against the aggression, as governments are understandably responsible for retaliating against State-sponsored aggression. And companies in, say, Australia cannot predict which company will become the target of Chinese ire in response to a statement or action by Canberra. Indeed, companies cannot know which part of their supply chain, or their markets, might become a target, or even if any specific company faces particular risk.

All these factors make Western companies highly vulnerable. The global footprint most of them maintain, through their own production, their customer base, or their supply chain, makes them more vulnerable still. They are, however, not in a position to defend themselves against the aggression, not least because the aggression is not limited to them. The fact that the aggression is mostly not prompted by any actions undertaken by the company itself makes it even more challenging for companies to steady themselves against hostile acts. Unlike with risks companies habitually plan for, businesses are therefore not in a position to prepare for the aggression through crisis-management exercises, nor are they in a position to predict it. Part of the beauty of grey zone aggression—from the aggressor's perspective—is that it can be applied to any aspect of another country's civil society, usually with plausible deniability.

---

[43] See ibid.

574   COUNTERING HYBRID AND GREY ZONE THREATS

A straightforward way of corporate participation in defence against grey zone aggression would be for Western governments to maintain an ongoing dialogue with business leaders. Such a dialogue would involve top civil servants and C-level executives and would see the government updating the business participants about geopolitical concerns. The business leaders, in turn, would highlight any risks or changes their companies have observed in their countries of operation. Thanks to this regular exchange, business leaders would have a good understanding of the geopolitical environment in which their companies operate, and governments would receive insights from the grey zone front line that their own agencies are not able to provide. In addition, the regular interaction would provide both sides with trusted partners whom they can call in to provide information or to discuss specific geopolitical concerns. Given that most executives do not have security clearances, and that the discussions would at any rate focus on larger trends, the engagement could take place on an unclassified basis. Keeping the exchange unclassified (though confidential) would also help allay any concerns about intelligence spreading outside the government. Today there are no such structured dialogues, though the Finnish government has for years maintained an informal discussion with industry leaders regarding Russia. The closest other example are the regular conversations the US Department of Energy maintains with energy-utility executives.[44]

Another way in which to enable the private sector to participate in defence against grey zone aggression is through military-business grey zone exercises. While most large companies conduct crisis-management exercises, by virtue of being individual companies they are not set up to conduct exercises involving larger crises that affect multiple parts of society. Correspondingly, while governments—through the armed forces—regularly exercise war scenarios, they should also exercise contingencies short of war and involve private companies in these exercises. That is particularly important as companies in Western countries operate a string of functions critical to society: from power plants to supermarkets. Through joint military-business grey zone exercises, government would be able to better plan for national contingencies, as response will involve not just the armed forces and other parts of the government but businesses as well. Conversely, it is in businesses' interest to participate in such exercises as they need to be better prepared for grey zone aggression and other national contingencies than is currently the case. Countries' chaotic response in the first weeks of COVID-19 delivered irrefutable evidence of the need for such preparedness.

---

[44] For more details, see Braw (n 2) ch. 10.

HOW TO INVOLVE CIVIL SOCIETY IN GREY ZONE DEFENCE   575

After I outlined the need for such exercises in a 2020 report[45] and described how they could be executed, the Czech Republic's Ministry of Defence immediately implemented the idea. In early 2021, the ministry conducted its first exercise. 'We had discovered, and especially given my responsibility for cooperation with the defence industry, which is 95 percent private, that we didn't even have the tools with which to involve them in exercising war-like scenarios—starting with threat assessment through to operationalization of measures against these threats', the country's then-deputy minister of defence for industrial co-operation, Tomáš Kopečný, told me in a subsequent interview.[46] His ministry has held several iterations of the exercise, each time inviting a different set of companies. 'After the first exercise companies called us up and said, 'why weren't we selected?'. Eight were selected, but we had more than twenty calling us asking why they hadn't been invited. There was genuine desire to be involved, either out of jealousy or because the exercise was organized by the MOD along with other parts of the government. I told them the truth, which is what there will be many more exercises', Kopečný said.[47] Having participated in such an exercise is, of course, also a valuable point as companies increasingly have to convince existing and potential shareholders and customers that they—the companies— are enhancing their resilience to disruptions. The companies able to demonstrate resilience will enjoy far higher shareholder and market confidence than those lacking such preparedness.

5. Conclusion

Grey zone aggression will continue to morph, evolve, and spread. During the course of 2021 and 2022, the world saw forms of grey zone aggression that included Chinese dredgers excavating Taiwanese sand and harming the Taiwanese seabed; China's long-distance fishing fleet continuing to deplete other countries' fish stocks and to harm its marine wildlife; Beijing punishing Western companies as proxies for their home governments; Belarus weaponizing migrants as a way of weakening the European Union; and Russia causing corporate and capital flight from Ukraine by posting tens of thousands of soldiers on the Ukrainian border. In the latter case, Russia followed up by invading Ukraine. It could, however, have kept its soldiers at the border and further exacerbated investors', companies',

---

[45] Elisabeth Braw, 'The Case for Joint Military–Industry Greyzone Exercises' (Royal United Services Institute, 28 September 2020) <https://rusi.org/explore-our-research/publications/briefing-papers/case-joint-military-industry-greyzone-exercises> accessed 25 February 2023.
[46] Video interview with the author, 17 February 2022.
[47] Ibid.

and international markets' confidence in Ukraine. Yet positioning soldiers on one's own side of a national border is not illegal. Until 24 February 2022, Russia was executing an extremely clever grey zone strategy against Ukraine, with this aspect aimed at harming the Ukrainian economy.[48]

Because grey zone aggression is extremely difficult to predict, it is also challenging to design deterrence-by-punishment measures and signalling for it. This makes deterrence by denial even more important than it is in defence against traditional military aggression, and because grey zone aggression targets civil society, the defence and deterrence signalling must likewise involve civil society. Such involvement can largely take place through voluntary citizen participation in schemes ranging from public-awareness campaigns to information-literacy courses and crisis-response training. Crucially, crisis-response training has to include participants' subsequent insertion into a command-and-control structure of government agencies and NGOs charged with crisis response. Graduates of such schemes would clearly be able to use their crisis-response skills even without insertion into a command-and-control system, but this would not benefit society-wide resilience and will thus be of little use in deterrence signalling. Indeed, individuals simply attending crisis-response training without afterwards being absorbed into a society-wide resilience effort would be seen by the West's adversaries as another example of Western societies' fragmentation. It would also risk feeding into the already proliferating prepper mindset.

There is also considerable potential in involving the private sector in grey zone defence and thus deterrence. Until recently, companies may have been reluctant to participate in national-security efforts unless legally obliged to do so, but because grey zone aggression harms them, they have an interest in better protecting themselves against it and in being part of government-led initiatives that change adversaries' cost-benefit calculus. Participating in societal resilience helps companies enhance their own performance in case of a grey zone-triggered crisis. In addition, because societal resilience underpins deterrence by denial, companies help protect their countries' economies against grey zone aggression. Because they depend on economies to thrive, participating in resilience efforts is in their interest for this reason too.

---

[48] Elisabeth Braw, 'Russia's 'Greyzone' Aggression Is Already Harming Ukraine', *Financial Times* (London, 9 December 2021) <https://www.ft.com/stream/89a963d8-cf76-3893-88c9-d121dc44b c5f> accessed 25 February 2023.

26

Security Assistance
by Liberal Democracies

Tensions in the Grey Zone

Mitt Regan and Sarah Harrison

1. Introduction

As liberal democracies consider how to compete effectively in the grey zone, one potential instrument for doing so is the provision of grant assistance to state security forces in various parts of the world. As two observers note, 'With China and Russia growing more assertive, parts of Asia, Africa [the] Middle East, and Europe are now contested through indirect approaches', such as 'providing military aid [and] advisors'.[1] The aims of such assistance are to 'promote domestic and regional stability, empower allies, broaden power, and provide deterrence'.[2] While different forms of support may have different labels and technical definitions, we will use the term 'security assistance' to encompass all programs intended to increase the capability and professionalism of state military and related forces.[3]

Our focus in this chapter is on the challenges that liberal democracies may face in providing security assistance to regimes that do not conform to liberal democratic principles in how they govern. One set of challenges arises from the fact that the goals and incentives of recipient States may not be fully aligned with those of donor States. This can result in what is called a 'principal-agency problem', which reflects the risk that recipients may use funds to further local goals that may be inconsistent with or even antithetical to donor State security interests.[4] A second set of challenges arises from the need for a donor State to

---

[1] Jahara Matisek and William Reno, 'Back to the Future' (*Modern War Institute*, 29 December 2021) <https://perma.cc/3FCK-EZR6> accessed 16 February 2023.
[2] Mara E. Karlin, *Building Militaries in Fragile States* (University of Pennsylvania Press 2018) 6.
[3] Department of Defense security assistance programs are typically referred to as 'security cooperation' while the State Department refers to its programs as 'security assistance'.
[4] Stephen Biddle, 'Building Security Forces and Stabilizing Nations: The Problem of Agency' (2017) 146 *Daedalus* 126.

Mitt Regan and Sarah Harrison, *Security Assistance by Liberal Democracies* In: *Hybrid Threats and Grey Zone Conflict.*
Edited by: Mitt Regan and Aurel Sari, Oxford University Press. © Oxford University Press 2024.
DOI: 10.1093/oso/9780197744772.003.0026

578   COUNTERING HYBRID AND GREY ZONE THREATS

consider how much divergence from liberal democratic principles it will tolerate in a recipient State for the sake of gaining recipient cooperation and maintaining influence.

The United States is by far the largest provider of security assistance, providing it in Fiscal Year 2020 to 133 states, or almost 70 per cent of independent states in the world. More than half of these states received at least $1 million in assistance.[5] We therefore will refer to the US experience in many cases as illustrative of the challenges that liberal democracies face when attempting to use this tool to further their national security interests.

2. Background

Security assistance can be attractive because it may enable a donor State to avoid the need to commit significant military resources to project power and directly confront potential adversaries around the world. Both the Soviet Union and the United States provided such assistance during the Cold War either to strengthen friendly governments or to support insurgents against unfriendly ones. This included indirect involvement in several developing states' civil wars, such as in Angola, Mozambique, Nicaragua, and El Salvador, as well as US support to South Vietnam that eventually led to direct US involvement in that conflict. After the fall of the Soviet Union, the United States furnished assistance to former Warsaw Pact states in an effort to bring them within the orbit of the West.

US security assistance has grown especially dramatically, however, since the 9/11 terrorist attacks. A large portion of this increase has been for counterterrorism and counterinsurgency operations, often to fragile states that the United States feared were vulnerable to becoming sanctuaries for terrorist organizations planning attacks in the United States and on US persons and facilities abroad. The number of security assistance programs increased from twenty-two in 2001 to thirty-six in 2020,[6] and funding increased from about $8.3 billion in 2001 to $16.2 billion in 2020.[7]

Also notable is the fact that the portion of funds provided under the authority of the Department of Defense (DoD) has grown significantly compared to the portion under the authority of the State Department. In 2001, the State

---

[5] Patricia L. Sullivan, 'Does Security Assistance Work? Why It May Not Be the Answer for Fragile States' (Modern War Institute, November 15, 2021) <https://perma.cc/SF5Q-CJRC> accessed 16 February 2023.

[6] Lauren Woods and Elias Yousif, 'Expanding the Scope of US Security Assistance Since 9/11' (Center for International Policy, September 2021) <https://perma.cc/E67A-LU57> accessed 16 February 2023.

[7] Ibid. 6.

Department managed about 79.1 per cent of total security assistance spending. By 2020, that had declined to about 46.7 per cent.[8] The increase in DoD authority reflects a particular emphasis on what is known as 'building partner capacity'—that is, 'training, mentoring, advising, equipping, exercising, educating and planning with foreign security forces primarily in fragile and weak states'.[9]

Recipient States that have the potential to use security assistance to further the interests of liberal democratic donor States depart to varying degrees from liberal democratic principles of governance. This can create challenges in ensuring that as a practical matter assistance to a recipient State will achieve donor State goals. It also requires donors to determine how best to weigh respect for state sovereignty on the one hand and the desire to avoid complicity in illiberal recipient State conduct on the other. As our discussion below elaborates, the forms that these challenges take may differ depending upon whether a recipient is a fragile or relatively stable state.

3. Fragile States

One challenge that a donor State may face is that the source of political authority in some states may not be a democratically elected unitary government with a monopoly on the use of force within its territory.

3.1 Multiple sources of authority

Instead, authority may rest with a set of local actors such as clans, tribes, ethnic groups, or warlords who have their own distinct sources of legitimacy, power bases, and militia groups. Although there may be a formal state, it will not represent a sense of national identity, will usually not be the only entity that provides public goods and services, and may be subject to considerable internal violent competition.

In these cases, State authority will rest upon bargaining among these groups and the coalitions that emerge, rather than on a sense of legitimacy based on providing benefits to and protecting the population. Attempts by Western states in these situations to use security assistance to create an apolitical military designed for a liberal democratic state will encounter substantial obstacles and may well destabilize the local political order. Providing security assistance to a group that

---

[8] Ibid. 2.
[9] Sullivan (n 5).

the donor regards as the ostensible version of a unitary national state would effectively mean taking a side in local political conflicts. This could undermine the legitimacy of the recipient and create incentives for groups to look to other sources for assistance.

A liberal democratic donor State may conclude that, while these conditions are not ideal, security assistance should accommodate them because of strategic national security interests. A donor State thus may permit assistance to go to multiple influential groups that comprise the local power structure, or competing components of a nascent government, rather than to a single recipient. The rationale for this would be the belief that this is the best way to maintain political stability and strengthen the military capabilities of groups that will provide a defence against the donor's adversaries.

A donor that provides security assistance under these conditions will need to keep in mind certain risks from doing so. First, various elites in this setting will have an incentive to utilize security assistance for patronage to reward loyalists and to undermine rivals. This may increase the power of certain militias or specific units in a fractured national military, and make even more difficult the eventual emergence of a State that can credibly claim to act in the interests of the population as a whole.

Second, recipient government officials who oversee security program recipients in some cases may be people who are involved in the criminal activity that security assistance is intended to combat. As Matisek and Reno declare, 'The risk is that their SFA [security force assistance] connections likely empower these people and their informal strategies that weak State officials use to exercise authority at the expense of long-term donor war aims'.[10]

Third, assistance may empower groups whose principal loyalty is to their leaders rather than to the more abstract concept of the State. Their commitment to resist the donor's adversaries therefore may be variable. It is conceivable that a donor adversary at a later point could offer more advantageous benefits that could lead a group to switch sides in order to further its own interest. Fourth, a donor State will need to be sensitive to the extent that providing assistance to different groups could create political instability by shifting the balance of power among them. This underscores the need for keen awareness of local political dynamics. Failure to take this possibility into account could result in the very instability that security assistance is meant to prevent.

Next, arming multiple groups raises the stakes of any failure to arrive at an acceptable power-sharing arrangement. Such arrangements can be temporary and provisional, and the prospect of violence as a response to perceived grievances

---

[10] Jahara Matisek and William Reno, 'Getting American Security Force Assistance Right: Political Context Matters' (2019) 92 Joint Forces Quarterly 65, 67.

may always lurk in the background. Security assistance may make such a response seem more feasible, which could make the consequences of disagreement more destructive than they would be in the absence of such assistance. This would make the restoration of stability even more difficult and could enhance the opportunities for adversaries to gain influence.

Finally, and more broadly, security assistance provided under these conditions can reinforce power structures that may be inconsistent to varying degrees with liberal democratic principles. These structures may systematically disfavour women or members of minority groups who have insufficient power to play a role in power-sharing arrangements. Receipt of services may be based on patronage rather than need, and power exercised on the basis of personal authority rather than rules that would ensure impartiality and accountability. In short, security assistance by liberal democracies to counter illiberal peer competitors may strengthen other illiberal regimes. A donor State may regard this trade-off as necessary, but this conclusion should be based on a clear understanding of the risks described above and the compromises that will be involved.

A notable example of how security assistance can be ineffective in the absence of a unified government is the collapse of the Afghan Army in the face of the Taliban offensive in August 2021. As one observer notes, 'political factions consistently tried to manipulate appointments to senior army, police, and security services positions to their advantage. Not only did this not serve the cause of 'meritocracy' in the Afghan security forces, but it also created a constant disruption to the chain of command, with opposing factions often refusing to cooperate with each other'.[11]

Early experience with the attempt to establish an Iraqi military after the fall of Saddam Hussein also illustrates these risks. Iraqi Prime Minister Nuri al-Maliki largely filled the military with Shiites and personal loyalists. The result was to undermine military cohesion, as reflected in the collapse of Iraqi armed forces in the face of Islamic State advances in 2013. As Matisek and Reno observe, 'Disenfranchised Sunnis found it relatively easy—besides for basic survival—to swap alliances from Baghdad to [Islamic State] because they had been abandoned politically and materially'.[12]

Similarly, these authors note that in Somalia, clan politics dominates how different elements of the Somali National Army (SNA) and other security institutions are organized. Thus, 'many Somali politicians receive different

---

[11] Antonio Giustozzi, 'Security Force Assistance: Bringing Local Politics Back In' (*RUSI*, 7 December 2021) <https://perma.cc/LH75-MZ4J> accessed 16 February 2023. See also Mike Jason, 'What We Got Wrong in Afghanistan' *The Atlantic* (12 August 2021) <https://perma.cc/64BP-6ZQH> accessed 16 February 2023.

[12] Matisek and Reno (n 10) 70.

582 COUNTERING HYBRID AND GREY ZONE THREATS

factions of the military as a threat to their personal rules and their family clan ties. In response to perceived threats, they empower their favorite armed groups (State-sanctioned and non-State) to attack other components of the government and security institutions.[13] This reflects the fact that 'each armed faction is vying for control of the government and also that each faction regards others as more of a threat than a viable component of a collective Somali State-building effort.[14]

Matthew Cancian's study of assistance and training provided to tens of thousands of Kurdish Peshmerga in the face of the Islamic State's attack on Kurdistan in 2014 suggests how difficult it can be to change these dynamics.[15] In response to the attack by ISIS on the Kurdistan region of Iraq, a coalition of Western countries provided military training to tens of thousands of Kurdish Peshmerga.

Apart from enhancing combat readiness, this program was intended to increase the professionalism of the Peshmerga. By professionalism, Cancian means a military whose goal is not to keep a particular regime in power but to defend it against external foes. In a professional military, advancement is based on competence and achievement rather than political loyalty. Prior to the initiative, different political parties controlled different Peshmerga military units. The United States organized certain brigades into units that integrated members from both parties, with the goal of establishing 'apolitical formations that reported to a unified government ministry.[16]

Cancian found, however, that integrated brigades did not differ from non-integrated ones in responses to questions such as, 'Is the support of a political party important for promotion?' and, 'Is your platoon commander in your tribe?' His use of various statistical techniques also indicated no appreciable difference between the two sets of brigades with respect to professionalism.[17] Cancian suggests that the Peshmerga 'represent an easy case because the engagement was well funded, the training was provided by a first-rate military (Americans), and the engagement went on for several years.[18] In addition, the Kurds were facing an existential threat from ISIS. He concludes soberly that if assistance 'cannot professionalize soldiers in this case, it is less likely to succeed in situations with a less deep engagement.[19]

---

[13] Ibid. 69.
[14] Ibid. 70.
[15] Matthew Cancian, *Trained to Win? Evaluating Battlefield Effectiveness and Sociopolitical Factors among Partnered Forces* (Joint Special Operations University Press 2021).
[16] Ibid. 2.
[17] Ibid. 38–39.
[18] Ibid. 39.
[19] Ibid.

3.2 Institution-building

While security assistance that accommodates a fragmented power structure may be regarded as necessary in some cases, experience indicates that it is unlikely to advance long-term donor security interests. It is exceedingly difficult to maintain a capable professional military in a fragile State if there are not host nation leaders who have the political willingness and ability to use assistance to build such a military rather than use it to dispense patronage. Tactical and operational education and training is unlikely to contribute to a sustainable professional military in the absence of social and political institutions that reinforce a sense of national identity. As Matisek and Reno put it, 'What good is a tactically proficient military, and expensive weaponry and considerable training, in a context where State officials lack political willpower and capacity to support such a force? This is a recipe for the expensive to build, yet easy to break, Faberge egg army'.[20]

Successful security force assistance programs therefore ideally should help strengthen efforts to engage in long-term State building, while at the same time avoiding efforts to impose a Western-style liberal democracy. In this respect, security assistance in weak States 'needs to be just as focused on doing politics as that of providing specific military training'.[21] Absent the ability to help establish institutions that will enable militaries to develop a professional ethos that stands apart from partisan politics, the most such assistance might do is build specialized components such as special operations forces to conduct specific tasks such as counterterrorism.

Achieving more ambitious goals will require attempts by a donor State to exert pressure for institutional reforms and to support local elites that embrace them. The hope is that, 'a more capable security sector will translate into a more effective State, and vice versa'.[22] A concern with this approach is that the process of 'mission creep' will involve security advisors in a range of activities beyond security assistance that may effectively constitute State-building. Donor State populations, however, tend to have little patience for the long-term commitment that such a process requires. In addition, the recipient State population may regard the donor State as overreaching or as engaging in coercion, which can undermine the legitimacy of the putative national authority that the donor is attempting to help establish.

Furthermore, donor States should not try to 'implant replicas of Western norms in places that lack a social base or popular demand for them'.[23] There may

---

[20] Ibid. 71.

[21] Ibid.

[22] Jahara Matisek and Joshua D. Williamson, 'Limited Wars in the Periphery: The Dilemma of American Military Assistance' (Marine Corps University Press, 15 June 2020) <https://doi.org/10.36304/ExpwMCUP.2020.03> accessed 21 February 2023.

[23] Matisek and Reno (n 1).

well be limits to the extent that any relatively stable state that emerges will completely conform to Western liberal democratic principles. Gender and sexual orientation equality and ethnic diversity may reduce the likelihood of civil conflict over the long run, but insisting on immediate reforms to achieve them can create significant tensions between the government and a more traditional population.

In addition, reforms that attempt to impose a Western-style civilian-military relationship might do more harm than good in a fragile state. Military elites may act as coequals with other political actors and societal elites rather than as subservient to them. As Matisek and Reno observe, in weak States, 'political cohesion is at a premium, and if this requires the development of militaries that are more politically involved in state building, it is better to have them engaged in positive state building rather than being used as tools against domestic rivals'.[24] They note that some states such as Rwanda, Uganda, and Ethiopia have been able to develop effective militaries 'precisely because their armies have "partnerships" with the state and are strategically integrated into the "shared vision" for statebuilding'.[25] At the same time, there is the risk that this could legitimize military leaders who might then feel empowered to conduct a coup if the civilian political actors are not adequately addressing security crises.

The effort by liberal democracies to use security assistance in fragile states to help establish a government that is regarded as legitimate and exercises a monopoly over violence in its territory therefore poses significant challenges. Focusing on training a security sector without regard to the larger political and institutional context may well be unsuccessful. A professional apolitical military is unlikely to emerge in a state with fragmented sources of power that inhibit the establishment of a government that reflects a shared sense of national identity.

At the same time, donor State attempts to help shape the larger political context can result in efforts to engage in state-building that are unlikely to be accompanied by long-term donor State commitment. In addition, such attempts may trigger the charge that liberal democracies are violating their own values by engaging in neocolonialism. Successful security assistance in a fragile state therefore requires a delicate balance of support and encouragement for institutional reform and respect for the ultimate authority of local partners to determine the shape of their political institutions, while avoiding heavy reliance on the provision of security assistance as the primary means to advance the donor State's interest.

---

[24] Matisek and Reno (n 10).
[25] Ibid. 71–72.

4. Relatively stable States

A second challenge is that a regime in a recipient State may be wary that a more professional military will pose a threat to its ability to remain in power.

4.1 Government resistance

The government in this case may resist changes that could create a rival centre of power that is able to use force more effectively. It also may fear that security assistance will include imbuing members of the military and other security forces with more of an ethos of meritocracy and professional independence. While such a regime may desire assistance, it may use it for its own purposes and thwart the creation of more efficient professional security forces. In other words, it may attempt to use security assistance to 'coup-proof' its hold on power.

Resistance may take the form of refusing to accept donor recommendations for changes in personnel or how military forces are organized, as well as declining invitations for military officers to engage in educational and training programs in liberal democracies. An authoritarian regime also may ensure that the benefits of assistance programs go mainly to officers perceived as loyal to the government. As the discussion below describes, the United States historically has been reluctant to insist on personnel or organizational changes in its provision of assistance because of the desire to create a close relationship with the recipient government.

A consequence of providing security assistance under such circumstances is of course that it may well undermine donor interests by impairing the development of a more capable military that is able to deter or restrain adversaries of the donor State. The recipient government will have an incentive to claim that additional assistance is necessary for improvement, even as it uses this assistance for its own purposes and continues to place obstacles in the way of military professionalization. Absent an actual conflict, it may be difficult to assess progress, and will be necessary to some extent to rely on the government's assurance that it is occurring.

The result may be a partner on whom the donor State may not be able to rely to counter adversary initiatives. As Rachel Tecott observes, 'Combat effectiveness depends on patterns of decisions political and military leaders make around personnel, command structures, training, and corruption. Recipients of SFA who are not interested in building better militaries will take US assistance while simultaneously implementing policies that keep their militaries weak'.[26]

---

[26] Rachel Tecott, 'All Rapport, No Results: What Afghanistan's Collapse Reveals about the Flaws in US Security Force Assistance' (Modern War Institute, 26 August 2021) <https://perma.cc/9LB5-5PZK> accessed 21 February 2023.

586 COUNTERING HYBRID AND GREY ZONE THREATS

US advisors are discouraged, however, from vigorously attempting to influence recipient State decisions by setting conditions for assistance. As Tecott notes:

> US military advising doctrine and training encourages advisors to develop trust and rapport with partner leaders, to inspire them to emulate the American approach through the power of their example, and to convince them to implement US advice on the strength of their logic. Advisors are actively discouraged from using carrots and sticks to incentivize their counterparts to follow their advice.[27]

Mara Karlin makes a similar point in discussing the US military's decades-long effort to build partner militaries: 'For decades, the US military has spent substantial time and treasure trying to build partner militaries in fragile states. These programs pointedly focus on training and equipping, emphasizing hardware as the solution, and limiting the US role. They take a hands-off approach to sensitive issues in these partner militaries, such as organizational structure and personnel appointments'.[28] Karlin says that the prescription to take a limited role is based on the belief that 'the program to strengthen the state's military should be wholly grounded in local ownership by the partner state', which can be undermined by a donor State's efforts to influence decisions about personnel and organizational matters.[29] Yet, as Tecott suggests, 'It is difficult to understand, however, why local military officers would decide to strike ghost soldiers from the rolls and pocket less money for themselves and their families, simply because their American friends asked nicely'.[30]

Karlin's case studies of US security assistance for foreign internal defence to Greece, South Vietnam, and Lebanon in the early 1980s and mid-2000s find that 'deep US involvement in a partner state's sensitive military affairs is critical for transforming a military'.[31] This is because

> [a]t least some partner state military personnel will be reluctant to adopt reforms that might limit their power. These disincentives to change are one reason why a deep U.S. role in sensitive partner state military issues, such as personnel affairs, is so critical. The role, shape, and mission of the organization, as influenced by its personnel, will therefore have an impact on the military's actions.[32]

---

[27] Ibid.
[28] Karlin (n 2) 4.
[29] Ibid. 8.
[30] Tecott (n 26).
[31] Karlin (n 2) 13.
[32] Ibid.

SECURITY ASSISTANCE BY LIBERAL DEMOCRACIES   587

Karlin cautions that active involvement in decisions about personnel and organizational structure will not guarantee effective security assistance, but failing to do so is unlikely to achieve it.[33]

As measured by the ability of a recipient State eventually to exercise and sustain control over its territory and monopolize violence, Greece was perhaps the most notable success and South Vietnam the most notable failure of US security assistance among Karlin's case studies. In Greece, the United States took an active role in matters involving 'sensitive Greek military affairs, including the military's structure and its personnel'.[34] As Karlin describes this role:

> In addition to training, equipping, offering tactical and strategic advice, assisting with planning and operations, and dealing with personnel affairs, [US] staff made organizational changes to the Greek military. They amended the order of battle, suggested changes to its 'laws and decrees', and Greek commanders regularly requested and followed [US] advice during the summer offensive— including collaboration on after-action reports examining [Greek army] troop performance [and] officer performance, and [offered] recommendations for improvement.[35]

By contrast, the United States took a much more limited role in South Vietnam throughout the 1950s and early 1960s, until the weakness of the South Vietnamese military eventually prompted the United States to become directly involved in combat. President Diem was personally involved in all major military appointments and promotions, which were based on loyalty rather than capability. Karlin says, 'As one former senior South Vietnamese military official reflected, 'the true mission of the armed forces . . . was repeatedly neglected in favor of the unspoken concern to prevent an overthrow of the government'.[36] This politicization resulted in an ineffective command-and-control structure, described by one US official as 'fraught with 'conflicting, duplicating channels' that ensured Diem's ultimate power'.[37]

Karlin maintains that for General Samuel Williams, head of the US Military Assistance Advisory Group-Indochina (MAAG) in the crucial years from 1955 to 1960, '[E]stablishing a warm, trusting relationship with the South Vietnamese was his immediate priority'.[38] As a result, 'MAAG generally refrained from

---

[33] Karlin maintains that a second crucial variable is the strength of external actors attempting to influence events in the recipient state.

[34] Ibid. 63.

[35] Ibid. 47.

[36] Ibid., 79.

[37] Ibid. 78.

[38] Ibid. 84.

588 COUNTERING HYBRID AND GREY ZONE THREATS

becoming deeply involved in sensitive military affairs such as command and control operations, politicization, and personnel assignments'.[39] She observes:

> Williams's commentary on critical problems—including the continued challenge posed by an incoherent chain of command, weak subordinates, and the low-priority training received—were almost always vague and lacked specific examples where Diem should make changes.
>
> In that vein, he urged Diem to establish a formal system for promotions and for 'demotions and elimination of unqualified 'personnel', but he failed to offer specific recommendations unless they were in the most innocuous areas, such as moving training centers. Therefore, the South Vietnamese military leadership remained weak as personnel decisions and command and control continued entirely in the hands of Diem and his cohort.[40]

Karlin concludes, '[The US] would commit millions of troops, suffer tens of thousands of casualties, and spend billions of dollars. Had its effort in South Vietnam to strengthen this partner military been organized differently—had it not been a spectacular failure—much of that may have been avoidable'.[41]

Active efforts to influence recipient State decision-making on military personnel, organization, and operations thus tend to be important for successful security assistance programs in some states. These efforts may include attaching conditions on some assistance and insisting on donor State participation in decision-making. At the same time, this approach may generate resentment on the part of recipient State officials who regard it as their prerogative to make decisions on issues that may be politically and culturally sensitive. As Karlin acknowledges, 'increasing US involvement in the details of a foreign country's military is rife with colonial undertones and therefore might be difficult to digest. To minimize pushback, US officials should watch how they communicate and avoid creating the perception that they are bullying those they seek to assist'.[42]

Aside from practical considerations, playing such an active role may square uneasily with liberal democratic respect for state sovereignty and a population's right of self-determination. Indeed, the US military's historical approach to its role arguably is based at least in part on this principle. Donor states that seek more influence may believe that they can acquire it by providing apolitical technical military expertise. The military, however, is a highly significant institution in a state's political order, not simply a neutral instrument whose mode of organization has no implications for that order. Donor States therefore must

---

[39] Ibid.
[40] Ibid. 104.
[41] Ibid. 107.
[42] Ibid. 199.

weigh the intrusion into another State's decision-making with regard to its political institutions against the extent to which security assistance will help counter broader illiberal forces.

4.2 Authoritarian repression

An especially acute challenge for liberal democratic security assistance is the risk that an authoritarian regime may use such assistance to enhance its ability to repress opponents and dissidents. Leaders of such regimes can reinforce the loyalty of military elites and armed forces by directing funds to favoured officers and units, and by enhancing military capability to quell domestic unrest. As Patricia Sullivan describes, 'Aid thus reinforces the privileged position of the military, empowering it relative to other state institutions and giving it an incentive to work with the ruling regime to repress liberalization efforts that would redistribute power and resources away from the military'.[43]

Research by Sullivan and her colleagues finds that this risk is especially high in countries emerging from conflict. A study of 171 internal conflicts that ended between 1956 and 2012 concluded that there is 'strong evidence that governments become more repressive when they receive military aid or major conventional weapons transfers in the decades after conflict termination'.[44]

Sullivan and other theorists suggest that leaders in post-conflict states face choices between two ideal types of strategies for maintaining the support of constituents. One strategy is to direct scarce state resources to provide public goods to further economic growth and thereby gain legitimacy among a large proportion of the population. The polar opposite strategy is to minimize the number of supporters a regime needs to stay in power, direct state resources to those supporters in the form of private goods, and use force to repress potential challengers to authority.[45]

Security assistance can tip the balance towards the latter strategy. Governments that rely on taxing the population to generate revenue have incentives to provide public goods and services in return and must be responsive to the views of the public. Receipt of security assistance makes the government less dependent on taxation to generate revenue. This can decrease its incentive to provide for the needs of the population and protect its human rights, and can lessen the cost of government repression.

---

[43] Sullivan (n 5).

[44] Patricia Sullivan, Leo J. Blanken, and Ian C. Rice, 'Arming the Peace: Foreign Security Assistance and Human Rights in Post-Conflict Countries (2020) 31 Defence and Peace Economics 177, 196.

[45] Bruce Bueno de Mesquita and Alastair Smith, 'Leader Survival, Revolutions, and the Nature of Government Finance' (2010) 54 American Journal of Political Science 936; Sullivan et al (n 44) 180.

In addition, receipt of security assistance enables a regime to 'secure the allegiance of military elites by distribut[ing] military training, weapons, equipment, and funding as private goods'.[46] Such allegiance is crucial in societies in which civilian control over the military has not been institutionalized. This 'reinforces the privileged position of the military, empowering it relative to other State institutions and giving it an incentive to work with the ruling regime to repress liberalization efforts that are likely to redistribute power and resources away from the military'.[47]

The result may be that security assistance is used by a government to violate the human rights of its population. Such use is antithetical to liberal democratic values, and States to varying degrees require review of human rights performance as a condition to providing assistance. In the United States, for instance, human rights vetting of foreign security forces receiving US assistance is primarily done through two laws that govern security assistance granted by the Department of State and DoD.[48]

Both laws prohibit assistance from the departments if there is credible information that a receiving unit of a foreign security force has committed a gross violation of human rights. The restriction regarding the Department of State applies specifically to assistance provided under the Foreign Assistance Act and the Arms Export Control Act, while all funds appropriated to DoD are subject to the restriction if used for 'training, equipment, or other assistance' for the recipient unit.[49] Credible information, as interpreted by both departments, is determined by assessing a list of factors, considering the integrity of the source and the allegation. Some of these factors include whether the source has a previous history of accurately reporting allegations, how the information was gathered, any potential bias in the source, and information that contradicts the allegation.

The process of vetting units is conducted by State Department personnel[50] for compliance with both Leahy laws[51] and the policy for Leahy vetting is overseen

---

[46] Sullivan (n 43).

[47] Sullivan et al (n 44) 181.

[48] 22 U.S.C. § 2378d (2018); and 10 U.S.C. § 362.

[49] 10 U.S.C. § 362(a)(1).

[50] Congress appropriates direct funds for the Department of State to conduct vetting, see Nina Serafino and others, '"Leahy Law" Human Rights Provisions and Security Assistance: Issue Overview' (Congressional Research Service, 29 January 2014) <https://perma.cc/359Q-HCSH> accessed 21 February 2023.

[51] The DoD law requires the Secretary of Defense to consult with the Secretary of State prior to a decision to provide training, equipment or other assistance to a unit in order to give full consideration to any credible information available to the Department of State relating to a human rights violation by such unit. While vetting is not explicitly required in the Leahy Law, vetting of units by the State Department for the DoD ensures compliance with this requirement and helps to implement the law's requirements.

by the Department of State's Bureau of Democracy, Human Rights, and Labor (DRL).[52] If the Department of State determines that there is credible information the unit committed a gross violation of human rights, the unit will not be eligible to receive the proposed assistance.[53] Such a determination will be recorded in a database and, as required by law, a list of ineligible units will annually be made public by the Department of State.[54] If the unit is considered 'clean' because there is no credible information showing it committed a gross violation of human rights, it is eligible to receive assistance for up to twelve months before another round of vetting must occur.[55]

In 2015, the Departments of State and Defense issued a joint policy on remediation that provides guidance to both departments on the steps required for a tainted unit of a foreign security force to regain eligibility for assistance.[56] When determining whether appropriate remediation measures have taken place, the departments assess the totality of the circumstances in each case. Officials in both State and DoD will convene to analyse a list of factors in the joint policy, mainly whether (1) there has been a credible, impartial, and thorough investigation;[57] (2) a credible and impartial judicial or administrative adjudication has addressed the gross violations of human rights, affording due process to the accused; and (3) there has been appropriate and proportional sentencing to the crime committed.[58]

---

[52] The Bureau of Democracy, Human Rights, and Labor maintains guidance for Leahy vetting and provides training to those conducting Leahy vetting across the department. See Liana Rosen, 'Global Human Rights: Security Forces Vetting ("Leahy Laws")' (*In Focus, Congressional Research Service*, 5 August 2022) <https://perma.cc/5AGK-NMXX> accessed 21 February 2023.

[53] The Leahy Law requires that units determined to be ineligible for assistance be made 'publicly available, to the maximum extent practicable' (i.e. a unit must be listed publicly unless the Secretary of State determines, on a case-by-case basis, and reports to Congress, that the disclosure is not in the national security interest of the United States). The Secretary of State must also provide a detailed justification for such determination, which may be classified. See 22 U.S.C § 2378d(d)(7); and 22 U. S.C. § 2378d(e)(1).

[54] If, during vetting, the State Department determines that an entire force is tainted, and if it can be shown that a subunit was not responsible for any violations, then that subunit can be considered 'clean' for vetting purposes and, thus, eligible to receive assistance.

[55] US Department of State, 'Public Release of Foreign Security Forces Units Ineligible for Foreign Assistance Act of 1961 and Arms Export Control Act Assistance Pursuant to the State Leahy Law CY2020' (Bureau of Democracy, Human Rights, and Labor, Security and Human Rights) <https://perma.cc/7HFQ-BW25> accessed 21 February 2023.

[56] 'Joint Department of Defense (DoD) and Department of State (DoS) Policy on Remediation and the Resumption of Assistance under the Leahy Laws', in Secretary of Defence, 'Additional Guidance on Implementation of Section 8057(b), DoD Appropriations Act, 2014 (Division C of Public Law 113-76)('the DoD Leahy Law') and New or Fundamentally Different Units' (memorandum, OSD001632-15/CMD001915-15, 10 February 2015) <https://perma.cc/3YXF-NRZD> accessed 21 February 2023.

[57] Ibid. Attachment 2. If a credible investigation has commenced, the departments can determine, under the joint policy, to continue assistance to the unit, as long as the investigation proceeds without undue delay and the alleged perpetrators do not remain in the unit.

[58] Ibid. sec. 1b(3). The assessment of the sentencing may take into account the 'legal, judicial and administrative systems of the foreign government'.

592 COUNTERING HYBRID AND GREY ZONE THREATS

Executive branch officials, human rights activists, and lawmakers continue to debate the effectiveness of human rights vetting, especially vetting conducted under the Leahy laws. Although Leahy vetting generally maintains a positive record of ensuring that the United States does not work with tainted units, some argue that there can be more improvements in the process and possibly clarifications in law.

One main area of criticism is inconsistency in application of the vetting policies established by DRL. In 2013 and 2016, the US Government Accountability Office (GAO) found inconsistency in application of vetting policy, or, in some instances, complete disregard for the policy. The 2013 report resulted in DRL requiring embassy standard operating procedures (SOP) for Leahy vetting. However, it has taken years for every embassy to establish SOPs for Leahy vetting, lending credence to the argument that vetting is not consistently administered. Despite these and other challenges, the increase in US security assistance globally will continue to require human rights vetting of hundreds of units of foreign security forces every year. The increase will also continue to incentivize rights groups to encourage Congress to strengthen the Leahy laws or inject other kinds of human rights considerations into US security assistance decisions.

Security assistance to authoritarian regimes that pose a risk of human rights violations is perhaps the most pronounced instance of what a report by Thomas Carothers and Benjamin Press for the Carnegie Endowment for International Peace describes as the 'democracy-security dilemma'.[59] As they characterize this dilemma with regard to the United States:

confronting partner governments over their political shortcomings risks triggering hostility that would jeopardize the security benefits that such governments provide to Washington. Yet giving them a free pass on democracy and rights issues undercuts the credibility of U.S. appeals to values, bolstering the damaging perception that America only pushes for democracy against its adversaries or in strategically irrelevant countries.[60]

This dilemma was especially acute during the Cold War. US assistance designed to thwart an authoritarian Soviet Union sometimes led to partnerships with anticommunist autocrats who ruthlessly suppressed political opposition and democratic movements in their own States. In recent years, a broader set of

---

[59] Thomas Carothers and Benjamin Press, 'Navigating the Democracy-Security Dilemma in U.S. Foreign Policy: Lessons from Egypt, India, and Turkey' (Carnegie Endowment for International Peace, November 2021) <https://perma.cc/95QL-NGHX> accessed 21 February 2023.

[60] Ibid. 1. See also Rhonda Callaway and Elizabeth Matthews, *Strategic US Foreign Assistance: The Battle Between Human Rights and National Security* (Routledge 2008); Ted Piccone, Tom Malinowski, and Daniel Byman, 'U.S Security Assistance and Human Rights' (Brookings Institution, moderated panel, 12 December 2016) <https://perma.cc/67EQ-YZZV> accessed 21 February 2023.

SECURITY ASSISTANCE BY LIBERAL DEMOCRACIES   593

national security aims have led to the perceived need to provide security assistance to regimes that depart from liberal democratic values and engage in some violations of human rights.

As Carothers and Press note, there are three US current national security objectives in particular that reflect this phenomenon. First, international efforts to combat terrorism have resulted in 'counterterrorism cooperation with eighty-five countries between 2018 in 2020, most of which are democratically deficient.[61] Second, the desire to maintain regional stability in the Middle East has led the United States to rely significantly on autocratic states throughout the region.[62] Finally, concern about the increasing influence of China has resulted in deepening security ties with 'the range of democratic backsliders, like India and the Philippines, as well as some outright autocracies like Thailand and Vietnam.[63]

US relationships with Egypt and India offer useful illustrations of the dynamics of the democracy-security dilemma. Egypt became a close security partner of the United States in the Middle East after arriving at a peace agreement with Israel in the late 1970s. As Carothers and Press put it, 'Egypt's continued peaceful co-existence with Israel has largely trumped whatever concerns US administrations have had about the authoritarian politics that have prevailed in Egypt for most of the last forty years.[64]

During the Arab spring, for instance, the Obama administration was reluctant to call publicly for the removal of Egyptian President Hosni Mubarak, suggesting to him that he resign only when continuing in power seemed impossible. The administration sought to work constructively to promote democracy with Mubarak's elected successor Mohamed Morsi. After the military overthrow of Morsi in July 2013 brought Abdel Fattah el-Sisi to power, however, the United States notably elected not to publicly designate the overthrow as a coup due to sensitivity to a US law that would imperil continuing security assistance to Egypt.[65]

In the next appropriations bill, Congress effectively removed the coup restriction on security assistance to Egypt, but conditioned the $1.3 billion in military assistance on taking specific steps towards a transition to democracy, including parliamentary and presidential elections. After Egypt began participating

---

[61] Carothers and Press (n 59) 6.
[62] Ibid.
[63] Ibid.
[64] Ibid. 7.
[65] The Department of State's annual appropriations bill includes 'the coup restriction', which restricts certain kinds of assistance, including security assistance, when a country's 'duly elected head of government is deposed by military coup d'etat or decree'. The most recent version of the provision is in Division K, Section 7008 of the Department of State, Foreign Operations, and Related Programs Appropriations Act for Fiscal Year 2022. See Consolidated Appropriations Act, 2022 Pub. L. No. 117-103, 136 Stat. 49, 593. The Obama administration never stated publicly that a coup occurred in Egypt in 2013, but internally officials were aware that security assistance was restricted under Section 7008.

in military operations against the Islamic State, however, the administration resumed assistance to the country. In addition, it provided $650 million in foreign military financing to Egypt notwithstanding the Secretary of Defense's determination that the United States was 'not yet able to certify that Egypt is taking steps to support a democratic transition'.[66]

The Obama administration continued to waive human rights conditions for military aid in succeeding years on the ground of national security. As Carothers and Press note, 'By 2015, the White House was openly pushing for human rights and democracy aid conditionality to be removed from appropriations legislation so that it would not have to issue an awkward certification of political progress that was clearly not actually happening'.[67]

The Trump administration generally did not press Egypt on human rights issues, but the Biden administration kept its distance from the Sisi regime for a few months after President Biden took office. The State Department issued a report in March 2021 citing a host of serious human rights abuses in the country, including:

> unlawful or arbitrary killings, including extrajudicial killings by the government or its agents and terrorist groups; forced disappearance; torture and cases of cruel, inhuman, or degrading treatment or punishment by the government; harsh and life-threatening prison conditions; [and] arbitrary detention.[68]

The report also found 'serious restrictions on free expression, the press, and the internet, including arrests or prosecutions of journalists, censorship, site blocking, and the existence of criminal libel laws, which were not enforced; [and] substantial interference with the rights of peaceful assembly and freedom of association'.[69]

In May 2021, however, the United States asked Egypt to negotiate a cease-fire between Hamas and Israel in the face of increasing hostilities. When Egypt was able to do so, President Biden responded with phone calls to Sisi, and Secretary of State Blinken visited the country to meet with him. Both raised human rights concerns with Sisi, but with little success.

The Secretary of State historically had waived for Egypt each year the statutory requirement that it certify Egypt's progress toward improving human rights on the ground that the waiver was important for the national security interests of

---

[66] Carothers and Press (n 59) 8–9.

[67] Ibid. 9.

[68] US Department of State, '2020 Country Reports on Human Rights Practices: Egypt' (Bureau of Democracy, Human Rights, and Labor, 30 March 2021) <https://perma.cc/9A2P-KABG> accessed 22 February 2023.

[69] Ibid.

the United States. In January 2022, however, the Secretary refused to issue such a waiver for $130 million of the $1.3 billion military assistance package to Egypt. The administration reportedly conditioned release of the aid on Egypt's end to prosecutions against civil society organizations and dismissal of charges against or release of sixteen individuals whose cases the United States has repeatedly raised with Sisi in the past.[70]

Human rights organizations criticized this step as too modest and unlikely to influence Egypt's practices. One analyst at Human Rights Watch, for instance, said:

> That sends a signal to the Egyptian government that they can definitely get what they want with time, and that they don't really have to meet any concrete benchmarks, and that the release of just a few activists can serve as the fig leaf to the Biden administration and others who want to continue doing business as usual.[71]

A State Department spokesperson, however, said, 'Our relationship with Egypt is multifaceted, and Egypt is a valuable partner across many fronts. The United States remains committed to engaging with Egypt on human rights issues'.[72] Together, these statements serve as a good illustration of the tensions in the democracy-security dilemma. As Carothers and Press put it, 'In short, Biden's determination to elevate the place of democracy and rights in US policy toward Sisi's Egypt has already clashed sharply with the deeply rooted habit of maintaining close security ties with the country. The result so far has been more continuity than change'.[73]

India has become an important US partner more recently than Egypt, but similar issues have begun to arise in that relationship. The two countries started to move closer during the George W. Bush administration, but cooperation has accelerated in recent years. US concern about rising Chinese influence in South Asia and the Indian Ocean region led it in early 2015 to announce with India a Joint Strategic Vision for the Asia-Pacific and Indian Ocean Region. President Obama described India as a major defence partner, and entered into several defence and arms agreements with it. Along with the United States, Australia, and Japan, India also is now a member of the Quadrilateral Dialogue, established to provide a coalition of democratic states to address Chinese ambitions.

---

[70] Lara Jakes and Mona El-Naggar, 'U.S. Blocks $130 Million in Aid for Egypt over Rights Abuses' *New York Times* (New York, 28 January 2022) <https://perma.cc/TBA6-JGLD> accessed 22 February 2022.

[71] Ibid. para. 23, quoting Amir Magdi.

[72] Ibid. para 19.

[73] Carothers and Press (n 59) 11.

596 COUNTERING HYBRID AND GREY ZONE THREATS

All this has been made possible by Indian Prime Minister Narendra Modi's willingness to embrace a close partnership with the United States, in contrast to many of his predecessor's wariness about such a relationship. At the same time, however, Modi has adopted increasingly illiberal policies at home based on sectarian Hindu ideology. These have included the use of incendiary Islamophobic rhetoric and large-scale voter suppression.

In advance of the 2019 election, for instance, Modi removed an estimated 120 million eligible voters from the electoral roll by demanding residency documentation. 'The aim', says an observer, 'was to erase religious groups that are seen as non-Indian in the Hindutva ideology, leading to the removal of some 70 million Muslims and Dalits'.[74] The observer concluded that Modi's style of leadership 'poses an existential threat to the world's largest democracy. Through his wildly successful promotion of Hindutva ideology, Modi is poised to remake India into a Russian-style 'managed democracy'—one retaining all the trappings of democracy while operating as a de facto autocracy'.[75]

The US State Department's March 2021 report on human rights practices in India stated that 'significant human rights issue' in the country included

> unlawful and arbitrary killings, including extrajudicial killings perpetrated by police; torture and cases of cruel, inhuman, or degrading treatment or punishment by some police and prison officials; arbitrary arrest and detention by government authorities; harsh and life-threatening prison conditions; political prisoners or detainees in certain states; [and] restrictions on freedom of expression and the press, including violence, threats of violence, or unjustified arrests or prosecutions against journalists.[76]

The report said, 'Despite government efforts to address abuses, a lack of accountability for official misconduct persisted at all levels of government, contributing to widespread impunity'.[77]

While the United States privately raises concerns about these practices, its public pronouncements tend to emphasize shared democratic aspirations between the United States and India rather than to levy direct criticism. At a civil society roundtable in New Delhi, for instance, Secretary Blinken said that:

---

[74] Azeem Ibrahim, 'Modi's Slide Toward Autocracy', *Foreign Policy* (13 July 2020) <https://perma.cc/X6Y4-33L2> accessed 22 February 2023.

[75] Ibid.

[76] US Department of State, '2020 Country Reports on Human Rights Practices: India' (Bureau of Democracy, Human Rights, and Labor, 30 March 2021) <https://perma.cc/5QLV-9WXN> accessed 22 February 2023.

[77] Ibid.

both of our democracies are works in progress. As friends, we talk about that, because doing the hard work of strengthening democracy and making our ideals real is often challenging. We know that firsthand in the United States, where we aspire to be, in the words of our founders, a more perfect union. That's an acknowledgement from day one of our country that in a sense we will always fall short of the mark, but that the way to make progress is by constantly trying to achieve those ideals.[78]

As Carothers and Press put it, the United States is in the process of 'seeking a path forward that balances democracy, rights, and values with the increasing geostrategic importance of the US-India relationship'.[79]

Some may contest the assertion that there is a tension between interest in security and democracy, and argue that over the long term, democratic reforms will reduce grievances that can lead to destabilizing extremism that jeopardizes donor State security interests.[80] This may be true in the long run, if donor States are actually able to effectuate some kind of meaningful influence, and it suggests that liberal democracies should seek ways to encourage recipients of assistance to undertake such reforms. As a practical matter in the near to medium term, however, acknowledging and attempting to navigate the democracy-security dilemma will be a crucial challenge.

Carothers and Press suggest a set of questions that the United States should ask when considering security assistance to states about which there may be human rights concerns. First, what are the particular security interests that assistance is designed to advance?[81] There may be different views within the government about the answer to this question. Furthermore, 'bureaucratic autopilot' may result in people accepting without rigorously examining putative interests that are based on outdated assumptions.[82]

Second, what is the relationship between US security interests ostensibly furthered by assistance and the recipients' failure to fully adhere to democratic principles?[83] There may be no close relationship, US security interests may benefit from local partner democratic reforms, or those interests may be impaired by such reforms.

A common view within the foreign policy community is that there is no relationship between the two—that Egypt is helping serve serving US security

---

[78] Antony J. Blinken, 'Opening Remarks at a Civil Society Roundtable' (US Department of State, New Delhi, 28 July 2021) <https://perma.cc/6VBJ-MHF8> 22 February 2023.

[79] Carothers and Press (n 59) 19.

[80] See e.g. Sarah Leah Whitson, 'The Human Rights vs. National Security Dilemma Is a Fallacy' (Foreign Policy, January 10, 2022) <https://perma.cc/7CGS-9XYL> accessed 22 February 2023.

[81] Carothers and Press (n 59) 20.

[82] Ibid.

[83] Ibid.

598 COUNTERING HYBRID AND GREY ZONE THREATS

interests regardless of its illiberal policies.[84] Some would even go further and argue that increasing democratization in Egypt might negatively affect US security interests, such as occurred with the election of the Muslim Brotherhood and the Morsi government.[85] Others, however, especially civil society organizations, maintain that that Sisi's unwavering repression over time could alienate the population and lead to greater radicalization and eventual instability that would undermine US interests in the long run.[86] This divergence of opinion underscores the way in which the cyclical nature of leadership in democracy potentially can lead to a focus on short-term goals at the expensive of longer-term strategic thinking.

With respect to India, the movement away from liberalism under Modi has not affected India's ability or willingness to further US national security interests as a member of the Indo-Pacific partnership. Some may contend that Modi's party's political dominance in fact has given it the opportunity to depart from historical Indian reluctance to align with the United States and its national security goals. Reasonable people may disagree, but as the Carnegie Endowment report emphasizes, 'The point is that one must examine the relationship closely rather than proceed on the basis of a priori assumptions'.

The third question is how US security interests might be threatened if the United States exerts pressure on a security partner to make democratic reforms.[87] Many in the US foreign policy bureaucracy assume that doing so will make a partner less willing to help further US security interests. The likelihood of this will depend, however, on the extent to which the partner has interests that are aligned with the United States. India's willingness to be more confrontational with China, for instance, reflects its own self-interest in the region and not simply acquiescence in US wishes. Thus, 'The notion that the security partner is taking a given stance on a certain issue as a favour to Washington—and thereby may abandon that stance if Washington is not nice to it—is frequently incorrect'.[88] An important consideration in contemplating whether to raise human rights issues therefore is the extent to which the United States has leverage because partner interests are aligned with those of the United States.

In addition, restraint in discussing human rights issues will not necessarily guarantee that a security partner will cooperate with the United States on most issues. US reluctance to express disapproval of Philippine President Rodrigo Duterte's illiberal actions have not stopped him from periodically threatening to discontinue cooperation with the US. Again, the point is that decision-making

[84] Ibid.
[85] Ibid.
[86] Ibid.
[87] Ibid. 21.
[88] Ibid.

should not automatically assume that exerting pressure will lead a partner to resist taking steps to further US interests.

A fourth question is how the United States can best attempt to exert influence on democracy and human rights issues in ways that enhance the likelihood that a partner will undertake meaningful progress on them.[89] Carothers and Press suggest that appeals to self-interest can be especially effective, rather than simply invoking general liberal democratic principles. This requires framing arguments in terms that are sensitive to the local context. The United States also should be clear in advance about the limits of what it will tolerate and have a menu of responses available in case those limits are transgressed.

Finally, the United States must analyse what it can reasonably hope to accomplish by pushing more aggressively on a partner to improve its performance on democratic and human rights issues.[90] The answers to this are likely to differ depending on whether the partner is an entrenched authoritarian government or a state that has some democratic features but is beginning to backslide. The United States will also have to take into consideration the recipient State's capacity or lack thereof to improve performance (e.g. considering whether a state would need assistance in establishing accountability measures for security forces that commit human rights violations).

In addition, it is important to consider not only the effects of pressure on the government but on other members of the domestic political community who may gain more visibility and legitimacy as a result of criticism or calls for reform. These elements may complement US efforts and have more local political legitimacy than a donor State. At the same time, the United States must avoid crossing the line from support to actual or perceived interference in the partner's political process. Pushing for greater electoral integrity, for instance, may be more effective than expressing support for certain candidates or groups.

Finally, while Carothers and Press do not specifically elaborate on it, another consideration in assessing whether to exert pressure on human rights issues is how likely a partner will turn to illiberal donors that are much less sensitive to such issues. This is especially a concern if such a donor is a peer or near-peer competitor of the United States such as China or Russia, or an aspiring regional hegemon like Iran. China, for instance, maintains that its foreign policy is rooted in tolerance and respect for sovereignty. As a practical matter, this means that Beijing is generally indifferent to the characteristics of the regimes to which it provides various forms of support.

Liberal democracies' decisions about security assistance to relatively stable but democratically deficient states thus require managing tensions between

---

[89] Ibid. 22.
[90] Ibid. 23.

strengthening security and promoting democracy. There is unlikely to be any simple resolution of these tensions, but careful analysis of each context can provide donor States with a clear-eyed assessment of trade-offs that may be necessary.

5. Conclusion

Providing security assistance to partner states by liberal democracies has the potential to serve as an effective instrument of competition in the grey zone. It ideally can extend donor State influence while avoiding direct intervention and confrontation with adversaries. At the same time, liberal democracies face challenges in ensuring that such assistance effectively meets their security needs in ways that are consistent with liberal democratic values. Navigating these challenges requires that States be sensitive to the practical demands of enhancing partner State capabilities, and the values that may be in tension as they attempt to do so. This chapter has suggested a framework for identifying these challenges and appreciating the trade-offs that they may require.

27
The Practice of Legal Resilience
Insights from the Maritime Incident of 31 May 2010

Marlene Mazel

1. Introduction

Since its inception, Israel has been involved in numerous armed conflicts against different adversaries. The nature of these conflicts has evolved—from State to non-State adversaries, from open to urban warfare, from states of war to grey zone conflict. With the advent of hybrid warfare,[1] which is often interpreted to include legal warfare,[2] Israel has become cognizant of the need to integrate more closely its military and non-military goals, addressing the expansion of the battlefield to different arenas, including the court of law and the court of public opinion.

Legal 'battles' are very important to win. Legal tactics are often used to influence public opinion.

Over the past two decades, there has been an increase, on a global level, in the strategic use of legal terminology and legal proceedings by States, non-State actors, non-governmental organizations (NGOs), and other actors in what is often termed 'lawfare'; that is, the use of legal institutions and mechanisms to achieve tactical and strategic goals, both on and beyond the battlefield. The use of legal strategies is becoming an integral part of conflict. These strategies influence how State and non-State actors frame not only their military strategy but also

---

[1] Though hybrid warfare has multiple definitions, a helpful definition in the context of understanding lawfare is that hybrid warfare is 'the synchronized use of multiple instruments of power tailored to specific vulnerabilities across the full spectrum of societal functions to achieve synergistic effects'. See Patrick J. Cullen and Erik Reichborn-Kjennerud, 'Understanding Hybrid Warfare' (MCDC Countering Hybrid Warfare Project 2017) <https://assets.publishing.service.gov.uk/gov ernment/uploads/system/uploads/attachment_data/file/647776/dar_mcdc_hybrid_warfare.pdf> accessed 27 April 2023. The law is one of the instruments of power that may be used in hybrid warfare.

[2] Avichai Mandelblit, 'Lawfare: The Legal Front of the IDF' (2012) 4 Military and Strategic Affairs 51. The former Military Advocate General of the Israel Defense Forces emphasized the importance of the Israeli Defense Forces (IDF) giving due consideration to the legal front, in particular in asymmetrical confrontations in densely populated urban areas. Mandelblit noted that historically two key fronts were military and political, but it is no longer sufficient for the military just to prepare for these two fronts as strategic gains are also sought on two additional fronts—the media front and the legal front.

Marlene Mazel, *The Practice of Legal Resilience* In: *Hybrid Threats and Grey Zone Conflict.* Edited by: Mitt Regan and Aurel Sari, Oxford University Press. © Oxford University Press 2024. DOI: 10.1093/oso/9780197744772.003.0027

602 COUNTERING HYBRID AND GREY ZONE THREATS

their legitimacy narrative. The growing use of lawfare has led Israel, the United Kingdom, Spain, France, Belgium, and the North Atlantic Treaty Organization (NATO) to broaden their understanding and expertise in this expanding arena.[3]

The purpose of this chapter is to share a practitioners' perspective on how the law is used for strategic purposes, both on and off the kinetic battlefield, in national and international legal fora. First, the chapter will describe some of the operational legal tools, strategies, and terminology used against Israel and Israeli officials, and measures taken by the Israeli government to respond to this emergent phenomenon. Second, the chapter will describe how Israel's adversaries use legal tools to promote their political and/or military agenda, and how the use of these tools may affect not only the conflict but the development of law. Third, the 31 May 2010 maritime incident, an illustrative case study, reflects how legal strategies are deployed. The chapter will share some insights drawn from this incident, and from Israel's experience, regarding how States and organizations can increase and strengthen their capacity and resilience in this critically important domain.

1.1 The use of legal operations against Israel

On 18 June 2001, in the midst of a relentless campaign of Palestinian terrorist attacks in Israel, which came to be known as the Second Intifada, a 'shot' was fired in Belgium, aimed at a target thousands of miles away. Rather than using a firearm, these adversaries drafted a criminal complaint, targeted at the Prime Minister of Israel at the time, Ariel Sharon.[4] This complaint marked the opening

---

[3] See e.g. United Kingdom Ministry of Defence, 'UK Defence Doctrine', Joint Doctrine Publication 0-01 (6th edn, 2022) <https://assets.publishing.service.gov.uk/government/uploads/system/uplo ads/attachment_data/file/1118720/UK_Defence_Doctrine_Ed6.pdf> accessed 4 April 2023. See also Ministère des Armées, 'Strategic Update 2021' (2021) para. 4 <https://cd-geneve.delegfrance. org/IMG/pdf/strategic_review_2021_-_10_key_points-3.pdf?2350/133c682f3374f15bc786c19b6 b0a1d10eb0656f7> accessed 4 April 2023.

[4] For a full discussion of the *Sharon* case see, Rephael Ben-Ari, 'Universal Jurisdiction: Chronicle of a Death Foretold' (2015) 43 Denver Journal of International Law and Policy 165, 174. The complaint was filed against former Prime Minister Ariel Sharon and the Director-General of the Ministry of Defense, Amos Yaron, for genocide, crimes against humanity and war crimes, alleging that these officials were responsible for the massacre carried out by Lebanese Christian Phlange in Lebanon in 1982. The political nature of the complaint was evident in several ways. First, the decision to file the complaint in Belgium, which was soon to assume the European Union (EU) presidency. Second, the fact that the complaint was filed a mere three months after Prime Minister Ariel Sharon was elected, and more than two decades after the incident. Third, that the complaint was neither filed in Lebanon nor filed against the Lebanese Christian Phlange. Fourth, it was accompanied by a well-orchestrated media campaign, including a website dedicated to the case. Israel challenged the legality of the Belgian law under international law on several grounds, including immunity and that the incident was fully examined in Israel. Belgium amended its law to limit its exercise of universal jurisdiction to cases with jurisdictional links to Belgium. The case against Israeli officials was dismissed on

THE PRACTICE OF LEGAL RESILIENCE   603

salvo in what has since developed into a concerted and coordinated legal battle directed against the State of Israel and its officials in various national and international fora around the world.[5]

Though the legal domain is not new, perhaps what has changed is that as more legal and media tools have become available, the law can be more effective in framing the narrative in hybrid warfare.[6] In this domain, the law is often used to undermine the legitimacy of the adversary's military campaign. Legal strategies are employed to produce a psychological effect on the public and on soldiers, commanders, and/or officials participating in the campaign. Some scholars have termed this 'reputational lawfare.'[7] It seems that there is increasing use of the legal sphere as legal strategies can have significant impact in framing the narrative and mobilizing support before, during, and long after the battle has ended.

As adversaries of the State of Israel actively sought to use the law to promote their military and political objectives, Israeli government attorneys began to work in this domain as far back as 2001. The government set up a team of attorneys within the Ministry of Justice specifically tasked with defending Israel and Israeli officials in the international legal arena. Government attorneys work as part of several inter-agency committees and study and contend with this emerging domain. Over time it became clear to practitioners working in Israel, in other States, and in organizations such as NATO that understanding the legal domain is critical to protecting national and global security.

---

immunity and jurisdictional grounds. See also Irit Kohn, 'The Suit against Sharon in Belgium: A Case Analysis' (Jerusalem Center for Public Affairs, 2007) https://jcpa.org/article/the-suit-against-sharon-in-belgium-a-case-analysis/, accessed 9 February 2023; Irit Kohn, 'Lessons Learned in Belgium' (article on file with the author); Barak M. Seener, 'Targeting Israelis via International Law: Israel and Its Enemies' (2009) 16 Middle East Quarterly 43.

[5] One of the non-governmental organizations active in this field, the Palestinian Centre for Human Rights (PCHR), published a summary of its legal arguments and information regarding the cases filed against Israel and Israeli officials on the basis of universal jurisdiction: Palestinian Centre for Human Rights, 'The Principle and Practice of Universal Jurisdiction: PCHR's Work in the occupied Palestinian territory' (2010) <https://www.fidh.org/IMG/pdf/PCHR_Work_Report_Web.pdf> accessed 1 February 2023.

[6] Though it seemed to Israeli government officials handling the Sharon complaint in Belgium that this was a new phenomenon, scholars have opined that the use of the law to promote military or political goals has always existed, including in the context of the Middle East conflict, and such use even predated the existence of the State. See Steven E. Zipperstein, *Law and the Arab–Israeli Conflict: The Trials of Palestine* (Routledge 2020) 82; dating the first use of law in the conflict to the year 1727, when residents claimed Jewish prayer at the Western Wall disturbed them, resulting in an order forbidding Jews to pray there.

[7] Amelie Ferey, 'Towards a War of Norms? From Lawfare to Legal Operations' (Securities Studies Center, 2022) 15 <https://www.ifri.org/sites/default/files/atoms/files/ferey_lawfare_2022_us.pdf> accessed 2 April 2023. Ferey defined reputational lawfare as 'mobilizing legal arguments to adversely affect the reputation of a practice and the parties involved in it. Legal arguments are therefore also communication tools'.

1.2 Lawfare terminology

At around the same time, the legal campaign against Israel was getting off the ground, Col. Charles J. Dunlap, Jr., a former US Air Force Judge Advocate General, published a seminal article identifying 'lawfare' as an emerging and potentially worrisome trend in international military conflicts and the laws that govern them. Dunlap came to define lawfare as 'the strategy of using—or misusing—law as a substitute for traditional military means to achieve a warfighting objective'.[8]

Terminology and definitions regarding these issues are not uniform, neither in doctrine nor in government practice. In Israel, the term most frequently used by practitioners is 'לוחמה משפטית', which can be translated as 'legal warfare' or 'legal operations in warfare'. The Hebrew terminology often used is similar, in its intent, to that used by NATO, Supreme Headquarters Allied Powers Europe (SHAPE), which uses the term 'legal operations' to describe the use of the legal domain to achieve objectives at the tactical, operational, or strategic/political levels.[9] Other experts in the field, such as Aurel Sari, have adopted or used the term 'legal resilience'.[10]

Another emerging term used in the field is 'legal gamesmanship' which also seems to be framed in broader terms than the mere use of the law during military conflict itself. Legal gamesmanship as defined:

> refers to actions by a state or attributable to a state that aim to leverage or exploit the structural, normative, or instrumental functions of law to achieve national objectives in a competitive environment. These instruments can apply in contexts broader than war, including the full spectrum of peace, gray zone, and conflict, and broader than the military context, including the use of all instruments of national power. 'Legal gamesmanship' is not a pejorative, most

---

[8] Charles J. Dunlap, Jr., 'Law and Military Interventions: Preserving Humanitarian Values in 21st Conflicts' (paper presented at Harvard University, Carr Center, Humanitarian Challenges in Military Intervention Conference 2001) <https://people.duke.edu/~pfeaver/dunlap.pdf> accessed on 2 April 2023. See also Orde F. Kittrie, *Lawfare, Law as A Weapon of War* (Oxford University Press 2016), 4–8, discussing the meaning and study of lawfare and a brief overview of lawfare literature.

[9] Major General Barre R. Seguin, Deputy Chief of Staff, NATO Strategic Employment Supreme Headquarters Allied Powers Europe, 'The Use of Legal Operations in a Context of Hybrid Threats and Strategic Competition', as delivered in January 2020 at the *Waging and Defending against Lawfare Symposium*, <https://sites.duke.edu/lawfire/2020/03/13/a-warfighters-perspective-on-lawfare-in-an-era-of-hybrid-threats-and-strategic-competition> accessed 2 April 2023. Major General Barre noted that 'the use of legal operations allows our potential adversaries to have a significant impact—while avoiding the use of kinetic means—and remaining under the use of armed force threshold. Several States and non-State actors are increasingly using the legal domain in order to achieve their strategic objectives and interests—effectively by tampering with the rules-based international order (RBIO)—and destabilizing international relations'.

[10] Aurel Sari, 'Legal Resilience in an Era of Grey Zone Conflicts and Hybrid Threats' (2020) 33 Cambridge Review of International Affairs 846.

if not all state actors engage in legal gamesmanship from time to time. Not all legal gamesmanship constitutes violations of law; not all violations of law are legal gamesmanship.[11]

The terminology of legal gamesmanship aptly describes the strategic aspects of the legal domain, though in addition to States and actions attributable to state actors, there may also be other actors active in the legal domain.

1.3 The lawfare battlefield as a distinct professional field

It seems that Israel was the first State to create a team of governmental attorneys specifically tasked to address this arena.[12] Though some are of the view that there is no need for a specific new field, as the legal domain merely describes the ordinary practice of State legal advisers who have the requisite expertise, there is no additional staffing or specific expertise required. However, in recent years, a shift has occurred as some States and experts practicing in the field have found that allocating human and financial resources to better understand and navigate this legal domain is both wise and constructive. Moreover, practitioners found that using terms such as 'lawfare', 'legal operations', 'legal resilience', or 'legal gamesmanship' enables them to explain, both domestically and internationally, the strategic importance of the field. Two decades of robust global practice in this field reflects that resourcing the legal domain as a separate domain with attorneys that have the requisite expertise is not only important, it is critical to increasing the State's domestic capacity and effectiveness in this expanding arena.

As the United Kingdom explained in its 2022 Defence Doctrine:

> Law is central to conflicts. The use of UK and international law by those opposed to the UK government's conduct of Defence activities, so called 'lawfare', has a real impact on how we do our business. Lawfare influences our priorities and informs permissions. The law can be used by adversary states to undermine the legitimacy of the UK government's position directly, or by civil society proxies through vexatious litigation to prevent or slow activities. We must ensure that our legal frameworks continue to allow us to meet our ethical standards while

---

[11] Pavel Kriz et al, 'Legal Gamesmanship and Rules-Based Order?' (17 May 2022) Strategic Competition Seminar Series #9, No. 06.

[12] Another State active in the field early on was China. Legal warfare (along with media/public opinion and psychological warfare) is one of the three modes of warfare China incorporated into its military strategy alongside kinetic warfare in 2003. See Kittrie (n 8) 162; Jill I. Goldenziel, 'Law as a Battlefield: The US, China and the Global Escalation of Lawfare' (2021) 106 Cornell Law Review 1084, 1092.

606   COUNTERING HYBRID AND GREY ZONE THREATS

reflecting the realities of the operating environment and its tempo. Furthermore, maintaining legitimacy is crucial to campaign authority. It builds morale and promotes cohesion, both within a force and between coalition partners, and confers both the freedom to act and constraints on military activity. We must be mindful of the risk of vicarious liability when operating with partners.[13]

Understanding, acknowledging, and resourcing the legal domain has several significant advantages. First, it is helpful in creating what Andrés B. Muñoz Mosquera, NATO Commander's Legal Advisor and Director of the Allied Command Operations (ACO) Office of Legal Affairs, SHAPE, has described as a 'lawfare state of mind'.[14] Just as military commanders have found that the methodical study of prior military battles and battlefield strategies increases their ability to think operationally, both on and off the battlefield, lawyers have found that the methodical study and monitoring of the legal domain enriches and expands their strategic thinking. This expansive approach and unique expertise became apparent to participants of the Israel-NATO ongoing legal dialogue, which enriched our respective understanding of legal operations in hybrid warfare and grey zone conflict.[15]

Second, as NATO, Allied Command Operations Office of Legal Affairs explained in their directive, the task of legal advisers in this domain is to 'maintain a persistent and comprehensive understanding of the legal environment which helps to anticipate and identify legal threats, enablers and hostile legal operations in the legal domain'.[16]

---

[13]   United Kingdom Ministry of Defence (n 3).

[14]   Remarks of Andrés B. Muñoz Mosquera at Allied Command Operations Legal Affairs Conference in Sevilla, Spain, May 2019 (not published).

[15]   Since 2018, NATO and the State of Israel have engaged in an ongoing strategic legal resilience dialogue, further to the Individual Partnership and Cooperation Programme (IPCP). The legal resilience dialogue includes the study of the legal domain and developing operational strategies and doctrines. Recognizing the importance of the dialogue, NATO awarded two Israeli government lawyers the *Serge Lazareff* Prize for contributing to NATO's work in the legal field, see Yonah Jeremy Bob, 'Israel Gov't Lawyers Help NATO Fight Lawfare, Receive Awards', *Jerusalem Post* (Jerusalem, 2 September 2019) <https://www.jpost.com/israel-news/israel-govt-lawyers-help-nato-fight-lawfare-receive-awards-600346> accessed 9 February 2023: "The dialogue, which is part of Israel's broader cooperation with NATO, involved in-depth discussions regarding how the law can be used to promote a military and political campaign, and what measures democratic states can take when these strategies are used against them or their officials by terrorist actors and enemy states promoting a political agenda," the (Justice) ministry said in a statement to the [Jerusalem] Post. (. . .) Muñoz described the dialogue that started in March 2018 as "bliss, because [NATO] started discovering that we were not inventing or making up anything, that lawfare or legal operations or hostile legal operations were really happening" ' Multilateral discussions regarding the Law of Armed Conflict are also important, and the IDF hosts a biannual International Conference on the Law of Armed Conflict (LOAC), see <https://www.idf.il/en/mini-sites/military-advocate-general-s-corps/conferences-on-the-law-of-armed-conflict/#:~:text=The%20most%20recent%20IDF%20International,20%20countries%2C%20organizations%20and%20institutions> accessed 9 February 2023.

[16]   ACO Legal Operations Directive 080-119 (5 May 2022).

Third, as the United Kingdom Ministry of Defence noted, maintaining legitimacy of military operations, and the perception of military operations in the public sphere are 'crucial to campaign authority'. Besides providing the public with an ongoing assessment supporting the legality of the military's conduct, the UK Defence Doctrine suggests that the military should proactively articulate the legal authority for their military operations to their own soldiers and to relevant audiences, anticipate the use of the law in operational planning, and 'robustly' call out the adversary's abuses of the law.[17]

1.4 The rule of law and lawfare

There is an ongoing robust debate regarding the legitimacy of the use of lawfare. I am of the view that like warfare, the use of lawfare, in of itself, is neither legitimate nor illegitimate. As reflected in the definition of legal gamesmanship, the term is not considered 'a pejorative'. It is the evaluation of a specific legal operation, which will enable a determination of its legitimacy, and whether the law is being abused. As the UK stated in their 2022 Defence Doctrine:

> Legitimacy encompasses the legal, moral, political, diplomatic and ethical propriety of the conduct of military forces at both an organization and individual level. Legitimacy is based upon both subjective perceptions, such as the values, beliefs and opinions of a variety of audiences, and demonstrable, objective legality. Therefore, the audiences and their perceptions of legitimacy will vary with each operation. It follows that the authority for military action, both legal and political, should be articulated clearly to members of our Armed Forces, the public, international audiences, and to our opponents and their domestic populations. The potential for the law to be used against us must be anticipated in operational planning. Equally, we must be robust in calling out our adversaries' abuses of the law.[18]

Moreover, it is worth recalling, as the former Military Advocate General of the Israel Defense Forces, Dr. Avihai Mandelblit, stated, that it is of vital importance to investigate credible claims of violations within the State's domestic legal system. Such complaints are constructive, and also assist law-abiding armies improve their procedures and actions.[19]

---

[17] See United Kingdom Ministry of Defence (n 3) para. 2.51.
[18] Ibid.
[19] Mandelblit (n 2) 56.

608 COUNTERING HYBRID AND GREY ZONE THREATS

When a campaign includes the filing of complaints in foreign jurisdictions, raising allegations against armed forces, identifying a legal case or tactic as 'lawfare' as part of a defensive counter-lawfare campaign, is in no way a tool in the service of impunity. Nor does it reflect an opinion with regard to the merits of such complaints. As States have an independent obligation to fully examine credible allegations of violations of the laws of armed conflict, Israel implements the laws of armed conflict and is under an obligation to examine alleged violations in accordance with international law in its domestic system.[20]

As Andrés B. Muñoz Mosquera and Nikoleta Chalanoul state in their chapter in the present volume, discussing the grey zone and the law:

> While continued compliance with the applicable rules of international law may seem to put States and organizations targeted by grey zone actions at a disadvantage, respect for the rule of law in the face of illegality is also source of strength. Hostile actors circumventing and abusing the law expose themselves not only to international condemnation, thereby putting their reputation at risk, but in doing so also offer a justification and rationale for appropriate countermeasures, for instance in the form of sanctions and embargoes. Moreover, countering lawfare and other malign legal activities requires measures in the legal domain, including strengthening legal interoperability and cooperation, which in turn demands respect for the rule of law.[21]

As adversaries, who themselves do not abide by the rule of law, use legal terminology and abuse legal institutions for political and military gain, States and organizations should take proactive measures to safeguard the legitimacy of their actions. In doing so, they also preserve the integrity of bedrock principles of international law. Moreover, States and scholars have expressed concern that failure to do so may impair the functioning of the rules-based international system, thereby compromising the integrity of international law and institutions.

---

[20] Marlene Mazel, 'Compliance with the Law of Armed Conflict: An Israeli Perspective', in *Military Self-Interest in Accountability for Core International Crimes*, Morten Bergsmo and Song Tianying (Torkel Opsahl 2015). See also Gilad Noam, 'Some Reflections on the Role of Military Justice Mechanisms in the International Criminal Justice System', in *Quality Control in Criminal Investigation*, edited by Xabier Agirre Aranburu et al (Torkel Opsahl 2020) 1035. Israel has oversight procedures for compliance with the Law of Armed Conflict, which includes training IDF forces in the law of armed conflict and operational compliance. IDF lawyers, subject only to the Military Advocate General, are available at different command levels to provide advice before, during, and after operations. The MAG's legal advice is subject to review in the civilian judicial system, by the Attorney General and by the Supreme Court of Israel. Israel has also taken numerous measures to improve its domestic system of examining alleged violations of the laws of armed conflict.
[21] See Andrés B. Muñoz Mosquera and Nikoleta Chalanouli, chapter 15, in this volume, 19–20.

2. Piercing the legal operational veil—strategies and methods

2.1 Identifying strategic litigation

Strategic litigation, in the context of the legal domain, is when a legal complaint and proceeding is used as a vehicle to achieve a goal that is beyond or unrelated to what can be achieved in the context of the litigation itself. The filing of complaints, at the same time that a democratic State or organization is undertaking a factual examination of specific allegations may be an indicator of strategic litigation. Various analytical tools may be used to help recognize whether a specific complaint filed in one jurisdiction may be part of a broader domestic and/or international strategic litigation campaign.

Israel and other States and practitioners in the field have identified several indicators that may be of assistance in identifying strategic litigation. These can include when:

1. after examination of the complaint, there is no factual basis to believe that there has been a violation of the law or of the laws of armed conflict;
2. the purpose of filing the complaint is to attract media attention and/or to advance the adversary's narrative and influence public opinion;
3. a doctrine or legal principle is employed in bad faith or inconsistently with its designated purpose to achieve strategic gain;
4. the potential impact sought through the action;
5. understanding the use of proxies and who is behind the claim;
6. whether the legal action is genuine or part of a broader legal goal;
7. whether the plaintiff is acting in bad faith or with 'unclean hands', for example, when alleging that his adversary violated a legal rule while the plaintiff is wantonly violating the very same rule themselves;
8. whether the plaintiff exhausted domestic remedies by first filing a complaint with the relevant competent domestic authority;
9. whether there is a surge of similar complaints simultaneously filed in multiple jurisdictions immediately after an incident, by the same attorney or group, and before the examination of the competent domestic authority has been completed; and
10. delegation of the power of attorney by alleged victim(s) to represent them in strategic litigation before their participation in an incident/event.

Analysis of factors such as these enables a more effective consideration as to whether and how to respond to the legal operation. The manner in which these

610 COUNTERING HYBRID AND GREY ZONE THREATS

lawfare strategies are deployed, and during which stages of a military operation, will be illustrated in section 3.

2.2 Mitigating reputational damage

As referenced earlier, lawfare campaigns, including the campaign against Israel, often seek to frame the military of the adversary as alleged criminals in the media in order to impinge on campaign authority and legitimacy and to cause reputational damage. Israel and other States or organizations seek methods to mitigate such harm. Helpful responses include when States and the executive authorities of targeted States acknowledge the vexatious political nature of the complaint when dismissing the complaint; explain, when implementing safeguards to their domestic law, that they need to do so to prevent misuse of their legal system; issue timely statements and/or reports debunking false information and misinformation; expose the actor behind the legal campaign and its strategic aim; publicly articulate the legality of their military's action; and timely and publicly support the legality of actions taken by States acting in accordance with the laws of armed conflict.

Several States have proactively taken effective measures to mitigate the effect of reputational damage not only of their officials but also of officials of foreign states, targeted by their adversaries' lawfare campaigns. However, additional strategies and doctrine could assist States and organizations to mitigate these reputational effects more quickly. For example, individuals can request that social media companies remove content if the content violates the company's terms of use. Social media companies could also remove such content on their own accord, within a reasonable time frame, and preserve the removed content. Such actions could not only assist those targeted but would also preserve the rule of law and its use in appropriate cases.

2.3 The use of legal principles in lawfare

An understanding as to how legal principles are identified and used as strategic tools or weapons in the legal domain is crucial. The study of the field reflects that just as a military commander seeks to identify the optimal weapon for a specific military operation on the kinetic battlefield, a legal adviser may seek the most appropriate legal vehicle or doctrine that can be effectively used to assert a claim that will achieve a strategic objective on the legal battlefield.

In the aftermath of World War II and the Holocaust, in which more than six million Jews were killed, the international community sought the use of legal

THE PRACTICE OF LEGAL RESILIENCE   611

tools that could be used to end impunity and bring individuals suspected of committing genocide and other grave crimes to justice. Many States ratified the Genocide Convention and some enacted broad universal jurisdiction laws in their domestic legal systems. These laws were intended to enable States to try alleged perpetrators for war crimes, crimes against humanity and genocide, even if the act had no link to the territory.

In the early 1990s, following the atrocities in Rwanda and Yugoslavia, the international community sought additional tools to pursue the laudable goal of combating impunity and deterring atrocities. These efforts included the creation of international tribunals such as the International Criminal Tribune for Rwanda (ICTR) and the International Criminal Tribunal for the former Yugoslavia (ICTY), and the establishment of the International Criminal Court in 2002.

It seems that many States did not forsee that these legal tools could also be used strategically for political gain in the legal domain.[22] As discussed earlier, the campaign against Israeli officials and officials from other democratic States began in the early 2000s, and involved the filing of complaints alleging violations of law during their visits to European countries. Complainants would frequently hold a press conference to accompany the public filing, to leverage the media effect.

At first, it was unclear why certain States such as Belgium, Spain, and the United Kingdom encountered such complaints, while other States did not. An in-depth legal analysis revealed that campaigners targeted States that enacted broad domestic universal jurisdiction laws. They also identified which domestic legal systems would allow them to file a complaint and request the issuance of an arrest warrant to an investigating magistrate or domestic court, without requiring the prior approval of the executive authorities of the State. It was found that some legal frameworks, in primarily common-law countries, allowed claims to be filed by individuals, acting as private prosecutors directly to a magistrate. Similarly, continental legal systems, such as Belgium and Spain allowed individuals to file a complaint directly to an investigating magistrate.

As States began to be flooded with complaints from around the world, it became apparent that their legal systems were being used to advance political agendas. States began to explore how to maintain the integrity of their legal system, while also preserving their ability to promote accountability. Several States introduced legislative amendments to incorporate safeguards in this regard.

---

[22] Henry Kissinger, 'The Pitfalls of Universal Jurisdiction', Foreign Affairs (July/August 2001). See also Steven Erlanger, 'Leader Celebrates Founding of Hamas With Defiant Speech' (*The New York Times*, 9 December 2012) <https://www.nytimes.com/2012/12/09/world/middleeast/khaled-meshal-hamas-leader-delivers-defiant-speech-on-anniversary-celebration.html> 13 March 2023.

612 COUNTERING HYBRID AND GREY ZONE THREATS

In the UK, the legal strategy of filing vexatious complaints against Israeli officials did not succeed. In fact, the complaints filed against Israeli officials in the UK led to both a public acknowledgment of these ideologically motivated court cases by the UK Prime Minister and Foreign Secretary[23] and a legislative amendment that incorporated legal safeguards, intended to prevent further malicious complaints of this kind.[24] The UK government explained that changes to its universal jurisdiction statute were necessary as such claims were often filed on the basis of 'scant evidence to make a political statement or to cause embarrassment'.[25]

The UK Foreign Secretary at the time, William Hague, commenting on the Police Reform and Social Responsibility Bill, which proposed to amend the law that requires the consent of the Director of Public Prosecutions before the issuance of an arrest warrant in a universal jurisdiction case filed by a private prosecutor, noted:

> This government has been clear that the current arrangements for obtaining arrest warrants in respect of universal jurisdiction offences are an anomaly that allow the UK's systems to be abused for political reasons. The proposed change is designed to correct these and ensure that people are not detained when there is no realistic chance of prosecution. It is now important that the amendment is considered by Parliament in line with normal constitutional practice.[26]

As such, the complaints filed in the UK against former Israeli officials, such as Shaul Mofaz, Doron Almog, Ehud Barak, Tzippi Livni, and others, were rightfully subsequently dismissed.[27]

---

[23] See The Prime Minister's Office, 'David Cameron's Speech to the Knesset in Israel' (12 March 2014) <https://www.gov.uk/government/speeches/david-camerons-speech-to-the-knesset-in-israel> accessed 13 March 2023. See also Ian Black, 'Gordon Brown Reassures Israel over Tzipi Livni Arrest Warrant', *The Guardian* (London, 16 December 2009) <https://www.theguardian.com/world/2009/dec/16/tzipi-livni-israel-arrest-warrant> accessed 19 March 2023.

[24] Sec. 153, Police Reform and Social Responsibility Act 2011. Requiring consent of the Director of Public Prosecutions for issuing of an arrest warrant in case of a private prosecution of international crimes committed outside the UK. See also Sec. 1A (3) Geneva Convention Act 1957 (Sec. 1A enacted 2001), requiring consent of the Attorney General for the institution of proceedings regarding grave breaches of the Geneva Conventions.

[25] United Kingdom Ministry of Justice, 'Press Release on Universal Jurisdiction' (15 September 2011) <https://www.gov.uk/government/news/universal-jurisdiction> accessed 5 February 2023. For further information, see Sally Almandras, 'Private Prosecutions', House of Commons Research Paper (6 September 2010) <https://researchbriefings.files.parliament.uk/documents/SN05281/SN05281.pdf> accessed 5 February 2023.

[26] Foreign and Commonwealth Office, 'Foreign Secretary Comments on Universal Jurisdiction' (1 December 2010) <https://www.gov.uk/government/news/foreign-secretary-comments-on-universal-jurisdiction> 16 May 2023.

[27] Decisions on file with the author. Many decisions of domestic prosecutors based on universal or extraterritorial jurisdiction are unpublished, making it more difficult to combat the disinformation contained in many complaints. However, numerous decisions of dismissal are publicly available in multiple jurisdictions.

THE PRACTICE OF LEGAL RESILIENCE   613

Other States, such as Spain, also dismissed complaints filed against Israeli officials and took steps to prevent the misuse of their domestic legal systems by actors promoting a political ban arrowing its domestic universal jurisdiction law, explained to the European Court of Human Rights (ECHR) that it amended it's domestic law due to the explosion of cases it received which were unrelated to Belgium and caused an excessive workload; as a result of diplomatic tensions; and to curb 'blatant political abuse'. The ECHR upheld the legality of the amendment.[28]

Some States legislated safeguards when they first enacted their laws, while others introduced safeguards at a later stage in order provide protection from vexatious use of legal systems. Yet, despite such safeguards and the eventual dismissal of cases filed, it is also important to unwind the reputational harm which may be caused by such campaigns. One of the main tools to mitigate reputational harm is to expose the actors behind the legal campaign and/or a specific complaint, as will be discussed in the following section. Additional tools should be considered as well.

2.4 Identifying the actor(s) deploying the legal strategy

A key to understanding the lawfare campaign that raised allegations of violations of international law against Israel officials, which included filing complaints in foreign jurisdiction, was to first identify who was deploying these tactics and what their strategic objectives were. Hamas, designated as a terrorist organization by Israel, the United States, and the EU[29] and by other States, seemed to be behind and/or to publicly endorse the filing of many of these complaints.[30] Over

---

[28] *Hussein and Others v. Belgium*, App. No. 45187/12, Judgment (16 March 2021). See European Court of Human Rights, 'Limitation in 2003 of the Jurisdiction of Belgian Courts regarding Crimes against International Humanitarian Law: No Violation of the Convention' (16 March 2021) <https://hudoc.echr.coe.int/fre#{%22itemid%22:[%22003-6965146-9374638%22]}> accessed 18 April 2023.

[29] See the EU list of designated persons and organizations at <https://eur-lex.europa.eu/legal-cont ent/EN/TXT/HTML/?uri=OJ:L:2022:025:FULL&from=EN> accessed 5 February 2023; the US list at <https://www.state.gov/foreign-terrorist-organizations/> accessed 14 March 2023; Israel's list at <https://nbctf.mod.gov.il/en/designations/Pages/downloads.aspx> accessed 14 March 2023. Many additional states also designated Hamas as a terrorist entity including the United Kingdom, Canada, and Australia. Other States designated specific military wings of Hama or designation for a specific purpose. See, Intelligence and Terrorism Information Center, 'International Activity Against Hamas since the Outbreak of Operation Iron Swords' (23 November 2023) <https://www.terrorism-info. org.il/en/international-activity-against-hamas-since-the-outbreak-of-operation-iron-swords/> accessed 24 November 2023.

[30] See the report about the Hamas legal committee Al-Tathwiq by the Intelligence and Terrorism Information Center, 'Al-Tathwiq and its Anti-Israel Campaign' (17 December 2009) <https://www. terrorism-info.org.il/Data/pdf/PDF_09_349_2.pdf> accessed 12 March 2023. In 2009, the head of the Al-Tawthiq committee claimed to have found more than one thousand five hundred allegations of war crimes for seven hundred and fourteen potential lawsuits (ibid. 4).

the years, Israel, NATO, and other States began to allocate resources to identify such strategies in order to understand and expose who is employing them and how they are employed.

After Operation Cast Lead, Hamas launched a propaganda media campaign using legal terminology to brand Israeli commanders as 'war criminals'. On 21 January 2009, Ismail Haniyea, the Head of the Hamas Administration in the Gaza Strip, set up a committee called 'the central committee for documentation and prosecuting Israeli war criminals', or Al-Tawthiq (documentation) for short. It was given an exclusive mandate to deal with the issue in the Gaza Strip (Hamas' Daily Felesteen, 27 January 2009).[31]

The Al-Tawthiq committee was appointed by Mohammad Faraj al-Ghoul, former Minister of Justice of the de facto Hamas Administration, current member of the Palestinian Legislative Council for the Hamas list and Chairman of the Council's Legal Committee, and on the US sanctions list.[32] Faraj al-Ghoul appointed Judge Diaa al-Din al-Madhoun, to chair the Al-Tawthiq committee, and Diaa al-Din defined the committee's mission as: 'documenting and gathering evidence connected with Israel war crimes, tracking [the so-called Israeli "war criminals"] and prosecuting them in international, national, and local courts'.[33] It seems that significant resources were allocated to this effort, as in a local interview, al-Madhoun explained that 160 Palestinians were divided into teams which were sent to the various districts of the Gaza Strip (Felesteen, 27 January 2009).[34] Additionally, efforts were made to file complaints against Israeli officials in UK courts.[35]

The lawfare efforts of Hamas also continued over the years. In a speech in December 2012, Chairman of the Hamas Political Bureau Khaled Mash'al described the methods to fight Israel as including legal methods:

> Fifth, Jihad and armed resistance are the proper and true path to liberation and to the restoration of our rights, along with all other forms of struggle—through politics, through diplomacy, through the masses, and through legal channels. All these forms of struggle, however, are worthless without resistance.[36]

Not only have these efforts not abated over the years—it seems that there is an increasing use of lawfare by Hamas. On 18 March 2023, a conference entitled

---

[31] Ibid. 1.
[32] See Office of Foreign Assets Control, 'Specially Designated Nationals and Blocked Persons list' <https://sanctionssearch.ofac.treas.gov/Details.aspx?id=9707> accessed 30 April 2023.
[33] Intelligence and Terrorism Information Center (n 30) 2.
[34] Ibid. 1–2.
[35] Ibid. 3–5.
[36] See Erlanger (n 22).

THE PRACTICE OF LEGAL RESILIENCE   615

'*Jurists Confronting the Occupier*' was held in the Gaza Strip. The conference was organized by the International Center for Law Studies, an organization headed by Faraj al-Ghoul, the former Minister of Justice who appointed the Al-Tawthiq committee, currently Chairman of the Legal Committee of the Palestinian Legislative Council.[37]

Conference speakers, including two members of Hamas' Political Bureau, discussed lawfare and its importance, claiming that 'legal weapons are no less important than military, security, and political weapons'.[38] The recommendations adopted at the conclusion of the conference included a call to use lawfare as one of the basic methods of 'resistance' against Israel.[39] A copy of the conference agenda, and summary of the various speeches given during the conference, was published by the Meir Amit Intelligence and Terrorism Information Center (hereinafter: 'the Center'). The Center commented that the use of the law as a weapon is not new and that the Palestinians have been using it for years as a part of their efforts to delegitimize Israel. The Center emphasized that the goals of the lawfare campaign waged against Israel are to

a. constrain Israel's ability to defend itself against terrorism;
b. defame Israel, particularly among other democratic states, by alleging it committed war crimes and damaging Israel's foreign relations;
c. erode confidence in Israeli institutions, including its military and legal system; and
d. defame the Israeli leadership.[40]

Conference speakers also noted lawfare efforts against Israel include appealing to international courts of law, such as filing claims to the International Criminal Court; General Assembly referrals to the International Court of Justice for Advisory opinions; and encouraging international commissions to investigate Israeli activity in the territories.[41] At the same time, speakers at the conference claimed that international law allowed for 'every form of resistance'.[42]

Ironically, Hamas raises spurious and manifestly unfounded allegations of 'war crimes' against Israeli officials in the media and in foreign courts, even as

---

[37] Intelligence and Terrorism Information Center, 'A Weaponizing the Law Conference' (26 March 2023) <https://www.terrorisminfo.org.il/app/uploads/-2023/03/E_063_23.pdf> accessed 27 April 2023. Conference speakers included Faraj al-Ghoul, Chairman of the International Center for Law Studies and of the Legal Committee of Hamas' Legislative Council as well as Mahmoud al-Zahar and Musa Abu Marzouq, members of Hamas' political bureau. The report includes a broad range of topics discussed at the conference.
[38] Ibid. 3–4.
[39] Ibid. 6.
[40] Ibid. 1.
[41] Ibid. 3–6.
[42] Ibid. 5.

616 COUNTERING HYBRID AND GREY ZONE THREATS

Hamas, on countless occasions, indiscriminately targets Israeli civilians, and uses Palestinian civilians, including children, as human shields.[43] This has never been more clear than on the painful day of 7 October 2023, when Hamas and Islamic Jihad attacked Israel; slaughtered over one thousand and two hundred Israelis and foreign citizens; wounded over five and a half thousand; committed acts of widespread torture, maiming, burning alive, rape, sexual violence, and mutilation of corpses; and abducted over two hundred and forty seven hostages, held them as human shields in Gaza, while also firing thousands of rockets at civilians residing in cities and towns in Israel. As noted by the Ministry of Foreign Affairs of Israel:

> Some of these crimes may also constitute genocide, as they are carried out with the 'intent to destroy in whole or part, a national, ethnical, racial or religious group' in furtherance of Hamas's declared genocidal agenda. Israel continues to face indiscriminate firing of rockets from Gaza and repeated attempts to infiltrate Israel to murder more Israelis, while the hostages taken by Hamas remain without ICRC visits or communication with the outsideworld.[44]

It seems neither Hamas nor its legal committee(s) have taken good faith measures to assure their own compliance with the very norms they strategically allege Israel violated. Hamas flagrantly and brutally violates the law. Hamas official, Ghazi Hamad, stated shortly after the massacre, on 23 October 2023, that the events of 7 October is just the first of the Al Aqsa flood events and that there will be a second, third, and fourth, as their goal is to teach Israel a lesson as Israel has no place on their land. At the same time, Hamas continues to use legal tools and terminology to promote their genocidal political agenda to gain operational manoeuvrability and legitimacy in the international sphere.[45]

---

[43] Government of Israel, 'The 2014 Gaza Conflict—Factual and Legal Aspects' (2014) 73–101 <https://mfa.gov.il/ProtectiveEdge/Documents/HamasCrimes.pdf> accessed 5 February 2023. See also Yoav Mor (ed), 'Human Shields: The deliberate Abuse by Terrorists of Children and Civilians. A Testimonial Report by IDF Soldiers' (My Truth, 2018) <https://mytruth.org.il/en/human-shields/> accessed 5 February 2023.

[44] Government of Israel, 'Hamas-Israel Conflict 2023: Key Legal Aspects' (2 November 2023) <https://www.gov.il/en/departments/general/hamas-israel-conflict-2023-key-legal-aspects#ANNEX%202> accessed 24 November 2023. See also, Government of Israel, Israel Defense Forces, 'The Shifa Hospital: Live Updates Regarding All Terrorist Infrastructure Located' (20 November 2023) <https://www.idf.il/en/mini-sites/hamas-israel-war-23/all-articles/the-shifa-hospital-live-updates-regarding-all-terrorist-infrastructure-located/> accessed 24 November 2023. See also 'Israel Lowers Oct. 7 Death Toll Estimate to 1,200' (10 November 2023) <https://www.nytimes.com/live/2023/11/10/world/israel-hamas-war-gaza-news/israel-lowers-its-official-oct-7-death-toll-to-1200?smid=url-share> accessed 28 November 2023.

[45] Memri, 'Hamas Offical Ghazi Hamad We Will Repeat October 7 Attack Time and Time Again until Israel is Annihiliated; We are Victims – Everything We Do is Justified' (1 November 2023) <https://www.memri.org/reports/hamas-official-ghazi-hamad-we-will-repeat-october-7-attack-time-and-again-until-israel> accessed 24 November 2023.

Exposing that the adversary, a designated terrorist organization, rather than a private individual, is behind the filing of a lawfare complaint can be termed 'lawfare gold', a type of 'smoking gun' in legal operations, as it exposes the cynical and political use of the law to promote an agenda which incorporates terror attacks and violence. Understandably, States are wary of allowing such actors to misuse their legal systems to promote their own agendas and have taken action to limit such use.[46]

2.5 Piercing the lawfare veil on the kinetic battlefield

Another useful strategy to expose an adversary's lawfare campaign is to seek to identify evidence, which reflects that and how the law is being used, or often misused, to promote a military or political agenda. For example, Hamas's own training manual, recovered by the IDF during Operation Protective Edge in 2014, instructs its fighters about the law of armed conflict and how to exploit Israel's adherence to international humanitarian law (IHL) to its advantage. Hamas explicitly notes that under the IHL principles of proportionality and distinction:

> soldiers and commanders [of the enemy] must limit their use of weapons and tactics that lead to the harm and unnecessary loss of people and [destruction of] civilian facilities', which 'poses difficulties [to the enemy].[47]

Aware of this restriction, Hamas consistently embeds their military activities among the civilian population and exploits hospitals, United Nations facilities, schools, mosques, and homes for military operations as a matter of military strategy, while directing attacks deliberately at civilians in Israel.[48] At the same time, while violating the core principles of IHL, Hamas, as discussed, ironically created its own committee to investigate Israel's violation of IHL.[49] In a slightly different take, Al-Qaeda training material advised captured fighters to claim they were tortured,[50] relying on the effect that such a claim would have on democratic state opponents.

---

[46] For considerations regarding the impact of political complaints, see United Kingdom Ministry of Justice (n 25); Almandras (n 25).

[47] Government of Israel (n 43) 153.

[48] Ibid. 73–75. This strategy continues to be deployed by Hamas during the current Hamas-Israel 2023 conflict, see n 44.

[49] See Intelligence and Terrorism Information Center (n 30) 1.

[50] Chapter 18 of the Al Qaeda Training Manual, found on a computer in Manchester in 2000, in English translation at <https://www.airuniversity.af.edu/Portals/10/CSDS/Books/alqaedatraining manual2.pdf> accessed 12 March 2023.

618 COUNTERING HYBRID AND GREY ZONE THREATS

Another strategy Hamas and other actors use in their legal operations is to contend certain means or strategies used by law-abiding militaries to minimize harm to civilians while targeting terrorists embedded in civilian areas, such as precision strikes or the 'roof knock' policy are per se illegal under international law.[51] Hamas uses such arguments in an attempt to impose legal limitations on Israel's ability to target terrorists embedded in a civilian population.

Similarly, in the maritime incident discussed in section 3, the allegation was made by one of the principal organizations involved that Israel was unlawfully imposing a maritime blockade to intentionally restrict the flow of civilian goods to Gaza and to collectively punish its civilians. The campaign sought to weaken Israel's position that the blockade was a legal measure under international law as it sought to restrict the flow of weapons to Hamas, weapons being fired on Israeli civilians, cities, and towns.

Israel, and increasingly other States facing such tactics and allegations have taken measures which included publishing the basis for their legal position in the public domain through either press statements or official speeches of their legal advisers. Israel published legal position papers regarding Operation Cast Lead,[52] Operation Protective Edge,[53] Cyber Operations,[54] and on the Hamas-Israel 2023 Conflict[55] the position of the government filed to the Israeli High Court of Justice relating to a broad range of issues, including regarding the legality of the actions of the military on issues such as targeted killings; the legality of the security fence; provisions of humanitarian aid. These responses, particularly if published in a timely fashion, are helpful in combatting this lawfare disinformation tactic, as the tactic is more effective when the area of law is 'grey' or when the public is not familiar with the legal terminology and relevant laws.

States and organizations, particularly in recent years, are increasingly proactive not only in explaining their legal policy and the legality of their actions. They are also proactive in calling out their adversary's violation of international law, while seeking to debunk disinformation regarding unfounded allegations raised against them. For example, United States senior officials gave numerous speeches on the legal framework for targeting terrorist overseas, the legality of

---

[51] Israel responded to this criticism by explaining the purpose and importance of the 'roof knock' policy, see Government of Israel (n 43) 180.

[52] Government of Israel, 'The Operation in Gaza: Factual and Legal Aspects' (2009) <https://embassies.gov.il/MFA/FOREIGNPOLICY/Terrorism/Pages/Operation_Gaza_factual_and_legal_aspects_use_of_force_Hamas_breaches_law_of_armed_conflict_5_Aug_200.aspx> accessed 17 May 2023.

[53] Government of Israel (n 43).

[54] Roy Schöndorf, 'Israel's Perspective on Key Legal and Practical Issues Concerning the Application of International Law to Cyber Operations' (*EJIL:Talk!* 8 December 2020) <https://www.ejiltalk.org/israels-perspective-on-key-legal-and-practical-issues-concerning-the-application-of-international-law-to-cyber-operations> accessed 20 April 2023.

[55] See n 44.

THE PRACTICE OF LEGAL RESILIENCE   619

drones,[56] and the US approach to the war against terrorism. On 26 February 2022, a mere two days after the Russian invasion, Ukraine submitted an application to the International Court of Justice to counter Russia's claim that Ukraine was committing genocide in its Eastern Regions.[57] Modern militaries not only have websites, but Facebook, Twitter, YouTube, Instagram, and other social media accounts to assist them in disseminating information to counter legal campaigns as swiftly as possible, often with the assistance of their legal advisers.

3. The maritime incident of 31 May 2010

Practitioners of lawfare 'learn on the job' how to identify lawfare strategies and what counter-strategies can be used in response. Developing both short- and long-term strategies to address the legal domain is important. Case studies can be an effective tool in this regard.

This section provides a glimpse of the operational and legal challenges Israel has faced, and continues to face, in the course of lawfare campaigns waged against it, using the 2010 maritime incident as an illustrative example. The flotilla organizers and some participants engaged in legal manoeuvring as an intrinsic part of the planning and execution of the operation. After the fact, the State of Israel faced legal challenges on various national and international fronts, in a multitude of legal fora, and against a variety of counterparties. A review of this incident, with a lawfare lens, could serve as a useful tool for states and practitioners in the field in their efforts to address similar campaigns.[58]

---

[56] Ben Wittes and Kenneth Anderson, *Speaking the Law: The Obama Adminstrations' Speeches on National Security Law* (Hoover Institution Press 2015). Congressional hearings can also be used to gather testimony from former government officials, academics, or experts regarding the legality of a specific policy. See, for example, the testimony of John Bellinger in Committee on the Judiciary, House of Representatives, *Drones and the War on Terror: When can the U.S. Target Alleged American Terrorists Overseas?* (US Government Printing Office 2013) <https://www.govinfo.gov/content/pkg/CHRG-113hhrg79585/html/CHRG-113hhrg79585.htm> accessed 25 April 2023.

[57] *Allegations of Genocide under the Convention on the Prevention and Punishment of the Crime of Genocide (Ukraine v. Russian Federation)*, Application Instituting Proceedings (26 February 2022) <https://www.icj-cij.org/sites/default/files/case-related/182/182-20220227-APP-01-00-EN.pdf> accessed 25 April 2023. Ukraine stated that 'the Russian Federation has falsely claimed that acts of genocide have occurred in the Luhansk and Donetsk oblasts of Ukraine, and on that basis recognized the so-called Donetsk People's Republic and Luhansk People's Republic, and then declared and implemented a "special military operation" against Ukraine with the express purpose of preventing and punishing purported acts of genocide that have no basis in fact. On the basis of this false allegation, Russia is now engaged in a military invasion of Ukraine involving grave and widespread violations of the human rights of the Ukrainian people'.

[58] The flotilla incident has been studied by scholars and practitioners, and is used as case study by NATO SHAPE to illustrate how legal operations can be an integrated part of military strategy. See also Kittrie (n 8) 312–18.

620 COUNTERING HYBRID AND GREY ZONE THREATS

3.1 Factual background

After Hamas took violent control of the Gaza Strip in 2007, and continuously fired thousands of rockets and mortars at Israeli towns, Israel imposed a maritime blockade in early January 2009. The blockade was imposed in order to prevent Hamas from continuing to build up its military capabilities, smuggling terrorists and weapons, and staging attacks from the sea. The Israeli government, in accordance with its policy, continued to facilitate the transfer of civilian goods into Gaza via land crossings, for humanitarian purposes.[59]

However, the Israeli government soon became aware of plans to breach the maritime blockade through the use of flotillas headed towards Gaza. Several European-based NGOs called on civilians to join the flotillas ostensibly to bring humanitarian aid to Gazan civilians.[60] In early March 2010, intelligence information has been published regarding Insani Yardim Vakfi (IHH), a Turkish organization that is designated a terrorist organization in Israel[61] and Germany,[62] and its involvement in the organization of the flotilla.

Using diplomatic measures, the Israeli government met with foreign governments and asked them to dissuade their citizens from joining an effort to breach the maritime blockade, and informed them that pursuant to Israel's policy on the entrance of goods to Gaza through land crossings, it would transfer any humanitarian aid through Israeli ports. Thus, allowing the Israeli authorities the opportunity to screen the goods for illegal weapons prior to it being transferred via land crossings to Gaza.[63]

In addition, through a combination of diplomatic, security, and political measures, the Israeli government was able to prevent several of the flotillas from departing their port of origin, and intercept the relevant ships without the use of force.[64] Upon interception, these boats were transported to a port in Israel, and

---

[59] The Turkel Commission, after a review of allegations raised that insufficient humanitarian aid was reaching Gaza before the maritime incident to meet the needs of the civilian population, concluded: 'On the contrary, considerable evidence was presented to the Commission to show that Israel allows the passage of objects essential for the survival of the civilian population and that it provides humanitarian aid as required by the rules of international humanitarian law in those areas that human rights organizations identify as a source of concern'. See Jacob Türkel et al, 'The Public Commission to Examine the Maritime Incident of 31 May 2010' (2019) (*Turkel Commission Report*) para. 80.

[60] Ibid. 102–03, 109, 116, para. 116.

[61] Ibid. para. 116.

[62] German list of outlawed organizations at <https://www.verfassungsschutz.de/DE/themen/islamismus-und-islamistischer-terrorismus/verbotene-organisationen/verbotene-organisationen_artikel.html> accessed 20 March 2023.

[63] The Turkel Commission concluded after a full review that Israel met its obligations under customary international law insuring that humanitarian aid reached the civilian population during the maritime blockade. See *Turkel Commission Report* (n 59) 64–102.

[64] Ibid. paras 26–27.

THE PRACTICE OF LEGAL RESILIENCE   621

humanitarian supplies on board were transferred to the Gaza Strip via accessible land crossings.[65]

At the end of May 2010, a flotilla of six ships from Ireland, Turkey, and Greece, departed with the stated destination of Gaza. There were approximately seven hundred people on board when the vessels approached the Israeli coastline.[66] The State of Israel continued its numerous diplomatic efforts prior to the departing of the flotilla to convince States to dissuade their citizens from joining the flotilla.[67] Prime Minister Netanyahu noted:

> During the month of May, a continual diplomatic effort to this end was made by the Ministry of Foreign Affairs vis a vis many countries, including countries whose citizens were onboard or whose harbors could be used by the flotilla at any stage of its voyage—including Egypt, Greece, Cyprus, Ireland, Britain, the United Nations, and above all with Turkey. The Minister of Defense even participated in these efforts.[68]

On 30 May 2010, as the vessels neared eighty nautical miles from the shore by Lebanon, the IDF transmitted communications warning the vessels that they were entering an area in which a naval blockade had been imposed, clarifying that if they were carrying humanitarian aid they would like to relay to Gaza, the humanitarian aid would be relayed via the Israeli port and land crossings.[69] At the end of the warnings stage and when the flotilla vessels were at a distance of approximately seventy miles west of the coast of the city of Atlit, the order was given to take over the flotilla vessels.[70]

In the early hours of 31 May 2010, the IDF intercepted and boarded the largest of the ships, the *Mavi Marmara*, which had approximately 590 crew members and passengers on board.[71]

However, upon boarding and taking control of the ship, the IDF soldiers were unexpectedly confronted with severe violence,[72] including a soldier being

---

[65] Ibid. paras 2 and 25.

[66] Ibid. paras 3 and 113.

[67] See Herb Keinon, 'Israel Increases Diplomatic, PR Offensive against Flotilla' (*Jerusalem Post*, 28 May 2010) <https://www.jpost.com/Israel/Israel-increases-diplomatic-PR-offensive-against-flotilla> accessed 13 March 2023.

[68] See Prime Ministers' Office, 'PM Netanyahu's Statement before the Turkel Commission' (9 August 2010) <https://www.gov.il/en/Departments/news/eventturkel090810> accessed 13 March 2023.

[69] *Turkel Commission Report* (n 59) para. 123.

[70] Ibid. para. 126.

[71] Ibid. para. 3.

[72] Prior to the incident, the IDF planned for the potential military interception of the flotilla vessels, in which force should only be used as a last resort. See *Turkel Commission Report* (n 59) para. 243: 'The finding that the IHH activists were taking a direct part in hostilities is important, because it places their actions in the proper legal context. However, due to the Israeli government's lack of

622 COUNTERING HYBRID AND GREY ZONE THREATS

forcibly taken to the hold of the ship, and suffering gunshot wounds and other serious physical injuries. In response to being attacked, the IDF soldiers used force of various types: stun grenades, less lethal weapons such as paintball guns, and after being attacked, live fire.[73] As a result of the clashes, ten of the participants were killed, and fifty-five participants as well as nine IDF soldiers were wounded. On the decks of the other ships, the IDF soldiers encountered less or no resistance, and there were no lives lost.[74] Knives and other weapons were later recovered on the *Mavi Marmara*, while no humanitarian supplies were found on this ship.[75]

Following the incident, on 14 June 2010, the Government of Israel decided to establish an independent public Commission to examine various aspects of the incident. Supreme Court Justice Emeritus Jacob Türkel was appointed to chair the Commission. Israeli experts were appointed as members along with two distinguished international observers (hereinafter 'the Turkel Commission'). The Commission examined and addressed the actions taken by Israel in connection with the flotilla incident and the conformity of those actions with the rules of international law.

On 23 January 2011, the Turkel Commission issued an interim report, entitled 'Report of the Commission for Examining the Maritime Incident of May 31, 2010' (hereinafter 'the Report'). The Report lays out the examination conducted by the Commission on (1) the security circumstances surrounding the imposition of the naval blockade on the Gaza Strip and the conformity of the naval blockade with the rules of international law; (2) the conformity of the actions taken by Israel to enforce the naval blockade on 31 May 2010, with the rules of international law; and (3) the actions taken by the organizers of the flotilla and its participants, as well as their identity. In conducting its examination, the Turkel Commission investigated all reported incidents of the use of force by the IDF, as well as Israel's treatment of the flotilla participants from the time the participants disembarked in the Port of Ashdod until the time the foreign participants were deported from Israel.[76]

---

information with regards to the IHH organization and the intentions of the flotilla organizers, the IDF was not aware of that group's plan until the first soldier fast-roped down towards the roof. During the planning of the Israeli military operation, the possibility that the passengers aboard the vessels might be direct participants in hostilities was not expected and was not taken into account. The Rules of Engagement (ROE), which outlined the authorized levels of force to be used by the Israeli soldiers, reflected that approach'.

[73] Ibid. para. 132.
[74] Ibid. para. 113.
[75] Ibid. para. 145. Humanitarian supplies where found on only two of six seized vessels, and building materials on a third. Ibid. paras 147–51.
[76] Ibid. para. 4.

THE PRACTICE OF LEGAL RESILIENCE 623

3.2 Lawfare aspects of the incident

When reviewing the maritime incident through a lawfare lens, it becomes apparent that the organizers of the flotilla carefully considered and planned the operation so that it would be able to launch legal challenges in national and international fora after the incident.

The legal planning began long before the ships set sail. First, it seems the organizers took action to ensure some of the ships were flagged and registered to State parties to the Rome Statute,[77] so they could subsequently challenge the events in the International Criminal Court (ICC). In particular, IHH, one of the principal organizers of the flotilla, purchased the *Mavi Marmara* and several other Turkish-flagged ships for use in the flotilla.[78] However, just two days prior to the incident, IHH changed the registration of the *Mavi Marmara* from Turkey to the Union of the Comoros, and then, curiously, changed it back six months later.[79] Given the purpose for which the ship was purchased, the re-flagging appears to have been a premeditated manoeuvre to ensure the jurisdiction of the ICC, to which Turkey is not a State party.[80] Other vessels in the flotilla sailed under the flags of Greece and Cambodia, which are also State parties.[81]

Second, the IHH recruited the members of the flotilla, some of whom were not associated with IHH prior to setting sail, to become active participants in the lawfare campaign against Israel. Upon being evaluated and vetted by the IHH Gaza Flotilla Committee, individuals were required to sign, as a condition of their participation in the flotilla, a document stating that 'I will not obey by the

---

[77] Three of eight participating ships were registered in State parties (Greece, Comoros, and Cambodia). See 'Referral of the "Union of the Comoros" with respect to the 31 May 2010 Israeli raid on the Humanitarian Aid Flotilla bound for Gaza Strip, requesting the Prosecutor of the International Criminal Court pursuant to Articles 12, 13 and 14 of the Rome Statute to initiate an investigation into the crimes committed within the Court's jurisdiction, arising from this raid' (14 May 2013) para. 32 <https://www.icc-cpi.int/sites/default/files/iccdocs/otp/Referral-from-Comoros.pdf> accessed 13 March 2023; The Office of the Prosecutor, *Situation on Registered Vessels of Comoros, Greece and Cambodia* 'Article 53(1) Report' (6 November 2014) para. 14 <https://www.icc-cpi.int/sites/default/files/iccdocs/otp/OTP-COM-Article_53(1)-Report-06Nov2014Eng.pdf> accessed 13 March 2023.

[78] IHH, 'Ship purchased for Gaza campaign' (29 March 2010) <https://www.ihh.org.tr/en/news/ship-purchased-for-gaza-campaign-231> accessed 13 March 2023 and 'Gaza Cargo Ship Arrived in Istanbul' (6 April 2010) <https://www.ihh.org.tr/en/news/gaza-cargo-ship-arrived-in-istanbul-171> accessed 13 March 2023.

[79] International Criminal Court, 'Annex III to the Transmission of Three Documents received from the Shurat Ha-Din – Israel Law Center', ICC-01/13-82-AnxIII (1 February 2019) <https://www.icc-cpi.int/sites/default/files/RelatedRecords/CR2019_00595.PDF> accessed 13 March 2023.

[80] See also International Criminal Court, 'Annex I to the Transmission of Two Documents received from the Shurat Ha-Din—Israel Law Center', ICC-01/13-84-AnxI (8 February 2019) paras 30–32 <https://www.icc-cpi.int/sites/default/files/RelatedRecords/CR2019_00597.PDF> accessed 13 March 2023.

[81] The Office of the Prosecutor (n 77) para. 14.

624   COUNTERING HYBRID AND GREY ZONE THREATS

decisions, warnings or demands of the governments of countries in the region regarding this ship'.[82]

Interestingly, in planning the operation, the IHH devised tools to create a legal framework that would ensure flotilla participants would not heed the warnings of any Israeli governmental authorities concerning the flotilla, and that they would also not be fully forthcoming or truthful in their statements to authorities examining the incident, to the extent that they had criticism or eye witness testimony or evidence against the actions of the IHH.[83] Moreover, by requiring participants to sign a power of attorney form before they boarded the ships, the IHH assured that only the organization would be entitled to legally represent participants until their return to dry land. IHH thus employed legal tools through which they sought to control not only the factual narrative but the legal strategy as well.

Third, as with most lawfare operations, this one had a significant media aspect to it. Israeli naval intelligence collected prior to 31 May 2010 ascertained the flotilla organizers 'intended to create a media event in real time' and were aware of the Israeli navy's intention to prevent the flotilla from reaching Gaza.[84]

3.3 The ensuing (pre-planned) legal campaign

Interestingly in this case study, the legal operation has lasted far longer than the military operation. Though the incident was over within approximately forty-eight hours, the legal proceedings went on for years and thus offered continuous opportunities to hold conferences, webinars, and similar events, during which the IHH promulgated its narrative both domestically and internationally.[85]

---

[82] Geoffrey Palmer et al, 'Report of the Secretary-General's Panel of Inquiry on the 31 May 2010 Flotilla Incident' (September 2011) (The Palmer Report) para. 88, <https://digitallibrary.un.org/record/720841?ln=en> accessed 13 March 2023, citing in footnote 303 the 'Turkish Point of Contact Response to the Palmer Commission of 11 April 2011, Appendix 1, *Palestine Our Route, Humanitarian Aid Our Load: Gaza Flotilla Individual Participation Form*, Guarantee ["Guarantee"] ¶ 12'.

[83] Ibid. paras 10 and 13.

[84] Ibid. para. 116. The aim of the 2010 flotilla and similar ones was revealed by the organizers years after the incident. See Intelligence and Terrorism Information Center, 'A Hamas-affiliated Palestinian in Britain admitted the flotilla project to the Gaza Strip was not intended to "break the siege" and bring humanitarian aid, but rather to promote the battle for hearts and minds against Israel' (17 September 2017) <https://www.terrorism-info.org.il/app/uploads/2017/09/E_186_17.pdf> accessed 9 February 2023, citing an interview of Flotilla activist Zaher Birawi with the Felesteen Daily Newspaper in 2017.

[85] See, for example, this press conference in Turkey in 2014: IHH, 'Mavi Marmara Victims Ask for Justice' (28 March 2014) <https://ihh.org.tr/en/news/mavi-marmara-victims-ask-for-justice-2218> accessed 26 July 2022; or the academic event at the London School of Economics in 2016: IHH, 'International Panel Held In LSE about Mavi Marmara' (29 November 2016) <https://ihh.org.tr/en/news/international-panel-held-in-lse-about-mavi-marmara> accessed 26 July 2022; anniversary events: IHH, '10 Years Since Blessed Voyage' (27 May 2020) <https://ihh.org.tr/en/story/10-year-since-blessed-voyage> accessed 26 July 2022; the flotilla being a topic at this conference in 2016: Huwaida Arraf, '2016 PANEL 3: Holding Israel Accountable for the Gaza Flotilla Raid' (May 2016) <https://www.wrmea.org/016-may/panel-3-holding-israel-accountable-for-the-gaza-floti

THE PRACTICE OF LEGAL RESILIENCE   625

After the incident, the organizers held meetings in Turkey. During one press conference, the 'three legs' of the legal campaign were spelled out: 'first one is the legal action taken against the Israeli officials within Turkey by the families of martyrs and victims, the second leg is about the activities carried out to mobilize the international community and authorities to take action and the third leg is about the legal action to be taken in the countries of each flotilla activist'.[86]

Attorneys who represented the participants in different countries declared during a conference that they would follow 'a joint roadmap of legal action in their defense of the activists'.[87]

As the IHH had planned, their attorneys and/or other attorneys recruited, encouraged, and assisted flotilla participants to file private domestic criminal complaints against Israeli officials who had participated in the military operation in various jurisdictions, including in Germany, Spain, Greece, and France. These complaints were subsequently dismissed for various reasons.[88] In addition, domestic civil claims were filed in the United States in California and Washington, DC, sometimes years after the incident. These cases were also dismissed by these federal courts.[89]

On a State level, Turkey initiated a domestic criminal investigation against the heads of the Israeli navy, air force, and military intelligence.[90] Istanbul's 7th High

---

lla-raid-huwaida-arraf.html> accessed 26 July 2022; or this list of events: Freedom Flotilla Coalition, 'Flotilla Informational Events', <https://freedomflotilla.org/flotilla-informational-eve nts/> accessed 1 September 2022.

[86] IHH, 'Forensic Reports on Flotilla Martyrs' (28 June 2010) <https://ihh.org.tr/en/news/foren sic-reports-on-flotilla-martyrs-258> accessed 22 March 2023. The legal campaign was explained in detail by Gulden Sonmez, Attorney, Vice President of MAZLUMDER, a Turkish Human Rights NGO: 'Following the attacks, first legal step was to carry out the forensic examinations and to obtain the testimonies from foreign passengers before they return to their own countries. Then, non-Turkish nationals have been following up with the legal procedures in their own countries. Each and every victim is in a position to take legal action against Israeli officials. Together with attorneys who are specialized in international law, we are working to take the case to the International Criminal Court. Efforts have been carried out not only in the countries of victims but also in a lot of other countries to start an investigation in the ICC. We are also working on to mobilize the UN to establish an investigation committee . . .' (Ibid.).

[87] IHH, '60 Attorneys Gathered in Istanbul to Discuss Flotilla Lawsuits' (16 July 2010) <https:// ihh.org.tr/en/news/60-attorneys-gathered-in-istanbul-to-discuss-flotilla-lawsuits-154> accessed 22 March 2023.

[88] Regarding Germany, see Claus Kreß, 'The Law of Naval Warfare and International Criminal Law: Germany's Federal Prosecutor on the Gaza Flotilla Incident' (2019) 48 Israel Yearbook on Human Rights 1 and Germany, Federal Prosecutor, *Complaint regarding the Israeli Actions against the Maritime Flotilla for the Gaza Strip (Gaza Flotilla Incident Case)*, Case No 3 ARP 77/10-4, Decision not to instigate investigation, 29 September 2014 (2019) 181 International Law Reports 488.

[89] Two cases regarding the flotilla were filed in the United States: in 2015, *Dogan v. Ehud Barak* [2019] No. 16-56704; D.C. No. 2:15-cv-08130-ODW-GJS (US Court of Appeals for the Ninth Circuit), and in 2016, *Schermerhorn v. Israel* [2017] No. 17-7023 (US Court of Appeals for the DC Circuit).

[90] See the summary of proceedings in Turkey and in international fora published by IHH, 'The Mavi Marmara Case: Legal Actions Taken against the Israeli Attack on the Gaza Freedom Flotilla

626 COUNTERING HYBRID AND GREY ZONE THREATS

Criminal Court approved an indictment against these Israeli officials in May 2012, contending they were guilty of wilful killing, among other charges. Turkish President Erdogan also sought to use the indictments to achieve a political objective, stating he would withdraw the indictments issued against Israeli officials if Israel apologized for the incident.[91]

In 2015, the governments of both Israel and Turkey agreed to take steps concerning the flotilla incident to ease diplomatic tensions. In addition to an oral apology, the State of Israel agreed to pay Turkey $20 million to compensate the alleged victims' families. In exchange, Turkey agreed to close existing criminal cases against Israeli officials, and both countries agreed to reappoint ambassadors.[92]

On the international level, the Union of the Comoros filed a State referral to the ICC, claiming the ICC had jurisdiction to investigate and prosecute alleged crimes which took place on the *Mavi Marmara*, since the ship constituted Comorian territory.[93] The ICC Prosecutor declined to open an investigation into the matter and yet was required by the ICC Pre-Trial and Appeals Chambers to reconsider the decision twice at the behest of the Comoros.[94] Each time, the ICC Prosecutor stood by her decision not to open an investigation, citing the grounds of insufficient gravity.[95] In her third decision not to open an investigation, the

---

on 31.05.2010' (31 December 2012) <https://ihh.org.tr/en/publish/detail/the-mavi-marmara-case> accessed 28 February 2023.

[91] See Alex Fishman, 'Turkey Dropping Marmara Lawsuits' (*YNET*, 13 January 2012) <https://www.ynetnews.com/articles/0,7340,L-4175182,00.html> accessed 13 March 2023.

[92] Isabel Kershner and Tim Arango, 'Israel and Turkey Agree to Restore Diplomatic Ties', *The New York Times* (New York, 18 December 2015) <https://www.nytimes.com/2015/12/18/world/middleeast/israel-turkey-mavi-marmara-gaza.html> accessed 13 March 2023.

[93] The Office of the Prosecutor (n 77) paras. 14–18.

[94] *Situation on the Registered Vessels of Comoros, Greece and Cambodia*, 'Decision on the admissibility of the Prosecutor's appeal against the "Decision on the request of the Union of the Comoros to review the Prosecutor's decision not to initiate an investigation"', ICC-01/13 OA (6 November 2015) <https://www.icc-cpi.int/Pages/record.aspx?docNo=ICC-01/13-51> accessed 13 March 2023; *Situation on the Registered Vessels of Comoros, Greece and Cambodia*, Judgment on the appeal of the Prosecutor against Pre-Trial Chamber I's 'Decision on the "Application for Judicial Review by the Government of the Union of the Comoros"', ICC-01/13 OA (2 September 2019) <https://www.icc-cpi.int/Pages/record.aspx?docNo=ICC-01/13-98> accessed 13 March 2023.

[95] International Criminal Court, 'Statement of the Prosecutor of the International Criminal Court, Fatou Bensouda, on concluding the preliminary examination of the situation referred by the Union of the Comoros: "Rome Statute legal Requirements Have Not Been Met"' (4 November 2014) <https://www.icc-cpi.int//Pages/item.aspx?name=otp-statement-06-11-2014> accessed 13 March 2023; International Criminal Court, 'Statement of ICC Prosecutor, Fatou Bensouda, on the Situation on registered vessels of the Union of the Comoros et al'. (30 November 2017) <https://www.icc-cpi.int/news/statement-icc-prosecutor-fatou-bensouda-situation-registered-vessels-union-comoros-et-al> accessed 13 March 2023; The Office of the Prosecutor, *Situation on the Registered Vessels of Comoros, Greece and Cambodia*, Final Decision of the Prosecutor concerning the "Article 53(1) Report" (ICC-01/13-6-AnxA), dated 6 November 2014, as revised and refiled in accordance with the Pre-Trial Chamber's request of 15 November 2018 and the Appeals Chamber's judgment of 2 September 2019 (2 December 2019) <https://www.icc-cpi.int/RelatedRecords/CR2019_07299.PDF> accessed 13 March 2023.

THE PRACTICE OF LEGAL RESILIENCE   627

prosecutor noted that all five of the domestic prosecuting authorities (outside Israel), which she was aware had opened inquiries into the matter, had discontinued their inquiries, in some cases without even opening a criminal investigation into the alleged incidents.[96]

It is notable that the requests by the Union of the Comoros for review of the ICC Prosecutor's decisions not to open an investigation was challenged, and re-challenged, and re-challenged, by the Comoros until the case was finally dismissed. Pre-Trial Chamber I noted:

> On 29 November 2017, the Prosecutor notified PTC I of her 'final decision', as required by rule 108(3). Having carried out a thorough review of all the submissions made and all the information available, including information newly made available in 2015-2017, the Prosecutor remained of the view that the information available did not provide a reasonable basis to proceed with an investigation. The final decision filed with the Court provided extensive reasoning in support of this conclusion.[97]

The legal wrangling to demand further investigation of the flotilla incident by the ICC appears to have been part of a concerted strategy to challenge Israel in as many domestic and international legal fora as possible, and for as long as possible.

3.4 Legal scrutiny in international fora

In tandem with complaints filed in national and international courts, there were actions taken in other fora as well. Some members of the international community condemned the takeover of the flotilla; Turkey recalled its ambassador from Israel to Ankara; and the UN Security Council denounced Israel's actions on the day that the incident took place, even before the complete facts of the incident were known.[98]

Notwithstanding that Israel had promptly opened an investigation of the incident within two days of it taking place, on 2 June 2010, the UN Human Rights Council (UNHRC) established its own fact-finding mission. Notably, the UNHRC's mandate to 'investigate violations of international law . . . resulting from the Israeli attacks on the flotilla of ships carrying humanitarian assistance'

---

[96] The Office of the Prosecutor (n 77) para. 52.

[97] International Criminal Court, *Registered Vessels of Comoros, Greece and Cambodia*, 'Preliminary Examination' <https://www.icc-cpi.int/comoros> accessed 25 April 2023.

[98] United Nations Security Council, 'Statement by the President of the Security Council', UN Doc. S /PRST/2010/9 (1 June 2010).

628 COUNTERING HYBRID AND GREY ZONE THREATS

(the 'UNHRC Mission'), appeared to pre-determine certain factual aspects of the incident, as well as legal conclusions.[99]

Israel examined the incident on its own, and for several reasons including the bias of the UNHRC and its mandate in this matter, refused to cooperate. The UNHRC completed its examination without waiting to consider the findings of Israel's inquiry into the events. Consistent with its pre-determined mandate, the UNHRC concluded that the naval blockade was illegal and that Israel committed violations of international law, finding the flotilla 'presented no imminent threat but that the interception was motivated by concerns about the possible propaganda victory that might be claimed by the organizers'.[100] On 29 September 2010, the UNHRC voted to endorse the report, with thirty of forty-six countries voting in favour, the United States voting against, and fifteen countries abstaining.[101]

During the same period that the UNHRC Commission was taking place, on 2 August 2010, the UN Secretary General at the time, Ban Ki-Moon, convened a Panel of Inquiry, led by Sir Geoffrey Palmer, the former Prime Minister of New Zealand, and President Alvaro Uribe, the former President of Columbia. Israel and Turkey cooperated with the inquiry. The panel produced a report known as the Palmer Report, which focused on how to avoid similar incidents in the future, and among other findings, found that the Israeli naval blockade of Gaza was legal.[102]

As we have set out in this chapter, the flotilla case study reveals that a military operation can be planned *ab initio* with multiple strategic legal goals at the forefront. One goal as mentioned by Israel's adversaries is to use the law to delegitimize Israel's military and its leaders, through filing strategic litigation in foreign courts. Another goal was to seek a declaration that Israel's actions in imposing the maritime blockade of Gaza were unlawful. In this regard, States and organizations should take note that had Israel lost its case in domestic or international courts, and the maritime blockade declared illegal, such a judgement could have had serious detrimental effects on the ability of all States to stop the flow of weapons from enemy states or organizations through the maritime channel.

---

[99] United Nations General Assembly Human Rights Council, 'Resolution 14/1: The grave attacks by Israeli forces against the humanitarian boat convoy', UN Doc. A/HRC/RES/14/1 (23 June 2010).

[100] United Nations General Assembly Human Rights Council, 'Report of the international fact-finding mission to investigate violations of international law, including international humanitarian and human rights law, resulting from the Israeli attacks on the flotilla of ships carrying humanitarian assistance', UN Doc. A/HRC/15/21 (27 September 2010) paras. 57, 59–61, and 265.

[101] United Nations General Assembly Human Rights Council, 'Resolution 15/1: Follow-up to the report of the independent international factfinding mission on the incident of the humanitarian flotilla', UN Doc. A/HRC/RES/15/1 (6 October 2010).

[102] See The Palmer Report (n 82) 4: 'The fundamental principle of the freedom of navigation on the high seas is subject to only certain limited exceptions under international law. Israel faces a real threat to its security from militant groups in Gaza. The naval blockade was imposed as a legitimate security measure in order to prevent weapons from entering Gaza by sea and its implementation complied with the requirements of international law'.

4. Conclusion: increasing legal resilience

As non-democratic States and terrorist organizations increase their use and reliance on lawfare, States and organizations facing these strategies or threats should take proactive steps to increase their legal resilience. The Israeli experience and the experience of other States and organizations reflect three core strategies, which can be used.

First, designating legal advisers in relevant ministries tasked with monitoring the legal arena, including an interagency process comprised of attorneys from the Ministry of Defence, the Ministry of Justice, the Ministry of Foreign Affairs, and the Ministry of Economy or other relevant ministries with expertise. These legal advisers should receive formal or practice-oriented training regarding how to identify, monitor, analyse, and strategically address the emerging challenges of legal operations, which arise both on and off the kinetic battlefield.

Second, trained legal advisers can counter legal influence campaigns in order to limit their impact. Attorneys, working with media personnel, can formulate strategies such as debunking factual or legal disinformation and misinformation; calling out false interpretations or applications of legal principles, and/or exposing adversaries that file strategic litigation via proxies.

Third, though lawfare practitioners often develop an 'I know it when I see it' intuition, States and organizations could benefit from pooling their knowledge and experience, sharing best practices, and working together to address these new challenges in an integrated, coordinated, and multidisciplinary fashion.

Israel's experience and the experience of other States and organizations in this arena reflect that the failure to take heed of the growing practice of the use of 'legal' tactics is unwise. Doing so may compromise not only the national security of the state or of allied states but also the fundamental integrity of international and domestic legal institutions, and of international law. If the law is seen by non-democratic States and designated terrorist organizations as a tool of strategic importance to be employed against their adversaries, possibly greater than the political or military arena, democratic states must proactively respond. Increasing national capacity and engaging in comprehensive academic and practice-oriented studies of this field are all crucial measures to enhance and strengthen resilience in the legal domain.

Acknowledgements

This article is written in a personal capacity and does not necessarily reflect the views of the State of Israel. Ms. Mazel received the *Serge Lazareff Prize*, awarded by NATO, in recognition of her significant contribution in matters relating to the legal aspects in hybrid environments and of her expertise in this field. The author would like to thank Ben Wahlhaus, former Senior Legal Advisor in the International Law Department of the Israel Defense Forces, and colleagues former Deputy Attorney General Dr. Roy Schöndorf, Tal Werner-Kling, and Shahar Sverdlov for their invaluable insights.

28

Legal Resilience from a Finnish Perspective

Tiina Ferm

1. Introduction

Following Russia's armed aggression against Ukraine, the security environment of Finland has deteriorated and become more difficult to predict than at any time since the end of the Cold War.[1] The shock after Russia launched its full-scale invasion on 24 February 2022 was described well by Finland's President Sauli Niinistö at a press conference held on the same day: 'Now the mask has come off. Only the cold face of war is visible.'[2] With this, the president referred to Russia's long-standing practice of exploiting ambiguity and clandestine military force in Ukraine.

Russia's actions and their consequences required strengthening Finland's security and resilience on a fast schedule. Finland's foreign and security policy was reassessed in a comprehensive report presented to Parliament on 13 April 2022.[3] In the report, the Government underlines that 'Finland is preparing for the possibility of becoming a target of exceptional, extensive, and multifaceted hybrid influence activities both in the short and in the long term. These activities may involve the use of military pressure or military force.'[4] Vigilance is needed even

---

[1] Finnish Government, 'Government Report on Changes in the Security Environment', Publications of the Finnish Government 2022:20 (2020) <http://urn.fi/URN:ISBN:978-952-383-811-6> accessed 15 March 2023.

[2] President of the Republic of Finland, 'President Niinistö: Finland Strongly Condemns Russia's Actions and Warfare' (24 February 2022) <https://www.presidentti.fi/en/news/president-niinisto-finland-strongly-condemns-russias-actions-and-warfare/> accessed 15 March 2023.

[3] Finnish Government, 'Government Report on Finnish Foreign and Security Policy', Publications of the Finnish Government 2020:32 (2020) <https://julkaisut.valtioneuvosto.fi/handle/10024/162515> accessed 15 March 2023.

[4] Finnish Government (n 1) 30. In Finland, hybrid influencing is generally understood as an act where a State or other external actor systematically employs a variety of methods, concurrently or in sequence, with an aim to influence the target's vulnerabilities to reach its goals. See Finnish Government (n 3) 14. See also the Government's Defence Report, which views hybrid threats from the military perspective, considering and defining them to be broad-spectrum influencing. In broad-spectrum influencing, the adversary may attempt to use military methods and the threat of using them, while still remaining below the threshold of open conflict. Finnish Government, 'Government's Defence Report', Publications of the Finnish Government 2021:80 (2021) 18 <http://urn.fi/URN:ISBN:978-952-383-852-9> accessed 15 March 2023.

Tiina Ferm, *Legal Resilience from a Finnish Perspective* In: *Hybrid Threats and Grey Zone Conflict*. Edited by: Mitt Regan and Aurel Sari, Oxford University Press. © Oxford University Press 2024. DOI: 10.1093/oso/9780197744772.003.0028

632 COUNTERING HYBRID AND GREY ZONE THREATS

more after Finland took the historic step, together with Sweden, of applying for membership of the North Atlantic Treaty Organization on May 17, 2022.

However, Finland did not need to start strengthening its security from scratch. During the Second World War, the whole of Finnish society was forced to participate in the defence of the country's existence. This created the basis of the operating model of Total Defence that Finland practiced during the Cold War years.[5] Total Defence refers to a comprehensive set of military or civilian activities to secure the nation's independence and the livelihood of the Finnish people against both external threats and other threats. It proved to be a natural and cost-effective choice for Finland. After the Cold War, the preparedness of Finnish society was based on the Concept for Comprehensive Security described in the Security Strategy for Society 2017.[6] It brings a broader approach to bear on preparedness, offering more possibilities for private companies, non-governmental organizations, and citizens to participate in joint planning and exercising.[7] The Concept for Comprehensive Security is a cooperation model in which the vital functions of society are jointly safeguarded by the authorities, business operators, organizations, and citizens.[8] This makes a major contribution to enhancing Finland's preparedness to respond to hybrid threats by increasing its ability to coordinate efforts across all relevant actors in society.

For example, we are increasingly becoming dependent on critical infrastructure that crosses borders and therefore is no longer under the control of a single State. Finland thus welcomes the European Union's Critical Entities Resilience Directive[9] and the Network and Information Security 2 Directive (NIS 2)[10] as common frameworks for European (EU) member States to secure and provide digital and physical resilience to providers of critical services. On 10 March 2022, the government appointed a Ministerial Working Group on Preparedness to form a comprehensive picture of the impacts of Russia's attack on Ukraine and to guide efforts to prepare against threats posed to critical infrastructure.[11] These

---

[5] Security Committee, 'The Concept of Comprehensive Security—Building National Resilience in Finland', <https://turvallisuuskomitea.fi/concept-of-comprehensive-security-building-national-resilience-in-finland/> accessed 15 March 2023.

[6] Finnish Government, 'Security Strategy for Society 2017', Government Resolution (2 November 2017) <https://turvallisuuskomitea.fi/wp-content/uploads/2018/04/YTS_2017_english.pdf> accessed 15 March 2023.

[7] Ibid.

[8] Ibid. 5.

[9] Directive (EU) 2022/2557 of the European Parliament and of the Council of 14 December 2022 on the Resilience of Critical Entities and Repealing Council Directive 2008/114/EC [2022] OJ L333/164.

[10] Directive (EU) 2022/2555 of the European Parliament and of the Council of 14 December 2022 on Measures for a High Common Level of Cybersecurity across the Union, amending Regulation (EU) No 910/2014 and Directive (EU) 2018/1972, and repealing Directive (EU) 2016/1148 (NIS 2 Directive) [2022] OJ L333/80.

[11] Ministry of Finance, 'Government Appoints Ministerial Working Group on Preparedness' (10 March 2022) <https://valtioneuvosto.fi/en/-//10623/government-appoints-ministerial-work

threats materialized at the end of September 2022 in the form of the deliberate sabotage of the gas pipelines Nordstream 1 and Nordstream 2 in international waters in the Baltic Sea, demonstrating that Europe's critical infrastructure is not immune from disruption.[12]

In this chapter, I address legal resilience from the Finnish perspective in the context of countering and responding to hybrid threats. Security and the protection of fundamental rights should not be conflicting aims, but certain forms of hybrid threats and malign influencing demand innovative solutions in a rule of law-governed country such as Finland. I highlight two particularly significant legislative amendments that have entered into force in July 2022. One was adding hybrid threats to the basis for emergency conditions in the Emergency Powers Act. The other was the amendment to the Border Guard Act concerning the management of the instrumentalization of migration. I will also review amendments to the legislation which aims to mitigate the vulnerabilities arising from the open economy. Finally, I examine the interdependence between internal and external security. As the Head of Countering Hybrid Threats during the years of 2018–2020 and as the Senior Ministerial Adviser for Legislative Affairs in the Ministry of the Interior, I have been at the heart of the efforts to enhance the preparedness to counter hybrid threats in our legislation, seeing firsthand that the ever-changing threat landscape requires constant assessment and adaptation.

2. Identifying Achilles' heels

Hybrid threats have attracted sustained attention in Finland for several reasons.[13] Even before Russia launched its full-scale aggression against Ukraine, its illegal annexation of Crimea and its actions undermining the stability of Southeastern

---

ing-group-on-preparedness> accessed 15 March 2023. For other incidents, see also Malte Humpert, 'Nord Stream Pipeline Sabotage Mirrors Svalbard Cable Incident' (*High North News*, 29 September 2022) <https://www.highnorthnews.com/en/nord-stream-pipeline-sabotage-mirrors-svalbard-cable-incident> accessed 15 March 2023.

[12] Council of the EU, 'Declaration by the High Representative on behalf of the European Union on Leaks in the Nord Stream Gas Pipelines' (28 September 2022) <https://www.consilium.europa.eu/en/press/press-releases/2022/09/28/declaration-by-the-high-representative-on-behalf-of-the-european-union-on-leaks-in-the-nord-stream-gas-pipelines/> accessed 15 March 2023. See also North Atlantic Treaty Organization, 'Statement by the North Atlantic Council on the Damage to Gas Pipelines' (29 September 2022) <https://www.nato.int/cps/en/natohq/official_texts_207733.htm> accessed 15 March 2023.

[13] According to the Finnish intelligence service (SUPO), 'Finland is subject to the continuous and wide-ranging intelligence operations of foreign powers. Finland's national security is conducted mainly by intelligence organizations of Russia and China'. In spring of 2021, SUPO identified a State-sponsored cyber espionage operation targeting the core of Finnish policymaking in Parliament. See Finnish Security and Intelligence Service, 'Yearbook' (2021) 18 <https://supo.fi/en/year-book> accessed 15 March 2023.

634 COUNTERING HYBRID AND GREY ZONE THREATS

Ukraine since 2014 have raised a great deal of concern. Hybrid influencing may also be part of normal lawful activities, yet still pose similar threats in the future.

The Finnish Security Committee coordinated the first national Hybrid Threat Survey (HTS) as early as 2015, working together with the relevant ministries and government agencies. Observed and plausible hostile actions were mapped and evaluated against our Achilles' heels, including structural weaknesses and vulnerabilities, in each of the DIME (diplomacy, information, military, and economics) areas. The survey assessed vulnerabilities and examined different means that would likely be useful in responding to hybrid activities or managing situations caused by them. The survey also highlighted the need for urgent legislative amendments. Since then, proactively addressing gaps in our legislation has been one of the cornerstones of Finland's efforts to counter hybrid threats.

One of the more surprising Achilles' heels identified as a result of these mapping exercises were the legal vulnerabilities arising from the principle of a free and open democratic society and the rule of law. In 2015, the first and most urgent area of work was to ensure that authorities such as the Defence Forces, the police, and the Border Guard had clear powers to respond in operative situations. In circumstances of hybrid influencing, the malign activities involved may be difficult for a targeted country to identify as coercive uses of force, as they are typically designed to stay below deterrence or response thresholds.[14] In a rule-of-law-governed country, the lack of clear powers to act may prevent or at least slow down the authorities' ability to respond, in particular in situations marked by ambiguity. The use of soldiers without insignia is a good example of such ambiguity that could hamper a timely response.[15]

2.1 Amendments to the Territorial Surveillance Act relating to Soldiers without Insignia

One of the first tasks was to minimize a hostile State's ability to exploit the legal environment as a force multiplier to achieve its goals.[16] To avoid destabilization of the borders, it was necessary to deal with the threat posed by 'little green men',[17] that is, the deployment of hostile forces without national insignia or other identification marks that would link them to a foreign State. This required

---

[14] Ibid. 3.

[15] See also Andrew Mumford, 'Ambiguity in Hybrid Warfare' (European Centre of Excellence for Countering Hybrid Threats 2020).

[16] Ibid. 3.

[17] The phrase 'little green men' refers to the military personnel deployed by the Russian Federation during the illegal annexation of Crimea 2014 without their national distinctive signs.

LEGAL RESILIENCE FROM A FINNISH PERSPECTIVE   635

reinforcing the powers of the territorial surveillance authorities so that they would be better equipped to handle situations where a military group without insignia violates Finland's territorial integrity. In the amended Territorial Act,[18] the phrase 'soldiers without insignia' refers to a group similar to a military detachment that is working on behalf of, for, or with the consent of a foreign State and is militarily organized, equipped, or armed and the State origin of which cannot be identified.

A key objective of the new powers was to ensure that territorial surveillance authorities have the opportunity, without delay, to take all necessary measures to combat hostile action that poses an immediate and serious threat to national security, including in the case of an unidentified military threat. As a result of the amendments, the Defence Forces and the Border Guard are now entitled to use military force if necessary to protect Finland's territorial integrity against soldiers without insignia. The use of military force may interfere with several fundamental rights, such as the right to life, personal liberty, integrity,[19] and the protection of property. In extreme cases, the right to life of those targeted may be jeopardized by the use of such force. However, the Constitutional Law Committee, a standing committee of the Finnish Parliament responsible for considering the constitutionality of bills and their compatibility with international human rights instruments,[20] considered that there were acceptable grounds for the new powers, as they were designed to be used against groups that are comparable to the military groups subject to the existing powers in Territorial Surveillance Act.[21]

2.2 Hybrid threats as the basis for emergency conditions

Developments in Russia's war against Ukraine have demonstrated in a very concrete way how hybrid tools can be used both as means of warfare and in support of hostilities. In response to the escalation of the conflict in February 2022, the Finnish Government decided to urgently review the current Emergency Powers Act to better counter serious hybrid threats, placing a legislative proposal before

---

[18] Territorial Surveillance Act (755/2000), sec. 3 <https://www.finlex.fi/en/laki/kaannokset/2000/en20000755> accessed 15 March 2023.

[19] According to the Constitution of Finland (731/1999), sec. 7, <https://finlex.fi/en/laki/kaannokset/1999/en19990731> accessed 15 March 2023, everyone has the right to life, personal liberty, integrity, and security. The personal integrity of the individuals shall not be violated, nor shall anyone be deprived of liberty arbitrarily or without a reason prescribed by an Act.

[20] Parliament of Finland, 'Constitutional Law Committee' <https://www.eduskunta.fi/EN/valiokunnat/perustuslakivaliokunta/Pages/default.aspx> accessed 15 March 2023.

[21] Constitutional Law Committee, 'Committee statement PeVL 25/2017 vp' (9 May 2022) <https://www.eduskunta.fi/FI/vaski/Lausunto/Sivut/PeVL_25+2017.aspx> accessed 15 March 2023.

Parliament in April 2022.[22] The main practical purpose of the Act is to provide public authorities additional powers in emergency conditions. In addition to conferring emergency powers, the Act includes provisions on procedure, right to compensation, legal protection, and criminal penalties. The Emergency Powers Act is a cross-sectoral piece of legislation covering all branches of government.

In a hybrid environment, an adversary may act in a way that does not trigger the conditions for the use of additional powers through the Emergency Powers Act, as originally adopted. To address this, the purpose of the government proposal was to ensure that the Finnish authorities can respond effectively and in a proportionate manner to hybrid threats following the prevailing security environment,[23] for example, to cover situations in which vital functions of society are affected by a disturbance that is difficult to trace unambiguously to a deliberate attack carried out by another party. The task was not easy, because hybrid threats as the basis for emergency conditions had to be described in a manner that is acceptable from the constitutional point of view. This demands that the concept of hybrid threats should be as precise and clearly defined as possible. The European Court of Human Rights has also set certain general conditions for the concept of public emergency,[24] while at the same time granting the State fairly extensive discretion in determining emergency conditions. In general, the bodies of the European Convention on Human Rights have allowed the national authorities to assess whether a state of emergency prevails in the country.

Parliament closely scrutinized the inclusion of the hybrid provision in the definition of a state of emergency. It paid particular attention to the fact that based on the provisions of emergency conditions, such as the Emergency Powers Act, essential and profound derogations can be made from people's fundamental rights that directly or indirectly affect even the fundamental prerequisites for a life of dignity and the rule of law.

Eventually, a new definition of a state of emergency was inserted in addition to the five definitions already stated in the Emergency Powers Act. The new definition aims to ensure that a state of emergency can be declared, if necessary, in case of serious hybrid influencing against Finland,[25] though without defining either

---

[22] Finnish Government, 'Proposal to Parliament on Amending Section 79 of the Emergency Act and the Conscription Act', HE 63/2022 (10 May 2022) <https://www.eduskunta.fi/FI/vaski/Hallit uksenEsitys/Documents/HE_63+2022.pdf> accessed 15 March 2023.

[23] Finnish Government (n 1) 30.

[24] See European Court of Human Rights, 'Factsheet—Derogation in Time of Emergency' <https://www.echr.coe.int/documents/fs_derogation_eng.pdf> accessed 15 March 2023.

[25] The new category of exceptional circumstances consists of a threat, activity, event or their combination, which affects the (a) decision-making capability of the public authorities; (b) maintenance of border security or public order and security; (c) accessibility of essential health, social and rescue services; (d) availability to energy, water, food, medicine or other essential commodities; (e) access to essential payment and securities services; (f) the functioning of transport systems critical to society; or (g) the functionality of information and communications technology services or information systems maintaining the functions listed in subparagraphs (a) to (f), as a result of which functions vital

the concept of hybrid threats or hybrid influencing. Also, a few new provisions on emergency powers were added to the Act. For example, movement and sojourn may be restricted or prohibited in certain localities in order to maintain border security and public order and security.

The work was also challenging because normally the Emergency Powers Act requires following the procedure for constitutional enactments, which means two parliamentary terms. However, the aim was to revise the Act during a single term and on a very tight schedule. The amendment was enacted in the urgent procedure for constitutional enactment that requires a majority of five sixths of the parliament. In connection with the amendments to the Constitution, the Constitutional Law Committee[26] emphasized the importance that the urgent amendment procedure referred to in section 73, subsection 2 of the Constitution[27] is not used for other than necessary and compelling reasons. In this context, the Committee paid attention to the changes that have taken place in Finland's security environment and the uncertainties associated with them, which underlined the need to produce objectively validated and analysed information on security threats against Finland in support of both political decision-making and decisions made by the security authorities. The Committee stressed that the international security environment has deteriorated in the short term. At the same time, global tensions and factors of uncertainty emerging in Finland's neighbouring areas have increased. These also increase the risk in Finland of multisectoral, asymmetric, and, in part, difficult-to-identify threats and disturbances severely endangering society's ability to function. The Committee stated that it is imperative that the authorities are granted adequate powers beyond those available in normal conditions. The amendment to the Emergency Powers Act was approved and came into force in July 2022.

2.3 Responses to the instrumentalization of migration

The instrumentalization of migration was one form of hybrid influence activity at the centre of public debates and attention at the time when the Government prepared its report on security changes in March 2022 after Russia launched

---

to the functioning of society are materially and extensively prevented or paralyzed or which in some other manner comparable to these seriously and materially endangers the functioning of society or the livelihood of the population.

[26] Constitutional Law Committee, 'Committee statement PeVL 29/2022 vp' (25 May 2022) <https://www.eduskunta.fi/FI/vaski/Lausunto/Documents/PeVL_29+2022.pdf> accessed 15 March 2023.
[27] Constitution of Finland (731/1999) sec. 73.

638 COUNTERING HYBRID AND GREY ZONE THREATS

its full-scale invasion in February.[28] Similarly to other hybrid activities, instrumentalized migration underlined the importance of putting into place the necessary operative, legal, and diplomatic tools to respond in a timely fashion.[29] Finland had already experienced the small-scale instrumentalization of migration between September 2015 and February 2016, when the number of third-party citizens crossing into Finland without visas seeking asylum at the northern section of the Finnish-Russian border increased suddenly. A similar development took place at the Norwegian-Russian border earlier in 2015. The EU has progressively imposed sanctions on Russia since 2014, following the illegal annexation of Crimea. Respectively in the autumn of 2021, Belarus used migrants to pursue its political objectives at the borders of Latvia, Lithuania, and Poland. The European Council Conclusions of 21 and 22 October 2021 declared that the EU will not accept any attempt by third countries to instrumentalize migrants for political purposes.[30] EU leaders stated that the Union remained determined to ensure effective control of its external borders.

In light of these incidents, Finland should be prepared for border incidents that are difficult to anticipate.[31] It is worth noting that the length of Finland's border with Russia, which is also an external border of the European Union, is 1,340 km or 830 miles. Accordingly, the Finnish authorities recognized the need to find appropriate legal means to counteract the instrumentalization of migration, above all in the form of a clear legislative basis and sufficient powers to enable the authorities to act proactively during incidents that exploit migration.

The work towards this goal began in a working group led by the Ministry of the Interior in November 2021.[32] The task was to draw up a report to assess Finland's preparedness for hybrid influence activities that instrumentalize migration, taking into account the impact on fundamental and human rights. The report presents EU legislation and the international treaties that underlie the national provisions, as well as the applicable case law, which set the framework conditions for the measures available. Measures aimed at preventing the large-scale instrumentalization of migration involves legal issues arising under EU law and the international treaties binding on Finland that are difficult to resolve. Specifically, the report found that it is not easy to reconcile Article 18 of the

---

[28] Finnish Government (n 1) 32.

[29] Ibid.

[30] European Council, 'European Council Meeting (21 and 22 October 2021)—Conclusions', EUCO 17/21 (22 October 2021).

[31] Finnish Government (n 1) 28.

[32] Ministry of the Interior, 'New Project to Examine Needs for Legislative Amendments to Address Use of Migration in Hybrid Influencing' (24 November 2021) <https://intermin.fi/-/muuttoliiketta-hyvaksi-kayttavaan-hybridivaikuttamiseen-varaudutaan-kartoittamalla-lainsaadannon-muutost arpeita?languageId=en_US> accessed 15 March 2023.

Union's Charter on Fundamental Rights[33] and the principle of non-refoulment. Robust border controls would be legitimate, but all measures adopted to this end must always respect fundamental rights, including the right to asylum and the principle of non-refoulment. One of the key questions arising in this context is how far and by what mechanisms Finland would be entitled, under applicable EU and international law, to close its border in response to a possible instrumentalization of migration, bearing in mind that a large-scale incident could compromise the functioning of society.

In the meantime, the European Commission published its proposals[34] to support the member States in responding to cases of instrumentalized migration. The proposal sets up an emergency migration and asylum management procedure which could allow a member State concerned to register an asylum application and offer the possibility for its effective lodging only at specific registration points located in the proximity of the border, including the border crossing points designated for that purpose.[35] The proposal underlines that 'where the Member States concerned are confronted at their external border with violent actions including in the context of attempts by third country nationals to force entry *en masse* and using disproportionate violent means, the Member States concerned should be able to take the necessary measures in accordance with their national law to preserve security, law and order, and ensure the effective application of this Decision.[36] The European Commission also published a proposal for emending a Union Code on the rules governing the movement of persons across borders.[37] The proposal defines in Article 2 what should be understood by instrumentalization.[38] However, the change in the security environment required that additional powers to respond proactively would be done urgently and Finland could not wait for the new EU legislation to be enacted.

---

[33] European Convention on Human Rights, 213 UNTS 222 (4 November 1950) Art. 3.

[34] European Commission, 'Proposal for a Council Decision on Provisional Emergency Measures for the Benefit of Latvia, Lithuania and Poland', COM (2021) 752 final (1 December 2021) and European Commission, 'Proposal for a Regulation of the European Parliament and of the Council addressing Situations of Instrumentalisation in the Field of Migration and Asylum', COM (2021) 890 final (14 December 2021).

[35] European Commission, 'Instrumentalisation in the Field of Migration and Asylum' (n 34) 4.

[36] European Commission, 'Provisional Emergency Measures' (n 34) final point 25.

[37] European Commission, 'Proposal for a Regulation of the European Parliament and of the Council amending Regulation (EU) 2016/399 on a Union Code on the Rules governing the Movement of Persons across Borders, COM (2021) 891 (14 December 2021).

[38] For these purposes, the instrumentalization of migrants refers to a situation where a third country 'instigates irregular migratory flows into the Union by actively encouraging or facilitating the movement of third country nationals to the external borders, onto or from within its territory and then onwards to those external borders, where such actions are indicative of an intention of a third country to destabilize the Union or a Member State, where the nature of such actions is liable to put at risk essential State functions, including its territorial integrity, the maintenance of law and order or the safeguard of its national security'.

The working group preparing Finland's response to instrumentalized migration was also mindful of a case pending in the Court of Justice of the European Union concerning the compatibility of the Lithuanian Aliens Act with the Reception Condition Directive 2013/33/EU and Asylum Procedures Directive 2013/32/EU. According to the Amendment of Lithuania's Aliens Act in 2021, the new provisions limit the possibility of applying for international protection when a situation of emergency is declared. The Court judgement was not available at the time the working group addressed the subject. Subsequently, however, the Court ruled that the provisions regarding detention and restrictions on the right to seek asylum in the new Lithuanian Aliens Act were not compatible with EU law. The judgement confirmed that a member State that has declared a state of emergency due to a mass influx of migrants cannot refuse to lodge for asylum applications; nor does EU legislation allow the detention of asylum applicants solely on the grounds of their irregular entrance or stay.[39]

After intense preparation, the Government of Finland submitted its proposal for amending the Border Guard Act to Parliament.[40] The Constitutional Law Committee has declared in previous legislative statements that border control, decisions on border crossing points, and regulation of border traffic are, as a rule, within the scope of the State's territorial sovereignty.[41] According to the established principles of international law, the State has the right to regulate the entry and residence of aliens.[42] Based on these principles, the Constitutional Law Committee considered it important that measures targeting the instrumentalization of migration take into account the State's right to decide on the security of its external borders and who has access to the State's territory.[43] However, the Committee also stressed that measures regulating entry must comply with Finland's international obligations to respect fundamental and human rights, and ensure that the asylum seekers are treated in dignified manner.[44] The Committee further stated that in connection with regulations such as the one being assessed, particular attention had to be paid to the case law of the European Court of Human Rights.[45]

---

[39] Case C-72/22 PPU, *Valstybės sienos apsaugos tarnyba*, Judgment, ECLI:EU:C:2022:505 (30 June 2022).

[40] Finnish Government, 'Proposal to Parliament Amending Border Guard Act (HE 94/2022)' (9 June 2022) <https://www.eduskunta.fi/FI/vaski/HallituksenEsitys/Documents/HE_94+2022.pdf> accessed 15 March 2023

[41] Constitutional Law Committee, 'Statement (PeVL 37/2022 vp)' (22 June 2022). <https://www.eduskunta.fi/FI/vaski/Lausunto/Documents/PeVL_37+2022.pdf> accessed 15 March 2023.

[42] *M.N. and Others v. Belgium*, Application No 3599/18, ECLI:CE:ECHR:2020:0505 DEC000359918 (5 May 2020).

[43] Constitutional Law Committee, 'Statement (PeVL 15/2022 vp)' (24 March 2022) <https://www.eduskunta.fi/FI/vaski/Lausunto/Documents/PeVL_15+2022.pdf> accessed 15 March 2023.

[44] Ibid.

[45] Ibid.

After intense political discussions in the Parliament, the amendments to the Border Guard Act entered into force on 15 July 2022.[46] According to the provisions where it is deemed necessary to prevent a serious threat to public order, national security or public health, the government may decide to close the border crossing points for a fixed period or until further notice. The government may also centralize the reception of asylum applications at to one or more designated border crossing points along the Finnish national border if an exceptionally high number of migrants present themselves at the border within a short period of time or if there are reasonable grounds to believe that foreign State or other actor is influencing the entry.[47] If the government has made such a decision, international protections may be applied only at the border crossing points along the Finnish national border where the application for international protection is centralized. An exception to this can be made in individual cases, taking into account the rights of children, persons with disabilities, and other persons in a vulnerable position.[48] According to the provision, border crossing points may not be closed and the applications for international protection may not be centralized more than what is necessary to prevent a serious threat to public order, national security, or public health. The decision shall be repealed when it is no longer necessary to prevent the threat in question.

As noted before, it is difficult to reconcile responding to instrumentalization of migration in an effective manner on the one hand and respect for the right to seek international protection on the other hand. According to the new provisions in the Border Guard Act, it is possible to close border crossing points along the Finnish national border and centralize applications for international protection to one or more border crossing points, but the proportionality of such action must be ensured and at the same time ensure genuine and effective access to international protection must be available. The question of what is a reasonable amount of border crossing points will have to be assessed on a case-by-case basis. All measures should always respect fundamental rights, including the right to asylum. For example, if a person has already crossed the border, one cannot push them back from the territory. Robust border control, however, is legitimate and includes, for example, physical prevention to cross the border. At the end of 2022, the Finnish Border Guard launched the implementation of the eastern border barrier project. In February 2023, the

---

[46] Ministry of the Interior, 'Amendments to Border Guard Act help prepare for Incidents' (8 July 2022) <https://valtioneuvosto.fi/en/-/1410869/amendments-to-border-guard-act-help-prepare-for-incidents> accessed 15 March 2023.

[47] Border Guard Act (Rajavartiolaki 578/2005), sec. 16 <https://www.finlex.fi/fi/laki/ajantasa/2005/20050578 - L3P16> accessed 15 March 2023.

[48] Ibid.

642 COUNTERING HYBRID AND GREY ZONE THREATS

construction of a barrier fence to the most important target areas in the eastern border started.[49]

2.4 Restrictions on foreign real estate ownership and foreign corporate acquisitions

Finland has also taken steps recently to reform the relevant legislation for screening foreign real estate purchases[50] and corporate acquisitions.[51] National security may be threatened by the exploitation of critical infrastructure or real estate ownership in a crisis involving Finland and its citizens. Foreign acquisitions may enable attempts by a State actor to exert influence.[52] Acquisition of critical infrastructure, such as harbour installations and railways, or branches of the high technologies, could make a country dependent upon a foreign-controlled supplier of goods or services crucial to the functioning of society and other national interests. For example, 5G technology creates possibilities to expose intelligence and information that can threaten national security. Finland has regularly amended its legislation in order to better prevent such threats to national security.

The amended act regulating foreign real estate acquisitions entered into force on 1 January 2020.[53] It improved the authorities' situational awareness of real estate ownership outside the European Economic Area (EEA) and created opportunities to intervene in purchases that endanger Finland's security. A permit must be acquired and issued by the Ministry of Defence when a buyer of real estate is a private individual who is a citizen of a State other than a member State of the EU or EEA.[54] A permit is also needed from a company or other entity domiciled outside an EU or EEA country.[55]

The threat landscape requires constant review of the screening process and another proposal to update the relevant legislation was submitted to Parliament

---

[49] Finnish Border Guard, 'The Construction of a Pilot of the Eastern Border Barrier Fence has begun in Imatra' (28 February 2023) <https://raja.fi/-/itarajan-esteaidan-pilotin-rakentaminen-on-alkanut-imatralla?languageId=en_US> accessed 15 March 2023.

[50] Act on Transfers of Real Estate Requiring Special Permission (Laki eräiden kiinteistöhankintojen luvanvaraisuudesta 470/2019) <https://www.finlex.fi/fi/laki/ajantasa/2019/20190470> accessed 15 March 2023.

[51] Act on the Monitoring of Foreign Corporate Acquisition (Laki ulkomaalaisten yritysostojen seurannasta 172/2012) <https://www.finlex.fi/fi/laki/ajantasa/2012/20120172> accessed 15 March 2023.

[52] Finnish Government (n 1) 48.

[53] Act on Transfers of Real Estate Requiring Special Permission (470/2019), sec. 2.

[54] Act on Transfers of Real Estate Requiring Special Permission (470/2019) sec. 1(2) https://finlex.fi/en/laki/kaannokset/2019/en20190470> accessed 15 March 2023.

[55] Ibid. sec. 3.

on 20 October 2022.[56] According to the new provisions, which entered into force on 1 January 2023, national security must be better taken into account in the consideration of requests for permits to purchase real estate. A permit for a non-EU/EEA buyer to acquire real estate should be issued only if the acquisition is not considered to endanger national defence, territorial surveillance, border control, border management, or the security of supply.[57] In its statement on the proposals, the Defence Committee of the Finnish Parliament underlined that hybrid influencing may include the use of legal means, which may involve both preparedness for future influencing in a crisis and actual influencing.[58] According to the Committee, this could be the case, for example, in real estate acquisitions that do not seem to have a commercial logic or a logic related to the normal usage of the property. A real estate owner acting on behalf of a foreign State may, for example, construct structures on their property that the hostile actor could use in a crisis to close transport routes or accommodate troops without insignia.[59]

Furthermore, the Ministry of Defence on 4 November 2022[60] set up a new project to examine the need to further restrict real estate transactions by Russian nationals. The working group submitted its report to the Ministry of Defence on 1 March 2023. The report includes a number of possibilities to develop the monitoring of real estate ownership of buyers outside the EU and the EEA.[61]

2.5 Vetting a person's foreign interests

Vetting an individual's foreign interests was made a clearer part of the security clearance procedures by the amendments to the Security Clearance Act in 2017. These interests may concern such matters as foreign citizenship, working in another country, and any foreign property holdings or business operations. Vetting a person's foreign interests, as defined in the Act,[62] is important because those

---

[56] Finnish Government, 'Proposal Amending the Act on Transfers of Real Estate Requiring Special Permission (HE 222/2022)' (20 October 2022) 5 <https://www.eduskunta.fi/FI/vaski/Hallit uksenEsitys/Documents/HE_222+2022.pdf> accessed 15 March 2023.

[57] Ibid.

[58] Defence Committee, 'Statement (PuVM 6/2022 vp)' (December 2, 2022) 5. <https://www. eduskunta.fi/FI/vaski/Mietinto/Documents/PuVM_6+2022.pdf> accessed 15 March 2023.

[59] Finnish Government (n 56) 5.

[60] Ministry of Defence, 'Project Set Up by Ministry of Defence to Examine Additional Restrictions on Foreign Real Estate Ownership' (4 November 2022) <https://www.defmin.fi/en/topical/press_re leases_and_news/project_set_up_by_ministry_of_defence_to_examine_additional_restrictions_ on_foreign_real_estate_ownership.13164.news - 33811ab2> accessed 15 March 2023.

[61] Ministry of Defence, 'Working Group Concludes It Is Possible to Tighten Monitoring of Foreign Real Estate Ownership' (3 January 2023) <https://www.defmin.fi/en/topical/press_releases_and_n ews/working_group_concludes_it_is_possible_to_tighten_monitoring_of_foreign_real_estate_ow nership.13444.news#e9699c32> accessed 15 March 2023.

[62] Security Clearance Act (Turvallisuusselvityslaki 726/2014) <https://finlex.fi/fi/laki/ajantasa/ 2014/20140726> accessed 15 March 2023, sec. 3(9) refers to foreign interests which may be a person's

interests may serve as an opportunity for the relevant person to be pressured, bribed, or otherwise lured to act in a manner that compromises the objectives protected by the Security Clearance Act. Close links to a foreign actor may create conflicts of interest, for example, through family members or property. The vetting of a person's foreign interests is performed where the individual concerned is entrusted with duties that require a heightened level of reliability, such as protecting national security, preparedness for a state of emergency, and maintaining public security and safety. The purpose of vetting foreign interests is to prevent inappropriate attempts by foreign States or other parties to influence such individuals.

Security clearance vetting is conducted when applying to the studies leading to officer posts at the National Defence University, police duties at the Police University College, studies leading to the post of a border guard at the Border and Coast Guard Academy, and studies leading to foreign affairs tasks. One of the issues to be considered in vetting is dual citizenship. The question was considered in 2020 by the Supreme Administrative Court in a case brought by an applicant who was refused admission to the Police University College on the basis that she did not meet the necessary reliability requirements. The applicant and her mother were dual Finnish and Russian citizens. The Supreme Administrative Court ruled that the Police University College had the right to reject the applicant. According to the Court, the refusal to accept the student was not based solely on her dual citizenship, but on an overall consideration of her specific circumstances.

3. The intertwined internal and external security

In this era of hybrid threats, understanding the nexus of internal and external security is crucial. Hybrid threat phenomena have changed the traditional dichotomy between the internal and the external aspects of security.[63] It is increasingly difficult to distinguish the two from each other. In fact, in dealing with hybrid threats, internal and external security are inextricably linked, which means that measures to tackle such threats often straddle the two dimensions of security.

---

current and previous citizenships of another State; employment, participation in business activities or holding assets in another State; continuous and close contacts with citizens of another State as well as other interests in another State or its citizens and communities.

[63] Tiina Ferm, 'Laws in the Era of Hybrid Threats' (European Centre of Excellence for Countering Hybrid Threats 2017) 3.

From the perspective of the rule of law, it should be noted that the roles and division of responsibilities between civilian and military authorities must be defined as clearly as possible in the legislation. One of the persistent challenges arising in this context is that malicious hybrid activity is often disguised, making it difficult to recognize as such. Law enforcement authorities, however, are often in a position that enables them to identify, in the course of their investigations, that an activity may be motivated by something that can be characterized as malicious intent. The activities of criminal and terrorist organizations must also be assessed from this perspective, since the motives and nature of their activities may also be connected to hybrid threats.

The internal security authorities thus play an important role in detecting and responding to hybrid threats, especially because less visible influencing activities may occur at the early stage and in normal, peacetime conditions that fall outside the usual responsibilities of the armed forces. Nevertheless, in Finland, there is a long tradition for the authorities responsible for internal security to engage in close cooperation with the Defence Forces. The joint use of equipment and capabilities, the regular exchange of information, and the development of a shared situational understanding are key strengths of this relationship.[64] The need for close cooperation between the security authorities, and its importance for the security of Finland as a whole, is also reflected in the relevant legislation. Thus, revised legislation concerning executive assistance given to the police by the Defence Forces entered into force on 15 June 2022. Pursuant to the revised legal framework, the police have the right, with the assistance of the Defence Forces, to use military force to prevent or interrupt the commission of a terrorist offense as laid down in the Act on Executive Assistance to the Police by the Defence Forces.[65]

The current energy crisis, rising electricity prices, and high inflation bring new uncertainties to internal security, testing the overall resilience of society. Severe disruptions to the electricity, energy, water, or logistics networks caused by a cyberattack or sabotage, for example, may quickly lead to economic harm and social discontent. Hybrid threats are widely feared to involve attempts to cause social instability, including a significant risk of large-scale, uncontrolled, and violent internal unrest that may be boosted by malign disinformation campaigns. To detect malicious hybrid activities including cyberattacks and to better understand the possible links between seemingly unconnected events that may point

---

[64] Finnish Government, 'Government Report on Internal Security', Publications of the Finnish Government 2022:12 (24 February 2022), 23 <http://urn.fi/URN:ISBN:978-952-383-669-3> accessed 15 March 2023.
[65] Act on Executive Assistance to the Police by the Defence Forces (Laki Puolustusvoimien virka-avusta poliisille 342/2022) <https://www.edilex.fi/saadoskokoelma/20220342.pdf> accessed 15 March 2023.

646 COUNTERING HYBRID AND GREY ZONE THREATS

towards such attempts to stoke social unrest, close cooperation and information sharing between government, industry, and civil society (a whole-of-society approach) is key.[66]

4. Conclusion

Finland's comprehensive security concept provides an example of how one member State is preparing for hybrid threats and organizing the activities of its competent authorities to this end. The key is the established and close interagency cooperation and cooperation between the government, the business community, and civil society.[67]

Countering hybrid threats is largely a matter of national competence. Resilience is at the heart of our national approach to safeguarding functions that are vital to our society in all situations. The rule of law and respect for fundamental rights are key principles of the Constitution of Finland. This applies also to Finnish foreign and security policy and internal security, which means that the human rights impacts of all actions taken in the conduct of foreign and security policy[68] and internal security operations are continuously assessed.[69]

However, countering hybrid threats also requires international cooperation. Finland is proud to host the European Centre of Excellence for Countering Hybrid Threats (Hybrid CoE) in Helsinki. The Centre has been a real boost for the cooperation between the EU and NATO, bringing the two institutions together to work on a range of activities and matters, from hostile influencing to hybrid warfare. At the national level, the Centre is seen as part of the efforts to further increase society's preparedness. For example, effective deployment of best practices in national preparedness arrangements requires training and exercises, which is one of the Centre's tasks. In addition, the Centre produces valuable information on hybrid threats and countermeasures, builds mutual trust, and facilitates the exchange of information through a network of experts.

Clearly, the Finnish approach is working: besides being the happiest country, Finland is also the safest and most stable country in the world.[70] It should be

---

[66] Finnish Government (n 6).

[67] The Security Strategy uses the national risk assessment as a basis for its preparedness risk analysis. The risk assessment is updated approximately every three years, with the next update due to be carried out in 2023. Ministry of the Interior, 'National Risk Assessment 2018', Publications of the Ministry of the Interior 2019:9 (5 February 2019) <http://urn.fi/URN:ISBN:978-952-324-249-4> accessed 15 March 2023.

[68] Finnish Government (n 3) 10.

[69] Finnish Government (n 64) 8.

[70] Finland tops the list of safest countries in the world compiled by the World Economic Forum (WEF) (2017, 2018, 2019), figures as the most stable State in the Fragile States Index (2017, 2018, 2019), and ranks as the top European country in Eurostat's assessment of trust in the police and

highlighted that one of the seven vital functions of Finnish society is psychological resilience, which is expressed in the citizens' will to defend their country's independence as well as in the determination to maintain their livelihood and security of the population in all situations.[71] Trust in security authorities is high among Finnish people.[72] A strong feeling of safety and security protects society from new types of threats bearing in mind that in crises and emergency conditions, the legality of all activities is central so that trust in the eyes of citizens remains high.

---

legal system (2018, 2019). Finland also does well in the World Internal Security and Policing Index (WISPI) (2016) and in Transparency International's index of the least corrupt nations in the world (2016, 2017, 2018). See Statistics Finland, 'Independence Day 2019' <https://www.stat.fi/tup/poi mintoja-tilastovuodesta/itsenaisyyspaiva-2019_en.html> accessed 15 March 2023.

[71] Finnish Government (n 6).
[72] Ministry of the Interior, 'Police Barometer 2020', Publication of the Ministry of the Interior 2020:12 (15 July 2020) <https://julkaisut.valtioneuvosto.fi/handle/10024/162345> accessed 15 March 2023.

29
The Path to Legal Resilience

Andrés B. Muñoz Mosquera, Jean Emmanuel Perrin, Panagiotis Sergis,
Rodrigo Vázquez Benítez, and Borja Montes Toscano

1. Introduction

Recent years have seen the development of the concept of hybrid threats and its materialization in grey zone and hybrid warfare environments.[1] With the increased use of, and hence attention to, asymmetric or non-conventional warfare techniques, both in 'peacetime' and during crises and war, the legal domain has become a 'battlefield'.

The use of the legal domain for strategic competition is not new. The Chinese general and strategist Sun Tzu already stated in the fifth century BC that the 'supreme art of war is to subdue the enemy without fighting'.[2] In 1975, John Carlson and Neville Yeomans first introduced the term 'lawfare' as a replacement of warfare, so that 'the duel is with words rather than swords'.[3] The term 'lawfare' as it is understood today was conceptualized by Major General Charles J. Dunlap (ret.) in 2001.[4] He defined the term as the 'strategy of using—or misusing—law as a substitute for traditional military means to achieve a warfighting objective'.[5]

In this context, the law is used as a tool or as a weapon in an international armed conflict to achieve traditional military objectives. However, this definition, which has been extensively commented on and developed in academic writing, does not have in itself a practical application to security and defence activities, including the planning and conduct of operations, whether in a conventional confrontation or in the context of hybrid threats.

There remains, therefore, an imperative need to set the objectives for tackling and operationalizing what it is perceived and assessed to be a very credible threat.

---

[1] For more detail, see Muñoz Mosquera and Chalanouli, chapter 15, in this volume.

[2] Sun Tzu, *The Art of War, The Book of Lord Shang* (Wordworth Editions Limited 1998), 25.

[3] John Carlson and Neville Yeomans, 'Whither Goeth the Law—Humanity or Barbarity', in *The Way Out: Radical Alternatives in Australia*, edited by M. Smith and D. Crossley (Lansdowne Press 1975).

[4] Charles J. Dunlap, Jr., 'Law and Military Interventions: Preserving Humanitarian Values in 21st Conflicts' (Carr Center for Human Rights Policy 2001) <https://people.duke.edu/~pfeaver/dunlap.pdf> accessed 6 February 2023.

[5] Charles J. Dunlap, Jr., 'Lawfare Today . . . and Tomorrow' (2011) 87 International Law Studies 315.

Andrés B. Muñoz Mosquera, Jean Emmanuel Perrin, Panagiotis Sergis, Rodrigo Vázquez Benítez, and Borja Montes Toscano, *The Path to Legal Resilience* In: *Hybrid Threats and Grey Zone Conflict*. Edited by: Mitt Regan and Aurel Sari, Oxford University Press. © Oxford University Press 2024. DOI: 10.1093/oso/9780197744772.003.0029

650 COUNTERING HYBRID AND GREY ZONE THREATS

In this vein, and in an attempt to escape controversies regarding the concept of lawfare, the North Atlantic Treaty Organization (NATO) Allied Command Operations Office of Legal Affairs (NATO ACO OLA), located at the Supreme Headquarters Allied Powers Europe (SHAPE), developed its own terminology to describe the subject with the help of the term 'legal operations'. The notion and its definition were incorporated in May 2022 into ACO policy in the following terms:

> Legal Operations is the use of law as an instrument of power. The term may encompass any category of actions in the legal environment by State or non-State actors aimed at, among others, gaining/undermining legitimacy, advancing/undermining interests, or enhancing/denying capabilities, whether at the tactical, operational and/or strategic/political levels. They may occur across the entire spectrum of peacetime, crisis and conflict either alone or in conjunction with any other Diplomatic, Information, Military, Economic, Financial, Intelligence or Legal (DIMEFIL) instruments of power in order to create the same or similar effects as those traditionally sought from conventional military action or in the context of strategic competition or as part of a hybrid strategy.

However, legal operations is only a concept and needs to be supported by effective actions and tools to achieve legal resilience. On this note, legal vigilance and awareness are essential actions and activities to detect at early-stage hostile legal operations and their potential effects and the risks they pose. Legal vigilance and awareness are also intended to calibrate and refine the continued assessment of legal developments to enable taking appropriate measures in response to hostile legal operations. This requires suitable tools to discriminate between 'legal business as usual' and the use of law with ulterior motives. The insertion of legal operations in the operational planning process and the conduct of such operations, as well as intensive legal training and a 360-degree legal interoperability approach, are also indispensable elements of this approach to legal resilience.

The conduct of legal operations, like other activities in hybrid environments, require the contribution of a variety of actors and the use of all relevant instruments of power. These actors and instruments would need to 'interoperate'. For this reason, planning, training, and exercising are essential for awareness and readiness to confront hostile legal actions and actors. This chapter will deal with the 'Matrix for the Identification of Legal Operations' (MILO) as a method to identify hostile legal actions and to strengthen deterrence and resilience. The latter is seen as a component of preparedness essential for developing an effective deterrence posture and defence capacity.[6] Resilience is essentially an effect to be

---

[6] North Atlantic Treaty Organization, 'NATO's Response to Hybrid Threats', 21 June 2022, <https://www.nato.int/cps/en/natohq/topics_156338.htm> accessed 6 February 2023.

attained and maintained. In this sense, legal deterrence is the external projection of a robust internal and external legal resilience within a given organization.

If its adversaries realize that an organization is able to swiftly identify or even anticipate hostile legal operations and deliver a fast and appropriate response, using its own resources or relying on its member States, to defend itself, its opponents will be discouraged from conducting new actions, and, therefore, the organization is projecting legal deterrence.

The following sections will chart in more detail the path towards legal resilience. Section 2 addresses the concept of legal resilience, while section 3 discusses the significance of interoperability in coalitions and alliances. Section 4 focuses on the operationalization of legal operations. Finally, section 5 covers the vital question of training.

2. Legal resilience: an overview

2.1 General resilience

In a security and defence context, resilience in a general sense requires continuous preparation to develop the capacities necessary for adaptation and recovery. These capacities and related means are instrumental for presenting a credible deterrence posture and an efficient and effective defence, and therefore make all the difference between success and failure.

Following the illegal annexation of Crimea by the Russian Federation in 2014, NATO adopted a strategy on countering hybrid warfare. Since 2016, both NATO and the European Union (EU) have developed a joint framework on countering hybrid threats, having designated this field as a priority for their mutual cooperation.[7] It is also important to note that NATO's Strategic Concept of 2022 acknowledged that: '[H]ybrid operations against Allies could reach the level of armed attack and could lead the North Atlantic Council to invoke Article 5 of the North Atlantic Treaty'.[8]

The European Centre of Excellence for Countering Hybrid Threats suggests that hybrid threats are methods and activities that are targeted towards vulnerabilities of the opponent with the aim of achieving a particular strategic

---

[7] For further details, see Andrés B. Muñoz Mosquera and Sascha Dov Bachmann, 'Lawfare in Hybrid Wars: The 21st Century Lawfare' (2016) 7 Journal of International Humanitarian Legal Studies 63, 70–71; Axel Hagelstam, 'Cooperating to Counter Hybrid Threats', *NATO Review*, 23 November 2018 <https://www.nato.int/docu/review/articles/2018/11/23/cooperating-to-counter-hybrid-threats/index.html> accessed 6 February 2023.

[8] North Atlantic Treaty Organization, NATO's Strategic Concept, <https://www.nato.int/strategic-concept/> accessed 6 February 2023.

objective.[9] In this vein, NATO considers resilience a component of preparedness for an effective deterrence posture and defence capacity, including against hybrid threats.[10]

In grey zone and hybrid warfare environments, the lines of effort to enhance *legal* resilience must focus, in the following order of precedence, on:

a. maintaining the cohesion of the instruments of power[11] available to a State or an alliance like NATO;
b. putting in place and strengthening the legal authorities required to safeguard democratic institutions and the general public's faith in them; and
c. countering an opponent's narratives to deprive it of legitimacy.

Continuous preparation and training under the banner of legal resilience enables States and international organizations to better resist 'hostile legal actions'. This leads to a situation of legal deterrence, where hostile actors understand that such hostile legal actions or lawfare will have limited impact on their target and therefore refrain from taking such action in the first place.[12]

2.2 The need for legal resilience

At its core, legal resilience is concerned with defending the rules-based international order (RBIO) against the threats emanating from malign revisionists.[13] The RBIO is based on principles and rules of coexistence developed over centuries, but it also reflects the values, preferences, and interests of liberal democracies.[14]

---

[9] See European Centre of Excellence for Countering Hybrid Threats, 'Countering Hybrid Threats' <https://www.hybridcoe.fi/hybrid-threats/> accessed 6 February 2023.

[10] North Atlantic Treaty Organization (n 6).

[11] J. P. McDonnell, 'National Strategic Planning: Lining DIMEFIL/PMESSII to a Theory of Victory' (master's thesis, Joint Forces Staff College, Joint Advanced Warfighting School 2009). See also Cale Horne, Stephen Shellman, and Brandon Stewart, 'Nickel and DIMEing the Adversary: Does it Work or PMESII them off?' (International Studies Association Annual Convention, San Francisco 2008); Brett Daniel Shehadey, 'Putting the "D" and "I" Back in DIME' (American Military University, 27 October 2013) <https://amuedge.com/putting-the-d-and-i-back-in-dime/>, accessed 6 February 2023 ('[D]IME [Diplomacy, Information, Military and Economics] is a recent military term reinvigorated to remind the leadership and policy makers above them to consider national power as not limited to the military power alone. It was because of the political over-use of "M" that led to the push for a "whole-of-government" (WoG) approach within the national security apparatus; and particularly, the DoD. DIME (FIL) was added to include statecraft resources of financial, intelligence and law enforcement dynamics to be applied to the operational environments.' Note that today 'L' stands for legal in general and not only law enforcement.)

[12] For further detail, see Muñoz Mosquera and Dov Bachmann (n 7).

[13] Fostering the rule of law is one of the key factors guaranteeing the way of life of Western societies and their internal and external stability. *Cf.* Lindsey R. Sheppard et al, 'By other Means: U.S. Priorities in the Gray Zone (Part I)' (Centre for Strategic and International Studies 2019) 20.

[14] See Michael J. Mazarr et al, *Understanding the Current International Order* (RAND 2016).

THE PATH TO LEGAL RESILIENCE   653

Some of these norms are under threat from revisionist actors, such as Russia, China, and Iran,[15] who exploit lacuna in the law and legal systems, operate across legal boundaries and under-regulated spaces, and exploit legal thresholds to pursue their interests.[16] These actions result in violations of the law, apart from generating confusion and ambiguity in the legal community. The aim of legal resilience is to uphold the integrity of these principles and the RBIO more generally against the threats that revisionists pose, in particular, by putting into place appropriate adaptation and recovery mechanisms.

Legal resilience is not a matter that concerns only lawyers and legal advisors, but all actors with a stake in the RBIO. The successful conduct of legal operations, which we will address in section 4, therefore is not the exclusive responsibility of legal experts, but requires an effort across the whole of government. Countering attacks on the RBIO is a multidisciplinary enterprise. In the military context, all echelons contribute to the achievement of legal resilience. However, as the necessary expertise and capabilities to confront a hostile legal operation may reside with other departments, the defence of the RBIO requires broader awareness and understanding of the stakes involved across government. Of particular relevance are ministries of foreign affairs, given their responsibility for the conduct of foreign policy, and authorities involved in the administration of the law, which have to deal with hostile legal operations trying to manipulate domestic legal procedures. International organizations, like NATO, whose tasks are at the forefront of the defence of the RBIO, also have a role to play within their sphere of competence in repelling hostile legal actions.

2.3 Legal resilience requirements

2.3.1 Environments
Legal resilience must be pursued in all types of hostile environments found across the spectrum of conflict, from times of peace to conventional war. Situations that

---

[15] While they pursue different goals, what unites these different revisionist or 'revanchist' actors is a shared sense of dissatisfaction with the existing legal order, including the values and underlying balance of power it is based upon. See Royal Institute of International Affairs, 'Challenges to the Rules-Based International Order' (The London Conference 2015) <https://www.chathamhouse.org/sites/default/files/London%20Conference%202015%20-%20Background%20Papers.pdf> accessed 8 February 2023. On China, which is one of the leading revisionist actors seeking to revise the RBIO to reflect its strategic priorities, see Andrés B. Muñoz Mosquera and Nikoleta Chalanouli, 'China, an Active Practitioner of Legal Warfare' (*Lawfire*, 2 February 2020) <https://sites.duke.edu/lawfire/2020/02/02/guest-post-andres-munoz-mosqueras-and-nikoleta-chalanoulis-essay-china-an-active-practitioner-of-legal-warfare/#_ftn1>, accessed 8 February 2023.

[16] Parliamentary Assembly of the Council of Europe, Legal Challenges related to Hybrid War and Human Rights Obligations, Resolution 2217, 26 April 2018.

fall between these two extremes, including grey zone competition and hybrid warfare, are of particular interest.

Grey zone and hybrid warfare actors are motivated by the principle of the economy of force and seek to avoid attribution of their actions. This creates uncertainty with regard to the applicable legal regimes, as illustrated by the events in Crimea[17] or Russian preparations in the Arctic.[18] The point is underlined by Lt. Col. Frank Hoffman's description of hybrid warfare as a situation where an 'adversary simultaneously and adaptively employs a fused mix of conventional weapons, irregular tactics, terrorism and criminal behaviour in the battle space to obtain their political objectives'.[19] However, the use of legal instruments and actions to support or impede other instruments of power also turns the legal domain itself into a 'battleground'.[20]

Due to their nature, grey zone and hybrid warfare situations are perfect environments for the malign use of law. Lawfare is a prominent tool in both cases. However, lawfare is not confined to grey zone competition and hybrid warfare, but also features in times of peace and in conventional war. Legal resilience efforts must therefore address the entire spectrum of conflict. Indeed, in peacetime, such efforts may make a significant contribution to preventing a crisis from escalating into grey zone conflict, hybrid warfare, or ultimately conventional war. While the exact dividing line between these different stages may be elusive, this should not be an impediment to develop legal effects and deploy legal actions, enablers, and tools in pursuit of legal resilience and thereby support rapid decision-making and allied cohesion.

2.3.2 Asymmetric regulatory environments

'Legal asymmetry' can be defined as the phenomenon whereby hybrid adversaries, as a rule, deny responsibility for hybrid operations as a means to escape the legal consequences of their actions.[21] Examples include Russian, Chinese, and Iranian efforts to directly or through the use of proxies benefit from situations of legal asymmetry in Crimea, the South and East China Seas region, and the Middle East, respectively. While legal resilience efforts

---

[17] Muñoz Mosquera and Dov Bachmann (n 7).

[18] Sascha Dov Bachmann and Andrés B. Muñoz Mosquera, 'Battleground Arctica: Precarious Arctic Law and Lawfare Opportunities' (2016) 108 *Amicus* Curiae Journal of the Society for Advanced Legal Studies 19.

[19] Frank G. Hoffman, 'The Contemporary Spectrum of Conflict: Protracted, Gray Zone, Ambiguous, and Hybrid Modes of War', in *2016 Index of U.S. Military Strength: Assessing America's Ability to Provide for the Common Defense*, edited by Dakota L. Wood (The Heritage Foundation 2015) 25, 29.

[20] On the legal domain, see Andrés B. Muñoz Mosquera, Sascha Dov Bachmann, and J. Abraham Muñoz Bravo, 'Hybrid Warfare and the Legal Domain' (2019) 31 Terrorism and Political Violence 98, 102.

[21] See Parliamentary Assembly of the Council of Europe (n 16).

may not be able to eliminate this tactic or immediately reverse grey zone gains resulting from its use, they may nevertheless diminish their effectiveness and appeal. For example, it is vitally important to reinforce rules in key areas of interest, such as attribution in the context of cyber defence, in order to strengthen the regulatory framework and prevent possible hostile legal actions by adversaries.

2.3.3 Effects, actions, tools, and enablers

Legal resilience demands the development of a complex set of capacities and procedures to enable a holistic, comprehensive approach designed to achieve a 360-degree set of effects. Specifically, it requires a series of tools, actions, and enablers in order to identify, assess, anticipate, and respond to hostile legal actions. Relevant tools include legal vigilance, legal awareness, and legal intelligence to keep track of developments in the legal domain. All of these must incorporate a clear articulation of what should be treated as threats in this context, distinct response thresholds, and unequivocal strategic goals. The relevant tools are employed during legal operations, which are a set of activities designed to identify the intent, instruments, and impact of hostile legal actions. Conducting legal operations demands unambiguous mandates and robust procedures. Legal training and all-level legal interoperability meanwhile are the enablers of these tools and actions. The following sections develop these elements of legal resilience in greater depth.

2.3.4 Preparedness and capacities

In essence, legal resilience is about being prepared and ready to respond to possible and 'impossible' situations in all conceivable scenarios and environments and to build the necessary adaptation and recovery capacities. The legal domain is open 24/7 and relevant legal developments, including hostile legal actions, may happen fast. Having the ability to take both defensive and more proactive action at a speed of relevance is essential. Access to relevant tools and procedures is an obvious precondition for prompt action. However, these tools and procedures also require subject matter experts trained to use them. Proficiency in both general international law and specific practice areas, including humanitarian law and human rights law, in relevant aspects of domestic law and familiarity with specific challenges, such as questions of attribution, targeting, the protection of civilians, the use of human shields and detention rules, are key training objectives. In addition, preparedness for legal resilience must also include, inter alia, media training on selected topics, interoperability with other expert and practitioner communities, and liaison with the judiciary and other authorities.

2.3.5 Respect for the rule of law

The ultimate aim of legal resilience is to preserve the RBIO. While taking robust and proactive steps to this end may be perfectly compatible with the rule of law, care must be taken not to mirror the techniques employed by hostile actors. Relying on similar methods may be particularly tempting in situations where hostile legal actions exploit asymmetries in the regulatory environment. However, accepting this asymmetry is the price of upholding the rule of law and operating within the parameters of legality as defined by the international community in the form of the applicable conventional and customary norms. While respecting the RBIO and the rule of law may seem like a weakness, the aim is to turn it into a source of strength: to use legal resilience to impose reputational and other costs, such as legal and other sanctions, on actors that contravene the rules.[22]

2.4 Legal domain and legal resilience

Legal resilience must take place along two vectors: time and space. Regarding the first vector, Fagan and Levmore present perspectives on how time influences law's architecture and the incentives for legal change, and how legislatures balance the risk between commitment to the rules that make up the legal order and maintaining flexibility to adapt those rules.[23] It is on these risks that legal resilience works, by anticipating and identifying hostile legal actions through developing prudent planning, promoting multidisciplinary legal interoperability, and training legal experts to respond to various legal scenarios.

The second vector is not limited to geographical spaces. One of the principal legal difficulties in the present context is the use of law as a non-kinetic weapon in grey zone and hybrid warfare environments. These environments are manifestations of hybrid threats and involve the use of methods and techniques across multiple domains, mainly those that do not require kinetic activities, such as cyberspace, 'neuromarking', or information operations. Law and legal interactions too offer such economy of force. As Kittrie underlines, hostile actors therefore rely on 'law to create the same or similar effects as those traditionally sought from conventional kinetic military actions'.[24]

Treating the law as a distinct domain assists States and organizations targeted by hostile legal actions[25] to better articulate and understand the defining features

---

[22] See also Muñoz Mosquera and Chalanouli, chapter 15, in this volume.
[23] Frank Fagan and Saul Levmore, *The Timing of Law Making* (Edward Elgar 2017).
[24] Orde F. Kittrie, *Lawfare: Law as a Weapon of War* (OUP 2015), 8.
[25] Muñoz Mosquera and Dov Bachmann (n 7) 76–77.

THE PATH TO LEGAL RESILIENCE   657

of competition and conflict carried out through legal means and methods.[26] It helps to visualize hostile activities in a spatial sense, connecting dots and placing them into the wider context of grey zone and hybrid warfare environments. Treating law as a domain thus turns legal resilience into a three-dimensional objective.

3. Ensuring legal interoperability in complex hybrid scenarios

There is no doctrinal definition of legal interoperability within NATO. In a general sense, interoperability in an alliance context refers to the ability of its members to act together coherently, effectively, and efficiently within the framework of the organization. Interoperability is one of the four methods of standardization together with compatibility, interchangeability, and commonality in the fields of operations, administration, and material, which aims to achieve tactical, operational, and strategic objectives.[27]

3.1 Legal interoperability's main purpose

Legal interoperability can thus be defined as the ability of States to work together coherently, effectively, and efficiently within the legal domain in pursuit of common objectives.

The underlying rationale for legal interoperability is a general commitment to comply with international obligations, as reflected in more specific rules, such as the duty to respect and to ensure respect for the law of armed conflict in all circumstances. The main challenge that multinational environments and operations pose to legal interoperability concerns the transformation of the potentially divergent obligations of individual States that derive from the various conventional and customary norms applicable to them into operational guidance and directives. Often, challenges for legal interoperability arise not merely because different States are subject to different legal obligations, but also due to divergent

[26] Andrés B. Muñoz Mosquera and Abraham Muñoz Bravo, 'The Legal Domain: A Need for Hybrid Warfare Environments' (2017) 2 Newsletter of the NATO Legal Community: NATO Legal . . . Matters 1, 9. See also Aurel Sari, 'Blurred Lines: Hybrid Threats and the Politics of International Law' (European Centre of Excellence for Countering Hybrid Threats, 2018).
[27] Andrés B. Muñoz Mosquera and Ulf-Peter Häussler, 'An Approach to Legal Interoperability' (2008) NATO Legal Gazette, Special Issue, 2. See also North Atlantic Treaty Organization, 'NATO Term – The Official NATO Terminology Database' <https://nso.nato.int/natoterm/Web.mvc> accessed 9 February 2023.

interpretations and understandings of what commonly applicable rules and principles require.[28]

Several examples of legal interoperability, which will be briefly analysed, have been studied by NATO legal advisors to identify normative gaps that require further action. Preparedness to deal with such gaps is particularly important in the context of complex operational scenarios, especially those involving the deployment of smaller contingents, as these usually do not deploy their own legal advisers to assist with the implementation of applicable instruments, including international agreements and operational documents.[29]

3.2 Caveats

Caveats[30] are 'reservations' entered by troop-contributing nations when designing rules of engagement (ROEs) with the aim of imposing limits on the use of their personnel or assets for the execution of particular tasks within the mission, including limits on the use of force. There are four grounds for caveats:

a. to ensure compliance with national law;
b. to ensure compliance with State's differing interpretations or obligations regarding international law;
c. because the State interprets the mandate of the operation differently; or
d. to impose additional restrictions or limitations on the use of State's forces, such as geographical limitations or prohibitions on the use of certain ammunitions.[31]

Caveats can offer an alternative to imposing restrictions on the entire force and thus prevent ending up with ROEs that reflect the lowest common denominator.[32] In this sense, national caveats facilitate legal interoperability by enabling

---

[28] E.g. Kirby Abbott, 'A Brief Overview of Legal Interoperability Challenges for NATO Arising from the Interrelationship between IHL and IHRL in Light of the European Convention on Human Rights' (2014) 96 International Review of the Red Cross 107, 110–11, and 117.

[29] On this issue, see Marina Jurić Matejčić, 'Legal Interoperability—A Croatian Perspective' (2008) NATO Legal Gazette, Issue 16, 27, 29.

[30] NATO defines caveats as '[a]ny limitation, restriction or constraint of any nation on its military forces or civilian elements under NATO Command and Control or otherwise available to NATO, that does not permit NATO commanders to deploy or employ these assets fully in line with approved military operational plan'. See North Atlantic Treaty Organization (n 27) 24.

[31] Sylvain Fournier, 'NATO Military Interventions Abroad: How ROE Are Adopted and Jurisdictional Rights Negotiated', in Criminal Law between War and Peace: Justice and Cooperation in Criminal Matters in International Military Interventions, edited by Stefano Manacorda and Adán Nieto Martin (Universidad de Castilla-La Mancha 2009) 117.

[32] Terry Gill et al. (eds), Leuven Manual on the International Law Applicable to Peace Operations (CUP 2017) 85.

individual troop-contributing nations to participate in certain aspects of a joint operation in a manner that respects their individual legal commitments.

In addition, caveats reduce legal uncertainty that arises from unresolved differences in legal positions adopted at the national level. Such differences may be a source of conflict and misunderstanding, which may undermine the successful accomplishment of a mission. For this reason, they are a vulnerability that adversaries and other hostile actors may be able to exploit. While caveats do not necessarily resolve these differences, they bring legal clarity to the situation and may enable these differences to coexist, whilst still allowing the operation to succeed. As such, caveats reflect both legal obligations and political considerations.

Common differences in national legal positions relate to the use of force or certain types of weapons. For example, with regard to anti-personnel mines under the Ottawa Convention[33] or cluster munitions under the Dublin Convention,[34] questions identified within the NATO ACO OLA[35] include situations where non-signatories States, such as the United States of America, might transport these weapons through the territory of a signatory State. What would be the consequences if a NATO commander from a signatory State were to approve the use of cluster munitions? Would they be 'bypassed' or will there merely be a 'national contribution' to achieve a NATO effect?

Significant differences may also exist in relation to the use of force. States may resort to the use of armed force in accordance with the requirements of the *jus ad bellum*,[36] including the right of the individual and collective self-defence.[37] However, during the conduct of hostilities, discrepancies may come to light regarding the meaning of 'hostile act' and 'hostile intent' for the purposes of authorizing the use of deadly force by individual units or the meaning of the notion of direct participation in hostilities under the law of armed conflict for the purposes of targeting.[38]

Regarding the notions of hostile act and hostile intent, the United States and NATO differ with regard to the requirement of imminence. While the US ROEs include hostile act and hostile intent within the concept of self-defence, NATO

---

[33] Convention on the Prohibition of the Use, Stockpiling, Production and Transfer of Anti-Personnel Mines and on Their Destruction, 18 September 1997, 2056 UNTS 211 (Ottawa Convention).

[34] Convention on Cluster Munitions, 30 May 2008, 2688 UNTS 39 (Dublin Convention).

[35] The content of this subsection is based on research done by Lt. Col. Joshua Shuey (Operational Law Branch, NATO ACO Office of Legal Affairs, SHAPE).

[36] The *travaux préparatoires* of the Charter of the United Nations suggest that its drafters assumed that any unilateral use of force would be exceptional and secondary to Article 2(4) of the Charter. See Ian Brownlie, *International Law and the Use of Force by States* (OUP 1963) 275.

[37] Yoram Dinstein distinguishes between *preventive* self-defence (where an armed attack has not arisen) and *interceptive* self-defence (where an armed attack has been launched but has not yet affected its target), arguing that the former is not permissible. See Yoram Dinstein, *War, Aggression and Self-Defence* (5th edn, CUP 2012) 203.

[38] Marten Zwanenburg, 'International humanitarian law Interoperability in Multinational Operations' (2013) 95 International Review of the Red Cross 681, 693.

660 COUNTERING HYBRID AND GREY ZONE THREATS

ROE use these terms outside the scope of the self-defence regime.[39] This is relevant as NATO ROEs cannot restrict the lawful use of force in self-defence.

Other areas that have posed challenges for legal interoperability in NATO include the conduct of certain military activities in non-international armed conflicts (NIAC). The conventional rules of the law of NIAC have little to say on detention, the principles governing targeting, or the geographical scope of hostilities in the context of multiple transnational armed conflicts.[40] In the particular context of NATO, there have been different attempts to address the question of detention, for example, including the 2006 Standard Operating Procedures (SOP 362) on Detention of non-ISAF Personnel, the 2013 Handbook on Treatment and Handling of Captured Persons (HB), a 2017 General Orientations on Detention Operations, and the 2019 Functional Planning Guides on the Treatment and Handling of Captured Persons. Despite these efforts, there are still gaps that need to be addressed by States to ensure interoperability, such as the classification of different categories of detained persons or who bears responsibility for their detention, which remains a matter falling within national competence but also one that NATO commanders have to deal with it.

3.3 How to ensure legal interoperability

Responsibility for ensuring legal interoperability rests on several levels and actors, including the level of commanders and at the political and strategic level.

As we have noted, ROEs are one of the key instruments for enhancing interoperability in the context of specific operations, as they determine when and where force may be used, how much force may be used, and against whom. They may also regulate other acts, such as the positioning of forces near the border of neighbouring States, the boarding of foreign vessels or aircraft, or the illumination of potential target. ROEs may be further complemented through additional guidance such as tactical directives, standard operating procedures (SOPs),[41] or clear legal annexes in operational documentation. This is essential when covering issues such as the national position on the force mandate and sensitive matters such as targeting and detention.[42] Ensuring that ROEs are in compliance

---

[39] Dustin Kouba (ed), *Operational Law Handbook* (17th edn, Judge Advocate General's Legal Center and School 2017) 478.

[40] See Aurel Sari, 'Hybrid Law, Complex Battlespaces: What's the Use of a Law of War Manual?', in *The United States Department of Defense Law of War Manual: Commentary and Critique*, edited by Michael N. Newton (CUP 2019) 410.

[41] Camilla Gudahl Cooper, 'Rules of Engagement Demystified: A Study of the History, Development and Use of ROEs' (2014) 53 Military Law and the Law of War *Review* 189, 194, and 196.

[42] A. P. V. Rogers, 'Command Responsibility and Legal Interoperability' (2008) NATO Legal Gazette, Issue 16, 17.

THE PATH TO LEGAL RESILIENCE   661

with national legislation and international commitments is first and foremost the responsibility of troop-contributing nations.

One key area of uncertainty where interoperability needs to be strengthened relates to the concurrent exercise of effective control over armed forces and their actions by both States and international organizations. Article 7 of the 2011 Draft Articles on the Responsibility of International Organizations leaves the question open, while Article 48(1) of the Draft clearly contemplates multiple attributions.[43] For this reason, commanders must always give specific guidance to subordinates,[44] so as to ensure uniform, legally compliant action and behaviour and to prepare subordinate commanders to take the legal measures required by the situation.[45]

Matters are complicated by the concurrent application of different legal regimes. In the conduct of hostilities, some matters are governed by international humanitarian law, others by international human rights law, while others fall within the scope of both regimes.[46] There are no NATO doctrines that guide its members on how to approach the relationship between these two bodies of rules. In addition, the applicability of international humanitarian law has to be determined on *case-by-case* basis, taking into account the prevailing circumstances and the mandate of the operation in question. Clearly, a common understanding and interpretation of the applicable law and how it should be applied in practice is key to legal interoperability. Operational plans and host nation support policies and agreements can go some way to ensure a common approach.

The hostile instrumentalization of international law also poses a challenge to the international rule of law.[47] Hence, in addition to ensuring compliance with applicable norms, operational plans and ROEs need to be carefully revised and

---

[43] International Law Commission, Draft Articles on Responsibility of States for Internationally Wrongful Acts (October 24, 2001) UN Doc. A/56/10. See David S. Goddard, 'Understanding the Challenge of Legal Interoperability in Coalition Operations' (2017) 9 Journal of National Security Law and Policy 211, 218–19.

[44] Andrew J. Carswell (ed), *Handbook on International Rules Applicable to Military Operations* (International Committee of the Red Cross 2013) 260. As noted by Muñoz and Häussler: '[M]ilitary commanders are obliged to ensure that their staffs and decision-making processes are organized in a manner repressing serious violations of international humanitarian and human rights law, that personnel under their command are appropriately trained, and that subordinate Commanders who have demonstrated their inability to prevent serious violations are no longer assigned tasks or mission in the course of which such violations are likely to occur' (n 27) 6. See also A. P. V. Rogers, 'Command Responsibility and Legal Interoperability' (2008) NATO Legal Gazette, Issue 16, 17.

[45] Orde F. Kittrie, pointing to the example of the Israeli responses to Hamas, suggests that the expansion of the role of military attorneys would be sufficient to maximize compliance with international humanitarian law. However, creating new tactics that would reduce casualties would be desirable and this should be taken into consideration by the chain of command when designing OPLANs and deploying forces. See Kittrie (n 24) 307.

[46] *Legal Consequences of the Construction of a Wall in the Occupied Palestinian Territory*, Advisory Opinion (2004), ICJ Rep. 136, para. 106.

[47] Aurel Sari, 'Legal Resilience in an Era of Grey Zone Conflicts and Hybrid Threats' (2020) 33 Cambridge Review of International Affairs 846, 857.

662   COUNTERING HYBRID AND GREY ZONE THREATS

designed, where relevant, to contribute to upholding the rule of law. This requires adopting clear mandates and delegating appropriate authorities to take appropriate measures to this end. Closer to home, rule-of-law concerns may also arise regarding operational claims connected with the stationing of troops in a host State. On this issue, Pierre Degezelle points out the complexity of the compensation system for third-party claims, for instance, in cases where assets belonging to one member State are used by the personnel of another.[48] Therefore, it is advisable that before deploying assets and capabilities, troop-contributing nations enter into arrangements regarding the use of their assets and capabilities in anticipation of possible future claims.

4. The operationalization of legal operations within NATO

As indicated, NATO ACO OLA defines legal operations as the use of law as an instrument of power. Although using law for instrumental purposes is well-established, a point reflected in the concept of lawfare, it is not sufficient to merely acknowledge this reality: its practical implications must be addressed too. This is what the MILO, developed by the NATO ACO OLA seeks to achieve.

4.1 Introduction

MILO is both a methodology and a tool or matrix which attempts to operationalize the concept of legal operations. Lawfare has for some time occupied the realm of theory, while hostile actors have actually proceeded to put it into practice.[49] This includes the conduct of hostile legal actions targeting NATO. The goal, therefore, is to enable the Alliance to prepare a response that is appropriate, in its kind and intensity, to the threats it is facing in this context. Ultimately, identifying and counteracting hostile legal operations contributes to the organization's ability to maintain its proper functioning and resilience and safeguard its reputation and conduct of its security and defence activities without impairment. However, to attest to the existence of hostile legal operation targeting a State or organization, certain parameters and criteria enabling their objective identification must be put into place. This is the primary purpose of MILO.

---

[48] Pierre Degezelle, 'General Principles of the NATO Claims Policy' (2012) NATO Legal Gazette, Issue 28, 17.

[49] See Stephan Halper, 'China: The Three Warfares' (University of Cambridge, May 2013) 11 <https://cryptome.org/2014/06/prc-three-wars.pdf> accessed 10 February 2023.

4.2 Practical examples

In order to build this new tool for analysis and action, the NATO ACO OLA began mapping existing examples of legal operations initiated by particular actors. This research identified many cases, particularly varied and very informative situations, in which the law has been used for operational or strategic purposes. The first example, which was directed against NATO, concerns the example of accusations made by an individual before the German judicial authorities of criminal misconduct by a senior NATO military official. During the military operations carried out by the Russian Armed Forces in Crimea, General Philip M. Breedlove, then exercising the functions of Supreme Allied Commander Europe, had taken the initiative of a communication campaign aimed at attributing these actions to the Russian Federation. Shortly after, the NATO ACO OLA was informed of a complaint in Germany against General Breedlove, which was likely to undermine not only his reputation but also NATO's standing as an organization. An investigation into the origins of the complaint showed the action had links with Russia and was, in all likelihood, sponsored by the latter.

The doctrinal documents developed by some terrorist organizations show another example on how opponents have a tangible interest in the use of the law as a tool of lawfare. For example, an Al-Qaeda manual found in Manchester in 2001 by the Metropolitan Police, known as the 2001 Manchester Manual,[50] instructs members of the organization to use Western legal procedures for their benefit and to claim in all circumstances to have been tortured to challenge the legality of their arrest and detention.

Vladimir Putin's declaration by which he recognized the independence of the Republics of Donetsk and Lugansk constitutes the most recent stage in a process of instrumentalization of the law, many of the sources of which have been identified during the annexation of Crimea by Russia in 2014. The attachment that the head of the Russian State seems to have for the legal justification of the recognition of the independence of these two provinces could appear surprising, even grotesque, as it may seem excessive. However, it shows a real sophistication of discourse and constitutes, in many respects, a textbook case of the instrumentalization of international law for political and military purposes. The existence of an act of recognition and treaties supports the theory of remedial secession or self-determination in response to alleged genocide, and in doing so Russia is following very closely the modus operandi set in the annexation of

---

[50] 'Al-Qaeda Training Manual' (Global Security 2001) <https://www.globalsecurity.org/intell/libr ary/reports/2001/al-qaeda_manualpart1.pdf> accessed 10 February 2023.

664 COUNTERING HYBRID AND GREY ZONE THREATS

Crimea, when the same steps preceded its occupation and annexation by force, with the consent of a supposed newly independent State.[51]

The Russian Federation has thus deployed considerable efforts to dress the de facto annexation of the provinces of Lugansk and Donetsk with the trappings of possible international legality. While the legal arguments put forward by the Russian authorities, whether referring to genocide, the protection of its nationals, the signing of international treaties, or the implementation of an operation to maintain peace, represent a legal dressing up of the reality of Russia's annexation; this has certainly not prevented the member States of the European Union, or the United States and the United Kingdom, from sanctioning Russia—which also relies on the use of law as an instrument of power—for the violation of Ukraine's sovereignty and territorial integrity.

These different cases demonstrate the power and effectiveness of the legal weapon when used smartly, in the most appropriate circumstances and at the right time. Furthermore, the relatively low cost of some of these legal actions put them within the reach of a large number of actors.

4.3 The three i's and the Matrix

In 2019, NATO ACO OLA, with the strong support of the University of Exeter, the NATO International Military Staff, and NATO partners, developed in-depth three distinct criteria, referred to as the three i's, to respond to the need implement the concept of legal operations in practice. A given legal action may be qualified as hostile if the existence of an *intention* to harm the organization, its reputation, or its operations is identified; it involves the use of particular *instruments*, in particular actions belonging to the legal domain; and finally this legal action has a particular *impact* on the organization, its reputation, or operations.[52]

The intent was to create a series of combinations in order to produce a 'legal operations score' which will indicate the severity and likelihood of the legal threat or legal hostile action, as well as what instruments of power need to be activated to produce an effective response and to support, keep, or restore the agreed levels of legal resilience. The nature and strength of the countermeasure conducted in response to the legal action will be largely defined by the result of

---

[51] See, for instance, Marko Milanovic's analyses of Russia's elaborate justifications: Marko Milanovic, 'What Is Russia's Legal Justification for Using Force against Ukraine?' (*EJIL:Talk!*, 24 February 2022) <https://www.ejiltalk.org/what-is-russias-legal-justification-for-using-force-agai nst-ukraine/> accessed 10 February 2023; Marko Milanovic, 'Recognition' (*EJIL:Talk!*, 21 February 2022) <https://www.ejiltalk.org/recognition/> accessed 10 February 2023.

[52] The term 'operations' is considered here in its broadest sense and includes, in particular, all security and defence activities undertaken by NATO.

the combined reading of the three i's. It is at this stage of the identification of the legal operation that the objectification process mentioned takes place.

The NATO ACO OLA has built a complex matrix that details comprehensively each of the three i's. Overall, the matrix allows more than 7,400 possible combinations between the three i's, the result of which is a score, defined as the 'Legal Operations Score'. Using the matrix in order to assess the Legal Operations Score of an event helps to assess its effectiveness and relevance.

4.4 Response and legal resilience

The composition of the Legal Operations Score allows early consideration of the relevance, nature, and intensity of an appropriate response. The Score also allows early consideration of the relevance, nature and intensity of an appropriate response. However, while the results of the matrix can detect the existence of a hostile legal operation and specify its nature, it is not designed to conclusively determine the form of the response and the means to be used to guarantee the best possible efficiency. Once the legal action is identified, it is necessary to define the vectors that will carry the response, which can be mainly of a political, legal, informational, or operational nature, or a combination of them.

The response itself is characterized by its proportionality to the legal action and takes into account not only the political orientations in force at the time of the incident, but also the intention of the commander of the operation within the legal domain. It could either be a purely passive response, including a choice not to react to a hostile legal operation. Inaction may be the result of a deliberate and assumed decision, rather than the result of a lack of awareness or decision-making. The response could also be limited, constrained merely to deal with the harmful effects of a hostile legal action, or it could involve a real countermeasure whose purpose would be not only to diminish the effects of a hostile legal operation but also to address its causes. Depending on the desired effect, the mix of political, media, legal, and operational components will be different in nature. The development of a tailored response as an antidote to a hostile legal action could thus be compared to the manufacture of a vaccine developed to contain the effects of a specific virus.

Measuring the effectiveness of both the legal hostile actions and the response contributes to operationalizing the concept of legal resilience. The term 'resilience' was originally used in the field of material physics to define the resistance of these materials to shocks; resilience is also defined as the capacity of an organization, an ecosystem, a species, or an individual to resume its normal operation or development after a significant disruption or alteration of its activity. Applied to the field of legal operations, resilience occurs when a given organization, after

666 COUNTERING HYBRID AND GREY ZONE THREATS

having suffered a hostile legal action that has created real damage, recovers its nominal functioning, whether it has been restored with or without the assistance of a legal response.

4.5 Operational readiness for legal operations

The preparation for the conduct of legal operations can be divided into three main areas. The first concerns legal information and the way in which an organization and its staff deals with the 360 degrees of legal information collected. The second is called legal vigilance and translates into the establishment of active means for seeking legal information in certain clearly identified areas of interest. The third is the inclusion of legal operations in the operational planning process and in the conduct of operations, especially when they are effects-based.

Collecting legal information is an essential part of the process of identifying hostile legal actions against NATO. It is not only a matter of establishing a map of the existing legal order, such as legislative developments and judicial decisions likely to impact the organizations' operations and activities, but it is also about carefully following the adoption, modification, or denunciation of any new legal or regulatory provision or international agreement which may have a potential impact on the organization's centres of gravity or lines of operations.

In order to obtain a sufficient level of legal information for the conduct of NATO's legal operations, it is desirable that a certain number of legal intelligence tools be put in place within the organization. Starting from all the open legal information available, as distinguished from classified or information not releasable to the public, it is desirable to target the part of this information that will be considered relevant to the achievement of the objective pursued. Legal vigilance helps to orient search sensors on a limited number of topics with high added value for the Alliance. This approach is based on a geographical, functionalist, and thematic approach.

First of all, the mapping of geopolitical tensions makes it possible to refocus research efforts on the activities undertaken by a particular State that merit a high level of vigilance due to the threat they present for the organization. The functionalist approach invites us, either cumulatively with the geographical approach or independently of it, to focus the organization's vigilance in the legal field according to the function performed by a given entity or structure, for example, a non-governmental organization or a think tank, whose respective functions have an impact, positive or negative, on the course of NATO's operations.

Legal vigilance may concentrate on an organization, a State, or even an individual, based on the practices, use, or interpretation of international or national law that are likely to harm the interests of the organization. This thematic

THE PATH TO LEGAL RESILIENCE 667

vigilance may be directed in particular at an organization whose recurrent practice consists in delivering false analyses of international humanitarian law, for example. Legal vigilance may also focus on persons or entities making false claims against NATO, members, or personnel. Once vigilance is focused on certain persons or entities of interest because of their propensity to adopt hostile behaviours and to express them through legal tools, it is particularly useful to deepen our knowledge on the modes of action implemented, in particular to anticipate and, if possible, neutralize the hostile activities.

The political, military, economic, social, infrastructure, and information (PMESII) construct provides a useful means of describing the 'system' of a potential adversary. In general, planners apply friendly elements of national power against the various components of the PMESII construct. The DIMEFIL model for national instruments of power offers a useful shorthand for describing these different elements, as it adds intelligence and legal instruments to the traditional national elements of power. The bottom line is that the Alliance's DIMEFIL national instruments of power are applied against the adversary's PMESII elements. The confrontation of the DIMEFIL and PMESII constructs helps to identify the preferred modes of action of NATO's potential adversaries and the way in which they can use various legal instruments of power in order to affect the political, economic, legal, social, and military organization systems of NATO's member States.

Applying the DIMEFIL and PMESII constructs systematically to the legal domain can be extremely revealing, especially in the early stages of a potential crisis, and highlight the Alliance's own weaknesses. Using the two constructs should therefore encourage the organization to harden the systems identified as being the most vulnerable to legal aggression from potential adversaries. There is also no doubt that some of NATO's potential adversaries are already practicing this kind of systemic analysis by confronting 'their' DIMEFIL instruments with the 'Alliance' PMESII elements.

Another area of activities is concerned with better integrating legal issues into the planning process and into the conduct of military operations. In order to prepare for complex multinational operations, it is absolutely necessary to plan the conduct of these operations by integrating all the factors contributing to their success. The planning process is geared towards achieving a desired end state and pursuing strategic-level military and non-military objectives within the framework defined by the political authorities. However, in the same way that specific developments on strategic communications are developed in each OPLAN, for instance, it should be possible in the future to identify in the same OPLAN specific developments related to legal operations.

Another way to implement legal resilience is to further integrate the planning and conduct of legal operations into the strategic-level targeting

668 COUNTERING HYBRID AND GREY ZONE THREATS

component of the OPLAN. Such an initiative would be completely consistent within the effects-based operations concept which makes it possible to reach a desired strategic end state or an effect on the enemy through the synergistic and cumulative application of the full range of military and non-military capabilities at all levels of conflict. Effects-based operations focus first on the ultimate objectives pursued, as well as on the means available to achieve those objectives. Legal tools should be considered one of the instruments available to achieve the defined strategic objectives, alongside more traditional instruments of war, such as, for example, the use of military force, diplomacy, or economic power.

5. Training

Hostile legal actions that undermine the international legal system are not a new phenomenon.[53] However, this instrumentalization of law is part of a wider approach to multidomain operations.[54] This reinforces the need for a new synthesis of skills and attitudes not only among the ranks and files of the military, especially among military legal advisors, but also among other relevant services and sections of government.

5.1 Creating new skills and attitudes through training

Training is an essential means to improve the ability of States and international organizations, such as NATO, to defend themselves and the RBIO against hostile legal action and to conduct legal operations. For these purposes, training may be understood broadly as the '[p]lanned process to modify attitude, knowledge, skill or behaviour through a learning experience to achieve effective performance in any activity or range of activities'.[55]

The case of military legal advisors may serve as an excellent illustration of the magnitude of the adaptation required through training. Generally, every legal advisor has traditionally three, inter-linked, principal roles: advising,

---

[53] E.g. the United States Freedom of Navigation (FON) program was developed in 1979 as a response to attacks on core principles of the law of the sea.

[54] This development necessitated responsive reaction from status quo States. E.g. see United States Army Training and Doctrine Command, 'The US Army in Multi-Domain Operations 2028' (U.S. Army, 2018) <https://api.army.mil/e2/c/downloads/2021/02/26/b45372c1/20181206-tp525-3-1-the-us-army-in-mdo-2028-final.pdf> accessed 10 February 2023.

[55] Manpower Services Commission, *Glossary of Training Terms* (HMSO 1981) 62. Moreover, '[i]ts purpose, in the work situation, is to develop the abilities of the individual and to satisfy current and future manpower needs of the organization'.

negotiating, and litigating.[56] These functions are barely sufficient for the current strategic environment characterized by the assaults against the RBIO. Using law as a weapon to purposefully undermine the legal order necessitates a different approach to the role of the military legal advisors, who should be incorporated fully in the operations planning process. Apart from their traditional role, they should be able to take the lead on the performance of all activities pertaining to the execution of the operationalization of legal operations, in order for their command, State, or organization to be able to properly deter or defend against a hostile legal operation.

5.2 Designing training to achieve legal resilience

Training is a key driver for every organization such as NATO to attain legal resilience. In order to create an effective training outcome, a structured methodology has to be implemented. The first phase of the systematic attitude towards training is the clear identification of the training needs[57] and the consequent training objectives. In the present context, the training needs, or in simpler terms what has to be trained, are a straightforward consequence of the aim to put into practice, or operationalize, the notion of legal operations. The performance analysis is the most appropriate tool in order to clearly articulate the delta between, on the one hand, the current functions performed by the organization and, on the other hand, the new requirements emanating from the practical execution of legal operations. This gap should serve as the basis in order to establish the training objectives. In general terms, training objectives for legal operations may include the following:

a. Legal advisors are able to identify hostile legal operations, in close coordination with the intelligence branches.
b. Legal vigilance and legal awareness are maintained throughout the organization.
c. The procedures established in the context of the operationalization of legal operations are well understood by all stakeholders, who are comfortable with their execution.
d. The decision makers are familiar with the procedures pertaining to strategic choices and possible responses to hostile legal actions based on the vector analysis.

---

[56] David Anderson, 'The Functions of the Legal Adviser: Advising, Negotiating, Litigating', in *The Role of Legal Advisers in International Law*, edited by Andraž Zidar and Jean-Pierre Gauci (Brill 2016) 13.
[57] Several tools are available for analysing training needs. For an overview, refer to Jean Barbazette, *Training Needs Assessment: Methods, Tools, and Techniques* (Pfeiffer 2006) 8.

670 COUNTERING HYBRID AND GREY ZONE THREATS

The next stage is to devise a training program that attains the training objectives. For present purposes, it suffices to mention the two broad categories pertaining to NATO: individual training and collective training and exercises. The former is primarily suitable for the enhancement of the personnel's technical skills. Accordingly, the familiarization with MILO, the vector assessment, and more generally a competence in legal operations procedures should inform the content of individual training. Collective training could help spread a 'culture of legal readiness', legal vigilance, and legal awareness across the organization.

Regarding individual training, a new 'legal operations' discipline should be created bringing coherence to the effort to create the necessary skills in this novel area of activity. This will facilitate the conduct of in-depth training objectives analysis, with a clear identification of training audiences and creation of performance statements, which will eventually lead to the establishment of new courses and the proper adaptation of the existing ones. Moreover, there is a two-way relationship between individual and collective training. On the one hand, the content of the individual training should inform the scenarios of the major joint exercises. Exercise planners should be supported by the content of individual training to successfully incorporate into the exercises the appropriate incidents and vignettes in order to train legal operations. On the other hand, lessons identified from the exercises could support the evaluation of the individual training.

The implementation of any training program should always be followed up with an evaluation of the training delivered.[58] This is a long-term and challenging effort in understanding the casual linkages between the outcomes and the training conducted.[59] This systematic approach to training could be followed *mutatis mutandis* by other organizations and entities, whether domestic or international. Obviously, the training architecture should be tailored to the specific characteristics of each organization, including its size, structure, and organizational culture.

6. Conclusions

This chapter has explored the steps necessary to operationalize the idea of legal resilience against hostile legal operations in complex scenarios. Legal resilience

---

[58] The most renowned model to access the effectiveness of training was introduced by Donald and James Kirkpatrick. Reaction, learning, behaviour, and results constitute the four levels of evaluating a training program. For more details on the subject, see Donald L. Kirkpatrick and James D. Kirkpatrick, *Evaluating Training Programs: The Four Levels* (3rd edn, Berrett-Koehler 2006).

[59] For example, poor training results are not always a straightforward consequence of the quality of training but could be attributed to other factors.

has as its main goal the creation of a state of preparedness to defend the RBIO. As has been exemplified in this chapter, revisionist powers and non-State actors do not hesitate to resort to the hostile instrumentalization of the law. Such hostile legal actions against particular States, organizations, or the international rule of law more generally are not new. While much of what falls under this banner has been discussed in the literature under the heading of lawfare, ACO prefers the notion of 'legal operations' that is, 'the use of law as an instrument of power'.[60]

Legal interoperability is a mandatory enabler to reach effective interaction among the different instruments of power within and among States. A coalition or an alliance like NATO can be legally interoperable if all member States rely on the same, or at least mutually compatible, legal regimes and understandings to regulate the use of force during armed conflict and to shape the OPLAN, ROEs, and other mission-specific instruments making up the legal framework of an operation.

Legal resilience cannot be attained in this context without the operationalization of the notion of legal operations. NATO ACO Office of Legal Affairs, with the support of key partners, has identified examples of legal operations ran by different actors, either on their own or in combination with other tools in the DIMEFIL spectrum, and has reacted to them by defining three distinct criteria to identify a hostile legal action in the form of the three i's: intention; the use of particular instruments; and their impact on the target. In this overall effort, legal interoperability, training, operationalization, and legal vigilance are essential activities.

At the end of the path to legal resilience lies the ability of a State or organization to successfully implement a solid response against, or in anticipation of, a hostile legal operation, effectively disabling it or mitigating its effects. The operationalization of legal operations contributes to greater legal certainty among the different actors involved and reinforces the rule of law in the face of hostile activities that disregard, debase, or abuse it.[61] Just as importantly, if an organization is legally resilient, meaning that it is able to effectively defend itself against hostile actions in the legal field while respecting its own legal obligations and the international rule of law, it will project legal deterrence against its adversaries.

Acknowledgements

This text was drafted in a personal capacity. The views and opinions of the authors expressed herein should therefore not be interpreted as stating or reflecting

---

[60] Kittrie (n 24) 8.
[61] Muñoz Mosquera and others (n 20) 102.

those of their respective employers, universities, associations and organizations of which they are members. In writing this chapter, Andrés Muñoz Mosquera has worked on section 2 (Legal resilience: an overview), Jean-Emmanuel Perrin on section 4 (The operationalization of legal operations within NATO), Panagiotis Sergis on section 5 (Training), Rodrigo Vázquez Benítez on sections 1 and 6 (Introduction and Conclusions) and Borja Montes Toscano on section 3 (Ensuring legal interoperability in complex-hybrid scenarios).

Index

For the benefit of digital users, indexed terms that span two pages (e.g., 52–53) may, on occasion, appear on only one of those pages.

Tables and figures are indicated by *t* and *f* following the page number

ABA Journal, 532
Abqaiq, refinery at, 358
Abu Marzouq, Musa, 615n.37
academia, infiltration of, 450–51
accountability, evasion of, 148
Acheson, David, 514–15
Achilles' heels, identifying, 633–44
active measures, 36–37, 166, 341
activities, below the threshold of war, 448
'act of aggression', 112
acts *ultra vires*, 121
adaptability, 536–38, 540–41
adaptation, 544–45, 547–48, 553–54
adapting institutions, 537–38
adaptive preferences, 68, 84
ad bellum criteria, 496n.6, 499–500, 504, 506
advanced persistent threat (APT) groups, 194–95
adversaries
    choices of, 342
    vs. competitors, 36
ad vim framework, 500
aerial domain, international standards and, 329
Afghan Army, 581
Afghanistan, 360–61, 481, 482, 483, 483n.40, 486–87
    Iran and, 488–90
    Mujahideen in, 463
    Russian invasion of, 346
    Soviet Union and, 35–36, 432
    terrorist groups in, 363
    US and, 53, 432
Africa, civil wars in, 471
African Union, 334
agents
    influencing, 158–59
    in lines of effort, 158
aggression. *See also specific forms of aggression*
aggressions, 45–46, 321–22, 321n.8
    attribution of, 37–38
    crime of, 126–27
    start-stop-start, 85

aggressiveness, 321–22
agonism, 371–72
    'agonistic' competition, 371
    'agonistic' relationships, 371–72
Airiston Helmi case, 426n.7
Albert, Prince, 454–55
Aldrich, R. J., 260
Alexander, David, 546–47
algorithms, 422, 423
Al-Khasawneh, Awn, 436n.51
alliance, 27
Almog, Doron, 612
al-Qaeda, 53, 54, 360–61, 362, 471, 486–87, 617
Al-Tawthiq committee, 614–15
'alteneu' endeavour, 323
ambiguity, 31–32, 168n.39, 321, 450, 529–30
    grey zone(s) and, 39–40, 374, 375, 466
    lying and, 375
    role of, 17–18
ambivalence, paralysis in response to, 71
American Federation of Labor (AFL-CIO), 462–63
Amnesty International (AI), 211
analogical reasoning, 138–48
Andreou, Chrisoula, 73, 74n.17
Angola, 578
anonymity, 62, 62n.2, 419–20
Ansar Allah Houthis, 333
Ansar al-Sham, 443–44
Antarctic Treaty System (ATS), 282, 282n.46
Anthem, 226–27
anti-5G movement, 563, 567–68
anticipatory defence, cyberattacks and, 505–7
antipropaganda laws, 164–65
anti-Roma sentiment, 479–80
anti-satellite (ASAT) tests, destructive, 293, 295, 302, 307–8
anti-Semitism, 479–80
anti-vaxxer movement, 563, 567–68
Anzilotti, Dionisio, 529–30
Apollo Moon Landing site, preservation of, 306–7

674 INDEX

Application of the Convention on the Prevention and Punishment of the Crime of Genocide (Bosnia and Herzegovina v. Serbia and Montenegro), International Court of Justice (ICJ), 436–38, 436n.51
application programming interfaces (APIs), 419–20
APT1, 202
APT10, 188–89
APT40, 194–95
APT41, 189–90
Arab League, 334
Arab Spring, 447, 464–65, 593
Arbitral Tribunal in the South China Sea Arbitration, 262–63
arbitration tribunals, 126–27
the Arctic
China and, 20–21, 271–87, 272n.8
fishing in, 276–77, 282, 285n.60
as global commons, 282–83
governance of, 280–82, 281n.42, 283, 284–87 (*see also* Arctic Council)
grey zone(s) in, 271–87
Indigenous peoples of, 282–83, 284–85
lawfare in, 280
NGOs and, 282–83
Norway and, 371–72
resources in, 276–77
Russia and, 53–54, 271, 332–33, 371–72
shipping regulation in, 285n.60
UN and, 284–85
US and, 53–54, 271, 273n.10, 277–78, 282–83, 286
Arctic-8, 277–78, 285
Arctic Council, 272, 273, 273n.10, 280–82, 284–85, 286–87, 371–72
Arctic Sunrise case, 268–69
Arendt, Hannah, 169–70, 174–75, 179
armed attack
'armed attack' threshold, 97
definition of, 119
armed conflict
institutionalized, 470–71, 472, 475–76 (*see also* conventional warfare; warfare)
subjectivity of, 119–25
armed forces, grey zone competition and, 325–26
armed non-State actors (ANSAs), 428, 429–35, 445
definition of, 429–30n.21
Geneva Conventions and, 429–32, 429–30n.21, 431n.29, 433–34
IHL and, 429–31

insurrectional movements, 432, 433, 434–35
legislative jurisdiction and, 432
responsibilities of, 434
States and, 431–32
armed resistance, 614
arms control treaties, 312–13, 352, 367. *See also specific treaties*
arms proliferation, as threat to peace, 113–14
arms trade treaties, 442–44
Arms Trade Treaty, 440, 442–44, 445
Arnold, Craig Anthony, 541
Arquilla, John, 42–43
Art, Robert J., 345
Artemis Accords, 293, 303–8, 315
deconfliction of space activities and, 307–8
emergency assistance and, 305–6
foundational principles of, 304–8
interoperability and, 306
peaceful purposes and, 305
preserving outer space heritage, 306–7
registration of space objects and, 306
release of scientific data and, 306
safety zones and, 307–8
space resources and, 307
transparency and, 305
Artemis Gateway, 304, 306
Articles on Responsibility of States for Internationally Wrongful Acts
Article 8, 435
Article 10, 432, 433
Artificial Intelligence (AI), 100, 198–99, 274–75
ASAT tests, 308–12
Asia, 59
Assad, Bashar al-, 55, 410, 443–44, 491–92
assertives, 377
Assurance Game, 83
Asylum Procedures Directive 2013/ 32/ EU, 640
asymmetrical combat, 517
Attack Lifecycle, 200
attacks
vs. espionage, 19, 180, 183, 190–91
exploiting intransitive preferences, 74–76
on infrastructure, 149
attribution, 451
challenges of, 451
cyberspace and, 401
effective control test, 437–38, 440
information operations and, 423
overall control test, 437–38, 440
problem of, 496n.5
proper attribution test, 438
of responsibility, 428–44
Atwater, Lee, 166–67n.35

INDEX   675

audience, in lines of effort, 158
Aurora Observatory, 278
Aust, Helmut, 534
Australia, 56, 208, 230, 252–53, 573
  2020 Defence Strategic Update, 253–54
  Artemis Accords and, 304
  China and, 230, 233–34, 265–66, 560–61, 573
  Quadrilateral Dialogue and, 595
Austria, Freedom Party (FPÖ), 478
authoritarianism, 1–3, 35, 490, 585
  in China, 207–8, 234
  democracies and, 447–48, 472, 547–48
  hybrid influencing and, 633–34
  liberal democracies and, 589–600
  media manipulation and, 175
  repression and, 589–600
  in Russia, 207–8
  technology and, 472–73
authority
  legitimate, 405–11
  lines of, 73–74
  multiple sources of, 579–82
autocracies
  vs. democracies, 1–4, 8–9, 14–15, 35, 234
  democracies and, 593
  hybrid threats and, 12
  rule of law and, 7
  transgressive competition and, 4
automated identification system (AIS), 267
Auxiliary Territorial Service (ATS), 564–65
aviation domain, 207, 215, 216–21, 484–85
Axelrod, Robert, 352

bad opponent action, 85
Bahrain, 304, 481
balance of power, 346
BALIKATAN 2016, 56–57
Balkans, 57–58, 425. *See also* Yugoslavia
Ban Ki-Moon, 628
Baqués, Josep, 326
Barak, Aharon, 516–17
Barak, Ehud, 612
Barela, Steven J., 22–23, 141–42, 141n.73,
  393–424
bargaining, 85
  bargaining problems, 61–62, 65, 79, 83
  bargaining theory, 83
Barium, 189–90
Barnsby, Robert, 100–1
Barr, William, 226–27
Barrett, Ed, 24
Barrett, Edward, 495–511
Basics of International Law for Modern Soldiers, 211

Bay of Pigs, 472, 484–85
Bechtol, Bruce, 205
BeiDou-2 navigation satellite system, 278–79
Beijing Olympics, 172
Belarus, 562, 575–76
  EU and, 562, 575–76
  migration and, 637–38
Belgium
  lawfare and, 601–2, 611, 613
  Second Intifada and, 602–3
  suit against Sharon in, 602–3n.4, 603n.6
Belt and Road Initiative (BRI), 174, 274–75, 347
Benkler, Yochai, 165
Bennett, R. B., 455
Bennett, W. Lance, 166–67n.35, 167, 170n.51
Berlin Wall, fall of, 449–50, 476
Bernays, Edward, 157, 163–64, 164n.23, 165
Bevin, Ernest, 516
Bicchieri, Cristina, 351–52
Biden, Joe, 35, 67n.9, 72n.13, 208, 594, 595
  administration of, 1–2, 35, 594
'big lie', 169–70, 179, 411–12
Bilms, Kevin, 35
bin Laden, Osama, 53, 54, 486–87
biodata, bio-technologies and, 243
biodiversity loss, 2–3
Biological Toxin and Weapons Convention
  (BTWC), 240, 245, 246
biological weapons, 240
bio-technologies
  biodata and, 243
  current conventions and dilemma of control,
    245–46
  disruptive effects of, 237–49
  emerging, 237–49
  gene editing, 241–43
  grey zone engagements and, 237–49
  nanoengineering, 244
  towards address, mitigation, and prevention,
    246–48
Bjarnason, Björn, 286n.64
Bjarnason-report, 286n.64
Black Sea, 263–64, 267
Blechman, Barry M., 355
Blinken, Antony, 594–95, 596, 597
Blue Origin, 305–6
blurred line between peace and war, 4–5, 6,
  12–13, 18, 32–36, 38, 43–44, 104, 119, 124,
  126, 339, 373–74, 447, 450, 451, 495–96
  in international law, 125
BNU-1, 278
Bolshevik Revolution, 451–52
Bolsheviks, 453

676 INDEX

Border Guards, 635
Borisova, Tatiana, 545
Bormes-les-Mimosas, France, 565
Bosnia, 443–44
Bosnian Muslims, 51, 57–58
Bosnian Serbs, 51, 52, 57–58
bots, 130, 136–37, 147, 162–63n.16, 419–20
Bourbeau, Philippe, 537–38
Bradshaw, Samantha, 175
brain-machine interfaces, 241
brain sciences, 240
Brands, Hal, 321n.8, 336
Braun, Megan, 499–500
Braw, Elizabeth, 25–26, 295, 450, 557–76
Brazil, 304
'breach of the peace', 112, 126–27
Bremseth, L. R., 20, 237–49
Brexit, 143
Brezhnev, Leonid, 352, 367
Bridenstine, Jim, 311
bridging, 554–55
Brier, Robert, 460n.44
British Army, 564–65
British Government, *Integrated Review of Security,
Defence, Development and Foreign Policy*, 2–3
Broadcasting Board of Governors, 164–65
broad-spectrum influencing, 631n.4
Brooking, Emerson T., 170, 175
Brown, Floyd, 166–67n.35
Brown University, 'Costs of War Project', 363
Brunstetter, Daniel, 357, 499–500
'brute force' objectives, vs. compliance
objectives, 342
Bucha, Ukraine, massacre in, 38–39, 212
Buchanan, Ben, 190–91, 196, 198, 200
Buck, Tim, 454–55
Building Blocks for the Development on
an International Framework on Space
Resource Activities, 307
building capacity, need for, 551
Bulgaria, 443–44
bullshitting, 162–63n.16
Burgess, Mike, 230
Bush, George H. W., 50, 166–67n.35
administration of, 50–51n.15
Bush, George W., administration of, 595
businesses, 569–70
Bynum, Terrell Ward, 415n.130

Caltagirone, Sergio, 191
Cambodia, 173, 623
Cambridge Analytica, 137, 420
Cambridge Five, 458

Camel's Nose warfare, 65n.5
campaigns, cyber operations and, 200–4
Campbell, Angus, 252–53
Canada, 403–4, 456–57
the Arctic and, 272–73, 273n.10, 277–78,
282–83, 286
Artemis Accords and, 304
Cold War and, 33
Criminal Code, 452–53
dissent in, 452–53
goal of avoiding 'another bloody century', 35
NATO and, 521, 522
Red Scares in, 447–48, 452–53, 466
strikes in, 452
'Workers' Revolt' in, 452
Canrong, Jin, 347
capability, credibility and, 344
'capability-intention dilemma', 345
capacity building, 464–65
Cape Breton coalfields, 452
capitalism, 451–52, 453, 454
capital punishment, 501, 502, 504–5
capitulation, vs. toleration, 371–72
Carlin, John, 198
Carnegie Endowment for International Peace,
188–89, 592, 598
Carothers, Thomas, 592, 593, 594, 595, 597, 599
Carr, Sam, 457–58
Carruthers, Susan L., 176, 177
Carter, Ash, 56
Carter, Jimmy, 377
Casey, William, 461–62, 486
Casey Accords, 485–86
Castro, Fidel, 484–85
casus belli, need for, 106
Catholic Church, 163–64
Catholic Relief Services, 462–63
causal nexus problem, 147–48
'cause for war' threshold, 495
caveats, 658–60
Cedras, Raoul, 51
Center for Strategic and International Studies
(CSIS) 'Gray Zone Project', 341
Central African Republic, 439–40
Central Arctic Ocean Fisheries Agreement
(CAOFA), 282
Central Europe, 443–44, 459–65. *See also
specific States*
Central Intelligence Agency (CIA), 197, 447–48,
474, 484–86
operation QRBERETTA, 462n.51
operation QRHELPFUL, 447–48, 461–62,
461n.47, 462n.51

Solidarność (Solidarity) movement and, 461, 461n.48, 462–63, 464
Central Military Commission (China), 330
Central Passage, 276–77
'Century of Humiliation', China and, 172
Chainalysis, 189
Chalanoul, Nikoleta, 21–22, 319–37, 608
challenges moving forward, 148–52
Challenging the Grey Zone: The Changing Character of Warfare and the Application of International Law hosted by The Judge Advocate General's Legal Center and School in Charlottesville, Virginia, 15–16
Chambers, John, 321
Chang, Welton, 23–24
change, 538
   resistance to, 546–47
   vs. stasis, 547–48
charitable organisations, 450–51
Charter 77, 449, 449n.6
Chechen fighters, 441
Chechen Wars, 476
Chechnya, 425, 476
chemical weapons, 54–55, 240
Chemical Weapons Convention (CWC), 240, 245, 551
Chenoweth, Eric, 462–63
Chesney, Bobby, 140
Chile, United States and, 398
China, 35, 321–22, 558–59
   AI and, 198–99
   the Arctic and, 20–21, 271–87, 272n.8, 277n.23, 282n.47
   Asian neighbours of, 207–8, 234
   attempts to steal vaccine research, 509
   Australia and, 230, 233–34, 265–66, 560–61, 573
   authoritarianism in, 207–8, 234
   Belt and Road Initiative (BRI) and, 174, 274–75, 347
   'Century of Humiliation' and, 172
   claims to South China Sea, 4–5, 14, 20–21, 24–25, 39, 53–54, 216–21, 234, 251, 255, 257, 260–61, 262–63, 264, 265–66, 267–69, 272–73, 272n.8, 330, 331, 517–18, 518n.15
   concept of 'the Greater Arctic', 282–83
   control of media by, 331
   COVID and, 389–90, 566
   cyber operations and, 188–90, 194–95, 198, 200–1, 202, 203
   defence spending by, 49
   destructive anti-satellite (ASAT) tests and, 308–9

   as donor State, 599
   escalating rhetoric and actions of, 208
   European Union and, 188–89
   GDP of, 213
   genocide accusations and, 172
   goal of national rejuvenation and, 287
   grey zone activities and, 19–20, 21–22, 32, 36–37, 38–40, 207–35, 322, 329–31, 337, 471–72, 491, 559–61, 562, 573, 575–76
   grey zone lawfare and, 207, 216–30
   as grey zone 'purist', 329–30, 337
   GZOs and, 471–72, 491
   hacking of databases by, 226–27
   human rights and, 7
   human rights NGOs and, 211
   India and, 598
   industrial espionage and, 188–89
   information technology domain and, 207, 212, 221–30
   Institute of Remote Sensing and Digital Earth, 278
   international commerce and, 213
   international law and, 7, 173–74, 175n.62
   International Lunar Research Station and, 304
   international standards and, 274–75
   internet in, 226, 234
   IP theft and, 188–89, 198, 222–24, 509, 559–60, 561
   Iran and, 481–82
   island building by, 57
   Japan and, 231
   on jurisdiction of the Arbitral Tribunal in the South China Sea Arbitration, 255
   lack of transparency and, 234
   land reclamation by, 57
   lawfare, 234
   lawfare and, 19–20, 207–35, 280, 605n.12
   lawfare doctrine of, 209, 214–16
   law in, 215
   legal warfare and, 605n.12
   Lithuania and, 560–61
   Macau and, 172
   'Made in China 2025', 274–75, 559–60
   as main competitor, 1–2
   maritime domain and, 331, 517–18, 518n.15
   maritime militia of, 267–68
   'military-civilian fusion' (MCF) strategy, 275–76, 276n.20
   narratives and, 171–72
   National Security Law, 274n.12
   NATO and, 207–9
   as 'near-Arctic State', 274

678 INDEX

China (*cont.*)
new opportunities in the Arctic, 284–86
normal competition and, 4
norm-challenging behaviours of, 53–54
Norway and, 560–61
Philippines and, 262, 263, 331, 517–18
'Polar Silk Road' and, 274–75
pressure on South Pacific maritime
boundaries, 319
private sector in, 234
purchase of US companies by, 227–28
as revisionist power, 331
rising influence in South Asia and Indian
Ocean, 595
rules-based order narrative and, 173–74
Russia and, 207–8, 284
Russia-China joint statement of February
2022, 284
'salami-slicing' strategy of, 331, 517
science and technology (S/T) and, 246–47,
275–76, 559–60
social media in, 226
Solomon Islands and, 253–54
South China Sea and, 33, 56–57, 87–88, 172,
207
South Korea and, 232
space domain and, 296, 302
Starlink/China Space Station incident and,
289–93
State immunity and, 546n.82
Taiwan and, 39, 50, 58, 208, 232–33, 371, 487,
559–61, 575–76
Taiwan Strait and, 33
technical standards strategy, 228–30
technology and, 559–60
Threat of Use of Force Against Outer Space
Objects initiative and, 312–13
Trump and, 389–90
UK and, 2–3, 172
UNCLOS and, 268–69
UN Convention of the Law of the Sea
(UNCLOS) and, 517–18, 518n.15
US and, 3, 19–20, 50, 53–54, 56–57, 58, 67n.9,
104, 172, 173–74, 207–8, 211, 215, 221–30,
272–73, 275–76, 279, 286, 289–93, 302,
304, 330, 347, 378–79, 593
use of law enforcement assets, 330, 331
use of maritime militia, 87–88
use of naval and paranaval assets, 4–5
use of trade regulatory authorities, 209,
231–34
US military and, 56–57
US Treasury securities owned by, 213

Uyghurs in, 172
willingness to challenge current international
order, 208–9
Wolf Amendment and, 304
China-Finland Arctic Monitoring and Research
Centre, 278
China Space Station, 289–93
China Standard 2035, 228
Chinese balloon over US airspace, 378–79
Chinese Coast Guard, 267–68
Chinese Communist Party (CCP), 227–28
Central Committee, 330
'Three Warfares' of, 214, 215, 273n.9, 330,
527, 605n.12
Chinese Embassy, 223
Chinese military, 50, 267–68, 321–22, 329–30
Chinese air force, 321–22
Chinese Central Military Commission, 214
Chinese Coast Guard, 219–20
Chinese People's Liberation Army (PLA),
329–30
People's Liberation Army (PLA), 39, 56,
495–96
People's Liberation Army Navy (PLAN), 56,
219–20
choice(s)
of action, 61
choice scenarios and dilemmatic
structures, 61
difficult conditions of, 61
under risk, 61
vagueness and, 61–62, 65–76, 85
of values, 61
Chojecki, Mirosław, 462–63
Christian political philosophers, 106
Churchill, Winston, 564–65
Cibralic, Beba, 19, 157–78
Cicero, 106, 377, 515, 522–25
citizen education, 567–69, 570–72
citizen involvement, 565
Citron, Danielle, 140
civilian infrastructure, targeting of, 488–90,
491–92
civilians, minimizing loss of life among, 486–87,
490–91, 499–500
civil participation, declining, 563–64
civil service, 474
civil society, 459–61, 597–98
funding and direction of organisations,
450–51
grey zone aggression targeting, 558–63
grey zone defence and, 25–26, 557–76
social media and, 465–66

Solidarność (Solidarity) movement and, 464
  as target of hybrid and grey zone threats, 25–26
  weaponization of, 23, 447–67
civil unrest, promotion of, 450–51
civil wars, 471
Clark, Richard, 204–5
Clausewitz, Carl von, 8, 33–34, 40, 103–5, 340–
  42, 524
Clay, Marcus, 39
Clean Hands doctrine, 24–25, 515, 528–31
climate change, 1–3, 275–76, 566–67
  Clinton, Hillary, 368
  2016 presidential election and, 143, 146,
    162–63n.16, 368, 408
Clinton, William J., 51–52, 57–58, 521
  administration of, 50–52, 58–59
Clodius, 524
Coats, Daniel, 222
coercion, 18–19, 22–23, 38, 130, 131–32,
    131n.13, 133–34, 148, 149, 339–72, 397–98
  as action that deprives State of sovereign will,
    134, 137
  classical theories of, 346
  'coercive force', 343
  coerciveness, 319–37
  consequentiality and, 142–43, 151–52, 418,
    419
  cyber operations and, 129–53, 321–22, 364–
    65, 366–67, 400, 401, 418, 419
  definition of, 134, 145, 395, 417, 418, 423–24
  diplomacy and, 321–22
  doxing as, 141–42
  economy and, 321–22
  effects of, 142–43
  election interference and, 141–42, 416–17,
    417n.137, 420, 421
  grey zone(s) and, 119, 134, 140–41
  hybrid threats and, 119
  incorporating empirical content, 416–23
  information operations and, 369, 370, 423
  information space and, 321–22
  intervention and, 401
  law and, 321–22
  logic and grammar of, 343–44, 346
  lying and, 144
  manipulation and, 141–42, 145
  military force and, 355–59
  non-intervention and, 141, 145, 423–24
  non-State actors and, 359–61
  as outdated standard, 140–45, 149, 151–52
  short of violence, 339
  as *sine qua non* in context of non-
    intervention, 133

socio-technological change and, 150
State actors and, 359–60
strategies of, 346
targets of, 345
through bots, 147
vs. warfighting, 342, 343
Cold War, 61–62, 104, 346, 484, 486, 490–91,
    592–93, 631
  'democracy-security dilemma' and, 592–93
  Deterrence Paradox game and, 84
  disinformation during, 368
  end of, 1, 35–36, 49, 559
  Finland and, 632
  Grey War and, 84
  grey zone(s) and, 33, 183, 448, 449–50,
    484–86
  GZOs and, 484–86
  leaflets, 565, 566
  lines of effort during, 161, 162–63
  OST and, 294
  political ideology and, 472
  political warfare during, 40, 41, 472
  prosecuted on logic of strategic rationality, 61
  Solidarność (Solidarity) movement and, 459–
    65, 461n.48
  Soviet Union and, 465, 472, 578, 592–93
  space domain and, 297
  strategic rationality and, 17–18
  superpowers and, 472
  US and, 472, 578
  weaponization of dissent during, 23
'Cold War 2.0', 104
collaboration, space technology and, 302
collateral damage
  justification of, 499–500
  proportionality constraint and, 500–1n.26
collateral harms, counter-terror operations and,
    363–64
collective self-defence, NATO and, 519, 521,
    522
Colombia
  Artemis Accords and, 304
  narco-wars in, 471
Colonial Pipeline ransomware attack, 189, 367,
    561
'colour revolutions', 447–48, 465, 467
combat readiness, 88
commercial space sector, 295–96
Committee to Support Solidarity (CSS), 462–63
common-law countries, 611
communicable diseases, 1–2
communications sector, cyber operations
    in, 184

680 INDEX

communications technology, 274–75
  new platforms of, 130
Communism, 453, 454–55, 457, 472
  in Cuba, 484–85
  in Eastern Europe, 449
  fall of, 465–66
  spectre of, 451–52
Communist International (Comintern), 451–52, 454, 457
Communist Parties, 171, 451–52, 452n.18, 457
Communist Party of Canada (CPC), 454
Communist Party of Canada (PCP), 452–53, 452n.18, 454, 455–59, 456n.32, 466
Communist Revolution, 215
companies. *See also* private sector
  grey zone aggression and, 573, 574, 575, 576
  losing intellectual property to Chinese competitors, 561
  targeted by China as proxies for their governments, 560–61
  vulnerability of, 573, 574, 575
  Western, 573, 575–76 (*see also* tech companies; *specific companies*)
competition, 104–5, 321–22
  advances in science and technology and, 2–3
  agonism and, 371–72
  competitive activities, 319–20
  vs. cooperation, 296–97
  coordination and, 389–91
  geographical arenas of, 20–21
  grey zone(s) and, 24–25, 179–206, 373–74
  inevitability of, 371
  international law and, 5–9
  law and, 16
  in legal domain, 9
  need to embrace, 515
  normal, 4
  norms and, 354
  peace and, 183
  renewed intensity of, 4–5
  right to, 371
  rising tide of, 486
  rule of law and, 8, 515
  short of armed conflict, 3–5, 36, 183–84, 426
  space domain and, 296–97
  through peaceful means, 6
  tools of, 354
  transgressive, 4
  use of force and, 3
'Competition Continuum', 470n.2
competitors, vs. adversaries, 36
complexity, 538

compliance
  securing, 553–54
  without compulsion, 406
compliance-leverage disparity lawfare, 211
compliance objectives, vs. 'brute force' objectives, 342
compound wars, 427n.13
computational propaganda, 165
computer-aided dispatch (CAD) systems, 504–5
Confederates, 523–24
Conference on Disarmament (CD), Prevention of an Arms Race in Outer Space (PAROS), 310–11, 312–13
conflict, increasing risk of, 1–2
conflict classification, 93–95
  conflict continuum, 469, 470–71, 470n.2
  lower and upper thresholds of, 319
  political warfare in, 472
conflicts, 104–5
  as permanent characteristic of international system, 36
  rule of law and, 515
  short of armed conflict, 34–35, 37–38, 40–41, 45–46, 62n.1, 88, 89–90, 93–94, 95, 96–98, 101, 107, 115–16, 319, 321, 325–26, 331
consent by the harmed, 24, 496, 497
consequentalists, 501–3
consequentiality approach, 142–43, 151–52
consultant lobbying, 549–50
Contagion, 567
content, disguising origin of, 162–63
contestation, 1–5
  below the threshold of open conflict, 4–5
  varied pace of, 4
context, in lines of effort, 158
Conti, 189
Contra rebels, 362, 436, 436n.51
control, deniability and, 23
conventional warfare, 3, 11–12, 93
  aims of, 33–34
  instruments used in, 33–34
Convention on the Law of the Sea (UNCLOS), 210–11, 218, 220–21, 262, 263–65, 267, 268–69, 280–81, 331, 371–72
  China and, 517–18, 518n.15
  hybridity and, 261–65
  maritime grey zone and, 261–65
  maritime hybrid threats and, 261–65
Convention on the Rights of the Child, Optional Protocol, Article 4, 431–32
Convention on the Settlement of Investment Disputes between States and Nationals, 434

cooperation, 83, 298–99, 301, 527, 554–55
  advances in science and technology and, 2–3
  Assurance Game and, 83
  vs. competition, 296–97
  diminishing space for, 1–2
  good faith, 389
  need for international, 1–2
  norms and, 351–53, 354
  Prisoner's Dilemma and, 82–84, 85
  shareable surplus of goods yielded by, 61,
    82–83, 85
  space domain and, 296–97, 315
  between States and NSAs, 426–27, 445
coordination, competition and, 389–91
coordination games, 351–52
coordination of plans of action, 389
*Corfu Channel, Tehran Hostages, Military and
  Paramilitary Activities in and against
  Nicaragua,* and *DR Congo v. Uganda,*
  117–18, 133
Cormac, R., 260
corporations, transnational, as non-State actors,
  434, 445
COSCO, 276–77, 282–83
COSMOS 1408, 311–12
Costa Rica, 91
Costa Rica v. Nicaragua, 91
cost-benefit analyses, retaliation and, 72
Council of the European Union, 421–22
  Directive (EU) 2016/ 1148, 552
counterinsurgency (COIN), 34, 578
counterintelligence operations, cyber
  operations and, 192, 197
counter-terrorism (CT), 34, 362, 363–64, 486–
  87, 490, 578, 583
  collateral harms and, 363–64
  military force and, 363
Court of Justice of the European Union, 640
covert operations, international law and, 37–38
Covid, 389–90, 393–94, 563, 564, 567–68, 570–
  71, 574
  China and, 566
  disinformation about, 509–10
  in South Korea, 509
  in Taiwan, 509
  in US, 509
  vaccines and, 509–10
Cozy Bear, 137
CrashOverride attack, 505
Crawford, James, 553–54
credibility, capability and, 344
crime
  crimes against humanity, 610–11

cyber crime, 476–77, 502–3, 507–8
  vs. statecraft, 19, 180, 183, 187–90
Crimea, 12, 14, 42–43, 55–56, 57, 80–81, 87–88,
  148–49, 332–33, 332n.50, 373, 374, 375,
  450, 495–96, 551, 633–34, 637–38
criminality, transnational, 488–90
crises
  conflict continuum and, 470
  definition of, 348
  relationships and, 348–49
  short of war, 566–67
crisis communication satellites, 302
crisis education, 25–26, 566–68, 570–72, 576
crisis-response training, 25–26
CRISPR/Cas-based gene editing, 241–43, 244
critical infrastructure, 207, 339, 364, 365, 450–
  51, 475, 486, 491–92, 554–55, 632–33
critical interconnectedness, 19, 179, 180–82,
  204
Croatia, 443–44, 487
Crootof, Rebecca, 138–39
cryptocurrency, 187–88, 189, 561
Cuba, 175n.61, 484–85
Cuban Missile Crisis, 465
customary international law, 130, 220–21
  emerging, 150–51
  new, 148
  non-intervention and, 129
  norm on non-intervention and, 150
  socio-technological change and, 129–53
  State lying and, 378–79
customary law, altered after terrorist attacks of
  11 September 2001, 118
customs, violations of, challenges to,
  undermining of, 495–96
'customs of war', 120
cyber arena, international law and, 224–25
cyber attacks, 18–19, 130, 364, 450–51, 476, 486,
  487–88, 491, 571–72
  anticipatory defence and, 505–7
  to degrade, 203–6
  to deny, 203–6
  to destroy, 203–6
  to disrupt, 203–6
  on Estonia, 328–29, 359
  Finland and, 633–34
  grey zone aggression and, 573
  Iran and, 561
  North Korea and, 561
'cyber biosecurity', 246
cyber capabilities, evolving use of, 487
cyber crime, 476–77, 502–3, 507–8
cyber defence, 329

682 INDEX

cyberdomain, international law and, 14–15
cyber espionage, 184, 190–91, 192, 193–95,
    196–200, 224–25, 366
  economic costs of, 507–8
  Finland and, 633–34
cyberhacking, 62n.1
cyber norms, 366–67
cyber operations, 22, 34–35, 145, 180–82, 255–
    56, 350, 354, 357, 358–59, 395–96, 400,
    423–24, 450–51, 475, 487, 488–90, 618. *See
    also* cyber attacks
  in 2016 US presidential election, 326
  as 'armed force', 366–67
  attribution of aggression and, 37–38
  campaigns and, 200–4
  China and, 188–90, 194–95, 198, 200–1, 202,
    203
  coercion and, 142, 364–65, 366–67, 400, 401,
    418, 419
  in communications sector, 184
  countering, 329
  counterintelligence operations and, 192, 197
  cyber influence operations, 326, 395
  to degrade, 197, 198
  democratic institutions and, 184
  destabilization through, 185, 190
  disruption and, 184, 190, 364, 365, 367
  economic costs of, 507–8
  election manipulation, 508–9 (*see also specific
    elections*)
  in energy sector, 184
  espionage and, 184, 190–91, 192, 193–200,
    366 (*see also* cyber espionage)
  in financial services sector, 184
  financial services sector and, 189–90
  goals of, 190–91, 196–200, 203–6
  grey zone competition and, 179–206
  grey zone(s) and, 19, 179–206, 328, 364–66
  as grey zone tool, 328
  hacking of databases, 226–27
  harm caused by entropy, 413
  in healthcare sector, 184
  impactful from below the threshold, 192–206
  ineffectiveness of, 365–66
  influence operations and, 199–200
  interference and, 141, 142, 149
  international law and, 358–59
  international norms and, 523
  interpretation of goals of, 190–91
  IP theft and, 198
  Iran and, 365–66
  Israel and, 365–66
  in IT sector, 184

  manipulation of, 142
  non-attribution and, 364–66
  normative implications, 366–67
  North Korea and, 187–88, 197, 205–6
  outcomes of, 201–2, 203
  physical damage inflicted through, 185, 190,
    366–67
  proportionate response to, 508–9
  Russia and, 189, 191, 193–94, 196–97, 204
  sabotage and, 192
  scale and scope of, 204–5
  in security sector, 184
  short of armed conflict, 183–84, 186–87,
    190–91, 192–206
  State actors and, 366–67
  strategic outcomes and, 201–2
  subversion and, 192
  thriving in grey zone(s), 182–92
  as tool of statecraft, 185, 190
  UK and, 194–95
  US and, 365, 367, 487–88
cyber proxies, 487
cybersciences, 240
cybersecurity
  AI and, 198–99
  intelligence and, 192, 193
cyberspace, 13–14, 18–19, 100, 130, 131, 135–
    48, 180–82, 399–400
  attribution and, 401
  coercion and, 129–53, 321–22
  defence problems in, 179–206
  dependence on, 180–82
  geostrategic competition in, 180
  global interconnectivity of, 180–82
  as grey zone for non-intervention by design,
    140
  international law and, 5–6, 14–15, 138
  lack of transparency and, 150
  non-intervention and, 134
  problem of non-transparency and, 129–53
cyber technologies, 339, 358–59
cyber threats, 137, 450–51
cyber warfare, 255–56. *See also* cyber attacks;
  cyber operations
Cyprus, 621
Czechoslovakia, 381, 449–50, 459–61
Czech Republic, 443–44, 479–80, 575

Daesh. *See* Islamic State of Iraq and Syria (ISIS)
Damon, Matt, 567
Danube Circle (*Duna Kör*), 449
Darfur, 425
Darkside, 189

INDEX 683

data access, 422, 423
data analytics companies, 137
databases, hacking of, 226–27
data collection, 368, 419–20, 422n.163
data sharing, privacy and, 422, 422n.164
'Day Without Space' exercise, 294
DCLeaks, 408
decentralized networks, 93
deception, 472–73
  definition of lying, 376
  information operations and, 370
  intention to deceive, 388–89
  lying in the grey zone, 373–92
decisional paralysis, 61
decision lines, bright, 61
decision-making, manipulation of, 144, 161
decision-theoretic tools, 61–85
decision theory, 61–62, 65
Declaration of Friendly Relations, 133
Declaration of Independence (US), 532
Declaration on Non-Interference, 146–47
Declaration on the Inadmissibility of
  Intervention and Interference, 146–47
Declaration on the Promotion of International
  Law of 2016, 7
'declarations of war', 115, 119, 120–21
de-colonization, 87–88
deep fakes, 18–19, 100, 130, 136–37, 140, 368
de-escalation, 370
defence, justified ends of harm, 501
defence posture, 337
defence spending, 49
defend forward strategy, 201–2
defensive harm, justified, 496–98, 511
DeFranco, Joseph, 20, 237–49
Deloite, 194
demands
  calibrating, 344–45
  value of, 344
Demers, John, 227
democracies/democracy, 173, 451–52, 472, 513,
  527–28
  appropriation of meaning of, 7
  authoritarianism and, 447–48, 472, 547–48
  vs. autocracies, 1–4, 8–9, 14–15, 35, 234, 593
  cyber operations and, 184
  defence of, 519
  as defenders of integrity of law, 24–25
  degradation of democratic processes, 488–90
  'democracy-security dilemma', 592–93
  distinctive vulnerabilities of, 16, 19
  election process in, 415
  ethical considerations and, 14–15, 24

foreign influence and, 157
free flow of information in, 19
goal of avoiding 'another bloody century', 35
grey zone competition and, 24–25
GZOs and, 471–72
hybrid threats faced by, 337
information and, 527
Islamic extremists and, 54
legal considerations and, 24, 634
partner states of, 26
persuasion and, 157
practical considerations and, 24
propaganda and, 163–64
resilience and, 25
rule of law and, 7, 14–15
Russian undermining of, 561
scrupulousness as a weakness of, 14–15
security and, 597, 598, 599–600
security assistance provided by, 26, 577–600
subversion of democratic processes, 1–2
United States as steward of, 52–53
US military as policeman, 1990-1999, 50–53
voting rights and, 508
vulnerability of, 148, 149, 157, 472–73, 478,
  527–28
Democratic National Committee (DNC)
  doxing of, 130, 141–42
  hacking of, 148–49, 368
Democratic Republic of Congo, 258
democratization, of power, 135, 136–37,
  152–53
demagoguery, propaganda and, 165–66
deniability, 37, 39–40, 96–97, 450, 451, 465–66,
  478, 488–90
  control and, 23
  GZO and, 471
  plausible, 550–51, 573
denial-of-service attacks, 496
denial(s), 477, 481–82, 559
  deterrence by, 576
  of involvement, 471
Denmark, 225, 529–30
  the Arctic and, 272–73, 273n.10, 277–78,
    282–83, 286, 286n.64
  military service in, 572
deontic attitudes, 76–77, 76n.21
descriptive norms, 353–54
desire, desire satisfaction, 69
desires, 68–69
  desire satisfaction, 68–69
desire satisfaction, 68–69, 83–84
destabilization, 478
d'Estaing, Valéry Giscard, 381

684 INDEX

destructive anti-satellite (ASAT) tests, 293, 295, 302, 307–12
deterrence, 35, 50, 99, 337, 501, 502–3, 559
  by denial, 25–26, 576
  deterrence signalling, 563, 575–76
  deterrence theory, 61
  enhancing, 24–25
  failure of, 346
  grey zone aggression and, 559, 576
  international law and, 519
  rule of law and, 519
  through force, 3
Deterrence Paradox game, 84
'dezinformatsiya', 166
De Zwart, Melissa, 21
Diem, Ngo Dinh, 587, 588
DiEuliis, Diane, 20, 237–49
diffusion of power, 148, 149, 152–53
Dig for Victory campaign, 564–65
digital communications technology, 212
digital contexts
  physical concepts and, 138
  territorial concepts and, 138
digital election interference, 18–19, 130
Digital Services Act (DSA), 421–22
digital sovereignty, 136
dignity, 496
diplomacy, 24–25
  coercion and, 321–22
  diplomatic efforts, 474
  diplomatic measures, 474
  warfare and, 40
diplomatic, information, economic, and military (DIME) practices, 41, 634
diplomatic, information, economic, financial, intelligence, and law enforcement (DIMEFIL) spectrum, 21–22, 33–34, 319–20, 322–23, 326–29, 331–32, 335, 336–37, 470–71, 473–74
disaster avoidance, 70
discrimination, 371
disinfo-ops. See disinformation operations
disinformation operations, 130, 136, 137, 158, 161, 166–70, 166–67n.35, 167n.38, 168n.39, 393–94, 395–96, 404, 407, 409, 411–16, 423–24, 465–66, 569. *See also* information operations
  about COVID vaccines, 509–10
  across international borders, 22–23
  amplification of, 423
  during Cold War, 368
  compelling evidence as antidote to, 41
  creating vs. retransmitting, 167n.36

debunking, 618–19
definition of, 166, 167, 179
disinformation campaigns, 161
domaine réservé and, 415, 416
in Eastern Europe, 393–94
election process and, 415, 416 (*see also* election interference; *specific elections*)
enabling of, 423
GZO and, 471
harm caused by, 413
identifying, 423
intent and, 167, 168n.39
vs. misinformation, 166, 167, 168n.39
online, 136–37, 139, 145
vs. Propaganda, 166
Russia and, 516–17, 561
skepticism and, 167, 168, 168n.39
social media and, 130, 134, 516–17
teenagers exposed to, 569
2016 presidential election (*see also* 2016 presidential election)
twenty-sixteen2016 presidential election and, 147
2020 US presidential elections, 370 (*see also* 2020 US presidential elections)
usage of, 167
disinformers, 166
disruption, 149, 203–6, 358–59, 499–500
  as alternative standard for wrongful intervention, 148, 151–52
  bio-technologies and, 237–49
  cyber operations and, 364, 365, 367
  election interference and, 417n.137
  of essential services, 184, 190
  information operations and, 369
  interference through, 142
  online, 145
  technology and, 237–49
  vulnerability to, 149
dissembling, vs. lying, 377
dissent
  in Canada, 452–53
  weaponization of, 23, 447–67
dissidents, 449–50, 449n.6, 459–65
dissimulation, 377
distrust, sowing of, 146–47
disturbance, 546–47
divided authority, 73–74
doctrine of estoppel, 380, 382–83, 385, 386, 389, 390–91
domaine réservé, 18–19, 22–23, 130, 131–33, 131n.13, 134, 136, 137, 147, 148, 149, 397–98, 401, 402–3, 418, 423–24

concept of, 403–4
difficulty of delineating, 139–40
disinfo-ops and, 415, 416
grey zone(s) and, 140
incorporating axiological content, 395, 402–16
incorporating empirical content, 395
information ethics and, 411–12
interference and, 140–41
as outdated standard, 149
Domber, Gregory F., 462–63, 462n.49, 463n.54, 463n.55
domestic law, non-State actors and, 99
Donbas, 332–33, 332n.50, 479
donor States, security assistance and, 577–600
Double Dragon, 189–90
double effect, 499–501, 499n.17
double standards, accusations of, 8–9
doublethink, 125
doxing, 130, 136–37, 141–42, 146, 416
Draft Treaty on the Prevention of the Placement of Weapons in Outer Space, 312–13
drones, 42–43, 123–24, 225
drone strikes, 486–87, 487n.49
legality of, 618–19
drug trafficking, 482–83
drug wars, 32–33
DSC system, 278–79
dual citizenship, 644
due process, justified defensive harm and, 511
Dukakis, Michael, 166–67n.35
Duke of Edinburgh Awards, 570–71
Dunford, Joseph, 252–53
Dunlap, Charles Jr., 356
Dunlap, Charles, Jr., 209–10, 225, 254–55, 604
Duterte, Rodrigo, 598–99
duty to obey, 405

early warning satellites, 302
earthquakes, 566–67
East Asia, 48. *See also specific States and locations*
East China Sea, 330
Eastern Europe, 443–44, 459–65. *See also specific States and locations*
communism in, 449
disinformation operations in, 393–94
grey zone conflicts in, 37
hybrid warfare in, 37
meddling in, 459–65
Russia and, 37, 347
US military exercises in, 55–56

Eastern Greenland case, International Court of Justice (ICJ), 529–30
East Germany, 459–61
ecological resilience, 535–36, 538, 542, 544
ecology, 538–39
economic interdependence, lawfare and, 210, 212–14
economics. *See also* economic interdependence
coercion and, 321–22
creation and exploitation of dependencies, 328
economic and financial measures, 328
economic associations, 450–51
economic hegemony, 472
economic leverage, 450–51
economic measures, 253
economic sanctions, 350
as grey zone tool, 328
Economy of Force, 526
Edelman Trus Barometer, 569–70
education
citizen education, 567–69, 570–72
crisis education, 566–68, 570–72, 576
effective control test, 436–38, 440
'effective control' threshold, 97
Efony, Dan, 141, 150
Egan, Brian, 140, 150–51
Egypt, 621
human rights in, 593, 594–95, 597–98
US and, 593–95, 593n.65, 597–98
Eisenhower, Dwight D., 484–85
election interference, 18–19, 137, 142, 143–44, 145, 161–62, 162–63n.16, 199–200, 393–94, 407–8, 416–17, 447–48, 475, 486, 496, 508–9. *See also specific elections*
coercion and, 141–42, 416–17, 420, 421
disruption and, 417n.137
non-intervention and, 146, 147, 416–17
proportionate response to, 508–9
Russia and, 416n.133, 416n.134, 417n.137, 420, 561
social media and, 143, 147, 420
election process, 132–33, 415, 416. *See also* election interference
election processes, 22–23
electoral coercion, 416–17, 417n.137
electric grids, logic bombs in, 505–7
Elizabeth II, 564–65
El Salvador, 578
embargos, 51
emergencies, 565, 566
emergency dispatch attack, 504–5
Emergency Powers Act (Finland), 634–36, 637

686 INDEX

emerging technologies (Ets), 148, 149, 246, 248, 274–75
  authoritarianism and, 472–73
  emerging technologies as threats (ETT), 239–40, 241, 246, 248
  ethical standards and, 20
  grey zone conflicts and, 20
  international law and, 138
  power diffusion and, 149
ends, in lines of effort, 158
energy sector, cyber operations in, 184
energy shortages, 1–2, 566–67
engineering, 240
engineering resilience, 535–36, 538, 542
entropy, 413, 413n.121
environmental law, 538–39, 541, 546–47
environmental matters, resilience and, 538–39
epistemic security, undermined by foreign influence, 157
epistemic unreliability, 167
equality, 298–99
Equifax, 226–27
equilibria, 357–58, 363–64, 367, 370, 519, 535–36, 537–38, 544–45. *See also* Nash Equilibrium
  'reflective', 372
  stable, 546–47
equity, 530–31
Erdogan, Recep Tayyip, 625–26
Ericsson, 229, 560–61
escalation, 61–62, 99, 348
  alternatives to, 349
  avoidance of, 37–38, 186–87, 319, 323, 357, 364–65, 370, 372, 562
  common structures to escalation-prone grey zone problems, 79–80
  defusing, 85
  escalatory spirals, 348
  games of chicken and, 82
  grey zone conflicts and, 22, 79–84
  intransigence and, 84
  inviting, 349
  limits on, 22, 83, 341–42, 349
  managing, 348–50
  minimizing, 371
  prevention of, 370
  probability of, 499–500
  problem of, 76–78
  risk of, 3, 23–24, 319, 346
  risks of, 61
  use of force and, 355–56, 357
Esper, Mark, 222
espionage, 190–91, 457–58, 466

vs. attacks, 19, 180, 183, 190–91
  cyber operations and, 184, 190–91, 192, 193–200, 366
  economic, 450–51
  ends and means of, 195–203
  industrial espionage, 188–89
  influence operations and, 199–200
  IP theft and, 188–89, 222–24
  political, 450–51
  Soviet Union and, 452
  State-sponsored, 189–90
Estonia, 403–4, 487
  cyber attacks in, 328–29, 359, 364, 365, 366–67
  OPERATION ATLANTIC RESOLVE and, 55–56
estoppel, doctrine of, 380, 382–83, 382–83n.64
EternalBlue, 197
ethical considerations, 14–15
  democracies and, 24
  emerging technologies and, 20
  ethical framework for assessing grey zone responses, 495–511
  legal categories and, 16
  US and, 20
Ethiopia, 584
Ethiopia- Eritrea Claims Commission, 96
ethnic cleansing, in Yugoslavia, 51
Euro-Atlantic security, 208
European Centre of Excellence for Countering Hybrid Threats (Hybrid CoE) in Helsinki, 646
European Code of Conduct for Activities in Outer Space, 312–13
European Commission, 167, 167n.38, 639
European Convention, 636
European Convention ofn Human Rights, 428–29, 636
European Court of Human Rights (ECHR), 613, 636
European Digital Media Observatory, 422n.164
European Economic Area (EEA), 642–43
European Parliament, Digital Services Act (DSA), 421–22
European Union (EU), 114–15, 123, 421–22, 555, 639, 640, 642–43. *See also specific States*
  Belarus and, 562, 575–76
  Charter on Fundamental Rights, 638–39
  China and, 188–89
  Critical Entities Resilience Directive, 632–33
  Greece and, 328
  Hamas designated as terrorist organisation by, 613–14

INDEX 687

Information Security 2 Directive (NIS 2), 632–33
migration and, 562
Morocco and, 334
NATO and, 646
Russia and, 368, 479–80, 637–38
Europol, 14
evidence, 402
exceptional circumstances, new category of, 636–37
exclusive economic zones (EEZs), 218, 219, 220, 267, 517–18
ex delicto non oritur actio principle, 529, 530
expectations, norms and, 351, 353
expected utility principle, 74
maximization of, 61
Expeditionary Sea Base, 266
exploitation, online, 136
external security, internal security and, 633

fabricated content, 167n.38
Facebook, 143, 161, 175, 226, 420, 421, 422, 527–28, 618–19
facial recognition, 225
fake news, 167, 167n.38, 168, 326, 416–17
Falk, Barbara J., 23, 447–67
false connections, 167n.38
false context, 167n.38
false news, 416–17
falu zhan, 214
Fancy Bear, 137, 162–63n.16
Faraj al-Goul, Mohammad, 614–15, 615n.37
Farer, Tom, 417
Faris, Robert, 165
fascism, 454
Federal Bureau of Investigation (FBI) (US), 474
Federal Communications Commission (US), 229–30
Federal Republic of Yugoslavia (FRY), 436–37
Federal Security Service (FSB) (Russia), 476–77, 479
FedEx, 204
Feliciano, Florentino, 142–43, 151–52, 418
Feng Gao, 285
FengYun 1C weather satellite, destruction of, 309
Ferey, Amelie, 603n.7
Ferm, Tiina, 26–27, 631–47
Ferrero, Guglielmo, 407–8
'Fifth Column' activities, 459
financial services sector, cyber operations and, 184, 187–88, 189–90
Financial Times, 188–89

Finish Parliament
Border Guard Act in, 640
Constitutional Law Committee, 635, 637, 640
Finland, 565
amendments to Territorial Surveillance Act, 634–35
amendment to Border Guard Act, 633
the Arctic and, 272–73, 273n.10, 277–78, 282–83, 286, 286n.64
Arctic Space Centre, 278
Border Guard Act in, 26–27, 640, 641–42
Border Guards, 634
Cold War and, 632
Constitution of, 646
critical infrastructure and, 632–33
cyber attacks and, 633–34
cyber espionage and, 633–34
Defence Forces, 634, 645
Emergency Powers Act in, 26–27, 633, 635–36, 637
Finnish Security Committee, 634
hybrid influencing in, 631n.4
hybrid threats and, 631–32, 631n.4, 633–44
intelligence service of, 634–35
intertwined internal and external security in, 644–46
legal resilience and, 26–27, 631–47
migration and, 633, 637–42
Ministerial Working Group on Preparedness, 632–33
Ministry of Defence, 642–43
NATO and, 285, 631–32
Parliament of, 635
restrictions on foreign real estate ownership and foreign corporate acquisitions in, 642–43
Russia and, 426n.7, 574, 631–32, 637–38, 643, 644
as safest and most stable country in the world, 646–47, 646–47n.70
Security Clearance Act, 643–44, 643–44n.62
security environment of, 26–27
Security Strategy for Society 2017, 632, 646n.67
Supreme Administrative Court, 644
Territorial Act, 635
territorial integrity and, 635
Total Defence model in, 632
World War II and, 632
FireEye, 189–90, 194, 197
First Gulf War, 526, 530
first principles, need to revert to, 513–14, 525–28

688 INDEX

'First' Red Scare, 451–52
Fischer, Benjamin B., 461, 461n.47, 461n.48, 462n.49, 463
Fischerkeller, Michael, 201
Fishburne, Laurence, 567
5G technology, 182, 228, 230, 234, 274–75, 642. *See also* anti-5G movement
Floridi, Luciano, 412, 413, 413n.121, 414, 414n.126
fog of war, 237–38
food insecurity, 1–2
force
  deterrence through, 3
  force thresholds, 90–93
  as instrument of international power, 3
  prohibition of use of, 6
Foreign Agents Registration Act, 549–50
Foreign Assistance Act and the Arms Export Control Act, 590
foreign corporate acquisitions, 642–43
foreign influence
  democracies and, 157
  foreign influence efforts (FIEs), 157–58, 162–63
  topography of information based, 157–78
Foreign Intelligence Service (SVR) (Russia), 479
foreign interests of individuals, vetting, 643–44
foreign interference, 18–19
  civil liberties and, 14–15
  disinformation operations and, 22–23
  globalization and, 3–4
  information-based, 19
  by Russia, 23
foreign internal defence (FID), 34
foreign policy, violence as tool of, 486
foreign real estate ownership, 642–43
foreign service, 474
forged actors, 419–20
4G technology, 182
Fox News, 175
fragmentation, 514
France, 402–3, 462, 560–61, 625
  2017 elections in, 199–200
  the Arctic and, 281n.42
  Artemis Accords and, 304
  interference in elections in, 393–94
  lawfare and, 601–2
  missile strikes in Syria and, 9n.37
  Morocco and, 334
  Nazi occupation of, 565
  Nuclear Tests case and, 381
  suspension of conscription in, 559
  universal national service (SNU) in, 570

Franck, Thomas, 110
Frankfurt, Harry, 162–63n.16
free and open democratic society, 634
freedom, 298–99
freedom of navigation (FON, 172
freedom of navigation (FON), 172
Freedom of Navigation Operations (FONOPs), 56–57, 58
freedom of speech, 150, 472–73
Freedom Party (FPÖ) (Austria), 478
Free Syrian Army, 443–44
free trade laws, violation of, 231
French Polynesia, 381
Frowe, Helen, 500
F-Secure, 194–95
Fukuyama, Francis, 1
Fulbright, J. William, 164–65
Fulda Gap, 515–16
future warfare, 11–12

G-20, 224
Galeotti, Mark, 447n.2, 447–48n.3
games of chicken, 61–62, 65, 79–80, 82
game theory, 61–62, 65
Gartzke, Erik, 201
Gates, Robert, 42
Gauthier, David, 83
Gaza Strip, 333, 614–15, 620–22, 620n.59, 628
Gdańsk, Poland, 459–61
Gdańsk Accord, 459–61
Gehl, Robert W., 162, 162–63n.16
gene editing, 241–43
General Data Protection Regulation (GDPR), 422
Geneva Conventions (GCs), 120, 121–22, 123, 429–32, 433–34, 437–38, 440–42, 558–59
  1864, 89–90
  1949, 90, 93–94, 94n.39, 107–8
  1977, 93–94
  Additional Protocol (APs), 120, 123
  armed non-State actors (ANSAs) and, 429–30n.21, 431n.29
  common Article 2 of, 120–21
  IV, 121
  proxies and, 442–43
  Second Additional Protocol, 429–31
  'war' as legal concept in, 120
genocide, 610–11
Genocide Convention, ratification of, 610–11
genomics. *See* gene editing
geopolitical advantage, in pursuit of, 179–206
Georgia
  Fact-Finding Commission in, 91

INDEX 689

hybrid warfare in, 425
Rose Revolution in, 467
Russia and, 58, 329–30, 332, 425, 516–17
Russian incursion into, 55–56
Geospatial Intelligence (GEOINT), 183
geostrategic competition, in cyberspace, 180
Gerasimov, Valery, 36, 38, 447–48, 447n.2, 447–48n.3
'Gerasimov Doctrine', 447–48, 447n.2, 447–48n.3
Germany, 171, 232–33, 348, 381–82, 401, 403–4, 451–52, 625
Federal Volunteer Service in, 570n.34
interference in elections in, 393–94
invasion of Soviet Union, 457
maritime incident of 31 May 2010 and, 620
suspension of conscription in, 559
UK and, 348
'Voluntary Social Year' in, 570–71
Giedroyc, Jerzy, 463n.54
Giordano, James, 20, 237–49
glasnost, 449
Glennon, Michael J., 109
'global battlefield', notion of, 123–24
global connectivity, 339, 368
global governance, 495
globalization, 210, 396–97
foreign interference and, 3–4
lawfare and, 210, 212–14
liberal democracies and, 558–59
Global Maritime Distress Safety System, 278–79
Global Navigation Satellite Strategy (GNSS) technology, 294
global power, changing nature and distribution of, 2–3
global stability, 24–25
Goebbels, Joseph, 177
Goertz, Gary, 351
Goldman, Emily, 201
Goldwater-Nichols Act (US), 485–86
Gonzales, Roberto, 152
good faith
in coordination of plans of action, 380, 383–85
good faith co-operation, 389–91
principle of, 381–83, 383–84n.74, 384, 385–86, 387, 388, 389–90, 530–31
good governance, 7
'good-neighbor policy', 398
Google, 226, 422, 573
Gorbachev, Mikhail, 449, 459–61
Gouzenko, Igor, 457–58

governance
global, 495
good governance, 7
governance structures, competition to shape, 2–3
government resistance, 585–89
gradation in law enforcement, 150
gradualism, grey zone conflicts and, 38
Granatstein, Jack, 458
Grant, Ulysses S., 523–24
Gray, Christine, 111
Gray, Colin, 35
Great Britain. *See* United Kingdom
Great Power Competition, 1–5, 33, 350
grey zone conflicts and, 16
hybrid threats and, 16
Greece, 621, 623, 625
EU and, 328
Russia and, 328
US and, 586, 587
Greenhill, Kelly M., 345
Greenland, 529–30
Grego, Laura, 296
Grey War, 61–62, 84
grey zone actors, 329–34
China, 330–31
Iran, 333
Russia, 331–33
grey zone aggression, 557–76
China and, 573, 575–76
companies and, 573, 574, 575, 576
cyber aggression and, 573
defining, 562, 563
deterrence and, 559, 576
as 'geopolitical gaslighting', 295
private sector and, 573, 574, 575, 576
retaliation for, 562
targeting civil society, 558–63
tech companies and, 573
technology and, 559–60, 562
grey zone approaches
avoidance of escalation and, 37–38
DIMEFIL spectrum and, 326–29, 331–32
revisionist powers and, 37, 319
grey zone attacks
exploiting intransitive preferences, 61–62
not requiring response, 61–62
paralysis in response to, 61
precautionary principle and, 61–62
requiring choices under conditions of vagueness, 61–62, 72–74
requiring response, 67–72
with responses dictated by cost-benefit analyses, 61–62

690 INDEX

grey zone attacks (*cont.*)
responses to, 61, 67–72
retaliation to, 72
vs. terrorism, 63
that may be misperceived as not requiring
response, 61–62
uncertainty and, 61
grey zone behaviours, 474–75
diplomatic measures and, 474
grey zone cases
COVID vaccines, 509–10
economic costs of cybercrime and cyber
espionage, 507–8
election manipulation, 508–9
emergency dispatch attack, 504–5
logic bombs in electrical grids, 505–7
a thousand cuts, 507–8
grey zone challenges, US military responses to,
1991-2020, 49–57
grey zone competition, 19, 179–206
armed forces and, 325–26
cyber operations and, 179–206
definition of, 322–23
democracies and, 24–25
DIMEFIL spectrum and, 21–22
elusiveness of the concept, 322–23
vs. hybrid warfare, 323–26
liberal democracies and, 526
grey zone conflicts, 10–13, 31–32, 43–44, 104,
126–27, 237–38, 373–74, 515. *See also* grey
zone warfare
aims of, 33–34
ambiguity and uncertainty and, 13–14, 17–
18, 39–40, 61–85
analytical utility of concept, 16–17
based on premise that Western interests and
institutions are outdated, 514–15
benefits offered by concept of, 16–17
bio-technologies and, 237–49
caused by revisionists, 64
character of, 61–65
China and, 19–20
Cicero's prescriptions for, 522–25
coercion and, 38, 119
common structures to escalation-prone grey
zone problems, 79–80
concept of, 514
as conflicts short of war, 36, 37–38
countering adverse effects of, 15
decoding of, 21–22, 319–37
definition of, 10–13, 62, 319, 450–51n.13
DIMEFIL spectrum and, 335, 336–37
in Eastern Europe, 37

emerging technologies and, 20
escalation and, 79–84
ethically permissible responses to, 24
exploitation of vulnerabilities of democracies
by, 16
general form of solution to escalation-prone,
80–84
gradualism and, 38
great power competition and, 16
vs. hybrid warfare, 41–43
IHL and, 127
incentivization of, 18
infrequency of, 17
instruments used in, 21–22, 33–34 (*see also*
grey zone tools)
international law and, 13–14, 103–27, 513–32
international norms and, 513–32
vs. irregular warfare (IW), 34
law and, 13–14, 19–20, 103–27, 513–32
lawfare and, 19–20
legal resilience and, 542–48
limits on escalation and, 22
LOAC and, 124–25
methods used in, 21–22
military affairs and, 45–60
as the new norm, 62n.1
non-intervention and, 134, 135–48
in outer space, 21
Principles of Warfare and, 526
Prisoner's Dilemma and, 17–18
regulation of, 13–14
revisionism and, 38, 64
Russia and, 38
short of armed conflict, 34–35
specific advice for manoeuvring in, 61–62
State lying and, 22
tactics used in, 21–22
technologies as enabling tools in, 239–46
thought of as an enemy, 63–64
unconventional tools of, 38
US and, 17, 237
used by the West, 72n.13
utility of the concept, 34
war and peace and, 108
weaponization of dissent and civil society
and, 23
grey zone defence, civil society and, 557–76
grey zone norms, vs. warfighting norms, 339–72
grey zone operations (GZOs), 45–46, 253–
54, 254n.9, 469–92. *See also* grey zone
aggression; grey zone approaches; grey
zone conflicts
ambiguity and, 374, 375

INDEX 691

China and, 36–37, 39, 329–30, 337, 471–72, 491
Cold War and, 484–86
comparative, 488–91
definition of, 476
democracies and, 471–72
deniability and, 471
DIMEFIL spectrum and, 473–74
disinformation and, 471
framing of, 46
funding of, 482–83
grey zone cyber operations, 179–206
GZO measures taxonomy, 473–74, 473n.6, 473*f*
implications for military affairs, 47–48
information operations and, 471
vs. institutionalized armed conflict, 475–76
international law and, 373–74
Iran and, 333, 476, 480–84, 487–91
legal uncertainty and, 259, 260
as less costly, less risky than conventional war, 34
logic and grammar of, 22
maritime, 259
means chosen, 47
Middle East and, 334
military-business, 574, 575, 576
military operations and, 475–76, 480–90, 489*t*, 575, 576
non-State actors and, 471
norms governing, 22
North Africa and, 334
in outer space, 289–315
paramilitary operations and, 476–90, 489*t*
political objectives of, 373–74
political warfare and, 472–73
proxies and, 471
recently viewed as systemic threat, 46
regime change and, 459–65
Russia and, 36–37, 329–30, 331–33, 337, 471–72, 476–80, 487–91
short of armed conflict, 373–74, 499–500
Solidarność (Solidarity) movement and, 464, 465
term created and used by liberal democracies, 471–72
three common elements of, 373–74
uncertainty and, 259, 260, 373–74
US and, 45–60, 476, 484–91, 489*t*
US Congress and, 485–86
US foreign policy and, 45–60
US presidency and, 485–86
Western, 459–65

grey zone responses, ethical framework for assessing, 495–511
grey zone(s), 31–32, 101, 448–51
as alternative to war, 341
ambiguity and, 466
as analytical construct, 58–59
in the Arctic, 271–87
avoiding risks of inaction, 335–36
blurred line between peace and war, 32–36, 38, 43–44
China and, 32, 38–40, 207–35
coercion and, 134, 140–41
Cold War and, 33, 183, 448, 449–50
competition and, 373–74
concept losing popularity, 36
as 'contested arena' between war and peace, 339
between crime and statecraft, 180, 183, 187–90
crime vs. statecraft, 19
cyber operations and, 19, 182–92, 364–67
definition of, 31–32, 34–35, 38, 43–44, 59, 182–83, 319, 323–24, 448, 449–50, 450–51n.13, 466, 495–96
domaine réservé and, 140
emerging from socio-technological change, 129–53
between espionage and attacks, 180, 183, 190–91
espionage vs. attacks, 19
exploitation of, 148–49, 395–96
future of, 43–44
grey zone cases, 504–10
hybrid conflict and, 17, 321–26, 450
hybrid threats and, 260–61, 336–37, 465–66
hybrid warfare and, 43–44
inclusion critieria of, 59
indistinct edges of, 336–37
information operations and, 368–69
international law and, 23, 98–101, 126, 148–49, 425–45
law and, 98–101, 126, 148–49, 207–35, 335, 425–45, 608, 618
lawfare and, 207–35, 618
lessons of the, 334–36
lethal responses in, 495–96, 499–500, 504–11
limits of revisionism, 335
logic, grammar, and norms of, 339–50
losses in, 371
lying in the, 373–92
maritime domain and, 20, 252–55
MENA region as, 334
military dimension of, 23–24, 469–92

692 INDEX

grey zone(s) (*cont.*)
  military operations and, 469–92
  need to resist efforts to erode human dignity and institutional integrity, 532
  non-intervention and, 130, 135–48
  non-State actors and, 23, 359–64, 425–45
  normative challenges and implications of, 339–72
  norms and, 350–70
  between peace and war, 12–13, 183–87, 496 (*see also* blurred line between peace and war)
  persistence of, 36–38
  as perspective-dependent, 322–23
  phenomenon of, 17
  piercing veil of ambiguity, 336
  vs. political warfare, 17, 40–41
  revisionism and, 323
  Russia and, 31–32, 38–40
  security assistance and, 577–600
  as series of actions with revisionist intent, 323
  in space between war and peace, 36
  States and, 445, 466
  between strategic competition and good faith cooperation, 390
  sublethal responses in, 495–96, 500–11
  tensions in, 577–600
  Ukraine in, 38–39
  as used by Central and Eastern European dissidents, 449–51
  use of the term, 182–83, 258–59
  utility of the concept, 59
  war vs. peace, 19
  weakness of the concept, 32–33, 37
grey zone tactics, 322, 515. *See also* grey zone approaches; grey zone operations (GZOs)
  ethical implications, 14–15
  legal tactics employed as part of, 14
  maritime domain and, 322
grey zone threats
  civil society as defence against, 25–26
  legal aspects of, 87–101
  in outer space, 315
  prevalence of, 321
  responses to, 315
  rights-based framework and, 495–511
grey zone tools, 21–22, 328
  challenging the territorial status quo, 329
  cyber operations as, 328–29
  instruments used in, 21–22, 33–34
  lawfare as, 327
  media and information operations, 326
  uncoded, 326–29

grey zone warfare. 515, *See* grey zone conflicts
  based on premise that Western interests and institutions are outdated, 514–15
  concept of, 514
  international law and, 513–32
  international norms and, 513–32
  thought of as an enemy, 63–64
  used by the West, 72n.13
Griffith, Melissa K., 19, 179–206
Gromyko, Andrei, 378
Gross, Michael, 354
Grotius, Hugo, 107, 376, 377, 391–92, 519, 522–23, 525
group think, 63–64
Grozny, 476
Guatemala, 398
Guccifer 2.0, 408
guerrilla operations, 11–12, 87–88, 469n.1, 484–85
Gulf of Maine, 386
Gunderson, Lance H., 541
Guyana/Suriname arbitration, 528–29
GZO measures taxonomy, 473–74, 473f, 473n.6

Haataja, Samuli, 22–23, 393–424
hack-and-leak operations, 197, 199–200
hackers, 96–97, 148–49
hacking, 162–63n.16, 561
  below the threshold of war, 179–206
  cognitive, 416n.133
  of databases, 226–27
  hacking groups, 137
  by Russia, 368
Hague, William, 612
Hague Institute for the Internationalisation of Laws, 554
Hague International Space Resources Governance Working Group, 307
Haiti, 50–51, 57–58
Hamas, 211, 360–61, 594, 613–14, 620
  lawfare and, 614–16, 615n.37, 617
  maritime incident of 31 May 2010 and, 620–22
Hamilton, Ian, 527
Haniyea, Ismail, 614
Hannibal, 526
Harknett, Richard, 62n.1, 201, 202
harm(s)
  collateral harms, 363–64
  consent by the harmed, 24, 496, 497
  intentional defensive harm, 24, 496–98
  justified defensive harm, 496–98, 511
  justified harm, 496–98, 511

INDEX 693

punitive harm, 501–3, 502n.29, 511
tallying, 85
Harrison, Sarah, 26, 577–600
Harvard University, Institute for Quantitative
    Social Science, 421
healthcare sector, cyber operations in, 184
Help America Vote Act (US), 415
Helsinki Accords, 459
Helsinki Watch groups, 449
Hercegovina, 443–44
Herngren, Felix, 557–58
Hezbollah, 211, 319, 333, 483
Hicks, Kathleen, 339
Higgins, Rosalyn, 140–41
Hindutva ideology, 596
Hiss, Alger, 458
Hitler, Adolf, 381
HMS *Albion*, 265–66
Hobbes, Thomas, 104–5
Hobbesian world view, 107
Hoffman, F. G., 256n.25
Hoffman, Frank, 11–12, 40–41, 42, 100
Holling, Crawford, 534–37
Hollis, Duncan, 417n.137
Hollywood, 567
Hollywood Ten, 458
Holocaust, 610–11
Hopkins, Stephen, 532
Horton William R., 166–67n.35
Houthi rebels, 55, 333, 358, 365
Howard, Philip N., 165, 175
Hua, Zhu, 188–89
Huawei, 228, 229–30, 234
Hudson Institute, 198
Hull, Cordell, 398n.32
human dignity, 24–25, 513
Human Intelligence (HUMINT), 183
humanitarian obligations, disincentives to
    comply with, 100–1
human liberty, 527–28
Human Machine Interfaces, 186
human rights, 7, 8, 94, 428–29, 496n.7, 501–2,
    518–19, 527, 592
    peacetime standard of, 357, 363–64
    security assistance and, 598–600
    US as steward of, 52–53
    violations of, 113–14, 590–91
human rights jurisprudence, 516–17
human rights law, 127, 544–45
    NSAs and, 428–29, 434–35
human rights NGOs, 211
human rights treaties, 428–29
Human Rights Watch, 211, 595

human trafficking, 32–33
Hungarian National Front (MNA), 479–80
Hungary, 479–80
Hussein, Saddam, 225, 342–43, 356–57,
    388n.90, 581
hybrid activities, short of armed conflict, 126
hybrid competition, 19
hybrid conflicts, 17, 31–32
hybrid influencing, 631–32, 631n.4, 634, 638–
    39, 642–43
    authoritarian States and, 633–34
    definition of, 636–37, 636–37n.25
    in Finland, 631n.4
hybridity, 11–12, 253–54, 256. *See also* hybrid
    threats; hybrid warfare
    framed as hybrid threats, 11–12
    UN Convention of the Law of the Sea
        (UNCLOS) and, 261–65
hybridization, of warfare, 88
hybrid operations
    in outer space, 289–315
    space and, 294–97
hybrid scenarios, legal interoperability in,
    657–62
hybrid threats, 10–13, 32, 42, 43–44, 104, 126–
    27, 179, 450–51n.13, 495–96, 543, 549–50.
    See also grey zone competition
    ambiguity and uncertainty and, 13–14, 17–18
    analytical utility of concept, 16–17
    as basis for emergency conditions, 635–37
    benefits offered by concept of, 16–17
    coercion and, 119
    concept of, 636
    countering adverse effects of, 15
    definition of, 10–13, 255–57, 636–37
    deterrence of, 99
    disguised, 645
    ethical implications, 14–15
    ethically permissible responses to, 24
    exploitation of vulnerabilities of democracies
        by, 16
    faced by liberal democracies, 337
    Finland and, 631–32, 631n.4, 633–46
    great power competition and, 16
    grey zone(s) and, 260–61, 336–37, 465–66
    IHL and, 127
    incentivization of, 18
    instruments used in, 21–22
    international law and, 13–14, 18, 87–101,
        103–27
    at intersection of *jus ad bellum* and *jus in
        bellow*, 95–98
    Iran and, 333

694 INDEX

hybrid threats (*cont.*)
  legal aspects of, 13–14, 18, 87–101, 103–27,
    542–48
  LOAC and, 124–25
  maritime domain and, 20, 252–57
  as a matter of national competence, 646
  methods used in, 21–22
  in outer space, 21
  regulation of, 13–14
  'shroud of legitimacy' and, 265–66
  tactics used in, 21–22
  unregulated, 126
  war and peace and, 108
Hybrid Threats in the Grey Zone held by the
  Center for Ethics and the Rule of Law
  (CERL) at the University of Pennsylvania,
  15–16
Hybrid Threat Survey (HTS), 634
hybrid warfare, 11–12, 43–44, 93, 104, 126–27,
  341, 445. *See also* hybrid conflict
  definition of, 41–43, 255–56, 322–23, 601n.1
  in Eastern Europe, 37
  elusiveness of the concept, 322–23
  future of, 43–44
  vs. grey zone competition, 323–26
  vs. grey zone conflicts, 41–43
  grey zone(s) and, 43–44, 321–26, 450
  hybrid warfare threats, 11–12
  IHL and, 127
  international law and, 103–27
  Iran and, 333
  vs. irregular warfare (IW), 42
  irregular warfare (IW) and, 43
  Israel and, 601
  LOAC and, 124–25
  narrative framing and, 603
  NSAs and, 425, 427
  Russia and, 38, 42, 329–30, 425
  Syria and, 425
  technology advances and, 100, 101
  Turkey and, 425
  Ukraine and, 42
  US and, 43, 425
  war and peace and, 108
  as war by many means, 41–43
hydrazine fuel, 309

Iceland, 272–73, 273n.10, 277–78, 282–83, 286,
  286n.64
IDF (Israeli Defense Forces), 635
If Crisis or War Comes, 565, 566
illiberal States, rise of, 516
Imagery Intelligence (IMINT), 183

impact, 664–65
'imperfect war', 107
Imperial College of London, 510
imposter content, 167n.38
impure coordination problems, 61–62, 65, 78
inaction, avoiding risks of, 335–36
in bello criteria, 500, 504
incrementalism, 50
indecision, 514, 518–19, 523
India, 471
  China and, 598
  destructive anti-satellite (ASAT) tests and,
    308–11
  human rights in, 596, 597
  Mission Shakti, 309–11
  Quadrilateral Dialogue and, 595
  US and, 593, 595, 596, 597, 598
Indian Ocean, 595
Indian Space Research Organisation (ISRO),
  309–10
Indigenous institutions, 463
Indigenous peoples, of the Arctic, 282–83,
  284–85
'indirect and asymmetric methods', 38
indirect participants, targeting of, 501, 503–4
individual non-State actors (NSAs), 428–29
Individual Partnership and Cooperation
  Programme (IPCP)., 606n.15
individuals
  as NSAs, 428–29, 434–35, 445
  rights of, 428–29
Indo-Pacific region, 2–3, 253–54, 265–66, 517.
  See also specific States
Industrial Control System (ICS), 191
industrial espionage, 188–89
infiltration, 450–51, 452–53
inflation, 1–2
influence campaigns, 162–63
influence debate, narratives and, 174
influence operations, 157–58, 162
  across three dimensions, 160
  anonymous political influencing, 62n.1
  aspects of, 166
  cyber operations and, 199–200
  definition of, 159n.3, 160
  espionage and, 199–200
  foreign, 157–78
  information-based foreign influence, 157–78
  involving information, 157–58
  socio-technological change and, 150
'infodemic', 393–94
information. *See also* information operations
  freedom flow of, 157

influence involving, 157–58
international law and, 14–15
manipulation of, 139
military application of as instrument of war, 32–33
political warfare and, 41
veracity of, 159
as vital women in arsenal of democracy, 527
weaponization of, 146
information age, 136
parity in, 135–36, 152–53
power diffusion in, 135–36, 152–53
informational context, 161
information and communication technologies (ICTs), 138, 165, 393–424
information and intelligence lines of effort (LOE), 474–75
information-based foreign influence, 19, 157–78
information campaigns, 157–58, 160, 491. *See also* information operations
definition of, 164, 164n.24
vs. information operations, 160
vs. propaganda, 164, 164n.24, 166
information environment, 472–73
information ethics, 22–23, 404, 411–16
information flows, breaking and distortion of, 407
information-literacy courses, 25–26, 567–69, 570–71
information measures, 474–75
information operations, 22, 157–58, 160–61, 350, 354, 357, 447, 488–90, 496, 527, 569
attribution and, 423
coercion and, 369, 370, 423
data collection and, 368
deception and, 370
definition of, 161, 161n.12, 162n.13
disruption and, 369
global connectivity and, 368
grey zone(s) and, 326, 368–69, 471
vs. information campaigns, 160
normative challenge of, 369–70
precision of, 368
Russia and, 368, 370
technologies and, 368
Ukraine and, 369, 370
uncertainty and, 369
information space, coercion and, 321–22
information technology (IT) sector, 100, 184, 274–75. *See also* cyber operations; information technology domain

information technology domain, 215
China and, 212, 221–30
as Cold War battlefield, 221–22
lawfare and, 209
US and, 207, 212, 221–30
US-China grey zone lawfare in, 207, 221–30
information technology revolution, 210, 211–12. *See also* information technology domain
information warfare, 475, 477, 516–17
'infosphere', 412, 413, 416
infrastructure
critical, 207, 339, 364, 365, 450–51, 475, 486, 491–92, 554–55, 632–33
targeting of civilian, 488–90
Insani Yardim Vakfi (IHH), 620, 621–22n.72, 623–27
instability, conflict continuum and, 470
Instagram, 143, 226, 422, 618–19
institutional actors, 478–79
institutional crises, 169–70, 170n.51
institutionalized armed conflict, 470–71, 472, 475–76
institution-building, 1, 583–84
instruments, 664–65
in conventional warfare, 33–34
in grey zone conflicts, 21–22, 33–34 (*see also* grey zone tools)
in grey zone tools, 21–22, 33–34
in hybrid threats, 21–22
in lines of effort, 158
military instruments of power, 33–34
insurgency, 11–12
insurrectional movements, 432, 433, 434–35
Integrated Review of Security, Defence, Development and Foreign Policy (UK), 2–3, 8–9
integrative S/ T intelligence (InS/ TINT), 247
Intel, 194
intellectual property (IP) theft, 188–89, 198, 221–22, 224, 486, 496
China and, 198, 222–24, 509, 559–60, 561
Russia and, 509
US and, 222–24
intelligence, cybersecurity and, 192, 193
intelligence actors, 479. *See also specific actors*
intelligence collection
cyber operations and, 195–200
grey zone competition and, 325–26
intelligence measures, 474–75, 477
Intelligence Oversight Act (US), 485–86
intensity indicators, 121–22, 122n.104, 123–24
intention, 664–65

696 INDEX

intentional defensive harm, 24, 496–98
　lesser evil justifications, 496–97
　three possible justifications for, 496–98
interconnectedness, critical, 179, 180–82, 204
interference. *See also* interference operations
　definition of, 131n.13
　international law of, 393–424
interference operations, 131–32, 150, 466
　covert nature of, 129–53
　cyber operations and, 141, 142, 149
　dictatorial, 134
　domaine réservé and, 140–41
　domestic, 143
　forcible, 134
　ICTS and, 393–424
　means of, 136–37
　new standard for wrongful intervention,
　　151–52
　new technologies of, 129–53
　new tools of, 135, 136–37, 152–53
　propaganda as, 146–47
　with social media, 136
　socio-technological change and, 141, 149
　technology advances and, 141
　through disruption, 142
Interim National Security Strategic Guidance
　(INSSG), 35
internal security, external security and, 633
International Activities Division (IAD), Soviet-
　East Europe group, 461n.47
international armed conflict, threshold for, 89–
　90, 94, 95, 96–98, 101
international armed conflicts (IACs), 120–21,
　122–23, 438
International Atomic Energy Agency, 342–43
International Brigade, 456–57
International Center for Law Studies, 614–15,
　615n.37
international comity, 527
international commerce, China and, 213
International Committee of the Red Cross
　(ICRC), 120–21, 437–38
International Court of Justice (ICJ), 116, 118,
　126–27, 140–41, 362, 399, 404, 517–18,
　518n.15, 615, 618–19
　*Application of the Convention on the
　　Prevention and Punishment of the Crime
　　of Genocide (Bosnia and Herzegovina v.
　　Serbia and Montenegro)*, 436–38, 436n.51
　Clean Hands doctrine and, 528–29
　concept of estoppel and, 382–83
　*Corfu Channel, Tehran Hostages, Military
　　and Paramilitary Activities in and against*

　　Nicaragua, and *DR Congo v. Uganda,*
　　117–18, 133
　Costa Rica v. Nicaragua, 91
　Eastern Greenland case, 529–30
　Gulf of Maine, 386
　Guyana/Suriname arbitration, 528–29
　Land, Island and Maritime Frontier Dispute
　　judgement, 382–83, 382–83n.64
　*Military and Paramilitary Activities in and
　　Against Nicaragua*, 436
　Nicaragua v. US, 91–93, 95–96, 132, 133, 362,
　　397–98, 400, 403–4
　Nuclear Tests case and, 381, 383, 384
　Palestinian Wall advisory opinion, 92–93
　State lying and, 380
　Yukos arbitration, 528–29
International Criminal Court (ICC), 210–11,
　428–29, 611, 615, 623, 626–27
International Criminal Tribunal for Rwanda
　(ICTR), 611
International Criminal Tribunal for the
　Former Yugoslavia (ICTY), 95, 121–23,
　362, 611
　Prosecutor v. Duško Tadić, 120–21, 437–38
international humanitarian law (IHL), 105–6,
　108, 119–20, 127, 371, 403, 428–29, 438.
　See also law of armed conflict (LOAC)
　Hamas's exploitation of, 617
　NSAs and, 428–29, 434–35
　proxies and, 441, 443–44
international law. *See also* international
　humanitarian law (IHL); international
　space law; lawfare; *specific laws, treaties,
　and doctrines*
　blurred line between peace and war in, 125
　China and, 173–74, 175n.62
　competition and, 5–9
　covert operations and, 37–38
　customary, 93–94 (*see also* customary
　　international law)
　cyber operations and, 5–6, 14–15, 138, 221–
　　22, 224–25, 358–59
　deterrence and, 519
　in digital age, 393–424
　emerging technologies and, 138
　existing rules and institutions of, 13–14
　gap with respect to non-intervention, 135
　goals of, 24–25, 531
　as good faith instrument to oppose lawless
　　invocations of convenience during grey
　　zone conflicts, 525
　grey zone actions and, 373–74
　grey zone conflicts and, 103–27, 513–32

grey zone(s) and, 23, 98–101, 126, 148–49, 425–45
hybrid threats and, 18, 87–101, 103–27
hybrid warfare and, 103–27
increased number and reach of, 210–14
information and, 14–15
of interference, 393–424
international investment law, 434
legal uncertainty and, 88
line between war and peace and, 18
need to defend integrity of, 525
nineteenth-century, 135
normative conflict and, 515–16
NSAs and, 23, 425–45
of pre-digital era, 5–6
principle of non-intervention and, 129, 130
proposed law on State lying, 373–92
proxies and, 435–44
reason for existence of, 513
role and relevance of, 5–9
Russia and, 173–74, 175n.62
security threats and, 25
self-defence and, 357–58
space domain and, 291, 295, 300, 315 (*see also* international space law)
State-centric principles vs. human rights, 7
State lying and, 22
strengthening ability to foster peace and prevent war, 126
as subterfuge for grey zone adversaries, 525–26, 527–28
uncertain and normative drift in international legal system, 7
underlying weaknesses exploited, 14–15
use of force and, 321, 355–56
violations of, challenges to, undermining of, 495–96
war vs. peace and, 103–27
International Law Commission, 381–82
Fragmentation Report, 515–16
international legal system. *See also* international law
following World War I, 107–8
nineteenth-century, 107
peace as norm in, 125, 126
structural problems of, 18
vulnerability of, 101
World War II, 107–8, 109
International Lunar Research Station, 304
International Military Tribunal, 532
international norms, 350–70
challenges to, 339
China's invocation of, 517–18
competition for, 531–32

cyber operations and, 523
grey zone warfare and, 513–32
need to recommit to defending, 514–15, 518–19, 523–24, 525, 531–32
regimes and, 351
international order, 518–19
China's willingness to challenge, 208–9
competition to shape, 1–2
defending against revisionist actors, 27
illiberal model of, 1–2
need to reaffirm Western vision of, 513–14
peace in, 32–33, 36
rules-based, 9
threatened by grey zone warfare, 514
utility of the concept, 59–60
before World War II, 339
international relations, regime theorists and, 537–38
international space law, 291, 292, 295, 297–303, 315
evolution of, 297–303
International Space Station Intergovernmental Agreement, 304
International Space Station (ISS), 295–96, 302, 304, 307–8, 311
International Space Station Intergovernmental Agreement, 304
international standards, 274–75
aerial domain and, 329
maritime domain and, 329
international standards development organisations (ISDOs), 228
International Tribunal for the Law of the Sea (ITLOS), 210–11, 262, 263–65
Arctic Sunrise Case, 268–69
Kerch Strait and, 263–65
international tribunals, increased number and reach of, 210–14. *See also specific tribunals*
internet, 175, 369–70, 464–65
in China, 226, 234
growth of, 181
regulation of, 234
internet of things (IoT), 182
Internet Research Agency (Russia), 143, 487–88
interoperability, 315, 554–55
interpretation, dilemma of, 190–91, 192
intervention, 131–32, 401
below the threshold of force, 131–32
coercion and, 401
military force and, 131–32
new standard for, 148, 149, 151–52
prohibition of, 400
as 'Protean concept', 396–97
'right of', 133
violations of, 395–96

698 INDEX

The Interview, 366–67, 561
intransigence, 79–80, 82, 84
intransitive preferences, 74–76, 75n.20, 85
intra-State conflicts, 104
Intrusion Model, 200
Iran, 3, 329–30, 469, 483–84
  Afghanistan and, 488–90
  China and, 481–82
  cyber operations and, 365–66, 487–88, 561
  Department 400 (Misaq Unit), 481
  as donor State, 599
  grey zone activities and, 333
  as grey zone actor, 333, 562
  grey zone instruments and, 21–22
  grey zone tactics and, 322
  GZOs and, 476, 480–84, 487–91
  hybrid threats and, 333
  hybrid warfare and, 333
  influence in Middle East, 48, 59
  Iraq and, 488–90
  IRGC-QF and, 488–90
  Israel and, 186, 333, 365–66
  JCPOA and, 366
  Lebanon and, 488–90
  maritime domain and, 333
  military activities of, 23–24, 58
  military and paramilitary cooperation in, 480–84
  military GZOs and, 480–84
  nuclear proliferation and, 333, 364–65, 366
  paramilitary GZOs and, 480–84
  proxies and, 356, 357–58, 362, 480–81
  as revisionist power, 333
  Russia and, 481–82
  Saudi Arabia and, 333, 358, 359, 365
  Stuxnet attack on, 364–65
  support for Hezbollah in Lebanon, 319
  Syria and, 480–81, 482, 483, 488–90
  Turkey and, 359, 365
  UK and, 358
  US and, 53, 55, 58, 333, 356, 357–58, 371, 398, 481–82
  Yemen and, 488–90
Iran-Contra Scandal, 173
Iranian Navy, 55
Iraq, 371, 481, 483
  counter-terror operations and, 362
  invasion of, 6, 58, 104, 173, 176–77
  Iran and, 357–58, 362, 488–90
  ISIL in, 363–64
  no-fly zones in, 50, 53
  nuclear proliferation and, 48, 50
  terrorist groups in, 362, 363

terrorist organisations in (*see also specific organisations*)
troop withdrawal and, 54
US and, 53, 54, 58, 342–43, 356–58, 363
Iraqi military, 581
Iraq War, 53, 225, 342–43, 356–57
Ireland, 621
irrationality, vs. rationality, 75n.20
irregular forces, 469n.1
irregular warfare (IW), 34, 87–88, 93, 100, 101, 341
  vs. grey zone conflicts, 34
  vs. hybrid warfare, 42, 43
Isenberg, Arnold, 376
Islam, 515–16n.9
Islamic extremists, 54
Islamic Republican Guard Corps, Qods Force.
  See Islamic Revolutionary Guards Corps-Quds Force (IRGC- QF)
Islamic Revolutionary Guards Corps- Quds Force (IRGC- QF), 356, 357–58, 481–82, 483, 483n.40, 488–90
Islamic State of Iraq and Syria (ISIS), 118, 123, 170, 175, 360–61, 363–64, 443–44, 471
Islamic State of Iraq and the Levant (ISIL). *See* Islamic State of Iraq and Syria (ISIS)
island building, 57, 58, 331
Isla Perejil (Leila or Tura) incident, 334
Israel, 26, 594, 620n.59
  2010 maritime incident case study, 26
  Artemis Accords and, 304
  cyber operations and, 364, 365–66
  Hamas designated as terrorist organisation by, 613–14 (*see also* Hamas)
  hybrid warfare and, 601
  Iran and, 186, 333, 365–66
  lawfare and, 26, 601–3, 602–3n.4, 603n.5, 603n.6, 604–8, 610–13, 617–19, 623–24
  Law of Armed Conflict and, 608n.20
  legal resilience and, 601–30, 606n.15
  legal warfare and, 601–30
  Maritime Incident of 31 May 2010 and, 601–30
  maritime incident of 31 May 2010 and, 619–28
  Ministry of Justice, 603
  NATO and, 606, 606n.15
  Second Intifada and, 360–61
  Stuxnet operation and, 186, 204–5
  Syria and, 364
Israeli Defense Forces (IDF), 601n.2, 608n.20, 617, 621–22, 621–22n.72
Israeli High Court of Justice, 618

Israeli Supreme Court, 516–17
Italy, 462
    Artemis Accords and, 304
    interference in elections in, 393–94
    Lega Nord, 478
    suspension of conscription in, 559
Iterated Prisoner's Dilemmas, 83

Jack, Caroline, 168n.39
Jackson, Robert, 532
January 6, 2021, attack on US Capitol, 563,
    567–68
Japan, 56, 208
    Artemis Accords and, 304
    China and, 231
    Quadrilateral Dialogue and, 595
Japanese imperialism, 172
Jaruzelski, Wojciech, 459–61
Jaysh al-Shabi (People's Army), 483
Jensen, Benjamin, 365
Jigsaw (Google), 568
Jihad, 614
John Paul II, 462–63
Johnson, Christopher, 307–8
Johnson & Johnson, 509
Joint Comprehensive Plan of Action (JCPOA),
    366
Joint Strategic Vision for the Asia- Pacific and
    Indian Ocean Region, 595
Jones, Seth G., 461–63, 462n.49, 462n.50,
    462n.52
Jordan, Hamilton, 377
Jordan, Javier, 319–20, 443–44
journalism, distrust of, 569–70
journalists, canceling of credentials of, 331
Jowett, Garth S., 165
jurisprudence, importance of, 496
'Jurists Confronting the Occupier', 614–15,
    615n.37
jus ad bellum, 88, 97–98, 101, 105–6, 108, 119–
    20, 356–57, 497, 499–500, 514, 516–17,
    523–24, 525
    vs. *jus in bello*, 89–90, 95–98
    use of force thresholds under, 90–93
jus ad vim, 356–57, 363–64, 499–500
jus cogens, 527
jus contra bellum, 111
jus extra bellum, 329
jus in bello, 88, 101, 105–6, 108, 119–20, 124,
    125, 126–27, 357, 514, 516–17, 522–23,
    525
    conflict classification for, 93–95
    vs. *jus ad bellum*, 89–90, 95–98

jus in vi, 357
jus post bellum, 514, 519, 523–24, 526
just cause, 499–500
just cause *ad bellum*, 499
justice, war and, 106
justified defensive harm, 496–98, 511
Just War tradition, 24, 88, 369–70, 371, 496, 500
    criteria for, 106, 106n.17, 499–500
    'Just War Doctrine', 106, 107

Kadryov, Ramzan, 441
Kadyrovtsy, 441
Kaempf, Sebastian, 176
Kagan, Robert, 1
Kahn, Herman, 371
Kahn, Tom, 462–63
Kant, Immanuel, 495, 501–2
Kaplan, Stephen S., 355
Kapusta, Philip, 31–32, 34–35, 37–38
Kardashians, 170
Karlin, Mara, 578, 586, 587–88, 587n.33
Karpiński, Jakub, 462–63
Kashmir, India-Pakistan standoff in, 471
Kellogg-Briand Pact, 107–8
Kennan, George, 40–41, 45, 253, 472
Kennedy, John F.
    administration of, 484–85
    foreign policy toward non-intervention, 485
Keohane, Robert, 352, 353
Kerch Strait, 263–65, 329, 551
Kerr, Jackie, 160
Khruschev, Nikita, 378
Kill Chain, 200
Kilovaty, Ido, 18–19, 129–53, 161, 417n.137
Kim Jong Un, 561
    Trump, Donald J. and, 390
kinetic methods, 63. *See also specific methods*
King, Mackenzie, 455
Kingston Penitentiary riot, 454, 455
Kirchofer, Charles, 360–61
Kirland, Lane, 462–63
Kissinger, Henry, 172
Kittrie, Orde F., 19–20, 207–35
Kleber, Emil, 456–57
Kleczkowska, Agata, 23, 425–45
Knopf, Jeffrey W., 359–60, 361
knowledge, 157
Kołakowski, Leszek, 463n.54
Kolb, Robert, 385
Kong Kong, 172
Kopečny, Tomáš, 575
Koplow, David, 299–300, 313–14
Korean War, 472

700 INDEX

Kosovo, 52
Kraska, James, 216
Kremlin, 449, 465, 478, 479, 480, 490
Kuwait, 342–43

Laatikainen, Antti, 194–95
Labour-Progressive Party (LPP), 457
Land, Island and Maritime Frontier Dispute judgement (IJC), 382–83n.64
land reclamation, 57, 58
Laos, 355
large-scale combat operations (LSCO), 41–42, 43–44
Lasota, Irene, 462–63
Latin America, 333, 485. *See also specific States*
Latvia, 570
  migration and, 637–38
  OPERATION ATLANTIC RESOLVE and, 55–56
law. *See also* lawfare; *specific categories*
  in China, 215
  coercion and, 321–22
  competition and, 16
  current legal framework of warfare, 88–95
  defence of integrity of, 24–25
  denounced as maladaptive, 546–47
  as a domain, 14
  grey zone(s) and, 14, 19–20, 87–101, 335, 608
  hybrid threats and, 14, 87–101
  instrumentation of, 14, 16, 27, 546
  internationalization of, 554
  as object of geopolitical contestation, 14
  resilience and, 534–41
  rule of (*see* rule of law)
  in Russia, 545
  as strategic tool, 26
  struggle for, 515–19
  vulnerabilities of, 543
Law, Jude, 567
law enforcement, 99, 474
  China's use of, 330, 331
  norms of, 357
law enforcement standards, law enforcement standards vs. military standards, 363–64
lawfare, 62n.1, 207–35, 254–55, 273n.9, 601–2, 605, 617–19
  in the Arctic, 280
  asymmetrical, 417n.137
  Belgium and, 611, 613
  China and, 19–20, 207–35, 280, 605n.12
  criticism of the term, 255
  debate on legitimacy of use of, 607–8
  definition of, 209–10, 450–51, 604

  as distinct professional field, 605–7
  economic interdependence and, 210, 212–14
  globalization and, 210, 212–14
  as grey zone tool, 327
  Hamas and, 614–16, 615n.37, 617
  identifying actor(s) deploying, 613–17, 629
  increase in power and prevalence of, 209–14
  information technology domain and, 209, 210
  Israel and, 26, 602–3n.4, 603, 603n.5, 603n.6, 604, 614–16, 615n.37, 617
  'lawfare state of mind', 606
  legitimacy of, 607–8
  maritime domain and, 210–11, 623–24
  maritime incident of 31 May 2010 and, 623–24
  media and, 611, 624, 624n.84
  NATO and, 209, 603, 604, 606, 606n.15, 613–14
  NGOs and, 210, 211
  non-democratic States and, 629
  reputational, 603, 603n.7
  rule of law and, 607–8
  Russia and, 213, 332–33, 618–19, 619n.57
  Spain and, 611, 613
  terminology, 604–5
  terrorist organisations and, 629 (*see also specific organisations*)
  UK and, 605–6, 611, 612
  Ukraine and, 618–19, 619n.57
  US and, 19–20, 209, 211, 221–30, 234–35
  use of legal principles in, 610–13
  use of the term, 209–10, 254–55
lawlessness, drift toward, 339, 340
law of armed conflict (LOAC), 119–25, 371
  Israel and, 608n.20
  NGOs focused on, 211
law of insincere State utterances, 373, 380–83
law of nations, 107
law of the sea, 220–21, 517–18, 518n.15
Law of the Sea Tribunal, 517–18, 518n.15
law of treaties, 380, 381, 383, 385, 389, 390–91
Law of War versus Law of Peace, 522–23
law on State lying (proposed), 373–92
law on unilateral declarations, 380, 381, 382, 383, 385, 389, 390–91
Lawson, Sean T., 162, 162–63n.16
Lazarus group, 187–88
leaflets, 565, 566
League of Nations, 1, 107–8
Leahy laws, 590–91, 591n.52, 591n.53, 592
Lebanese Christian Phlange, 602–3n.4
Lebanon, 319, 333, 481, 482, 586, 602–3n.4, 621
  Iran and, 488–90

Lee, Roderick, 39
legal advisors, 629
legal categories, ethical concerns and, 16
legal clarification, through development of
    jurisprudence, 95–98
legal considerations. *See also* legal
    interoperability
    democracies and, 24
    legal indeterminacy, 523
    policy planning processes and, 25
legal domain, 601–30, 656–57. *See also* legal
    operations
    identifying hostile legal actions, 27
    legal attribution, 439–40 (*see also* attribution)
    legal equilibrium, 544–45
legal integration. *See also* legal interoperability
    need for, 515
    strategic seams and, 519–22
legal interoperability, 24–25, 27, 520–21
    in complex hybrid scenarios, 657–62
    how to ensure, 660–62
    main purpose of, 657–58
legalism, 47
legality, 406
legal norms, 20. *See also* norms
legal operations, 27, 604, 604n.9, 605. *See also*
    lawfare; legal warfare
    legal gamesmanship, 604–5, 607
    military operations and, 607
    North Atlantic Treaty Organization (NATO)
        and, 662–68
    operationalization of notion of, 27
    operational readiness for, 666–68
    piercing veil of, 609–19
    used against Israel, 602–3
legal paradigms, exploitation of seams between,
    514
legal positivism, 107
legal preparedness. *See also* legal resilience
    addressing legal vulnerabilities, 549–51
    contributing to societal resilience, 552–53
legal principles, used in lawfare, 610–13
legal resilience, 26–27, 533–56, 604, 605
    analytical benefit of, 543–45
    asymmetric regulatory environments and,
        654–55
    definition of, 542
    effects, actions, tools, and enablers, 655
    environments and, 653–54
    in eye of beholder, 545–47
    Finland and, 26–27, 631–47
    grey zone conflicts and, 542–48
    hybrid threats and, 542–48

increasing, 629
Israel and, 601–30, 606n.15
legal domain and, 656–57
NATO and, 27
need for, 652–53
as normative concept, 546–47
normative dimension of, 545–48
an overview, 651–57
path to, 649–72
in practice, 548–55
practice of, 601–30
preparedness and capacities, 655
requirements, 653–56
respect for rule of law, 656
response and, 665–66
as status quo strategy, 546–47
training and, 668–70
understanding and awareness and, 549
utility of, 534
Legal Resilience in an Era of Hybrid Threats
    convened by the Exeter Centre for
        International Law (ECIL) at the University
        of Exeter in the United Kingdom, 15–16
legal resilience strategies, 25
legal scholarship, resilience thinking in, 538–41
legal strategy, identifying actor(s) deploying,
    613–17
legal systems, 546–47
legal thresholds, misalignment of, 88, 98, 100–1
legal uncertainty
    international law and, 88
    maritime domain and, 259, 260
    maritime grey zone and, 264–65
legal vulnerabilities
    addressing, 549–51
    of democracies, 634
    understanding of, 25
legal warfare, 214, 273n.9, 330, 601n.2, 604. *See
    also* lawfare
    China and, 605n.12
    Israel and, 601–30
Lega Nord, Italy, 478
legislative jurisdiction, armed non-State actors
    (ANSAs) and, 432
legitimacy, 22–23, 405–11, 423–24
    concept of, 404
    erosion of, 409–11
    of lawfare, 607–8
legitimate authority, 405–11, 499
Le Maire, Bruno, 560–61
Lenin, Vladimir, 452–53
Lenin shipyard, 459–61
lesser evil, attaining, 24, 496–97

702 INDEX

lethal aid, 477–78, 480
lethal responses, in the grey zone, 495–96, 499–500, 504–11
Letts, David, 20, 251–70
lex ferenda, 373, 378–80, 389–90
lex lata, 373, 378–80, 514
lex specialis, 522–23
liability, 24, 497–98, 503n.32
    four preconditions of, 498, 499
    instrumental nature of, 497–98
Liability Convention, 301–2
Liang, Qiao, 214
liberal democracies, 559–60
    attacks on, 496
    authoritarianism and, 589–600
    vs. authoritarian regimes, 547–48
    described by Putin as 'obsolete', 514–15
    as donor States, 577–600
    first principles of order binding, 513–14
    globalization and, 558–59
    grey zone competition and, 526
    need to defend integrity of law, 525
    need to recommit to defending norms, 514–15, 523–24, 525, 526
    security assistance by, 577–600
    self-defence and, 527
    vulnerability of, 496, 558–59
Liberals, 455
liberal theory, 496
Libicki, Martin, 201
libraries, 568–69, 568n.28
Libya, 439–40
    NATO and, 54–55
    US and, 54–55
    US military and, 54–55
Lieber, Francis, 89–90
liminality, 12–13, 32–36, 38, 43–44, 319–20, 321, 339, 373–74, 447, 450, 451, 465–66, 495–96
limitations, enforcement of, 47, 48
limit-testing, 50
Lin, Herbert, 160
Lincoln, Abraham, 89–90
line between strategic competition and good faith cooperation, 390
line between war and peace, 32–36, 38, 43–44, 103–27, 319–20, 321, 373–74, 447, 450, 451, 495–96
    blurred, 4–5, 6, 12–13, 18, 32–36, 38, 43–44, 104, 119, 124, 125, 126, 339, 373–74, 447, 450, 451, 495–96
lines of effort (LOE), 19, 157–63, 470–71, 473–74
    agents in, 158

audience in, 158
during Cold War, 161, 162–63
context in, 158
definition of, 158
DIMEFIL spectrum, 473–74
discrete, 159
ends in, 158
epistemic consequences of, 158
information and intelligence, 474–75
instruments in, 158
military, 477
Linkos Group, 204
Lipmann, Walter, 164
Lithuania, 232–33, 487
    China and, 560–61
    migration and, 637–38
    military service in, 572
    OPERATION ATLANTIC RESOLVE and, 55–56
    resurrection of military service in, 559
Lithuanian Aliens Act, 640
litigation, strategic, 609–10
Livingston, Steve, 166–67n.35, 167, 170n.51
Livni, Tzippi, 612
Li Zhenfu, 282–83
lobby groups, 450–51
lobbying, 549–50
Lockheed Martin, 200
loss, role in shaping permissions, 371
Lotus era, 529–30
Lotus principle, 390–91
Low Earth Orbit (LEO), 309–10, 311, 313
'low intensity of violence' threshold, 97
Luban David, 162–63n.16
Luch satellite, 295n.25
Luxembourg, Artemis Accords and, 304
lying, 527
    ambiguity and, 375
    coercion and, 144
    definition of, 376
    vs. dissembling, 377
    law of insincere State utterances, 373, 380–83
    law on State lying, 373, 378–80
    moral theory and, 379
    State actors and, 385–89
    traditional vs. modern lies, 169–70, 174–75

MacArthur, Douglas, 526
Macau, 172
MacCormick, Neil, 377
Machiavelli, Niccoló, 379
machine-learning algorithms, 140, 143–44
MacIntosh, Duncan, 17–18, 61–85

Mackenzie-Papneau Battalion, 455–56
Macron, Emmanuel, 565, 570
Made in China 2025, 559–60
Madhoun, Diaa al-Din al-, 614
Maersk, 204
Main Intelligence Directorate (GRU), 408, 476–77, 479–80
Malaysia, 58
Mali, 439–40
malign interference, 13–14
Maliki, Nuri al-, 581
malware, 189, 194–95, 364, 365, 505–7
Malzahn, Dick, 461n.47
Managed Service Providers, 188–89
Mandelblit, Avichai, 601n.2, 607
Mandiant, 200, 202
Maness, Ryan C., 365
manipulated content, 167n.38
manipulation, 136, 143, 149
  as alternative standard for wrongful intervention, 148, 151–52
  coercion and, 141–42, 145
  definition of, 144, 164n.27
  domestic, 143
  non-intervention and, 143–44
  online, 136–37, 139, 142, 143–44, 145
  propaganda and, 143–44, 164
  through social media, 143
  vulnerability to, 149
Manoeuvre, 526
Mao Zedong, 215
mapping exercises, 634
Marcus Aurelius, 514–15
maritime domain, 100, 215–16, 251–70, 274–75
  China and, 207, 216–21, 331, 517–18, 518n.15
  Chinese grey zone lawfare in, 207, 216–21
  grey zone(s) and, 20, 252–55, 257–66, 322 (*see also* maritime grey zone)
  hybrid threats and, 20, 252–57, 260–66 (*see also* maritime hybrid threats)
  international standards and, 329
  Iran and, 333
  lawfare and, 207, 210–11, 216–21
  legal uncertainty and, 259, 260
  new solutions and responses, 267–69
  political warfare and, 252–55
  unique nature of, 267
maritime grey zone, 20, 252–55, 322
  definition of, 257–61
  legal uncertainty and, 264–65
  positivist approach to defining, 257–58
  'shroud of legitimacy' and, 265–66
  UNCLOS and, 261–65

maritime hybrid threats, 20
  definition of, 255–57, 260–61
  'shroud of legitimacy' and, 265–66
  UNCLOS and, 261–65
maritime incident of 31 May 2010, 601–30, 619n.58
  ensuing (pre-planned) legal campaign, 624–27
  factual background, 620–22
  Hamas and, 620–22
  Israel and, 619–28
  lawfare aspects of, 620–22
  legal scrutiny in international fora, 627–28
Maritime Interception Operations (MIO), 475
Marsh, Christopher, 17, 31–32
Martin, Diego, 162–63
Marx, Karl, 451–52
Marxism, 215
Mash'al, Khaled, 614
maskirovka ('camouflage', or deceptive operations), 36–37
Mass, 526, 527
mass media, 160
Matisek, Jahara, 580, 581, 583, 584
matrix, 664–65
Mattis, James, 11–12, 42, 410
Mavi Marmara, 621–22, 623, 626–27
Mazarr, Michael J., 17–18, 34, 38, 61–62, 64, 65, 66, 80, 81–82, 323, 324–25, 331, 346
Mazel, Marlene, 26, 601–30
Mazerall, Edward, 457–58
McCallum, Ken, 222
McCarthyite witch hunt, 451–52
McDougal, Myres, 142–43, 151–52, 418
McMahan, Jeff, 497–98
McMaster, H. R., 42
Mearsheimer, John, 379
Measurement and Signature Intelligence (MaSINT), 183
measures short of war, 4–5, 107, 115–16
meddling, 466. *See also* interference
media. *See also* media warfare; *specific organisations*
  authoritarian manipulation and, 175
  definition of, 175
  distrust of, 569–70
  exploitation of, 450–51
  as grey zone tool, 326
  influence of, 177
  lawfare and, 611, 624, 624n.84
  media channels, 162–63
  open houses hosted by, 569–70
  State control over, 177n.76, 331
  warfare and, 177, 178

704 INDEX

mediation, definition of, 175
mediatization, 158, 174–77
 definition of, 175, 179
 warfare and, 176
media warfare, 214, 215, 330
Meir Amit Intelligence and Terrorism
 Information Center, 615
Meisels, Tamar, 354
meta-conflict, 80
Mexico, 456–57
 Artemis Accords and, 304
 interference in elections in, 393–94
 narco-wars in, 471
Microsoft, 194–95
Microsoft Exchange Server, 194–95, 198–99,
 200–1
micro-targeting, 136–37, 143, 419–20
Middle Ages, war and peace in, 106
Middle East, 78, 329–30, 481. *See also specific
 States*
 grey zone activities and, 334
 grey zone instruments and, 21–22
Middle East and North Africa (MENA) region,
 329–30, 334, 593. *See also* Middle East;
 North Africa; *specific States*
migrants, weaponization of, 575–76
migration
 Finland and, 633, 637–42
 instrumentalization of, 637–42, 639n.38
 responses to instrumentalisation
 of, 637–42
 weaponization of, 562
Militarized Compellent Threats dataset, 341
military, 13–14, 22, 350, 355, 447. *See also
 military operations; military service;
 specific military organisations*
 coercion and, 355
 counter-terror operations and, 363
 grey zone(s) and, 23–24, 45–60, 480–90, 489t
 GZOs and, 480–84, 490
 intervention and, 131–32
 'military activities exception', 262
 normative implications, 355–59
 paramilitary forces and, 484–88
 posturing and, 357
*Military and Paramilitary Activities in and
 Against Nicaragua* (IJC), 436
military doctrines, development of, 88
Military Industrial Kurier, 447
'Military Information Support Operations'
 (MISO), 160
military instruments of power, 33–34
military occupation, 121

military operations
 grey zone analytic framework for, 469–92
 GZOs and, 475–76
 high-risk, 475–76
 Iran and, 480–84
 legal operations and, 607
 'military operations other than war'
 (MOOTW), 50
military service
 in Denmark, 572
 expanded to women, 572
 in Lithuania, 572
 in Norway, 572–73
 resurrection of, 559
 return to mandatory, 572
 selective, 572
 suspension of, 559
 universal national service (SNU) in France, 570
military standards, vs. law enforcement
 standards, 363–64
military tactics, evolutions in, 88
militias, 92, 96–97, 99–100, 219–20. *See also*
 paramilitary forces
Milo, 524
Milosevic, Slobodan, 51, 52
'ministries of war', renamed 'ministries of
 defence', 115
ministry of grey zone conflict, 63
mirroring, 66–67
miscalculation, risk of, 3
Mischief Reef, 218–19
misinformation, 167, 167n.38, 465–66, 472–73
 definition of, 166, 167
 vs. disinformation, 166, 167, 168n.39
 teenagers exposed to, 569
misinformers, 166
misleading content, 167n.38
misrepresentation, 62
Mission Shakti, 309–11
Mitrokhin archives, 462n.49
mixed-motivation games, 351–52
mobile telecommunications networks, growth
 of, 182
mobilization, general appeals for, 97
Moderna, 509
modern lies, 169–70, 174–75
Modi, Narendra, 309–10, 596, 598
Mofaz, Shaul, 612
Moldova, Russia and, 516–17
Monselinzef, Nicolay (Maxim), 456–57
Montego Bay, Jamaica, 261
Montenegro, 443–44, 479–80, 487
Montes Toscano, Borja, 27, 649–72

INDEX 705

Montevideo Convention on the Rights and
Duties of States, 398
Moon, 304, 313, 315
Moon Agreement, 301–2, 304–5
Moonlight Maze, 193–94
Moore, Daniel, 187
moral agents, 496
moralism, 47
moral norms, 353–54
moral psychology, 69, 69n.12
moral theory, lying and, 379
moral worth, 496
Morocco, 334
Morsi, Mohamed, 593, 597–98
'Moscow Gold', 452, 452n.18
Mouffe, Chantal, 371–72
Mozambique, 578
Civil Contingencies Agency (MSB), 566
Mubarak, Hosni, 593
Mueller, Robert, 407–9, 411n.112
Mueller Report, 147, 407–9, 411n.112
Muirhead, Russell, 167, 168
Mujahideen, 432, 463
multipolarity, move toward, 2–3
Munich Agreement, 381–82
Muñoz Mosquera, Andrés B., 21–22, 27, 319–
37, 606, 606n.15, 608, 649–72
Murdoch, Rupert, 177n.76
Muslim Brotherhood, 597–98

Naimski, Piotr, 462–63
Nakasone, Paul, 201–2
naming and shaming, 62n.1
nanotechnology, 244
nanocarriers/capsules, 244
nanodevices, 244
nanoengineering, 244
nanomaterials, 244
nanoparticles, 244
Napoleon Bonaparte, 526
Napoleonic Wars, 1
narco-trafficking, 482–83
narco-wars, 471
narratives, 158, 170–74, 177, 178
as campaigns or constructs, 170
definition of, 170–71
influence debate and, 174
narrative framing, 603
reality and, 174–75
truth and, 174, 179
Nash Equilibrium, 351–52
Nasu, Hitoshi, 18, 87–101
Natanz facility, 186, 204–5

National Aeronautics and Space Administration
(NASA) (US), 311–12
Artemis Accords and, 303–8
Mission Shakti and, 311
National Congress (Poland), 459–61
national crisis response, command-and-control
structure of, 25–26
National Endowment for Democracy (NED),
447–48, 462–63, 462n.52, 463n.55
National Home Guard (NHG), 479–80
nationalism, 99–100
National Research Council, National
Academies of Science (US), 245
National Security Act (US), 484
National Security Agency (NSA), 196, 197
National Security Strategy (US), 1–2, 3, 8
national service, 573. See also military service
natural law, 106
natural resources, 472, 486
navigation, 278–79
freedom of, 54–57
Navtex systems, 278–79
Nazis, 457, 565
Nazism, 457
necessity in bello, 499
Nedashkovskaya, Michelle, 162–63
Neff, Stephen C., 106
neocolonialism, 584
Netanyahu, Benjamin, 621
Netflix, 226
network propaganda, 165
neurobiological substances, 245
neurosciences and technologies (neuroS/T),
240, 241, 245–47
neurotechnologies, 245
'new generation warfare', 38
news organisations. See also media; specific
organisations
distrust of, 569–70
open houses hosted by, 569–70
New Space industry, 295–96
Newton, Michael A., 24–25, 513–32
new tools, of interference, 152–53
'new world order', 50
New York Times, 168, 226
New Zealand, 208, 304, 381, 403–4
Nicaragua, 91–93, 95–96, 398, 436, 436n.51,
485–86, 578. See also Nicaragua v. US
(IJC)
Nicaragua v. US (IJC), 91–93, 95–96, 132, 133,
397–98, 400, 403–4
niceness, 66
Niinistö, Suali, 631, 637–38

706 INDEX

Nikoliavitch, Ivan, 456–57
  Partial Test Ban Treaty, 299–300
Nix, Maegen, 23–24
Nixon, Richard, 352, 367
no-fly zones, in Iraq, 53
Nokia, 229
Non-Aggression Pact (Soviet Union and
    Germany), 457
non-attribution, cyber operations and, 364–66
non-contact warfare, 329–30
non-democratic States, lawfare and, 629
non-governmental organisations (NGOs),
    450–51, 569–70, 576. *See also specific
    organisations*
non-governmental organisations (NGOs)
  the Arctic and, 282–83
  focused on LOAC and HRL, 211
  human rights, 211
  lawfare and, 210
  maritime incident of 31 May 2010 and, 620
  rise of, 210, 211
non-international armed conflicts (NIACs),
    121–22, 123–25
  criteria for, 121–22, 123–24
  extra-territorial, 123
  threshold for, 89–90, 94, 95, 96–98, 101
non-intervention, 131–34, 131n.13, 138–48
  advancements in cyber context, 399–401
  coercion and, 130, 131–32, 131n.13, 133–34,
    140–41, 145, 148, 149, 423–24
  at crossroads, 135
  cyberspace and, 134, 140
  definition of, 131
  domaine réservé and, 130, 131–33, 131n.13,
    134, 140–41, 147, 148, 149
  election interference and, 146, 147, 416–17
  future of, 131
  grey zone conflicts and, 134, 135–48
  grey zone(s) and, 130, 134, 135–48
  historical understanding of, 395–99
  manipulation and, 143–44
  new standard for wrongful intervention,
    151–52
  non-transparency problem and, 150–51
  as norm, 129–53
  outdated standard of, 148, 149, 150–51
  power diffusion and, 148
  principle of, 5–6, 7, 13–14, 18–19, 22–23, 129,
    130, 131–34, 135, 329, 395–401, 403–4,
    423–24, 638–39
  propaganda and, 146–47
  proposal for legal resilience, 402–23
  scope of, 135

shifting notions of what constitutes, 135
socio-technological contexts and, 129–53
two constitutive elements of, 130, 131–32,
    131n.13, 148
US foreign policy and, 485
violation of, 131–32
non-kinetic activities, 31–32, 34–35, 41, 63. *See
    also specific activities*
non-lethal aid, 477–78, 480, 482
non-linear warfare, 260, 329–30
non-maximizing action, 73
non-refoulment, principle of, 638–39
non-State actors (NSAs), 22, 32–33, 96–97, 362
  armed, 428, 429–35, 445 (*see also* armed non-
    State actors (ANSAs))
  coercion and, 359–61
  competitive activities of, 319–20
  definition of, 428
  democratization of power and, 137
  deterrence and, 360–62
  domestic law and, 99–100
  grey zone(s) and, 23, 322, 359–64, 425–45,
    471
  growing capability to undermine States'
    domaine réservé, 137
  GZOs and, 322, 471
  hybrid warfare and, 425, 427
  individuals as, 428–29, 434–35, 445
  international law and, 23, 425–45
  normative implications and, 359–64
  norms and, 427
  operating independently from States,
    428–35
  PMC Wagner Group, 43
  political warfare and, 41
  as proxies, 322n.11, 359, 426–27, 435–44, 445
  self-defence and, 117–18, 119
  State actors and, 139, 148, 319–20, 362–64,
    425, 426–27, 445
  as 'systems' rather than unitary organisations,
    361
  technology advances and, 135
  three categories of, 428–35, 445
  threshold legal questions and, 97, 98, 101
  transnational corporations as, 428, 434–35, 445
  treaties and, 445
non-symmetric warfare, 329–30
non-transparency problem, 150–51
non-violent means, synergistic use of, below the
    threshold of open conflict, 12, 13–14
Nordstream pipelines, 632–33
  sabotage of, 491–92, 632–33
Norman, Herbert, 458

INDEX 707

normative challenges
information operations and, 369–70
international law and, 515–16
non-State actors and, 362–64
norms
actors governed by, 350–70
challenges to, 339
competition for, 531–32
cooperation and, 351–52
enforcement of, 47, 48
evolution of, 350–54
expectations and, 351, 353
grey zone(s) and, 339–72
grey zone vs. warfighting, 339–72
international, 350–70
legal norms, 20 (*see also* norms)
moral norms, 353–54
need to recommit to defending, 531–32
of non-intervention, 129–53
NSAs and, 427
peace as, 106–8, 109, 111–12, 125, 126, 127
of reprisal, 358–59
of responsible behaviour, 312–14
self-interest and, 352–54
social norms, 353–54
vs. standards of behaviour, 111–12
violations of, challenges to, undermining of,
495–96
of warfare, 357, 358–59
North Africa, 21–22, 329–30, 334. *See also
specific States*
North Atlantic Council, 522
North Atlantic Treaty. *See also* North Atlantic
Treaty Organization (NATO)
Article 5, 36–37, 325, 516n.11
Article 51, 553–54
signing of, 514–15
North Atlantic Treaty Organization (NATO),
35, 59, 99, 515–16, 519–21, 555, 632
ACO Matrix for the Identification of Legal
Operations, 609
Allied Command Operations, Office of Legal
Affairs, 27
Arctic Council and, 285
China and, 207–9
Cold War and, 33
collective self-defence and, 519, 521, 522
countering hostile cyber operations, 329
at end of Cold War, 49
European Union and, 646
Finland and, 285, 631–32
goal of avoiding 'another bloody century', 35
hybrid threats and, 10, 12

hybrid warfare and, 12
Israel and, 606, 606n.15
lawfare and, 209, 601–2, 603, 604, 606,
606n.15, 613–14, 662–68
legal operations and, 662–68
legal resilience and, 27
Libya and, 54–55
new 'Strategic Concept' of, 208
operationalization of legal operations within,
662–68
OPERATION ATLANTIC RESOLVE and,
55–56
rule of law and, 27
Russia and, 70, 71, 77–78, 104, 175n.61, 286,
347, 348, 368, 369, 479–80
SHAPE, 619n.58
Strategic Communications Centre of
Excellence, 450–51n.13
Sweden and, 285, 631–32
three i's and, 664–65
Wales Summit, 12
Yugoslavia and, 51–52
Northern Sea Route, 276–77
North Korea, 3, 232, 470
aggression by, 187–88, 366–67, 561, 562
cyber operations and, 187–88, 197, 205–6,
561
grey zone tactics and, 322, 561, 562
hacking of Sony, 366–67
nuclear proliferation and, 48, 50, 53, 55, 58
US and, 53, 55, 58, 390
North Macedonia, 487
North Vietnam, 355
Northwest Passage, 276–77
Northwest Rebellion, 452
Norway, 403–4, 462, 529–30
the Arctic and, 272–73, 273n.10, 277–78,
281–83, 281n.43, 286, 286n.64, 371–72
China and, 560–61
military service in, 572–73
Norwegian television, 567
Russia and, 371–72, 637–38
Norwegian fisherman, targeted by China as
proxies for their government, 560–61
NotPetya, 197, 204–5
NPR (National Public Radio) (US), 198–99
nuclear deterrence, satellites and, 302
nuclear proliferation, 50, 59, 333
Iran and, 364–65, 366
Iraq and, 48
North Korea and, 48, 53, 55, 58
nuclear tests, 381
Nuclear Tests case (ICJ), 381, 383, 384

708 INDEX

nullus commodum capere de sua injuria
  propria, 529
Nussbaum, Martha, 465n.61
Nye, Joseph, 136

Obama, Barack, 54–56, 146, 224, 228, 593, 595
Obama, Barack, 172
  2016 presidential election and, 146, 411n.112
  administration of, 58–59, 561
obedience, 407
  deficit in, 409–10
  natural flow of, 409–10
objective(s), 526
  'brute force' vs. compliance, 342
  principle of, 525–26
occupation, 121
Occupied, 567
October Revolution, 545
O'Donnell, Victoria 165
Offensive, 526
Office of the Director of National Intelligence
  (ODNI Report) (US), 146
officials, bribery and corruption of, 450–51
Official Secrets Act (Canada), 457–58
Ohlin, Jens, 417n.137
oil industry, 358
online communications, interference with, 133
online communities. social engineering of, 162–
  63n.16, *See also* social media
ontological equality principle, 412, 413
Open- Ended Working Group, UN General
  Assembly, 313, 315
Open-Source Intelligence (OSINT), 183
'operational assertions', 265–66
operational flexibility, 179, 191
operational manoeuvre, evolutions in, 88
OPERATION ATLANTIC RESOLVE, 55–56
Operation Burnt Frost, 309
Operation Cast Lead, 614, 618
Operation Enduring Freedom, 118
Operation Protective Edge, 617, 618
Operation QRBERETTA, 462n.51
Operation QRHELPFUL, 447–48, 461–62,
  461n.47, 462n.51
operations. *See also specific kinds of operations*
  below the threshold of war, 448
  vs. campaigns, 200
  'operations of war', 120
Operation Skeleton Key, 198–99
opinio juris, 110–11, 140, 141, 150–51, 378–79
Oppenheim, Lassa, 134
oppositional narratives, 45, 46–47, 53
optionality, 150

Orange Revolution, in Ukraine, 467
Organization of American States (OAS), 398
organized criminality, 2–3, 11–12
Ormond, D. M̃., 454–55
Ormuz strait, 333
Orpo, Petteri, 637–38
Orwell, George, 103, 106
  1984, 125
Ottawa Landmines Convention, 521, 522
outer space, hybrid and grey zone operations in, 21
Outer Space Treaty (OST), 289–91, 294, 298, 307
  Article I, 298, 306
  Article II, 307
  Article III, 298, 305, 306–7
  Article IV, 299–300, 305
  Article IX, 290, 301, 307–8
  Article V, 289, 290, 291–92, 305–6
  Article VI, 289–90
  Article VII, 300
  Article VIII, 300–1
  Article X, 299
  Article XII, 299, 305
  non-State commercial activity and, 300
overall control test, 437–38, 440

pacta sunt servanda, 381–82
Pakistan, 363, 471, 483
Palantir, 137
Palestinian Centre for Human Rights (PCHR),
  603n.5
Palestinian Legislative Council, 614–15
Palestinians, 602–3, 614–15
Palestinian Wall advisory opinion, 92–93
Palmer, Geoffrey, 628
Palmer Report, 628, 628n.102
Palo Alto Networks, 194–95
Paltrow, Gwyneth, 567
Pamment, James, 165
Paracel Islands, 265–66
parallel tracks, 150
paramilitary forces, 469n.1, 480–84. *See also*
  specific forces
  GZOs and, 476–90, 489t
  military force and, 484–88
paratrooping, 484–85
Paris Club, 463
parity, 135–36, 152–53
  diffusion of, 135–36
  in information age, 135, 136, 152–53
Parliamentary Assembly of the Council of
  Europe, 543
parody, 167n.38
partial-conflict scenarios, 61–62, 81, 85

INDEX 709

Partial Test Ban Treaty, 297
participatory propaganda, 165
Pathet Lao, 355
patron States, proxies and, 435–44, 445
Paul, Christopher, 160–61, 161n.12, 162n.13
'Pax Americana', 104, 172
peace. *See also* war and peace
  as ability to handle conflict by peaceful
    means, 32–33
  as absence of violence, 104–5
  competition and, 183
  conflict continuum and, 470
  definition of, 104–5, 127
  'general conclusion of peace', 122n.104
  in international order, 32–33, 36
  negative peace, 470
  as norm, 106–8, 109, 111–12, 125, 126, 127
  peaceful ordering, 1
  'positive peace', 104–5
  'quality peace', 104–5, 127
  secure peace, 470–71, 470*f*
  stable peace, 470–71, 470*f*
  as temporary cessation of fighting, 36, 45
  vs. war, 4–5, 6, 12–13, 18, 19, 32–36, 43–44,
    103–27, 183–87, 319–20, 321, 339, 373–74,
    447, 450, 451, 495–96
  war in the name of, 112–15
  war with, 112–15
peacekeeping forces, 51
Pearl Harbor, attack on, 484
Pedrozo, Raul, 219
peer-to-peer communications, 393–94
penetration, 162–63n.16
People's Armed Forces Maritime Militia
  (PAFMM), 219–20
People's Armed Forces Maritime Militia
  (PAFMM), 267–68
People's Republic of China (PRC). *See* China
perestroika, 449
'perfect war', 107
Permanent Court of Arbitration (PCA), 517–18
Permanent Court of International Justice
  (PCIJ), 129
  Nationality Decrees Issued in Tunis and Morocco,
    402–3
Perrin, Jean Emmanuel, 27, 649–72
Persian Gulf, 267
persistence criteria, 542, 545, 546–47
persistent competition, 1–5
persistent engagement strategy, 201–2
personalized data, 207, 419–20
  available online, 211, 212
  control over, 221–22

personal liberties, 472, 513, 527–28, 594
persuasion, democracies and, 157
Pfaff, C. Anthony, 22, 339–72
Pfizer, 509
pharmacological agents, 241
Philip, Prince, Duke of Edinburgh, 570–71
Philippines, 58, 598–99
  China and, 262, 263, 331, 517–18
  exclusive economic zone (EEZ), 56
  Philippine military, 262
  United States and, 598–99
phishing, 368
physical concepts
  digital contexts and, 138
  socio-technological contexts and, 138
physical force, 406
PMC Wagner Group, 43
Poland, 51, 457
  Artemis Accords and, 304
  indigenous institutions in, 463
  martial law in, 463
  migration and, 637–38
  NATO and, 521
  OPERATION ATLANTIC RESOLVE and,
    55–56
  Solidarność (Solidarity) movement in, 23,
    447–48, 449, 459–65
  underground publishing in, 464–65
'Polar Silk Road', 274–75
policy planning processes, legal considerations
  and, 25
political challenges, 450–51
political consulting firms, 137
political disruptiveness, 167
political ideology, Cold War and, 472
political independence
  principle of, 129
  principle of non-intervention and, 135
political influencing, anonymous, 62n.1
political institutions, sowing of distrust in,
  146–47
political pluralism, 7, 8
political processes, sowing of distrust in, 146–47
political warfare, 32, 43–44, 471–72
  during Cold War, 40, 41, 472
  in conflict continuum, 472
  definition of, 40–41, 252, 253–54, 472
  grey zone(s) and, 17, 40–41, 472–73
  GZOs and, 472–73
  information and, 41
  maritime domain and, 252–55
  US and, 40, 41
  utility of the concept, 40

710 INDEX

politics, social media and, 135
'positive peace', 104–5
post-traumatic stress disorder, 499–500
Powell, Colin, 388n.90
power, 135–36, 148
  conferral of, 423–24
  democratization of, 135, 137, 152–53
  diffusion of, 135–36, 137, 148, 149, 152–53
  emerging technologies and, 149
  employment of, 407
  exercise of, 423–24
  granting of, 407
  in information age, 135, 136
  legitimacy of, 423–24
  new tools of interference and, 137
practical considerations, 24, 25–26
Prague Spring, 449
precautionary principle, 61, 70–71, 74, 85
  grey zone attacks and, 61–62
precautionary principle sub-structures, 74
precision strikes, 618
preparedness, 574, 575
Press, Benjamin, 592, 593, 594, 595, 597, 599
pretexting, 162–63n.16
Prevention of an Arms Race in Outer Space
    (PAROS), 312
  Conference on Disarmament (CD), 310–11,
    312
Prigozhin, Yevgeniy, 439–40
principles of war, 24–25, 515, 525–28
print culture, social media and, 464–65, 464n.58
Prisoner's Dilemma, 17–18, 61, 65, 82–84, 85,
    352, 384
prisoners of war, 120, 122–23
private information, control over, 221–22,
    225–28
Private Military Company (PMC), 476–77
private sector
  grey zone aggression and, 573, 574, 575, 576
  involvement in defence and deterrence,
    25–26
private space operators, 305–6
procrastination, 73, 73n.16
pro-democracy organisations, 447–48
prohibition of use of force, undermining of, 6
propaganda, 158, 161, 163–66
  coined by Catholic Church, 163–64
  concepts of, 165–66
  definitions of, 163–66, 164n.24, 179
  democracy and, 163–64
  demagoguery and, 165–66
  vs. disinformation, 166
  vs. information campaigns, 164, 164n.24, 166

  as interference, 146–47
  manipulation and, 143–44, 164
  non-intervention and, 146–47
  online, 136–37
  vs. State-sponsored media, 166
proper attribution test, 438
property destruction, 499–500
proportionality, 371
  calculation of, 499–500
  proportionality constraint on sublethal
    collateral damage, 500–1n.26, 503–4
  proportionality criteria, 500
  proportionality principle, 500–1, 516–17, 523
  proportionality requirement, 499
  proportionate goods, 499n.16
  'stringency account' of proportionate
    response, 498
Prosecutor v. Duško Tadić (ICTY), 437–38
protest, promotion of, 450–51
Protestantism, 163–64
proxies, 39–40, 92, 477, 481–82, 487
  Arms Trade Treaty and, 440, 442–44
  definition of, 426–27, 426n.9, 426n.10
  Geneva Conventions and, 440–43
  GZO and, 471
  IHL and, 441, 443–44
  international law and, 435–44
  Iran and, 356, 357–58, 362, 480–81
  NSAs and, 322n.11, 359, 426–27, 435–44, 445
  patron States and, 435–44, 445
  responsibility for actions of, 440–44, 445
  Russia and, 37, 441, 487, 490
  State actors and, 359, 428, 435–44, 445
  States' responsibility for actions of, 440–44
proxy wars, 93
psychographic profiling, online, 136–37
psychological operations (PSYOPS), 157–58,
    160, 214, 253, 330
public-awareness campaigns, 25–26
public influence campaigns, 393–94
public opinion
  influence over, 157
  manipulation of, 165
  non-intervention and, 130
  sowing of distrust and, 146–47
public power, 22–23
punishment, 501, 511. See also punitive harm;
    punitive war
punitive harm, 501–3, 511
  consequentalist justifications for, 501–3
  retributivist justifications for, 501–2,
    502n.29
punitive war, 502

INDEX 711

Putin, Vladimir, 38–39, 42–43, 70, 82, 332–33, 350–51, 374, 465, 478–79, 514–15
  2016 presidential election, 146
  Xi and, 207–8
Putnam, Robert, 563

Qaddafi, Moammar, 54–55
Qatar, 199–200
Qiao Liang, 321–22
Quadrilateral Dialogue, 595
'quality peace', 104–5, 127
Quong, Jonathan, 498

Radek, Karl, 453, 454–55
radical levelling technologies (RLTs), 239–40, 241, 246, 248
radio, 175
Radio Free Europe, 164–65, 462–63, 463n.54
Raimondo, Gina, 229
RAND, 41, 159n.3, 160
ransomware, 188–89
  ransomware-as-a-service, 188–89
  ransomware attacks, 189, 367
  ransomware groups, 189, 194–95
Rasmussen, Anders Fogh, 42
rational agents, 68–69, 70, 73, 74–75, 75n.20
rationality, 72–75
  vs. irrationality, 75n.20
  theory of, 71, 72–73
'ratlines', 462
Rauta, Vladimir, 426n.9
Rawls, John, 372
Reagan, Ronald, 32–33, 462–63, 486
realist international relations theorists, 36
reality, narratives and, 174–75
Reception Condition Directive 2013/ 33/ EU, 640
recipient States, security assistance and, 577–600
Red Army, 456–57
Red Cross, 571
Red Cross movement, 89–90
'Red Menace', 452–53
Red Scares, 451–59
  in Canada, 447–48, 452–53, 466
  'First' Red Scare, 451–52
  infiltration and, 452–53
  in literature, 452n.15
  'Second' Red Scare, 451–52
reefs, 218–19, 220–21
Reeves, Shane, 100–1
'reflective equilibrium', 372
reflexive control, 157–58, 161–62
reform, 502–3

Regan, Mitt, 26, 42, 577–600
regime change, grey zone activities and, 459–65
regimes
  international norms and, 351
  'sovereignty regime', 351
regime theorists, international relations and, 537–38
Registration Convention, 301–2, 306
Reith, John, 177
relationships, crisis and, 348–49
religious orders and denominations, 450–51
Rendezvous and Proximity Operations, 295, 295n.25
Reno, William, 580, 581, 583, 584
Report on the Investigation into Russian Interference in the 2016 Presidential Election ('Mueller Report'), 147. *See also* Mueller Report
repression, authoritarian, 589–600
reprisal, norm of, 358–59
Republic of China (ROC). *See* Taiwan
reputational damage, 613
  mitigating, 610
reputational lawfare, 603, 603n.7, 610
Rescue and Return Agreement, 301–2, 305–6
resilience, 559, 651–52. *See also* legal resilience
  definitions of, 533–34, 535–37, 538
  ecological resilience, 535–36, 538, 542
  engineering resilience, 535–36, 538, 542
  environmental matters and, 538–39
  grey zone aggression and, 563
  law and, 534–41
  legal, 533–56
  modalities of, 547–48
  as normative principle in international environmental law, 538–39
  notion of, 25
  reception of in legal scholarship, 538–41
  resilience thinking, 535–38
  in Russia, 545
  societal resilience, 559, 576
  vs. stability, 535
  as theory about systems, 543
  usage of, 538
  vulnerability and, 546–47
resilience theory, 540–41, 555–56
resilience thinking, 534, 535–38, 555
  in legal scholarship, 538–41
  origins of contemporary, 534–35
  utility of, 25, 534
resistance, 615
  adaptation and, 553–54
  government, 585–89

712 INDEX

resistance actors, 477–80
resistance support operations, 478–79
response, legal resilience and, 665–66
responsibility
  of armed non-State actors (ANSAs), 434
  attribution of, 428–44
responsible behaviour, development of norms
    of, 312–14
retaliation
  cost-benefit analyses and, 72
  for grey zone aggression, 562
'retorsion', 62n.1
retribution, 502–3
retributivists, 501–2, 502n.29
revisionism, 1–2, 4–5, 8, 34, 38, 126, 329, 547–
    48. *See also* revisionist powers
  grey zone conflicts and, 64
  grey zone(s) and, 323
  incremental, 64
  limits of, 335
revisionist powers, 322, 329
  China as, 331
  grey zone approaches and, 37, 319
  Iran, 333
  Russia as, 331–32
  vs. status quo powers, 8–9
revolutions, 454
Rice, Condoleezza, 196
Richardson, John, 267–68
Rid, Thomas, 192, 365–66, 368
right intention, 499
'right of intervention', 133
rights, universality of, 497–98
rights-based framework, 24
  grey zone threats and, 495–511
rights forfeiture, 24, 499, 500–1
  justification of, 497–98
rights violation, defence against, 496
right to command, 405
risk, choice under, 61
Roberts, Hal, 165
robotics, 274–75
ROCOSMOS, 311
Rodin, David, 499n.16
Rogers, Mike, 198
ROKS *Cheonan*, 470
Romania, 443–44
  Artemis Accords and, 304
Rome Statute, 521, 623, 623n.77
'roof knock' policy, 618
Roosevelt, Franklin, 398
Rose, Fred, 457–58
Rosenberg, Ethel, 458

Rosenberg, Julius, 458
Rosenblum, Nancy, 167, 168
Rose Revolution, in Georgia, 467
Rosneft, 204
Roundtable Talks, 463
Rovner, Joshua, 196, 201
Royal Canadian Mounted Police (RCMP)
    Security Service, 452–53, 455–57
Royal Mounted qualifying purchase, 456–57
Ruhl, J. B., 540–41, 544, 555–56
Rule 66, 400, 403–4
rule of law, 14, 519, 645, 646
  autocracies and, 7
  competition and, 8, 515
  conflicts and, 515
  democracies and, 7
  deterrence and, 519
  lawfare and, 607–8
  NATO and, 27
  respect for, 656
  thick understanding of, 7, 14–15
Rule of Law in Armed Conflicts project, 124
rules-based order narrative, 173
rules of engagement (ROE), caveats and,
    658–60
Russel, Daniel, 228
Russia, 33, 35, 67n.9, 68–69, 268–69, 350–51, 454,
    469, 483–84, 572. *See also* Soviet Union
  2014 efforts to annex Ukrainian territory,
    374, 375, 471, 479
  aggression against Ukraine, 1–2, 3, 6, 7, 8–9,
    14, 20–21, 26–27, 33, 34, 36–37, 38–40,
    42–43, 67n.9, 68–69, 68n.10, 70–71,
    72n.13, 75n.20, 77–78, 80–81, 82, 104, 111,
    114–15, 125–26, 148–49, 212, 332–33, 425,
    480, 530, 631–32
  ambitions in Europe, 48
  annexation of Crimea, 12, 14, 42–43, 55–56,
    57, 87–88, 148–49, 373, 374, 375, 450, 495–
    96, 633–34, 637–38
  the Arctic and, 53–54, 271, 276–78, 282–83,
    284–86, 332–33, 371–72
  Arms Trade Treaty and, 444
  Artemis Accords and, 304
  attempts to steal vaccine research, 509
  authoritarianism in, 207–8
  Chechen fighters and, 441
  Chechnya and, 425
  China and, 207–8
  Code of Criminal Procedure and, 264–65
  Crimea and, 551
  cyber attacks on Estonia, 359, 364, 365,
    366–67

cybercrime groups in, 476–77
cyber operations and, 189, 191, 193–94, 196–97, 204, 359, 364, 365, 366–67
cyber proxies and, 487
declaration under UNCLOS Article 298, 263–64
destructive anti-satellite (ASAT) tests and, 308–9, 311–12
disinformation operations and, 370, 516–17, 561 (*see also specific operations*)
as donor State, 599
Eastern Europe and, 37, 347
economic war with, 560–61
efforts to annex Ukraine since 2014, 22, 34
efforts to restore status quo ante of 1991, 331–32, 332n.50
Europe and, 48, 368, 479–80
EU Sanctions on, 637–38
exploitation of grey zones in international law by, 148–49
Finland and, 426n.7, 574, 631–32, 637–38, 643, 644
foreign interference by, 23
FSB in, 476–77, 479
geopolitical goals of, 331–32
Georgia and, 329–30, 332, 425, 516–17
'Gerasimov Doctrine' and, 447–48
Greece and, 328
as grey zone actor, 331–33, 561, 562
grey zone conflicts and, 38
grey zone instruments and, 21–22
grey zone(s) and, 21–22, 31–32, 36–37, 38–40, 322, 329–30, 331–33, 337, 476, 561, 562
grey zone tactics and, 322
GZOs and, 36–37, 329–30, 331–33, 337, 471–72, 476–80, 487–91
hacking by, 368
hacking of DNC, 368
human rights and, 7, 211
human rights NGOs and, 211
hybrid measures toward Ukraine before invasion, 256–57
hybrid warfare and, 38, 42, 329–30, 337, 425
incursion into Georgia in 2008, 55–56, 58
information operations and, 368, 370
intellectual property (IP) theft and, 509
interference in 2016 US election, 130, 139, 146, 147, 161–62, 162–63n.16, 199–200, 368, 370, 407–9, 411n.112, 416n.133, 416n.134, 417n.137, 420, 447–48, 561
interference in 2020 US election, 370
international law and, 7, 173–74, 175n.62

International Lunar Research Station and, 304
invasion of Afghanistan, 346
invasion of Ukraine, 158, 189, 207–8, 213, 273–74, 284–85, 286–87, 313–14, 337, 347, 369, 370, 372, 376, 441, 447–48, 471, 547–48, 553–54, 560–61, 566–67, 575–76, 631–34, 635–36, 637–38
Iran and, 481–82
ITLOS and, 262, 263–65, 268–69
Kerch Strait and, 329
lawfare and, 213, 332–33, 618–19, 619n.57
law in, 545
legal model for annexation of Crimea and the Donbas, 332–33, 332n.50
'little green men' (often SPETSNAZ), 476–77
lying by, 373
as main competitor, 1–2
Main Intelligence Directorate (GRU), 408, 476–77, 479–80
maskirovka ('camouflage', or deceptive operations) used by, 36–37
military activities of, 23–24
military and paramilitary cooperation in, 490
Ministry of Defense, 439–40
Moldova and, 516–17
as most acute direct threat to the United Kingdom, 2–3
narratives and, 175n.61
NATO and, 70, 71, 77–78, 104, 175n.61, 286, 347, 348, 368, 369, 479–80
normal competition and, 4
norm-challenging behaviours of, 53–54
Norway and, 371–72, 637–38
as nuclear power, 331–32
paramilitary GZOs and, 476–80
proxies and, 37, 438, 439–40, 441, 487, 490
resilience in, 545
as revisionist power, 331–32
rules-based order narrative and, 173–74
Russia-China joint statement of February 2022, 284
Russian special forces (*Spetnaz*), 375
Sahel region and, 517–18
Salisbury poisoning incident and, 4–5
separatists' downing of MH-17 in Ukraine, 336
space domain and, 295n.25
SVR in, 476–77
Syria and, 486, 491–92, 517–18
Threat of Use of Force Against Outer Space Objects initiative and, 312–13
UK and, 2–3, 374, 375

714 INDEX

Russia (*cont.*)
    Ukraine and, 1–2, 3, 6, 7, 8–9, 12, 14, 20–21, 26–27, 33, 34, 36–37, 38–40, 42–43, 55–56, 57, 67n.9, 68–69, 68n.10, 70–71, 72n.13, 75n.20, 77–78, 80–81, 82, 87–88, 104, 111, 114–15, 125–26, 148–49, 158, 189, 207–8, 212, 213, 273–74, 284–85, 286–87, 313–14, 329–30, 332–33, 337, 347, 369, 370, 372, 373, 374, 375, 376, 425, 441, 447–48, 450, 471, 479, 480, 495–96, 516–17, 530, 547–48, 551, 553–54, 560–61, 566–67, 575–76, 631–34, 635–36, 637–38
    UNCLOS and, 268–69
    US and, 38, 48, 53–54, 55–56, 57, 104, 130, 139, 146, 147, 161–62, 162–63n.16, 173–74, 175n.61, 199–200, 213, 367, 368, 370, 398, 407–9, 411n.112, 416n.133, 416n.134, 417n.137, 420, 447–48, 561
    US-led financial sanctions against, 213
    violation of prohibition of use of force, 111
    war crimes committed by, 212
    Western nations and, 516–17
Russia-Georgia war, 471
Russian Coast Guard, 263–64
Rwanda, 584
    atrocities in, 57–58, 611

safe havens, 51
safety zones, 307–8
Sahel region, 517–18
Saint-Gobain, 204
Saint Vincent de Paul Penitentiary, Quebec, riot at, 454–55
'salami-slicing' strategy, 323, 331, 517
Salisbury poisoning incident, 4–5, 551
samizdat, 464–65, 464n.58
Sandworm, 204
San Francisco, California, 566–67
Sarajevo, Yugoslavia, bombing of, 51
Sari, Aurel, 25, 83n.34, 255, 295, 373–74, 533–56, 604
satellites
    crisis communication satellites, 302
    early warning satellites, 302
    nuclear deterrence and, 302
    Starlink/China Space Station incident, 289–93
satire, 167n.38
Saudi Arabia, 443–44
    Iran and, 333, 358, 359, 365
Scarborough Shoal, 56
Schadlow, Nadia, 319–20
Schelling, Thomas J., 66, 343–45, 346

Schmitt, Michael, 132–33, 134, 143–44, 145, 146, 148–49, 150–51, 395–96, 416n.134, 417n.137, 423–24
science, advances in, 2–3. *See also* science and technology (S/T)
science and technology (S/T)
    China and, 246–47, 275–76, 559–60
    integrative S/T intelligence (InS/TINT), 247
    three vistas of future development, 247
    uses of, 247
    warfare, intelligence, and national security (WINS) operations, 247–48
Science of Military Strategy, 208–9
Sea of Azov, 263–64, 267, 329
Searle, John, 380
Second Gulf War, 176–77
Second Intifada, 360–61, 602–3
'Second' Red Scare, 451–52
Second Thomas Shoal, 262, 263
secrecy, 488–90
Secure World Foundation, 308–9
security
    democracy and, 597, 598, 599–600
    internet of things (IoT) and, 182
    intertwined internal and external, 644–46
security assistance
    background, 578–79
    grey zone(s) and, 577–600
    human rights and, 598–600
    by liberal democracies, 577–600
    US Department of Defense (DoD) and, 578–79
    US State Department and, 578–79
security assistance to other States, 26
security clearance vetting, 643–44
Security Council, 526
security sector, cyber operations in, 184
Security Strategy for Society 2017 (Finland), Concept for Comprehensive Security, 632
security threats, international law and, 25
Segal, Adam, 202
Seguin, Barre R., 604n.9
self-defence, 24–25, 92–93, 107, 109, 115–16
    anticipatory, 116–17, 119
    as catch-all justification, 115–19
    Cicero on, 524, 525
    collective, 553–54
    definition of, 116, 119
    international law and, 357–58
    invocation of for many unilateral uses of force, 119
    as justification for use of force, 115–16, 125
    liberal democracies and, 527
    NSAs and, 117–18, 119
    'pre-emptive'/'preventative', 116–17

right of, 6, 90–91, 95–97, 105–6, 119
UNSC and, 115–16
use of force and, 116–18, 119, 356–58
self-determination, 513, 588–89
violations of, 395–96
self-interest, norms and, 352–54
semiconductors, 198–99, 207–8, 213, 229–30
Sen, Amartya, 465n.61
Senkaku/Diaoyu Islands, 172
Serbia, 425, 443–44
Serbs
grey zone tactics used by, 51, 52
Serbian forces, 362
Serbian nationalists, 479–80
Sergis, Panagiotis, 27, 649–72
Sessions, Jeff, 408–9
SF72, 566–67
Shadow Brokers, 197
Shany, Yuval, 141, 150
Shapiro, Jacob, 162–63
Sharon, Ariel, 602–3, 602–3n.4, 603n.6
Shiites, 581
Shilong, Zhang, 188–89
short-of-war techniques, 62n.1
'shroud of legitimacy', 265–66
Sierra Madre, 262
Signal, 226
Signals Intelligence (SIGINT), 183
Šiklova, Jiřina, 449–50, 449n.6
Simplicity, 526, 527
Singapore, Artemis Accords and, 304
Singer, Peter Warren, 170, 175
Sinovac, 509
Sisi, Abdel Fattah el-, 593, 594, 595, 597–98
Sisson, Melanie W., 17, 45–60
6G technology, 182
skepticism
disinformation and, 167, 168
pervasive, 167, 168, 169–70
Skerker, Michael, 497
Skripal, Sergei, 514–15, 514n.6
Slaughter, Anne-Marie, 414n.129
Slovakia, 443–44
Smeets, Max, 201, 202
Smith, Cecil, 456–57n.36
Smith-Mundt Act, 164–65
social change, 3–4
social engagement, 570
social engineering, 157–58, 162, 162–63n.16
definitions of, 163n.17
of online communities, 162–63n.16
social media, 13–14, 149, 150, 162–63, 165, 175, 226, 368, 369–70, 563, 569, 618–19. See also specific platforms

anonymity and, 419–20
in China, 226
civil society and, 465–66
definition of, 464–65
disinformation and, 130, 134, 516–17
election interference and, 143, 147, 420
emerging power of, 148
exploitation of, 450–51, 527–28
growing role of, 130
interference with, 136
manipulation through, 143
parity with States and, 136
politics and, 135
power of, 135, 136
print culture and, 464–65, 464n.58
tech companies and, 419–20, 419n.148, 421–22
trolling on, 62n.1
weaponization of, 174–77
social norms, 353–54
Social Science One, 421, 422
Societal Collapse, 557–58, 567
society
cohesion of, 564
divisions within, 564
how to involve, 564–75
societal resilience, 552–53
societal welfare, 24–25
socio-ecological resilience, 536–38, 540–41
socio-technological change, 130, 131, 137, 138–48, 149
customary international law and, 129–53
definition of, 135
grey zone(s) emerging from, 129–53
interference and, 141, 149
non-intervention and, 129–53
norm of non-intervention and, 129–53
what constitutes, 135
socio-technological contexts
non-intervention and, 138–39
physical concepts and, 138
territorial concepts and, 138
SolarWinds, 191, 194, 196–97
Soleimani, Qassem, 115–16, 356, 357–58, 483, 486–87
Solidarność (Solidarity) movement, 23, 447–48, 449, 459–65, 460n.45, 467
American support for, 462–63
CIA and, 461n.48, 462–63, 464
civil society and, 464
Cold War and, 461n.48
grey zone activities and, 464, 465
Solomon Islands, 253–54
Solzhenitsyn, Aleksandr, 527–28

716 INDEX

Somalia, 50–51n.15, 581–82
Somali National Army (SNA), 581–82
Sony, 366–67, 561
Sørenson, Camilla T. N., 20–21, 271–87
sorites, 61–62, 72–74
Sorites Problems, 72–73
South Asia, 595
South China Sea
 arbitration of, 251, 255, 262–63, 264, 265–66, 268–69
 China and, 4–5, 14, 20–21, 24–25, 33, 39, 53–54, 56–57, 87–88, 172, 207, 216–21, 234, 257, 260–61, 262–63, 267–69, 272–73, 272n.8, 330, 331, 517–18, 518n.15
Southern Lebanon War, 87–88
South Korea, 172, 231–32, 444, 470
 Artemis Accords and, 304
 China and, 232
 Covid in, 509
 Institute for Defense Analysis, 187–88
 at NATO summit, 208
 US and, 53
South Pacific, maritime boundaries in, 319
South Vietnam, 578, 586, 587–88
sovereign equality, 7, 129
sovereign prerogatives, 131–33
sovereignty, 397–98, 400, 401, 402–3n.61, 506, 529–30, 588–89
 China's manipulation of concept, 517
 lawful exercise of, 95–96
 principle of, 403–4
 respect for, 362, 363
 right to, 363
 States and, 495
 violations of, 363, 395–96, 400
'sovereignty regime', 351
Soviet-East Europe group, International Activities Division (IAD), 461n.47
Soviet Union, 449, 452, 454, 545, 592–93. *See also* Russia
 active measures used by, 166
 in Afghanistan, 432
 Afghanistan and, 35–36
 changes in Western perception of, 457–58
 Cold War and, 33, 465, 472, 578, 592–93
 collapse of, 49, 50
 Communist Parties and, 452n.18
 Cuba and, 484–85
 destructive anti-satellite (ASAT) tests and, 308–9
 at end of Cold War, 49, 50
 espionage and, 452
 fall of, 175n.61, 578
 geographic sphere of, 331–32

invaded by Germany, 457
maskirovka ('camouflage', or deceptive operations), 36–37
Solidarność (Solidarity) movement and, 459–61
space domain and, 300, 302
sphere of influence, 464
US and, 297, 346, 378–79, 398, 592–93
Soyuz capsules, 311
space. *See also* space domain
 hybrid and grey zone operations in, 21, 289–315 (*see also* Outer Space Treaty (OST))
 hybrid operations and, 294–97
 military uses of, 299–300
 space debris, 302, 313–14, 315
 as unique environment for grey zone operations, 293
 as 'warfighting domain', 293
space domain, 215, 289–315
 absence of consensus on use of, 295
 ambiguity of attribution in, 296
 asymmetry of assets and interests regarding, 294, 296
 China and, 296, 302
 Cold War and, 297
 competition and, 296–97
 cooperation and, 296–97
 cooperation in, 315
 development of norms and, 315
 as domain of international law, 295 (*see also* international space law)
 first UNGA Resolution on, 297
 high level of secrecy associated with the, 294
 hybrid operations in, 296–97
 international law and, 291, 300, 315
 international space law and, 315
 proliferation of space debris in, 302
 security in, 289–315
 Soviet Union and, 300, 302
 space debris and, 313–14, 315
 unique physical attributes of, 296
 US and, 296, 300, 302
space law, 292, 295, 297–303
space race, 296–97, 371–72
Space Surveillance Network, 309
space sustainability, 302
space technology, 274–75
 collaboration and, 302
 development of, 302
 dual-use nature of, 313–14
 as inherently dual use, 294
 interoperability and, 315
 technology-sharing arrangements, 315
SpaceX, 289–93, 305–6

INDEX 717

SpaceX Dragon Capsules, 311
Spain, 455–57, 625
    interference in elections in, 393–94
    lawfare and, 601–2, 611, 613
    Morocco and, 334
speaker-identity deception, 162–63
spear-phishing, 416n.133
Special Counsel's Office, 147
speech, freedom of, 150
Spitsbergen Treaty, 280–82
spoofing, 416
Spratly Island chain, 331
Sputnik X, 509
stability, 104, 535, 546–47
    factors in, 103
    vs. resilience, 535
    US military as policeman, 1990-1999, 50–53
stability operations, 34
stakes, raising, 346–47
Stalin, Josef, 453
Standage, Tom, 464–65
standards, enforcement of, 47, 48
standards of behaviour, vs. norms, 111–12
standing armies, development of, 107
Stanley, Jason, 164, 165–66
Starlink/China Space Station incident, 289–93
start-stop-start aggressions, 85
stasis, vs. change, 547–48
the State
    State responsibility, 402
    State sovereignty, 362
State actors
    coercion and, 359–60
    cyber operations and, 366–67
    grey zone tactics and, 322
    law of insincere State utterances, 373, 380–83
    laws on State lying, 373, 378–80
    lying and, 385–89
    NSAs and, 139, 148, 319–20, 362–64
    political warfare and, 41
    proxies and, 359
    rogue, 322
state-building, 583
statecraft
    vs. crime, 19, 180, 183, 187–90
    cyber operations as tool of, 185, 190
    dissimulation and, 377
    vs. warfare, 339
State lying, 373, 385–89
    customary international law and, 378–79
    as existential threat to international law
        system, 391–92
    role and legal status in grey zone conflicts, 22

state of emergency, 636–37, 636–37n.25
State-sponsored media, vs. propaganda, 166
the State/States, 585–600
    armed non-State actors (ANSAs) and,
        431–32
    beliefs of, 387–88, 387n.89
    as biggest beneficiaries of grey zone, 445
    control over proxies, 435–40
    fragile, 579–84
    free, 528
    grey zone(s) and, 466
    as information entity, 413–15, 423–24
    as 'multiagent system', 414, 414n.126
    non-democratic, 629
    NSAs and, 425, 426–27, 445
    patron States, 426–27, 426n.10, 435–44, 445
    proxies and, 428, 435–44, 445
    relatively stable, 585–600
    responsibilities for actions of proxies, 428,
        445
    responsibility for proxy actions on the
        grounds of treaties, 440–44
    rise of illiberal, 516
    sovereignty and, 495
    stable, 544
    State authority, 579–82
    State immunity, 546n.82
    targeted by hybrid warfare, 445
    targeted by NSAs, 445
    Weber's definition of, 406
status quo
    challenges to, 329
    support for, 8
    survival of, 347
    valuing the, 347
status quo powers, vs. revisionist powers, 8–9
Sterling, Bruce, 181
Stern, Manfred, 456–57
St Petersburg Declaration of 1868, 353, 354
Strait of Hormuz, 55
Strait of Malacca, 276–77
strategic competition, 35
    good faith cooperation and, 390
strategic competitors, 33
strategic environment, challenges that define
    the present, 1–2
strategic litigation, identifying, 609–10, 629
strategic rationality, 61
'strategic seams', 24–25
strategic seams
    legal integration and, 519–22
    winning at, 513–32
strikes, 451–52

718 INDEX

Stuxnet operation, 186, 198, 204–5, 364–65, 366
Subi Reef, 218–19
sublethal responses
  to deter and reform wrongdoers, 502–3, 504
  in grey zone(s), 495–96, 500–11
sublethal threats, 24
sub-threshold conflicts, 45–46, 48, 49, 50–57
success, reasonable change of, 499–500
Sudan, 360–61, 425
Sudentenland, 381
Suez Canal, 276–77
Sullivan, Clair, 366–67
Sullivan, Patricia, 342, 589
Sunni forces, 443–44
Sun Tzu, 207, 208–9, 215, 237
superpowers, Cold War and, 472
Supervisory Control and Data Acquisition (SCADA) network, 505
Surprise, 526
surveillance, grey zone competition and, 325–26
surveillance balloons, 378–79
Svalbard, Norway, 281n.43, 282
Svalbard Science Forum, 281–82
Sweden, 278–79, 462
  the Arctic and, 272–73, 273n.10, 277–78, 282–83, 286, 286n.64
  Cold War defence and, 562
  Liberal Party in, 572
  likely NATO-membership of, 285
  North Atlantic Treaty Organization (NATO) and, 631–32
  resurrection of military service in, 559
  suspension of conscription in, 559
Swedish Civil Contingencies Agency, 565
Swedish National Television, 557–58, 567
Switzerland, 403–4
Symantec, 182
symmetry-breaking techniques, 85
Syria, 443–44, 481, 530
  conflict in, 123
  Daesh in, 363–64
  hybrid warfare in, 425
  Iran and, 480–81, 482, 483, 488–90
  Israel's cyberattacks on, 364
  missile strikes in, 9n.37
  Russia and, 486, 491–92, 517–18
  US and, 54–55, 486
  US military and, 54–55
  Wagner Group in, 439–40
  WMDs in, 491–92
systemic competition, 2–3

Tadić Tribunal, 95n.45, 120–21
Tahrir Square uprising, 464–65
Taiwan, 3, 58, 232–33
  China and, 39, 50, 208, 232–33, 371, 487, 559–61, 575–76
  COVID in, 509
  US and, 208, 487
Taiwan Strait, 33, 219
Taliban, 483n.40, 581
Tallin Manual Project, 400
Tallinn Manual 2.0 on the International Law Applicable to Cyber Operations, 134, 141, 145, 358–59, 366–67, 400, 401, 402–3n.61, 403–4, 416–17, 419
Tallinn Manual Process, 395–96
tamizdat, 464–65, 464n.58
tech companies, 135, 150, 188–89. *See also specific companies*
  grey zone aggression and, 573
  power of, 136
  responsibility for content users post, 421–22
  social media and, 419–20, 419n.148, 421
technical standards, 228–30
technologies, 100, 131. *See also* cyber operations; *specific technologies*
  advances in, 2–4, 18–19, 93, 100, 101, 130, 135, 138–48
  authoritarianism and, 472–73
  bio-technologies, 237–49
  China and, 559–60
  cyber technologies, 339
  disruption and, 237–49
  emerging technologies (ETs), 20, 130, 131, 135–48, 149, 237–49, 274–75, 472–73
  emerging technologies as threats (ETT), 239–40, 241
  as enabling tools in grey zone engagements, 239–46
  5G technology, 182, 228, 230, 234, 274–75, 642 (*see also* anti-5G movement)
  4G technology, 182
  geostrategically significant, 198–99
  grey zone aggression and, 559–60, 562
  information and communication technologies (ICTs) and, 393–424
  information operations and, 368
  interference and, 141
  international law of interference and, 393–424
  leveraged for coercive effect, 1–2
  neurotechnologies, 244, 245
  new technologies, 130, 321

INDEX 719

non-intervention and, 135
non-State actors and, 135
quickening pace of technological change, 2–3
radical levelling technologies (RLTs), 239–40, 241
6G technology, 182
socio-technological change, 130, 131, 137, 138–48, 149
space race and, 371–72
space technology, 294, 302, 313–14, 315
technology-sharing arrangements, 315
US technological advantage in space domain, 296
Tecott, Rachel, 585, 586
teenagers, 569, 570–71
Tehran Hostage Rescue Mission, 377
telecommunications, battle over whose pipelines supply the world, 228–30
telecommunications equipment, Chinese-made, 228
telecommunications networks, 207. *See also specific networks*
television, 175
Terminal High Altitude Area Defense (THAAD), 172
Territorial Act, 635
territorial concepts, socio-technological contexts and, 138
territorial expansion, 323–24
territorial integrity, 375, 635
  principle of, 58
  principle of non-intervention and, 135
  violations of, 31
territorial sovereignty, principle of, 129
territorial status quo, challenging, 329
territorial surveillance, 635
Territorial Surveillance Act (Finland), 634–35
territory, battle for, 559–60
terrorism, 1–3, 11–12, 361, 362, 363, 471, 488–90
  degradation of, 363
  deterrence and, 360–62
  disruption of, 360–61, 363
  vs. grey zone attacks, 63
  terrorist attacks of 11 September 2001, 53, 73–74, 116–17, 118, 360–61, 486, 578
  as threat to peace, 113–14
  war on, 54, 104
terrorist organisations, 211, 360–61, 362, 363, 613–14, 629. *See also specific organisations*
  lawfare and, 629
Third International, 451–52, 457. *See also* Communist International (Comintern)

Third United Nations Conference on the Law of the Sea, UN Convention of the Law of the Sea (UNCLOS), 261
threatening intent, signalling of, 23–24
Threat of Use of Force Against Outer Space Objects, 312–13
threats, credibility and capability of, 344, 345, 346
'threat to peace', 113–14, 126–27
three i's, 664–65
'Three Warfares', 214, 215, 273n.9, 330, 527, 605n.12
'three non-warfares', 329–30
threshold legal questions, 89–90, 93–94, 95, 96–98, 101
Tiananmen Square massacre, 172
Tianjin State Security Bureau, 188–89
TikTok, 226, 422, 569
'time of war', 120
TNT Express, 204
Tokyo, Japan, 566–67
toleration, vs. capitulation, 371–72
tolls, 147
'tools of obfuscation', 100, 101
Toronto Daily Star, 453
total-conflict scenarios, 61–62, 81–82, 85
Total Defence model (Finland), 632
track domains, 215
trade authorities, Chinese grey zone lawfare and, 231–34
trade wars, 62n.1
traditional lies, 169–70, 174–75
traditional warfare, decline of, 559
training, legal resilience and, 668–70
trajectory, 148–52
transcription activator-like effector (TALE), 242
transitive preferences, 74–76, 75n.20
transnational challenges, 1–3
transnational corporations, 428, 434–35, 445
transnational organisations, 450–51
transparency, 549–50
  lack of, 150
Transpolar Passage, 276–77, 277n.23
trashing, 162–63n.16
treaties, 130, 210–11, 442–44. *See also specific treaties*
  arms trade treaties, 442–44
  new, 150
  non-State actors and, 445
  proxy actions and, 440–44
Treaty on Principles Governing the Activities of States in the Exploration and Use of Outer Space, including the Moon and Other Celestial Bodies, 298. *See also* Outer Space Treaty (OST)

720 INDEX

Treaty on the Functioning of the European
Union, 553–54
Article 215, 553–54
trolley problem, 'Bridge' version, 496–97
trolls, 136–37, 162–63n.16, 368, 416n.134,
419–20
Truman, Harry S., 516
Trump, Donald J., 54, 168
2016 presidential election and, 143, 146, 408,
410
2020 presidential elections and, 411
accuses China of underreporting Covid
cases, 389–90
'Big Lie' and, 411
Kim Jong Un and, 390
Trump administration, 55, 303–8, 410, 594
Artemis Accords and, 303–8
truth, 157
narratives and, 174, 178
Tufekci, Zeynep, 464–65, 465n.61
Türkel, Jacob, 622
Turkel Commission, 620n.59, 620n.63, 621–
22n.72, 622
Turkey, 443–44
hybrid warfare and, 425
Iran and, 359, 365
maritime incident of 31 May 2010 and, 621,
623, 625–26, 627, 628
Turnball, Malcolm, 230
2016 presidential election, 146, 199–200, 408–9
disinformation and, 147
interference in, 393–94
Obama and, 146
Russian interference in, 130, 139, 146, 147,
161–62, 162–63n.16, 368, 370, 407–9,
411n.112, 416n.133, 416n.134, 417n.137,
420, 447–48, 561
Trump and, 143, 146, 408, 410
US and, 326
2020 US presidential elections
'Big Lie' about, 411
interference in, 393–94
Russian disinformation targeting, 370
Trump and, 411
Twitter, 143, 147, 226, 421, 422, 527–28, 618–19

U-2 incident, 1960, 378–79
Uganda, 584
UK House of Commons, 564–65
Ukraine, 487
Artemis Accords and, 304
atrocities in, 441
CrashOverride attack on, 505

declaration under UNCLOS Article 298,
263–64
in grey zone, 38–39
hybrid warfare and, 42, 425
information operations and, 369, 370
international armed conflict (IAC) in, 438
'Internet Army' in, 158
ITLOS and, 262, 263–65, 268–69
Kerch Strait incident and, 329
lawfare and, 618–19, 619n.57
Ministry of Digital Transformation, 158
Orange Revolution in, 467
Russia and, 329–30, 516–17, 551
Russian aggression against, 1–2, 3, 6, 7, 8–9,
14, 20–21, 26–27, 33, 34, 36–37, 38–40,
42–43, 68n.10, 70–71, 72n.13, 75n.20, 77–
78, 80–81, 82, 104, 111, 114–15, 125–26,
158, 189, 207–8, 212, 213, 273–74, 284–85,
286–87, 313–14, 332–33, 337, 347, 369,
370, 372, 376, 425, 441, 447–48, 471, 480,
530, 547–48, 553–54, 560–61, 566–67,
575–76, 631–34, 635–36, 637–38
Russian hackers and, 204
Russian proxies in, 438, 439–40
Russian separatists downing of MH-17 over,
336
Russia's 2014 efforts to annex Ukrainian
territory, 22, 34, 55–56, 57, 148–49, 374,
375
Russia's hybrid measures before invasion,
256–57
territorial integrity of, 375
2014 Russian efforts to annex Ukrainian
territory, 471
US and, 38–40
Western arms supplies to, 39–40
the uncanny, 451
uncertainty, 525–26, 527, 529–30, 538, 551. *See
also* ambiguity
grey zone actions and, 373–74
grey zone attacks and, 61
information operations and, 369
role of, 17–18
UN Compensation Commission (UNCC), 530
UN Conference on Disarmament, 297
unconventional warfare (UW), 34
UN Convention on State Immunity, 546n.82
undecidedness, grey zone warfare and, 61–85
underground publishing in, in Poland, 464–65
Union Code, 639
Union of the Comoros, 623, 626–27
United Arab Emirates, 199–200, 304, 443–44
United Kingdom, 348, 401, 402–3, 570–71, 621

INDEX 721

2022 Defence Doctrine, 605–6, 607
Arms Trade Treaty and, 443–44
Artemis Accords and, 304
China and, 2–3, 172
cyber operations in, 194–95
*Integrated Review of Security, Defence,
Development and Foreign Policy*, 2–3, 8–9
interference in elections in, 393–94
Iran and, 358
lawfare and, 601–2, 605–6, 611, 612
Ministry of Defence, 607
missile strikes in Syria and, 9n.37
NATO and, 516, 521
Police Reform and Social Responsibility Bill,
612
referendum on secession from European
Union (Brexit), 143
Russia and, 2–3, 374, 375
Russia as most acute direct threat to, 2–3
Salisbury poisoning incident and, 4–5
United Nations (UN), 484–85, 621, 628. *See also
specific bodies, divisions, and groups*
the Arctic and, 284–85
collective security system, 107–8, 112
establishment of, 90
Group of Governmental Experts on
Developments in the Field of Information
and Telecommunications, 138
High-Level Panel Report, 113
invasion of Iraq and, 58
Refugee Agency, 160
Security Council, 90–91, 105–6, 109
space treaties developed by, 301–2, 304–5,
306, 311–12 (*see also* international space
law; Outer Space Treaty (OST); *specific
treaties*)
special rapporteur on extrajudicial killings,
356, 357–58
Yugoslavia and, 51
United Nations Charter, 4–5, 107–8, 109, 115,
120, 125–26, 298
Article 2(1), 396
Article 2(4), 5–6, 31, 35, 90, 109, 110–12,
117–18, 131–32, 131n.15
Article 39, 112
Article 41, 112
Article 42, 112
Article 51, 116–18, 325, 355–56, 495
Chapter VII, 442
Group of Governmental Experts (GGE) on
Developments in the Field of Information
and Telecommunications in the Context of
International Security, 399–400

Oxford Commentary on, 110
principle of non-intervention, 5–6
United Nations Committee on the Peaceful
Uses of Outer Space (UNCOPUOS), 289,
290–91, 292, 297, 302, 307
Transparency and Confidence Building
Measures, 311, 312
transparency and confidence building
measures and, 310–11
Working Group on the Long Term
Sustainability of Outer Space Activities,
302
United Nations General Assembly
condemnation of Russia's war in Ukraine, 111
Russian war in Ukraine and, 114–15
United Nations General Assembly (UNGA)
Declaration on the Inadmissibility of
Intervention, 397
Declaration on the Inadmissibility of
Intervention and Interference, 397
Declaration on the Principles of Friendly
Relations, 397
first Resolution on use of outer space, 297
GA Res. 68/262, 375
GA Res. ES-11/4, 376
PAROS and, 312
Resolution 69/32, 310–11
Resolution 1884, 297
Resolution 1962 (XVIII), 298–99
Resolution 3314 (XXIX), 325
resolution 'Reducing Space Threats
through Norms, Rules and Principles of
Responsible Behaviour, 313
Resolutions of, 298
resolutions of, 297, 298–99, 310–11, 313,
325, 397
resolutions on interference and intervention,
397
United Nations Group of Governmental
Experts (GGE), 312
United Nations Guidelines for the Long- term
Sustainability of Outer Space Activities,
307–8
United Nations Human Rights Council
(UNHRC), 627–28
United Nations Open-Ended Working Group
(OEWG), 313, 315, 399–400
Open-Group of Governmental Experts
in the Field of Information and
Telecommunications in the Context of
International Security, 367
UN Open Ended Working Group on
Responsible Behaviours, 293

722 INDEX

United Nations Security Council (UNSC), 112, 115, 125, 196, 332n.50, 378, 442–43
  disagreement of scope of powers, 113
  language of, 126–27
  maritime incident of 31 May 2010 and, 627
  Powell's address to, 388n.90
  Russian war in Ukraine and, 114–15
  self-defence and, 115–16
  'threat to peace' and, 113–14
  UNSCR 2098, 258
United States (US), 35, 172, 355, 456–57, 469, 549–50, 565, 593, 625. *See also* US foreign policy; US military
  1919 bombing campaign in, 451–52
  absence from UNCLOS, 268–69
  Afghanistan and, 53, 432
  the Arctic and, 53–54, 271, 273n.10, 277–78, 282–83, 286
  Arms Trade Treaty and, 443–44
  Artemis Accords and, 304
  attempts to limit civil casualties, 486–87, 490–91
  BALIKATAN 2016 and, 56–57
  Balkans and, 57–58
  Chile and, 398
  China and, 3, 19–20, 50, 53–54, 56–57, 58, 67n.9, 104, 172, 173–74, 207–8, 211, 215, 221–30, 272–73, 275–76, 279, 286, 289–93, 302, 304, 330, 347, 378–79, 593
  Cold War and, 33, 472, 578, 592–93
  control of private information in, 225–28
  covert operations by, 37–38
  COVID in, 509
  cyber operations and, 365, 367, 487–88
  default tending towards non-GZO engagement, 490
  defence spending by, 49, 50
  destructive anti-satellite (ASAT) tests and, 308–9
  diplomacy and, 37–38
  disinformation targeting 2016 elections, 370
  as donor State, 578–79, 585, 586, 587–89, 590, 592–95, 593n.65, 596, 597–99 (*see also specific recipient States*)
  East Asia and, 48, 265–66
  Egypt and, 593–95, 597–98
  election process in, 415
  at end of Cold War, 49, 50–53
  ethical standards and, 20
  goal of avoiding 'another bloody century', 35
  Greece and, 587
  grey zone conflicts and, 17, 221–30
  grey zone lawfare and, 221–30

Guatemala and, 398
GZOs and, 237–38, 476, 484–91, 489*t*
Haiti and, 57–58
Hamas designated as terrorist organisation by, 613–14
hybrid warfare and, 43, 425
India and, 593, 595, 596, 597, 598
information technology domain and, 207, 212, 221–30
interference by, 398
interference in elections in, 370, 393–94, 407–9, 411n.112, 416n.133, 416n.134, 417n.137, 447–48
Interim National Security Strategic Guidance (INSSG), 35
invasion of Iraq and, 342–43, 356–57
IP theft and, 222–24
Iran and, 48, 53, 55, 58, 333, 356, 357–58, 371, 398, 481–82
Iraq and, 48, 53, 54, 58, 357–58, 363
lack of lawfare strategy in, 234–35
land reclamation and, 57, 58
Latin America and, 485
lawfare and, 19–20, 209, 211, 234–35
Libya and, 54–55
military activities of, 23–24
military advantage of, 49
military and paramilitary cooperation in, 484–88, 489*t*
military GZOs and, 490
missile strikes in Syria and, 9n.37
moratorium on ASAT testing, 311–12
narratives and, 172, 173
national security objectives of, 593
National Security Strategy, 1–2, 3, 8
NATO and, 516, 521, 522
Nicaragua and, 91–93, 95–96, 398, 436, 436n.51, 485–86, 578 (see also *Nicaragua v. US* (IJC))
Nicaragua v. US and, 91–93, 95–96
North Korea and, 48, 53, 55, 58, 390
OPERATION ATLANTIC RESOLVE and, 55–56
Operation Burnt Frost, 309
Operation Enduring Freedom, 118
Ottawa Landmines Convention and, 521, 522
Philippines and, 598–99
as policeman, 1990-1999, 51
political warfare and, 40, 41
position on NIACs, 121
al-Qaeda and, 360–61
Quadrilateral Dialogue and, 595
as realist power, 37–38

INDEX 723

rules-based order narrative and, 173–74
Russia and, 38, 48, 53–54, 55–56, 57, 104,
173–74, 175n.61, 213, 367, 398, 407–9,
411n.112, 416n.133, 416n.134, 417n.137,
447–48
Russian interference in 2016 election, 407–9,
411n.112, 416n.133, 416n.134, 417n.137,
447–48
shoots down Chinese balloon, 378–79
South Korea and, 53
South Vietnam and, 587–88
Soviet Union and, 297, 346, 378–79, 398,
592–93
space domain and, 296, 300, 302
Starlink/China Space Station incident and,
289–93
strike to kill Soleimani, 115–16
Stuxnet operation and, 186, 204–5
Syria and, 54–55, 486
Taiwan and, 208, 487
technological advantage in space domain,
296
2016 presidential election, 130, 139, 146, 147,
199–200, 326, 393–94, 410, 561
2016 presidential election, 370, 407–9,
411n.112, 416n.133, 416n.134, 417n.137,
447–48
2020 presidential election, 393–94, 411
Ukraine and, 38–40
Vietnam War and, 35–36, 346
war on terrorism and, 123–24, 618–19
Unity of Command, 526
Universal Declaration of Human Rights, 442
universal jurisdiction laws, 610–11
University of Cambridge, 568
unlawfulness, outdated standard
for, 149–50
unreliability, 167
Unrestricted Warfare, 214
'unrestricted warfare' strategy, 495–96
Uribe, Alvaro, 628
US Air Force, 291n.10
US Airforce, China Aerospace Studies
Institute, 39
US Army Field Manual, 2022, 103–4
US Bureau of Land Management, 386
US-China Economic Security Review
Commission, 224–25
US Civil War, 89–90
US Commercial Space Launch Competitiveness
Act 2015. Title IV, 303
US Committee on Foreign Investment in the
United States, 227

US companies, Chinese purchase of, 227–28
US Congress, 240, 474, 593–94
grey zone operations (GZO) and, 485–86
House and Senate Armed Services
Committee ((HaSC/SASC), 484
House and Senate Permanent Select
Committees on Intelligence, 485–86
Zelenskyy's speech to, 635–36
US Cyber Command, 487
US Department of Commerce, 194, 213–14,
229–30
US Department of Defense (DoD), 36, 161, 176,
219–20, 252–53, 450, 474, 486
on China's military presence in the Arctic,
279
Cyber Command, 201–2
as donor State, 590–91, 591n.54
grey zone engagements and, 237–38
hybrid warfare and, 42
security assistance and, 578–79, 590
Tenets of Responsible Behaviour in Space,
314
US Department of Energy, 194, 574
US Department of Homeland Security, 194
US Department of Justice, 188–89, 229–30
Special Counsel's Office, 407–9, 411n.112
US Department of Treasury, 194, 213–14
use of force. *See also* military force
banning of, 107–8
on continuum scale, 104n.2
customary rule prohibiting, 110–11
discrimination in, 357
escalation and, 355–56, 357
international law and, 321, 355–56, 375
outlawed under UN Charter Article 2(4),
90–91, 110–12
permeable ban on, 109–12
prohibition of, 90–91, 109–12, 375
proportionality in, 357
self-defence and, 115–16, 125, 356–58
short of armed conflict, 325, 356–57
threat of, 107–8
thresholds under *jus ad bellum*, 90–93
use of power, short of armed conflict, 495–96
US foreign policy
attachment to unhelpful binaries, 45, 46–47
grey zone activities and, 45–60
non-intervention and, 485
US Government Accountability Office (GAO),
592
US Intelligence Community, Worldwide
Threat Assessment of, 239. *See also specific
agencies*

724 INDEX

US Marine Corps, 475
Combat Development Command, 42
US military, 484. *See also* US Department of
Defense (DoD); *specific branches*
China and, 56–57
exercise in Eastern Europe, 55–56
grey zone conflicts and, 45–60
Haiti and, 50–51
Libya and, 54–55
media and, 176
old efforts, new rules, 2011-2020, 54–57
as policeman, 1990-1999, 50–53
responses to grey zone challenges, 1991-
2020, 49–57
in Somalia, 50–51n.15
Syria and, 54–55
Yemen and, 55
Yugoslavia and, 50–52
US Military Assistance Advisory Group-
Indochina (MAAG), 587–88
US National Counterintelligence and Security
Center, 222
US National Defense Strategy of 2018, 322
US Naval War College, 219
US Navy, 219, 266, 267–68, 484–85
in East Asia, 265–66
Freedom of Navigation Operations
(FONOPs) and, 56–57, 58
USNS auxiliary ships, 266
USNS *Impeccable*, 267–68
USN Warships, 266
US Office of Personnel Management, hacking
of, 226–27
US Office of the Director of National
Intelligence's 2021 Annual Threat
Assessment, 205–6
US presidency, GZOs and, 485–86. *See also*
specific elections
US Senate, 486
data access and, 422
Judiciary Committee, 458
Red Scare and, 458
Select Committee on Intelligence (SSCI)
report, 420
USS *Lassen*, 265–66
USSOCOM (United States Special Operations
Command), 38
US Space Command, 290–91, 291n.10,
311–12
US Space Surveillance Network, 291n.10
USSR. *See* Soviet Union
US State Department, 194, 196–97, 213, 215,
253, 311–12, 474, 593, 594, 595

Bureau of Democracy, Human Rights, and
Labor (DRL), 590–91, 591n.52, 592
International Security Advisory Board, 390
North Atlantic Treaty and, 519
report on human rights in India, 596
security assistance and, 578–79, 590–91, 591n.54
US stock exchange, 213
US Terminal High Altitude Area Defense
(THAAD), 231–32
US Treasury Department, 213, 474
US Treasury securities, owned by China, 213
US v Nicaragua, 362. See also *Nicaragua v US* (IJC)
utilitarianism, 107
Uyghurs, in China, 172

vaccine research, theft of, 509
vaccine skepticism, 509
vagueness
choice amid, 61–62, 65–76, 85
true vagueness substructure, 61–62, 72–74
Valeriano, Brandon, 365
Van Passen, Pierre, 453, 454–55
Vattel, Emer de, 385–86, 525
Vault, 197
Vázquez Benítez, Rodrigo, 27, 649–72
Venezuela, 482
Vermeulen, Mathias, 422n.164
Very High Frequency (VHF) radio connectivity,
278–79
Vestner, Tobias, 18, 103–27
vetting foreign interests of individuals, 643–44
Vietnam, 58. *See also* North Vietnam; South
Vietnam; Vietnam War
Vietnam War, 35–36, 173, 175n.61, 176, 346,
472
violence
short of war, 4–5, 10–14, 31–32, 36–37, 45–
46, 107, 115–16, 126, 499–500
as tool of foreign policy, 486
Virgin Galactic, 305–6
Voice of America, 164–65
Vostok-2018, 331–32
Votel, Joseph, 40
voter fraud, 508–9
voter rolls, hacking of, 130
voting rights, 508
vulnerabilities, 546–47, 549–51

Wagner Group, 439–40, 476–77, 479
Wall Street Journal, 226
Walzer, Michael, 356–57, 358, 363, 371, 499–500
Wang Xiangsui, 208–9, 321–22
Wanless, Alicia, 165

INDEX   725

WannaCry, 197
war and peace, 125
   four eras of thinking on, 106
   future of, 126
   grey zone conflicts and, 108
   hybrid threats and, 108
   hybrid warfare and, 108
war crimes, 212, 610–11
Wardle, Claire, 167n.38
warfighters, personal information of, 225–28
warfighting, 350
   vs. coercion, 342, 343
   warfighting norms vs. grey zone norms,
      339–72
Warner, Michael, 192, 196, 201
war on terrorism, 54, 104, 123–24, 486, 618–19
Warsaw Communiqué, 519–20
Warsaw Pact, 175n.61, 515–16
Warsaw Pact states, 578
war vs. peace, international law and, 103–27
war/warfare, 4–5. *See also* conventional warfare;
      irregular warfare (IW); war and peace;
      warfighting
   as absence of peace, 104–5
   conflict continuum and, 470
   current legal framework of, 88–95
   definition of, 31–32, 104–5, 127
   destructiveness of, 495
   diplomacy and, 40
   evolving character of, 33
   hybridization of, 88
   hyper-personalization of, 207, 225–28
   justice and, 106
   language of, 126–27
   as legal concept, 120
   logic of, 341–42
   media and, 177, 178
   mediatization and, 176
   moral perceptions of, 106, 107
   in the name of peace, 112–15
   non-contact warfare, 329–30
   non-symmetric, 329–30
   norms of, 357, 358–59
   outlawed by Kellogg-Briand Pact, 107–8
   vs. peace, 4–5, 6, 12–13, 18, 19, 32–36, 38,
      43–44, 103–27, 183–87, 319–20, 321, 339,
      373–74, 447, 450, 451, 495–96
   with peace, 112–15
   principles of, 515, 525–28
   psychological (*see* psychological operations
      (PSYOPS))
   vs. statecraft, 339
   wars, 2000-2010, 53–54

Washington Post, 168
Watts, Sean, 418
   Wciślik, Piotr, 464–65
weakness of will, 73–74
wealth, 472
weaponization, 4–5
weapons of mass destruction (WMDs), 297,
      299–300
   countering, 490
   in Syria, 491–92
weapons plans, theft of, 496
weather events, 566–67
Weber, Max, 406
Wenger, Andreas, 360
Wentzell, Tyler, 23, 447–67
Western imperialism, 172
Western States. *See also specific States*
   covert operations by, 37–38
   military primacy of, 35–36
   overstepping international legality, 8–9
   Russia and, 516–17
Western values, 527–28
West Germany, 462
WhatsApp, 226
Wheatley, Steven, 22, 144, 373–92
Whelan, Theresa, 185–86
White Star Lines, 455–56
white zones, 37–38
Wicked Panda, 189–90
Wicked Spider, 189–90
Wiener, Norbert, 415n.130
Wight, Martin, 405
WikiLeaks, 408, 417n.137
Willams, Samuel, 587–88
Williams, Bernard, 496–97
'willing dupes', use of, 450–51
Wilner, Alex, 360
Wilson, Brian, 216
Wilson Center, 198–99
Winnipeg General Strike, 452, 455–56
Winnti, 189–90
Winslet, Kate, 567
win-win games, 61–62, 80, 81, 85
Wittgenstein, Ludwig, 380
Wolf Amendment, 304
Wooley, Samuel C., 165
Workers' Defence Committee (KOR), 463
working-from-home trend, 563
World Trade Organization (WTO), 210–11,
      231–32, 393–94
World War I, 34–35
   international legal system following, 107–8
   as 'war to end all wars', 103–4

726 INDEX

World War II, 34–35, 172, 484, 564–65
  aftermath of, 610–11
  allies of, 519
  Finland and, 632
  international legal system following, 107–8,
    109
Wray, Christopher, 198, 222, 223, 224, 226
Wright, Quincy, 142, 378
wrongful intervention
  disruption or manipulation as new standard
    for, 148
  new standard for, 151–52
Wuerth, Ingrid, 218–19

Xiangsui, Wang, 214
Xi Jinping, 171, 224, 347
  goal of national rejuvenation and, 287
  on 'peacetime employment of military force', 39
  Putin and, 207–8

Yaron, Amos, 602–3n.4
Yemen, 333, 365, 443–44, 482
  Iran and, 488–90
  US military and, 55
Young Communist League, 455–56

YouTube, 226, 527–28, 618–19
Yugoslav Army, 362
Yugoslavia, 95, 362, 436–38. *See also*
    International Criminal Tribunal for the
    Former Yugoslavia (ICTY)
  atrocities in, 611
  ethnic cleansing in, 51, 57–58
  NATO and, 51–52
  no-fly zones in, 51
  UN and, 51
  US military response to, 50–52
Yukos arbitration (IJC), 528–29

Zagare, Frank C., 347
Zahar, Mahmoud al-, 615n.37
Zaneth, Tony, 455–56
Zapad-2017, 331–32
Zawahiri, Ayman al-, 486–87
Zelenskyy, Volodymyr, 38–39, 158, 635–36
zero-sum games, 61–62, 80–82, 85
Zhao Lijian, 291–92
Zolenska, Olena, 158
Zolotarev, Pavel, 139
Zorniksy, Edward, 164–65
ZTE, 229, 234